OXFORD EC LAW LIB

General Editor: F. G. Jacobs
Formerly Advocate General, The Court of Justice
of the European Communities

GOYDER'S EC COMPETITION LAW

OXFORD EC LAW LIBRARY

The aim of this series is to publish important and original studies of the various branches of EC Law. Each work provides a clear, concise, and original critical exposition of the law in its social, economic, and political context, at a level which will interest the advanced student, the practitioner, the academic, and government and Community officials.

Other Titles in the Library

The European Union and its
Court of Justice
Second edition
Antony Arnull

The General Principles of EU Law
Second edition
Takis Tridimas

EC Company Law
Vanessa Edwards

EU Anti-Discrimination Law
Evelyn Ellis

EC Securities Regulation
Third edition
Niamh Moloney

EC Agricultural Law
Second edition
J.A. Usher

Intellectual Property Rights in the EC
Volume 1 Free Movement and
Competition Law
David T. Keeling

EC Customs Law
Second edition
Timothy Lyons

EC Employment Law
Third edition
Catherine Barnard

EU Justice and Home Affairs Law
Second edition
Steve Peers

Directives in EC Law
Second edition
Sacha Prechal

External Relations of the European
Union Legal and Constitutional
Foundations
Piet Eeckhout

The Law of Money and Financial
Services in the EC
Second edition
J.A. Usher

Workers, Establishment, and Services
in the European Union
Robin C.A. White

GOYDER'S EC COMPETITION LAW

Fifth Edition

D. G. GOYDER

Solicitor; Visiting Professor in Law at King's College London

JOANNA GOYDER

*Barrister, England and Wales, MA (Cantab.), Lic. Spec. (ULB, Brussels),
LLM (EUI, Florence)*

ALBERTINA ALBORS-LLORENS

*Licenciatura en Derecho (Valencia (Spain));
LLM (London); PhD. (Cantab.)*

OXFORD

UNIVERSITY PRESS

OXFORD

UNIVERSITY PRESS

Great Clarendon Street, Oxford OX2 6DP

Oxford University Press is a department of the University of Oxford.
It furthers the University's objective of excellence in research, scholarship,
and education by publishing worldwide in

Oxford New York

Auckland Cape Town Dar es Salaam Hong Kong Karachi
Kuala Lumpur Madrid Melbourne Mexico City Nairobi
New Delhi Shanghai Taipei Toronto

With offices in

Argentina Austria Brazil Chile Czech Republic France Greece
Guatemala Hungary Italy Japan Poland Portugal Singapore
South Korea Switzerland Thailand Turkey Ukraine Vietnam

Oxford is a registered trade mark of Oxford University Press
in the UK and in certain other countries

Published in the United States
by Oxford University Press Inc., New York

British Library Cataloguing in Publication Data

Data available

Library of Congress Cataloging in Publication Data

Data available

Typeset by Newgen Imaging Systems (P) Ltd., Chennai, India
Printed in Great Britain
on acid-free paper by
CPI Antony Rowe, Chippenham, Wiltshire

ISBN 978-0-19-923230-7 (pbk.)
ISBN 978-0-19-953531-6 (hbk.)

1 3 5 7 9 10 8 6 4 2

Dedicated to
Sir Arthur fforde
(1900–1985)
Lawyer, Headmaster, and Poet

GENERAL EDITOR'S FOREWORD

It is a pleasure to welcome the fifth edition of this book, which was the first to be published in the Oxford EC Law Library and is now the first to reach the milestone of a fifth edition. Dan Goyder was a remarkably efficient author who regularly up-dated, and indeed thoroughly revised, his book every five years.

It is sad that we must now record Dan Goyder's untimely death. He was a straightforward man and an excellent colleague. He brought a fresh voice to his work, which was always direct and original in its approach.

It is good that Dan Goyder's work on this book has been carried forward by an excellent team of authors including his daughter Joanna, herself a leading scholar and practitioner in European competition law. Albertina Albors-Llorens is also a most appropriate co-author, having been a close colleague and friend of Dan Goyder during his time teaching at Cambridge University.

Moreover the new team has maintained the well-established virtues of the book. While bringing the work completely up to date, they have succeeded in providing, within a reasonable compass, a fresh and practical book which still covers all the principal aspects of EC competition law and policy.

The book not only remains up to date, but also looks to the future. At the same time, as before, it stresses the interconnections between law and economics; it places the law firmly in its historical perspective so that the current law can be better understood; and it treats the subject not only from the viewpoint of the lawyer and the corporate adviser, but also from that of the official and the court.

The book will be of value therefore to the student, the practitioner, the administrator and the judge; and especially to those who seek not merely to look up particular points or to discover the rules, but to understand the system of which the rules form a part.

November 2008   Francis G. Jacobs

AUTHORS' PREFACE TO THE FIFTH EDITION

New editions of this work have appeared every five years since its first publication in 1988, and in his preface to the fourth edition, published in 2003, shortly before his death, Dan noted that 'EC competition policy in its early days was a small stream whose features could be quite easily and briefly described...however, this stream has grown into a mighty river with an impact far beyond the surrounding European landscape, at times running smoothly but at other moments disturbed by sudden squalls and fierce currents'. That mighty river has continued in full spate over the last five years, and Dan would have relished the task of bringing his book up to date once again, but sadly that was not to be.

We are both privileged to have been asked to continue his work, and our overriding aim, while updating the text thoroughly, has been to maintain all the qualities for which this book has been appreciated during the years since its first appearance. We have continued Dan's historical approach, retaining material which relates to the earlier development of individual topics, and also his practice of describing important cases in detail. One new feature that we have introduced is the inclusion of lists of further reading material at the end of each chapter of Part II.

There have been very many legal and policy developments for us to incorporate, not least the ever increasing influence of economic analysis in EC competition law. To mention but a few specific developments, there is Regulation 1/2003, effecting radical modernisation of Article 81 and 82 enforcement procedures, which represented only a theoretical concept when Dan wrote about it in 2003, whereas it has now been in force for over four years and has become part of everyday life for competition lawyers. A new merger regulation has also come into force, bringing with it most notably a new substantive test and a considerable increase in flexibility in terms of referrals of mergers to and from the Commission and national authorities. The Commission has devoted much attention to developing thinking and stimulating debate in a number of other areas, including in particular both private enforcement through litigation in national courts, and enforcement policy in respect of Article 82. The latter has proved especially fraught with difficulty, though as we write this the Commission has just succeeded in publishing guidance on its Article 82 enforcement priorities, providing a useful summary of its policy. Meanwhile the importance and influence of EC competition law expanded considerably during this period, with the accession to the Community of twelve new Member States.

In order to maintain the book at approximately the same length as before, we have regretfully omitted the chapter dealing with intellectual property rights in the context of the EC Treaty rules on the free movement of goods. Though this chapter is not concerned with competition law in the strict sense, we know that users of this book have found the chapter immensely valuable, so we have updated it and it is available through the on-line resource centre for this book. The resource centre, accessible at www.oxfordtextbooks.co.uk/orc/goyder5e, also provides a list of useful links, and the chronological table of events that appears also at the start of the book.

In referring to Articles of the Treaty of Rome whose numbering was altered by the Treaty of Amsterdam in 1997, we have continued the practice of the previous edition of referring only to the new number, e.g. 'Articles 81 and 82' rather than 'Articles 81 (ex. 85) and 82 (ex. 86)'. The only exception is where a court judgment has referred to an Article under its old number; here we have changed the reference to the current numbering but left it in square brackets to indicate the change. If and when the Lisbon Treaty enters into force this will effect yet another renumbering of these Articles, but the fate of that Treaty is currently uncertain following its rejection by popular referendum in Ireland. Likewise for consistency we have described the Directorate General for Competition throughout as 'DG Comp', though strictly speaking the change of name from 'DG IV' occurred only in 1999; merger decisions prior to that change have been left under the reference of IV/M with only cases post-September 1999 as Comp/M.

We have not done all this work ourselves, and we are particularly grateful to Andrew Renshaw, colleague of Joanna's and partner at Freshfields Bruckhaus Deringer in Brussels, for taking time from his practice to thoroughly update Chapters 16 to18 on merger control and joint ventures. We think Dan would have been glad to have this task carried out by someone with Andrew's wealth of knowledge and experience in this area. We would also like to thank Philip Marsden, Director of the Competition Law Forum and Senior Research Fellow at the British Institute of International and Comparative law, who updated Chapter 22 on the international aspects of EC competition law, which he had contributed to the fourth edition

Joanna also thanks all her other colleagues in the competition practice at Freshfields Bruckhaus Deringer, who allowed her time to work on this project, and from whom she learns on a daily basis. Albertina would like to thank Pantelis, Alexander and Nicholas for their patience and support while this new edition was being prepared. We both also warmly acknowledge the support of Dan's wife Jean, who has encouraged us throughout.

Finally we would both like to thank Ruth Ballantyne and Alex Clabburn and their colleagues at Oxford University Press. They are highly professional and a pleasure to work with, and they did all that was needed to ensure that the book appeared on time.

Notwithstanding all the help received and acknowledged we are responsible for the contents of the book and any errors contained in it; and all views expressed are personal unless otherwise indicated in the text.

This book remains dedicated, as it was by Dan, to Sir Arthur fforde. However, we ourselves dedicate this fifth edition to Dan himself. This book still really belongs to him, and we record here our great gratitude to him for what he gave us as father, colleague, friend and competition law enthusiast.

Thanks to the flexibility shown by our publishers in allowing us to make some late changes, we have been able to state the law as we understand it on 1 December 2008.

J.R.G. and A.A.L.
December 2008

AUTHOR'S PREFACE TO THE FIRST EDITION

The actual process of writing a book is necessarily solitary: in spite of Voltaire's belief that 'the happiest of all lives is a busy solitude', there are moments when one could wish for a more gregarious task. Fortunately, however, there are other stages (both at the beginning and the end of the process) which cannot be completed without the help of many others, and that has been especially true on this occasion.

Before writing a general account of the European Community's competition law, it seemed to me important to interview a number of the officials of Directorate-General IV of the Commission, which is responsible for the administration of Community competition policy, particularly as some of the more senior among them would shortly be reaching retirement. I am grateful to all those officials who allowed me to share their memories of the pioneer days of DG IV, as well as their views of past and present events and policy issues. Some of them also later read and commented on individual chapters. As those who helped me in this way were numerous, I have elected not to name them individually, with but two exceptions. The first is Aurelio Pappalardo, now retired from the Commission, who made it possible for me to spend time in DG IV and conduct these interviews; the second is Karen Williams, formerly a colleague at the University of Essex, who after her move to Brussels to join DG IV continued to give me enthusiastic encouragement and practical help on many aspects of the work.

I was also fortunate to be able to spend time in Brussels in the offices of Cleary, Gottlieb, Steen & Hamilton, where Don Holley and his colleagues made me welcome, allowed me the use of their excellent library, and kept me going with copious cups of black coffee. I am also grateful to Don for reading the drafts of several chapters and for his wise comments upon them. Professor Arved Deringer allowed me on a visit to Cologne to benefit from his unrivalled knowledge of the historical roots both of the Treaties of Paris and Rome, and also of the circumstances in which Regulation 17 was enacted in 1962. The Leverhulme Trust awarded me a research grant to help meet part of the travelling and other expenses involved in the writing of the book, and I am pleased to acknowledge their help.

I must also express my thanks to Byron and Eleanor Fox, Barry Hawk, Sir Alan Neale, Noel Ing, Philippa Watson, Francis B. Jacobs (of the European Parliament's Secretariat), and Chris Docksey, all of whom gave me help, in a variety of different ways, during the writing of the book. Most of this writing was done in the Library of the University of Essex at Colchester where Peter Luther ensured that I had all the relevant authorities. I must also express my appreciation to my colleagues, both in Ipswich and at the University Law Department, for their tolerance of my preoccupation with this project at times when they must have wished it was less time-consuming.

All the typing of the manuscript has been done by my former secretary, Elaine Golledge, whom I was fortunately able to persuade to return from premature domestic retirement; she and her husband Brian have tolerated the presence of a word processor in their dining room for eighteen months, which has enabled her to produce a series of consistently accurate typescripts to a succession of increasingly unreasonable deadlines.

My relationship with Oxford University Press has been pleasant, and I would like to thank Richard Hart for ensuring a smooth production process. My final expressions of thanks must, however, be directed towards three people in particular; to my Consulting Editor, Professor Francis Jacobs of London University, for cheerful and admirably constructive advice throughout; to my daughter Joanna, Barrister, for her help, especially with French language material; and finally to my wife Jean, without whose unfailing support this book could certainly not have been written.

This book is dedicated, with the approval of Lady fforde, to Sir Arthur fforde, who died in 1985. After a distinguished career as a City of London solicitor and wartime civil servant, he came as headmaster to Rugby School from 1948 to 1957. Many of us who were in the school during that time remember him with particular respect and affection. I am glad to have this opportunity to acknowledge my own debt of gratitude to him; his inquiring and subtle mind would, I like to think, have enabled him to enjoy the intricacies of EC competition law.

I have finally to issue the customary disclaimers. Though I have received help from many sources, responsibility for the contents of the book and for any errors within it are exclusively mine. Neither the contents nor the errors are to be attributed in any way to any of the persons or organizations referred to in this Preface, nor to any other body with which I am, or have been, associated.

The law is stated as at 31 March 1988.

D.G.G.

20–26 Museum Street
Ipswich, Suffolk   April 1988

CONTENTS

Table of Cases from the ECJ and CFI   xxxi

Table of European Commission Decisions   xli

Table of Cases from Other Jurisdictions   xlvii

United Kingdom Monopolies and Mergers Commission Reports   xlix

Table of European Community Treaties   li

Table of Agreements and Conventions   liii

Table of European Community Secondary Legislation   lv

Table of Legislation from Other Jurisdictions   lix

Chronological Table (1951–2008)   lxi

Abbreviations   lxxv

PART I THE EARLY YEARS

1	**INTRODUCTION**	3
	1 The Scope of the Book	3
	2 The Structure of the Book	5
2	**COMPETITION POLICY AND THE ROLE OF ECONOMICS**	8
	1 The Definition of Competition	8
	1.1 The Basic Concept	8
	1.2 The Advantages of Competition	9
	2 The Nature and Aims of Competition Law	10
	2.1 Introduction	10
	2.2 Economic Welfare	11
	2.3 The 'Single Market Imperative'	11
	3 The Role of Economics in Competition Law	12
	3.1 Introduction	12
	3.2 Market Power	12
	3.3 Market Shares and Market Definition	13
	3.4 Economic Welfare and Legal Certainty	14
	4 Monopoly, Oligopoly, and Workable Competition	15
	4.1 Perfect Monopoly and Perfect Competition	15

	4.2	Oligopoly and Workable Competition	16
	4.3	The Difference between Horizontal and Vertical Agreements	18
5	The Role of Competition Policy in the Community		19
	5.1	Introduction	19
	5.2	Restrictive Agreements	19
	5.3	Single Firm Dominance	20
	5.4	Collective Dominance	20
	5.5	The Essential Elements of Effective Competition Policy	21

3   THE ORIGINS OF EUROPEAN COMPETITION LAW   24

1	The Treaty of Paris and the Formation of the European Coal and Steel Community		24
	1.1	OEEC and the Council of Europe	24
	1.2	The Schuman Plan and the Treaty of Paris	26
2	The Treaty of Rome and the Formation of the European Economic Community		31
	2.1	The Benelux Memorandum	31
	2.2	The Spaak Report	32
	2.3	Negotiations over the Terms of Articles 81 and 82	33
	2.4	The Text of Articles 81 and 82	36
	2.5	The Two Sets of Competition Rules Contrasted	37

4   THE EARLY YEARS OF DG COMP   40

1	The Need for a Procedural Framework		40
	1.1	The Requirements of Article 83	40
	1.2	The Negotiations over the Draft Regulation	41
	1.3	The Involvement of the European Parliament	42
	1.4	The Enactment of Regulation 17/62	44
2	The Provisions of Regulation 17		45
	2.1	Recitals	45
	2.2	Articles 1 to 9 of the Regulation	46
	2.3	Articles 10 to 14 of the Regulation	49
	2.4	Articles 15 to 25 of the Regulation	51
3	The Implementation of Regulation 17: The Early Experience of DG Comp		52
4	The *Grundig* Case and its Consequences		53
	4.1	The Facts of *Grundig*	53
	4.2	The Consequences of *Grundig*	55

5   THE ADVENT OF THE BLOCK EXEMPTION   57

     1   Early Case-Law Experience   57

          1.1   The First Cases on Distribution Systems   57

          1.2   The Next Step—The Need for Block Exemptions   59

     2   The Enactment of Council Regulation 19/65   60

          2.1   The Scope of the Enabling Regulation   60

          2.2   The Introduction of Regulation 19/65   61

          2.3   The Italian Challenge to the Regulation   62

          2.4   The *STM* Case—A Broad Interpretation of Article 81(1)   63

     3   The First Ten Years of DG Comp: A Review   65

          3.1   The Value of the Early Case Law   65

          3.2   The Attitude of Industry to Competition Rules   66

          3.3   Relationships between the Commission and Other Community
                 Institutions   67

          3.4   The First Block Exemption Regulation 67/67   68

PART II THE SUBSTANTIVE LAW OF
THE EUROPEAN COMMUNITY

6   ARTICLE 81(1): ANALYSIS (1)   73

     1   Introduction   73

     2   The Concept of an Undertaking   74

          2.1   A Basic Definition   74

          2.2   Insurance and Social-Security-Fund Cases   76

          2.3   Employees and Trade Unions   77

          2.4   Agents   77

          2.5   A Summary: The Limits to its Scope   79

     3   Group Economic Units   80

     4   Agreements   82

          4.1   Introduction: The Broad Scope of Article 81(1)   82

          4.2   Network Agreements and Unilateral Conduct   84

          4.3   The *Bayer* Case   86

     5   Concerted Practices   88

          5.1   The Early Case Law   88

          5.2   The Burden of Proof: The Commission's Task   91

          5.3   The *Woodpulp* Case   92

          5.4   Other Examples of Concerted Practices between Competitors   94

| | 5.5 | Concerted Practices in the Chain of Distribution | 95 |

6	Decisions by Associations of Undertakings		96
	6.1	The Definition of a Trade Association	96
	6.2	Different Categories of Association	97
	6.3	The Definition of a 'Decision'	99

7   ARTICLE 81(1): ANALYSIS (2)   101

1	'Which May Affect Trade between Member States'		101
	1.1	Early Cases	101
	1.2	The Impact of the Notices on Agreements of Minor Importance	104
	1.3	The New Commission Guidelines on the Effect on Trade Concept Contained in Articles 81 and 82 EC	105
	1.4	The Meaning of 'Trade'	107
	1.5	Articles 81 and 82 Compared	109

2	'Which Have as their Object or Effect the Prevention, Restriction, or Distortion of Competition within the Common Market'		110
	2.1	A Strict or Liberal Interpretation?	110
	2.2	Leading Cases on its Interpretation	112
	2.3	The *Wouters* and its *Meca-Medina* Cases	115
	2.4	Markets Where Competition is Inherently Restricted	116
	2.5	'Object or Effect' of Restricting Competition	118
	2.6	Restrictions on Competition by Non-Resident Parties	122
	2.7	Summary of the Commission's Task	122

3	Ancillary Restrictions on Competition		123
	3.1	Vendors and Purchasers	123
	3.2	Ancillary Restrictions in Trade Association Rules: *Gottrup Klim*	124
	3.3	Other Ancillary Clauses	125
	3.4	Ancillary Restraints and the 2004 Commission Guidelines on the Application of Article 81(3) EC	126

4	The Width of the Coverage of Article 81		126
	4.1	Introduction	126
	4.2	Defence	127
	4.3	Coal and Steel: Nuclear Energy	127
	4.4	Collective Bargaining	128
	4.5	Agriculture	129
	4.6	Air Transport	131
	4.7	Maritime Transport	134

4.8   Road and Rail Transport and Inland Waterways   136

8   ARTICLE 81(3): DISAPPLYING THE ARTICLE 81(1)
     PROHIBITION   138

1   The Changing Role of the Commission   138
     1.1   Introduction   138
     1.2   The Directorate General for Competition (DG Comp)   140

2   Block Exemptions   141
     2.1   Major Current Examples   141
     2.2   The Preparation of Block Exemptions   141
     2.3   The Form of Block Exemptions   142

3   The Article 81(3) Conditions   144
     3.1   The Application of Article 81(3) in the Old System of Enforcement   144
     3.2   The Application of Article 81(3) Post Modernization   146
     3.3   The Interpretation and Application of the Four
            Article 81(3) Conditions   146
     3.4   The Individual Conditions   148
     3.5   The Rule of Reason   156

4   Case Law and Practice on the Application of Article 81(3) in Individual
     Cases: Some Examples   156
     4.1   Multi-Party Agreements   157
     4.2   Insurance Cases   161
     4.3   Television-Rights Cases   162
     4.4   Financial Cases   164
     4.5   Environmental Cases   164
     4.6   Beer-supply Cases   165
     4.7   Horticultural Cases   166
     4.8   The Use of Conditions   167

5   Nullity: The Effect of Article 81(2)   168
     5.1   The Scope of the Basic Rule   168
     5.2   The 'Shimmering' Nature of the Prohibition   169

9   HORIZONTAL AGREEMENTS: CARTELS   171

1   Introduction   171
     1.1   Categories of Horizontal Agreements   171
     1.2   The Approach of the Commission to Cartels   172

2   Price-fixing and Market-sharing Agreements   173
     2.1   Early Cases   173

	2.2	Leading Cases of the 1980s	176
	2.3	A New Commission Approach—The Leniency Notices	179
3	Cartels Involving Shipping Lines	182
4	Crisis Cartels	184
5	Cartels Controlling National Markets	187
6	Cartels Operated by or through Trade Associations	189
	6.1	Dutch Trade Association Cases	189
	6.2	Cartels Operating through the Exchange of Information	190
	6.3	Cartels Operated by Trade Associations Controlling Standards and Certification	194
	6.4	Other Forms of Trade Association Restrictions on Competition	195

10 DISTRIBUTION AGREEMENTS AND PRACTICES   198

1	Introduction	198
2	Distribution through an Agent	199
	2.1	Article 81 and Agency	199
	2.2	The 1962 Notice	199
	2.3	The Policy Dilemma	201
	2.4	Current Policy on Agency Agreements	202
3	Distribution Agreements: The Early Years	205
	3.1	Exclusive Distribution	205
	3.2	Exclusive Purchasing	208
	3.3	The 1983 Block Exemptions	209
4	The 1996 Commission Green Paper on Vertical Restraints	210
5	Distribution Agreements: Policy Since 1999	213
	5.1	When will a Distribution Agreement Infringe Article 81(1)?	214
	5.2	Resale Price Maintenance (RPM)	215
	5.3	Exclusive Distribution and Territorial Protection	217
	5.4	Exclusive Purchase and Non-compete Clauses	219
	5.5	Other Restrictions on Distributors	220
	5.6	Parallel Networks	221
6	The 1999 Block Exemption Regulation 2790/99	221
	6.1	Elimination of the 'White List'	221
	6.2	The 30 per cent Market-Share Cap	222
	6.3	Wider Scope of Agreements Covered	223
	6.4	Prohibited or 'Black-listed' Clauses	224
	6.5	Single-branding (Non-compete) Clauses	226

	6.6	Parallel Networks	226
	6.7	Beer and Petrol	227
	6.8	Withdrawal by National Authorities	227
	6.9	Individual Exemption under Article 81(3)	228
	7	Distribution and Abuse of a Dominant Position	228
11		DISTRIBUTION: SELECTIVE DISTRIBUTION AND FRANCHISING	230
	1	Selective Distribution Systems	230
	1.1	Introduction	230
	1.2	Selective Distribution: The Early Years—*Metro/Saba (No. 1)* and Other Cases	231
	1.3	Refusal to Honour Guarantees	234
	1.4	Selective Distribution of Perfume and Cosmetics	235
	1.5	Refusal to Deal	237
	1.6	Selective Distribution: The 1999 Block Exemption	239
	1.7	Individual Exemption for Selective Distribution: The Current Policy	242
	2	Motor-vehicle Distribution and Servicing Networks	243
	2.1	The Historical Background	243
	2.2	The First Motor Vehicle Distribution Block Exemptions: Regulations 123/85 and 1475/95	245
	2.3	The New Block Exemption: Regulation 1400/2002: The Debate over its Adoption	245
	2.4	Details of Regulation 1400/2002	247
	3	Franchising	249
	3.1	Franchise Systems: The Early Years	249
	3.2	The *Pronuptia* Case	252
	3.3	The Adoption of the Block Exemption 4087/88	255
	3.4	Franchise Systems: The 1999 Block Exemption 2790/1999	257
	3.5	Franchise Systems: The 2000 Guidelines	258
12		INTELLECTUAL PROPERTY RIGHTS: LICENSING	261
	1	Introduction	261
	1.1	The Nature of Intellectual Property Rights	261
	1.2	The Exploitation of Such Rights	262
	2	Early Commission Attitudes to Patent Licensing	263
	2.1	The 1962 Christmas Message	263
	2.2	The Commission's Changing Attitude to Exclusivity	265
	3	The Evolution of the Patent Block Exemption	267

3.1   Travaux Préparatoires and the *Maize Seed* Case   267
3.2   The Block Exemption Regulation (Reg. 2349/84)   271
3.3   The *Windsurfing* Case   271

4   Know-How Licenses and the Know-How Block-Exemption
     Regulation 556/89   274
4.1   The Subcontracting Notice   274
4.2   The Know-How Regulation 556/89   276

5   The First Technology Transfer Block-Exemption Regulation 240/96   277
5.1   The Travaux Préparatoires   277
5.2   The First Technology Transfer Block Exemption in Detail   278

6   The Current Technology Transfer Block-Exemption
     Regulation 772/2004   281
6.1   Background   281
6.2   The Travaux Préparatoires   282
6.3   The Current Technology Transfer Rules in Detail   284

7   Trade-Mark Licences   287
7.1   Early Cases on Trade Marks   287
7.2   Trade-Mark Licences under Regulation 772/2004   289

8   Copyright and Software Licences   290
8.1   Copyright Licences   290
8.2   Software Licences   292
8.3   Other Forms of Intellectual Property Rights   293

13 ARTICLE 82: THE CONCEPT OF DOMINANCE   295
1   The Definition of Dominance   295
1.1   Introduction   295
1.2   *United Brands* and *Hoffmann- La Roche*   296
1.3   Its Applicability to Small Markets as well as Large   299
1.4   Super-Dominant Companies: Their 'Special Responsibility' 301
1.5   Companies with Lower Market Shares   301
1.6   Factors Involved in Assessing Dominance   302

2   The Definitions of Relevant Geographic and Product Markets   302
2.1   The Geographic Market   303
2.2   The Product or Service Market   304

3   Leading Judgments of the European Court on Market Definition 305
3.1   *Ahmed Saaed*   305
3.2   *Hilti*   306

	3.3	*Tetrapak (No. 2)*	307
4		Mergers and Market Definition	308
5.		The 1997 Commission Notice on Market Definition	309
6.		Some Problems in Assessing Dominance	311

14   ARTICLE 82: ABUSE   314

1		Introduction	314
	1.1	The Nature of Abuse	314
	1.2	Categories of Abuse	315
2		Excessive Pricing	316
	2.1	Early Cases	316
	2.2	Further EC and UK Cases	317
3		Predatory Pricing	319
	3.1	The *AKZO* Case	319
	3.2	The *Compagnie Maritime Belge* Case	321
	3.3	The *Deutsche Post* Case	321
	3.4	Predatory Pricing and the 2005 Commission Discussion Paper on Exclusionary Abuses	323
4		Discriminatory Pricing	324
	4.1	*United Brands*	324
	4.2	A Price Squeeze	325
	4.3	*Tetrapak (No. 2)* and *Irish Sugar*	325
	4.4	Discrimination in Airport Charges	326
5		Discounts and Rebates	327
	5.1	Early Cases: *Hoffmann* and *Michelin*	327
	5.2	Recent Cases: *Michelin II* and *British Airways*	329
6		Refusal to Deal (In Goods or Services)	333
	6.1	*Commercial Solvents*	333
	6.2	*United Brands*	335
	6.3	Treatment of Occasional Customers	336
	6.4	Objective Justification and Proportionality	337
7		Abuses by Individual Owners of Intellectual Property Rights	341
	7.1	The Early Cases: The IBM Settlement	341
	7.2	Refusal to Supply Spare Parts	343
	7.3	The *Magill* Saga	344
	7.4	The Effects of *Magill*	347
	7.5	*IMS Health*	348

7.6	*Tetrapak (No. 1)*	350
8	**Abuses by Collective Owners of Intellectual Property Rights**	352
8.1	Restrictive Rules of Collecting Societies	352
8.2	Excessive Charges	355
8.3	The Commission's Reluctance to Intervene	357
9	**Refusal of Access to Essential Facilities**	358
9.1	The 'Harbour' Cases	358
9.2	Other Categories of Essential Facilities	360
9.3	The Tide Turns: *Bronner*	361
10	**Refusal to Supply Interoperability Information**	362
11	**Tying Practices**	364
12	**Other Forms of Abusive Conduct**	366
12.1	Acquisitions by Dominant Companies	366
12.2	Imposition of Unreasonable Terms	367
12.3	Nationality Discrimination	367
12.4	Abuse of Legal Proceedings	368
15	**ARTICLE 82: ITS RELATIONSHIP WITH ARTICLE 81**	370
1	**Their Common Features and Differences**	370
1.1	Six Distinctions between the Articles	370
1.2	Three Similarities between the Articles	372
1.3	Issues of Exclusivity Involving Both Articles	373
2	**Case Law on the Relationship between Article 81 and 82 EC**	374
2.1	*Continental Can* and *Italian Flat Glass*—Collective Dominance Emerges as a Concept	374
2.2	The *CMB* Case—The Development of Collective Dominance	376
3	**The Influence of Merger Decisions on the Concept of Collective Dominance**	379
4	**Collective Dominance in a Vertical Relationship**	381
5	**The Relevance of Individual or Block Exemptions to Article 82**	382
16	**MERGERS (1)**	384
1	**The Origins of Council Regulation 139/2004**	384
1.1	The Need for Merger Control	384
1.2	*Continental Can* and its Consequences	385
1.3	Early Drafts of the Merger Regulation	387
1.4	The *Philip Morris* Case	388

	1.5	Final Negotiations for the Regulation	389
	1.6	Initial Steps Towards Reform	390
	1.7	The 2002 Crisis	390
2	Merger Regulation 139/2004: The Commission's Jurisdiction over Concentrations with a Community Dimension		391
	2.1	The Regulation: Its Jurisdictional Scope	391
	2.2	The Identification of Relevant Turnover	393
	2.3	Articles 5(3) and 5(4)	396
3	The meaning of a 'Concentration'		398
	3.1	The Meaning of 'Control'	398
	3.2	The Meaning of 'Concentrative' Joint Ventures	398
	3.3	The Meaning of 'Decisive Influence'	399
	3.4	Joint Control	400
	3.5	The Issue of Physical Location	401
4	Notification of Concentrations		401
	4.1	The Task of Notification	401
	4.2	The Need for Pre-Notification	402
5	Criteria for Assessment of a Concentration		403
	5.1	Compatibility of Concentrations with the Common Market: Article 2(1)	403
	5.2	The Choice: 'Dominance Significantly Impeding Competition' or 'a Substantial Lessening of Competition'?	404
	5.3	The Definition of Collective Dominance in *Airtours*	405
	5.4	Article 2(2) and (3)	406
	5.5	The Application of the Criteria	406
	5.6	The Merger Regulation in Practice	407
6	Definition of the Relevant Product or Service Market		408
	6.1	The Commission's General Approach	408
	6.2	Issues of Demand and Supply Substitutability	409
7	Definition of the Relevant Geographic Market		412
	7.1	The Commission's General Approach	412
	7.2	The Range of Possible Geographical Markets	413
8	The Prohibition of Mergers		416
	8.1	Application of the 'SIEC' Test	416
	8.2	Dominance of a Single Company	417
	8.3	Non-Coordinated Effects Cases	419
	8.4	Coordinated Effects: The Early Days	420
	8.5	Coordinated Effects: *Kali und Salz*	422

8.6	Coordinated Effects: *Gencor and Airtours*	422
8.7	Coordinated Effects: the Horizontal Merger Guidelines	424
9	**Vertical and Conglomerate Mergers**	425
9.1	The Harm that can be Caused by Non-Horizontal Mergers	425
9.2	Conglomerate Mergers in Practice: *GE/Honeywell*	426
9.3	Vertical Mergers in Practice: *GE/Honeywell*	427
10	**The 'Efficiencies' Defence**	427
11	**The 'Failing Company' Defence**	428

17 MERGERS (2)   430

1	**Referrals of Concentrations between the Commission and Member States**	430
1.1	The 'One-Stop Shop'	430
1.2	Pre-Notification Referrals from the Commission to Member States (Article 4(4))	431
1.3	Pre-Notification Referrals from the Member States to the Commission (Article 4(5))	432
1.4	Post-Notification referrals from the Commission to the Member States (Article 9)	433
1.5	Post-Notification referrals from Member States to the Commission (Article 22)	435
2	**Member State Protection of Legitimate and Defence Interests**	436
2.1	The Legitimate Interest Exception—Article 21(4)	436
2.2	The Defence Exception—Article 296 of the EC Treaty	437
3	**Merger Regulation Investigatory Procedures and Powers**	438
3.1	Time Limits	438
3.2	The Framework of a Commission Investigation	439
3.3	Modification by the Parties of the Original Concentration Plan	440
3.4	Form CO	441
3.5	The Inquiry Process: Powers of the Commission	442
3.6	The Simplified Procedure	443
3.7	Power to Impose Conditions and Obligations—Article 8(2)	443
3.8	The Administrative Powers of the Commission	444
3.9	The Blocking of Mergers	445
4	**Remedies—Conditions and Obligations Imposed as the Price of Clearance**	446
4.1	The Purpose of Remedies	446
4.2	Structural and Behavioural Remedies—The Case Law	447
4.3	Divestiture—A Structural Remedy	449

5	Ancillary Restraints	450
	5.1 The Concept	450
	5.2 The 2005 Notice	451
	5.3 Non-Compete Clauses	451
	5.4 Intellectual Property Right Licences	452
	5.5 Purchase and Supply Agreements	453
6	The Relationship between the Merger Regulation and Articles 81 and 82	454
7	Appeals to the CFI and ECJ	455
	7.1 Competition Law Appeals in General	455
	7.2 Appeals under the Merger Regulation	456
	7.3 The Expedited Appeal Procedure of the CFI: *Schneider* and *Tetra*	*458*

18	JOINT VENTURES AND HORIZONTAL COOPERATION AGREEMENTS	460
1	Introduction	460
	1.1 Why Joint Ventures are Formed	460
	1.2 Control of a Joint Venture	461
	1.3 The Distinction between Joint Ventures that Are Concentrations and those that are not	462
	1.4 The Effect of Regulation 1/2003 on Joint Ventures	463
2	The Definition of Joint Ventures which are Concentrations under the Merger Regulation	464
	2.1 The Merger Regulation Article 3(1) and (2): Definition of a Concentration	464
	2.2 The Effect of Regulation 1310/97	465
	2.3 Joint Control	465
	2.4 Performance of the 'Positive Condition': Full-Function Joint Ventures	467
	2.5 The Abolition of the 'Negative Condition'	470
3	Joint Ventures which are Concentrations: Their Treatment under the Merger Regulation	470
	3.1 Article 2(1) to (3): The Application of the Normal Merger Regulation Criteria to Joint Ventures	470
	3.2 Article 2(4) and (5): The Application of the Special Rules Applicable to Coordination between the Parties to Joint Ventures	472
	3.3 Case Law under Article 2(4) and (5)	474
4	Article 81 and Joint Ventures which are not Concentrations	475
	4.1 Introduction	475
	4.2 Application of Article 81(1) to Joint Ventures: Basic Principles	476

4.3   Application of Article 81(3) to Joint Ventures: Basic Principles   477
4.4   The Commission 2001 Notice: New Guidelines for
      Horizontal Cooperation Agreements   480
4.5   Joint Purchasing and Joint Selling   482
4.6   Standardization and Environmental Agreements   483

5   Joint Ventures which are not Concentrations: Block
    Exemptions for Specialization and R&D Agreements   484
    5.1   Introduction   484
    5.2   Specialization Agreements: Early Case Law   484
    5.3   Introduction of Block Exemption Regulation 417/85
          and its Successor No. 2658/2000   489
    5.4   Specialization Agreements: The Guidelines   490
    5.5   R&D Agreements: The 1968 Notice on Co-operation between
          Enterprises   491
    5.6   Early Case Law on R&D Agreements   492
    5.7   Introduction of Block Exemption Regulation 418/85
          and its Successor 2659/2000   494
    5.8   R&D Agreements: The Guidelines   496

6   Recent Trends in Joint Venture Proposals   497
    6.1   The Changing Background   497
    6.2   Telecommunications Joint Ventures: Some Case Law   498
    6.3   B2B Exchanges   500
    6.4   Energy Joint Ventures   501

19 ENFORCEMENT OF COMMUNITY LAW BY NATIONAL
    AUTHORITIES   502

1   Introduction: The Original Division of Responsibility   502
    1.1   The Need for Member State Participation in Community
          Competition Policy   502
    1.2   The Terms of the Treaty of Rome   503
    1.3   Regulation 17/62 and the Need for Cooperation   504
    1.4   European Court Case Law on 'Dawn Raids'   506
    1.5   Other Means of Member State Involvement   506

2   Article 81(3) and the Issue of Supremacy   507
    2.1   The Walt Wilhelm Case and its Three Rules   507
    2.2   The BMW and Volkswagen Cases   512
    2.3   The New Regulation Resolves the Issue   513

3   National Competition Authorities as Active Enforcers of
    Community Law   515

	3.1	The Debate on National Competition Authority Participation	515
	3.2	The 1997 Notice on Cooperation	516
	3.3	The Modernization White Paper of 1999	517
	3.4	Adoption of Regulation 1/2003 and the Modernization Package	518
4		The New Role for National Competition Authorities	519
	4.1	Introduction	519
	4.2	United Kingdom Competition Authorities	520
	4.3	National Competition Authorities in Other Member States	522
5		National Competition Authorities under Regulation 1/2003—The New Era	525
	5.1	Introduction	525
	5.2	The Content of Regulation 1/2003	525
	5.3	Case Allocation between the Commission and National Authorities	527
	5.4	The European Competition Network	528

20   NATIONAL COURTS AND THE DIRECT APPLICATION OF COMMUNITY LAW   531

1		Introduction and Early Case Law	531
	1.1	*Hasselblad* and *BRT* v. *Sabam*	531
	1.2	*Delimitis* and *Masterfoods*	533
	1.3	The 1993 Notice on Co-operation with National Courts	534
	1.4	The Basis for Private Damages Claims	535
	1.5	The *Garden Cottage* Case	536
2		Remedies Available in the UK Courts Before *Crehan*	538
	2.1	Progress at the ECJ: *Francovich* and *Brasserie du Pêcheur*	538
	2.2	Later High Court Cases	538
3		Remedies Available in the UK Courts after *Crehan*	540
4		The Impact of Regulation 1/2003 on National Courts	542
	4.1	The Recitals of Regulation 1/2003	542
	4.2	The Relevant Articles of Regulation 1/2003	543
	4.3	The Combined Effect of *Crehan* and of the New Regulation	544
5		The Green and White Papers on Private Damages Claims	545
	5.1	The Need for Further Action	545
	5.2	Antitrust Litigation in the United States	547
	5.3	The 2005 Green Paper	547
	5.4	The 2008 White Paper	548
	5.5	The 'Passing On' Defence	549

21 MEMBER STATES AND EC COMPETITION RULES   552

    1   Articles 81 and 82: Obligations of Member States   552

    2   National Laws Affecting Price-Fixing: Some Leading Cases   553

        2.1   The First Rule: Member States Must Not Legislate to
              Create or Protect Agreements or Give Privileges in
              Breach of Article 81 or 82   553

        2.2   The Second Rule: Undertakings Do Not Escape Article 81 or
              82 Merely Because of State Action Affecting Their Markets   557

        2.3   Mandatory Tariffs for Sectors of the Economy   560

        2.4   The *Aluminium Cartel* Case   561

    3   Article 86(1) and (2): Public Undertakings Subject to the
        Treaty Rules on Competition   562

        3.1   The Purpose of these Articles   562

        3.2   Public Undertakings and Undertakings with Special or
              Exclusive Rights   563

        3.3   The Limited Exemption in Article 86(2)   565

        3.4   The Grant of Exclusivity   567

        3.5   Services of General Economic Interest—A Definition   569

    4   Article 86(3): Directives and Decisions of the Commission   570

        4.1   The Initial Use of Such Directives: Telecommunications 570

        4.2   Other Related Initiatives of the Commission   573

        4.3   Council and European Parliament Directives—Other Sectors   573

        4.4   Commission Decisions under Article 86(3)   575

22 INTERNATIONAL ASPECTS OF EC COMPETITION LAW   578

    1   Introduction   578

    2   Extraterritoriality and the Effects Test   580

        2.1   The Principle of Extraterritoriality   580

        2.2   The Group Economic Unit Doctrine   581

        2.3   The Concept of Implementation of an Agreement: *Dyestuffs*
              and *Woodpulp (No. 1)*   582

        2.4   The Merger Regulation: Concentrations with a
              Community Dimension   585

    3   Enforcement Cooperation through Bilateral Measures   587

        3.1   The Need for Cooperation   587

        3.2   Bilateral Agreements Made by the Community   587

        3.3   The Principle of Notification   589

        3.4   Traditional Comity   590

3.5	Positive Comity	590
3.6	The Issue of Confidentiality	591
3.7	Substantive Differences in Law	593
3.8	The Limitations of Bilateral Cooperation	594

4 Proposals for Multilateral Measures — 595

4.1	The Community's Approach	595
4.2	The US Approach	597
4.3	The 1996 WTO *Reference Paper*: Pro-Competitive Regulatory Principles	598
4.4	Application of the *Reference Paper*—Mexican Telecoms	601
4.5	The International Competition Network (ICN)	603

PART III CONCLUSIONS AND PROSPECTS

23 FIFTY YEARS OF THE TREATY OF ROME — 607

1 The Commission's Task 1958–2008 — 607

| 1.1 | The Basic Priorities for the Commission | 607 |
| 1.2 | The Changing Economic Background | 608 |

2 The Commission's Legislative Programme — 610

| 2.1 | The Initial Choices | 610 |
| 2.2 | Block Exemptions | 611 |

3 The Problem of Resources — 613

3.1	Staffing Levels of DG Comp	613
3.2	The Root of the Problem—Notification	614
3.3	The Handling of Complaints	614

4 The Commission and the Community Courts — 615

| 4.1 | The First Thirty Years (1958 to 1988) | 615 |
| 4.2 | The Period from 1989 Onwards | 617 |

5 The Achievements and Failures of the Commission — 619

5.1	The Background	619
5.2	Greater Transparency	621
5.3	Substantive Achievements and Failures	621

24 THE FUTURE OF EUROPEAN COMPETITION LAW — 629

1 Introduction — 629

| 1.1 | Looking Back: Reforms Suggested in the Fourth Edition | 629 |
| 1.2 | The Progress of Reform Since 2003 | 630 |

2   Competition Law: Its Status in the Community Legal Order   631
3   Modernization: The New Order   633
   3.1   The European Competition Network   634
   3.2   Convergence of National Competition Laws   634
   3.3   Powers yet to be Used   637
   3.4   Block Exemptions   638
   3.5   Setting Priorities in 2008   639
   3.6   The Commission's Relationships with National Courts   640
   3.7   The Judicial Architecture of the Community   642
4   Mergers   643
   4.1   Heightened Pressure on the Commission   643
   4.2   Economic Nationalism   645
5   Cartels and Private Enforcement   645
   5.1   Higher and Higher Fines?   645
   5.2   Settlement   647
   5.3   Multiple Leniency Applications   647
   5.4   Private Enforcement   648
6   Dominance   649
7   The Role of Economics and Economists   651
8   The New Economy   652
9   The International Dimension   654

Sources of Law and Bibliography   656
Index   663

TABLE OF CASES FROM THE EUROPEAN COURT OF JUSTICE AND COURT OF FIRST INSTANCE

A. Ahlström Oy v. Commission (Woodpulp I) [1988] ECR I-5193: [1988] 4 CMLR 901 . . . 93, 122, 195, 401, 582–585

A. Ahlström Oy v. Commission (Woodpulp II) [1993] ECR I-1307: [1993] 4 CMLR 407 . . . 93

Aalborg Portland AS v. Commission (Cases C-204, 205, 211, 213, 217 and 219/00P) [2004] ECR I-123 . . . 95, 192

AEG Telefunken v. Commission (Case 107/82) [1983] ECR 3151; [1984] 3 CMLR 325 . . . 86, 88, 233

Aéroports de Paris v. Commission (Case C-82/01P) [2002] ECR I-9297: [2003] 4 CMLR 609 . . . 326

AGCM v. Ente Tabacchi Italiania (Case C-280/06) [2008] 4 CMLR 277 . . . 524, 642

Ahmed Saeed (Case 66/86) [1989] ECR 803; [1990] 4 CMLR 102 . . . 81, 305–306, 570

Airtours v. Commission (Case T-342/99) [2002] ECR II-2585: 5 CMLR 317 . . . 379, 380, 381, 405, 457, 618–619, 625, 630, 643

AKZO v. Commission (Case C-62/86) [1991] ECR I-3359; [1993] 5 CMLR 215 . . . 298, 311, 319–320, 322, 323, 418, 627

Albany International (Case C-67/96) [1999] ECR I-5751; [2000] 4 CMLR 446 . . . 77, 79, 115, 126, 128, 129

Almelo (Case C-393/92) [1994] ECR I-1477 . . . 373

Alpha Flight Services v. Commission (Case T-128/98) [2000] ECR-II-3929: [2001] 4 CMLR 1376 . . . 326

Alsatel v. Novasam (Case 247/86) [1988] ECR 5987; [1990] 4 CMLR 434 . . . 304

Ambulanz Glockner (Case C-475/99) [2002] 4 CMLR 726 . . . 75

Anseau-Navewa v. Commission see IAZ International Belgium v. Commission (Cases 96–102, 104–5, 108, 110–82)

ANTIB v. Commission (Case 272/85) [1987] ECR 2201; [1988] 4 CMLR 677 . . . 137

Arduino (Case C-35/99) [2002] ECR-I-1529 4 CMLR 866 . . . 556

Argos and Littlewoods v. Office of Fair Trading [2004] CAT 24 . . . 96

Asia Motor France (No. 3) (Case T-387/94) [1996] ECR-II-961; 5 CMLR 537 . . . 82

Asnef-Equifax v. Asociación de Usuarios de Servicios Bancarios (Case C-238/05) [2006] ECR I-1125: [2007] 4 CMLR 6 . . . 193

Atlantic Container Line v. Commission (C-149/95P) (R) [1995] ECR I-2165: [1997] 5 CMLR 167 . . . 183

Atlantic Container Line v. Commission (TACA) (Case T-395/94) [2002] ECR II-875: [2002] 4 CMLR 1008 . . . 118, 155, 156, 184, 298

Automec v. Commission (No. 1) (Case T-64/89) [1991] 4 CMLR 177 . . . 46

Automec v. Commission (No. 2) (Case T-24/90) [1992] ECR-II-2223; 5 CMLR 431 . . . 357, 515, 532, 534, 615

B & I Line v. Sealink Harbours [1992] 5 CMLR 255 . . . 359

Bagnasco (Case C-216/96) (Italian Banks) [1999] ECR I-135; 4 CMLR 621 . . . 106

Banks v. British Coal Corporation (Case C-128/92) [1994] ECR I-1209; 5 CMLR 30 . . . 538

BASF (L+F)-Accinauto (Cases T-175 to 176/95 [1999] ECR II-1581; [2000] 4 CMLR 33 . . . 119–120

Bassano (Cases C-140 to 142/94) [1995] ECR I-3257; [1996] 4 CMLR 157 . . . 560

BAT and R. J. Reynolds v. Commission and Philip Morris (Cases 142 and 156/84) [1987] ECR 4487; [1988] 4 CMLR 24 . . . 384, 388, 389

BAT Cigaretten-Fabrieken v. Commission (Case 35/83) [1985] ECR 363; 2 CMLR 470 . . . 289
see also Toltecs-Dorcet Trade Marks in *Table of Commission Decisions*

Bayer/Adalat (Cases C-2/01 and C-3/01P) [2004] ECR I-23: [2004] 4 CMLR 653 . . . 218, 340, 618, 630, 640

Bayer AG v. Commission (Case T-41/96) [2000] ECR II-3383; [2001] 4 CMLR 126 . . . 12, 86, 87

Bayer v. Sülhöfer (Case 65/86) [1988] ECR 5249; [1990] 4 CMLR 182 . . . 272

BBC v. Commission (Case T-69/89) [1991] ECR
II-535; 4 CMLR 669 . . . 300

Becu (Case C-22/98) [1999] ECR I-5665; [2001] 4
CMLR 968 . . . 77, 79

Béguelin (Case 22/71) [1971] ECR 949: [1972]
CMLR 81 . . . 168

Belasco v. Commission (Case 246/82) (Roofing
Felt) [1989] ECR 2117; [1991] 4 CMLR
96 . . . 106

Belgian Radio and Television v. SABAM
(Case 127/73) [1974] ECR 51, 313; 2 CMLR
238 . . . 353, 371, 533, 537, 545, 563

BEMIM v. Commission (Case T-114/92) [1995]
ECR-II-147; [1996] 4 CMLR 305 . . . 532

Bertlesmann AG and Sony Corporation of
America (Case C-423/06P), 10 July 2008, not
yet reported . . . 380, 458, 619

Binon v. Agence et Messagieres de la Presse
(AMP) (Case 243/83) [1985] ECR 2015; 3
CMLR 800 . . . 85, 240

BKA see Bundeskartellamt v. Volkswagen (VW)
(Case C-266/93)

BMW Belgium SA v. Commission (Cases 32 and
36–82/78) [1979] ECR 2435; [1980] 1 CMLR
370 . . . 84

BMW v. ALD Autoleasing (Case C-70/93) [1995]
ECR-I-3439; [1996] 4 CMLR 478 . . . 512

BNIC v. Aubert (Case 136/86) [1987] ECR 4789;
[1988] 4 CMLR 331 . . . 560

BNIC v. Clair (Case 123/83) [1985] ECR 391: 2
CMLR 430 . . . 558, 559

Bodson v. Pompes Funèbres (Case 30/87) [1988]
ECR 2479; [1989] 4 CMLR 984 . . . 304, 318

Boehringer Mannheim v. Commission
(Case 45/69) Quinine Cartel) [1970] ECR
769 . . . 173, 174

BP see British Petroleum v. Commission (Case
77/77)

BPB see British Plasterboard v. Commission
(Case C-310/93)

Brasserie de Haecht v. Wilkin-Janssens (No. 1)
(Case 23/67) [1967] ECR 407; [1968] CMLR
26 . . . 83, 102, 208

Brasserie de Haecht v. Wilkin-Janssens (No. 2)
(Case 48/72) [1973] ECR 77; CMLR 287 . . . 42

Brasserie du Pécheur v. Germany (Case C-46/93)
[1996] ECR I-1029; 1 CMLR 889, AER (EC)
301 . . . 538

Brentjens v. SBVHB (Cases C-115 to 117/97)
[1997] ECR I-6025; [2000] 4 CMLR
566 . . . 129

British Airways v. Commission (Case T-219/99)
[2003] ECR II-5917: [2004] 4 CMLR 19:
Case C-95/04, 15 March 2007, not yet
reported . . . 298, 332, 627, 650

British Leyland v. Commission (Case 226/84)
[1986] ECR 3263; [1987] 1 CMLR 185 . . . 299

British Petroleum v. Commission (Case 77/77)
[1978] ECR 1513; 3 CMLR 174 . . . 336, 338

British Plasterboard (BPB) v. Commission
(Case C-310/93) [1995] ECR I-865; 4 CMLR
718 . . . 327

Bronner (Oscar) v. MediaPrint (Case C-7/97)
[1998] ECR I-7791; [1999] 4 CMLR
112 . . . 361, 362, 524, 600, 619, 626

BRT see Belgian Radio and Television v. SABAM
(Case 127/73)

BT Telespeed see Italy v. Commission (Case
41/83)

Bundeskartellamt (BKA) v. Volkswagen (VW)
(Case C-266/93) [1995] ECR I-3477; [1996] 4
CMLR 505 . . . 202, 204, 512

Carra (Case C-258/98) [2000] ECR I-4217;
[2002] 4 CMLR 285 . . . 567

Cassis de Dijon see Rewe-Zentral v.
Bundesmonopolverwaltung für Branntwein
(Case 120/78)

CBEM v. CLT & IPB (Case 311/84)
(Telemarketing) [1985] ECR 3261; [1986] 2
CMLR 558 . . . 358

Cement Cartel (Cases T-25 to 104/95) [2000]
ECR II-491; 5 CMLR 204 . . . 90, 94, 97, 189,
192

Centrafarm BV v. Sterling Drug Inc (Case 15/74)
[1974] ECR 1147; 2 CMLR 480 . . . 81, 583

Centrafarm BV v. Winthrop BV (Case 16/75)
[1974] ECR 1183; 2 CMLR 480 . . . 81

Chemiefarma NV v. Commission (Case 41/69)
[1970] ECR 661: [1970] CMLR 43 . . . 82

CIF v. Autorita Garante della Concorrenza del
Mercato (Case C-198/01) 30 January 2003 see
Consorzio Industrie Fiammiferi v. AGCM
(Case C-198/01)

Cipolla (Case C-94/04) [2006] ECR
I-11421 . . . 556

CMB see Compagnie Maritime Belge v.
Commission (Case C-395/96P)

CNL-Sucal v. Hag (Hag No. 2) (Case C-10/89)
[1990] ECR I-3711; 3 CMLR 571 . . . 455

Coca-Cola Company v. Commission (Cases
T-125 and 127/97) [2000] ECR-II-1733; 5
CMLR 467 . . . 411–412, 457

Coditel v. Cine Vog Films (No. 1) (Case
62/79) [1980] ECR 881; [1981] 2 CMLR
362 . . . 290–291

Coditel v. Cine Vog Films (No. 2) (Case 262/81)
[1982] ECR 3881; [1983] 1 CMLR 49 . . . 291

Commercial Solvents see Istituto
Chemioterapico Italiano and Commercial

Solvents Corporation v. Commission (Cases 6 to 7/73)

Commission v. BASF AG (Case C-137/92P) see PVC

Commission v. CNST (Case T-513/93) [2000] ECR II-1870; 5 CMLR 614 . . . 561

Commission v. France (Case 167/73) (French Merchant Seaman) [1974] ECR 359; 2 CMLR 216 . . . 43, 134

Commission v. France (Case C-146/00) [2001] ECR-I-9767: 6 December 2001 . . . 573

Commission v. France (Case C-159/94) [1997] ECR I-5815; [1998] 2 CMLR 2373 . . . 570

Commission v. Italy (Case C-35/96) [1998] ECR I-3851; 5 CMLR 889 . . . 561

Commission v. Netherlands (Case C-157/94) [1997] ECR I-5699; [1998] 2 CMLR 373 . . . 570

Commission v. Portugal (Case C-163/99) [2001] ECR I-2613: [2002] 4 CMLR 1319 . . . 326

Commission v. UIC (Case C-264/95P) [1997] 5 CMLR 49 . . . 136–137

Commission v. UK, Denmark, Sweden, Finland, Belgium, Luxembourg, Austria, and Germany (Cases C-466 to 469, 471–2, 475–6/98 (Open Skies), Judgment of 5 November 2002) . . . 133

Commission v. Volkswagen AG [2006] ECR I-6585 . . . 87

Compagnie Générale Maritime v. Commission (Far Eastern Freight Conference) (CaseT-86/95) [2002] ECR II-1011: 4 CMLR 1115 . . . 183

Compagnie Maritime Belge v. Commission (Cases T-24/93 etc [1996] ECR II-1201: [1997] 4 CMLR 273: on appeal, Case C-395/96P [2000] ECR I-1365; 4 CMLR 1076 . . . 301, 302, 311, 322, 373, 376, 378, 379, 380, 381, 618

Compagnie Royal Asturienne des Mines and Rheinzink v. Commission (CRAM and Rheinzink) (Cases 29 and 30/83) [1984] ECR 1679; [1985] 1 CMLR 688 . . . 92, 118, 160

Concordia see De Norre v. Brouwerij Concordia (Case 47/76)

Confederación Española de Empresarios de Estaciones de Servicio v. Compañía de Petróleos SA [2006] ECR I-11987, [2007] 4 CMLR 866 . . . 79

Consorzio Industrie Fiammiferi v. AGCM (Case C-198/01), [2003] ECR I-8055: [2003] 5 CMLR 829 . . . 519, 526, 554

Consten and Grundig v. Commission (Cases 56 and 58/64) [1966] ECR 299: [1966] CMLR 418 . . . 54, 109, 119, 131, 200, 205, 207, 265, 266, 267, 616

Continental Can see Europemballage Corporation and Continental Can Co. Inc v. Commission (Case 6/72)

Conti v. Rossi (Case C-221/99) [2002] ECR I-9359: 4 CMLR 269 . . . 556

Cöoperative Stremsell-en Kleurselfabriek v. Commission (Case 61/80) (Rennet) [1981] ECR 811: [1982] 1 CMLR 240 . . . 152

Corbeau (Case C-320/91) [1993] ECR I-2533; [1995] 4 CMLR 621 . . . 566

Corsica Ferries (No. 1) (Case C-18/93) [1994] ECR I-1783 . . . 367, 565

Corsica Ferries (No. 2) (Case C-266/93) [1998] ECR I-3949; 5 CMLR 402 . . . 566

Courage v. Crehan (Case C-453/99) [2001] ECR I-6297: 5 CMLR 28 . . . 166, 168, 169, 540, 542, 543, 544, 545, 621, 632

Cullet v. Leclerc (Case 231/83) (Leclerc Petrol) [1985] ECR 305; 2 CMLR 524 . . . 554, 556

DaimlerChrysler (Case T-325/01) [2005] ECR II-3319: [2007] 4 CMLR 559 . . . 203, 204

Dan Air v. Commission Case T-2/93 [1994] ECR II-121 . . . 435, 456

Dassonville see Procureur du Roi v. B & G Dassonville (Case 8/74)

de Geus v. Robert Bosch (Case 13/61) [1962] ECR 45; CMLR 1 . . . 42, 63

Delimitis v. Henninger Bräu (Case C-234/89) [1991] ECR I-935; [1992] 5 CMLR 210 . . . 49, 102, 121, 143, 166, 210, 220, 221, 455, 533, 534, 542, 543–544, 545

Demo-Studio Schmidt v. Commission (Case 210/81) [1983] ECR 3045; [1984] 1 CMLR 63 . . . 238

De Norre v. Brouwerji Concordia (Case 47/76) [1977] ECR 65; 1 CMLR 378 . . . 209

Deutsche Telekom v. Commission (Case T-271/03), 10 April 2008, not yet reported . . . 325, 558, 627, 650–651

DGG see Deutsche Grammophon v. Metro (Case 78/70)

Diego Cali & Figli v. Servicio Ecologici Porto di Genova (Case C-343/95) [1997] ECR I-1547; 5 CMLR 484 . . . 75, 79

Distillers Co v. Commission (Case 30/78) [1980] ECR 2229; 3 CMLR 121 . . . 104, 154

Dow Benelux v. Commission (Case 85/87) [1989] ECR 3137; [1991] 4 CMLR 410 . . . 49

Dow Chemical Iberica v. Commission (Cases 97–99/87) [1989] ECR 3165; [1991] 4 CMLR 410 . . . 49, 506

Dutch Books see VBVB and VBBB v. Commission (Cases 43 and 63/82)

Dutch Courier Services (Cases C-48 and 66/90)
[1992] ECR I-565; [1993] 5 CMLR 316 . . . 300

Dyestuffs *see* ICI and Others *v.* Commission
(Cases 48, 49, 51–7/69)

EBU *see* European Broadcasting Union (Cases
T-528, 542–3, 546/93 and Case T-206/99)

Ecco Swiss China Time (Case C-126/97) [1999]
ECR I-3055: [2000] 5 CMLR 816 . . . 168

Echirolles Distribution (Case C-9/99) [2000]
ECR I-8207 . . . 554

ECO Swiss *v.* Benetton (Case C-126/87) [1999]
ECR I-3055; [2000] 5 CMLR 816 . . . 169

EDP *v.* Commission (Case T-87/05) [2005] ECR
II-3745, [2005] 5 CMLR 1436 . . . 458

EMI Electrola *v.* Patricia (Case 341/87) [1989]
ECR 79; 2 CMLR 413 . . . 356

EMI Records Ltd *v.* CBS United Kingdom
Ltd (Case 51/75) [1976] ECR 811; 2 CMLR
235 . . . 288

Endemol *v.* Commission (Case T-221/95) [1999]
ECR II-1299 . . . 418, 435

ENU *v.* Commission (Cases T-458 and 523/93)
[1995] ECR II-2459 . . . 128

Erauw-Jacquery *v.* La Hesbignonne (Case 27/87)
[1988] ECR 1919: 4 CMLR 576 . . . 293

ERT (Case C0260/89) [1991] ECR I-2925; [1994]
4 CMLR 540 . . . 567–568

ETA Fabriques d'Ebauches *v.* DK Investment SA
(Case 31/85) [1985] ECR 3933; [1986] 2 CMLR
675 . . . 207

Eurocontrol *see* SAT *v.* Eurocontrol (Case
C-364/92)

European Night Services (Cases T-374 to 375,
384, 388/94) [1998] ECR II-3141: 5 CMLR
718 . . . 104, 108, 113, 114, 137, 482, 618

Europemballage Corporation and Continental
Can Co Inc *v.* Commission (Case 6/72) [1973]
ECR 215: CMLR 199 . . . 38, 73, 317, 366,
374–376, 385, 386–387, 454, 617, 632, 650

Fédération Française des Sociétés d'Assurance
(Case C-244/94) [1995] ECR-I-4013; [1996] 4
CMLR 536 . . . 76

Fedetab (Cases 209–15, 218/78) (Van
Landewijck) [1980] ECR 3125; [1981] 3 CMLR
134 . . . 149, 557, 558, 617

Fenin *v.* Commission (Case T-319/90) 4 March
2003 . . . 75–76, 79

FFSA/Albany International . . . 79

Fiatagri UK and Others *v.* Commission
(Cases T-34 and 35/92) (Agricultural
Tractor Registration Exchange) [1994] ECR
II-905 . . . 191

Flemish Travel Agents *see* VZW Vereniging
van Vlaamse Reisebureaus *v.* VZW Sociale
dienst van de Plaatselijke en Gewestelijke
Overheidsdiensten (Case 311/85)

FNK and SCK *v.* Commission (Cases T-213/95
and 18/96) [1997] ECR-II 1739: [1998] 4
CMLR 259 . . . 97, 195

Fonderies Roubaix-Wattrelos *v.* Fonderies
Roux (Case 63/75) [1976] ECR 111; 1 CMLR
538 . . . 207

Ford *v.* Commission (Cases 25–26/84) [1985]
ECR 2725; 3 CMLR 528 . . . 85, 88

France Télécom *v.* Commission (Case T-340/03),
30 January 2007, not yet reported . . . 309,
320, 321, 324

France *v.* Commission (Case C-202/88)
(Terminal Equipment) [1991] ECR I-1223;
[1992] 5 CMLR 552 . . . 571, 575

France *v.* Commission (Case C-327/91) [1994]
ECR I-3641; 5 CMLR 517 . . . 587

France *v.* Commission (Cases 19–20/74)
(Kali und Salz) [1975] ECR 499; 2 CMLR
154 . . . 188

France *v.* Commission (Cases C-68/94 and
30/95) (Kali und Salz (No. 2)) [1998] ECR
I-1375; 4 CMLR 829 . . . 379, 406, 428, 446,
625

Francovich and Bonifaci *v.* Italy (Cases C-6
and 9/90) [1991] ECR I-5357; [1993] 2 CMLR
66 . . . 538, 556

French Mercant Seaman *see* Commission *v.*
France (Case C-167/73)

FRUBO *v.* Commission (Case 71/74) [1975] ECR
563; 2 CMLR 123 . . . 130, 196

Gebhard (Case C-55/94) [1995] ECR
I-4165 . . . 338

Gencor Ltd *v.* Commission (Case T-102/96)
[1999] ECR II-753; 4 CMLR 971 . . . 258, 379,
380, 381, 393, 401, 447, 456, 585, 618, 625

General Electric *v.* Commission (Case T-210/01)
[2005] ECR II-5575: [2006] 4 CMLR
686 . . . 427

General Motors Continental *v.* Commission
(Case 26/75) [1975] ECR 1367; [1976] 1 CMLR
95 . . . 299, 316

General Motors *v.* Commission (Case
C-551/03P) [2006] ECR I-3173 . . . 120

Genzyme Limited *v.* Office of Fair Trading
[2004] CAT 4 . . . 325

German Ice Cream *see* Lagnese-Iglo *v.*
Commission (Case T-7/93) and Schöller
Lebensmittel *v.* Commission (Case T-9/93)

German Property Insurers *see* Verband des
Sachversicheres *v.* Commission (Case 45/81)

Germany v. Delta (Case C-153/93) [1994] ECR I-2517; [1996] 4 CMLR 21 . . . 560

Glaxo (Case T-168/01) . . . 219

GlaxoSmithKline v. Commission (Case T-168/01) [2006] ECR II-2969: [2006] 5 CMLR 1623, on appeal Cases C-501 and others . . . 11, 87, 120, 122–123, 151, 154, 155, 340, 618

Gøttrup Klim v. DLG (Case C-250/92) [1994] ECR I-5641; [1996] 4 CMLR 191 . . . 96, 99, 124, 298, 373

Greenwich Film Productions v. SACEM (Case 22/79) [1979] ECR 3275; [1980] 1 CMLR 629 . . . 354

GVL v. Commission (Case 7/82) [1983] ECR 483; 3 CMLR 645 . . . 355

Hag No. 1 see Van Zuylen Frères v. Hag (Case 192/73)

Hag No. 2 see CNL-Sucal v. Hag (Hag No. 2) (Case C-10/89) [1990] ECR I-3711; 3 CMLR 571

Hasselblad v. Commission (Case 86/82) [1984] ECR 883; 1 CMLR 559 . . . 207

Hercules v. Commission (Case C-51/92P) [1999] (Polypropylene) ECR I-4235; 5 CMLR 976 . . . 178

Hercules v. Commission (Case T-7/89) (Polypropylene) [1991] ECR II-1711; [1992] 4 CMLR 84 . . . 83, 94, 178

Hilti v. Commission (Case T-30/89) [1991] ECR II-1439; [1992] 4 CMLR 16: [1994] ECR I-667: 4 CMLR 614 . . . 299, 306, 338, 350, 368

Hoechst v. Commission (Cases 46/87 and 227/88) [1989] ECR 2859; [1991] 4 CMLR 410 . . . 49, 506

Hoffman-La Roche (Case 85/76) (Vitamins) [1979] ECR 461; 3 CMLR 211 . . . 297, 305, 311, 312, 314, 315, 320, 327–328, 330, 331, 351–352, 378, 417

Höfner and Elser v. Macrotron (Case C-41/90) [1991] ECR I-1979; [1993] 4 CMLR 306 . . . 74, 567

Hudson's Bay and Annings v. Danish Fur Breeders' Association (No. 1[1988] OJ L316/43: [1989] 4 CMLR 340 . . . 195

Hugin v. Commission (Case 22/78) [1979] ECR 1869; 3 CMLR 345 . . . 109, 300, 336

Hydrotherm Gerätebau v. Andreoli (Case 170/83) [1984] ECR 2999; [1985] 3 CMLR 224 . . . 78

IAZ International Belgium v. Commission (Cases 96–102, 104–5, 108, 110–82) [1983]

ECR 3369: [1984] 3 CMLR 276 . . . 121, 194, 564

Ice Cream see Langnese-Iglo v. Commission (Case C-279/95)

ICI and Others v. Commission (Cases 48, 49, 51–57/69) (Dyestuffs) [1972] ECR 619; CMLR 557 . . . 89, 96, 174, 176, 177, 508, 581, 582–585, 616

Ijsselcentrale v. Commission (Case T-16/91) [1992] ECR II-2417; [1997] 4 CMLR 453, (Case C-19/93P) [1995] ECR I-3319: [1997] 4 CMLR 392 . . . 568

Impala v. Commission (Case T-464/04) [2006] ECR II-2289, overturned on appeal Case C-413/06 P, 10 July 2008 (not yet reported) . . . 380, 423, 455, 644

IMS Health (Case C-418/01) [2004] ECR I-5039: [2004] 4 CMLR 1543 . . . 348, 349, 350, 363

Inail (Case C-218/00) [2002] ECR I-6911: 4 CMLR 833 . . . 76, 79

Industrie des Poudres Spheriques v. Commission (Case T-5/97) [2001] 4 CMLR 1020 . . . 318

INNO v. ATAB (Case 13/77) [1977] ECR 2115; [1978] 1 CMLR 283 . . . 553–554, 557

IPS see Industrie des Poudres Spheriques v. Commission (Case T-5/97)

Irish Sugar v. Commission (Case T-228/97) [1999] ECR-II-2969; 5 CMLR 1300, on appeal Case C-497/99R [2001] ECR I-5333: 5 CMLR 1082 . . . 81, 326, 379, 381

Istituto Chemioterapico Italiano and Commercial Solvents Corporation v. Commission (Cases 6 to 7/73) [1974] ECR 223; 1 CMLR 309 . . . 109, 333, 336, 583

Italian Banks see Bagnasco (Case C-216/96) (Italian Banks) [1999] ECR I-135; 4 CMLR 621

Italian Flat Glass (Cases T-68, 77, 78/89) [1992] ECR II-1403; 5 CMLR 302 . . . 373, 374–376, 378, 618

Italy v. Commission (Case 41/83) (BT Telespeed) [1985] ECR 873; 2 CMLR 368 . . . 565, 566

Italy v. Council and Commission (Case 32/65) [1966] ECR 389; [1969] CMLR 39 . . . 62, 173, 200

ITT Promedia v. Commission (Case T-111/96) [1998] 5 CMLR 491 . . . 368

Javico v. Yves St Laurent (Case C-306/96) [1998] ECR I-1983; 5 CMLR 172 . . . 68, 108

JJB Sports/All Sports v. Office of Fair Trading [2004] CAT 17 . . . 96

Job Centre Co-op (Case C-55/96) [1997] ECR I-7119; [1998] 4 CMLR 708 . . . 567

John Deere v. Commission (Cases 7 and 8/95)
  [1998] ECR I-3111; 5 CMLR 311 . . . 191
Joynson v. Commission (Case T-231/99) [2002] 5
  CMLR 123 . . . 166

Kali und Salz see France v. Commission (Cases
  19–20/74)
Kali und Salz (No. 2) see France v. Commission
  (Cases C-68/94 and 30/95)
Kesko/Tuko (Case T-22/97) [1999] ECR II-3775;
  [2000] 4 CMLR 335 . . . 435
Koelman v. Commission (Case T-575/93) [1996]
  ECR II-1; 4 CMLR 636: on appeal Case
  C-59/96P [1997] ECR I-4809 . . . 357

La Crespelle (Case C-323/93) [1997] ECR
  I-5077 . . . 568
Ladbroke Tierce (Case T-504/93) [1997] ECR
  II-923; 5 CMLR 309 . . . 348, 361
Lancóme v. Etos (Case 99/79) (Perfume) [1980]
  ECR 2511; [1981] 2 CMLR 164 . . . 233
  see also Perfume Cases (Procureur de la
    République v. Giry and Others)
Langnese-Iglo v. Commission (Case T-7/93)
  (German Ice Cream) [1995] ECR II-1533;
  5 CMLR 602: Case C-279/95) (Ice Cream)
  [1998] ECR I-5609 . . . 220
Leclerc (Case T-19/92) [1997] 4 CMLR
  995 . . . 237
Leclerc Books (Case 229/83) [1985] ECR 1: 2
  CMLR 286 . . . 216, 554, 555
Leclerc Petrol see Cullet v. Leclerc (Case 231/83)
  (Leclerc Petrol) [1985] ECR 305; 2 CMLR 524
Leyland Daf v. Automotive Products [1993] BCC
  389: [1994] BCLC 245 . . . 337
Limburgse Vinyl v. Commission (Cases T-305
  to 307, 313–16, 318, 325, 328–9, 335/94) [1999]
  ECR II-931; 5 CMLR 303; (2003) 4 CMLR
  397 . . . 178

Magill v. Radio Telefis Eireann (RTE) (Cases
  T-69–70/89) RTE, ITP, BBC v. Commission
  [1991] ECR II-485: [1991] 4 CMLR 586; on
  appeal (Case C-241/91P) [1995] ECR I-743: 4
  CMLR 718 . . . 300, 344, 347, 348, 349, 362,
  363, 371, 439, 455, 618, 627
Maize Seed see Nungesser v. Commission (Case
  258/78)
Manfredi (Cases C-295–98/04) [2006] ECR
  I-6619: [2006] 5 CMLR 980 . . . 168
Mannesman v. High Authority (Case 19/61)
  [1962] ECR 357 . . . 74
Maritime Container Network v. Commission
  (Case T-229/94) [1998] 4 CMLR 220 . . . 361

Masterfoods (Case T-65/98) [1998] 5 CMLR
  530: [2003] ECR II-4653: [2004] 4 CMLR 14:
  Case C-344/98) [2001] 4 CMLR 449 . . . 365,
  373–374, 534, 542, 543, 544, 619, 621
Matra Hachette v. Commission (Case T-17/93)
  [1994] ECR-II-595 . . . 150
Maxicar and Others v. Renault (Case 53/87)
  [1988] ECR 6211; [1990] 4 CMLR 265 . . . 300,
  344, 345, 347, 352
MDB v. SPVH (Case C-219/97) [1999] ECR
  I-6121; [2000] 4 CMLR 599 . . . 129
Meca-Medina (Case C-519/04P) [2006] ECR
  I-6991: [2006] 5 CMLR 1023 . . . 115, 116
Meng (Case C-2/91) [1993] ECR I-5751 . . . 556
Merci Convenzionali Porto di Genoa v. Gabrielli
  (Case C-179/90) [1991] ECR I-5889; [1994] 4
  CMLR 422 . . . 564
Metropole (M6) v. Commission (Cases T-185,
  216, 299–300/00) [2002] ECR II-3805: [2003] 4
  CMLR 707 . . . 164
Metropole v. Commission (Cases T-528, 543
  and 546/93) [1996] ECR II-649: 5 CMLR
  386 . . . 162
Metropole v. Commission (Case T-112/99)
  [2001] ECR II-2459: 5 CMLR 1236 . . . 114,
  126
Metropole v. Commission (Case T-206/99)
  [2001] ECR II-1057: [2001] 4 CMLR 39 . . . 164
Metro v. Cartier (Case C-376/92) [1994] ECR
  I-15; 5 CMLR 331 . . . 207, 234, 235
Metro v. Saba (No. 1) (Case 26/76) [1977] ECR
  1857; [1978] 2 CMLR 1 . . . 51, 231, 238
Metro v. Saba (No. 2) (Case 75/84) [1986] ECR
  3021; 1 CMLR 118 . . . 301
Michelin v. Commission (Case 322/81) [1983]
  ECR 3461; [1985] 1 CMLR 282 . . . 303, 305,
  327–329
Michelin II (Case T-203/01) [2003] ECR II-4071:
  [2004] 4 CMLR 923 . . . 330, 331, 332, 333,
  627, 650
Micro Leader Business v. Commission (Case
  T-198/98) [2000] ER II-3989: 4 CMLR
  886 . . . 108
Microsoft v. Commission (Case T-201/04) [2007]
  5 CMLR 11: [2008] 29 ECLR 117 . . . 293, 343,
  363, 618, 627
Miller International v. Commission (Case 19/77)
  [1978] ECR 131: 2 CMLR 334 . . . 119, 207
Ministère Public v. Asjes (Cases 209–213/84)
  (Nouvelles Frontières) [1986] ECR 1425: 3
  CMLR 173 . . . 49, 132, 555
Ministère Public v. Tournier (Case 395/87)
  [1989] ECR 2521; [1991] 4 CMLR 248 . . . 355,
  357

Musik-Vertrieb Membran and K-tel International v. GEMA (Cases 55 and 57/80) [1981] ECR 147; 2 CMLR 44 . . . 356–357

Musique Diffusion Française v. Commission (Case 100/80) (Pioneer) [1983] ECR 1825; 3 CMLR 221 . . . 95

MyTravel v. Commission (Case T-212/03), 9 September 2008 (not yet reported) . . . 644

Napier Brown v. British Sugar [1990] 4 CMLR 196 . . . 325

National Carbonizing Co v. Commission and NCB (Case 109/75R) [1975] ECR 1193; 2 CMLR 457 . . . 325

National Panasonic (UK) v. Commission (Case 136/79) [1980] ECR 2033; 3 CMLR 169 . . . 49

Neste Markinouti v. Youtuuli Ky (Case C-214/99) [2001] 4 CMLR 993 . . . 121–122

Nestlé/Perrier v. Commission (Cases T-96/92 and 12/93) [1995] ECR II-1213/ECR II-1247 . . . 456

Nouvelles Frontières see Ministère Public v. Asjes (Cases 209–213/84) (Nouvelles Frontières) [1986] ECR 1425: 3 CMLR 173

Nungesser v. Commission (Case 258/78) (Maize Seed) [1982] ECR 2015; [1983] 1 CMLR 278 . . . 268, 269, 271

O2 (Germany) v. Commission (Case T-328/03) [2006] ECR II-1231: [2006] 5 CMLR 5 . . . 114, 116

Open Skies see Commission v. UK, Denmark, Sweden, Finland, Belgium, Luxembourg, Austria, and Germany (Cases C-466 to 469, 471–2, 475–6/98 (Open Skies), Judgment of 5 November 2002)

Orkem and Solvay v. Commission (Case 374/87) [1989] ECR 3283; [1991] 4 CMLR 502 . . . 49, 506

Oude Luttikhuis (Case C-399/93) [1995] ECR I-4515; [1996] 5 CMLR 178 . . . 96

Parke, Davis v. Probel (Case 24/67) [1968] ECR 55: CMLR 47 . . . 266, 341, 343, 344, 352

Parker Pen (Case T-77/92) [1994] ECR II-549; [1995] 5 CMLR 435 . . . 119

Pavlov (Cases C-180/98 and 184/98) [2001] ECR I-6451: 4 CMLR 30 . . . 74, 77, 129

Perfume Cases (Procureur de la République v. Giry and Others)(Cases 253/78, 37, 99/79) [1980] ECR 2327, 2481, 2511: [1981] 2 CMLR 99 . . . 233, 236, 240, 253, 535
see also Lancóme v. Etos (Case 99/79)

Peroxygen see Commission v. Solvay and Laporte (Case 81/74) (Peroxygen) [1985] 1 CMLR 481

Peugeot v. Ecosystems (Case T-9/92) [1993] ECR II-493: [1995] 5 CMLR 696 . . . 245

Philip Morris see BAT and R. J. Reynolds v. Commission and Philip Morris (Cases 142 and 156/84) [1987] ECR 4487; [1988] 4 CMLR 24

Pioneer see Musique Diffusion Française v. Commission (Case 100/80) (Pioneer) [1983] ECR 1825; 3 CMLR 221

Pitney Bowes v. Francotype [1990] 3 CMLR 466 . . . 300

Polypropylene see Hercules v. Commission (Case C-51/92P) [1999] (Polypropylene) ECR I-4235; 5 CMLR 976

Poucet and Pistre (Cases C-159 and 160/91) [1993] ECR I-637 . . . 76, 79

Primecrown see Merck & Co v. Primecrown (Cases C-267 and 268/95) ECR I-6285; [1997] 1 CMLR 83

Pronuptia de Paris GmbH. v. Pronuptia de Paris Irmgard Schillgallis (Case 161/84) [1986] ECR 353: 1 CMLR 414 . . . 124, 250, 252, 255

Publishers Association (Case 360/92P) [1995] ECR I-23: 5 CMLR 33 . . . 149, 154

Quantel International v. Quantel SA [1993] 5 CMLR 497 . . . 124

Quinine Cartel see Boehringer Mannheim v. Commission (Case 45/69) Quinine Cartel) [1970] ECR 769

Reiff (Case C-185/91) [1993] ECR I-5801: [1995] 5 CMLR 145 . . . 560

Remia and Nutricia v. Commission (Case 42/84) [1985] ECR 2566: [1987] 1 CMLR 1 . . . 124

Renault see Maxicar and Others v. Renault (Case 53/87) [1988] ECR 6211; [1990] 4 CMLR 265

Rennet see Cöoperative Stremsell-en Kleurselfabriek v. Commission (Case 61/80) (Rennet) [1981] ECR 811: [1982] 1 CMLR 240

Rewe-Zentral v. Bundesmonopolverwaltung für Branntwein (Case 120/78) (Cassis de Dijon) [1979] ECR 649: 3 CMLR 494 . . . 338

Rheinzink see Compagnie Royal Asturienne des Mines and Rheinzink v. Commission (CRAM and Rheinzink) (Cases 29 and 30/83) [1984] ECR 1679; [1985] 1 CMLR 688

Roofing Felt see Belasco v. Commission (Case 246/82) (Roofing Felt) [1989] ECR 2117; [1991] 4 CMLR 96

Roquette (Case C-94/00) [2002] ECR I-9011: [2003] 4 CMLR 46 . . . 506

RTT v. GB/INNO (Case C-18/88) [1991] ECR I-5941 . . . 564

Ruling on the Physical Protection of Nuclear Materials (Case C-1/78) [1978] ECR 2151 . . . 128

Sacchi (Case 155/73) [1974] ECR 409; 2 CMLR
177 . . . 563

SACEM v. Debelle (Case 241/88) [1989] ECR
2811: [1991] 4 CMLR 248 . . . 355

SACEM v. Lucazeau (Case 110/88) [1989] ECR
2811: [1991] 4 CMLR 248 . . . 355

SACEM v. Soumagnac (Case 242/88) [1989] ECR
2811: [1991] 4 CMLR 248 . . . 355

Salonia v. Poidomani and Baglieri (Case 126/80)
[1981] ECR 1563: [1982] 1 CMLR 64 . . . 106,
240

Sandoz v. Commission (Case 227/87) [1990] ECR
145: 4 CMLR 242 . . . 84

SAT v. Eurocontrol (Case C-364/92) [1994] ECR
I-43: 5 CMLR 208 . . . 75, 79

Scandlines Sverige v. Port of Helsingborg [2006]
4 CMLR 1298 . . . 317

Schneider Legrand v. Commission (Case 351/03)
[2008] 4 CMLR 1533: Case C-440/07 . . . 458,
619, 625–626, 643, 644

Schöller Le Bensmittel v. Commission (Case
T-9/93) (German Ice Cream) [1995] ECR
II-1611: 5 CMLR 602 . . . 220

Shaw and Falla v. Commission (Case T-131/99)
[2002] ECR II-2023: 5 CMLR 81 . . . 166

Silvano Raso (Case C-163/96) [1998] ECR I-533:
4 CMLR 737 . . . 564, 565

Sirena v. Eda (Case 40/70) [1971] ECR 69: CMLR
260 . . . 288, 287

Société de Vente de Ciments et Bétons de l'Est
(SVCB) v. Kerpen and Kerpen (Case 319/82)
[1983] ECR 4173: [1985] 1 CMLR 511 . . . 188

Société Technique Minière v. Maschinenbau
Ulm (STM Case) (Case 56/65) [1966] ECR
235: CMLR 357 . . . 63–65, 101, 104, 118, 205,
214

Spain and Others v. Commission (Cases C-271,
281, 289/90) [1992] ECR I-5833 . . . 571

Spanish Banks (Case C-67/91) [1992] ECR
I-4785 . . . 50, 529

Spanish Petrol Stations (Case C-217/05) [2006]
ECR I-11987: [2007] 4 CMLR 181 . . . 203, 204

Spanish Petrol Stations (Case C-279/06), 12
September 2008 (not yet reported) . . . 203,
204

Spediporto v. SMG (Case C-96/94) [1995] ECR
I-2883: 4 CMLR 613 . . . 560

SPO (Case T-29/92) [1995] ECR II-289 . . . 190

SPO v. Commission (Case C-137/95P) [1995]
ECR I-1611 . . . 156

SSI see Stichting Sigaretten Industrie v.
Commission (Cases 240–2, 260–2, 268–9/82)

Stichting Sigaretten Industrie v. Commission
(Cases 240–2, 260–2, 268–9/82) (SSI) 1985]
ECR 3381: [1987] 3 CMLR 661 . . . 557, 558

STM see Société Technique Minière v.
Maschinenbau Ulm (Case 56/65) (STM case)

Stork v. High Authority (Case 1/58) [1959] ECR
17 . . . 42

Sugar Cartel see Suiker Unie v. Commission
(Cases 40–8, 50, 54, 111, 113–14/73) (Sugar
Cartel) [1975] ECR 1663: [1976] 1 CMLR 295

Suiker Unie v. Commission (Cases 40–8, 50, 54,
111, 113–14/73) (Sugar Cartel) [1975] ECR
1663: [1976] 1 CMLR 295 . . . 78–79, 90, 94,
96, 117, 176, 177, 201, 303, 558, 616

Sunday Trading see Stoke on Trent BC v. B & Q
(Case C-169/91) (Sunday Trading) [1990] 3
CMLR 897: [1993] 1 CMLR 426: 2 CMLR 509

SVCB see Société de Vente de Ciments et Bétons
de l'Est v. Kerpen and Kerpen (Case 319/82)

Syfait (Case C-53/03) [2005] ECR I-4609 . . . 12,
219, 338, 340, 642n

see also Syfait II (Sot.Lelos KaiaSia EE v.
GlaxoSmithKline) (Cases C-468/06 to
C-478/06), 16 September 2008, not yet
reported

Syfait II (Sot.Lelos KaiaSia EE v.
GlaxoSmithKline) (Cases C-468/06 to
C-478/06), 16 September 2008, not yet
reported . . . 12, 339–340, 640

TAA (Case T-395/94R) [1995] ECR II-2895:
[1997] 5 CMLR 195 . . . 183

Telefónica (Case C-280/08), appeals pending
Cases T-336/07 and T/398/07 . . . 651

Telemarketing see CBEM v. CLT & IPB (Case
311/84) (Telemarketing) [1985] ECR 3261;
[1986] 2 CMLR 558

Telespeed see Italy v. Commission (Case 41/83)
(BT Telespeed) [1985] ECR 873; 2 CMLR 368

Terminal Equipment see France v. Commission
(Case C-202/88) (Terminal Equipment) [1991]
ECR I-1223; [1992] 5 CMLR 552

Tetra/Laval/Sidel (Case T-5/02) [2002] ECR-II-
4381: 5 CMLR 1182: Case C-12/03 [2005] ECR
I-987 . . . 407, 426, 457, 458, 619, 625, 626, 630,
643

Tetrapak (No. 1) (Case T-51/89) [1990] ECR II-309:
[1991] 4 CMLR 334 . . . 350, 352, 382, 510

Tetrapak (No. 2) (Case C-333/94 P [1996]
ECR I-5951: [1997] 4 CMLR 662/(Case
T-83/91) [1994] ECR II-755: [1997] 4 CMLR
726 . . . 301, 307, 308, 311, 320, 321, 338, 364,
371, 618

Transocean Marine Paint Association v.
Commission (Case 17/74) [1974] ECR 1063: 2
CMLR 459 . . . 44, 157

Tremblay v. Commission (Case C-91/95P)
[1996] ECR I-5547: [1997] 4 CMLR 211: Case

T-224/95 [1997] ECR II-2215: [1998] 4 CMLR 427 . . . 357, 532

Tremblay v. Commission (Case T-5/93) [1995] ECR II-185: [1996] 4 CMLR 305 . . . 532

United Brands v. Commission (Case 27/76) [1978] ECR 207: 1 CMLR 429 . . . 296, 297, 298, 302, 303, 305, 309, 317, 324, 335, 338, 352, 417

UPS Europe v. Commission (Case T-175/99) [2002] 5 CMLR 67 . . . 322

Vand den Bergh Foods v. Commission [2003] ECR II-4653: [2004] 4 CMLR 1 . . . 374

Van der Woude (Case C-222/98) [2000] ECR I-7111: [2001] 4 CMLR 93 . . . 129

Van Eycke v. ASPA (Case 267/86) [1988] ECR 4769: [1990] 4 CMLR 330 . . . 555

Van Gend en Loos (Case 26/62) [1963] ECR 1: CMLR 105 . . . 533

Van Landewijck see Fedetab (Cases 209–15, 218/78) (Van Landewijck) [1980] ECR 3125; [1981] 3 CMLR 134

van Marwijk v. FNK and SCK [1996] 4 CMLR 565 . . . 195

Van Schijndel (Case C-430 to 431/93) [1995] ECR I-4705: [1996] 1 CMLR 801 . . . 169

Van Zuylen Frères v. Hag (Hag No. 1) Case 192/73) [1974] ECR 731: 2 CMLR 127 . . . 455

VBA/Florimex (Case C-265/97P) [1999] ECR I-2061 . . . 130

VBVB and VBBB v. Commission (Cases 43 and 63/82) (Dutch Books) [1984] ECR 19: [1985] 1 CMLR 27 . . . 145, 215

Verband des Sachversicheres v. Commission (Case 45/81) (German Property Insurers) [1987] ECR 405: [1988] 4 CMLR 264 . . . 161

Vereeniging van Cementhandelaren v. Commission (Case 8/72) [1972] ECR 977: [1973] CMLR 7 . . . 83, 106

Vichy (Case T-19/91) [1992] ECR II-415 . . . 236–237

Viho Europe BV v. Commission (Case C-73/95P) [1996] ECR I-5457: [1997] 4 CMLR 419 . . . 80, 581

Vitamins see Hoffman-La Roche (Case 85/76) (Vitamins) [1979] ECR 461; 3 CMLR 211

Völk (Frans) v. Verbaecke (Case 5/69) [1969] ECR 295: CMLR 273 . . . 103

Volkswagen (Case C-338/00) [2003] ECR I-9189: [2004] 4 CMLR 351 . . . 246

Volkswagen (Case T-62/98) [2000] ECR II-2707: [2000] 5 CMLR 853 . . . 246

Volkswagen (Case T-208/01) [2003] ECR II-5141 [2004] 4 CMLR 727 . . . 87

Volvo v. Veng (Eric) (Case 238/87) [1988] ECR 6039: [1989] 4 CMLR 122 . . . 300, 336, 343–344, 345, 347, 352

VZW Vereeniging van Vlaamse Reisebureaus v. VZW Sociale dienst van de Plaatselijke en Gewestelijke Overheidsdiensten (Case 311/85) (Flemish Travel Agents) [1987] ECR 3801: [1989] 4 CMLR 213 . . . 201, 203, 555

Wilhelm (Walt) v. Bundeskartellamt (Case 14/68) [1969] ECR 1: CMLR 100 . . . 382, 508, 509, 510, 511, 534

Windsurfing International v. Commission (Case 193/83) [1986] ECR 611: 3 CMLR 489 . . . 86, 105, 271–273

Woodpulp see A. Ahlström Oy v. Commission (Woodpulp I) [1988] ECR I-5193: [1988] 4 CMLR 901

Wouters (Case C-309/99) [2002] ECR I-1577: 4 CMLR 913 . . . 96, 107, 113, 115, 116

Züchner v. Bayerische Vereinsbank (Case 172/80) [1981] ECR 2021: [1982] 1 CMLR 313 . . . 91, 568

Zunis Holding (Case T-83/92) [1993] ECR II-1169: Case C-480/93P [1996] ECR I-1: 5 CMLR 219 . . . 456

Zwarteveld (Case 2/88) [1990] ECR II-3365: 3 CMLR 457 . . . 50

TABLE OF EUROPEAN COMMISSION DECISIONS

ABG v. Esso and Others [1977] OJ L117/1: [1977] 2 CMLR D1 ... 336–337

Accor/Wagons-Lits (Case IV/M126) [1992] OJ C204/1: [1993] 5 CMLR M13 ... 398, 428

ACEC/Berliet [1968] CMLR D35 ... 486, 489

Adecco/Manpower/Vediorbis (Case M.3419), 5 November 2004 ... 469

Aer Lingus/British Midland Airways [1992] OJ L96/34 ... 360–361

Aerospatiale/Alenia/De Havilland (Case IV/M53) [1991] OJ L334/42; [1992] 4 CMLR M2 ... 409, 412, 427

Agricultural Tractor Registration Exchange [1992] OJ L68/19: [1993] 4 CMLR 358 ... 191–192

Ahlstrom & Others (Woodpulp) [1985] 3 CMLR 474 ... 92

Airtours/First Choice (Case IV/M1524) [1999] 5 CMLR 971 ... 423, 424, 434, 440

Alcan/Pechiney Il (Case COMP/M. 3225), 29 September 2003 ... 411

Alcatel/AEG-KABEL (Case IV/M165) OJ C6/23: [1992] 4 CMLR 80 ... 421

Alcatel/Telettra (Case IV/M18) [1991] 4 CMLR 778 ... 415

Aluminium Cartel [1987] OJ L92/1: 3 CMLR 813 ... 177, 561

American Cyanamid/Shell (Case IV/M354) [1993] 5 CMLR 312 ... 413

AOIP v. Beyrard [1976] OJ L6/8: 1 CMLR D14 ... 267

ARG/Unipart [1988] 4 CMLR 513 ... 201

Arjomari/Wiggins Teape (Case IV/M25) [1991] 4 CMLR 854 ... 397, 399

Armagnac see Pabst and Richarz KG v. BNIA

Astra see BT/Astra

Atka A/S v. BP Kemi A/S and Danske Spritfabrikker [1979] 3 CMLR 684 ... 82, 187

B & I Line v. Sealink Harbours [1992] 5 CMLR 255 ... 359

BA/Virgin [2000] OJ L30/1: 4 CMLR 999 ... 298, 330, 331

BASF/(L+F)-Accinauto [1996] 4 CMLR 811 ... 119–120

BASF/Pantochin/Eurodiol (Case Comp/M2314) [2002] OJ L132/45 ... 428

Bass [1999] OJ L186/1: 5 CMLR 782 ... 166

BAT/Reynolds ... 366

Bayer/Adalat [1996] OJ L201/1: 5 cMLR 416 ... 86

Bayer/Aventis (Case Comp/M2547), 17 April 2002 ... 449

Bayer/Gist-Brocades [1976] 1 CMLR D98 ... 488

Bayo-n-ox [1990] OJ L21/71: 4 CMLR 905 ... 153

Beecham/Parke, Davis [1979] OJ L70/11; 2 CMLR 157 ... 478, 493

Belgian Architects' Association, 24 June 2004 (unpublished) ... 556

Belgian Tiles Cartel (Convention Faïnce case) JO 1167/64 ... 58–59

Bettercare [2002] CAT 7 ... 76

Blackstone/Acetex (Case Comp/M.3625, 13 July 2005 ... 416

Blokker/Toys 'R' Us (Case IV/M890) [1998] OJ L316/1 ... 435

BMW [1975] 1 CMLR D44 ... 243, 244

Boeing/McDonnell Douglas (Case IV/M877) [1997] OJ L336/16; 5 CMLR 270 ... 393, 416, 448, 586, 590

Bosch (Robert)/Rexroth (Case Comp/M2060), 13 December 2000 ... 449

BP/E. on (Case Comp/M2533), 20 December 2001 ... 434

BP/Kellogg [1986] 2 CMLR 619 ... 478–479

British Aerospace/VSEL (Case IV/M528/ CM2851) [1994] OJ C348/6; [1995] 4 CMLR 323 ... 437

British Dental Trade Association [1988] OJ L233/15: [1989] 4 CMLR 1021 ... 196

Brown Boveri/NGK Insulators [1989] 4 CMLR 610 ... 48

BSCH-Champalimaud (Case IV/M1799), 29 November 2001 ... 437

BT/MCI [1994] OJ L223/36; [1995] 5 CMLR 285 ... 590

BT/SES/Astra [1993] OJ L20/23: [1994] 5 CMLR 226 ... 154

Campari [1978] 2 CMLR 397 ... 289

Carbon Gas Technology [1984] 2 CMLR 275 ... 493–494

Cartonboard [1994] OJ L243/1: 5 CMLR 547 . . . 179

CECED Washing Machines [2000] OJ L187/47; 5 CMLR 635 . . . 150, 165, 620

CECIMO (No. 3) [1990] 4 CMLR 231 . . . 196

Cementregeling voor Nederland (Netherlands Cement) [1972] OJ L303/7: [1973] CMLR D149 . . . 187

Charles Jourdan [1989] 4 CMLR 591 . . . 256

Cimbel [1972] OJ L303/24: [1973] CMLR D167 . . . 187

Citric Acid Case [2002] 5 CMLR 1070 . . . 83

Cobelpa VNP [1977] OJ L242/10: 2 CMLR D28 . . . 151, 191

Commission v. Degeto Film [1990] OJ L284/36: 4 CMLR 841 . . . 291

Compari [1978] 2 CMLR 397 . . . 289

Concordato Italiano [1990] OJ L15/25: [1991] 4 CMLR 199 . . . 161

Convention Faïnce see Belgian Tiles Cartel (Convention Faïnce case) JO 1167/64

Courtaulds/Snia (Case IV/MI13) [1992] 4 CMLR 349 . . . 453

Deutsche Bahn 1 P/01/1415 (15 October 2001) . . . 365

Deutsche Telekom [2003] OJ L263/9 . . . 325

Digital/Phillips (Case IV/M129) [1991] 4 CMLR 737 . . . 416

Distillers [1978] OJ L50/16: 1 CMLR 400 . . . 10

Dong/DUC (Commission Press Release IP/03/566, 24 April 2003) . . . 501

Du Pont/ICI (Case IV/M214) [1995] 5 CMLR M41 . . . 410, 441

Dutch Banks [1999] OJ L271/28, [2000] 4 CMLR 137 . . . 107

Dutch Courier Services [1990] OJ L10/47: 4 CMLR 947 . . . 300

EACEM [1998] OJ C12/2: AR 152: [1998] 4 CMLR 502 . . . 165

EBU see European Broadcasting Union

Elactrabel/Energia Italiana/Interpower (Case M.3003), 23 December 2002 . . . 469

Electricité de France (EDF)/London Electricity (Case IV/M1346), 27 January 1999 . . . 434

Eridania/ISI (Case IV/M62) [1991] OJ C204/12; 4 CMLR 663 . . . 397, 399

Eudim [1996] OJ C111/8: [1996] 4 CMLR 871 . . . 192–193

European Aeronautic Defence and Space Company/Nortel Networks (Case Comp/M2546), 10 October 2001 . . . 438

European Broadcasting Union (EBU) [2000] 5 CMLR 650 . . . 164

Exxon/Mobil (Case IV/M1383), 29 September 1999 . . . 449

Far Eastern Freight Conference [1994] OJ L378/17 . . . 183

Fatty Acids [1987] OJ L3/17: [1989] 4 CMLR 445 . . . 190–191

FEG/TU [2000] OJ L39/1: 4 CMLR 1208 . . . 190

Fenex [1996] OJ L181/28: 5 CMLR 332 . . . 100

Floral Düngemittelverkaufs (Floral sales) [1980] OJ L39/51: 2 CMLR 281 . . . 83, 157

FNSEA [2003] OJ L 209/12 . . . 77

1998 Football World Cup [2000] see Nineteen-Ninety-Eight

Ford/Volkswagen [1993] OJ L20/14: 5 CMLR 617 . . . 150

France Telecom/Deutsche Telekom [1996] OJ L239/29, [1997] OJ L47/8; [1997] 4 CMLR 89 . . . 498

Franco-Japanese Ballbearings [1974] OJ L343/19: [1975] 1 CMLR D8 . . . 122

French/West African Ship Owners Conference [1992] OJ L134/1: [1993] 5 CMLR 446 . . . 182

FT/DT see France Telecom/Deutsche Telekom

GE Engine Services/Unison Industries (Case Comp/M2738), 17 April 2002 . . . 435

GE/Honeywell (Case Comp/M2220), 3 July 2001 . . . 364, 416, 426, 426–427, 446, 594

GEMA (No. 1) [1971] CMLR D35 . . . 353–354

Gencor/Lonrho (Case IV/M619) [1996] 4 CMLR 742 . . . 393, 422–423

General Electric Company/VSEL (Case IV/M529/CM2852) [1994] OJ C368/23; [1995] 4 CMLR 323 . . . 437

German Green Dot Scheme (DSD) [2001] OJ L166/1: 5 CMLR 609 . . . 367

GISC [2001] Comp AR 62 . . . 115

Glaxo/SKB (Case IV/M1846), 8 May 2000 . . . 411

Glaxo/Wellcome OJ L302/1; [2002] 4 CMLR 335 . . . 87

Grohe/Ideal Standard 14th Annual Report, p. 61 . . . 240

Grundig/Consten JO [1964] 161/2575; CMLR 489 . . . 53–56, 59, 60, 65, 68, 85, 102, 104, 105, 109, 119, 131, 238

Hag (No. 2) [1990] 3 CMLR 571 . . . 288

Harbour Cases see B & I Line v. Sealink Harbours; Sea Containers v. Stena Sealink and Stena v. . . . DSB

Henkel/Colgate [1972] OJ L14/14 . . . 492

Holland Media Group *see* RTL/Endemol/
Veronica (Case IV/M553)

Hudson's Bay and Annings *v.* Danish Fur
Breeders' Association (No. 1) [1989] OJ
L316/43: 4 CMLR 340 . . . 195

Hummel/Isbecque JO 2581/65; [1963] CMLR
242 . . . 57, 61, 64

IBM Personal Computers [1984] 2 CMLR
342 . . . 168, 233, 238, 347

ICI/BP Chemicals [1985] 2 CMLR
330 . . . 488–489

ICI/Tioxide (Case IV/M73) [1991] 4 CMLR
792 . . . 400

ICI/Wasag [1979] 1 CMLR 403 . . . 480

ICL/Nokia (Case IV/M105) [1991] 4 CMLR
817 . . . 453

IEA *see* International Energy Authority

IFTRA [1974] OJ L160/1: [1975] 2 CMLR
D20 . . . 100

Ijsselcentrale [1992] OJ L28/32: 5 CMLR
154 . . . 568

Interbrew [1996] 5 CMLR 519 . . . 81

International Energy Authority (IEA) [1984] 2
CMLR 186; [1994] 4 CMLR 521 . . . 161, 620

Irish Continental Group *v.* CCI Morlaix
(Harbour) [1995] 5 CMLR 177 . . . 360

Italian Flat Glass [1989] OJ L33/44: [1990] 4
CMLR 535 . . . 375

Italian Raw Tobacco cartel (Case
COMP/C.38/281/B.2) . . . 181

Jaz/Peter [1970] CMLR 129 . . . 485, 489

Johnson & Johnson/Pfizer Consumer
Healthcare (Case Comp/M.4314), 11
December 2006 . . . 427

Kabel und Metallwerke Neymeyer/Luchaire
[1975] OJ L221/24: 2 CMLR D40 . . . 151

Kali und Salz/MDK (Case IV/M308) [1994] OJ
L186/38; 4 CMLR 526 . . . 422

KEWA [1976] 2 CMLR D15 . . . 487, 620

Knorr-Bremse/Allied Signal (Case IV/M377)
[1993] 5 CMLR 535 . . . 409

Kodak [1970] CMLR D19 . . . 80

Langnese-Iglo [1993] OJ L183/1: [1994] 4 CMLR
51 . . . 143

LDPE Cartel [1990] OJ L74/21: 4 CMLR
382 . . . 178

Lehman Brothers/Starwoord/Le Meridien (Case
M.3858), 20 July 2005 . . . 469

Leroy Merlin/Brico (Case Comp/M.2898), 13
December 2002 . . . 432

Lyonnaise/Northumbrian Water (Case IV/
M567) [1995] 4 CMLR 614 . . . 436, 437

Magill (Case 214/91) [1989] 4 CMLR 757 . . . 439

Magneti Marelli/CEAC (Case IV/M43) [1992] 4
CMLR M61 . . . 409, 413

Maison Jallatte/Voss JO 37/66; [1966] CMLR
D1 . . . 57, 61, 64

Maize Seed [1978] 3 CMLR 434 . . . 268

Mannesmann/Hoesch (Case IV/M222) [1992] 5
CMLR 117 . . . 414

Marconi/British Aerospace (Case IV/M1438), 25
June 1999 . . . 438

Maritime Container Network [1994] OJ
L104/34 . . . 361

Martell-DMP [1992] 5 CMLR 582 . . . 81

Masterfoods [1998] OJ L246/1: 5 CMLR
530 . . . 365, 374

MBB/Aerospatiale (Case IV/M17) [1992] 4
CMLR M70 . . . 400

Mediobanca/Generali (Case IV/M159) [1994] 4
CMLR M1 . . . 456

Mercedes Benz-Kässbohrer (Case IV/M477)
[1995] 4 CMLR 600 . . . 409, 414, 415, 427

Michelin (No. 2) [2002] OJ L143/1: 5 CMLR
388 . . . 329

Mitchell Cotts/Sofiltra [1987] OJ L41/31; [1988] 4
CMLR 111 . . . 479

Moosehead/Whitbread [1990] OJ L100/32;
[1991] 4 CMLR 391 . . . 258, 277, 290

National Sulphuric Acid Association [1980] OJ
L260/24: 3 CMLR 429 . . . 178

Nederlandse Cement-Handelsmaatschappij
[1973] CMLR D257 . . . 187

Nestlé/Perrier (Case IV/M190)[1992] OJ L356/1;
[1993] 4 CMLR M17 . . . 410, 415, 421

Nestlé/Ralston Purina (Case Comp/M2337), 27
July 2001 . . . 448

Netherlands Cement *see* Cemenreling voor
Nederland

1998 Football World Cup [2000] 4 CMLR
963 . . . 367

Norske Skog/Parenco/Walsum (Case Comp/
M2499) [2002] 5 CMLR 1309 . . . 423

Northrop Grumman/TRW (Case Comp/
M.2781), 13 September 2002 . . . 438

Odin [1990] OJ L209/15; [1991] 4 CMLR
832 . . . 480

Omega Watches [1970] CMLR D49 . . . 240

Optical Fibres [1986] OJ L236/30 . . . 48, 480

Owen-Illinois/BTR Packaging (Case IV/M1109), 21 April 1998 . . . 444

P & I Clubs [1999] OJ L125/12; 5 CMLR 646 . . . 162

Pabst and Richarz KG v. BNIA (Armagnac) [1976] OJ L231/24: 2 CMLR D63 . . . 558

Paribas/MTH/MBU (Case IV/M50) [1991] OJ C277/18 . . . 400

Penney's Trade Mark [1978] 2 CMLR 100 . . . 289

PepsiCo/General Mills (Case IV/M232) [1992] 5 CMLR 203 . . . 408

Pernod Richard/Diageo (Case Comp/M2268), 8 May 2001 . . . 448

Peroxygen [1985] OJ L35/1: 1 CMLR 481 . . . 94, 176

Phoenix (Global One) [1996] OJ L239/57; [1997] 4 CMLR 147 . . . 150, 499–500

Pilkington/SIV (Case IV/M358) [1994] OJ L158/24 . . . 421

Piloting Tariffs [1998] 4 CMLR 91 . . . 565

Pirelli Edizone/Telecom Italia (Case Comp/ M2574), 29 September 2001 . . . 450

Pittsburgh Corning Europe [1973] CMLR D2 . . . 79, 200

Polypropylene Cartel [1988] OJ L230/1: 4 CMLR 347 . . . 178

Polyvinyl Chloride (PVC) Cartel [1989] OJ L74/1: [1990] 4 CMLR 345 . . . 94, 178

Proctor & Gamble/VPS (Case IV/M430) [1995] 5 CMLR 146 . . . 410

Promatech/Sulzer (Case Comp/M2698), 24 July 2002 . . . 435

Prym/Beka [1973] CMLR D250 . . . 486–487

PVC Cartel [1990] 4 CMLR 435 see Polyvinyl Chloride (PVC) Cartel

Quinine Cartel [1969] CMLR D41 . . . 173

Reuter v. BASF [1976] OJ L254/40: [1976] 2 CMLR D44 . . . 123

Reuters/Telerate (Case Comp/M.3692), 23 May 2005 . . . 432

Rewe/Meinl (Case IV/M1221) 3 February 1999 . . . 418

RTL/Veronica/Endemol (Case IV/M343) [1999] 5 CMLR 611 . . . 435

Sabre-Amadeus . . . 591, 593

Sammelrevers and Einzelrevers [2002] 4 CMLR 1278 . . . 216n

Sandoz/Ciba/Geigy (Case IV/M737), 2 May 1996 . . . 411

Scottish & Newcastle [1999] OL L186/28: 5 CMLR 831 . . . 166

Sea Containers v. Stena Sealink (Harbour) [1994] OJ L15/8 . . . 359

Servicemaster [1989] 4 CMLR 581 . . . 256

Shell/BASF [1998] OJ C81/5 (Case IV/M1041), 23 December 1997 . . . 472

Shell/DEA (Case Comp/M2389), 20 December 2001 . . . 434

Sicasov [1999] OJ L4/27: 4 CMLR 192 . . . 166, 167, 294

Siemens/Fanuc [1988] 4 CMLR 945 . . . 122

SKB/Block Drug (Cases Comp/M2192–3), 11 January 2001 . . . 410–411

SLW/TDV [1972] CMLR D11 . . . 385

Smith & Nephew/Beiersdorf (Case IV/54), 30 January 2001 . . . 471

Spanish Courier Services [1991] 4 CMLR 560 . . . 300

Sprint/France Telecom/Deutsche Telekom (Case Comp/M1741) [1996] OJ L239/57; [1997] 4 CMLR 147 . . . 590

Stena Sealink v. DSB (19940 OJ L55/52 . . . 360

Stichting Baksteen [1994] OJ L131/15: [1995] 4 CMLR 646 . . . 186

Strabag/Walter Bau (Case Comp/M.3754), 23 June 2005 . . . 435

Synthetic Fibres [1984] OJ L207/17: [1985] 1 CMLR 787 . . . 185, 186, 620

Tarmac/Steetly (Case IV/M75) [1992] 4 CMLR 343 . . . 433–434

Telia/Telenor/Schibsted (Case JV/1), 27 May 1998 . . . 474

Tesco/Catteau (Case IV/M301) [1993] 4 CMLR 238 . . . 452

Tetra Pak/Alfa-Laval (Case IV/M68) [1992] 4 CMLR M81 . . . 418

Tetra/Sidel (Case Comp/M2416): [2002] 5 CMLR 1182 . . . 412

Thales/Finmeccaniaca/AAS/Telespazio (Case M.4403), April 2007 . . . 471

Toltecs-Dorcet Trade Marks [1983] 1 CMLR 412 . . . 289

Total/Petrofina (Case Comp/M.1464), 26 March 1999 . . . 431

Totalfina/Elf Acquitane (Case Comp/M1628) [2001] 5 CMLR 682 . . . 415

United International Pictures [1990] 4 CMLR 749 . . . 188

United Reprocessors [1976] 2 CMLR D1 . . . 487

UPM-Kymmene/Heindl (Case Comp/M.2499) [2002] 5 CMLR 1309 . . . 423

UPS/Deutsche Post [2001] OJ L125/27; 5 CMLR 99 . . . 321, 331

URG [1976] 2 CMLR D1 . . . 620

Varta/Bosch (Case IV/M12) [1992] 5 CMLR M1 . . . 445

Viag/Continental Can (Case IV/M81) [1991] 4 CMLR 739 . . . 414

Villeroy-Boch [1985] OJ L376/15 . . . 240

Vimpoltu [1983] OJ L200/44: [1983] 3 CMLR 619 . . . 99

VISA [2002] OJ L293/24; 4 CMLR 168; [2002] OJ L318/17; [2003] 4 CMLR 283 . . . 164

Volkswagen [1998] OJ L124/60, 5 CMLR 33 . . . 217, 246

Volvo/Renault (Case IV/M4) [1991] 4 CMLR 297 . . . 400, 410, 414

Volvo/Scania (Case Comp/M1672) [2001] OJ L143/74 . . . 414, 445

WEA-Filipacchi Music SA [1973] CMLR D43 . . . 84, 119

Wegener/PCM (Case M.3817), 7 July 2005 . . . 474–475

Whitbread [1999] OJ L88/26: [1999] 5 CMLR 118 . . . 166

Woodpulp see Ahlstrom & Others (Woodpulp) [1985] 3 CMLR 474

1998 World Cup [2000] see Nineteen-Ninety-Eight

Zanussi [1979] 1 CMLR 81 . . . 207

TABLE OF CASES FROM OTHER JURISDICTIONS

NETHERLANDS

Grundig, 12 January 1962 (Supreme Court) . . . 53

UNITED KINGDOM

Bettercare [2002] Comp AR 226 . . . 76

Coin Controls v. Suzo [1997] FSR 660 . . . 532

Cutsforth v. Mansfield Inns [1986] 1 All ER 577 . . . 537, 545

Garden Cottage Foods Ltd v. Milk Marketing Board [1982] All ER 292; QB 1114 (CA); [1983] 3 WLR 143; 2 All ER 770; 3 CMLR 43; [1984] AC 130 (HL) . . . 536

Gibbs Mew v. Gemmell [1998] EuLR 588 . . . 539

Hasselblad (GB) v. Orbinson [1985] 1 All ER 173; 2 WLR 1: QB 475 . . . 532n

Iberian v. BPB [1996] 2 CMLR 601; [1997] EuLR 1 . . . 539

Inntrepreneur v. Crehan [2006] UKHL 38 . . . 544n

MTV Europe v. BMG Records [1997] EuLR 100; 1 CMLR 867 . . . 542

Napp Pharmaceuticals v. Director General of Fair Trading [2002] Comp AR 13; European Commercial Cases 177 . . . 318–319, 322

National Sulphuric Acid Association's Agreement [1963] 3 All ER 73; LR 4 RP 169; [1966] LR 6 RP 210 . . . 178

Passmore v. Morland [1999] 3 All ER 1005: [1999] 1 CMLR 1129 . . . 169, 170, 540

Pearce v. Ove Arup [1997] FSR 641 . . . 532n

Premier League [1999] UKCLR 258 . . . 641n

At the Races Ltd v. The British Horseracing Board [2007] UKCLR 309 . . . 317n

Williams v. Welsh RFC [1999] EuLR 195 . . . 542

UNITED STATES

Brooke Group Ltd v. Brown & Williamson Tobacco Corp, 509 US 209 (1993) . . . 321n

California Dental Association v. FTC 119 S Ct Reports 1604 [1999] . . . 116

Hanover Shoe v. United Shoe Machinery Corp 392 US 481 (1968) . . . 549, 550

Illinois Brick Co v. State of Illinois 431 US 720 (1968) . . . 549, 550

Leegin Creative Leather Products v. PSKS Inc., 171 Fed. Appx 464 (5th Cir., March 20 2006) . . . 215, 639, 651–652

MCI Communications Corp v. AT&T 464 US 891 (1983) . . . 600n

Monsanto v. Sprayrite 104 S Ct Reports 1551 (1984) . . . 89

Perma Life Mufflers v. International Parts Corp 392 US 134 (1968) . . . 541

US v. Dupont ('Cellophane' case) 351 US 377: 76 S Ct 994 (1956) . . . 310

US v. Jerrold Electronics 187 F Supp 545 (EDPa) 1960 . . . 364n

US v. Microsoft, 253 F, 3d 34 DC Circ. 2001 . . . 364n

US v. Terminal Railroad Association of St Louis 224 US 383 (1912) . . . 16

US v. White Motors 372 US 253 (1963) . . . 63

UNITED KINGDOM MONOPOLIES AND MERGERS COMMISSION REPORTS

British Aerospace/VSEL Cm. 2851 (1995) . . . 437n

Collective Licensing, Cm. 530 (1988) . . . 353n

GEC/VSEL Cm. 2852 (1995) . . . 437n

Performing Rights Society, Cm. 314 (1996) . . . 353n

TABLE OF EUROPEAN COMMUNITY TREATIES

Constitutional Treaty 2004 . . . 632

Single European Act 1987 . . . 5, 656n

Treaty of Amsterdam 1997 . . . 5n, 569, 656n
   Art. 3(1)(g) . . . 8n, 553, 554
Treaty of Lisbon 2007 . . . 631, 632, 633, 656n
Treaty of Nice 2003 . . . 5n, 642, 656n
Treaty of Paris 1951 (ECSC Treaty) . . . 5, 24n,
   27, 28
   Art. 1 . . . 27
   Art. 2 . . . 27
   Art. 3 . . . 27, 34
   Art. 4 . . . 27, 34
     (d) . . . 27, 28
   Art. 5 . . . 27, 34
   Art. 65 . . . 28, 33–34, 37, 38, 83, 118, 128
     (1) . . . 28–29
     (2) . . . 29
     (4)–(5) . . . 29
   Art. 66 . . . 28, 29, 33, 34, 38, 128
     (1)–(5) . . . 38
     (3) . . . 29
     (7) . . . 30, 38
   Art. 67 . . . 30

Treaty of Rome 1957 (EC Treaty) . . . 4, 5, 22, 32,
   33, 655
   Art. 1 . . . 34
   Arts. 1–7 . . . 34
   Art. 2 . . . 34, 456, 510, 511
   Art. 3 . . . 19, 34
     (f) . . . 8n, 34, 386, 503
     (1)(g) . . . 8, 34n, 511, 607, 610, 632
   Art. 6 . . . 367
   Art. 7 . . . 355
   Art. 10 . . . 534, 535, 539n, 553, 554, 556, 560n,
   561, 562, 637
   Art. 12 . . . 34, 367, 533n
   Art. 16 . . . 569
   Art. 28 . . . 87, 262, 265, 266, 357, 554, 571
   Arts. 28–30 . . . 6, 266, 345, 356
   Art. 29 . . . 262

Art. 30 . . . 55, 87, 262, 265, 266, 341, 346, 554
Art. 31 . . . 562
Art. 33 . . . 130
Art. 36 . . . 129
Art. 37 . . . 129
Art. 39 . . . 77, 134, 135, 562, 564
Art. 43 . . . 562
   (2) . . . 267n
Art. 46 . . . 567
Art. 49 . . . 562
Art. 59 . . . 291
Art. 70 . . . 135
Arts. 70–80 . . . 131
Art. 80(2) . . . 135
Art. 81 . . . 6, 8, 21, 24, 29, 33–35, 36–37, 39,
   40, 41, 42, 43, 45, 46, 48, 50, 51, 53n, 57,
   58, 59, 62, 63, 64, 65, 66, 67, 73, 74, 75, 76,
   77, 78, 79, 80, 81, 83, 88, 90, 91, 96, 97, 98,
   99, 101, 103, 104n, 105–107, 107, 109–110,
   111, 113, 114, 115, 116, 117, 121, 122, 125,
   127, 128, 129, 130, 132, 133, 135, 136, 137,
   138, 139, 144, 147, 169, 170, 173, 176, 180,
   184, 188, 193, 194, 196, 199, 200, 202, 204,
   207n, 208, 216, 217, 218, 219, 220, 221, 222,
   230, 235, 238, 242, 246, 253, 259, 261, 264,
   265, 274, 275, 283, 285, 286, 288, 292, 294,
   295, 296, 303, 318, 339, 357, 367n, 370–383,
   372, 373, 375, 376, 384, 385, 386, 387, 388,
   389, 403, 406, 408, 439, 444, 453, 454, 455,
   463, 464, 465, 467, 471, 473, 475–484, 480,
   490, 491, 497, 498, 500, 502, 503, 504, 506,
   507, 508, 510, 513, 514, 517, 518, 519, 520,
   521, 522, 523, 525, 527, 531, 532, 533, 534,
   535, 537, 539, 540, 541, 543, 544, 545, 546,
   552–553, 553, 555, 556, 557, 558, 559, 560,
   560n, 561, 562, 568, 571, 573, 574, 575, 578,
   578n, 609, 610, 611, 611n, 614, 615, 616, 617,
   618, 622, 623, 629, 630, 634, 636–637, 637,
   638, 641, 650, 651, 654, 657
   (1) . . . 3, 6, 35, 37, 46, 48, 49, 54, 55, 56, 60,
   61, 63–65, 73–100, 101–137, 112, 138–
   170, 139, 144, 145, 170, 171, 172, 175, 177,
   178, 181, 182, 187, 188, 189, 190, 195, 196,
   200, 201n, 202, 204, 205, 206, 209, 210,
   214–215, 217, 218, 220, 221, 225, 230–231,
   232, 233, 234, 235, 236, 237, 239, 250,
   253, 254–255, 256n, 258, 263, 264, 265,
   266, 267, 269–270, 272, 273, 279, 281,

284, 285, 289, 290, 291, 294, 337, 373, 374,
382, 384, 399, 451, 453, 462, 463, 464,
470, 472, 473, 474, 475, 476–477, 479,
480, 481, 482, 483, 491, 492, 494, 497,
500, 504, 507, 509, 512, 513, 514, 516, 517,
518, 526, 533, 534, 535, 540, 541, 543,
544, 557, 560, 615, 620, 622, 623

(a) . . . 118, 173, 215

(b) . . . 118, 184

(c) . . . 118

(d)–(e) . . . 118

(2) . . . 6, 46, 55, 56, 131, 168–170, 253, 371,
389, 514, 518, 533, 614

(3) . . . 3, 6, 19, 23, 35, 38, 41, 44, 45, 46, 48,
49, 51, 57, 58, 59, 60, 61, 62, 63, 64, 65,
68, 85, 86, 87, 99, 112, 113, 114, 115, 116,
117, 126, 130, 132, 135, 138–170, 178, 183,
186, 187, 188, 189, 194, 196, 206, 209,
213n, 219, 228, 232, 234, 235n, 237, 242,
244, 255, 259, 263, 264n, 267, 269, 270,
281, 285, 289, 292, 293, 294, 337, 340n,
371, 374, 383, 399, 453, 462, 463, 464,
470, 472, 473, 474, 475, 477, 478, 479, 480,
481, 482, 483–484, 486, 487, 490, 493,
496, 497, 498, 503, 504, 507–514, 511,
513, 514, 515, 516, 517, 518, 519, 525, 526,
533n, 534, 540, 542, 543, 544, 546, 565,
568, 618, 620, 623, 624, 633, 638, 641

(c) . . . 372

Arts. 81–82 . . . 69n, 267n, 350n, 352n

Arts. 81–86 . . . 38, 503n

Arts. 81–89 . . . 5, 33, 35, 40, 127–128, 552

Art. 82 . . . l, 5, 13n, 21, 24, 30, 33–35, 36–37,
38, 39, 40, 41, 43, 45, 46, 49, 50, 51, 62, 63,
65, 67, 73n, 75, 76n, 77, 81n, 86, 97, 105–107,
109–110, 128, 132, 133, 135, 136, 137, 139,
144, 176, 196, 197, 219n, 222, 228, 237, 261,
263, 264, 278, 288, 292, 293, 295–313, 307,
314–368, 370–383, 372, 385, 386, 387, 389,
403, 404, 406, 407, 408, 417, 420, 427, 439,
444, 454, 455, 502, 503, 504, 506, 508, 513,
514, 516, 517, 518, 519, 520, 521, 522, 523, 525,
526, 527, 531, 532, 533, 534, 535, 537, 539,
543, 544, 545, 546, 552–553, 554, 557, 558,
560, 561, 562, 564, 565, 567–568, 571, 573,
574, 575, 576, 578, 578n, 609, 610, 614, 615,
616, 617, 618, 626–627, 629, 630, 631, 633,
634, 637, 638, 641, 649, 650, 651, 654, 657

(57) . . . 196

(a) . . . 316, 367

(a)–(d) . . . 372

(c) . . . 324, 576

(d) . . . 364

Art. 83 . . . 35, 40–41, 45, 60, 132, 141, 372,
503n, 504, 571

(1) . . . 40

(2) . . . 41

(a)–(b) . . . 41

(e) . . . 37, 38, 503

Arts. 83–6 . . . 610

Art. 84 . . . 35, 37, 38, 41, 49, 132, 372, 504, 555

(2) . . . 134

Art. 85 . . . 35, 37, 38, 41, 52, 132, 133, 372,
504, 555

Arts. 85–86 . . . 30n

Arts. 85–90 . . . 503n

Art. 86 . . . 35, 77, 324n, 360, 502, 515, 564,
565, 566, 567, 568, 570, 571, 575, 576

(1) . . . 562–570, 565

(2) . . . 116n, 128, 163, 353, 562–570,
565–567

(3) . . . 7, 150, 296, 315, 497, 515, 563, 569n,
570–576, 575–576, 609, 613, 626–627

Arts. 86–89 . . . 35

Art. 87 . . . 503n

Arts. 87–89 . . . 30, 35

Art. 95 . . . 571, 573

Art. 128(4) . . . 217

Art. 130(a) . . . 456

Art. 211 . . . 40, 140

Art. 220 . . . 643

Art. 225 . . . 643

Art. 225a . . . 643

Art. 226 . . . 571

Art. 229 . . . 45, 51

Art. 230 . . . 51, 68, 140, 146, 253, 315, 455, 615,
616, 642, 644

(2) . . . 455

Art. 232 . . . 140

Art. 234 . . . 53n, 64, 68, 75, 78, 91, 101, 103,
106, 108, 125, 131, 132, 168, 188, 207n, 209,
221, 233, 234, 236, 253, 288, 304, 305, 315,
339, 341, 349, 353, 355–356, 358, 362, 373,
455, 507, 524, 532, 533, 534, 540, 542, 544,
553–554, 555, 560, 560n, 566, 567, 569, 615,
616, 617, 619, 621, 630, 642, 643

Art. 288 . . . 644

Art. 295 . . . 55, 562

Art. 296 . . . 127, 430, 431, 437–438

Art. 298 . . . 127

Art. 305

(1) . . . 127

(2) . . . 128

Art. 308 . . . 387

Treaty on European Union 1993
(Maastricht) . . . 5n, 8n, 386n, 656n

Art. 4(1) . . . 553

TABLE OF AGREEMENTS
AND CONVENTIONS

EC Treaty of Co-operation—Canada 1999 . . . 588, 591, 628

EC Treaty of Co-operation—Japan . . . 588, 628

EC Treaty of Co-operation—Russian Federation 1997 . . . 589

EC Treaty of Co-operation—South Africa 1999 . . . 589

EC Treaty of Co-operation—USA 1991 . . . 587–590, 591, 628

EEA Agreement
Arts. 53–54 . . . 578

Euro-Mediterranean Agreement (EC and Israel) 2000 . . . 588

European Convention on Human Rights . . . 25
Art. 6 . . . 617n

General Agreement on Tariffs and Trade (GATT)

Art. III . . . 598

General Agreement on Trade and Services (GATS) . . . 599, 602
Art. XVII . . . 598

Luxembourg Patent Convention 1975
Art. 43(2) . . . 267

MOU between Korea and Commission 2004 . . . 588–589

Partnership and Cooperation Agreement between EC and Ukraine 1998 . . . 589

Political Coordination and Cooperation Agreement—EC and Mexico 2000 . . . 588

Potsdam Agreement 1945 . . . 26

Vienna Convention on the Law of Treaties 1969 . . . 602

TABLE OF EUROPEAN COMMUNITY
SECONDARY LEGISLATION

These are listed in chronological order of year

DIRECTIVES

Dir. 80/723 Transparency of Relationships ... 563n

Dir. 88/301 Terminal Equipment ... 570, 571, 572, 575

Dir. 89/104 Trade Marks ... 293n

Dir. 90/388 Telecommunications Services ... 571, 572

Dir. 91/250 Software Protection ... 292

    Art. 6 ... 347

Dir. 93/98 Term of Copyright Protection ... 287n

Dir. 94/46 Telecommunications ... 564, 571, 572

Dir. 95/51 Cable TV Networks ... 572

Dir. 96/2 Mobile Telephones ... 572

Dir. 96/19 Full Competition Telecommunications ... 150, 572

Dir. 96/92 Electricity ... 573

Dir. 97/67 Postal Services ... 574

Dir 98/30 Gas ... 573

Dir. 2002/77 Electronic Communications Networks and Services (Antitrust) ... 572–573

Dir. 2006/111 Transparency of Financial Relations ... 563

REGULATIONS

Reg. 17/62 ... 5, 21n, 41, 44–45, 45–52, 52–53, 57, 61, 62, 63–65, 67, 69, 112, 135, 138, 140, 144, 168, 200, 205, 264, 266, 281, 320, 372, 464, 465, 477, 488, 503, 504–505, 506, 507, 513, 515, 517, 525, 527, 531, 616

    Art. 2 ... 145

    Art. 4 ... 52

        (1) ... 144

        (2) ... 145

    Art. 9

        (1) ... 146, 504

        (3) ... 516

    Art. 1 ... 42n, 46, 525

    Art 1–9 ... 49

    Art. 2 ... 46

    Art. 3

        (2) ... 46

        (3) ... 46

    Art. 4 ... 46, 48

        (1) ... 46, 47

        (2) ... 47

    Art. 5 ... 46, 48

    Art. 6 ... 46, 48

    Art. 8 ... 48

    Art. 9 ... 49

        (1) ... 144

        (3) ... 49, 533

    Art. 10 ... 50, 51, 504

        (2) ... 50, 505

        (3) ... 50, 505

    Art. 10–14 ... 49–50

    Art. 11 ... 50, 144

        (1) ... 505

    Arts. 11–14 ... 505

    Art. 12 ... 65, 573

    Art. 13 ... 50

        (1) ... 505

    Art. 14 ... 49, 144, 505, 506

        (2) ... 49n, 505

        (3) ... 49n, 181, 505

        (6) ... 505

    Art. 15 ... 51

        (6) ... 51

    Arts. 15–25 ... 51–52

    Art. 16 ... 51

    Art. 19 ... 51

        (3) ... 51

    Art. 20 ... 529

    Art. 21 ... 52

Reg. 26/62 Competition Rules—Agricultural Sector ... 131

    Art. 1 ... 130

    Art. 2 ... 130

        (1) ... 131

Reg. 27/62 Notification Arrangements ... 53

Reg. 99/63 Hearings of Individual Cases ... 53

    Art. 2 ... 53

Reg. 19/65 Block Exemptions—Exclusive
  Distribution and Exclusive Purchasing
  and Industrial Property Rights
  Licences . . . 60–65, 141n, 142, 213n, 228n,
  264, 266, 282n, 510
  Art. 7 . . . 62
Reg. 67/67 Block Exemptions—Specified Forms
  of Exclusive Distribution and Purchasing
  Arrangements . . . 68–69, 73, 78, 205, 206,
  208, 209, 252n, 253, 254, 611
  Recitals . . . 205n
Reg. 1017/68 Competition Rules—Road, Rail
  and Inland Waterways Sectors . . . 137, 141n,
  183
  Arts 3–4 . . . 136
Reg. 2821/71 on Horizontal
  Agreements . . . 141n
Reg. 2822/71 amending Reg. 17/62 . . . 47
Reg. 4056/82 Block Exemption—International
  Maritime Transport Services . . . 108
Reg. 1983/83 Block Exemption—Exclusive
  Distribution Agreements . . . 143, 209, 264n,
  611
Reg. 1984/83 Block Exemption—Exclusive
  Purchasing Agreements . . . 143, 209, 220, 227,
  256, 264n, 533, 539, 611, 612
Reg. 2349/84 Patent Block Exemption . . . 264n,
  271, 276, 278, 351, 382
Reg. 123/85 Block Exemption—Automotive
  Dealers . . . 245, 512, 532, 612
Reg. 417/85 Block Exemption—Specialization
  Agreements . . . 489–490
Reg. 418/85 Block Exemption—R & D
  Agreements
  Art. 6 . . . 496
Reg. 4056/86 Competition Rules—Maritime
  Transport . . . 135–136, 141n, 182, 183, 376,
  377, 638
  Art. 8 . . . 378
Reg. 3975/87 Competition Rules—Air
  Transport . . . 133
Reg. 3976/87 Competition Rules—Air
  Transport . . . 133, 141n
Reg. 4087/88 Block Exemption—Franchise
  Agreements . . . 255–257, 611
  Art. 2 . . . 255
  Art. 8 . . . 256
  Art. 16 . . . 51
Reg. 556/89 Block Exemption—Know-how
  Licensing Agreements . . . 274–277, 290
Reg. 4064/89 Merger Regulation (ECMR) . . . 7,
  133, 140n, 374–375, 379, 390, 430, 431, 463, 609
  Art. 1 . . . 390

  (3) . . . 391
  Art. 2 . . . 278, 379n, 391
  Art. 9
  (3) . . . 431n, 432n
  Recitals
  13 . . . 456
Reg. 1534/91 for insurance sector
  agreements . . . 141n
Reg. 479/92 Block Exemption—Liner Shipping
  Agreements . . . 136
Reg. 151/93 amending Reg. 417/85 . . . 489
Reg. 1617/93 Block Exemption—
  Agreements for Air Services (Technical
  Co-ordination) . . . 133
Reg. 2894/94 concerning Arrangements for
  Implementing Agreement on EEA . . . 589n
Reg. 870/95 Block Exemption—Liner
  Shipping Agreements (Maritime Transport
  Services) . . . 136
Reg. 1475/95 Block Exemption—Motor Vehicle
  Distribution Agreements . . . 245, 246, 612
Reg. 240/96 Block Exemption—Technology
  Transfer Agreements . . . 48n, 142, 142n,
  277–281, 281–287, 612, 630, 638
  Art. 1(1) . . . 279
  Art. 2 . . . 279, 280
  Art. 3 . . . 280
  Art. 4 . . . 280
  Art. 5 . . . 281
Reg. 1310/97 amending Reg. 4064/89 . . . 465
  Art. 1
  (b) . . . 393n
Reg. 1582/97 Notification of Mergers . . . 143n
Reg. 447/98 extending Reg. 418/85 . . . 494–496
Reg. 1215/99 amending Reg. 17/62 . . . 213n,
  228n
Reg. 1216/99 amending Reg. 17/62 . . . 44–45, 47,
  145, 614, 620
Reg. 2790/99 Block Exemption—Vertical
  Restraints . . . 6, 48, 113, 126, 141, 143, 145,
  213n, 221–228, 227, 230, 239–242, 246–247,
  257–258, 281, 289, 451, 453, 489, 517, 527, 612,
  614, 620, 621, 638
  Art. 1 . . . 226n
  (d) . . . 241
  Art. 2
  (1) . . . 223, 257
  (3) . . . 224, 257, 258, 259
  (4) . . . 223n
  Art. 3 . . . 222
  Art. 4 . . . 143n, 224, 226

(a) ... 225

(b) ... 225, 241

(c) ... 225, 241

(d) ... 225–226, 241

(e) ... 226

Art. 5 ... 143n, 224, 226, 227

(a) ... 227

(b) ... 258

(c) ... 242

Art. 6 ... 143n, 242

Art. 7 ... 143n, 227–228

Art. 8 ... 226, 242

Reg. 823/2000 Liner Shipping Agreements for Maritime Transport ... 136, 141

Reg. 2658/2000 Block Exemption—Specialization Agreements ... 113, 141, 281, 484, 489–490, 612

Art. 2 ... 490, 495

Art. 4 ... 490

Reg. 2659/2000 Block Exemption—Research and Development Agreements ... 113, 141, 281, 484, 494–496, 612

Art. 1 ... 495

Art. 5 ... 496

Art. 6 ... 495

Reg. 1400/2002 Block Exemption—Motor Vehicles ... 141, 224n, 245–247, 247–249, 612, 622

Art. 3(1) ... 247, 248

Art. 4(1)(b) ... 235

Recital 17 ... 235

Reg. 1/2003 Modernization Regulation ... 6, 21n, 105, 114, 133, 136, 139, 144, 146, 284, 320, 372, 444, 445, 450, 451, 454, 463–464, 465n, 481, 503, 504, 513, 518–519, 522, 523, 525–530, 530, 542–545, 546, 615, 624, 630, 635, 638, 639, 640–641, 642

Art. 1 ... 525

Art. 2 ... 146, 526

Art. 3 ... 454, 513, 526, 529, 543, 633

(1)–(2) ... 513, 514

Art. 5 ... 526

Art. 6 ... 543, 544

Arts. 7–9 ... 526

Art. 11 ... 526

(3)–(4) ... 528

(6) ... 528, 633, 638

Art. 12 ... 529, 637

(2) ... 529

Art. 13 ... 528

Arts. 13–16 ... 526

Art. 14 ... 140n, 142

Art. 15 ... 529–530, 544, 641

(1) ... 544

(2) ... 544, 641

Art. 16

(1) ... 544

(2) ... 529

Art. 17 ... 527, 633

Arts. 17–21 ... 527

Art. 19 ... 527

Art. 20

(4) ... 181

Arts. 20–1 ... 320n

Art. 22 ... 527

Art. 29 ... 143n

Art. 29(2) ... 527

Art. 30 ... 637n

Recitals ... 542–543

3–4 ... 543

7 ... 543

14 ... 637

21 ... 543

22 ... 543

27 ... 543

38 ... 637

Reg. 358/2003 Block Exemption ... 141, 639

Reg. 139/2004 Merger Regulation ... 7, 19, 125, 140n, 375n, 379, 384–391, 391–398, 405, 424, 431, 439, 457, 462, 463–464, 481, 613, 626, 631, 657

Art. 1 ... 387, 392, 443, 462, 464, 470–471, 585

Art. 2 ... 366, 374, 386, 403, 404, 406, 427, 447

(1) ... 403–404, 406

(1)–(3) ... 470–472

(2) ... 404, 406, 416, 463, 470

(3) ... 404, 406, 416

(4) ... 399, 463, 470, 472–475

(5) ... 470, 472–475

Art. 3 ... 432, 456

(1) ... 398, 464–465

(1)(b) ... 465

(1)(g) ... 374, 386n

(2) ... 398, 464–465, 500

(4) ... 465

(5) ... 400–401

Art. 4 ... 442–443

(1) ... 442

(4) . . . 431–432, 433
(5) . . . 431, 432–433
Art. 5 . . . 392, 464, 470–471
 (1) . . . 394, 585
 (2) . . . 392
 (3) . . . 396–398
 (4) . . . 394, 396–398, 399, 400
 (4)(b) . . . 397, 399
Art. 6 . . . 403
 (1) . . . 470
 (1)(a) . . . 403
 (1)(b) . . . 403, 437, 447, 450
 (1)(c) . . . 403, 447, 471
 (2) . . . 446, 471
 (3) . . . 449
Art. 7
 (2) . . . 442
Art. 8
 (1) . . . 477
 (2) . . . 443–444, 446, 450
 (3) . . . 445, 449
Art. 9 . . . 431, 433–435, 436, 439
 (1) . . . 433
 (3) . . . 434
Art. 10 . . . 439
 (5) . . . 446
Art. 11 . . . 443
Art. 13
 (2) . . . 444
Art. 14 . . . 444, 455
 (2)(d) . . . 449
Arts. 14–16 . . . 445
Art. 15 . . . 444, 455
 (1)(c) . . . 449
Art. 16 . . . 455
Art. 17 . . . 444–445
Art. 18 . . . 445
Art. 19 . . . 445
Art. 21 . . . 437
 (1) . . . 430, 454
 (2) . . . 455
 (4) . . . 431, 436–437
Art. 22 . . . 431, 435–436

Recital 21 . . . 450, 451
Recital 25 . . . 416
Recital 32 . . . 301
Reg. 772/2004 on Technology Transfer
 Agreements . . . 126, 141, 142n, 281–287,
 289–290, 453, 612, 638
 Art. 1
  (1)(b) . . . 289
 Art. 2 . . . 284
 Art. 3 . . . 284–285
 Art. 4 . . . 285–286
 Art. 5 . . . 286
  (1)(c) . . . 290n
 Art. 6 . . . 286–287
 Art. 8 . . . 287
Reg. 773/2004 on conduct of proceedings by
 Commission . . . 518
Reg. 802/2004 implementing Reg.
 139/2004 . . . 402, 439
 Arts. 1–6 . . . 439
 Arts. 7–10 . . . 439
 Arts. 11–16 . . . 439–440
 Art. 14 . . . 440
 Art. 15 . . . 440
 Art. 17 . . . 440
 Art. 18 . . . 440
 Art. 19 . . . 440–441
 Art. 20 . . . 440–441
 Arts. 21–25 . . . 441
Reg. 847/2004 on the Air Service Agreements
  Art. 1 . . . 134
  Art. 2 . . . 134, 135
  Art. 3 . . . 135
Reg. 1184/2006 Competition Rules—
 Agricultural Sector
 Art. 1 . . . 130
 Art. 2 . . . 130
Reg. 1419/2006 Competition Rules—Maritime
 Transport . . . 108n, 135, 141n, 182n
Reg. 1459/2006 Block Exemption—
 Agreements for Air Services (Technical
 Co-ordination) . . . 133, 638
Reg. 622/2008 on Settlement Procedures
 regarding Cartels . . . 647n

TABLE OF LEGISLATION FROM OTHER JURISDICTIONS

AUSTRALIA

Trade Practices Act 1974

    s. 46 . . . 600n

BELGIUM

Royal Decree on tax relief on the income of holders of deposits in savings accounts . . . 555

Royal Decree requiring travel agents not to depart from official tariffs . . . 555

CANADA

Competition Act 1985 . . . 592–593

    ss. 78–79 . . . 600n

Foreign Extra-territorial Measures Act 1985 . . . 581n

FRANCE

Code du Travail Maritime . . . 134

MEXICO

Ley Federal de Competencia Económica

    Art. 8 . . . 601n

    Art. 10 . . . 601n

NETHERLANDS

Economic Competition Act . . . 189

UNITED KINGDOM

Competition Act 1980 . . . 520

Competition Act 1998 . . . 22, 262n, 317n, 520, 539n

    Chapters 1 and 2 . . . 318, 514, 520, 521, 522, 545

    s. 60 . . . 76, 318, 521n

Copyright Designs and Patents Act 1988

    s. 144 . . . 262n

    ss. 237–239 . . . 262n

Enterprise Act 2002 . . . 21, 404, 514, 520, 521, 522, 545

    s. 16 . . . 545

    ss. 18–19 . . . 545n

    ss. 243–244 . . . 529

    s. 188 . . . 636n

    Sched. 8 . . . 514

European Communities Act 1972

    s. 2(1) . . . 536

    s. 3 . . . 536

Fair Trading Act 1973 . . . 21, 520

    s. 84 . . . 521

Patents Act 1977

    ss. 44–45 . . . 262n

    ss. 48–54 . . . 262n

Protection of Trading Interests Act 1980

    Chapter 11 . . . 581n

Restrictive Trade Practices Acts 1976 and 1977 . . . 178, 520

UNITED STATES

Clayton Act 1914 . . . 404

    s. 3 . . . 364

    s. 7 . . . 21

F. Hoffman-La Roche Ltd v. Empagran S.A. 124 S. Ct. 2359 (2004) . . . 585

Foreign Trade Antitrust Improvement Act 1982 . . . 580n

Sherman Act 1890 . . . 541, 542, 611n

    s. 1 . . . 21, 111, 116, 121, 189

    s. 2 . . . 21, 296, 315, 600n

Webb-Pomerene Export Trade Act 1918 . . . 195

CHRONOLOGICAL TABLE (1951–2008)[1]

Year	Date	Chronological table of events	European Community Council and Commission Regulations	Commission: leading decisions	European Court of Justice leading decisions
1951	18 Apr.	Signature by France, Germany, Italy, and Benelux countries ('the Six') of Treaty of Paris establishing European Coal and Steel Community (ECSC).			
1953	10 Feb.	Common Market in coal comes into force.			
	1 May	Common Market in steel comes into force.			
1957	25 Mar.	Signature of Treaty of Rome establishing European Economic Community by the Six (and establishing EURATOM).			
1958	1 Jan.	Treaty of Rome comes into force.			
1961	7 Sept.	European Parliament report (the Deringer Report) on the draft of Reg. 17 published.			
1962	13 Mar.	First Council Reg. 17 implementing Articles 85 and 86 of the Treaty of Rome comes into force.	COUNCIL Reg. 17/62 Commission's powers and procedures in competition matters.		*Bosch/van Rijn*
	11 May		COUNCIL Reg. 27/26 Notification arrangements.		
	30 July		COUNCIL Reg. 26/62 applying certain competition rules to agriculture.		
	1 Nov.	Deadline for notification of multilateral agreements under Reg. 17/62 (approx. 800 lodged).			
	26 Nov.		COUNCIL Reg. 141/62 retrospectively from 13 Mar. 1962 excluding transport from scope of Reg. 17/62.		

[1] For reasons of space, some abbreviations have been used and names are occasionally given in either abbreviated or 'popular' form. Names of cases may change when taken on appeal to the Court from the Commission. Numbers of Treaty articles have not been updated.

Year	Date	Chronological table of events	European Community Council and Commission Regulations	Commission: leading decisions	European Court of Justice leading decisions
1962	24 Dec.	'The Christmas Message' issued by DG IV; Notices on patent licensing and commercial agents.			
1963	31 Jan.	Deadline for registration of bilateral agreements under Reg. 17/62 (approx. 34,000 lodged).			
	24 July	First informal decision by DG IV prohibiting agreement under Article 85(1), the *'Convention Faience'* recommendations.			
	25 July		COMMISSION Reg. 99/63 governing procedures of hearings of individual cases by the Commission.		
1964	13 May	First publication of Notice of proposed decision (the *'Convention Faience'* case) under Article 19(3) of Reg. 17/62.		*Grosfillex–Fillistorf; Grundig–Consten; Bendix–Mertens & Straet; Nicholas–Vitapro*	
1965	2 Mar.	First Council Reg. authorizing the granting of block exemptions by the Commission.	COUNCIL Reg. 19/65 conferring power on Commission to issue block exemptions for Exclusive Distribution and Exclusive Purchasing and Industrial Property Rights licences.	*DRU-Blondel Hummel–Isbecque; Maison Jallate-Voss*	
	8 Apr.	Signature of Treaty on amalgamation of executives of ECSC, EC, and EURATOM.			
1966	13 July	First European Court Justice decision on Art. 85, (*Grundig–Consten/ Commission*)		*Grundig–Consten/ Commission; Italy/Council Commission; STM/ Maschinenbau Ulm*	
1967	1 May	First Commission Reg. granting block exemption comes into force.	COMMISSION Reg. 67/67 block exemptions for specified forms of Exclusive Distribution and Exclusive Purchasing Agreements.	*Transocean Marine Paint (No. 1)*	*Brasserie de Haecht (No. 1)*

Year	Date	Chronological table of events	European Community Council and Commission Regulations	Commission: leading decisions	European Court of Justice leading decisions
	1 July	Effective date for amalgamation of executives of ECSC, EC, and EURATOM.			
1968	1 July		COUNCIL Reg. 1017/68 rules of competition applied by Council to rail, road, and inland waterway transport.	*Eurogypsum; ACEC/Berliet; Cobelaz*	*Parke, Davis/ Probel*
	29 July	Commission issues Notice concerning co-operation between undertakings.			
1969	16 July	First fines imposed by Commission for a substantive violation of Article 85 of the Treaty of Rome (the *Quinine Cartel*).		*Quinine Cartel; Jaz/Peter; Dyestuffs; Christiani–Nielsen*	*Walt Wilhelm/ BKA; Völk/ Vervaecke*
1970	27 May	Commission issues first Notice concerning Agreements of Minor Importance.		*Omega; Kodak; ASBL; German Ceramic Tiles*	*Quinine Cartel*
1971	2 June	First formal decision of Commission on Article 86 (*GEMA*).		*GEMA; Continental Can*	*Sirena/Eda; DGG/Metro*
	7 June	European Parliament first requests the Commission to prepare an Annual Report on Competition Policy.		*VCH; Burroughs– Del-planque; Henkel–Colgate*	*Béguelin/GL Import*
	20 Dec.		COUNCIL Reg. 2821/71 conferring power on Commission to issue block exemptions for specialization agreements; Reg. 2822/71 relieving some specialization agreements from the requirements of notification by amending Reg. 17/62.		
1972		First *Annual Report* on Competition Policy issued.	COMMISSION Reg. 2591/72 extending Reg. 67/67 for a further ten years. Reg. 2779/72 group exemption for specialization agreements	*Saviem/MAN; Raymond/Nagoya; Davidson Rubber; Cimbel; Pittsburgh Corning; Commercial Solvents; WEA–Filipacchi; GISA*	*Dyestuffs*

Year	Date	Chronological table of events	European Community Council and Commission Regulations	Commission: leading decisions	European Court of Justice leading decisions
	19 Dec.		COUNCIL Reg. 2743/72 introducing minor amendments to Reg. 2821/71.		
1973	1 Jan.	UK, Ireland, and Denmark enter the Community.		Sugar Cartel; Kali–Salz; Prym–Beka; Transocean Marine Paint (No. 2)	Continental Can; Brasserie de Haecht (No. 2)
1974			COMMISSION Reg. 2988/74 bringing in rules relating to limitation of actions from 1 Jan. 1975.	GM Continental; Europair–Durodyne; SHV/Chevron; Belgian Wallpapers; FRUBO; Franco-Japanese Ballbearings; BMW	BRT/SABAM; Commercial Solvents; Van Zuylen/Hag; Centrafarm; Sterling and Winthrop; French Merchant Seamen
1975	1 Jan.			Bayer/Gist–Brocades; KEWA/United Processors; United Brands; IFTRA Rules; AOIP/Beyrard; Bomée Stichting	Sugar Cartel; GM Continental; Belgian Wallpapers; FRUBO; Kali–Salz
	15 Dec.	European Patent Convention signed.			
1976				Vitamins (Hoffman); Pabst–Richarz/BNIA; Junghans; Gerofabriek; Reuter/BASF; Miller International	Fonderies Roubaix; EMI/CBS; Terrapin/Terranova
1977			COMMISSION Reg. 2903/77 amending and extending Reg. 2779/72 on specialization agreements.	ABG; Hugin/Liptons; Cobelpa/VNP; Campari; GEC/Weir; Vacuum Interrupters (No. 1); De Laval/Stork	Concordia; Metro/SABA (No. 1); Inno/ATAB
1977	29 Dec.	Amended Notice concerning Agreements of Minor Importance.		Spices; Distillers; BMW Belgium	
1978	7 Feb.	Publication by Commission of new draft Reg. amending 67/67.		Fedetab; Maize Seed; Black Powder; Zanussi Guarantee	Miller International; United Brands; BP Commission; Hoffman-La Roche/Centrafarm; Centrafarm/American Home Products

Year	Date	Chronological table of events	European Community Council and Commission Regulations	Commission: leading decisions	European Court of Justice leading decisions
1979	3 Mar.	Publication by Commission of new draft Regs. containing block exemption for patent licences.		*Floral Sales; Atka/ BP Kemi; Rennet; Pioneer; Beecham, Parke Davies*	*Vitamins (Hoffman); Hugin/Lipton; BMW Belgium; Greenwich/ SACEM*
1980				*Italian Cast Glass; Hennessy–Henkell*	*Fedetab; Perfumes; Camera Care; Distillers; Coditel (No. 1)*
1981	1 Jan.	Greece enters the Community.		*Anseau–Navewa; VBVB–VBBB; Hasselblad; Michelin*	*Coöperative Stremsel; Salonia/ Poidomani; Züchner/ Bayerische Vereinsbank*
1982	1 Sept.	Post of Hearing Officer for DG IV created.		*AROW/BNIC; Amersham/ Buchler; AEG/ Telefunken; SSI; Rolled Zinc (CRAM); Toltecs/ Dorcet*	*Maize Seed (Nungesser); Polydor/ Harlequin; Keurkoop/Nancy Kean; Coditel (No. 2)*
1983	1 Jan.	New specialization agreement block exemption comes into force.	COMMISSION Reg. 3604/82 amended block exemption for specialization agreements replacing Reg. 2779/72, and Regs. 1983/83 and 1984/83 replacing Reg. 67/67 and providing block exemptions for Exclusive Distribution and Exclusive Purchasing Agreements, with special provision for beer and petroleum products.	*Remia–Nutricia; Vimpoltu; Ford; Saba (No. 2); Rockwell/Iveco; Carbon Gas Technology; Int. Energy Authority; Windsurfing International*	*Anseau–Navewa; GVL; Michelin; Pioneer; AEG/ Telefunken; Demo-Studio Schmidt; Kerpen & Kerpen*
1983	1 July	New Exclusive Distribution and Exclusive Purchase block exemption Regs. come into force.			
1984				*Synthetic Fibres; Zinc Cartel; Peroxygen; Woodpulp; Aluminium; IBM Personal Computers; BPCL/ ICI; Carlsberg/ Grand Met.*	*VBVB–VBBB; Hasselblad; Ford of Europe (interim measures); Rolled Zinc (CRAM); Hydrotherm*

Year	Date	Chronological table of events	European Community Council and Commission Regulations	Commission: leading decisions	European Court of Justice leading decisions
1985	1 Jan.	Commission Reg. granting block exemption for patent licences comes into force.	COMMISSION Reg. 2349/84 block exemption for patent licences.	*Grundig; Villeroy–Boch; Olympic Airways; BP/Kellogg; ECS/*	*British Telecom; CBEM–CLT; Toltecs; Ford of Europe (selective*
	1 Mar.	Specialization and R & D block exemptions Regs. come into force.	COMMISSION Reg. 417/85 Specialization Agreements block exemption replacing 3604/82.	*AKZO; Ivoclar*	*distribution system); Leclerc (Books); Leclerc (Petrol); BNIC/*
	1 July	Automotive Dealers Distribution Agreements block exemptions Regs. come into force.	COMMISSION Reg. 418/85 R & D block exemption COMMISSION Reg. 123/85 Automotive Dealers block exemption.		*Clair (Cognac); Binon; ETA Fabriques; Pharmon v. Hoechst; Remia–*
	5 Aug.		COMMISSION Reg. 2526/85 amending Reg. 27/62 by introducing a new Form A/B for notification purposes.		*Nutricia; SSI*
1986	1 Jan.	Spain and Portugal enter the Community.		*Polypropylene; Optical Fibres; Meldoc; Fatty Acids; Pronuptia; Yves Rocher; Belasco;*	*Nouvelles Frontières; Pronuptia; Windsurfing; International; Metro/SABA*
	17 and 28 Feb.	Signature by all Member States of the Single European Act (amending certain provisions of the Treaty of Rome).		*Boussois/ Interpane Mitchell -Cotts/Sofiltra*	*(No. 2); British Leyland*
	9 Sept.	Commission Notice on Agreements of Minor Importance issued.			
	22 Dec.		COUNCIL Reg. 4056/86 applying competition rules to maritime transport.		
1987	1 July	Single European Act comes into force.		*Sandoz; Hilti*	*Phillip Morris (merger)*
	1 July	Reg. 4056/86 applying competition rules to maritime transport comes into effect.			
1988	1 Jan.		COUNCIL Regs. 3975–3976/87 applying competition rules to air transport.		

Year	Date	Chronological table of events	European Community Council and Commission Regulations	Commission: leading decisions	European Court of Justice leading decisions
				Bayer/BP Chemicals; VBA; BSC/Napier Brown; Delta Chemie; BPB Industries; PVC/ LDPE Cartels; ServiceMaster	*Allen & Hanbury/ Generics; Erauw– Jacquery; Bodson; Van Eycke/ Aspa Woodpulp* (Jurisdiction only) *Novasam/ Alsatel; Renault/ Maxicar; Volvo/ Veng*
	30 Nov.	New Commission Regulations adopted for franchising and know-how licensing.			
1989	1 Feb.	Commission Reg. granting block exemption for franchise agreements comes into force.	COMMISSION Reg. 4087/88 block exemption for franchise agreements.	*Dutch Banks; Dutch Courier Services; Italian Fire Insurance;*	*Ahmed Saeed Ottung/Klee Belasco; Hoechst/ Dow/Solvay*
	1 Apr.	Commission Reg. granting block exemption for know-how licensing agreements comes into force.	COMMISSION Reg. 556/89 block exemption for know-how licensing agreements.	*APB; Bayo-n-ox; Welded Steel Mesh; UIP*	
	1 Sept.	Establishment of Court of First Instance (CFI) in Luxembourg.			
	21 Dec.	New Council Regulation adopted on control of concentrations (mergers).			
1990	14 Aug.	Commission notices on concentrative/ co-operative joint ventures published.		*Alcatel/ANT; Elopak/Metal Box (Odin); Moosehead/ Whitbread*	*Sandoz; Tetrapak (CFI); Hag (No. 2)*
	21 Sept.	Council Regulation on control of mergers, and Commission Regulation on merger procedures comes into force.	COUNCIL Reg. 4064/89 on control of mergers. COMMISSION Reg. 2367/90 on merger procedures.		
1991	2 Oct.	First Prohibition decision under Merger Regulation (*Aerospatiale-Alenia*).		*Vichy; Ecosystems; Aerospatiale-Alenia* (merger)	*Delimitis/ Henninger Bräu; ECS/AKZO; Magill/RTE* (CFI)
1992	23 Dec.	New internal procedures adopted for co-operative joint ventures.	COUNCIL Reg. 479/92. Authorizing Commission to issue block exemptions for liner shipping conferences (amending Reg. 4056/86)	*Fiat/Hitachi; Ford/VW; Accor/ Wagons Lit* (merger); *Nestlé/ Perrier* (merger); *du Pont/ICI* (merger)	*Spanish Banks; Automec (No. 2)* (CFI); *Italian Flat Glass* (CFI); *PVC cases* (CFI)

Year	Date	Chronological table of events	European Community Council and Commission Regulations	Commission: leading decisions	European Court of Justice leading decisions
1993	1 Jan.	Legislative programme for Single Market completed.	COMMISSION Regs. 1617/93 and 3652/93 amending Reg. 3976/87 by providing block exemption for certain air transport agreements.	*Sea Containers; Port of Rødby; Kali und Salz* (merger)	*Woodpulp; Reiff*
	1 Nov.	Maastricht Treaty enters into force.			
		Publication of Notice on Co-operation between Commission and national courts in applying Articles 85 and 86	COMMISSION Reg. 151/93 amending Regs. 417/85 and 418/85.		
1994	1 Jan.	European Economic Area EEA comes into existence.	COMMISSION Regs. 3384/94 introducing amended Merger Regulation procedures (replacing Reg. 2367/90), 3385/94 introducing amended procedures for Article 85 and 86 (replacing Reg.27/62).	*Cartonboard, Steel Bar and Cement Cartels; Pasteur/Merck; Shell/Montecatini* (merger); *MSG Media* (merger); *Mannesman/ Vallourec/Ilva* (merger);*PG/VP Schickendanz* (merger)	*France v. Commission* (US/EC Agreement); *IHT/Ideal Standard; Gottrup-Klim; Tetrapak II* (CFI)
	July	EC Competition Newsletter begins publication.			
	12 Dec.	Commission Decision widening terms of reference of Hearing Officer.			
	31 Dec.	Issue of amended Interface Notice on Concentrative/ Co-operative joint ventures			
1995	1 Jan.	Austria, Finland, and Sweden join the EU. World Trade	MOTOR VEHICLES DISTRIBUTION Reg. 1475/95 (replacing 123/85).	*Nordic Satellite* (merger); *Crown Cork* (merger); *RTL/Veronica;* (merger);	*Publishers Assoc.; Magill/ RTE; Bosman; Langnese/Schöller* (CFI);
		Organization (WTO) comes into existence.	Reg. 870/95 (block exemption for Liner Shipping Consortia).		
	10 Apr.	EC/USA Co-operation Agreement enters into force after ratification by Council.		*Mercedes Benz/ Kässbohrer* (merger)	*Soda Ash* (CFI)
1996	1 Apr.	Reg. 240/96 comes into force.	COMMISSION Reg. 240/96. Technology Transfer Block Exemption, replacing 2349/84 (patents) and 556/89 (know-how).	*Atlas/Phoenix; Gencor/Lonrho* (merger); *Kesko/ Tuko* (merger); *St Gobain/ Wacker* (merger); *Kimberley Clark/ Scott* (merger); *Viho Europe*	*Tetrapak II; Eurimpharm; CMB* (CFI); *Metropole* (CFI); *Leclerc/ Commission* (perfumes); *Kruidvat/ Commission* (perfumes)

Year	Date	Chronological table of events	European Community Council and Commission Regulations	Commission: leading decisions	European Court of Justice leading decisions
	18 Jul.	Notice on leniency published			
1997	22 Jan.	Publication of Commission Green Paper on Vertical Restraints.	COUNCIL Reg. 1310/97 amending Merger Reg. 4064/89.	*Boeing/McDonnell Douglas* (merger); *Irish Sugar; Guinness/Grand Met* (merger)	*SCK/FNK* (CFI) *Diego Cali* (CFI) *UIC* (ECJ) *Deutsche Bahn* (CFI)
	2 Oct.	Signature of Treaty of Amsterdam (amending Treaty of Rome).	Commission Reg. 1582/97 extending life of Regs. 1983/83 and 1984/83 to 31 Dec. 1999.		
	15 Oct.	Publication of Notice on Co-operation between Commission and national competition authorities.			
	9 Dec.	New Notice on Agreements of Minor Importance published.	COMMISSION Reg. 2237/97 extending life of Regs. 417/85 and 418/85 to		
	9 Dec.	Notice on Market Definition published.	31 Dec. 2000.		
1998	1 Jan.	Full liberalization of Telecommunications Sector, under Directive 96/19.		*Pre-Insulated District Heating Pipes; VW Audi; TACA; Van der*	
	14 Jan.	Notice on Calculation of Fines published.		*Bergh; Sicasov*	*Kali und Salz* (ECJ); *Oscar Bronner* (ECJ); *European Night Services* (CFI)
	1 Mar.	Reg. 1310/97 comes into force	COMMISSION Reg. 1310/97 amending Merger Reg. 4064/89.	*World Com/MCI* (merger)	
	21 Mar.	Reg. 447/98 comes into force.	COMMISSION Reg. 447/98 replacing Reg. No. 3384/94 on Merger Regulation procedures.		
1999	1 Jan.	Euro becomes common currency for 12 Member States.			
	1 Feb.	Reg. 2842/98 comes into force.	COMMISSION Reg. 2842/98 comes into force (dealing with procedure at hearings) and replacing Reg. 99/63.	*Seamless Steel Tubes; BA/Virgin; FEG/TU; Airtours* (merger); *Exxon/Mobil* (merger); *Telia/Telenor* (merger).	*Albany International* (ECJ); *CMB* (ECJ); *Gencor/Lonrho* (CFI); *Irish Sugar* (CFI)

Year	Date	Chronological table of events	European Community Council and Commission Regulations	Commission: leading decisions	European Court of Justice leading decisions
	28 Apr.	White Paper on Modernization of Article 81 and 82 published			
	1 May	Treaty of Amsterdam came into force (altering numbering of Articles of Treaty of Rome)			
	18 June	Regs. 1215/99 and 1216/99 come into force.	COUNCIL Reg. 1215 and 1216/99 amending Art. 4(2) of Reg. 17/62.		
	22 Dec.	Reg. 2790/99 adopted.			
2000	26 Apr.		COMMISSION Reg. 823/2000 renewing 870/95 (block exemption for liner conferences)	*Volvo/Scania* (merger); *Vodafone/ Mannesman* (merger); *MCI World Com/Sprint* (merger); *AOL/ Time Warner* (merger)	*Masterfoods* (ECJ); *Bayer Adalat* (CFI)
	1 June	Reg. 2790/99 comes into force.	COMMISSION Reg. 2790/99 replacing 1983 and 1984/83 and 4087/88 as block exemptions for vertical restraints.		
	29 Nov.	Regs. 2658 and 2659/00 adopted.			
2001	1 Jan.	Regs. 2658/2000 and 2659/2000 come into force.	COMMISSION Regs. 2658 and 2659/00 replacing 417 and 418/85 respectively as block exemptions for specialization and R&D agreements.	*Vitamins and other major cartel cases; SAS/ Maersk; Michelin (France); Deutsche Post I and II; Volkswagen; UPM Kymmene* (merger); *GE/ Honeywell* (merger)	*Courage/Crehan* (ECJ); *IMS Health* (CFI/ECJ) *interim measures*
	23 May	New Mandate for Hearing Officers.			
	11 Dec.	ECMR Green Paper published.			
	22 Dec.	New Notice on Agreements of Minor Importance published.			
2002	19 Feb.	Revised Notice on leniency published			
	23 July	Treaty of Paris establishing ECSC expires.			

Year	Date	Chronological table of events	European Community Council and Commission Regulations	Commission: leading decisions	European Court of Justice leading decisions
	1 Oct.	Motor Vehicle Distribution Block Exemption Reg. 1400/202 comes into force.	COMMISSION Reg. 1400/002 replacing 1475/95 as block exemption reg. for motor vehicles.		*Ambulanz Glockner* (ECJ); *TACA* (CFI); *Cartonboard Cartel* (CFI); *Airtours* (CFI); *Schneider/le Grand* (CFI); *Tetra/Laval* (CFI)
	9 Dec.	Agreement at Copenhagen by Council and Heads of Member States to admit 10 new Member States from 1 May 2004, subject to ratification.			
	16 Dec.	Modernization Regulation adopted.			
2003	1 Feb.	Treaty of Nice enters into force.	COUNCIL Reg. 1/2003 replacing 17/62 as procedural regulation for Arts. 81 and 82.	*Carbon and graphite and other major cartels; Telenor/Canal+/ Canal Digital; Yamaha*	*FENIN* (ECJ); *Volkswagen* (CFI); *Volkswagen* (ECJ); *Ven den Bergh Foods* (CFI); *British Airways* (CFI)
	1 Apr.	Reg. 358/2003 enters into force.	COMMISSION Reg. 358/2003 replacing block exemption Reg. 3932/92 on insurance agreements.		
2004	5 Feb.	Horizontal merger guidelines published.	COUNCIL Reg. 411/2004 on air transport.		
	1 May	Cyprus, the Czech Republic, Estonia, Hungary, Latvia, Lithuania, Malta, Poland, the Slovak Republic and Slovenia join the EU.	COMMISSION Reg. 463/2004 amending block exemption Reg. 823/2000 on liner shipping consortia.	*Six major cartel cases; Air France/ Alitalia; REIMS II, Microsoft; Oracle/PeopleSoft (merger); ENI/ EDP/GDP (merger)*	*AOK Bundesverband* (ECJ); *Bayer Adalat* (ECJ); *British Sugar* (ECJ); *IMS Health* (ECJ); *Meca-Medina* (CFI)
	1 May	Reg. 1/2003 and Commission implementing Regulation enter into force and six guidance Notices are published.	COMMISSION Reg. 773/2004 on procedure under Reg. 1/2003.		

Year	Date	Chronological table of events	European Community Council and Commission Regulations	Commission: leading decisions	European Court of Justice leading decisions
	1 May	Reg. 139/2004 and Commission implementing Regulation enter into force.	COUNCIL Reg. 139/2004 replacing Reg. 4064/89 on merger control. COMMISSION Reg. 802/2004 replacing Reg. 2367/90 on merger control procedure.		
	1 May	Reg. 772/2004 enters into force and technology transfer guidelines are published.	COMMISSION Reg. 772/2004 replacing block exemption Reg. 240/96 on technology transfer agreements.		
2005	5 Mar.	Notice on ancillary restraints in mergers published.	COMMISSION Reg. 611/2005 extending liner shipping consortia block exemption.	*Cartel cases Monochlor. acid, Industrial thread, Italian raw tobacco, Industrial bags and Rubber chemicals; Peugeot; AstraZeneca*	*Many cartel appeals; DaimlerChrysler* (CFI); *Piau* (CFI); *Syfait* (ECJ); *Tetra Laval* (ECJ); *General Electric* (CFI); *EDP* (CFI)
	19 Dec.	Publication of Commission Green Paper on damages actions.			
	19 Dec.	Publication of DG Comp Discussion Paper on Art. 82.			
2006	28 June	Revised fines guidelines published.	COUNCIL Reg. 1184/2006 on agriculture. COUNCIL Reg. 1419/2006 repealing block exemption Reg. 4056/86 in maritime transport.	*Seven major cartel cases; Tomra; T-Mobile /Tele. ring (merger)*	*Many cartel appeals; Asnef-Equifax* (ECJ); *Cipolla* (ECJ); *FENIN (2006); General Motors* (ECJ); *GlaxoSmithKline* (CFI); *Manfredi* (ECJ); *Meca-Medina* (ECJ); *Spanish Petrol Stations* (ECJ); *O2 (Germany)* (CFI); *Volkswagen* (ECJ); *Selex Sistemi* (CFI); *Schneider* (CFI); *Cementbouw Handel* (CFI); *easyJet* (CFI); *Impala* (CFI); *Endesa* (CFI);
	7 Dec.	Revised Notice on leniency published.	COMMISSION Reg. 1459/2006 Block exemption on air transport agreements.		

Year	Date	Chronological table of events	European Community Council and Commission Regulations	Commission: leading decisions	European Court of Justice leading decisions
2007	1 Jan.	Bulgaria and Romania join the EU.		*Eight major cartel cases; Visa; Groupement de Cartes Bancaires; Telefonica; Ryanair/Aer Lingus (merger)*	*Many cartel appeals; Wanadoo* (CFI); *Microsoft* (CFI); *British Airways* (ECJ); *Schneider* (CFI); *Alrosa* (CFI); *Akzo Nobel* (CFI)
	10 Jul.	Consolidated merger control jurisdictional Notice published.			
	28 Nov.	Guidelines on non-horizontal mergers published.			
	13 Dec.	Signature of Treaty of Lisbon (amending Treaty of Rome).			
2008	1 Jan.	Slovenia joins the Euro currency area.		*Rubber cartel; Removals cartel; Sodium chlorate cartel; Wax cartel; Banana cartel; Car glass cartel; Microsoft (non-compliance with previous Art. 82 decision)*	*Many cartel appeals; Deutsche Telekom* (CFI); *Sony and Bertelsmann* (ECJ); *Syfait II* (ECJ); *MyTravel* (CFI)
	3 Apr.	Publication of Commission White Paper on damages actions.			
	1 Jul.	Cartel settlements procedure enters into force.	COMMISSION Reg. 622/2008 amending Reg. 773/2004 to provide for settlement.		
	22 Oct.	Revised merger remedies notice published.			

ABBREVIATIONS

All ER	All England Law Reports
Antitrust Bull	Antitrust Bulletin
BCC	British Company Cases
BCLC	Butterworths Company Law Cases
CAT	Competition Appeal Tribunal
CFI	Court of First Instance
CMLR	Common Market law Reports
CML Rev	*Common Market Law Review*
Comp LJ	*Competition Law Journal*
CTM	Community Trade Mark
DG Comp	Directorate-General of the Commission responsible for Competition Policy
EC	European Community
ECJ	European Court of Justice
ECJ	European Competition Journal
ECLR	*European Competition Law Review*
ELRev	*European Law Review*
ECMR	European Community Merger Regulation
ECR	European Court Reports
ECSC	European Coal and Steel Community
ECU	European Currency unit(s)
EEA	European Economic Area
EEC	European Economic Community
EFTA	European Free Trade Association
EIPR	*European Intellectual Property Review*
EuLR	European Law Reports
EU	European Union
FSR	Fleet Street Reports
Fordham Corp L Inst	Annual Proceedings of the Fordham Corporate Law Institute
IAB	International Advisory Board
IATA	International Air Transport Authority
ICLQ	*International and Comparative Law Quarterly*
ICN	International Competition Network
IEA	International Energy Authority
IIC	*International Review of Industrial Property and Copyright Law*
MLR	*Modern Law Review*
MMC	Monopolies and Mergers Commission
MTF	Merger Task Force
OECD	Organization for Economic Cooperation and Development

OEEC	Organization for European Economic Cooperation
OFT	Office of Fair Trading
OHIM	Office for Harmonisation in the Internal Market
OJ	*Official Journal of the European Communities*
RPM	Resale Price Maintenance
SMEs	Small and Medium sized Companies
US	United States Supreme Court Reports
WLR	Weekly Law reports
World Comp	World Competition
WTO	World Trade Organisation
YEL	*Yearbook of European Law*
ZWeR	Zeitschrift für Wettbewerbsrecht

PART I

THE EARLY YEARS

Contemplation of the actual is succeeded at once by reflection on its implications and possibilities, so men say 'if this is what we have, we can and shall make something different'. We see the process going on all the time. For instance, in politics, governments are always telling us how they will change our world for the better, but when they have brought in their Acts of Parliament, they are very surprised by the consequences, and begin to ask anxiously what exactly is happening, why this new world is behaving in such a strange and unexpected way: and a new crowd of observers set to work to examine the new world, to see what it really is, and to write books and articles about it.

Joyce Cary, *Art and Reality*
(Cambridge University Press, 1958)

1

INTRODUCTION

1. THE SCOPE OF THE BOOK

The aim of this book is to provide in a clear, concise, and critical manner an account of Community competition law and its social, political, and economic context. It is hoped, therefore, that it will be read not only by legal practitioners and students of competition law but equally by administrators and civil servants within the Community and by businessmen and others interested in acquiring a general understanding of its origins, development, current status, and outlook.

Competition law is a complex and often highly technical subject, which does not lend itself to easy summary or concise clarification. In addition to these inherent complexities, further difficulties are caused by the fact that the institutions of the European Community necessarily operate through a number of languages, and the process of translation itself brings the risk of blurring or misunderstanding the point at issue. My objective, therefore, has been to make the understanding of the substantive law easier by explaining its historical origins and early development, and then illustrating the development of the main areas of substantive law arising both from the decisions and policy of the Commission itself and from the many decisions of the European Court of Justice and (since 1989) of the Court of First Instance. The radical modernization of the system of administering Articles 81(1) and (3), which took effect in 2004, is also described, both in connection with the individual chapters on substantive law in Part II and as part of the general overview of the subject contained in Part III. A chronological table is provided to illustrate the sequence of Treaty amendments, Council and Commission Regulations, major cases, and other notable landmarks over the period since 1951.

I have no doubt from my own experience that the study of EC competition law benefits substantially from comparison with other systems of competition law, particularly the wealth of cases found in, and the academic and professional commentary on, United States antitrust[1] law. However, this book is not a study in comparative law,

---

[1] 'Antitrust' is often used as a convenient portmanteau expression referring to US statute, case law, and administrative processes relating to monopoly and competition. The phrase derives from the technical device adopted in the late nineteenth century for vesting shareholdings (held by a number of enterprises) in individual trustees, who then issued trust certificates to those enterprises for whose benefit the pooling of interests had taken place, normally to facilitate the operation of cartels and other restrictive arrangements.

though the reader will discover that I occasionally found it difficult to resist the temptation to draw comparisons, normally confined to footnotes. Moreover, this is a book on substantive, rather than procedural issues, although some reference to important procedural questions is inevitable, particularly in connection with mergers and the modernization programme.

Competition law is a subject of great practical importance. It involves the establishment and development of legal principles and policies for the benefit of the public interest, enforced mainly (but not exclusively) through the work of public authorities; but these principles and policies are applied to a wide range of private agreements and arrangements which commercial undertakings have made for themselves, or with each other, on the basis of existing rights under contract and property law. Whilst the doctrine of restraint of trade has been familiar in the common law for several centuries,[2] the approach of the English courts has largely been that the basis for refusal to enforce the individual restrictive clauses in contractual documents was that they appeared unreasonable in respect of the parties involved, either as employer and employee, or as vendor and purchaser of a business, rather than because they offended against the interests of third parties, let alone those of the State or the public interest generally. Today, however, the justification, both of national and Community competition law, for interfering in such contractual and property rights derives far less from concern for the interests of the parties and far more from the need to protect the economic health of particular markets in individual Member States or the Community as a whole. Moreover, when the Treaty of Rome was first signed no Member State had a competition law of a comprehensive nature and proven effectiveness, whereas all twenty-seven Member States now have competition law and institutions to enforce it, albeit in some cases still limited in both scope and effectiveness of implementation.[3] In addition candidate States for Community membership are required in advance of joining to ensure the conformity of their competition law regimes with that of the Community. This means that the Community competition law rules are effectively 'exported', thereby having a direct impact beyond the borders of the European Union.

Community competition law (by which of course is meant competition law that applies to the whole of the European Economic Area (EEA) including Norway, Iceland, and Liechtenstein as well as the twenty-seven Member States as opposed to the national law of individual Member States) is now of great practical importance, because of its influence upon the everyday conduct of business and industry within the Community of the Twenty-seven; of course, this alone is not a valid reason why students should study it, especially as the subject provides but few simple answers. On the

---

[2] The history of restraint of trade is fully dealt with in J. D. Heydon, *The Restraint of Trade Doctrine* (Butterworths, 1971). See also *Chitty on Contracts* (29th edn, Sweet & Maxwell, 2004), Vol. 1., Ch. 16 on 'Illegality and Public Policy', and G. H. Treitel, *The Law of Contracts* (12th edn, Sweet & Maxwell, 2007), pp. 415–39.

[3] For a contemporary review of the competition laws of the Six in the early days of the Community, see S. A. Riesenfeld, 'Antitrust Laws in the EEC', (1966) 50 California Law Review 459. See Ch. 19, for a review of the current state of national competition authorities.

contrary, after fifty years of operation it still appears to raise a number of difficult and unsolved questions. Moreover, the active use by the Commission of its powers under Article 86(3) to issue Directives and Decisions in support of competition law and other Treaty policies has had the effect that Article 82 in particular has been applied through such Directives and Decisions to a number of new and highly important sectors. These have included telecommunications and energy, areas not much affected in the early days by Community competition policy; this, in turn, has raised fresh problems for the effective application of the Treaty in these sectors. It is therefore a subject eminently worth learning about within the general study of the legal framework of the European Community, and also because of the importance of its substantive rules for both government and business. However, it must be seen as part of the wider sphere of EC law, so that the importance of both the Treaty of Rome and the institutions of the Community can be fully appreciated in their application to many other fields of law as well as to the field of competition law.[4] For freedom of competition is only one of the principles underlying the Treaty of Rome and the Common Market, and may at times have to yield priority to the requirements of other social and political objectives.

2. THE STRUCTURE OF THE BOOK

The book contains three parts. Part I comprises a historical introduction to the subject. After a brief introduction to the economics of competition law in Chapter 2, Chapter 3 examines the early origins of Community competition law by considering the Treaty of Paris which established the European Coal and Steel Community (ECSC) in 1951, but which after a life of fifty years has now in effect been consolidated into the Treaty of Rome.

These events led directly to the negotiations in 1955 and 1956 which culminated in the signature of the Treaty of Rome on 25 March 1957. Reference is made to the influence of the Spaak Report upon whose firm foundations these final negotiations leading to the adoption of Articles 81 to 89 of the Treaty of Rome were based (dealing with various aspects of monopoly and competition) and to other important influences in establishing the final form of that part of the Treaty.

We next consider in Chapter 4 the early history of how the Commission began its task of implementing the Treaty's provisions on such matters, from its early days to the eventual development of the key procedural regulation known as Regulation 17 of 1962. For the next forty years it was upon this Regulation that all subsequent

---

[4] For the purposes of this book, it is assumed that the reader has at least an outline knowledge of the main provisions of the Treaty of Rome, as amended by the Single European Act and the Treaties of Maastricht (effective 1993), Amsterdam (effective 1999) and Nice (effective 1 February 2003) and of the institutions of the Community. The Bibliography at p. 656 lists a number of books to which reference can be made if this assumption proves unfounded, together with some comments on other sources of information about developments in EC competition law.

operations of the Directorate-General of the Commission responsible for competition policy, known as DG Comp,[5] were based. In view of its subsequent importance
to DG Comp and to the Community as a whole, detailed consideration is given to the
powers conferred by the Regulation and its influence on later developments in substantive law. Only after over forty years of operation was this Regulation replaced by
a new Regulation (No 1 of 2003), the key element in the modernization programme
for the elimination of notification of individual agreements and the sharing of the
administration of Article 81 in its entirety between the Commission and the Member
States, as described in Chapters 20 and 21. The early emphasis placed by DG Comp
on reviewing vertical agreements concerned with exclusive distribution leads to a
description in Chapter 5 of the origins of the first block exemption, applicable to such
agreements.

Part II, which comprises the largest part of the book, is an account of the current substantive competition law of the European Community, in the context of
its development since 1958. Chapters 6 and 7 analyse key features of Article 81(1),
including the concept of agreement, concerted practice, and decisions of associations, as well as those of agreements affecting trade between Member States
and restricting competition within the common market. Chapter 8 deals in some
detail with the conditions for exemption found in Article 81(3), and also with the
nullity sanction found in Article 81(2). Chapter 9 considers major case law under
Article 81(1) dealing particularly with horizontal agreements relating to price-fixing,
market-sharing, and other 'defensive' applications of the Article including 'crisis
cartels'.

Chapters 10 and 11 deal with vertical agreements relating mainly to the distribution
of goods and in particular with the important block exemption Regulation 2790/99.
This covers all forms of distribution and has been drafted so as to accord greater freedom to the parties to include terms appropriate to their commercial relationship, provided that they do not include any of a limited number of prohibited clauses, such
as export bans, minimum resale price restrictions, or certain forms of territorial or
customer restrictions.

Chapter 12 addresses a subject to which the Commission has devoted considerable attention, namely the basis upon which licences for patents and other
forms of intellectual property may be approved under Article 81(3) notwithstanding that they combine territorial exclusivity with other restrictions upon the
licensee.

Chapters 13 and 14 are concerned with Article 82, which prohibits abuse by undertakings of a dominant position within the Common Market which affects trade
between Member States. Although fewer cases have been dealt with by the Commission
and Court under this Article than under Article 81, they have been of major significance both in terms of their effect upon commercial practice and because of the

---

[5] Until 1999, known as 'DG IV' or 'DG 4'.

significant size of many of the companies involved. Chapter 15 discusses the relationship between Articles 81 and 82 which has now been considered in a number of cases. Chapters 16 and 17 provide an account of the system of merger control operated by the Community since 1990 under the terms of Council Regulation 4064/89 and its successor, Council Regulation 139/2004. Almost four thousand cases have been dealt with under these Regulations; the developing jurisprudence and procedural innovations (including strict time limits) have had an important impact on the administration by the Commission of its longer established responsibilities under Articles 81 and 82. Many joint ventures are also 'concentrations' within the terms of the Merger Regulation and are therefore dealt with in the following Chapter 18.

The next three chapters of Part II review the operation of the Community competition laws as a system, both in cooperation and occasionally in conflict with a variety of national Member State institutions, administrative, legislative, and judicial, whose actions have considerable effect on the workings and enforceability of Community competition policy. Chapter 19 deals with the relationship between the Commission and Member State competition authorities in their collective enforcement of competition policy, both under the earlier rules and as they have developed in consequence of the modernization programme. Chapter 20 concerns itself with the application of EC competition rules by national courts. Special attention is given to the approach of UK courts and tribunals. Chapter 21 deals with the extent to which Member States seek on occasion through national legislation to protect local commercial or professional interests against the provisions of Community competition law; it also explains the use by the Commission of its powers under Article 86(3) to bring legislative and case law pressure on Member States to comply both with existing legal requirements under the Treaty and with new Directives introduced to provide suitable rules for new sectors (such as energy and communications) where competition law principles had not previously been implemented. Part II concludes with Chapter 22, which considers the role of competition policy in the context of international trading relationships outside the Community, including the problem of extraterritorial jurisdiction, and the developing role and significance both of bilateral treaties of cooperation between the Community and other jurisdictions, including the USA, and of attempts through the World Trade Organization and other bodies to set up multilateral systems of cooperation.

Part III completes the book with two chapters which reflect on the past achievements of, and the future changes needed by, the Commission and other Community institutions in the field of competition law and policy. Chapter 23 records the Commission's ability to adapt over the years to new challenges and situations: these have included the introduction and effective implementation of merger control, the development and continuing revision of block exemptions for both vertical and horizontal agreements, and the influential use of its powers under Article 86(3). Chapter 24 finally assesses the likely future development of the Community's competition policy in the new circumstances in which so much change is taking place, and examines the way in which existing institutions at both Community and national level may have to adapt if effective enforcement is to be ensured.

2

COMPETITION POLICY AND THE ROLE OF ECONOMICS

1. THE DEFINITION OF COMPETITION

1.1 THE BASIC CONCEPT

The competition policy of the European Community is the underlying theme of virtually every chapter in this book. It may therefore be advisable to consider at this early stage what is meant in this context by the expression 'competition'. This chapter can attempt only a brief account of this highly complex topic. However, it may assist those meeting the subject for the first time to become familiar with some of its basic principles before starting to grapple with its application to Community competition law. In addition it is essential to understand both the role that economics plays in this area, and some economic concepts.[1] Those already familiar with the issues can, of course, pass straight to the following chapters.

The Treaty of Rome refers to 'competition' as a concept in both Articles 3(1)(g)[2] and 81, but perhaps wisely offers no definition. However, it is helpful to have at least a general understanding of how the word is used, and important to realize that Article 81 has no application unless the agreement, decision, or practice concerned has either the object or the effect of preventing, restricting, or distorting competition.

Competition is basically the relationship between a number of undertakings which sell goods or services of the same kind at the same time to an identifiable group of customers. Each undertaking having made a commercial decision to place its goods or services on the market, utilizing its production and distribution facilities, will by that act necessarily bring itself into a relationship of potential contention and rivalry with the other undertakings in the same geographical market, whose limits may be a single

---

[1] This description will necessarily be brief and simplified. Those who wish to know more about the different schools of economic thought that have been influential in this area may look for example at O Budzinski, 'Monoculture versus diversity in competition economics' [2008] 32 *Cambridge Journal of Economics* 295 and the references cited there.

[2] Originally Art. 3(f) of the Treaty of Rome referred to the activities of the Community as including 'a system ensuring that competition in the internal market is not distorted'; under the Treaty of Maastricht this provision was renumbered Art. 3(g) and later under the Treaty of Amsterdam Art. 3(1)(g). For discussion of the potential impact on this provision of the Lisbon Treaty, see Ch. 24, Section 2.

shopping precinct, a city, a region, a country, a group of countries, the entire European Community, or even the whole world. Whilst competition law tends to focus more on the activities of, and relationships between, sellers, it logically applies equally to the like activities and relationships between buyers, who also find themselves in contention in particular product and geographic markets. Moreover it applies not only to the markets for tangible goods and objects, but also to the fast-growing range of commercial and personal services available and necessary for the smooth operation of a developed modern economy, including banking and financial services, insurance, and the whole range of computer networks and services. There are of course important differences between, on the one hand, the operation of competition in economic theory and, on the other, its practical workings in real markets.

1.2 THE ADVANTAGES OF COMPETITION

Nevertheless, in spite of its imperfections, the existence of competition within markets is normally considered by economists to confer real advantages. Among these the following are often referred to:

(a) the part that it has played in allocating resources in the direction preferred by consumers, generally described as 'allocative efficiency'; this has the benefit of reducing the risk that goods or services produced will not be wanted, or not wanted at the price at which they are offered

(b) the continual pressure on all producers and sellers in the market to use raw materials and human capital in a way that keeps down costs, and therefore prices, for fear of losing custom to other sellers who find ways to attract business either by general price cuts or by special discounts to favoured buyers: this is 'productive efficiency'

(c) the constant process of dynamic adjustment to continual changes in consumer preferences is an incentive for producers to invest in research and development and to innovate, leading to the survival and growth of those companies which make the necessary changes in good time, whilst those that fail to do so inevitably fall behind: this is 'dynamic efficiency'.

Though the benefits of competition are great it should not be forgotten that its effect on the losers in that process may be financially disastrous for them. Nor will those effects always be without disadvantage even for consumers, as for example when local shops find themselves put out of business by the very success of the supermarket in the next town. It may be argued that it is not appropriate to take such concerns into account in the context of competition policy, and this is broadly the approach of mature competition law regimes today. However, sometimes laws that are labelled 'competition' laws are in fact either expressly drafted, or applied in practice, so as to serve policy purposes going beyond competition issues, resulting in measures that may be questionable from a pure competition policy standpoint. This variety of possible policy purposes is explored in the next section.

2. THE NATURE AND AIMS OF COMPETITION LAW

2.1 INTRODUCTION

Competition is not an aim in itself; rather it is a means to achieving certain outcomes that benefit society, these being essentially economic progress and the economic welfare of the people and organizations that make up society. In practice however it is often used to pursue other aims.[3] Apart from the aims of economic welfare and strengthening of the Single Market, both of which are discussed further below, many other policy aims have been and are still pursued through 'competition' laws by different governments and authorities. They include protection of smaller businesses, promoting economic freedom and ensuring 'fairness'. Social, political and environmental goals have also come into play, for example where a merger is prohibited because it would lead to job losses, or an agreement restricting the marketing of certain goods is allowed because it promotes sales of other goods that are less harmful to the environment.

Industrial- or trade-policy aims also sometimes drive competition law enforcement. Examples are seen in the resurgence in recent years of a tendency for some national governments in the European Union to adopt, under the guise of competition law, measures designed to protect or create national industrial champions, or to prevent them coming under foreign ownership.[4] This occurs for example where a national competition authority blocks, or imposes onerous conditions on, the acquisition of a national company by a foreign company.

In some instances the pursuit of non-economic goals may not be damaging, provided economic welfare considerations are also taken into account. For example, Community competition law has often been applied with a view to promoting an integrated single European market. Frequently, though not always, this aim meshes with that of economic welfare, with the enabling of cross-border trade stimulating competition. On the other hand, if economic considerations are neglected the paradoxical result may be that a measure intended to remove barriers to cross-border trade may in fact reduce competition, for example because a producer decides that he would prefer not to be present at all on a particular foreign market, rather than to compete there on terms dictated by single market considerations.[5] Other aims are likely to conflict with that of maximizing economic welfare, and in any case are arguably more effectively achieved through separate means. For example, if it is desired to preserve the local shops referred to above, it is probably preferable to do this by reducing their tax

---

[3] See M. Motta, *Competition Policy: Theory and practice* (Cambridge University Press, 2004) for detailed consideration of a broad range of objectives that may be subsumed within competition policy.

[4] For an explanation of why such policies tend to be economically damaging see L. Sørgard 'The Economics of National Champions' [2007] *ECJ* 49.

[5] A well known example of such an outcome is the Commission decision in *Distillers* [1978] OJ L50/16: [1978] 1 CMLR 400 which apparently contributed to segmentation of the European market. See V. Korah, *An Introductory Guide to EC Competition Law and Practice*, 9th edn (Hart Publishing 2007), Section 1.3.

burden, rather than by restricting the supermarkets' ability to compete, or allowing the local shops to engage in business practices that would normally be treated as anti-competitive.

2.2 ECONOMIC WELFARE

The main goal of developed competition law systems is economic welfare, sometimes referred to as economic efficiency. In the language of economics 'economic welfare' does not refer to a general state of economic well-being, but rather it is a technical term that refers to the degree to which available resources are allocated to producing as efficiently as possible the goods or services that will be most valued by consumers. Economists have theoretical models that allow them, on the basis of certain assumptions, to calculate in numerical terms the loss or gain in welfare brought about by particular changes in the market circumstances. That change might be, for example, the exit of a company from a market, or the imposition by a regulator of a minimum price for a particular good or service.

The welfare measure preferred by most economists is that of 'social welfare', which takes into account both the economic welfare of final consumers and the profits of producing companies. However, competition policy in the European Union, and in the United States, favours the maximizing of 'consumer welfare' which places importance only on the benefits to consumers.[6] In practice these two measures usually result in the same policy choice, though this will not always be the case. For example, a merger may allow considerable cost savings to the merging parties, but reduce competition and so lead to price rises. A consumer welfare approach would result in the merger necessarily being viewed in a negative light, whereas a social welfare approach would require a weighing up of the two effects.

A pure economic welfare approach is often described as aiming at protecting the process of competition, rather than protecting competitors. One of the criticisms most frequently levelled by US commentators at EU competition policy is that it protects competitors whereas it should focus on protecting competition. This may have been fair comment in the past, but is much less so today.[7]

2.3 THE 'SINGLE MARKET IMPERATIVE'

In Community law by far the most influential additional aim, after that of economic efficiency, pursued through competition policy is that of breaking down barriers to cross-border trade within the European Union. This is a feature unique to Community competition law. It is seen most clearly in cases where companies allocate different

---

[6] For a statement of this principle by the European Court of First Instance see Case T-168/01 *GlaxoSmithKline* v. *Commission* [2006] ECR II-2969: [2006] 5 CMLR 1623, on appeal Cases C-501 and others. See also speeches by Commissioner Kroes e.g. 'European Competition Policy—Delivering Better Markets and Better Choices' SPEECH/05/012, 15 September 2005.

[7] See J. Vickers, 'Competition Law and Economics: A Mid-Atlantic Viewpoint' [2007] *ECJ* 1.

national territories, either among themselves (in a horizontal market-sharing cartel), or to different distributors (in vertical distribution arrangements).[8] Though
consumer-welfare considerations are now in the ascendancy in the EU system,
European Commission hostility to such arrangements persists, and is perhaps most
obvious in cases in which the alleged infringement interferes with parallel trade. As
recently as 2004, judgment was given in cases in which the European Commission
had argued, though unsuccessfully, before the European courts that proof that a company's conduct was intended to hinder cross-border trade was sufficient in itself to
establish a competition law infringement.[9]

3. THE ROLE OF ECONOMICS IN
COMPETITION LAW

3.1 INTRODUCTION

It will by now be clear that, given the nature and purposes of competition policy, economics is an integral part of it, and that no sensible discussion of policy, law, or individual cases can take place in the absence of awareness of economic principles. At
European Community level, but also in individual member States and the broader
international community, in recent years significantly more prominence has been
given to economics and economists wherever competition issues are raised.

   In the European Community DG Comp has had a chief economist since 2003.
Many DG Comp officials have an economics background, and Commission decisions
taken today devote much more space to economic evidence and argument than do
those from even a few years ago. The large volume of guidance applicable to different
aspects of European competition law, published in the form of Commission notices
and guidelines, all emphasize the importance of the use of economic concepts in the
analysis of individual cases.

3.2 MARKET POWER

Of all the economic concepts that are relevant to competition law and policy, the most
important is that of market power. This is for the simple reason that competition concerns can only arise when one or more companies, acting either alone or with others,
has a certain degree of market power: firms can only act to restrict or distort competition if they have significant market power.

---

   [8] An early and influential example is the *Grundig* case, described in Ch. 4.
   [9] *Bayer* v. *Commission*, described in Ch. 6; see also the Opinions of Advocate Generals Jacobs and Ruiz-
Jarabo respectively in the two *Syfait* cases, Case C-53/03 [2005] ECR I-4609 and Cases C-468-378/06, 16
September 2008 (not yet reported), and the judgment in the latter.

Economists do not agree on an exact definition of significant market power, but the essential idea is that it is the ability profitably to limit output or raise prices in a way that would not be possible in a competitive market, or to exclude competitors from the market. There is no mathematical means to measure market power held by a particular undertaking. Instead there are a number of factors which contribute to the assessment. These include the undertaking's market share, and the number and market shares of its actual and potential competitors in the market. Entry and expansion barriers, meaning factors that prevent or hinder other firms from entering the market or expanding, are also very important in such an assessment. A company may have an extremely high market share, but if it is easy for a new entrant to come into the market then that company does not have significant market power, as it is constrained by the knowledge that if it restricts its output or raises its prices then others will quickly come into the market and win market share by charging lower prices. Other relevant factors include the nature of any interaction between the market players, and the extent to which consumers consider that the competing products differ from one another.

It is also important to remember that market power always needs to be looked at over a broad timescale, as it does not normally raise competition problems if it is short-lived. This is especially relevant in markets characterized by frequent innovation and consequently high levels of investment in research and development. If successful innovation is treated too harshly then investors and innovators will ultimately be deterred, which would be detrimental to consumer welfare. One way of looking at this is to say that in such circumstances there is little real market power. Another way of putting it is to say that the presence of market power, over a short period, may actually be economically beneficial.

Even once this exercise has been carried out, no figure can be put on market power, and there is no specific definition of a level of market power that can confidently be said to be too high. For that reason market shares, which have the virtue of being expressed as numbers, are sometimes used as a proxy for market power to establish general rules as to when intervention by competition law authorities may or may not be warranted.

3.3 MARKET SHARES AND MARKET DEFINITION

When assessing market power in an individual case it is often helpful, and in some cases it is a legal requirement, to define the relevant market in which that power may be held. This means identifying possible substitute products that act as competitive constraints.[10] For example, in order to know whether a producer of apples has market power it is necessary to establish whether he is constrained in raising his prices from a competitive level only by the fear that consumers will buy cheaper or better apples elsewhere, or whether he must also consider the risk that they respond to a rise in the price of his apples by buying pears instead. In the latter case the relevant product

---

[10] This is discussed further in Ch. 13 in the context of Art. 82.

market consists of at least apples and pears, and perhaps other fruits. Similarly, the geographic market, meaning the area over which competition takes place, needs to be established.

Market elasticity is a useful concept when analysing markets, and can be expressed by economists in numerical terms. 'Demand elasticity' refers to the extent to which demand decreases or increases when prices rise or fall, and is one indicator of market power; 'demand cross-elasticity' refers to the way in which a price change for one product affects demand for a different product and is helpful in assessing the extent to which one product acts as a competitive constraint on another.

Once a market has been defined, it is interesting to know what is the percentage share of that market held by the company in question. Market share has already been mentioned as a relevant factor in assessing market power. However, for an economist, and increasingly for competition law authorities, such a percentage is no more than a possible starting point for assessing the level of market power, as it is recognized that market shares do not necessarily equate to market power, as illustrated by the discussion above of the significance of entry barriers. Nevertheless, they are frequently used in competition law rules as a proxy for market power, in particular in order to provide a degree of legal certainty in the form of thresholds below which authorities may not, or are unlikely to, intervene. For example, the benefit of modern block exemptions is available only where certain market-share thresholds are not exceeded, and guidance in the area of merger control includes such thresholds to indicate when mergers are likely to be approved without difficulty.

3.4 ECONOMIC WELFARE AND LEGAL CERTAINTY

The fact that economics can provide forms of analysis that provide numerical results might lead one to suppose that making more use of economics to reach competition decisions would significantly enhance the certainty involved and make competition analysis generally easier to carry out. Unfortunately the opposite is true, for a number of reasons.

The legalistic approach, such as prevailed in Community law enforcement in its early years, though criticized for a rigidity that was not conducive to companies adopting optimally efficient business practices, did have the merit that it provided them with relatively clear rules of conduct. In addition it had the not inconsiderable advantage that an assessment of the legality of an agreement or legal arrangement could be carried out simply by examining its terms and assessing whether they were of a type that the law characterized as anti-competitive.

Economics, on the other hand, tells us that almost any contractual clause or business practice can be either beneficial or harmful to welfare, depending on all the surrounding market circumstances. This means that large volumes of empirical market data will often be needed to make a proper assessment of the impact on economic welfare of any particular agreement or practice. Economics calculations are based on theoretical models, which in turn are based on assumptions. Faced with a given issue, by selecting a different model, or varying the assumptions, it is possible to reach diametrically opposed conclusions. In order to decide which represents the situation most accurately, empirical market data is essential, and such data is frequently either difficult or impossible to obtain. When the European Commission first proposed the use of market-share thresholds in block exemptions there was strong opposition from business and its advisers, because of the uncertainty involved in concepts such as market definition, and the likely difficulty of obtaining the relevant data, despite the recognition that such an approach would provide greatly increased freedom to companies with little or no market power.

However it is generally recognised that on balance these disadvantages do not justify ignoring economics. Rather, it has to be accepted that the price of increased economic efficiency is a competition regime that is more onerous for both companies and authorities. Many policy debates in this area revolve largely around finding the proper balance between legal certainty and economic integrity. This has been particularly evident during the European Commission's review of its policy on enforcement of the rules on abuse of market dominance, as companies want both a clear legal framework, but also the freedom to engage in as broad a range of efficient market practices as possible. While it is not feasible for authorities to examine each individual case on its merits, it has proved very difficult to state general rules that do not offend too greatly against economic principles.

The pragmatic approach taken by many authorities is to adopt an economics-based approach while trying to ensure as high a level of certainty as possible, mainly by producing detailed guidance setting out the economic framework that they will apply in given circumstances.

4. MONOPOLY, OLIGOPOLY, AND WORKABLE COMPETITION

4.1 PERFECT MONOPOLY AND PERFECT COMPETITION

The economist illustrates the workings of the competitive process by reference to four models which are designed, on certain assumptions, to show what would be the rational behaviour of sellers under two extreme sets of conditions. The two extremes are perfect (or pure) monopoly and perfect competition: in the real world it is extremely rare to find either, but they represent the two ends of the spectrum between which markets in the real world operate. In a perfect monopoly the provider of goods or services has 100 per cent control of the market and so absolute market power. There are no close or even similar products or services to which buyers can turn.[11] This is normally

---

[11] Some types of market may appear to function as monopolies if considered at a particular point in time, but if a wider timeframe is taken into account it will be seen that the market takes the form of successive and

only possible through State intervention, when a public service or utility is provided either directly by a government department or agency, or through a nationalized body such as the Post Office, although even in these cases some form of competition may exist, such as private delivery courier services. The widespread movement within the Community towards the privatization of those sectors, such as telecommunications, transport, and energy, which were once State monopolies means that such examples are now much less common. Private monopolies controlling 100 per cent of a given market are also rare in their pure form, unless the control is over an essential facility or product which is simply not available elsewhere.[12]

The opposite of pure monopoly is pure (or atomistic) competition, which is also rare. For such a condition to exist, the number of competitors must be so great that the market share of each is tiny, so that none alone has sufficient influence to alter price levels or the balance of supply and demand. In such a market undertakings have no market power at all and could, at least in theory, remain totally uninterested in the actions or reactions of their rivals since the market simply responds to the 'invisible hand' whose operations were first explained to us by Adam Smith.[13] Moreover buyers and sellers must be fully aware of the transactions taking place in the market, so that they can make an immediate and appropriate response to ensure that the relevant product remains available at the current market price in both the short and medium term. The type of market most likely to approach this extreme is one consisting of many agricultural producers of the same crop, none of whom has a large enough percentage of total production in the relevant area to be able individually to influence market conditions or prices.

4.2 OLIGOPOLY AND WORKABLE COMPETITION

Far more important for us, however, are the other two principal types of market: oligopoly and workable competition. An oligopoly is a market in which some degree of competition remains but there are only a handful of competitive undertakings (not less than two and probably not more than eight). They may have significant market power, either individually or collectively, and the nature of the rivalry between them is substantially affected by this fact. Workable competition is found when there are fewer

relatively short-lived monopolies. For example, a pharmaceutical company that develops a blockbuster drug may enjoy an extremely high market share, but only until the patent expires, or another company develops a better product. It therefore remains subject to significant competitive pressure and has relatively little market power over time.

[12] In US antitrust law, this is often referred to as a 'bottleneck monopoly'. The classic example is the case of *United States* v. *Terminal Railroad Association of St Louis* 224 US 383 (1912), where the Association controlled the only rail approach from the west into St Louis and was ordered by the Supreme Court to make it available to all railroads which desired to serve St Louis, on non-discriminatory terms. See A. Neale and D. Goyder, *The Antitrust Laws of the United States*, 3rd edn (Cambridge University Press, 1980), pp. 128–34. The equivalent phrase under EC law is 'essential facility', discussed in Ch. 14, pp. 358–62. For the differences between the US and EC approaches see J. Venit and J. Kallaugher, 'Essential Facilities: A Comparative Law Approach' [1994] Fordham Corp L Inst 315–44.

[13] In his famous work, *The Wealth of Nations*, published in 1776.

rivals in the market than are needed for perfect competition, but where the numbers involved and other relevant circumstances mean that there is a sharper degree and different tempo of mutual reaction than in an oligopoly, and individual companies have very limited, if any, market power. However, it can on occasion be difficult to distinguish between oligopolistic and workably competitive markets, as the borderline is indistinct.

Some oligopolies are notable for distinct elements of competition among their members, whilst some forms of what appear to be workably competitive markets are necessarily affected significantly by oligopolistic tendencies. In an oligopolistic market there is nearly always a marked degree of interdependence, which is not a recognized feature in markets that enjoy workable competition. The vast majority of the markets which concern us within the Community fall within one of these last two categories. Throughout the remainder of this book references to 'competition' will normally mean 'workable competition', including markets with recognizable features of oligopoly.

Workable competition itself is not easily defined. Its operation may be quite easy to understand if the product is homogeneous, possibly offered for sale in identical form by all competitors within a market, or where product differentiation which suppliers claim to exist is not objectively based, or is merely marginal: for example the differences between various brands of petrol or oil placed on the market by competing oil companies. Other product differences may be tangible or objective, attributable to different physical or chemical formulations or other differences between the relevant ingredients and components of competing products. If the rival products being marketed are substantially identical, with no real or ostensible differentiation being perceived by buyers, then competition is likely to take place largely on the basis of price, and to a lesser extent in terms of the level of service or conditions of sale, or by enabling the simultaneous purchase of a wide variety of other products from the same outlets, as is now possible, for example, at service stations owned or controlled by major oil companies.

In many markets, however, competition is of a more complex kind, since the products, whilst generally appropriate for the same end uses, have distinct characteristics, perhaps unique to one product. Potential customers are asked to value and assess one of these heterogeneous products as better suited to their needs than any other brand. Into this category would fall such popular consumer products as cars, cameras, and television sets. Here the competitive struggle between undertakings is waged on a number of fronts.[14] At one time, the chosen weapon may be price cuts or secret discounts, whilst at other times it may be better warranties or service, changes in product specification, or an increase in the range of models or varieties offered, backed up by widespread advertising and promotion. For some consumer products particular kinds of distribution systems may be thought necessary to promote inter-brand

---

[14] For a full-scale analysis of the competitive process from the viewpoint of the undertaking itself, see M. E. Porter, *Competitive Strategy* (Harvard University Press, 1980) and id., *Competitive Advantage* (Harvard University Press, 1985), and *The Competitive Advantage of Nations* (Macmillan Press, 1990).

competition. With capital goods and other non-capital products which are sold by one industrial concern to another, rather than to individuals, the competitive struggle is usually waged at a more objective level. Such buyers usually have more information about the product which they wish to purchase and will be less susceptible to the blandishments of advertising and the promotional ingenuity of sellers. In the case of consumer goods, however, advertising and sales promotion and the establishment of consumer recognition for the seller's brand may be all-important, and market shares more influenced by the skill of such promotion than by the inherent quality of the product and its pricing, at least in the short term.

4.3 THE DIFFERENCE BETWEEN HORIZONTAL AND VERTICAL AGREEMENTS

If companies seek to eliminate or at least reduce competition between themselves, they will normally try to do so by some form of agreement or concerted practice; these are classified as 'horizontal' since they are made between undertakings operating at the same level, for example as manufacturers or as retailers. By contrast 'vertical' agreements are those where the relationships of the parties are complementary, for example when a supplier makes a distribution agreement with a dealer or a patent owner enters into a licence agreement with a licensee. Whilst this distinction can normally be made without difficulty, occasionally relationships between undertakings not currently in competition, but with a potential to compete with each other, may pose problems for competition policy; for example, should reciprocal exclusive distributorships be allowed between manufacturers in potential competition with each other? Although it is horizontal agreements that normally offer the greatest danger to competition, vertical agreements containing certain types of restriction can also damage both the Single Market itself and competition within it.

An important consideration for consumer-goods markets, involving the distribution of products through retail outlets, is whether manufacturers of such goods can compete fully with each other on an inter-brand basis. They can of course choose to sell direct to the public through wholly owned distribution channels: that is, on a vertically integrated basis. However, they will often prefer to sell at arm's length to independent dealers or distributors, who will then sell to consumers.

If each manufacturer has access to sufficient outlets of the required quality in appropriate locations, then even if these vertical agreements contain some degree of restriction, for example by requiring exclusivity, inter-brand competition should not be seriously affected. On the other hand, if there are not sufficient outlets available to some potential manufacturers then their consequent 'foreclosure' from the market and the subsequent reduction in competition may be damaging to consumer and manufacturer alike.

Foreclosure may occur as a result of excessive concentration in particular markets, leading to domination of wholesale and retail outlets by manufacturers. It can also occur if, although there are enough outlets available, manufacturers so arrange matters that only a few can obtain the goods which consumers actually require. Manufacturers may seek to justify that situation on the ground that too many dealer appointments would deter the best outlets from adequate investment in premises, equipment, staff, and promotional activities. The reason will be the fear that those who make a minimal investment, or enter the market at a later stage, will inherit as 'free riders' the benefit of the larger capital outlay made by the original entrants. Similar arguments can be made by licensees in the context of the terms upon which intellectual property rights are made available.

5. THE ROLE OF COMPETITION POLICY IN THE COMMUNITY

5.1 INTRODUCTION

The Treaty of Rome gave prominence to competition policy as one of the main activities of the Community listed in Article 3. The Commission has exercised its responsibilities in this area under three main headings, two conferred by the Treaty itself and the third by a subsequent Regulation. The two original Treaty obligations relate respectively to the control of the content of agreements between undertakings, of both a horizontal and vertical nature, and the control of abuse of dominance, i.e. of market power. The third is the control of 'concentrations' (mergers) under the authority currently provided by Council Regulation 139/2004.

5.2 RESTRICTIVE AGREEMENTS

For reasons explained in the following chapters of Part I, the initial focus of the Commission was the analysis and treatment of vertical agreements in the context of distribution. For a number of years a lower priority was given to horizontal agreements, partly because of the resources required for, and difficulties encountered in, the establishment of the relevant evidence, but also because of the Commission's perception that vertical agreements could be a considerable hindrance to cross-border trade. This is despite the fact that, as explained above, the former frequently enhance economic efficiency whereas the latter can generally be expected to be harmful.

The experience of the Commission over the fifty years since the Treaty came into effect has enabled it to simplify its approach towards vertical agreements, to which a succession of block exemptions under Article 81(3) have been applied. Now that the Single Market is well developed, it has proved possible to provide distribution agreements of various kinds with only a list of prohibited 'black' clauses, without having to spell out a long list of permitted 'white' restrictions; the parties are now free to choose the form of agreement that suits their own requirements, so long as the 'black' clauses are avoided. The only condition imposed on such undertakings is that their market share of the relevant goods or services in the particular market (usually a single Member State) must not exceed 30 per cent. A market share above that level is deemed to confer a degree of market power which renders foreclosure more likely, so that the effect of restrictive clauses in this situation is still for individual assessment. This will be further examined in Chapters 10 and 11.

Priorities began to change in the last two decades of the twentieth century; from the end of the 1990s improved techniques of handling cases involving major horizontal cartels were adopted and greater resources applied in targeting them. Today much of DG Comp's resources are devoted to detecting and punishing horizontal hard-core cartels, as described in Chapter 9.

5.3 SINGLE FIRM DOMINANCE

The greater degree of success in dealing with cases where an agreement or a concerted practice could be clearly identified did not lead to the finding of a solution for the yet more difficult problem, that of the oligopolistic market where the effect of such arrangements could be obtained without the need for any agreement.

By comparison, the application of Community competition policy to companies having 'single firm' dominance of particular markets proved—at least initially—less difficult, though the number of cases taken by the Commission was few and the economic rationale underlying them sometimes doubtful. In almost any market the competitive process itself will probably ensure that some of its participants will sooner or later gain a degree of market power. The acquisition of such market power may in turn enable undertakings to exercise strategic power over prices and levels of output and thus increase their profit margins. This increase in profitability may then allow them, either by taking advantage of economies of scale or by pursuing successful research and development, to gain still further advantage over their competitors. Moreover, such acquisition of market power places the holder in a stronger position to overcome adverse economic trading conditions, including a general economic recession as well as temporary falls in demand. In such circumstances, the likely weakening or demise of some competitors may strengthen its position even further. Competition law can deal with the problem of markets dominated by a single company by a number of remedies available under anti-monopoly legislation. These include divestiture of assets, regulatory control of prices and profits, and the prohibition of specific trading practices that contribute to a monopolistic position.

5.4 COLLECTIVE DOMINANCE

However, it is far more difficult to find appropriate and effective means of restoring and maintaining competition in an oligopolistic market. Because the number of undertakings in the market is relatively small, it is easier for them to adjust their commercial and pricing policies so as to achieve the effects of a horizontal agreement covering products, prices, conditions of business, and even, to some extent, the pace of technological advance, without actually having to enter into either agreements or concerted practices, even within the broad definition of Article 81. Their mutual interdependence enables an equilibrium to be established between them, at a higher price level than would be possible under conditions of even workable, let alone unrestricted, competition. Each competitor is aware that to cut prices will precipitate a response from the other oligopolists which would render such an initiative futile. The difficulty for competition policy is not only that the oligopolists can achieve these higher prices and profits without agreements or concerted practices, but that the market may at first sight appear to be competitive, in that prices are closely matched, although the process which underpins their proximity (and the level at which they stand) is not one of true competition. For these reasons, and despite the fact that many economists believe that in practice such systems are frequently unstable and short-lived, the concept of 'joint' or 'collective' dominance, that enjoyed by more than one company in the same market, has attracted great interest from the European Commission. The concept is considered in leading cases under both Article 82 and the Merger Regulation.[15] An important justification indeed for a strict system of merger control is that it helps to prevent the creation of market structures in which such joint dominance and consequent 'tacit collusion'[16] is possible. Oligopolistic markets however are undoubtedly the most difficult in which to apply an effective competition policy.[17]

5.5 THE ESSENTIAL ELEMENTS OF EFFECTIVE COMPETITION POLICY

The experience both of the Community and of other competition authorities shows that the effectiveness of competition policy depends on the combination of three elements. There has to be a substantive law setting out, not necessarily at great length, the basic rules to be applied. This is found in Article 81 of the Treaty of Rome, which is itself similar to section 1 of the Sherman Act in the United States, prohibiting agreements in restraint of competition to the extent that they also affect trade between Member States. It is also found in Article 82, prohibiting abuse of a dominant position, equivalent in broad terms to section 2 of the Sherman Act, to which the merger control rules, found in the EC Merger Regulation and in section 7 of the Clayton Act in the United States are an essential supplement. The second element is the adoption of procedures for ascertaining the relevant facts in each case, from which fair and properly reasoned conclusions can be drawn about the application of the substantive law to the case. A

[15] See Chs. 15 (Art. 82), 16, and 17 (mergers) respectively.

[16] This term is used by economists to mean collusion not involving communication such that the companies could be said to be operating a cartel.

[17] The broad terms of the UK Fair Trading Act 1973 (now contained in the Enterprise Act 2002) made possible sectoral inquiries into oligopolistic markets leading to a variety of possible remedies, both of a structural and behavioural character. By contrast Art. 82 with its emphasis on 'punishment' for past abuses is less well adapted for dealing with and providing appropriate remedies for such oligopolistic markets. It is puzzling that the Commission made little use of its investigatory powers into individual sectors of the economy under Reg. 17/62, but since 2004 it has made frequent use of the equivalent provision in Reg. 1/2003.

difficult balance has to be struck between the need of the competition authority to have sufficient powers to ascertain these facts, which may be elusive, and the rights of the undertakings involved to due process, including access to the allegations made against them[18] and a full right of response. The third element is the maintenance and development of institutions capable of enforcing the substantive rules in a way which is both fair and effective. Here the question of availability of resources is a perennial problem, notwithstanding the major increases in staff numbers for DG Comp over the years. Some would also see effective private enforcement, in particular through damages actions, as an essential adjunct to public enforcement. All these aspects of policy will be considered in the course of Parts II and III.

Over the last few years major changes have taken place in the world and Community economy which have had their impact on the implementation of competition policy. These have included:

- great advances in technology for many markets, such as communications, computers, software, energy, and the Internet revolution, enabling exchange of information between businesses and consumers on a scale previously unimaginable
- the growth of new markets such as those for sport and the media, to which the Commission had previously been able to pay little attention, but which now need investigation of their complex activities and networks
- the trend towards the opening up to competition of areas historically controlled by the State
- human-rights legislation under the European Convention of Human Rights, which has an impact on the procedures of the Commission
- an increase in the number and complexity of concentrations with a Community dimension, which has had the effect of making the Commission on occasion act almost as a world merger authority
- adoption by many Member States of national rules of competition law closely based upon both the principles and the language of the Treaty of Rome, including the UK in its Competition Act 1998
- the multiplying of competition laws beyond the Community, and the activities of international bodies such as the International Competition Network
- development of increased co-operation with both the United States and other competition authorities outside the Community, leading to increased pressures on the Commission for harmonization of its timetables, rules and policies in particular with those of the US
- the acceptance by fifteen out of the twenty-seven Member States of the euro as their common currency.

---

[18] Often referred to generally as 'access to file'.

The response of the Commission to all these significant changes, and to its own resource problems, was to alter its approach towards its original monopoly over the application of Article 81(3) in granting individual exemptions, and to propose and obtain Council acceptance for far-reaching changes. As a result Member States have since 2004 taken over far greater responsibility for enforcing Community as well as national competition rules.

FURTHER READING

S. BISHOP and C. WALKER, *The Economics of EC Competition Law* (2nd edn, Sweet & Maxwell, 2002).

N. BOEGER, 'Solidarity and EC Competition Law' [2007] ELRev 319.

O. BUDZINSKI, 'Monoculture versus Diversity in Competition Economics' [2008] 32 *Cambridge Journal of Economics* 295.

C.-D. EHLERMANN, 'The Contribution of EC Competition Policy to the Single Market' [1992] 29 CMLRev 257.

M. MOTTA, *Competition Policy: Theory and Practice* (Cambridge University Press 2004).

A. PERA and V. AURICCHIO, 'Consumer Welfare, Standard of Proof and the Objectives of Competition Policy' [2005] 1 ECJ 153.

L.-H. RÖLLER and P. A. BUIGES, *The Office of the Chief Competition Economist at the European Commission* (May 2005, available on DG Comp website).

L. SØRGARD, 'The Economics of National Champions' [2007] ECJ 49.

J. VICKERS, 'Competition Law and Economics: A Mid-Atlantic Viewpoint' [2007] ECJ 1.

3

THE ORIGINS OF EUROPEAN COMPETITION LAW

1. THE TREATY OF PARIS AND THE FORMATION OF THE EUROPEAN COAL AND STEEL COMMUNITY

1.1 OEEC AND THE COUNCIL OF EUROPE

The original central pillars of the competition law of the European Community were Articles 81 and 82 of the Treaty of Rome, which have been applied in many different situations and to a great variety of agreements and practices. To understand the ideas that underlie the drafting of these particular Articles the events which led up to the signing of the Treaty on 25 March 1957 have first to be considered.

The history of Western Europe during the period from the end of the Second World War up to the actual signature of the Treaty shows a recurring pattern of events.[1] An individual statesman puts forward an idea for European cooperation within a particular area of activity. Then follows acceptance by European nations of that idea as a broad political aim, with later development of that aim itself into a detailed international treaty. Upon the basis of this treaty permanent institutions are then formed in order to implement the broad political aim now established, but which themselves lack the authority or political will to ensure that the cooperation itself develops into any kind of supranational integration. The lack of any real progress in this direction leads other politicians then to propose new ideas, in the hope that these, in spite of the disappointing experience of the past, will have the result of bringing about more than mere cooperation between individual European nations.

The first of these European institutions was the Organization for European Economic Co-operation[2] established in 1948, primarily to allocate Marshall Aid, which was the inspired idea of General George Marshall, then United States Secretary

---

[1] For a detailed account of the negotiations leading up to the Treaty of Paris 1951 and the Treaty of Rome 1957, see R. Mayne, *The Recovery of Europe* (Weidenfeld & Nicolson, 1970), Chs. 8–10, and D. Swann, *The Economics of the Common Market* (5th edn, Penguin, 1984), Ch. 1.

[2] This body changed its name in 1960, when joined by the USA and Canada, to that of the Organization for Economic Co-operation and Development (OECD). Among other responsibilities it numbers the International Energy Authority (IEA) which was to feature in an important decision of the Commission referred to in Ch. 8. It plays an important role in coordinating the activities of European and a number of

of State. The object of this plan was the economic rehabilitation of Europe by the provision of much-needed financial assistance, not only for its immediate needs of food, fuel, and other necessities, but also the capital investment required for the modernization and re-establishing of much of the industrial capacity destroyed, or allowed to deteriorate, in the course of the Second World War and the depressed days immediately following. Whilst discussions for the implementation of a customs union were held within the framework of OEEC in the late 1940s, the essential political will to convert this organization into one with any elements of supranational integration was lacking. OEEC went on in the following years to play an important role in the liberalization of trade within Western Europe, but its constitution remained that of a permanent conference of sovereign States without any supranational powers. It lacked, therefore, the ability to effect any major changes leading to integration of the economies of the countries of Western Europe.[3]

The second major European institution, created soon afterwards, was the Council of Europe which, however, also lacked any supranational power. Its founders were chiefly Georges Bidault, French foreign minister, and Paul-Henri Spaak, the Belgian foreign minister, both of whom had attended the famous Congress of Europe at The Hague in May 1948. The original project agreed upon at that Congress had been of a European legislative Assembly to which some sovereign powers, even if of only a limited nature, could be transferred at a future date. British opposition ensured, however, that the Assembly would have a purely consultative rather than a legislative role. The Statute of the Council was signed in May 1949 and the Assembly first met in August that year under the presidency of Paul-Henri Spaak. Its Committee of Ministers could operate only on the basis of unanimity and its Assembly (composed of members of national parliaments) had no legislative powers.

To belittle the achievements of the Council over subsequent decades would be unjust. It was responsible in 1950 and afterwards for the signature by the great majority of European States of the European Convention for the Protection of Human Rights, whose influence has risen steadily over the intervening years. A large number of other conventions have been drafted and negotiated by the staff of the Council, with the support of the Assembly and the Committee of Ministers, covering a wide range of topics including narcotics, terrorism, data protection, enforcement of foreign judgments, family law, and a variety of other social issues. These conventions have had a significant influence on the adoption of related national legislation in the individual member countries participating in the Council. The Council, however, had no influence in the direction of greater

---

other national competition authorities, and publishes influential studies relating for example to cartels and other aspects of competition policy.

[3] Richard Mayne records in *The Recovery of Europe* that during the period 1947 to 1950, while France urged that OEEC should be given greater powers, it was the UK which repeatedly opposed all such moves (p. 127). Edmund Dell, in *The Schuman Plan and the British Abdication of Leadership in Europe* (Oxford University Press, 1995) emphasizes that while the USA wanted the OEEC to have executive powers so that it could become the primary instrument of European economic integration, the UK insisted on national vetoes and the denying of executive powers, fearing the 'federalistic implications of American ideas' (p. 49).

cooperation on purely economic and industrial issues. Progress, therefore, towards the economic or political integration of Western Europe during the period prior to 1950 through the creation of new international institutions was limited.

In the meantime, important developments had been taking place in Germany. At the end of the Second World War in 1945 the country was divided up by the Potsdam Agreement into four zones, the Eastern Zone being placed under the control of the USSR and the three Western Zones under the United States, the United Kingdom, and France respectively. As no agreement could be reached between the occupying powers as to the basis upon which German industry should be reorganized, each power gradually introduced its own legislative and administrative measures in respect of its zone. The original policy objectives behind these measures had been largely negative (to prevent Germany from again becoming a threat to peace) and restrictive, the 'decartelization' of the existing structures of industry in the various sectors (coal, iron and steel, chemicals, plastics, heavy engineering, banking, etc.). Some of the largest 'Konzerns' were split up; for example IG Farben (the huge chemicals combine) was split into three parts which became Bayer, Hoechst, and BASF respectively, and considerable reorganization took place in some other sectors. As democracy gradually returned, the more positive elements in the programme of the Western powers were given more prominence, in an attempt to ensure that the German economy recovered to a sufficient extent to provide an adequate standard of living for its people. The punitive element in the Allied programmes of reorganization gradually faded, and emphasis switched to the establishment of the most effective and efficient means of ensuring that the German economy could be stabilized and so linked on a non-discriminatory basis with the undertakings of France and other Western European nations. Coal and steel were the industries where the need of this reform was of the greatest urgency.

1.2 THE SCHUMAN PLAN AND THE TREATY OF PARIS

It was at this point that a fresh impetus to change was provided by Jean Monnet, a well-known French administrator and civil servant, who throughout his life provided a copious flow of original ideas of economic cooperation between nations both in war and peace.[4] His idea was the bold one of creating a common market for iron, steel, and coal in Western Europe by the removal of all customs duties, tariffs, quotas, and other market restrictions; these rules would be administered by an independent High Authority endowed with supranational powers to which all participating countries would be subject. These ideas were keenly supported and elaborated by Robert Schuman, then French foreign minister, and in April 1950 the detailed proposals for the implementation of Monnet's original ideas were put forward as the Schuman Plan.[5]

---

[4] Mayne, ibid. p. 177. See also Mayne's translation of the *Memoirs of Monnet* (Collins, 1978). A full account of Monnet's life is contained in '*Jean Monnet, the First Statesman of Interdependence*' by François Duchêne (Norton, 1994).

[5] See P Fontaine, *A New Idea for Europe: The Schuman Declaration—1950/2000* (2nd edn, European Commission, 2000), for additional background material.

Not surprisingly, in view of its past negative attitude to the development of other European institutions, the United Kingdom again refused to contemplate participating in any body with powers which could derogate from those of the United Kingdom Parliament. Notwithstanding the fact that the United Kingdom would not join them,[6] the Six (France, Germany, Italy, the Netherlands, Belgium, and Luxembourg) decided to proceed with the Schuman Plan influenced by both the economic and political advantages that the creation of a body with supranational powers could bring to industries so essential to the development of the industrial strength of Western Europe. On 18 April 1951, the Treaty of Paris was signed creating a new legal entity with a status in international law, the European Coal and Steel Community.

The Treaty of Paris was a document of one hundred clauses, three annexes, and a number of protocols. By its terms French and German production of coal and steel was placed under a common High Authority, whose decisions would be binding on the member countries. Its ratification by the governments of the Six was completed by the end of June 1952, and the Common Markets in coal and steel opened on 10 February and 1 May respectively in 1953. It was to have a life of fifty years, coming to an end on 23 July 2002. The objectives of the Treaty were set out in Articles 1 and 2 which defined the task of the Community as: 'to contribute, in harmony with the general economy of the Member States and through the establishment of a Common Market...to economic expansion, growth of employment and a rising standard of living in the Member States'. Article 3 set out the duties of the institutions of the Community: to ensure orderly supplies of materials in the Common Market, to promote the expansion and modernization of production and the rational uses of the raw materials available within the Community, and to promote international trade in those products. Article 4 continued by listing the following practices as incompatible with the new market and, therefore, to be 'abolished and prohibited', namely:

(a) import and export duties, or charges having equivalent effect, and quantitative restrictions on the movement of products

(b) measures which discriminate between producers, purchasers, or consumers relating to prices, delivery terms, or transport rates and conditions, or which interfere with the purchaser's free choice of supplier

(c) subsidies or aids granted by States

(d) restrictive practices 'which tend toward the sharing or exploiting of markets'.

Article 5 continued the reference to protection of competition contained in Article 4(d) with a positive obligation placed upon the Community to 'ensure the establishment, maintenance and observance of normal competitive conditions...'. Clearly, therefore, an early requirement for the new Community would be that its institutions should take responsibility for identifying any anti-competitive practices and eliminating

---

[6] At a later date the UK did enter into a Treaty of Association with the ECSC, but on terms which did not involve the yielding of any parliamentary sovereignty to the new High Authority. See Dell op. cit. n. 3, above, for a full assessment of the reasons for the UK's attitude to the Schuman Plan.

them. These institutions would include the executive body to be known as the High Authority, which had primary responsibility for carrying out the objectives of the Community.[7] Other relevant institutions created by the Treaty were an Assembly, a Special Council of Ministers, and significantly a Court of Justice required to ensure the implementation and application of the Treaty, to provide interpretation of its terms, and to give rulings binding both on the High Authority and Member States as well as on undertakings within the Community.

At this stage it is appropriate to consider the principal reasons for according so much importance to the value of pro-competitive measures within the framework of the Treaty. The chief element was of course that the absence of, or at least the major imperfections of, competition readily visible in the markets covered by the 1951 Treaty of Paris were felt to be major weaknesses in industries that needed the spur of rivalry in order to achieve a higher level of performance. Beyond that element, however, lay the known example of the United States, an economy that had apparently reached its position of pre-eminent industrial strength by its reliance over many decades on free competition, the principle that provided the mainspring of antitrust. If the Coal and Steel Community were to avoid the need for a form of supranational control, involving management on a completely centralized basis, then allowing to its undertakings a fuller freedom of exposure to the forces of competition was unavoidable. This conclusion was accepted even though the individual Member States had little tangible evidence from their own national experience to support a wholesale move away from the existing norm of industry regulated by governmental and private agencies towards the uncertainties of a freer and less regulated market.[8]

Nevertheless, the structure of the Treaty of Paris retained certain elements of central control; so long as supplies of coal or steel were in reasonable balance, competitive forces could operate, but if a serious imbalance arose between supply and demand, the Treaty permitted the High Authority to take measures to bring them back into closer accord. This would necessarily involve interference with the operation of the market. Moreover, the High Authority had jurisdiction under the terms of the Treaty to deal with restraints on competition wholly within an individual Member State, as well as those that affected trade between two or more States within the ECSC.[9]

Articles 65 and 66, therefore, provided detailed legislative backing for the enforcement of Article 4(d). Article 65 contained several provisions relating to the preservation of a competitive structure in the Community. First, paragraph (1) of Article 65 stated that agreements between undertakings, decisions by associations of undertakings, and

---

[7] The functions of the High Authority were set out in Arts. 8–19 of the Treaty. The functions of the Assembly (Arts. 20–5), the Council (Arts. 26–30), and the Court of Justice (Arts. 31–45) followed immediately after in the Treaty.

[8] On the other hand, the Freiburg School, favouring the social market economy as the only means of combining individual liberty with social justice, had substantial influence on the policies of the Christian Democrats under Ludwig Erhard at this time, which in turn led to the enactment of the German Law against Restraints of Competition with effect from January 1958.

[9] A point noted in the editorial preface to the first volume of Common Market Law Reports (1962), a rare example of such comment in the pages of a law report.

concerted practices were prohibited if they tended directly or indirectly to prevent, restrict, or distort 'normal competition' within the Common Market. Although the prohibition applied to all agreements, decisions, and concerted practices, the attention of the High Authority was drawn in particular to those which tended (a) to fix or determine prices, (b) to restrict or control production, technical development, or investment, or (c) to share markets, products, customers, or sources of supply.

Having laid down the basic rule in paragraph (1), paragraph (2) proceeded with some qualifications; specialization agreements or joint buying or selling agencies could be authorized by the High Authority if it found that the agreement (a) would make for substantial improvement in production or distribution, (b) was also essential to achieve such results and was not more restrictive than necessary for that purpose, and (c) was not liable to give undertakings power to determine prices or restrict production or marketing of a substantial part of the products within the Common Market or shield them against effective competition within the Market. Other agreements found to be 'strictly analogous' and meeting the same requirements were also to be permitted by the High Authority. Authorization of agreements could be both conditional and for a limited period, and could be amended or subsequently revoked if circumstances changed sufficiently.

The sanctions to be applied if agreements were made which did not obtain clearance under Article 65(2) were twofold. The first (contained in Article 65(4)) was that the relevant agreement, decision, or practice was 'automatically void' and could not be enforced in any court or tribunal in the Member States. The second sanction, contained in paragraph (5), was that a fine or penalty could be imposed by the High Authority on an undertaking which entered into or tried to enforce such an agreement. Such fines or penalties could be of a substantial nature rising to 10 per cent of annual turnover in respect of fines for past conduct or 20 per cent of daily turnover in the case of penalties imposed to prevent the continuation of an offending agreement.

Article 65, therefore, dealing with agreements, decisions, and concerted practices, anticipated in some respects the corresponding Article 81 of the Treaty of Rome. Article 66 by contrast dealt with the problem of future mergers or concentration of undertakings in the coal and steel markets; it is relevant to remember that problems of excessive concentration and oligopolistic structure were always a major issue in these markets which since the ending of the Second World War (and notwithstanding the efforts of the Western powers under their 'decartelization' programmes for Germany) had not enjoyed any period of genuine competition. Consent to such mergers could only be given by the High Authority if it found that the proposed transaction would not give power to the undertakings concerned to determine prices or to control or restrict production or distribution, or to hinder effective competition in a substantial part of the market, or otherwise to evade the rules of competition found in the Treaty so as to give an 'artificially privileged position involving a substantial advantage in access to supplies or markets' to any such undertakings. The High Authority was given authority by paragraph (3) of Article 66 to provide what in effect would be a form of group exemption from the need for prior consent for small undertakings wishing to

merge and was also given sweeping powers to impose fines or order divestiture if concentration took place without its consent.

Finally, paragraph (7) dealt with the problem of an undertaking, private or public,
which either *de facto* or *de jure* held a dominant position shielding it against effective competition in a substantial part of the Common Market and abused that position for purposes 'contrary to the objectives of the Treaty'. In such a situation, the
High Authority could make recommendations to such undertakings to prevent such
abuse of its position and in default could 'by decisions taken in consultation with the
Government concerned' determine the prices and conditions of sale that that undertaking must apply and draw up mandatory delivery or production programmes with
which it must comply. If it failed to comply, substantial fines could be imposed. In this
last paragraph (7), we find for the first time the concept of 'abuse of a dominant position' which would appear again in the equivalent Article 82 of the Treaty of Rome.[10]

Article 67 was headed generally 'Interference with conditions of competition' being
intended to cover the problem of assistance provided by Member States to undertakings within the coal or steel industry without the approval of the High Authority. The
High Authority was itself permitted to allow States to grant aid to individual undertakings but only on terms and for a period which it had laid down. This provision
foreshadowed similar clauses found in Articles 87 to 89 of the Treaty of Rome.

To complete the array of powers granted to the High Authority, Article 60 prohibited pricing practices which either involved price reductions of a predatory nature
which assisted the acquisition by an undertaking of a monopoly position or, alternatively, discriminatory pricing policies under which sellers applied different conditions
to comparable transactions, especially on the ground of the nationality of the buyer.
To enable it to cope with any such practices, the High Authority could order that price
lists and conditions of sale be made public.

This brief review of the powers conferred on the High Authority of the ECSC shows
how the original simple conception contained in the Schuman Plan for unifying
the coal, iron, and steel production and sales of the Six was converted through the
Treaty of Paris into a set of working rules binding under international law on the Six;
it embodied, for the first time in an international treaty, a set of rules of competition
tailored to the special circumstances of particular industrial sectors in a group of sovereign States. The executive authority for implementation of the rules lay firmly with
the High Authority, but subject to both the judicial control of an independent Court
of Justice and the political control of the Council of Ministers, with whom the High
Authority worked in close cooperation. These principles of cooperation, but with legislative powers vested exclusively in the High Authority, and with equality of Member
States, provided both an institutional framework and a set of substantive rules which,
as we shall see, proved an important model a few years later, when negotiations began

---

[10] Duchêne, op. cit. p. 213 records that the draftsman of Arts. 85–6 (now Arts. 81–2) was a US antitrust
lawyer, Robert Bowie.

which were destined to lead to the extension of the principles of the ECSC into a much wider field.

2. THE TREATY OF ROME AND THE FORMATION OF THE EUROPEAN ECONOMIC COMMUNITY

2.1 THE BENELUX MEMORANDUM

The first real step towards Western European integration in the economic area had now been taken. The success of the Six in agreeing upon a basis for cooperation within such crucial industrial sectors as coal and steel led naturally to further consideration of the possibility of the application of these principles of integration on a broader front. The progress made in establishing the Coal and Steel Community had, however, to some extent been overshadowed by the subsequent failure of the Six to agree to the terms for a European Defence Community, the French National Assembly having rejected this project at the end of August 1954. Notwithstanding the temporary depression which this setback cast over those who favoured closer industrial and commercial arrangements linking the Six, once again Jean Monnet was ready with proposals for the development of further cooperation, on a wider economic and political level. To his individual contribution further impetus was added by the Benelux Memorandum[11] which was to have long-term significance in the establishment and development of a Common Market on a wider basis even than the Coal and Steel Community. A key extract from this Memorandum reads:

All partial integration tends to solve the difficulties in one sector by measures which harm other sectors or the consumers' interests, and it tends to exclude foreign competition. That is not the way to increase European productivity. Furthermore, sector integration does not help to strengthen the feeling of Europe's solidarity in unity in the same degree as general economic integration. To strengthen this feeling, it is essential that the notion of the European States' joint responsibility for the common good be incorporated in an organization adapted to the pursuit of the general interest and whose executive body is responsible not to Governments but to a supranational Parliament...

That is why it seems opportune for the three Benelux governments to take a well prepared initiative which might usefully be announced at the ECSC Foreign Ministers' meeting. Such an initiative would aim at establishing a supranational community whose task it would be to achieve the economic integration of Europe in the general sense, proceeding by means of a customs union to the establishment of an economic union...

A positive response was obtained to this document from the German government, supporting the need for economic integration, liberalization of trade in goods and

---

[11] Submitted by Spaak on behalf of the Benelux nations to the Foreign Ministers of the Six on 6 May 1955 with a covering note to Monnet: 'herewith your child' (Mayne, *Recovery of Europe*, p. 232).

services, the elimination of tariffs, and the free movement of persons. The response also significantly emphasized the need for competition rules in order to establish normal market conditions within the integrated market, to protect competition from State intervention and also from private monopoly power.[12]

2.2 THE SPAAK REPORT

The result of this activity was the meeting held at Messina in Sicily on 29 and 30 May 1955 of the foreign ministers of the Six, principally to discuss the possibility of extending the principles of the ECSC on a wider front. The resulting Messina Declaration, which was substantially influenced by the Benelux Memorandum, set in motion a series of studies relating to the establishment of a European Common Market to be free from all customs duties and quantitative restrictions between its members. Preparation of treaties to shape these new ideas into detailed political and institutional form was entrusted to a group of senior officials under the presidency of Spaak. The importance of the preservation and promotion of a competitive structure of industry within such a Market was already well understood, and the final resolution of the Messina Conference contained, inter alia, the following passage: 'Its [i.e. The Treaty's] application necessitates a study of the following questions... *The elaboration of rules to ensure undistorted competition within the Community*, which will in particular exclude any national discrimination'. (Original emphasis)

The Spaak Report[13] is a seminal document of great importance, which comprises the most important of the various preparatory works (*travaux préparatoires*) upon which the subsequent Treaty of Rome is based. The necessity for freedom of competition within the new Market referred to by the Messina Declaration does not seem to have been in doubt, although the detailed drafting of the rules relating to competition to be contained in the Treaty was to be the subject of keen argument and negotiation between the different Member States involved, in particular between the French and German representatives.

The first paragraph of the Spaak Report sets the context within which competition policy will have to operate:

The object of the European Common Market should be to create a vast zone of common economic policy, constituting a powerful unit of production permitting continuous expansion and increased stability and accelerated raising of the standard of living and the development of harmonious relations between its Member States... These advantages of a Common Market, however, cannot be obtained unless adequate time is allowed and means are collectively made available to enable the necessary adjustment to be effected, unless practices whereby competition between producers is distorted are put to an end, unless co-operation

[12] J. Kallaugher, 'The Influence of German Competition Law on the Development of the Competition Law of the European Communities' (unpublished article). The permission of the author to refer to it is gratefully acknowledged.

[13] Kallaugher records in the same article that although the working group responsible for the report was chaired by Spaak, the chief draftsmen were a German, von der Groeben, and a Frenchman, Uri.

between states is established, to establish monetary stability, economic expansion, and social progress...

At paragraph 55 of the Report, we find reference to the detailed requirements for competition policy in such a market:

In the final period, the elimination of trade barriers will lead to the disappearance of the opportunities for discrimination by competing enterprises. The problem only remains because there are enterprises which, owing to their size or specialization or the agreements they have concluded, enjoy a monopoly position. The action against discrimination, therefore, links up with the action that will be necessary to counteract the formation of monopolies within the Common Market. The Treaty will have to lay down basic rules on these points... More generally, the Treaty will have to provide means of ensuring that monopoly situations or practices do not stand in the way of the fundamental objectives of the Common Market. To this end, it will be necessary to prevent—

- A division of markets by agreement between enterprises, since this would be tantamount to re-establishing the compartmentalization of the market.

- Agreements to limit production or curb technical progress because they would run counter to progress and productivity.

- The absorption or domination of the market for a product by a single enterprise since this would eliminate one of the essential advantages of a vast market, namely that it reconciles the use of mass production techniques with the maintenance of competition.

Already we can sense here an anticipation of the final wording of Articles 81 and 82, indicating that the new Treaty will go well beyond the more limited objectives of Articles 65 and 66 of the Coal and Steel Community Treaty. The Spaak Report was indeed a document that combined compelling logic with a considerable degree of imagination and was accepted with little amendment by the foreign ministers of the Six at the Venice Conference on 29 May 1956. The officials responsible for its preparation resumed work some weeks later at Val Duchesse (just outside Brussels) for the preparation of the Treaty that was to embody the greater part of the content of the Spaak Report, subject to those slight modifications agreed to at the Venice Conference. Preparation of the detailed draft of its Articles then took place continuously over the next ten months prior to the signature of the Treaty of Rome on 27 March 1957.

2.3 NEGOTIATIONS OVER THE TERMS OF ARTICLES 81 AND 82

The minutes and text of the relevant meetings during this period illustrate the ebb and flow of negotiations over the parts of the Treaty which deal with competition and related issues. The section of the Treaty dealing with competition rules is contained in Part III 'Policy of the Community: Title I—Common Rules: Chapter 1—Rules on Competition'. Chapter 1 covers the Articles which were subsequently numbered 81 to 89. Articles 81 and 82 are the main Articles covering the rules of competition applicable to undertakings. The negotiators had, of course, the recent model of Articles 65 and 66 of the Treaty of Paris to follow but the provisions adopted in that Treaty to apply to the mainly oligopolistic market situation for both coal and steel would clearly not be appropriate in their entirety to the far wider range of products, processes, and markets that the new Treaty would have to cover.

One of the earliest points discussed and accepted was that the Treaty should contain a specific prohibition, applicable across the range of industrial activity, against discrimination on grounds of nationality (now found in Article 12). This principle clearly had importance far beyond the rules of competition alone; and was ultimately not included in the later section concerned mainly with rules on competition but earlier in the Treaty, as a 'principle', to emphasize its importance and wide application to all aspects of Community activity rather than just as one of many rules relating to competition.

The more detailed rules contained in the section of the Treaty dealing with competition were in fact drafted before the final form of the agreement was reached on the 'principles' set out in Articles 1 to 7 and in particular before the adoption in its final form of Article 3(f). Articles 1 and 2 declared the establishment of the European Economic Community and proclaimed its tasks of establishing a Common Market to bring about, through the progressive approximation of economic policies, a harmonious development of economic activities, a continuous and balanced expansion, an increase in stability, an accelerated raising of the standard of living, and closer relations between States. Article 3 (equivalent to Article 3 of the Treaty of Paris) listed the policies of the Community necessary in order that the purposes set out in Article 2 could be achieved but in accordance with the wider objectives of the Treaty of Rome. They are considerably more comprehensive than in the earlier Treaty and in particular we find (as we do not in the Treaty of Paris) the following original Article relating to competition: '(f) The institution of a system ensuring that competition in the Common Market is not distorted'.[14]

In Article 4 were listed the institutions required to carry out the Community's tasks, namely the Assembly (subsequently known as the European Parliament), the Council, the Commission, and the Court of Justice (and in an advisory capacity only, the Economic and Social Committee); Article 5 laid down a further principle relevant to the maintenance of competition. In this, Member States are required:

To take all appropriate measures, whether general or particular, to ensure fulfilment of the obligations arising out of this Treaty or resulting from actions taken by the institutions of the Community. They shall facilitate the achievement of the Community's tasks. They shall abstain from any measure which could jeopardise the attainment of the objectives of this Treaty.

Under the terms of this Article, it is clear that Member States are required to take measures to ensure that competition in the Common Market is not distorted, this being one of the major objectives of Article 3, and in both a positive and negative sense to contribute to the implementation of competition policy.

[14] Now Art. 3(1)(g).

We come now to the Articles in the Treaty, numbers 81 to 89, which deal with 'Rules on Competition'. Of these, Articles 81 and 82 contained the main substantive principles of law applicable to undertakings. Article 83 provided for the making of subordinate regulations and directives, and Articles 84 and 85 for the responsibilities of both Member States and the Commission during the transitional period before such subordinate regulations had been enacted.

Since it would be unfair if Member States could at the same time effectively reduce the degree of competitive activity within their own economies by giving privileges to monopolies such as nationalized State bodies or authorities, Articles 86 to 89 inclusive provided rules governing the activities of Member States in maintaining public undertakings (Article 86), and in providing State aid in any form to undertakings (Articles 87 to 89).

The archives of the Council show that the wording of the Treaty of Rome dealing with the rules on competition was the subject of lengthy discussion and indeed disagreement between in particular the French and German officials. The German preference was for an authorization system, under which agreements which restricted competition would be automatically void, unless they had received prior authorization from an administrative body to which the agreement had been notified. The French by contrast preferred a system normally described as 'control of abuse', under which an agreement containing restrictions on competition would remain valid unless and until an adverse decision had been rendered against it.[15]

The final outcome of these negotiations was that wording was adopted for Article 81 which, while clearly rejecting the French proposals in respect of restrictive agreements (though accepting them in respect of abuses by undertakings of dominant position), did not accept the German position either. Instead the choice of how the 'prohibition' principle was to be applied was left over; two methods of implementing it were possible. The strict rule of prior authorization by an administrative or judicial body, following notification, was one; the other, less stringent, was that either an entire agreement, or certain clauses found within it if severable from the rest of the agreement, would be classified under a process of 'exception légale' as either legal or illegal, therefore valid or void. This process would be carried out by applying together the prohibition in 81(1) and the exemption in 81(3), without any need for prior notification; the mechanisms however by which such a legal exception rule would be carried out were left over for the Commission to decide at a later date.[16]

---

[15] Often referred to as the principle of 'exception légale'. The English equivalent of 'legal exception' though correct, is not in common usage.

[16] The issue of the intention of the draftsmen of Art. 81 became of relevance in the course of the debate over the modernization proposals of the Commission following their publication in April 1999. See G. Marenco, at pp. 145–96 of *European Competition Law Annual 2000: The Modernization of EC Antitrust Policy*, ed. C.-D. Ehlermann and I. Atanasiu (Hart Publishing, 2001). See also I. Forrester, at pp. 75–122 of the same volume. Both Marenco and Forrester reach a finding that the legislative history of the drafting of Art. 81 shows that the intention was to leave the Community free to choose at a later date between the two possible systems for implementing the principle of prohibition contained in that Article.

2.4 THE TEXT OF ARTICLES 81 AND 82

Articles 81 and 82 were finally adopted in the following form:

Article 81

1. The following shall be prohibited as incompatible with the common market: all agreements between undertakings, decisions by associations of undertakings and concerted practices which may affect trade between Member States and which have as their object or effect the prevention, restriction or distortion of competition within the common market, and in particular those which:

    (a) directly or indirectly fix purchase or selling prices or any other trading conditions;

    (b) limit or control production, markets, technical development, or investment;

    (c) share markets or sources of supply;

    (d) apply dissimilar conditions to equivalent transactions with other trading parties, thereby placing them at a competitive disadvantage;

    (e) make the conclusion of contracts subject to acceptance by the other parties of supplementary obligations which, by their nature or according to commercial usage, have no connection with the subject of such contracts.

2. Any agreements or decisions prohibited pursuant to this Article shall be automatically void.

3. The provisions of paragraph 1 may, however, be declared inapplicable in the case of:

    — any agreement or category of agreements between undertakings;

    — any decision or category of decisions by associations of undertakings;

    — any concerted practice or category of concerted practices;

    which contributes to improving the production or distribution of goods or to promoting technical or economic progress, while allowing consumers a fair share of the resulting benefit, and which does not:

    (a) impose on the undertakings concerned restrictions which are not indispensable to the attainment of these objectives;

    (b) afford such undertakings the possibility of eliminating competition in respect of a substantial part of the products in question.

Article 82

Any abuse by one or more undertakings of a dominant position within the common market or in a substantial part of it shall be prohibited as incompatible with the common market in so far as it may affect trade between Member States.

Such abuse may, in particular, consist in:

(a) directly or indirectly imposing unfair purchase or selling prices or other unfair trading conditions;

(b) limiting production, markets or technical development to the prejudice of consumers;

(c) applying dissimilar conditions to equivalent transactions with other trading parties, thereby placing them at a competitive disadvantage;

(d) making the conclusion of contracts subject to acceptance by the other parties of supplementary obligations which, by their nature or according to commercial usage have no connection with the subject of such contracts.

2.5 THE TWO SETS OF COMPETITION RULES CONTRASTED

The examples in Article 81(1) were certainly not intended to be exhaustive. They have some common features with, but cover a wider range than, those examples given in Article 65 of the ECSC Treaty, which are limited to agreements which fix prices, restrain production, technical development, or investment, or involve the sharing of markets, products, customers, and sources of supply. Of these provisions in Article 81(1), items (d) and (e) are unique to it, items (a) and (b) are more widely drawn than their equivalent in the ECSC Treaty, and (c) is rather more narrowly drawn. No great significance should, however, be read into these minor differences. Neither the Commission nor the Community Courts have subsequently placed any weight on the fact that any particular type of agreement has been omitted from this list. Whilst inclusion in the list may certainly be of minor relevance, in that it indicates the type of restrictive agreement which the framers of the Treaty may have had in mind, the wide scope remaining for a declaration of inapplicability under paragraph (3) minimizes the significance of even that factor.

The negotiators were well aware of the differences in national competition laws, particularly between French and German law, and were concerned primarily to establish basic principles and to allow the Commission thereafter to deal with the remaining issues. These basic principles corresponding to the three separate paragraphs of Article 81 were:

(1) that a defined category of agreement/concerted practice/decision of an association with anti-competitive objects or effects and the potential to affect trade between Member States would be prohibited and

(2) that if prohibited, the agreement/concerted practice/decision would be void and

(3) that the prohibition could nevertheless be declared (in some manner not yet specified) inapplicable, i.e. an exemption could be granted, if the agreement/concerted practice/decision satisfied four conditions.

A major difference between the new Treaty and the Treaty of Paris was clearly to be that the implementation of rules relating to competition would involve the cooperation of the relevant authorities in Member States, since the Commission would not be required nor indeed able (unlike the High Authority under the Treaty of Paris) to deal with the complete range of practices and agreements that would potentially fall under its jurisdiction. The content of Articles 83(2)(e), 84, and 85 soon made clear that in enforcing competition policy a basis for cooperation was required between the

Commission and Member States. At this time competition law in the Six was in a primitive state. Italy, Belgium, and Luxembourg had no such legislation. The Netherlands had only an Economic Competition Act, which required registration of restrictive agreements but granted exemptions on a relatively liberal basis. French competition law was almost entirely concerned with vertical agreements and in particular with preventing refusals to deal. Germany alone had a new and relatively comprehensive competition law and administrative procedures and machinery capable of enforcing it, which came into force on the same date as the Treaty of Rome.

It is the more remarkable, therefore, that whereas the High Authority had exclusive jurisdiction over competition issues under Articles 65 and 66, the Treaty of Rome contained provisions for sharing jurisdiction over the equivalent area of law between the Commission and the Member States. Clearly much work still had to be done after signature of the Treaty to work out how this relationship would be implemented. Article 83(2)(e) stated that the relationship between national and Community laws would have to be dealt with in regulations or directives to be adopted by the Council,[17] acting unanimously on proposals from the Commission and after consultation with the Assembly. Article 84 retained the right for authorities in Member States, until such regulations or directives had been adopted, to rule on the status of agreements, decisions and concerted practices, and on abuses of dominant positions within the Common Market in accordance with national law applying, however, the substantive terms of 81(3) and 82. The Commission itself was not allowed to be inactive during the interim period prior to the adoption of such regulations; Article 85 gave it authority to take steps to investigate cases of suspected infringement of the Treaty principles.

The Treaty of Rome came into effect on 1 January 1958. In Part II we shall analyse the substantive content of Articles 81 to 86, but it is already clear from this brief account of their origins that the legal provisions of these Articles, whilst influenced by Articles 65 and 66 of the Treaty of Paris, went considerably beyond them both in width of application and in the specification of the only grounds upon which exemption could be granted. On the other hand, the differences in the relative content of Article 66 of the Treaty of Paris and the new Article 82 appeared to have the result that under the latter Article the Commission lacked any control over concentrations or mergers as such, merely having jurisdiction over abuse of a dominant position by individual undertakings. It seems that those who negotiated Article 82 did not intend that it should provide the Commission with a control mechanism over concentrations; had they intended to do so, it might have been expected that they would have made use of wording adapted from that already available in Article 66, paragraphs 1 to 5, rather than the more limited wording using only the terminology of paragraph 7 actually adopted.[18]

---

[17] Dell (op. cit.) notes that the existence of the Council of Ministers as the legislative body under the Treaty of Rome represented the High Authority model under the Treaty of Paris (p. 184).

[18] See, however, the European Court's judgment in Case 6/72 *Europemballage Corporation and Continental Can Co. Inc.* v. *Commission* [1973] ECR 215: CMLR 199.

In spite of this limitation, it was widely believed that these Articles in the Treaty, and in particular Articles 81 and 82, contained far-reaching and important rules affecting a wide range of agreements and practices that could affect trade between the Member States of the Six. The primary task of that Directorate of the Commission responsible for enforcing competition policy (referred to throughout the rest of the book as 'DG Comp') would be to establish the detailed content of these rules and exemptions, as well as procedural machinery adequate for enforcing them.

4

THE EARLY YEARS OF DG COMP

1. THE NEED FOR A PROCEDURAL FRAMEWORK

1.1 THE REQUIREMENTS OF ARTICLE 83

It is a sobering thought that the detailed application of important international treaties and basic constitutional documents, however lofty their inspiration or impressively ceremonial their inauguration, is determined largely by the subsequent thoughts and debates of anxious men and women sitting around a table, blank sheets of paper before them. In other words, the conversion of relatively abstract treaty principles into enforceable procedural and substantive rules adequate to implement the ideals which underlie the constitutional framework can be achieved only through the hard and unromantic task of drafting detailed working documents, and then obtaining sufficient acceptance of their provisions from all interested parties. In this process, the skill involved is to pay enough attention to those parties' special or national interests to obtain their consent without at the same time risking undue compromise over the basic underlying principles of the original Treaty.

The implementation of the Articles of the Treaty of Rome relating to competition itself involved this time-consuming, but necessary process. The Treaty had established the Commission as the basic executive body responsible under Article 211 for carrying out the implementation of the Treaty; this Article lays down a fourfold task for the Commission. Of these tasks, two were directly relevant to DG Comp with its particular responsibility for implementing Articles 81 to 89. The first was to ensure that the provisions of the Treaty, as well as measures taken by the Community institutions under its authority, were applied; the second that it should exercise powers, to be conferred on it at a later date by the Council, for the implementation of subordinate legislation which the Council would prescribe. These general obligations were supplemented by the more specific references contained in Article 83. Paragraph (1) provided that the Council was to adopt appropriate regulations and directives to give effect to the principles set out in Articles 81 and 82 'within three years of the entry into force of this Treaty'. If that period elapsed without the regulations being adopted, then the requirement for unanimity ceased, and a qualified majority of the Council could authorize the adoption of regulations; in both cases, however, regulations must be based on a proposal from the Commission, and the Parliament had the right to be consulted.

Such regulations were envisaged by Article 83(2) to deal with five items. These ranged from the general to the highly specific. The general requirements referred to the need to define the outer range of the jurisdiction of the provisions of Articles 81 and 82 so that the extent of their application to transport, agriculture, and other specialized sectors could be clarified. A further general requirement was the need to determine the relationship between national laws and the provisions of the Treaty, and the third general aim was to ensure that the respective functions of the Court of Justice and the Commission were clearly defined.

Two specific objectives were also defined under headings (a) and (b) of Article 83(2). Compliance with the requirements of these two Articles 81 and 82 could clearly only be enforced if sanctions could be applied by the Commission to undertakings failing to comply with the requirements of the Articles or with decisions made by the Commission in implementing its jurisdiction. It was therefore necessary that fines and periodic penalty payments be provided as sanctions and also that the application of the procedural rules for exemption of agreements contained in Article 81(3) was spelled out. This would require the Commission itself to regulate the proper implementation of these rules, balancing the importance of its effective supervision against the need to keep administrative procedures as simple as possible, in compliance with the requirements of the Treaty.

For this reason, whilst Articles 84 and 85 provided for the temporary enforcement of the rules on competition pending the adoption of the relevant regulations by both Member States and the Commission itself, the preparation of a comprehensive procedural regulation was felt from the earliest days by the officials of DG Comp to be an essential foundation for the exercise of its powers. The initial resources of DG Comp were very small, growing slowly from a handful of senior officials appointed during the first year of its operations, gradually rising to about 20 by the end of the second year, and increasing steadily but slowly to 78 by April 1964 and to just over 100 by ten years later. To put these figures in proportion, in 2008 there are approximately 800 DG Comp officials, around half of whom are 'A' grade staff.[1]

1.2 THE NEGOTIATIONS OVER THE DRAFT REGULATION

The first four years of its existence were therefore mainly committed to the preparation of this procedural regulation, later to become familiar as 'Regulation 17', which would need to provide answers to those questions about the application of the competition rules, for which the Treaty itself either provided no specific answer or one that was plainly inadequate. It had first to conduct a review of the existing national laws of Member States which, as we have seen, varied from the non-existent to the comprehensive but untried. Consultation had to take place on a wide basis with Member States

---

[1] Some of these are engaged however in State aid work rather than in competition matters.

and with numerous experts and organizations: meetings and conferences were held
to discuss both the existing systems of law in Member States and the best method of
adopting features from them for inclusion in the Regulation. The influence of German
lawyers was particularly strong at this time, partly because they had recently seen the
introduction of the German competition statute after long and fierce internal debate.[2]
The German approach was to favour a system under which specified agreements in
restraint of competition were void unless and until exemption was conferred upon
them by the constitutive act of the Commission, which alone could have the power
of granting exemption from the basic prohibition of the law. In direct contrast, the
French preference was for specific exemptions which would be automatically applied
if the necessary conditions were satisfied, without the need for any intervention or
imprimatur by the Commission. This conflict was eventually resolved by the Council
on a basis necessarily involving a compromise between the two approaches.

Those negotiating the wording of Article 81 had, as we have seen in Chapter 3,[3] left
over the method of implementation, for resolution at a later date. On the other hand,
the terms of the Regulation as finally adopted left open the possibility that agreements
in existence at the date of the adoption of the Regulation could be declared invalid
following investigation by the Commission, not necessarily with retrospective but
simply with prospective effect, and that exemptions could be granted on a retrospective basis rather than merely prospectively. This situation was in due course clarified
by the European Court of Justice in *Brasserie de Haecht (No. 2)*[4] when the doctrine
of provisional validity for agreements in existence at the implementation date of the
Regulation was upheld, and the full rigours of the German preference for total illegality and unenforceability of all agreements pending the granting of the exemption not
accepted. Equally however it was felt at that early date, in the absence of national courts
or competition authorities experienced in making rulings in competition cases, that
the French preference that no prior decision of the Commission was required before a
restrictive agreement could be declared void by a national court was unacceptable.

1.3 THE INVOLVEMENT OF THE EUROPEAN PARLIAMENT

Once the draft of the Regulation had been agreed internally within DG Comp, following
these protracted negotiations, it had to be approved by the full Commission, and then
submitted also to the Economic and Social Committee and the European Parliament.
At the instance of the Parliament, whose committee reviewing the Regulation had

[2] J. Kallaugher, 'The Influence of German Competition Law on the Development of the Competition Law
of the European Communities' (unpublished article).

[3] See Ch. 3, fn. 16.

[4] Case 48/72 *Brasserie de Haecht* v. *Wilkin-Janssens (No. 2)* [1973] ECR 77: CMLR 287. This decision of the
Court of Justice followed the same general lines as earlier cases decided by it on cases arising under the ECSC
rules (Case 1/58 *Stork* v. *High Authority* [1959] ECR 17) and on the interpretation of Art. 1 of Reg. 17 (Case
13/61 *de Geus* v. *Robert Bosch* [1962] ECR 45: CMCR 1). The German view can be said to have prevailed to the
extent that the Court's decision excluded the possibility of provisional validity for new agreements.

as rapporteur Professor Arved Deringer, a German lawyer and expert on competition law, some important additional proposals were made. The early paragraphs of the Deringer Report contain a careful analysis of the three possible approaches which the Commission could adopt in its approach to the implementation of Articles 81 and 82 in providing the answers to the essential questions which the Articles themselves for the most part had not dealt with. The first was that adopted in the then current Dutch national legislation, under which all restrictive agreements had to be notified, but by notification obtained a presumption of validity until the competition authority was able to prove that any particular agreement constituted an abuse, and then with prospective effect only. The second was the *French* approach, under which undertakings would themselves decide if their agreements were in accordance with the law, but the competition authorities could elect to challenge them and, if successful, declare them unenforceable under the principle of 'legal exception' with retrospective effect. The third was the *German, and ECSC*, approach of preventative control, under which exemption from the general law prohibiting agreements restraining competition was only effective if notification had been effected and an individual or group exemption then pronounced or applied by the competition authorities.

After discussing the various advantages and disadvantages of these systems, the Parliamentary Committee accepted the third alternative as most consistent with the actual terms of the Treaty, and as the system most likely to give the Commission the widest knowledge of the types of agreement being made by undertakings within the Community. The Committee suggested that Article 82 should also be brought within the procedural framework of the new Regulation, although it had originally been intended to apply only to Article 81, and this was accepted in the final form of the Regulation. Notwithstanding the lesser probability that undertakings would wish to notify to DG Comp the existence of dominant positions held by them in individual markets and possible abuses of which they were guilty, the inclusion of Article 82 within the scope of the Regulation enabled the powers given to the Commission in respect of investigations and the imposition of fines and penalties to be applied likewise to abuses of a dominant position as well as in the control of agreements, decisions, and concerted practices.

It has certainly proved more convenient for the Commission that both Articles are dealt with in the same procedural Regulation. Numerous other suggestions were made by the Parliament's Report, including the introduction of a negative clearance procedure. No such facility existed under German competition law, but this was accepted as part of the procedural machinery of DG Comp, where it has proved its practical usefulness. It enabled the Commission to certify that the relevant Articles of the Treaty did not apply in an individual case because the jurisdictional requirements of Articles 81 or 82 were not satisfied. This might be because of insufficient effect on trade between Member States, or because the sector concerned was not covered by Article 81, or because the agreement was insufficiently restrictive to have any effect detrimental to competition in the Common Market, perhaps having an effect purely within one Member State. A negative clearance, however, would be valid only so long as the facts upon the basis of which it had been granted remained unchanged. If these altered, then the original negative clearance would automatically, and without further decision of the Commission, cease to have effect.

The concept of the 'negative clearance', therefore, had to be contrasted with the effect of granting a formal exemption under the provisions of 81(3). Once the Commission had taken a notified agreement through this procedure and satisfied itself that all four conditions for exemption had been satisfied, the parties were enabled, as with negative clearance, to continue to operate the agreement without fear of fines, penalties, or legal unenforceability in the courts. Unlike the position with negative clearance, however, DG Comp retained control over the agreement since it would only have been exempted for a specific period of time (not normally exceeding ten years) with a continuing right for the Commission to obtain information from time to time relating to its operation, and subject to renewal at a future date when the renewal conditions might be varied by DG Comp in the light of any change in circumstances since the date of the original exemption.[5] If there were a major change in any material circumstances affecting the exemption, or the recipient could be shown to have provided false information to obtain it, then it could be withdrawn at once, if necessary retroactively.

The negotiations over the terms of Regulation 17 were long-drawn-out, encountering a full measure of both legal and political difficulties. The Commission's attitude to the draft Regulation was understandably ambivalent. On the one hand it was alarmed by the sheer size and scope of the jurisdiction which the Treaty provided in this area, so that it welcomed the ability to share it to some extent with Member States and their national authorities. On the other hand, it was concerned not to allow Member States or their national courts to operate the exemption provisions nor to operate a system based on the 'abuse' rather than the 'prohibition' principle, for fear that loss of Commission control over the system would weaken both its effectiveness and its consistency.

1.4 THE ENACTMENT OF REGULATION 17/62

The final text of the Regulation was approved by the Council on 6 February 1962 and published in the Official Journal on 21 February, with the result that it became effective on the following 13 March. For many years it remained in force unaltered save for minor amendments and provided a strong procedural base for the Commission's administration of Community competition policy. It gave the Commission powers which were undoubtedly greater than those granted by the Treaty to any other Directorate General. Not until the very end of the twentieth century would the first significant changes be made to its content, by the widening under Regulation 1216/99

---

[5] Thus, in the well-known *Transocean Marine Paint Association* case, the conditions imposed on renewal of the exemption were considerably more stringent than in the original decision. The two decisions of the Commission can be found at [1967] CMLR D9 and [1974] 1 CMLR D11 respectively, part of the latter being the subject of appeal by the Association to the court as Case 17/74 [1974] ECR 1063: 2 CMLR 459. The exemption was renewed again in 1980 and 1988.

of the categories of agreement to which exemption could be granted without the need for prior notification. Only at the end of April 2004 would it finally be replaced as part of the modernization programme, under which the Commission's monopoly of granting individual exemption under 81(3) would be removed to be shared with national courts and competition authorities, and the process of notification to the Commission abolished.

2. THE PROVISIONS OF REGULATION 17

2.1 RECITALS

Even though Regulation 17/62 has been repealed with effect from 1 May 2004, it is still necessary to be familiar with its content, because of the great influence which it had over the development of Community competition law and policy for over forty years.

It opened with lengthy recitals setting out the background to the adoption of the Regulation by the Council. Under civil law as well as under the practice of the European Court, it is open to courts interpreting such a Regulation to look to the terms of any recitals for assistance in interpreting points of difficulty arising from the construction of individual clauses. The Commission and the Council have both adopted the practice, in regulations governing competition law, of setting out long (some would say overlong) recitals giving the background to the circumstances in which they were adopted and their detailed objectives, apparently in order to assist the European Court of Justice and national courts in their interpretation. Some of the recitals in Regulations were purely precautionary, referring back to relevant Articles of the Treaty of Rome (notably 81, 82, 83, and 229) which establish the powers (*vires*) of the Council or Commission to act and set the framework within which the Regulation has to operate. However, lengthy references are also made to practical and policy issues which concern the implementation by the Commission through DG Comp of competition policy. Thus Regulation 17 referred to the fact that the number of agreements, decisions, and concerted practices to be investigated would probably be too numerous to be examined at the same time, whilst others might have special features rendering them less prejudicial to the development of a Common Market so that there was a need to provide more flexible arrangements for the treatment of certain categories of agreement. There was also reference to the need for liaison with the competent authorities of the Member States both in acquiring information and in carrying out investigations required to bring to light any agreements prohibited under Article 81 or any abuse of dominant position in breach of Article 82. Reference was also made to the need for procedural requirements to ensure that third parties, whose interests may be affected by a decision, were given the opportunity of submitting their comments before decisions were formally taken. Mention was made of the right of the European Court under Article 229 to exercise its unlimited jurisdiction in respect of any decisions where the Commission imposed fines or periodic penalties.

2.2 ARTICLES 1 TO 9 OF THE REGULATION

After this introduction, Article 1 of Regulation 17 launched immediately into a dec-laration that agreements, decisions, and concerted practices covered by Article 81(1) and abuses of dominant position covered by Article 82 'shall be prohibited, no prior decision to that effect being required'. The drafting of Article 1 in this way was prob-ably required as a direct consequence of the terms of Articles 81 and 82 in the Treaty. Nevertheless, at least one national court (in the Netherlands) had declared in 1961 that, notwithstanding the terms of Article 81(2), agreements covered by the Article were not invalid until a decision to that effect had been taken by the Commission,[6] so that this Article was required to make clear to Member States and their courts that no Commission decision was required as a necessary condition of invalidity.

It was clearly beneficial to undertakings to be able to obtain confirmation where appropriate that their agreements or practices were not covered by Articles 81 or 82. Article 2 of the Regulation gave authority to the Commission to give such negative clearance. In practice, undertakings did almost invariably apply in the alternative for either negative clearance or an exemption under Article 81(3).

Article 3 covered the important subject of complaints; paragraph (2) states that either Member States or natural or legal persons claiming a legitimate interest in the subject matter of the complaint may make application to the Commission which is then bound to investigate, though of course the volume of complaints and notifica-tions to DG Comp gradually reached such a level that the Commission could not give priority to all applications and some had to be deferred for a considerable period. If, after investigation, the Commission wished to require the undertakings concerned to bring legal infringements to an end, the Article permitted them to do so by way of decision,[7] but paragraph (3) entitled the Commission to attempt to dispose of the complaint by way of informal negotiation and recommendation. In practice, the Commission did dispose of the majority of complaints in this way and indeed, given its limited resources, could not have operated in any other manner.[8]

Articles 4 and 5 set the framework for the notification of both existing agreements and agreements coming into existence after the operative date of the Regulation. New agreements under Article 4(1) had to be notified to the Commission and could not, until after notification, receive the benefit of any exemption under Article 6. The clear intention of the Article was that new agreements should be notified when or imme-diately after they were made. The only original exception related to three groups of

---

[6] The original decision in this case had been given by the District Court of Zutphen in 1958, the decision being upheld by the Arnhem Court of Appeal in 1961.

[7] For an analysis of the Commission procedures in considering complaints including a definition of when a 'decision' is given, see Case T-64/89 *Automec* v. *Commission (No. 1)* [1991] 4 CMLR 177. See also the *20th Annual Report* (1990), pp. 117–18.

[8] DG Comp gradually developed the practice of negotiating settlements and undertakings from the parties to agreements and practices in order to avoid having to issue formal decisions in every case and also to avoid having to make extensive use of its powers to grant interim measures of relief prior to formal decisions.

agreement which by their nature are considered less likely to affect competition or trade between Member States, namely:

(1) agreements where the only parties are undertakings from one Member State and the agreements do not relate either to imports or exports between Member States

(2) where only two undertakings are party to the agreement which itself either:

(a) merely restricts the freedom of one party to the contract in determining prices or conditions of business upon which goods purchased from the other party are to be resold or

(b) imposes restrictions on industrial property licensees or persons obtaining know-how under contract or licence relating to the use and applications of industrial processes

(3) where the agreements have as their sole object standardization of joint research and development or specialization agreements and where the products the subject of the specialization do not in a substantial part of the Common Market represent more than 15 per cent of the volume of business done in that market, so long as the total annual turnover of the participants does not exceed 200 million units of account.[9]

For many years Article 4(2), listing the exceptions to 4(1), remained unchanged apart from a very small extension of the turnover maximum under Regulation 2822/71. Not until the end of the twentieth century did Regulation 1216/99 extend the scope of freedom from notification as a condition precedent to exemption to virtually all distribution agreements, both bilateral and multilateral, and bilateral assignments or licences of intellectual property rights. In all these cases, as notification was voluntary, grant of an exemption at a later stage could be retrospective to the date when the agreement was made rather than, as with all other agreements, simply with effect from the date of notification.

One essential element of this Regulation was to establish a timetable for notification of the many existing agreements in force at the date when the Regulation became effective. The Commission elected to receive the forms of agreement required to be notified by two instalments. Multilateral agreements had to be notified to the Commission by 1 November 1962 whilst bilateral agreements (which were to comprise the vast majority of notifications) had to be lodged by the slightly later date of 1 February 1963, other than those, of course, for which exemption from notification had been given under Article 4. These rather short time limits within which agreements had to be notified were the subject of criticism from both United States and European

---

[9] Art. 4(2). Amendments to the terms of this clause under Reg. 2822/71 included an increase in the maximum annual turnover permitted to benefit from the Regulation. The Commission's interpretation of the wording of Art. 4(2) tended to be strict. Of course many agreements that might benefit from it came also within the categories covered by block exemption and were freed from the obligation to notify for that reason.

industrial and commercial concerns. They claimed that the volume of agreements to be notified would make it impossible in practice for the Commission to deal with them adequately, given its limited resources. This criticism turned out to be well founded. Originally, the draft of Article 5 dealing with the timetable and supported by the Deringer Report provided also that all agreements notified within the time limit which were not specifically opposed by the Commission within a period of six months from notification should remain provisionally lawful, and therefore enforceable in the courts of Member States. Opposition procedure is a concept known to German law, under which the German Cartel Authority (the *Bundeskartellamt*) has to object to agreements within a fixed period from receipt of notification if it finds any objectionable features. The Commission had originally suggested that agreements of lesser importance (as listed in Article 4) should be subject to a similar procedure, the time limit being six months, with the consequence that if opposition were not raised by DG Comp the agreements were deemed provisionally (not finally) to be outside the scope of Article 81(1)'s prohibition.

While this proposal certainly had its attractive features (particularly on the score of administrative convenience), it was felt that such a proposal would move too far away from the principle embodied in Article 81 that all restrictive agreements (except those covered by the specified exemptions) were prohibited; for the effect of the opposition procedure being introduced could have been that agreements were allowed to be enforced by national courts, even in cases where no exemption was ultimately given. Another reason why the Commission ultimately declined at this stage to accept the opposition procedure as a basis for reducing its workload was that it was difficult for any administrative body to operate such a procedure without adequate case-law experience of the range of restrictive clauses and agreements which it may encounter. At this time, of course, the Commission had had almost no experience of the kind of agreements which would be notified to it for assessment. Opposition procedures did, later on, become more common in block exemptions adopted by the Commission.[10] Not much use of them was made in practice and they are not found in recent block exemptions such as Regulation 2790/99 dealing with vertical restraints.

Articles 6 and 8 dealt with the important subject of exemption under 81(3). It was clear from the combined effect of these Articles that any exemption granted must operate from a specific date, which could not be earlier than the date of notification (except for the 'less harmful' agreements referred to in Article 4), for a specified period, and quite possibly upon detailed conditions. No maximum time limit was attached, though in practice it rarely exceeded ten years.[11] Conditions and obligations imposed by DG Comp had also to be those necessary to ensure compliance with the conditions set out by 81(3) and to make possible supervision of the conditions and general workings of

---

[10] See, e.g. the 'opposition' procedure to be found in the first block exemption regulation covering technology licences (Reg. 240/96).

[11] An exception has been made in some joint venture cases where a fifteen-year exemption has been permitted, e.g. *Optical Fibres* [1986] OJ L236/30, *Brown Boveri/NGK Insulators* [1989] 4 CMLR 610, and see *Electricidade de Portugal, 1993 Annual Report*, pp. 139–41.

the agreement by DG Comp. Thus, information could be requested as to the names of parties involved in joint buying or selling arrangements or participating in distribution systems exempted on such a basis. Once these Articles entered into force, jurisdiction over the application of Article 81(3) was removed from national authorities of Member States and left entirely in the hands of the Commission (Article 9);[12] although under Article 9(3), until the Commission actually initiated proceedings against an undertaking, the application of Article 81(1) or Article 82 by a Member State could continue.[13]

The combined effect of Articles 1 to 9 was therefore to establish a procedural machinery under which both old and new agreements were to be notified and thereby brought within the knowledge of the Commission; they established both a timetable for notification and a procedure for declaring either that the agreement infringed the Treaty or was entitled to exemption, with or without obligations attached. Breach of such obligations entitled DG Comp to bring action to cancel the exemption.

2.3 ARTICLES 10 TO 14 OF THE REGULATION

Articles 10 to 14 contained powers required by the Commission to carry out its duties effectively. Article 14 was particularly important since it gave authority to the Commission to undertake all necessary investigations, empowering its officials: (a) to examine books and other business records, (b) to take copies of books or business records, (c) to ask for oral explanations on the spot from undertakings investigated, and (d) to enter any premises or vehicle or land belonging to undertakings. These powers could be exercised either voluntarily with the consent of the undertaking or compulsorily if a decision of the Commission to such effect was granted.[14] Liaison was required with the competent authority of the Member State in the territory of an undertaking if an on-the-spot search was to be made:[15] a power absent from Article 14 was one to require employees or directors of undertakings to attend a hearing (in

[12] This would apply of course only to those sectors covered by Reg. 17 and not to any which were expressly removed by Regulation from its scope, e.g. air and sea transport, where under Art. 84 Member States' existing national authorities would retain jurisdiction to grant exemption until applicable regulations had been made. See the Cases 209–213/84 *Nouvelles Frontières* [1986] ECR 1425: 3 CMLR 173.

[13] The inability of national courts to grant individual exemption to agreements under Art. 81(3) was confirmed by the European Court in Case C-234/89 *Delimitis* v. *Henninger Bräu*, [1991] ECR I-935: [1992] 5 CMLR 210.

[14] The voluntary and compulsory methods of proceeding are found in Art. 14(2) and (3) respectively, and the Commission has complete discretion which to adopt in any particular case, Case 136/79 *National Panasonic (UK)* v. *Commission* [1980] ECR 2033: 3 CMLR 169.

[15] The European Court, in leading cases decided in 1989, laid down important principles controlling the way in which these rights of the Commission are to be carried out. In particular, Commission officials have no right to use force to obtain entry to business premises in order to examine documents, but must obtain appropriate authority from national courts: Cases 46/87 and 227/88 *Hoechst* v. *Commission* [1989] ECR 2859: [1991] 4 CMLR 410; Case 85/87 *Dow Benelux* v. *Commission* and Cases 97–99/87 *Dow Chemical Iberica* v. *Commission* [1989] ECR 3137, 3165 [1991] 4 CMLR 410; Cases 374/87 and 27/88 respectively *Orkem and Solvay* v. *Commission* [1989] ECR 3283, 3355 [1991] 4 CMLR 502. See Ch. 19, p. 506.

Brussels or elsewhere) and to bring relevant documents for that purpose.[16] This power would have been of considerable use to the Commission, but it was no doubt felt that Member States would regard its exercise as too great an infringement on the rights and liberties of their nationals.

Considerable emphasis was placed on the obligation of the governments in Member States and their competent authorities[17] to cooperate with the Commission. This obligation was found both in Article 11 (dealing with the right of the Commission to request information from governments and competent authorities of Member States and undertakings in those Member States), and also in the right to require investigation by authorities of Member States under Article 13. Article 10 required Member States to be sent copies of all relevant documents in each case involving an allegation of infringements of Article 81 or 82 or where notification has been made for purposes of obtaining negative clearance or exemption. Article 10(2) provided that all these procedures of DG Comp must be carried out 'in close and constant liaison' with competent authorities, and that 'such authorities shall have the right to express their views upon that procedure'.

Article 10(3) was a clause which caused considerable difficulty during negotiations. It was the wish of France that the Member States would collectively have a veto upon the original decision of DG Comp, before it was sent up for approval by the Commission, by requiring that any decision be supported by the majority of the Advisory Committee. This proposal was strenuously resisted by the Commission officials and by the German negotiators because it was felt that it would both prevent development of competition law criteria applicable uniformly to all Member States and tend to make it far more difficult for the Commission to issue either decisions or exemptions in cases that were politically sensitive. The solution finally adopted was to make the relevant committee, consisting of representatives of Member States, advisory only, without the power of veto, the committee having the right only to express its views, not to pronounce any formal decision. In general the Commissioners, called at their meetings to arrive at final decisions in competition cases, will attach weight to the opinions expressed by the members of this committee. Nevertheless, some decisions of the Commission have apparently been issued notwithstanding an adverse vote (apparently on occasions even a unanimous vote) in the Advisory Committee, but this is rare. Proceedings of the Advisory Committee are, however, confidential, and it is therefore only possible to speculate how often this has occurred.[18]

---

[16] This would be a power equivalent to that possessed by English courts to require witnesses to attend with relevant documents (know as a 'subpoena *duces tecum*').

[17] The definition of such authorities is referred to in Ch. 19, p. 525. Both they and the Commission were limited in the use of information acquired under Arts. 11 to 14 for the purposes of the relevant request or investigation (Case C-67/91 *Spanish Banks* [1992] ECR I-4785). Nevertheless in Case 2/88 *Zwarteveld* (1990) ECR II 3365, 4405: 3 CMLR 457 the European Court held that normally the Commission must supply national courts with confidential information in its possession, unless the Court itself directs that the provision of such information would be detrimental to the functioning and independence of the Community.

[18] In contrast, the opinions of the Advisory Committee on draft decisions under the Merger Regulation can be published if the Committee so request, and this has occurred in a number of cases.

2.4 ARTICLES 15 TO 25 OF THE REGULATION

The remaining Articles of the Regulation contained a number of clauses of value to the Commission in its administrative task. Articles 15 and 16 dealt with the ability of the Commission to impose substantial fines and penalties respectively. A fine was imposed for past conduct where undertakings had participated in agreements or practices forbidden under Article 81 or 82, or where incorrect or misleading information had been supplied in the course of investigation. The former type of fine might be of a very substantial amount, not exceeding 10 per cent of the turnover in the preceding business year of each of the undertakings found so to have participated. In fixing the fine, regard was to be had to the duration of the infringement and its seriousness.[19] Fines were not imposed in respect of any period after notification had been made unless a preliminary warning had been given under Article 15(6) that, in the view of the Commission 'after preliminary examination', application of the exemption provisions in 81(3) could not be justified. This procedure has been of value in the course of some investigations where the Commission was satisfied that no exemption would ultimately be available, but where the preparation of the necessary decision required a substantial amount of work, and it was hoped in this way to put pressure upon the undertakings concerned to terminate the agreement or practices, without waiting for the issue of the formal decision. Penalties under Article 16 dealt, not with the past, but with the future, and were payable in respect of each day upon which an undertaking continued to refuse to put an end to an infringement condemned by a decision of the Commission, or to supply information required by a decision of the Commission in the course of its investigation. Proposed fines and penalties were also considered by the Advisory Committee under Article 10, and the Commission's decision was in turn subject to the unlimited jurisdiction of the Court under Article 229, quite apart from the right of an undertaking to seek review of a decision under Article 230. The Court had powers to cancel, reduce, or increase the fine imposed.

Article 19 dealt with the important issue of natural justice. Undertakings were entitled to be heard on matters where the Commission proposed to raise a statement of objections, and rights were also given to other natural or legal persons with a sufficient interest. This concept was generously interpreted and gave competitors and customers standing to object to decisions by the Commission which were claimed to have prejudiced them.[20] Article 19(3) required the Commission to publish any proposed decisions relating to either negative clearance or exemption in the Official Journal, allowing all interested parties to submit their observations within a time limit of not less than a month. All final decisions, whether for negative clearance exemption or prohibiting the

---

[19] The size of fines imposed has increased substantially in recent years especially in cartel cases. Tables of fines are set out in *EC Competition Law Handbook* (Sweet & Maxwell, published annually), and in practitioners' handbooks. In 2006 the Commission published its latest Notice setting out the basis on which fines are to be calculated: [2006] OJ C210/2. Reductions in or total remission of fines may be possible for undertakings which take advantage of the Commission's Leniency Notice (see Ch. 9, p. 179).

[20] See e.g. *Metro* v. *Saba (No. 1)* Case 26/76 [1977] ECR 1875: [1978] 2 CMLR 1.

infringement with or without fine, had, under Article 21, to be published in detail in the Official Journal subject only to the requirements of business secrecy.

3. THE IMPLEMENTATION OF REGULATION 17: THE EARLY EXPERIENCE OF DG COMP

The entry into force of this new Regulation was a major psychological boost for DG Comp. At last it had a firm procedural foundation for its inquiries and investigations. The Directorate had previously felt itself inhibited in making inquiries and in carrying out investigations because of its lack of specific powers, notwithstanding the provisions of Article 85. Up to March 1962, therefore, the Commission had investigated only thirty-three cases and had issued no formal decisions, although in some cases it had tried to persuade the parties involved to end particular practices. In one case a boycott of a trader by a producer holding a dominant position was terminated as the result of such pressure, as was also the reservation of one national market to local producers and some preferred foreign producers to the exclusion of other producers within the Community. A magazine taking advertisements from various manufacturers refused to accept advertisements from competing manufacturers in other States; this practice was also brought to an end after intervention by DG Comp.

Whilst in early 1962 officials in DG Comp were therefore generally pleased with the scope of their new powers, they had no doubt that the future pattern of administration would become a great deal more demanding than the comparatively tranquil period that had prevailed since its formation four years previously. Indeed, the Regulation could be (and was) criticized for bringing within coverage for notification too many routine and relatively innocuous agreements, without enabling DG Comp to focus its attention on the kind of horizontal market-sharing and other cartels which are normally considered to have most effect on the health of the competitive process. The mesh of the net for catching notifications was so fine that it was anticipated that the number of agreements likely to be registered, particularly of a vertical nature, would be extremely high, notwithstanding the provisions of Article 4 for exemption from notification of agreements of apparently less immediate threat to competition. The view of the critics was that the Commission, in its natural desire to assert a wide jurisdiction over undertakings within the Common Market, had really attempted 'to bite off more than it could chew'; they claimed that it should have proceeded more gradually in selecting the criteria applicable to notification requirements.

The inherent consequences therefore of the approach adopted by Regulation 17 was to take DG Comp in the direction of having to devote far too much of the energies of its limited staff to vertical agreements relating to distribution of goods and the licensing of intellectual property rights, leaving too few resources to handle horizontal agreements and cartels which might be said to have a 'particularly adverse effect' on the development of the Common Market referred to. The Commission's own response to such criticism at the time would certainly have been that the integration of the Common Market itself positively required an emphasis on vertical agreements relating to distribution and licensing, the very numbers of restrictive agreements of that kind compelling the priority given to them.

The result of the time limits contained in the Regulation was that a total of 920 *multilateral* registrations were filed by the closing date of 1 November 1962, but the much larger and daunting total of 34,500 *bilateral* agreements were filed by 1 February 1963. The 'mass problem' of which the Commission had been warned had indeed arrived: for some months all DG Comp officials had to concentrate simply on giving a preliminary review to as many as possible of the vast number of documents which had arrived and were now piled throughout their offices. The notification form itself (known as 'form A/B') had been prescribed by a Regulation (No. 27 of 1962) made by the Commission under the authority of Council Regulation 17, and a further Regulation (No. 99 of 1963) was shortly afterwards adopted setting out procedures for investigations and oral hearings.

Under Article 2 of this latter Regulation, the Commission was required, when considering a decision against an undertaking, to send a statement of objections raised against it; the undertaking was then entitled to reply, setting out all matters relevant to its defence and attaching any relevant documents. This reply having been considered by the Commission, an oral hearing was called if the undertaking desired it. At the hearing the parties themselves and any other parties with a sufficient interest (in technical terms) might attend and address the Commission. Representatives of the Advisory Committee were also present at this hearing and might question the parties. The procedural framework for carrying out investigations was now at last in place,[21] and over the following years decisions of the Commission began to be issued, though initially at a very slow rate.

4. THE *GRUNDIG* CASE AND ITS CONSEQUENCES

4.1 THE FACTS OF *GRUNDIG*

Without question the most important decision to be issued by the Commission in 1964, its first full year of active operation as a decision-making body, was the *Grundig* case. The outcome of this case,[22] following the appeal from the Commission's decision

---

[21] The leading textbook on the procedural aspects of Community competition law is C.S. Kerse and N. Khan, *EC Antitrust Procedure* (5th edn, Sweet & Maxwell, 2005).

[22] *Grundig–Consten* JO [1964] 161/2545: [1964] CMLR 489. On 12 January 1962 the Dutch Supreme Court had already declared an export ban imposed by Grundig on its Dutch distributor to be unenforceable because it violated Art. 81 and had struck down an injunction imposed by a lower court on parallel importers of Grundig products. The Dutch court had refused to refer the case to the European Court under Art. 234. For a contemporary assessment of the case, see C. Fulda (1965) 65 *Columbia Law Review* 625.

to the European Court of Justice,[23] was to have a major influence on the development of the competition policy of the Commission. The facts of the case are therefore set out in some detail.

The well-known German manufacturer, Grundig, had appointed a firm called Consten as its sole distributor in France, the Saar, and Corsica in respect of a range of products including wireless and television sets, tape recorders, and dictating machines. Consten accepted an obligation to place minimum orders, to set up a repair workshop with an adequate stock of spare parts, and to provide an effective guarantee and after-sales service. It agreed not to sell goods competitive with the Grundig range, and also agreed that it would not make deliveries into other territories, having received an assurance from Grundig that similar restrictions had been placed on Grundig distributors in other countries. Consten was then enabled by Grundig to register under its own name in France the trade mark GINT which was carried on all Grundig appliances including those sold on the German domestic market. However, if Consten ceased to be the sole distributor for France, this trade mark had to be re-assigned to Grundig.

A French competitor of Consten was UNEF, which found itself able to buy Grundig appliances in Germany, for resale to French retailers, at more favourable prices than those available to them in France from Consten. Consten therefore brought an action in the French courts against UNEF both for unfair competition and for infringement of the trade mark GINT. As the result of a complaint by UNEF to the Commission, an investigation was carried out and a statement of objections filed against Grundig in accordance with the requirements of Regulation 17. The resulting decision of the Commission, issued on 23 September 1964, was that the agreement between Consten and Grundig violated Article 81(1). The Commission ruled that the rights of Consten under both the distribution agreement and the linked trade-mark licence must be limited so that they did not enable Grundig and Consten to prevent parallel imports of these products into France from other Member States. The Commission, therefore, declared the whole agreement between Consten and Grundig to be void and unenforceable.

An appeal was brought against this decision to the European Court. The Court heard the opinion of the Advocate General appointed to the case before considering its own decision. The opinion of Advocate General Roemer was that the numerous complaints of Consten and Grundig against the procedure of DG Comp in investigating the case were justified, as in his view it had not been sufficiently thorough. He believed that it should be reopened to enable the parties to deal more fully with the allegations made. However, the Court disagreed and upheld the Commission's decisions other than on two important points. The points upon which the Court overruled the Commission concerned the Commission's finding that exclusivity alone in a distribution system was sufficient to raise artificial barriers between Member States of the Common Market. It concluded first that such a finding was too sweeping and could

---

[23] Cases 56 and 58/64 *Consten and Grundig* v. *Commission* [1966] ECR 299: CMLR 418.

not be justified. Nor, in its view, should the Commission have ruled that the clauses of the agreement which did not relate to restrictions on the parallel imports of goods be annulled. Notwithstanding the reference in the wording of Article 81 striking down 'all *agreements* between undertakings...', and the like wording in paragraph (2) ('any *agreements*...prohibited...shall be automatically void') the annulment should apply solely to restrictive clauses and the remainder of the agreement remain fully in force. The remaining findings of the Court, however, wholly supported the approach of the Commission and would have a major influence on future case law and competition policy; they can be summarized as follows.

The Court's first ruling was that the expression 'affecting trade' in Article 81(1) meant that the Commission should consider whether the agreement was capable of endangering, directly or indirectly, in fact or potentially, freedom of trade between Member States in a direction which could harm the attainment of the object of a single integrated market. Such an effect could be found even if the result of the agreement was to favour a large increase in Grundig trade through its appointed distributor, Consten, if at the same time other undertakings (such as UNEF) were prevented from importing Grundig products into France or if Consten itself was prevented from re-exporting. If intra-brand competition between Grundig dealers were weakened by the agreements, then it was no answer for Grundig simply to claim that inter-brand competition between manufacturers would thereby be increased.

Secondly, the Commission was commended for taking into account in its decision the whole 'system' set up in France for absolute territorial protection, including the assignment of the GINT trade mark to Consten. Trade-mark rights should not be used in such a way as to defeat the effectiveness of EC law in this area, nor should the domestic law of Member States relating to unfair competition or intellectual property rights be used for such a purpose. Other Articles of the EC Treaty had been cited in favour of Grundig and Consten to support their use of trade marks to protect the exclusivity of the distribution arrangement: in particular, Article 30 had been referred to in the course of the case because of its reference to the protection of 'industrial and commercial property', and Article 295 because of its statement, as a general principle, that the Treaty was not in any way to 'prejudice the rules of Member States governing the system of property ownership'. Neither Article, however, was adjudged sufficiently far-reaching in its scope to affect the Court's ruling.

4.2 THE CONSEQUENCES OF *GRUNDIG*

The whole Commission had realized that the issues posed by the *Grundig* case were of central importance and that a clear ruling of the Court was needed to provide a sound basis for its future policy, emphasizing the elimination of export bans that would have the effect of segregating national markets, particularly if combined with ancillary restrictions on the use of intellectual property rights such as trade marks. This is but the first of a number of situations in which a clear and authoritative ruling from the Court at a timely moment has enabled the Commission to develop its own policy strengthened by the Court's support on a key issue. In our subsequent review in Part II of various areas of the development of competition policy we shall see how important the role played by the Court has been in assisting the development of the Commission's own confidence in the application of its policies. In particular, the wide interpretation given by the Court to the expression 'which may affect trade between Member States' has enabled the reach of the Commission to be extended more broadly than would have been possible if the Court's interpretation of these words had been more restrictive. It enabled the Commission to exercise jurisdiction in a number of areas where it had previously been thought that the effect on trade between Member States would be insufficient, even when the markets affected were mainly national with comparatively minor effect on imports or exports. Later chapters show that subsequent case law has further developed the principles laid down in the *Grundig* case.

The two points on which the Commission's judgment had been overturned were not damaging to it. The decision that only the restrictive clauses would be struck out and void under 81(2) was not itself limiting to the exercise of the Commission's jurisdiction, although it did appear to run contrary to the apparently categorical wording of Article 81(2). Nor did the refusal of the Court to accept that exclusivity arrangements alone would automatically breach Article 81(1) cause major problems. DG Comp had already started to develop principles for distinguishing those situations where an element of exclusivity in distribution systems could in fact assist the process of inter-brand competition and would eventually enable a large number of the bipartite distribution arrangements notified to it at the beginning of 1963 to receive exemption. To arrange for this to happen, however, would require the introduction of new administrative machinery to permit exemption by category rather than simply on an individual basis.

5

THE ADVENT OF THE BLOCK EXEMPTION

1. EARLY CASE-LAW EXPERIENCE

1.1 THE FIRST CASES ON DISTRIBUTION SYSTEMS

During its first few years of operation DG Comp began to carry out its implementation of Article 81, utilizing its new powers under Regulation 17/62, in a number of minor cases. These included:

Hummel/Isbecque:[1] An agreement between a German manufacturer and a Belgian distributor for the sale of small tractors and other products contained a restriction that the manufacturer, Hummel, could not sell to anyone else in Belgium apart from Isbecque, thereby preventing other Belgian distributors from bypassing Isbecque and buying direct. Individual exemption was granted because the requirements of Article 81(3) were held to be met. The exclusivity granted to Isbecque was not such as to prevent parallel imports from Germany, and the restrictions imposed on it were limited to those required to ensure that the economic benefits of exclusivity were obtained. There was substantial competition in Belgium for the range of products covered by the agreement. The period of exemption given was six years.

Maison Jallatte/Voss:[2] Here a French manufacturer of safety shoes appointed exclusive distributors for Germany (Voss) and also for Belgium (Vandeputte). Vandeputte had agreed an exclusive purchasing clause under which they consented not to acquire safety shoes from any of Maison Jallatte's competitors, a restriction which had not featured in any previous agreement considered under Article 81. An exemption was granted for an eight-year period, on the basis that the clause would require Vandeputte to exercise its representation of Maison Jallatte in a more vigorous manner, having to make its profit from one range of shoes alone; the range of safety shoes which the distribution agreements would enable customers to buy in these two markets would be considerably wider than those available without the existence of the agreements. Parallel imports remained available for both countries.

---

[1] JO 2581/65: [1965] CMLR 242.   [2] JO 37/66: [1966] CMLR D1.

Belgian Tiles Cartel:[3] Inevitably the Commission found itself moving on from relatively simple bilateral agreements to more complex multilateral agreements. This case involved arrangements between two Belgian trade associations representing tile layers and tile dealers, as well as twenty-nine manufacturers of ceramic tiles throughout the Community. Under the agreements notified, all these manufacturers were required to sell in Belgium only to dealers and tile layers accorded the status under the arrangements of 'recognized customers'. These dealers and layers in turn had a reciprocal obligation to buy their tiles only from manufacturers who were parties to the relevant agreements. General contractors and their agents were barred from membership so that manufacturers could not sell direct to them, nor to other large potential buyers of tiles, such as government departments, hospitals, or factories. The admission of any new manufacturer to the agreements required the unanimous consent of all other manufacturers, and the admission of any new trade associations of tile layers or dealers required the consent of the two existing associations.

As we shall see from later cases decided by the Commission and the European Court, this type of cartel was frequent in the Common Market at the time of the signature of the Treaty of Rome, particularly in Belgium and Holland. The justification claimed for the arrangements, and the basis for requests for exemption under Article 81(3), was that it brought about improvements in the proper use and distribution of ceramic tiles because of the higher standards it was supposed to set for tile layers and dealers. The weakness of this argument was that the rules of the cartel actually contained no reference to minimum technical standards, nor requirements for technical education, so that a manufacturer was actually free to sell tiles to any tile layer or dealer with no control over their end use. The cartel could have achieved its proclaimed objectives only by prescribing minimum technical standards for its distributors and placing other requirements on them for the benefit of their customers, such as the maintenance of a reasonable stock of tiles.

It was clearly impossible for the Commission to find that such a cartel satisfied the four conditions of Article 81(3). Not only was there no apparent improvement in the distribution of goods, there was certainly no benefit reserved for consumers, and the restrictions imposed on both manufacturers and recognized customers went far beyond the level required for the improvement of technical standards. The conclusive argument against exemption however was that, with such arrangements in force, the elimination of competition in the Belgian tile market was not only the aim but the almost certain achievement of the cartel. The association, therefore, had to amend its rules on the definition of customers and on membership.

This important early decision shows that the Commission realized that the established European preference (in certain markets at least) for confining the operation of a national market to a group of approved undertakings (manufacturers and middlemen), which themselves retained a veto on the admission of new members at their respective levels, ran completely contrary to the provisions of Article 81. It was a particularly clear case since the parties to the arrangement included manufacturers not

---

[3] JO 1167/64. It is also referred to as the 'Convention Faïence' case.

only from Belgium itself but from four other Member States. Later cases extended the principle of this case even to situations where all members of the relevant association were trading within one Member State. The recommendation that entry to the categories of recognized customers should be open to all qualified entrants, assessed on an objective basis, itself had long-term effects on the jurisprudence of the Commission, notably in the area of selective distribution. The case also illustrated the point that horizontal agreements between competitors, especially when combined with restrictions on vertical relationships covering distribution of a product, could also affect the integration of national markets within the Community, as could vertical agreements of the *Grundig* type.[4]

1.2 THE NEXT STEP—THE NEED FOR BLOCK EXEMPTIONS

The way in which the Belgian tile cartel was disposed of, by recommendation rather than formal decision, illustrates that quite early in its operations DG Comp recognized that the volume of cases to be decided made the availability of informal methods of disposal essential. A decision required a number of formal steps, including the preparation of a statement of objections to the parties, probably an oral hearing of the issues, and a presentation of the draft decision to the Advisory Committee, leading up to the Commission's formal decision. All this took considerable time. On the other hand, an informal negotiated settlement could be dealt with far more speedily; it was particularly suitable where only some clauses of an agreement were regarded as contrary to Article 81, which the parties were often willing to remove if it led to a comparatively quick clearance or exemption for the remainder of the agreement.

Neither the mere handful of official decisions in these early years, however, nor even a number of settlements could make substantial inroads into the large number of notified agreements. This problem had weighed heavily, not only in the filing cabinets, but on the minds of the officials in DG Comp from the beginning of 1963 onwards, when for some months all other tasks had to be laid aside whilst an attempt was made to list and assess on a preliminary basis the great numbers of notified agreements. A very substantial proportion of these notifications were exclusive-distribution agreements; the next largest category were patent licences.

Clearly, the way forward would have to be the laying down by the Commission of broad criteria under which block exemption[5] could be given to these forms of agreement (particularly in the area of exclusive distribution where the largest number of notifications had occurred) which were regarded as having many pro-competitive features, and restrictions which on the whole fell within the letter and spirit of Article 81(3). To apply to the Council for a block exemption, however, would be fruitless unless at least some experience of the particular form of agreement for which the exemption was sought could be shown. The experience of the Commission through 1963 and 1964 on the nature and content of exclusive distribution was not extensive, but the experience

---

[4] See in particular cases referred to in Ch. 6 on trade associations.
[5] Specifically referred to in Art. 81(3) as 'exemption by category'.

gained from the *Grundig* case and the other minor cases already referred to had at least begun to show the nature of the distinctions that could be drawn. On one hand, there were relatively straightforward distribution agreements containing mainly the basic clauses essential to any system of exclusive distribution and which would not damage the competitive process so long as parallel imports remained possible; on the other hand there were a variety of more complex and restrictive agreements governing distribution where individual scrutiny of the particular circumstances of the product and the parties' market share would remain necessary before exemption could be allowed. The great advantage of the block exemption, moreover, was that undertakings would have an incentive to frame their new agreements in terms that complied with it. They would thus eliminate all need for notification and thereby reduce further the administrative burden on DG Comp.

2. THE ENACTMENT OF COUNCIL REGULATION 19/65

2.1 THE SCOPE OF THE ENABLING REGULATION

Work had begun as early as the end of 1963 on the preparation of a draft regulation which the Council could adopt under the terms of Article 83, giving the Commission power to grant exemptions on a group or block basis by reference to objective criteria. Under normal consultative arrangements within the Community, once a draft was approved within DG Comp and by the Commission, it had to be circulated by the Council to the Economic and Social Committee and also to the European Parliament. Once their comments had been considered, and any consequential amendments suggested by the Commission, the Council could enact the final version.

Picking up the reference in Article 81(3) to 'any agreement or category of agreements between undertakings' the draft Regulation prepared and circulated for approval referred to two particular types of agreement to which DG Comp wished to be able to declare that Article 81(1) should be inapplicable. These two categories were:

(a) where one party agreed with the other to supply only to that other goods for resale within a defined area of the Common Market; or where one party agreed with the other to purchase only from that other goods for resale; or where two undertakings entered into reciprocal obligations with each other for exclusive supply and purchase of goods for resale

(b) where restrictions were imposed on the acquisition or use of industrial property rights (patents, utility models, designs, or trade marks) or on rights arising out of contracts for assignment of or the right to use methods of manufacture or knowledge relating to the use or the application of industrial processes.

The draft made clear that the block exemption to be given by the Commission would only apply to bilateral agreements; each exemption covering a particular category was required to specify both the individual clauses not to be contained in such agreements, and those minimum clauses which had to be contained in the exempted agreements.

With regard to (a), the intention was clearly to cover cases such as those of *Hummel/Isbecque* and *Maison Jallatte–Voss* of which the Commission had already gained some experience. On the other hand, to issue a block exemption for defined categories of patent licences (obviously the main type of agreement covered by (b)), would be more contentious, and considerably more experience would be required before the terms of a published block exemption could be decided upon.[6]

2.2 THE INTRODUCTION OF REGULATION 19/65

The Council recognized the difficulties of DG Comp with regard to the 'mass problem', and authorized relatively quickly the enactment of Regulation 19/65, giving to the Commission authority to grant block exemptions for both categories of agreement. The recitals of this Regulation are important. After formal recitals referring to the authority of the Treaty, the proposal made by the Commission and the necessary opinions received from the Parliament and Economic and Social Committee, reference is then made to the large number of notifications received under Regulation 17. It was considered desirable 'in order to facilitate the task of the Commission' that the Commission should be able to declare by way of Regulation that the provisions of Article 81(1) do not apply to certain categories of agreement. Reference is then made to the importance that the Council should lay down the conditions under which the Commission can grant such exemption 'in close and constant liaison with the competent authorities of the Member States' and also that such exemptions are exercised only 'after sufficient experience has been gained in the light of individual decisions and it becomes possible to define categories of agreements…in respect of which the conditions of Article 81(3) may be considered as being fulfilled'.

This point is often overlooked by subsequent commentators, who have criticized the Commission for not obtaining authority from the Council at an earlier stage for a wide range of block exemptions covering not only vertical but horizontal agreements. This ignores the fact that it was neither possible nor sensible for a body such as DG Comp to issue broad criteria for exemption until they had gained sufficient familiarity with the types of agreement being entered into and the types of restriction which they contain. Only by dealing with a reasonable number of individual requests for negative clearance or exemption could the Commission acquire the necessary experience to publish and implement an effective block exemption, based on criteria that would both make economic and commercial sense and command a broad measure of acceptance and understanding from European commerce and industry.

---

[6] The first draft of a block exemption for patent licences was in fact not published until 1979. See Ch. 12 for detailed consideration of this topic.

The Regulation went on to authorize the Commission to make its own Regulation setting out block exemptions in categories (a) and (b) only, for a specified period of time. Before it could be issued it would have to be considered by the Advisory Committee and published in the Official Journal so that any interested party could submit comments. The Commission was also authorized by Article 7 to withdraw the benefit of the block exemption from any agreement to which it had been applied if it found that the agreement exempted had 'nevertheless certain effects…incompatible with the conditions laid down in Article [81(3)] of the Treaty'.

2.3   THE ITALIAN CHALLENGE TO THE REGULATION

The enactment of this Regulation was of course essential for the Commission because it provided the necessary powers for the issue of 'category-type' exemptions which could deal at a stroke with a large number of those bilateral agreements on its books. However, it was not created without challenge. Not long after its enactment on 2 March 1965 Italy brought a case to the European Court of Justice claiming that the Regulation should be annulled.[7] Italy's challenge was based on the ground that the passing of the Regulation by the Council was itself a *détournement de pouvoir* (abuse of power) in that it purported to extend the scope of Article 81 of the Treaty. Amongst other arguments raised by Italy were that the Regulation raised a presumption that those agreements not expressly referred to in it as eligible for group exemption were illegal, and that Article 81 was in any case intended to govern only horizontal relationships between actual competitors, rather than vertical relationships concerning distribution or licensing to which Article 82 alone would apply.

Neither Advocate General Roemer nor the Court had much difficulty in rejecting these arguments. The Advocate General began by pointing out that the case was primarily concerned with a question of principle, not the mere application to a particular case of the Community law of competition. The passing of Regulation 19/65 was the direct result of the large number of notifications received under Regulation 17, and the consequential demand from both DG Comp and European commercial and industrial interests for a speedier treatment of the requests for exemption. The Advocate General continued:

For anyone who knows the difficulties of the law relating to agreements, it soon becomes clear that this is an area which does not lend itself at all to using legislative means to find a complete and comprehensive solution for all the problems which may occur. Therefore, the institutions empowered to deal with these matters are acting rightly in proceeding by stages. In proceeding thus, they are also acting rightly in directing their attention first to cases, such as exclusive dealing agreements, where relatively harmless restrictions on competition are involved and which, because of their number, call for a set of rules whereby they can be dealt with speedily in the interests of simplifying administration. Although it is not possible to avoid some initial uncertainty as regards various agreements not covered

---

[7]   Case 32/65 *Italy v. Council and Commission* [1966] ECR 389: [1969] CMLR 39.

by Regulation 19/65 until decisions about them are taken individually, it must be admitted that difficulties of this sort are inevitable in the very complex matter of the law relating to agreements, particularly at the beginning of its evolution.[8]

He also pointed out that the Treaty was based on a wide concept of competition including not only horizontal but also vertical agreements, of particular economic importance in that the costs of distribution represented an important element in the total costs of consumer goods. He found no distinction in Article 81 between horizontal and vertical agreements, nor any limitation of Article 82 to vertical agreements, and indeed pointed out that the Court in *de Geus* v. *Robert Bosch*[9] had already decided that Article 81 did apply to vertical agreements. He concluded by pointing out the duty of the Commission to make a conscientious examination of all relevant economic factors before granting an exemption under Article 81(3), whether individual or block.[10]

The Court in its judgment emphasized that in adopting Regulation 19/65 the Council had not enlarged the field of application of Article 81. It had merely given the Commission procedural powers to grant exemption to specific categories of agreement and concerted practices, a step clearly contemplated by the drafting of Article 81 with its reference to 'categories'. The definition of a category, however, provided only a framework for the Commission and DG Comp and did not mean that all agreements of that type which failed to comply with the specific obligations laid down for block exemption would be automatically prohibited or ineligible for individual clearance. Moreover, the Court said it would be wrong to read the Regulation as creating any presumption of law about the way in which Article 81(1) was to be interpreted or as limiting the freedom of the Commission to spell out those conditions which an agreement had to satisfy in order to gain a block exemption. Italy's application for annulment of the Regulation was therefore rejected.

2.4 THE *STM* CASE—A BROAD INTERPRETATION OF ARTICLE 81(1)

This case shows that the Court was fully aware of the administrative difficulties under which DG Comp had been placed by the perhaps over-ambitious scope of Regulation 17, and of the immense task which DG Comp would have in continuing to deal with, and prescribe appropriate criteria for, the large number of notified agreements. For the Court to have rejected the validity of the Council's Regulation would have been to place an impossible weight on the Commission's shoulders, forcing it to proceed solely by way of individual decision. It happened that the decision of the Court was issued on the very same day as its *Grundig* decision, and the combined effect of the

---

[8] [1966] ECR 416.   [9] Case 13/61 [1962] ECR 45: CMLR 1.
[10] It is interesting that, in support of his opinion, the Advocate General drew attention to the recent *White Motors* case in the US Supreme Court, which had laid down precisely the same rule for Federal district courts in the USA when examining vertical agreements: 372 US 253 (1963).

two cases was of importance not only in terms of the substantive law but also in rais-ing the morale of the officials in DG Comp. Moreover, only some two weeks earlier,[11] the Court had delivered a preliminary ruling under Article 234 in the case of *Société Technique Minière* v. *Maschinenbau Ulm*[12] on appeal from the Court of Appeal in Paris which would also prove of importance to it. Maschinenbau Ulm had supplied large earth levellers to STM, a French company engaged in the distribution of equip-ment for public works. STM had difficulties in finding purchasers for all the levellers, of which it had agreed to buy a substantial number over a two-year period. It had also agreed to organize a repair service and a spare parts stock and to meet the whole of the demand for the product in France, promising not to sell any competing products without Maschinenbau Ulm's agreement. In return, Maschinenbau Ulm had granted STM exclusive rights to sell these machines exclusively in both France and certain overseas territories. When Maschinenbau did not receive payment, it sued STM in France; STM defended the claim on the basis that at least some clauses in the agree-ment were void under Article 81. The Court of Appeal asked the European Court of Justice to decide which, if any, clauses were so affected.

Both the Advocate General and the Court took the view that agreements of this kind could normally be exempt under Article 81(3). The Advocate General pointed out that it would be impossible in many cases for undertakings of a modest size to risk entering foreign markets if they could not concentrate their distributive efforts in one set of hands, especially if the product were technical, requiring assembly and repair services and supplies of spare parts at short notice to keep the machines working. The offer of exclusivity was in practice, therefore, essential to the setting up of a satisfactory distribution system and would not normally threaten the competitive process because of the same factors seen in the earlier Commission cases such as *Hummel/Isbecque* and *Maison Jallatte–Voss*, namely that it would be difficult for the manufacturers to ensure that only products circulated and distributed through official channels could reach the relevant market.

The Court's view was that one had to look at the severity of the restrictive element in the clauses granting the exclusive right, and decide whether these clauses could have the effect of partitioning the market between the Member States. However, the Court, went on to make an important statement about the interpretation of the words 'agreements...which may affect trade between Member States' in Article 81(1). The test laid down by the Court was that 'it must be possible to foresee with a sufficient degree of probability on the basis of a set of objective factors of law or of fact that the agreement in question may have an influence, direct or indirect, actual or potential, on the pattern of trade between Member States'.[13] On this basis, the potential jurisdiction of DG Comp was clearly not to be limited to agreements between undertakings in

---

[11] On 30 June 1966.   [12] Case 56/65 [1966] ECR 234: CMLR 357.

[13] [1966] ECR 249: CMLR 375. As the case was a reference to the Court under Art. 234, the Court was not required to decide the issues between the parties but merely to provide a reply to the questions raised by the Paris Court. For further consideration of the words 'may affect trade between Member States', see Ch. 7, Section 1.

different Member States but could apply equally to agreements operating within one Member State but having wider effects, particularly on imports into or exports from that State.

3. THE FIRST TEN YEARS OF DG COMP: A REVIEW

3.1 THE VALUE OF THE EARLY CASE LAW

The combined effect of these early Court decisions and its own experience in handling individual cases had in 1967 brought DG Comp to a point, some ten years after the signing of the Treaty of Rome, where it could be seen to be applying general principles reached as a result of its own experience and to start operating on a legislative basis, rather than simply applying the Treaty's general rules to the merits of individual notifications. Clearly progress had not been as speedy as might have been hoped, and the achievements of these first ten years were limited, if assessed solely by the number of cases decided either formally or informally. Nevertheless, at the end of its first decade there was no doubt that progress had been made in the establishment of relevant principles which would provide sound foundations for DG Comp and the Commission as a whole in years to come. Apart from a number of informal settlements and recommendations, it had reached formal decisions during this period on four negative clearances and four Article 81(3) exemptions. It had issued Notices relating to commercial agency and patent licences, and carried out a single sectoral investigation under Regulation 17, Article 12 into the margarine industry. In the *Grundig* case it had obtained not only outright support for the disallowing of export bans but also a clarification of the expression 'which have as their object or effect...'. The Court had accepted the Commission's argument that it was sufficient to establish that the *purpose* of the restrictive arrangement or agreement was to separate national markets for distribution purposes, and that it was only necessary to consider separately the *effects* of the restrictive clauses in the agreement if no such purpose could be found. It was also clear that the Court would not prevent Community law from having a restrictive influence on the free exercise of industrial property rights under national law, and that rights flowing from such national laws could not be used for purposes contrary to the basic principles of competition law laid down in Articles 81 and 82. The competition which the Court was protecting in dealing with vertical agreements was generally not competition between the parties to that agreement (whose functions would normally complement each other) but competition between those and other parties at both manufacturing and distribution level who desire to compete for that particular product. Article 81(1) was, therefore, to be applicable to both horizontal and vertical agreements.

As to the meaning of the phrase 'which may affect trade between Member States', the Court, as we have seen in the *STM* case, had applied a very broad test with the effect of maximizing the jurisdiction of the Commission. It is clear from *Grundig*, moreover, that in making this assessment the Court would not operate a 'balancing test'; even

if the volume of trade between particular countries had increased as a result of a particular agreement, the restrictive clauses in that same agreement could nevertheless
be held to have affected trade in breach of Article 81. What had still to be worked out
was the extent to which exclusive distribution agreements would be permitted when
they no longer contained an absolute ban on exports but where other restrictions were
included which might more indirectly make parallel imports, and therefore intra-
brand competition, more difficult. This was indeed one of the problems which faced
the Commission when considering the exact phrasing required for the block exemption, on exclusive distribution, shortly to be introduced.

3.2 THE ATTITUDE OF INDUSTRY TO COMPETITION RULES

Of course, many other problems in the interpretation and application of Article 81
remained unsolved. In two major respects, however, the first decade could be said to
have achieved important steps forward. The first of these related to the expectation of
industrialists and businessmen operating within the original Common Market. In
the early years after the Treaty, there had been some expectation, and indeed hope,
amongst European businessmen unfamiliar with a totally (or even substantially) competitive environment that the administration of Articles 81 and 82 would be relatively
lenient, and that the interpretation given to the application of the exemptions and the
interpretation of the phrase 'agreements...which may affect trade between Member
States and which have as their object or effect the prevention, restriction or distortion of competition within the Common Market' would catch only clear and obvious
anti-competitive cartels involving price-fixing or market-sharing between horizontal
competitors. This view had been encouraged by the relative weakness of the national
competition laws in the Six Member States at that time, with the possible exception
of the new German competition law, which was only gradually gathering effectiveness over its first decade of operation in parallel with the growth of the Commission's
own jurisdiction. The European tradition had been one which respected close links of
loyalty between suppliers and their customers, and such relationships between manufacturers and their dealer or distributor systems were generally thought of greater
importance than the free play of competitive influences. Maintenance of associations
of manufacturers or dealers with a firm commitment to dealing on a regular basis with
each other and excluding undertakings outside the scope of the agreement was considered respectable and normal, rather than as an artificial and objectionable division
of national markets into 'insider' and 'outsider' groups. Agreements not to compete or
not to export particular categories of product for fear of reprisals by competitors in
neighbouring States had also been considered normal.

Against this traditional fear of an outright rivalry between undertakings, expectation at the outset had been that change, though necessary, would be gradual—even
gentle.[14] Although it was some years before the effect of the change in atmosphere

---

[14] For an account of the European attitude to competition in the early 1960s, see E. Minoli, 'Industry's
View of Trade Regulations in the EEC' [1962] Fordham Corp L Inst.

was perceived, it had become clear by the middle of the 1960s that Articles 81 and 82, and the Regulations to be made under them, were going to introduce a totally new situation. Undoubtedly, a major influence was that the Commission realized that a system of centralized planning of industrial and commercial objectives (akin to the centralized planning of agriculture carried out by the Commission to implement the Common Agricultural Policy) was impossible, first because of the size of the bureaucracy needed to enforce such a scheme throughout the Community, and secondly because the ground rules for such common policies could never have been agreed among the Member States in view of their widely differing views on industrial structures and their differing interpretations of national interest.

3.3 RELATIONSHIPS BETWEEN THE COMMISSION AND OTHER COMMUNITY INSTITUTIONS

The second important step was that over this period DG Comp had found it essential to establish working relationships with the other DGs, and also with two other Community institutions, the Economic and Social Committee and the European Parliament. Although the Parliament had only limited powers at this time (well before the introduction of direct elections) it was able to continue to apply pressure on the Commission as a whole by means of questions tabled for answer by the relevant Commissioner relating to development of competition policy. The questions recorded illustrate the continuing concern of members of the Parliament that DG Comp should continue its forward movement in the development of its policies.[15] The value of the continuing individual questioning of the Commission as a means of ascertaining information about its progress and as a means of goading it on to further efforts should not be underestimated. In later years the Parliament has continued to take a keen interest in the development of competition law reflected in particular in the fact that it comments each year on the Annual Report of DG Comp. This Report, which came into existence only as the result of persistent requests from Parliament itself, was first published in 1972 and now appears in early summer with a review of the previous year's activities and developments in competition policy.

Relationships between the Commission and the Council had also matured substantially over the period. Whilst the Council is essentially a political body consisting of ministers for the individual Member States, it had concluded during the early 1960s that substantial powers under Articles 81 and 82 would need to be delegated to the Commission if progress was to be made in enforcing the Articles; it would also be inappropriate for the Council, given its other responsibilities and the technical nature of most of the work to be carried out by DG Comp in implementing Articles 81 and 82, to involve itself in individual cases. Few other Directorates received such wide delegated powers at that stage in the life of the Community as DG Comp with Regulation 17/62. Their existence however enabled DG Comp to continue its progress in enforcing policy both through its administrative (both investigatory and

---

[15] The questions, and the answers provided by DG Comp, are recorded in the Official Journal.

quasi-judicial) and legislative functions, even at times when political deadlock made it difficult for the Council to reach decisions on many other matters, to the general frustration of those working in other areas of the Commission. To this extent DG Comp has been fortunate in that at a critical stage in its development it did receive these far-reaching delegated powers, not only to investigate but also to make decisions which would be final, subject only to appeal to the Court at Luxembourg[16] on the grounds set out in Article 230 of the Treaty.

It was however the developing relationship of DG Comp with the European Court of Justice that was the most important single factor in this first ten years of its life. There is no doubt that the support given by the Court to the work of the Commission was of critical importance in enabling its main lines of policy to be established. The outcome of the *Grundig* case was to lay a firm legal foundation supporting the Directorate in its aim to establish market integration as the foremost principle to be considered in applying Article 81(3), to the extent that an export ban found in an agreement imposed on a distributor would alone certainly make it impossible for exemption to be obtained, unless the export ban were simply to countries outside the Common Market itself without any possibility of subsequent re-export of goods into the Market because of the existence of substantial tariff barriers or transport costs.[17] So familiar has this concept become with the passage of time that it is perhaps too easy to overlook the serious consequences had the European Court not firmly supported the Commission on this key issue. The Court's assistance was rendered, of course, through decisions under Article 234 on requests for preliminary rulings from national courts as well as in cases on direct appeal from the Commission's own decisions under Article 230. In the next five years (1967–72), a period when political progress was slow, largely owing to the influence of General De Gaulle, the role of the Court would nevertheless continue to grow in importance in the establishment of further substantive legal doctrine in this area.

3.4 THE FIRST BLOCK EXEMPTION REGULATION 67/67

The end of this first decade was marked by the passage of the first Regulation by the Commission itself, namely Regulation 67/67 setting out the conditions for group exemption of exclusive distribution agreements, to be considered in detail in Chapter 10. At this point the Commission should have been given adequate resources to consider the smaller number of multilateral agreements now notified, many of which involved horizontal agreements having at least an element of market-sharing on a national basis. Such agreements represented a greater danger to the competitive process than the mass of bilateral agreements, largely relating to exclusive distribution and patent licensing, whose early notification by 1 February 1963 imposed so heavy a

---

[16] Initially to the European Court of Justice, but from 1989 to the Court of First Instance with further appeal to the Court of Justice on points of law only. See Ch. 23, Section 4.

[17] See, e.g., Case C-306/96 *Javico* v. *Yves St Laurent* [1998] ECR I-1983: 5 CMLR 172.

burden on the workings of DG Comp for many years afterwards. It is arguable, though by no means certain, that this could have been done without doing substantial damage to the principle of market integration, usually put forward as the essential reason for the early concentration on the bilateral vertical agreement. In the event, not until some years later did the Commission get to grips with some of the major horizontal cartels that had operated with impunity for some years within the Community.

DG Comp had, however, developed its policies towards vertical agreements far more quickly than towards horizontal agreements and cartels. It is a justifiable criticism of the policy of the Commission during its first ten years that the terms of Regulation 17 inevitably forced this initial concentration on vertical rather than horizontal agreements because of the extent to which the mass notification of the vertical agreements in accordance with the Regulation's requirements limited DG Comp's freedom of action.[18] With hindsight, it might have been better for the Commission to have phased in the notification of such vertical agreements over a longer period of time.

---

[18] This is confirmed by the subsequent figures produced by the Commission itself a decade later. The *9th Annual Report* (1979), pp. 15–16, confirms that 40,000 notifications were received by the Commission during the first years of application of Arts. 81–2, of which as many as 29,500 concerned exclusive dealing agreements, and of which more than 25,000 were eventually disposed of on the basis of Reg. 67/67.

PART II

THE SUBSTANTIVE LAW OF THE EUROPEAN COMMUNITY

Each man's experience starts again from the beginning. Only institutions grow wiser: they accumulate collective experience, and owing to this experience and this wisdom, men subject to the same rules will not see their own nature changing, but their behaviour gradually transformed.

Jean Monnet, quoting the Swiss philosopher Henri-Frédéric Amiel (1821–81),
in the course of a speech to the Common Assembly of the
European Coal and Steel Community in 1955.

6

ARTICLE 81(1): ANALYSIS (1)

1. INTRODUCTION

Part I contains a historical account of the early implementation by DG Comp of the policies relating to competition contained in the Treaty of Rome. In retrospect, the first ten years can be seen as a slow-moving, but essential, gestation period for the development of a distinct Community competition policy. The tempo of development begins to increase sharply with the implementation of the block exemption contained in Regulation 67/67 at the end of this first stage. Because of the sheer volume and complexity of substantive-law developments since that time, it is not possible to give an account of the substantive law or the development of policy simply by reviewing cases as they occur in successive years. Instead, it is necessary to consider the law under a number of different subject headings, reviewing under each of them relevant major cases and policy developments.

To all these subjects the structure of Article 81 is of central importance. It is therefore logical to begin our examination of the substantive law by analysing its content. Article 81 has not been interpreted by the European Court of Justice, nor by the Court of First Instance, nor indeed by the Commission, in the way that an English court or administrative agency would interpret an English statute. It has been treated in a far more teleological way—that is, in a manner which gives great weight to the particular part that it is considered to play within the general framework of the Treaty,[1] allowing the content of other Articles to influence its interpretation within the general scheme of the Treaty. Correspondingly, whilst keeping this always in mind, less importance is placed on exact analysis of individual words and phrases within the Article. It is probably helpful, nevertheless, to analyse the Article under five separate headings, namely:

(1) the meaning of 'undertaking,' including the concept of 'group economic unit'

(2) the meaning of 'all agreements, decisions by associations of undertakings and concerted practices'

---

[1] The best known example of the teleological approach is an Art. 82 case: Case 6/72 *Europemballage Corporation Can Co. Inc.* v. *Commission* [1973] ECR 215: [1973] CMLR 199, but it can be found also in a number of Art. 81 cases. For comment on the general approach of the ECJ in competition cases, see Ch. 23, Section 4 'The Commission and the Community Courts'.

(3) the meaning of 'which may affect trade between Member States'

(4) the meaning of 'which have as their object or effect the prevention, restriction or distortion of competition within the common market'

(5) the scope of its coverage, with special reference to sectors partially or totally excepted.

The first two items are dealt with in this chapter; the last three are considered in the following chapter.

2. THE CONCEPT OF AN UNDERTAKING

2.1 A BASIC DEFINITION

The definition of an undertaking is the first essential step in the analysis of Article 81(1). An undertaking, of course, must be a body capable of having legal rights and duties and acting in cooperation with other parties. For the purpose of the ECSC the European Court had defined it as 'a single organization of personal, tangible and intangible elements attached to an autonomous legal entity and pursuing a given long-term economic aim'.[2] An examination of the substantial number of cases under the Treaty of Rome in which the term has actually been considered (or held to apply without detailed consideration) illustrates that such a broad definition has been largely accepted, with the exclusion of activities carried on by a State in the exercise of its sovereign function (as opposed to merely commercial functions) and, at the other extreme, of those that neither involve the conduct of any kind of business nor the coordination of commercial activities to be carried on by others.[3] It can therefore apply to State bodies engaged in commerce, nationalized industries operating as separate legal entities, municipalities, federations, trade associations (regardless of specific function), publicly owned undertakings, and undertakings with special rights granted by the State; it also includes private individuals engaged in any form of business, commerce, profession, partnerships, cooperatives, companies, and performing-rights societies. To be engaged in an economic activity is necessary[4], but the objective of making a profit is not essential. The European Court has explained that 'any activity consisting in offering goods or services on a given market'[5] is an economic activity. Identification of an 'undertaking' for the purposes of Article 81 should in the majority of cases thus not present any difficulty, but nevertheless there have been some exceptional cases at the borderline.

From such borderline cases considered by the European Court it is clear that the key element is the nature, not of the body but of the activities which it carries out. In

---

[2] Case 19/61 *Mannesman* v. *High Authority* [1962] ECR 357, 371.

[3] For an extensive analysis of the concept of undertaking under Art. 81 EC, see Odudu, 7 *Cambridge Yearbook of European Legal Studies* [2004–2005] 211.

[4] Case C-41/90 *Höfner and Elser* [1991] ECR I-1979.

[5] Joined Cases C-180/98 to C-184/98 *Pavlov* [2000] ECR I-6451: [2001] 4 CMLR 93.

Eurocontrol,[6] that international organization, responsible for air traffic control over much of Europe, sought to collect charges from a German airline which had claimed that Eurocontrol had been acting in breach of Articles 81 and 82; the Court ruled that this could not be the case since Eurocontrol was not an 'undertaking' to which the Article applied. Whilst the concept of 'undertaking' covered any entity engaged in an economic activity, regardless of legal status and the way it was financed, in this case the function of Eurocontrol was to control and supervise airspace, a task undertaken in the public interest for the safety of air passengers. Collection of route charges could not be separated from the organization's other activities which, taken as a whole, were more like those of a public authority than an economic concern. A similar outcome occurred in the case of *Diego Cali* v. *SEPG*.[7] SEPG was a company formed to perform services in the Port of Genoa relating to the prevention and removal of pollution, particularly oil spills. Italian law required that these tasks were performed by the port operator; SEPG acted on behalf of the port operator and charged users a fee based either on the tonnage of the vessel or the volume of petroleum products being transported. Diego Cali was a shipping company which claimed that it did not require the services of SEPG because it maintained anti-pollution and cleaning-up facilities on its vessels. The Court nevertheless found in favour of SEPG, because its activities involved the performance of a task in the public interest which formed part of the central functions of the State, protecting the marine environment. That the company had been formed under Italian private law did not affect the outcome of the case, which turned on the nature of the activities which it carried out; the fact that a charge was made for those activities, as in *Eurocontrol*, did not render SEPG an undertaking for purposes of the Article. The decisions in these cases appear to suggest that an organization can be an undertaking in respect of some of its activities but not in respect of others, if its first set of activities were essentially commercial but the second involved the performance of functions of a public character equivalent to those carried out by Eurocontrol or SEPG. In contrast was the finding in *Ambulanz Glockner*[8] heard by the ECJ under Article 234 on a request from a higher administrative court in Germany for a ruling, inter alia, on the status of an ambulance service which provided both emergency transport and also routine patient transport. The service received payment for both services both from the Land (Rhineland-Palatinate) and from insurers. The ECJ ruled that, since the provision of goods and services (even emergency services) is an economic activity, *Ambulanz Glockner* was an undertaking, regardless of the source of the payments which it received.

More recently, the decision of the Court of First Instance in *FENIN*, confirmed on appeal by the European Court of Justice,[9] held that the public bodies running the

---

6 Case C-364/92 *SAT* v. *Eurocontrol* [1994] ECR I-43: [1994] 5 CMLR 208.

7 Case C-343/95 *Diego Cali & Figli* v. *Servicio Ecologici Porto di Genova* [1997] ECR I-1547: [1997] 5 CMLR 484.

8 Case C-475/99 [2001] ECR I- 8089: [2002] 4 CMLR 726.

9 Case T-319/99 *FENIN* v. *Commission* [2003] ECR II-357: [2003] 5 CMLR 34.110, on appeal, Case C-205/03P *FENIN* v. *Commission* [2006] ECR I-6295: [1996] 5 CMLR 7. See also the Opinion of Advocate General Poiares Maduro who summarized the case law on the concept of undertakings.

Spanish health service were not undertakings even though they purchased large quantities of products from commercial suppliers, as their principal purpose was to carry out functions of a public character. The goods bought were not resold but used in the performance of a social function and therefore the Spanish authorities were not undertakings within the meaning of Article 81 EC.[10]

2.2 INSURANCE AND SOCIAL-SECURITY-FUND CASES

A number of the leading cases here involved insurance funds. The first two were a pair of French cases. In the first, *Poucet and Pistre*,[11] the Court held that a fund running a compulsory social-security scheme based on principles of 'solidarity' was not an undertaking. Under its sickness and maternity insurance scheme, benefits were paid of an identical size to all recipients but contributions were made proportionate to income. Pension rights paid out under the fund were also not proportionate to contributions. There were also other elements of cross-subsidy which enabled those parts of the fund that were in surplus to assist those parts which were in deficit. By contrast, *Fédération Française des Sociétés d'Assurance*[12] concerned a voluntary old-age-pension scheme for agricultural workers, supplementing the basic compulsory scheme. Certain private insurers challenged the French law which established this scheme on the basis that it had an effective monopoly. The Court held that the insurance company managing the pension scheme was indeed an undertaking. The mere fact that it was non-profit making was irrelevant since it was competing with private insurance companies, and managed according to normal principles of insurance contributions: members received payments linked to the contributions made. Provisions on deferment of contributions because of illness were similar to those found in private insurance schemes, and there was no element of cross-subsidy between different categories of beneficiary.

The *Inail* case[13] from Italy was closer in its facts to *Poucet and Pistre*, since it involved a compulsory scheme covering accidents at work which the managing partner of a firm refused to join, because it had already covered these risks by private insurance and he objected to the monopoly nature of the official scheme. The ECJ ruled that, although the social aims of such a scheme did not rule it out automatically from being classed as an undertaking, the rules of this scheme were strongly redistributive; payments made did not reflect the level of contributions, and were fixed by the State. It

---

[10] The decisions in *FENIN* can be contrasted with the judgment of the UK Competition Appeal Tribunal in *Bettercare* [2002] CAT 7 which held that purchases of services from the private sector for the maintenance of old-peoples' homes by a public statutory trust were economic activities of an undertaking. The UK Competition Appeal Tribunal was set up by the Competition Act 1998 to hear appeals against decisions of the Office of Fair Trading under provisions of the Act equivalent to Arts. 81 and 82. Under s. 60 of the Competition Act, the Tribunal and UK courts are required to apply EC principles and case law in deciding appeals.

[11] Cases C-159, 160/91 [1993] ECR I-637.

[12] Case C-244/94 [1995] ECR I-4013: [1996] 4 CMLR 536.

[13] Case C-218/00 [2002] ECR I-691: [2002] 4 CMLR 24.

was therefore not an undertaking. On the other side of the line fell *Pavlov*,[14] where the consultants at a Dutch hospital had objected to being forced to belong to a pension fund, which had not been set up in the context of collective bargaining, but which was held to be an undertaking because it was carried on in competition with other insurance companies and their equivalent funds. It made no difference, in the view of the Court, that the compulsory nature of the fund did restrict competition to a limited extent, as the payments to the fund had only a marginal effect on the cost of the consultants' services.

In a number of Dutch cases involving pension funds these were held on the same grounds to be undertakings, but nevertheless outside the scope of Article 81(1) because of the fact that they had been established as part of collective bargaining arrangements between employers and employees in a particular industry. (See Chapter 7, section 4.4.)

2.3 EMPLOYEES AND TRADE UNIONS

The position of employees is clear. They are not undertakings, but 'workers' within the meaning of Article 39, because they perform their duties for and under the direction of the undertaking. In *Becu*[15] a company operating a grain-warehousing business in the Ghent port area used registered dockers for loading and unloading grain vessels, but other (less highly paid) workers in its warehouse on other duties. When prosecuted by the Belgian authorities for alleged breach of the Royal Decree giving monopoly rights to registered dockers in respect of dock work (which included the work carried out in the warehouse), the company claimed that the dockers protected by the Royal Decree were individually acting in breach of Articles 82 and 86. The Court however rejected this argument; the dockers were not undertakings. The status of such employees is moreover unaffected by the fact that they may be linked to other groups of workers employed by the same undertaking by some form of association, so that trade unions are not themselves undertakings[16] (except to the extent that they enter into separate commercial activities involving breaches of Article 81).[17]

2.4 AGENTS

The position of agents however depends very much on the extent of their activities. An agent could be classified as an undertaking if the activities in which it is engaged fall outside the normal range of services performed by an agent for its principal so that, to

---

[14] Joined Cases C-180/98 to C-184/98, fn. 5 above.

[15] Case C-22/98 [1999] ECR I-5665: [2001] 4 CMLR 968. See also the opinion of Jacobs A-G in Case C-67/96 *Albany* [1999] ECR I-5751: [2000] 4 CMLR 446 at para. 217.

[16] See the Opinion of Jacobs A-G in *Albany* at paras. 219–27.

[17] See, for example, the decision of the Commission in *FNSEA* (O.J. [2003] L 209/12 at paras. 109–17), which involved some French farmers unions engaged in price fixing agreements with slaughterers.

use the language of the Commission Guidelines on Vertical Restraints,[18] the agency is no longer a 'genuine' one. When the agency remains genuine then Article 81 is in any case unlikely to have application, since two independent undertakings are required for an agreement or concerted practice to come into being. A genuine agent only accepts a limited amount of risk and does not usually invest its own monies for the benefit of its principal. An agent is normally restricted by its principal as to the territory in which it may operate, the customers to whom it may sell, and the prices and conditions applicable to those sales; an agent without these limitations on his conduct may be at risk of passing over the line into independent status as an undertaking.

Whilst individuals operating their own businesses, alone or in partnership, are undertakings this status will not necessarily be accorded to individuals who are controlling shareholders in companies. On the other hand an individual who controls a number of businesses may be classified as a single undertaking. The issue was raised by a German court under Article 234: a German company, Hydrotherm, claimed that a manufacturing and distribution agreement was void under Article 81(1).[19] The other parties to the agreement were a firm known as Compact and a company called OSA, both owned by an Italian individual, Dr Andreoli. Hydrotherm had agreed to place a substantial order with Compact for the purchase of aluminium alloy radiators; it was claimed that Hydrotherm had not placed an order as large as that required by the contract and the Italian parties sued Hydrotherm for breach of contract before the German court. An issue in the case was whether the agreement could have been covered by the block exemption contained in Regulation 67/67; the Court held that the term 'undertaking' designated an economic unit, even if in law that economic unit consisted of several persons, natural or legal. Regulation 67/67 required that only two undertakings be parties, but the Court held that this condition was satisfied even if one of the parties contracted through the medium of several undertakings with identical interests and controlled by the same natural person. In this case Dr Andreoli controlled all the relevant businesses in his operations, and the Court, adopting the economic analysis suggested by Advocate General Lenz, found that the agreement had been made by only two undertakings, namely Hydrotherm on one side and Andreoli and his businesses on the other.

The issue of agency was considered by the European Court in the *Sugar Cartel* case,[20] where some of the undertakings involved acted as agents for each other in the sugar market, and also as principals on their own account, and were adjudged by the Court to be essentially independent traders to whom Article 81 applied. An element in this decision was clearly the ambiguous relationship between those particular undertakings and their alleged principals; it does not seem to be the Commission's practice to refuse the status of agent to a business simply because it also trades on its own account

---

[18] [2000] OJ C291/1: [2000] 5 CMLR 1074, at paras. 12–17. See also Ch. 10, Section 6.
[19] Case 170/83 *Hydrotherm Gerätebau v. Andreoli* [1984] ECR 2999: [1985] 3 CMLR 224.
[20] Case 40/73 *Suiker Unie v. Commission* [1975] ECR 1663: [1976] 1 CMLR 295.

or for other principals in respect of other products. The actual economic function of the so-called agent must be fully analysed in each case.[21]

It is clear that the mere description of an individual or company as an 'agent' is insufficient to prevent the application of Article 81. In *Pittsburgh Corning Europe*,[22] certain distributors for Pittsburgh Corning, which supplied cellular glass in Belgium and Holland, were described in relevant documents as agents, although the evidence showed that they were actually distributors. The Commission found that the term 'agent' in the agreement between Pittsburgh Corning and its Belgian representative company was in fact used only for tax reasons.

2.5 A SUMMARY: THE LIMITS TO ITS SCOPE

It may be useful to sum up the situations in which it is unlikely that an individual or other entity will be adjudged to be acting as an undertaking:

- Where the nature of the activities carried out, even if they involve the receipt of payment for services rendered, form part of the functions of the State or other public authorities (*Eurocontrol, Diego Cali*). An entity performing such functions may nevertheless be classified as an undertaking in respect of other, purely commercial, functions.

- Where the purchase of goods or services is not aimed at resale but carried out in the fulfilment of a social function (*FENIN*).

- Where the function is not one of a commercial nature, since it is a compulsory social security system or insurance fund based on the principles of internal solidarity (*Poucet, Pistre* and *Inail*) as opposed to being a fund where benefits are paid proportionately to contributions collected from members (*FFSA/Albany International*). Even where the latter situation applies the terms of the fund (though an undertaking) may be outside Article 81(1) if established in the context of a collective bargaining agreement. (*Albany International* and other pension fund cases cited in Chapter 7, section 4.4.)

- Where the relevant person is simply an integral part of a larger organization (which itself may well be an undertaking) and had therefore no separate or independent economic role on the market. This will apply to employees (*Becu*) and to genuine agents who do not accept unusual risks on behalf of their principal nor act in practice as principals (*Pittsburgh Corning*).

---

[21] Recently, in Case T-325/01 *DaimlerChrysler* [2005] ECR II-3319: [2007] 4 CMLR 559, the Court of First Instance summarized the principles of the case law by stating that an agent would lose the character of an independent commercial operator only if it did not bear the risks resulting from the contracts negotiated for its principal and operated as an auxiliary organ forming an integral part of the principal's undertaking. These principles were developed further in *Confederación Española de Empresarios de Estaciones de Servicio v. Compañía Española de Petróleos SA* [2006] ECR I-11987, [2007] 4 CMLR 866. Both decisions are discussed in detail in Ch. 10, pp. 203–04.

[22] *Pittsburgh Corning Europe* [1972] OJ L272/35: [1973] CMLR D2.

3. GROUP ECONOMIC UNITS

The second important issue concerning the definition is whether individual corporate bodies comprised within a group are separate undertakings, or whether the group itself constitutes the relevant undertaking. The view usually taken by the Commission and the Court, (which is consistent also with the approach taken to the status of an agent in relation to its principal) is that each company within a group, either as parent or wholly owned subsidiary, is treated as an undertaking capable of entering into an agreement or concerted practice. On the other hand, the essential condition that both entities concerned must be capable of independent economic policymaking for a relationship between them to be classified as an agreement or concerted practice is not satisfied if the agreement or concerted practice reflects no more than the allocation of functions within a corporate group under the legal and actual control of one company. An early example was the *Kodak* case.[23] This involved a request for negative clearance by various wholly owned European subsidiaries of the United States company Eastman Kodak, following the introduction of new uniform conditions of sale which permitted export sales by them to other Member State countries at the same price as was charged there by the local Kodak subsidiary, whilst imposing restrictions on sale outside the Community. The Commission took the view that, since these subsidiaries could not act independently of their parent company, their individual agreements within the group were not made between independent economic policymaking units, and therefore no effect on competition was either likely or possible.

In *Viho Europe* v. *Commission*,[24] the European Court confirmed that this was the correct interpretation of Article 81. Viho had sought to buy Parker pens direct from that company but Parker had refused to supply direct, though willing that Viho should obtain supplies on less favourable terms from their distributors in Europe, who were all directly owned Parker subsidiaries. It was clear that Parker Pen in Europe traded as a single economic unit, within which subsidiaries did not enjoy autonomy, since their distribution strategies on product ranges, advertising margins, and prices were all centrally controlled. Moreover, the Court made clear that, even if the effect of the internal allocation of functions within a corporate group is 'to contribute to preserving and partitioning the various national markets and in so doing to thwart one of the fundamental objectives to be achieved by the Common Market', it still did not breach Article 81. What would amount to such a breach would be a requirement by the Group that its individual subsidiaries dealt with third parties only on terms which limited price competition or restricted free movement of goods.

---

[23] *Kodak* [1970] OJ L147/24: [1970] CMLR D19).
[24] Case C-73/95P [1996] ECR I-5457: [1997] 4 CMLR 419.

Thus the Commission was able in the *Interbrew* case[25] to prevent a Belgian brewery group with a dominant position in Belgium from entering into arrangements with its wholly owned subsidiaries under which each of them had to obtain a 'destination clause' from its customers: effectively a promise not to export the beer supplied by the subsidiary. Such an arrangement went far beyond mere 'internal allocation' of duties between subsidiaries of the group.

This approach by the Commission (often referred to as the doctrine of the 'group economic unit') had also been referred to by the Court in its *Centrafarm*[26] and *Ahmed Saeed* cases[27] in 1974 and 1983 respectively, where the Court indicated that Article 81 might well be applicable if a company is accorded a measure of independence, either de facto or *de jure*; it may well then fall within the scope of the Article, even if the degree of independence is restricted. Difficult issues can also arise in joint venture cases, where the degree of independence of the joint venture company from its parents can present analytical problems for the Commission.

In *Martell-DMP*[28] fines were imposed both on the French cognac producer Martell and on DMP, its 50-per-cent-owned subsidiary which distributed the product in France, for conspiracy to prevent parallel exports to Italy (where prices were substantially higher). The parties had acknowledged to the Commission that they regarded themselves as separate, rather than as parts of the same economic unit. Moreover, the other 50 per cent owner of DMP, Piper-Heidsieck, had exactly the same shareholding and representation on the supervisory board of DMP as had Martell. DMP also distributed brands not belonging to its two parent companies and acted independently from them in determining the terms of sales to syndicates in France.

The adoption by the Court of the 'group economic unit' theory has a dual advantage for the Commission. It enables it to apply a test to the relationship between undertakings within a corporate group which gives a realistic degree of emphasis to the actual economic relationship between them, rather than relying on formal tests relating to legal indicia which might more easily be manipulated by the parties. It also enables the Commission (and the Court) to justify the extension of its jurisdiction to parent companies apparently operating from outside the Community, so long as they actively control subsidiary companies resident or doing business within it, an issue discussed further in Chapter 22.

---

[25] [1996] 5 CMLR 518. Although this informal settlement concerned a company with a dominant position under Art. 82, it nevertheless indicates the Commission's approach under Art. 81 to such arrangements or agreements between the individual subsidiaries of Interbrew and their customers.

[26] Cases 15 and 16/74 *Centrafarm BV* v. *Sterling Drug Inc. and Winthrop BV* [1974] ECR 1147, 1183: [1974] 2 CMLR 480.

[27] Case 66/86 [1989] ECR 803: [1990] 4 CMLR 102.

[28] [1992] 5 CMLR 582. In an Art. 82 case, Case T-228/97 *Irish Sugar* v. *Commission* [1999] ECR II-2969: [1999] 5 CMLR 1300, a subsidiary in which Irish Sugar held 51 per cent of the share capital was nevertheless accepted as not forming part of a group economic entity.

4. AGREEMENTS

4.1 INTRODUCTION: THE BROAD SCOPE OF ARTICLE 81(1)

Article 81(1) was drafted to cover three related, though conceptually distinct, situations: agreements, decisions by associations of undertakings, and concerted practices. Undertakings can be said to have reached an *agreement* when there can objectively be said to be a sufficient consensus between them as to the bargain to which they have mutually committed themselves. It is clear from cases such as *Asia Motor France (No. 3)*[29] that the parties' lack of autonomy in their choice of commercial arrangements may deprive these of the character of a voluntary 'agreement'. On the other hand, the reasons which induced the making of an agreement need not be identical on all sides. The interests of distributors in being able to supply their principal territory, and also to export product into other territories where higher prices may prevail, may of course be at variance with the interest of the manufacturer in preventing parallel imports.

Identification of such consensus is ultimately a matter for courts of law, not for the undertakings themselves. This task is easier if the contract is written, but a purely verbal, or partly written and partly verbal agreement may exist and be recognized by a court or administrative body, even if the parties claim that, whatever the agreement's outward form, it was not intended to be legally binding but simply a 'gentlemen's agreement'.[30] The Commission decision in BP *Kemi-DDSF*[31] illustrates that even if the relevant document has been neither signed nor dated, it will still be treated as an agreement if it has been acted upon by both parties. In this case, De Danske Spritfabrikker (DDSF) was the only producer in Denmark of synthetic and agricultural ethanol, used in the production of several products including vinegar and cosmetics. About 45 per cent of the total synthetic ethanol production in the Common Market in 1971 was manufactured by BP, and it had begun to supply certain customers in Denmark through its Danish subsidiary (BP Kemi). To protect its market position, DDSF then sought an exclusive purchasing and cooperation agreement with BP and its subsidiaries; a document was drawn up, though never signed nor dated, under which:

(1) DDSF would only buy the product from BP Kemi, up to an agreed maximum, provided that BP Kemi had the opportunity of supplying it also with excess quantities on similar terms

(2) BP Kemi would be entitled to sell yearly in Denmark up to 25 per cent of the combined aggregate sales of the product; but if BP Kemi exceeded this limit, it would pay compensation to DDSF.

---

[29] Case T-387/94 [1996] ECR II-961: [1996] 5 CMLR 537.
[30] Case 41/69 *Chemiefarma NV* v. *Commission* [1970] ECR 661: [1970] CMLR 43.
[31] [1979] OJ L286/32: [1979] 3 CMLR 684.

There were subsidiary agreements on the pricing of the product (which was to be kept identical by both companies) and on rules for allocating customers within Denmark. Atka, a competitor of DDSF, challenged these arrangements, and the Commission ruled that the mere application by the two parties of identical prices (which continued after the termination of the original agreement) would not necessarily prove the continuing effect of the agreement, but was strong evidence of it if pricing of the product was likely to have been different in normal market competition.

A *decision* by an association of undertakings is any provision of the rules of a trade association (having members which are either trade associations or, more often, separate undertakings) or any decision or recommendation made under those rules either for or by its members, or arrived at informally within the framework which they provide.[32] Again, it is normally quite easy to identify the existence of such decisions.

The concept of *concerted practices*, however, is more fluid; it is unquestionably the widest, and the vaguest, of the three expressions, intended to cover any kind of cooperative activity between undertakings which falls short of an actual agreement. For safety's sake, 'concerted practices' are often alleged by the Commission as an alternative even when some kind of 'agreement' probably also exists, as for example in the sales cartel operated in the *Floral* case.[33] In an early decision, *Brasserie de Haecht* v. *Wilkin-Janssens (No. 1)*,[34] the European Court had indicated that the three concepts need not be separately distinguished in the Commission's analysis of the situation; the constituent elements of the three forms of relationship could be considered together if they were factually hard to disentangle.

In this area, Article 81 has again drawn part of its content from Article 65 of the ECSC Treaty, where all three expressions are found. Of these, both 'agreements' and 'concerted practices' require that at least two undertakings be party to the agreement or practice; by contrast, a 'decision' by a trade association could involve the association alone (which may be a single legal person) although in practice it will usually involve the participation of a number of undertakings, almost certainly the members of that association. Although two undertakings must be party to agreements or concerted practices, restrictions need only affect one party.

The Commission and the Court have dealt with numerous cases on both horizontal and vertical agreements. As we have seen, horizontal agreements are those made between undertakings that compete with each other (or at least are believed to do so) because each operates at the same level, whether as manufacturer, wholesaler, distributor, or retailer. On the other hand, vertical agreements are those made between undertakings at different levels in the commercial chain, whose relationship to each other is complementary. The vertical agreement may therefore be between manufacturer and

---

[32] Case 8/72 *Vereeniging van Cementhandelaren* v. *Commission* [1972] ECR 977: [1973] CMLR 7.

[33] *Floral Düngemittelverkaufs* [1980] OJ L39/51: [1980] 2 CMLR 285. In the *Citric Acid* Case [2002] OJ L239/18: [2002] 5 CMLR 1070, the Commission confirmed that the concepts of 'agreement' and 'concerted practice' are fluid and may overlap. See also Case T-7/89 *Hercules* v. *Commission* [1991] ECR II-1711: [1992] 4 CMLR 84.

[34] Case 23/67 *Brasserie de Haecht* v. *Wilkin-Janssens (No. 1)* [1967] ECR 407: [1968] CMLR 26.

distributor, or wholesaler and retailer, or in another context patentee and licensee. Both types of agreement are covered by Article 81.[35]

4.2 NETWORK AGREEMENTS AND UNILATERAL CONDUCT

Even a document which looks less like an agreement than unilateral instruction may be held to constitute an agreement, if the recipient of the instructions has been required to acknowledge its receipt, even if the recipient was not expressly required to acknowledge its contents. An early example of this approach was provided by the Commission in its decision in *WEA-Filipacchi Music* SA[36] where WEA, a subsidiary of the US corporation Warner Brothers, was engaged in the sale of pop records. It sent a circular to its various French distributors informing them that sales of such records outside France were forbidden. In sending this circular, WEA was influenced by the fact that the French price was considerably lower than the price in Germany, so that sales or distribution by way of 'parallel imports' into Germany could have proved extremely profitable for the French distributors. The distributors were merely asked to affix their official stamp to the circular by way of acknowledgement, without being asked specifically to acknowledge that they were bound by the terms communicated.

In the case of *Sandoz*[37] invoices for the supply of pharmaceuticals used by this producer bore the words 'export prohibited'. In practice that restriction had been accepted by its trade customers. This was held by the European Court (confirming the Commission decision) to represent, not simply a unilateral request, but part of an agreement of which the words endorsed were the documentary evidence.

In *BMW Belgium SA* v. *Commission*,[38] a circular urging dealers to discourage exports of cars to Germany was distributed (without authority from the parent company in Germany) by the Belgian BMW subsidiary. The circular went out after consultation with, and under the signatures of, the BMW Belgium dealers' trade association's executive committee, and a number of Belgian BMW dealers acknowledged its receipt in writing. These were held by the Commission to have acknowledged participation in the arrangements, so that fines were imposed for the attempt which the circular represented to prevent exports of BMW vehicles from Belgium. It is also clear that, once such an agreement has been made, the Commission cannot easily be satisfied that it has been completely terminated: even if the parties claim that this is so, its effect may continue to influence their conduct. In such circumstances

---

[35] As we have already seen in Ch. 5, pp. 62–3, an early attempt by Italy to have vertical agreements read out of the Article failed.

[36] [1973] CMLR D43.   [37] Case C-227/87 [1990] ECR I-45: [1990] 4 CMLR 242.

[38] Cases 32 and 36–82/78 [1979] ECR 2435: [1980] 1 CMLR 370. It is noteworthy that in this case the BMW subsidiary was fined, but its German parent which had played no part in the arrangements was not even made a defendant, showing that the doctrine of the 'group economic unit' is not, and should not be, applied automatically without analysis of the relevant facts. The rulings of the Commission were upheld by the Court.

it may therefore be held still to exist, or alternatively to have been transformed into concerted practices.[39]

An interesting development of the jurisprudence of the Court on the question of the definition of an 'agreement' has come in cases where a manufacturer has apparently taken unilateral action, but in a way so closely connected to an agreement that it has been interpreted, together with that agreement, as forming part of the general complex of contractual arrangements between the manufacturer and the various distributors or dealers with whom these individual agreements (even if notified or exempted) were made. In *AEG Telefunken* v. *Commission*,[40] AEG had its selective distribution system for consumer electronic products in Germany and other countries notified to the Commission and exempted under Article 81(3). This distribution agreement contained no right for AEG to lay down resale prices for its dealers. Numerous complaints were received by the Commission from small traders claiming that AEG had sought to discriminate against some of them, especially those who would not maintain resale prices at the level considered appropriate by AEG. The Commission imposed a substantial fine, which was upheld by the Court. The Court ruled that the activities of AEG Telefunken alone in ensuring that at least a substantial proportion of its dealers did not cut prices below the recommended level was not unilateral conduct, but formed an integral part of its contractual nexus with the distributors who, by remaining part of the distribution network, had confirmed their adherence to the AEG policy.

In *Ford* v. *Commission*,[41] Ford had likewise notified to the Commission its distribution system for Germany. Originally, the products covered by the agreement included both left-hand and right-hand drive cars. By a circular taking effect on 1 May 1982, right-hand drive cars were withdrawn, so that they would not be available for resale to British buyers for import into the United Kingdom at a lower overall price than then prevailed in the UK domestic market. The Commission alleged that exemption should be refused for the distribution system because its effect was to partition national markets, contrary to the well-known *Grundig* principle. Ford claimed that its decision was simply unilateral, having no necessary connection with the main dealer agreement for Germany, and that its distribution system was entitled to exemption under Article 81(3).

The Court upheld the Commission's decision on this issue and held that the decision to change the product covered by the dealer agreement was not simply unilateral. It was rather part of the whole contractual framework between Ford and its dealers; admission to the dealer network in Germany implied acceptance, in the view of the Court, by all parties of the policy pursued by Ford with regard to the choice of models to be delivered to the German market. The Court said that the Commission was entitled, in deciding whether to grant exemption, to take all the relevant facts into

---

[39] Another example is Case 243/83 *Binon* v. *Agence et Messageries de la Presse (AMP)* [1985] ECR 2015: 3 CMLR 800 where the effect of previous arrangements for the distribution of newspapers and periodicals in Belgium was held likely to continue even after a new system had been introduced.

[40] Case 107/82 [1983] ECR 3151: [1984] 3 CMLR 325.

[41] Cases 25 and 26/84 [1985] ECR 2725: [1985] 3 CMLR 528.

account, including the effect which Ford's refusal to supply right-hand drive cars to Germany could have on the partitioning of the Common Market.

In its decision, the Court also laid down an important general finding as to the correct approach to the interpretation of Article 81(1). The Court held that the Commission was not required to rule on each individual element of the agreement, so long as the agreement as a whole fell within the coverage of Article 81(1). Ford had claimed that the Commission must first identify each provision of the agreement in breach of the Article, and then consider that provision in isolation against all the relevant criteria, including the four conditions for exemption contained in Article 81(3). However, the Court, took the view that a more 'broad brush' approach was justified in such circumstances.[42]

4.3 THE *BAYER* CASE

The Commission obviously benefited from these decisions, which characterized the whole distribution network as individually and collectively responsible for both initial policy and subsequent changes of policy decided upon by their supplier. It however suffered a setback on October 2000, when its decision against *Bayer* in the *Adalat* case[43] was annulled by the CFI over the issue of supply quotas. The background to the judgment was the fact that the prices of most Bayer pharmaceuticals sold in France and Spain by its distributors were considerably lower than those prevailing for the same products in the United Kingdom. Adalat was a popular treatment for coronary heart disease, which had to be taken on a regular basis. It was not however the only drug available for this purpose, and Bayer did not have a dominant position for its market in any Member State in terms of Article 82. Bayer's French and Spanish wholesalers were keen to supply not only their regular customers in those countries but also the more lucrative parallel trade in the United Kingdom.

Bayer therefore tried to disrupt this parallel trade by its wholesalers in a number of ways. It reduced the quantities of Adalat supplied to the French and Spanish wholesalers to the level which it believed corresponded to local demand only; it made excuses for being unable to meet the larger orders that the wholesalers continued to place. The key element in the situation, and in the decision of the CFI, was that at no time did the wholesalers acquiesce in Bayer's efforts to reduce their supplies. Bayer did not monitor the levels of parallel trade between the territories involved, so that there was little incentive for the wholesalers to change their commercial strategy, nor were they offered any reward in the hope that they would change their policy. In the absence of such acquiescence, the CFI found no 'agreement' between Bayer and the wholesalers could be presumed, and the fine imposed on Bayer for having entered into such an 'agreement' was quashed.[44] The decision of the CFI was later upheld by the European Court.

---

[42] The Court adopted a similar approach in Case 193/83 *Windsurfing International* [1986] ECR 611: 3 CMLR 489, considered in detail in Ch. 12, pp. 271–3.

[43] [1996] OJ L201/1: [1996] 5 CMLR 416.

[44] Case T-41/96 *Bayer AG* v. *Commission* [2000] ECR II-3383: [2001] 4 CMLR 126. There appeared to be only a narrow distinction, if any, between the *Ford* and *Bayer* cases. See for critical comment Jephcott,

In a Commission decision taken after the judgment of the Court of First Instance in *Bayer, Glaxo-Wellcome*,[45] the manufacturer had sought an individual exemption under Article 81(3) for the terms of its distribution agreement with its Spanish wholesalers, in a similar commercial situation as in the *Bayer* case, except that the agreement covered a range of drugs. To discourage diversion of its drugs to the UK market the supplier sought to impose a dual pricing system, drugs purchased for national sale being priced at a lower level than those sold in other Member States. Most of the wholesalers had endorsed these new terms by returning signed copies of the General Sales Conditions to Glaxo. Although a few wholesalers voiced complaints against these instructions, they made no efforts to distance themselves from the agreement they had originally concluded with Glaxo and eventually complied with the new terms. The main argument raised by Glaxo was that the large-scale parallel imports were damaging not only patients in Spain, who were not receiving the full quantities of Glaxo products that they needed, but also Glaxo's own business in Europe. It claimed that it had been forced by the parallel imports to scale down its spending on research and development (R&D). The Commission, however, was unimpressed by this argument, pointing out that there was no evidence of any linkage between the volume of parallel imports and the R & D budget. It also stated that under Articles 28 and 30 of the Treaty differences in the treatment of intermediaries in different territories to prevent parallel imports were not allowed, and that Article 81(3) should not be utilized for such purposes. The Commission decision was challenged before the Court of First Instance.[46] Although the Court of First Instance annulled in part the Commission decision because it felt that the Commission had not carried out an adequate examination of the conditions of exemption laid down in Article 81(3), it confirmed the finding of the Commission that an *agreement* existed between Glaxo Wellcome and the Spanish wholesalers. In *Glaxo*, the express acquiescence of most of the wholesalers and the tacit compliance with the anti-competitive conditions by the others were therefore the crucial elements in determining the existence of a concurrence of wills between the parties.

The Glaxo decision can be usefully compared with the ruling of the Court of First Instance in *Volkswagen*, confirmed on appeal by the European Court,[47] which made it clear that the narrower approach taken by the Community judicature in *Bayer* on the classification of apparent unilateral conduct as a form of cooperation between undertakings is here to stay. In *Volkswagen*, a car manufacturer operated a lawful selective and exclusive distribution system throughout Europe. After the signature of the distribution agreements, the Commission found out that the manufacturer had sent circulars to its distributors aimed at influencing the discount policy that they should

---

'Commentary on Case T-41/96 *Bayer v. Commission*' [2001] 22 ECLR 469–76 and Jacobsen and Broberg 'The Concept of Agreement in Article 81: On the Manufacturers' Right to prevent Parallel Trade Within the European Community' [2002] 22 ECLR 127–41.

[45] [2001] OJ L302/1: [2002] 4 CMLR 335.

[46] Case T-168/01 *GlaxoSmithKline Services* v. *Commission* [2006] ECR II-2969: [2006] 5 CMLR 1589.

[47] Case T-208/01 [2003] ECR II-5141 [2004] 4CMLR 727 and, on appeal, Case C-74/04P *Commission* v. *Volkswagen AG* [2006] ECR I-6585.

apply to the sale of a particular car model—although there was no evidence that the instructions of the manufacturer had been implemented in practice. The Commission, on the strength of the *AEG* and *Ford* judgments, concluded that by remaining part of the distribution network, the dealers had tacitly acquiesced to the unlawful contractual variation proposed by the manufacturer. The Court of First Instance, however, annulled the Commission decision and held that the Commission had again stretched the notion of agreement too far. In the view of the Court, tacit acquiescence to a *subsequent*, *unforeseen*, and *unlawful* contractual variation proposed by a manufacturer could not be inferred from the simple fact that a dealer remained part of a distribution system. Therefore, the actions of Volkswagen in the case had the character of unilateral conduct falling outside the scope of Article 81 EC.

5. CONCERTED PRACTICES

5.1 THE EARLY CASE LAW

All systems of law which seek to restrain anti-competitive behaviour find that it is difficult to do so unless the prohibitions apply effectively not only to agreements, but also to the many ways which can be used to dispense with the need for actual agreements. Those who originally negotiated the terms of Article 81 would have been well aware of the likelihood that in many sectors of European industry and commerce (particularly where there was a strong oligopolistic element) effective concertation of commercial policy could be arranged without the need for formal agreement, indeed often without creating any external evidence at all. Desired results could often be achieved by far simpler or subtler methods.

The problem for DG Comp as an enforcement authority has been to find evidence of the arrangements made which have the effect of enforcing uniformity of price or other undesirable consequences falling within the range of Article 81. The best evidence, of course, in such cases would be documentation comprising, if not a formal agreement, at least letters, emails, fax copies, minutes of meetings, or other commercial documents: in other words the kind of document which is the routine product of the business office. To enable the Commission through DG Comp to reach these more informal arrangements, the concept of 'concerted practice' was introduced into the Treaty and, thanks to the wide definition given to it by the European Court, has proved vital to the implementation of the Commission's competition policy.

It is noteworthy that at the time of the enactment of the Treaty of Rome in 1957, none of the Member States, even if they had competition legislation in their domestic law, had a concept in their domestic law equivalent to 'concerted action' or 'concerted practice'. Its introduction can undoubtedly be attributed to the influence of US antitrust law, where the concept of 'concerted action' was already familiar in relation to both horizontal and vertical relationships. When parallel conduct by enterprises was found, which arose not because of independent business decisions but as a result of inter-dependent decisions raising the inference that there was a tacit agreement between the parties, then US Federal Courts were entitled, and inclined, to look for 'plus factors' to distinguish the latter situation from the former. Among the factors which they took into account were any actions taken by companies contrary to their own normal business interests. These might include raising prices at a time when there was a substantial supply available of the relevant product, artificially limiting the supply of products, imposing unusual conditions of sale, refusing to attend sales of goods by auction unless other leading competitors were present, or agreeing to price identical goods to be transported long distance only on identical fixed basing points.[48]

Proof of concerted practices was at issue in the first three major horizontal agreement cases to reach the Court, all being appeals brought against decisions by the Commission to impose fines on groups of manufacturers from a number of separate Member States. The first of these was the *Dyestuffs* case.[49] Between 1964 and 1967, there were three general and uniform increases in the price of dyestuffs sold by leading European producers. In January 1964, there was a 15 per cent increase for nearly all dyes based on aniline. In January 1965, there was a 10 per cent increase in prices for all dyes and pigments not covered by the increase of the previous year. Major Italian companies did not participate in this increase, so the other European companies did not maintain the price increase for the Italian market even though it had already been announced. In October 1967, the parties uniformly imposed an 8 per cent increase for dyes sold in Germany, the Netherlands, Belgium, and Luxembourg, and a 12 per cent increase in France.

Advocate General Mayras characterized the market for such products as oligopolistic, controlled by a small number of producers with national markets 'walled off' from competition. Customers tended only to have direct contact with producers in their own country, all contact with foreign producers being through their subsidiary companies' representatives or agents. There was therefore no true transparency of price or awareness on a Europe-wide basis for the individual customer. The Advocate General felt that in a more competitive market price increases would have followed on a less uniform basis; whereas oligopolistic pressures might account for downward movements of prices on a concerted basis, it would be less likely, without some form of

---

[48] The Supreme Court laid down clear guidelines to prevent the courts from inferring agreements merely from parallel conduct. The *Monsanto* v. *Sprayrite* case, 104 Supreme Court Reports 1551 (1984), finally established that a high degree of collaboration is required between a manufacturer and its distributors if a distributor whose appointment had been ended is to establish the necessary proof of an agreement. The mere fact that complaints have been made by other distributors against that distributor is insufficient, since it is the normal practice of distributors to discuss such matters with their manufacturer, and the mere making of a complaint is not necessarily decisive in the manufacturer's decision to terminate an appointment. Whilst it is not the practice of the European Court of Justice to refer in its decisions to Court decisions of any jurisdiction, let alone those outside the Community, there is no doubt that the US experience has influenced the significant development of the concept of concerted practice through the cases. Advocates General are not so restricted, and examples can be found of cases where their opinions have referred to relevant US cases, e.g. in the *Dyestuffs* case cited in fn. 49 below.

[49] Cases 48–57/69 *ICI and Others* v. *Commission (Dyestuffs)* [1972] ECR 619: [1972] CMLR 557.

agreement, to have been responsible for such concerted upward moves. He therefore felt sufficiently suspicious about the contacts between the parties to find that the price moves had been coordinated.

The Court agreed that there had been concerted practices by the defendants. There was an element of interconnection between the three separate price increases operating in a virtually simultaneous way. In 1964 the increase had proceeded as planned, but on the two later occasions the advance announcements from major undertakings had allowed each of them to observe the reaction of the others and to eliminate the risk that any one producer's increase might get out of line. Although every producer was legally free in changing its prices to take into account the present or foreseeable conduct of its competitors, it was a breach of Article 81 to cooperate with competitors in a way which enabled a coordinated course of action relating to price increases to be put into effect. It was an even greater breach to ensure the success of that course of action by deliberate prior elimination of all uncertainty about each other's conduct over such matters as percentages of increase, date, place, and exact range of products covered. The term 'concerted practice' was defined by the Court as a 'form of coordination between enterprises, that had not yet reached the point of true contract relationship but which had in practice substituted cooperation for the risks of competition'.[50]

In 1975, a more detailed definition of concerted practices was given by the Court in the *Sugar Cartel* case, as follows:

The concept... refers to a form of coordination between undertakings which, without having been taken to the stage where an agreement properly so-called has been concluded, knowingly substitutes for the risks of competition practical co-operation between them which leads to conditions of competition which do not correspond to the normal conditions of the market having regard to the nature of the products, the importance and number of the undertakings as well as the size and nature of the said market. Such practical co-operation amounts to a concerted practice, particularly if it enables the persons concerned to consolidate established positions to the detriment of effective freedom of movement of the products in the Common Market and of the freedom of consumers to choose their suppliers.[51]

This complex case[52] involved sugar manufacturers throughout the Community, and required the examination of the market situation in each of the relevant markets. Since sugar came within the scope of the Common Agricultural Policy, there was considerable Member State involvement in the marketing of sugar. In the case of Italy the Court found that the involvement was so substantial as to justify a finding that the restrictive

---

[50] Ibid., at paras. 64–5 of the judgment.

[51] Cases 40–8, 50, 54–6, 111, 113 and 114/73 [1975] ECR 1663: [1976] 1 CMLR 295.

[52] The case report in ECR is 491 pages long, and in CMLR 195 pages long. This probably means the report is rarely read in its entirety. It is the kind of case for which the existence of the Court of First Instance would have been invaluable: had it then been in operation, its detailed analysis of the complex facts would have allowed the European Court (if an appeal had been brought) to concentrate on the legal issues involved, rather than having to review so many factual issues individually. On the other hand Cases T- 25, 26, 30–2, 34–9, 42–6, 48, 50–71, 87, 88, 103 and 104/95P *Cement Cartel* [2000] ECR II-491: [2000]: 5 CMLR 204 were so lengthy that the CMLR report is only a summary—not the full text of the CFI judgment—which in the 2000 ECR report at ECR II, pp. 491–1, 682, amounts to nearly 1,200 pages!

practices of the parties in attempting to preserve the principle of *chacun chez soi* could not of themselves have affected the competitive position, so little room for manoeuvre having been left by the stringent domestic legislation. In other jurisdictions, notably Germany and the Netherlands, the scope for individual agreements and practices was greater and, after a painstaking examination, a number of findings of concerted practices were made, although by no means identical with the findings of the Commission. Some of the fines imposed were therefore reduced.

5.2 THE BURDEN OF PROOF: THE COMMISSION'S TASK

An important element in establishing the existence of concerted practices is contact between the parties, which must involve intentional communication of information between them, either directly or through an intermediary. There must be some positive intention on the part of one party to direct the information to the other, or at least to launch it into the area where the other is likely to receive it. It is also essential for the Commission to show that the party receiving the information is aware of having done so, not accidentally, but as a target. Such giving and receiving of information clearly goes beyond mutual awareness by competitors that the terms which they quote to their customers will subsequently become known to their competitors, who will naturally make use of this knowledge in their own pricing and other competitive strategies. If even awareness of what one's competitor is doing constitutes a sufficient level of contact to justify a claim of concerted practices, independent undertakings would be prevented from adapting intelligently to the conduct of other undertakings. This would be particularly serious in a market whose operations are normally relatively transparent and where there are a substantial number of competitors. The distinction is clearly drawn in the case of *Züchner* v. *Bayerische Vereinsbank*.[53] Herr Züchner had an account with the Bayerische Vereinsbank at Rosenheim and challenged the service charge made for the transfer of funds to Italy, on the basis that debiting what appeared to be a uniform charge by a number of banks constituted a concerted practice. The issue was referred under Article 234 to the Court, which confirmed that the banking services were indeed covered by Article 81 and that any such agreement, if proved, would have been in breach of it. The tests which the Court laid down for determining whether the banks had operated sufficiently independently in applying a uniform charge to customers making foreign transfers were:

(1) whether contacts between the various banks which had imposed such charges related only to charges made in the past, or also to those to be made in the future

(2) whether in a state of free competition different rates of charge would have applied

---

[53] Case 172/80 [1981] ECR 2021: [1982] 1 CMLR 313. See J. Faull and A. Nikpay, *The EC Law of Competition* (2nd edn, Oxford University Press, 2007), paras. 11.09–11.64.

(3) the number and importance of the participating banks in the market for monetary transfers between Member States

(4) the volume of transfers on which a uniform charge was imposed, as compared with the total number of transfers made.

In conclusion, the Court said that parallel conduct in debiting uniform charges on transfers by banks from one Member State to another could amount to a concerted practice if it were established not only that the parallel conduct exhibited features of coordination and cooperation characteristic of such a practice, but also that such conduct was capable of having a sufficient effect on competition.

In such cases, the Commission will normally allege that the facts established cannot be explained other than by concerted action. The parties must provide a rational explanation, which the Commission will accept or reject. This is well illustrated by the case of *Compagnie Royal Asturienne des Mines and Rheinzink* v. *Commission*.[54] These two companies supplied rolled zinc to a Belgian company, Schlitz. Schlitz resold the zinc to a German company, the market price in Germany being higher than that in Belgium. However, Schlitz had obtained its supplies from CRAM and Rheinzink by a false claim that the product would be resold to Egypt; CRAM found out the deceit and refused to make further supplies, and Rheinzink came to a similar conclusion to cut off Schlitz. Evidence showed that there was regular contact between CRAM and Rheinzink.

The Commission found that there was sufficient evidence of concerted practice between the two companies in refusing to continue supplies. The suggested motive was that they wished to continue their own profitable supplies to the German market and to prevent Schlitz from continuing to engage in it. Unfortunately for the Commission, the European Court found, to the contrary, that the reason for the refusal of supplies was in fact the poor credit record of Schlitz, finding sufficient evidence that this was the major ground for the decision to refuse supplies.

5.3 THE *WOODPULP* CASE

In summary, much case law illustrates the great importance of findings of 'concerted practices' from the viewpoint of the Commission as an enforcement agency. The most important case in this area was originally decided by the Commission in December 1984, in *Woodpulp*.[55] Bleached sulphate pulp, used in the manufacture of many different kinds of paper, can be made from either hardwood or softwood. Many companies were alleged to have concerted prices for this product, either directly or indirectly. The defendants included eleven United States, six Canadian, eleven Swedish, eleven Finnish, one Norwegian, one Portuguese, and one Spanish company who collectively supplied about two-thirds of the EC market. The Commission found that all the

---

[54] Cases 29–30/83 [1984] ECR 1679: [1985] 1 CMLR 688.
[55] The Commission decision is reported at [1985] OJ L85/1: [1985] 3 CMLR 474.

companies involved were subject to EC competition law because their conduct had an effect on the EC market, and that the deliberate transparency of prices charged on the European market by such a large number of competitors, although in theory making concertation more difficult, might in practice make it easier if carried out in ways which helped anticipation and knowledge of the pricing policy of competitors. Apparently prices were charged on a quarterly basis, the vast majority being quoted in US dollars rather than in the local currency of the company giving the quotation.

The Commission's decision was based on what it characterized as the 'deliberate transparency of prices'. It argued that in an open competitive market one would find a variety of approaches to pricing strategy, prices being quoted in different currencies with substantial reductions for quantities supplied and long-term contracts. It found a suspicious lack of variation between the quoted price levels and the transaction price, and that quoting prices in dollars made any variation from the arrangements easier to identify. Moreover, some of the European agents acted for a number of producers from different countries so as to discover quickly pulp prices and changes. The Commission accepted that the presumption of concerted practices could be displaced if evidence was produced of a genuine equilibrium of price required as the result of independent action by the participants or as a result of the existence of a market leader upon whom other firms had aligned their prices, but said it was not satisfied that these explanations held good.

The European Court's judgment[56] on the appeals raised by the companies ultimately overruled the Commission's findings in most of the cases. At the heart of its judgment was a finding (based on a report by economists appointed by the Court) that there was a convincing explanation for the alleged 'concertation' of announced prices. Concertation was not the only plausible explanation for the parallel conduct of the parties, which the economists said might instead be a rational response to the fact that the pulp market was a long-term one, in which both buyers and sellers sought to limit commercial risk. A system of quarterly price announcements had been established largely at the request of buyers some years before. The price announced was treated as the 'ceiling price' and transaction prices could then be negotiated at lower levels, so the market was characterized by much greater transparency than many other commodity markets, and links between buyers and sellers were close because of the importance of quality. Moreover, the market comprised a 'group of oligopolies' because of the method of manufacturing paper pulp; as each paper is a mixture of several pulps, every paper manufacturer can in practice only deal with a limited number of pulp producers, and conversely each pulp producer could supply only a limited number of customers. For all these reasons, the Commission's original decision was annulled, except in the cases of certain undertakings where there was specific evidence of contact and price agreements between individual producers.

---

[56] Cases 89, 104, 114, 116–17, and 125–29/85 *A. Ahlström Oy.* v. *Commission* (*Woodpulp II*) [1993] ECR I-1307: [1993] 4 CMLR 407. For the separate judgment on the issue of jurisdiction, see Ch. 22, pp. 582–5, and Cases 89, 104, 14, 116–17, and 125–29/85 *A. Ahlström Oy.* v. *Commission* (*Woodpulp I*) [1988] ECR 5193: [1988] 4 CMLR 901.

5.4 OTHER EXAMPLES OF CONCERTED PRACTICES BETWEEN COMPETITORS

An example of concerted practices between parties in competition with each other is the *Peroxygen* case.[57] This involved a limited number of producers in Europe of hydrogen peroxide and its derivatives, which are used as industrial bleaches. There was evidence that major European companies had for some years participated in agreements which had the effect of reserving each national market for supply by its major producer, these arrangements being enforced by regular meetings of the members, at which marginal disputes were resolved, arrangements similar to those found in the *Sugar Cartel* case.[58] Full exchanges were made of information about production, so that each knew the others' general commercial policy. It was held that these arrangements constituted a concerted practice: although the parties had not necessarily agreed a precise or detailed plan in advance, it was sufficient that by their mutual involvement they had departed from the basic requirement that each must determine independently the policy which it intended to adopt on the market.

When the participants in alleged widespread industry arrangements for identical basic products (such as particular chemicals) comprise virtually all the European manufacturers in this industry, the Commission has a major problem in finding evidence to link all the participants sufficiently closely to the arrangements. In cases such as *Polyvinyl Chloride (PVC)*,[59] the Commission considered it sufficient to show that all the parties had reached a consensus on a plan which limited, or was likely to limit, their commercial freedom, by determining the general lines of action (or indeed abstention from action) on the market. The fact that some participants attended meetings more assiduously or played a greater role than other companies (a factor possibly relevant in assessing fines) would not absolve the less frequent attenders from being found to have participated in a common enterprise. Responsibility for operating the cartel as a whole would in the view of the Commission apply to 'central' and 'fringe' players alike; this approach seems to be confirmed by the judgment of the Court of First Instance in the *Polypropylene* case in 1991.[60]

The *Cement*[61] cartel case provided the CFI with yet further opportunities to define those undertakings which are deemed to be participators in such practices. It ruled that a concerted practice could be found where there was any direct or indirect contact by an undertaking with participants in the discussions at which their course of conduct was disclosed, either in a formal or informal manner, and as a result of which uncertainty as to their future strategy had been removed or at least substantially reduced. Even though concerted practices normally implied reciprocity between

---

[57] [1985] OJ L35/1: [1985] 1 CMLR 481.

[58] Though here without the added complications of a common Community policy to give Member States a legitimate opportunity of becoming involved in the market 'arrangements'.

[59] [1994] OJ L239/14 at paras. 25–6 of the decision. Problems of proof are considerably reduced if one or more participants confess their involvement to the Commission, in return for a reduction in the fine imposed under the Commission's Leniency Notice. See Ch. 9, pp. 179–82.

[60] *Hercules* v. *Commission* Case T-7/89 [1991] ECR II-1711: [1992] 4 CMLR 84.

[61] Cases T-25 to 104/95 [2000] ECR II-491. See fn. 52, above.

the participants, even mere participation at relevant meetings is sufficient unless the undertaking had unequivocally and openly distanced itself from the plan agreed at a particular meeting.[62] The Commission need not prove the exact date on which, or the exact document by which the concerted practice was set in train so long as there is a clear concurrence of wills established on the basis of some documentary evidence.

5.5 CONCERTED PRACTICES IN THE CHAIN OF DISTRIBUTION

We have so far concentrated on the establishment of concerted practices between hori-zontal competitors. It is also important to define this concept for vertical arrangements. The leading authority is the *Pioneer* case.[63] Pioneer was a leading Japanese manufacturer of high fidelity equipment and had a number of European distributors in Germany, France, and the United Kingdom. Distribution agreements allowed dealers to export to other countries subject to the usual requirement not actively to solicit business outside their territories. Price levels in the French market were, however, considerably above those in Germany and the UK, so that there was an incentive for parallel importing into France from both those countries. A German distributor was approached for an order for delivery in France. Following pressure from the main distributor in Germany, Melchers, this contract was cancelled. Likewise, the United Kingdom distributor stopped various sub-distributors from exporting to France and Holland.

The parent company, through its Dutch coordinating company, Pioneer Electronic Europe NV, became concerned at this activity and called a meeting in Antwerp in January 1976. No records were kept of the meeting, which was attended by all the European distributors, but it was established that various matters were discussed relating to the distribution of Pioneer products, including parallel imports. The Commission obtained evidence that the main complainant was the French distribu-tor, who used the meeting as an opportunity to pass on complaints by other distribu-tors about parallel importing into France. Pioneer Electronic Europe NV then used its influence as coordinating Pioneer subsidiary for Europe to damp down the zeal for such sales. The Commission later investigated the arrangements and decided that a reduction in such sales was directly attributable to concerted practices between Pioneer and its distributors. Relationships here were not simply horizontal, since Pioneer Electronic Europe NV had a coordinating function to ensure that supplies were available to its various distributors and was not in direct competition with them, whereas in theory all the distributors, although allocated separate territories, were in competition with each other.

---

[62] This was confirmed in clear terms by the European Court on appeal, Cases C-204, 205, 211, 213, 217 and 219/00P *Aalborg Portland AS* v. *Commission* [2004] ECR I-123. The Court held that 'a party which tacitly approves of an unlawful initiative, without publicly distancing itself from its content or reporting it to the administrative authorities, effectively encourages the continuation of the infringement and compromises its discovery. That complicity constitutes a passive mode of participation in the infringement which is there-fore capable of rendering the undertaking liable in the context of a single agreement' (at para. 84 of the judgment).

[63] Case 100/80 *Musique Diffusion Française* v. *Commission* [1983] ECR 1825: [1983] 3 CMLR 221.

The Court naturally referred to its earlier judgments in both *Dyestuffs* and *Sugar Cartel*. In this case, concerted practices had been established by circumstantial as well as direct evidence. The presumption and inference from the facts set out above was that the coordinating Pioneer subsidiary had called the relevant meeting in Antwerp to deal with the problem of parallel imports as the result of which the practice had been substantially reduced, at least for a time. It is in the context of parallel imports that coordination between parties in a vertical relationship is most likely; the Commission is therefore alert to the possibility of establishing concerted practices in such situations.[64]

6. DECISIONS BY ASSOCIATIONS OF UNDERTAKINGS

6.1 THE DEFINITION OF A TRADE ASSOCIATION

Trade associations play an important part in the commercial life of the Community and its Member States. Article 81(1) recognizes this with its prohibition against 'decisions by associations of undertakings' which have the required effect on trade between Member States and on competition within the Common Market.

The normal use of the term 'association' in the Article describes a separate legal entity formed to pursue particular objectives for its members. Since in the context of Article 81 these objectives are almost invariably commercial, it is normal to refer to them as 'trade associations'. It is important, however, when using this term to remember that Article 81 applies to any kind of association which has some form of economic or commercial purpose, and that the association need not have a separate legal personality (or even any formal constitution) to be subject to the prohibitions of Article 81. It may also be a professional organization or association (*Wouters*).[65] The expression 'association' in Article 81 also covers a number of bodies not normally described as trade 'associations', from which they differ in important respects. In particular, cooperatives and other forms of trading association often found in the agricultural sector, which trade actively on behalf of members in both a buying and selling capacity, are subject as associations to the same legal rules under this Article as trade associations proper. This is clear from the *Gottrup-Klim* and *Oude Luttikhuis* cases[66] discussed in Chapter 7. The term also covers an association of which a number of other

---

[64] Recent judgments of the UK Competition Appeal Tribunal in *JJB Sports/All Sports* v. *Office of Fair Trading* [2004] CAT 17 and *Argos and Littlewoods* v. *Office of Fair Trading* [2004] CAT 24 offer interesting observations on the possible ramifications of this line of case law involving 'triangular' or 'trilateral' commercial relationships. See also the judgment of the Court of Appeal of England and Wales in these cases ([2006] UKCLR 1135).

[65] Case C-309/99 [2002] ECR I-1577: [2002] 4 CMLR 913. See Ch. 7, pp. 115–6.

[66] Case C-250/92 *Gottrup-Klim* v. *DLG* [1994] ECR I-5641: [1996] 4 CMLR 191 and Case C-399/93 *Oude Luttikhuis* [1995] ECR I-4515: [1996] 5 CMLR 178. See Ch. 7, p. 124 and p. 131.

associations are members, which again may be cooperatives, often in the agricultural sector. If the association is unincorporated, the prohibitions of that Article in effect fall upon its participating members, even though a decision of the Commission may be expressed to cover the association as well. If the association is incorporated the decision will be directed to it and to its participating members.[67]

Not all the bodies loosely referred to by this title necessarily fall within the scope of Article 81 or indeed Article 82. Employers' organizations and Chambers of Commerce or Trade will rarely do so, unless carrying on a particular economic activity, such as an airport, nor will national business organizations such as the Confederation of British Industry.

It is important to emphasize that many, and probably most, trade associations raise no problem for authorities, such as the Commission, required to enforce competition law. The constitutions of such bodies will be carefully drawn to limit their authorized range of activities so as to avoid any suggestion of facilitating agreements between their members that would offend the provisions of competition law; efforts will also be made to avoid any suggestion that, regardless of its constitution, the association could in practice provide a useful cover for coordination of business activities between competitors. Legal advisers to such associations are aware that the boundary line between the legitimate and the illegitimate in this context, though recognizable, needs careful and regular monitoring.

Nevertheless in some cases the so-called trade association may be actually a cartel seeking to dress itself in respectable clothes. For example, in the *Cement Cartel* case discussed in Chapter 9,[68] the role played by Cembureau as the trade association for European cement manufacturers participating in the cartel appeared to fall within this description. It is with such cases, that this chapter is primarily concerned. The Commission has in many cases had little difficulty in penetrating the disguise, either because the rules or practices of the association are blatantly restrictive or because they clearly create a market situation where members are encouraged to regard the unity of the industry as more important (as a matter of 'solidarity') than the advantages each might gain from strenuous competitive effort.

6.2 DIFFERENT CATEGORIES OF ASSOCIATION

The trade association will normally have a written constitution and relatively predictable rules, which will cover at least:

- the objectives of the association
- qualifications for membership

---

[67] Whatever the legal structure of an 'association', fines levied upon it for breaches of Arts. 81 or 82 are calculated against the aggregate turnover of its members, at least in cases where its rules are binding on them. In other cases they are calculated against the turnover of the undertaking or association alone. See Cases T-213/95 and 18/96 *FNK and SCK* v. *Commission* [1997] ECR-II 1739: [1998] 4 CMLR 259.

[68] At p. 192.

- rules for the conduct of the association, including the appointment of its governing body
- rules for the termination of membership.

There may also be by-laws containing detailed rules for the procedural conduct of the affairs of the association.

A trade association, especially in a sector where there is little product differentiation and an oligopolistic market structure, may be tempted to use the association to eliminate as many as possible of the uncertainties inherent in the competitive situation, especially those relating to pricing. This temptation can arise even when the association represents merely a single interest group within the industry, e.g. all manufacturers or wholesalers, or all retailers. If information can be passed to the membership about the way in which each member establishes its costs, sets its prices, obtains its orders, and achieves a particular level of profit and turnover, this will considerably assist the business planning of its fellow members and reduce the uncertainties that will otherwise exist. A member's uncertainty is not simply as to the factual nature of the business of its actual competitors (about which it will normally be fully informed) but also as to the likely reaction of those competitors to any change of policy which the individual member might decide to initiate—a far less easily acquired type of information. The form in which this data is disseminated will, as some recently decided cases illustrate, make a considerable difference to the extent of competition between the members.

However, it has been made very clear by cases decided by both the Commission and the Court that those associations which have the greatest potential for anti-competitive activities are not those where a single interest only is represented in the membership. The potential is greatest where one association includes persons or undertakings with different roles within the same industry, or alternatively, where an association of associations has been created to regulate the basis for a particular industry which almost totally eliminates the element of uncertainty and arm's length negotiation that would otherwise exist between the different levels. These arrangements, of which particularly notable examples have been found in cases involving Belgian and Dutch trade associations discussed in this chapter, normally provide for 'collective exclusive dealing'; another appropriate description for such entities might be 'closed-circuit associations', where a high percentage of the market is insulated from outside entry by rigid and complex rules. On the other hand, trade associations whose membership includes not only producers but also 'consumers' at different levels of the relevant product may enable the 'consumers' to monitor anti-competitive restrictions by the producers.

Having analysed the basic structure of the trade association, it becomes possible to define more exactly what is meant by the expression 'decision' in Article 81. Within the context of such an association, a 'decision' normally means a resolution by the authorized organ of the association (usually a board of management or council with authority delegated by the members under the terms of its constitution) to impose restrictions and obligations on its members, which have the effect of reducing their freedom of action. These obligations and restrictions may prescribe the persons with whom members may deal, and may also control to a greater or lesser extent the terms upon which any business can be carried out. A wide variety of examples can be found among cases decided by the Commission and the Court. It is also clear that the rules of an association can themselves constitute a 'decision' without any form of resolution or recommendation by the board of management. Rules such as those which impose financial penalties on members seeking to leave an association or cooperative, or prohibiting current members from acting in ways believed to be prejudicial to its stability have been the subject of Commission decisions, though such rules have not always been found to breach Article 81. The essential principle set out in *Gottrup-Klim* already mentioned is that the rule must always be proportionate to the needs of the association to carry out its normal function and that, in particular, the interests of those members of the association with relatively limited buying power are treated with respect by both the Commission and the European Court, especially where the price of the products concerned is highly dependent on volumes purchased, as in that case with fertilizers or pesticides. Decisions by associations implemented by agreements between more than one association will, of course, fall within the category of 'agreements'.

6.3 THE DEFINITION OF A 'DECISION'

In *Vimpoltu*,[69] the Dutch trade association was an importer of farm tractors. Sources of purchase here were not restricted, but all members were required to observe decisions of the association. All Dutch tractors were imported from abroad and local demand was gradually declining, although prices remained higher in Holland than in most parts of the Community. For these reasons, the association was anxious to negotiate with the association of dealers in agricultural machinery for a maximum discount by dealers to farmers of 25 per cent. It was agreed that fines would be imposed on any dealer breaking this limit. Importers were required to exchange price lists with each other so that none were able to 'cheat' by importing goods at lower prices than others,[70] and standard terms of business were adopted. In both cases, the rules of the association were found to breach Article 81(1), and the lack of any benefit to consumers from the arrangements meant that no exemption was available under Article 81(3).

However, decisions of a trade association need not formally bind its members for Article 81(1) to apply. An informal decision of a trade association, even one made outside its rules altogether, may be sufficient. However, there must be at least some evidence that the conduct of members has been or might in the future be influenced by information received from the association. A clear example was the decision of the

---

[69] [1983] OJ L200/44: [1983] 3 CMLR 619.

[70] The Commission decision suggested that even the exchange of recommended prices between importers might reduce competition between them, since each would derive from the list a better idea of the likely pricing policy of other importers (para. 38 of the Decision).

Commission in the *IFTRA* case[71] where European manufacturers of virgin aluminium had adopted a standard contract which contained fair trading rules, known as
the IFTRA rules. The rules purported to set out principles of trading to be adopted
by the members to prevent 'unfairness', but in practice gave members an opportunity
to take joint action against normal competitive actions and reactions by individual
undertakings.

The *Fenex* case[72] illustrates that even non-binding recommendations can be 'decisions'. Here the association of Dutch freight forwarders had for many years authorized
a committee to prepare on its behalf a list of suggested charges for various services
such as the forwarding of goods and customs clearance. The non-binding tariffs were
sent to members each year with a circular which expressed the desirability of compliance in strong terms. Although the Commission was only able to obtain evidence
from one member of the association that he had adopted these tariffs, the Commission
nevertheless concluded that not only the members of Fenex but also non-member
competitors would as a result of the publication of the tariffs in the trade press know
considerably more about the structure and movement of such tariffs and would have
been influenced in their general approach to pricing by them.

FURTHER READING

P. HENTY, 'Agency Agreements—What
are the Risks? The CFI Judgment in
DaimlerChrysler AG v. Commission'
[2006] ECLR 102.

V. KORAH, 'Concerted Practices' [1973] 36
MLR 220.

P. S. JAKOBSEN and M. BROBERG, 'The
Concept of Agreement in Article 81(1) EC:
On the Manufacturer's Right to Prevent
Parallel Trade within the European
Community' [2002] 23 ECLR 127.

A. JONES, 'Woodpulp: Concerted Practice
and/or Conscious Parallelism' [1993]
ECLR 273.

O. ODUDU, 'The Meaning of Undertaking
within Article 81 EC' [2004–2005] 7
Cambridge Yearbook of European Legal
Studies 211.

G. VAN GERVEN and E. N. VARONA, 'The
Woodpulp Case and the Future of
Concerted Practices' [1994] 31 CMLRev
575.

---

[71] [1974] OJ L160/1: [1975] 2 CMLR D20. An unusual feature of the case is that the 'Fair Trading Practice
Rules' were written in such appalling English that the editor of Common Market Law Reports was moved (at
p. 22) to disclaim any responsibility for it. An extract gives the flavour of this remarkable document (p. 26):
'Rebates which are granted openly for competitive reasons without any connections to quantities or functions are not unfair as such, but could easily lead to a claim of reactions boomeranging on the instigator.'
[72] [1996] OJ L181/28: [1996] 5 CMLR 332.

7

ARTICLE 81(1): ANALYSIS (2)

1. 'WHICH MAY AFFECT TRADE BETWEEN MEMBER STATES'

1.1 EARLY CASES

Agreements, decisions, and concerted practices have no significance under Article 81 unless they are capable of affecting trade between Member States, quite apart from the second and further requirement (considered in the next section of this chapter) that they should have as object or effect the prevention, restriction, or distortion of competition within the Common Market. It is important to remember that the two requirements are both separate and cumulative, and that analysis of the effect of an agreement or concerted practice on interstate trade and on competition should be carried out as two distinct exercises. Both the Community Courts and Commission however have on occasion (for example in all the Notices on Agreements of Minor Importance except the latest in 2001) used language that has blurred, rather than clarified, the difference between these two requirements.

The interpretation of this phrase developed gradually. Initially it was believed that agreements and practices that had effect merely within a single Member State, and upon undertakings whose business was operating only there, could always claim to be outside the scope of the Article. On the other hand, if an agreement contained a transnational element, either because one or more of the undertakings involved was incorporated or resident in a different Member State of the Community, or because the agreements concerned altered the actual or potential flow of goods or services between Member States, then the requirement of the Article was satisfied. This was clearly set out in one of the earliest preliminary rulings given under Article 234 by the European Court, in the *STM*[1] case of 1966 where the phrase was interpreted as follows: 'For this requirement to be fulfilled, it must be possible to foresee with a sufficient degree of probability on the basis of a set of objective factors of law or of fact that the agreement in question may have an influence, direct or indirect, actual or potential, on the pattern of trade between Member States.'

---

[1] Case 56/65 *Société Technique Minière* v. *Maschinenbau Ulm* [1966] ECR 234, 249: [1966] CMLR 357, 375.

Scarcely two weeks later the European Court supplemented this ruling by its findings in the *Grundig*[2] case: after pointing out that the purpose of this requirement is to establish the boundary between Community law and that of Member States in the context of the competition rules, it continued by stating that:

it is only to the extent to which an agreement may affect trade between Member States that the deterioration in competition caused by the agreement falls under the prohibition of Community law contained in Article [81]: otherwise it escapes the prohibition. In this connection, what is particularly important is whether the agreement is capable of constituting a threat, either direct or indirect, actual or potential, to freedom of trade between Member States in a manner which might harm the attainment of the objectives of a single market between States. Thus the fact that an agreement encourages an increase, even a large one, in the volume of trade between States is not sufficient to exclude the possibility that the agreement may 'affect' such trade in the above-mentioned manner.

Of course, little difficulty was found in that case in establishing the necessary effects on volume of trade because Consten was clearly restricted from exporting Grundig products to other countries of the Common Market, whilst purchasers of Grundig products in Germany were restrained from exporting Grundig products into France.

At that time, the tests apparently required as the result of these two cases appeared fairly simple to apply. The necessary approach involved imagining a complete overview of trade within the Common Market, as a series of flows and counter-flows crossing and re-crossing national boundaries, under the effect of seasonal and other changes in supply and demand, costs, prices, and other external factors. It was necessary to compare this picture, with no restriction on competition, with the picture after the restriction had been introduced; in theory such a comparison should produce a definite answer. It is not necessary however for the agreement at issue actually to have affected trade between Member States so long as it can be shown to be capable of having that effect. This comparatively simple test was later however complicated by further qualifications to the basic rule.

In these early days, the Court also clarified the application of this requirement to networks of agreements. It decided that where there is a network of agreements, it is not permissible to treat them individually, ignoring the existence of the network. This was emphasized by the Court in *Brasserie de Haecht (No. 1)*.[3] A brewery in Belgium made loans to a married couple called Wilkin-Janssens, proprietors of a café in Esneux. In return, the café owners had agreed to take all their requirements for beer, lemonade, and other drinks exclusively from the brewery for the term of the loan plus a further two years. The brewery subsequently discovered that the agreement had been broken and sued for the return of the loan and damages. The Wilkin-Janssens claimed that

---

[2] [1966] ECR 299, 341: [1966] CMLR 418, 472. For an account of the development of the meaning attached to this phrase see J. Faull, 'Effect on Trade Between Member States', in [1991] Fordham Corp L Inst 485.

[3] Case 23/67 *Brasserie de Haecht* v. *Wilkin-Janssens (No. 1)* [1967] ECR 407: [1967] CMLR 26. In a subsequent case, however, the Court emphasized that even if an agreement is part of a network of similar agreements the individual contribution of that particular agreement has also to be taken into account: Case C-234/89 *Delimitis* v. *Henninger Bräu* [1991] ECR I-935: [1991] 5 CMLR 210. See Ch. 10, pp. 220–1.

the agreement was void under Article 81(1), and the Belgian court at Liège asked the Court for a ruling whether, in assessing whether 81(1) applied, it was possible to take into account the economic context of the agreement and the surrounding circumstances affecting this particular type of agreement in the Belgian beer market. The Court, closely following in this case the opinion of its Advocate General Roemer, ruled that when assessing whether an individual agreement was in breach of Article 81(1), it was necessary to look not only at the individual agreement but also the context, both economic and legal, in which the agreement had been made. It placed importance on the degree to which the effect of the network would be to foreclose the brewer from finding sufficient outlets for its own products, whether by sales to existing pubs or cafés or through the acquisition of its own chain of outlets. Therefore, if the whole network of similar brewery 'tying' agreements made in Belgium was shown to have an effect on trade between Member States, e.g. if it made it more difficult for breweries in France or Germany to arrange for export of their beers into Belgium, then this fact could be taken into account both in determining whether the original agreement with the Wilkin-Janssens affected trade between Member States, and also with regard to its effect upon competition.

The Commission was soon faced with a more immediate problem: how to exclude from the coverage of Article 81 a number of agreements considered to be of relatively minor importance, which it was especially anxious to remove from consideration in view of the volume of notified agreements received at the beginning of 1963, whose continuing effect was felt throughout the following years. It received some assistance from the decision of the European Court, under an Article 234 reference from the Munich Oberlandsgericht in the case of *Frans Völk* v. *Vervaecke*.[4] Völk was a small German company that manufactured washing machines and entered into an exclusive distribution agreement for Belgium with Vervaecke, on normal terms including an obligation on the Belgian distributor to take minimum quantities. Subsequently, Vervaecke was sued in Germany by Völk for alleged breach of contract. The question raised by the German Court under Article 234 was whether, in interpreting Article 81, it was entitled to pay attention to the very modest fraction of the relevant geographic market (Belgium) in which the product was sold.

The Court answered that, in principle, insignificant agreements could escape the prohibition of Article 81, since it was essential to be able to show a reasonable expectation that the agreement would exercise an influence direct or indirect, actual or potential, on trade trends between Member States to an extent that would harm the attainment of the objectives of a single market between States. The total market share obtained by Völk in West Germany was about 0.2 and 0.05 per cent in 1963 and 1966 respectively, and the number of machines annually sold in Belgium and Luxembourg by Vervaecke was about 200. The essence of the decision was that a *de minimis* rule could be applied in such cases. This would mean that in assessing effect on trade flows between Member States, agreements affecting a market share of 1 per cent or below

---

[4] Case 5/69 [1969] ECR 295: [1969] CMLR 273.

would be most unlikely to have the required effect. However, it should be noted that both parties in this case were small undertakings, and the same generosity of treatment may not be accorded to major public companies even where their market share of the relevant product is less than 1 per cent.[5]

1.2 THE IMPACT OF THE NOTICES ON AGREEMENTS OF MINOR IMPORTANCE

The Commission followed up this case with its 1970 Notice concerning 'Decisions and concerted practices of minor importance which do not fall under Article [81(1)] of the Treaty'. This stated that agreements whose effects on trade between Member States and on competition are negligible did not fall under the ban of Article 81(1), which only applies if the agreements 'have an appreciable impact on market conditions, that is if they appreciably alter the market position, in other words the sale and supply possibilities, of non-participating firms and of consumers'. This definition followed carefully the approach of the Court in the *STM* and *Grundig* cases. In this Notice the maximum market share was quantified as 5 per cent of the relevant market in a substantial part of the Common Market, with a maximum turnover of 20 million units of account for distributors or 15 million units of account for manufacturers; these figures were raised by the later 1986 and 1994 versions of the Notice to 200 and 300 million respectively, whilst the 5 per cent figure remained unchanged.

By a further Notice in 1997 the maximum aggregate turnover requirement was removed, whilst the percentages remained at 5 per cent for horizontal and mixed horizontal–vertical agreements but were raised to 10 per cent for vertical agreements. The only exceptions were hard core agreements, those whose object was the fixing of prices or the sharing of markets or the setting of production or sales quotas. But the changing priorities of the Commission meant that this Notice too was soon replaced, with effect from 22 December 2001. On this occasion the new Notice[6] stated expressly that it did not deal with the impact of an agreement on interstate trade, but only with a definition of what did not constitute an appreciable restriction of competition.[7] It acknowledged that all earlier Notices on this subject had been 'somewhat ambiguous' on this point, and pointed out that market share percentages were a much better indicator of whether effects on competition were appreciable than in measuring an effect on interstate trade. For the latter, which was an issue directly linked to market integration, a turnover threshold, combined with a much lower market share threshold,

[5] Case 30/78 *Distillers Co.* v. *Commission* [1980] ECR 2229: [1980] 3 CMLR 121. Here the Court stated that Art. 81 would apply and that no exemption would be granted even for a product like Pimm's, which held only a fraction of 1 per cent of the relevant market, if it was only one product of a large company which sold a wide range of products and whose total sales as a percentage of the combined markets exceeded the *de minimis* level. See also the CFI judgment in *European Night Services*, at p. 113 in this chapter.

[6] [2001] OJ C368/13. See, in particular, para. 3 of the Notice.

[7] The requirement that an agreement must have an appreciable effect on competition and the guidance provided by the 2001 Notice on Agreements on Minor Importance in this respect are discussed in this chapter in section 2.2.

would be a better indicator. The new Notice did however emphasize that in any case agreements between SMEs (small and medium sized companies) are rarely capable of appreciably affecting trade between Member States.

After the Commission stated that its latest Notice no longer applied to the 'effect on trade' requirement in Article 81, the natural question that arose was how was that gap to be filled? The answer was to be found with the arrival of the new and fully decentralized system of application of Article 81 introduced by Regulation 1/2003—which is described in detail in Chapters 19 and 20. Under the new system of automatic exception, the role of national courts and national competition authorities in the application of Article 81 EC was substantially enhanced and hence it was of the utmost importance that they were offered clear guidance on how to interpret the 'effect on trade' requirement found both in Articles 81 and 82 EC. The guidance came in the form of a new Commission Notice, published in 2004[8] which not only reflects the pattern of interpretation accorded to the requirement by both the case-law jurisprudence of the Community courts and the Commission but also provides help in the application of the requirement to common types of agreements and abuses.

1.3 THE NEW COMMISSION GUIDELINES ON THE EFFECT ON TRADE CONCEPT CONTAINED IN ARTICLES 81 AND 82 EC

The Commission Notice confirms the nature of this requirement as a jurisdictional criterion that defines the scope of application of Community competition law in relation to national law—as laid out by the Court in early cases like *Grundig*—and also reflects the increasingly widening reach given to it by subsequent decisions of the Community courts. For example, paragraph 14 of the Notice reflects the findings in the *Windsurfing* case,[9] where the Court gave important assistance to the Commission; it said that in examining an individual agreement it need not look at every clause restricting competition to see if it individually could be shown to have an effect on trade between Member States. Provided that the agreement taken as a whole had such effect, Article 81 would be applicable.[10]

The Notice also reflects decisions of the Community judicature and of the Commission holding that agreements or practices covering several Member States are, by their very nature, capable of affecting intra-Community trade but also that agreements or practices, apparently confined to the territory of one Member State or even to part of that territory can still affect trade between Member States.

Some cases had concerned trade associations operating horizontal cartels or vertical agreements extending to the whole of national markets. The Commission and the Court took the view that such agreements had the natural effect of partitioning national markets and hindering the penetration of imports, a result that was at

---

[8] Guidelines on the effect on trade concept in Arts. 81 and 82 EC [2004] OJ C101/81.
[9] Case 193/83 *Windsurfing International* v. *Commission* [1986] ECR 611: [1986] 3 CMLR 489.
[10] See Ch. 12, pp. 272–3.

variance with the market-integration goal of the Treaty and which naturally meant that there was an effect on trade between Member States.[11] Further confirmation that even agreements of an apparently domestic nature within a Member State, and without the element of attempting to control the operation of a substantial part of an *entire* national market, could affect trade between Member States is also seen in later cases like *Salonia* v. *Poidomani and Baglieri*,[12] a reference under Article 234 by a Court in Ragusa, Sicily. Salonia was the proprietor of a retail business in Ragusa which dealt in stationery, newspapers, and books. She wanted to be supplied with both newspapers and periodicals by Poidomani and Baglieri from their wholesale warehouse in Ragusa. They refused on the ground that she was not on the list of retailers approved by the Italian publishers' association. Mrs Salonia brought an action in Italy to force the defendants to supply her with newspapers and periodicals, claiming that failure to do so constituted unfair competition.

The European Court was troubled by some uncertainties as to the factual situation in the case, particularly whether the agreement laid down by the publishers' association in Italy was still in existence, and whether the defendants adhered to it. Nevertheless, in dealing with the issues involved, it held that a distribution system operated in accordance with a national trade agreement restricting the supply of relevant products to approved retailers would infringe Article 81 if it were shown that authorized retailers were not chosen by objective criteria, such as their abilities as retailers or their suitability with regard to staff, trading premises, and experience.

A number of Commission decisions on this issue involved the banking sector, in which it held that a number of the services provided by banks and related agreements between them in individual Member States (even if involving some foreign banks) did not have a sufficient effect on interstate trade. In particular agreements relating to automatic cash machines, safe custody services, and the conditions governing current accounts have all been treated as primarily domestic. The Commission's approach in this type of case was however challenged by Ruiz-Jarabo Colomer A-G in *Bagnasco (Italian Banks*[13]*)* where debtors of certain Italian banks claimed that the onerous standard-form guarantees which they had given had a sufficiently appreciable effect on interstate trade to be subject to Article 81. In support of their arguments, he suggested that the existing Single Market in banking across Europe meant that the imposition by a Member State of particular forms of agreement more restrictive than those generally in use in other Member States had a tendency to compartmentalize national markets and damage the provision of financial services on a Community-wide basis. The ECJ however did not adopt his opinion, but ruled that the restrictive terms of the

---

[11] See Case 8/72 *Vereniging van Cementhandelaren* v. *Commission* [1972] ECR 997, [1973] CMLR 7. Another example of the same principle is Case 246/82 *Belasco* v. *Commission* [1989] ECR 2117: [1991] 4 CMLR 96, involving a cartel of Belgian roof manufacturers.

[12] Case 126/80 [1981] ECR 1563: [1982] CMLR 64.

[13] Case C-216/96 [1999] ECR I-135: [1999] 4 CMLR 624.

guarantees required to support the opening of current accounts with Italian banks did not have an appreciable effect on interstate trade.[14]

It is doubtful if this case by itself indicates any significant shift in the approach of the Court to its definition of agreements having an effect on interstate trade. However, now that most Member States have national competition laws that can deal with those agreements which have their principal effect in local markets, there is perhaps less need for the Commission or the Community Courts to seek to characterize as falling within Article 81 all those categories of relatively routine agreements that may have only a minor impact on interstate trade.

The most innovative aspect of the Notice is not the statement that the actual or potential effect on intra-Community trade must be 'appreciable'—a condition that was already gleaned from, if not clearly defined, in the early cases and Commission Notices on Agreements on Minor Importance—but the provision of criteria for the quantification of this 'appreciability'. This has the important effect of creating a much clearer separation than had existed before between the requirements that an agreement should have a significant effect on *competition* and that it should be capable of appreciably *affecting trade between Member States*. The Commission is careful to note that a case-by-case analysis remains necessary but that, in principle, there is a negative rebuttable presumption that an agreement that fulfils two cumulative conditions will not be capable of appreciably affecting trade between Member States. These conditions are: (1) that the aggregate market share of the parties on any relevant market within the Community affected by the agreement should not exceed 5 per cent *and* (2) that the aggregate annual Community turnover in the products covered by the agreement of the undertakings concerned (in the case of horizontal agreements) or of the supplier (in the case of vertical agreements) does not exceed €40 million. Where the turnover of the parties covered by the agreement exceeds €40 million and the agreement concerns imports or exports or covers several Member States, the Notice establishes a rebuttable positive presumption that this agreement is, by its very nature, capable of appreciably affecting trade between Member States. Paragraphs 58–109 of the Notice provide examples of the application of these principles to frequently occurring forms of agreements and abuses.

1.4 THE MEANING OF 'TRADE'

'Trade' has received a wide interpretation in the case law to include not merely the normal industrial and commercial activity of manufacture and distribution, but also commercial services of all kinds including not only banking, insurance, and financial services but also shipping and all forms of transport. As the Guidelines state, the notion includes all cross-border economic activity, including establishment.[15] A

---

[14] See also, in the same vein, the subsequent decision of the Commission in *Dutch Banks* [1999] OJ L271/28, [2000] 4 CMLR 137.

[15] Case C-309/99 *Wouters* [2002] ECR I-1577: [2002] 4 CMLR 913.

number of important cases have involved transportation, and in particular shipping services. The fact that the routes involved have been to non-Member States has not persuaded the Commission or the Community Courts to refrain from finding an effect on trade between Member States, in particular given the existence and purpose of Regulation 4056/86 to provide shipping lines with a limited measure of exemption from the requirements of Article 81 in view of the well known instability of the business.[16] Other leading cases have involved rail services; in *European Night Services*[17] the Court of First Instance overruled a Commission decision that a proposed joint venture between four national rail companies to operate a night sleeper service through the Channel Tunnel affected trade between Member States to the required extent, after determining that the overall market share for passenger traffic held by the participants was no more than 4 per cent (or slightly more, if a narrower route by route definition was taken). The Court emphasized that, when market shares were so small, it was necessary for the Commission to provide a statement of reasons showing why nevertheless the agreement did have an appreciable effect on interstate trade.

The phrase has also been applied to a variety of other activities of a commercial nature including, for example, the provision of exhibitions and trade fairs, performing rights societies, television programmes, sport, and cultural activities. Futhermore, its application is not limited to trade between the twenty five Member States, but extends also to trade with those EFTA countries still outside the Common Market (Iceland, Norway, and Liechtenstein) which form part of the European Economic Area (EEA). It extends also to other countries (such as Switzerland) and associated territories having free trade agreements with the Community.

Finally, it is possible for trade between Member States to be affected even if the relevant agreement on its face appears to prohibit such activity. In *Javico v YSL*,[18] YSL had appointed Javico as its authorized distributor of luxury cosmetics in Russia, Ukraine, and Slovenia. The facts took place before Slovenia became a member of the European Union. The contract contained an express prohibition on Javico selling these products outside the authorized territories, either by direct marketing or through re-exports from them. On a reference from a French court under Article 234 the ECJ held that the national court's decision on whether such a clause could itself be in breach of Article 81 must depend on the information available as to the likely outcome of any such breach. Only if the products intended to be sold in the Community were likely in any case to amount to a very small percentage of the total market for the product then could the Article be held inapplicable without further examination of the economic and legal context of the agreement; in all other cases this would have to be considered before a decision could be reached as to the effect on trade between Member States.

---

[16] This Regulation has now been replaced by Reg. 1419/2006, see below section 4.7.
[17] Cases T-374–75, 384, 388/94 [1998] ECR II-3141: [1998] 5 CMLR 718.
[18] Case C-306/96 [1998] ECR I-1983: [1998] 5 CMLR 172. See also Case T-198/98 *Micro Leader Business* v. *Commission* [1999] ER II-3989: [2000] 4 CMLR 886.

1.5 ARTICLES 81 AND 82 COMPARED

In the light of all these developments, the early debates over the correct interpretation of the word corresponding to 'affect' in the English translation of Article 81 now appear somewhat academic. At a time when there were only the four original authoritative languages for the Treaty of Rome, it was apparent that whilst the Dutch word required an unfavourable influence to be shown on trade between Member States, the equivalent expression in German and Italian was more ambiguous, and the French term 'affecter' had both a neutral and a pejorative sense. The combined effect of the slightly different flavours of these four translations left the impression that an effect upon trade of a purely neutral kind, i.e. having both good and bad consequences, would not necessarily be covered by Article 81(1). Deringer,[19] commenting on these expressions some ten years after signature of the Treaty, indicated that he found the wording alone of the Article insufficient to support a definite conclusion, and that the best means of interpretation was to consider the essential purpose of the expression. This was to promote and protect the free flow of trade within the Common Market, unhampered by private restraints on competition. If the restraint changed the intensity or the direction of flow of goods, artificially diverting it from its normal and natural course, then the Article would certainly come into play, and the question of whether the effect was adverse or neutral would not normally arise. The Court's approach in *Grundig* v. *Consten* was consistent with this view.

Similar wording is found in Article 82, prohibiting the abuse of dominant positions within the Common Market. The two leading cases in which the European Court has confirmed the interpretation of these words in the context of Article 82 are *Commercial Solvents* v. *Commission*[20] and *Hugin* v. *Commission*.[21] In the former case the Court stated that if an undertaking within the Common Market exploited its position in a way likely to eliminate a competitor, it did not matter whether the conduct complained of related specifically to the exports to be made by the competitor or its general trade within the Common Market, provided it was established that its elimination by the dominant company would have an effect on competitive structures within the Common Market. However, the conduct complained of in the case was a refusal to supply a particular chemical substance essential to the business of the smaller company and for which there was no other source of supply, so that complete elimination from the market would have followed for that smaller company.

By contrast, the *Hugin* case was one of those rarities where the Court decided that there was no sufficient effect on trade between Member States to justify a finding of abuse or breach. The facts were rather unusual, since the product market was of spare

---

[19] A. Deringer, *The Competition Law of the European Economic Community: A Commentary on the EEC Rules of Competition* (CCH Editions, 1968), pp. 22–3.

[20] Cases 6–7/73 *Istituto Chemioterapico Italiano and Commercial Solvents Corporation* v. *Commission* [1974] ECR 223: [1974] 1 CMLR 309.

[21] Case 22/78 *Hugin* v. *Commission* [1979] ECR 1869: [1979] 3 CMLR 345.

parts for cash registers manufactured by Hugin, a large Swedish company, having at the time some 13 per cent of the United Kingdom market for the registers. Lipton was a company acting in the servicing and maintenance of such machines; following disagreements between the parties further supplies of spare parts were refused, preventing Lipton from carrying on its independent business of servicing them. Lipton claimed that Hugin's refusal to supply spare parts violated Article 82 as, without them, Lipton was unable to carry on its business. No objective reason had been offered for the refusal to supply the parts, now supplied only to Hugin's own subsidiaries. The Court agreed that there was no reason in theory why these facts should not justify a finding of abuse of a dominant position, but found that there was insufficient effect on trade between Member States since Lipton only traded in its capacity as a service company within a 50-mile radius of London and made no exports of any kind. Moreover, the characteristics of the market were that Hugin produced many different models for various countries in Europe which were affected by the different requirements of language and currency, so that the exporting of machines or spare parts from one Member State to another was uneconomic and unlikely. The Court found that an independent undertaking such as Lipton would not benefit from buying spare parts in other Member States rather than from the parent company in Sweden. There was, in the Court's view, no normal pattern of trade in such spare parts between Member States that could be disrupted by the commercial decision made by Hugin not to supply.

The principles developed by these and other cases are now reflected in the 2004 Commission Guidelines on Effect on Trade. The Notice provides that it is the overall strategy pursued by dominant undertakings that should be assessed—rather than each element of their behaviour—when applying this requirement. Thus, if various practices pursue the same aim—e.g. the elimination or foreclosure of a competitor—it is sufficient that one of them is capable of affecting intra-Community trade to trigger the application of Article 82 EC. Finally, and on the basis of the relevant Article 82 EC case law, the Notice provides guidance on the application of this requirement to cases concerning abuses of dominant position covering several Member States, one single Member State or part of it and to abuses involving undertakings in non-Member States.

2. 'WHICH HAVE AS THEIR OBJECT OR EFFECT THE PREVENTION, RESTRICTION, OR DISTORTION OF COMPETITION WITHIN THE COMMON MARKET'

2.1 A STRICT OR LIBERAL INTERPRETATION?

The difficulties inherent in defining competition were discussed in Chapter 2. If the competition referred to in this Article were to be of that rarely encountered atomistic variety, requiring a very large number of market participants unable by their own policies to influence prices or the level of demand, then to test whether any particular agreement or concerted practice between undertakings would have an effect on the competition within that market would be comparatively simple: its effect would be clearly and immediately perceptible, like the result of throwing a stone into a smooth pond. However, since virtually all the product and service markets encountered within the Community are imperfectly competitive, the task of assessing whether an agreement or practice does cause or have as its object the prevention, restriction, or distortion of competition becomes considerably more problematic.

Another problem is the interpretation of the words 'prevent, restrict, or distort competition within the Common Market'. Too strict a definition might cover almost every agreement for the sale of goods or services. Too liberal a definition would reduce the jurisdiction of the Commission, excluding from its control a substantial number of agreements that may, either individually or cumulatively, have an effect on competitive structures or processes. In determining the correct approach to these words within Article 81(1) it is necessary to decide whether the Article is primarily designed to assert jurisdiction, or whether it seeks to provide an assessment of whether individual agreements can be justified. An Article that seeks to establish initial jurisdiction would normally be expected to be more comprehensively interpreted than one concerned simply with the assessment or substantive justification of the agreements. After all, it is obvious that many more agreements will need scrutiny by the Commission than will ultimately fail to pass whatever substantive criteria are applied to them. This will not necessarily imply, however, that a 'jurisdictional' Article should be read with total adherence to a strictly literal meaning, bringing within its grasp every kind of agreement or concerted practice with the smallest impact on competition. It is clearly sensible for some limit to be placed on the scope even of such a phrase read in a broad sense.

While the European Court has taken the view that Article 81(1) is a jurisdictional clause, there are increasing indications in its decisions that the Court is prepared to accept that there are a number of cogent reasons why Article 81 should not be interpreted literally, so as to bring within its scope such a wide range of commercial agreements and restrictive clauses found within them that the Commission is unable to deal with them effectively. This limit to the scope of Article 81 is sometimes described as 'the rule of reason', although it is misleading to use this phrase because it is not properly to be compared directly with the same phrase used in describing the interpretation by US Federal Courts of section 1 of the Sherman Act.[22] Section 1 of the Sherman Act is, of course, a combination of both a 'jurisdictional' and an 'assessment' clause, and the expression 'restraint of trade' requires a more liberal approach. Over its one hundred years and more of existence the section has seen a variety of different approaches from courts; the liberal approach to interpretation has been in the ascendant in recent decades, particularly in the treatment of vertical agreements.

---

[22] See A. D. Neale and D. G. Goyder, *The Antitrust Laws of the United States* (3rd edn, Cambridge University Press, 1981) on this issue, at pp. 23–30. See also R. Whish and B. Sufrin, 'Article 81 and the Rule of Reason', YEL 1987 1–38.

The assessment element in Article 81 is found in paragraph (3), and only to a more limited extent in paragraph (1). To discuss the alleged 'rule of reason' in the context of 81(1), especially in the context of the scope of 'prevention, restriction, or distortion of competition', leads to confusion rather than clarity. What is important for a clear understanding of these words is the way in which the Commission and, more importantly, the European Court and the Court of First Instance have interpreted them in a variety of different contexts. Initially interpretation was strict, but in recent years has been more flexible, although never giving an escape from the control of the Article to more than a narrow range of clauses found primarily in joint ventures and certain licensing agreements. Only after the reader has considered the application of this phrase in all the different contexts which decided cases present will it be possible to determine whether there exists under Community law a single principle to explain all the exceptions to Article 81(1) and to which a general title such as 'rule of reason' could be given, if misleadingly; or whether these examples will remain as relatively limited exceptions to a normally rigorous general interpretation of these words in Article 81(1). This debate was very important in the system of enforcement of Article 81 laid down by Regulation 17/62—the first enforcement regulation—which applied for over forty years and before the introduction of the 2004 Modernization Programme. That regulation had given the Commission the monopoly in the application of the Article 81(3) conditions and, therefore, an interpretation of Article 81(1) providing scope for the assessment of pro- and anti-competitive effects of an agreement offered obvious procedural advantages when Article 81 was applied by national courts and national competition authorities.[23]

2.2 LEADING CASES ON ITS INTERPRETATION

A good starting point for our review of the way in which this phrase has been interpreted and applied is the 2001 Commission Notice on Agreements of Minor Importance, already referred to in the previous section.[24] For the first time the Notice deals only with the meaning of 'prevent, restrict, or distort competition within the Common Market' and not with the effect of the agreement on interstate trade. The 5 per cent and 10 per cent thresholds of the previous Notice for horizontal and vertical agreements respectively are now increased to 10 and 15 per cent; and for the first time a 5 per cent market-share threshold is introduced for networks of agreements producing a cumulative anti-competitive effect, which can apply in sectors such as beer and petrol, to which previously the Notice could not apply, because of its specific exclusion of agreements operating in markets where 'competition is restricted by the cumulative effects of parallel networks of similar agreements established by several manufacturers or dealers'.

---

[23] The differences between the old system and the new system of enforcement are considered in Ch. 8.
[24] See fn. 6.

As before, however, a list of hardcore restrictions incapable of benefiting from the Notice is set out, though in some respects it differs from the list in previous Notices. Those applicable to vertical agreements have deliberately been made identical to those in the Vertical Restraints Block Exemption 2790/99 (discussed in Chapter 10), whilst those relating to horizontal agreements are identical with those in the Horizontal Co-operation Block Exemptions 2658 and 2659/2000 for agreements on specialization and R&D (discussed in Chapter 18). The overall effect of the Notice is to remove a large number of agreements, especially in the area of distribution, from the scope of Article 81(1) altogether; and when this change is added to the more generous terms of these block exemptions as compared with their predecessors, the Article is likely to affect a lower proportion of agreements than before.

Unfortunately the importance of maintaining a clear distinction between the 'jurisdictional' and the 'assessment' element of Article 81 has not always been strictly observed by the ECJ—especially in dealing with cases involving vertical agreements, discussed in Chapter 10, and in *Wouters* (considered in the next section)—which in this respect has not matched the more convincing analytical approach of the Court of First Instance. This was typified by the Court of First Instance's well-known *European Night Services* judgment referred to in the previous section,[25] in which it annulled a Commission decision of doubtful validity. The joint venture in question had been granted an exemption by the Commission on onerous terms, including an obligation to supply locomotives and train crews to any potential competitor which sought to offer the same night-sleeper service through the Channel Tunnel between the United Kingdom and Europe. The period for the exemption was only eight years, notwithstanding the large capital investment required. The Commission claimed that the agreement would restrict competition:

(a) between the parties themselves, even though the evidence showed that none of these railway companies, for both financial and operational reasons, could have operated the service on their own

(b) between the parties and other rail operators, who might have been potential competitors in the provision of the service.

After a full review of the facts and relevant commercial issues, the Court of First Instance ruled that the agreement did not restrict competition on either basis to a sufficiently appreciable extent, so that neither 81(1) nor (3) applied. However, it made at paragraph 136 of its judgment an apparently significant statement on the relationship between (1) and (3):

It must be borne in mind that in assessing an agreement under Article [81(1)] of the Treaty, account should be taken of the actual conditions in which it functions, in particular the economic context in which the undertakings operate, the products or services covered by the agreement and the actual structure of the market concerned ... unless it is an agreement

---

[25] See fn. 17.

containing obvious restrictions of competition such as price-fixing, market-sharing or the control of outlets ... in the latter case, such restrictions may be weighed against their claimed pro-competitive effects only in the context of Article [81(3)] of the Treaty, with a view to granting an exemption from the prohibition in Article [81(1)].

Some commentators have suggested that the last of the sentences in this quotation may indicate that the Community Courts may now be more willing to balance the 'pro' and 'anti' arguments relating to restraints on competition under 81(1), in all cases except those involving hardcore restrictions. The actual wording of Articles 81(1) and (3) would seem hard to square with such an approach; and the continuing need to preserve the distinction between the two separate paragraphs was underlined by the Court of First Instance in another case some three years later, that of *Metropole* v. *Commission*.[26] Here a group of French television companies had formed a joint venture to challenge in the French pay-TV market the market leader, Canal+. After notification to the Commission this group appealed to the Court of First Instance against the conditions imposed by the Commission under 81(3), and in particular that only for a three-year period were restrictions allowed on the use by the joint venture participants of 'general interest' and 'special interest' television channels, other than through the joint venture itself. The joint venture claimed that the Commission should have assessed the restrictions under the 'rule of reason', balancing their pro- and anti-competitive elements under Article 81(1), rather than under 81(3) alone.

In rejecting this claim the Court of First Instance referred to the *European Night Services* judgment but emphasized that it was only in the 'precise framework' of Article 81(3) that the balancing of these issues could be carried out. The fact that some earlier judgments of Community Courts had found certain agreements outside Article 81(1) was not to be explained by the existence of a so-called 'rule of reason' but rather by the characterization of some restraints on the parties as merely restrictions on *conduct* rather than on *competition*.

Recent support for this approach is found in the decision of the Court of First Instance in the *02 (Germany)* v. *Commission* case,[27] where the Court made it clear again that the task of the enforcement authorities under Article 81(1) EC was to consider the impact of an agreement on existing and potential competition and the competition situation in the absence of the agreement but not to assess the positive and negative effects of an agreement on competition.

This approach seems correct and preferable in terms of the structure of the Article, even if its application to individual cases still remains difficult. Given that under the new decentralized system of application of Article 81 introduced by Regulation 1/2003, the Commission has surrendered its monopoly in the application of the Article 81(3) conditions, any procedural benefits that might have been available to national courts and national competition authorities in balancing pro- and anti-competitive elements under Article 81(1) will no longer be as significant as before. National courts and

[26] Case T-112/99 [2001] ECR II-2459: [2001] 5 CMLR 1236.
[27] Case T-328/03 [2006] ECR II-1231: [2006] 5 CMLR 5.

national competition authorities are now able to apply the Article 81(3) conditions in the same manner as they have always applied the elements in Article 81(1) EC.[28] However, it remains important to understand the substantive scope of application of the first and third paragraphs of Article 81,[29] a distinction that has not always been made clear by the European Court, as the *Wouters* and *Meca-Medina* decisions neatly illustrate.

2.3 THE *WOUTERS* AND *MECA-MEDINA* CASES

Wouters[30] involved a dispute between two Dutch lawyers and the Dutch Bar Council. The Bar Council had a rule that its members could only enter into partnerships with members of other professions if the Council's consent had been given. Wouters and another lawyer each wanted to join a firm of chartered accountants, but were refused consent by the Council. On appeal the case was referred to the ECJ; its judgment confirmed that the rule was 'the decision of an association', and therefore subject to Article 81, and moreover that the rule did have an effect on competition in the market for legal services. Nevertheless it held that the rule was not in breach of Article 81(1), because it had been introduced for reasons of 'public interest', not merely in the interests of the Dutch legal profession. It could (said the Court in its judgment which contrasted strongly with the opinion of Leger A-G) be regarded as a reasonable exercise of the Bar Council's concern to ensure that lawyers acted for clients with complete independence and without any risk of conflict of interest which multidisciplinary partnerships might raise.

The problem with this decision is that, while it could well have been taken, had the rule been notified to the Commission (which it had not) under the provisions of Article 81(3), on the basis that the concerns of the Bar Council might have been considered to represent an 'improvement' of legal services in the Netherlands,[31] it was actually taken under Article 81(1), after balancing the acknowledged restriction of competition that it involves against the stated public interest arguments of the Bar Council. It is noteworthy that the judgment did not expressly state that in the context of the varied aims of the Treaty, both social and economic, rules relating to the provision of professional services should be treated as outside Article 81(1), as agreements which were the product of collective bargaining between employers and employees have been (as in *Albany International* and other cases mentioned later in this chapter).

---

[28] See further Ch. 8, pp. 138–9.

[29] It must not be forgotten, for example, that the burden of proof to show the fulfilment of the Art. 81(3) conditions falls on the party invoking the benefit of that provision while the burden of proof to show the existence of an anti-competitive agreement falls on the party that argues the illegality of the agreement.

[30] Case C-309/99 [2002] ECR I-1979: 4 CMLR 913. The first substantive decision of the UK Competition Commission Appeal Tribunal, in *GISC* [2001] Comp AR 62, raised some similar issues.

[31] Furthermore, the application of Art. 81(3) EC would have raised interesting issues such as the consideration of benefits produced by an agreement which are not purely economic. In this respect, see further Ch. 8, Section 3.4.

A similar reasoning was adopted by the European Court in the later case of *Meca-Medina*[32] where it held that certain anti-doping rules adopted by the International Olympic Committee and implemented by the International Swimming Federation did not constitute restrictions of competition within the meaning of Article 81(1) because they were *justified* by a legitimate objective—i.e. the proper conduct of competitive sport and the guarantee of healthy rivalry between athletes. Again the justification seemed to have been considered entirely within the analysis of Article 81(1) and with no reference to the role of Article 81(3).

Cases like *Wouters* and *Meca-Medina* have ignited a lively academic debate as to whether non-economic justifications can be balanced against anti-competitive aspects of an agreement in the application of Article 81(1).[33] It is submitted that what appears to have happened in these cases is that Article 81(1) and (3) may have been conflated and operated as if they were a single provision (in the same way as under section 1 of the Sherman Act in a case like *California Dental Association* v. *FTC*[34] and not an application of a 'rule of reason' approach. Recent confirmation that the weighing of pro-competitive and anti-competitive effects of an agreement is regarded by the Commission as reserved for Article 81(3) can be found in the 2004 *Commission Guidelines on the application of Article 81(3) EC,* which are discussed in Chapter 8.[35] The Guidelines, however, make no mention of the appropriate framework for the assessment of public interest justifications such as the ones at issue in *Wouters* and in *Meca-Medina* and it remains to be seen whether the apparently global approach taken to Articles 81 in these decisions will be applied to other cases involving associations with regulatory powers.[36]

2.4 MARKETS WHERE COMPETITION IS INHERENTLY RESTRICTED

The meaning of 'prevent, restrict, or distort' becomes clearer if one considers the normal mental processes of any businessman seeking to enter a specific geographic and product market. If there are no agreements or concerted practices then he will have complete freedom of choice as to the territories in which he can sell, the availability of outlets through whom he can distribute his goods, the prices and conditions of sale at which he can distribute, and a range of choices in other matters such as marketing techniques. However, if there are agreements between other undertakings which have the effect of limiting his freedom of choice so that, for example, he is foreclosed from using his first choice of distributors, cannot (because of earlier exclusive appointments) be

---

[32] Case C-519/04P [2006] ECR I-6991: [2006] 5 CMLR 1023.

[33] See G. Monti, 'Article 81 and Public Policy' 38 CMLRev [2002] 1057.   [34] 119 S. Ct 1604 (1999).

[35] [2004] OJ C101/97 at para. 30. See also the ruling in *O2 (Germany)*, discussed in section 2.2 of this chapter.

[36] Commentators have also pointed out that Art. 86(2) (see below Ch. 21) might have provided a better framework for analysis in these cases. See A. Jones and Brenda Sufrin, *EC Competition Law,* (3rd edn, OUP, 2007), p. 266 and V. Korah, *An Introductory Guide to EC Competition Law and Practice* (9th edn, Hart Publishing, 2007), p. 83.

appointed a franchisee for particular goods, cannot be appointed an exclusive dealer himself because there is a quantitative limit on those nominated within a given territory, or if he cannot manufacture successfully in a particular Member State because sole or dominant suppliers have entered into agreements which restrict their ability to sell to him, then in all these cases the restraint of trade is directly responsible for the reduction in freedom imposed on his business by the agreements in existence between others already in the market. The object of Article 81 is to eliminate or reduce the number of such agreements, and to try to distinguish between agreements without sufficient redeeming virtues and those whose effect on competition, or whose purpose of reducing competition, is nevertheless accompanied by substantial advantages of the kind referred to in Article 81(3).

In some cases, the restraint will affect all manufacturers or all wholesalers or retailers of a particular product in a particular Member State: in other cases, the range of undertakings affected will be smaller. An important preliminary point, however, is that fully free competition is not possible in all markets because of government intervention in their workings.

The best-known example of this is the *Sugar* cartel case.[37] The Italian government had laid down complex rules governing the marketing of sugar; the Italian public authority in charge of sugar prices, the CIP, adopted a series of regulations intended mainly to benefit Italian sugar-beet producers and exporters. Aids were financed by a levy applied to both Italian sugar manufacture and imported sugar, but permitting reduction of the levy in a few cases to encourage a certain level of imports so as to fill up the gap between Italian production and the target level of demand. Foreign producers were invited to tender to supply certain quantities of sugar for import, and complicated regulations determined the extent to which the levy was charged in full or only in part. The effect of the regulations together with the risks attaching to the invitations to tender was that foreign manufacturers often agreed to allocate between themselves the right to supply into Italy, because they otherwise risked being individually excluded from the market altogether. Certain imports were permitted outside the formal system of invitations to tender, but only in limited quantities, and further regulations controlled the price that could be obtained by foreign concerns for imports into Italy. The regulations also had the result of concentrating demand in Italy in the hands of the large producers, since they alone were likely to be able to fulfil on a reliable basis the requirements of purchasers. The real consequence of these regulations was to match supply closely to demand, which itself removed a vital element of normal competition, and had a considerable effect on both the buyer's freedom to choose his supplier (and vice versa) and the price at which the goods were supplied. The Court concluded that:

All these considerations show that Italian regulations and the way in which they have been implemented had a determinative effect on some of the most important aspects of the course of conduct of the undertakings concerned which the Commission criticises, so that it appears

---

[37] Case 40/73 [1975] ECR 1663: [1976] 1 CMLR 295.

that, had it not been for these regulations and their implementation, the co-operation which is the subject matter of these proceedings, either would not have taken place, or would have assumed a form different from that found by the Commission to have existed.[38]

The Court's ruling in this instance was, therefore, that the sugar producers concerned, who themselves operated restrictive agreements in response to the Italian 'sugar regime', did not prevent, restrict, or distort competition because of the limited scope left for it by the result of the Italian State intervention.[39]

2.5 'OBJECT OR EFFECT' OF RESTRICTING COMPETITION

It was established in the early days of the Court that an agreement could satisfy the requirements of these words if it had as its object a restriction on competition, or if (whatever its object) the restriction had that effect; it was unnecessary to prove both object and effects in any individual case.[40] This wording is significantly different from the terms of Article 65 of the ECSC Treaty, which referred to agreements 'tending directly or indirectly' to the prevention, restriction, or distortion of competition. The requirement for either an 'object' or 'effect' of such a restriction in the EC Treaty is more specific. The agreement must either be intended to have such a result on competition or, regardless of the parties' intentions, actually to have such a result. Over the years, this has proved both a comprehensive and workable definition.

The Court stated that it was first necessary to look at the object or purpose of the agreement by reference to its express provisions. Other relevant factors also included its economic context and the behaviour of the parties.[41] Only if it did not appear that the purpose of the agreement was to restrain competition was it necessary to consider its effects. If effects had to be considered, then the issue was whether the agreement restricted competition perceptibly, comparing the results of the agreement with the state of affairs likely to exist in the absence of that restriction.[42] Restrictions had always to be considered in the circumstances of their economic background.

The case law has established that some contractual restrictions are, prima facie, so likely to affect competition that this effect will be presumed. Clearly, those categories of agreements which are listed under sections (a) to (e) of Article 81(1) would probably fall into this category. This is so despite the fact that these are only examples, and in no sense an exhaustive list of the kinds of agreement which the Article prohibits. Later chapters consider some individual examples of agreements falling within these categories.

---

[38] [1975] ECR 1923: [1976] 1 CMLR 410.

[39] Ch. 21 considers other leading cases where the degree of competition, in particular national markets, was reduced by governmental measures, without necessarily allowing undertakings affected by it to avoid the application of Art. 81(1).

[40] See *STM* (fn. 1 above). A case in which this point is emphasized is Case T-395/94 *TACA* [2002] ECR II-875: [2002] 4 CMLR 1008.

[41] Cases 29/83 and 30/83 *CRAM and Rheinzink* [1984] ECR 1679 at para. 26.

[42] See *STM* (fn. 1), p. 249.

The category which has come closest to being called illegal per se is the agreement which, like the restrictions in *Grundig*,[43] directly bans parallel imports by imposing export bans on distributors—and therefore attempts to partition the markets of the Community—or which, in arrangements between horizontal competitors, bans the export of goods to other countries within the Common Market or into territories outside the Market from which they were in practice likely to be re-imported into the Market.

A number of cases illustrate this important feature of the case law deriving from the original judgment of the European Court in *Grundig*, which has proved to be so important. Thirty years ago, in the *WEA-Filipacchi* case,[44] German manufacturers sought to restrain various French dealers in pop records from reselling the records outside France, particularly in Germany. One of the arguments raised by the manufacturers was that in practice they would not have been able to enforce these restrictions, and that they were therefore without effect. The Commission held, however, that any restriction in an agreement which effectively operated as an export ban was so inherently the type of agreement that would have as its objective the prevention of free movement of goods across national boundaries by way of parallel imports that it was unnecessary to consider the further issue of whether the manufacturer concerned had the actual power to enforce such restrictions. A similar decision was reached by the Court itself in *Miller International* v. *Commission*.[45] Again a record company had imposed an export ban on its French distributors. On this occasion the Court disregarded the opinion of the Advocate General, who had recommended a cancellation of the fine imposed by the Commission and remission of the case to the Commission on the ground that the undertakings has been misled by advice given by its lawyer. The Court found that the export ban was by its very nature a restriction on competition, whether adopted at the instigation of the supplier or of the customer, since the whole basis of the agreement between the parties was an endeavour to isolate a part of the market.

Export ban cases, perhaps surprisingly, continue to arise and to attract fines from the Commission, despite the relevant principles of law being established and well known to both business and legal communities. For example, in *Parker Pen*,[46] Parker had made an agreement with Herlitz, a German dealer, with a clause prohibiting sales of its products outside Germany. Herlitz claimed that it had no interest in any 'export ban' since it was only interested in providing a wide range of stock for independent department stores in Germany and other Member States. It claimed not to have implemented the export ban in a number of cases. The Court of First Instance ruled, nevertheless, that the mere existence of the 'export ban' in such an agreement had a 'visual and psychological' effect which could contribute to the partitioning of the market. The same point was made by the Commission in *BASF(L + F)—Accinauto*[47] where a dealer

---

[43] For a detailed discussion of the *Consten and Grundig* decision, see Ch. 4, Section 4.

[44] [1973] CMLR D43.   [45] Case 19/77 [1978] ECR 131: [1978] 2 CMLR 334.

[46] Case T-77/92 [1994] ECR II-549: [1995] 5 CMLR 435.

[47] [1995] OJ L272/16: [1996] 4 CMLR 811, appeal to the CFI dismissed (Cases T-175/176/95 [1999] ECR II-1581, 1635: [2000] 4 CMLR 33, 67).

in car finishing paints manufactured by BASF had under his agreement to refer all orders received from outside his contract territory to BASF, so that BASF could allocate them between its official dealers in the relevant territories and prevent parallel importers acquiring goods. It was clear that the dealer had not always complied with this contractual restriction, yet a substantial fine was nevertheless imposed on BASF and a nominal fine on the dealer. Other examples can be found, as in the *Bayer* case, where the Commission recognizes that dealers are not always enthusiastic supporters of such clauses.[48]

Despite the clarity of the standing case law on the point that agreements that intend to limit parallel trade have an anti-competitive object; the recent decision of the Court of First Instance in *GlaxoSmithKline* v. *Commission*[49] has introduced a degree of confusion. This case concerned a clause inserted by a pharmaceutical supplier in its General Conditions of Sale which purported to restrict parallel trade (by establishing price differences between drugs sold at national level and those sold for export to other Member States). The Commission had taken the view that the agreement had both the object and the effect of restricting competition. The Court of First Instance disagreed with the Commission's conclusion that such an agreement had an anti-competitive object. It noted that the pharmaceutical market had very special features and that the prices of medicines were not determined by the interplay between supply and demand but by the regulatory authorities of the Member States. While in most markets an agreement limiting parallel trade would have an anti-competitive object, the same automatic conclusion could not be inferred in the pharmaceutical market where parallel trade could not be presumed to reduce prices. As a result, it was necessary to examine whether the agreement had an anti-competitive *effect*. It would seem therefore that an agreement limiting parallel trade could be presumed to be restrictive by object only if it effectively deprived consumers of the traditional advantages of parallel trade—i.e. reduction in prices. Although the Court held that there was a restrictive effect on competition and hence a breach of Article 81(1), its reasoning sat ill at ease with previous decisions which had clearly decided that agreements containing export bans, dual-pricing systems or other limitations of parallel trade were restrictive of competition 'by object'. The judgment has been appealed before the European Court of Justice and it remains to be seen whether it will be confirmed. If upheld, it might well alter the analysis of export bans provided in the existing case law.

Most of the case law, however, indicates that certain types of restrictive clauses and/or agreements are regarded as having an object which is so manifestly anti-competitive that consideration of their effects is unnecessary, for example the hardcore restrictions

---

[48] Some rulings have confirmed that agreements that clearly intend to treat parallel trade unfavourably—even it they do not seek to prohibit it altogether—are also regarded in principle as having an anti-competitive object (see Case C-551/03P *General Motors* v. *Commission* [2006] ECR I-3173 at para. 67 of the judgment).

[49] Case T-168/01 [2006] ECR II-2969: [2006] 5 CMLR 1589 (see Ch. 6, Section 4.3, for a full description of the facts).

listed in the 2001 Notice on Agreements of Minor Importance,[50] which may be either horizontal or vertical. Such horizontal restrictions include:

- market sharing agreements (of territory or of customers)
- quotas or limitations of production or sales.

Vertical restrictions include:

- minimum resale price restrictions
- customer allocation clauses (with some exceptions).

The majority of these clauses would be described by a US antitrust lawyer as per se breaches of section 1 of the Sherman Act, equivalent to Article 81. Is it ever necessary then to go on to seek to ascertain the subjective intent of the parties? The answer is yes, but only rarely; in the majority of cases the 'object' of the agreement is clear on its face. Occasionally, however, the subjective intent of the parties may need to be sought, for example where the Commission are aware of an industry-wide scheme that purports to have beneficial objectives such as improved standards, but where these may prove after investigation to be cosmetic only.[51] Such cases, however, will be few, compared to the number where the object clearly stands out from the very nature of the agreement itself.[52]

In many cases however, where the object of an agreement is not clearly anti-competitive, it will be necessary to examine the economic context of the agreement and the actual *effect* that the restrictive clauses will have or possibly have already had, if it has been implemented already. The classic authority for this is the well-known *Delimitis* case.[53] The contractual restriction on the tenant of a Frankfurt café was that he had to purchase all his supplies of beer from Henninger Brau, the owner of the café, though there were advantages to both the tenant and his landlord in the arrangements. The cumulative effect of the brewery's network had to be assessed, the number of outlets tied by the brewery, and the degree of loyalty of tenants generally to it. The option for the tenant to purchase beer from outside Germany should also be considered. The actual contribution of the individual tenant's agreement to the blocking effect on potential new entry was also relevant.

A more recent case dealt with by the ECJ involved exclusive purchasing agreements by petrol stations in Finland. In *Neste Markkinointi* v. *Yötuuli Ky*,[54] Neste was an oil company with a large national chain of petrol stations, and a market share of petrol and diesel-fuel sales in that country of 33.5 per cent and 44.2 per cent respectively. Some of these stations had agreements for as long as ten years, others for much shorter periods such as a year. The ECJ held that, in the case of an agreement for a year only,

---

[50] See fn. 6.

[51] As, e.g. in the *IAZ* cases, Cases 96–102, 104–5, 108, 110/82 [1983] ECR 3369: [1984] 3 CMLR 276.

[52] For a very interesting analysis of the importance of subjective intent in restrictions by object, see Odudu, 'Interpreting Article 81(1): Object as Subjective Intention' [2001] 26 ELRev 60.

[53] Case C-234/89 [1991] ECR I-935: [1992] 5 CMLR 210. The facts are set out in Ch. 10, p. 221.

[54] Case C-214/99 [2000] ECR I-1121: [2000] 4 CMLR 993.

the degree to which such agreements foreclosed the access of rival oil companies to the retail market was too limited to fall within the range of Article 81.

2.6 RESTRICTIONS ON COMPETITION BY NON-RESIDENT PARTIES

To restrict competition within the Common Market, it is not necessary that all parties to the agreement are resident within it. This is illustrated by Commission decisions relating to trade between the Common Market and Japan. In *Siemens/Fanuc*,[55] the Commission imposed a fine on both a German and a Japanese company which had entered into reciprocal exclusive dealing agreements covering numerical controls for machine tools for Asia and the EC respectively, and under which a substantial range of restrictions was imposed and extremely high prices charged to all customers, who could not obtain the controls from other sources. In the Commission decision in *Franco-Japanese Ballbearings*,[56] it was proved that meetings had taken place between the manufacturers of ball bearings in France and Japan to discuss the sales and pricing policy of Japanese manufacturers with regard to imports into France. Considerable pressure was applied upon the Japanese manufacturers to bring export prices to France into line with French prices, and to inform the French manufacturers of the prices and discounts that the Japanese would grant to purchasers in France. Here the restraint on competition was clear and its result was that customers for the ball bearings would find themselves paying a higher price to Japanese manufacturers than would otherwise have been the case. The flow of trade between Member States within the Common Market would also be affected, since Japanese ball bearings were supplied to other Common Market countries and the likely effects would be a reduction in direct imports from Japan and an increase in parallel imports to France from other Common Market countries, and possibly an overall reduction in the purchase by France from Japanese sources. The Court of Justice in the *Woodpulp* case[57] focused on the place where the agreement was implemented, regardless of where it was made or where its parties were situate.

2.7 SUMMARY OF THE COMMISSION'S TASK

In conclusion the Commission must in nearly all cases conduct a market analysis of the effect of particular restrictions or agreements on the patterns of trade. There will be occasions when it may be excused from doing this in detail, because the objective of the agreement is so clearly anti-competitive that the Commission does not need to analyse the effects of the restriction. The decision in *GlaxoSmithKline*, however, has muddied the waters in relation to the classification of export bans as restrictions of

---

[55] [1985] OJ L376/29: [1988] 4 CMLR 945.   [56] [1974] OJ L343/19: [1975] 1 CMLR D8.
[57] See Ch. 22, Section 2.3.

competition by object because it suggests that this assumption can be disproved in exceptional circumstances, such as the ones present in the pharmaceutical market.

3. ANCILLARY RESTRICTIONS ON COMPETITION

3.1 VENDORS AND PURCHASERS

One of the ways in which the Court of First Instance and European Court have been able to restrict the scope of Article 81(1) has been by characterizing a wide range of restrictions on conduct contained in commercial agreements as 'ancillary'. Ancillary restrictions can occur in a wide variety of situations. Their essential characteristic is that without the restriction the proposed transaction would not take place because one party would be unable to prevent the other from acting subsequently so as to deprive the transaction of its main commercial benefit.

Some of these cases involve restrictive covenants on vendors which have sold their businesses, imposed by purchasers acquiring their goodwill as well as their business assets. In *Reuter* v. *BASF*,[58] Dr Reuter sold to the German chemical company, BASF, a business which involved the manufacture of polyurethanes, synthetic products used in the manufacture of plastics and varnishes. As part of the agreements, Dr Reuter accepted a number of covenants restricting his own future activities, and which he subsequently complained were contrary to Article 81. The principal covenant restrained him for eight years from engaging directly or indirectly either in Germany or elsewhere in research, development, manufacture, use, or distribution of any chemical product required in the production of polyurethanes or related products. He was also prevented for eight years from disclosing any confidential technical matters known to him before the sale. The Commission ruled that any restrictive covenant on the sale of a business or of know-how must be limited in length and width to an extent proportionate to the goodwill and business sold. In assessing reasonable duration and extent for such a covenant, the factors to be considered included the nature of the know-how, opportunities for its use, and the transferee's own technical knowledge. Such a clause should normally be restricted to the markets in which the vendor was active before the sale or in which he could be regarded as a potential competitor; any clause covering new developments could not be of greater length than those properly inserted to protect existing markets. If clauses were limited in this way they might well not even be caught by the provisions of 81(1), and would not therefore be subject to the individual exemption process.

Applying these principles to Dr Reuter's agreement, the Commission held that the contractual clauses were invalid because they covered non-commercial as well as commercial research and development, and went beyond what was required to safeguard

---

[58] [1976] OJ L254/40: [1976] 2 CMLR D44.

the interests of the purchaser in preserving the value of the goodwill and assets acquired. Moreover, it was felt that the obligation on Dr Reuter to keep information confidential for as long as eight years might be used to prevent him from competing with the purchaser later through his further development of basic know-how not covered by the sale agreement. The Commission also ruled that a competition-restraining agreement between a vendor and a purchaser, even if situate in the same Member State, would be likely to affect trade between Member States if it affected goods or services which if put on sale by the vendor of the business could be the subject of trade between Member States. The Commission ultimately ordered that the agreement should stand for a period of only five years, instead of the eight-year period originally imposed.

A similar intervention occurred in *Remia and Nutricia*,[59] involving the sale of two businesses in Holland for the production of sauces and pickles. Here the Court upheld a Commission decision that covenants restraining the vendors from competitive activity should be reduced from ten to four years in one case, and from five to two years in another, on the basis that even such apparently normal clauses may impose restraints upon trade between Member States which the Commission is required to consider. The Court, however, emphasized that clauses of this kind whose length, scope, or geographical application do no more than is necessary to permit the agreement in which they occur are not caught by 81(1), but are simply ancillary to a necessary and legitimate business transaction.[60]

3.2 ANCILLARY RESTRICTIONS IN TRADE ASSOCIATION RULES: *GOTTRUP KLIM*

The concept of the ancillary restraint can also arise in connection with the rules of trade associations or cooperatives. *Gottrup Klim* v. *DLG*[61] involved the rules of a Danish farmers' cooperative, DLG, which was open to both individuals and associations of farmers, and its treatment under those rules of smaller associations which sought to terminate their membership. The plaintiffs were various smaller associations which remained members of DLG, but had elected to buy the majority of their requirements of fertilizers and pesticides direct from suppliers. The consequent reduction of orders placed through DLG led to discounts for its members on those products being reduced. DLG then decided to change its rules so that membership of any association that competed with it in the purchase of pesticides and fertilizers would lead to expulsion of its members from DLG. Members of such small associations could

---

[59] Case 42/84 *Remia and Nutricia* v. *Commission* [1985] ECR 2566: [1987] 1 CMLR 1. The Court pointed out that the effect of such sales of businesses is to increase the number of potential competitors in the market. However, a clause of this kind which seeks to protect the *vendor* against the competing activities of the *purchaser* in particular territories is never regarded as ancillary: *Quantel International* v. *Quantel SA* [1993] 5 CMLR 497.

[60] Another clear example of this pattern of reasoning can be found in Case 161/84 *Pronuptia* [1986] ECR 353: [1986] CMLR 414 , which involved restrictions of competition that were necessary for the proper functioning of a franchising agreement. The *Pronuptia* judgment is discussed in Ch. 11.

[61] Case C-250/92 [1994] ECR I-5641: [1996] 4 CMLR 191.

however continue to buy their individual requirements either direct from suppliers or through DLG.

The small associations expelled as a result of the change of rules brought an action in the Danish courts, and under Article 234 a number of issues relating to the DLG rules were raised with the European Court. The Court ruled that a provision in the statutes of an organization like DLG prohibiting its members from joining competing cooperatives to acquire certain products did not necessarily constitute a restriction of competition within the meaning of Article 81, provided that the rule was restricted to what was necessary to ensure that the cooperative functioned properly and was able to maintain its contractual power in relation to suppliers. Such was the case with the DLG rules, where (a) the prohibition only covered products (principally fertilizers and pesticides) where there was a direct relationship between sales volume and price, (b) non-members of the cooperative were allowed to buy from it the whole range of products sold on by it on the same terms and at the same prices as its members, and (c) members of DLG were allowed to buy those products direct outside DLG provided, as mentioned above, that they did not buy through a competing cooperative. The issue in determining whether Article 81(1) applied was whether the rules containing such restrictions were necessary to ensure that the cooperative functioned properly and maintained its contractual power in relation to producers, in the interests of its ordinary individual members.

3.3   OTHER ANCILLARY CLAUSES

Ancillary clauses can however be found in many different types of agreement apart from sales of businesses. In joint ventures the parent companies may quite reasonably impose covenants upon each other not to compete with the business of the joint venture, usually for a period of years, and not to take other action that might prejudice it. Franchisers normally seek to restrict the business methods adopted by their franchisees so as to protect their business secrets; and suppliers of certain products and services may wish to adopt certain quality standards for their selective distributors. The owners and licensors of some specialized intellectual property rights may also with justification seek to protect themselves during the early years of the commercial development of a particular plant or seed by imposing export bans for a period, with the object of controlling the extent of widespread licensing. Nevertheless the Commission will be unwilling to accept the classification of a restrictive clause as ancillary without clear evidence that its adoption is a *sine qua non* of the transaction of which it forms part.

The question of whether a contractual restriction can be properly described as ancillary also arises under the Merger Regulation, and the detailed contents of the 2005 Commission Notice on this subject is to be found at Chapter 17 at p. 451. The treatment of such restrictions under this Regulation focuses on whether, in the absence of such a clause, the particular merger could be implemented at all, or only under more uncertain conditions or at substantially higher cost. Whilst some of the ancillary clauses found in merger agreements are similar to those mentioned in this section, the range of clauses included in merger agreements, usually in an attempt to preserve the continuity and stability of the merged undertaking, is wider. The Notice is specific as to the maximum length of non-compete clauses which can be treated as ancillary, two years when goodwill alone is transferred and three years if both goodwill and know-how are conveyed. The Notice however mentions that, even if a particular clause appears in a merger agreement, this does not prevent it from benefiting from the provisions of Article 81(3) or of a block exemption such as Regulation 772/2004 on Technology Transfer Agreements or Regulation 2790/99 on Vertical Agreements.[62]

3.4 ANCILLARY RESTRAINTS AND THE 2004 COMMISSION GUIDELINES ON THE APPLICATION OF ARTICLE 81(3) EC[63]

The principles distilled from the cases considered in the previous sections are reflected in the 2004 Commission Notice. There, the Commission has noted that:

The assessment of ancillary restraints is limited to determining whether, in the specific context of the main non-restrictive transaction or activity, a particular restriction is necessary for the implementation of that transaction or activity and proportionate to it. If, on the basis of objective factors, it can be concluded that without the restriction the main non-restrictive transaction would be difficult or impossible to implement, the restriction may be regarded as objectively necessary for its implementation and proportionate to it.[64]

Furthermore and echoing the findings of the Court of First Instance in *Metropole*,[65] the Commission was also careful to emphasize that the analysis based on objective justification and proportionality which is entailed in the application of the doctrine of ancillary restraints[66] is different from a balancing of pro- and anti-competitive effects that should take place *only* in the context of the application of the third paragraph of Article 81.

4. THE WIDTH OF THE COVERAGE OF ARTICLE 81

4.1 INTRODUCTION

The general approach of the Treaty is to provide for only a very limited number of sectoral exceptions to the general application of the competition rules[67] and the Community

---

[62] For a detailed examination of these Regulations see Chs. 12 and 10 respectively.

[63] These Guidelines are considered in detail in Ch. 8.   [64] See para. 31 of the Guidelines.

[65] See fn. 26 above.

[66] Some authors, like Professor Whish, interpreted the judgment in *Wouters* as an extension of the doctrine of ancillarity. See R. Whish, *Competition Law* (6th edn, 2008), p. 126–30.

[67] See Jacobs A-G's Opinion in Case C-67/96 *Albany International* [1999] ECR I-5751: [2000] 4 CMLR 446 at paras. 120–6.

Courts have interpreted these exceptions in a restrictive way. It is therefore sensible to approach a discussion of the coverage of the Article by listing those particular sectors which have been specifically excluded from its scope rather than by trying to enumerate all those which it covers. In some cases exclusion from its coverage has meant that there is partial or complete exemption for a sector from the competition rules; but in other cases the exclusion from coverage by Article 81 has been comprehensive so as to provide an alternative set of competition rules. Some of the exclusions or exceptions result directly from specific provisions in the Treaty, while others arise from the adoption of Regulations made under the authority of the Treaty.

4.2 DEFENCE

The competition rules may be excluded under Article 296 from applying to any product included in the list of Defence items prepared by the Council of Ministers. This Article gives Member States the right to take necessary measures to protect their essential security interests connected with the production of or trade in arms, munitions, and war materials; the only qualification is that 'such measures shall not adversely affect the conditions of competition in the Common Market regarding products which were not intended for specifically military purposes'. This distinction is presumably drawn so as to ensure that while undertakings may be allowed to enter into agreements otherwise within the scope of Article 81 but for the fact that they relate, for example, to the supply of rifles or tanks, similar arrangements made to cover, for example, the supply of boots (potentially suitable for army or civilian use) are not so excluded. The tendency of the Commission in recent years has been to narrow the scope of this exemption. Moreover, under Article 298 the Commission is entitled to intervene if it believes that a Member State is abusing its rights under Article 296 with the effect of distorting conditions of competition within the Common Market.

Perhaps the greatest reliance by Member States on Article 296 has arisen in the context of mergers, where the Commission has accepted their right in several such cases to deal with those cases themselves, without the individual undertaking having to supply the Commission with information relating to their defence activities. The Commission has in each case so far stated publicly that the measures taken by the Member State in such a case were necessary for the protection of its essential security interests and had little effect on competition or suppliers. It should not be assumed, however, that all Defence cases and notably mergers involving companies in the Defence industry, will be dealt with solely by Member States, as in a number of cases under the Merger Regulation the Commission has nevertheless taken jurisdiction under the Regulation of non-Defence areas of the business being acquired.

4.3 COAL AND STEEL: NUCLEAR ENERGY

Article 305(1) states that the provisions of the Treaty of Rome (including, of course, Articles 81–9 containing the rules on competition) shall not affect the ECSC Treaty 'and in particular the rules laid down by that Treaty for the functioning of the Common Market in coal and steel'. Articles 65 and 66 of the ECSC Treaty clearly therefore formed part of those rules and were applied by the Commission in parallel with Articles 81 and 82 of the Rome Treaty. As from 23 July 2002, however, the fifty-year life of the ECSC came to an end and a Communication from the Commission set out the transitional arrangements in respect of pending ECSC cases, and also those for the future application of the competition rules of the Treaty of Rome to the coal and steel sector. This change is perhaps less dramatic than might have been expected. Over its fifty-year life the size of the Community coal and steel industry sharply reduced, even while the Community increased from six to twenty seven Member States, and the approach of the Commission in its application of the ECSC rules under the Treaty of Paris had for many years been converging with its practices under the Treaty of Rome. In future national competition authorities and national courts will be competent to deal with coal and steel cases in parallel with the Commission, in the same way as they can deal with other cases under Articles 81 and 82.

By contrast the nuclear energy industry continues to retain its separate regime under Article 305(2) which states that the Treaty of Rome shall not derogate from the provisions of the Treaty establishing the European Atomic Energy Community, which in practice means that Articles 81 and 82 are applied to this sector if required. The relationship between the two treaties was considered by the Court of First Instance in *ENU* v. *Commission*[68] and by the European Court in its *Ruling on the Physical Protection of Nuclear Materials*.[69]

4.4 COLLECTIVE BARGAINING

No specific exemption is found in the Treaty for agreements that form part of the collective-bargaining process within the Community, but on social-policy grounds the ECJ has ruled in several cases that such agreements fall outside the scope of Article 81. The leading case is *Albany International*.[70] Companies in the Dutch textile industry were required to provide supplementary pensions for their employees. Albany already had its own such scheme (which it claimed was more generous than the compulsory scheme) and claimed also that the compulsory scheme was in breach of Article 81 so that it could not be required to participate in it. The ECJ however rejected Albany's claim; whilst Article 81 was applicable to the scheme because of its compulsory nature the scheme was justified under the terms of Article 86(2) of the Treaty because of the social-policy objectives which the Treaty embodied. For the same reason, however, Article 81 did not apply to the collective agreement between employers and employees for the establishment and maintenance of the scheme. The Court followed the strong lead given by Jacobs A-G, whose opinion laid down conditions for holding such agreements outside the scope of Article 81. These were that the agreement was made as part

---

[68] Case T-458 and 523/93 [1995] ECR II-2459.
[69] Case C-1/78 [1978] ECR 2151.   [70] Case C-67/96 [1999] ECR I-5751: [2000] 4 CMLR 446.

of normal collective bargaining, that it was made in good faith rather than to conceal restrictions of competition, and that it dealt with the core subjects of collective bargaining, such as wages or other conditions of work, and did not affect third parties or third markets.

There have been a number of other cases, also mainly from the Netherlands, in which similar conclusions have been reached by the courts. Whether the actual agreement establishing a trust fund or a social security scheme against industrial accidents is covered by the competition rules is of course a different question from whether the fund itself is an undertaking; the answer in several of the cases has been that the trust fund or scheme created by collective agreement was itself an undertaking but that nevertheless for the reasons of social policy mentioned above, Article 81 had no application to it. Thus on the same day as the *Albany* case was decided, the Court reached a similar finding in *Brentjens* v. *SBVHB*[71] where the appellant was a wholesaler in the buildings-material sector. It likewise wished to withdraw from the industry compulsory scheme on the grounds that it had already provided a scheme of equivalent value for its employees. Funds that are not the outcome of a collective bargaining process may well however fall within the scope of Article 81 as in the *Pavlov* case discussed above (in Chapter 6 at p. 77).

4.5 AGRICULTURE

The position of agricultural products is covered by Article 36 of the Treaty. This declares that the competition rules shall only apply to agriculture to the extent that the Council determines, within the framework of and subject to the requirements of the Common Agricultural Policy, which is set out in outline in Article 37. The detailed objectives of Article 33 are to be taken into account in framing these Regulations. The objectives set out in Article 33 for the Common Agricultural Policy include:

(a) increasing agricultural productivity by promoting technical progress, and by ensuring the rational development of agricultural production and the optimum utilization of the factors of production, in particular labour

(b) ensuring a fair standard of living for the agricultural community

(c) stabilization of markets

(d) assurance of the availability of supplies

(e) ensuring that supplies reach consumers at reasonable prices.

In working out these policies account is to be taken of the particular nature of agricultural activity, including: its social functions and the disparities between different regions, the need to effect the appropriate adjustments gradually, and its close links

---

[71] Cases C-115–117/97 [1999] ECR I-6025: [2000] 4 CMLR 566. Other similar Dutch cases were Case C-219/97 *MDB* v. *SPVH* [1999] ECR I-6121: [2000] 4 CMLR 599 and Case C-222/98 *Van der Woude* [2000] ECR I-7111: [2001] 4 CMLR 93.

with the rest of the economy of Member States. Some of these objectives, especially (c) and (d), appear inevitably to require substantial intervention in free markets, and indeed the terms of the Common Agricultural Policy at present in force illustrate this. Accordingly, Regulation 26/62 was adopted by the Council, which in substance permitted the competition rules to apply (Article 1) subject to two substantial exceptions set out in Article 2. The first of these was any agreement which formed an integral part of a national market organization. Such organizations are now rare since the marketing rules for agricultural products have, for a number of years, been dealt with on a Community-wide basis. Occasionally however such organizations are still created. The second exception was any agreement 'necessary for the attainment of the objectives set out in Article 33 of the Treaty' as set out above. Regulation 26/62 has now been replaced by Regulation 1184/2006,[72] but Articles 1 and 2 of the new regulation are substantially identical to its counterparts in Regulation 26/62 and hence the same general principle and exceptions apply. The Commission's interpretation of the exceptions has been invariably strict.

An example of the attitude taken by the Commission and Court towards the interpretation of Regulation 26 is the *FRUBO* case.[73] This involved an agreement between a trade association of Dutch fruit importers and another association of Dutch fruit wholesalers. Under the agreement, wholesalers were not allowed to seek alternative sources of supply into the Common Market of fruit and vegetables originating from outside the Community, other than through the Rotterdam fruit auctions. As a result, of all the apples, pears, and citrus fruit imported into Holland, at least 75 per cent usually came in through the Rotterdam auctions, making it extremely difficult for Dutch importers to seek long-term import agreements with other parties within the Common Market. A rather half-hearted argument was put forward by the associations that, under Dutch law, the practices of the associations did not constitute contractual relationships between their members, comprising only a 'gentlemen's agreement'; even if this argument had been successful, such an agreement would in any case be caught by the provisions of Article 81. The contractual nature of these rules was emphasized by the fact that they contained penalties for their breach with the possibility of the exclusion of defaulters from participation in the Rotterdam fruit auction, a serious detriment for the importers.

Both the Commission and the European Court of Justice rejected the argument that these arrangements were an integral part of a national market organization or necessary for the attainment of the objectives of Article 33. The Court concluded that the agreements might possibly improve the distribution of fruit in Holland, and even that consumers might receive the benefit of price reduction as a result, though it remained sceptical on this issue. Nevertheless, the exemption under Article 81(3) was unavailable, for the restrictions placed on the parties were not indispensable to the agreements' claimed purpose: the improvement of fruit distribution throughout Holland.

---

[72] [2006] OJ L214/7.

[73] Case 71/74 *FRUBO* v. *Commission* [1975] ECR 563: [1975] 2 CMLR 123. See also Case C-265/97P *VBA/ Florimex* [1999] ECR I-2061.

The restrictions also, of course, contravened the 'integration' principle laid down in *Grundig*, under which the wholesalers should have been left free to search for alternative sources of supply outside their own country rather than being kept effectively 'segmented' from the rest of the Common Market. The effect of the restriction was substantial: in practice it meant that a Dutch wholesaler could not act as an importer and that importers established in the other Member States could not, without joining the association and participating in the fruit auction, deliver fruit to Dutch wholesalers. At least in the area of marketing agricultural products, Article 81 clearly has considerable application, and has also been utilized, for example, in the sugar, vegetable, and dairy products sectors.[74]

Subsequent cases have explained the role of national courts in determining whether the exemption found in Article 2 is applicable. In the *Dijkstra, Van Roesell*, and *Luttikhuis* cases[75] the European Court had to deal with a number of issues on this Article raised by Dutch courts under Article 234. In each case, farmers had left milk producers' cooperatives and argued that rules which required them to pay money to the cooperative on withdrawal were void as being in breach of Article 81(1). The Court's ruling was that national courts were competent to determine whether the payment obligation on the withdrawing member comprised an infringement of Article 81(1) (and was therefore void under Article 81(2)) if it was clear to that court that the terms of Article 2(1) of Regulation 26/62 could not be met. However, if it had any doubt on the matter it should suspend proceedings in order to enable the Commission to make its own decision under Regulation 26. In any case, the restrictions imposed by agricultural cooperatives on their members must be limited to those necessary to ensure that the cooperatives function properly with a sufficiently wide commercial base and a reasonable degree of stability.

4.6 AIR TRANSPORT

As a mark of its importance to the economy of the Common Market the transport sector was given special mention within the Treaty in Articles 70 to 80. Article 80(1) states that the provisions of this title apply to road, rail, and inland waterway transport and paragraph (2) states that the Council may decide whether appropriate provisions may also be laid down for sea and air transport, for which a qualified majority has been required since the Single European Act.

The position of air transport has always been special. There were a number of international treaties and conventions setting out the basis upon which such services were to be carried out, going back to the Chicago Convention, entered into as long ago as 1944 which had led to the creation of the International Air Transport Authority (IATA) to play a leading role in the worldwide coordination of fixing both its services and

---

[74] The marketing of Dutch milk was the subject of the *Meldoc* decision [1986] OJ L348/50: [1989] 4 CMLR 813.

[75] Cases C-319/93, 40/94, and 224/94 *Dijkstra and Van Roesell* [1995] ECR I-4471: [1996] 5 CMLR 178; Case C-399/93 *Oude Luttikhuis* [1995] ECR I-4515: [1996] 5 CMLR 178.

fares. The perceived need to support national airlines had naturally led Member States themselves to become much involved in the fixing of details relating to the revision of air services. For a considerable period therefore no competition rules applied to air transport. Numerous references were found in the early Annual Competition Reports to Commission proposals for the introduction of regulation in the sector. Owing to strong opposition by some Member States, the Commission then sought alternative means of opening up the sector to a greater degree of competition and the position was firmly clarified by the *Nouvelles Frontières* case.[76] This to some extent strengthened the position of the Commission, although it did not give it the full authority for which it had hoped to impose the complete range of competition rules on Member States and air undertakings within them. The case arose after the Tribunal de Police in Paris asked the Court for a ruling under Article 234 on whether it was contrary to the Treaty for Member States to require courts to apply the criminal law to undertakings which had failed to comply with mandatory tariffs for air transport 'if it were established that those tariffs were the result of an agreement, decision or concerted practice between undertakings contrary to Article [81]'.

The Court, noting that no regulation had been made for air and sea transport under Article 83, nevertheless concluded that Articles 84 and 85 remained applicable. Article 84 required authorities in the Member States to apply Article 81, including paragraph (3), and Article 82 until relevant regulations had been adopted. However the authorities referred to in Article 84 did not include criminal courts (whose task was simply to punish infringement of the law) but merely administrative bodies charged with administering competition law and civil courts having jurisdiction over such authorities or to apply such laws. Neither the French authorities nor the Commission had in fact exercised any of their powers under Articles 84 and 85 with regard to the air transport tariff agreements which had allegedly been broken by the defendant travel agents in the criminal proceedings before the Tribunal de Police.

The Court, following earlier cases, held that the two Articles were 'not of such a nature as to ensure a complete and consistent application of Article 81' so as to permit the assumption that Article 81 had been fully effective from the date of entry into force of the Treaty. The principle of legal certainty, to which the Court had always attached great importance, therefore meant that these agreements remained provisionally valid unless and until the Member State, or the Commission, took action under those Articles (84 and 85 respectively) which gave transitional powers to them. Only when such a ruling had been given could the French courts be required to hold, as a matter of Treaty obligation, that no criminal liability could be imposed for breach of the relevant requirement of the French Code of Civil Aviation, which required sales of air tickets to be at official approved prices.

As a result of *Nouvelles Frontières*, it became clear that, until the Council adopted a regulation dealing with air transport, the Commission would be able to make progress only by implementing Article 81. The Commission subsequently gave notice

---

[76] Cases C-209–213/84 *Ministère Public* v. *Asjes* [1986] ECR 1425: 3 CMLR 173.

during the summer of 1982 that it would be implementing Article 81 against ten airline undertakings in Member States with regard to certain forms of agreement, although it would prefer the Council to adopt a group of measures under which the rules of competition would be introduced initially to a limited extent only, applying first to fare and capacity agreements between airlines, and then gradually to the full range of agreements between them. The Commission prepared separate reasoned decisions against three leading European airlines under Article 85, requiring them to end agreements on setting fares and sharing route capacity and revenues. This had the desired effect of persuading those airlines to modify their agreements to the extent required by the Commission. In December 1987 the Council adopted a package of measures applying Articles 81 and 82, including two Regulations (3975 and 3976/87),[77] two Directives and a Decision. The collective effect of these was to place some limits on the terms of route- and capacity-sharing agreements between airlines, to enable some new discount fares to be offered, and to authorize the Commission to issue block exemptions for some categories of agreement whose effect on competition is only minor. The Commission adopted Regulation 1617/93, a block exemption regulation covering passenger-tariff consultations and slot allocations at airports. Regulation 1617/93 was replaced by Regulation 1459/2006[78] but this applied only until 31 October 2007. Following consultation with interested parties in the industry and Member States and after the introduction of the system of directly applicable exception by Regulation 1/2003,[79] the Commission has taken the view that there are no longer grounds to exempt this type of agreements by regulation. Following the expiry of the transitional period, self-assessment of these agreements by the airline industry replaces the block exemption. Other Regulations have been issued dealing with computer reservation systems and ground-handling services.

Regulations 3975 and 3976/87 apply only to domestic and international air transport between Community airports, and Article 81 also applies only to such routes, and not to international routes to or from non-Member States. By contrast, under the old Merger Regulation 4064/89, the Commission intervened in a number of proposed mergers involving such routes where it perceived potentially anti-competitive effects. It is very conscious of the need to extend the scope of its jurisdiction under Article 81 to such important international routes. The Commissioner for Competition therefore introduced proposals in May 1997 under which Regulation 3975/87 would be extended to cover such routes, so that the Commission could apply Article 81 to them without the need to use the cumbersome and transitional regime of Article 85.

The Commission has however not yet been able to obtain the specific agreement of Member States that Article 81 should apply to international routes to and from the Community; it has however made some progress as a result of the judgment of the ECJ in the *Open Skies* case.[80] Here the Commission had challenged a number of Member

---

[77] [1987] OJ L374/1 and [1987] OJ L374/9 respectively.   [78] [2006] OJ L272/3.

[79] See Ch. 8, section 1.1.

[80] Cases C-466, 476/98 *Commission* v. *UK, Germany, and others* [2002] ECR I-9427: [2003] 1CMLR 143.

States, which had signed bilateral aviation service agreements with the USA, claiming that they had acted in breach of the Treaty. The Court's judgment was partially in favour of the Commission. It accepted its claim that the 'nationality' clauses in the agreements deprived other Community airlines of their Treaty rights not to be discriminated against on the grounds of nationality; it also agreed that in respect of those matters, e.g. airport slots and computer reservation systems, where the Council had authorized the Commission to act for the Community as a whole, Member States no longer retained jurisdiction. Following the judgment, the Council and the Parliament adopted Regulation 847/2004 on the negotiation and implementation of air service agreements between Member States and third countries.[81] Given that some aspects of air service agreements fell within the scope of Community competence and others within that of the Member States, the main purpose of the regulation was to clarify the obligations of the Member States[82] when these entered into negotiations with third countries with a view to ensure the coordination of these negotiations, a harmonized approach in the implementation of the agreements and their compatibility with Community law.

4.7 MARITIME TRANSPORT

Article 84(2) of the Treaty had provided that it was for the Council to decide whether appropriate provisions should be laid down for sea transport and for some years, as with air transport, the Commission were unsuccessful in introducing any Community legislation where a permanent exemption for sea transport was unacceptable given its importance to the economies of Member States. Nonetheless, some Member States were prepared to argue that the rules of competition did not apply to this sector at all, at least until an appropriate regulation had been adopted by the Council. Originally, the only case that appeared relevant to this issue was that of the *French Merchant Seaman*.[83] This case, which came before the European Court of Justice, had considered whether the French government was in breach of Article 39 prohibiting discrimination based on nationality between workers of individual Member States affecting their rights to employment and conditions of work. The French Code du Travail Maritime had laid down that French merchant ships should be manned by not less than three Frenchmen to each seaman of other nationality. The French government claimed that instructions had been given to the naval authorities to treat other EC nationals as if they were French, but that such instruction was a matter for unilateral French discretion rather than Treaty compulsion.

The Court ruled, to the contrary, that as the Treaty was in principle applicable to the whole range of economic activities; these Treaty rules could be rendered inapplicable only as a result of an express clause in the Treaty to that effect. The Court also said

---

[81] [2004] OJ L157/7.

[82] These obligations included notification to the Commission (Art. 1) or equal treatment of all Community carriers involved in the negotiations (Art. 2).

[83] Case 167/73 *Commission v. France* [1974] ECR 359: [1974] 2 CMLR 216.

that the reference to the 'objectives' of the Treaty in Article 70 meant those set out in Articles 2 and 3. So far as air and sea transport was concerned, both remained subject to the general rules of the Treaty until the provision of a transport policy under Article 80(2); in the interim period, the other Treaty provisions continued to apply, unless an express exception was granted, including the principle of freedom of movement for workers contained in Article 39. The Court therefore ruled that the French legislation was discriminatory against foreign seamen in breach of this Article.

The Council eventually adopted the detailed Regulation 4056/86,[84] applying to regular international maritime transport services from or to a Community port, but not to tramp-vessel services. It included both procedural rules under which the Commission could carry out its duties under Articles 81 and 82, with powers largely equivalent to those conferred upon it under Regulation 17—the old enforcement regulation—and special substantive provisions applicable to liner conferences.[85] In particular, Council Regulation 4056/86 declared Article 81(1) inapplicable to technical agreements and created a block exemption, subject to certain conditions, for agreements between members of liner conferences fixing prices and carrying capacity, as well as for some other agreements coordinating timetables and sailings, determining the frequency of sailing, regulating carrying capacity, and allocating cargo. The rationale for this exemption was the assumption that liner conferences had a stabilizing effect and ensured the reliability of services and that such result could not be achieved by means less detrimental to competition.

In practice, however, this regulation appeared to provide some incentive to members of liner conferences (as evidenced by a number of cases) to build a web of anticompetitive practices around the limited exemption created by Regulation 4056/86. The practices condemned in subsequent cases brought by the Commission included attempts to fix prices for the entire door-to-door conveyance of containers (whereas the Regulation provides an exemption only for the sea portion of the journey) and a variety of other practices designed deliberately to exclude competitors from particular routes, through the introduction of 'fighting ships' subsidized by members of the liner conferences and by the provision of quotas upon which given routes were shared between members of that conference (see Chapter 9, section 3 for a description of cases in this sector). Recently, Council Regulation 1419/2006[86] repealed Regulation 4056/86 in its entirety on the strength of the argument that a full review of the industry demonstrated that liner shipping conferences no longer fulfilled the conditions for exemption laid down in Article 81(3) EC or deserved protection from competition more than other industries. Some of the provisions of Regulation 4056/86 continue to apply

---

[84] [1986] OJ L378/4.

[85] Liner conferences are defined by the Regulation as 'a group of two or more vessel operating carriers which provides international liner services for the carriage of cargo on a particular route or routes within specified geographical limits and which has an agreement or arrangement, whatever its nature, within the framework of which they operate under uniform or common freight rates and any other agreed conditions with respect to the provision of liner services'.

[86] [2006] OJ L269/1.

until 18 October 2008 but thereafter the Article 81(1) EC prohibition applies in full to liner shipping conferences. In preparation for the new competitive regime, the Commission published on 1 July 2008 a set of Guidelines designed to help undertakings to assess whether their agreements are compatible with Article 81(1) EC.[87]

In 1992, the Council adopted Regulation 479/92,[88] enabling the Commission to adopt block-exemption regulations and the Commission used this power to adopt Regulation 870/95,[89] and block-exempt liner shipping consortia. Such consortia are agreements between shipping companies which relate to cooperation in a technical and operational area, applicable to regular international cargo services principally by container to or from Community ports. However, the fixing of prices or rates was not protected by the regulation. Regulation 870/95 was succeeded by Regulation 823/2000,[90] introducing some changes to its operation and which is due to apply until 25 April 2010.

4.8 ROAD AND RAIL TRANSPORT AND INLAND WATERWAYS

This was the first of the transport sectors to receive its own specialized Council Regulation, 1017/68,[91] which laid down both substantive and special enforcement rules for rail, road, and inland-waterway transport. This regulation confirmed that Articles 81 and 82 were to apply to undertakings dealing with road, rail and inland waterway traffic, with the following qualifications:

(1) Article 3 declared Article 81(1) inapplicable to agreements for standardization of equipment or other technical matters, including the coordination of timetables and routes, and organization of combined transport operations. This amounted to a declaration that such agreements fell outside the scope of Article 81(1)—or were *excepted* from the application of this provision.

(2) Article 4 created a special block *exemption* for agreements between small and medium-sized undertakings where the undertakings individually and the grouping do not exceed some maximum carrying capacities.

Regulation 1017/68 was amended several times, most recently, by Regulation 1/2003, which now applies the general enforcement regime to this sector. The Commission has submitted a proposal for a new Parliament and Council Regulation that would replace Regulation 1017/68 which essentially reflects the substantive exception and exemption provided, respectively, in Articles 3 and 4 of Regulation 1017/68.[92]

As a result of Regulation 1017/68, Articles 81 and 82 apply only marginally less to the field of road, rail, and inland waterways than to industry in general, though the Commission must be careful to proceed under the appropriate Regulation if challenging agreements claimed to be restrictive of competition. This was confirmed in *Commission* v. *UIC*.[93] UIC was an international association of national railway

---

[87] SEC (2008) 2151 final.   [88] [1992] OJ L55/3.   [89] [1995] OJ L89/7.
[90] [2000] OJ L100/24.   [91] [1968] OJ L175/1.   [92] COM (2006) 722 final of 27 November 2006.
[93] Case C-264/95P [1997] ECR I-1287: [1997] 5 CMLR 49.

organizations which had laid down rules about selling tickets for international journeys. These included a 10 per cent standard-rate commission on ticket sales, an obligation on agents to sell tickets only at the official rate, and other restrictions on the
activities of travel agents engaged in the sale of these tickets. After the Commission
had imposed a fine in respect of this agreement under Article 81, UIC appealed successfully to the Court of First Instance (whose decision was upheld by the European
Court) claiming that the Commission should have proceeded, not under Article 81,
but under Regulation 1017/68. The Court of First Instance had stressed that the key criterion for deciding whether 1017/68 applied was whether the agreement had the object
or effect of fixing transport rates or limiting the control of the supply of transport; this
does not necessarily mean that all activities related to rail transport would necessarily fall outside Article 81. Articles 81 and 82 have indeed been applied to a number of
important agreements, including joint ventures for major trans-European networks
and key transport links such as the gas inter-connector pipeline across the North Sea,
and other major rail and road projects. The Court of Justice has, for example, applied
the Regulation to prevent the application in France of a levy on barge operators which
effectively discriminated against non-French operators.[94]

There have also been other leading cases in this sector notable among which is the
European Night Services case[95] in which the Commission's grant of individual exemption to a proposal to provide night sleeper services through the Channel Tunnel
between the United Kingdom and Europe was quashed by the Court of First Instance
on grounds that its effects on restriction of competition were insufficient to breach
Article 81.

FURTHER READING

J. FAULL, 'The Effect on Trade between Member States' [1991] Fordham Corp L Inst 485.

E. GONZALEZ DIAS, 'Some Reflections on the Notion of Ancillary Restraints under EC Competition Law' [1995] Fordham Corp L Inst 325.

A. JONES, 'Analysis of Agreements under US and EC Antitrust Law—Convergence or Divergence' [2006] 51 *Antitrust Bull* 691.

V. KORAH, *An Introductory Guide to EC Competition Law and Practice* (9th edn, Hart Publishing, 2007).

O. ODUDU, *The Boundaries of EC Competition Law: The Scope of Article 81* (Oxford University Press, 2006).

O. ODUDU, 'Interpreting Article 81(1): Demonstrating Restrictive Effect' [2001] 26 ELRev 261.

R. WHISH and B. SUFRIN, 'Article 81 and the Rule of Reason' [1987] YEL 1.

---

[94] Case 272/85 *ANTIB* v. *Commission* [1987] ECR 2201: [1988] 4 CMLR 677.   [95] See fn. 17.

8

ARTICLE 81(3): DISAPPLYING THE ARTICLE 81(1) PROHIBITION

1. THE CHANGING ROLE OF THE COMMISSION

1.1 INTRODUCTION

Article 81 is structured in three paragraphs. As seen in previous chapters, the first paragraph contains a prohibition on anti-competitive forms of cooperation which have or may have an appreciable effect on intra-Community trade. The second paragraph sets out a sanction of nullity for agreements, decisions, or concerted practices which infringe the Article 81(1) prohibition.[1] The third paragraph of Article 81 provides for the possibility that certain agreements, decisions or concerted practices which, in principle, fall foul of Article 81(1), may escape the application of the prohibition if they fulfil certain conditions laid down in Article 81(3).

For over forty years and since the entry into force of Regulation 17/62, the first enforcement Regulation, the main task of the Commission in the area of competition policy was to apply and enforce the two balanced paragraphs 81(1) and 81(3), the former setting out the prohibition, and the latter limiting its application. The system of enforcement provided by Regulation 17/62 gave the Commission the monopoly in the application of Article 81(3) EC. It is understood that the reason for bestowing this exclusive competence on the Commission was a wish to guarantee the uniform application of the Article 81(3) conditions throughout the Community. National courts and national competition authorities could apply the first and the second paragraph of Article 81 but only the Commission could apply the third paragraph of this provision. It was a system of notification and authorization where undertakings had to notify their individual agreements to the Commission for these to benefit from an *individual* 'exemption'—or in other words from a declaration from the Commission that an agreement satisfied the criteria set out in Article 81(3).

In practice, the Commission only granted a few formal exemptions each year, dealing with most requests through a system of 'comfort letters'—or informal letters letting

---

[1] The effect of this sanction of voidness is considered at the end of this chapter (see Section 5).

the interested undertakings know of its intention to close the file. Of more practical importance in most cases than the grant of individual exemptions were the legislative provisions under which Council and Commission promulgated block exemptions which applied to particular categories of agreements—the so-called block-exemption regulations. These related primarily to vertical agreements, such as exclusive distribution and purchasing arrangements and other forms of distribution and to technology transfer licences, but a few dealt with horizontal agreements, including research and development and specialization agreements. If an agreement fell squarely within the scope of a block-exemption regulation, then the Article 81(1) prohibition was automatically disapplied without the need of individual notification to the Commission. National courts and national competition authorities were therefore able to apply the provisions of the block-exemption regulations.

The partially decentralized system of enforcement set out by Regulation 17/62 placed a great strain on the Commission's resources—given that thousands of notifications were received every year—and also significantly restricted the enforcement of Article 81 by national courts and authorities. In 1999, the Commission published a *White Paper on the Modernisation of the Rules Implementing Articles 81 and 82*.[2] There, the Commission suggested the surrender of its monopoly in the application of Article 81(3) and the replacement of the system of notification and individual exemption by a system of directly applicable *legal exception*. Essentially, this meant that agreements, decisions by associations of undertakings, and concerted practices that fell under the Article 81(1) prohibition but satisfied the conditions in Article 81(3) would be automatically valid, without the need of an enabling administrative decision. The new system therefore would shift from one of prior authorization to one of *ex post* control. Undertakings would now bear the burden of the self-assessment of individual agreements falling outside the scope of a block-exemption regulation. This self-assessment was to be exercised in the light of the guidance provided by the Commission and by years of case law of the Community judicature and a decision on the legality of an individual agreement or practice would only be necessary if a complaint or contractual dispute between the parties arose. At that point, not only the Commission, but also the national courts and national competition authorities would have the power to apply the conditions in Article 81(3). This was a momentous change that not only aimed to enable the Commission to allocate its resources more efficiently but also to give national courts and national competition authorities a full enforcement role in the application of Article 81. The White Paper proposals were later laid down in legislative form in Council Regulation 1/2003,[3] the new enforcement regulation which entered into force on 1 May 2004. Regulation 1/2003 replaced Regulation 17/62 and has confirmed the character of Article 81(3) as a directly applicable legal exception, which coexists with a system of block exemption regulations that apply to certain categories of agreements.[4]

---

[2] [1999] OJ C132/1, [1999] 5 CMLR 208.   [3] [2003] OJ L1/1.

[4] The impact of this Regulation on the application of EC Competition Law by national courts and competition authorities is discussed in Chs. 19 and 20.

1.2 THE DIRECTORATE GENERAL FOR COMPETITION (DG COMP)

The Commission exercises its powers through a number of Directorates-General,[5] which in turn are divided into directorates. Each Directorate-General has, under Article 211 and subsequent regulations made by the Council, some policymaking functions. In some areas, e.g. the harmonization of corporate and tax laws of Member States or environmental-pollution control within the Community, little can be achieved by an individual Directorate-General without active support on issues of policy from the Council of Ministers and, increasingly, the European Parliament. This is so even if all twenty-seven Commissioners are supportive of the proposals put forward. This means that the staff of a directorate within a Directorate-General may consult widely and work up proposals over a long period, only to find that their draft suggestions (negotiated in detail over many months with individual Member States and relevant organizations) are ultimately ignored or rejected or, at the least, postponed because of political difficulties arising at the Council or at the Parliament.

It is notable that DG Comp, as the Directorate-General responsible for competition matters, has managed to avoid some, if not all, of this frustration and in many respects operates differently from other DGs. The reason is mainly that, through Council Regulation 17/62, it obtained early a procedural statute delegating considerable powers from the Council to the Commission itself, including complete monopoly over the grant of individual exemption to agreements under Article 81(3). The Commission normally acts on the advice and recommendation of the Commissioner having special responsibility for competition.[6] The Commissioner in turn will normally be guided by the advice of his/her officials, thoroughly discussed in advance with the Commissioner's 'cabinet'—the group of individual officials operating as the Commissioner's private office—and having been the subject of prior consideration by the Advisory Committee, which comprises official representatives of Member States entitled to comment both on proposed individual decisions and on proposed Community legislation on competition issues.[7]

So far as competition issues are concerned, the Council will now normally become involved only if new legislation is needed for which authority has not already been given to the Commission.[8] In general, therefore, the Commission conducts its regular decision-making function without political intervention. All decisions taken by the Commission are, however, subject to a right of review for interested parties under Article 230 of the Treaty and in respect of alleged failure by the Commission to act under Article 232.

---

[5] Normally abbreviated to DG both orally and in writing.

[6] Though there have been some cases of concentrations under the previous Merger Regulation (Reg. 4064/89) where the Commissioners have not accepted the original draft decision of DG Comp.

[7] See Art. 14 of Reg. 1/2003.

[8] For example in adopting the Merger Regulations (Reg. 4064/89, the first EC Merger regulation adopted after many years of negotiations) and the current EC Merger Reg. 139/2004, discussed in Chs. 16 and 17.

2. BLOCK EXEMPTIONS

2.1 MAJOR CURRENT EXAMPLES

These have increased in both number and importance over the years, and are made either by the Council under the authority of Article 83 or by the Commission under delegated authority from by the Council.

As discussed in Chapter 7, the Council adopted some substantive regulations containing block exemptions in special sectors, such as maritime transport[9] and road, rail, and inland-waterway transport.[10] However, most Council regulations were simply enabling regulations granting the Commission the power to adopt block-exemption regulations.[11] Accordingly, Regulations made by the Commission providing block exemptions are more numerous. Following a very extensive review of its policy towards vertical and horizontal restraints that took place between 1996 and 2004, the Commission replaced the old system of block-exemption regulations by a new set of regulations. The principal ones in force are as follows:

Reg. No.	Year	Subject Matter
2790	1999	Vertical restrictions in distribution agreements (goods and services)
823	2000	Liner consortia
2658	2000	Specialization agreements
2659	2000	Research and development agreements
1400	2002	Motor vehicle distribution agreements
358	2003	Insurance agreements
772	2004	Technology transfer agreements

2.2 THE PREPARATION OF BLOCK EXEMPTIONS

Finalizing the terms of any regulation is a lengthy process. It involves a great deal of consultation with interested parties including the authorities of all Member States (through the Advisory Committee) and relevant commercial and industrial interests. If the Regulation is to be made by the Council, it is originally drafted by the staff of DG Comp (with specialist advice from the Legal Service of the Commission) who themselves consult widely with Member States and other interested bodies before sending a draft to the Commissioner. Once the Commissioner has given his approval, it reaches the agenda of the full Commission and once approved goes on to the Council. The draft then goes from the Council for approval by the European Parliament, who

---

[9] See Reg. 4056/86 now repealed by Reg. 1419/2006 (Ch. 7, p. 135).

[10] See Reg. 1017/68; see Ch. 7, pp. 136–7.

[11] See, e.g., Reg. 19/65 [1965] OJ L36/533 in the field of vertical agreements, Reg. 2821/71 [1971] OJ L285/46) for certain types of horizontal agreements, Reg. 1534/91 for agreements in the insurance sector ([1991] OJ L143/1) or Reg. 3976/87 for certain air transport agreements ([1987] OJ L374/9).

return it with their comments for reconsideration by the Commission. Though the Commission is not legally bound to accept comments or suggestions made by these other bodies, it normally pays close attention to them, and the final draft sent forward to the Council for approval will normally be in a revised form.[12]

On the other hand, if the Regulation is to be made by the Commission under delegated powers, it does not go to the Council but to the Advisory Committee of representatives of Member States as established under Article 14 of Regulation 1/2003, usually both before and after its publication in the Official Journal. The Economic and Social Committee and the European Parliament are also shown the draft on a consultative basis. It is important for DG Comp to obtain approval from the Advisory Committee for any draft regulation it puts forward, because when it later comes before the Commission it can be shown to confirm that the national interests of individual Member States have been taken into consideration.[13]

Both Council and Commission members are aware that the adoption of a new block exemption or the revision of an existing one is a protracted process, involving the need to establish consensus with the many interests concerned. Sufficient interest has to be paid to the preferences, susceptibilities, and suspicions of individual Member States. Moreover, those commercial, industrial, and professional interests must also be consulted and the benefit of their experience gained. Obtaining agreement on the form of the block exemption can be a laborious process; the rules must not only meet the policy needs of the Commission but also comply with the requirements of the many interested regional, national, and sectoral pressure groups which have a voice in the process. The process of adoption of the block-exemption regulations[14] showed the importance which the Commission places on gaining the assent of these interest groups, particularly in respect of the more technical block exemptions. The final version of these exemptions showed many and important differences from earlier drafts, as the description of their legislative process records.[15]

2.3 THE FORM OF BLOCK EXEMPTIONS

Block exemptions once had a clearly recognizable form. After extensive recitals setting out the policy considerations which led to the introduction of the measure, there followed a statement of the basic scope of the exemption. Next would come a list of restrictions permitted to be included in the exempted agreements (popularly called 'the white list'),[16] matched immediately afterwards by a list of those restrictions whose

---

[12] This is a simplified account of the normal legislative process. For a fuller account see Hartley, *The Foundations of European Community Law* (6th edn, Oxford University Press, 2007) pp. 36–42.

[13] The recitals to Reg. 19/65 refer specifically to the need for the Commission to prepare its block-exemption regulations in close and constant liaison with the competent authorities of Member States.

[14] The first block exemption regulation on Technology transfer agreements (Reg. 240/96) was replaced by the current Regulation on Technology Transfer Agreements (Reg. 772/2004). See section 2.1 above.

[15] See Ch. 12.

[16] The number of clauses contained in the 'white lists' grew substantially in the block exemptions, up to and including the transfer of technology block exemptions (240/96).

inclusion would prevent the block exemption from applying ('the black list'). Some but not all block exemptions also contained a provision for 'opposition'. This means that the parties to the agreement might put forward clauses restraining competition which are found in neither the 'white' nor the 'black list', and which therefore might be described as 'grey'. Since the enactment of Regulation 2790/99 however the normal form of block exemptions no longer includes a 'white list' nor an opposition procedure. They do still contain a 'black list' of clauses whose inclusion will either totally prevent the block exemption from applying, or would at least be themselves void (even if the validity of the rest of the agreement is unaffected).[17] It is also now more likely that a condition precedent for undertakings seeking to benefit from the block exemption is that their market share for the relevant market does not exceed a given percentage, normally in the range of between 20–30 per cent, though this will vary between different block exemptions.

The new regulations are likely also to include a wider provision for the withdrawal of the block exemption from particular agreements, if either the Commission or even individual Member States believe that the exemption is no longer appropriate.[18]

It should also be noted that block exemptions must have a time limit. This is normally for ten years, or at most fifteen. Review occurs as the expiration date approaches, and changes to the terms of the regulation are normally proposed. The experience of its operation may in some cases lead to pressure for change or even, in extreme cases, for non-renewal of the regulation as a whole. If the Commission has difficulty in completing its consultation, negotiation, and drafting process before the date on which the Regulation should expire, an extension of one or even two years may be given to the existing Regulation. An example was the extension of both the Exclusive Distribution and Exclusive Purchasing block exemptions (Regulations 1983/83 and 1984/83) from the end of 1997 to the end of 1999,[19] pending the implementation of Regulation 2790/99 on vertical agreements from the start of 2000.

One final point should be made about block exemptions. They are not interpreted with the same liberality as Article 81. The European Court made it very clear that it expected them to be interpreted strictly and, unless a particular agreement complied exactly with the precise terms of the relevant legislation, it could not have the benefit which that legislation provided. This was established in *Delimitis*,[20] concerning an exclusive purchasing arrangement between a brewery and a cafe owner, where the principle of strict interpretation was laid down. The formalism of the old block-exemption regulations coupled with the strict interpretation followed by the Community Courts meant that undertakings were severely constrained in the configuration of their

---

[17] Note, e.g. the difference in treatment of 'black' clauses listed respectively under Arts. 4 and 5 of Reg. 2790/99.

[18] See Art. 29 of Reg. 1/2003 and Arts. 6 and 7 of Reg. 2790/99. Member States can only exercise this power in relation to their territory or part of it. Under both the old and the current system, the Commission has scarcely used this power. A rare example of its use occurred in the *Langnese-Iglo* decision ([1993] OJ L183/1: [1994] 4 CMLR 51).

[19] By Reg. 1582/97.   [20] See Ch. 10, p. 221 for a full account of this case.

agreements—if they wanted to invoke the benefit of a block exemption. However, it must be underlined that the new system of block-exemption regulations has removed to a great extent the so-called 'straitjacket effect' caused by the old regulations—which had set out not only the restrictive clauses that were forbidden but also the *only* restrictive clauses that were permitted in the relevant agreements. In the new regulations, only forbidden clauses are laid down and thus much more contractual freedom is allowed to the parties.

3. THE ARTICLE 81(3) CONDITIONS

3.1 THE APPLICATION OF ARTICLE 81(3) IN THE OLD SYSTEM OF ENFORCEMENT

Under the old system, one of the chief administrative functions of DG Comp was to deal with notifications of individual agreements. From the adoption of Regulation 17/62 the Commission held the monopoly of granting such individual exemptions under Article 9(1). However, under the new regime introduced by Regulation 1/2003, discussed in detail in Chapters 19 and 20 and Part III, responsibility for applying Article 81 is now shared by the Commission with national courts and with national competition authorities which previously had legal power to apply only Article 81(1) and not 81(3). Moreover, the mechanism of individual notification of agreements containing clauses that may be in breach of Article 81(1), and the requesting in the alternative of negative clearance or individual exemption for them, no longer operates. It is nevertheless essential to understand how the system of notification of agreements operated for so many years and the reasons why it was brought to an end.

The basic framework of Regulation 17/62 has already been described in Chapter 4; it gave the Commission extensive powers to carry out its responsibilities under both Article 81 and 82, in particular under Article 11 to send out requests for information to Member States and to authorities and to commercial undertakings of all kinds, and by Article 14 to carry out 'dawn raids' at the premises of undertakings. In addition Article 12 gave the Commission powers to carry out general enquiries into any economic sector where it believed that competition was being restricted; the powers under this last Article had been little used for many years though there were signs in more recent times that the Commission was at last more willing to make such enquiries.[21]

The original intention behind the Regulation was, as we have seen, that notification of all individual agreements would be made to the Commission by undertakings which had entered into them, and that the granting of an exemption under Article 81(3) could only apply to actually notified agreements (Article 4(1)). The only

---

[21] The 1999 *Annual Report* recorded that a sectoral inquiry had been opened into three areas of telecommunications (leased lines, the 'local loop' and mobile 'roaming' services), paras. 74–6.

exception to this principle, set out in Article 4(2) was a very limited list of bilateral agreements, essentially those concerned with either the distribution of goods or the licensing of technology. This position however changed radically with the adoption of Regulation 1216/99 whose effect was to extend Article 4(2) of Regulation 17/62 to all categories of vertical agreements (bilateral or multilateral) concerned with the production or distribution chain and to virtually all bilateral licences for the transfer of technology. This meant that all such vertical agreements could be exempted retrospectively back to the date when they were first made (even if prior to the implementation of Regulation 1216/99), rather than simply from the date of notification to the Commission. The effect of this was to protect the Commission from possible mass notification of vertical agreements, following the introduction of the new block exemption for vertical agreements 2790/99, and, moreover, prepared the way for the introduction of the new system which has eliminated the need for notification of any agreement to the Commission

To understand the way in which DG Comp operated it is essential to realize that the process which it set in hand usually involved negotiated settlement, such that formal or informal clearance could be given to an agreement or concerted practice after removal of those features which appeared unacceptable under the terms of Article 81(1) and 81(3). As the European Court itself put it in the 1984 *Dutch Books* case:[22] 'The purpose of the preliminary administrative procedure is to prepare the way for the Commission's decision on the infringement of the rules on competition, but ... also presents the opportunity for the undertakings concerned to adapt the practices at issue to the rules of the Treaty.' Only exceptionally was an agreement, not covered by a block exemption and individually notified, found either so harmless that it could be approved in its entirety, or so restrictive and anti-competitive that it had to be rejected by a formal decision to that effect. The majority of agreements notified individually fell between those two extremes and were therefore suitable to form the subject for negotiation.

The range of choices for DG Comp when considering an individual agreement was therefore as follows. First, it could decide that the agreement fell outside Article 81(1) altogether, and thus entitled to what was described in Article 2, Regulation 17/62 as a 'negative clearance'. There could be sometimes insufficient evidence of an agreement or concerted practice between undertakings, or that the relevant trade association made a decision or recommendation; sometimes it was not possible to show a sufficient effect on trade between Member States or on competition within the Common Market. The parties to the agreement could be small and their agreement covered by the *de minimis* rule of the current Notice on Minor Agreements; or they could be covered by one of the other Commission Notices interpreting the application of Article 81(1) to particular types of agreement. If the agreement did fall within the scope of Article 81(1), the next question was whether it was covered by an existing block exemption. If so, its restrictions could be disregarded because Article 81(1) had by that block exemption

---

[22] Cases 43 and 63/82 *VBVB and VBBB* v. *Commission* [1984] ECR 19, 68: [1981] 1 CMLR 27, 95.

been determined as inapplicable; indeed there was no need for an agreement falling within that category to be notified at all. Only if it was decided that the agreement was within Article 81(1), but not covered by the terms of an existing block exemption, was the availability of individual exemption relevant until 1 May 2004.

Regulation 17, Article 9(1) gave DG Comp authority to grant individual exemption, subject to the right of Community judicature to review any such decision under Article 230. Once a procedure had officially been started by the Commission, the jurisdiction of a Member State to pronounce such an agreement, even to be within or without Article 81(1), ceased.

3.2 THE APPLICATION OF ARTICLE 81(3) POST MODERNIZATION

Under the new regime established by Regulation 1/2003 both the Commission and national courts and national competition authorities may consider the provisions of Articles 81(1) and 81(3) together rather than having to deal with them separately. Notifications and individual exemptions no longer exist. This important change in the *enforcement* of Article 81(3), however, should not mean that the outcome of the *substantive* examination of any individual agreement will be different, because the national court or authority will still need to apply each of the four cumulative conditions in Article 81(3). Whether national courts in particular find it difficult to apply the provisions of Article 81(3) to individual agreements is an issue which will be discussed in Chapter 20.

According to Article 2 of Regulation 1/2003, the undertakings or association invoking the benefit of Article 81(3) bear the burden of proving that those conditions are fulfilled and failure to do so will lead to the individual agreement coming under the scope of the Article 81(1) prohibition. As part of the modernization package, the Commission issued a series of Notices in 2004, one of which provides substantive guidelines on the application of the Article 81(3) conditions to individual agreements[23] and is discussed later on in this chapter.

If an agreement falls squarely within the scope of a block-exemption regulation it is assumed that it automatically satisfies the Article 81(3) criteria and the parties invoking the benefit of the exemption are relieved from the burden of showing that each one of the conditions is fulfilled.

3.3 THE INTERPRETATION AND APPLICATION OF THE FOUR ARTICLE 81(3) CONDITIONS

The conditions set out in Article 81(3) are essentially four separate conditions. In each case, four separate questions have to be asked and answered: the disapplication of the Article 81(1) prohibition can be available only if an affirmative answer is given to the first pair and a negative answer to the second pair. *Positive condition 1* is: 'Does the

---

[23] [2004] OJ C101/97.

agreement, decision, or concerted practice improve the production or distribution of goods or promote technical or economic progress?' *Positive condition 2* is: 'If so, does it also allow consumers a fair share of the resulting benefit?' *Negative condition 1* is: 'Does the agreement impose restrictions on the undertakings not indispensable to the attainment of the objectives already referred to?' Finally, *negative condition 2* asks: 'Does the agreement afford the undertakings the possibility of eliminating competition in respect of a substantial part of the products?.'

If Article 81 were a United Kingdom statute, we would have to conduct a textual analysis of each of these conditions and examine how they have been applied by the Commission and Community Courts. However, this is not a useful or productive way of understanding how they are dealt with by either the Commission or the Courts. The four conditions are treated more like provisions in a civil code, as broad statements of principle to be read in the context of the remainder of Article 81 and the other Treaty provisions, as well as in the light of the many cases in which they have already been applied. On the other hand, there is no principle of *stare decisis* binding on all subsequent cases. In theory (though not always in practice), the Commission, and post-modernization also national courts and national competition authorities, are free to look at each case individually. They will, however, apply well-established principles of interpretation, based on the underlying objectives of Article 81 as a whole, to the particular restrictive clauses encountered.

There was some ambivalence in the way in which DG Comp addressed the analysis of individual agreements during the years it held the monopoly in the application of that provision. Its general approach, which would appear to be required by the terms of Article 81(3), was to take each condition separately and to consider logically whether an appropriate answer can be given to each of the four questions. Only if the appropriate answer could be given in each case did the question of non-applicability of 81(1) arise. On the other hand, one frequently obtained the impression from the terms of Commission decisions that the positive conditions 1, and to a lesser extent, 2 demanded priority of attention; if a satisfactory answer could be given to those questions from analysis of the factual background, then lesser difficulties were raised in many cases by negative conditions 1 and 2. Again, reports of decisions sometimes gave the impression that the Commission deliberately chose the phrasing of its answers to the first two questions in order to make it easier to give an appropriate answer to the two following negative questions.

In practice, the Commission first analysed the agreement to see if it was outside the terms of any block exemption and therefore liable to individual notification, and if so whether it contained any of those restrictive clauses which had, as the result of analysis in earlier cases, become almost automatically deemed to lead to the splitting up or segmentation of geographical markets. This might be caused either by a specific clause to that effect between parties in competition with each other, or as the result of export bans contained in vertical agreements, perhaps patent licences or distribution agreements, which prevented the free movement of goods at a lower level of the distribution stage from country to country within the Single Market by way of parallel imports. If any such clause was found in the agreement, then it was unlikely that the requirements of even the first positive condition in Article 81(3) could be satisfied.

Only if no such presumptively illegal clause appeared did DG Comp proceed to the next stage of the inquiry, to analyse the main objectives and effects of the agreement, and to carry out the balancing test—in the context of Article 81(3)—of whether the anti-competitive restraints were outweighed by the advantages claimed as likely to result from them. In carrying out this process, the four questions were approached in order. If, after a first review, the agreement did not seem tainted by any restrictions or restraints on competition within it, an attempt was made to save it by removing undesirable features. This process was not a court hearing but a review by an administrative body seeking to apply the provisions of paragraph (3) in a flexible way, in the light of the objectives of the Treaty and the Regulations made under it, also taking into account the considerable case law that existed as the result of both Court and Commission decisions.

Post-modernization, the 2004 Commission Guidelines on the application of the Article 81(3) conditions describe comprehensively the Commission's policy on the interpretation of these criteria. The Guidelines mostly reflect the case law developed under the old system but also provide some additional guidance on issues not yet considered by the Community Courts.

3.4 THE INDIVIDUAL CONDITIONS

Positive Condition 1: 'Which contributes to improving the production or distribution of goods or to promoting technical or economic progress'

Of the four conditions, this is considered first and has probably been the most important in the eyes of DG Comp. It is essential that the economic benefit is clearly identified—the 2004 Guidelines refer, by way of example, to cost and qualitative efficiencies. The 'improvements' or 'progress' may arise either immediately following the production by the undertakings, or at a later date, following processes in which value has been added or distribution has taken place. In other words, the 'improvement' or 'progress' need not be at the same level (e.g. manufacturing) as that in which the parties to the agreement are involved. 'Improvement' can include almost any kind of beneficial alteration to the operation of industry or commerce, including the elimination of barriers to entry, increased output from a given number of inputs, better quality in production, greater speed or quality control in manufacturing output, a greater range of products produced from the same inputs, or the possibility of making a wider range of products on the same plant or range of machine tools. As we saw in early Commission cases, distribution systems likely to improve the service of local markets with their particular features also qualify.

Whilst such improvements are fairly tangible, the assessment of the alternative benefit, 'technical' or 'economic' progress, has proved to be a good deal more shadowy. It is an expression familiar in French law, requiring a reasonable conjecture to be made about the likely outcome of an agreement. Initially, it was not clear whether this expression involved a broad social balancing of economic advantages and disadvantages. This was illustrated by *Fedetab*.[24] This case involved the majority of those engaged in the tobacco trade in Belgium, including manufacturers, wholesalers, and retailers, where Belgian legislation relating to excise tax and price controls made it virtually impossible for undertakings selling cigarettes and tobacco retail to compete with each other on selling prices. Nevertheless, the Commission found, and the Court agreed, that the legislation did not prevent competition entirely, since this was still possible on terms of payment, profit margins for both wholesalers and retailers, and on rebates payable. The rules of Fedetab for classification of wholesalers and retailers into a number of categories, fixing discounts for each category, and laying down in great detail the terms of business between each level of distribution, brought rigidity even to those areas which had been left unaffected by the government regulations. A justification put forward for the restrictive systems involved was that it enabled a very large number (approximately 80,000) of retail outlets to be preserved, and it was argued that this enabled the retailer to offer customers a much larger number of brands of cigarettes and cigars than would otherwise have been the case, as well as improving the freshness of products for the customer. The Commission took the view that if the services which specialized wholesalers and retailers offered were as valuable as the association maintained, customers and retailers would ensure by their buying practices that wholesalers and retailers of this specialized nature survived, and that it was therefore unnecessary for the association to give them more favourable treatment to ensure their survival (especially if there was no guarantee that in return for this special treatment they would actually provide services of the desired standard).

It had been hoped that the European Court would confirm in the *Fedetab* case whether 'social' arguments relating to the protection of small businessmen and shopkeepers in the tobacco trade were relevant considerations properly to be taken into account by the Commission in applying Article 81(3). The Commission obtained no clear answer, because the Court avoided the question. The same question arose in the *Publishers Association* case[25] and the tone, if not the precise terms, of the judgment seemed to indicate that social objectives, including avoiding the decrease in the number of stockholding booksellers and book sales, leading to smaller print runs and higher prices, could be taken into account, as they had been in UK proceedings by the Restrictive Practices Court at an earlier date.[26] The European Court also stated that the benefits from the agreement under scrutiny occurred not only in the territories of the parties to the agreement, and could be taken into account even if taking place in other Member States. In *Fedetab*, however the Court was divided and unable to reach a clear-cut decision upon it, though such indications as it gave were that it would not allow such an argument to be adopted under 81(3). Of some significance was the

---

[24] Cases 209–215, 218/78 [1980] ECR 3125, 3278: [1981] 3 CMLR 134, 247.

[25] Case 360/92P [1995] ECR I-23: [1995] 5 CMLR 33.

[26] For an account of the previous proceedings in the Restrictive Practices Court, see in particular paras. 2–31 of the ECJ's judgment.

statement that 'the number of intermediaries and brands is not necessarily an essential criterion for approving distribution within the meaning of Article 81(3) which has above all to be judged by its commercial flexibility and capacity to react to stimuli from both manufacturers and consumers'. The Court preferred to decide the case on the fact that restrictions gave the parties the possibility of almost entirely eliminating competition on the Belgian cigarette market, so that there was no need in upholding the Commission's decision to decide whether any of the other three conditions were specifically satisfied.

In more recent years, however, the Commission's decisions indicated a rather more expansive approach to this condition. Thus in *Ford/Volkswagen*[27] the social benefits to be expected from increased employment likely to be generated by the proposed joint venture for the construction of a multipurpose vehicle in Northern Portugal was referred to as a positive element in the favourable exemption decision granted; and the Court of First Instance, in dealing with an appeal by a third party contesting that exemption decision (*Matra Hachette v. Commission*), did not criticize the Commission's approach in this respect.[28] In a number of the 'crisis cartel' cases reviewed at Chapter 9, pp. 184–187, the Commission likewise treated favourably an agreement which would enable structural changes to take place in an orderly and socially acceptable manner. Environmental benefits have also on occasion been taken into account as constituting important technical and economic progress as is illustrated by the *CECED* and related cases considered in detail in the next section of this chapter.

Historically, therefore, this condition has been given a broad interpretation, extending to a wide variety of situations and responsive to many different types of economic progress and technical advance. In particular, this condition has been generously interpreted in a large number of proposed joint ventures in advanced technological areas, such as telecommunications, computers, and multi-media, and to major transport-network proposals within the Community. However, the most radical application, was that in the *Phoenix-Atlas* joint venture decision (see Chapter 18), where an application by the French and German governments for a joint venture in telecommunications on both a domestic and a worldwide basis was exempted only when new conditions were included, which not only changed the terms of the agreement but required liberalization of the French and German telecommunications markets in accordance with the 'Full Competition' Directive of the Commission (96/19) issued under Article 86(3).

The 2004 Guidelines reflect broadly the Commission's methodology in the application of this condition, but suggest a departure from previous practice because they appear to refer solely to 'efficiency gains' or economic benefits and do not seem to leave much scope for the consideration of general public benefits like social or environmental benefits—which were clearly taken into account in several Article 81(3) cases and decisions.[29] It remains to be seen how the Community judicature will interpret

---

[27] [1993] OJ L20/14: [1993] 5 CMLR 617.   [28] Case T-17/93 [1994] ECR II-595.
[29] Para. 42 of the Guidelines provides that goals pursued by other Treaty provisions can be taken into account in the application of Art. 81(3) but only 'to the extent that they can be subsumed under the four

the condition, following the introduction of this limitation.[30] Furthermore, some commentators have observed that the Notice contains criteria for the calculation of economic efficiencies which are significantly more elaborate than those used by the Commission in its decisions under Article 81(3) and that this could undermine the value of these decisions as sources of guidance for national courts and national competition authorities.[31]

Positive Condition 2: 'While allowing consumers a fair share of the resulting benefit'

At one time there was considerable debate as to whether it was strictly 'consumers' or 'users' who were entitled to benefit, in the light of the language used in the four original versions of the Treaty. It soon became clear, however, that the word was to be interpreted broadly and would not be limited to final consumers or retail purchasers. The use in the French text of the expression *utilisateurs* was always a cogent indication that the class of 'consumers' was wide enough to cover those who acquired the goods at any stage of the distribution process, whether in order to add value or merely to make use of the product for any purpose. This was later confirmed by the Commission[32] and has now been reflected in the 2004 Commission Notice.[33] Again, a broad definition of 'benefit' is taken, not limited to reductions in purchase price, but including any other economic advantage which a consumer may enjoy, such as an increase in the number or quality of outlets from which the goods can be purchased, better guarantee and service facilities, quicker delivery, greater range of goods, or more responsive distribution systems. The agreement need only be capable of producing some or all of these advantages in the course of normal trade; proof it has done so is not required, provided that there is some connection between the agreement and the subsequent 'benefit' to users of the relevant goods or services. The Guidelines clarify that the notion of a 'fair share' means that the benefits passed to consumers must at least compensate for the negative effect caused by the restrictions of competition embodied in the agreement.[34]

Finally, the 'improvement' or 'progress' required must not simply benefit the parties themselves but have an overall beneficial effect on consumers in the relevant market. This was clearly laid down in the case involving exchanges of information between the Dutch Paper Industry Federation (VNP) and its Belgian counterpart (Cobelpa).[35] Nearly all the important manufacturers of stationery were members, accounting for approximately 80 to 90 per cent of domestic output in both countries. The Commission found a clear breach of Article 81(1) and refused exemption under paragraph (3). The

---

conditions in Article 81(3)'. Depending on how this important clause is interpreted, non-competition benefits may or may not continue to play a prominent role in the application of Art. 81(3).

[30] In Case T-168/01 *GlaxoSmithKline* v. *Commission* [2006] ECR II-2969: [2006] 5 CMLR 1589, the Court of First Instance used the language of pure economic efficiencies in the application of the first condition in Art. 81(3) EC.

[31] See in particular P. Lugard and L. Hancher, 'Honey I Shrunk the Article! A Critical Assessment of the Commission's Notice on Article 81(3)' 25 ECLR [2004] 410.

[32] E.g. in *Kabel und Metallwerke Neumeyer/Luchaire* [1975] OJ L221/24: [1975] 2 CMLR D40.

[33] See para. 84 of the Art. 81(3) Guidelines.   [34] Para. 85 of the Art. 81(3) Guidelines.

[35] *Cobelpa VNP* [1977] OJ L242/10: [1977] 2 CMLR D28.

extent of the information exchanged between the association and its members was so detailed and so readily identifiable to the transactions of specific companies that it had become more than simply the provision of an information service for a trade association. It had become rather so detailed a source of information as to provide artificial market stability, which in turn eliminated a large number of the competitive risks involved for members of both associations. This was particularly so as the benefit of the information accrued solely to sellers of paper, not to buyers, so that transparency of prices and terms of trading were still absent from one side of the market.

Both associations claimed that their arrangements meant that progress and improvements were available to members of the association, who were able to plan output and investment on a more stable basis because of the information in their possession about future trends in the market and prices being charged by their competitors. The Commission ruled that such benefit could not be taken into account since, to be treated as an improvement or as progress, a benefit must have the potential at least to help third parties, whether the benefit was short term or one whose results would take longer to become apparent. The fact that the improvement of production or distribution or the promotion of economic or technical progress was only one of the effects of the agreement is not necessarily fatal to an exemption, however, provided that the overall balance of detriment and benefit is sufficiently favourable to have some recognizable value for such third parties.

Negative Condition 1: 'Which does not impose on the undertakings concerned restrictions which are not indispensable to the attainment of these objectives'

The first negative condition deals with the effect of the restrictions on the undertakings. The objectives referred to in the condition are those set out as justification for the exemption under the first positive condition. It is essential for undertakings to show that the individual restrictions, individually and collectively, are tailored strictly to the valid purposes of the agreement, and that subsequent damage to the competitive process does not spill over to wider effect. The concept of necessity is very closely related to the principle of proportionality, familiar as a general principle of law which plays an important part in the jurisprudence of the European Court of Justice.[36] In this more limited context too, proportionality is highly relevant. As the 2004 Commission Guidelines explain, the question to be asked in the application of this condition is 'whether more efficiencies are produced *with* the agreement or restriction than in the absence of the agreement or restriction'.[37] Often, agreements able to satisfy the two positive conditions fail to clear the hurdle of this condition, sometimes because the effect of the restrictions has not been carefully enough analysed by the parties to the agreement.

A case where the two positive conditions were satisfied, but where the agreement failed on this first negative condition was *Rennet*.[38] A cooperative at Leeuwaden

---

[36] See P. Craig and G. de Búrca, *EU Law* (4th edn, OUP, 2008), pp. 544–51.

[37] See para. 74 of the Guidelines.

[38] Case 61/80 *Cöoperative Stremsel-en Kleurselfabriek* v. *Commission* [1981] ECR 851: [1982] 1 CMLR 240. In other cases involving farmers' cooperatives some restrictions in their rules have been held to fall outside Art. 81(1) altogether. See Ch. 7, fn. 61.

produced animal rennet and colouring agents for cheese. It accounted for 100 per cent of the Dutch national output of rennet and 90 per cent of colouring agents; of this production, 94 per cent of the rennet and 80 per cent of the colouring agents went to its members, who between them accounted for over 90 per cent of the total output of Dutch dairy products. The members were obliged to purchase all their requirements from the cooperative, and on breach of this obligation were fined heavily. Members who resigned from the cooperative were subject to a financial penalty, calculated on the average quantity of rennet which they had purchased in each of their last five years' membership. Resignation was therefore made extremely expensive, whether its purpose was because the member wanted to obtain supplies from another source, or to produce his own rennet in competition with the cooperative. Although the Commission agreed that the first two conditions were satisfied by the restrictive clauses, which promoted greater efficiency in rennet production within Holland and some benefit in terms of price to purchasers, it considered that the two negative conditions (including the issue of indispensability) were not satisfied. The economic advantages could be obtained by less sweeping restrictions on the members: for example, an obligation to take a smaller percentage of its requirements, or to give reasonable notice of intention to withdraw, would have been adequate to protect the interests of the cooperative, without the infliction of a large fine. The Commission's decision was upheld by the Court.

Another well-known example is the early *Grundig* case[39] where, although the distribution contract under which Consten was entitled to distribute Grundig products on an exclusive basis in France was found likely to lead to an improvement in distribution, the use of trade-mark law to ensure absolute territorial protection constituted unnecessarily broad restrictions of competition for the benefit of the distributor. It was felt that Consten could have derived sufficient strength simply from its exclusive appointment, without the additional protection conferred and the attempted use of French unfair-competition law to keep out all parallel imports from Germany and other Member States.

In *Bayo-n-ox*,[40] Bayer had manufactured a growth-promoting product for piglets, which was normally added to their feed. The relevant patents had expired and Bayer was concerned that parallel imports of the product were increasing. It therefore sought to sell it to feed manufacturers subject to the express condition that they should only use it in the preparation of their own mixes, and not sell it on separately. Bayer's claimed justification for this restrictive clause was that it was necessary to prevent the mixing of the products with other products of lower quality, with possible ill effects to the piglets. The Commission refused an individual exemption, pointing out that the restriction was actually so wide as to have prevented feed manufacturers from supplying the product even to reputable undertakings in Germany and elsewhere in Europe, to whom Bayer would have had no reason to refuse direct supplies. The restriction was therefore too widely drawn to allow an individual exemption to be granted, even if

---

[39] Cases 56 and 58/64 [1966] ECR 299: [1966] CMLR 418.
[40] [1990] OJ L21/71: [1990] 4 CMLR 930.

Bayer's original objective of limiting parallel imports of the product had been considered valid (itself most unlikely).

A totally different type of agreement was presented to the Commission in *BT/SES/Astra*.[41] BT had proposed a joint venture with SES, the Luxembourg operator of the Astra satellite, to sell space for programmes on the satellite and to provide an 'up-link' for television programmes produced in the United Kingdom. SES could have approached potential UK customers direct, but under the agreement all marketing was done by BT. BT was not allowed to offer more favourable terms on other satellites at its disposal to those customers who were signed up to Astra. Moreover, SES was prevented by the arrangement from negotiating direct with customers on up-link terms in respect of non-UK territories. The Commission ruled that there was no distinct advantage to the customers from these arrangements to justify the restrictions, as in its view SES could well have provided its up-link service in the United Kingdom without BT's involvement in this manner and the consequent restrictions. By contrast, in *Publishers Association*[42] the Commission, and indeed the Court of First Instance, were held by the European Court to have failed to show that a collective system of fixed prices for books was not indispensable, especially as earlier rulings by the Restrictive Practices Court in the United Kingdom had held that such an agreement was indispensable on public interest grounds for the book trade in the United Kingdom.

Negative Condition 2: 'And which do not afford such undertakings the possibility of eliminating competition in respect of a substantial part of the product in question'

This final condition relates to the external effect of the agreement and clearly indicates that, as with the application of Article 81(1), there is a need for market analysis by the Commission on both the product range and the geographic range of that market. In spite of the volume of economic and legal writings on the subject, analysis of markets is far from an exact science,[43] and the Court has made it clear that it will only interfere if the Commission abuses the wide discretion given to it for the purposes of paragraph (3). It is probably primarily the result of this condition (as well as the first positive condition) that specific market-sharing arrangements between competitors, as well as export bans in vertical arrangements, will fail to obtain exemption because of the priority given rightly by DG Comp to retaining the possibility of parallel imports as a controlling influence upon price levels. Similar considerations apply in respect of dual pricing, under which goods for export are priced at a level different from those for home consumption, since DG Comp normally regards these also as likely to discourage exports.[44] This however, might change (at least in reference to certain markets)

---

[41] [1993] OJ L20/23: [1994] 5 CMLR 226.   [42] See fn. 25.

[43] The Commission has published its own Notice on market definition: [1997] OJ C372/5. See also Ch. 13, Section 2, and Ch. 16, Sections 6.

[44] Case 30/78 *Distillers* v. *Commission* [1980] ECR 2229: [1978] 3 CMLR 121: See also the decision of the Commission in *Glaxo Wellcome* [2002] 4 CMLR 335, which was, however, annulled by the Court of First Instance in Case T-168/01 *GlaxoSmithKline* v. *Commission* (fn. 30 above).

depending of the outcome of the appeal against the judgment of the Court of First Instance in *GlaxoSmithKline*, a case concerning an agreement imposing dual pricing in the pharmaceutical market and discussed in Chapter 7, section 2.5. The Court of First Instance annulled a Commission decision based on Article 81(3) on the grounds that the Commission had not examined properly whether the agreement produced an economic benefit. In particular, again making reference to the special features of the pharmaceutical market, the Court explained that the contribution of such an agreement to innovation—which was an essential element in that market—had not been properly assessed by the Commission.

The Commission looks at the nature of the market involved, which could be the entire Common Market, one or more Member States, or simply a substantial region of a Member State. The absolute size of the enterprises concerned, and their market shares in the relevant product, are then considered; and the structural condition of that market will be taken into account; DG Comp is always interested in knowing whether the market trends are pro-competitive or in the opposite direction. It will be necessary to ask whether particular forms of competition exist, possibly in promotion or product innovation, which may be especially damaged by the agreement. The Commission here is normally concerned with inter-brand competition; reductions in intra-brand competition, i.e. between rival distributors of the same brand of goods, will not normally weigh heavily so long as there is still reasonable competition between the different brands and the possibility of these brands crossing national boundaries. This framework of analysis is reflected in the 2004 Commission Guidelines.[45]

It is insufficient for the Commission, however, simply to allege that some degree of competition will be eliminated by the restrictions, in a case where the parties account collectively for a substantial part of the market already. Nor are the terms of this condition intended to be equivalent to a statement that parties to an agreement who collectively could be said to have a dominant position in a market can never satisfy it. This was illustrated by the judgment on the *TACA* appeal[46] from an adverse decision of the Commission refusing individual exemption to an agreement between a number of shipping companies involved in container transport on the North Atlantic routes. Although these companies had some 75 per cent of the container transport on these routes, the Court examined in detail the way in which the Commission had itself investigated the extent to which there was both actual and potential competition on the route; the Court only found against the TACA on this point because none of the independent shipping companies were shown to have sufficient power on the market to exert 'real pressure' on it.

---

[45] See paras. 108–15 of the Art. 81(3) Guidelines.

[46] Case T-395/94 [2002] ECR II-875 at para. 330: [2002] 4 CMLR 1008, 1091 ('The prohibition on eliminating competition is a narrower concept than that of the existence or acquisition of a dominant position').

3.5 THE RULE OF REASON

It is often asked whether the implementation of Article 81(3) by the Commission amounts to the equivalent of the 'rule of reason', for many years applied by Federal Courts in the United States to a wide variety of agreements not covered by the per se rule. If the US rule of reason is relevant at all it is (as already explained in Chapter 7) more appropriate to compare it with Article 81(3) than with 81(1). A superficial answer is that the broad effect of the decisions rendered over the years since DG Comp was first established has been similar to that of the case law jurisprudence of these US courts; the restrictions to which Article 81(1) has been applied have been analysed in the context of their particular markets, product and geographic, and in their function and consequences (trivial or weighty) within the framework of the relevant agreement. The Commission, like the United States Courts, has in applying Article 81(3) been aware of the importance of distinguishing between restrictions which are merely ancillary to a legitimate commercial purpose, and those others which provide a measure of relief for the participants from the rigours of competitive struggle.

Nevertheless, at a deeper level, the difference between the two jurisdictions remains pronounced. The US courts may take into account all the positive and negative features of the restraint, as well as the context in which it is applied, remaining as free from statutory restriction as the courts of common law in assessing the real validity of contractual restraints between vendor and purchaser or employer and employee. By comparison, the Commission must operate within a rigid conceptual framework which allows less freedom of manoeuvre and requires the restriction to pass, not one single balancing test, but a cumulative series of four separate tests. Credit obtained by a restraint for passing any particular condition by a considerable margin cannot be taken advantage of at a later stage (at least in theory) if the restraint fails to satisfy a subsequent condition for exemption. There cannot be an 'overall' balancing of debits and credits under the system laid down by Article 81(3). If the consumer does not receive a fair benefit from the improved production or distribution of goods, or if the restrictions appear to outweigh the benefits obtained, even if shared fairly with consumers, then in principle no 'rule of reason' can prevail to exempt the restriction.[47]

4. CASE LAW AND PRACTICE ON THE APPLICATION OF ARTICLE 81(3) IN INDIVIDUAL CASES: SOME EXAMPLES

Following the 2004 modernization programme, the Commission no longer has the exclusive competence in the application of Article 81(3) but it may be helpful to review some of the decisions of the Commission and of the Community judicature in this

[47] See, e.g., the CFI judgment in *TACA* (see note 46 above) at p. 1078 citing in this context the ECJ judgment in Case C-137/95 P *SPO* v. *Commission* [1996] ECR I-1611.

field. These, together with the 2004 Notice will doubtless be of great importance in providing guidance to national courts and competition authorities.

4.1 MULTI-PARTY AGREEMENTS

To understand how the Commission and Community Courts have interpreted these conditions it is useful to consider the application of Article 81(3) in a number of different individual cases, in some of which exemption was granted, some refused, or made subject to onerous conditions. A straightforward example of an agreement which failed to satisfy any of the four conditions was illustrated in the decision of the Commission in *Floral Sales*[48]; here, exemption was refused to an agreement between the three leading French manufacturers of fertilizer who cooperated to form a German subsidiary company to carry out their export to Germany of compound fertilizer. Although these three French undertakings sold to their German subsidiary at varying prices, the product was resold in Germany at a uniform price and on uniform terms and conditions.

The parties argued that the formation of the joint sales subsidiary was necessary to improve the efficiency of their export sales, but it was not an argument accepted by the Commission. They were the largest producers of these fertilizers in France, with excess production capacity and, as the market in France was itself oligopolistic, the effect of their joining together was an appreciable limitation of competition *inter se*. The joint selling arrangements had not only no compelling commercial justification, but also no beneficial effects on either production or distribution to offset the competitive disadvantages. Use could have been made of the normal wholesale and retail distribution facilities provided for the sale of the straight compound nitrogenous fertilizers which they sold, and no reduction in buying price resulted for customers in Germany which could be regarded as a consequent benefit to 'consumers'.

Clearly, the market strength and share of these companies weighed heavily against them; the case may therefore be contrasted with the weak market position and small size of the companies involved in *Transocean Marine Paint*[49] often cited as a good example of the flexible use of Article 81(3) in allowing joint sales arrangements between small companies with a weak market position, even where these amount to a horizontal market-sharing agreement. However, the restrictions imposed must be the minimum essential for carrying out effective marketing, and must only apply to products where there are technical reasons for allowing allocation of territories, as in the case of *Transocean Marine Paint*, when customers would be travelling from port to port and would need a range of standard quality paints available at a number of ports of call. The Commission in that case accepted that such an arrangement would not be possible for small companies without this kind of market-sharing agreement. On renewal of an individual exemption, however, restrictions exempted on an earlier

---

[48] *Floral Düngemittelverkaufs* [1980] OJ L39/51: [1980] 2 CMLR 285.
[49] Case 17/74 *Transocean Marine Paint Association* v. *Commission* [1974] ECR 1063: 2 CMLR 459. See also Ch. 4, fn. 5.

occasion may be considered to have become unnecessary for the achievement of the original objectives of the agreement.

The approach of the Commission to the application of these four conditions can be further illustrated by a unique and complex example, the 1983 decision relating to the Energy Programme of the International Energy Authority (IEA).[50] The OECD had established a separate agency known as the International Energy Authority which carried out this International Energy Programme. Its objectives were to take common measures effective to meet any oil-supply emergency by providing a plan for self-sufficiency that would restrain demand and allocate available oil on an equitable basis between the members. It was agreed that, since each country's supply position was slightly different, any crisis leading to shortages would affect them differently. Some would have a large refining capacity and would normally import mainly crude oil, whilst others would normally import only refined products. Some countries would have oil provided from only one source, others from many, and others again might be largely self-sufficient, having their own production. Supply rights were established by IEA for each country; in the event of disruption in any part of the world the rights of each country would be compared with the overall supplies available in the world. If it was determined that the country had more than its equitable share, it would be deemed to have an 'allocation obligation', if less, an 'allocation right'. Those with allocation obligations would yield up excess supplies to those with allocation rights.

To make this system function, an International Advisory Board (IAB) had to be established from the oil industry to assist the IEA in providing effective emergency measures. On the IAB were represented sixteen oil companies and two oil company trade associations; altogether forty-six oil companies were reporting regular information relating to imports, exports, levels of production, refining, etc. to both the IEA and national governments during any crisis period. Other non-reporting companies were also asked to submit data to their national governments, who would then pass the aggregated information on to the IEA.

A group of expert oil-company employees coordinated these arrangements on a monthly cycle in the event of a crisis. Transactions were placed in three categories. Type 1 was a voluntary rearrangement of supply between a reporting and a non-reporting company. A type 2 transaction was the rearrangement of supplies by reporting companies in response to a specific request from the IEA. It could be effected either by special arrangements between two companies or by the company receiving the request making an open offer to provide supplies capable of acceptance by any company having an allocation right. Type 3, the rarest transaction, was required to supplement the voluntary system, if the situation was sufficiently serious that participating countries had to meet and discuss further allocations, if and only if type 1 and type 2 arrangements could not meet the deficit.

---

[50] [1983] OJ L376/30: [1984] 2 CMLR 186. The members of the IEA were the then twenty-one members of OECD, including all the Member States of the Community other than France. The Community itself had observer status at the IEA. The exemption was renewed for a further ten years in February 1994: [1994] 4 CMLR 506.

These arrangements came into force only when the overall shortfall to all countries within the plan was at least 7 per cent; when this level of supply was reached again, the allocation process ceased. Nevertheless, members of the oil industry, because of their knowledge of the market, were involved in the scheme before it was activated and remained involved after it had been laid to rest. It was clear that the International Energy Programme could not operate satisfactorily without the assistance of the oil companies in carrying out the emergency oil-allocation system. The oil companies' agreement to participate in the system was at least a concerted practice, if not an agreement *stricto sensu*, even though the rules had been laid down by the IEA on an intergovernmental basis. The involvement of the major oil companies had a specific objective, namely the redistribution of oil products that would enable the allocation rights and obligations to be met and ensure that no company and no country were unfairly treated. To achieve this result, extensive information would be needed as to sources of oil, both in general and as to particular cargoes, with supporting detail on its quality, the location of tankers, refinery capacity, and storage capacity. This exchange of information would inevitably provide company representatives with much data from their rivals which would normally have remained confidential.

Clearly, such concerted practices could have had the effect of distorting competition. Oil under type 2 and 3 arrangements would be sent to destinations it would not have gone to in a free market and the sharing of information with many companies, who would not normally know it, might cause oil companies to behave otherwise than would have been the case if the scheme had not existed. If fully implemented, an International Energy Programme would probably involve redistribution of about 10 to 15 million tonnes of oil every month out of a total monthly supply to IEA members of approximately 120 million tonnes.

Not surprisingly, many of the oil companies, notably those from the United States, were unwilling to participate in such arrangements unless a specific clearance under Article 81(3) was obtained. The oil industry has a long history of cartel arrangements, and the size and power of many of the participants in the industry was substantial by any standard. Nevertheless, after complex negotiations an exemption was granted by DG Comp. It was tailored as carefully as possible to the precise needs of the International Energy Programme. Some of the conditions imposed to ensure that the agreement did not contain any unnecessary broad restraints were the following:

(1) The programme did not apply to any exchange of price information except in so far as it was absolutely necessary for negotiating a specific bilateral transaction, e.g. the price of a single cargo available in a tanker at a particular port on a particular date. More general price information could not be exchanged.

(2) These arrangements could only be put into effect while the emergency oil-allocation system was operating, except that consultation was allowed in preparation for the commencement of an actual allocation period. Test runs to ensure the efficiency of the system could also be dealt with on this basis.

(3) To ensure that discussions on oil prices and other sensitive commercial information did not stray beyond the permitted limits, the Commission was itself entitled to attend meetings of the International Advisory Board and to be shown copies of relevant documentation.

With these restrictions a decision was ultimately issued that the requirements of Article 81(3) were satisfied. The concerted practices were said to contribute to improving oil distribution throughout Western Europe, and thereby promoting economic progress and substantially reducing the inconvenience (possibly even major economic distress) that would be caused if supplies to any one participating country were substantially interfered with. Consumers would benefit because they knew that their own country would receive proportionately equal supplies in any such crisis, and the agreement would minimize the impact of shortages on the general economy of each country involved. Great care had been taken to ensure that the restrictions imposed were limited to those indispensable to the scheme, and that competition in respect of 90 per cent of oil supplies would remain on the same basis as before. In fact, with the majority of type 1 and type 2 transactions the companies themselves would still establish the commercial terms for supply of the product. The negotiation of this agreement represents a considerable achievement for the Commission and the other participants. To adjust an agreement of such importance to the members of OECD within the 'four conditions' without either compromising the integrity of those conditions or imposing impossible requirements upon the oil companies and governments participating was no small task.

However, it would be wrong to assume from the IEA case that the Commission's interpretation of Article 81(3) is such that any programme of mutual assistance will be upheld. In *Rheinzink*,[51] a reciprocal supply agreement between three large suppliers of rolled zinc was not given an exemption. The arrangement was that if the companies suffered disruption which caused a loss of supply of 20 tonnes per day, or a total of 200 tonnes, each of the other parties would make good the shortfall up to a total of 1,500 tonnes so long as its own production was not disrupted. This agreement would be for a contract year and automatically renewed for another year. The Court in assessing the arrangements concluded that the agreement would deprive the parties of their independence of action, their ability to adapt individually to circumstances, and the possibility of benefiting by increasing direct sales to customers, from production stoppages or reductions in output sustained by other undertakings. The contract could also compel the parties to supply each other with considerable tonnages. The Court concluded that a contract of such general scope and of such long duration 'institutionalizes mutual aid in place of competition and was likely to prevent any change in the respective market position'.[52] However, it indicated that it would not necessarily have disallowed a mutual-supply agreement applicable simply to cases of *force majeure*, that

---

[51] Cases 29 and 30/83 *Compagnie Royal Austurienne des Mines and Rheinzink* v. *Commission* [1984] ECR 1679: [1981] 1 CMLR 688.
[52] Para. 33 of the Court's decision.

is, loss of supplies directly attributable to an external natural disaster or act outside the control of the parties. Here it was fearful that the agreement in question could be implemented otherwise than in the limited circumstances which the parties claimed to have envisaged.

It is in this perhaps that the agreement differs from the *IEA* case, even though the extent of assistance to be provided in the latter case was also substantial. Nevertheless, some points of difference can be seen. First, the involvement of national governments in the *IEA* case made it unlikely that the agreement could be used as a cover for market-sharing arrangements wider than those specifically referred to in the actual agreement. Second, the threshold of a 7 per cent reduction in supplies before the crisis arrangement came into force meant that circumstances had to be at least moderately critical before the cooperation arrangements were triggered. Finally, the external factors causing the intervention were more clearly defined in the IEA case, as being an interruption of supplies in circumstances falling normally within the *force majeure* situation.

4.2 INSURANCE CASES

In agreements relating to services the Commission has to go through precisely the same analytical process as with those relating to goods. This is illustrated by the *Concordato Incendio* case.[53] This involved an agreement between twenty-eight Italian insurance companies setting up a non-profit association in order to coordinate some aspects of their activities in the industrial fire insurance sector, which controlled about 50 per cent of the Italian industrial fire-insurance market. Originally members who did not use a standard form of agreement had to notify the association, but this obligation was removed at the request of the Commission. The association's responsibilities included the definition of various key terms relevant to the policy, the preparation of relevant statistics required for the calculation of premiums, the updating of the required premium rates in the light of the risks shown, and a study of preventive measures to reduce risks. Membership of the association was open to all insurance undertakings in Italy, initially for a term of two years.

The Commission had no difficulty in concluding that the agreement fell within Article 81(1); its effect would undoubtedly be to limit competition between members, which would tend to standardize premiums, and in general to use the recommended terms and conditions. There would be an effect on trade between Member States because of the existence of foreign insurers operating in these markets in Italy, as well as the fact that some of the property insured by members of the association would be owned by undertakings outside Italy. In reviewing the application of the four conditions the Commission stated that the acquisition of specialized knowledge by the association was a means of improving the services provided, and that the statistical

---

[53] [1990] OJ L15/25: [1991] 4 CMLR 199. The facts were different in Case 45/81 *Verband des Sachversicheres* v. *Commission* [1987] ECR 405: [1988] 4 CMLR 264 where recommendations on actual percentage increases were made to association members.

and other assistance which the association could provide could make it easier for new entry to the market to quote sensible premiums for industrial fire cover. Consumers would therefore have a wider choice of insurance cover. The existence of standard conditions would also make it easier for them to compare the policies offered by different insurers, both in terms of extent of cover and premium paid. No part of the agreement permitted the different insurance companies to agree the final premium to be quoted to potential customers.

The Commission took the view that the restrictions on competition contained in the agreement were indispensable to the attainment of the association's objectives. Only by establishing certain common practices with regard to the premiums and conditions would the insurers and their clients have a proper basis for evaluating the quality of management and of service offered by the individual companies. This should lead to higher standards within the fire-insurance industry in Italy. The Commission did not feel that the agreement would afford the members the possibility of eliminating competition for a substantial part of the services. Members were free to fix their own premium rates and could vary the terms of the standard policies to suit particular cases. In addition a number of powerful insurance companies outside the agreement were in active competition with members of the association. Exemption for a period of ten years from the date of notification was therefore granted.

Another example of the application of Article 81(3) to the insurance sector was the renewal by the Commission in 1999 of the earlier exemption granted to *P & I Clubs*.[54] Mutual non-profit-making insurers offered pooled cover on a worldwide basis to ship owners for a wide variety of risks. Shipowners joined individual clubs belonging to the International Group, whose rules allocated the basis upon which claims would be met. At certain levels the claims were shared equally between the clubs whilst claims at a higher level were shared according to the percentage of each club in claims, tonnage, and total calls. At higher levels still, reinsurance cover was applicable. Some amendments to the rules were made by the Commission in view of complaints that the minimum cover required by the clubs to be taken out by each member was too high. Moreover, the exemption granted by the Commission could be withdrawn if the members of the International Group collectively came to hold a market share larger than twice the minimum scale economically required to provide the level of cover agreed to at the time with that Group.

4.3 TELEVISION-RIGHTS CASES

The saga of the European Broadcasting Union (EBU) rules[55] illustrates the application of the four conditions in a complex and multilateral context. In 1993 the Commission had granted the EBU an individual exemption for five years for its Eurovision rules for sports broadcasting. At the time of the decision EBU had sixty-seven members from forty-seven countries, mainly public-sector broadcasters, and a few private companies.

[54] [1999] OJ L125/12: 5 CMLR 646.
[55] Cases T-528, 542, 543 and 546/93 *Métropole* v. *Commission* [1996] ECR II-649: [1996] 5 CMLR 386.

Only from 1988 had its membership criteria included a requirement that the member provide a broadcasting service of 'national character and national importance'. Their members agreed that through Eurovision they would share, on an exclusive basis, major sports and other programmes, though limited contractual access would be given to non-members of the Union. Screensport, a television company, was refused access to these programmes and complained to the Commission of non-admission to membership as well as the refusal to license these programmes unless exemption had been given from the rule. The Commission in reaching this decision had apparently used as its main criterion the question of whether the EBU was fulfilling a particular 'public mission' within the concept of Article 86(2), but had failed sufficiently to examine other relevant aspects of the case. These included whether the exclusivity required under its rules was indispensable to allow members a fair return on their investment, and whether it was possible to introduce a system of financial compensation for the burdens and obligations imposed on its members as a result of the 'public mission' aspects of their business.

The Court of First Instance found that EBU members were not required by its statutes to comply with a 'public mission' requirement, and referred in particular to Canal Plus in France. In the Court's view, the Commission had failed to examine whether the rules were objective and sufficiently determinate to be applied uniformly and in a non-discriminatory way to potential members of EBU. The criteria in EBU's own statutes were too vague for application to ensure non-discrimination. Moreover, the voluntary acceptance by some members of the different obligations of a public nature was insufficient as a basis for the grant of an individual exemption. For these reasons the restrictions in the rules were held not to be indispensable to the essential function of EBU. In granting an exemption the Commission had wrongly given priority to Article 86(2) over Article 81(3), even though it was agreed that Article 86(2) had no application to this particular organization. The pursuit of public-interest goals was not irrelevant to Article 81(3) but could not outweigh the importance of the indispensability requirements.

The EBU had therefore to redraft its rules so as to meet the terms of the Court of First Instance judgment and duly notified these amended rules to the Commission. Since the original decision of the Court of First Instance the EBU had suffered a substantial loss of market share in Europe at the hands of commercial television companies against a background of sharply rising prices paid for major sports on television such as football. These factors were taken into account by the Commission in assessing the fourth condition. In a number of respects, however, the revised rules offered better opportunities to non-members of the EBU to have access to broadcasts of major sporting events. Although the EBU would still submit bids for major events on behalf of all its members there would now be greater opportunities for small member companies, often in small countries, to have access to such transmissions. Competition between the members and non-members of the EBU was not eliminated because of this sub-licensing arrangement for non EBU members; the technical rules covering the use of the Eurovision signal had been amended to improve distribution and coverage for major events throughout Europe. Moreover non-members could also acquire the right to broadcast on their individual pay TV channels events identical or comparable to those presented on the EBU's members channel. The period of the exemption[56] granted was until 2005 but the EBU were required as a condition of the exemption to provide the Commission regularly with information about the application of its rules to particular major sporting events. Unfortunately not all of the European free-to-air television companies were happy with the revised sub-licensing arrangements: French, Spanish, and Portuguese companies appealed to the CFI against this second decision on the grounds that the sub-licensing rules gave insufficient access to transmission rights for sporting events to non-members of EBU. The rights were generally sold on an exclusive basis and were not freely available to third parties; whilst the restrictions imposed were at their most severe for live transmissions, even deferred coverage was subject to editing and embargo time limitations. Ruling in favour of the complainants, the Court of First Instance also struck out the second grant of exemption by the Commission.[57]

4.4 FINANCIAL CASES

It is noticeable that in recent years many of the leading decisions in respect of individual exemptions under Article 81(3) have involved multilateral networks operating across Europe, where the need to establish stable relationships and deal with inevitable technical problems have had to be balanced against the inherent risk that such networks will incorporate an unreasonable degree of exclusivity and also cause some prejudice to consumer choice. The *VISA* rules for Multilateral Interchange Fees (MIF) illustrate that even agreements that provide for the fixing of prices to be charged by undertakings in competition with each other can in exceptional cases be exempted. The banks from numerous Member States participating in the VISA debit- and credit-card systems would not normally have been able, without a breach of Article 81(1), to make these arrangements, but the ability to be able to fix a standard fee applicable to all cross-border payment transactions at retail outlets meant that many more banks were, in fact, able to join the network without incurring substantial transaction costs of negotiated fees with all other banks participating. An important element in the granting of the exemption, however, was the placing by the Commission of a 'cap' on the amount of the MIF, which related to the audited costs of services which the banks would be rendering to the retailers and their own customers.[58]

4.5 ENVIRONMENTAL CASES

A group of related decisions underlined the importance which the Commission will attach to environmental benefits even for agreements that had an industry-wide basis.

---

[56] [2000] 5 CMLR 650 (The Commission's second decision).

[57] Case T-206/99 *Métropole* v. *Commission* [2001] ECR II-1057: [2001] 4 CMLR 39 and Cases T-185, 216, 299–300/00 *Métropole (M6)* v. *Commission* [2002] ECR II-3805: [2003] 4 CMLR 707.

[58] [2002] OJ L318/17: [2003] 4 CMLR 283. The remaining elements of its credit card system had already received negative clearance from the Commission [2002] OJ L293/24: 4 CMLR 168.

In the *CECED Washing Machines* case,[59] the agreement was made between members of a trade association of washing machine manufacturers who covered some 90 per cent of the manufacturing market in the EEA. The members of this association included nearly all the major manufacturers of such machines; and the purpose of the agreement was to discontinue the manufacture and import of certain makes and models that had only a low energy efficiency, and to set a new target under which all machines produced in future would reach a particular level of efficiency through improved technology. The new, more efficient models would also reduce the amount of water required in each washing cycle. It was accepted that the agreement would in some ways narrow-down consumer choice and restrict competition. But it imposed no rules as to manufacturers pricing in future (indeed as costs might be increased by the arrangement, prices too might increase) nor for reduction of their output; but the agreement would have the benefit both of reducing customers' electricity bills and overall electricity demand.

In weighing the benefits of the agreement the following matters were taken into account:

- Energy consumption of the new models would be at least 15–20 per cent lower and would cause less pollution.

- The additional costs of machines would be recouped by the average domestic user between nine and fourteen months after purchase.

- All the restrictions were indispensable for the fulfilment of the objective benefits and it would not have been adequate simply to agree a target for the industry without the accompanying detailed restrictions.

- There was no elimination of competition, which was active in this market.

The period of exemption granted was four and a quarter years. This case proved a precedent for other related agreements relating to water heaters, household dishwashers and low-voltage motors used in a range of pumps and ventilators.[60] In each case the members of the association agreed to phase out production of the least efficient categories of machine, and thereby reduce overall electricity and water consumption by users. It will be interesting to see how the Community judicature will react to similar cases now that the 2004 Commission Guidelines appear to have narrowed the scope for the use of non-competition benefits in the application of Article 81(3).

4.6 BEER-SUPPLY CASES

A large number of exemption decisions have also been rendered in respect of bilateral agreements between United Kingdom brewers and their tenants, these having been notified in considerable numbers to the Commission during the 1990s. It

---

[59] [2000] OJ L187/47: [2000] 5 CMLR 635. Certain restrictions, e.g. as to exchange of information were held to fall outside Art. 81(1) altogether. See also the decision in *EACEM* [1998] OJ C12/2.

[60] [2001] 5 CMLR 1401, 1405.

was the argument of the tenants that many of such agreements (drawn up in almost entirely standard form) did not meet the requirements of the existing block exemption (No. 1984/83) and were therefore void. After considerable delays the Commission did eventually issue formal decisions providing individual exemptions for certain standard tenancy agreements of a number of British breweries. Following the start of litigation in which tenants claimed that the standard leases which they had signed with the breweries were void because they infringed Article 81(1), Whitbread, Bass, and Scottish & Newcastle notified their agreements to the Commission with a view to obtaining negative clearance or individual exemption.

The Commission first considered whether the agreements infringed Article 81. The principal restrictions were found to be the exclusive purchasing obligation and the 'beer tie' or non-compete clause, and these were found to have a considerable effect on the opportunities for other breweries to gain access to the retail market, given that such restrictions applied to about half the market by volume. The Commission went on to find that the agreements of each brewery made a significant contribution to this foreclosure effect, as the most recent UK retail market share figures showed shares of 6.12 per cent, 13.7 per cent, and 9.44 per cent respectively. Therefore both limbs of the *Delimitis* test were satisfied and there was an infringement of Article 81(1).

Because the agreements did not fit precisely within the terms of the block exemption in force at the time the Commission had to decide whether the conditions of Article 81(3) were satisfied. It held that although the tenants (with 'tied houses') paid higher prices for their beer than the so-called 'free houses', they benefited from compensating measures such as subsidized rents, bulk buying, and procurement services and other forms of financial and operational support. An individual exemption was granted to each brewery.[61]

4.7 HORTICULTURAL CASES

In more recent years the Commission also showed itself noticeably more willing to reach a finding that the effect of a notified agreement on competition had been insufficiently appreciable to bring Article 81(3) into play at all. The Commission was willing in such cases to give a formal or informal confirmation of a negative clearance, in some cases to the entire agreement, in others to important features of it. This for example was the outcome in *Sicasov*,[62] an application by an organization of French breeders of plant varieties and seeds for negative clearance or exemption for their standard-form agreements. Both Regulations and Directives had been made by the Community

---

[61] See the decisions of the Commission in *Whitbread* [1999] OJ L88/26: [1999] 5 CMLR 118; *Bass* [1999] OJ L186/1: [1999] 5 CMLR 782; and *Scottish & Newcastle* [1999] OJ L186/28: [1999] 5 CMLR 831. See also Case T-131/99 *Shaw and Falla* v. *Commission* [2002] ECR II-2023: [2002] 5 CMLR 81 and Case T-231/99 *Joynson* v. *Commission* [2002] ECR II-2085: [2002] 5 CMLR 123. Not all notified beer supply agreements, however, met the requirements of Art. 81(3), and a number of such notifications were withdrawn. See Case C-453/99 *Courage* v. *Crehan* [2001] ECR I-6297: [2001] 5 CMLR 28.

[62] [1999] OJ L4/27: [1999] 4 CMLR 192.

giving protection for individual plant varieties (broadly equivalent to patent protection) which laid down conditions for the production and marketing of seeds. Seeds had to be certified as to their identity and purity and could only be marketed if this had been done. A distinction was made between 'basic seed' used only for producing additional seed of a later generation and 'certified seed' (commercial seed intended for sale to farmers for sowing which could not normally however be used for the production of further seeds). The role of Sicasov in France was to manage its members' rights by granting licences for the reproduction and sale of plant breeders' rights and the marketing of seeds. The standard agreement contained restrictions on 'multipliers' who purchased basic seed from members of Sicasov preventing them from reselling such seeds to third parties outside France. This was a safeguard against possible technical mishandling of the seed. The restriction applied also to purchasers within France of basic seed from the original multiplier/purchaser; the multiplier was required to prevent purchasers of certified seed from using it as a 'basic seed' in their own country whose propagation rules may not have been as strict as those in France.

The export of 'certified seeds' from France could be banned under these agreements for four years from the date of original registration, though foreign purchasers could acquire them indirectly through intermediaries established in France; this export ban was held to be covered by Article 81(1) but nevertheless exemption was granted for a ten-year period. The benefit which the overall agreement provided was that it facilitated the dissemination of new varieties from France to other Member States by encouraging undertakings in those countries to accept the risks involved in marketing new varieties selected by French breeders, without having the concurrent risk of contending with the competition of direct exports from France by multipliers during the first years of trial. The four-year restriction on the sales of basic seed by such multipliers forced the multipliers to concentrate on the French market but, nevertheless, purchasers from such multipliers were able to acquire seed indirectly. The period of four years before the export ban was lifted was regarded by the Commission as a reasonable one to allow the establishment or dissemination of new varieties. It was noted that parallel imports from France through purchasers having branches or subsidiaries established in that country remained possible.

4.8 THE USE OF CONDITIONS

It is important to note when considering the practice of the Commission in this field, however, that a decision granting an exemption did not need to be absolute, but could be subject to a number of conditions. These could relate to the period of exemption, to supervision by the Commission, or to reporting and even attendance conditions. The exemption was normally for a fixed period, usually a minimum of three years and up to twelve or fifteen years. The supervision required by DG Comp varied according to the circumstances and could in some cases be limited to the simple provision of annual accounts by undertakings, or of lists of members in—or persons refused membership of—an association, ranging up to detailed review by the Commission of individual contracts or the business dealings of the parties exempted. Reporting requirements could be imposed on the working of particular aspects of an agreement and, as in the *IEA* case, the attendance of representatives of the Commission could be made a specific term of approval. In at least one case, *IBM*,[63] it was a condition of the settlement that the operation of the relevant business transactions of IBM were reported annually to the Commission, which enabled close contact to be maintained between the company's senior executives and the supervising officials of the Commission.

5. NULLITY: THE EFFECT OF ARTICLE 81(2)

5.1 THE SCOPE OF THE BASIC RULE

Between the basic rule of prohibition found in Article 81(1) and the exemption or 'non-applicability' provision of Article 81(3) lies the short and deceptively simple paragraph (2) which states that any 'agreements or decisions prohibited pursuant to this Article shall be automatically void'. For a considerable period neither the ECJ nor the CFI had, in spite of its importance as a matter of both national and Community law,[64] thrown light in any judgment on the correct approach to the interpretation of this paragraph. Finally, however, in *Courage* v. *Crehan*[65] the ECJ in an Article 234 reference from the English Court of Appeal confirmed the effect of this paragraph. The effect of the automatic nullity of an agreement which falls within the prohibition of Article 81(1), without benefiting from 81(3), is that the agreement has no effect as between the parties to it, nor can it be set up as a defence to a claim by third parties.[66] This principle has, of course, to be understood in the light of the earlier ruling in *Grundig* that, if severance of the clauses held void is possible under relevant national law, then only those clauses themselves rather than the entire agreement are unenforceable.

It is of course possible to conclude from the bare words of the text of Article 81(2) that the quality of voidness should apply to the entire agreement containing prohibited clauses, and this was the original attitude adopted by the Commission in the *Grundig* case. The Court however adopted a different interpretation, finding that those clauses of the agreement which did not contain restraints in breach of Article 81(1) were not rendered void either by the terms of Article 81(2) or Regulation 17.

---

[63] See Ch. 14, pp. 341–3, and the *14th Annual Report* (1984), pp. 77–9, and DG Comp Competition Policy Newsletter (1998) No. 3, pp. 7–11.

[64] As the European Court noted in Case C-126/97 *Ecco Swiss China Time* [1999] ECR I-3055: [2000] 5 CMLR 816, the importance of the Art. 81(1) prohibition for the functioning of the Common Market is such that the drafters of the Treaty attached a sanction of nullity to any practices that came under the scope of that provision.

[65] Case C-453/99, see fn. 61 above.

[66] See also Cases C-295-98/04 *Manfredi* [2006] ECR I-6619: [2006] 5 CMLR 980 at para. 57, citing the judgment of the Court in Case 22/71 *Béguelin* [1971] ECR 949: [1972] CMLR 81.

It is however for the national court to rule in each individual case whether it is possible for the contract to remain in being after removal, i.e. severance of the clauses held in breach of Article 81(1). Authority from the UK cases is limited but it appears that judges are often unwilling to make a finding that the inclusion in a contract of clauses of breach of Article 81(1) necessarily renders the whole agreement unenforceable. To reach such an unpalatable conclusion from the viewpoint of the parties seems to require a finding by the Court that as a result of the removal of the offending clauses the parties have been left with a contract so different from that with which they began their relationship it would be unconscionable to hold them to it. The main finding in *Courage*, however, was that the automatic invalidity imposed by paragraph (2) could not itself prevent an undertaking or person which is a party to such a contract from relying upon the contract and its illegal clauses in order to claim damages in the appropriate national court from the other party. Further discussion of this important case is found in Chapter 20 (pp. 540–2). An important question is what is the legal position if the parties to an agreement fail to raise in court the question of the application of Article 81 to contractual restrictions. The European Court has held in *Van Schijndel*[67] that the court hearing the case must of its own initiative raise the issue. Moreover, in *ECO Swiss* v. *Benetton*[68] the Court confirmed that, as Article 81 has direct application in national courts as a rule of public policy, an arbitrator must apply Article 81(2) so as to render an agreement or restriction prohibited by it unenforceable; and an award of damages made on the basis of such an agreement would therefore be a nullity, even if the issue was not raised by the party at the arbitration hearing or on appeal.

5.2 THE 'SHIMMERING' NATURE OF THE PROHIBITION

The effect therefore of *Courage* has been to overrule a number of Court of Appeal and High Court decisions in the UK where claims for damages have been made by parties to contracts containing restrictive clauses, many of which involved the brewers and their tenants. It does not however affect the outcome of another judgment given by the UK Court of Appeal as to the application of Article 81(2). In *Passmore* v. *Morland*,[69] Passmore had been a tenant of Inntrepreneur, a large national pub-owning company which entered into a long lease of the pub with Passmore containing the usual requirements that he purchase all his beer exclusively from Inntrepreneur. At some point in the tenancy Inntrepreneur transferred the lease to a much smaller brewery company with a *de minimis* share of the national beer market. Passmore sought to argue that the tie fell within Article 81(2) and therefore could not be enforced against him. The response of the new brewery landlord, Morland, was to argue that the prohibition in Article 81(2) is not a 'once for all' consequence but simply a provisional 'shimmering' prohibition, effective only so long as the economic circumstances of the agreement remain unchanged. Since the effect of the restrictive clause on the beer market once

[67] Case C-430/93 [1995] ECR I-4705: [1996] 1 CMLR 801.
[68] Case C-126/97 [1999] ECR I-3055.   [69] [1999] 3 All ER 1005: [1999] 1 CMLR 1129.

the tenancy was in the hands of Morland was not appreciable, Morland claimed that the enforceability of the contract was no longer an issue, even if this had been void under Article 81(1) at the time when it was originally granted.

The Court of Appeal agreed with the argument of Morland and logically it seems hard to fault. It raises however the possibility of difficult issues having to be resolved in future cases where, for example, either the relevant agreement has been transferred from one party to another, as in the *Passmore* case, or even when the agreement has remained between the original parties but where their relative bargaining position and other economic circumstances changed, so that the Court may find itself imposing the finding of nullity at a later stage in the performance of the contract even though, at the time it was made, no finding of nullity would have been appropriate. The Court of Appeal was considerably influenced by the fact that Article 81 is essentially dealing with the 'effects' of particular contracts that may restrict competition, which may later change, rather than with their legal form which remains unaltered.

FURTHER READING

H. R. BASRAN, 'How should Article 81 Address Agreements that Yield Environmental Benefits' [2006] ECLR 479.

B. HAWK, 'System Failure: Vertical Restraints and EC Competition Law' [1995] 32 CMLRev 973.

L. KJØLBYE, 'The New Commission Guidelines on the Application of Article 81(3): an Economic Approach to Article 81' [2004] 25 ECLR 566.

P. LUGARD and L. HANCHER, 'Honey, I Shrunk the Article! A Critical Assessment of the Commission's Notice on Article 81(3) of the EC Treaty' [2004] 25 ECLR 410.

O. ODUDU, 'Article 81(3), Discretion and Direct Effect' [2002] 23 ECLR 17.

B. SUFRIN, 'The Evolution of Article 81(3) of the EC Treaty' [2006] 51 *Antitrust Bull* 915.

9

HORIZONTAL AGREEMENTS: CARTELS

1. INTRODUCTION

1.1 CATEGORIES OF HORIZONTAL AGREEMENTS

At first sight any horizontal agreement between undertakings which are actual, or at least, potential competitors to each other would seem less likely to escape prohibition under Article 81(1) than those agreements which are vertical, where the function of the parties are complementary to each other.[1] Nevertheless, there is an important distinction to be drawn at the outset between two principal categories of horizontal agreements.

The first of these categories is where the agreement has a primary objective which is not substantially anti-competitive, even though its detailed terms may include restrictions possibly falling within the range covered by Article 81(1). It includes agreements for cooperation and specialization, sharing research and development, establishing industry standards, and also some types of joint venture. The task for DG Comp with this category, if the requirements of a particular block exemption are not met, is to analyse the alleged benefits arising from the agreement and the extent to which they are, in turn, likely to be passed on to consumers—while at the same time considering whether the anti-competitive restrictions are no more widely drawn than necessary for its objectives to be obtained.

The second category is the agreement whose primary objective is the reduction or elimination of competition between the parties, the protection of existing market positions, or the prevention of a feared deterioration. It may be brought on by other causes such as shortages, lack of demand, or simply lack of confidence in the future of the industry in a competitive environment. Cartels and market-sharing agreements are often found here, sometimes as a response to over-capacity in a sector where demand has fallen substantially and is unlikely to revive. Often the enforcement of this kind of agreement is marked by machinery for tight control with sanctions to ensure that all participants stay in line. External and internal influences on individual members

---

[1] Chs. 10 and 11 deal with vertical agreements for distribution; Ch. 12 with vertical agreements involving licensing of intellectual property rights.

of the cartel may mean that they are fragile and in time either collapse completely or become only partially effective. Sometimes a cartel arises largely from corporate greed in an attempt to extract more from the customers of the industry than would be paid under competitive conditions.

1.2 THE APPROACH OF THE COMMISSION TO CARTELS

Cartels are most often found in respect of products which are standard commodities, such as sugar, cement, steel, and basic chemicals, where price is the principal criterion for competition, though the recent experience of the Commission shows that they can spring up in an almost infinitely wide variety of markets. The OECD has played a leading role in coordinating the activities of the competition authorities in its Member States in combating such arrangements. Although there were important cartel cases in the early years of the Treaty of Rome, it is since the 1990s that investigation by the Commission has been substantially increased and accompanied by an important change in strategy. One of the principal problems in establishing the existence of cartels has always been that of obtaining the necessary evidence against the participants, who will normally have taken careful steps to conceal their activities even if these have not always been totally successful. Although additional resources had been allocated by the Commission to pursue cartels as early as the 1980s, the need to establish sufficient evidence in respect of such concerted practices and agreements led to a major change of strategy in the 1990s, which has considerably improved the record of the Commission in successfully finding and punishing such arrangements.

Of course, many types of horizontal agreements contain clauses embodying restraints of trade to which Article 81(1) may apply. Sometimes, as discussed in Chapter 7, a restraint of trade is merely a minor (indeed a normal) element in a routine contract: for example, the sale of an existing business including its goodwill. The covenant restraining the subsequent trading activities of the vendor may be strictly ancillary to the need of the purchaser to protect the goodwill sold under the agreement. However, in most cases coming before the Commission for individual exemption the anti-competitive restraint plays a more significant part. The analysis of such restraints has to be thorough, probing, and sensitive to the nuances and special circumstances of particular industries. The parties may seek to conceal a naked cartel in the fine clothes of what appears to be a legitimate trade association or creative joint venture—the officials of DG Comp have to be ready and able to distinguish substance from surface. This chapter examines next some examples from the first category of agreements, those having a primarily defensive quality, and then considers some of the leading cases where Article 81(1) has been applied by the Commission and the Courts. The Commission has, since the end of the 1980s, taken a more vigorous approach towards major cartels. It has found additional resources for conducting such cases, often difficult to complete—with their many defendants and a complex web of evidence spanning a number of years. It has established a unit within DG Comp to specialize in this kind of case and this has achieved some notable successes in identifying breaches of Article 81 and imposing heavy fines in a number of such cases.

The Article itself provides examples of the kind of agreement which will normally fall within its prohibition; however, it provides little assistance as to the basis upon which the benefits and burdens of the restraints are to be assessed, referring simply to certain general types of agreement. Whilst it is sometimes possible to allocate notified agreements neatly within these headings, there is little value in trying to do so in every case since many agreements fall within more than one category.

2. PRICE-FIXING AND MARKET-SHARING AGREEMENTS

2.1 EARLY CASES

Category (a) in Article 81(1) refers to agreements which 'directly or indirectly fix purchase or selling prices or any other trading condition'. We know from *Italy* v. *Council and Commission*[2] that both horizontal and vertical agreements fall within the prohibition. Clearly, however, category (a) deals primarily with agreements or concerted practices made between horizontally related competitors on prices to be charged, markets to be allocated, or conditions of sale to be applied. It could also apply to such agreements between rival manufacturers to enforce resale price maintenance within a particular sector, or even to an agreement between a manufacturer and a distributor or dealer requiring resale price maintenance over sales by the latter. One of the earliest cases on horizontal cartels within category (a) dealt with by the Commission (whose decision was later upheld by the Court) was that of the *Quinine Cartel*.[3]

The participants in this cartel were companies in France, Germany, and Holland. The companies were engaged in the sale of quinine, used for making medicines to treat malaria, and also in synthetic quinidine, an ingredient for making other medicines. Both products are obtained from cinchoma bark, which grows in a number of third-world countries. Cooperation between the companies in the European industry dated back to 1913 when agreements were made in an attempt to stabilize market conditions for the supply of the raw material. After the Second World War, new plantations of cinchoma were established in Congo and Indonesia; supplies of the bark then rose steadily, with the result that by 1958 prices had reached a lower level than had prevailed twenty years before. At the same time the US government elected to dispose of surplus held by the General Services Administration (GSA) at auction, having accumulated

---

[2] Case 32/65 [1966] ECR 389: [1969] CMLR 39.

[3] Case 45/69 *Boehringer Mannheim* v. *Commission* [1970] ECR 769; [1972] CMLR D121. UK companies were mentioned in the report as participating in the agreement, but were not proceeded against by the Commission. The Commission's decision is reported at [1969] CMLR D41.

very large stocks over the previous year. In the face of this unstable market situation, the defendant companies decided in 1958 to put together a defensive cartel, involving collaboration on the prices to be paid for the bark, the allocation of purchases of the GSA stockpile, and the protection of individual national markets for their respective national producers. It was also decided that particular export markets would be reserved for particular companies, and that quotas would be allocated in respect of those markets when they were permitted to 'compete' there.

The original agreement was for a period of five years and, in order that compliance with the agreement could be policed, members had to notify each other of their quarterly sales and prices. If a company was unable to reach its quota for export sales, compensating sales would then have to be made to other members which would be supervised by the Dutch company (Nedchem) which took prime responsibility for administration of the cartel and for the enforcement of restrictions on the manufacture of quinidine by companies other than the German and Dutch participants.

Some of these arrangements were contained in so-called 'export agreements' and others in so-called 'gentlemen's agreements'. Although the Common Market was excluded from the scope of the export agreement, in practice all companies set their Common Market prices on the basis of those charged for exports outside the Market so that, as a result of the arrangements, pricing effects were felt within Europe. Market prices within Europe at the time were generally higher than those in world markets. Later in 1961, a buying pool was set up to stabilize the cost of the cinchoma bark and quotas were allocated. The evidence in the case deals interestingly with the reaction of the participants to the entry into force of the Treaty of Rome. They had to decide whether to notify the agreements, terminate them, or keep them in existence secretly. They determined to amend the agreements slightly, but to keep them in force without notification to the Commission. Subsequently market conditions changed sharply as bark supplies were reduced, and the prices charged by all companies rose substantially. A contributing factor was the demand by the United States Defence Department for use in Vietnam during the early 1960s. The arrangement eventually came to an end in 1965.

The Commission had imposed substantial fines on the participants, and these were only slightly reduced on appeal to the European Court, on the basis of a finding as to the period during which the principal agreement had affected the market price within the industry. The Court made it clear, however, that it would not accept any legalistic distinctions between the effects of the export agreement and those of the gentlemen's agreement, and stated that it regarded both as a single set of concerted practices.

We saw in Chapter 6 that the definition of 'concerted practices' lay at the heart of the next important horizontal cartel case decided by the Court: the *Dyestuffs* case.[4] Undoubtedly, the evidence was more circumstantial than in the *Quinine Cartel* case, and in particular the proof of concerted practices between the dyestuffs manufacturers depended largely on inferences drawn from the similarities of price increases and subsequent retraction of individual increases as a response to withdrawals of the

---

[4] Cases 48, 49, 51–7/69 *ICI and Others* v. *Commission* [1972] ECR 619: [1972] CMLR 55.

increases by other parties to the agreement. As with quinine, the dyestuffs agreement was intended both to protect national markets from outside intervention and to maintain price levels generally. The number of companies engaged in the Common Market in the dyestuffs business was relatively small (probably less than a dozen) but all were of a very substantial size, and the nature of the market was distinctly oligopolistic. Whereas *Quinine* had dealt with a small number of related medicinal products, dyestuffs manufacturers produced between them several thousand different dyes, with a large variety of different customers having slightly different needs. The manufacturers considered it essential to maintain control of their local markets by ensuring that local national producers maintained direct contact with all their large national customers, being attentive to their needs and having natural advantages of location and nationality over foreign producers, who were likely to be represented locally only by subsidiaries, representatives, or agents who could not give the same complete service as the local manufacturers. The price of dye is only a small element in the total price of clothing and other items to which it is applied; therefore the market was not very price elastic, quality of service counting for much in the competitive process. Each leading manufacturer within its own country tended to behave as a price leader, but always faced the risk that undertakings from outside the country would make a positive effort to penetrate the national market by selective price cutting. The purpose of the cartel was to remove this risk.

In its judgment, the Court considered the need for competition in such markets against the perceived needs and wishes of the producers for stability. With regard to the former, it stated that:

the function of competition in relation to prices is to maintain prices at the lowest possible level, and to encourage the movement of products between Member States so as to permit an optimum sharing out of activities on the basis of productivity and the adaptive capacity of undertakings. The variation of price rates encourages the pursuit of one of the essential aims of the Treaty, namely the inter-penetration of national markets, and hence the direct access of consumers to the sources of production of the whole Community.

However, the purpose of the cartel was deliberately designed to counter these aims:

in these circumstances, having regard to the characteristics of the market in these products, the behaviour of the applicant, in conjunction with other undertakings...was designed to substitute for the risks of competition, and the hazards of their spontaneous reactions, a co-operation which amounts to a concerted practice prohibited by Article 81(1) of the Treaty.

The manufacturers argued that uniform price changes in 1964, 1965, and 1967 were the result of price leadership by different undertakings making their choice of pricing policies, which in turn produced a response required to maintain the equilibrium between the major manufacturers. The weakness in this explanation of the conduct of the parties was pointed out by Advocate General Mayras, namely that while such equilibrium could perhaps have explained a downward adjustment of price to keep in line with the price leadership, it was less probable that substantial parallel increases would be explained in this way, especially when there were so many different varieties of dyestuffs at such a range of prices.

Elimination of the risks of competition lies at the heart of many horizontal cartels. It was central to the *Sugar Cartel* case,[5] though here the factual complexities were compounded by the Commission's decision to proceed under both Articles 81 and 82, because some European sugar producers had engaged in unilateral action to protect or extend dominance within specific Member States (or important regions of Member States), quite apart from the concerted practices adopted by the parties with a view to protecting national markets and price levels. The European Court judgment considered each of these geographical markets in turn and (as in the *Dyestuffs* case) found that the principle of *chacun chez soi* (to each his own) dominated the attitude of the participants. The lengthy judgment takes us through a variety of individual national or regional markets, examining the evidence to an extent, at the time, unique for the European Court. Italy had proved a special case, where the degree of government intervention meant that the residual element left for restraints of competition by arrangement between the sugar companies was so limited that it was not sufficient to affect competition to an extent that would constitute a breach of Article 81.[6] In the remaining jurisdictions, the position was that whilst Common Market agricultural policy, including the intervention and target prices set for producers, provided the background to the arrangements, there was still considerable scope for competition between them. There was indeed a considerable surplus of sugar production over demand within the Common Market. France and Belgium, in particular, had surplus capacity and in a freer market would have been able to sell substantial quantities to major end-users and sugar brokers or wholesalers within the Community; there were also collusive arrangements for obtaining tenders for sales into export where export refunds were available from the Commission to cover the difference between world prices and Community prices. The purpose and the effect of the cartel was to restrain the degree to which sugar was bought and sold across national boundaries within the Common Market and to allocate the export sales between the participants.

In giving strong support to most of the Commission's findings in these important cases early in the history of the Community's competition policy, the Court gave an important boost to the confidence of the Commission in preparing and bringing substantial cartel cases. The wide definition which the Court was prepared to give to concerted practices, and its willingness to take a broad view of the exercise of the Commission's discretion in reaching conclusions from the evidence available, encouraged the Commission to bring other cases of similar magnitude in following years. Such cases often require several years' investigation and preparation before decisions can be issued.

2.2 LEADING CASES OF THE 1980S

The 1980s brought several important cases. In the *Peroxygen* case,[7] European hydrogen peroxyde producers were found to have participated for several years in an allocation

---

[5] Cases 40–8, 50, 54, 56, 111, 113, 114/73 *Suiker Unie* v. *Commission* [1975] ECR 1663: [1976] 1 CMLR 295.
[6] See Ch. 7, p. 117.   [7] [1985] OJ L35/1: [1985] 1 CMLR 481.

of markets which (as in *Sugar* and *Dyestuffs*) gave preference to home producers on their own national markets. As a result prices for these products were kept at a higher level than would have prevailed under competitive conditions. There were arrangements for meetings between the companies to settle any disputes about the allocation of territories or about sales made over quota. Production and sales details were also freely exchanged between companies so that the operation of the cartel could be easily controlled. The Commission pointed out in its decision that if the parties were prepared to take such trouble to enter into and maintain such arrangements, and to concert their policies and practices so as to produce such convenient results, it could be presumed that they believed it gave them an actual trading benefit. Therefore, the mere fact that the end result in terms of prices might be much the same as could have been expected from an oligopolistic market without the exchange of information would not itself provide any defence to a claim under Article 81(1).

In the *Aluminium Cartel* case,[8] the Commission had the opportunity to consider a particularly long-lived arrangement between several European and North American producers between 1963 and 1976. The object here was not to protect individual home markets for specific companies but to protect Western markets generally from supplies of aluminium ingot produced in Eastern Europe, which could have undercut Western producers on a price basis and force world prices down if released onto the market without control. To prevent this, Western producers arranged through a broker, Brandeis Goldschmidt and Co. Ltd and its Swiss subsidiary, that all the Eastern European production would be purchased by this broker, who would then allocate it to the participants in the cartel, in a ratio corresponding to the share of each in Western European sales. To disguise the source of the metal, and in order to check whether the Eastern Bloc countries still managed to export any metal direct to the West, all participants agreed that the Eastern metal purchased through Brandeis Goldschmidt would not be resold outside the cartel until it had been melted down.[9]

Many aluminium producers are also engaged in the production of semi-manufactured items such as aluminium plates, sheets, strips, and foil (known generally as rolled products) as well as rods and sections, tubes, and wire (known as extruded or drawn products). Those remaining manufacturers of aluminium products without access to the raw material of aluminium ingot, and who wished to produce semi-manufactured or manufactured items (rolled or extruded) in aluminium, were heavily dependent upon the integrated producers for their supplies; this control enabled the integrated producers within the cartel to increase substantially the prices they charged for semi-manufactured products. Moreover, the parties in the cartel did all they could to prevent aluminium being traded freely or quoted on the London Metal Exchange, since this again could have weakened the effect of the main agreement by introducing greater volatility to prices. The agreement had a substantial impact on competition in

---

[8] [1985] OJ L92/1: [1987] 3 CMLR 813. See also the *14th Annual Report* (1984), pp. 58–9 and Ch. 21, p. 561.

[9] Technical arguments were raised by the participants that the metal from Eastern Bloc sources had to be mixed with other aluminium of a higher grade before commercial use.

Western Europe, directly affecting the price of between 13 and 20 per cent of the total consumption in that territory. No fines were imposed by the Commission, allegedly for technical reasons relating to the age of the agreement, and this no doubt influenced the decision of the participants not to appeal.

In the late 1980s there were several important cases involving the great majority of large chemical producers in Western Europe, where it was alleged that price cartels had existed and that important production information had been exchanged by the manufacturers of polypropylene, polyvinylchloride (PVC), and low-density polyethylene (LDPE) respectively. In each of these cases[10] the Commission imposed substantial fines on participants; regular meetings of the leading producers were proved, though clearly there were both 'leaders' and 'followers' in respect of each product, and not all producers were always as closely involved in the industry's continuing efforts to protect its price levels against the background of oversupply and excessive production capacity. Uniform price increases and closely matching list prices appeared to be the outcome of these arrangements. The individual cases were taken on appeal to the Court of First Instance and subsequently on legal issues to the European Court itself.[11] It would be wrong, though understandable, to assume that agreements affecting the price to be paid for raw materials will always be struck down under Article 81(1) by the Commission. The agreement may satisfy the Article 81(3) conditions if there are any compensating advantages which relate to improvement of production or distribution and where consequent benefits arise not only for the participants but also for purchasers and consumers. The *National Sulphuric Acid Association* decision of the Commission[12] is an example. Sulphur in solid form is heavy and expensive to transport from the United States, where almost all of it is produced. Manufacturers of sulphuric acid in the United Kingdom had formed a buying pool for sulphur, which nearly all the producers within the United Kingdom had joined. The existence of the buying pool had made it much easier for substantial dock installations to be built in England enabling sulphur to be imported by tankers in liquid form, enabling the smaller undertakings within the pool to receive small loads at convenient ports; the agreement also enabled the price of sulphuric acid to be reduced and continuity of supplies protected. However, the Commission successfully objected to restrictions in the original agreement imposed on resales to non-members and against use being made of the sulphur for other than acid-making purposes. Moreover, the members of the pool were not obliged under the amended agreement to take more than 25 per cent of their total needs from the pool, whereas this figure had originally been 100 per cent.

[10] The original Commission decisions were *PVC Cartel* [1989] OJ L74/1: [1990] 4 CMLR 345; *LDPE Cartel* [1989] OJ L74/21: [1990] 4 CMLR 382; and *Polypropylene Cartel* [1986] OJ L230/1: [1988] 4 CMLR 347.

[11] See, for example, Case T-7/89 Hercules v. *Commission (Polypropylene)* [1991] ECR II-1711: [1992] 4 CMLR 84 and, on appeal, Case C-51/92P *Hercules* v. *Commission* [1999] ECR I-4235: 5 CMLR 976. The *PVC Cartel (No. 1)* decision of the Commission was later annulled by the ECJ on procedural grounds, but a subsequent Commission decision (*PVC Cartel (No. 2)*) was upheld by the CFI in Cases T-305–7, 313–16, 318, 325, 328–9, and 335/94 *Limburgse Vinyl* v. *Commission* [1999] ECR II-931: [1999] 5 CMLR 303.

[12] [1980] OJ L260/24: [1980] 3 CMLR 429. The UK 'buying pool' had been upheld by the UK Restrictive Practices Court under the Restrictive Practices Acts. See *National Sulphuric Acid Association's Agreement* [1963] 3 All ER 73: LR 4 RP 169 and [1966] LR 6 RP 210.

In practice some 30 per cent of the sulphuric acid produced by pool members was sold to third parties and competition between members of the pool was thus maintained. The terms of the final agreement, whilst maintaining the essential advantages of the pool, limited the restrictions contained in it to those which the Commission found to be necessary for its objects to be achieved. The result might have been different had the buying pool given the buyers disproportionate market power over the sellers.

2.3 A NEW COMMISSION APPROACH—THE LENIENCY NOTICES

It is however during the second half of the 1990s that the campaign on cartels began to achieve a succession of important victories and in which a change of strategy by the Commission has played an ever-increasing role, starting with the *Cartonboard* case.[13] Cartonboard is manufactured in large mills and sold to converters who transform it into folding cartons for use in food and other industries. Over the period 1982 to 1991 some twenty-three companies in Scandinavia and Western Europe had met regularly as 'the Product Group Paper Board' to discuss market shares and production quotas. Regular price rises were implemented every six months and confidential information exchanged. The results of this concertation was that the parties' market shares remained stable and prices, following annual rises of between 6 and 10 per cent, stayed well above those that would have existed if true competition had prevailed, even at times when raw material prices were falling. The minutes of the Product Group Paper Board and its various sub-committees which enforced the cartel provided convincing evidence of the existence of the agreements and concerted practices, both by their contents and significant omissions.

The Commission's ability to acquire relevant evidence in this case was substantially assisted by the fact that one of the participants, Stora, cooperated with them from an early stage. Stora none the less received a substantial fine at the conclusion of the case, though it would have been still higher absent its cooperation. Following this case the Commission issued a Notice in July 1996 making official its policy towards 'whistle-blowers' in this type of case, previously dealt with only unofficially. Three levels of cooperation with the Commission were officially identified:

- an undertaking which was the first to provide full and documentary evidence of a cartel *before* DG Comp had started its own investigation and which immediately ceased participation in it could benefit by a reduction of between 75 to 100 per cent of the potential fine

- an undertaking which acted in this way *after* the Commission's investigation had begun could benefit by a reduction of between 50 to 75 per cent of the potential fine

- other undertakings providing co-operation at a later stage could benefit from a reduction of between 10 to 50 per cent of the potential fine.

---

[13] [1994] OJ L243/1: [1994] 5 CMLR 547.

The number of cartels involving major companies discovered and against whom decisions were reached under Article 81 rose sharply towards the end of the twentieth century. Such decisions were given in a wide variety of sectors including lysine and amino acids, graphite electrodes, vitamins, citric acid, sodium gluconate, zinc phosphate, heating pipes, banking, breweries, carbonless paper, sugar, and airlines. A number of these cases were not merely European in their scope but arose after successful investigations by the Department of Justice or Federal Trade Commission in the United States. Once the proceedings had been completed in the United States the information available in the public domain was normally sufficient that the parties did not seek to contest cases brought consequentially under Article 81, even if in some cases they refused to waive rights of confidentiality in respect of all matters uncovered in the US investigations. An influential part of the practice of the US authorities was the application of the principles of immunity and leniency offered to those undertakings prepared to break ranks with their fellow members and disclose details of the restrictive agreement at a sufficiently early stage in the enquiries.

But it soon became apparent that the original 1996 Notice required revision. It is true that in statistical terms the Notice had proved successful. It had been applied in some sixteen cases and over eighty companies had sought to benefit from its terms. Reductions in fines on undertakings found to have been engaged in cartels had amounted to some 1,400 million euros with reductions ranging from 100 per cent in certain cases to 10 per cent in cases where the information was provided only at a late stage and after pressure from the Commission. The exercise by the Commission of its discretion under the Notice, in respect of the contribution made to the resolution of the case by the disclosures of individual undertakings in this way, was upheld by the Court of First Instance in more than one case.

Nevertheless in spite of this degree of success the Commission learnt from experience that the Notice did not always produce results as satisfactory as might have been hoped. Undertakings apparently felt that the degree to which their cooperation with the Commission would secure a substantial reduction in those fines was uncertain; the evidence provided had to be decisive and supplied before any other undertaking within the cartel had revealed it. Nor was the full benefit of the Notice available to any company which had been a ringleader, i.e. had played a determining role within it. These uncertainties meant that much of the information provided to the Commission came too late in the case to have much 'added value'.

For these reasons the revised Notice of 2002[14] gave, by way of incentive, yet larger rewards to the undertaking which first brought the existence of the cartel to the attention of the Commission. The Notice also tried to make the reduction in fines obtainable by other participants more closely related to the value of their cooperation. Immunity from fines—rather than a mere reduction on the level of fines—was made available to the *first* company to approach the Commission in respect of the particular cartel.

---

[14] [2002] OJ C45/3. An explanatory article can be found in DG Comp Competition Policy Newsletter [2002] No. 2, pp. 15–22.

However, in order to qualify for immunity, the evidence which this company had to bring had either to enable the Commission:

(a) to carry out an investigation under Article 14(3) of Regulation 17/62 (now Article 20(4) of Regulation 1/2003) or

(b) to find an infringement of Article 81(1).

Under the 2002 Notice, therefore, two different situations could lead to the grant of immunity. The Commission could be totally unaware of the existence of a cartel and the information provided to it under (a), while insufficient to enable it to make a finding of a breach of the Article, could yet be reliable enough for it to launch a successful 'dawn raid'. On the other hand under (b), the Commission may have already carried out a 'dawn raid' without finding sufficient incriminating material, but is then enabled by the information provided to move to a finding under Article 81. Immunity could however only be given to the first company to contact the Commission and the company must continue to cooperate genuinely throughout the course of the case. The mere fact of being a 'ringleader' did not automatically block a claim for immunity, so long as no coercion was used to induce other companies to take part in the arrangements (though the establishment of such matters will always be a difficult question of proof). A decision to grant immunity would normally be available from the Commission within a few weeks of receipt of the original disclosure.

For those companies which did not qualify for immunity, which were of course necessarily the majority of participants in the cartel, a revised leniency tariff was still available. The criterion applied by the Commission was whether the information provided had significant 'added value', and the greater reductions went to those first to reach the Commission with their evidence. Tariffs were from a 30–50 per cent reduction in fine for the first company in this category, 20–30 per cent for the next and only up to 20 per cent for any subsequent providers of such information.[15]

In 2006, the Commission adopted the current Leniency Notice[16] which reflects the essential features of the 2002 Leniency Notice but also introduces some small changes. In particular, it sets out in greater detail the kind of information and evidence that an undertaking must submit in order to benefit from immunity.[17] Furthermore, it introduces a discretionary 'marker' system, which allows an applicant for immunity to secure a place in the queue by submitting only limited information about the cartel at first. This permits the applicant to gather all the information and evidence necessary to meet the relevant immunity threshold at a later stage.[18] Finally, and in order to protect the effectiveness of the leniency programme, the Notice lays down the protection from disclosure that is available to corporate statements submitted by undertakings

---

[15] For a recent example of a cartel where fines were reduced for two participants under the terms of the 2002 Leniency Notice, see the Decision of the Commission of 20 October 2005 in the *Italian Raw Tobacco cartel* (Case COMP/C.38.281/B.2).

[16] [2006] OJ C/298/11.   [17] See paras. 8–11 of the 2006 Notice.

[18] See paras. 14–15 of the 2006 Notice.

applying for leniency.[19] This protection is based on the fact that undertakings may be less than willing to provide information to the Commission if this can later be used in civil proceedings against them before national courts. The recent 2008 Commission White Paper on Damages[20] has recognized the importance of maintaining a balance between guaranteeing the attractiveness of leniency programmes and encouraging a culture of private enforcement of the Competition rules before national courts.[21] To achieve this, it suggests not only the protection of corporate statements submitted by applicants for leniency under EC *and* national leniency programmes but also the limitation of the civil liability of a successful applicant for immunity to claims submitted by his direct and indirect contractual partners.[22] Thus, the White Paper proposes that a successful applicant for immunity should remain liable in a civil action brought by those injured parties but not in relation to damage suffered by other victims of the cartel.

3. CARTELS INVOLVING SHIPPING LINES

In Chapter 7 (at p. 135) reference was made to a block exemption from Article 81(1) found in Council Regulation 4056/86.[23] This block exemption applied only however to certain categories of agreements between ship-owners operating as a liner conference on specific routes under which the same tariff is applied to each freight shipper. It had no application if there was discrimination in rates charged, nor to passenger services. A number of shipping conferences were subsequently found to have been operating cartels as to prices and capacities on particular routes which did not comply with the block exemption. The Commission therefore brought proceedings against a number of them. In 1992 fines were imposed against members of the *French/West African Ship Owners Conference*[24] for activities falling outside those permitted by the Regulation. Under arrangements between members of these Conferences, all commodities travelling between France and the eleven West and Central African States involved were allocated: 40 per cent to French companies, which had a fixed percentage of that amount, 40 per cent to African companies, and 20 per cent to others. Any cargo for which a line had insufficient capacity could be transferred only to other members of the Conferences. The effect of these arrangements was that the French companies were able to carry the majority of the cargoes on these routes, against the intention of the UNCTAD Code of Conduct for Liner Conferences which sought to

---

[19] See paras. 31–5 of the 2006 Notice.

[20] COM (2008) 165. The White Paper was published on 3 April 2008 together with a Staff Working Paper (SEC (2008) 404) which provided a full commentary of the initiatives suggested in the White Paper.

[21] On damages actions before national courts, see Ch. 20.

[22] See the 2008 White Paper on Damages at para. 2.9 and Ch. 10 of the Staff Working Paper.

[23] This Regulation has now been repealed by Reg. 1419/2006 (see Ch. 7, p. 135).

[24] [1992] OJ L134/1: [1993] 5 CMLR 446.

guarantee for carriers from developing countries a greater percentage of the markets previously dominated by carriers from the developed world; such arrangements were not within the scope of the exemption in Regulation 4056/82. None of the requirements for individual exemption under Article 81(3) were satisfied.

The Commission has also taken action against multi-modal price-fixing by such Conferences. This practice arises because shippers of goods prefer to obtain a single quotation for the cost of sending goods from A to B, covering the overland journeys as well as the sea voyage itself. Liner conferences have therefore been giving quotations, and agreeing rates with other members of Conferences for covering the entire route, not simply the sea voyage. Later in 1994 the Commission reached its first decision in this area, against the *Far Eastern Freight Conference*,[25] imposing a nominal fine on fourteen undertakings for breaches of Regulation 1017/68 relating to price-fixing for road and rail transport routes. The Commission claimed that exemption could not apply to such an arrangements because the existence of such land tariffs limited competition between the shipping lines to provide the best and cheapest service on those routes; the more competitive shipping companies were, because of the arrangements, unable to offer better terms to shippers, which in turn affected the trade carried on at particular Community ports. No member of a Conference was contractually obliged to quote only the rates set by the Conference but in practice it would normally follow the tariff recommendation of the Conference. An appeal to the Court of First Instance[26] was unsuccessful. The Court held that there was no evidence that the fixing of rates for inland transport would actually improve the stability of the shipping business, and the restrictions on competition which the agreement imposed were not indispensable in any case to its ostensible objectives.

A similar case was brought against the Transatlantic Agreement operated by members of the relevant shipping Conferences leading to a further decision in October 1994.[27] The Association here provided rules for establishing freight rates on services contracts under which customers undertook to ship a minimum quantity over a given period in exchange for a discounted freight rate and on a capacity management programme, designed to limit the supply of transport in order to stabilize the market; these freight rates related to inter-modal transport as well as to maritime freight. Following the decision the members of the Conference applied to the Court of First Instance[28] for interim measures pending the hearing of a full appeal; the Conference members claimed that their inability to fix jointly their inter-modal rates as in the past would lead to a collapse in maritime transport rates generally, which could affect the regularity of service so that some carriers would actually have to terminate operating their lines. On this occasion the Court ruled that the immediate application of the Commission decision risked such serious and irreparable damage to the shipping

---

[25] [1994] OJ L378/17.

[26] Case T-86/95 *Compagnie Générale Maritime* v. *Commission* [2002] ECR II-1011: [2002] 4 CMLR 1115.

[27] (1994) OJ L267/1.

[28] Cases T-395/94R [1995] ECR II-2895: [1997] 5 CMLR 195 and C-149/95P (R) [1995] ECR I- 2165: [1997] 5 CMLR 167.

lines that the balance of interest required that its operation be suspended, insofar as it prohibited them from jointly exercising rate-making authority for the inland portions of intermodal transport services. The substantive appeal was eventually heard by the CFI, where the Commission's findings were upheld, save in one minor respect.[29]

4. CRISIS CARTELS

The effect of many of the agreements referred to so far could have been to 'limit or control production', within the terms of Article 81(1)(b). Perhaps the clearest example of agreements that have this effect directly are so-called 'crisis cartels' whose participants agree to close down part of their productive capacity in the event that demand falls so far that normal competition is thought to be impossible. This arises because of the disparity between the total productive capacity of the industry and the actual demand for output of those factories. Without some form of industry-wide agreement the weaker units in the sector may close down altogether, leaving only a small number of active undertakings, leading inevitably to a sharp increase in unemployment and social dislocation.

Under normal economic theory, the productive capacity of such an industry would have to decline to the point where it matched available demand, notwithstanding the painful nature of that transition period. The Treaty of Rome came into being at a time when economic expansion seemed set to continue indefinitely, and no qualifying clauses limit the operation of Article 81 in the event of such crises arising. The agreement entered into to mitigate the effect of such substantial falls in demand would be essentially 'defensive', rather than creative, and therefore open to suspicion. Moreover, it was not immediately apparent how the four conditions could be applied without considerable strain upon their language. In particular, it was difficult to see how a crisis cartel could be shown to 'improve the production or distribution of goods' or 'promote technical or economic progress' if consumers had to receive a fair share of the resulting benefit. The furthest that the Commission went during the first years of its operation was to reduce or dispense with fines in cases where proven agreements or concerted practices were made during crises in various industries affected by major recession in demand, such as iron and steel, lead, glass, and cement.

The continuation of the recession through the late 1970s eventually led to a reconsideration of policy which surfaced officially in the *12th Annual Report*,[30] in which the Commission gave guidance on how far solutions for restructuring individual industries were compatible with Article 81. The Commission defined the situation in which it would tolerate restructuring agreements, but not in the form of official notices, of the kind issued in respect of commercial agencies and subcontracting on earlier

---

[29] Case T-395/94 *Atlantic Container Line* v. *Commission* [2002] ECR II-875: [2002] 4 CMLR 1008.

[30] (1982), pp. 43–5, where the issues that such cases place before the Commission are well stated. A more recent statement of the Commission's attitude is found in the *23rd Annual Report* (1993), pp. 47–50.

occasions, nor in the form of a block exemption, as this would have required preparation of a draft whose content would have posed particular difficulties and which would in any case have been subject to the usual extended consultation. The announcement in the *12th Annual Report* was on a more informal basis, indicating that the Commission's approach was to treat such agreements more generously, and providing guidelines to alert those preparing such agreements to the limitations the Commission would impose upon them.

The minimum requirement laid down by the Commission for this kind of agreement was that a structural overcapacity must be shown to exist which had caused all the undertakings concerned, over a prolonged period, a significant reduction in their rate of capacity utilization leading to a drop in output accompanied by substantial operating losses with no expectation of lasting improvement in the medium term. The conditions upon which the Commission would insist before granting exemption for an agreement containing mutual reductions in capacity and output would include the following:

(a) the reduction in overcapacity must be permanent and irreversible and of an amount which would enable the existing participants in the industry to compete at this lower level of capacity[31]

(b) the cutback must facilitate moves to specialization by individual companies

(c) the timing of the reduction in capacity must be carried out so as to minimize the social dislocation caused by the inevitable loss of employment.

Since the first announcement of the policy change, there have been a number of decisions by the Commission permitting agreements in this category. A leading example is the *Synthetic Fibres* case.[32] The companies involved manufactured synthetic fibres, principally polyester and polyamide. The factories owned by the undertakings had been operating for the period 1981 to 1983, with between 54.7 and 77.6 per cent of the various markets for the different fibres, and comprised 81 per cent of the installed production capacity for the EC. As a result of a serious imbalance between this capacity and existing demand, they had already tried in 1978 to implement a 13 per cent reduction in capacity, but clearance had been refused by the Commission because of the extent to which production and delivery quotas were an integral part of the scheme. The scheme, although refused clearance, had nevertheless been provisionally implemented. The subject of the new Commission decision was a supplementary agreement signed in 1982 which had also already been partly implemented. Under this each company would commit itself to achieving its own reduction in capacity by a given date and would agree not to increase this until the end of 1985. All the figures would be checked by independent experts and the overall target for the period would be a reduction of 18 per cent of the capacity originally scheduled to remain in existence at the end of the operation of the 1978 agreement.

---

[31] So that it would not simply become an allocation of existing production levels between them.
[32] [1984] OJ L207/17: [1985] 1 CMLR 787.

In its decision approving the exemption, the Commission referred to the definition given in the *12th Annual Report* of continuing over-capacity, and to the fact that market forces had tried but failed to achieve the reduction necessary to re-establish and maintain a long-term, effective competitive structure. In these circumstances, the need to organize on a collective basis an adjustment to the new levels of demand could, taking a longer view, be argued to be to the benefit of consumers: the industry that would emerge from the restructuring would, at least in theory, have potential for fresh competition, the capacity remaining could be more intensively operated, and trends to specialization encouraged once profitability had returned, since the least profitable plants were those which were likely to be scheduled for closure under the scheme. There was little possibility that the parties would increase prices as the result of approval of the plan because they operated in what was a very competitive market under pressure from available substitute products. Unlike the earlier 1978 agreement, there were no restrictions on the parties' level of production from the reduced capacity or the total deliveries which they could make. Whilst the number of decisions of this kind has remained small in recent years it would be wise to remember that economic circumstances can change and that the principles applied in cases like *Synthetic Fibres* may well become relevant once again. That this area of the law remains far from a dead letter is shown by *Stichting Baksteen*[33] in 1995. Here the Dutch brick industry found itself in crisis at the beginning of the 1990s with a considerable surplus of brick production capacity which had led to large stock piles. The surplus had been caused by a combination of larger plants producing bricks at a higher rate and a fall in demand owing to recession in the building industry in the Netherlands. The high capital cost of brickworks means that they are only economic if run close to full capacity; to bring supply and demand into balance through price adjustments was impossible because of the inelasticity of demand. The only rational solution was the closure of the oldest and least efficient brick plants. This could only be achieved by an agreement between all the Dutch producers, under which a levy was paid by each of them in order to compensate those producers whose plants had to be permanently closed down under the industry plan.

The Commission had objected to the original industry plan which involved the implementation of production quotas backed by a system of fines in order to support the permanent closure of some works. The later revised plan was however approved and it was agreed that no new capacity would be brought on-stream for a period of at least five years.

The history of the alteration of Commission policy towards crisis cartels shows the flexibility inherent in Article 81(3) and in particular that the results of its application may vary at different times against differing economic backgrounds. These cases, however, do pose major difficulties in DG Comp and the Commission generally, because of the substantial political pressures which inevitably accompany such cases. Such pressures may come not only from national and industrial sources, but

---

[33] [1994] OJ L131/15: [1995] 4 CMLR 646.

also from other DGs within the Commission, whose differing responsibilities may result in them urging policy arguments which in their view should take precedence over normal application of Article 81(1).

5. CARTELS CONTROLLING NATIONAL MARKETS

The Commission has struck out numerous horizontal agreements which have attempted to provide either exclusive purchasing arrangements or exclusive selling agreements between manufacturers in competition with each other. By contrast, bilateral arrangements made for the distribution of goods in particular territories have generally been regarded in a more favourable light by the Commission. A case however of exclusive purchasing unfavourably received by the Commission was *Atka A/S v. BP Kemi A/S and Danske Spritfabrikker*.[34] Here, the element in the agreement to which the Commission objected was the fact that DDSF was required to purchase all its requirements of synthetic ethanol from BP Kemi up to a maximum amount, and BP Kemi had the opportunity of supplying excess quantities on similar terms. This would give BP Kemi a substantial advantage over all other competitors in the market, especially because in return for its assurance of supplies, BP Kemi was guaranteed by DDSF at least one-quarter of the combined sales of ethanol in Denmark; if these exceeded certain percentages, compensating payments had to be made to DDSF in return. In effect this was a market-sharing agreement which assured supplies to DDSF for a period of six years and would in practice relieve it from having to seek supplies from any other foreign source.

Restrictive agreements of a horizontal nature affecting national sales are commonly found in the cement industry. In *Netherlands Cement*,[35] a sales agency was formed by a number of German cement manufacturers to handle the sale of their cement in that country. These manufacturers bound themselves to sell only through this company, at the price fixed by the trade association of Dutch cement traders. Quotas were granted to individual German suppliers, and detailed provisions governing the conditions of sale, quality guarantees, freight charges, and many other contractual details were imposed, with penalties to be paid if a member deviated from the rules. The manufacturers retained no freedom as to the prices to be charged and had to follow the decision of the Dutch cement traders. The application for exemption under Article 81(3) was refused by the Commission because the obligation of the manufacturers in Germany to sell only on these conditions restrained their freedom substantially, whereas each was perfectly capable of selling direct into Holland. The buyers, rather than having a number of suppliers, would have to deal with only a single supplier, and the volume of business was again controlled not by the individual manufacturers responding to

---

[34] Discussed in Ch. 6, p. 82.

[35] *Cementregeling voor Nederland* [1972] OJ L303/7: [1973] CMLR D149. See also *Cimbel* [1972] OJ L303/24: [1973] CMLR D167 and *Nederlandse Cement-Handelsmaatschappij* [1973] CMLR D257.

demand but by a single agency working in close association with the traders' association. Even if the arrangements did make the distribution process more efficient, there was little evidence that it would benefit buyers.

By contrast, the case of *Société de Vente de Ciments et Bétons de l'Est (SVCB)* v. *Kerpen and Kerpen*[36] involved a bilateral agreement. The French plaintiff company (which later went into liquidation) agreed to supply 40,000 tonnes of cement to Kerpens in Germany annually for the next five years. The German company agreed as a condition of the contract that it would not resell the cement in Saarland and would also pay attention to the interests of the works partly owned by the supplier at Karlsruhe if asked to make deliveries in that area. When the liquidator of SVCB claimed payment for the cement, the defendant argued that the contract was void under Article 81. In a preliminary ruling under Article 234, the Court held that the agreement was indeed void since it had as its object the reduction of competition in a part of the Common Market; moreover as the total quantity on an annual basis amounted to between 10 and 15 per cent of all exports of cement by France to Germany, this was adjudged sufficient to have an appreciable effect on trade between Member States.

However, not all such arrangements necessarily fall within the prohibition of the Article. In the *Kali und Salz* cases,[37] the Commission had ruled that Article 81(1) applied to an agreement under which Kali-Chemi sold its surplus potash production, which it did not require for the manufacture of compound fertilizer, to a much larger company, Kali und Salz. This was the only other German potash manufacturer, having approximately 90 per cent of the total production, Kali-Chemi having the other 10 per cent. There had been a gradual decline in the surplus quantities made available by Kali-Chemi to Kali und Salz, and in defending the agreement Kali-Chemi argued that it could not have disposed of the potash in any other way because of the expense involved in setting up a separate sales organization solely for the sale of potash. The Court held that the Commission's decision had failed to give sufficient weight to the fact that the surplus supplies which Kali-Chemi had agreed that Kali und Salz should dispose of were gradually reducing and to the expense involved for Kali-Chemi in establishing a separate sales organization. For this reason the decision was annulled.

In other sectors, the benefit to purchasers was held sufficient for joint selling arrangements to meet the Article 81(3) criteria, notwithstanding the Commission's normal long-standing objection to such arrangements. In *United International Pictures*,[38] three major US film producers (Paramount, MGM, and MCA) with a total market share of 25 per cent in the Common Market had formed a joint sales company for distributing their films. Each shareholder/producer had to give the sales company a right of first refusal for the distribution of its films, and could require it to distribute particular films if it chose. The Commission found that the agreement had not eliminated all competition between the three producers since each retained considerable control over distribution in certain Member States; however, it did enable more effective

---

[36] Case 319/82 [1983] ECR 4173: [1985] 1 CMLR 511.
[37] Cases 19–20/74 [1975] ECR 499: [1975] 2 CMLR 154.   [38] [1990] 4 CMLR 749.

distribution through the Community as a whole so that consumers in each Member State could enjoy a wider range of films.

The flexibility of Article 81(3) in its application to horizontal agreements relating to national markets is shown by subsequent developments in this case. Originally the Commission had intimated to the parties that it would be unwilling to continue the individual exemption after its expiration in 1993. Subsequent investigations, however, indicated to the Commission that competition in the film exhibition business in the Member States of the Community had substantially improved, with a number of new cinemas having been opened. The balance of power between the European and the US films had apparently not been affected by the horizontal agreement between the major producers approved in the original decision, and indeed the market share of the UIP consortium had fallen over the 1990s. It had not been used to coordinate release dates in an anti-competitive way; the renewal of the arrangements was actually supported by a large number of the industry players including independent producers and exhibitors. A comfort letter was therefore issued in this case continuing the exemption subject to certain changes in the agreement under which for example UIP's right of first refusal in respect of the films made by the three participants had to be applied on a national basis rather than for the entire Community as one territory. The film-makers for their part gave an undertaking to maintain the highest possible degree of independence in the conduct of their filming businesses.

6. CARTELS OPERATED BY OR THROUGH TRADE ASSOCIATIONS

6.1 DUTCH TRADE ASSOCIATION CASES

The experience of competition authorities in both the EC and the United States has led to the conclusion that often trade associations are very closely associated with agreements or concerted practice in breach of Article 81(1) or its US equivalent, section 1 of the Sherman Act. In cases such as the *Cement* case, mentioned below,[39] a trade association has often been created primarily to provide the necessary administrative links for the operation of the cartel and may indeed have no other real reason for existence. In other cases, however, the trade association does have a valid primary purpose, of representing the interests of its members and of providing facilities of value to their business. Many of such agreements have not involved necessarily a background of recession or fall in demand but have been maintained simply on a basis of protectionism.

The absence until 1998 of a Dutch national law dealing with cartels meant that the Commission had to intervene in a number of national cartels in that Member State.

[39] At pp. 192–3.

The *SPO* case[40] involved the Dutch building-industry association, on which large fines were imposed by the Commission which were confirmed by the Court of First Instance in early 1995. The rules of this Association provided that when its members tendered for a building contract a meeting of the tenderers should be held to determine which undertaking would deliver the lowest competitive bid. The tenderer chosen would then be protected in various ways from competition by the other members and would also have to add certain sums to the tendered price to cover reimbursement by it to the other tenderers of their own unsuccessful tender costs. The Court confirmed the finding of the Commission that this exchange of information was unlawful since it limited the party's freedom to negotiate and increased the price payable by the building customer. Benefits from the arrangements were enjoyed by the members of the association, not by the customers. The restrictions of competition were also held not to be indispensable to achieve their alleged aims, namely improvement of the market balance between demand and supply; limiting transaction costs for tenderers would ruin competition between them. In particular, the Court believed that contract awarders who knew their requirements best were effectively excluded from the system.

The *FEG/TU* case[41] concerned the Dutch Association of Wholesalers for Electrical Fittings such as cables, switches, switchgear equipment and trunking (FEG) and its largest and most influential member TU. A British company found difficulties in obtaining supplies on the Dutch market because it was not a member of the FEG and was refused membership (on the grounds that its turnover in The Netherlands was insufficiently high!) as the rules of FEG prohibited supply to non-members. FEG and TU had combined their market leverage to engage in collective exclusive dealing agreements both with individual suppliers and with NAVEG (the importers' association) for such fittings so as to prevent non-members of FEG entering the market. Moreover in relation to its own wholesale members FEG fixed increases in retail prices and regulated discounts prohibiting loss-leader advertisements. All these practices had the single aim of improving the profit margins of the FEG members. The Commission found the practices a clear breach of Article 81(1) and imposed fines on both FEG and TU.

6.2 CARTELS OPERATING THROUGH THE EXCHANGE OF INFORMATION

One of the most effective ways of reducing competition within an industry is by the detailed exchange of confidential information between its members, and trade associations are often involved in such activities.

Nevertheless, it is important to realize that such agreements may exist between undertakings without any form of common membership in an organization, while an organization may have only a tenuous existence as a trade association if dominated by a few large producers in an oligopolistic setting. The *Fatty Acids* decision[42] shows that the Commission is capable of sophisticated analysis of this type of arrangement and

---

[40] Case T-29/92 [1995] ECR II-289.   [41] [2000] OJ L39/1: [2000] 4 CMLR 1208.
[42] [1987] OJ L3/17: [1989] 4 CMLR 445.

is able to distinguish the 'pure exchange' of information from that which is linked to anti-competitive involvement in the details of a competitor's trading arrangements, including market shares, pricing, and order book. In the *Fatty Acids* case, three leading European manufacturers of oleine and stearine were fined for information exchanges which allowed them to adjust their production and marketing policies with knowledge of each other's plans and thereby avoid 'destructive' competition.

The case of *Cobelpa/VNP*[43] raised new issues relating to the exchange of financial information between associations. Important manufacturers in two countries belonged to the relevant federations, and the information exchanged between them and their individual members included notification of relevant prices, naming individual companies, their general terms of supply, sales, and payments, including discounts granted to particular customers, rebates, and changes in price levels. The original object of their coordination was claimed to have been to align prices with those of manufacturers in countries to which they exported, but it gradually developed into a widespread collection, analysis, and distribution of virtually all the data that would have been required by undertakings within the two countries so as to anticipate the trading and pricing policies of their rivals.

The Commission's view was that the collection and analysis of figures from individual members of the association, with the object of preparing output and sales statistics, was itself a legitimate purpose for a trade association,[44] nor could there be objection to national associations or federations exchanging the same type of statistical information giving a general picture of the output and sales of the individual federation. Real objections, however, arise when individual undertakings within the body are identified, or where the simple exchange of aggregated information about the collective fortunes of the industry is replaced by a supply of information about the trading of individual members of the associations. In this case, the exchange was so detailed that it allowed members to plan export-sales policy with exact knowledge of the prices charged by the local manufacturers in that market for various grades of paper. Even if some of the pricing information could have been obtained from other sources, the convenient form in which it was provided saved the parties a considerable amount of time. Whilst there was some price legislation in effect, the exchange of information went far beyond mere exchange of those prices subject to control.

More recently the decision of the Commission in UK *Agricultural Tractor Registration Exchange*[45] emphasized the importance of the extent to which, in the context of a national market, the exchange of information identifies individual undertakings.

---

[43] [1977] OJ L242/10: [1977] 2 CMLR D28. The federations were of paper manufacturers in Belgium and The Netherlands.

[44] This view had been cautiously expressed by the Commission as long ago as the 1968 Notice on Co-Operation between Enterprises, where the distinction was drawn between the provisions of aggregated data on the one hand and 'conclusions given in a form that they induce at least some of the participating enterprises to behave in an identical manner on the market' on the other.

[45] [1992] OJ L68/19: [1993] 4 CMLR 358. The decision of the Commission was upheld by the Court of First Instance in Cases T-34 and 35/92 *Fiatagri UK and Others* v. *Commission* [1994] ECR II-905 and later by the European Court in Cases 7 and 8/95 *John Deere* v. *Commission* [1998] ECR I-3111: [1998] 5 CMLR 311.

The seven manufacturers or sole importers of agricultural tractors into the United Kingdom between 1975 and 1988 had systematically exchanged information through their association about their individual sales. This information was extremely detailed, broken down into sales at national, regional, county, dealer territory, and post-code level. This meant not only that manufacturers' sales performance could be measured but even the performance of individual dealers in their territories. The information included the exact number of particular models sold by each member, as well as the volume of retail sales and market share held by each for particular horsepower groups. These facts were passed by each manufacturer to all its own dealers, creating a market with almost complete transparency.

In a fully competitive market it could of course be argued that such transparency would aid competition. The UK tractor market, however, was oligopolistic, the four largest suppliers holding some 80 per cent, and the remaining three members of the association only 2 or 3 per cent each, whilst non-members held no more than 13 per cent (a figure that had not increased since the information exchange began in 1975). Moreover, in some areas the smaller suppliers were not represented at all. Barriers to entry were high, because of the need for suppliers to provide a large network of dealers to carry out repairs and service quickly for farmer customers. Sales volumes were quite low (about 20,000 tractors per annum) and brand loyalty had made it hard even for existing members, let alone new entrants, to increase their market share.

In its decision upholding the Commission decision terminating the exchange, the Court of First Instance found that there was an effective agreement between the members of the association that each would organize their sales territories in a way that facilitated this exchange, and that this knowledge enabled them to reduce competition between members and between their dealers, the element of uncertainty in respect of sales strategy and performance having been almost completely eliminated.

The value of the exchange of relevant information can be equally important at an international level. In the *Cement Cartel* case[46] Cembureau had compiled for its members, cement producers and associations of producers across Western Europe, a wide range of information on prices prevailing for cement in different markets as well as the supply and demand balance at different times. In some cases this information would not have been available at all to the members, in others only as a result of considerable expenditure of time and money. Nevertheless the Commission has shown itself willing to give individual exemption or even negative clearance to information exchanges when these are limited to associations of relatively weak undertakings which may be purchasers in an oligopolistic market, especially if the exchange does not include the most sensitive categories of data such as current sales information or identification of customers. In *Eudim*,[47] a group of wholesalers supplying plumbing, heating, and sanitary equipment exchanged information on general market conditions in various

---

[46] Cases 25–104/95 [2000] ECR II-491: [2000] 5 CMLR 204. See, on appeal, Cases C-204/00P, etc. *Aalborg Portland* v. *Commission* [2004] ECR I-123: [2005] 4 CMLR 251.

[47] [1996] OJ C111/8: [1996] 4 CMLR 871.

Member States where they operated and especially about prices being charged by their suppliers, mainly large companies. It was agreed, however, as part of the exemption of the agreement by the Commission that a restriction preventing members from trading outside their own national territories would be eliminated.

It is possible from these decided cases to identify those elements in an information exchange scheme which are most likely to damage the competitive structure of individual markets. First, the extent to which the information provided is aggregated by taking a large number of individual companies, and producing global figures for individual regions or countries, by contrast with information provided about individual undertakings so that their costs, turnover, and even profits can be calculated with some accuracy by rivals. The second relevant factor is the extent to which information as to relevant products are split into their individual grades or classes, or are aggregated so as to make calculation of individual statistics more difficult. The third element is the extent to which this information is made available to the public, and in particular to end-users and consumers; the more widely disseminated the information, the less likely that it will provide the basis for anti-competitive coordination. The fourth, and perhaps most important issue, is the timescale and the extent to which information is provided on a current basis or in arrears. The more current the basis upon which the information is provided, the more valuable it is as an aid in eliminating the uncertainty of competitive reaction in planning pricing policy. Other relevant factors are whether restrictions are placed on the identity of those to whom it may be communicated and the purpose to which it may be put. Significant also would be whether current conditions of sale are notified as well as lists of discounts, rebates, and other special deals, and whether the association includes interpretative comments with the figures. Probably of minor importance only is whether the research has been carried out by the association itself, through its own staff or on information provided by members, or whether a third party such as a market-research organization or firm of independent chartered accountants carried out the research and provided it on an arm's length basis. An effective anti-competitive price-information scheme could, however, be implemented on either basis, although members of the association will be able to place greater reliance on the accuracy of the figures if certified by such an independent agency.

A recent decision of the European Court concerned the exchange of information between some Spanish financial institutions on the solvency of their customers.[48] This information took the form of a register which revealed the identity and economic activity of debtors and reflected special situations such as bankruptcy or insolvency. The Spanish Supreme Court made a reference to the Court asking whether such exchanges would fall foul of Article 81. In its ruling, the Court gave a helpful steer. It emphasized that exchanges of information between undertakings could not be considered in the abstract. In particular, the economic conditions prevalent on the relevant market, the

---

[48] Case C-238/05 *Asnef- Equifax* v. *Asociación de Usuarios de Servicios Bancarios* [2006] ECR I-1125: [2007] 4 CMLR 6.

purpose of the information exchange scheme, the type of information, and its relevance in the fixing of prices or conditions of service were all important considerations. For instance, in markets where the supply was highly concentrated, the exchange of information was likely to increase the awareness of the market participants of the position and strategy of their competitors—and hence to have a restrictive effect on competition—while the sharing of information in fragmented markets could be 'neutral, or even positive'.[49] Furthermore, and in relation to the register in question, the Court set out two conditions for the scheme to escape the application of Article 81. Firstly, the individual identity of the competing financial institutions should not be revealed directly or indirectly and, secondly, the conditions of access and use of the information should not be discriminatory.

6.3 CARTELS OPERATED BY TRADE ASSOCIATIONS CONTROLLING STANDARDS AND CERTIFICATION

Another way in which trade associations may seek to reduce competition and raise barriers to new entry is by controlling standards and certification. Standards and certification rights are often originally linked with objective standards of health and safety whose enforcement is delegated to the associations by national government or authorities. Such privileges, however, can be abused.

In the case of *Anseau-Navewa*,[50] fines were imposed by the Commission, and upheld by the Court of Justice, on associations of manufacturers, importers, and distributors of washing machines and dishwashers in Belgium, as well as an association of water supply companies in that country which had statutory duties to approve appliances to be connected to the public water supply. Under these arrangements machines could only be installed if they had a certificate of conformity, available only from particular associations. These in turn restricted their membership to manufacturers and sole importers, so that general importers and dealers found themselves unable to obtain the necessary certificates. It was clear that the intention of these arrangements was to make it more difficult for parallel imports of such appliances to occur, and exemption under Article 81(3) was therefore refused. The Commission and Court both held that where a trade association is a party to a restrictive agreement of this kind but does not have formal power to order its members to conform, if its recommendations are in practice followed because of the grave practical problems which the manufacturers and dealers will otherwise encounter, then the agreement will be regarded as binding on the members and treated as a 'decision' under Article 81. The grave practical disadvantage in this case was that foreign manufacturers of washing machines were forced to use sole agents to handle imports into Belgium; any other kind of importer, e.g. a distributor of a variety of such machines, would not be eligible to obtain the necessary certificate.

---

[49] See para. 58 of the judgment.
[50] Cases 96–102, 104–5, 108, 110/82 [1983] ECR 3369: [1984] 3 CMLR 276, reported at the European Court level as *IAZ International Belgium* v. *Commission*.

Difficulties in certifying the safety of cranes which foreign mobile crane operators wished to introduce to the Netherlands were raised in *van Marwijk* v. *FNK* and *SCK*[51] Here the trade association of Dutch mobile crane operators (FNK) also controlled the certification agency, SCK. Both national and Community rules required safety checks to be made on mobile cranes and certification that these had been met. Participation in certification by SCK was much cheaper for national members of the local trade association FNK than for non-members including foreign operators. The certification procedure by SCK was not totally open and transparent and gave no weight to equivalent guarantees produced by certification systems in other Member States. Under the system of *inhuurverbod*, firms were not allowed to hire mobile cranes from undertakings not affiliated to SCK. The rules of the certification scheme were adjudged to breach Article 81(1), and fines were imposed.

6.4 OTHER FORMS OF TRADE-ASSOCIATION RESTRICTIONS ON COMPETITION

Where the membership of a trade association consists largely of producers of the same goods or services, its rules may seek to limit the competition between them. *The Danish Fur Breeders' Association* provided a number of facilities for its members who sold fox and mink furs, including a production centre for pelts and an auction house. Use of the facilities was conditional upon the observation of a number of rules limiting the use by members of other auction houses for disposal of their pelts, and their ability to act as collecting agents for competing sales organizations. Each member also had to agree to a certain percentage of its production being sold at one of five auctions held annually by the Association. These rules were not surprisingly found to be in breach of Article 81 and a fine was imposed.[52]

Particular problems are also caused when members of trade associations combine in connection with exports. The law of individual States often permits export associations to make agreements that would normally be illegal if carried out purely for domestic markets. The oldest and best-known example is the United States Webb-Pomerene Export Trade Act 1918, which provides that nothing in the Sherman Act shall make illegal 'an association entered into for the sole purpose of engaging in export trade and actually engaged solely in such export trade'. The *Woodpulp I* decision[53] of the European Court had to consider the status of such an agreement by the Kraft Export Association, to which several pulp manufacturers in the United States belonged and who were accused by the Commission of having agreed prices for sulphate pulp.

---

[51] [1996] 4 CMLR 565, a Commission decision upheld by the CFI as Cases T-213/95 and 18/96 [1997] ECR II-1739: [1998] 4 CMLR 259.

[52] *Hudson's Bay and Annings* v. *Danish Fur Breeders' Association (No. 1* [1988] OJ L316/43: [1989] 4 CMLR 340; on appeal some of the Commission's findings were overruled and the fine reduced (Case T-61/89 [1992] ECR II-1931).

[53] Cases 89, 104, 114, 116–17, 125–9/85: [1988] ECR 5193: [1988] 4 CMLR 901.

The Court's finding was that this Association could not be held responsible for any agreements on pricing made between its members since it made no separate recommendations to them but simply announced the terms of pricing agreements made by them in a number of separate meetings. The Association had also always distanced itself from the implementation of those agreements.

In considering the effect of restrictions that trade associations may seek to impose on their members, the degree of their influence and their power of exclusion from national or regional markets will be closely considered by DG Comp. Therefore, if an association is able to control public markets or 'bottleneck' facilities, any restrictive provisions which cause detriment to members, non-member traders, or consumers are likely to be in breach of Article 81(1). The *FRUBO* case[54] is a clear example. Here, the associations of fruit importers and wholesalers between them controlled 75 per cent of the sales of apples, pears, and citrus fruits in the Netherlands. The associations were able to impose the sanction of total exclusion from such auction on any importer or wholesaler who dared to break the associations' rules, which with very limited exceptions provided that the Rotterdam auctions should be the only route for importing fruit into the Netherlands. The object and the likely effect of these restrictions, if unchecked, would have been to give Rotterdam a virtual monopoly over the import of fruit into the Netherlands and to prevent wholesalers from using alternative sources of supply of fruit originating from outside the Community.

Trade associations also frequently attempt to make rules for their members covering the holding of international trade fairs and exhibitions, since they claim that an absence of guidelines applied to the organization of and attendance by exhibitors at such occasions could seriously affect the reputation of individual major events by limiting the full range of products displayed, reducing the special impact which the exhibition may have on its market. The Commission has attempted to apply Article 81(3) to such restrictions in a reasonable way, in order to provide in effect a 'rule of reason' for their assessment, distinguishing between, on one hand, those ancillary to the need for some limitation on the 'free for all' that could exist if no restrictions were allowed and, on the other hand, restrictions which are unduly and unnecessarily onerous. Examples from a number of industries, including motor cars, exhibitions, engineering, and dental products, can be found in various Annual Reports: a common thread running through the cases is the importance of preventing discrimination in the relevant rules on a national basis. Commission decisions which illustrate the way in which it applies this principle include those in *British Dental Trade Association*[55] and *CECIMO (No. 3).*[56]

The reader may be surprised that the cases cited in this chapter are invariably dealt with under Article 81 rather than Article 82.[57] The main reason is that the wide definitions given by the Court and Commission to 'decision' and to 'concerted practices'

---

[54] Case 71/74 [1975] ECR 563: [1978] 2 CMLR 123. The facts were considered in Ch. 7, p. 130.
[55] [1988] OJ L233/15: [1989] 4 CMLR 1021.   [56] [1990] 4 CMLR 231.
[57] Ch. 14, Section 8, considers the use made by the Commission of Art. 82 against a particular form of trade association; namely, collective owners of intellectual property rights.

makes the use of Article 82 unnecessary in the great majority of cases, since the structure and rules of the association will usually ensure that any practices which it authorizes, or rules which it enforces or suggests, will come within one or more of these definitions. There will be no need for the Commission to perform the possibly more difficult task of showing that the association is 'dominant' in some particular market and that it is abusing its dominance.

FURTHER READING

E. F. Bissocoli, 'Trade Associations and Information Exchange under US and EC Competition Law' [2000] 23 *World Competition* 29.

C.-D. Ehlermann, 'Reflections on a European Cartel Office' [1995] 32 CMLRev 471.

M. Jephcott and T. Lübbig, *The Law of Cartels* (Jordans, 2003).

N. Levy and R. O'donoghue, 'The EU Leniency Programme comes of age' [2004] 27 *World Comp* 75.

10

DISTRIBUTION AGREEMENTS AND PRACTICES

1. INTRODUCTION

The development of any product for sale involves a substantial investment of both time and money. This may be wasted if an appropriate system is not available for distributing the product to the point of sale. This is particularly true of consumer goods, e.g. lawnmowers, clothing, or cutlery, sold in large numbers primarily through wholesalers, then to a variety of retail establishments including specialist shops, department stores, cash-and-carry outlets, supermarkets, and discount houses. The same applies to goods for industrial use, whether sold for use or consumption by industrial concerns or for incorporation by purchasers in their own manufacturing operation, e.g. screws, valves, or iron bars. In every case, commercial success depends largely on the choice of an appropriate distribution system.

Any manufacturer considering how to distribute products in the European Union or any of its Member States has a wide range of choice. The main decision is how far its distribution system should be integrated with the rest of its organization. The greatest degree of control is generally obtained by making its own employees (whether based at home or abroad) responsible for ensuring distribution of its goods to the chosen form of outlet in the relevant geographical markets within the Community. Reliance on one's own employees for sales can, of course, be combined with other means of promotion such as exhibiting at trade fairs, maintaining a local showroom or warehouse, and mailing catalogues and other sales information to prospective customers.

In many cases, however, direct representation may not be the best method of ensuring effective distribution in a foreign country. The advantages of organizing distribution through those familiar with local markets, languages, and conditions may well mean that a local representative is chosen, either an agent or a distributor. A manufacturer's relationship with an agent is quite different from that with a distributor; an agent is a person or company with the task of bringing its principal (the manufacturer) into contractual relationships with customers. Agents are normally paid by a percentage commission on the sales which they effect. By contrast, the distributor stands at arm's length from the manufacturer, purchasing goods from it on agreed terms, normally at its own risk, and reselling either direct to the public or indirectly through its choice of wholesalers and dealers.

2. DISTRIBUTION THROUGH AN AGENT

2.1 ARTICLE 81 AND AGENCY

Although competition policy in the Community has been far more concerned with the relationship between manufacturers and their distributors, particularly exclusive distributors, a review of the law relating to distribution of goods must begin with a brief consideration of the legal position of the commercial agent. There are, of course, many varieties of commercial agent. These include the simple commission agent, who does not hold stocks of the product but merely passes orders back to the manufacturer, who delivers goods direct to the customer. Another is the 'stocking agent' who, in addition to his selling function, provides warehousing facilities for a certain amount of the manufacturer's stock, for which he receives a fixed payment, but without acquiring ownership of the goods. An agent may also give other kinds of help to the manufacturer, such as the provision of service facilities for which he will often have to carry a stock of spare parts purchased from the manufacturer. The agent may also take on a *del credere* responsibility, under which he will accept liability for payment of accounts by those customers whom he introduced to the manufacturer, relieving the manufacturer of the risk of non-payment, for the cost of an additional commission percentage.

The mere appointment of an agent, however, does not itself bring in Article 81 unless it involves some express or implied restriction upon either the agent or his principal. If an agent is appointed simply to act as an agent for a product in a particular territory, Article 81 has no application, since the essential restriction upon competition is lacking. Whilst manufacturers do sometimes retain the right to appoint a number of agents in parallel in one territory, competing with each other, and agents are sometimes under no restriction as to the supply of competing products to customers, this is comparatively rare. It is far more usual in the European Union to find that either manufacturer or agent, or both, accept restrictions on their commercial freedom. The restriction on the manufacturer may be that having appointed an agent for a given territory, say France, it agrees to appoint no other agent for that territory; for its part, the agent may agree that within France it will represent no other manufacturer selling identical or competing products.

2.2 THE 1962 NOTICE

It is with this latter kind of agency agreement that the 1962 Commission Notice on exclusive agency contracts made with commercial agents was concerned. This stated that the decisive criterion which in the view of the Commission distinguished an agent from the independent trader was the extent of the agent's responsibility for the financial risks connected with the performance of his obligations. If the agent undertook any element of risk on his own account, then his function became more similar to that of an independent trader and, for the purposes of the competition rules, he was to be treated as an independent undertaking. On the other hand, if the agent simply performed the basic role of seeking customers for its principal, the agent's restriction to the goods of its principal was acceptable as the inherent consequence of the agency relationship.

The timing of the 1962 announcement was significant: it appeared only five weeks before the deadline for notification of bilateral agreements under Regulation 17/62 (1 February 1963). It was the first of a number of Notices issued by the Commission providing guidance to enable undertakings to decide their legal position under Article 81(1) and to discourage them from filing unnecessary and purely precautionary notifications. The legal basis for the Notice had already been challenged by the Italian government in proceedings at the European Court in the *Consten-Grundig* case[1] in 1966. The Court, rejecting the suggestion that Article 81 applied only to arrangements between parties in direct competition with each other, ruled to the contrary that this Article referred generally to all agreements which distorted competition within the Community. The Article made no distinction at all between agreements between undertakings competing at the same level of production and those between non-competing undertakings operating at different levels. The Court went on to say that a distortion of competition could occur within the meaning of Article 81(1) not only where agreements limited competition between the parties but also where agreements prevented competition between one of them and third parties.

It was also established early that the Commission will always look at the economic reality of a commercial relationship, rather than the legal description applied by the parties to their agreements. This principle is highlighted by the decision in *Pittsburg Corning Europe*.[2] In this case, a Belgian subsidiary of a United States corporation manufactured cellular glass and distributed it in Belgium, Holland, and Germany. The prices which it was able to obtain for this product in Germany were some 40 per cent higher than those which could be obtained in Belgium and Holland. It therefore tried to insist that orders from its Belgian and Dutch distributors always indicated the ultimate country of destination of the goods ordered (the glass normally being used in the construction of a new building), so as to deter distributors from sending goods by way of parallel imports into Germany and undercutting the prices being obtained by its German distributors. Because parallel imports into Germany had occurred, the system of control was later tightened still further by increasing prices for glass sold into Belgium and Holland substantially, subject to a reduction if it could be shown later that the glass had actually been installed in a site in Belgium or Holland rather than Germany.

The arrangement, if made between independent undertakings, clearly represented a concerted practice under which a single territory with a high price level for this product was separated from other territories with a lower price level. The argument raised

---

[1] Cases 56 and 58/64 [1966] ECR 299: CMLR 418. See also *Italy* v. *Council and Commission*, discussed in Ch. 5, p. 62.

[2] [1973] CMLR D2. This case was briefly referred to in Ch. 6, p. 79.

by Pittsburg Corning Europe was that the Belgian distributor, Formica Belgium, was merely an agent; the written agreement described Formica Belgium in this way. After examining the facts, the Commission concluded that the designation 'agent' in this agreement was accorded merely for tax reasons and did not reflect the actual relationship. For this reason, the agency concession contained in the Notice was inapplicable, and a fine was imposed on Pittsburg Corning Europe for breach of the provisions of Article 81 by its arrangements for differential pricing between the separate national markets.

The question also arose as to whether the benefit of the Notice could apply to agents who act for more than one principal. The argument has been made that a principal cannot claim to have integrated an agent into its own sales network (as the Notice appears to contemplate) if that agent devotes only part of its time and effort to promoting the products of that principal, reserving a substantial commitment also to competing manufacturers. The approach taken by the Court in the complex *Sugar Cartel* case[3] suggests that so long as the agent only undertakes a limited function, it does not matter whether it performs this function solely for a single principal (with whom it normally becomes closely associated in the course of dealing) or whether it spreads its efforts over a number of principals for each of which it will remain only partially involved, provided only that it accepts no risk in any of them. If, however, the appointment is accepted by the agent, not as its sole occupation, but while it is also engaged as a broker or manufacturer, then this split status would tend to weaken the likelihood that the Notice could benefit it.[4] Also the Notice probably did not apply if the company claiming to act as agent was so large and powerful that in practice it was sufficiently independent not simply to obey the requirements of the principal but to have substantial influence on the distribution policy of the principal. It was also essential that the appointment of an agent did not involve the appointment of an actual or potential competitor, since the required integration of function clearly was not possible if the economic interests of the two undertakings were opposed to each other.

2.3 THE POLICY DILEMMA

Over the years following the publication of the Notice it became clear that the Notice no longer reflected the law. Court decisions and Commission practice had diverged appreciably from it, perhaps most noticeably over the significance of an 'agent' working for more than one principal[5] and it became clear that a revised Notice was needed. In fact it was not until 2000 that the Commission published official revised guidelines.

---

[3] Case 40/73 [1975] ECR 1663: [1976] 1 CMLR 295. See also Ch. 6, p. 78.

[4] See also the Commission's decision in *ARG/Unipart* [1988] 4 CMLR 513, a case where the agent's role varied according to the category of product (various kinds of spare parts for cars) in which it dealt. Art. 81(1) was held to apply to all the relationships except that where the agent accepted no risk at all. However, an individual exemption for seven years was granted to all the arrangements, which included wholesaling functions for some products as well as agency relationships for others.

[5] In particular in Case 311/85 *Flemish Travel Agents* [1987] ECR 3801: [1989] 4 CMLR 213.

While a principal reason for the lack of progress in this area was the low priority accorded by the Commission to agency matters as compared with issues of exclusive distribution and purchasing, mergers, and joint ventures, there was also a clear policy dilemma.

The problem was reflected in the Opinion of Advocate General Tesauro in *BKA/VW*.[6] This Article 234 case concerned the issue of whether the requirement by VW on its German dealers to develop their activities as agents for leasing out VW cars exclusively through VW's own leasing subsidiary (VAG Leasing) was caught by Article 81(1). VW argued that the German VAG dealers, as agents for VAG Leasing, formed a 'single economic unit' with both VW and VAG Leasing. The Court rejected this argument, principally on the basis that the commercial risks taken by the dealers were greater than under the normal form of agency; the agency was not voluntary but an obligatory adjunct to their status as selective distributors of VW cars for sale. No VW dealer had the alternative available to it of running its own leasing company.

The Advocate General's opinion dealt with issues that went to the heart of the Commission's dilemma in framing general principles on agency issues. It summarized the Commission's attitude to agency as having identified three situations where Article 81 would apply to such a relationship. First when the agent bore, at least in part, the financial risks involved; second when the agent competed on its own account directly against its principal in the same market; and third when the agent acted for a number of competing principals in the same market. The Commission's problem is that it was the restrictive clauses which the agent entered into in its Volkswagen contract which actually prevented it from taking part in activities under the second and third categories, which Volkswagen argued made it more of an 'integrated agent'; but these very restrictions were themselves anti-competitive. For this reason Tesauro A-G rightly concluded that the concept of the 'economic unit' by itself provided no general solution to the problem of deciding which agency contracts fall under Article 81; he stated that 'search for universal parameters capable of providing a general answer to all agency contracts ... is doomed to fail'.

2.4 CURRENT POLICY ON AGENCY AGREEMENTS

Review of the 1962 Notice was repeatedly postponed, and it is perhaps a measure of the difficulty of this issue that even in its 1996 Green Paper[7] in which it proposed radical reform of the competition rules on distribution agreements, the Commission chose not to discuss agency at all. But presumably the consultations following its publication convinced the Commission that the issue was too important to be postponed yet again, because the resulting Guidelines, though primarily focused on distribution by independent distributors, did deal with it. Despite Tesauro A-G's scepticism as to the appropriateness of making special provision for agency agreements,

---

[6] Case C-266/93 [1995] ECR I-3477: [1996] 4 CMLR 505, 514.
[7] Green Paper on Vertical Restraints in EC Competition Policy COM(96)721.

paragraphs 12 to 20 of the Commission's Guidelines on Vertical Restraints[8] do just this. But because the Guidelines do not accord in all respects with the European Courts' case law, which is of higher legal authority, the law is left somewhat confused. It is crucial to read the Guidelines in conjunction with the relevant judgments, and in particular those given subsequently to the Guidelines in *DaimlerChrysler*[9] and *Spanish Petrol Stations*.[10]

In those cases the Court of First Instance and the Court of Justice respectively emphasize first that the key question is whether there is 'economic unity' between principal and agent. Agents must 'operate as auxiliary organs forming an integral part of the principal's undertaking', meaning that in concluding contracts they essentially carry out their principal's instructions, without being able to influence the principal's terms of sale, and without bearing risk in the sale. This 'integration' criterion is fundamental for the Courts.

Strangely, the Guidelines do not refer to 'integration' or 'economic unity' at all, but only focus on the question of risk. In practice, insistence on establishing integration, in addition to looking at risk, will rarely affect the outcome of the analysis, given that a key element in establishing integration is the question of whether the agent bears financial risk on the contracts entered into for his principal. However, a different result might well be reached where an agent acts for more than one principal. The Guidelines say that it is irrelevant whether the agent acts for one or several principals, which is in direct contradiction to the earlier cases such as *Flemish Travel Agents*.

After considering the integration criterion, the Courts emphasize that the agent must not bear any of the risks resulting from the contracts negotiated on behalf of the principal. This does accord with the Guidelines, which state that, as under the 1962 Notice, the crucial criterion for the more favourable treatment under Article 81 is that of financial and commercial risk. According to the Guidelines, the relevant types of risk which will prevent an agent being regarded as a 'genuine agent' are categorized as either relating to the contracts negotiated or concluded, such as financing of stocks, or relating to market-specific investments which are required to enable the agent to negotiate or conclude the type of contract concerned, and which are unlikely to be recouped if he leaves that field of activity, and a non-exhaustive list of both kinds of risk is given. Where an agent bears any significant risk of either type he is regarded as an independent dealer who must be free to determine his own marketing strategy and Article 81 applies in full to arrangements made between him and his principal, just as it would to any other distribution arrangement. On the other hand, the kind of risks borne by anyone in business, such as those inherent in leasing premises, or related to his degree of success as an agent, are not relevant.

However, the approach to risk of the Court of First Instance in *DaimlerChrysler* diverged from the Guidelines. It seemed to introduce a hierarchy of risks, in which

[8] [2000] OJ C291/1: [2000] 5 CMLR 1074.
[9] Case T-325/01 [2005] ECR II-3319: [2007] 4 CMLR 559.
[10] Case C-217/05 [2006] ECR I-11987: [2007] 4 CMLR 181, and see the similar judgment in Case C-279/06, 12 September 2008 (not yet reported).

the crucial issue was who bore the sales risk, whereas other types of risk would only affect the analysis if they were very significant. It therefore found that the car dealers were genuine agents despite the fact that they bore some limited risk in respect of transport costs, purchase of demonstration vehicles and carrying out repair work on vehicles under guarantee. The Court of Justice in *Spanish Petrol Stations* was responding to a request for a preliminary ruling, and so did not apply the law to specific facts. However, it appears to endorse an approach much closer to that of the Guidelines, looking at risk as a broad category and saying that Article 81 will apply where the agent 'assumes, to a non-negligible extent, one or more financial risks linked to the sale to third parties'.

The Guidelines are silent in respect of other criteria of agency that have been applied by the Court, and which may be seen as an aspect of an integration criterion. For example, in a number of cases the Commission has referred to 'independence of action' of the agent as precluding genuine agency. This may be because of the size or economic strength of the agent, or the fact that it has a number of other profitable businesses, and particularly businesses which compete with the principal, which prevent it from being economically dependent on the principal. The Court in *BKA/VW* mentioned as a factor precluding genuine agency the fact that the agents' 'principal business of sales and after-sales services is carried on, largely independently, in their own name and for their own account'. On the other hand, in *DaimlerChrysler* one of the reasons given by the Court for deciding that the risks in respect of transport costs, purchase of demonstration vehicles and carrying out repair work on vehicles under guarantee did not bring the agency relationship within the scope of Article 81 was that these activities took place in markets other than the market for the sale of new cars.

Even in the case of genuine agency, the Guidelines do not allow all aspects of the contract between agent and principal to escape the application of Article 81. They state that in such cases, Article 81 does not apply to 'obligations imposed on the agent as to the contracts negotiated and/or concluded on behalf of the principal'. These include limitations on the area in which or the customers to whom the agent may sell goods or services, and the prices and conditions which the agent is required to apply.

Other restrictive terms in the agency agreement, such as territorial or customer exclusivity, or a prohibition on the agent acting as agent for competing goods, are in principle subject to Article 81, even in the case of genuine agency. Although this is hard to reconcile with the Court's concept of a genuine agent as a single economic entity, integrated into its principal, which suggests that Article 81 should not apply at all to a genuine agency agreement, the Court of Justice expressly endorsed this approach in *Spanish Petrol Stations*.

The Guidelines state that exclusivity clauses do not normally have anti-competitive effects, but non-compete clauses may infringe Article 81(1) if they foreclose the market to competing products. This is consistent with the position that an agent may act for several principals, because if agents were required to work for one principal only, then a non-compete clause, or at least the absence of such competition, would be a requirement of 'genuine agency'.

3. DISTRIBUTION AGREEMENTS: THE EARLY YEARS

3.1 EXCLUSIVE DISTRIBUTION

Before considering current law and policy relating to distribution it is useful to summarize events leading up to it. The present state of the law is more easily understood once the development of the subject during the early years has been explained.

The number of bilateral distribution agreements filed after the coming into force of Regulation 17 was so large that the Commission's priority was to prepare a block exemption eliminating the need to review too many individual agreements. It chose exclusive distribution as the subject of its first block exemption, Regulation 67/67, in part because early on it had recognized the advantages of exclusivity agreements for both manufacturer and distributor. Some of these advantages were set out by the Commission in the recitals to the original block exemption which it issued in 1967:

> The entrepreneur is able to consolidate his sales activities…he is not obliged to maintain numerous business contracts with a large number of dealers, and the…fact of maintaining contacts with only one dealer makes it easier to overcome sales difficulties resulting from linguistic, legal and other differences;…exclusive dealing agreements facilitate the promotion of the sale of a product and make it possible to carry out more intensive marketing and to ensure continuity of supplies, while at the same time rationalising distribution; moreover the appointment of an exclusive distributor…who will take over, in place of the manufacturer, sales promotion, after-sales service and carrying of stocks, is often the sole means whereby small and medium-sized undertakings can compete in the market…[11]

Another important factor was that such agreements amounted to nearly three-quarters of all bilateral agreements notified. Of course, the Commission had already issued a certain number of decisions on exclusive distribution agreements. The primary influence on the content of the Regulation was *Consten-Grundig*, which provided a clear model for future patterns of distribution by exclusive distributors. The principles laid down by the Commission in its decision, approved with only minor adjustments by the Court, formed the foundation for the original block exemption Regulation.

It is important to note that the European Court had established very early on, before Regulation 67/67 was adopted, that not all distribution arrangements, nor even all exclusive distribution arrangements, fall within Article 81(1). In the 1966 case of *Société Technique Minière (STM)* v. *Maschinenbau Ulm*,[12] the Court had ruled that some exclusive distribution agreements did not contain the elements necessary

---

[11] Recital 10 of Reg. 67/67, which came into force on 1 May 1967.
[12] Case 56/65 [1966] ECR 234: CMLR 357.

to bring them within Article 81(1), and that in determining this issue the following should be considered:

(1) the nature of the products covered, and whether the supply was of limited or unlimited amount

(2) the importance of both the supplier and the distributor with respect to the relevant markets

(3) whether the agreement was isolated or one of a network of agreements covering at least a substantial area or region of a Member State

(4) the degree of territorial protection afforded by the agreement, in particular whether the agreement aimed to give absolute territorial protection, and whether parallel imports could be brought into the territory by third parties.

If, after applying these tests, it appears that there is either no effect on trade between Member States or no object or effect of imposing any restriction on competition within the Community, then the Commission's interest should cease. If, however, as is often the case, there is significant impact in both these respects, then Article 81(1) applies and exemption, either through a block exemption or individual application of Article 81(3), is needed.

Regulation 67/67 exempted agreements:

(i) between one supplier (S) and one distributor (D)

(ii) under which S agreed to supply only D with the relevant defined goods (G) for resale within a specific territory (T) forming part or all of the Community

(iii) if D agreed to purchase such goods for resale in T only from S, and not to sell competing goods during the term of the agreement or for one year afterwards. (D could not be restricted as to unrelated types of goods)

(iv) if S could place no restriction on D as to prices or customers but could subject D to certain obligations, namely to purchase complete ranges of goods or minimum quantities, to sell goods under S's trade marks and packaging, and to take promotional measures including provision of an adequate sales network, stock, guarantee services and adequate trained staff

(v) it was essential that S remain free to supply other dealers or users outside T, even if he knew they intended to use or resell them in T and

(vi) D had to be free to sell G outside T provided that it received the orders passively, not advertising or having branches or depots outside T.

Finally:

(vii) S and D could not be competing manufacturers granting each other reciprocal distribution rights

(viii) nor could they exercise industrial property rights or otherwise act so as to make it difficult for dealers or consumers to obtain G from elsewhere.

These eight elements comprised the original model for automatically permitted exclusive distribution; they were subsequently interpreted and developed by both Commission and Court decisions[13] during the period between the first implementation of the Regulations in 1967 and their replacement in 1983.

After 1967 a large proportion of notified exclusive distribution agreements were brought under the terms of the block exemption, enabling DG Comp to turn to the other individual notifications already made: many other distribution agreements that could not benefit from the exemption remained for consideration. Some kinds of clauses could make individual exemption difficult or impossible. The central importance of the integration of the national markets into a single market meant that the existence within such an agreement of any form of ban on exports, direct or indirect, was fatal to a claim for individual exemption. The strong line adopted from the outset by the Commission in this area was fully supported by the Court. This, of course, runs directly contrary to the immediate interests of the distributor, who would prefer to have absolute territorial protection for his own area so that neither the manufacturer nor any other distributor appointed for another Member State could enter it. This had been precisely the hope of Consten in the *Grundig* case, in which such protection had been sought deliberately both by the use of the 'GINT' trade mark coupled with French unfair competition law and by the contractual export restriction on distributors in Germany. Even now, any absolute ban on exports in an exclusive distribution agreement will almost certainly have to be deleted for exemption to apply. This has been laid down in a number of cases before the Commission and by several European Court rulings.[14]

Distribution could also be hindered indirectly rather than directly by clauses creating a disincentive to export. If consumer goods were sold within one Member State, the Commission regarded it as essential that there be no restriction on their resale which discouraged their export to other Member States. For example, in the case of consumer goods, this resale was less easy if a purchaser in another Member State was unable to rely on the original guarantee.[15]

[13] For example, the Commission originally assumed that exclusive distribution agreements affecting only one Member State, and made between parties solely from that State, would fall outside Art. 81 because of the lack of effect on trade between Member States; however, the European Court took a different view in Case 63/75 *Fonderies Roubaix-Wattrelos* v. *Fonderies Roux* [1976] ECR 111: 1 CMLR 538.

[14] Case 19/77 *Miller International* v. *Commission* [1978] ECR 131: 2 CMLR 334. See Ch. 7, p. 119.

[15] *Zanussi* [1979] 1 CMLR 81. See also Case 31/85 *ETA Fabriques d'Ebauches* v. *DK Investment SA* [1985] ECR 3933: [1986] 2 CMLR 674, an Art. 234 case involving cheap Swiss watches. On the other hand, it is not a breach of Art. 81 for a retailer to provide a special service for goods acquired through official distributors so long as the standard manufacturer's guarantee is available to all purchasers: Case 86/82 *Hasselblad* v. *Commission* [1984] ECR 883: 1 CMLR 559. Nor are manufacturers of goods sold through selective distributorships obliged to provide guarantees on their products that have been sold to the public other than through their official dealer network: Case C-376/92 *Metro* v. *Cartier* [1994] ECR I-15: 5 CMLR 331. See Ch. 11, p. 234.

3.2 EXCLUSIVE PURCHASING

One of the issues arising under Regulation 67/67 was the extent to which it covered exclusive purchasing (that is, a requirement on D to purchase all of his supplies of G from S) and non-compete clauses (that is, where D is prohibited from selling within T goods which compete with G), in the absence of exclusive distribution: in other words whether (ii) above was essential if an agreement was to benefit from automatic exemption.

An exclusive distribution agreement will normally include a promise by the distributor to its manufacturer not to distribute or manufacture competing goods made by other manufacturers. It may in addition be required to purchase all its needs for contract goods from the other party, and not, say, from other distributors. In the exclusive distribution agreement, the exclusivity relates to a specific territorial area. In a pure exclusive purchasing or non-compete agreement, no territorial area is named, and the purchaser remains in competition with all other parties entering into similar agreements, though of course the manufacturer will normally take care to ensure that the number of distributors granted this concession is not unrealistically high, so that all can enjoy a reasonable level of turnover. Undoubtedly, such agreements offer potential economic advantages to both parties. The manufacturer is enabled to calculate the likely demand for his product over the period of the agreement. The distributor, in return for committing himself for a reasonable length of time, often receives special prices, preference in supply if shortages occur, and perhaps the provision of technical and financial assistance. In particular, the acceptance of an exclusive purchase arrangement, perhaps together with a non-compete obligation, is often the principal condition for making loans on favourable terms to individual businesses which cannot easily acquire these funds on comparable terms from other sources.

At an early stage in the development of competition policy, the European Court had taken a relatively relaxed attitude to non-compete agreements. In *Brasserie de Haecht v. Wilkin-Janssens (No. 1)*[16] the Court of Justice stated that:

agreements whereby an undertaking agrees to obtain its supplies from one undertaking to the exclusion of all others do not by their very nature necessarily include all the elements constituting incompatibility with the Common Market as referred to in Article 81(1) of the Treaty. Such agreements may, however, exhibit such elements, where taken either in isolation or together with others, and in the economic and legal context in which they are made on the basis of a set of objective factors of law or of fact, they may affect trade between Member States and where they have either as their object or effect the prevention, restriction or distortion of competition.

In this case a Belgian brewery brought a claim against its tenants for breach of their agreement to sell only beers produced by the brewery; the tenants claimed that the agreement was null and void under Article 81 because it prevented them from selling other beers and thereby restricted trade between Member States, since it limited the

---

[16] Case 23/67 [1967] ECR 407: [1968] CMLR 26; discussed in Ch. 7, p. 102.

outlets in Belgium for foreign breweries. Although the effects would be trivial for an agreement affecting a single café or inn, the Court of Justice held, on this reference for a preliminary ruling under Article 234, that the effects of such a tying agreement must not be considered in isolation but in the light of the fact that it formed part of a network of similar agreements. On the other hand, if one or more parties to the agreement were powerful in their particular markets, and had important market shares, their agreement considered in isolation might be caught under 81(1) so that the issue of exemption under the four conditions of 81(3) would become relevant. If additional restrictions were placed upon the dealer, particularly those affecting the terms and conditions upon which he could resell or his choice of customers, these were likely to weigh against the validity of the agreement. However, if market entry by manufacturers through the opening up of new outlets (or finding alternative forms of distribution such as hyper-markets) was in practice available, then clearly the exclusionary effect of the purchasing arrangements would be less pronounced.

Whilst Commission consideration of the amendments to be introduced to Regulation 67/67 was still in progress, the Court held in the *Concordia* case[17] that the Regulation could apply even when there was no specific geographical area referred to in the contract within which resale of the product was permitted.

3.3 THE 1983 BLOCK EXEMPTIONS

In fact Regulation 67/67 was replaced in 1983 by two separate block-exemption Regulations. Regulation 1983/83, like its predecessor, exempted certain types of exclusive distribution agreements, while Regulation 1984/83 exempted certain exclusive purchasing agreements. The new Regulations aimed to reflect the Commission's experience of distribution agreements and the Court's judgments, but they proved controversial and went through a number of drafts, the first dated February 1978, and only finally entered into effect on 1 July 1983.

Regulation 1983/83 retained the same basic thrust as Regulation 67/67, but there were a number of detailed amendments to the rules. Regulation 1984/83 covered both exclusive purchasing and non-compete obligations (that is, both the requirement on D to obtain all his supplies of G from S, and not to manufacture or distribute goods competing with G) but imposed a maximum duration of five years. It also included special rules applicable to beer and petrol distribution, which presented particular problems in the light of the cumulative effect of the many large exclusive purchase networks in these sectors.

In addition, for the first time, at the request of numerous industrial and commercial organizations and trade associations, the Commission issued guidelines on its interpretation of the individual clauses of the Regulations. Though these did not prevent a national court interpreting the Regulations independently, and still less did they stop the European Court from making its own, legally binding, interpretation, they were

---

[17] Case 47/76 *De Norre v. Brouwerij Concordia* [1977] ECR 65: 1 CMLR 378.

extremely useful to any lawyer or businessman seeking to interpret the Regulations, and usually had at least persuasive influence. Not least, they were also an invaluable aid to the DG Comp officials applying the rules. The practice of issuing Guidelines in support of new Block Exemption Regulations is now well established.

At one level these block exemptions worked well, providing welcome legal certainty, and for many sectors they were adopted as the operating model. The extensive use of the legislation, however, had the effect of placing the legal structure of distribution in a 'straitjacket', which was not commercially desirable, especially as distribution methods continued to change in the light of advancing technology. The European Court had already made clear in the *Delimitis* case[18] that even a minor or technical departure from the permitted model of the block exemption in the form of an additional obligation or restriction on the distributor or supplier made the benefit of the exemption totally unavailable.

These and other factors led to the system becoming the object of some trenchant criticism. In a seminal article published in 1995 Barry Hawk characterized the Commission's treatment of vertical restraints as a complete failure.[19] He pointed to its overly broad application of Article 81(1) to agreements having little or no anti-competitive affect, which he saw as incoherent and not based on proper economic analysis, as well as being inconsistent with Court judgments. He described how this had led to extraordinary legal uncertainty, which the Commission had tried to address through the adoption of block exemptions, and which resulted in excessive legal formalism and a failure to focus on the actual competitive harms and benefits of a particular agreement or practice. While undoubtedly uncomfortable reading for Commission officials, this article is widely seen as a catalyst of the policy reform that was to follow. Support gradually grew for a more flexible, economics-based approach, which was officially discussed for the first time in the Commission's 1996 Green Paper.

4. THE 1996 COMMISSION GREEN PAPER ON VERTICAL RESTRAINTS

The question of the approach to be adopted towards vertical agreements for the distribution of goods was a principal concern within DG Comp throughout the second half of the 1990s, not least because of the criticism referred to above. The discussion ranged much more widely than exclusive distribution and purchasing, encompassing also franchising and selective distribution,[20] both of which were by then very popular forms of distribution, and went to the heart of the Commission's policy in this area.

The process of reform of the block exemption for licences for technology transfer, as described in Chapter 12, had shown the Commission the importance of substantive

---

[18] Case C-234/89 [1991] ECR I-935: [1992] 5 CMLR 210.

[19] B. Hawk, 'System Failure: Vertical Restraints and EC Competition Law' [1995] 32 CMLRev 973.

[20] Discussed in Ch. 11.

and far-reaching consultation with all interested groups before making formal proposals for amendment of existing legislation. It was found necessary in that case to
take into account not only the wishes and views of industry, of the professions, and
of Member States, in the light of the experience of how the block exemption for technology transfer had worked over a number of years, but also to consider the ability
of the Commission to operate an effective system while it remained unable to deal
promptly with individual notification of agreements because of lack of resources. It
was therefore decided that a Green Paper should be published setting out the options
for the future shape of such block exemptions; after some delay, caused by disagreements within the Commission, this was published in 1996.[21]

The Green Paper set out its aim of providing a detailed consultation process on the
approach to be adopted by the Commission to distribution in the light of three major
factors, namely:

- that the existing block exemption covering forms of distribution would expire
  shortly and that review was necessary to prepare for its renewal, with any changes
  considered necessary

- that the Single Market legislation was now largely in place so that in future private barriers, that is arrangements between undertakings, might gain in importance relative to public barriers as a cause of partition of the Single Market

- that there had been major changes in both the structure of final distribution and
  the organization of distribution logistics, largely due to the application of information technology.

Of the Green Paper's eight chapters, Nos. 1 and 7 provided an interesting account
of the changing patterns of the distribution of goods, reflecting evidence submitted
from a number of sources. The distinction between manufacturing, wholesaling, and
retail functions was now less clearly defined than before: increasingly the chain of supply is treated as indivisible, without clear demarcation points; suppliers often provide
wholesaling services whilst retailers are often integrated backwards into wholesaling
or even manufacture. Distribution is a major activity within the Community: at the
beginning of the 1990s there were over 4 million undertakings involved in it, of which
some three-quarters were retailing businesses.

The Commission acknowledged that it is not always easy to define what wholesaling means under modern circumstances. The central concept, however, is that of a
'bridge' between the supplier and the retailer which brings about the necessary conversion from the goods leaving the production line in one form into the quantities
to be supplied through location, timing, and price in a form acceptable to retailers.
The existence of wholesalers in any market plays an important role in maintaining
its competitive nature. Technological change meant that wholesalers no longer operated as a separate form of undertaking; in particular the point of sale information
now available to retail chains enabled them to forecast demand with great accuracy

---

[21] See fn. 7.

and thus to exercise precise control over their stock levels and delivery requirements. The principles of delivery 'just in time' which has led to factories requiring component deliveries for production lines merely hours, in some cases even minutes, prior to actual use had for this reason spread to the distribution market. This forced very close cooperation between all parties in the chain of supply.

Undertakings specializing in warehousing and physical distribution for a number of larger manufacturers had also come into existence, and could now provide some of the services previously offered by wholesalers, without necessarily acquiring title to the goods which they handle. Small buyers, for example local grocery shops, often formed buying groups or cooperatives under which a single trading style was applied to all its members to enable bulk purchases and keener pricing. Alternatively, such retail outlets obtained much of their stock, not by delivery from manufacturers or wholesalers, but by themselves visiting local cash-and-carry warehouses. Retailing itself had become more specialized for products such as garden and recreational equipment, furniture, clothing, and toys. On the other hand, it was clear that many retailers remained hesitant about obtaining goods from parallel import sources because of the lack of certainty of continuity of supply and fear of retaliatory action by manufacturers.

Chapter 2 of the Green Paper contained an economic analysis of the way in which a variety of contractual restraints contained in distribution contracts had affected the growth of the Single Market. It was clear that the process of integration still had some way to go and that it was still possible to find significant price differences between Member States. The statistics produced did show some convergence in consumer goods and services, though considerably less in sectors such as energy and construction where the Single Market had developed more slowly. The Paper stated that vertical restraints, e.g. exclusivity of territory, may in many circumstances have had a beneficial effect on relationships between suppliers and distributors, enabling distributors to focus their efforts on the products of particular manufacturers and to minimize 'free riding' by other dealers at the expense of those dealers who do make the required investment. On the other hand, the structure of exclusive distribution itself can make intra-brand competition less lively than may be desirable. Competing manufacturers seeking to come into such a market at a later date may not in such circumstances be able to find sufficient competent distributors in strategic locations.

The rest of the Green Paper described existing law and practice at Community and national level, and finally set out possible options for change, ranging from maintaining the existing system more or less unchanged, to the replacement of the existing rules by a generally applicable block exemption available where the parties' market shares fell below 40 per cent.

In November 1998 this discussion text was followed by the Commission's 'Follow-up to the Green Paper on Vertical Restraints',[22] which set out the Commission's intention to adopt a single, broadly applicable block-exemption Regulation, to include market-share limits on its application. Though the detail of this proposal was

---

[22] [1998] OJ C365/3 [1999] 4 CMLR 281.

somewhat changed by the time it was adopted, the broad framework proposed by the Commission remained. The details of the current policy will be discussed in the following sections.

5. DISTRIBUTION AGREEMENTS: POLICY SINCE 1999

Some three years after the Green Paper was published, the solution finally adopted was the replacement of the block exemptions on exclusive distribution, exclusive purchasing, and franchising with a single block exemption Regulation[23] intended to cover these three types of agreement, as well as selective distribution agreements, which had not previously benefited from any block exemption.[24] It entered into force on 1 June 2000. The Regulation was accompanied by very detailed Guidelines[25] on the application of the Regulation, and on the treatment of distribution agreements falling outside the scope of the Regulation.

The current policy on vertical restraints is still of course governed by Article 81 and the Court's jurisprudence. However, while the Commission works within the bounds of this framework, its general approach is now clearly grounded more firmly in economics than in the past, and a generally more relaxed attitude to such restraints is in evidence. This can be seen in the policy statements in the Guidelines, and in the new block exemption, which provides a much greater degree of freedom for firms without market power than did the earlier block exemptions. As a result of this change, the number of notifications to the Commission of vertical agreements dropped substantially.

Firms above the 30 per cent market threshold laid down by the Regulation, on the other hand, are now in a worse position than before, as they can never benefit from a block exemption. If they enjoy over 40 per cent and are dominant in their market their situation is even worse: not only can they no longer benefit from any block exemption, but the Commission has said in its Guidelines that the vertical restraints of such firms are unlikely to satisfy the criteria for exemption.[26]

Nevertheless, despite these profound changes, there are those who argued that the reform should have been more radical, and who would advocate an even more liberal

---

[23] Regulation 2790/99 on the application of Art. 81(3) of the Treaty to categories of vertical agreements and concerted practices [1999] OJ L336/21 [2000] 4 CMLR 398. Although the title of the Regulation refers to vertical agreements, in fact it is only intended to deal with supply and distribution, and not with other types of vertical agreements such as intellectual property licences.

[24] Before the Commission could adopt such a broad block exemption the Council enabling Reg. 19/65 had to be amended to give it the necessary powers: Reg. 1215/99, [1999] OJ L148/1.

[25] See fn. 8.

[26] This aspect of the Guidelines is expected to be softened when they are revised before the block exemption expires in 2010. But the fact remains that the introduction of the market share threshold did make life more difficult for companies with high market shares.

policy towards distribution agreements, and to vertical restrictions generally.[27] The relevant arguments can be expected to be extensively canvassed during 2009, when the Commission will consult on its future policy in the light of the expiry of the Regulation on 31 May 2010.

The following discussion will deal with distribution agreements in general, and much of what is said here applies to selective distribution and franchising agreements. However, as there is much to be said in addition which specifically relates to these particular types of distribution arrangement, they will also be discussed separately in the next chapter.

5.1 WHEN WILL A DISTRIBUTION AGREEMENT INFRINGE ARTICLE 81(1)?

For obvious practical reasons there is a tendency to approach distribution-law issues as block-exemption issues: that is, to start by seeing whether the arrangement in question fits within the scope of the applicable block exemption. However, as the European Court established in 1966 in *STM* v. *Maschinenbau Ulm*,[28] distribution agreements, even exclusive ones, do not necessarily infringe Article 81(1). In the case of many agreements no exemption is therefore necessary. As DG Comp's practice has evolved, particularly in recent years, to look increasingly at the economic effects and less at the contractual wording of agreements, it has become confirmed in its view that most distribution agreements deserve generous treatment.

Economics classifies distribution agreements as 'vertical' (because they concern parties acting, at least for the purposes of the agreement, at different levels in the supply chain) and as a general rule, from an economic point of view, these pose less of a threat to competition than do 'horizontal' agreements (between competing firms). The Commission's approach, stated expressly in the Guidelines, is that restrictions in distribution agreements are frequently economically beneficial as long as inter-brand competition remains strong.[29] Most restrictive clauses need to be looked at in their market and economic context in order to establish whether they do in fact constitute an appreciable restriction on competition. Relevant factors include market shares and market structure, product differentiation, barriers to entry, the existence of potential competition, collusion or oligopolistic behaviour between competing firms, buyer power, and the cumulative effects of a number of similar networks.

Restrictions on inter-brand competition are normally viewed with more concern than restrictions on intra-brand competition. Where a supplier has a strong market presence then exclusive purchase and non-compete clauses will raise issues, because

---

[27] See e.g., R. Subiotto and F. Amato, 'The Reform of the European Competition Policy concerning Vertical Restraints' (2000) 69 Antitrust Law Journal 147–93. See also J. Lever and S. Neubauer, 'Vertical Restraints: Their Motivation and Justification' [2000] 21 ECLR 7–23. For a comparison of EC policy with the more generous US policy on anti-competitive agreements see A Jones, 'Analysis of Agreements under US and EC Antitrust Law—Convergence or Divergence?' [2006] Antitrust Bull 691.

[28] Case 56/65 (1966) ECR 235: CMLR 357.   [29] Paras. 5 and 100–2.

of the risk to inter-brand competition where competing suppliers cannot find distributors for their products. Foreclosure of other buyers may occur where a powerful distributor operates an exclusive distribution system, but because the effects will be felt on intra-brand competition, they are less likely to raise concerns, unless inter-brand competition is weak.

Only maximum resale price maintenance and absolute export prohibitions are treated as infringing Article 81(1) per se. These, and various other clauses which are judged on the basis of their economic effects, will now be considered in turn.

5.2 RESALE PRICE MAINTENANCE (RPM)

Resale price maintenance is expressly prohibited by Article 81(1)(a) and is treated by the Commission and Court as a per se infringement of Article 81(1), though it is a practice whose effects are variously regarded by economists.[30] It may be horizontal, where it is agreed between suppliers, or vertical where a supplier imposes it on his distributor. A whole range of justifications for the latter have been claimed. The manufacturer or supplier may argue that if prices are cut, the prestige or luxury connotations of the product, e.g. perfume, may suggest to consumers that it is of less value.[31] A related argument is that without resale price maintenance, dealers may sell popular brands at unreasonably low prices as loss leaders, even below cost (thereby in the manufacturer's view 'devaluing the brand') in order to attract to its premises customers who will then buy other goods at high prices. It is suggested that without resale price maintenance, the more aggressive retailer will drive smaller dealers out of business, depriving smaller communities of competition at the retail level and permitting the remaining dealers to raise their prices to unreasonable levels.

Another argument in support of the practice is that resale price maintenance is necessary to guarantee dealers a generous profit margin, so that services can be provided which are of value to both customers and the cultural life of the community. In this category could be placed the profit required for electronic consumer goods, where extensive demonstration and advice from the dealer involves substantial expense, which may be incurred without any return if the customer then purchases the goods from a discount store or department store not offering such services but merely the same goods at a lower price. This is an example of the 'free rider' argument often raised as justification for exclusive or selective distribution systems. Alternatively, the manufacturer may claim that a large number of outlets are required for the best distribution

---

[30] The literature on this topic is extensive. For citations see n. 7 of the opinion of Advocate General VerLoren van Themaat in Cases 43–63/82 *Dutch Books (VBVB-VBBB)* [1984] ECR 19: [1985] 1 CMLR 27. US law, which previously took a similarly strict approach, changed in 2007 so that vertical resale price maintenance is now assessed under the 'rule of reason', *Leegin Creative Leather Products v PSKS Inc.*, 171 Fed. Appx. 464 (5th Cir., March 20, 2006). For arguments against the change see e.g. P. Jones Harbour, 'An Open Letter to the Supreme Court of the United States' (available in the speeches section of the US Federal Trade Commission website).

[31] The same argument has been used to justify certain forms of selective distribution, as described in Ch. 11 at p. 235.

of its product, which can only be obtained by offering guaranteed margins. Resale price maintenance may be of value in helping new entrants in a particular trade to obtain dealers who will be encouraged to promote their products if the margins are generous. Of course, contrary arguments are available to most of these grounds for supporting resale price maintenance. The most important is that legalizing the practice prevents retailers from competing with each other on price, and hence tends to raise the overall level of prices that consumers are required to pay. It tends also to have the effect that, if as its consequence inefficient dealers are protected against their inefficiency, efficient dealers are thereby prevented from taking the advantage to which they are entitled from their superior performance.

In its early years DG Comp spent much energy establishing the principle that, even where resale price maintenance was legal at national level, Article 81 applied whenever a system prevented consumers or intermediaries from obtaining products wherever they chose within the Community. But the general trend of recent decades in Member States of the Community and beyond has been to reduce the extent to which resale price maintenance is an acceptable economic practice. By 1997 RPM was generally prohibited in almost all OECD countries, subject only to certain exceptions for books, newspapers, and medicines.[32] This means that retail price maintenance is now rare in the Community.

However, in the publishing sector, arguments based on the cultural imperatives of protecting small bookshops unable to afford to discount 'bestseller' titles, and encouraging the continued publishing of books with a small print run, have to some extent prevailed.[33] These arguments have strong political support, particularly in Germany where it has been argued in some quarters that this is a cultural issue falling outside the Commission's jurisdiction. Where the system is imposed by law then the Community free-movement rules are relevant but, where it is composed of agreements between publishers and retailers, Article 81 is potentially applicable.

In 2000 the Commission concluded lengthy negotiations on the legality of German and Austrian RPM systems for German-language books. The version of the agreement eventually accepted by the Commission as not infringing Article 81 applied only within national borders, and could not be applied to exported and re-imported goods. However, it did apply to such goods where they had been exported solely for the purpose of avoiding the national RPM arrangements, a result unlikely to be reached in any other product sector.[34] The special and sensitive nature of this market is underlined by a 1999 Council Resolution which called on the Commission 'whilst applying European competition rules to agreements in cross-border linguistic areas, to take account of

---

[32] OECD Report: Resale Price Maintenance, OCDE/GD(97)229.

[33] Even in the book sector RPM is becoming rarer. In the UK, RPM for books formally came to an end in 1997, when the publishers' agreement known as the Net Book Agreement was declared illegal by the Restrictive Practices Court. However, in practice it had been abandoned in 1995 when several major publishers had withdrawn from it.

[34] *Sammelrevers and Einzelrevers* [2002] 4 CMLR 1278. Such 'U-turn' transactions have also been held not to be real cross-border transactions for the purposes of free movement of goods: Case 229/83 *Leclerc Books* [1985] ECR 1: 2 CMLR 286.

the provisions and implications of Art. 128(4) of the Treaty, of the special cultural role of the book market and of the specific value of the book as a cultural object, as well as of relevant national cultural policies', and a similar Resolution in 2001.[35]

The Commission's current Guidelines repeat the general rule that RPM affecting trade between Member States is prohibited by Article 81(1), and express considerable reserve with regard even to recommended or fixed maximum prices where a supplier has a strong market position.[36] It considers that in such circumstances these practices may result in most distributors charging the same price (that is, de facto RPM), and also that they may facilitate collusion between suppliers. Interestingly, an earlier draft of the Regulation had proposed exempting recommended and fixed maximum price clauses without any market share limit.

5.3 EXCLUSIVE DISTRIBUTION AND TERRITORIAL PROTECTION

Despite its acknowledged benefits, in practice the granting of an exclusive territory to the distributor also is generally treated by the Commission as infringing Article 81(1), and the greater the degree of territorial protection granted, the more serious is the infringement. Absolute protection, so that a distributor is completely protected from competition from other distributors, even those based outside his territory, is normally treated as a per se infringement of Article 81(1) and is unlikely to be exempted. Lesser degrees of protection will also normally infringe Article 81(1), though they may benefit from exemption. This is partly because of the potential for intra-brand competition to be limited, but more importantly because of the danger it is perceived as posing to creation of a single European market.

As we have already seen, the aim of Community market integration has meant that vertical restraints which divide up territories have been severely treated, and this has tended to obscure the general principle that vertical restrictions are frequently benign. As already discussed, both the Commission and the Court have been severe in their treatment of clauses which either directly or indirectly tend to divide up markets along national frontiers.

In its Vertical Restraints Guidelines the Commission makes particular mention of the importance it attaches to consumers' freedom to purchase in any Member State,[37] and it has imposed extremely high fines in cases where this freedom has been restricted. Despite the benevolence with which DG Comp generally regards distribution agreements, in 2002 it imposed a €149 million fine on Nintendo for colluding to prevent exports from the UK to Germany, the Netherlands, and other European countries, which at that time was one of the highest fines it had ever imposed on a single company.[38] Another example is the €102 million fine imposed on Volkswagen for hindering parallel imports between Germany and Italy.[39] Indeed, the Commission

---

[35] [1999] OJ C42/3; [2001] OJ C73/3. [36] Paras. 111–12.
[37] Para. 103. [38] [2003] OJ L255, appeal pending Case T-13/03.
[39] [1998] OJ L124/60. The fine was reduced to €90 million on appeal. See Ch. 11, fn. 43.

has been particularly active in rooting out such practices in the car market, and this will be discussed in more detail in the next chapter.

An exception to the per se prohibition of absolute territorial protection mentioned in the Guidelines is when it is used temporarily to launch a new product or penetrate a new area of the Community. The Commission states that such restrictions, provided that they do not last more than two years from the first marketing of the product, will not generally infringe Article 81(1) at all.[40] In addition, recent judgments have established that not all conduct aimed at preventing exports infringes Article 81. An example illustrating the way in which the Court has tempered the Commission's zeal is the *Bayer* case.[41]

Like all pharmaceuticals producers, Bayer has to contend with the existence of different national health policies in different Member States, and in particular with the differing extents to which national governments intervene to set pharmaceutical prices at lower than market rate. In the case of the heart disease drug Adalat, the prices fixed by the Spanish and French health services at the relevant time were, on average, 40 per cent lower than in the United Kingdom. As a result, Spanish and French wholesalers exported to the United Kingdom, causing Bayer's direct sales there to fall dramatically. To combat this parallel importing, Bayer ceased fulfilling the increasingly large orders which these wholesalers were placing with its Spanish and French subsidiaries. Wholesalers complained, and the Commission held that Bayer's conduct amounted to an export prohibition and infringed Article 81(1). It fined Bayer €3 million and ordered it to inform its wholesalers that exports within the Community were not restricted and would not be penalized.

The Court of First Instance took the unusual step of suspending operation of the decision pending the appeal, and eventually annulled the Commission's decision on the grounds that there was no agreement or concerted practice, which is an essential element of Article 81(1); this aspect of the case is discussed in Chapter 6. In reaching its decision, which was later upheld by the Court of Justice, the Court examined the conduct of Bayer, its national subsidiaries, and its wholesalers in minute detail, before finding that there was not in fact the necessary concurrence of wills for an agreement. But the detail in which the facts are examined suggests that, had they been slightly different, for example had Bayer put an exports monitoring system in place, or threatened uncooperative wholesalers with sanctions, it might well have lost the case. This is because such conduct could have indicated the existence of an export ban which the wholesalers had implicitly accepted by continuing to deal with Bayer, rather than only a unilateral reduction by Bayer of quantities supplied.

Amongst the many Commission arguments that the Court rejected was the contention that a distribution system operated with the aim of hindering parallel imports necessarily infringes Article 81. While this judgment shows that this is not the case, that there are limits to the Commission's ability to promote parallel imports using

---

[40] Para. 119.   [41] Cases C-2 and 3/01P, discussed in Ch. 6, p. 86.

Article 81, and that the Court will uphold those limits, it also shows the lengths to which DG Comp is prepared to go in pursuit of the market integration aim.

In a similar case the Court of First Instance placed yet further limits on the Commission's ability to protect parallel trade through Article 81, at least in pharmaceutical markets. It had to rule on a dual-pricing scheme put in place by Glaxo to deal with a parallel import problem between Spain and the United Kingdom. The written sales conditions notified to and accepted by wholesalers gave different prices according to the market for which the products were intended, so there was clearly an agreement in this case. The Commission held that this amounted to an export restriction which had as its object and effect the restriction of competition, and that grounds for exemption under Article 81(3) had not been shown. The Court rejected this in part, holding that in a highly regulated market of this kind, in which prices are to a large extent shielded from market forces, a restriction on parallel trade could not be assumed to have an anti-competitive object. This is because in such a situation it cannot be presumed that parallel trade reduces prices to final consumers. Furthermore, where an anti-competitive object or effect is established, serious consideration must be given to whether the restriction is justified under Article 81(3), in particular if, given the very specific characteristics of the pharmaceuticals market, it may safeguard incentives to innovate.[42]

5.4 EXCLUSIVE PURCHASE AND NON-COMPETE CLAUSES

As already discussed, a combination of exclusive purchase and non-compete clauses have recognized economic benefits. However, the Commission is well aware that in certain market conditions they pose the risk of foreclosure of the market to competing and potential suppliers, facilitation of supplier collusion, and reduction in inter-brand competition.

An 'English clause', which requires the distributor to report any better offer to his supplier, and giving the supplier the opportunity to match that offer, will often have a similar, if perhaps weaker, effect. So will 'quantity forcing', which refers to incentives agreed between the parties which tend to make the distributor concentrate his purchases with that supplier, such as minimum purchase requirements and loyalty rebate schemes.

In deciding whether Article 81 is infringed, the Commission will look at the usual factors such as the market strength of the supplier, but also in particular at the duration of the restriction. The Guidelines give the rule of thumb that non-compete obligations shorter than one year entered into by non-dominant companies can normally be assumed not to infringe Article 81, but that they may do so if concluded for longer than this, depending on other factors.[43]

---

[42] Case T-168/01, discussed in Ch. 6, p. 87. For a similar approach when applying Art. 82 see the opinion of Advocate General Jacobs in Case C-53/03 *Syfait*, though the ECJ did not follow him.

[43] Para. 141.

The *Ice Cream* cases[44] illustrate the kind of situation in which exclusive purchasing arrangements will infringe Article 81(1). Schöller Lebensmittel and Langnese-Iglo had substantial shares in the German market for 'impulse' ice cream. Each operated through a large number of exclusive purchase agreements with retail outlets under which these would buy all their ice cream requirements exclusively from their supplier. For their part both Schöller and Langnese provided freezer cabinets to the retailers without charge provided they were only used for the suppliers' own product and not for those of rival manufacturers. These arrangements were challenged by Mars, which had a very small share of the German 'impulse' ice-cream market and sought to win additional market share, inter alia, by offering an original range of products under the trade names of well-known chocolate bars. The Court of First Instance upheld the Commission's decision in Mars' favour, and ruled that the existing exclusive purchase arrangements operated by Schöller and Langnese not only breached Article 81(1) but were also ineligible for block exemption under Regulation 1984/83 and individual exemption.

In reaching its decision the Court of First Instance referred to the important earlier case of *Delimitis*,[45] which principally concerned the legality of beer supply under ties. In that case the European Court had laid down the principles for the assessment of exclusive purchase agreements generally against Article 81(1). It stressed the importance of looking in a realistic way at the anti-competitive effect of an individual agreement, taking into account both its own terms against the background of the retail market and the circumstances in which the agreements operated generally as part of an overall network.

The relevant factors in the *Ice Cream* cases were the percentage of the market controlled by the tied supplies from the manufacturers in question, and the length of the exclusive-purchase obligations agreed to by which trade between Member States was affected. The Court found that there was an appreciable effect on competition as a result of these exclusive-purchase arrangements leading to foreclosure of Mars from access to the German market, an effect to which the provision of freezers for exclusive use by retailers for those two suppliers' ice cream made a major contribution. Trade between Member States was affected in that imports from the French subsidiary of Mars were considerably reduced as a result of the exclusive purchase arrangements operated by the two German suppliers.

5.5 OTHER RESTRICTIONS ON DISTRIBUTORS

Article 81 may be infringed where a supplier imposes other restrictions on the way in which his distributors market his goods. The Commission's concerns will be similar to those raised by exclusive distribution and territorial protection though they will be less when there is healthy competition in the relevant market from suppliers of competing goods. Such restrictions might include exclusive customer allocation, where a

---

[44] Case T-7/93 *Langnese-Iglo* v. *Commission* [1995] II ECR 1533: 5 CMLR 602 upheld in Case C-279/95 [1998] I ECR 5609 and Case T-9/93 *Schöller Lebensmittel* v. *Commission* [1995] ECR II-1611: 5 CMLR 602.

[45] Case C-234/89 *Delimitis* v. *Henninger* [1991] ECR I-935: [1992] 5 CMLR 210, see Section 5.6 below.

distributor may only distribute to a restricted group of customers (though this will not necessarily infringe Article 81 in the context of selective distribution, as explained in the next chapter).

Another example is the practice of 'tying' whereby the supplier makes the supply of one product to the distributor conditional upon the purchase of another product, where the second is one that customers do not normally want or expect always to purchase together. The Commission's main concern here is about possible foreclosure of the market for the tied product, in particular where tying is combined with a non-compete clause.[46] It will look in particular at factors such as the supplier's strength on the market for the tying product, and the existence of buyer power, to establish whether Article 81(1) is infringed.

5.6 PARALLEL NETWORKS

The leading case on the effect of parallel networks is *Delimitis* v. *Henninger Bräu*.[47] A dispute had arisen between Delimitis, a former tenant of a café in Frankfurt, and Henninger Bräu, the brewery which owned the premises, as to the sums owing between the parties. Delimitis claimed before the Oberlandesgericht that the exclusive purchase clauses which his agreement with Henninger Bräu contained were not protected by the block exemption and were therefore void under Article 81(1). A number of important issues were raised in the resulting Article 234 reference.

As far as the parallel networks were concerned, the judgment first stated that there were advantages to both brewery and its tenant in having an exclusive distribution agreement, provided that it neither was intended to make, nor made, it difficult for competitors to enter the beer market in competition with the brewery. The cumulative effect of the brewery's network was, as earlier case law had established, one factor to take into account, looking at the number of the outlets so tied, the duration of that tie, and the degree of loyalty of tenants to the breweries. In addition, however, the actual contribution of the disputed contract to the blocking effect on potential new entry had also to be weighed up. This had perhaps not been sufficiently emphasized in the earlier cases.

6. THE 1999 BLOCK EXEMPTION REGULATION 2790/99

6.1 ELIMINATION OF THE 'WHITE LIST'

Perhaps the single most liberating change in approach in the current block-exemption Regulation as compared with earlier block exemptions is the fact that

---

[46] Guidelines, paras. 215–24.   [47] See fn. 45.

Regulation 2790/99 operates on the basis that everything which is not expressly prohibited is permitted. In other words there are no 'white' and 'grey' lists of clauses to
which the parties must limit themselves.

The new rules, involving as they do concepts such as market share, are less clear-cut
than those in the previous block exemptions which focused more on the wording of
clauses, but the Guidelines offer substantial and detailed assistance to those applying
them.

To a large extent the new Regulation removed the 'straitjacket' effect for which the
earlier regimes had been criticized, but the unavoidable concomitant of this was a lower
level of legal certainty. During consultations, the aim of only subjecting agreements
between parties with significant power to individual examination by the Commission
was not controversial, but the uncertainty inherent in the economic concepts necessary to achieve this were the subject of much argument.

6.2 THE 30 PER CENT MARKET-SHARE CAP

In line with its aim of treating distribution in an economics-based, rather than a formalistic, manner, Regulation 2790/99 is intended to grant exemption to distribution
agreements between parties without substantial market power. Market power being
difficult to measure, market share is taken as an approximate indicator of market
power. So the block exemption incorporated for the first time a market share threshold above which automatic exemption is unavailable, and the Regulation is available
only where the supplier (or, in the case of exclusive distribution where the exclusive
territory covers the whole of the Community, the distributor) does not have a relevant market share exceeding 30 per cent (Article 3). Above this threshold, individual
assessment of the agreement is necessary.

The introduction of a market-share cap was one of the most hotly contested aspects
of the Regulation. Industry and its lawyers argued long and vigorously that such a rule
would be unworkable, since it is so difficult to establish market shares with any degree
of precision, particularly in rapidly developing markets. However, the Commission
insisted that there was no better means of ensuring that the benefit of the new, more
generous, block exemption, did not go to firms with too much market power, and the
market-share cap stayed, albeit in the form of a single threshold of 30 per cent, rather
than two of 20 per cent and of 40 per cent which had been proposed in an earlier draft.
One factor which may have assisted the Commission in prevailing was the fact that
while discussions on the block exemption were going on, it published its White Paper
on procedural modernization in the application of Articles 81 and 82, which proposed
the abolition of the notification system altogether. This may have led some to feel less
strongly about the content of the block exemption.

The Guidelines[48] deal in considerable detail with the theoretical question of how
to establish market share, and further assistance is available from the Commission's
Notice on Market Definition.[49] The question can be particularly difficult in innovative

---

[48] Paras. 88–99.   [49] [1997] OJ C372/5: [1998] 4 CMLR 177.

markets involving new technologies, where market definitions and shares shift rapidly with each new technological development. On the one hand, the first to market a new product may, at least for a short time, hold a 100 per cent market share. On the other hand, the phenomenon of 'convergence' whereby it becomes possible to receive phone messages or watch films on a personal computer, means that product market definitions change rapidly. However, in most markets the difficulty often lies not so much in theoretical market definition, as in the absence of the kind of statistics and information required, since companies frequently do not have records broken down in a suitable way, and even where they do, the information for different product and geographical markets may be scattered in different places and hard to track down.

Where a company has a market share above the threshold for some of its products and below the threshold for others, the question arises as to whether they need to be split up into different agreements in order to benefit from the Regulation in respect of some products. In practice the Commission is quite relaxed about this, and allows the Regulation to apply in respect of those goods or services for which the conditions of application are fulfilled, even where other goods and services are also covered by the same agreement.

In fact, during the years following the entry into force of the Regulation, the Commission received very few queries in connection with the market-share rule. Nor did the flood of notifications from parties with large market shares, predicted by some during the consultations which led up to adoption of the Regulation, materialize. The lengthy consultations leading up to adoption of Regulation seem generally to have resulted in a very reasonable compromise, and one which does not appear to have given rise to any major problems.

6.3 WIDER SCOPE OF AGREEMENTS COVERED

Block exemption Regulation 2790/99 is fundamentally different from its predecessors in other ways too. The fact that there is no list of permitted restrictions, so that everything which is not expressly prohibited is permitted, creates a radically different environment from that of earlier exemptions. Parties and their advisers used to have to draft agreements to fit in with the framework provided by a block exemption, and to ensure that no restrictions beyond those expressly permitted were included, failing which the benefit of the block exemption was lost entirely. Now, their situation depends on whether they are below or above the 30 per cent threshold: if below, they are reasonably free to draft as they wish, provided they bear in mind certain forbidden 'hard core' restrictions; if above they cannot benefit from the block exemption at all.

If the market-share requirement is satisfied, Article 2(1) provides a broad general exemption where 'two or more undertakings each of which operates, for the purposes of the agreement,[50] at a different level of the production or distribution chain, and relating to the conditions under which the parties may purchase, sell, or resell certain

---

[50] Though agreements between competitors may fall within this general definition, the extent to which these can benefit from the Regulation is circumscribed by the additional requirements of Art. 2(4).

goods or services'. This means that many types of agreement which previously did not fall within the scope of any of the narrowly drafted previous block exemptions can now enjoy such automatic exemption. The definition cited above includes, for example, agency agreements, agreements for the supply of services and intermediate goods, industrial supply agreements, customer allocation agreements, and many forms of selective distribution. On the other hand, it does not cover motor vehicle distribution agreements[51] nor technology transfer agreements such as intellectual property licences. Nor does it cover rental or leasing contracts, and this can lead to difficulties of interpretation where, for example, access to a telecommunications network is granted, as this can be seen as leasing of the lines, or as supply of a service.

Though the exemption is broadly drawn, the presence of clauses dealing with intellectual property rights can preclude its application altogether, because the agreement is within its scope only where the rights concerned are 'directly related to the use, sale or resale' of the goods or services being supplied to the buyer and are not the 'primary object' of the agreement (Article 2(3)). One consequence of this is that the Commission considers software distribution to fall outside the scope of the Regulation where the distributor is licensed to reproduce the software, but within it if he resells diskettes or CD-Roms containing the software. On the other hand, where software is incorporated in hardware being sold, even where the software is protected by copyright, the Regulation will normally apply.[52] This limitation is also of particular importance in the context of franchising and will be discussed in the next chapter.

6.4 PROHIBITED OR 'BLACK-LISTED' CLAUSES

As in previous block exemptions, Article 4 sets out a list of elements whose presence in an agreement will make the benefit of the block exemption unavailable to the whole agreement. This is in contrast to the types of clause set out in Article 5, which only entail lack of enforceability of the specific clause, and not of the whole agreement. Interestingly, all the black clauses concern limitations on intra-brand competition, which the Commission has said are usually less detrimental to competition than limitations on competition between different brands. In fact it is not just such express clauses which are caught, but any means which 'directly or indirectly, in isolation or in combination with other factors under the control of the parties', have the same object, which means that companies and their advisers will need to look further than the bare wording of the agreement, even in the context of black clauses. Taking this together with the fact that, although shorter than some of its predecessors, the black list is fairly complex in its wording, it is perhaps not surprising that, of all the aspects of the new policy, it is the black list that has been the subject of the most unofficial queries to DG Comp. The five types of 'black-listed clauses' or 'hard-core restraints' covered by Article 4 are discussed below.

---

[51] These are covered by a sector specific Reg. 1400/2002 described in the next chapter.
[52] Guidelines, paras. 39–41.

6.4.1 Fixed or minimum resale prices (Article 4(a))

The first prohibition mentioned is that on fixed or minimum resale prices, whether these are directly or indirectly enforced. As we have already seen, resale price maintenance has always been treated as a per se infringement of Article 81(1), so it was bound to be excluded from any block exemption. The Guidelines mention as an example of possible indirect price-fixing the pre-printing of recommended prices on the packaging of goods.[53]

6.4.2 Restrictions on the buyer as to where or to whom he may sell (Article 4(b))

The second prohibition, on restrictions on the buyer as to where or to whom he may sell, is the most complex, as it encompasses a rule against such restrictions and four exceptions to that rule. As a first exception, there may be a ban on active sales into an exclusive territory allocated to another buyer or exclusively reserved to the supplier, or on active sales to certain customer categories reserved to another buyer or to the supplier. Exemption of such customer restrictions is a new feature which has not before appeared in block exemptions.

It can be difficult to assess whether a given restriction is, or has the effect of, an active sales ban,[54] in particular where modern electronic forms of distribution are involved. Use of a website to reach customers is not normally considered active selling, and this applies regardless of the language used. This means that, for example, although it is clear that placing advertising in a German newspaper or on a billboard in Germany constitutes active selling, the Guidelines[55] seem to indicate, for example, that the placing of German language advertising on the Internet site of a French company that can be accessed in Germany does not constitute active selling into Germany. This is perhaps surprising, for the main reason for including the German language advertising will almost certainly be to reach customers in Germany.

Second, wholesalers may be stopped from supplying end-users. The third exception relates only to selective distribution and will be discussed in the next chapter, and the fourth allows the buyer to be banned from reselling components, which have been sold to him for incorporation into another product, to competing manufacturers.

6.4.3 Prohibition on selective distribution retailers making active or passive sales to any end-users (Article 4(c))

Selective distribution cannot therefore be combined with an exclusive distribution obligation on the buyer, except to the extent that the use of location clauses can be used to limit the buyer's freedom of action.[56]

6.4.4 Prohibition on cross-supplies between members of a selective distribution network (Article 4(d))

---

[53] Para. 7.   [54] See Guidelines, paras. 49–52.   [55] Para. 51.

[56] This is discussed in Ch. 11, Section 1.6.3, with other issues relating to selective distribution.

6.4.5 Restrictions on the sale of parts to end-users and independent repairers by suppliers to OEM manufacturers (Article 4(e))

The fifth hard-core restriction listed in Article 4 means that OEM manufacturers cannot prevent suppliers selling parts to end-users and independent repairers who are not part of the manufacturer's network. Note that this is the only type of hard-core restriction listed in Article 4 which involves a restriction on the supplier rather than the buyer.

6.5 SINGLE-BRANDING (NON-COMPETE) CLAUSES

The rules on non-compete[57] and related clauses are contained in Article 5 and have in one respect been tightened up in comparison with the previous block exemptions. In the context of exclusive distribution and franchising an exemption was available under them irrespective of the duration of such a clause, but now its duration must be limited to five years, whatever the type of agreement.

On the other hand, such clauses have a special status as compared with other types of prohibited restriction in that they are severable for the purposes of the Regulation, and so their inclusion does not mean that the whole agreement is ineligible for exemption under it. Furthermore, the way in which 'non-compete' is defined would appear to mean that pure exclusive purchase clauses (relating only to where the buyer should source his stocks of the supplier's product, and not mentioning competing products) are not mentioned in the Regulation at all, and so are exempted regardless of duration or the percentage of supplies concerned.

6.6 PARALLEL NETWORKS

In Article 8, a novel provision which caused unease at the time of its proposal and adoption, the Commission is given the power, where 'parallel networks' account for over 50 per cent of a market, to exclude, by means of a specific regulation, its application to certain types of agreement in that market.[58] Six months' notice of such an intended withdrawal, which may apply to specific product and geographic markets as well as to particular types of clause, has to be given. Though it was claimed at the outset by some that this provision amounted to permission for the Commission to rewrite the block exemption at will, and to reintroduce sector-specific rules, to date it has not been used at all.

---

[57] In Art. 1, 'non-compete' is defined for the purposes of the Regulation so as to include non-compete and requirements clauses which bind a buyer to sourcing over 80 per cent of the type of product in question from the supplier.

[58] The motor vehicle block-exemption Regulation (discussed in the next chapter) is a good example of a sector which the Commission sees as requiring extra legal safeguards in the light of the cumulative effect of the high number of near-identical distribution networks.

6.7 BEER AND PETROL

There are, of course, several features common to these two sectors. Both involve liquid products, widely regarded as essential to the maintenance of normal life, which are consumed or utilized on a regular basis in relatively small quantities by individual consumers, but which have to be provided on a wide geographical basis from a large number of outlets. Brand preference is an important factor, so that heavy promotional expenditure is incurred in order to ensure brand loyalty from customers and to attract support for new products; product differentiation is a major element in the competitive struggle between manufacturers. In both cases outlets have to be regularly visited by the supplier's vehicles carrying fresh supplies, and tanks, pumps, and equipment have to be provided. Any interruption in these supplies (as the result of strikes or other cause) may be commercially disastrous, particularly if local competitors are able to take advantage.

The cost of acquiring sites for retail outlets and of rendering them attractive to customers is substantial and often beyond the financial resources of those who will run them. Therefore it is necessary for suppliers to ensure that these outlets can be let to tenants at rents ultimately linked with the level of turnover they can obtain, or alternatively run by managers employed to run them effectively. Substantial financial assistance to tenants of the outlets is often needed for fitting out the premises to an appropriate standard. This assistance is also made available on favourable terms to owners of premises who are prepared to accept a partial or total tie to the lender's products in return for such loans.

These factors have led to the development in both industries of many large exclusive purchasing and non-compete agreements, and when it was drafting Regulation 1984/83 the Commission decided that specific provisions were needed to cover these special sectors with their own particular problems. Since then market developments have persuaded the Commission that there is no longer any need for this, and when that Regulation was replaced by Regulation 2790/99 the beer and petrol industries more or less lost their special regimes and were brought within the general rules.

The only remaining vestiges of these sector-specific regimes appear in Article 5 of the vertical-restraints block exemption. Article 5(a) provides that the usual limit on exemptable exclusive purchase and non-compete clauses of five years' duration does not apply 'where the contract goods or services are sold by the buyer from premises and land owned by the supplier or leased by the supplier from third parties not connected with the buyer, provided that the duration of the ... obligation does not exceed the period of occupancy of the premises and land by the buyer'. In practice this exception is most likely to apply in the beer and petrol markets.

6.8 WITHDRAWAL BY NATIONAL AUTHORITIES

At the procedural level a major change is that, in any specific case, Article 7 allows withdrawal of the benefit of exemption in respect of all or part of a Member State by the relevant national authorities.[59] Previously, this could only be done by the Commission, and this change anticipated the procedural modernization measures which came into force on 1 May 2004, and which devolved certain enforcement responsibilities from the Commission to national courts and competition authorities.

6.9 INDIVIDUAL EXEMPTION UNDER ARTICLE 81(3)

The application of Article 81(3) has been considered in detail in Chapter 8. In its Guidelines, the Commission stresses that there is no presumption of infringement of Article 81(3) where the relevant market share is over 30 per cent.[60] The Guidelines refer to benefits arising from restrictions in distribution arrangements including increased inter-brand competition, more efficient market penetration, and the streamlining of distribution logistics.[61] The Commission also summarizes what it sees as the four main negative effects of vertical restraints:[62]

(1) 'foreclosure of other suppliers or other buyers by raising barriers to entry'

(2) 'reduction of interbrand competition between the companies operating on the market, including facilitation of collusion amongst suppliers or buyers'

(3) 'reduction of intrabrand competition between distributors of the same brand'

(4) 'the creation of obstacles to market integration, including, above all, the freedom of consumers to purchase goods or services in any Member State they choose'.

7. DISTRIBUTION AND ABUSE OF A DOMINANT POSITION

We have seen that firms with market shares exceeding 30 per cent face a more stringent legal regime than those below the 30 per cent threshold, and that this is a change introduced for the first time by the 1999 block-exemption Regulation.

Firms with market shares exceeding around 40 per cent may, depending on the market situation, be regarded as having a dominant position. Article 82 prohibits firms with a dominant market position from abusing that position, and that applies to their distribution practices just as it does to their behaviour in other areas of their business. A number of the potentially abusive practices dealt with in Chapter 14 relate to distribution, including refusal to deal, discriminatory pricing, excessive and predatory pricing, operating discount and rebate systems and tying.

---

[59] In order to allow the Commission to include this clause the Council enabling Reg. 19/65 had to be amended to give it the necessary powers: Reg. 1215/99 [1999] OJ L148/1.

[60] Para. 62.   [61] Paras. 115–17.   [62] Guidelines para. 103.

FURTHER READING

S. BISHOP and D. RIDYARD, 'E.C. Vertical Restraints Guidelines: Effects-Based or Per Se Policy?' [2002] ECLR 35–8.

B. HAWK, 'System Failure: Vertical Restraints and EC Competition Law' [1995] 32 CMLRev 973.

A. JONES, 'Completion of the Revolution in Antitrust Doctrine on Restricted Distribution–*Leegin* and its Implications for EC Competition Law' [2008] Antitrust Bull (forthcoming).

P. JONES HARBOUR, 'An Open Letter to the Supreme Court of the United States' (available in the speeches section of the US Federal Trade Commission website).

J. LEVER and S. NEUBAUER, 'Vertical Restraints: Their Motivation and Justification' [2000] 21 ECLR 7–23.

L. PEEPERKORN, 'E.C. Vertical Restraints Guidelines: Effects-Based or Per Se Policy? A Reply' [2002] ECLR 38–41.

L. PEEPERKORN, 'Resale Price Maintenance and its Alleged Efficiencies' [2008] 4 ECJ 1.

E. ROUSSEVA, 'Modernizing by Eradicating: How the Commission's New Approach to Article 81 EC Dispenses with the Need to Apply Article 82 EC to Vertical Restraints' [2005] CMLRev 587–638.

R. SUBIOTTO and F. AMATO, 'The Reform of the European Competition Policy concerning Vertical Restraints' (2000) 69 Antitrust Law Journal 147–93.

R. WHISH, 'The New Regulation 2790/99: the Commission's new style block exemption for vertical agreements' [2000] 37 CMLRev 887.

11

DISTRIBUTION: SELECTIVE DISTRIBUTION AND FRANCHISING

Selective distribution and franchising are forms of distribution. Moreover, since 2000 they have been covered by the same Regulation 2790/99 and its accompanying Guidelines which apply to distribution agreements generally, so that much of the previous chapter is relevant to such systems. However, both the Regulation and Guidelines also include rules and guidance referring specifically to selective distribution and franchising, and these will be discussed in this chapter, together with the relevant Commission decisions and European Court judgments. There is also a section on motor-vehicle distribution agreements, which normally involve selective distribution, and which have long been subject to a sector-specific regime.

1. SELECTIVE DISTRIBUTION SYSTEMS

1.1 INTRODUCTION

Selective distribution systems differ from both open and exclusive distribution systems in that, whilst no specific territorial area is allocated to the dealer, a unique restriction is placed upon him, namely a prohibition on the resale of contract goods to other dealers unless these other dealers have themselves already been admitted to the selective system. The essence of selectivity, therefore, is not simply that the supplier selects its main distributors or wholesalers, for if this were the only restrictive element, it would be hard to see how Article 81 could apply at all to such a unilateral act of commercial policy. It is rather that the supplier limits the distribution of goods to only those wholesalers and retailers which satisfy appropriate criteria and as a result have been allowed to join the system. Wholesalers will normally sell to any wholesaler or retailer within the system, whereas retailers may sell to consumers or users, and also, sometimes, to dealers within the approved list.

The establishment of a distribution system utilizing such restrictions might appear at first sight to raise problems under Article 81(1), if the other requirements of the

Article were also present. In fact, both Commission and Court have taken a tolerant view of such systems, which provide perhaps the only example of an important group of commercial agreements with specifically restrictive provisions being allowed to remain outside the scope of Article 81(1), for the sake of the advantages which they are said to confer for the distribution of certain types of product. However, this is conditional upon the systems being operated in accordance with limits placed upon them to minimize their overall effect on competition.

1.2 SELECTIVE DISTRIBUTION: THE EARLY YEARS—
METRO/SABA (NO. 1) AND OTHER CASES

Selective distribution developed particularly in respect of products that fell into one of two categories. The first category, and the most important, was consumer products requiring a high degree of after-sales service because of their inherent complexity and the purchaser's reasonable requirements for both initial guarantee and later sales and service coverage. In this category came motor cars, electric and electronic equipment (such as high-fidelity equipment and personal computers), and (perhaps unexpectedly) false teeth. The second category comprised goods which were not necessarily highly complex but which were expensive and sold under prestige brand names which had been extensively promoted; their manufacturers believe that continuing control over the environment in which the goods are sold is important to their goodwill and continuing success. Into this latter category come watches and clocks, jewellery, perfume, and some borderline items such as porcelain and possibly even newspapers.

The Commission first began to give active consideration to the legal basis for the assessment of such systems of distribution for both technical and luxury products in the early 1970s. The earliest cases arose in the perfume, automobile, and electrical goods markets. The most important early decision was *Metro/Saba (No.1)*[1]. Saba was a German company specializing in electrical and electronic equipment including high-fidelity equipment and television sets. It had established a distribution network in Germany which involved the appointment of wholesalers who would purchase the Saba products and resell them to approved specialist dealers, whose turnover had to be obtained mainly from the sale of electric and electronic equipment of this kind. Department and discount stores would therefore normally have difficulties in obtaining appointment. Other qualifications related to the premises, the acceptance of substantial minimum supply figures, and the stocking of a full range of products, whilst distributors' employees had to have a suitable level of technical expertise. In other EC countries, sales by Saba were made direct to its sole distributor, dealing also only with approved specialist dealers, who in turn served the public.

In the original forms of agreement, there were numerous prohibitions on the sole distributors (and wholesalers) and the specialist dealers. These included prohibition against export to other EC countries, prohibition against cross-supplies (wholesaler

---

[1] Case 26/76 [1977] ECR 1875: [1978] 2 CMLR 1.

to wholesaler or retailer to retailer), return supplies (retailer to wholesaler), and direct supplies by wholesalers or sole distributors to consumers. The Commission exempted the agreements but rejected all these restrictions except the last, which was accepted on the ground that a separation of the function of wholesalers from those of retailers was appropriate to the multilevel distribution system that Saba operated.

The Commission's decision was challenged by Metro, a self-service wholesaler, running a cash and carry business for retailers which had been unable to obtain admission to the Saba system.[2] Metro challenged the decision of the Commission, claiming that the prohibition on making supplies available to private customers should not be permitted under the exemption afforded by Article 81(3). It also challenged the requirement imposed by Saba that the turnover of wholesalers engaged in a number of different sectors and having a special department for such electrical goods must be on a level comparable with that of a specialized wholesaler. The decision of the Court, given in October 1977, provided the first authoritative judicial pronouncement on the criteria which the Commission had applied to selective distribution systems. The Court held that Metro, whilst entitled to challenge the ruling of the Commission, had failed to adduce sufficient evidence to overturn it. Pointing out that Saba's market share in relation to the various products concerned was in no case greater than approximately 10 per cent (and in some cases less) the Court stated that the nature and intensiveness of competition in such markets would vary to an extent dictated by the nature of the products as well as by the structure of the relevant market itself.

The Court emphasized that price competition was not the only form of competition for specialist wholesalers and retailers. The acceptance of a certain level of prices consistent with consumers' interests in retaining a network of specialist dealers alongside a parallel system of wholesalers operating self-service and other methods of 'low price, no frills' distribution formed a rational objective for the Commission. The availability of this choice for the consumer was considered appropriate especially in sectors covering the production of high quality and technically advanced consumer durable goods, where a relatively small number of large and medium-sized producers offered a varied range of readily interchangeable items. While the Commission exempted the various restrictions of the selective distribution system under Article 81(3), the Court took a slightly different approach and ruled that some of those restrictions did not fall under Article 81(1) at all, being normal requirements in the distribution of the sale of consumer durables. Any marketing system based on the selection of outlets necessarily involved the obligation on wholesalers to supply only appointed resellers; therefore, the right for Saba to verify that the wholesalers had carried out these obligations fell outside 81(1), as also the restriction on the sale only to dealers already approved as members of the system.[3]

---

[2] Metro was later admitted to the system on condition it complied with the restrictions applicable to wholesalers, which included a ban on sales to both private customers and institutional customers such as schools and hospitals.

[3] Separation of functions as a part of the system also entitled Saba to prohibit wholesalers from selling direct to the large institutional customers which Metro had wished to serve.

This decision seemed to give a green light to the approval of such systems, provided that the choice of dealers within the system was based on the qualitative grounds adopted by Saba. On the other hand, the terms of the judgment suggested that a system based on other grounds, e.g. on limiting the total number of distributors within a given Member State or particular area, could only be justified by way of individual exemption, if at all. To keep the agreement outside Article 81(1), the criteria applied had to relate to the technical qualifications of the retailer and its staff and the suitability of its trading premises. Moreover, all conditions had to be laid down uniformly for all potential dealers and not in a discriminatory way, as subsequently confirmed by the Court both in an Article 234 reference in the *Perfumes* cases[4] and in the later *AEG/Telefunken* case,[5] where the Court said:

It is common ground that agreements constituting a selective system necessarily affect competition in the Common Market. However, it has always been recognized in the case law of the Court that there are legitimate requirements, such as the maintenance of a specialist trade capable of providing specific services as regards high-quality and high-technology products, which may justify a reduction of price competition in favour of competition relating to factors other than price. Systems of selective distribution, in so far as they aim at the attainment of a legitimate goal capable of improving competition in relation to factors other than price, therefore constitute an element of competition which is in conformity with Article [81(1)]. The limitations inherent in a selective distribution system are, however, acceptable only on condition that their aim is in fact an improvement in competition in the sense above mentioned. Otherwise they would have no justification inasmuch as their sole effect would be to reduce price competition.[6]

The application of these principles can be well illustrated by the subsequent 1984 decision of the Commission in the *IBM Personal Computers* case.[7] IBM had created a selective distribution system for which it wished to recruit a large number of dealers capable of offering skilled pre- and post-sales service acting as independent undertakings to sell personal computers in direct competition with IBM's own sales force. Criteria had been published for such appointment and IBM had publicly announced that it would appoint any applicant who satisfied them. The distribution system would then consist of all these authorized dealers who would be required to sell the goods only to each other or to consumers, not to unauthorized dealers. IBM had also appointed wholesale distributors to operate alongside and in competition with its own wholesale subsidiary company. It stated that it would also appoint other wholesalers in such a capacity as long as they could also provide a service of the required standard. Given the high level of skill required from dealers, the criteria laid down for their appointment being matched appropriately to the nature of the product, and IBM's commitment to its uniform application without discrimination, the Commission gave negative clearance to the system.

---

4 E.g. Case 99/79 *Lancôme v. Etos* [1980] ECR 2511: [1981] 2 CMLR 164.
5 Case 107/82 [1983] ECR 3151: [1984] 3 CMLR 325.   6 Paras. 33–4.
7 [1984] 2 CMLR 342. See also the *14th Annual Report* (1984), pp. 60–1.

The essential element in this system was that, although the restriction on selling to unauthorized dealers was retained, entry to the system was 'open' for any qualified dealer, so that any restriction on competition flowing from the restrictions on resale outside the approved circle was kept to a minimum. If such agreements are to remain outside Article 81(1), it is essential that the obligations imposed on the retailer do not exceed those absolutely necessary to maintain the quality of the goods or to ensure they are sold under proper conditions. Obligations that go beyond this, e.g. to purchase complete ranges of the product or prescribing substantial minimum turnover figures over a particular period of time, would be regarded as 'quantitative' restrictions of competition meaning that, if they were to be included, they would have to be exempted under Article 81(3). Likewise, no discrimination can be practised by a manufacturer between, on one hand, specialized retailers and, on the other, department and discount stores, provided that each is able to meet the criterion of ability to sell the relevant products at the required standard. Nor may the manufacturer exercise its power of selection on the basis that a particular dealer has either exported or imported the goods outside official channels or has failed to comply with any particular pricing policy.[8]

1.3   REFUSAL TO HONOUR GUARANTEES

A particular issue which has come up in the context of selective distribution concerns selective dealers who find themselves in competition with others selling identical goods purchased from the manufacturer in another country (normally at lower prices) which have been brought in as parallel imports. The question before the European Court in *Metro* v. *Cartier*[9] was whether Cartier, a manufacturer of luxury watches sold throughout the Community by selective distribution, was entitled to refuse to honour guarantees on its watches obtained in non-Community countries such as Switzerland where there were gaps in the selective distribution system. Since 1984 Cartier had refused to provide a guarantee for watches not obtained from its authorized dealers within the selective system, and Metro had applied for a declaration that Cartier was nonetheless under an obligation to give this guarantee because there would otherwise be a breach of Article 81(1). The issue was raised under Article 234 by the German Bundesgerichtshof; the European Court ruled that, if the goods in question were appropriate for a selective distribution system, manufacturers were able to prevent trade sales to unauthorized dealers and were logically, therefore, entitled also to limit the benefit of guarantee on the product to those sold through such dealers. Moreover, whether or not the particular distribution system was 'impervious', i.e. had no gaps

---

[8] However, such agreements might escape the reach of Art. 81(1) altogether if the market share of the producers operating the system is very small.

[9] Case C-376/92 [1994] ECR I-15: 5 CMLR 331. The issue of whether the system is 'impervious' may nevertheless under Community law be relevant to the issue of whether a trade-mark owner in the Community can be deemed to have made it impossible for sales within the EEA to have taken place outside official distribution channels.

in it, enabling products to be sold outside the officially authorized sales network was irrelevant to the issue under Article 81, though treated as essential to validity of the system under German law. This rule in *Metro* v. *Cartier* does not apply to cars where these are distributed under the terms of the block exemption 1400/2002 (Article 4(1)(b) and recital 17), because the block exemption requires authorized repairers to honour guarantees for any motor vehicle acquired within the Community, regardless of the Member State in which it was bought and whether it has passed through the hands of dealers not part of the official chain.

1.4 SELECTIVE DISTRIBUTION OF PERFUME AND COSMETICS

A common link between many of the sectors where selective distribution systems have been approved is that the goods are expensive, technically complex, and require sales and service facilities of sufficient standard to ensure that customers obtain satisfaction from their purchases. To find that selective distribution is also used for perfume and cosmetics comes initially as a surprise, and the legal basis for using selective distribution for goods which, although expensive, lack complexity or the need for after-sales service or repair requires explanation. The requirement for selectivity in retail outlets for such products is based on a claim by manufacturers that their products can only be satisfactorily sold in a suitable atmosphere or ambience, where the luxurious quality of the products is not spoilt by association with more mundane and less expensive goods.

The Commission's 1974 *Annual Report*[10] refers to the examination by DG Comp of the distribution systems adopted by Christian Dior and Lancôme, which organized the sale of perfume and other beauty and toiletry goods through a selective distribution network limited to a restricted number of approved retailers supervised by their general agent in each Member State. The Commission[11] insisted on the deletion from the agreement of several clauses imposing, in its view, severe restraints on competition. These included, for example, restrictions on resale prices to be charged by Dior and Lancôme dealers when supplying any other retail outlet, either inside or outside their own country. The retailers were also prevented from obtaining supplies from any source other than their national general agent. If such clauses had not been removed, the individual national market would have been partitioned securely; their removal meant that the retailers were enabled within their trade network to sell or purchase to or from any approved agent or retailer in any EC country, and obtained freedom as to the resale prices charged on goods obtained from any source. The Commission commented that it expected this to lead to an alignment of prices for such products in the different Member States, and also that the market for these products is characterized

---

[10] pp. 60–1.

[11] The Commission in this case granted negative clearance from Art. 81(1) by informal settlement rather than by formal decision. Given the high prices charged, and the apparent lack of consumer benefit from the systems, granting formal exemption under Art. 81(3) might well have presented difficulties to the Commission.

by the existence of a fairly large number of competing firms, none of which held much more than 5 per cent of the market.

In the following year, the *5th Annual Report* referred to further consideration of these distribution arrangements. A large number of other companies in the industry had been involved in negotiations with the Commission seeking approval of simi-lar distribution terms. We find the Commission here complimenting itself for having been able to apply a 'uniform general arrangement throughout an entire industry, the perfume industry, without having to issue formal decisions'.[12]

However, litigation over the selective distribution system did arise, and was ultim-ately referred by French courts to the European Court for an Article 234 ruling. The case arose in the French courts because the Commission, though having approved the arrangements for the industry, had done so merely by a 'comfort letter' confirming that the system was not considered to be in breach of Article 81(1). Various perfume shops which had tried unsuccessfully to obtain supplies from Lancôme, Guerlain, and other leading suppliers brought action under the French law, which forbids refusal to supply. The perfume manufacturers argued that the existence of the 'comfort let-ter' provided a complete defence to this claim, but the European Court rejected this argument.[13] It held that national courts are quite free to reach their own findings on the standing of such agreements. National courts may, of course, act on the basis of all information available to them, and although they are not bound by the 'comfort letter', they may take its contents into account.

In principle, a system which relies, as did the perfume manufacturers, not merely on qualitative criteria for admission to the system but upon a quantitative selection of retailers would fall within the prohibition of Article 81(1). Nevertheless, in consider-ing whether either an individual agreement or a set of agreements distorted competi-tion, the Court ruled that it was necessary to consider the context within which they were established. Relevant factors here were the nature and quantity of the product, the position and importance of the parties on the market, and whether the retail outlet was isolated or formed part of a large network. The judgment of the Court contains an interesting explanation of the rationale for allowing selective criteria in the choice of outlets for luxury goods. The Court indicated that a selective system could be accepted provided it was laid down uniformly for all potential resellers, and that the objective criteria for selection were not applied in a discriminatory fashion. It was also necessary to examine whether the product required 'for the purpose of preserving its quality and ensuring that it is used correctly' such a system. National courts should also take into account whether national legislation already covered such requirements by specifying conditions of sale or qualifications for entry into the occupation of such a reseller.

Another case raised the issue of whether the sale of cosmetics, often found in the same retail outlets as perfumes, can be limited to those shops where a qualified pharmacist is present. In its 1991 *Vichy* decision[14] the Commission found that the

---

[12] p. 51.
[13] The *Perfume* Cases 253/78, 37, 99/79 [1980] ECR 2327, 2481, 2511: [1981] 2 CMLR 99, 143, 164.
[14] [1991] OJ L75/57, upheld by the CFI in Case T-19/91 [1992] ECR II-415.

basis on which the French company operated lacked consistency. In France it supplied cosmetics through a variety of outlets, but outside France only to retail pharmacies run by a qualified pharmacist. Vichy argued that this requirement was objective,
necessary, and proportionate, that it improved quality control and the services given to
customers, and enhanced inter-brand competition with other cosmetic manufacturers. The Commission rejected these arguments. Its finding was clearly assisted by the
difference between the distribution systems adopted by Vichy in France and in other
Member States, and was based principally on the ground that the benefits claimed
could be obtained by less restrictive means.

Important also was the Court of First Instance decision in *Leclerc* at the end of
1996.[15] On this occasion, the Leclerc group, a frequent litigator in competition cases,
challenged a 1991 negative clearance provided to the distribution system of Yves
St Laurent (much as Metro had challenged Saba's exemption for electrical goods). Its
principal argument was that the criteria applied by the Commission in its decision
would preclude the sale of Yves St Laurent cosmetics by retail outlets in the Leclerc
group. The outcome of the case, however, was as unsatisfactory for Leclerc as Metro's
experience had been. The Court upheld the Commission's decision in all but one
respect: its approval of a clause that Yves St Laurent would treat applications from
retailers less favourably if their total sale of perfumes was less than 60 per cent of
their overall sales. Such a ruling was held to be unnecessarily discriminatory, since it
favoured applications by specialist perfumeries at the expense of multiproduct shops,
even if the latter had specialized areas laid out so as to meet all the criteria specified by Yves St Laurent for the sale of their luxury cosmetics. In all other respects
the Commission confirmed the earlier case law to the effect that such systems were
outside Article 81(1) so long as the criteria specified were objective, uniform, and non-
discriminatory. It emphasized that it was for national courts and competition authorities to decide if the criteria were being properly applied to particular markets, and
indicated that any subjective or discriminatory application of the criteria would lead
to restrictions being held within Article 81(1) but without the possibility of individual
exemption under 81(3).[16]

1.5 REFUSAL TO DEAL

Refusals by a supplier to deal with or supply a distributor are normally purely unilateral and so fall outside Article 81.[17] Selective distribution by its nature requires
that members of the network be in a position to refuse to supply non-authorized distributors, and this will be reflected in the agreements concerned. Nevertheless, since

---

[15] Case T-19/92 [1997] 4 CMLR 995.

[16] Case T-19/92 [1997] 4 CMLR 995. It is clear that the Commission attaches importance to procedures
and criteria by which applicants in this sector are assessed and will expect arbitration to be available for
unsuccessful applicants. See Commission *Press Release* IP/95/736 of 11 July 1995. The Commission prefers
that the supply chain incorporates wholesalers as well as retailers. Arbitration procedures are also recommended in the *Fine Fragrances Report* of the MMC, 1993 (Cm. 2380), Ch. 8, para. 188.

[17] Art. 82 may apply if the supplier is dominant in the relevant market.

selective distribution systems are outside the range of Article 81 if they comply with the requirements set out in the *Metro/Saba (No. 1)* case, involving qualitative criteria only in the selection of their dealers, the inherent nature of selectivity means that some refusals to deal are acceptable and will not invalidate the system so as to bring it back within the range of the Article. It is also inherent in the system that a manufacturer or wholesaler or retailer cannot refuse to deal with qualified applicants and that the criteria must be applied without discrimination to all qualified applicants. Moreover, as we have seen, the criteria need often not be applied by the manufacturer itself but can be applied by a wholesaler or sole distributor, normally within a short time limit as in the *IBM Personal Computers*[18] and *Grundig*[19] cases.

An interesting, and not finally decided, issue is the effect of a refusal to deal with a qualified applicant who has been admitted to the distribution system. If the refusal to deal is part of a deliberate policy by a manufacturer to introduce into the distribution system a discouragement to certain outlets (perhaps because it feels that they are too inclined to cut prices) or in other ways to depart from the manufacturer's policy, then if it is likely that the refusal to deal is more than an isolated incident the Commission may be justified in withdrawing any negative clearance or exemption given, as in *AEG/Telefunken*.

The case of *Demo-Studio Schmidt* v. *Commission*[20] deals by contract with the rights of applicants to be appointed as selective distributors. Schmidt, a designer in a German machinery factory, decided to set up his own electronic-equipment business as a sideline to his salaried activities. He opened a small shop in Wiesbaden with opening hours of a limited nature, selling a variety of consumer electronics made by Revox. Revox later discussed Schmidt's request to be supplied with its Series B products, which were its more expensive items and afforded a higher profit margin, and made it clear to him that supply would be conditional on his sales premises remaining open for the whole of the working day. Schmidt said he would take a salesman on for this purpose. Later, however, Revox told Schmidt they had decided he could not be appointed a specialist retailer entitled to deal in Series B equipment because he did not satisfy the conditions laid down by them relating to the technical qualifications of staff and the design of sales area, as well as the observance of normal opening hours.

Revox having refused supplies of Series B equipment to him, Schmidt complained to the Commission, who rejected his claim saying that it had no grounds under Article 81 to order Revox to supply him with products. Schmidt asked the European Court to annul this decision, but it also rejected his claim. Their view was that if a selective distribution system was properly adopted for highly technical electronic goods, it was reasonable for a manufacturer to require retailers to be open for normal shopping hours, and that supplies could be refused to a part-time establishment. Even if the selective distribution system had elements which made it incompatible with Article 81(1), this would not of itself entitle Schmidt to be appointed a dealer by Revox, nor to force Revox to supply any particular range of products to him. The case

---

[18] [1984] 2 CMLR 342.   [19] *15th Annual Report* (1985), pp. 66–7.
[20] Case 210/81 [1983] ECR 3045: [1984] 1 CMLR 63.

therefore does not seem to give a broad right to a manufacturer not to deal with any particular applicant (whether or not he satisfies the necessary criteria laid down for the relevant distribution system) but places a duty on the manufacturer (or distributor with delegated responsibility) fairly to assess the criteria in the case of each applicant, taking the facts as they were at the time when the application was made.

1.6 SELECTIVE DISTRIBUTION: THE 1999 BLOCK EXEMPTION

During all this time selective distribution had remained the only common type of distribution arrangement not covered by a block exemption, and there was discussion as to whether a new block Regulation should be adopted for the benefit of such systems. Though there was some support for this, others considered that it was not necessary, given that, according to the Court's case law, many such systems fall outside the scope of Article 81(1) anyway. Others were against it on the grounds that selective distribution arrangements vary so widely that one block exemption could not take into account all the necessary possibilities and types of goods without becoming unwieldy. But both objections could be countered by pointing to other block exemptions in place at the time. Many exclusive distribution and franchising agreements fall outside Article 81(1), but block exemptions existed for such agreements. As to the varied nature of selective distribution agreements, the motor vehicle block exemption covers, amongst other things, selective distribution.[21]

1.6.1 Qualitative and quantitative criteria

Early drafts of what became the block exemption on vertical agreements, Regulation 2790/99, included selective distribution within its scope, but proposed different market share thresholds depending on whether the system was based on qualitative or quantitative criteria.

As we have seen, the first category involves products whose suppliers impose selectivity upon outlets which can be restrained from trading freely with non-approved outlets so long as entry to this 'family circle' is open to all suitably qualified undertakings. These tests for suitability relate to objective factors such as technical expertise, suitability of premises, adequacy of staff, and financial stability. These tests should be applied quickly, i.e. within a few weeks, and not simply by the manufacturer but at a delegated level, i.e. that of the wholesaler or sole distributor, so as to prevent a supplier from finding excuses to exclude undertakings more inclined to aggressive promotional innovation or even price cutting.

The second category involves products where the technical requirements for pre- and post-sales services and guarantee work justify additional restrictions being imposed by the supplier, namely quantitative limits on the number of appointed dealers within a Member State.[22]

---

[21] See p. 243—though admittedly this Regulation is particularly complex and detailed.

[22] Though the dividing line between the two permitted classes is itself indistinct: close examination of the case law shows considerable ambiguity as to what is 'qualitative' and what is 'quantitative'. Thus, in

It was initially proposed that the latter could benefit from automatic exemption only below a 20 per cent market share threshold, with the former being subject to a 40 per cent threshold. But in the Regulation as finally adopted no distinction of this sort was made, and the same 30 per cent threshold was applied to all selective distribution as to other types of distribution agreement.[23]

1.6.2 Product type

There had also been speculation that any block exemption covering selective distribution would be restricted to certain product types, as early cases had stressed that selective distribution was appropriate only for certain classes of goods. But over the years exemption had been granted in such a wide variety of different sectors, starting with watches and clocks in the *Omega Watches* case[24] that the distinction no longer seemed sustainable.

The principal reason for the blurring of the distinction is probably the Commission's acceptance, based on the judgment of the European Court in the *Perfume* cases, of the principle that selectivity can be justified by the circumstances in which goods are thought to have to be sold, as much as by their actual technical requirements. Thus, as we have seen, the privilege of classification as a selective distribution system has been accorded to a variety of products, not simply because of the nature of the product—justification also being drawn from other extraneous circumstances and alleged commercial needs, which many commentators feel lack validity. In this category, for example, are claims by newspapers, as in *Salonia* v. *Poidomani*[25] and *Binon*[26] where it seemed that the justification for permitting selectivity turned largely on the problems of financing the return of unsold newspapers.[27] Whilst the Commission appears to have heeded the requirement imposed by the European Court in the *Perfume* cases that consideration should be given to whether national law provides sufficient safeguards so that selectivity of distribution outlets is unnecessary—and applied it in the *Grohe/Ideal Standard*[28] cases relating to bathroom fittings (and refused to accept that the sale of normal household furniture requires the setting up of such systems[29])—the criteria still appear unpredictable.

In practice therefore, product type has now ceased to be a criterion for clearance or exemption of a selective distribution system. Rather, it has come to be required

---

Grundig (*15th Annual Report* (1985), pp. 66–7), exemption was granted to the Grundig selective distribution system for consumer electronic goods, where a number of restrictions were described by the Commission as quantitative which could as well have been classified as qualitative, and vice versa. It is in fact difficult to find a totally consistent thread of principle throughout the cases.

[23] But in the motor vehicles block exemption qualitative and quantitative systems are subject to different market share thresholds (see p. 247).

[24] [1970] CMLR D49.   [25] Case 126/80 [1981] ECR 1563: [1982] 1 CMLR 64.

[26] Case 243/83 [1985] ECR 2105: 3 CMLR 800.

[27] Another questionable example is the *Villeroy-Boch* case, where a selective distribution system relating to the sale of high-class porcelain was approved: *15th Annual Report* (1985), p. 66, [1985] OJ L376/15.

[28] *14th Annual Report* (1984), p. 61.   [29] *15th Annual Report* (1985), p. 66.

only that the selection criteria applied be appropriate to the goods or services con-cerned. This is reflected in the treatment of selective distribution under the vertical-restraints block exemption, which makes no mention of product type as a criteria of exemption.

1.6.3 Black-listed clauses

In order to benefit from automatic exemption under the vertical-restraints block exemption selective distribution agreements have to satisfy all the general require-ments of the Regulation, such as the 30 per cent market-share threshold, and the prohibition on fixed or minimum resale prices. The particular nature of selective dis-tribution, however, means that in this context a restriction on sales to unauthorized distributors is not black-listed as it is in the context of other types of distribution sys-tem (Article 4(b)).

However, the Regulation also lays down some specific requirements in the case of selective distribution, which it defines as 'a distribution system where the supplier undertakes to sell the contract goods or services, either directly or indirectly, only to distributors selected on the basis of specified criteria and where these distributors undertake not to sell such goods or services to unauthorized distributors' (Article 1(d)). As we have seen, for the purposes of the application of the block exemption no distinc-tion is made on the basis either of the type of product being distributed, or of whether the criteria applied are qualitative or quantitative.

There is no prohibition on selective distribution being combined with the allocation of an exclusive territory. However, where both are combined Article 4(c) prohibits any ban on either passive or active sales to users outside the allotted territory. This means that the distributor must be free, for example, to advertise in all ways and to seek cus-tom by using an Internet site.[30] The exclusivity in such a case is an obligation on the supplier only, and not on the distributor: the supplier can agree not to supply anyone else at any level of trade within that territory. However, the dealer may be prohibited from opening additional sales outlets without his supplier's permission.

According to the Guidelines,[31] a prohibition on selling through an Internet site will count as a hard-core restriction and take the system outside the ambit of the exemp-tion, in the absence of 'an objective justification' for such a clause. In the context of selective distribution the Guidelines recognize that it may well be appropriate for a supplier to establish quality requirements in respect of the site, but it will be rare that there is objective justification for prohibiting use of an Internet site outright.

Nor can there be any ban on cross-supplies between authorized distributors at any level in the network (Article 4(d)), or on supply even to non-authorized dealers in ter-ritories where the supplier does not operate a selective distribution system.[32]

---

[30] In May 2001, the Commission issued a press release confirming that Yves Saint Laurent's selective distribution was exempted by the Regulation, making special mention of the fact that approved retailers already operating a physical sales outlet were authorized to sell also via the Internet IP/01/713.

[31] Paras. 50–51.   [32] This is the Commission's interpretation of Art. 4(*b*): Guidelines, para. 52.

1.6.4 Non-compete clauses

As we have seen, certain non-compete clauses will not benefit from exemption under the Regulation, but they are treated as severable and so do not compromise the exempted status of the rest of the agreement. In the case of selective distribution Article 5(c) gives an additional non-exempted clause: suppliers may not stop dealers from selling the brands of particular competing suppliers, though they may impose an absolute non-compete provision. The Commission believes that selective non-compete clauses can facilitate horizontal cooperation between competing suppliers using the same network of outlets, so as to foreclose specific competitors from the market.[33]

1.6.5 Parallel networks

As we have seen, the Commission is on the look out for any undesirable 'network effect', by which is meant the combined restrictive effect of a number of similar networks in a market. Article 6 of the Regulation gives the Commission the power to withdraw the benefit of the Regulation where particular agreements, despite falling within the scope of the Regulation, do not in fact satisfy the requirements of Article 81(3).[34] Further, Article 8 allows the Commission to enact Regulations declaring the block exemption inapplicable to vertical agreements containing specific restraints relating to the market where such networks account for over 50 per cent of the relevant market, though so far it has never done so.

1.7 INDIVIDUAL EXEMPTION FOR SELECTIVE DISTRIBUTION: THE CURRENT POLICY

As already discussed, many selective distribution systems do not infringe Article 81 at all and so do not require any kind of exemption. The Guidelines state that, as case law has established, qualitative selective distribution falls outside Article 81 altogether, provided that certain conditions (necessity of the system to preserve the quality and proper use of product, and necessary, objective, qualitative, non-discriminatory criteria) are satisfied.[35] Acceptable clauses in this context include the application of the qualitative criteria themselves, as well as those connected with their application. They mention that the Commission's main concerns in the context of selective distribution are the risk of a reduction in competition between competing brands of goods, and a reduction in competition as a result of the cumulative effects of a number of similar networks operating on the same market, either because of foreclosure of distributors from entering or remaining on the market, or because collusion between suppliers or buyers is facilitated.

Systems involving quantitative or other types of restriction, and which for some reason do not fall within the scope of Regulation 2970/99, may qualify for individual

---

[33] Guidelines, para. 61.

[34] The Regulation does not confine the application of Art. 6 to selective distribution systems, but the 13th recital to the Regulation states explicitly that such concerns may arise in connection with such systems.

[35] Para. 185.

exemption. The overriding consideration will be the market position of the supplier, as the Guidelines state explicitly that a loss of competition within the same brand is only problematic if competition between brands is limited.[36] Much importance will also be placed on the presence on the market of a number of similar distribution networks, and in such cases the risk of foreclosure will be closely examined, especially if non-compete or similar clauses are present.

As to the relevance of product type, the Guidelines refer to the need to combat 'free-riding' and to create brand image, and say that the argument for exemption is strongest for new products, complex products, products which are difficult to judge before consumption ('experience products') and products difficult to judge even after consumption ('credence products').[37] Though this is quite a different formulation from the older product categories, it clearly has its roots in the same reasoning. It also shows why product type is not a criterion included in the Regulation: concepts such as 'complex products' are too difficult to define clearly to be appropriate for use in a block exemption.

2. MOTOR-VEHICLE DISTRIBUTION AND SERVICING NETWORKS

2.1 THE HISTORICAL BACKGROUND

The motor car is probably the most complex consumer product of all, as well as being the most expensive purchase that many consumers ever make. These unique characteristics have been put forward by motor manufacturers as justifying special rules on the distribution of cars. The issue first reached the Commission in the *BMW* case. The importance of the Commission's decision is shown by the fact that some two and a half pages are devoted to it in the *4th Annual Report*.[38] The most notable feature of the exemption granted is that it permits a restriction on the number of dealers allowed in Germany, which is a quantitative, not a qualitative, criterion. The Commission justified its decision by saying that 'Motor vehicles, being products of limited life, high cost and complex technology, require regular maintenance by specially equipped garages or service depots because their use can be dangerous to life, health and property and can have a harmful effect on the environment'. It described the required cooperation between BMW and its dealers as going beyond the mere marketing of products and involving cooperation which not only promoted economic progress and the distribution of the vehicles but also gave benefits to consumers in the form of improved service. The Commission felt that this close cooperation and specialization by the dealers would not be possible if BMW were required to admit to the system, without limit of

---

[36] Para. 187.   [37] Para. 195.
[38] [1975] 1 CMLR D44, 56. The comments are found at pp. 57–9.

numbers, any dealer required merely to show he had adequate premises, staff, and other qualitative attributes.

The first official draft of a block exemption for car distribution was published in June 1983, and met strong opposition from the motor industry. Amongst their complaints were that it sought to bring about an artificial realignment of vehicle prices within the EC, sought to interfere without justification in the detailed relationship between manufacturer and dealer, and failed to provide sufficient legal certainty for both. The content of the original draft actually owed a considerable amount to the principles already laid down in the *BMW* case. The Commission acknowledged that in the motor-vehicle sector (covering cars, buses, and vans) many of the restrictions of competition approved in the *BMW* case fulfilled the requirements of 81(3). In particular, the benefit to the public claimed for a system of authorized dealers was that it provided more satisfactory maintenance and repair services; the degree of competition of an inter-brand nature between the major car manufacturers made competition on an intra-brand basis between their dealers rather less important. The Regulation would grant exemption for the placing of restrictions on the motor dealer against:

(1) selling another manufacturer's vehicles or parts

(2) actively seeking customers outside its allotted territory

(3) subcontracting distribution, servicing, or repairs without the manufacturer's consent

(4) selling the vehicles or parts to dealers outside the distribution network.

In return, the manufacturer would agree not to appoint other dealers in the allotted territory during the period of the contract.

Considerable concern, especially by consumers' organizations, had been expressed about difficulties placed in the way of purchasers desiring to make parallel imports of vehicles from Member States where cars could be purchased more cheaply, and the draft contained clauses designed to give some protection to the consumer. Thus, consumers were entitled to have servicing or repairs done under a manufacturer's warranty anywhere in the Community, and were entitled to order cars to the specifications required at the place where they were to be registered from a dealer in another Member State, provided that the manufacturer or his importer sold the relevant model through the official distribution network at both places. Spare parts supplied by third parties, matching the quality of those supplied by the manufacturer, could also be purchased by dealers in the official network without breach of their agreement with the manufacturer.

The original draft dealt specifically with this sensitive issue of the freeing of parallel imports, providing that if the difference between retail prices recommended in any two countries exceeded 12 per cent over a six-month period, the authorized dealers would be free to sell to dealers outside the network in that second country. This freedom would not apply if prices were artificially held at different levels as the result of very high Member State tax rates, or where there was a temporary legislative freeze on the fixing of prices or profit margins. Fierce debate continued right up to the last moment as to whether the overall terms of the Regulation were unduly onerous upon the car manufacturers or upon dealers.

2.2 THE FIRST MOTOR-VEHICLE DISTRIBUTION BLOCK EXEMPTIONS: REGULATIONS 123/85 AND 1475/95

When Regulation 123/85 was finally issued at the end of 1984, some important changes had been made to the original draft. Dealers were now entitled to a minimum period of four years' appointment in order that they would not be made over-dependent on the manufacturer or importer. Additional safeguards were included to make it difficult for manufacturers or importers to prevent sales in the United Kingdom of right-hand-drive versions of cars bought through official channels on the Continent. The Commission, however, had removed the reference to the original price differential of 12 per cent from the Regulation and transferred it to an accompanying Notice[39] issued by way of interpretation of the Commission's attitude to the Regulation.

The Regulation preserved the right for dealers to sell to intermediaries, as agents for individual customers; this was the subject of the Court of First Instance judgment in *Peugeot* v. *Ecosystems*.[40] The Commission decision in favour of the intermediary's right to act on behalf of customers was accompanied by a Notice[41] from the Commission limiting the number of vehicles which an individual dealer is entitled to dispose of annually in this way to 10 per cent of its total sales. The great majority of any dealer's sales still had to be made direct to individual purchasers; intermediary sales could constitute only a relatively minor part of its business.

Regulation 123/85 turned out to be unsuccessful in accommodating the conflicting interests of the different parties, and when it was replaced ten years later by Regulation 1475/95 the principal aim was to redress the balance in favour of dealers so as to give them more independence from their suppliers and to increase competition between them. Numerous changes to this end were made to the rules, including provisions allowing dealers to sell competing brands and giving them more freedom to sell outside their allotted territory, and granting better protection of independent suppliers of spare parts.

2.3 THE NEW BLOCK EXEMPTION: REGULATION 1400/2002: THE DEBATE OVER ITS ADOPTION

But when, five years on, the time approached to review the Regulation again, the Commission admitted that these aims had again not been achieved. It was dissatisfied with the situation on two main counts. First, its twice-yearly statistics-gathering exercises showed that the tightening up of the Regulation in 1995 had not brought about

---

[39] [1985] OJ C17/4.   [40] Case T-9/92 [1993] ECR II-493: [1995] 5 CMLR 696.
[41] [1991] OJ C329/20. This remained applicable under Reg. 1475/95, though not now under Reg. 1400/2002.

significant price convergence: prices for some models still varied by up to 50 per cent between Member States. Second, despite the special privileges accorded to the industry by the block exemption, a number of large manufacturers were found to be flouting the competition rules and, in particular, to be hindering parallel imports between Member States.

Volkswagen was the first of a number of manufacturers to be investigated and heavily fined for such behaviour. The Commission found that dealers in Italy had been discouraged by a number of means from exporting cars to Germany and Austria, where higher retail prices made importing from Italy an attractive proposition. Their means included tying dealer bonuses to the subsequent registration of vehicles in Italy, restricting supplies and penalizing exporting distributors.[42] The €102 million fine imposed on Volkswagen in 1998 was at the time the highest ever imposed by the Commission for breach of Article 81. This underlines the fact that although vertical restraints are generally less serious from a competition point of view than agreements between competitors, when they divide markets along national borders they will be regarded as extremely serious infringements. The Court of First Instance later reduced the fine to €90 million, but itself emphasized the gravity of the infringement.[43]

After Volkswagen, large fines were also imposed on Opel (€43 million in 2000), JCB (€39.6 million in 2000), DaimlerChrysler (€71.825 million in 2001) and Volkswagen again (€30.96 million in 2001) for similar behaviour.[44] Though it is not logically linked, such widespread conduct in the industry clearly influenced the Commission's thinking.

As required by Regulation 1475/95, in November 2000 the Commission made a report on its operation: this identified a number of specific drawbacks to the existing regime, and confirmed the Commission's impression that it had not achieved some of the aims it had set out in 1995. First, the fact that exclusive dealer territories could be combined with both quantitative and qualitative selective distribution meant that sales networks were closed to many potential distributors and too tightly controlled by manufacturers. Consumers had no alternative source of supply outside the networks, and still found it difficult to buy cars outside their home country. Furthermore, the development of new types of distribution channel such as supermarkets and Internet sites was being hampered.

At this point the Commission had three basic options to consider: extending the application of the existing Regulation, allowing the Regulation to lapse so that the motor-vehicle sector became covered by the general rules on vertical restraints, or drafting a new motor-vehicles block exemption.

The first option was rejected because of the failures identified by the Commission in its report. The second was also rejected, in part for similar reasons, since the application of Regulation 2790/99 would have allowed most networks to continue to function

---

[42] [1998] OJ L124/60, [1998] 5 CMLR 33.

[43] Case T-62/98, [2000] ECR II-2707: [2000] 5 CMLR 853; upheld in Case C-338/00 [2003] ECR I-9189: [2004] 4 CMLR 351.

[44] Some of these fines were annulled or reduced on appeal.

more or less unchanged, and would therefore not have alleviated these problems. Moreover, it would not have helped to open up the after-sales service market, nor would it have ensured the use of the so-called 'availability clause' which allows, for example, a British motorist to purchase a right-hand-drive model in Belgium.

The two years leading up to the adoption of the new Regulation 1400/2002 in July 2002 saw some of the fiercest lobbying of the Commission and Parliament since the abolition of duty-free sales. Manufacturers rehearsed the usual arguments, in particular that increased competition would threaten quality and safety standards as well as the viability of small dealerships. They argued especially strongly that, if a combination of exclusive and selective distribution were no longer permitted, manufacturers relying on selective distribution still needed to be able to impose a 'location clause' on dealers, preventing them from establishing a sales outlet or depot away from their main outlet. The Commission for its part saw the outlawing of location clauses as key to encouraging parallel imports.

2.4 DETAILS OF REGULATION 1400/2002

Regulation 1400/2002[45] as finally adopted in July 2002 to some extent follows the general trend towards more flexible and economics-based block exemptions. It does not exempt a combination of exclusive and selective distribution, but leaves manufacturers free to choose to use one or the other. Nor does it contain 'white' and 'grey' lists of permitted clauses: as under the vertical restraints block exemption, the principle is that anything not expressly prohibited is exempted. It also introduces market-share thresholds above which certain types of agreement are not exempted (Article 3(1)). However, the 'black list' of prohibited, hard-core restrictions is extremely detailed, and there are many additional clauses mentioning characteristics which distribution systems are required to have or not to have in order to qualify for exemption. This means that the 'straitjacket' effect, for which older generations of block exemptions have often been criticized, is in many ways still a feature of this new Regulation.

The Commission explains in the second recital to the new block exemption that stricter rules are needed in this sector than those provided for in Regulation 2790/99, and it is true that many more requirements are laid down by the motor-vehicle Regulation.[46] For example, a choice has to be made between exclusive and selective distribution, and the limits of this choice vary depending on whether the agreements concern motor vehicles, spare parts or repair and maintenance, or a combination of the three. The rules also vary according to whether they cover passenger cars or light commercial vehicles, or heavier vehicles.

---

[45] [2002] OJ L203/30. See also the Explanatory Brochure on the Regulation, an 83-page document available on DG Comp's website (www.europa.eu.int/comm/competition/publications/).

[46] It is ironic that whereas the first block exemptions overall provided car manufacturers with a more generous regime than was available in other markets, the latest imposes more restrictions on them than would be the case under the Regulation (2790/99) generally applicable to distribution agreements. Being regarded as a 'special case' has become a burden rather than a privilege!

However, in some respects the rules are more generous than those of Regulation 2790/99. Although Article 3(1) states that the exemption is generally available in respect of sale of new vehicles and spare parts, and repair services, as under the vertical restraints block exemption, up to a market share threshold of 30 per cent, it adds that quantitative selective distribution for new vehicle sales is exempted up to a 40 per cent threshold. Qualitative selective distribution is exempted irrespective of market share.

If exclusive distribution is the option chosen, dealers have to be left free to make passive supplies to anyone in any territory (and active sales into any territories where selective distribution is used), including supermarkets and Internet-based operators. Few manufacturers have taken this route. Almost all have chosen selective distribution, which may be both quantitative and qualitative. However, even here, it is not possible to discriminate against supermarkets if they satisfy the manufacturer's selection criteria. The criteria may be established so as to exclude operators working purely through the Internet, but not those with outlets which satisfy the criteria but which also deal via the Internet. Selective-distribution dealers must be allowed to make even active sales to any end-user in any part of the Community, except exclusive distributorship territories, in respect of which only passive sales have to be permitted.

Manufacturers are required to allow dealers to stock competing vehicles in the same showroom and may no longer require that competing products be sold in separate premises, under separate management, and by a separate legal entity. More freedom is also ensured for operators purchasing as intermediaries, who can no longer be refused supplies in volumes beyond 10 per cent of their total sales, as was the case under the previous block exemption.[47] There are also detailed requirements regarding the length and means of termination of agreements and settling of disputes, and transfer of dealerships, all designed to prevent manufacturers from exerting illicit pressure on dealers.

Distributors can no longer be forced to provide repair and maintenance services as well as distributing new motor vehicles, and they must be allowed to source components from the same producers that supply the manufacturer. Manufacturers have to make available to independent service providers the necessary spare parts, technical information,[48] training and tools, and a number of other detailed rules aim to free up the market for servicing and spare parts.

The new Regulation thus significantly tightened the rules for manufacturers, and contained only one significant concession to the powerful industry and political lobbying: manufacturers were allowed to use a location clause in respect of cars and light commercial vehicles until October 2005, whereas the rest of the Regulation became applicable on 1 October 2002.

---

[47] See fn. 41.

[48] This is the only aspect of the Regulation to have given rise to formal Commission Decisions. The Commission took detailed commitments from DaimlerChrysler, Fiat, General Motors and Toyota to make the necessary technical information available to independent repairers: [2007] OJ L329/52, L330/44, L332/77.

Though manufacturers are not legally required to operate through agreements that follow these requirements, if they choose to work outside them they forego the legal certainty provided by the block exemption. In practice, therefore, the scheme laid down by the new Regulation has, like its predecessors, been widely followed by the industry. Market shares in new vehicle sales will rarely exceed 30 per cent, and even more rarely will they exceed 40 per cent, which in practice is likely to be the threshold of interest to most producers, so there will be little incentive to adopt a different scheme. (The thresholds are more likely to be exceeded in the case of spare parts and repair services.) The Commission and consumer groups were optimistic that price differences across the European Union would decrease, as would prices themselves. Some producers however predicted that prices would rise, with prices across the Union becoming more closely aligned with the highest existing prices. The Commission's Evaluation Report,[49] published in May 2008, concluded that the situation had improved in respect of both competition on the market for new cars and better conditions for repair and maintenance providers. However, it also recognized that the Regulation has not had entirely positive effects, and it will continue to watch market developments carefully as it decides what the future of this block exemption should be.

3. FRANCHISING

3.1 FRANCHISE SYSTEMS: THE EARLY YEARS

Another method available for the large-scale distribution of goods or services is franchising. The basic idea is that, instead of appointing an independent distributor who takes on the risk of reselling the supplier's product within a particular area and is responsible for determining sales policy within the territory, the manufacturer (franchisor) appoints an independent undertaking (franchisee) to operate in a manner far more closely integrated with the franchisor; the franchisor supplies the franchisee not just with a product or service for sale, but with a standardized and highly detailed promotional framework within which the franchisee has to operate. This will probably include the following elements:

(1) a right for the franchisee to sell the relevant product or service from a location in a particular contract territory

(2) the provision of trade-mark and know-how licences to ensure that the presentation of the brand image of the product is identical to that of the franchisor and all other franchised outlets

(3) a requirement that the required products or services are obtained through or from the franchisor, and if from some third party then in accordance with detailed specifications

---

[49] Available on DG Comp's website.

(4) an obligation on the franchisee to pay both a lump sum for the know-how provided and royalties in respect of all sales made, as well as to adhere strictly to the terms of the franchisor's package (in terms of the layout of his retail premises and in all respects in which the business is conducted)

(5) a network of other franchise holders operating on an identical basis.

Franchises came into common use in the Community in the early 1970s, developing out of business models adopted from the United States. By May 1982, there were 200 franchise systems in the Federal Republic of Germany involving 120,000 franchisees; in France there were nearly 400 franchise systems at that time; in the Netherlands, 280 franchise systems in 1983. Similar developments took place in other Member States.[50]

There are three main varieties of business-format franchising which apply to the retail distribution of goods and services. The first, which most concerns us here, is a *distribution* franchise where the function of the trade mark is to assist the effective distribution of the franchisor's goods in a recognizable way. Other varieties of the same concept of 'business format franchising' are *service* franchising, which is similar to the distribution franchise except that any goods provided are only ancillary to the service offered, and *production* franchising, where the producer/franchisor arranges for the manufacture of the particular range of branded goods to be carried out by his franchisee. Within normal categories of service franchising are found restaurants and hotels, car hire, accounting bureaux, and data-processing services; in the field of production franchising are found clothes, cosmetics, footwear, and other mass production items.

Distribution franchising, however, can apply to almost every type of product. A normal franchise agreement for the distribution of goods is a lengthy document of up to 100 pages, presenting in great detail the way in which the parties are to carry out their mutual obligations. Inherent in most franchising arrangements are a number of clauses which restrict competition; and the issue immediately arises whether any of these clauses fall under Article 81(1) and if so whether exemption will be available. Since the essence of a franchise system, like that of exclusive distribution, is a network of agreements conferring partial or total territorial exclusivity on the franchisee in return for substantial payments by the franchisee, the franchisor may accept some or all of the following restrictions:

(1) not to appoint another franchisee in the territory allocated

(2) not to be involved in the sale of the franchise goods within the territory, e.g. by opening a rival shop

(3) not to sell, directly or indirectly, contract goods to persons who will resell them in the contract territory.

---

[50] These figures are taken from the opinion of Advocate General VerLoren van Themaat in the *Pronuptia* case (see fn. 52) which itself provides a full account of the economic role and development of the system of franchising.

The franchisee may have to accept a large number of restrictions, including:

(1) the obligation to sell franchise goods only to customers of his specified shops at named locations, which have to be fitted out exactly in accordance with the franchisor's requirements

(2) not to change the location of these shops nor to assign the agreement to third parties without the consent of the franchisor

(3) not to sell franchise goods to dealers outside the franchise network

(4) not to sell except at the prices (maximum or minimum) laid down or recommended by the franchisor

(5) not to deal in any competing goods, or possibly to deal with them only to a limited extent

(6) not for a period after the end of the franchise agreement to enter into competition with the franchisor in respect of the contract product.

The Commission originally had some difficulty in deciding how to classify franchise agreements, since they exhibited in varying degrees features commonly found in no less than three other categories of agreement with which DG Comp was familiar and for which it had, with the assistance of the European Court, developed detailed ground rules. These were: exclusive dealing agreements, selective dealing agreements, and patent and trade-mark licensing.

Although there were similarities between each of these three classes of agreement and franchising, franchising remained inherently distinct from each of them by virtue of the close control maintained over the manner in which the franchisee conducts his business. In the case of exclusive dealing agreements, by contrast, though the dealer could be required to sell goods under the supplier's trade mark and packaging under the terms of the block exemption then in force, the dealer retained considerable independence in its marketing policy and was normally free to sell from whatever outlets and in whatever way it chose. Moreover, also under the terms of the block exemption, it had to be free to respond to orders outside its territory so long as it did not promote sales actively there itself, and the supplier remained free to sell to other distributors or dealers outside the territory even if they would subsequently resell into the contract territory. Any licensing of know-how or trade marks was ancillary to these distribution rights.

The selective distribution systems discussed earlier in this chapter also showed considerable differences from franchising. Here again, the dealer normally remained free to sell competing goods in addition to the contract goods, and agreements did not usually prescribe specific territories beyond allocating territorial areas of primary responsibility. Nor did the Patent Licence Regulation or case law on trade-mark or know-how licences provide much assistance to the Commission. In such licences, the primary subject is the transfer of, for example, know-how, whereas in franchising these licences are often merely ancillary to the whole 'business package', which the franchisee usually acquires for a substantial payment.

It was argued that the Commission should adopt a tolerant attitude towards franchise agreements, and a strong case can indeed be made that they have some beneficial and pro-competitive aspects.[51] The close support received from the franchisor enables new retail outlets to compete strongly and immediately with other outlets, and it is also claimed that it contributes to the reduction of prices for manufacturers' goods without any sacrifice of quality. It can be argued to have a significant ability in the creation of an EC mass market and in breaking down frontiers, by allowing the coverage of large territories in a number of Member States without having to produce substantial product differentiation on a national level. The promotion of the 'brand image' enables recognition of the product to spread faster than would otherwise be the case, and thereby enables unit costs to be kept lower and prices possibly reduced. Whilst not all these arguments would necessarily be accepted, it was widely expected that the European Court would take a relatively positive attitude towards this form of distribution.

3.2 THE *PRONUPTIA* CASE

The opportunity arose in the *Pronuptia* case.[52] Mrs Schillgalis had entered into a franchise agreement in Germany several years previously to sell wedding dresses and other wedding items under the trade mark 'Pronuptia de Paris'. Her appointment covered three separate areas (Hamburg, Oldenburg, and Hanover) and contained restrictions on both her and Pronuptia. The main restrictions on Pronuptia were that:

(1) it would grant Mrs Schillgalis the exclusive right to use the trade name for the marketing of the contract goods in a specific territory

(2) it would not open any other Pronuptia shop in that territory or provide goods or services to third parties in the territory

(3) it would assist Mrs Schillgalis with regard to all commercial aspects of her business, including advertizing, staff training, fashion purchasing, marketing, and any other help needed to improve her turnover and profitability.

In return, Mrs Schillgalis accepted a large number of restrictions, which included the following:

(a) to sell wedding gowns under the trade mark 'Pronuptia de Paris' only in the shops specified, which had to be equipped and decorated exactly as the franchisor required and could not be transferred to another location or altered without the franchisor's agreement

---

[51] A useful early source of information on franchising, written from a US viewpoint before the Court delivered its *Pronuptia* judgment, and urging its liberal treatment on the ground that it has a significant ability to make retail markets more competitive, is R. J. Goebel, 'The Uneasy Fate of Franchising Under EEC Antitrust Laws' (1985) 10 EurLR 87–118.

[52] Case 161/84 [1986] ECR 353: 1 CMLR 414. When the relevant agreements were entered into Reg. 67/67 was still in force.

(b) to purchase 80 per cent of wedding dresses and accessories to be sold from Pronuptia direct, and to purchase at least a proportion of other dresses from the franchisor or from suppliers approved by the franchisor, and to make the sale of bridal fashions her main concern

(c) to pay an entry fee for the know-how of DM15,000 and thereafter a royalty of 10 per cent on the total sales of Pronuptia products

(d) to advertise only in a manner approved by the franchisor and in general to use the business methods prescribed by the franchisor, save that the fact that prices were recommended by Pronuptia did not affect her ultimate freedom to fix her own prices

(e) to refrain during the contract and for one year afterwards from competing in any way with Pronuptia outside her own contract territory.

When later sued for substantial arrears of royalty by Pronuptia, she claimed that the agreement was void under Article 81(2) and that she was therefore not required to pay. Her argument succeeded before the Frankfurt Court of Appeal (Oberlandgericht); the German Supreme Court (Bundesgerichthof) referred to the European Court under Article 234 the issue of whether Article 81 applied to franchise agreements, and if so whether Block Exemption 67/67 could also have applied to it.

In such Article 234 references the European Court does not review the case as a whole but merely answers the specific questions asked by the national court. It is, therefore, less likely in such cases that the European Court will find it possible to pronounce in general terms on the legal principles involved than, say, when it reviews a DG Comp decision under Article 230. Nevertheless, there have been occasions, such as the *Perfumes* case, when the Court has taken the opportunity of an Article 234 reference to state or restate basic principles relating to competition law, and it was hoped that it would take this opportunity to provide assistance to the Commission in dealing with the increasing numbers and types of franchise agreements now being notified to it.

Advocate General VerLoren van Themaat took a relatively relaxed view of such agreements; after careful review of the earlier Court jurisprudence on related areas (such as exclusive distribution agreements and licence agreements) he reached the general conclusion that franchising as a method of distribution had major advantages for both the franchisor and the franchisee, and in general should not fall within Article 81(1) unless:

(a) the agreement was made between a franchisor from one Member State or its subsidiary on one hand and one or more franchisees in one or more other Member States on the other hand and

(b) the franchisor had through its subsidiaries and franchisees in one or more of those Member States or a significant part of their territory a substantial share of the market for that product and

(c) the agreement had the effect or intention of restricting either parallel imports of the product into the contract territory or exports of those products by the franchisee to other Member States or

(d) the agreement resulted in the establishment of unreasonably high resale prices, that is prices which could not be charged if effective competition existed for them.

The Advocate General also considered that Regulation 67/67 did not apply to the Pronuptia franchises at issue, since no consideration had been given to the question of franchising when the Regulation was drawn up, and since in any case the issues of exclusive supply and exclusive purchasing covered by that Regulation are only minor factors in the normal franchise agreement.

The European Court, whilst agreeing that Regulation 67/67 was inapplicable, declined to give broad approval to franchise agreements in the way that the Advocate General had suggested. It accepted that such agreements gave substantial advantages to both franchisors and franchisees and allowed the franchisor to derive financial benefit from its expertise without having to invest its own capital. The franchisee benefited because it could receive, even without any past experience of the trade, access to trading methods which the franchisor had used successfully, and for which it had gained a reputation. In order for such a system to work, therefore, protecting the legitimate expectations of the franchisor, restrictive conditions could be accepted as falling outside Article 81(1) if they contributed to satisfying one of two conditions.

The first condition was that the franchisor must be able to pass on its know-how to franchisees and provide them with the necessary promotional and other assistance without running a risk that this might benefit its competitors. Under this heading, a clause preventing the franchisee both during and for a reasonable period after the agreement from opening a shop of the same or similar nature in another area (where he might compete with another member of the franchise network) was acceptable and outside 81(1), as also was any restriction on proposed transfer of the shop to another party without the franchisor's approval.

The second condition was that the franchisor must be allowed to take the necessary measures to maintain the identity and reputation of the franchise network, to the extent that it had to exercise control over it. This would cover obligations on the franchisee to apply the franchisor's business method and sell the goods covered by the contract only in premises laid out and decorated according to the franchisor's instructions, which were intended to ensure uniform presentation. Likewise, the franchisor could impose requirements as to the location of the shop and its subsequent transfer and prohibit the transfer by the franchisee of its rights and obligations without the franchisor's approval. In order that the goods supplied by each franchisee should be of the same quality, it was reasonable for the franchisor to require that the franchisee sell only products supplied by the franchisor or a supplier selected by it. The franchisee must be allowed to purchase such goods from other franchisees.

However, the judgment did indicate clearly that Article 81(1) would apply to a clause obliging the franchisee to sell goods covered by the contract only in specified premises, e.g. preventing him or her from opening up a second shop in his own territory when the franchisor is obliged to ensure the franchisee exclusivity in that territory; for if such a restriction were applied throughout the network, it would mean that a Member State would be divided up by the franchisor into a number of closed territories. If it was shown nevertheless by the franchisor that franchisees would not risk entering the network and investing substantial sums on the purchase of the franchise without such an assured exclusive territory, then these matters should be considered under Article 81(3). The Court ruled that provisions which shared markets between the franchisor and franchisee or between the franchisees themselves were likely to affect trade between Member States, even if entered into solely by undertakings established in one Member State, because of their ability to prevent franchisees in one Member State from establishing themselves also in another Member State.

Finally, on the question of control over resale prices by the franchisor, the Court took a more severe view than the Advocate General. He had indicated that resale price maintenance should not be illegal unless one party has a position of economic strength on the local market concerned where price maintenance was also applied by competitors or where the franchisor is a price leader on that particular market. The Court said that only recommendations on price were permissible, without distinguishing between maximum and minimum price recommendation, and indicated that price recommendations would only be acceptable so long as there was no concerted practice between the parties as to their application.

3.3 THE ADOPTION OF THE BLOCK EXEMPTION 4087/88

Pressure was now growing for the adoption of a draft block exemption, which was finally published in August 1987. Drawing substantially on the *Pronuptia* judgment, it adopted a generally favourable approach to the concept of both distribution and service franchises, without seeking to cover industrial or manufacturing franchising. Regulation 4087/88 came into force on 1 February 1989.

Its general shape followed the traditional pattern for block exemptions, with a definition of its coverage and lists of exempted and prohibited restrictions, the 'white' and 'black' lists, a list of relevant conditions that had to continue to apply throughout the duration of the exemption, an opposition procedure, and grounds for withdrawal of the exemption. Article 2 contained a particularly long list of restrictions exempted, including the exclusive right of the franchisee to operate his franchise in a particular territory from his contract premises only and without seeking to solicit customers outside that territory. The franchisee could be prohibited from selling competing goods or services. The 'white' list also included two main categories of clause which the Court had referred to in *Pronuptia*: first, those permitted in so far as they were needed to protect the franchisor's intellectual property rights, and second, those that maintained the common identity and reputation of the particular franchise network.

The 'black' list of clauses was comparatively brief. It naturally included any restriction on the franchisee's freedom to determine sale prices, no-challenge clauses against intellectual property rights, and any attempt to limit competition between franchisees or to impose restrictions on sources of supply for contract products. An opposition clause was included to enable additional restrictions not found in the lists to be presented to the Commission; and the 'safety valve' Article 8 listed a number of situations in which the Commission would be entitled to withdraw the benefit of the exemption from individual agreements, including any where franchisees engaged in horizontal price-fixing or obstruction to parallel imports, where goods or services faced no effective competition in the Common Market, or where the franchisor used its contractual rights and considerable influence over the franchisee for purposes wider than the proper protection of its identity and reputation within the framework of the contract.

During the time that the block exemption was being drafted, the Commission adopted a few individual exemptions.[53] In *Servicemaster*[54] the franchise covered the supply of housekeeping, cleaning, and maintenance services for both commercial and domestic customers. The Commission pointed out that, although the Regulation only referred to the distribution of goods, franchises dealing with services alone should be treated similarly. Characteristic features of the franchise included the relative importance of the know-how provided to the franchisee, and the fact that the services were normally provided at the customer's premises creating a personal relationship with him. Individual exemption was granted both here and in the case of the *Charles Jourdan*[55] franchise for the sale of a brand of French shoes and other leather goods. Charles Jourdan as franchisor reserved the right to approve individual managers who had been selected for the franchised shops and an exact territory was allocated to each franchisee. Franchisees all had to pay an entry fee, either to run the business from particular premises within the territory, or for being granted a 'franchise-corner', an area within a shop but with no exterior sign. The effect of the close control maintained by the franchisor was to give each franchisee relatively strong protection from competition within its territory against other franchisees. The Commission ruled, however, in granting the exemption that unless territorial exclusivity were given few prospective franchisees would be willing to make the necessary investment in this franchise. The product itself only had 10 per cent of the French market for medium- and top-quality shoes, and as little as 2 per cent of the whole Community market for such products. The decision showed that such arrangements could be exempted even if the goods had no great technical complexity and were sold alongside similar products not the subject of a franchise.

The comparatively liberal terms of the Regulation led to their widespread use as a model by companies throughout the Community, in some cases replacing use of the exclusive dealing block exemption Regulation 1983/83 with its far more limited list of

---

[53] Cynics have suggested that the franchising systems in question did not require exemption, but that exemption decisions were taken to prove that the Commission had the necessary 'experience' of franchise agreements to justify the adoption of a block exemption.

[54] [1989] 4 CMLR 581.

[55] [1989] 4 CMLR 591. The lesser restrictions placed on the 'franchise-corner' retailer were actually held to fall outside Art. 81(1) altogether.

permitted restrictions. In fact, during the whole eleven years that Regulation 4087/88 remained in force, there were no further Commission decisions or Court judgments on franchising agreements, nor have there been since. This meant that, when the Commission was drafting its 1997 Green Paper and later adopting the Vertical Restraints Block Exemption Regulation and accompanying Guidelines, franchising was expected to be one of the least controversial aspects of the exercise. Once it emerged that a block exemption applicable to vertical restraints generally was being drafted, it was assumed that franchise agreements would be covered, and would continue to enjoy the generous treatment they had so far received.

3.4 FRANCHISE SYSTEMS: THE 1999 BLOCK EXEMPTION 2790/1999

Franchise businesses were therefore disturbed to see the way that the scope of the new Regulation was defined. The general definition in Article 2(1) of 'vertical agreements' is broad enough to include many franchising agreements, including those involving agency or based on selective distribution. However, Article 2(3) provides that where vertical agreements contain provisions relating to the assignment to the buyer or use by him of intellectual property rights (IPRs), they would only be within the scope of the block exemption 'provided that those provisions do not constitute the primary object of such agreements and are directly related to the use, sale or resale of goods or services' by the buyer or his customers.

Some have argued that Article 2(3) is not a limitation on the general scope of the exemption, but rather an extension of it.[56] However, the more widely held view, and certainly the Commission's intention as expressed in its Guidelines,[57] is that it is an additional requirement which agreements must satisfy if they are to benefit from block exemption. On this view, it is true that at least on the face of the Regulation it would appear that some types of distribution and service franchises which were exempted by the old franchising block exemption are no longer exempted by the new Regulation.

The concept of the IPR provisions in an agreement being the 'primary object' of the agreement, rather than 'ancillary'[58] is far from clear and is nowhere defined. Moreover, the Commission itself stated in the recitals to the old franchising block exemption that 'franchising agreements consist essentially of licences of industrial or intellectual property rights relating to trade marks or signs and know-how', which suggests that such agreements should not generally be covered by the new Regulation. Certainly it seems hard to argue that service or distribution franchises involving IPRs, and where the franchisor does not himself supply goods or materials to the franchisee, have anything other than IPRs as their 'primary object'. In this context franchisors may be

---

[56] E.g. V. L. Korah and D. O'Sullivan, *Vertical Agreements: Distribution Agreements under the EC Competition Rules* (Hart Publishing, 2002), pp. 141ff.

[57] Paras. 30–6.   [58] This is the word used in recital 3 of the Regulation.

concerned by the Commission's decision in *Moosehead/Whitbread*,[59] where it found an exclusive licence for a little-known trade mark not to be 'ancillary' to a grant of know-how covering the production and promotion of a brand of beer.

On the other hand, if the franchise consists mainly of a business method which can be characterized as 'know-how' rather than IPRs, then it should be covered by the Regulation. The Regulation defines both IPRs and know-how separately and the limitation in Article 2(3) only mentions IPRs and so does not extend to know-how. The same rules apply in respect of non-compete and exclusive purchasing agreements in franchising agreements as apply to other distribution agreements. Indeed non-compete clauses in the context of franchising do not infringe Article 81(1) at all when they are necessary to maintain the common identity and reputation of a franchised network. Furthermore, Article 5(b), while not explicitly mentioning franchising, will frequently be to the benefit of franchisors. It is the rule which says that normally any restriction on the buyer making, purchasing, selling or reselling goods or services after the agreement has come to an end is not exempted, but that there is an exception where the obligation:

- relates to competing goods or services
- is limited to premises and land from which the buyer operated during the contract period and
- is indispensable to protect know-how transferred by the supplier to the buyer.

Even where these conditions are satisfied, the non-compete clause must apply for no longer than a year, unless the obligation relates to use and disclosure of know-how which has not entered the public domain.

3.5 FRANCHISE SYSTEMS: THE 2000 GUIDELINES

So far we have considered the text of the Regulation itself, and we now turn to the Commission's Guidelines.[60] These make clear the Commission's intention to include most distribution and service franchises within the scope of the Regulation and Community law requires legislation to be interpreted in the light of the intention of the legislator.[61] Nevertheless, it is unfortunate that these intentions are not clearly reflected in the wording of the Regulation.

Paragraph 44 of the Guidelines lists seven types of restrictions generally considered necessary to protect the franchisor's IPRs, but which the Regulation is intended to exempt if for any reason they do infringe Article 81(1). Paragraph 119 also indirectly

---

[59] [1990] OJ L100/32 [1991] 4 CMLR 391. See Ch. 12.   [60] [2000] OJ C291/1: 5 CMLR 1074\.

[61] For an example of the application of this principle, see Case T-102/96 *Gencor* v. *Commission* [1999] ECR II-753: [1999] 4 CMLR 971 at para. 148, where the Court of First Instance had to decide whether the EC Merger Regulation could be applied to situations of collective dominance. See Ch. 16, Section 8.6.

indicates the Commission's continuing support for franchising as a generally desirable distribution method justifying a number of restrictive contractual provisions where these are linked to the transfer of know-how, saying that the more a vertical restraint is linked to the transfer of know-how, the less likely it is to infringe Article 81.

The Guidelines also make it clear that distribution and service franchising is intended to be covered, though not 'industrial franchise agreements'. Paragraph 31 explains that the intention is to include agreements featuring IPRs where these allow the more effective distribution of goods or services. Paragraph 43 says that IPR licensing contained in franchise agreements escapes the application of Article 2(3) and remains within the scope of the Regulation if it satisfies the conditions listed in paragraph 30:

- The IPR provisions must be part of a vertical agreement, i.e. an agreement with conditions under which the parties may purchase, sell or resell certain goods or services.

- The IPRs must be assigned to, or for use by, the buyer.

- The IPR provisions must not constitute the primary object of the agreement.

- The IPR provisions must be directly related to the use, sale or resale of goods or services by the buyer or his customers. In the case of franchising where marketing forms the object of the exploitation of the IPRs, the goods or services are distributed by the master franchisee or the franchisees.

- The IPR provisions, in relation to the contract goods or services, must not contain restrictions of competition having the same object or effect as vertical restraints which are not exempted under the Block Exemption Regulation.

The Guidelines do recognize, however, that the block exemption will not apply to franchise agreements where the franchisor does not supply goods or services (including not only services passed on to consumers, but also commercial and technical assistance services to the franchisee) to his franchisees, and the franchise consists mainly or entirely of IPR licensing. It says that such franchises 'will be treated in a way similar to those franchise agreements which are covered' by the Regulation.

So far, franchise agreements have apparently not caused significant problems which have been brought to the attention of the Commission. Perhaps the main area of doubt concerns the fact that, depending on the nature of the product or service franchise concerned, it may well include a substantial intellectual property element, and some distribution and service agreements previously covered by the franchising block exemption may no longer benefit from any block exemption. However, since 2004, when the new modernization rules entered into force, Article 81(3) has applied automatically, so that failure to notify the agreement to the Commission is no longer a bar to application of the block exemption by analogy. This means that in practice such difficulties are now unlikely to arise.

FURTHER READING

R. Aleixo Gregório, 'Driving Competition: The Impact of Regulation 1400/2002 on Motor Vehicle Distribution' [2008] 31 *World Comp* 299.

J. Chard, 'The Economics of the Application of Article 85 to Selective Distribution Systems' [1982] ELRev 83.

R. Goebel, 'The Uneasy Fate of Franchising Under EEC Antitrust Laws' (1985) 10 ELRev 87–118.

R. Goebel, 'Metro II's Confirmation of the Selective Distribution Rules: Is this the End of the Road?' [1987] 24 CMLRev 605.

J. Venit, 'Pronuptia: Ancillary Restraints or Unholy Alliances?' [1986] ELRev 213.

S. Vezzoso, 'On the Antitrust Remedies to Promote Retail Innovation in the EU Car Sector' [2004] ECLR 190–201.

12

INTELLECTUAL PROPERTY RIGHTS: LICENSING

1. INTRODUCTION

1.1 THE NATURE OF INTELLECTUAL PROPERTY RIGHTS

The protection by national law of different types of intellectual property is common to all Member States. The range of that legislation however, and the classification of the rights thus protected, vary considerably between them. These rights include patents, registered and unregistered designs, trade marks, and copyright together with various other minor or specialized categories such as plant-breeders' rights. The methods of protection adopted themselves differ; some can be protected only by registration, after a more or less rigorous process of screening for acceptance, as with patents, trade marks, and registered designs. In other cases, rights can simply be acquired as the result of publication, as with artistic or literary copyright protected by Community Directives, by national legislation, and by a number of international conventions. Such proprietary rights can protect technical information of importance and value for commercial and industrial activities, or they may simply protect the identity and commercial individuality of an undertaking, as in the case of business names and trade marks.

There is an inherent conflict between, on one hand, the existence and exercise of any such rights, which will necessarily give a degree of exclusivity and protection to their owners, and on the other the competition policy of prohibiting restrictions of competition as embodied in Articles 81 and 82. Nevertheless, a key aim of both sets of rules is now generally accepted to be fostering innovation for the benefit of consumers. The challenge is therefore to achieve the right balance between incentivising and rewarding individual innovators, and keeping markets open to their competitors. In this chapter we review the way in which the Commission, in applying these Articles and Regulations made under the Treaty, has dealt with agreements that relate to the use and exploitation of industrial property rights, in particular patents and know-how, to which most of its attention in this area has been devoted.

There is a further limitation to the exploitation and enjoyment of industrial-property rights, arising from the very nature of the European Community as described in the

Treaty. This is the restraint placed upon owners of such rights in Member States to prevent their use in a way that hinders the free movement of goods and services within the Community. Articles 28 and 29 of the Treaty set out the basic prohibitions on quantitative restrictions on imports and exports, and all measures having equivalent effect (a number of which arise as a direct consequence of the protection of industrial and commercial property), whilst Article 30, inter alia, preserves the right of a Member State nevertheless to impose prohibitions or restrictions on imports and exports required to protect industrial and commercial property, so long as those restrictions or prohibitions are neither a means of arbitrary discrimination nor a disguised restriction on trade between Member States. The interpretation of these concepts, which have been considered by the European Court in many cases, is outside the scope of this book.

1.2 THE EXPLOITATION OF SUCH RIGHTS

The owner of intellectual property rights naturally desires the greatest possible freedom to negotiate the basis upon which their exploitation can be arranged. However, whilst the manufacturer of goods will select a particular system of distribution through which its sales can be maximized, in the exploitation of intellectual property the owner normally finds that it is best to part with only a limited interest in the asset, giving a licence to a third party for its use, whilst still retaining ownership of the asset. Transfer of the owner's rights to a third party by assignment always remains a possible alternative.

The owner of an intellectual property right has a wide choice over the exploitation of its asset. A patent can, of course, be used simply to assist the owner's own manufacturing activities, a defensive shield preventing others from making use of the data comprised within its protection. Provided that the owner itself is making adequate use in its own processes of the information, then it is highly unlikely that licences for use of that right will be compulsorily issued under any national legislation, since this procedure can normally only be adopted when a patent owner conspicuously fails to make adequate use of its patent.[1] On many occasions, however, mere defensive use of the right will prove insufficiently profitable to its owner, who may wish to obtain additional revenue by licensing one or more other undertakings that will pay to utilize the information or process for their own purposes.

Three kinds of licence are found. The simplest is the *non-exclusive* licence, where no licensee receives any guarantee from the licensor as to the exclusivity of the rights provided, which the owner remains free to grant also to other undertakings. Clearly, the value of each such licence is thereby reduced and the percentage payable by way of royalty is normally less than for an equivalent exclusive licence. The *exclusive* licence,

---

[1] For the legal position in the UK see the Patents Act 1977, ss. 48–54 and *Terrell on the Law of Patents* (16th edn, Sweet & Maxwell, 2006), Ch. 11. Compulsory licensing of design rights and copyright may now also be required in certain circumstances. See the Copyright Designs and Patents Act 1988, ss. 144 and 237–9. Sections 44 and 45 of the Patents Act 1977 declaring certain practices by patentees illegal were repealed by the 1998 Competition Act, which now governs such practices.

an equally common method of exploitation of industrial property, contains the same two-way bargain found in exclusive distribution arrangements. The owner agrees that it will not itself license any undertaking within the particular territory apart from the chosen exclusive licensee, and agrees that it will itself not exploit that particular right in that territory. An exclusive licence where the owner of the right reserves for itself the right to compete in the licensed territory, but must refrain from licensing any third parties situate there, is known as a *sole* licence.

In the earlier editions of this work the development of Community policy towards the licensing of intellectual property was treated in detail and on a historical basis, setting out the various stages through which the thinking of the Community and its Member States have passed. Now that more than forty-five years have passed since the 'Christmas Message' first announced its initial attitude towards patent licensing, it seems appropriate to treat the earlier developments of the subject more briefly, and to focus on the more recent developments in the licensing not only of patents, but of know-how, trade marks, copyright and software. Some other competition law issues raised by intellectual-property-right licensing, and in particular the circumstances in which conduct such as refusal to licence, or setting royalty charges too high, may constitute abuse of a dominant position, are covered in the Chapters on Article 82.

2. EARLY COMMISSION ATTITUDES TO PATENT LICENSING

2.1 THE 1962 CHRISTMAS MESSAGE

In spite of predictions from some sources that national patent systems in Europe would become obsolete as a result of the ever quickening pace of new technical developments, arriving at both their high point of value and subsequent obsolescence more quickly than could be adequately coped with by relatively cumbersome national patent systems, a large number of patents have continued to be granted both in Member States and, since 1975, by the European Patent Office in Munich on behalf of the individual Member States. From the viewpoint of DG Comp, therefore, a method of controlling and dealing with the large number of patent licences became an important element in early competition policy. Many of the problems which it faced were similar to those which arose as the result of the very large number of exclusive distribution arrangements notified. A substantial number of such individual agreements might fall within the terms of Article 81(1) and would therefore need consideration for exemption under Article 81(3). This in turn would mean a demand from industrial sources for an early block exemption in order to avoid the delay inherent in individual consideration of a very large number of patent licence agreements.

Just as with exclusive distribution, block exemptions could only be provided, both as a matter of good administration and under the express terms of

Regulation 19/65,[2] when sufficient experience had been gained of individual case law. This meant in practice that a first block exemption covering patents was not issued until well over twenty years after the adoption of Regulation 17. However, it would be unfair to DG Comp not to point out that, by comparison with exclusive distribution and purchasing, patents and other intellectual property rights and their licensing present considerably more complex issues. This is not only because of their individual protection under national legislation but also because they normally involve a greater degree of exclusivity, which in turn requires the consideration of a larger variety of restrictions upon licensees.[3] Given the inherent tension between the provisions of national laws on one hand and the requirements of Articles 81 and 82 on the other, it was not surprising that the problem of reconciliation took a considerable time.[4]

Amongst the very large number of agreements notified to the Commission at the end of 1962 and the beginning of 1963 under the provisions of Regulation 17 were many thousands of such licences. Considerable prior discussion had already taken place in DG Comp as to the basis upon which patent licences would be dealt with. It was accepted from the start that a certain number of restrictions would inevitably be imposed by licensors on their licensees as the direct result of the inherent nature of patents, and of the fact that, in granting a licence, the licensor is not disposing of its entire asset but only a limited interest whose bounds have to be carefully delineated. A difficult policy choice, which the Commission could not avoid, was the need to distinguish between those restrictions which merely reflected this right of the patentee to spell out the extent of the licence, and other restrictions which would actually restrict competition between the licensee and other licensees in respect of specific territories, and in particular would interfere with the basic principle of the need for integration of the Common Market itself by the free movement of goods across national boundaries.

A few weeks before the closing date for the notification of bilateral agreements under Regulation 17 came the publication of the 'Christmas Message' on 24 December 1962, the first public statement by the Commission of the approach that it would adopt to patent licences. This Notice contained four sections. The first set out the list of clauses which it regarded as falling outside Article 81(1). These were:

- obligations imposed on the licensee having as their objects either limitation of the exploitation of the invention to manufacture, use, or sale, and limitations to certain fields of use

---

[2] The relevant recital reads 'Whereas it should be laid down under what conditions the Commission ... may exercise such powers after sufficient experience has been gained in the light of individual decisions and it becomes possible to define categories of agreement and concerted practices in respect of which the conditions of Art. 81(3) may be considered as being fulfilled'.

[3] This is clearly illustrated by the considerably greater detail and complexity of the Patent Block Exemption Reg. 2349/84 compared with those on Exclusive Distribution (Reg. 1983/83) or Exclusive Purchasing (Reg. 1984/83).

[4] This does not mean, however, that the block exemption need ultimately have taken as long as it actually did, namely, some eight years (1977–84) from the publication of the first draft to the implementation of the exemption.

- limitations imposed as to the quantity of products to be manufactured, the period and territorial area for which they were permitted to be used, and limitations on the licensee's powers of disposal, e.g. on sub-licensing
- obligations as to marking of the product with a patent number and the observance of quality standards necessary for the technically perfect exploitation of the patent, also non-exclusive improvement undertakings on a reciprocal basis between licensor and licensee
- undertakings to ensure that the exclusivity of the grant to the licensee was protected.

The second section confirmed that all other clauses would be looked at on their individual merits, and that in any case a general 'appraisal' was not possible for agreements relating to joint ownership of patents, reciprocal licensing, or multiple parallel licensing, or to any clauses which purported to extend beyond the period of validity of the relevant patent. The third section of the Notice confirmed that patent licences containing only those clauses referred to in the first part of the Notice did not require to be notified. The fourth stated that the basis of the Notice was that the clauses referred to 'entail only the partial maintenance of the right of prohibition contained in the patentee's exclusive right in relation to the licensee who in other respects is authorized to exploit the invention. The list…is not an exhaustive definition of the rights conferred by the patent.'

This Notice initially received little adverse comment, especially as the approach which it had adopted corresponded generally to current attitudes in Member States. The acceptance of the principle of exclusive licensing of patents was strongly influenced by the attitude of German law, whose statute against restraints of competition had adopted a relatively mild approach to such exclusivity. Moreover, the Commission had at that time only very limited case-law experience and was chiefly occupied with notifications relating to exclusive distribution agreements.

2.2 THE COMMISSION'S CHANGING ATTITUDE TO EXCLUSIVITY

A distinct change of policy occurred over the latter part of the 1960s. By the end of the decade, DG Comp no longer regarded an exclusive patent licence as prima facie outside the scope of Article 81(1) and was already starting to take a stricter view, namely that exclusivity had to be justified by the particular circumstances of the licensing arrangements. A number of suggestions have been made as to the reason for this change in policy, including the influence of *Grundig-Consten*[5] decided by the European Court in 1966. Under this argument, the distinction drawn in that case between the *existence* of a right of intellectual property, protected by Article 30 of the Treaty, as opposed to the exercise of that right, which is subject not only to Article 28 but also to Article 81, led inevitably to a more rigorous examination of the justification

---

[5] Cases 56 and 58/64 [1966] ECR 299: CMLR 418. For the facts of the case see p. 53.

for exclusivity of licensing. The alternative explanation for the change in policy was that the Commission was influenced by cases decided by the European Court relating to the interpretation of Articles 28 to 30, as applied to the free movement of goods, and the broad interpretation by the Court of Article 28, as compared with the narrower approach adopted to the limitations and exceptions set out in Article 30.[6]

Neither of those two suggestions is completely convincing. Whilst the *Grundig-Consten* case, as the leading influence on policy within DG Comp during the 1960s, undoubtedly influenced the thinking of officials and ensured the pre-eminence of the principle of market integration, more than this would have been necessary to effect the major shift apparent from the original Christmas Message of late 1962 to the position adopted in the cases decided in 1971. Moreover, nothing in the judgment leads inevitably to a conclusion that exclusive patent licences fall inherently within the scope of Article 81(1); the strictures of the Court apply specifically to such uses of those rights as may defeat the effectiveness of the Community law on agreements that are restrictive of competition. It can be argued that the limitation placed by the *Grundig* decision on the use of intellectual property rights, in this case trade-mark rights, to make it hard for distributors to effect parallel imports was indeed covered by the terms of the Christmas Message, and that the case alone could not be the foundation for such a complete change of attitude to exclusivity in patent licences.[7]

We therefore need to find other explanations for the change of policy. It would surely be reasonable to conclude that it occurred primarily because of the weight of experience accumulating within DG Comp as the result of examining a large number of patent agreement notifications during the six or seven years following Regulation 17's implementation at the start of 1963. Some evidence of this is the very full treatment given to this topic in the *First Annual Report* of the Commission.[8] It was clearly felt at that time that an explanation was needed of the course of development of policy relating to patent licences since the Christmas Message, and an account is given of the examination of some 500 such licences. The Commission explained that these agreements were analysed in order to determine which clauses most often occurred, also to ascertain which of the restrictions imposed were made essential either by the inherent nature of national patent rights, or to maintain the secrecy of related know-how, or which for other reasons did not have the effect of restricting competition. The Report stated that the analysis was being used in the preparation of a draft block exemption covering two-party agreements such as patent licences, which was permitted by the terms of Council Regulation 19/65, which also gave the Commission powers to introduce the existing block exemption for exclusive distribution agreements.

---

[6] See L. Gormley, *Prohibiting Restrictions on Trade within the EEC* (North-Holland, 1985), esp. pp. 184–9 and 230–3.

[7] While the subsequent European Court decision in Case 24/67 *Parke, Davis* v. *Probel* [1968] ECR 55: CMLR 47, confirmed the application of *Grundig-Consten* to patents, it took the issue of exclusivity no further.

[8] This appeared in 1972 and covered the work of DG Comp to the end of 1971. See pp. 65–74 of the Report.

The growing awareness of the Commission of the scope for application of Article 81(1) to exclusive patent licensing is perhaps most clearly shown by its decision in *AOIP/ Beyrard*.[9] Beyrard was a French inventor who granted an exclusive patent licence to AOIP to manufacture and market in France and in certain foreign French territories rheostats and speed changers for electric motors. In the decision, the principle of exclusivity itself was challenged. The clauses declared by the Commission to be in breach of 81(1), and not capable of exemption under Article 81(3), included the exclusivity of the rights granted, and an export prohibition applying to any country where Beyrard had either licensed his patent or assigned his rights to third parties. Among other clauses held illegal were a no-challenge clause and an obligation to pay royalties during the lifetime of the most recent original or improvement patent, whether or not the patent was being exploited by the licensee. Finally, there was an obligation on the licensee to refrain from any kind of competition with the licensor in the field covered by the agreement. If the licensor invented new processes or devices in the field (even if based on different principles but which could be used for the same purpose) such processes and devices automatically fell within the scope of the agreement. On the other hand, if the licensee made any such devices by processes other than those of the licensor, he still had to pay royalties on them. All these restrictions were treated as inherently incapable of exemption.

3. THE EVOLUTION OF THE PATENT BLOCK EXEMPTION

3.1 TRAVAUX PRÉPARATOIRES AND THE *MAIZE SEED* CASE

Commission policy had now travelled so far from the 1962 Christmas Message that some official clarification of the content of patent licences acceptable to the Commission was clearly necessary. The principal point of difficulty was the extent to which the licensor could establish a group of exclusive licensees within the Common Market with territorial protection from each other, and whether this territorial protection could be made complete, or would be invalid to the extent that it impeded the movement of parallel imports under the *Grundig-Consten* principle. In the view of the Commission, all such arrangements involving any degree of exclusivity had to be considered under Article 81(3), thus raising the possibility in every case that a claim for exemption would be rejected.[10]

---

[9] [1976] OJ L6/8: [1976] 1 CMLR D14.

[10] A problem raised for the Commission was that the 1975 Luxembourg Patent Convention included an express provision (Art. 43, para. 2) that the exclusive territorial licence for a part of the Community formed part of the Community's patent regime, and was therefore immune from Arts. 81–2. The Commission never accepted that this was a correct statement of the legal position.

This uncertainty about the status of exclusive licences could not continue indefinitely. A draft Regulation was submitted at the end of 1977 for consideration by the
Member States, and made public for consultative purposes. In this early draft it was
indicated that the inclusion of any of the following clauses, amongst others, would be
likely to prevent the application of a block exemption:

(1) no-challenge clauses, debarring the licensee from challenging the patent

(2) non-competition clauses between licensor and licensee in respect of matters not
    directly covered by the relevant patents and know-how

(3) extension of agreements beyond the life of the most recent patents covered by
    the agreement unless the agreement is terminable by the parties on reasonably
    short notice—also forbidden are requirements to pay royalties after the expiry
    of the last patent

(4) agreements requiring purchase of unpatented supplies for use with the patented
    process

(5) restrictions on the manner in which the product made with the licensed patent is
    sold, e.g. in small tubes or large bottles and in what kinds of packaging

(6) exclusivity of sales and export restrictions exceeding the period necessary for
    a new product having to penetrate its market. The amended draft introduced
    the condition that the combined licensed territory for individual licensees (or
    licensees within the same group) have a maximum population of one hundred
    million.

Criticism that the draft was too stringent continued from industrial sources; objection was taken to the limit on the extent to which field of use restrictions could be
imposed, which would, it was claimed, make the proposed Regulation unattractive
to most potential licensors. The restriction of one hundred million population for a
territory within which exclusive licensing would be allowed incurred particular criticism as unnecessarily arbitrary;[11] in response the Commission indicated that it was
prepared to consider replacing it by a more generous qualification.

Further indications of the views of the Commission on the preferred content of
the draft Regulation were shown by its decision in the *Maize Seed* case.[12] This case
arose out of the assignment by a French State agency for agricultural research (Inra) of
plant breeders' rights in a variety of maize seed to Eisele, a German resident, who proceeded to register them in Germany. Eisele and Inra also later concluded an arrangement under which Eisele received the exclusive right to distribute Inra's maize seed
varieties in Germany, and under which Inra accepted an obligation to prevent other
imports of its own maize seed into Germany. Subsequently Inra assigned to a French

---

[11] Similar objections had also been raised to the proposed application of such limitation on the areas for
which exclusive distribution agreements could be permitted.

[12] The report of the original Commission decision is at [1978] 3 CMLR 434. The decision was appealed in
Case 258/78 *Nungesser* v. *Commission* [1982] ECR 2015: [1983] 1 CMLR 278. The rights originally granted to
Eisele were later transferred to Nungesser KG, a business controlled by him.

company, Frasema, an exclusive licence for commercial exploitation of its maize seed and vested all its own rights in that company. Meanwhile, Eisele agreed to purchase two-thirds of the maize seed which he sold in Germany from Inra, whilst in respect of the remaining third he was free either to produce it or to arrange for its production under his supervision. Eisele also agreed not to sell competing seeds and to set prices in agreement with Inra, although in practice this last arrangement was apparently not enforced. Eisele had enforced his rights in the German court against at least one parallel importer and had obtained a settlement under which the importer agreed not to sell Inra's maize seed in Germany without Eisele's permission.

The decision of the Commission in 1978 was that all the restrictive terms referred to above and those incorporated in the settlement in the German court were in violation of Article 81(1). The claim for exemption under Article 81(3) was rejected. Eisele appealed to the Court of Justice against all the findings of the Commission except those relating to the requirements clause, the non-competition clause, and the resale price maintenance requirement. The Commission's viewpoint is summed up by the following extract from the subsequent Court decision:

The Commission considered that, as in the case of a patent, exclusive propagation rights granted by the owner of breeders' rights to a licensee within the Common Market are, in principle, capable of being considered to have satisfied the tests for exemption under Article [81(3)]. There are even circumstances in which exclusive selling rights linked with prohibitions against exporting might also be exempted, for example when the exclusivity is needed to protect small or medium-sized undertakings in their attempt to penetrate a new market or promoting a new product provided that parallel imports are not restricted at the same time.[13]

In *Maize Seed*, however, the Commission felt that the absolute territorial protection afforded to Eisele did not satisfy these tests, especially as the prices paid for the seed in Germany were as much as 70 per cent higher than those paid in France.

The first official publication of a draft block exemption, already considerably revised since a draft had first been shown to the Advisory Committee, appeared in 1979. In spite of its publication, further progress was apparently blocked by the need for the Commission's procedures to be under-pinned by the Court's judgment on the pending appeal on the Commission's *Maize Seed* decision. Moreover, the complexity of the subject and the different interests involved inevitably caused some delay in its resolution; this was exacerbated by procedural difficulties encountered by the European Court of Justice in finalizing the hearings on the case, where its final decision was not rendered until summer 1982. The Court's ultimate decision reversed some parts of the Commission's 1978 decision, ruling that the following restrictions did not per se amount to a violation of Article 81(1):

(1) the obligation upon Inra (or those deriving rights through it) to refrain from producing or selling relevant seeds in Germany through other licensees; and

---

[13] [1982] ECR 2023–4.

(2) the obligation upon Inra (or those deriving rights through it) to refrain from producing or selling the relevant seeds in Germany themselves.

The Court upheld the remainder of the Commission's decision, namely that a violation of 81(1) was involved by the obligation upon Inra or those deriving rights from it to prevent third parties from exporting the relevant seeds into Germany without Eisele's authorization, as also by Eisele's concurrent use of his own contractual and proprietary rights to prevent all imports into Germany of the seed. These violations resulted from the fact that the licensee had obtained absolute territorial protection not only from the licensor, but from fellow licensees in other territories, as a result of the combined effect of the licensor's undertaking to prevent exports by third parties into Germany and by Eisele's own use of his exclusive rights to challenge parallel imports in the German courts. The Court also confirmed that an agreement which permitted such 'blanket' protection would not receive exemption under 81(3). The Court also indicated that a German court had previously approved settlement between the licensee and David, a parallel importer, requiring David to obtain Eisele's consent before marketing seed in Germany, which settlement itself violated Article 81(1).

The Court drew an important distinction between, on one hand, an 'open' exclusive licence in which the licensor only agreed not to grant rights to other licensees for the same territories without affecting the ability of third parties, such as parallel importers and licensees for other territories, to compete and, on the other hand, exclusive licences accompanied by absolute territorial protection aimed at eliminating competition from third parties, especially parallel importers. Whilst absolute territorial protection could never receive negative clearance under Article 81(1), the grant of exclusivity under an open licence had to be considered in the light of a number of factors, including the nature of the product, the novelty and importance of the relevant technology, the investment risks assumed by the licensee, and the development of inter-brand competition. These last two factors deserved to carry most weight. It is, however, unlikely that the Court intended this definition of an open exclusive licence outside the reach of Article 81 to include licences containing clauses protecting the licensee for even limited periods from competition from other licensees of the same technologies in other territories. Such restrictions would surely have had to be assessed in each case under the terms of Article 81(3), whether under the terms of the relevant Block Exemption or by way of individual exemption.

Commentators on the case felt that its effect would be very considerably to widen the scope for argument by the owners of intellectual property rights, and that the Commission should thereafter show a more generous attitude towards restrictive clauses necessary to protect the interests of licensors and licensees in exclusivity. The Court had after all made it clear that it regarded its decision as relevant, not only to the narrower field of plant breeders' rights, but to the more general application of patent licences. In late 1983 a further draft of the block exemption appeared, incorporating a number of amendments, followed by a 1984 version containing still more alterations, mainly extending the number of restrictions that could be imposed. It also introduced the concept, already familiar in the block exemption of exclusive distribution, that a licensee could be prevented from making active sales outside the territory while remaining able to satisfy unsolicited sales orders from outside its territory.

3.2 THE BLOCK EXEMPTION REGULATION (REG. 2349/84)

The major features of the new Block Exemption as finally adopted in 1984 included the following:

(1) It applied only to bilateral agreements (for which alone the Council Regulation 19/65 had given authority to the Commission to adopt such category exemption).

(2) Its coverage was for patent licences only, but including those which also had a licence of secret know-how which enabled better exploitation of the licensed patent.

(3) The licensor could grant the licensee exclusive rights to make itself items covered by the patent throughout its duration.

(4) The licensee could be given absolute territorial protection for five years from the date when the patented product was first marketed in the Community.

(5) A long list of 'black' clauses was set out which could not be included, as well as an even longer list of permitted 'white' clauses containing restrictions which were allowed, though in some cases subject to qualification. The 'white' list included a number of clauses deemed permissible by the ECJ in the *Maize Seed* case.

(6) Any restrictions found in neither the 'black' nor 'white' list could be notified to the Commission as 'grey' clauses under a procedure known as 'opposition'; if the Commission failed to object to such a clause within six months after notification, the block exemption was deemed to apply to it.

(7) It applied only where the licensee was actually manufacturing the products, directly or through subcontractors, not if it was engaged only in distribution.

(8) Benefit of the block exemption could be withdrawn if the licensee refused without any objectively valid reason to meet unsolicited demands from users or resellers in the territory of other licensees, or made it difficult for users or resellers to obtain products from other resellers in the Community.

3.3 THE *WINDSURFING* CASE

After the implementation of the Patent Regulation, the number of notifications of individual agreements substantially reduced, as DG Comp had hoped, though there remained a number of patent licences which for one reason or another did not fall within the framework of the block exemption. An indication of the likely treatment of such agreements was given by the Court decision in *Windsurfing International* v. *Commission*.[14] The importance of this case was that it was the first occasion since the introduction of the block exemption when the Court had an opportunity of laying down rules for the assessment of individual patent licences. The Commission had imposed a fine, albeit a small one, on a patent licensor, Windsurfing International. The licences under challenge were those between Windsurfing International and its German licensees. The Court accepted the Commission's finding that the coverage of the German patent obtained by Windsurfing International was not for a complete sailboard but only for the rig (mast, sail, and spars) attached to the board. There was a market for the rig alone, though usually boards and rigs were sold as an integrated unit. Several restrictions in the licence were stated by the Commission to be in breach of Article 81(1), as follows:

(1) The licensed product having been specified as a complete sailboard, the licensor's approval was nevertheless needed for any type of board on which the licensee intended to place the rig.

(2) There was an obligation on the licensee to sell only complete sailboards, i.e. the patented rig and an approved board.

(3) The licensee was obliged to pay royalties on the entire selling price of the complete sailboard (rather than solely on that of the patented rig).

(4) The licensee was required to fix a notice on the board stating that it was 'licensed' by the licensor.

(5) There were no-challenge clauses with respect to the licensor's trade mark and patent.[15]

(6) There was a restriction against the licensee manufacturing the sailboard except at certain factories in Germany.

Advocate General Lenz disagreed with a number of findings made by the Commission and himself undertook a very thorough investigation of the facts. In his lengthy opinion, he concluded that only three of the restrictions could be held to be in breach of Article 81(1), namely numbers (1), (2), and (3) above. With regard to the others, his opinion was either that the restrictions could not have any effect on competition or that they would in practice have insufficient effect on trade between Member States. He therefore recommended that the fine be reduced.

The Court took a stricter view, concurring with the views of the Commission on all except item (3) above, and reduced the fine slightly. The reasons given by the Court

---

[14] Case 193/83 [1986] ECR 611: 3 CMLR 489. The founder of the company, Mr Hoyle Schweitzer, was one of the leading figures in the development of the sailboard.

[15] On the other hand, the Court subsequently held that a no-challenge clause cannot restrict competition if the licence itself is free, since the licensee then suffers no competitive disadvantage by any payment of royalties: Case 65/86 *Bayer* v. *Sülhöfer* [1988] ECR 5249: [1990] 4 CMLR 182.

were important for the future. With regard to restriction (1), the Court found that Windsurfing International had failed to show that their control over the manufacture of non-patented components, such as boards, related to any objective criteria to do with the patented rig as no technical method of verifying the quality of the board was provided by the agreement. The Court found that its real interest lay 'in ensuring that there was sufficient product differentiation between its licensee's sailboards to cover the widest possible spectrum of market demand'. If any passing off of other boards as Windsurfing International boards by the licensees was found, this could have been dealt with by an action in the national courts. The distinction drawn by the Court in respect of item (3) was that the method of calculating royalties on the entire sailboard might have a small effect in restricting competition with regard to the board, but would have no effect on the sale of rigs, especially as the royalties levied on the sale of complete sailboards proved to have been no higher than that laid down for the sale of separate rigs.[16] With regard to restriction (6), the Court rejected the argument by Windsurfing International that the restriction of manufacturers to one location was required by quality control. The Commission's argument to the contrary was accepted, that in fact numerous licensees throughout Germany were manufacturing components for the rig, and that Windsurfing International in any case would have had no say in the quality control of such manufacturers. The Court also gave an important general ruling on the interpretation of Article 81(1): it said that the Commission need not examine each clause restricting competition to see if each could be shown to have an effect on trade between Member States. Provided that the agreement taken as a whole had such an effect, Article 81(1) would be applicable to it. The Court appears to have found the necessary effect on trade from the levels of imports into the Community of both complete sailboards (about 20 per cent of national markets) and of their individual components (where the corresponding figure was about 10 per cent).

This case also importantly illustrates that the Court will generally support the Commission in its analysis of restrictions imposed by the holders of an intellectual property right (here a patent, but equally applicable to other forms of such rights). It will divide them into those (comparatively limited in number) which flow from the inherent subject matter of the right (and can, therefore, be said to form part of the right itself) and those which represent an attempt to extend the holder's rights beyond, even if only marginally. It will also respect the Commission's findings as to the scope of the right (provided that the findings appear reasonable in the light of all the evidence presented); crucial in this case was its finding that the patent covered only the rig and not the complete sailboard, a factor that influenced most of the adverse rulings against Windsurfing International.

---

[16] The licensee acknowledged that it would be equitable to accept a higher rate of royalty if it were calculated on the price of the rig alone.

4. KNOW-HOW LICENCES AND THE KNOW-HOW BLOCK-EXEMPTION REGULATION 556/89

4.1 THE SUBCONTRACTING NOTICE

Much technical information exists that is essential, or at least of substantial import-ance, to manufacturing operations or other industrial activities. Although undoubt-edly a form of industrial property, it cannot be protected by registration, notification, or symbol; it either exists alone or forms part of a 'package' of technical information which includes patents and other intellectual property rights. It is well defined by Hawk as 'a catch-all expression embracing a broad and ill-defined spectrum of unpatented and unpatentable inventions, techniques, processes, formulae, devices, blueprints, technical and production skills, etc'.[17] Since no time limit applies to the protection, it has been argued that it should be more strictly treated by the Commission than patents. It could also be argued that a great deal of what starts as technical know-how will reach the public domain relatively quickly, so that in practice its commercial value for exploitation will last for a considerably shorter period than patents, trade marks, or copyright. These factors could be put forward in support of a shorter period of protec-tion for know-how than for such other rights.

Light was shed on the Commission's attitude to the related topic of know-how after the termination of a licence for its use by the publication in December 1978 of a Notice on subcontracting agreements. This topic had been under discussion for four or five years with interested industrial groups, trade associations, and Member States. Under such agreements, a main contractor, often but not necessarily as the result of an order it had received from a third party, would order from a subcontractor goods or services that had to be integrated closely with its own manufacturing or service operations. A typical example is the supply by a subcontractor of components for assembly and incorporation in complex mechanical and electrical machinery or apparatus such as aircraft, motor cars, or computers. Similarities exist between such subcontracts and patent/know-how licences, although subcontracts normally last for a shorter time than patent licences, so that the main contractor would be particularly concerned to restrict future use by the subcontractor of the patented or unpatented information provided to him for the purposes of the subcontract. It is also important to ensure the close integration of the subcontractors' manufacturing processes with those of the main contractor. Article 81 is relevant to the restrictions under which the main contractor seeks to protect his interests by limiting the use of this information by the subcontractor once the contract has been terminated.

---

[17] B.E. Hawk, *United States, Common Market and International Antitrust: A Comparative Guide* (2nd edn, Harcourt Brace Jovanovitch, 1994 Supplement), Vol. ii, p. 691.

The solution eventually adopted was a compromise: the publication in December 1978 of a Notice.[18] This, of course, had less value in terms of legal certainty than a block exemption. However, it did at least indicate DG Comp's views on the restrictions available for placing within a subcontract and enabled greater scope to be given to the main contractor's wish to restrict the subsequent use of know-how by its previous subcontractors. The Notice can be summarized as follows:

(1) Article 81 would not apply to a subcontracting agreement where the subcontractor received either industrial property rights or unpatented secret data (know-how) or documents, dies, or tools belonging to the contractor and which permitted the manufacture of goods in a manner which differed in form, function, or composition from other goods on the market, unless the subcontractor was able to obtain access to the relevant technology and equipment needed to produce the relevant goods from sources in the public domain.

(2) If the relevant conditions were satisfied, then Article 81 would not apply to a clause whereby the technology or equipment provided by the contractor, and necessary for the subcontractor to carry out its obligations, could not be used except for the purposes of the subcontracting agreement or made available to third parties, and whereby goods or services resulting from its use should be supplied only to the contractor.

(3) Further ancillary restrictions would be permitted, namely that during the period of the subcontract the parties would not disclose confidential information, and that the subcontractor might enter into an obligation not to reveal the relevant know-how of a secret nature even after the expiration of the agreement, and to pass on to the main contractor improvements which the subcontractor has discovered, on a non-exclusive basis. On the other hand, the mere previous existence of a subcontracting agreement should not be allowed to displace the subcontractor's ability to compete in the future with the main contractor, utilizing independently its own technical information and know-how even if this had developed from experience gained during the main contract.

The Notice attempted to strike a fair balance between the interests of the main contractor in preventing unfair activity at a subsequent date by the subcontractor in utilizing the main contractor's information, whilst relieving the subcontractor from onerous restrictions placed upon it after the termination of the contract, that would restrict it from utilizing the benefits of the research and development which it may have carried out, and which may in turn have substantially contributed to its own specialized input to the contract. The difficulty of balancing these equally legitimate interests in the subcontracting area well illustrated the difficulties that faced the Commission in preparing the framework of model agreements acceptable as block exemptions for both patented and unpatented material.

---

[18] [1979] OJ C1/2.

4.2 THE KNOW-HOW REGULATION 556/89

It was by now clear that the model of the Patent Licence Block Exemption 2349/84 would not be wholly suitable for the many licences whose principal subject matter was non-patented know-how. At this time the Commission did obtain some experience from individual applications for exemption in respect of know-how licences in a variety of different markets, whose outcome suggested that it would be quite liberal in the level of protection it would give to licensees of know-how against the sales activities of other licensees in different territories.

The Know-how Block Exemption Regulation came into force on 1 April 1989. Its main features were as follows:

(1) It applied both to pure know-how agreements and also to mixed agreements covering both know-how and patents, which did not come within the Patent Licence Block Exemption.

(2) It applied only to bilateral agreements.

(3) The agreement had to contain at least one of eight restrictions which included an obligation on the licensor itself not to exploit know-how in the licensed territory nor to license other undertakings to do so and an obligation on the licensee not to actively market the know-how in territories licensed to others.

(4) A list of 'black' clauses were largely modelled on those contained in Regulation 2349/84, and included no-challenge and non-competition clauses, and restrictions on the customers to be supplied, maximum production quantities and price restrictions.

(5) A long list of 'white' clauses included those making the licence exclusive to the licensee, but prohibiting sub-licensing and limiting the use of know-how to particular fields of use, while the licensee could enjoy the benefit of a 'most favoured licensee' clause to ensure that no other licensee received better terms.

(6) The periods of protection allowed were shorter than those in the Patent Licence Block Exemption; ten years for the licensor against his licensee and vice versa and for the licensee against the active selling by other licensees into its territory, calculated from the date when the first licence was granted by the licensor in any Member State; five years by contrast for the licensee against passive selling into its territory.

The recitals followed the normal pattern, setting out at great length the policy considerations underlying its introduction. After emphasizing the growing importance of know-how within the Community, they stress the need to limit with precision what is to be properly covered by this very general phrase. Not all useful information is to benefit; it must be secret, substantial, and identified. It originally included the requirement that it must be of 'decisive importance' to the technology involved, but this was later discarded. None of the three definitions is totally straightforward. 'Secret' means not that all the information is totally unknown (save to the licensor), but that, taken as a whole, it is not generally known or easily accessible so that its use can give the licensee lead time once communicated to it. 'Substantial' means that it has important value for the whole or a significant part of a manufacturing process or a product or service or its development. In practical terms it must be useful to the licensee in its commercial operations. 'Identified' means that the package of information is described or recorded in sufficient detail for the other obligations of substantiality and secrecy to be verified and to clarify for the licensee where its existing knowledge stops and the new know-how package begins. The exemption did not cover licences connected to franchising or distribution (as opposed to production technology).[19]

5. THE FIRST TECHNOLOGY TRANSFER BLOCK-EXEMPTION REGULATION 240/96

5.1 THE TRAVAUX PRÉPARATOIRES

By the end of the 1980s, therefore, the would-be licensor in intellectual property, patented or unpatented, had block exemptions to provide a model for licences so long as they were relatively straightforward and did not fall into the awkward no-man's-land where the know-how involved was neither ancillary to the licence patent (so covered by the Patent Regulation) nor more than ancillary to them (covered by the Know-how Regulation), even if by concession the Commission did not take this particular point in the great majority of cases. The licensor had also however to consider whether any of the other intellectual property rights covered by a licence were commercially more important than either the patents or know-how which it licensed, as for example in the *Moosehead/Whitbread* case considered in Section 7 below. If these other rights were more significant than either the patents or know-how concerned, then individual exemption would be necessary.

A desire to eliminate these other awkward points covering both groups of licence led the Commission in 1993 to consider how to amalgamate the two block exemptions into a single instrument. The fact that the block exemption for patent licences was due to expire on 31 December 1994 was an incentive for action, and the fact that the Know-how Regulation was not due to expire until the end of 1999 seemed no obstacle to an amalgamation. The original target date for the entry into force of the new joint Regulation was 1 January 1995, but difficulties were encountered in obtaining final approval to the draft referred to below, so that this was postponed on several occasions, ultimately to 1 April 1996.

---

[19] Apart from transitional arrangements when a licensee acted temporarily as a distributor prior to commencing manufacture with the aid of the know-how.

The main problem in drafting the Regulation was the Commission's concern that it should not benefit either licensors or licensees with a particularly substantial market share in a particular product or service market in a given geographical area (normally that of a single Member State). The Commission suggested in early drafts for this reason that no exclusivity should be allowed if the licensee alone had more than 40 per cent of that relevant market, nor if, holding at least 10 per cent itself, was one of a number of oligopolists or if three or less had 50 per cent of the market, or if five or less had two-thirds of that market. Moreover, territorial restrictions on both licensor and licensee against selling their output arising from the licence into competing markets were limited to cases where they had less than 20 per cent of the market share. What the Commission failed to take sufficiently into account in making these proposals was that, as case law under Article 82 and the Merger Regulation had already made clear, the establishment of definite market shares for either licensors or licensees in particular geographical markets is more than a matter of quantitative analysis. The Commission's 1997 Notice on defining relevant markets illustrates that the task involves judgment, not merely statistical calculations, taking account of both demand- and supply-side substitutability in assessing actual and potential competition, and very detailed consideration of relevant price changes. The product to be licensed might be new, for example a new drug with characteristics not possessed by existing products, or it might have multiple uses, again not paralleled by its existing competitors. For such reasons, it is turnover, a relatively objective measure, that can be calculated reasonably quickly without so many delicate judgments, which is normally preferable as a jurisdictional test in merger-control cases, even though market shares might be thought to have far more connection with the issues of market power and dominance with which Article 2 of the Merger Regulation is concerned, and upon which the examination of the merger will concentrate.

For these reasons there was almost total opposition from industry, commerce, and professional advisers to these 'market share' proposals, expressed in particular at the public hearing on the Commission's proposals, just as for Regulation 2349/84 previously. Even after the original proposals had been substantially watered down there was still considerable opposition and finally, at the end of 1995, the Commission drew back from confrontation. In its final draft it withdrew all but some minor references to market shares.

5.2 THE FIRST TECHNOLOGY TRANSFER BLOCK EXEMPTION IN DETAIL

As it finally emerged, Regulation 240/96 reflected a less doctrinaire approach to licensing by the Commission and a greater willingness to accept that the block exemption must contain sufficient incentives for licensors to grant licences as well as a reduction of the restrictions which they can be allowed to place on licensees, which could have limited the ability of licensees to compete. The recitals reflected many provisions of the two predecessor Regulations, but made clear that they applied to licences of patents (national, Community, and European) as well to know-how licences and mixed agreements which combine both forms of property. The principal elements of this Regulation were as follows:

(1) It applied primarily to exclusive licences but in practice also covered a large number of non-exclusive licences, since these inevitably tended to contain a number of restrictions included in the eight listed in Article 1(1) which brought the licence within the scope of the block exemption, for example an obligation on the licensee not to exploit the licence technology in the territory of the licensor or of other licensees.

(2) It still applied only to bilateral agreements and not, for example, to patent pools or multiple cross licensing.

(3) It covered patent licences, know-how licences, mixed patent/know-how licences; licences for other intellectual property rights, such as trade marks, design rights, and copyright were covered only if ancillary to the principal licence.

(4) It provided a substantial measure of territorial protection to the licensee, potentially longer in duration for the patent licensee than the know-how licensee, against both the licensor and other licensees of the same licensor.

(5) It permitted field of use restriction, provision for minimum royalties and minimum quantities, as well as tying where this was needed to ensure technically proper exploitation of technology.

(6) It did not however permit customer allocation nor price restrictions on the licensee nor, subject to certain qualifications, no-challenge clauses nor non-compete obligations.

Article 2 contained the 'white list', which was rather longer than either of the predecessor Regulations. The substantive content did not differ greatly from the earlier Regulations, and those changes that were made tended to give greater freedom to the parties.

One change was that, although the licensee still could not use the know-how other than for its own purposes, e.g. it could not utilize it to build factories for third parties, it could, however, set up additional facilities of its own 'on normal commercial terms', including payment of additional royalties. Problems could arise if licensors were unwilling to commit themselves when the licence was first drawn up to a specific rate of royalties. This is not surprising since when the original licence was drawn up the circumstances in which subsequent additional sites were to be built may have been unknown. One of the omissions from the Regulation was clear provision with regard to the extent to which site licences were permitted. In 1997 the Commission opened proceedings in a case where the original licence, limited to a particular factory site in Spain, stated that the parties should negotiate mutually acceptable terms for future site licences, on the basis that, since the licence did not guarantee the licensee the right to utilize the technology at a new site, the licence was in breach of Article 81(1) and possibly outside the rather ambiguous terms of the block exemption. After the parties, ARCO and Repsol, had compromised their dispute, the Commission abandoned the case, unfortunately leaving the basic issues unresolved.[20]

Article 3 contained the 'black list', which was rather shorter than in the earlier block exemptions. These included the following clauses:

(1) restrictions on the determination of prices for the licensed products

(2) a restriction of one party from competing with the other in respect of products that compete with the licensed product, though this prohibition was qualified by the licensor's right to include a clause obliging the licensee to use his best endeavours to promote the licensed products and to convert an exclusive licence to non-exclusive if the licensee started to compete with him in this way

(3) a restriction that required a party without any objectively justified reason to refuse to meet orders from users or resellers in their respective territories who would market products in other territories within the Common Market, or made it difficult for such users or resellers to obtain products from such other resellers within the Common Market

(4) restrictions between competing manufacturers on categories of customer to be supplied, with prohibitions on employing certain forms of distribution

(5) unqualified restrictions on the quantity of licensed products produced (save as permitted specifically by the 'white list') or unqualified obligations of the licensee to assign the benefit of improvements to the licensed technology to the licensor save as permitted under Article 2 under the circumstances specified there.

Article 4 provided an opposition clause; certain 'grey' restrictions not falling within either the 'white' or the 'black list' could be put forward to the Commission for approval, with a time limit for objections to be raised, in a more streamlined form than before. However, the procedural innovation suggested on the severability of such clauses was not retained in the final version. This would have allowed an agreement to retain the benefit of the block exemption even if it contained such a 'grey' clause, merely by ignoring the clause as if it did not appear in the agreement at all, without affecting the validity of the remainder of the agreement. The lack of such a provision meant that a licence agreement which contained a single 'grey' clause which had not been accepted by the Commission through the opposition procedure remained totally ineffective, even if in all other respects it met the requirements of the new Regulation. Perhaps the novelty of such a provision appeared less attractive to the Commission in comparison with the familiar opposition procedure.[21]

[20] See M. Dolmans and M. Odriozola, 'Site Licences under EC Competition Law' [1998] 19 ECLR 493–500 and in reply J. Townend, 'The Case for Site Licences' [1999] 20 ECLR 168–74.

[21] A few years later the Commission's approach changed and block exemptions adopted since 1999 do not include an opposition procedure. In some of them, clauses which might be regarded as 'grey' are now simply declared to be unexempted, but do not prevent the application of the block exemption to the rest of the agreement. For an example in the context of distribution agreements see Ch. 10, Section 6.5.

Article 5 listed five categories of licence to which the block exemption did not apply, including patent or know-how pools, joint ventures between competitors or agreements between competitors involving reciprocal rights, sales licences and licences of intellectual property rights other than patents.

6. THE CURRENT TECHNOLOGY TRANSFER BLOCK EXEMPTION REGULATION 772/2004

6.1 BACKGROUND

A few years after the adoption of Regulation 240/96 the original timetable under which it would have remained in force until 2006 began to look unrealistic, because of three important developments relevant to its future.

The first was that the approach of the Commission to block exemptions in general changed, so as to become less prescriptive and to focus much more on setting out the restrictive clauses which are *not* allowed without seeking to list in detail other restrictive clauses which the parties may wish to include, provided that the market share of the licensor is below the threshold at which substantial market power can be assumed to exist. Regulation 2790/99 was the model for this, as described in Chapter 10, in which there is neither a 'white' nor 'grey' list but simply a relatively short 'black' list. The concern of the Commission is much more with the effects of the restriction, rather than with its legal form; for this reason it seeks to place more reliance on both the market share threshold and the publication of extensive guidelines to accompany the Regulation than on seeking to control in detail the precise content of the agreement in a way that places a straitjacket on the parties. It also seeks to place more emphasis on the encouragement of inter-brand competition rather than intra-brand competition.

The second change is that new block exemptions introduced after Regulation 240/96 had been adopted themselves introduced provisions which affected its content. In the area of vertical agreements covering distribution, Regulation 2790/99 included within its scope the assignment or licence of intellectual property rights which are ancillary to the distribution arrangements for goods or services and are directly related to the use for sales of goods by the distributor. In the area of horizontal agreements, Regulations 2658/2000 and 2659/2000 also provided new rules for ancillary rights in intellectual property which form part of a principal agreement covered by these measures on specialization and R&D respectively (see Chapter 18).

The third, and perhaps the most important, change is that the modernization programme of the Commission and the replacement after some forty years of Regulation 17/62 was to bring with it in 2004 the end of the granting by the Commission of individual exemption to licences of intellectual property rights, even though the block exemptions themselves were to remain of essential importance. Article 81(1) and (3) was to be applied by national courts and national competition authorities as well as the Commission. This in turn meant that considerable clarification and simplification of the rules applied to transfers of technology of all kinds was needed.

6.2 THE TRAVAUX PRÉPARATOIRES

In the light of these changing circumstances the Commission at the end of 2001 produced a comprehensive report on the operation of Regulation 240/96 and the changes that might be needed to it. The Report called for full consultation on the issues; it was clear from the responses received that any replacement block exemption in this area would have to incorporate radical changes if the challenge already raised by these major shifts in Commission policy were to be satisfactorily met. The Commission itself suggested some of the principal changes that might be needed, namely:

- a broader range of licensing agreements to be covered, including copyright licences
- an extension of its scope to include multi-party agreements[22]
- the elimination of the concept of 'white' and 'grey' clauses and further simplification of the list of 'black' clauses
- a distinction between licences between non-competitors, where a number of the present 'black list' restrictions could be eliminated, and those between competitors, where they would need to be maintained
- a market share threshold to determine which licensors would be entitled to benefit from the block exemption, which might be set at a higher level, say 30 per cent for non-competitors or say 25 per cent for undertakings in competition with each other.

Informal consultations with industry and other interested parties took place throughout 2002 and, after the draft texts had been discussed with the Member States, a proposal was formally published in October 2003. Though it represented a radical break with Regulation 240/96, the approach taken was hardly surprising as the Report had created the expectation of a proposal that followed closely the pattern set only a few years earlier by the new rules on vertical and horizontal restraints. The proposal was indeed for a new block exemption of broader scope than before, accompanied by detailed guidelines. It was to be based more on economic principles than on the legal formalism that had informed earlier block exemptions, and in particular the benefit of the exemption was to be available only where certain market share thresholds were not exceeded.

The key features of the draft regulation were:

(1) It applied not only as before to patent and know-how licences (pure and mixed) but also to software copyright licences and design licences (other types of

---

[22] In fact the new block exemption Reg. 772/2004 as finally adopted applies only to two-party agreements, because this is all that is permitted by enabling Reg. 19/65 which is the legal basis for its adoption. For the same reason it could not be extended to cover copyright in general or database licensing.

copyright remained excluded from its scope, except to the extent that they were ancillary to the main agreement).

(2) Market-share thresholds limited the application of the block exemption to situations where the parties' combined share was not more than 20 per cent (in the case of an agreement between competitors) or no individual party had more than 30 per cent (where the parties were not competitors).

(3) Agreements between non-competitors were treated differently from agreements between competitors, with separate 'black lists' for each category; this would mean a more generous regime for the former, but the loss of block exempted status for some of the latter, in particular as far as territorial restrictions were concerned.

The draft guidelines included detailed guidance not only on these proposed provisions, but also on the application of Article 81 to such agreements when they fell outside the scope of the block exemption, and included assessment of royalty obligations, exclusive licensing, non-compete obligations, tying, and sales, output and field of use restrictions. They also set out criteria for assessing settlement agreements and non-assertion agreements, as well as certain arrangements not covered at all by the block exemption such as technology pools.

Despite the innovative nature of the proposed new regime and general recognition that it represented substantial and welcome progress as compared with the existing rules,[23] the draft nevertheless attracted criticism on a number of points. In January 2004 Commissioner Monti announced that the final version of the block exemption would incorporate changes responding to many of these criticisms,[24] and indeed Regulation 772/2004 as eventually adopted is significantly different from the original draft on a number of points. It is unusual, and testament to the effective dialogue that took place between the Commission and the many interested parties, for such far-reaching changes to be made to a formal Commission proposal of this sort.

One criticism had been that parties might not be competitors at the time a licence was entered into, but might, as a result of later events, become competitors, for example because the licensee develops its own technology and starts to license it, thereby causing a different 'black list' to apply to the agreement. The regulation was amended to provide that in such circumstances the 'black list' for non-competitors would continue to apply for the full life of the agreement. It was also amended to give more generous treatment than originally proposed to field of use restrictions, exemption being granted to all such agreements, even where reciprocal between competitors. The scope for exemption of non-reciprocal restrictions between competitors was also extended so as to make exemption available to certain territorial and customer restrictions. As

---

[23] Many were pleased in particular to see that the proposed regime would bring about significant convergence between European and US rules on technology licensing, though differences were to remain, in particular in the approach to intra-technology restrictions.

[24] See M. Monti, 'The New EU Policy on Technology Transfer Agreements', speech available on the website of DG Comp, 16 January 2004.

to agreements between non-competitors, the extent to which active and passive sales could be restricted was also increased. Output limitations in non-reciprocal agreements between competitors were exempted, under certain circumstances. On the other hand the Commission stood firm on both the principle and the levels of the market share thresholds, though the texts were amended so as to emphasize that these only provide a safe harbour, and that there is no presumption of illegality when they are exceeded.

Regulation 772/2004 entered into force on 1 May 2004, the same day that Regulation 1/2003 entered into force in implementation of the Commission's competition law modernization programme referred to above,

6.3 THE CURRENT TECHNOLOGY TRANSFER RULES IN DETAIL

The principal features of Regulation 772/2004 are as follows:

(1) It has no 'white' or 'grey' lists, with the important consequence that, provided a licence agreement falls within its scope, any clause not expressly prohibited may be included without jeopardizing the exempted status of an agreement.

(2) It applies only to bilateral agreements.

(3) It covers patent and know-how licences (pure and mixed), and also software copyright licences and design licences.

(4) Availability of the block exemption depends on the parties' combined market share on the relevant technology and product markets being no more than 20 per cent (in the case of an agreement between competitors) or no individual party having more than 30 per cent on the relevant technology and product markets (where the parties are non-competitors);

(5) There are separate 'black lists' according to whether an agreement is between competitors or non-competitors.

(6) The rules on territorial and customer restrictions have been made more coherent than under Regulation 240/96.

(7) A more liberal approach than before is taken to non-compete clauses, tying and output restrictions.

Article 1 sets out definitions of a number of terms appearing in the block exemption, including 'technology transfer agreement'. Article 2 is the core of the regulation, stating that technology transfer agreements entered into by two undertakings permitting the production of contract products are exempted from the application of Article 81(1).

Article 3 sets out the market-share thresholds. Market definition and quantification of market shares is frequently not easy; nor, often, will it be simple to assess whether parties are competitors, in particular in fast-developing industries such as information technology and computer software. The Commission provides substantial guidance on these issues in its guidelines, but the application of the rules to given facts often raises significant difficulties. The guidelines stress that there is no presumption of illegality where the thresholds are exceeded, and they give an additional, informal, safe harbour, which reflects a similar rule in US law: regard will be had to the number of competing technologies in existence, and infringement of Article 81 is unlikely where there are four other independently controlled substitutable technologies.

Article 4 sets out the two 'black lists'; the inclusion of any of these restrictions in an agreement takes the whole agreement outside the scope of the block exemption. Such restrictions normally infringe Article 81(1) and do not fulfil the criteria for exemption under Article 81(3). The 'black list' for agreements between competitors mentions the following restrictions:

- resale price maintenance, irrespective of whether the agreement concerns fixed, minimum, maximum or recommended prices
- output limitation, except limitations on the output of contract products imposed on the licensee in a non-reciprocal agreement or imposed on only one of the licensees in a reciprocal agreement
- market or customer allocation except:
  (i)   field of use or product-market restrictions imposed on the licensee
  (ii) in non-reciprocal licences, field of use, product-market or territorial restrictions on the licensor or licensee where that field, market, or territory has been exclusively allocated to the other party
  (iii) the obligation on the licensor not to license the technology to another licensee in a particular territory
  (iv) in non-reciprocal licences, bans on sales by the licensee or licensor into exclusive territories or customer groups allocated to the other
  (v)   in non-reciprocal licences, bans on active sales by the licensee into territories or customer groups allocated to a non-competing licensee
  (vi) the requirement that the licensee produce the contract products only for its own use provided that the licensee is not restricted in selling the contract products as spare parts for its own products; and
  (vii) the obligation in a non-reciprocal agreement to produce the contract products only for a particular customer, where the licence was granted in order to create a second source of supply for that customer
- the restriction of the licensee's ability to exploit its own technology or the restriction of the ability of the parties to the agreement to carry out research and development, unless this is essential to prevent the disclosure of the licensed know-how to third parties.

As regards non-competitors, the 'black list' includes:

- resale price maintenance, although a maximum or recommended price is permitted provided it does not amount to a fixed or minimum price

- the restriction of the territory into which, or of the customers to whom, the licensee may passively sell the contract products, except:

  (i)   the restriction of sales into an exclusive territory or to an exclusive customer group reserved for the licensor

  (ii) the restriction of sales into an exclusive territory or to an exclusive customer group allocated by the licensor to another licensee during the first two years that the other licensee is selling the contract products in that territory or to that customer group

  (iii) as (vi) above

  (iv) as (vii) above

  (v)   the restriction of sales to end users by a licensee operating at the wholesale level of trade

  (vi) the restriction of sales to unauthorized distributors by the members of a selective distribution system

- the restriction of active or passive sales to end users by a licensee which is a member of a selective distribution system and which operates at the retail level, though a member of the system may be prohibited from operating out of an unauthorized place of establishment.

Article 5 lists certain restrictions that are not themselves exempted, but that are treated as severable and so do not affect the availability of exemption for the rest of the agreement. Such restrictions are not necessarily prohibited, but fall to be assessed individually under Article 81. The first three apply without distinction to agreements between competitors and those between non-competitors. The relevant restrictions are:

- any exclusive grant back obligation on the licensee in favour of the licensor or to a third party designated by the licensor in respect of its own severable improvements to or its own new applications of the licensed technology

- any obligation on the licensee to assign, in whole or in part, to the licensor or to a third party designated by the licensor, rights to its own severable improvements to or new applications of the licensed technology

- any no-challenge obligation, though it is possible to provide for termination of the technology transfer agreement in the event that the licensee challenges the validity of the licensed intellectual property rights

- where the undertakings are non-competing, any obligation limiting the licensee's ability to exploit its own technology or limiting the ability of the parties to the agreement to carry out research and development, unless such latter restriction is indispensable to prevent the disclosure of the licensed know-how to third parties.

Article 6 allows the Commission or a national competition authority to withdraw the benefit of exemption from an agreement under certain circumstances, and Article 7 allows the Commission to declare the regulation inapplicable to specific restraints in a given market, where parallel networks of similar technology transfer agreements cover over 50 per cent of that relevant market. The latter provision in effect allows the adoption of a stricter, sector-specific block exemption.[25]

Article 8 contains rules for applying the market-share thresholds, and in particular provides for some flexibility for up to two years where the market-share thresholds are exceeded.

The single key difficulty posed by the current rules is that they remain very complex, both in principle, and in their application to concrete situations. Moreover, the relatively low levels at which the market thresholds have been set mean that in practice a large number of agreements fall outside the scope of the block exemption. In practice therefore the guidelines are an extremely important resource for those who have to assess the legality of technology transfer agreements, and indeed, by analogy, other intellectual property licences.

On the other hand, the current block exemption and guidelines undoubtedly provide a more liberal framework, and more flexibility for those drafting licences, than did the earlier block exemptions. Like those now applicable in other areas of competition law, they are strongly grounded in economics and in the market effects of licensing arrangements, with economic consumer welfare the overriding concern. However, this means that any assessment exercise must take into account all the surrounding facts and market circumstances: it is no longer possible to assess an agreement simply by examining its terms. Moreover it is necessary to continue to monitor the situation during the lifetime of an agreement, because a change in market circumstances, such as market shares, may entail a change in the legal status of an agreement.

7. TRADE-MARK LICENCES

7.1 EARLY CASES ON TRADE MARKS

Both trade marks and copyright are familiar types of intellectual property rights which often carry considerable commercial value: their development and protection are justified by the time, effort, and expenditure that their owners have incurred in their creation. Both, of course, have potentially much longer lives than patents; indeed while the legal protection of copyright does ultimately expire,[26] the use of trade marks can continue indefinitely. In early European Court jurisprudence a feeling can be detected (notably in *Sirena* v. *Eda* discussed below) that trade marks are perhaps not as worthy of protection as other forms of intellectual property. In later cases, however,

---

[25] The Commission has not yet made use either of this provision, or of any of the similar provisions in other block exemptions.

[26] The duration of copyright protection in the Community has been harmonized (and for many Member States extended) by Directive 93/98.

notably *Hag (No. 2)*,[27] a firm basis was provided for treating trade marks as no less important than any other form of intellectual property. Their chief importance is that they enable a manufacturer who consistently produces high-quality goods to extend his reputation from one market to another without having to start from scratch in every case. Earlier suggestions by the Commission that it was considering the issue of a draft block exemption for trade marks have not, however, been followed up.

Early European Court cases were concerned mainly with horizontal agreements relating to trade-mark rights. The early case of *Sirena* v. *Eda*[28] shows the width of application of Article 81 in this context. In this case, an Italian Court sought, by an Article 234 reference, to know whether Articles 81 and 82 prevented an Italian company (Sirena) from asserting its registered trade mark, 'Prep', so as to prevent the sale in Italy under the same trade mark of similar hairdressing products made in Germany by another manufacturer. Both the Italian and the German undertaking claimed to have rights to the use of this trade mark, by assignments from an American company as long as thirty years previously. The problem had arisen because the German product had been imported into Italy for resale at prices lower than those at which the Italian product was sold, and Sirena wished to prevent these imports by relying on its registration of the mark in Italy. The Italian importer of the German product naturally contested the action on the basis that such a finding would be in breach of Article 81, claiming that the previous assignment of the two licences constituted an agreement between the United States owner and the licensees in their two separate markets, even though these assignments had taken place a considerable number of years previously.

As in all Article 234 cases, the Court was not required to rule on the merits of the case between the parties, only to answer questions on legal issues submitted to it by the national court responsible for deciding the case. The terms of the opinion given, however, were substantially in favour of the importer of the German product. The Court agreed with its argument that the effect of licences or assignments relating to trade marks can be that of preventing imports, notably through allocating particular watertight areas to individual undertakings, and that it would be a breach of Article 81 if such arrangements actually had such an effect, even if not intended to do so. The result of *Sirena* v. *Eda* initially caused some alarm, since Article 81 seemed to be applicable without reference to the length of time that had passed since the original trade mark rights had been allocated. However, the potentially wide effects of the decision were substantially reduced by *EMI Records Ltd.* v. *CBS United Kingdom Ltd.*[29] where the Court confirmed that, to bring Article 81 into play, the original allocation of trade marks had to be accompanied by a continuing relationship between the original owner of the trade mark and its licensees or assignees.

[27] [1990] 3 CMLR 571.

[28] Case 40/70 [1971] ECR 69: CMLR 260. Had the case reached the European Court at a later date, after the development of the extensive case law relating to the effect upon national intellectual property rights of Arts. 28–30, it would probably have been decided (with much the same ultimate result) by reference to those Articles, rather than to Art. 81.

[29] Case 51/75 [1976] ECR 811: 2 CMLR 235.

A case which reached the European Court in 1985 related to a trade-mark agreement between BAT (the German subsidiary of the multinational British-American Tobacco Ltd) and a small Dutch tobacco manufacturer, Segers.[30] This limited the use of trade marks which were alleged, rather unconvincingly, to be of a confusingly close nature. BAT owned a German trade mark, 'Dorcet', which had never been utilized for any particular tobacco product; Segers owned a mark in Holland, 'Toltecs Special', in respect of fine-cut tobacco. Segers had applied to have its trade mark registered in Germany (as well as in some other countries). BAT opposed this on the ground of potential confusion. The compromise, set out in the relevant agreement, involved withdrawal of opposition by BAT if Segers restricted the application of Toltecs to the sale of its fine-cut tobacco and agreed not to market its tobacco under the Toltecs mark in Germany except through BAT's approved importers. Moreover, Segers was not to exercise his trade-mark rights against BAT even if the Dorcet mark remained unused for a period of over five years. The Commission had found that in reality there was no serious risk of confusion between the two trade marks, and imposed a fine on BAT for agreeing the no-challenge clause, even though a five-year period of non-use had already expired. The Court annulled the fine on technical grounds, ruling that the restriction on Segers limited only the use of the mark, not trade in goods or services, but confirmed that BAT had, by attempting to control the distribution of Segers's products in this way, misused their trade-mark rights available under national German law. Not all settlements of trade-mark disputes involving the allocation of territories between competitors will be in breach of Article 81(1).[31]

7.2 TRADE-MARK LICENCES UNDER REGULATION 772/2004

The more liberal terms of the block exemption 772/2004 encompass a broader range of agreements covering both patented and unpatented material and other intellectual property rights. Provided that the principal purpose of the licence is technology transfer as defined in the Regulation, the inclusion within the licence of other rights (such as trade marks) does not prejudice the granting of exemption provided that these other rights can properly be defined as ancillary (Article 1(1)(b)). In many cases this will mean that trade-mark licences will be covered by the Regulation when part of a package of rights granted to the licensee, just as with Regulation 2790/99 in its treatment of ancillary intellectual property rights.[32]

In determining whether individual exemption applies to trade-mark licences under Article 81(3), the same principles are likely to be applied as under Regulation 770/2004, and useful guidance is also available in the technology transfer guidelines.

---

[30] Case 35/83 *BAT Cigaretten-Fabrieken* v. *Commission* [1985] ECR 363: 2 CMLR 470. The original Commission decision is reported as *Toltecs-Dorcet Trade Marks* [1983] 1 CMLR 412.

[31] See, e.g., *Penney's Trade Mark* [1978] 2 CMLR 100.

[32] In *Campari* [1978] 2 CMLR 397, a network of exclusive licences to a variety of undertakings from the original manufacturers of that well-known aperitif was granted individual exemption once tying and export ban clauses had been removed.

In particular, the equivalent clauses to those contained in the 'black list' of the block exemption are unlikely to be acceptable, for example, where the licensee is placed under restrictions as to price, customer, or quantity.

On the other hand it seems clear from the *Moosehead* case[33] that 'no challenge' clauses as to ownership will be acceptable since the issue of trade-mark ownership lies only between licensor and licensee, not between third parties. Any no-challenge clause as to the general validity of the mark would fall however within Article 81(1), since it could affect third parties, but it might nevertheless obtain exemption unless it was believed to be potentially damaging to competitors.[34] In the *Moosehead* case, Moosehead, a Canadian brewery, wished to sell its beer in the United Kingdom but could not justify the capital costs of setting up its own production and distribution facilities there. By entering into a licence with Whitbread, a well-established UK public company with its own brewing and distribution facilities, Moosehead could obtain access to the UK market. Under the arrangements, know-how was to be provided to Whitbread to enable them to produce and sell Moosehead beer. The principal object of the agreement, however, was the exploitation of the Moosehead trade mark, rather than this know-how, so that the block exemption then in force, Regulation 556/89, could not apply. The Commission, however, granted individual exemption to a number of restrictive clauses, including the exclusive use of the trade mark in the United Kingdom and prohibitions on Whitbread against actively selling the product outside the UK or dealing in competing brands of lager.[35]

8. COPYRIGHT AND SOFTWARE LICENCES

8.1 COPYRIGHT LICENCES

The importance of copyright in protecting a wide variety of commercial rights continues to grow. It applies to books, magazines, and other printed matter, and the varied products of the entertainment and music industry, such as compact discs, DVDs, videos, cassettes, CD-ROMs, films, programs, and the diverse new digital products created by advanced technology. A number of pieces of Community legislation reflect its importance. The willingness of the European Court to look at the special characteristics of copyright was illustrated early by the *Coditel* cases. In

---

[33] [1991] 4 CMLR 391.

[34] Reg. 772/2004 expressly excludes from the benefit of block exemption any clause prohibiting challenge to the validity of an intellectual property right, though it is permitted to provide for termination in the event of such challenge (Art. 5(1)(c)).

[35] The Commission also ruled that a 'no challenge' clause to the validity of a trade mark may constitute a restriction of competition within the terms of Art. 81(1), as a successful challenge could bring the mark into the public domain for use by everyone, but only if the mark were already well known (not the case with Moosehead in the UK) and its use an important advantage to a company competing in a particular market, so that its unavailability would be a barrier to entry.

Coditel (No. 1)[36] the European Court ruled that Article 59, protecting the freedom to provide services, did not prevent the granting of a seven-year exclusive copyright licence in a film by the French producer to a Belgian distributor (Cine Vog) thus entitling Cine Vog to prevent Coditel, a Belgian cable-television company, from intercepting the transmission of the film and re-showing it to its subscribers, even with the consent of the original French producer. In the sequel case (in this context more important), *Coditel (No. 2)*,[37] the Court went on to rule that an exclusive grant of copyright in a film did not automatically bring the licence within Article 81(1) since there were many special circumstances relating to the film industry; the difficulties in obtaining a return on investment in a film, which did not apply to other goods and services, entitled the Court to make a full economic analysis of the effects of the particular agreements before reaching a conclusion.

The Court stated that the exercise of exclusive rights would fall within Article 81(1) only if economic analysis showed that it gave the parties to the licence the opportunity: (1) either to create artificial barriers to the market or to charge fees exceeding a fair return on the investment, (2) to provide exclusivity for a disproportionate period of time, or (3) on a more general note, that it enabled the parties in a particular Member State to prevent or restrict competition in that country. The Court seemed to accept, reflecting its earlier conclusions in the *Maize Seed* case referred to above,[38] that original investment in films is far more likely if accompanied by the possibility of an exclusive licence being granted. Given also the comparatively short commercial life of many films, it seems reasonable to accord them greater protection for that short period than is reasonable for other products, for example, those protected by plant breeders' rights in the *Maize Seed* case.

Again no block exemption has been provided by the Commission but in analysing licences of this kind the Commission and the Court will take into account not only the geographic and product markets concerned but also the duration of the licence granted and the particular characteristics of the industry involved.[39] In the German TV films case *Commission/Degeto Film*,[40] the proposed licence related to a large number of feature films owned by MGM/United Artists Corporation. The original intention was to license these exclusively to Degeto, a subsidiary of the association of public broadcasting companies in Germany. The exclusivity apparently covered some 1,350 of the 3,000 films owned by MGM/UAC and would have lasted for terms of approximately fifteen years starting on different dates. During these exclusive periods, third parties would have no access to the films. Degeto would also have rights over new films produced by

---

[36] Case 62/79 *Coditel* v. *Cine Vog Films (No. 1)* [1980] ECR 881: [1981] 2 CMLR 362.

[37] *Coditel* v. *Cine Vog Films (No. 2)* Case 262/81 [1982] ECR 3381: [1983] 1 CMLR 49.

[38] At p. 268.

[39] Since 2004 useful guidance as to the Commission's approach has been available in the technology transfer guidelines, which state that, although Reg. 772/2004 'does not cover copyright other than software copyright, the Commission will as a general rule apply the principles set out in [that regulation] and these guidelines when assessing such licensing of copyright under Article 81' (para. 51).

[40] [1989] OJ L284/36: [1990] 4 CMLR 841.

MGM/UAC during the period of the agreement. The Commission found that feature films played an important part in television programming, as they were very popular with audiences and often of a higher artistic standard than films produced specifically for television. The licence period of fifteen years, however, was at least five years longer than the normal permitted period for such agreements, and the total number of films covered extremely large; both these factors caused concern to the Commission.

The licence was eventually given Article 81(3) exemption following substantial amendments to it; 'windows' were introduced to the agreement, permitting the licensing of the films to third parties for particular periods during its lifetime. These 'windows' would last for periods of two to six years, considerably reducing the degree of exclusivity. Exemption was granted because with these amendments some advantages could be obtained for German viewers who would have greater access to a larger number of films. The package deal provided would reduce the price per film licensed, and thus also the operating costs of public broadcasting organizations. The remaining degree of exclusivity was accepted as necessary in order to allow MGM/UAC a fair return for their original investment.

8.2 SOFTWARE LICENCES

Many computer-software licences are now eligible for protection under the technology-transfer block exemption, as discussed above, and where a licence does not qualify for block exemption, the technology transfer guidelines will be of assistance.

Nevertheless, the protection of computer software does raise special issues. The existence of Software Directive 91/250, adopted on 4 May 1991, which required Member States to adopt national laws implementing the Directive by 1 January 1993, makes clear that the basic form of intellectual property for protection of software is to be copyright.[41] The Directive itself specifies the rights of the software owners, which are the right on an exclusive basis to prevent copying, both permanent and temporary, and against translation, alteration, and distribution. The only exception to these rights is where the work carried out by the licensee in this way is necessary for the use of the program in its intended purpose. Moreover, subject to certain limits set out in the Directive, the licensee is entitled to decompile and reverse-engineer in order to obtain sufficient information to create other programs to interface with the licensed programs. Of course, the provisions of a Directive cannot change the terms of Articles 81 or 82. However, it would be reasonable to expect the Commission, in assessing such licences, to recognize and follow the policy contained in the Directive, which recognizes the particular characteristics of this form of property, including its necessary exclusivity and the vital need for the control of copying, often reinforced by licensing of particular work sites rather than in general terms. It is perhaps surprising that no

---

[41] Nevertheless, in February 2002, the Commission published a proposal that, under Community law, patent protection should be granted to a limited category of software; mainly computer-implemented inventions (Com. (2002) 92 final). This proved very controversial and the proposal was abandoned in 2005.

individual case on the validity of a software licence has yet been dealt with, at least by way of formal decision.

In assessing the range of restrictions which might be imposed on a licensee for the use of software, and which might satisfy the criteria for individual exemption under Article 81(3), it is undoubtedly appropriate to take into account its special features, which in some respects make it more difficult to safeguard than other forms of intellectual property. The licensor of software might properly define the field of use in which a particular program or group of programs is to be used, since if the licensee were to make a broader application than the licensor intended, the licensor might lose substantially in terms of the royalties to be obtained.

On the other hand, although decompilers will normally seek to rely on the rights given to them by the Directive, they may well find situations in which these rights do not apply, but they believe they should be entitled to decompile, for example, whether the decompiling right extends to obtaining and using interface information to enable the designing of hardware to interface with the relevant software. The recitals of the software Directive do say that the Directive does not prejudice the application of Article 82 'if a dominant supplier refuses to make information available which is necessary for inter-operability'. The *Microsoft* case, described in Chapter 14, is an example of a refusal to supply interoperability information being held to be an abuse of dominance.

One final general point needs to be made which applies to all forms of licensing of intellectual property. The terms of the licence cannot be used to extend the inherent right of the owner of the particular form of intellectual property or his period of ownership. The Commission has in recent years been attempting to harmonize these rights, and the software Directive referred to above is one attempt to lay down common standards, not only for these rights but also for the terms upon which software licences may be granted. The duration of copyright has itself been determined for all EC countries by a Directive. The Council's first Directive on Trade Mark Licences[42] also sought to specify the rights which the owner of a trade mark may regard as his under Community principles. This includes a definition of trade marks, enumerates when they cannot be accepted for registration, and defines the rights which they are capable of conferring. They also provide that non-use for a five-year period after registration can lead to revocation of a proprietor's rights.

8.3 OTHER FORMS OF INTELLECTUAL PROPERTY RIGHTS

Special rights exist for other types of property. For example, it is clear from *Erauw-Jacquery* v. *La Hesbignonne*[43] that the rights of the owners of basic seeds may well include protection against improper handling and the control of propagation by those establishments regarded as suitable. For this reason, and to this extent, a clause prohibiting a licensee from selling or exporting basic seeds would not come within the

---

[42] Directive 89/104 [1989] OJ L40/1.   [43] Case 27/87 [1988] 1919: 4 CMLR 576.

prohibition of Article 81(1), even though an equivalent clause would not be permitted in a copyright or know-how licence. The Court pointed out that the breeder of basic seeds is in some respects more similar to a franchisor than to the owner of a copyright, and that the breeder's control over use of the seeds was essential to prevent its know-how becoming too easily available to its competitors. The same products were the subject of a more recent *Sicasov* case, the facts of which are discussed in Chapter 8 at p. 166. Here the rights of the French plant breeders to control the use made of their basic seeds (used only for propagating new seed) were held outside Article 81(1), whilst restrictions on the export of certified seeds (available for use in sowing by growers and farmers) fell within Article 81, even though on the facts an individual exemption under Article 81(3) was granted. The validity of licence terms in types of intellectual property yet to be developed may well also be influenced substantially by the nature of the right being licensed, and the benefits to both licensors and consumers from the restrictions imposed.

FURTHER READING

M. Dolmans and M. Odriozola, 'Site Licences under EC Competition Law' [1998] 19 ECLR 493–500 and, in reply, J. Townend, 'The Case for Site Licences' [1999] 20 ECLR 168–74.

C.-D. Ehlermann and I. Atanasiu (eds.), *The Interaction Between Competition Law and Intellectual Property Law: European Competition Law Annual 2005.*

F. Fine, 'The EU's New Antitrust Rules for Technology Licensing: A Turbulent Harbour for Licensors' [2004] 29 ELRev 766.

I. Lianos, 'Competition Law and Intellectual Property Rights: is the Property Rights Approach Right?' [2005–6] *Cambridge Yearbook of European Legal Studies* 153.

M. Patterson, 'Revision of the New Technology Transfer Block Exemption: Convergence or Capitulation?' in Hans Ullrich (ed.), *The Evolution of European Competition Law* (Edgar Elgar Publishing, 2006).

13

ARTICLE 82: THE CONCEPT OF DOMINANCE

1. THE DEFINITION OF DOMINANCE

1.1 INTRODUCTION

Articles 81 and 82 EC have the common aim of ensuring that competition in the Common Market is not distorted. They have, however, different scopes of application: Article 81 EC aims to control anti-competitive behaviour that results from cooperation between undertakings while Article 82 EC has the purpose of curbing abuses of dominant position by one or more undertakings. The wording of Article 82 EC suggests that in order to find a breach of this provision it is necessary to prove, firstly, that a company is dominant, secondly, that it has abused that position of dominance and finally, that such abuse has or may have, an effect on intra-Community trade. This chapter will consider the first of these elements, namely the determination of a position of dominance or economic strength. Given that dominance cannot exist in an abstract context, but only in relation to a particular market, an essential prerequisite to assess market power is the definition of the relevant market where the undertaking operates. Dominance and market definition are therefore the main objectives of this chapter while the notion of abuse and the different forms that it may take will be considered in Chapter 14.

Following the important and economics-driven reforms that took place in the context of Article 81 EC and in the field of merger control in the late 1990s and the early years of the twenty-first century, there was a general expectation that the reform of Article 82 EC would become a priority for the Commission. More so, when both the Commission and the European Court had come under close scrutiny as a result of their rather formalistic method of application of Article 82 EC. The review of this provision was duly initiated by DG Competition in 2003 and reflected in the publication in 2005 of a *Discussion Paper on the Application of Article 82 EC to Exclusionary Abuses*. The main purpose of this Paper was to develop practical rules in tune with economic reality that would assist the Commission and national agencies in the application of Article 82 EC. The scope of the Discussion Paper was limited to exclusionary abuses and did not cover exploitative or discriminatory abuses. At the time, it was expected that the Commission would turn its attention to these other forms of abuse in 2006 but this never materialized. Following the publication of the 2005 Discussion Paper, a period of public consultation was opened and DG Competition received plenty of comments—and some intense criticism—in relation to several aspects of its proposal. At the time of writing, it was expected that the Commission would publish some more definitive guidance on the application of Article 82 EC. Despite the non-binding nature of the Discussion Paper, this document remains a useful tool to understand the pattern of analysis used in the application of Article 82 EC as well as providing a helpful summary of the case law that has interpreted this provision.

1.2   *UNITED BRANDS* AND *HOFFMANN-LA ROCHE*

Preceding chapters have dealt almost exclusively with the development of the law relating to Article 81, and its application to both horizontal and vertical agreements and concerted practices. Although the resources devoted by DG Comp to the administration of Article 81 have far exceeded those spent on Article 82, this second of the twin pillars of the competition policy established under the Treaty has nevertheless given rise to decisions of great significance, from both the Commission and the Community Courts. Article 82 is increasingly important to the Commission in its continuing enforcement of competition policy; it has potential for further development and application by way of control, in a great variety of circumstances, of the problem of the abuse by undertakings of dominant positions in specific markets. It has proved particularly valuable to the Commission as it has through its powers under Article 86(3) issued directives bringing more competition to key Community markets, including energy, telecommunications, transport, and postal services.

   Article 82 is itself brief. It states that abuse by one or more undertakings of a dominant position within the Common Market (or a substantial part of it) should be prohibited, in so far as it may affect trade between Member States.

   Dominance is an abstract word but, used in a commercial context, it refers to a position of substantial power for an undertaking in relation to a specific product market and within a relevant geographical market, both of which must be defined. Fortunately dominance was considered in detail by the European Court in one of its early cases arising out of this Article, *United Brands*.[1] The market power of this company (engaged in the large-scale international fruit business) derived principally from the degree to which it had integrated its various activities. Although it also had a market share in the four relevant Member States of between 40 and 45 per cent, its strength and dominance derived from the fact that at each stage of the production and distribution process it was able from its own resources to accept and react to variations in demand. It alone was capable of carrying over two-thirds of its production in its own fleet of specially

---

[1] Case 27/76 [1978] ECR 207: [1978] 1 CMLR 429. This chapter deals with dominance by a single undertaking or corporate group. Joint dominance by two or more undertakings is dealt with in Ch. 15. A comprehensive account of the significant differences between Art. 82 and Section 2 of the Sherman Act is found in P. Jebsen and R. Stevens, 'Assumptions, Goals, and Dominant Undertakings: the Regulation of Competition under Article [82] of the EU' (1996) 64/3 ALJ 443–516.

designed ships. It alone was able to advertise the 'Chiquita' brand name and to revolutionize the commercial exploitation of the banana. Its large capital investment in purchasing and equipping its plantations allowed it to increase its source of supply, so as to overcome any effects from disease or bad weather. It was enabled by the scale of its capital investment to introduce a distribution system for a highly perishable commodity through the extensive use of refrigeration facilities, giving it a strategic advantage over all its competitors. In particular, the ability to control the timing of the ripening process close to the ultimate retail market within the Community gave it an important element of strategic leverage, placing all its competitors at a disadvantage. The combined effect of these measures led the Court to characterize the concept of dominance as follows: 'the position of economic strength enjoyed by an undertaking enabling it... to behave to an appreciable extent independently of its competitors and customers and ultimately of its consumers. In general, it derives from a combination of several factors which taken separately are not determinative.'[2]

Not long after in the *Hoffmann-La Roche* case, the Court gave a rather more extended definition to the concept of dominance:

The dominant position... relates to a position of economic strength enjoyed by an undertaking which enables it to prevent effective competition being maintained on the relevant market by affording it the power to behave to an appreciable extent independently of its competitors, its customers and ultimately of the consumers. Such a position does not preclude some competition which it does where there is a monopoly or quasi-monopoly but enables the undertaking which profits by it, if not to determine, at least to have an appreciable influence on the conditions under which that competition will develop, and in any case to act largely in disregard of it so long as such conduct does not operate to its detriment.

... The existence of a dominant position may derive from several factors which taken separately are not necessarily determinative but among these factors a highly important one is the existence of very large market shares.[3]

Such comments by the Court need to be illustrated by reference to specific markets in cases decided by it. In *Hoffmann-La Roche*, the Court found that La Roche held the following market shares within the Community:

Vitamin A—47 per cent

Vitamin B2—86 per cent

Vitamin B3—64 per cent

Vitamin B6—95 per cent

Vitamin C—68 per cent

Vitamin E—70 per cent

Vitamin H—95 per cent

---

[2] Case 27/76, above at para. 65 of the judgment.

[3] Case 85/76 [1979] ECR 461, at paras. 38–9 of the judgment: [1979] 3 CMLR 211, 274, often called the *Vitamins* case.

In 1974, the turnover of the company in the Common Market comprised 60 per cent of the total sale of vitamins worldwide. The group had altogether some 5,000 customers, many of whom were large multinational companies who purchased in large orders the entire range of vitamins produced, particularly under pressure of the fidelity rebate scheme already discussed. On the basis of these figures, for all except Vitamin A there was an overwhelming presumption of dominance from the market share alone, which gave Hoffman-La Roche a position of strength, allowing it freedom of action in responding to changes in market conditions. In the case of Vitamin A, where the market share was lower, the factors upon which the Court placed heavy reliance were the great disparity between its market share and that of its next largest competitors, and the wide technological lead which it enjoyed over them. The absence of real challenge in many of the markets, and the extent to which the Roche sales network was more highly developed than any of its competitors, were also factors that could be taken into account.

On the other hand, whilst the Commission had placed weight on the size of the company and the volume of turnover it provided, the Court itself did not accept that size and turnover alone could establish dominance. The Court also placed far less reliance than the Commission on both the range of products produced by Roche and the fact that it had retained market share over a continuous period of time, pointing out that this could be explained by a large number of other factors, including simply its ability to compete effectively in a normal manner.

The existence of very high market shares is therefore likely to be a good indication of dominance unless there are special circumstances. Thus, the European Court of Justice and the Court of First Instance have held that a market share of 50 per cent or more will normally be indicative of dominance, provided this position has been maintained for some time and that the immediate competitor or competitors of the supposedly dominant undertaking have a much smaller market share.[4] Dominance has also been found in cases where the market share of an undertaking was below 50 per cent but above 40 per cent[5] and the Court has even recognized that dominance might exist—albeit very exceptionally—where the market share of a company falls below 40 per cent, depending on the strength and number of its competitors and other relevant factors.[6]

---

[4] Case C-62/86 *AKZO* v. *Commission* [1991] ECR I-3359: [1993] 5 CMLR 215 and Case T-395/94 *Atlantic Container Line* [2002] ECR II-875.

[5] Case 27/76 *United Brands*, see fn. 1.

[6] Case C-250/92 *Gøttrup Klim* v. *Dansk Lanbrugs* [1994] ECR I-5641, [1996] 4 CMLR 191. See also the judgment in Case T-219/99 *British Airways* v. *Commission* [2003] ECR II-5917 where the Court of First Instance upheld a Commission Decision (*Virgin/BA* OJ [2000] L 30/1: [2000] 4 CMLR 999) that concluded that British Airways was a dominant purchaser in the market for travel agency services in the United Kingdom with a market share of 39.7%. The next largest competitor airline had sales of only 5.5% and a number of other relevant factors like the number of routes operated to and from the United Kingdom and BA's large holding of slots at major airports were also taken into account. The finding of dominance was later confirmed on appeal by the European Court of Justice on appeal: see Case C-95/04 *British Airways* v. *Commission* (Judgment of 15 March 2007, not yet reported).

However, market shares must be used with caution. Not only it is necessary to consider the ratio between the market share of the undertaking in question and that of its nearest rivals and whether a large market share has been maintained for some time, but also, as DG Competition observed in its *Discussion Paper on Exclusionary Abuses*, it must not be forgotten that 'market share is only a proxy for market power, which is the decisive factor'. In other words, while market share provides a starting point for the analysis of market power other factors—like for example the degree of product differentiation in a given market—may ultimately influence the extent to which it determines a finding of dominance.[7]

1.3 ITS APPLICABILITY TO SMALL MARKETS AS WELL AS LARGE

The concept of dominance is not limited to large-scale markets but is also found in markets that are narrow; where one undertaking has, through legislation or other circumstances, obtained a monopoly or a very strong position which completely or substantially reduces competition. The earliest example was *General Motors Continental*.[8] This involved granting type approval for GM cars manufactured in Germany but which required certification before import into Belgium; the cars in question were parallel imports for whose certification GM Continental had charged excessive prices. After the complaints had been raised, GM reduced their charges to actual cost and refunded the excess, before the Commission's investigation had even begun. On appeal from the Commission's decision, the European Court of Justice annulled the decision, indicating that it felt the Commission had been unjustified in raising under the Article what appeared to be so trivial a case, especially as General Motors had corrected the overcharge made. Nevertheless, the case had a certain value as a precedent, though actually more relevant to market integration than to excessive pricing.[9]

Any undertaking which holds an exclusive legal right for the performance of a statutory duty, delegated by a State or public authority, must in carrying out its duties not abuse the powers conferred so as to enhance its other objectives, such as rendering less attractive the possibility of parallel imports. In *Hilti* v. *Commission*[10] the Court of First Instance ruled that it was an abuse of dominant position for a company owning a patent, required by national legislation to grant a licence of right, to demand a fee six times higher than that ultimately awarded by the Comptroller of Patents,

---

[7] See further Azevedo and Walker, 'Dominance: Meaning and Measurement' [2002] 23 ECLR 363 and Monti, 'The Concept of Dominance in Article 82' [2006] 2 European Competition Law Journal 31.

[8] Case 26/75 [1975] ECR 1367: [1976] 1 CMLR 95.

[9] A direct descendant of *General Motors Continental* is Case 226/84 *British Leyland* v. *Commission* [1986] ECR 3263: [1987] 1 CMLR 185, where the Commission's fine on British Leyland was upheld. The actions of which the Commission complained were BL's refusal to issue national type approval certificates for Leyland cars imported into the United Kingdom other than through official channels, and for charging £150 for certificates of conformity to those national type approvals for those dealers and individuals who sought to import Metros with left-hand drive from the Continent.

[10] Case T-30/89 [1991] ECR II-1439: [1992] 4 CMLR 16.

thereby prolonging the proceedings needlessly. *Hugin* v. *Commission*[11] shows that dominance can occur even in a market for spare parts. In this case, the product market was Hugin cash registers, although the European Court of Justice ruled that no effect on trade between Member States had been shown by its practices. An example of narrow geographical markets in which dominance is shown are the 'essential facilities' cases discussed in the next chapter, where even a single harbour or airport within the Community may be held to be a market of sufficient significance for Article 82 to be applicable.

The ownership of intellectual property rights sometimes provides a dominant position in a product covered by the relevant rights. In *Volvo* v. *Eric Veng (UK)* the car makers Volvo sued Veng for breach of its registered designs covering a front wing panel for a particular Volvo model. The prime issue in the case (an Article 234 reference from the High Court) was whether Volvo's refusal to grant a licence to Veng to manufacture such panels was an abuse by Volvo of its undoubted dominant position with regard to that part; in a parallel case decided on the same day the Court also rendered its opinion under an Article 234 reference in the *Renault* case.[12] Renault had claimed monopoly rights under Italian law for its ornamental body panels. It was accepted by the Court in these cases that, although under national law Volvo or Renault could validly secure the exclusive right to manufacture these panels and thereby obtain complete dominance of that product, this alone did not justify an adverse finding under Article 82. Dominance alone, even as to 100 per cent, is insufficient as it is not the monopoly or quasi-monopoly that can be challenged but its abuse.[13]

One hundred per cent control of a particular product or service market may arise under other national legislation; in the *Magill* case, finally decided by the European Court in 1995,[14] the law of copyright gave RTE in the Republic of Ireland complete control of the compilation of programme schedules for radio and television, which were therefore not available (absent the grant of an appropriate licence by their owners) to those entrepreneurs who wished to publish weekly magazines including such details. National legislation conferring a monopoly may also place a business in such a position of dominance; an example was the granting of sole rights in the Netherlands and Spain for certain categories of letter delivery to the national postal authorities to the exclusion of commercial organizations who wished to compete for this business.[15]

---

[11] Case 22/78 [1979] ECR 1869: [1979] 3 CMLR 345.

[12] Case 53/87 *Maxicar and Others* v. *Renault* [1988] ECR 6039: [1990] 4 CMLR 265: Case 238/87 *Volvo* v. *Veng* [1988] ECR 6211: [1989] 4 CMLR 122.

[13] For an example of the same principle applied by the English High Court, see *Pitney Bowes* v. *Francotype* [1990] 3 CMLR 466.

[14] Case C-241/91P [1995] ECR I-743: [1995] 4 CMLR 718. At earlier stages there had been similar Community cases involving the BBC and ITP in the United Kingdom: see Cases T-69 and 70/89 [1991] ECR II-535, 575: [1991] 4 CMLR 669, 745.

[15] *Dutch Courier Services* [1990] OJ L10/47: [1990] 4 CMLR 947. The Commission decision was however annulled by the European Court on procedural grounds: Cases C-48 and 66/90 [1992] ECR I-565: [1993] 5 CMLR 316. See also *Spanish Courier Services* [1991] 4 CMLR 560.

1.4 SUPER-DOMINANT COMPANIES: THEIR 'SPECIAL RESPONSIBILITY'

The wording of Article 82 appears to state that an undertaking will either be in a dominant position in relation to a given market or will not, and no mention is made of any separate categories of dominance. Nevertheless there have been some cases where the market share of the defendant undertaking has been so large, amounting to a percentage in excess of 90 per cent, that the 'special responsibility' of dominant companies with very high market shares referred to by the ECJ in *Tetrapak (No. 2)*[16] has apparently led to a more onerous or comprehensive obligation being placed on them not to engage in particular practices, such as predatory or excessive pricing or refusal to deal. A recent example of this approach is found in *Compagnie Maritime Belge* v. *Commission*[17] which involved selective price cutting and use of 'fighting ships' by members of a shipping conference holding between them more than 90 per cent of the relevant market, in order to drive out a particular rival which had sought to compete with them. Fennelly A-G made this point with particular clarity: 'Article 82 cannot be interpreted as permitting monopolists or quasi-monopolists *to exploit the very significant power which their super dominance confers* so as to preclude the emergence of either a new or additional competitor.' Though the European Court itself did not make use of precisely the same language, it nevertheless placed emphasis in its judgment on the significance of the market share of the conference members being more than 90 per cent.

1.5 COMPANIES WITH LOWER MARKET SHARES

At the other end of the scale, the Court in *Metro (No. 2)*[18] made it clear that no question of dominance could arise when a supermarket chain had less than 10 per cent of the general electronic equipment market for leisure purposes and less than 7 per cent of the colour-television market. In practice, it seems unlikely that any undertaking having a market share of less than 25 per cent will be held to have a dominant position. Recital 32 of the EC Merger Regulation (Regulation 139/2004)[19] sets out a presumption that a concentration significantly impeding competition in the Common Market cannot be created if the parties' joint market shares do not exceed 25 per cent.[20] Over that percentage dominance can become an issue: then the larger the percentage share, the more difficult to avoid the presumption that the undertaking benefits from

---

[16] Case C-333/94 P [1996] ECR I-5951: [1997] 4 CMLR 662.

[17] Cases C-395/96 P [2000] ECR I-1365: [2000] 4 CMLR 1076.

[18] Case 75/84 [1986] ECR 3021: [1987] 1 CMLR 118.

[19] See Chs. 16–18 for a detailed consideration of the Community system of merger control.

[20] More ambiguously, the 2005 *Discussion Paper on Exclusionary Abuses* states that 'undertakings with market shares of no more than 25% are *not likely* to enjoy a (single) dominant position on the market concerned (emphasis added)' (para. 31 of the Discussion paper). This form of words appears to suggest that a finding of dominance cannot be ruled out in cases where undertakings hold a market share of less than 25%.

a lesser degree of control from normal competitive pressures. Notwithstanding the lesser emphasis placed by the Court than the Commission on levels of market share in *United Brands*, the Commission continues to place great emphasis on such percentages, and once these can be shown to reach 45 per cent it becomes almost impossible to claim that an undertaking lacks power unless there is another undertaking in the same market with a share of equivalent size.

1.6 FACTORS INVOLVED IN ASSESSING DOMINANCE

As indicated above, the identification of a dominant position is never solely a quantitative task. The Commission and courts have also to take into account that 'combination of several factors' which is the qualitative nature of the relevant market. The number and strength of competitors will always be important; if there is a wide gap between the market share and resources of the principal company in the market compared with the next largest companies, this will be significant. Also relevant will be the ability of competitors as the result of unused productive capacity to respond promptly to output reduction or expansion or price increases by the principal company or market leader. The likelihood of new entry will depend on the barriers that exist; these may be inherent in the nature of the market or have been brought about rather by the actions of the dominant company.

Barriers inherent in the nature of the market will include Community or Member State regulations, for example those dealing with health and safety, economies of scale or scope, and the risk of having to make large capital investments to enter the market that may turn out to be irrecoverable (referred to as 'sunk costs'). Barriers caused by the dominant company itself might involve the use of intellectual property rights such as patents and copyrights, the need for vertical integration for purposes of distribution, and the need (especially with consumer products) for heavy expenditure on marketing and brand promotion, and in some cases access to scarce raw materials. Sometimes dominance is alleged by the Commission to have been enhanced by the very acts which have been complained about since potential new entrants may fear to enter a market where incumbents are known to react vigorously against new entrants, for example, by predatory pricing as indeed was well illustrated in the shipping conference cases such as *Compagnie Maritime Belge*.

2. THE DEFINITIONS OF RELEVANT
GEOGRAPHIC AND PRODUCT MARKETS

As explained above, the definition of the relevant market where an undertaking operates is an essential prerequisite to any assessment of dominance. Market share percentages only have meaning when the market to which they relate has been defined. In its 1997 *Notice on Market Definition*,[21] the Commission highlighted that the purpose of market definition in both its product and geographical dimension is to identify the competitive constraints that operate on an undertaking. Given that dominance exists when it can be demonstrated that an undertaking is capable of operating, to an appreciable extent, independently of competitive pressures, it is necessary to determine these competitive pressures before market power can be properly assessed. The criteria used to define the relevant geographic and product markets will be examined in the following sections. Some important decisions of the Commission and of the Court as well as the 1997 Commission *Notice on Market Definition* will also be considered. The latter did not alter the parameters of legal assessment but simply consolidated the principles laid down by the Court and the Commission on market definition. These can be of application not only in Article 82 EC but also in Article 81 EC cases and in the context of merger control.

2.1 THE GEOGRAPHIC MARKET

The search for the relevant geographic market begins with the words of the Article: 'within the Common Market or in a substantial part of it'. A Member State's territory will often provide a natural geographic setting equivalent to the commercial area in which competition is taking place; in early cases the assumption was readily made that geographic markets would be, if not the entire area of the Community, then no smaller than an individual Member State. This tendency was first challenged in the *Sugar Cartel* case[22] when the Court accepted the Commission's contention that a substantial part or region of a Member State could also constitute a market given a sufficient volume of sales.

In each case the parties concerned and the Commission will advance economic arguments to justify their contention, including any existing barriers to the free movement of goods, consumer buying habits, and costs of transporting goods in from neighbouring areas. The easier it is to bring goods in from a distance, using the improved transport systems now found in many parts of the Community, the wider the likely market will be. It is usually in the interests of the undertakings to suggest that a market is a relatively wide area so that their individual shares are reduced. The Commission in contrast will normally argue that narrower areas form natural individual markets. The Commission will often reach a conclusion that, since undertakings organize their distribution arrangements on a national basis, this implies that they regard such national territories as separate markets, an approach adopted, for example, in both *United Brands*[23] and *Michelin I*.[24] If national legislation also creates different market conditions in individual Member States, this too will tend to establish them as separate markets.

[21] [1997] OJ C372/5.
[22] The Court here accepted Southern Germany as a geographic market for sales of sugar (Cases 40–48, 50, 54, 56, 111, 113, 114/73 [1975] ECR 1991–4: [1976] 1 CMLR 463–5).
[23] Case 27/76, see fn. 1.   [24] Case 322/81 [1983] ECR 3461; [1985] 1 CMLR 282.

The Court has shown in at least one Article 234 ruling that in this context it is prepared to look beyond the geographical focus of the immediate case and to define the geographic market more broadly if circumstances require. In *Alsatel* v. *Novasam*,[25] the original dispute arose when the Alsace Telephone Authority tried to enforce payment from Novasam, an employment agency, as compensation for Novasam's early termination of a long-term telephone rental installation. Under the terms of an admittedly onerous contract, Novasam as the price of early cancellation had to pay some three-quarters of the remaining payments for the original duration of the agreement. Moreover, the agreement stated that if the equipment provided was at any time supplemented so as to increase Novasam's annual rental by more than 25 per cent, then this automatically extended the contract for a further fifteen years. Alsatel alone was entitled to make any extension or modification to the equipment. The making and enforcement of such an onerous contract was found by the Court to be potentially abusive but the relevant geographic market was considered to be not simply Alsace (with which the immediate case was concerned) but the whole of France. Businesses such as Novasam were not limited to obtaining telephone equipment from Alsatel but could purchase or rent it from any part of France. In this wider market Alsatel had a market share well below that required to constitute dominance.

Another French case referred to the Court under Article 234 on this type of issue was the *Bodson* v. *Pompes Funèbres* case.[26] The Court did not reach a finding on the facts as to whether Pompes Funèbres had a dominant position, this being left for the national court to decide. Nevertheless, it pointed out that Pompes Funèbres held the exclusive concession for conducting funerals (apart from the provision of church services, flowers, and monuments) for some 2,800 of those 5,000 local communes in France in which the performance of external aspects of conducting funerals had been delegated exclusively to one specified private firm. These 5,000 communes covered 45 per cent of the entire French population. The contrast between this and the *Alsatel* case is that the individual purchaser of funeral services could in practice clearly not choose from a wide variety of enterprises but was obliged to use the firm or firms authorized by the local commune. The Court stressed that in assessing dominance (as well as the effect on trade between Member States) it was the share of the population affected by the exclusive allocation that was crucial, rather than simply the total percentage of communes affected, though in this case, this factor was not crucial to market definition.

2.2 THE PRODUCT OR SERVICE MARKET

The definition of product markets is, if anything, even more elusive. There are few products for which there are not substitutes of some kind, and the interrelationship of quality, price, and availability is in nearly all cases difficult to analyse with precision.

---

[25] Case 247/86 [1988] ECR 5987: [1990] 4 CMLR 434.
[26] Case 30/87 [1988] ECR 2479: [1989] 4 CMLR 984.

Cross-elasticity of demand between substitute products has been at issue in a number of cases, notably *United Brands*, in which the banana's unique characteristics were considered in meticulous detail in the context of an ultimately unsuccessful argument that it should be considered as part of a wider product market including fruit of different kinds. The Court upheld the Commission's view that in terms of year-round availability, price, suitability for particular types of consumer (notably the very young and very old), and other characteristics, the product market could not be said to include any other kind of fruit—a decision whose effect increased the market shares held by United Brands. This part of the decision has however been attacked by a number of commentators on the grounds that the analysis by the Court of substitutability of different fruits for bananas was based on inadequate economic data or surveys to show accurately the cross-elasticity of demand between the banana and such other fruits. The interchangeability of products was also considered by the Court in *Hoffmann-La Roche*, where the Court found, inter alia, that a simple product could be considered as belonging to separate product markets if applied for more than one end use. Generally, however, the more emphasis placed on the degree of market power possessed by the defendant, the clearer the process of identifying the relevant market.

Substitutability from the point of view of demand therefore appears as the key criterion for market definition in most Article 82 EC cases. However, in some cases, the Commission and the Court have also taken into account elasticity of supply as a second competitive constraint which may influence market definition. Thus, a finding of cross-elasticity of supply might determine a broader relevant market than the one defined when only demand substitutability is considered. A clear example is found in *Michelin I*,[27] where the Commission defined the relevant product market as the market of replacement tyres for heavy vehicles. After deciding that replacement tyres for heavy vehicles like lorries and buses would not be interchangeable with replacement tyres for light vehicles—like cars and vans—in the eyes of a consumer, the Commission then moved to examine whether it would be possible for a manufacturer of replacement tyres for heavy vehicles to easily change its conditions of production so as to be able to manufacture replacement tyres for light vehicles. On the facts, it was found that there was no cross-elasticity of supply.

3. LEADING JUDGMENTS OF THE EUROPEAN COURT ON MARKET DEFINITION

3.1 *AHMED SAAED*

One of the leading cases on market definition arose on an Article 234 reference from a German court. In *Ahmed Saaed*,[28] two travel firms in West Germany had sold airline

---

[27] Case 322/81, see fn. 24.   [28] Case 66/86 [1989] ECR 803: [1990] 4 CMLR 102.

tickets at prices which substantially undercut the official Federal government approved tariffs, exploiting anomalies in the pricing system. The tickets they purchased were for a journey from Portugal via a German airport to a third country at rates cheaper than the shorter journey from that German airport to the same foreign destination. Under German law, such opportunism is not encouraged, but is a criminal offence. On the appeal by the travel firm against their convictions for such ticket sales, the Court ruled that the product market in Article 82 cases was not limited to different forms of air travel, namely charter and scheduled flights, but included all other means of travelling between the same points, including rail and coach services. It emphasized, however, that every case would turn on its own facts.

3.2 HILTI

In two important later cases the market assessment of the Commission was directly in issue. In *Hilti* v. *Commission*[29] the Commission's definition was challenged before the Court of First Instance and the European Court, being regarded as crucial to the eventual outcome of the case. Hilti, a Luxembourg company, had patent protection for both its nail guns and the cartridge strips inserted into the guns, but not for the individual nails which the gun fired from that strip. Hilti argued that the product market here could not be limited to powder-actuated fastening systems (the technical description of the particular type of nail gun) but covered a variety of other fastening methods used on building sites. It pointed out that such fastenings could also be created in certain circumstances with hand or power drills, spot welding, screws, bolts, and nuts. The choice of method would depend on a variety of factors, including the technical problems of the particular materials to be fastened, the load it would need to bear, the skill of the operators, and the time available for carrying out work, quite apart from the cost of the fixing materials.

The Commission had regarded powder-actuated fastening systems in certain situations as giving builders particular advantages. These included versatility of use, easy portability, and speed of operations, even if there were some materials which these systems could not fix and some loads which such fixings could not sustain. Moreover, the nails and cartridges used were often considerably more expensive than alternatives, such as screws and bolts. Nevertheless, in its view powder-actuated fastening systems could be properly regarded as a product market separate from that of the alternatives because the cost of fixing represented only a very small element in the total cost of building; the relatively minor variation in cost attributable to the use of that system made it unlikely that a small change in the price of Hilti's own guns, cartridge strips, or nails would cause a shift by customers to an alternative product. The Court of First Instance upheld the Commission's decision and its fine of six million ECUs. Hilti's share in the UK market for nails was found to be between 70 and 80 per cent. The Court also confirmed that not only were guns, cartridge strips, and nails all

---

[29] See fn. 10. The ECJ report is Case C-53/92P [1994] ECR I-667: [1994] 4 CMLR 614.

separate product markets, but also that the powder-actuated fastening system which they comprised was sufficiently different from other fastening systems to justify a finding that the degree of substitutability between them was relatively low. In rejecting the appeal from the Court of First Instance the European Court emphasized that it would not normally disturb findings of fact by the lower court unless it had a clear sense that the evidence had become distorted, which was not the case here. Moreover, the Court ruled that if the Commission defines a product market on the basis of factual evidence, as opposed to supposition, the Court may require the appellant to prove that his different version of the market is correct and cannot merely rely on showing that the facts on which the Commission relied could be interpreted in a different way.

3.3 TETRAPAK (NO. 2)

An even more complex case on market definition was *Tetrapak (No. 2)*[30] in 1996. Tetrapak were alleged to have had a dominant position in four related markets: those for carton machinery and cartons for UHT (aseptic) milk, and carton machinery and cartons for ordinary milk. It is, of course, sold in glass and plastic bottles as well as in cartons, and market shares for these different types of container had varied over the fifteen years to 1991 with which the Commission had been concerned. The Commission found that each of the four markets was separate because the technology of carton manufacturing for aseptic and for ordinary milk was quite different. Under other forms of packaging, aseptic products presented little competitive threat to aseptic milk cartons. Tetrapak's argument that it provided an 'integrated' packaging system combining machinery and cartons with consequent public-health advantages was not accepted, on the basis that in the absence of mandatory consumer protection rules any undertaking should be free to manufacture consumable items, such as cartons, intended for use in equipment being manufactured by others.

The share held by Tetrapak in the four markets varied; in the two aseptic markets it had unquestioned dominance, with over 90 per cent of the markets for both cartons and machinery. In the two markets related to ordinary milk its market share was lower, about 55 per cent, giving it an overall market of some 78 per cent for cartons of all kinds. Rather than relying, however, on the lower market share for a finding of dominance separately in the non-aseptic markets, the European Court chose to uphold the Court of First Instance and the Commission in their finding that the aseptic and non-aseptic markets were so closely associated that, taking them together:

Tetrapak's practices on the non-aseptic markets are liable to be caught by Article 82 of the Treaty without its being necessary to establish the existence for a dominant position on those markets taken in isolation, since that undertaking's leading position on the non-aseptic markets, combined with the close associative links between those markets and the aseptic markets, gave Tetrapak freedom of conduct compared with the other economic operators

[30] The ECJ report is Case C-333/94P [1996] ECR I-5951: [1997] 4 CMLR 662. The CFI report is Case T-83/91 [1994] ECR II-755: [1997] 4 CMLR 726.

on the non-aseptic market, such as to impose on it a special responsibility under Article 82 to maintain genuine undistorted competition on those markets.

It is only fair to record that some leading commentators, including Korah,[31] have criticized this ruling on the basis that the finding of dominance in the second market as a result of its close association with a primary market is a dangerously wide doctrine, which could be used to support findings of dominance in secondary markets where the company really had relatively little market power. The facts in the *Tetrapak (No. 2)* case, however, were unusual and particularly strong. The products being packaged in the two markets were similar and many of the same companies acquired product from Tetrapak in both markets, even though only 35 per cent of Tetrapak's customers purchased both types of equipment. Tetrapak's control of the aseptic market was almost a complete monopoly, enabling it to do business on very favourable terms in the ordinary milk market. It is possible, however, that there would be few other cases where the links between the two relevant markets are so strong as to justify such a finding.

4. MERGERS AND MARKET DEFINITION

Market definition plays a key role not only in Article 82 cases, but also in cases brought under the Merger Regulation which are considerably more numerous. The need to carry out a large number of market-definition analyses from 1990 onwards under the old and the new Merger Regulations (with its strict time limits) has alerted the Commission to the importance of a methodical and consistent approach to market definition in all cases. There is, however, a significant difference between market definition in the two situations. In merger cases the focus is inevitably on the future consequences of the concentration and the probability, or even possibility, of important changes in the future, for example as a result of changes in distribution, patent, or technological advances.[32] In Article 82 cases the focus has to be on the past conduct of the particular undertaking and the Commission must be at least primarily concerned with the way markets have worked over that period. However, in many cases the decision as to the relevant market, in both product and geographical terms, will ultimately be reached on the same basis in both merger and Article 82 cases. The 1997 Commission Notice on Market Definition was not primarily intended to announce any revolutionary new approach to the process of analysis, but to provide reassurance that the Commission would seek a consistent methodology in both Article 82 and merger cases.

---

[31] V. Korah, '*Tetrapak (No. 2)*—Lack of Reasoning in Court's Judgment' (1997) 18 ECLR 98–102.
[32] See further Chs. 16–18.

5. THE 1997 COMMISSION NOTICE ON MARKET DEFINITION

In its 1997 Notice[33] the Commission sets out the basis upon which it defines both product and geographic markets, on the basis of the established case law. Thus, relevant product markets are defined as comprising 'all those products and/or services which are regarded as interchangeable or substitutable by the consumer, by reason of the product's characteristics, their prices and their intended use'. Relevant geographic markets are defined as 'the area in which the undertakings concerned are involved in the supply and demand of products or services, in which the conditions of competition are sufficiently homogeneous and which can be distinguished from neighbouring areas because the conditions of competition are appreciably different in those areas'.[34] The Commission begins by pointing out that this concept of relevant market is closely related to the particular objectives with which the individual case is concerned. In an Article 82 case, its focus is on whether the undertaking in question can behave, to an appreciable extent, independently of competitors and its customers; and this ability will often, though not invariably, follow from its possession of a large market share in the supply of products or services. The assessment inevitably has to work backwards in time since the determination of whether a breach of Article 82 has occurred is not made in the abstract but in respect of a particular past period, which may only cover a few months, but is more frequently a period of some years.

The Notice goes on to identify three main competitive constraints from which relevant product markets can be identified: demand substitutability, supply substitutability, and potential competition. Of these, demand substitution, with its focus on consumer preferences, is considered the most relevant and important. This follows the precedent of the United States Department of Justice Antitrust Division Merger Guidelines and of the practices of other leading antitrust authorities throughout the world. The key test is the 'SSNIP test' which considers the natural reaction of customers to a small (5 to 10 per cent) but permanent rise in prices;[35] if its effect is to cause customers to switch to readily available substitutes, or to suppliers located elsewhere, to the point that the original price rise becomes unprofitable owing to the loss of sales incurred, then these additional suppliers will be included in the scope of the relevant market. By contrast, if there is little or no such switching by customers, then the existing market patterns are likely to be adopted as the relevant market. This is the so-called SSNIP test, to which the Community Courts have made occasional references.[36]

However, the application of the SSNIP test can sometimes constitute an inaccurate tool for market definition in Article 82 EC cases. For example, in the case of a

---

[33] [1997] OJ C372/5: [1998] 4 CMLR 177.   [34] Case 27/76 *United Brands*, see fn. 1.
[35] SSNIP stands for 'small but significant non-transitory increase in price'.
[36] Case T-340/03 *France Télécom* v. *Commission* ([2007] ECR II-107) at para. 87 of the judgment.

dominant company already charging particularly high prices, it is possible that the prevailing price may already have been substantially increased above market levels and hence there is a danger that the market could be defined too widely by including products that are only in competition with those offered by the dominant company because the latter have been priced at monopoly levels. In other words, the market may include false substitutes. This is often referred to as the 'Cellophane fallacy'.[37]

By contrast, 'supply side' substitutability is a measurement of the degree to which suppliers can switch production to a new product quickly and market it without incurring significant additional costs or risks, in response to small and permanent changes in the relative prices of existing suppliers. When this occurs it will naturally have some 'disciplinary' effect on the pricing behaviour of the original suppliers in respect of all products with which the 'switchers' can compete. This form of competition may be adequate even if the new suppliers can only provide part of the range of products sourced from the original suppliers. By contrast, if the would-be new suppliers would not be able to enter the market without first building new factories or making other substantial investments over time, then these will not be regarded as part of the relevant product market. Examples are given of products where branding is important, such as soft drinks, where the value of the brand can only be built up by substantial advertising over time. For the same reason, potential—rather than actual—competition for supplies is not given great weight, unless there is some real evidence of a company with both the ability and the intention to enter the market in the foreseeable future.

The Commission goes on to list a number of factors which it regards as important in the assessment both of demand and supply. In some cases the issue will be relatively straightforward and narrow; if a particular product is not substitutable for another, then the required market shares will fall short of the necessary level and no further enquiries will be needed. In other cases a precise market definition will be required before the issue of dominance can be decided. Information will then be sought from the principal companies as to their activities, the range of prices they pay, and the increases they would be prepared to accept from existing suppliers. Consumer preferences may be relevant and existing data from market research studies can be utilized, though ad hoc surveys in response to a particular case are treated with more reserve. Evidence of past price changes in response to market 'shocks' will also be taken into account. There are particular barriers or costs associated with switching from one product to another. These will also be considered; they may include regulatory barriers or simply substantial capital cost incurred for the provision of the manufacturing capacity or promotional expenditure required.

---

[37] *US* v. *du Pont* (the 'Cellophane' case) 351 US 377: 76 S. Ct 994 (1956). The 2005 *Discussion Paper on Exclusionary Abuses* considers the problems that derive from the application of the SSNIP test (see paras. 14–17).

6. SOME PROBLEMS IN ASSESSING DOMINANCE

There is no lack of both Court and Commission case law on the interpretation and application of the concept of dominance. It would, however, be misleading to give the impression that the ascertainment in individual cases of whether dominance exists is necessarily straightforward. Whilst in some cases its existence is clear and indisputable, especially where market shares represent a very high percentage and there are barriers to entry, there are other cases where the basis on which dominance has been alleged by the Commission has given rise to strong criticism by both economists and legal commentators.

These difficulties begin with the initial definition provided by the ECJ in *Hoffmann-La Roche*, with its emphasis on 'economic strength . . . affording [the dominant company] power to behave to an appreciable extent independently of its competitors . . .'. It is clear that a large market share is important but not necessarily determinative. In other words, this definition embodies not only quantitative but also qualitative elements and the balance between them has to be worked out on a case by case basis. In presenting such a formula the Court seems to suggest that it will be possible to decide in each case whether an undertaking is or is not dominant.

In recent years however the approach of the ECJ and CFI has changed; 'the special responsibility' of all dominant companies not to abuse their position has been supplemented by a new requirement on the 'super dominant' as already mentioned and as pointed out by Whish.[38] The cases (*Tetrapak No. 2* and *Compagnie Maritime Belge*) in which this special obligation has been referred to, have all been in the 90–95 per cent market-share range; the concept is clearly to be applied with restraint, not simply to all companies with a market share well above the 50 per cent level. But this development, however desirable in its application to the particular facts of those cases, goes far beyond the *ECS/Akzo* presumption of dominance at the much lower level of 50 per cent and appears to contain the following message to undertakings. 'We can tell you in broad terms at what market share you may start to be dominant but your responsibility as a dominant company is not simply to refrain from particular activities; it is to refrain from all activities inappropriate to your individual market share considered in the context of all other circumstances'. As applied, for example in *Compagnie Maritime Belge*, this means that price cuts not actually below average variable costs but made for the purpose of excluding a competitor from the market might still for this reason be abusive, even if equivalent reductions made by a dominant company with a smaller market share would not have been.

While we have always known that undertakings with non-dominant positions are free to indulge in pricing or marketing strategies that a dominant company may not adopt, for example in the framing of discount or rebate schemes, it appears that it is the degree of dominance which may now determine the exact classifications of those

---

[38] R. Whish, *Competition Law* (6th edn, Butterworths, 2008), pp. 184–6.

actions or strategies that will be characterized as abusive—in other words a 'sliding scale' approach to dominance.

A further difficulty in the application of the concept of dominance is that the definition found in *Hoffmann-La Roche* is itself hard to apply to individual cases. This is because it does not analyse the way in which economic markets actually work, which is that even dominant companies find that their pricing strategy is to some extent controlled by consumers; the demand curve for their products in that market imposes a discipline or restraint upon even the company with a very large market share.[39] Competitors, even if considerably weaker than the dominant company, will themselves sometimes be able to force the dominant company to change its pricing strategy if they themselves reduce prices, and if the dominant company wishes to remain at a profit maximizing level. If it was possible in each market to determine what was the 'competitive price level' then it might also be possible to decide if at any particular time in that market the alleged dominant company was pricing above it; but in practice economists are unanimous in saying that the competitive price level in a given market is usually impossible to measure accurately. It may be possible to have a 'hunch' about it but legal prohibitions should have a firmer basis. A better test, which at least stays closer to the *Hoffmann-La Roche* definition, may be that the probability of the dominant company being able to act independently of the market is to be measured by its ability to restrict current output in the market, which may give it in turn power over price and ability thereby to hurt consumers. In conclusion therefore the problem with dominance as a concept is that it is often too complex to serve as a satisfactory criterion for determining jurisdiction; it may be difficult indeed to know if it exists until after completing a detailed examination of the market including the nature and effects of the alleged abusive acts. Clearly this is not always the problem as there are some situations where the existence of dominance is obvious. Nevertheless clearer guidelines are needed for the many situations where the answer is far from obvious and where present Court jurisprudence provides inadequate assistance for the guidance of companies with a reasonable degree of market power and their advisers.

FURTHER READING

B. ALLAN, 'Article 82: A Commentary on DG Competition's Discussion Paper' [2006] *Competition Policy International* 43.

C. W. BADEN FULLER, 'Article 86: Economic Analysis of the Existence of a Dominant Position' [1979] 4 ELRev 423.

V. KORAH, 'Concept of a Dominant Position within the Meaning of Article 86' [1980] 17 CMLRev 395.

V. KORAH, '*TetraPak II*: Lack of Reasoning in Court's Judgment' [1997] ECLR 98.

---

[39] See D. Ridyard, 'Exclusionary Pricing and Price Discrimination Abuses under Art. 82—An Economic Analysis' [2002] 23 ECLR 286–303.

R. O'DONOGHUE and J. PADILLA, *The Law and Economics of Article 82* (Oxford: Hart Publishing, 2006).

J. TEMPLE LANG, 'Monopolisation and the Definition of Abuse of a Dominant Position under Article 86 EEC Treaty' [1979] 16 CMLRev 345.

S. TURNBULL, 'Barriers to Entry, Article 86 EC and the Abuse of Dominant Position: An Economic Critique of European Community Competition Law' [1996] ECLR 96.

14

ARTICLE 82: ABUSE

1. INTRODUCTION

1.1 THE NATURE OF ABUSE

Article 82 does not attempt to provide a definition of abuse, but does give a number of examples, namely:

(1) directly or indirectly imposing unfair purchase or selling prices or other unfair trading conditions

(2) limiting production, markets, or technical development to the prejudice of consumers

(3) applying dissimilar conditions to equivalent transactions with other trading parties, thereby placing them at a competitive disadvantage

(4) making the conclusion of contracts subject to acceptance by the other parties of supplementary obligations which, by their nature or according to commercial usage, have no connection with the subject of such contracts.

The fundamental nature of the concept of abuse was addressed quite early by the European Court in *Hoffmann-La Roche*[1] and described as:

an objective concept relating to the behaviour of an undertaking in a dominant position which is such as to influence the structure of a market where, as the result of the very presence of the undertaking in question, the degree of competition is weakened and which, through recourse to methods different from those which condition normal competition in products or services on the basis of the transactions of commercial operators, has the effect of hindering the maintenance of the degree of competition still existing in the market or the growth of that competition.

This definition covers not only the illustrations of abuse set out in the text of the Article, but also a large number of other practices not specifically mentioned, but which have been considered in the case law of the Community Courts. The majority of these cases in which such practices have been defined and analysed have been appeals

---

[1] Case 85/76 *Hoffmann-La Roche* [1979] ECR 461, 541: [1979] 3 CMLR 211, 290.

from decisions of the Commission, under Article 230, which have often involved the imposition of a fine on the dominant undertaking. There have also been a small number of such cases brought to the ECJ under Article 234 from national courts, which have required the opinion of the ECJ on such issues.

Abuses are often classified as either exclusionary or exploitative, though the Commission regards the distinction as not of great importance. An exclusionary abuse is one of those of the kind referred to in the quotation above from *Hoffman-La Roche*, where its effects are primarily on the structure of the market, for example by weakening competitors through raising their costs, refusing to deal with them or denying access to essential facilities. By contrast exploitative abuses are aimed directly at consumers, for example by imposing excessive prices or unreasonable terms and conditions; of course a successful use of exclusionary abuses may well lead on to subsequent use of exploitative ones, or they may be used simultaneously and in combination. Under section 2 of the Sherman Act, however, mere exploitation abuses would not normally be prohibited.

1.2 CATEGORIES OF ABUSE

In reviewing the extensive case law relating to abuse, it is helpful to deal in turn with the principal categories, as follows:

(1) those connected with pricing, including excessive and predatory pricing, discriminatory and cross-subsidized pricing, and rebate and discount schemes with anti-competitive features

(2) those involving a refusal to deal by the dominant company in respect of goods or services, either absolutely or except on unreasonable terms (such as a 'tying' obligation)

(3) those involving a refusal either by an individual proprietor or collective societies to grant licences of intellectual property rights (or otherwise to abuse their exploitation)

(4) those involving a refusal to grant access to essential facilities

(5) those involving the refusal to supply interoperability information

(6) other miscellaneous acts, including abuse of legal proceedings or insisting upon unreasonable terms and conditions with contractual partners.

The Commission's ability to issue directives to Member States under Article 86(3) is of particular relevance here since it is able to identify aspects of conduct which it regards as likely to interfere with competition in markets where previous dominance by the national monopoly supplier, such as a national telephone company or other dominant undertaking, can now be challenged in such sectors as communications, energy, and transport. An example is the Notice[2] from the Commission on the application of

---

[2] [1998] OJ C 265/2 and [1998] 5 CMLR 821.

the competition rules to 'access agreements in the telecommunications sector'. The Notice not only summarizes the access principles derived from a large number of Commission decisions, some of which are considered below, but also explains how Article 82 should be applied consistently across various sectors involved in the provision of new multimedia communication services, especially in the principle of access to system 'gateways'. Many of the particular abuses referred to, including refusal to provide access to competitors, withdrawal of existing access, exclusionary practices within networks, tying, excessive or predatory pricing, and discrimination, reflect the case law under Article 82 from other sectors, discussed below.

It is also important to emphasize that many of the leading decisions of the Commission and judgments of the Community Courts in respect of this Article have been controversial and subject to criticism by both lawyers and economists, principally in respect of alleged failure to analyse in sufficient depth the various types of abusive conduct, in particular those dealing with price and with access to essential facilities. It has been alleged that some of the practices characterized as abusive reflect normal competitive practice for larger companies.

2. EXCESSIVE PRICING

2.1 EARLY CASES

The wording of Article 82(a) refers to the imposition of 'unfair' purchase or selling prices. The charging of excessive prices clearly falls within this description. The criteria by which prices can be assessed as 'excessive' are however in practice often difficult to establish and there is less authority from either the Commission or from Community Court cases to rely upon than might have been expected.

The Court first dealt with this issue in the rather unusual case of *General Motors Continental*[3] discussed in Chapter 13 (p. 299) but the circumstances of the case meant that its value as a precedent was limited. The charge made by General Motors for the approval certificates required by importers of its cars into Belgium (made only over a relatively short period) was accepted as being excessive by all parties and had been refunded by General Motors to those customers before the Commission's investigation had begun. In overruling therefore the finding of the Commission that on these facts a breach of Article 82 had occurred, the Court did not need to go into depth into the concept of an 'excessive' price. The decision was nevertheless valuable to the Commission in showing that in an appropriate case the use of the pricing mechanism by undertakings to interfere in the process of integrating national markets (by making parallel imports more difficult) would be treated as a breach of the competition rules.

---

[3] Case 26/75 [1975] ECR 1367: [1976] 1 CMLR 95.

Shortly afterwards the issue arose for the first time in a major case in *United Brands*, where one of the allegations made by the Commission was that the prices charged for bananas in some national markets were excessive. There, the Commission had relied on the prices charged for Ireland, which were the lowest, as a base line from which to claim that the higher prices in the other countries were demonstrably excessive. As in *Continental Can*[4] and other cases, the Court refused to accept the Commission's economic analysis on the basis that it lacked the depth and adequacy to substantiate the claims made. In particular, it indicated that it felt that the basis for the Irish prices had not been sufficiently investigated, to see if in fact they were loss-making prices. The Court confirmed that Article 82 could apply when the dominant undertaking directly or indirectly applied unfair prices to its customers. The Court stated that prices are excessive when they have no reasonable relation to the economic value of the product supplied, and that Article 82 could be breached if the consumer suffered as the result of such pricing policies, even if no effect on competition could be shown. It would perhaps have been too much to expect that the Court would indicate exactly how an individual price or range of prices could be assessed as excessive, a problem only too familiar to economists. Later decisions observed that a major difficulty in the analysis suggested by the Court in *United Brands* was the absence of detailed guidance on how to determine the 'economic value' of the product supplied.[5] The Court did, however, indicate that a detailed cost analysis was an essential preliminary requisite in every case, and that the next step was to compare the prices charged with those charged by competitors for the same product.[6] The finding of the Court on this issue was that the difference between the Chiquita bananas and those of its principal competitors was only 7 per cent, which evidence alone was insufficient to justify a finding of excessive prices. Hence, on this aspect of the case, United Brands were not adjudged to have acted in breach of Article 82. Other examples of excessive pricing are referred to in Section 2.2.

2.2 FURTHER EC AND UK CASES

There are of course a number of benchmarks against which prices can be examined to see if they are so far above the competitive price level for the relevant market as to be classified as 'unfair'. One approach is to examine the profit margin made by the seller over and above its costs (of all kinds), another to compare prices against those charged

[4] See Ch. 16, p. 385.

[5] See the Decision of the Commission in *Scandlines Sverige* v. *Port of Helsingborg* [2006] 4 CMLR 1298 at para. 218 of the decision. There is also an interesting discussion of this point in the judgment of the Court of Appeal for England and Wales in *At the Races Ltd* v. *The British Horseracing Board* [2007] UKCLR 309, a case brought under Chapter II of the UK Competition Act—which is almost identical in wording to Art. 82 EC.

[6] It has also been noted that the determination of the 'economic value' of a product, while it may start from a comparison of the cost of production with the price charged for a product it must also take into consideration non-cost related factors like the demand for a product or service. (See the Commission Decision in *Scandlines Sverige* at paras. 228 and 232). In *At the Races* v. *The British Horseracing Board*, the Court of Appeal explained that the value of a product or service for an end consumer was an essential element to take into account in the calculation of its economic value (see paras. 213–15 of the judgment).

for the same goods or services in other markets (as for example in *Bodson*).[7] The issues may arise in the context of another alleged abuse such as a refusal to allow access to an essential facility (see pp. 358–62) or in connection with the calculation of royalties to be paid under collective licensing schemes (see pp. 352–7).

One of the few cases in which cost and price analysis was carried out in detail both by the Commission and on appeal to the Court of First Instance was *Industrie des Poudres Spheriques (IPS)* v. *Commission*.[8] IPS wished to purchase supplies of primary calcium metal from Pechiney, in order to manufacture spherical balls of calcium metal through its own atomization process. Pechiney offered supplies at a price which IPS rejected as excessive; IPS then made a complaint to the Commission that Pechiney was in breach of Article 82 both because of the pricing policy and because of its participation in anti-dumping procedures aimed at preventing imports of primary calcium metal into the Common Market from third countries. Both the Commission and Court of First Instance, having examined the detailed costing of the Pechiney operations, came to the conclusion that the IPS allegations should be rejected.

There is still, however, a singular lack of case law on this subject which is perhaps surprising in view of its importance. For this reason it was welcome that the first major decision of the Competition Appeal Tribunal established by the 1998 Competition Act in the United Kingdom was on this topic, namely *Napp Pharmaceuticals* v. *Director General of Fair Trading*.[9] It dealt, inter alia, with issues of excessive pricing over a number of years for morphine supplied to the National Health Service. Section 60 of the Competition Act 1998 requires the Tribunal and the Director General to apply EC law in cases under both Chapter 1 of the Act (equivalent to Article 81) or Chapter 2 of the Act (equivalent to Article 82). Napp had been found by the DGFT to have abused its dominant position in the market for sustained release morphine, a painkiller used widely both in hospitals and in community medicine (sales by pharmacists). Napp was fined £3.21 million for predatory pricing in regard to hospital sales which represented some ten per cent of its overall sales by volume and for excessive pricing in sales to the community (which represented the other 90 per cent of its sales). Its position of dominance with over 90 per cent of the relevant market in the United Kingdom for some twenty years was not in issue. The main ground of Napp's appeal from the Director General's decision related rather to whether its pricing practices were abusive; the issue of predatory pricing is dealt with in the next section of this chapter. On the issue of whether the prices charged in the community were excessive, the Tribunal reached the conclusion on several grounds that they were indeed such. These grounds included:

- that the profit margin made on the product by Napp compared to other of its products was excessive (especially as its relevant patents had expired several years ago)

[7] Ch. 13, p. 304.   [8] Case T-5/97 [2000] ECR II-3755: [2001] 4 CMLR 1020.
[9] [2002] CAT 1. The predatory pricing allegations were the main issue in the case, and the excessive pricing claims might well not have been pursued apart from them. It can be argued that predatory pricing may have more serious effects, by driving out competitors, than excessive pricing, which may attract new entry.

- that its prices for community sales were some 33–67 per cent higher than for similar drugs sold by its competitors

- that the prices for such sales by Napp to the community outlets were on average 1400 per cent higher than average corresponding prices in the hospital market and indeed on some products even higher

- that the gross profit realized by Napp on this product was over 80 per cent whilst on other products it made no more than half that amount

- that such prices exceeded substantially the prices charged by Napp for export sales of the same product in competitive markets.

On the other hand the Tribunal did not adopt the DGFT's suggestion that Napp's cost of capital should be analysed and compared with the weighted average cost of capital regarded as normal for undertakings in the pharmaceutical sector, possibly perhaps because the evidence on the costs and profit side of the analysis was already so convincing. If a similar case were to reach the Commission or the Court of First Instance, it is to be hoped that it will also be able to carry out a detailed analysis of this kind, which is necessary if the outcome of the decision is to be regarded as authoritative.

3. PREDATORY PRICING

3.1 THE *AKZO* CASE

Predatory pricing is the pricing of goods and services at a very low level with the object of driving out competitors from the market who are unable to compete at that price level, with the likely consequence that price levels in that market will rise again after such competitors have been forced out. It is the dominant company in such a market which is likely to have both the inclination and the resources to finance such a strategy and such pricing can be as equally 'unfair' to competitors as excessive pricing.

The leading case in this area is *AKZO*.[10] This concerned an appeal by AKZO against a decision of the Commission taken as long ago as 1985 following a dispute with the original complainant, ECS, which was a small producer of benzoyl peroxide in the United Kingdom. ECS originally supplied its product for use as an additive to flour, a small market found only in the United Kingdom and Eire. It planned to expand its sales within the Community by marketing its product also to the plastics industry, a much larger potential market, and AKZO became unhappy about the prospect of this competition in Europe from ECS. According to the complaint by ECS, AKZO had threatened over a period of several years to take reprisals against it by way of selected price cuts unless ECS abandoned its intention of selling to the plastics market. AKZO was a much larger company, whose trade in the flour additive field was of

---

[10] Case C-62/86 [1991] ECR I-3359: [1993] 5 CMLR 215.

little importance compared to its trade with the chemical companies, and who could afford to undercut ECS substantially in the flour additives field, even to the extent of putting it out of business. It appeared prepared to do so to protect its position in the more important market.

Interim measures were applied for and granted to protect ECS, and the Commission issued a decision that AKZO's predatory pricing and use of threats to induce ECS to withdraw from the plastics market were breaches of Article 82. A substantial fine of 10 million ECUs was imposed on AKZO. However, the Commission refused to prescribe any specific pricing rules linked to costs, or to define the precise stage at which price-cutting by a dominant firm became abusive. It concentrated rather on the object-ives of a dominant company which were shown—from the evidence obtained by the Commission through the use of its investigatory powers under the old enforcement Regulation (Regulation 17)[11]—to have been intended to eliminate or damage ECS as a competitor in the relevant markets.

The Court's decision, however, went into considerable detail about the basis upon which the finding of abuse was to be confirmed. It stated in its judgment that, in apply-ing the *Hoffmann-La Roche* principles to AKZO's pricing, it was to be presumed that prices charged that were lower than average variable costs alone were intended to eliminate competitors since they would be necessarily loss-making.[12] Moreover, even at a higher level above average variable cost—but below average total cost—pricing would still be presumed abusive if it was part of a deliberate plan to eliminate a com-petitor with fewer financial resources. The two points of reference used in *AKZO* were, therefore, the notions of average variable costs (AVC) and of average total costs (ATC). The first is obtained by dividing all variable costs (but not fixed costs) by the number of units of output. The second is calculated by adding variable and fixed costs and dividing them by the number of units produced. Accordingly, predation is presumed to exist, under the *AKZO* criteria, where pricing takes place below average variable costs or even where it takes place above average variable costs but there is evidence of a predatory intention. This test has been confirmed in later decisions of the Community Courts.[13]

The Court also confirmed the Commission's findings about the use of threats against ECS and that offers of both benzoyl peroxide and other related chemicals had been made (at prices below average total costs) by AKZO to customers which nor-mally dealt with ECS. AKZO was also found to have sold its products cheaply in the flour market to some major customers in return for exclusivity of purchase by them. However, the fine was reduced to 7.5 million ECUs, mainly because of the novelty of the pricing issues and because ECS had not actually lost substantial market share as the result of AKZO's conduct.

---

[11] The new enforcement Regulation (Reg. 1/2003) provides for even more draconian powers of investiga-tion for the Commission (see Arts. 20–1 of the Regulation).

[12] See paras. 70–1 of the *AKZO* judgment.

[13] See Case C-333/94 *Tetrapak II* [1996] ECR I-5951 and more recently, Case T-340/03 *France Télécom*, [2007] ECR-107.

It is also clear from the European Court judgment in *Tetrapak (No. 2)*[14] that the Commission need not prove that the dominant company will actually succeed in subsequently raising its prices following the elimination or weakening of its competitor. It is sufficient for the Commission to show that the pricing practices were sufficiently below cost to be likely to eliminate competitors; a further test that the ability to recoup the losses in the future must be shown is not a requirement for a finding of abuse.[15]

3.2 THE *COMPAGNIE MARITIME BELGE* CASE

The case of *Compagnie Maritime Belge*[16] involved allegations of predatory pricing by members of the Central and West African shipping conference (CEWAL). CEWAL was a liner conference whose members benefited from the provisions of Regulation 4056/86 giving block exemption to such conferences which were permitted to fix shipping rates and schedules for particular services. When a non-member line sought to compete with them, members of the conference agreed to designate certain sailings to the ports covered by the conference as 'fighting ships' for which lower, though not loss-making, rates would be quoted to shippers. The challenger would thus be prevented from gaining freight business from the other members of the conference. The losses incurred for the fighting ships' lower charges would then be shared between all members of the conference. This targeted use of a pricing strategy to eliminate a competitor, even if the rates charged were not below cost but simply reduced earnings of the conference members, was held abusive. The analysis by Fennelly A-G of the application of Article 82 in these circumstances is essential reading for an understanding of the issues that can arise in such cases, where the object of price cutting strategy is clearly exclusionary even if the participants can show that they are not thereby actually making a loss.

3.3 THE *DEUTSCHE POST* CASE

However, it soon became clear that the rules stated in the *AKZO* case by the ECJ were by themselves inadequate for application in all kinds of predatory pricing cases. A welcome further decision in this area was therefore the *UPS/Deutsche Post*[17] case. Here Deutsche Post, in addition to its letter post monopoly in Germany, operated a business parcel service in competition with private operators. One of these private operators, United Parcel Services, complained to the Commission that Deutsche Post was cross-subsidizing its business-parcel services from its monopoly letter-mail revenues and thereby abusing its dominant position in both markets. The Commission's

---

[14] See Ch. 13 at p. 307.

[15] See also the judgment in *France Télécom*, cited above in fn. 13. This is an important difference with the American system, where a predatory pricing action will only succeed if it is shown that the dominant company has a strong probability of recouping its losses (see the decision of the U.S. Supreme Court in *Brooke Group Ltd* v. *Brown & Williamson Tobacco Corp.*, 509 US 209 (1993)).

[16] Ch. 13, fn. 17.   [17] [2001] OJ L125/27: [2001] 5 CMLR 99.

investigations established that for five years Deutsche Post had not covered the long-run incremental costs incurred in providing the business parcel service. No fine was imposed for this breach of Article 82 although a fine was imposed for a separate breach of the Article involving the granting of fidelity rebates to mail order customers. Deutsche Post was however required to reorganize its business so as to make its postal services' finances transparent. The parcels business would provide its services either from its own resources or through entering into a contract at full market prices with Deutsche Post or third parties. Deutsche Post for its part had to agree to supply any services provided to the parcels business at the same terms and prices as to third-party competitors. It was not however required to cease to make use of its existing infrastructure of freight centres and delivery offices so that any existing economies of scope arising from the joint provision of several services from these could continue to benefit customers.

The main principle which this case establishes was that a dominant company, especially one with a statutory monopoly, which then sets up a new business must cover the entire incremental cost incurred by the new venture entirely from its revenues from that new business. With this case however should be contrasted the ruling of the CFI in *UPS Europe* v. *Commission*[18] that the mere possession by a dominant company of the funds enabling it to make acquisition of a competitor is not itself evidence of abuse, provided that the funds obtained are not then used for excessive pricing or predatory pricing in breach of Article 82.

In the United Kingdom guidelines produced by the DGFT and sectoral regulators have also adopted a similar approach and to varying degrees explained that such 'avoidable costs' should be the approach to be adopted, taking into account marginal long-run or incremental costs of the particular service, including the necessary capital investment in fixed assets. The most contentious issue is the period over which these costs should be calculated, which will tend to vary from sector to sector according to the anticipated life of assets.

The *Napp* case referred to in the previous section also placed emphasis on two elements in determining whether predatory pricing is abusive. The first is the importance of the evidence of exclusionary intent, a factor also present in both *AKZO* and *Compagnie Maritime Belge*. The Tribunal found that over a period of years after Napp's patents for slow-release morphine had expired, it had methodically lowered its hospital prices to match those of its much smaller competitors, at least one of which was forced to leave the market. The second was the element of discretion enjoyed by the dominant company, in that the losses incurred by Napp on its sales to the hospital market (where some 10 per cent of sales were made) were more than balanced by the very high prices charged to general practitioners and pharmacies in the community making up the other 90 per cent of its sales.

---

[18] Case T-175/99 [2002] ECXR II-1915: [2002] 5 CMLR 67.

3.4 PREDATORY PRICING AND THE 2005 COMMISSION DISCUSSION PAPER ON EXCLUSIONARY ABUSES

The pattern of analysis used by the Community courts in predatory pricing cases was subject to criticism on several counts. In particular, the Community judicature appeared to adopt a formalistic approach to predation which did not take due account of the economic context where the practice occurred or of the impact that it had on consumers. For example, there might be some circumstances where it may make economic sense for a company to price below average variable costs. Directly related to this is the fact that a strong chance of recoupment of losses by the dominant company did not appear as a condition to show the existence of predation when in fact, it is unlikely that an undertaking would engage in pricing below cost unless there is a good chance to make up for the losses suffered in the short term. Finally, the *AKZO* test did not seem to consider the value of average avoidable costs (AAC) which refer to the avoidable cost involved in the production of one unit of output as a possible criterion that may be useful in a finding of predatory pricing.

As explained in Chapter 13, one of the main objectives driving the review of Article 82 EC and the publication by DG Competition of the *2005 Discussion Paper on Exclusionary Abuses* was to develop a system of rules in the application of Article 82 EC that would be more in tune with economic reality. The Discussion Paper was, of course, limited by the unambiguous case law of the Community courts on predation but some aspects of it merit special consideration. Principally, the Discussion Paper subtly introduces average avoidable costs as the main tool to establish a presumption of predation. Rather than assuming that any pricing below average variable cost is automatically predatory, it suggests that the appropriate benchmark is whether 'the dominant company, by charging a lower price for all or a particular part of its output over the relevant time period, incurred losses that could have been avoided by not producing that particular part of its output'.[19] In other words pricing below average avoidable costs (AAC) assumes the existence of predation instead of pricing below average variable costs (AVC). For pricing above AAC but below ATC, while the Discussion Paper maintains the presumption of predation if there is evidence of predatory intent, it gives guidance as to the kinds of direct and indirect evidence that can be used to prove the existence of a predatory strategy by the dominant company.[20] Finally, and on the issue of recoupment, the Discussion Paper does not appear to depart fully from the case law because it ultimately concludes that it is generally not necessary to provide separate proof of recoupment to show the existence of predatory pricing. Nonetheless, it suggests that it is sufficient to show the likelihood of recoupment and that this can be done by investigating the barriers to entry and the strengthened position of the dominant company in the market. Given that the existence of a dominant position would have already been established prior to an investigation of abuse, this would mean that the barriers to entry are high enough to presume the chance of recoupment of the

---

[19] See the Discussion Paper at paras. 106–8.   [20] See paras. 111–20 of the Discussion Paper.

profit that had been previously sacrificed. It also provides that a dominant company may rebut a presumption of predatory abuse by arguing that recoupment will never be possible.[21] The recent decision of the Court of First Instance in *France Télécom*[22] delivered after the publication of the Discussion Paper, however, has confirmed the standing case law that holds that proof of recoupment of losses is not a prerequisite for a finding of predatory pricing.

4. DISCRIMINATORY PRICING

4.1 *UNITED BRANDS*

Discriminatory pricing is closely related to predatory pricing and is itself an example of the third illustrative example in Article 82(c) 'applying dissimilar conditions to equivalent transactions with other trading parties thereby placing them at a competitive disadvantage'.

The first case involving such practices was *United Brands*.[23] The charge against United Brands was that it had charged discriminatory prices to its distributors in different Member States. It was shown that there were substantial differences in prices between, on one hand, Denmark and Germany where prices were relatively high, and, on the other hand, the Benelux countries and Ireland where they were much lower. It was apparently the practice of the Rotterdam management of United Brands to fix scale prices to the distributor so as to reflect as closely as possible the anticipated price obtainable in its territory for ripe (yellow) bananas in the following week. The ability of United Brands to obtain such prices from its different distributors, and therefore to disadvantage those distributors who purchased at the higher prices, served to underline the strength of the company in Western Europe. All the bananas were sold 'free on rail' (f.o.r.) from Rotterdam and costs were virtually identical in each case. United Brands claimed that the difference in the pricing resulted from a commercial decision as to what each part of the market could bear, but the Commission and the Court concluded that this was not an objective justification for the differences imposed.[24]

It is not clear from the terms of the Court's decision to what degree such a company, when determining its prices, may take into account market forces of supply and demand. It appeared to suggest that this would be permitted only in cases where the seller takes a substantial risk, having involved itself in local production and distribution to such an extent that market movements in that country are likely to affect it directly. The facts in this case were different, United Brands not being involved in the local markets as it was selling to all the distributors at Rotterdam, and in practice

---

[21] See paras. 122–3 of the Discussion Paper.   [22] Cited above at fn. 13.

[23] Case 27/76 [1978] ECR 207: [1978] 1 CMLR 429.

[24] The approach of the Court to geographical discriminatory pricing in *United Brands* has been subject to strong criticism (see, among others, Bishop, 'Price Discrimination under Article 86: Political Economy in the European Court' [1981] 4 MLR 284).

it was the distributors who bore the risks of the individual national markets. The Court's judgment left uncertain what was meant by 'involvement' in local markets, but gave the impression that United Brands might have had a stronger case, had the discrimination in pricing reflected pressures resulting from market conditions in the individual countries, i.e. 'market lead pressures', rather than appearing to arise from United Brands' own ability to impose higher prices on its distributors in those markets because of the absence of effective competition. Had United Brands itself been carrying out the distribution function in the Member States, then it would have been taking a greater risk and having a closer involvement with the national markets; to that extent its freedom to adjust its prices to local dealers would have been greater.

4.2 A PRICE SQUEEZE

Another category of price discrimination involves a 'price squeeze', meaning that a dominant company, which is active in a downstream market, charges prices to its competitors in that downstream market that prevent them from operating profitably. In *Napier Brown* v. *British Sugar*,[25] the Commission fined British Sugar three million units of account for abuse of dominant position for refusing to supply industrial sugar to Napier Brown. It gave the excuse that it had insufficient supplies but the true commercial reason was that it wished to make it more difficult for Napier Brown to compete with it in the market for retail consumers purchasing one-kilogram bags. British Sugar was also found to have engaged in other practices to make life difficult for Napier Brown, for example maintaining a margin between the price it charged Napier Brown for raw materials supplied and the charge which it made for its own consumer sales such that Napier Brown were unable profitably to transform the industrial sugar into consumer retail packets.[26] Moreover, it prevented customers from collecting industrial sugar from its factory and denied supplies of raw material of particular types and origin to Napier Brown, whilst still willing to supply these to other companies. It also offered rebates to other buyers on condition that they bought from it exclusively in future.

4.3 *TETRAPAK (NO. 2)* AND *IRISH SUGAR*

Similar practices were found in *Tetrapak (No. 2)*.[27] Here there were substantial variations in the prices charged for milk cartons and the machines for manufacturing

---

[25] [1990] 4 CMLR 196. The particular 'squeeze' in this case was easy to calculate. The same principle may however prove considerably more difficult to apply in the more complex markets, such as telecommunication services. See also Case 109/75R *National Carbonizing Co.* v. *Commission and NCB* [1975] ECR 1193: [1975] 2 CMLR 457.

[26] For another interesting example of a case concerning a 'margin squeeze', see the decision of the UK Competition Appeal Tribunal in *Genzyme Limited* v. *Office of Fair Trading* [2004] CAT 4. The concept is also frequently invoked by the Commission and also by national competition authorities in the telecommunications market (see the decision of the Commission in *Deutsche Telekom* [2003] OJ L263/9, upheld by the Court of First Instance in Case T-271/03 *Deutsche Telekom*, Judgment of 10 April 2008, not yet reported).

[27] Ch. 13, fn. 16.

them as between Member States; customers in particular in Italy were charged prices substantially lower than those in other countries in Western Europe, at a time when Tetrapak's main competitor, Elopak, was providing particularly fierce competition to it in that country. Another complex case in this area was *Irish Sugar*[28]. This company held over 90 per cent of the Irish market for both industrial and retail sugar and was the sole producer of sugar beet in that country. Its pricing strategies were held abusive in three separate respects. The first was by way of discriminatory prices offered to those industrial customers who agreed to export their sugar purchases rather than reselling on the Irish market in competition with the defendant. The second was by the offering of discriminatory prices (whether by special rebates or other means) to rival packers depending again upon whether they agreed to resell sugar in retail packs otherwise than in competition with Irish Sugar's own retail business. The third was a case of geographical discrimination under which retail purchasers in the border area of Ireland were given special rebates in order to make it difficult for cheaper supplies in Northern Ireland to enter the Irish market and thereby insulate it from this competition. The Court of First Instance upheld the Commission's decision and its judgment was in turn upheld by the European Court.

4.4 DISCRIMINATION IN AIRPORT CHARGES

A number of price discrimination cases also relate to charges for airport services made in several Member States, including Belgium, Finland, Spain, and Portugal. The normal situation to be found in these cases was that landing charges were calculated by the airport managers on a basis that favoured the national incumbent airline which would normally have the largest number of flights, disadvantaging all other airlines which would have a lower number, by the offering of substantial discounts at the higher level of flights. Community Courts have twice had to review Commission decisions in this area and on both occasions have fully supported its reasoning.

In the case of *Commission* v. *Portugal*[29] the discount structure at several Portuguese airports was held abusive partly because of the fact that the airport could show no economies of scale arising as a result of the greater number of flights made by Portuguese airlines. In *Aéroports de Paris* v. *Commission*,[30] where the European Court upheld an earlier decision of the Court of First Instance,[31] this discrimination was not in landing charges but in different charges made to the companies who provided catering and ground-handling services. Preferential terms were offered to a French company which disadvantaged its rival, Alpha, a subsidiary of a British public company. The Court held that dominant undertakings managing international airports must justify any different rates charged by establishing the existence of either objectively different situations or circumstances to justify the discrimination.

[28] Case C-497/99P [2001] ECR I-5333: [2001] 5 CMLR 1082.
[29] Case C-163/99 [2001] ECR I-2613: [2002] 4 CMLR 1319.
[30] Case C-82/01P [2002] ECR I-9297: [2003] 4 CMLR 609.
[31] Case T-128/98 [2000] ECR II-3929: [2001] 4 CMLR 1376.

5. DISCOUNTS AND REBATES

5.1 EARLY CASES: *HOFFMANN* AND *MICHELIN*

The granting of discounts and rebates by suppliers is closely linked with price discrimination, and indeed the discrimination itself may be effected through the terms of the discount or rebate scheme. A discount is normally a percentage reduction in the price of goods or services which appears on or closely associated with a supply invoice. A rebate, although sometimes offered in addition to a discount, is in effect an aggregation of discounts seeking to attract and bind customers to a particular supplier over a longer period. Its normal function is to encourage a customer to do business with a supplier on a regular basis by offering it a retrospective cash payment calculated on its purchases over the year or other fixed period. It has however the same commercial purpose over a longer period as does the offer of an individual discount on a single particular transaction: to encourage the buyer to do business with that seller rather than with its competitors.

Rebates are often used quite legitimately, even by dominant undertakings, particularly in markets where there is active price competition, and in cases where the seller can reasonably claim that its costs are lower if customers show loyalty by placing regular orders with it. Rebates can also however be used by a dominant company so as to make it difficult for customers without substantial countervailing market power to switch purchases between suppliers, to take advantage either of price fluctuations, or other changes in market conditions, or because some of the products of other suppliers are considered of better quality or suitability. The use of the rebate by a dominant company is often, therefore, linked with its desire to ensure 'fidelity' from its buyers, using the leverage of one product to compel buyers to acquire the remainder of their needs from it, involving a form of 'tying' on the buyer.

In a notice of a settlement made with the Coca Cola Export Company in 1988,[32] the Commission recorded that the use of fidelity rebates by a Coca Cola subsidiary having a dominant position on the Italian Cola market had been discontinued, it being accepted that the fidelity rebates were an abuse of its position in that market. In the text of the settlement, however, a distinction was drawn between certain types of unacceptable rebate, namely those conditional on targets linked to volume of purchases in the previous year, or linked to targets which relate to a group of products in different markets, as contrasted with rebates conditional on the purchase of a series of different sizes of product, or participation in advertising promotions, which were acceptable.

The treatment of such practices under Article 82 was first shown by two European Court cases, *Hoffmann-La Roche*[33] and *Michelin I.*[34] Hoffmann-La Roche is a

---

[32] Dated 13 October 1988: IP (88) 615. In Case 310/93 *British Plasterboard (BPB)* v. *Commission* [1995] ECR I-865: [1997] 4 CMLR 238), the abuse was found to consist of the payment of rebates in return for dealers agreeing not to handle plasterboard supplied by Spanish importers.

[33] See fn. 1.   [34] Case 322/81 [1983] ECR 3461: [1985] 1 CMLR 282.

multinational group whose parent company is based in Switzerland. As already discussed in Chapter 13, the Commission had decided that this company had abused
its dominant position for seven categories of vitamins. One abuse was committed by
entering into exclusive or preferential supply contracts with major industrial purchasers, containing 'fidelity rebates' which placed considerable pressure on the buyers
to obtain virtually all their vitamin requirements from Roche. A large fine had been
imposed and, although the Court reduced the fine by one-third, it substantially upheld
the main elements in the Commission's decision.

In *Hoffmann-La Roche*, as explained in Section 1.1 in this chapter, the Court took the
opportunity to give a general definition of 'abusive conduct'. It then drew a distinction
between quantity rebates (i.e. those related to the volume of the products purchased)
and loyalty or fidelity rebates (i.e. those that try to 'tie' a customer to the dominant
company and prevent it from obtaining supplies from competing suppliers). It held
that pressure applied by a dominant undertaking to its purchasers to obtain all or most
of their requirements from itself is an abuse, whether or not accompanied by a rebate
payable to the customer so long as the customer remains loyal for all (or at least a large
proportion of) its requirements. The Court ruled that the application of such pressure
is itself incompatible with the normal working of competition, since it has the effect
that orders are placed not because the buyer has made a simple commercial choice in its
own interests, but because the buyer, given his dependence on the dominant supplier,
simply cannot afford to spread his orders over a variety of suppliers and thus risk losing
the rebate offered by the dominant company. By contrast, this judgment suggested that
volume rebates fell automatically outside the scope of Article 82 EC.

Roche had placed considerable reliance in their argument on the price alignment
clause included in its agreements, widely known as the 'English clause'. Under this, a
customer who obtained a better price quotation from another producer was entitled to
ask Roche to align its prices to those prices. If Roche failed to do so, the customer could
then buy from the other producers without losing the benefit of the fidelity rebate. The
Court felt that this clause, rather than enabling competitive pressure to work effectively for the benefit of the buyer, actually had the effect of providing Roche with a great
deal of information about the state of the relevant vitamin markets, and the pricing and
marketing strategies open to it in the light of actions being adopted by its competitors.
The information which it received in this way further enhanced its ability to dominate;
the effect of the 'English clause' therefore was to weaken still further the competitive
structure of the market, which the Court regarded as an important factor.

The *Michelin I* case also concerned itself largely with fidelity rebates. Again
the initial decision of the Commission was upheld by the Court, although the fine
was reduced in this case by more than half. Michelin held a strong position in the
Dutch replacement-tyre market for heavy vehicles including trucks and buses. The
Commission's decision had been based on a number of grounds and had focused
particularly on the fact that the rebates fixed by Michelin in return for the achievement of sales targets of individual distributors were not sufficiently objective, and
the rebate schemes characterized by a general lack of transparency. There were also

findings that the relevant targets and rebates given for 1977 had linked two differ-ent tyre markets (heavy-vehicle and light-vehicle markets respectively) and then used Michelin's market dominance for heavy-vehicle tyres to promote sales of light-vehi-cle tyres. The Commission had ruled that, for the use of rebates to be acceptable as normal commercial practice for the purpose of Article 82, they must be both clearly known to the purchaser and defined on an objective basis, the sums payable to deal-ers being commensurate with the task they performed and the services which they actually provided.

Following the Commission's decision, fears were expressed by manufacturers that its effect would be to reduce considerably the extent to which manufacturers with a strong market position would feel able to use any form of rebate or bonus scheme. The terms of the subsequent Court decision to some extent reduced that concern. The Court did, however, concur with the Commission's view that the system adopted by Michelin for variable discounts linked to the attainment of individual sales targets, and the method of administering the scheme through frequent personal visits by Michelin representatives applying pressure to its distributors to attain those targets (particularly towards the end of the sales year) constituted an abuse, in view of the undue pressure placed on dealers. Michelin set out neither the rebate scale nor sales targets in writing; this would increase the disinclination of the dealers to deal with Michelin's competitors particularly towards the end of that relevant year. All these factors contributed to strengthening Michelin's market position and increasing the barriers to entry in the Dutch tyre market by its competitors.

These findings alone were sufficient to justify confirmation by the Court of the Commission's finding of abuse, even though some of the factual findings of the Commission were rejected. The Court did not, for example, accept that resellers of tyres would have hesitated to complain about the lack of written confirmation of sales targets, and also rejected allegations that both targets and rebates were related to the percentage that Michelin sales made by the client bore to the total sales of all makes by it, a formula known as 'temperature Michelin'. It also rejected the finding by the Commission that different rates of rebate, representing differences in treatment between dealers, were the result of the application of unequal criteria and had no basis in ordinary commercial practice.

5.2 RECENT CASES: *MICHELIN II* AND *BRITISH AIRWAYS*

Michelin were, in 2001, again involved in a decision of the Commission which related to the French market for retread and new replacement tyres for heavy vehicles where its market share in France was over 50 per cent.[35] It operated a complex system of quan-titative bonuses (linked to rebate schemes) for both products, which had the effect of discouraging dealers from choosing between Michelin and other manufacturers on their merits. Each Michelin dealer was allocated a 'base', that is the minimum number

---

[35] [2002] OJ L143/1: [2002] 5 CMLR 388. See B. Sher, 'Price Discounts and Michelin 2' [2002] 23 ECLR 482–9.

of tyres which it was expected to order in a year and rebates were awarded under a number of steeply graded 'steps' above the base level. In 1995 and 1996 the rebate was changed by reducing the number of steps within the scheme and by the retrospective application of the rebates to all tyres ordered over the whole period not merely any excess over the base.

In return for these schemes the dealers were obliged to provide Michelin with much information about their businesses and to remain faithful to it. There was little wholesaler activity in France nor evidence of parallel importing. The strength of the Michelin brand was such that it was an 'unavoidable partner' on the French market for tyre dealers and garages. The period of these rebate schemes was normally one year, far longer than the maximum of three months which the Commission surmised to be the reference period endorsed by the European Court. Profit margins on tyres were low and thus for the dealers the rebate was essential to their financial health. The fact that the loyalty element of the rebate scheme was implicit in its structure, rather than explicit, did not lessen its practical effect in keeping the dealers loyal. One element in the scheme was progress-related, in that it depended on the actual sales target of the tyres reached as a percentage above the level reached in the previous year, an important element in the *British Airways* case discussed below. The Court of First Instance upheld almost all the findings of the Commission.[36]

The ruling in *Michelin II* was significant on several counts. Firstly, and in contrast with the sweeping statement in *Hoffmann-La Roche*, which appeared to have made a clear distinction between volume rebates and traditional loyalty discounts, the Court observed that not *all* quantity rebates could automatically escape the application of Article 82 EC; in fact some of them could well have a loyalty-inducing effect. A quantity rebate would be compatible with that provision if it was economically justified either by the business it generated or by any economies of scale that it allowed the dominant company to generate. In other words, the decision in *Michelin II* placed the focus of the analysis of the loyalty inducing effect of quantity rebates on whether they truly create efficiencies or cost savings for the dominant company. If they do, then they would be permissible. If they do not, then they would come under the scope of application of Article 82 EC because it would be assumed that their only purpose would be the exclusion of rivals of the dominant company. On the facts, the quantity rebates offered by Michelin were held to be abusive because they could not be justified by any countervailing economic advantages but simply aimed to 'tie' dealers to the dominant company and prevent them from finding other sources of supply.

Secondly, it should be noted that while *Michelin II* offered a novel approach to the analysis of quantity rebates, which had appeared to be per se legal in *Hoffmann-La Roche*, it did not reassess traditional loyalty inducing rebates (i.e. openly linked to exclusivity) which were assumed to be per se abusive.

---

[36] Case T-203/01 [2003] ECR II-4071: [2004] 4 CMLR 923. The only significant point of departure was that the CFI disagreed with the Commission's statement that the Court had ruled that the reference period for the rebates should not exceed a maximum of three months.

Finally, the Court was faced with Michelin's argument that its activities did not have the *effect* of limiting competition, an essential element of the definition of abuse provided by the Court in *Hoffman-La Roche*. On this point, the Court held that for a breach of Article 82 EC to take place it is sufficient that the behaviour of an undertaking '*tends* to restrict competition or, in other words, that the conduct is *capable of having that effect*'.[37] The Court went on to state in even clearer terms that 'if it is shown that the object pursued by the conduct of an undertaking in a dominant position is to limit competition, that conduct will also be liable to have that effect'.[38] This statement appears to be dangerously broad in that it could allow a finding of abuse to be detached from any real analysis of the effects that the behaviour of the dominant company has in the relevant market and on consumer interests. It seems surprising, to say the least, that when the Court had been strongly criticized for their formalistic construction of the forms of abuse capable of coming under the scope of Article 82 EC, a lower than ever threshold for a finding of abuse should be favoured in *Michelin II*.

Overall, the result of these cases seemed to be that the use of rebates by dominant companies, although not prohibited outright, required very careful analysis of the services for which they were granted. It was not permitted to tie rebates simply to exclusive purchasing obligations, but they could be linked to the achievement of objective sales targets provided that the operation of the system was sufficiently objective and transparent so as not to impose undue pressure on dealers and did not discriminate between different categories of dealers on a basis that did not reflect cost savings to the supplier.

In *UPS/Deutsche Post*,[39] Deutsche Post had made contracts with its customers for both mail order and bulky parcels under which the contract prices offered were conditional on those customers providing exclusivity to Deutsche Post for all parcels in those categories, or in some cases linked to a very high percentage of their total requirements. This had the effect of preventing large mail-order companies from establishing their own postal arrangements which in time might have developed also into the provision of services for third parties in direct competition with Deutsche Post. A substantial fine was levied on Deutsche Post for imposing this scheme.

The extent to which 'fidelity' as a forbidden element in such schemes is now being imputed by the Commission from the inherent structure of those schemes rather than by express obligation of the customers is well illustrated by *BA/Virgin*.[40] Virgin had complained to the Commission that the British Airways commission scheme (equivalent to a discount scheme) provided a 'performance reward' to its travel agents, which the Commission regarded as making them sell an increasing number of BA tickets every year, thereby giving BA an unfair advantage against other airlines. A flat commission of 7 per cent was paid by BA to its agents for ticket sales but under the 'performance reward' additional commission payments of up to 3 per cent on international flights and 1 per cent on domestic flights could be earned, by matching the

---

[37] See para. 239 of the judgment. [38] See para. 241 of the judgment.
[39] See fn. 17.   [40] [2000] OJ L30/1: [2000] 4 CMLR 999.

agent's total sales in a given month against its sales in the corresponding month of the previous year. The increased commission was retrospective and applied to all sales within the relevant period, not merely for the excess after the previous year's level had been reached.

In its defence BA pointed out to the Commission that there were other similar commission schemes operated by major airlines in Europe and that there were cost savings and efficiencies which the performance reward scheme brought about; moreover there was little evidence that the scheme had a damaging effect on competing airlines. These arguments were rejected by the Commission, which ruled that the scheme was abusive in its calculation of commission on sales in the current year by reference to levels of performance in the previous year. In other words, the Commission felt that there was no possible economic justification for the rebates because they were not based on the volume of ticket sales but on the increase in sales by reference to the sales in the previous year. The discounts were therefore not based on any 'cost saving or efficiencies realised by BA'[41] and hence they were deemed to be abusive.

British Airways brought annulment proceedings against the Commission decision before the Court of First Instance. Four years later, the Court of First Instance delivered a judgment which confirmed all the Commission findings[42] and which was further appealed to the European Court of Justice,[43] again with little success for British Airways. Both Courts confirmed that the scheme operated by British Airways was discriminatory—because two agents selling the same number of tickets could receive different commission—and exclusionary because although there was no direct obligation imposed on the agents to deal exclusively with British Airways, the scheme effectively encouraged them to deal solely with British Airways. As a result, a foreclosing effect on the market could be presumed. In relation to the issue of any economic justification for the bonuses paid by British Airways, the European Court upheld the views of the Commission and of the Court of First Instance that the scheme was not objectively justified.

The decisions in British Airways show an increasingly sophisticated picture of the law concerning discounts offered by dominant companies. While Michelin II provided a new lead in the treatment of volume rebates, it did not consider traditional loyalty inducing rebates, which the case law appeared to classify as per se abusive. The judgment of the Court of First Instance in British Airways, however, seemed to extend the possibility of economic justification to the latter type of discounts.[44] Furthermore, the European Court referred to 'advantages in terms of efficiency which also benefit the consumer' when articulating the possibilities of objective justification for a system of rebates.[45] Since the Court was dealing with the case on appeal it could not review

---

[41] See the Commission Decision at para. 48.

[42] Case T-219/99 British Airways v. Commission [2003] ECR II-5917; [2004] 4 CMLR 19.

[43] Case C-95/04P, [2007] ECR I-2331; [2007] 4 CMLR 22.

[44] See Case T-219/99 at para. 271 of the judgment.

[45] See Case C-95/04P at para. 86 of the judgment. See also O. Odudu's case note on the British Airways litigation, (2007) 44 CMLRev 1781.

the findings of fact of the Court of First Instance on this point and simply confirmed that BA schemes were not objectively justified. Therefore, no clear guidance emerged from the judgment as to the circumstances when fidelity rebates would produce economic efficiencies that were *also* advantageous for consumers. This is an important issue, particularly given the low threshold for abuse set out in *Michelin II*, where the Court of First Instance held that it was only necessary to show that the behaviour of a dominant company was *capable* of restricting competition rather than *likely* to do so.[46] Unless consumer gains are rigorously taken into account at the stage of objective justification, the Court will continue to attract criticism for placing the main emphasis of its approach to exclusionary abuses on the mere protection of the process of rivalry between market players and not giving sufficient weight to the impact on consumer interests—which ought to be the ultimate objective driving an economically based control of abusive behaviour. In other words, if rebates granted by a dominant company yield price reductions for the consumer, such schemes should be carefully scrutinized before being labelled as abusive.

6. REFUSAL TO DEAL (IN GOODS OR SERVICES)

6.1 *COMMERCIAL SOLVENTS*

The first European Court case involving a refusal to deal was *Commercial Solvents*[47] in 1974. Nitropropane is a compound that results from the nitration of paraffin and is the base product for the industrial production of a substance called aminobutanol. This in turn is the base product for the industrial production of ethambutol, a compound used in the treatment of pulmonary tuberculosis. Commercial Solvents Corporation (CSC) had a world monopoly in the manufacture of products derived from the nitration of paraffin, including both nitropropane and aminobutanol. Although the relevant patents had largely expired, it was difficult for other enterprises to enter the market because of the difficulty of finding outlets for other products that could also be derived from the nitration of paraffin, and because of the high cost of research and development. The necessary manufacturing installations were also of considerable complexity and cost.

CSC had originally been willing to supply ethambutol to a smaller Italian company, Zoja, through its Italian subsidiary, Istituto Chemioterapico Italiano (ICI) over which it exercised complete control. After merger talks between ICI and Zoja had

---

[46] This approach can be compared with the more effects-based approach to exclusionary conduct heralded in the 2005 Discussion Paper, where the Commission laid down two elements encompassed in the proof of abusive conduct: capability to foreclose competitors *and* likely market distorting effect on the relevant market (see section 5, para. 58 of the Discussion Paper).

[47] Cases 6–7/73 *Istituto Chemioterapico Italiano and Commercial Solvents Corporation v. Commission* [1974] ECR 223: [1974] 1 CMLR 309.

broken down, ICI on the instructions of CSC raised its prices for ethambutol to Zoja and sought gradually to reduce the level of its supplies. Originally, aminobutanol remained available from other sources, but these gradually dried up. By the start of 1971 Zoja was unable to manufacture any further ethambutol and complained to the Commission that CSC and ICI were abusing their dominant position as world leaders in production both of nitropropane and aminobutanol. It claimed the object of this conduct was to eliminate Zoja from the market place in Europe as a producer of ethambutol. Ethambutol was important for the treatment of tuberculosis in conjunction with other drugs, and there was no valid reason why Zoja could not be supplied by CSC, which had adequate supplies. On the basis of these facts, the Commission imposed a fine of 200,000 units of account on CSC and ordered an immediate resumption of supplies by it to Zoja at a price no higher than the maximum price which it had previously charged for both nitropropane and aminobutanol.

The Advocate General, although finding that the facts established by the Commission were largely correct, would have cancelled the fine because prior to its decision CSC had offered to resume sufficient supplies to Zoja to carry on business within the Community. The Court, however, upheld the imposition of a fine, though reduced to 100,000 units of account, and in other respects upheld the findings of the Commission.

In particular, the Court agreed with the Commission that CSC and ICI between them held a dominant position in the relevant market of nitro-propane and aminobutanol. By abusing their dominant position in these markets, they were able to restrict competition in the market for the derivative obtained from those products, namely ethambutol. Such effect must be taken into account in considering the effect of CSC's action, even if the market for the derivatives was not self-contained but could be met from other sources. The refusal to supply Zoja involved an abuse of its market power, particularly as it had previously supplied it and then discontinued supply without adequate commercial reason. The case would, of course, have been less clear had CSC never supplied Zoja, and even more so if Zoja had been merely a potential entrant to the market rather than an actual competitor; in those circumstances it is doubtful if CSC would have had an obligation to supply.[48] Finally, the Court ruled that any undertaking that abuses its dominant position within a substantial part of the Common Market in a way likely to eliminate a competitor is in breach of Article 82, regardless of whether the conduct by the dominant company relates to its exports or to trade within the Common Market, so long as it can be established that the elimination of the competitor would itself have repercussions on the competitive structure of relevant markets within the Community. Whilst the case was also concerned with the detriment to consumers that would flow as the result of the action taken by CSC,

---

[48] A dominant company appears to have no obligation to supply an undertaking with which it had never previously dealt, even an actual or potential competitor, except in the case of access to essential facilities (see pp. 358–62).

the Court placed greatest emphasis on the likely effect on competitive structure of the conduct complained of.

6.2 *UNITED BRANDS*

The most important early case to come before the European Court under this Article was *United Brands*,[49] already considered in Chapter 13. This US multinational exported bananas from its own plantations in South America and had a substantial proportion of the banana market in the Community. The majority of bananas were shipped in the company's own fleet to Rotterdam where they were resold to national distributors in the various Member States, who purchased bananas on a 'free on rail basis' from Rotterdam at prices which varied significantly. United Brands held a substantial market share, amounting to some 40 to 45 per cent in each of the four geographic markets in issue: Germany, Benelux, Ireland, and Denmark. Its dominance in these markets was even greater than might have been expected simply as the result of its market share. The conduct of which the Commission complained involved several separate practices. The first two were:

(1) the prohibition against resale by distributors of green, i.e. unripe, bananas

(2) the refusal of supplies on certain occasions to a Danish distributor which had offended United Brands by promoting a competing brand of banana.

The facts established by the Commission showed that United Brands' policy was to try to sell its product at prices which, both by their absolute level and by their variation as between Member States, sought to extract the highest possible profit from all these countries. Its distributors were left with a relatively small margin for resale which nevertheless had to be accepted because of the market strength possessed by United Brands.

The Court had little difficulty in establishing abusive conduct. The prohibition against trade in green bananas had the effect of an export ban. The bananas arrived in the green, unripened form in Rotterdam, and only ripened at the time and at the speed required by ripeners in order to bring them into the right conditions of sale to suit local markets. In a freer market, the various distributors might well have exchanged supplies with each other in the face of the varying demands of different national markets. The limiting of such resales of unripened bananas meant that in practice the short periods between the attainment of ripeness and the subsequent onset of decay ensured that no exchange of supplies was possible. The Court acknowledged that a restriction of this kind, if imposed simply to maintain a certain quality level, would have been justifiable. However, a complete restriction on the transfer of all green bananas went far beyond such a legitimate aim, because its real purpose was clearly to weaken the bargaining position of the distributors with United Brands.

---

[49] Ch. 13, pp. 296–7, Case 27/76 [1978] ECR 207: [1978] 1 CMLR 429.

The second commercial practice found to violate Article 82 was a refusal to continue to supply Olesen, a Danish distributor. The alleged basis for this was that Olesen had been active in promoting sales of competitors' fruit. The Court found that the reaction of United Brands to Olesen's conduct was out of proportion to its alleged 'disloyalty', and ruled that it was not permissible for an undertaking with a dominant position to cut off supplies to a long-standing distributor, so long as its orders placed on the supplier had remained within the normal range.[50]

We have already met the case of *Hugin*,[51] in which a small firm in South East England had sought spare parts for repairing Hugin cash machines, and the action under Article 82 by the Commission failed only because there was no evidence that the refusal by Hugin to supply them had an effect on trade between Member States (the only geographical area affected was a relatively small radius around London). Subject to this qualification it will normally be abusive for spare parts to be refused by the maker of original equipment unless too long a period has passed for it to be commercially reasonable for these to be available (as emphasized in *Volvo/Veng*).[52]

6.3 TREATMENT OF OCCASIONAL CUSTOMERS

Use of the Article is relatively straightforward when the recipient of the abusive behaviour or treatment is a well-established customer, either as part of a distribution network (as in *United Brands*) or by way of a series of individual transactions (as in the *Commercial Solvents* case). Useful pointers on the permitted response of a dominant company to the requirements of customers falling within neither of these categories is found in the *BP* case.[53] This case arose as the result of oil shortages during the crisis period that started in November 1973. The Commission decided that BP had breached Article 82 by substantially reducing supplies of petrol during this period to a Dutch independent central-buying organization, ABG. The Commission relied on the evidence that whilst BP had reduced its supplies at this time to all its customers in the Netherlands, the percentage reduction to ABG was of the order of 73 per cent while the average reduction for its other customers was only about 12.7 per cent. The result of this apparent discrimination was that ABG had to buy its remaining needs on the open market or through the official marketing scheme established for the crisis period by the Dutch government. The Commission defined abuse in this context as 'any action which reduces supplies to comparable purchasers in different ways without objective justification, and thereby puts certain of them at a competitive disadvantage

---

[50] An interesting issue with which the Court did not deal is whether it would have been abusive conduct for United Brands to have insisted on the distribution of fruit through exclusive dealers or distributors: in practice exclusivity was unlikely to have been accepted by dealers and distributors in perishable products, whose handling raised many problems not encountered in selling consumer products with a reasonable or indefinite shelf life.

[51] Ch. 13, p. 300.   [52] But see also *Pelikan/Kyocera*, 1995 Annual Report, para. 87.

[53] Reported as Case 77/77 *British Petroleum* v. *Commission* [1978] ECR 1513: [1978] 3 CMLR 174. The Commission's decision is reported at [1977] OJ L117/1: [1977] 2 CMLR D1, as *ABG/Oil Companies*.

to others, especially when such action can result in change in structures of the particular market'. The Commission pointed out that BP had not supplied any objective reasons for the proportionately greater reduction in supplies to ABG and, after taking into account the extent, regularity, and continuity of commercial relationships between the parties, the conduct was ruled abusive.

The European Court, however, took a radically different view of the commercial relationship between BP and ABG. Accepting the findings of the Advocate General, it held that ABG was far from a regular customer, either by way of long-term contractual obligations or by reason of having made regular spot purchases. On the contrary, ABG was simply an occasional customer and BP was able to show that it had, owing to a reduction in its own crude oil supplies from Libya and Kuwait, reduced its contractual commitment to ABG twelve months before the oil crisis. It had actually requested ABG in future to obtain the greater part of its crude oil from other sources, though BP remained willing to refine this crude oil. Temporarily, in the earlier part of 1973, BP had 'lent' ABG some crude oil to be repaid at a later date. The Court ruled that it was clearly justifiable to remove these figures from the total oil sales between the parties; once this had been done, the percentage reductions in supplies to ABG during the crisis period became too small to justify any finding of abuse by BP of its market position. Nevertheless, in spite of the reversal of the Commission's decision on the particular facts, the duty of the dominant supplier to deal equitably with its regular customers is now clearly established, even though individual application of this rule will clearly raise difficulties in individual cases.

6.4 OBJECTIVE JUSTIFICATION AND PROPORTIONALITY

In other jurisdictions, one good defence to a claim for refusal to deal is the existence of a reasonable commercial justification. The best-known example is that involving a customer with a poor credit record. The supplier may refuse to supply simply because it does not believe that it will be paid for further deliveries, or it may seek through its refusal to apply pressure on the debtor to make partial alternative payment for earlier supplies. In the English High Court case of *Leyland Daf* v. *Automotive Products*[54] a refusal by Automotive Products to make further supplies to Leyland Daf, even though it would take Leyland Daf six to eight months to find an alternative supplier (because of stringent product liability requirements in the motor industry) was held to be justified by the Court of Appeal on this basis because of the substantial debt already outstanding from Leyland Daf.

Article 81(3) sets out four conditions which, if fulfilled, determine the inapplicability of the prohibition on anti-competitive forms of cooperation between undertakings laid down in Article 81(1). By contrast, Article 82 is drafted in terms of an absolute prohibition and no formal escape routes are provided. However, some decisions of the Community judicature have developed a form of reasoning based on objective

---

[54] [1993] BCC 389: [1994] BCLC 245.

justification and proportionality that has introduced some flexibility to the application of Article 82 EC and which may allow ostensibly abusive behaviour to fall outside
the scope of Article 82 EC. This is not a new exercise, but a technique broadly used
by the European Court in other areas of European Union Law like free movement of
goods and persons.[55] While this approach has not been developed systematically in
the context of Article 82 EC,[56] some of the rulings on refusals to supply provide useful
examples of this construction.

In *United Brands*, the European Court recognized that a dominant undertaking
could invoke the protection of its legitimate commercial interests as a justification
against a refusal to supply. In that case, as explained above, United Brands had discontinued its supplies to Olesen, a long-standing customer, because the latter had participated in an advertising campaign for one of its main competitors. While the Court
was prepared to accept that a dominant company could act to 'meet competition', it
felt that United Brands' refusal to supply was an *excessive* response to Olesen's actions.
This is, of course, the language of proportionality, an inseparable companion of objective justification in EU law. This concept[57] was inspired in German law and originally
required that public authorities should not impose obligations on citizens except to
the extent necessary for the attainment of a worthwhile public benefit. In cases like
United Brands, it was widened as a general principle of Community law to apply to
undertakings, whose response to competitive pressures should be limited to steps that
are appropriate and commercially necessary in the circumstances.

Another possible justification for outwardly abusive behaviour is exemplified in the
BP case,[58] also discussed above. There, the Court accepted that a practice which at first
sight appeared to be abusive—i.e. reduction of supplies to a casual customer—was in
fact justified by an objective and external cause: the shortage of supplies. This second
line of justification has also been argued in some of the tying cases where public health
or safety and reliability considerations have been invoked to justify potentially exclusionary behaviour –often with little measure of success.[59]

A particularly interesting development in this area of the law came through the
compelling Opinion of Advocate General Jacobs in *Syfait I*.[60] The facts of the case
were straightforward. Glaxosmithkline, a large pharmaceutical company, found out
that a large amount of the supplies that it made available to its Greek wholesalers were
being exported to other Member States, where the prices of these pharmaceuticals

[55] See for example the case law of the Court in the field of indirectly discriminatory measures having
equivalent effect to quantitative restrictions (Case 120/78 *Cassis de Dijon* [1983] ECR 203) or indirectly discriminatory measures that hinder the free movement of persons and services (Case C-55/94 *Gebhard* [1995]
ECR I-4165).
[56] Only the 2005 Discussion Paper of the Commission provides, for the first time, extensive coverage of
these concepts and of their application to the different forms of exclusionary abuse.
[57] See G. de Búrca, 'The Principle of Proportionality and its Application in EC Law' [1993] 13 YBEL 105.
[58] Case 77/77, fn. 53.
[59] Case T-30/89 *Hilti v. Commission* [1991] ECR II-1439: [1992] 4 CMLR 16 and Case T-83/91 *Tetrapak II*
[1994] ECR II-755: [1997] 4 CMLR 726.
[60] Case C-53/03 [2005] ECR I-4609.

were higher than in Greece. Glaxo decided to cut down the supplies and it was clear that its intention was to limit parallel trade because this had a detrimental effect on its commercial interests. Glaxo's actions gave rise to complaints by the Greek wholesalers that the company had acted in breach of Article 82. After examining the case law in detail, Advocate General Jacobs concluded that such refusal to supply would not be *necessarily* abusive, even when aimed at curbing parallel trade. This conclusion was highly relevant because limitations to parallel trade are essentially at variance with the single market objective of the Treaty—as are, for example, export bans in the context of Article 81—and yet the Advocate General went on to press his enquiry on the likely harm that Glaxo's practice would actually cause to competition and the free market. One of the key aspects of Advocate General Jacobs' Opinion was the analysis of whether Glaxo's behaviour could be objectively justified. In his view, there were several reasons why the pharmaceutical market was a special market in which normal conditions of competition did not prevail. Firstly, the price differentials between Member States were largely the result of government intervention and not of suppliers' decisions and the high degree of national regulation in the distribution of medicinal products meant that pharmaceutical undertakings were subject to some additional duties, such as maintaining an adequate level of supply in each Member State. This meant that attempts to rein in parallel trade by dominant companies were not aimed at consolidating differences in prices that they themselves had created across the Member States and that pharmaceutical companies did not always have the option to withdraw from the market of a Member State where low prices had been imposed. Secondly, in a market where high investment was required in research and development, undertakings could eventually decide not to invest in developing a new product in a 'low price' Member State if there was little prospect of making a suitable profit. Finally, there was evidence that distributors rather than consumers, benefited from parallel trade. As a result, the Advocate General opined that the refusal to supply could be justified by the need to lessen the harm caused by parallel trade to the commercial interests of the dominant company. He was, however, at pains to emphasize that this line of analysis could yield very different results in other markets. His cogent Opinion provided an exemplary template for the articulation of objective justification and proportionality in Article 82 EC cases, particularly in the context of special markets such as the one for pharmaceuticals. Disappointingly, the European Court declined jurisdiction to give a ruling under Article 234 EC on the grounds that the reference had been raised by the Greek Competition authority and that this authority was not a 'court or tribunal' entitled to make a reference under that provision.

In the meantime, however, the wholesalers brought an action before the Greek civil courts and the Athens Court of Appeal made a reference to the European Court under Article 234 asking substantially the same questions previously referred by the Greek Competition authority. The judgment of the European Court in *Syfait II*[61] was

---

[61] Cases C-468/06 to C-478/06 *Sot.Lelos KaiaSiaEE* v. *GlaxoSmithKline* (already known as *Syfait II*), (Judgment of 16 September 2008, not yet reported). Advocate General Ruiz-Jarabo Colomer gave his Opinion

delivered on 16 September 2008 and adopted a much more guarded approach, towards the protection of the commercial interests of dominant companies than that embodied in Advocate General Jacobs' Opinion in *Syfait I*. The Court sought to strike a balance between the protection of the single market objective of the Treaty and of the legitimate commercial interests of dominant companies. On the one hand, the Court stated that a dominant company's refusal to meet ordinary orders for supplies from wholesalers with a view to limit parallel trade would be prima facie abusive—doubtless because of the incompatibility of this behaviour with the common-market ideal.[62] On the other hand, it went on to recognize that State intervention in the pricing and distribution of products in the pharmaceutical sector created unusual opportunities for parallel trade and that dominant companies should be entitled to take proportionate steps to protect their commercial interests. The compromise formula adopted by the Court was that a dominant company would be entitled to refuse to meet orders for medicines from wholesalers in quantities which were '*out of all proportion* to those previously sold by the same wholesalers to meet the needs of the market in that Member State'.[63] It then left it to the national court to ascertain whether the orders placed by the Greek wholesalers in the case were out of the ordinary.[64] The difficulties with this reasoning are, of course, how to determine what an 'ordinary' order is and when an order would be 'out of all proportion'. These are difficult tasks devolved by the judgment to the national courts and on which will hinge the availability of objective justification for dominant companies in situations similar to those in the *Syfait* cases. Overall, however, it seems that although the Court upheld the importance of the single market ideal of the Treaty in *Syfait II*, this case together with the ruling in *Bayer*[65] and the decision of the Court of First Instance in *GlaxoSmithKline*,[66] suggest a less rigid assessment of the activities of pharmaceutical companies aimed at restricting parallel trade than that prevalent in earlier case law and Commission decisions.

Protection of legitimate commercial interests or the existence of an objective and external justifying cause therefore emerge from the case law as the two main possible heads of objective justification for potentially abusive behaviour. The 2005 Commission Discussion Paper adds a third head of justification based on efficiency considerations.[67] Although there is limited guidance on the use of this line of justification in the case law,[68] the judgment of the European Court in *British Airways*

---

in these cases on 1 April 2008, and reached the conclusion that Glaxo's behaviour could not be objectively justified either by the need to protect its commercial interests or on the basis of efficiency considerations.

[62] See paras. 65–6 of the judgment.　　　[63] See para. 76 of the judgment.

[64] In these cases, six out of eleven Greek wholesalers had asked for an increase of up to 20% in the quantities to be supplied, calculated in relation to the monthly average of medicines *sold* in the first ten months of 2000.

[65] Cases C-2 and 3/01 [2004] ECR I-23: [2004] 4 CMLR 653, see Ch. 6, pp. 86–8.

[66] Case T-168/01 *GlaxoSmithKline Services* v. *Commission* [2006] ECR II-2969: [2006] 5 CMLR 1589, see Ch. 6, p. 87.

[67] The efficiency defence set out in the 2005 Discussion Paper essentially replicates the Art. 81(3) conditions but adapted to the framework of the Art. 82 EC case law.

[68] For a recent consideration of this defence, see the Opinion of Advocate Genera Ruiz-Jarabo Colomer in *Syfait II*, (see n. 61) at paras. 116–19.

makes a clear allusion to the fact that efficiencies could justify potentially abusive discounts—even if the case did not discuss in detail the nature of these efficiencies.[69]

7. ABUSES BY INDIVIDUAL OWNERS OF INTELLECTUAL PROPERTY RIGHTS

7.1 THE EARLY CASES: THE IBM SETTLEMENT

The first ever case to reach the Court on the interpretation of Article 82 came in 1968 under an Article 234 reference from a Dutch court, the *Parke, Davis* v. *Probel* case,[70] and concerned the rights of an individual patent owner. Parke, Davis was the owner of a Dutch drug patent for an antibiotic process called chloramphenicol and sought to use its ownership of this patent to exclude from Holland drugs which had been produced in Italy, where patent protection was not then available for drugs or medicine. In so far as the Court's judgment reveals, Parke, Davis had had nothing to do with the production or marketing of the drugs in Italy. Such a normal use of patent protection under national law was held by the Court to be a right protected by Article 30, and by itself could not constitute abuse; abuse necessarily involved an element of impropriety in the way in which the patent right was exercised. Such impropriety could not be said to occur simply because Parke, Davis utilized its patent rights to exclude from Holland drugs which it had neither placed on the market in Italy nor allowed to be manufactured there by a third party. The mere fact that prices were higher in Holland for this particular drug than on the Italian market had no effect on the legal position; indeed, the likely reason for the ability of the Italian manufacturer to undercut the price charged in Holland was that the cost of the research and development of the drug had been incurred largely by Parke, Davis rather than the potential importers. The Court did, however, leave open an important issue, namely the extent to which the existence of the higher price level in one Member State might in some cases be relevant in determining the existence on other occasions of improper exploitation of market power.

Whilst, of course, it is decisions of the European Court and Court of First Instance which carry the greatest authority in this area, an important pointer for the future application of this aspect of the Article by the Commission was found in a case which never reached a formal decision. This was the widely publicized settlement involving International Business Machines (IBM). IBM was originally challenged with four practices claimed to be in violation of Article 82, though two of these charges were later withdrawn after IBM modified its marketing policies. The charges which were the subject of the final settlement involved: (a) IBM's practice of including the main memory function in the price of a central processing unit and refusing to supply it

---

[69] See Section 5.2.   [70] Case 24/67 [1968] ECR 55: [1968] CMLR 47.

separately, a practice known as 'memory bundling'; and (b) its policy of not disclosing important information about the interface of IBM computer systems until they
had actually been marketed, thereby placing at a disadvantage the manufacturers of
equipment that would have been compatible with the IBM hardware, who were unable
to obtain the necessary 'interface disclosure'. The terms of settlement were that the
Commission suspended its proceedings under Article 82 in return for an undertaking by IBM to amend its practices relating both to memory bundling and interface
disclosure. The Commission retained the right to reopen legal proceedings against
IBM should the relevant undertakings not prove in its view satisfactory; IBM agreed
to observe the terms of the undertaking at least until 1990, and to give twelve months'
notice of any intention to terminate the settlement.

IBM were alleged to have obtained market dominance in large mainframe computers and in the sub-market of the IBM Systems-370; the issue of 'memory bundling'
ultimately appeared to be less important than that of interface disclosure, because by
the time of settlement memory no longer formed a large part of the central processing unit. IBM indicated that it was willing to offer the EEC System-370 with no main
memory capacity, or at least only with the capacity required for reasonable tests to be
carried out. The more difficult issue of interface disclosure began with an allegation by
the Commission as to the foreclosure from competition of independent manufacturers
of peripheral equipment that would be compatible with IBM computers; this original
complaint was later extended to alleged non-disclosure of the IBM System-370 source
code permitting a company to design and prepare software programs that could work
in conjunction with IBM software, and also to practices adopted regarding its communications standard known as Systems Network Architecture (SNA). The Commission
had alleged in particular that the non-disclosure of interface information relating to
such architecture could conceivably have adverse effects on the data communication
industry's efforts to develop its own standard computer networking procedures, since
such non-disclosure would prevent other brands of computer equipment from being
able to be combined in a simple communications system with IBM products.

Under the terms of the complex settlement, IBM agreed to make interface information available within 120 days following the announcement of a new System-370
product intended for sale within the Community, and to make source code interface
information available to competitors as soon after the announcement of a new product
as the interface had been technically proved. IBM would also disclose adequate information to competitors to enable them to interconnect with System-370, using SNA,
once the relevant format and protocols were stable. However, the undertakings did not
extend to interfaces between two distinct products of a sub-system, from which the
design of the products could be detected.

This highly complex and technically demanding inquiry[71] may have been satisfactorily resolved from the viewpoint of the Commission and of IBM, for the completion

---

[71] The *14th Annual Report* (1984) contains details of the decision at pp. 77–9. A detailed assessment of the
operation of the settlement in the period 1984 to 1995 is found at DG Comp Competition Policy Newsletter
(1998) No. 3, pp. 7–11.

of any litigation to resolve the case would probably have taken several years and a disproportionate amount of the resources of DG Comp. It is clear that the Commission will place great importance on any activity of a dominant company which involves foreclosure of competitors from a particular market, either by insisting that two related products can only be purchased together, e.g. the CPU and its memory, or in cases of what is often called 'implicit tying', where smaller firms within an industry have adapted their products to those of the dominant firm and subsequently suffer a commercial disadvantage when the dominant firm redesigns its products so that competitors' complementary products cease to be compatible.

The undertaking remained in force until 1995 and seems to have been regarded by the Commission as a success. It enabled competitors of IBM entitled to receive interface information under its terms to give credible assurances to their own customers that their product would continue to be compatible with System-370 until at least 1990 (and in fact for a further five years). The making of the settlement in 1984, as opposed to the entering into litigation continuing for many years after that date, gave the required assurance at a much earlier time than would otherwise have been the case. The Commission believes that the incentive provided to IBM to improve its own products after 1984 was not reduced by the existence of its obligations under the undertaking.

If implicit tying is likely to lead to an allegation of abusive conduct, it seems to indicate that companies with a dominant position may not only have a negative obligation to refrain from action that places their smaller competitors at a disadvantage in this way, but that their dominant position imports a responsibility for maintaining a competitive market structure regardless of whether that commercial practice can be shown to have other justifications. This argument seems to be particularly relevant to the issue of non-disclosure of interface information relating to SNA, which was considered likely to restrict the development of markets for communication and area networks. However, its use may well be valuable to the Commission in future in other areas of advanced technology where a powerful company appears likely to be able, if left unchecked, to use its technical superiority to dampen the level of competition in its chosen markets.

The refusal to supply interface or interoperability information has been a major issue in the recent *Microsoft* litigation, which is discussed below.[72]

7.2 REFUSAL TO SUPPLY SPARE PARTS

The right of the owner of a patent, or other intellectual property right in a particular jurisdiction, to exercise it simply by excluding goods that infringed his territorial monopoly had been clearly confirmed in *Parke, Davis* v. *Probel* as not constituting an abuse. By analogy it appeared almost certain that such an owner would be entitled also to refuse to license his property to third parties. In *Volvo* v. *Eric Veng*[73] and its

---

[72] See section 10 below.   [73] Case 238/87 [1988] ECR 6211: [1989] 4 CMLR 122.

companion case *Renault v. Maxicar*[74] (two similar cases decided on the same day in October 1988) this principle was accepted but subject to a qualification so substantial as to considerably reduce its value. The Court agreed that the owners of protected design, in these cases for car body panels, had the right to prevent third parties from manufacturing, selling, or importing products which infringed the design and that this right to prevent third parties from entering the market comprised the very subject-matter of the exclusive right which national law had granted. Therefore, if Volvo and Renault were obliged as a matter of law to grant third parties a licence to supply products (even in return for reasonable royalties) then this would in effect deprive them of the substance of those exclusive rights. Hence a refusal to grant licences could not in itself constitute an abuse.

The qualification which the Court then stated reflected the underlying relationship between car makers on one hand and car owners on the other, who will need to have them maintained and repaired from time to time. The Court stated that any manufacturer who arbitrarily refused to supply spare parts to independent repairers, or fixed prices of spare parts at an unfair level, or made a decision to stop producing spare parts for particular models, even though many cars of that model were still in circulation, would commit an abuse of the dominant position which each manufacturer necessarily has in respect of many kinds of spare parts for its range of vehicles. The Court seems to be saying that there are situations where the relationship between the manufacturer-owner of intellectual property rights and the seller of the product which it has manufactured is such that the rights themselves cannot be used in a way which effectively reduces the value of the product supplied. However, the Court's final comment, reminiscent of the judgment in *Parke, Davis*, was that the mere fact that prices charged for spare parts by such manufacturers which enjoyed national protective rights for their designs were higher than those charged by independent producers did not necessarily indicate abuse, since the higher prices might be necessary to provide 'a return on the amounts invested in order to perfect the protected design'.

7.3 THE *MAGILL* SAGA

The line of reasoning adopted in the earlier cases was taken a stage further in the subsequent Court of First Instance and European Court decisions in *Magill v. Radio Telefis Eireann (RTE)*.[75] Here the intellectual property right concerned was the copyright in the compilation of weekly radio and television schedules. RTE, the Irish radio and television authority, had consistently refused to license Magill, an organization which wished to publish a weekly magazine containing these schedules. Basing its refusal on the grounds of copyright, it was only prepared to license the publication of twenty-four-hour schedules in newspapers (and forty-eight-hour at weekends) with

---

[74] Case 53/87 [1988] ECR 6039: [1990] 4 CMLR 265.
[75] Cases T-69–70/89 *RTE, ITP, BBC* v. *Commission* [1991] ECR II-485: [19991] 4 CMLR 586: (on appeal to the European Court) Cases C-241–242/91P [1995] ECR I-743: [1995] 4 CMLR 718.

some additional provision at public holidays. Magill claimed that this refusal to license the weekly programme details was an abuse of the monopoly which RTE held in them by virtue of its copyright. The Court of First Instance, largely adopting the reasoning of the Commission but after extensive citation of the earlier case law of the Court of Justice (both from cases concerning Article 82 and those involved with Articles 28 to 30 of the Treaty), confirmed that decision. After defining the relevant product market as RTE's own weekly programme listings and also the guide in which it published them (which of course had a monopoly) it pointed out that only weekly guides, with comprehensive listing for seven days, enabled viewers and listeners to decide in advance which programmes they wished to follow, and to arrange their leisure and domestic activities accordingly. Moreover, the existence of a demand for comprehensive weekly guides was shown by the fact that they were provided in nearly all other Member States irrespective of other available sources of programme information. RTE clearly had a monopoly in the listings themselves and in the right to reproduce and market them as it thought fit through its RTE guide. Third parties like Magill who wished to publish a general television magazine were in a position of economic dependence upon RTE, which could hinder the emergence of any effective competition.

The most interesting section of the decision, however, concerned the definition of abusive conduct. The Court of First Instance drew attention to the extensive case law, which balanced the need for free movement of goods against the protection of subject-matter of intellectual property rights, including copyright. It pointed out that the cases showed that the principle of the supremacy of Community law, particularly concerning such fundamental principles as free movement of goods and competition, normally prevailed over any rule of national intellectual property law contrary to those principles. It referred to the cases of *Volvo* and *Renault*, drawing an analogy between the hypothetical refusal there to supply spare parts to independent repairers or to provide parts at all for cars still in current use, and RTE's actual refusal to license a weekly magazine when there was a clear demand for it. By this action RTE was preventing the emergence on the market of a new product, namely a general television magazine, likely to compete with its own programme magazine. Copyright was being used in the programme listings which RTE produced as part of its broadcasting activities in order to secure a monopoly in the derivative market of weekly television guides, and the offer to provide information for brief periods only did not meet that need.

The Court of First Instance found that preventing the production and marketing of a new product for which there is a potential consumer demand and excluding competition from the market simply to secure a monopoly went well beyond the essential function of copyright as permitted under Community law. RTE's refusal to authorize such publications was justified neither by the specific needs of the broadcasting sector nor of the technical requirements of producing magazines containing the schedules.

When the appeal eventually reached the European Court in 1995, very considerable interest in the final outcome of the case had arisen, particularly in the basis upon which the ultimate finding would be made. Interest was heightened by the publication of the long and scholarly opinion of Gulmann A-G, who took the view that no breach of Article 82 had been committed. He accepted that, in certain special circumstances, the rights of owners of intellectual property have to be balanced against the interests of free competition (as indeed in many cases against the interests of the free movement of goods under Article 30) and the Court had to balance the 'essential function' of intellectual property rights against the other interests to arrive at a solution. In his view, however, the fact that a balance had to be struck did not mean that those interests had to be given equal weight. In his view the balance must always be in favour of intellectual property rights. 'The starting point set out in the Treaty is that intellectual property rights can be exercised even if that leads to obstacles to trade or restrictions of competition. Consequently if exercise of a given intellectual property right is necessary in order for that right to be able to fulfil its essential function, that exercise is not affected by the Treaty rules.'[76] In his view no such special circumstances existed in this case which would justify the removal of the copyright protection in the programme schedules, especially as any product which compulsory licensing would permit would be in direct competition with the programme guide published by RTE. He also distinguished the existing case law prohibiting refusal to supply to a competitor who wished to use a product on a derivative market, e.g. spare parts which the very design of the original car or other machinery made essential, with the different facts of this case where the refusal was to grant a licence to a competitor seeking merely to compete in a secondary market.

When the European Court decision appeared some months later it gave rise to considerable disappointment. This was not so much with the outcome of the case, in favour of the plaintiff, Magill, but with the fact that it concurred with almost the entire decision of the Court of First Instance without adding much detail or further analysis. It also made scarcely any reference to the main points of the Advocate General. Disappointment was also caused by its perceived failure to enunciate a clear doctrinal basis for refusals to license intellectual property rights, an issue of importance in many industrial sectors, notably pharmaceuticals and software.

The European Court in finding in favour of Magill placed weight on two main factors. The first was that there was no actual or potential substitute for the product (a comprehensive guide showing all programmes during the week) for which there was a substantial consumer demand, not currently being met by any broadcasting authority. The second reason was that there was no commercial or technical justification for the refusal to license which entitled the owners of the programme information to grant licences. It is notable that the European Court stressed that the material sought was essentially 'information' rather than intellectual property, the copyright protection arising almost accidentally or incidentally, rather than forming an essential part of the owners' business.

This decision is highly contentious. Interestingly, two powerful additional arguments justifying the Commission's decision were not referred to by the Court. The first is that in considering the concept of abuse, the normal practice to be found within

---

[76] Para. 80 of the Advocate General's Opinion.

Member States may be of considerable relevance. Here the facts found were that in all Member States, apart from the United Kingdom and Ireland, competing publications containing a full week's programmes of television and radio were commonly found. The fact that these publications existed not only proved that they represented a separate product market for which there was substantial demand, but also illustrated that there could be no overwhelming commercial or technical reason for refusing listeners and viewers the opportunity of planning their activities at least a week ahead. In other words, within the concept of abuse can be included an element of departure from norms of commercial conduct commonly found throughout the Community.

The second distinguishing feature of *RTE* v. *Magill* is that the copyright in the programme material only arose in the first place because of the existence of the statutory privilege or monopoly conferred on RTE to act as a broadcasting authority. It could therefore have been appropriately argued that RTE had not only a right to prepare programme schedules in which it had copyright but a duty to publicize in every reasonable manner the details of the programmes broadcast pursuant to this monopoly. In other words, the existence of a copyright obtained simply in order to enable the proper performance of a public function may be treated more severely by the Court than a copyright voluntarily acquired by the expenditure of creative effort. This point was not expressly taken by the Court, but may nevertheless have played an important part in its thinking.

7.4 THE EFFECTS OF *MAGILL*

It has been suggested that this decision may have far-reaching consequences in other sectors since it could be used as a justification for requiring owners of a wide variety of intellectual property rights, in software for example, to grant licences on reasonable terms if it can be shown that there is an existing demand for the material covered by the licences and no convincing technical or commercial reason for refusing to grant it on reasonable terms. It could therefore be used to remove from the owners of a variety of intellectual property rights even that limited protection from obligations to grant licences of relevant material to the extent that the *Renault* and *Volvo* cases had appeared to provide. The special features present in the *Magill* case, however, suggest that the Court will not be keen to apply such principles freely to other types of copyright such as computer programs or patents where similar factors may be absent.

Of course, the recitals to the Software Directive 91/250[77] confirm that its terms are without prejudice to the application of Article 82 when a dominant supplier refuses to provide information necessary for the interoperability of equipment, as in the *IBM* case. Moreover, Article 6 of the Directive allows a person authorized or licensed to use a program to 'decompile' it to allow communication with another program which the licensee has already created. However, this right of decompilation, which is achieved

---

[77] [1991] OJ L122/42. Decompilation can only apply when the owner of the program fails to disclose required interface information.

through reverse engineering, may not be used so as unreasonably to prejudice the legitimate interests of that program's owner, nor so as to conflict with his normal exploitation of his program. In the past, however, such an owner was free to refuse to license software to persons whom he suspects may seek to carry out 'decompilation'; following *Magill* (until it is reversed or distinguished in later cases) such a refusal on those grounds alone may be considerably harder to maintain. On the other hand, whilst second-hand cars cannot be operated without the availability of a full range of spare parts, and a television service without adequate published programme schedules is of limited value, the potential range and function of new software programs that licensees may wish to produce to communicate with (and expand the use of) their existing software is unlimited. The analogy with *Magill* may therefore not be straightforward.

Much anxiety has been expressed during and since *Magill* by the owners of intellectual property such as patented drugs or software that the decision might make it difficult for owners to refuse requests for licences. Thus the owners of a new patent for, say, a revolutionary drug to combat Aids might suddenly find itself besieged with requests for licences to manufacture the product all around the world, or the owners of a valuable software program who wish to exploit it themselves, might be prevented from doing so by being forced into widespread licensing. However, it appears that the Commission has treated the *Magill* judgment as having limited application, not requiring widespread compulsory licensing. Owners of intellectual property rights are normally entitled to decide whether to license or not. Merely to reach a negative decision is not to commit a breach of Article 82. A breach only occurs if there is no commercial justification for or explanation of the refusal and, moreover, the object or result of the refusal is to give the intellectual property rights owner some advantage in a derivative market which goes beyond the proper protection of 'essential function', as indicated in *Ladbroke* (see Section 9.3).

7.5   IMS HEALTH

A sequel to the *Magill* saga has been the *IMS Health* case.[78] Pharmaceutical companies require for their business a large amount of sales information at a local level. Because of data-protection legislation in Germany, this cannot be provided for groups of less than three pharmacies but needs aggregation at a local level into a number of units each covering at least four or five pharmacies. The system developed in Germany over a number of years, by cooperation between pharmaceutical companies and IMS, is currently known as the '1860 brick structure', under which the country is divided into that number of zones of equivalent size. Originally there were far fewer separate bricks in the system but by the joint efforts of all parties a more detailed system was gradually refined. Rivals to IMS unsuccessfully sought alternative methods for breaking down sales data in Germany and having failed, then sought licences from IMS to use its

---

[78]   Case C-418/01 [2004] ECR I-5039: [2004] 4 CMLR 1543.

copyright in the 1860 brick structure. When IMS refused, these rivals complained to the Commission which, following an investigation, granted their request for interim measures under which IMS would have been forced to give immediate licence of the 1860 brick system, in return for royalties set by an independent expert if the parties should fail to agree.

IMS appealed the interim measures decision of the Commission to the President of the CFI,[79] who overruled the Commission's order in a judgment that contained a number of significant comments on the interpretation of *Magill* and whose decision was subsequently upheld by the President of the ECJ.[80] The main ground for his decision was that the granting of interim measures requiring the granting of a licence by IMS would be more likely to cause 'serious and irreparable harm' to IMS, whereas the disadvantage to the complainants of not receiving an immediate licence was lesser. But in the course of his judgment, Judge Vesterdorf, without reaching a final decision on the merits of the case (which was still before the Commission), expressed serious doubts as to whether the *Magill* judgment necessarily meant that IMS would be required under Article 82 to grant compulsory licences in such circumstances. It seemed arguable that the 'exceptional circumstances' of *Magill* did not exist in the present case since IMS were not unilaterally preventing the creation of a market, but were operating a system which had through cooperation with the pharmaceutical industry become a de facto industry standard.[81] Judge Vesterdorf of the CFI emphasized the need for the plaintiff to show damage to competition, rather than mainly to competitors.

In the meantime, the German court dealing with the proceedings at national level made a preliminary reference to the European Court under Article 234 EC asking, inter alia, about the circumstances in which a refusal by a dominant company to grant a copyright licence could be abusive. As in earlier cases, the Court confirmed that a refusal to licence was abusive only in exceptional circumstances. It then set out three *cumulative* conditions which, if satisfied, would determine the abusive nature of this practice. These were that the refusal to supply (1) is preventing the emergence of a new product in the market for which there is a potential consumer demand, (2) is not objectively justified and (3) excludes competition in a secondary market.

The judgment essentially confirms *Magill* but provides some interesting observations on the interpretation of the requirement that the refusal to supply should exclude competition in a secondary market. Thus, while the Court emphasized that an upstream and a downstream market should be identified, it then held that it would suffice for the upstream market to be a 'potential or even a hypothetical market'.

On the facts, some of the key issues in the interpretation of those three conditions were whether the '1860 brick structure', the upstream market, was *indispensable* to the downstream supply of German regional-sales data for pharmaceutical products and whether the refusal to supply prevented the development of a new product for which

---

[79] Case T-184/01R [2001] ECR II-3193: [2002] 4 CMLR 58.
[80] Case C-418/01R [2002] ECR I-3401: [2002] 5 CMLR 44.
[81] The detailed arguments of the protagonists can be found in F. Fine, 'NDC/IMS: A Logical Application of the Essential Facilities Doctrine' [2002] 23 ECLR 457–68.

there was potential consumer demand. On this second point, the Court held that it was important to show that applicants for a licence did not simply intend duplicate the goods or services already offered by the copyright owner in the secondary market but that they were really intending to produce *new* goods or services. Given that the case was brought before the Court via a preliminary reference, the European Court had no jurisdiction to deal with the application of these criteria to the actual facts of the case, a task that was referred back to the national court. Unfortunately, this means that the full implications of the ruling will only become clear when these parameters are applied by the Commission and national enforcement agencies in future cases. However, it is possible to conclude that the *IMS* decision confirms the established case law, according to which a refusal to grant a licence will only be abusive in those cases where the intellectual property right holder is using his right with the sole purpose of preventing the development of a new market for which the licence is an indispensable input and, in doing so, is acting to the detriment of consumer interests.

7.6 TETRAPAK (NO. 1)

The abuse of power provided by intellectual property rights was also a central theme in other major cases, namely *Hilti*[82] and *Tetrapak (No. 1)*.[83] The facts in *Hilti* were essentially unremarkable; Hilti attempted to use its intellectual property rights, namely patent and copyright respectively in nail guns and cartridge strips (into which the nails were fixed before firing), in order to discourage other companies from manufacturing or buying the nails (which enjoyed no such protection) from third parties. Its methods included tying the sale of the nails to the purchase of the cartridges and upon sales of cartridges made without correspondingly large purchase of nails to reduce the discounts provided. The Commission and Community Courts rejected Hilti's argument that it was primarily concerned to prevent damage to users of its guns and cartridges by the use of nails from other sources. There was no evidence that the use of non-Hilti nails had led to accidents, and a complete absence of any current written complaints from Hilti about the quality of nails produced by competitors for use with Hilti's guns and cartridges.

The facts of the *Tetrapak (No. 1)* judgment by the Court of First Instance were altogether more unusual, and the decision is a landmark in the development of case law on abuse.[84] Milk can be provided for household consumption in two main ways. It can be sold fresh, normally in familiar 'gable-shaped' cartons, or it can come as UHT milk, which is aseptic (after sterilization by hydrogen peroxide) and normally sold in 'brick-shaped' cartons. Consumers find it much easier to open the gable-shaped carton and for some years Liquipak, a United States company, had been trying to develop

---

[82] Case T-30/89 [1991] ECR II-1439: [1991] 4 CMLR 16.

[83] Case T-51/89 *Tetrapak (No. 1)* [1990] ECR II-309: [1991] 4 CMLR 334.

[84] It is noteworthy that, in its first major case on this issue, the Court took the opportunity to lay down broad principles of the relationship between Arts. 81–2 rather than deciding the case on relatively narrow, technical grounds.

technology to produce machinery for manufacturing gable-shaped cartons in which UHT milk could be sold (thus eliminating the need for brick-shaped cartons). It had collaborated with—and had as its Community licensee—a Norwegian company, Elopak, and with this company it had carried out numerous trials in the development of the new product which it believed had been brought to the point of commercial full-scale development. In doing so it had had the help of an exclusive patent licence from the British Technology Group (BTG) granted in 1981 but in terms which complied with the subsequent Patent Block Exemption (Regulation 2349/84) introduced in 1984. By 1986 Elopak believed it was in a position to challenge Tetrapak, which had at that time some 90 per cent of the Community market in both the machinery for manufacturing the cartons and the cartons themselves.

In that same year, however, Tetrapak acquired the Liquipak group of companies and with them the exclusive licence for developing the gable-shaped aseptic milk carton and necessary filling machinery. Elopak raised a complaint under Article 82 with the Commission and after proceedings had been instituted against Tetrapak, Tetrapak abandoned any claim to exclusivity under the licence, which would have meant that BTG could license other would-be entrants (had it wished to do so) to the market for gable-shaped aseptic milk cartons. In spite of this, the Commission continued with the case because it raised important issues of principle. Tetrapak's acquisition of Liquipak had left only one other active competitor capable of producing aseptic filling machinery and cartons, enjoying only 10 per cent of the market; moreover, the technology of this company, PKL, was inferior to that of Tetrapak since it could only supply individually flattened blanks, and not cartons produced in continuous rolls. The market for the filling machinery was limited: dairies did not change their machines often as they had a life of at least ten years; moreover, milk was not a growing market. All these factors meant that the barriers to entry by new competitors were high.

The issue raised by the actions of Tetrapak was whether the acquisition of the exclusive licence previously owned by its main competitor could constitute an abuse; Tetrapak argued that this could not be so because the agreement itself benefited from an existing block exemption under Regulation 2349/84. It is clear from the Court's decision that the mere existence of the block exemption covering the licence agreement did not automatically prevent abuse. In his lengthy review of the earlier cases on abuse Advocate General Kirschner pointed out that undertakings with a dominant position were entitled to act in a profit-orientated way in order to expand their business activities. They were not required to act contrary to economic sense or their own legitimate interests. On the other hand, commercial steps which might be open to undertakings without a dominant position were, when effected by a dominant company, to be treated as abuse of its power; nor was it necessary to an Article 82 finding for the dominant company to have used that market power in order to obtain the benefit of the acquisition or licence agreement concerned. He referred back to the judgment in *Hoffmann-La Roche*,[85] and pointed to the concept of proportionality underlying

---

[85] Case 85/76 [1979] ECR 461, 520: [1979] 3 CMLR 211, 274, popularly called the *Vitamins* case.

the various kinds of abuse dealt with in earlier cases including *United Brands*,[86] *BRT v. SABAM*,[87] and other performing rights cases. In *Tetrapak (No. 1)*, a company with some 90 per cent of the market in the aseptic filling machines and the cartons made to be used with them acquired an exclusive licence from its main potential competitor endeavouring to break into that market. The effect of the acquisition of the Liquipak group was that the alternative technology protected by that patent was denied not only to Liquipak but to all Tetrapak's potential competitors. The acquisition of this exclusive licence was a disproportionate method of carrying on business since the acquisition of a non-exclusive licence would also have enabled Tetrapak to use its patented process to improve its own products, but without impeding access by competitors to the market over which Tetrapak enjoyed so dominant a position.

The Court speedily made clear that the principles laid down in *Parke, Davis*, as later qualified in the *Renault/Volvo* cases, would not help Tetrapak. A distinction was drawn between the development of technology in those cases by an individual company which it was then entitled to protect or refuse to license (other than in exceptional circumstances), and the acquisition in this case by Tetrapak of technology developed by others. The Court, dealing briefly with the concept of abuse because during the hearing of the case Tetrapak had withdrawn their appeal against the Commission's decision on this aspect (though not on other aspects)[88] of the case, found that the mere fact that an undertaking in a dominant position acquired an exclusive licence did not per se constitute abuse; on the other hand, in the specific circumstances of the acquisition, the exclusivity of the licence acquired had not only strengthened Tetrapak's already considerable domination of the market but also had the effect of preventing, or at the very least considerably delaying, the entry of new competitors into the market.

8. ABUSES BY COLLECTIVE OWNERS OF INTELLECTUAL PROPERTY RIGHTS

8.1 RESTRICTIVE RULES OF COLLECTING SOCIETIES

The application of Article 82 to performing rights societies within the Community raises some novel issues, and cases decided by the Court of Justice have illustrated the potential flexibility of the Article as applied to situations outside normal industrial and commercial markets. The role of performing rights societies, found in most Member States, is to collect and administer very large numbers of copyrights for music

---

[86] Case 27/76 [1978] ECR 207: [1979] 1 CMLR 429.

[87] Case 127/73 [1974] ECR 51: [1974] 2 CMLR 23 (the Court's judgment dealing with the direct effect in national courts of Art. 82) and 313 (the Court's judgment dealing with the issue of whether SABAM was exploiting its dominant position as a copyright authority in Belgium): [1974] 2 CMLR 238 is a consolidated report of both judgments.

[88] The Court's important ruling on the relationship between Arts. 81–2 is considered in detail in Ch. 15.

to be publicly performed, representing the creative work of composers and librettists, so as to enable the licensing of these works (often by way of a block licence) to all those undertakings which may require their use. These may range from broadcasting authorities and cable TV companies on one hand to individual proprietors of businesses such as discothèques and public halls on the other. Performing rights societies have two advantages: they enable the owners of the individual copyrights (which are often assigned to music publishers for exploitation) to obtain and monitor a greater number of performances of his work, with a corresponding increase in income, while enabling those paying the licence fees to obtain by a single payment a far greater range of copyright material than would be possible if individual negotiations were required for each copyright.

Nevertheless, performing rights societies have on occasion sought to introduce into their rules restrictions going beyond those reasonably necessary for the proper protection and promotion of their members' interests. Such restrictions have been challenged under the provisions of Article 82, involving performing rights societies and similar undertakings in Germany, France, and Belgium. The leading case is *BRT* v. *SABAM*.[89] Two Belgian radio employees decided to prove that even a 'nonsense song' could become a hit, and wrote a song entitled 'Asparagus Beans', assigning the copyright to Belgian Radio and Television (BRT). BRT then arranged for it to be recorded and for the discs to be sold. SABAM claimed rights in the song on the basis that under its standard form of agreement it obtained rights over the work of its former members (who included the BRT employees who had written the song) for five years after they had ceased to be members. BRT claimed that SABAM's claim was invalid because SABAM was a de facto monopoly, and the five-year restriction went so far beyond its reasonable requirements as to constitute an abuse of its dominant position. An Article 234 reference by a Belgian Court resulted in a ruling from the European Court that any undertaking entrusted with the exploitation of copyrights was likely to hold a dominant position, and that if it imposed on its members obligations not absolutely requisite for the attainment of its legitimate objects, it would be in breach of Article 82. Protection could not be afforded to that organization by reason of Article 86(2) since the responsibilities taken on by SABAM had not been assigned to it by the State, but merely involved the management of private interests, namely intellectual property rights protected by Belgian law. However, the extent to which the validity of any contract in dispute before a national court was thereby affected was for the national court to decide.

Cases had already been heard and decided by the Commission in connection with the rules of such organizations. In 1971, *GEMA (No. 1)* involved a challenge to the complex set of rules relating to the German Performing Rights Society. The Commission decided that in a number of respects the rules violated Article 82; they discriminated

---

[89] Case 127/73 [1974] ECR 51 313: 2 CMLR 238. Public interest issues arising in the operation of collective societies are considered in the MMC Reports on *Collective Licensing* (Cm. 530) (1988) and the *Performing Rights Society* (Cm. 314) (1996).

against nationals of other Member States, who were denied credit for royalties which they received from similar associations in the Community, when their status and eligibility for ordinary membership in GEMA were being considered.[90] Moreover, foreign nationals were unable to become members of GEMA's council, nor could music publishing houses outside Germany be admitted to membership. The rules also required higher royalties on records imported or reimported from other Member States than on records produced in Germany.

GEMA was also found to have imposed over-wide obligations on its individual members, requiring, inter alia, assignments of their rights in all categories of creative work, and for the whole world; it was made extremely difficult to withdraw from the association because membership had to be for a minimum period of six years. GEMA was therefore required to amend its rules and practices to remove the discriminatory and over-wide provisions.[91]

Subsequently, *Greenwich Film Productions* v. *SACEM*[92] raised further issues arising out of a dispute between the French Performing Rights Society (SACEM) and the producers of a film for which two members of SACEM had composed music. Under the terms of their membership, the copyrights in their work had been assigned to SACEM, though some performances would take place in territories over which SACEM had no direct jurisdiction, outside the Common Market. SACEM sued Greenwich for the royalties in respect of these performances, and Greenwich put forward Article 82 as the ground for non-payment. The issue before the Court was whether Article 82 could apply to the performance in non-EC countries of contracts entered into within the territory of a Member State by parties within the jurisdiction of that State. On an earlier occasion, SACEM had had to alter its rules to comply with Commission requirement that it reduce the restrictions which it imposed, on the same basis as the findings in *GEMA (No. 1)*. SACEM had therefore already eliminated from its rules discrimination against nationals of other Member States and reduced the period for which a member had to bind himself or herself to SACEM.

The results of the case proved unsatisfactory to the composers as well as to the Commission. The Court held that if Article 82 abuses were found, it was for French courts to decide to what extent the interests of the composers would be affected. The rules of the association were still in breach of Article 82, and the fact that such an abuse affected only the performance in non-member countries of contracts entered into in the territory of a Member State would not preclude the application of that Article. In the event, however, the French Cour de Cassation avoided any application of the ruling

---

[90] This was a more favourable category of membership than the extraordinary membership normally accorded to foreign nationals: [1971] CMLR D35.

[91] In a later Commission decision ([1982] 2 CMLR 482) there has been further review of the GEMA rules, and a negative clearance granted to an amendment aimed at preventing broadcasting companies from obtaining unfair advantages through special royalty-sharing arrangements with composers in return for 'song-plugging'. The Commission emphasized that practices which might in other contexts be an abuse of a dominant position would not necessarily be so if 'indispensable to carrying out the essential purposes of a collecting society'.

[92] Case 22/79 [1979] ECR 3275: [1980] 1 CMLR 629.

by the European Court to the particular case, claiming that the original membership of the two composers in SACEM antedated the application of Article 82 to the case, so that no effect on trade between Member States could be considered attributable to the conduct of SACEM. This unsatisfactory ruling (ignoring the direct effect in national law of Article 82 which was in force at the date when both composers joined SACEM) offers an example, fortunately rare, of a national court ruling which paid scant attention to the terms of the decisions of the European Court.

Article 82 has also been applied to an organization established in Germany for the protection of copyright in order to manage the rights of performers to royalties in respect of visual or sound recordings of their performances which are then shared on an equitable basis with the manufacturers of these recordings.[93] This type of right is normally called 'secondary exploitation' and is, of course, quite separate from the primary exploitation of the copyright in the music and words of the individual works. The defendant, GVL, was the only organization of its kind in Germany and, until November 1980, refused to conclude agreements with performers who were not resident in Germany. The relevant market was found by the Commission and Court to be the commercial management of the secondary exploitation rights of performers, and for this the Court ruled that residence was not a relevant factor. Therefore, the refusal of GVL to act for foreign performers was itself an abuse of their de facto monopoly position. Although no fine was imposed because GVL's internal decision had been reversed before the date of the Commission's decision, a valuable ruling had been obtained; in view of the express provisions of Article 7 of the Treaty forbidding discrimination on the grounds of nationality, however, the decision itself caused no surprise.

8.2 EXCESSIVE CHARGES

The question of the level of charges made by such organizations reached the European Court in four linked cases[94] involving the rules of SACEM, referred under Article 234 from French courts. In the first three cases SACEM sought payment of royalties from French discothèques in the Poitiers region which had refused to take out a licence from it; in the other case a disco owner sued Tournier as managing director of SACEM in respect of alleged unfair trading practices under French law. Since 1978 there had been a long-running dispute between SACEM and a large number of French discothèque owners who thought that its rates were too high, that it discriminated unfairly between categories of discothèque, and that it refused without objective justification licences for the only category of music in which they were really interested, namely dance music of predominantly Anglo-American origin such as rock. As it was an Article 234 reference the Court was not asked to resolve the specific disputes between

[93] In Case 7/82 *GVL* v. *Commission* [1983] ECR 483: [1983] 3 CMLR 645.

[94] The cases were Case 395/87 *Ministère Public* v. *Tournier* [1989] ECR 2521: [1991] 4 CMLR 248); Case 110/88 *SACEM* v. *Lucazeau*; Case 241/88 *SACEM* v. *Debelle*; and Case 242/88 *SACEM* v. *Soumagnac*—all at [1989] ECR 2811: [1991] 4 CMLR 248.

the parties but simply to reply to those questions which the French courts had raised. These questioned the compatibility of the practices of SACEM with respect to this kind of musical material, in the light of its undoubted dominance as a performing rights society within France and the various complaints about the manner in which this was carried out which the cases had raised.

In one aspect of the case the Court's ruling would have disappointed the discothèque owners. It found that SACEM's refusal to grant them licences simply for the foreign repertoire likely to be preferred by its patrons would not be a restriction of competition unless providing access to part only of the repertoire (at presumably reduced royalties) could also entirely safeguard the interests of composers without increasing the costs of managing and monitoring the use of such copyright works. In other ways, the Court judgment was more favourable to the discothèque owners. It pointed out that if an undertaking such as SACEM imposed special fees for its services which were appreciably higher than those in other Member States, that difference might indicate an abuse of SACEM's dominant position. The burden of proof would then be on SACEM to justify that difference by showing that there were objective differences between its position and that of equivalent organizations in other Member States. The Court mentioned that the level of operating expenses in SACEM appeared particularly high and wondered if this was attributable to lack of competition. However, it refused to rule on whether the amount charged to discothèques themselves, as compared to the rates charged to other large-scale users of recorded music such as TV and radio stations, were unfair discrimination, leaving that awkward question to the national court. The Court decision followed the spirit, though not all the detail, of Jacobs A-G's opinion; he emphasized the particularly dominant position of this kind of organization which had no need to fear competition from foreign performing rights societies and no likelihood of substantial regulation of its affairs by public authority, so that it had near absolute freedom of action, coupled with a clear inequality of bargaining power between it and discothèques which were completely dependent upon it.

The general attitude of the Court in such cases has been robust. It has swept aside a number of the arguments raised by the societies, including protests that they are not 'undertakings', and that the writing of songs and music is a cultural rather than economic activity, and that individual composers or publishers are therefore not entitled to the protection of Article 82. The Court has also refused to allow the rules of such societies to limit the free transfer of copyright items between Member States which have been placed in commercial circulation in a single Member State. Here Articles 28 to 30, of course, also come into the reckoning as illustrated by the case of *Musik-Vertrieb Membran and K-tel International* v. *GEMA*[95]. This involved the question of whether the German collecting society which owned the copyright in musical works reproduced on gramophone records was entitled to claim

---

[95] Cases 55 and 57/81 [1982] ECR 147: [1982] 2 CMLR 44. This case follows closely the earlier precedents of the Court in respect of patents and trade marks. The distinction between this and Case 341/87 *EMI Electrola* v. *Patricia* [1989] ECR 79: 2 CMLR 413 is that in the latter case the owner of the copyright had not given consent to the marketing of the records.

from a parallel importer a fee equal to the royalties ordinarily paid for marketing such records in Germany, less the lower royalties already paid in the United Kingdom, where the records were originally put into circulation by the copyright owner. The Court gave a negative answer emphasizing that sound recordings, even if incorporated in copyright material, are covered by the system of free movement of goods, so that it was contrary to Article 28 for the owner of the copyright in the records to rely on copyright legislation to prevent the import of a product lawfully marketed in another Member State by the owner or with his consent.

8.3 THE COMMISSION'S RELUCTANCE TO INTERVENE

It should also be emphasized that the Commission has not in recent years shown itself enthusiastic about seeking to adjudge the conduct of collecting societies against the standards of Article 82 and, particularly since *Automec (No. 2)*, has shown a willingness to return cases for assessment of their individual merits to national courts and competition authorities. In *Tremblay* v. *Commission*[96] and in the *Tournier* group of cases the continuing differences between the French discothèque owners and SACEM (mentioned above) were once again brought to the Commission, but on this occasion the European Court and the Court of First Instance supported the refusal of the Commission to deal further with the individual claims, since they only affected France and had no particular relevance to the functioning of the Common Market. The main interest of the complainant in this case was the recovery of damages that it may have incurred, and a decision of the Commission on such issues would not be binding on the national court or national competition authorities. The Court of First Instance adopted a similar attitude to the Commission's approach in *Koelman* v. *Commission*[97] where a claim by a Dutch composer that the rules of Dutch collecting society BUMA were in breach of Article 81 were found to be rules on which the Commission need not adjudicate, given that Koelman had suffered no financial or personal loss as a result of BUMA's activities.

Nevertheless the inherent nature of collecting societies, required to balance the interests of their many members with their very different priorities and circumstances, means that their rules and operations will always be the subject of complaint. This in turn leads the Commission necessarily to keep their operations under constant review, even if no formal proceedings have been begun. In many cases too the inevitably international nature of their operations will mean that the Commission may be unable to delegate responsibility for the investigations to national competition authorities.

---

[96] Case C-91/95P [1996] ECR I-5547: [1997] 4 CMLR 211 and Case T-224/95 [1997] ECR II-2215: [1998] 4 CMLR 427.

[97] Case T-575/93 [1996] ECR II-1: [1996] 4 CMLR 636: (on appeal to the ECJ) Case C-59/96P [1997] ECR I-4809.

9. REFUSAL OF ACCESS TO ESSENTIAL FACILITIES

9.1 THE 'HARBOUR' CASES

It is a characteristic of Article 82 that it can be applied in a variety of new situations to deal with apparently novel kinds of abuse. The development of the doctrine of 'essential facilities' illustrates this well. 'Refusal to deal' and 'discriminatory dealing' have been well-established examples of abuse for some time and a new category of abusive conduct has now been established which involves a combination of these practices. Essentially the conduct involved is the refusal by an undertaking, which owns or controls a facility or an infrastructure to which competitors require access in order to provide a service to their customers, to allow that access. Alternatively, the abuse may involve allowing access only on such unfavourable and discriminatory terms that it places new or existing competitors at a competitive disadvantage so that they cannot compete effectively.

This essential facility might be a port, harbour, or airport, a national telecommunications network, or a grid for electricity or gas. It might be an electronic system, such as a computer reservation system for airlines, a banking system enabling electronic transfer of funds, or a television network. For a variety of reasons, often connected with its strategic location or formal legislative protection, competitors may regard the particular facility as essential to their commercial needs and will complain to the Commission if they believe that the company controlling the facility is deliberately making it difficult or impossible for them to share it. There is substantial case law in this area; probably the earliest example is *Telemarketing (CBEM v. CLT & IPB)*.[98] IPB sold advertising time on Luxembourg television. It refused to accept advertisements that contained a telephone number from which further information could be obtained by potential customers unless the agency's own number was used. Under an Article 234 reference the European Court ruled:

if telemarketing activities constitute a separate market from that of the chosen advertising medium, although closely associated with it, and if those activities mainly consist in making available to advertisers the telephone lines and team of telephonists of the telemarketing undertaking, to subject the sale of broadcasting time to the condition that the telephone lines of an advertising agent belonging to the same group as the television station should be used, amounts in practice to a refusal to supply the service of that station to any other telemarketing undertaking.

Essentially the practice amounted to a refusal to supply except on terms which amounted to 'tying'.

The development of the doctrine was accelerated by a group of cases involving passenger ferries and their need to use particular harbours within the Community. The first two cases involved the port of Holyhead in Wales, the others, ports in Denmark

[98] Case 311/84 [1985] ECR 3261: [1986] 2 CMLR 558.

and France. The first case was *B & I Line* v. *Sealink Harbours*.[99] Both parties used Holyhead as the base for their Holyhead–Dublin ferry routes, but Sealink were also, through a subsidiary, the owner of the harbour. Unusually, B & I complained of an abuse affecting its business that involved physical interference with its use of the harbour. Schedules for the Sealink ferries were altered so that the Sealink ships passed close by B & I's ferry terminal on their way to the Sealink berths in the inner harbour. Because of the narrowness of the channel, the passing of these Sealink ships caused vertical and horizontal turbulence, such that the B & I linkspan for vehicles and passengers had to be disconnected and its loading period to be interrupted and shortened. The particular complaint of B & I was that Sealink had changed its schedules deliberately to cause more disruption to B & I. For its part, Sealink claimed that the plaintiffs could alter the stern shape of their ferry so that it would suffer less disruption from the passage of the Sealink ferries, and that they were already aware of the problem when they moved to their existing terminal.

The Commission ruled that the port of Holyhead was a substantial part of the Common Market and that Sealink had a dominant position there as owner of the port. The port controlled an important corridor for ferry services between Ireland and the United Kingdom. The Commission also ruled that Sealink as the dominant company must not change its schedules to put B & I at a disadvantage, because the physical limitations of the port and the narrowness of its channel meant that B & I's loading and unloading activities would be affected by Sealink's choice of schedules. By way of interim order the defendants were told to resume their original schedule.

The next case[100] involved the same defendants, Sealink, but a different plaintiff, Sea Containers, also operating out of Holyhead. On this occasion the Commission refused interim measures because the defendants were regarded as having provided sufficient offers of additional slot times to allow the plaintiffs to run a viable service. The activities complained of here were not physical movements of ships, but the loss of commercial access to suitable berths, causing financial loss. Sea Containers also complained that Sealink had developed the port so as to reduce its current capacity and thereby Sea Containers' ability to make a success of their use of it. Sea Containers were particularly worried about delay caused to its proposed introduction of a fast catamaran to the harbour. Although in the event no order was made, the Commission was clearly prepared to develop the doctrine of essential facilities raised in the previous case involving the same harbour. It stated that any dominant company providing an essential facility to competitors which abuses that facility, and refuses access without objective justification, or grants access only on terms less favourable than those which it provides its own services, breaches Article 82. The background to the case was that both parties were trying to introduce the first 'fast cat' wave-piercing catamaran service on the

---

[99] [1992] 5 CMLR 255.

[100] *Sea Containers* v. *Stena Sealink* [1994] OJ L15/8: [1995] 4 CMLR 84. The Commission held that Liverpool was not an effective alternative base for passenger ferry services to Ireland but Sea Containers eventually in 1998 opened its 'fast cat' service from Liverpool, which had better motorway access than Holyhead even if the sea crossing to Ireland was longer.

route to Ireland. The Commission believed that Sealink were not negotiating in good faith and had failed to set up adequate procedures for handling its responsibilities as harbour operators towards other users.

In the third case[101] roles are reversed: we find Stena Sealink as the plaintiff in a case involving the refusal by the Danish State railways (DSB) either to allow Stena to build a new private commercial port near Rødby in Denmark, or to operate from the existing port. Rødby-Puttgarden is apparently the best route for ferry crossings between Denmark and Germany and is so commercially attractive that it is used by some 70 per cent of passengers and 88 per cent of lorries between Denmark and Germany. Rødby Harbour was operated by DSB which also ran the ferry jointly with the German railways. Because of the State involvement an Article 86 case was brought in respect of DSB's practices. The Commission ruled that an undertaking owning or managing a port facility from which it provides a ferry service may not, without objective justification, refuse to grant facilities or access to a shipowner seeking to operate in competition on the same route. The case clearly marked a further advance in the doctrine since it was now applied not only to discriminatory treatment for existing customers of a port, but to potential customers who sought entry and were refused access. Clearly the right of access could not be unconditional, since there might be circumstances in which it would be unreasonable to expect the owner of the harbour to provide access, for example if it was already full or if there were genuine technical reasons why the new applicant could not be admitted. However, in the view of the Commission, this was not the case at Rødby.

The final case[102] of this quartet involved an Irish ferry line seeking to operate a route from Cork and Rosslare to Roscoff in Brittany, a port controlled by the local Chamber of Commerce, which held a minority interest in Brittany Ferries operating on the same routes between Ireland and Brittany. Roscoff to Cork was undoubtedly the most convenient route and Roscoff had the best harbour facilities at the French end. The Irish line had tried Brest as an alternative and found it unsatisfactory. A special factor here was that the Roscoff Chamber of Commerce had encouraged the Irish line to believe that facilities would be available for ferries in the 1995 summer season but subsequently changed their mind. On this occasion interim measures were ordered for the 1995 summer season, since otherwise the plaintiffs would have found themselves in a very awkward position, being unable to convey the passengers who had already booked in anticipation of a Roscoff service.

9.2 OTHER CATEGORIES OF ESSENTIAL FACILITIES

The Commission has been involved in other such cases connected with essential facilities in the transport sector. Thus in *Aer Lingus/British Midland Airways*,[103] Aer Lingus was in competition on the Dublin–London route with British Midland. Aer Lingus was

---

[101] *Stena Sealink* v. *DSB* [1994] OJ L55/52.
[102] *Irish Continental Group* v. *CCI Morlaix* [1995] 5 CMLR 77.   [103] [1992] OJ L96/34.

dominant on the route and decided not to 'interline' with British Midland. Interlining is a standard practice approved by IATA by which airlines agree to accept each other's tickets and receive a compensating proportion of revenue. The Commission ruled that for a new airline seeking to compete on a route, interlining is in practice essential since its absence forces a new entrant either to operate infrequent flights, or to offer frequent flights attracting passengers but accepting that initial passenger utilization of its aircraft will be low. The Commission did not order an indefinite obligation on Aer Lingus to interline but a period of two years; this was considered as sufficient for British Midland to acquire sufficient passenger loading to be able to survive without interlining, if Aer Lingus then decided not to continue with it.

In a decision involving the German Railway Authority, the Deutsche Bahn (DB),[104] DB was found to have discriminated against container cargo being transported through the Benelux Countries to ports there by charging lower freight rates in respect of containers forwarded by it to German ports. Operators of the cargo services through the Benelux countries could not provide rail services but had to obtain them from the German authorities. The Commission held that DB had used its dominant position on the rail transport market to impose higher prices than would otherwise have prevailed, on a discriminatory basis, in order to promote its own combined rail and shipping services as against those of other transport operators who could not provide rail services.

9.3 THE TIDE TURNS: *BRONNER*

This trend of cases came however to an end with the *Tierce Ladbroke* case.[105] This involved a complaint by Ladbroke which already held a substantial share of the horse-race betting market in Belgium but claimed that its operations were being obstructed by the refusal of the racecourse operators' association to allow it radio and television commentaries on race meetings in its betting shops. The CFI held that the provisions of these services were not an essential facility since it was not an essential part of the betting business (nor was their refusal preventing the introduction of a new product or service); and moreover that the racecourse operators were not themselves engaged in competition with Ladbrokes as in running a betting business. Soon after followed the more important case of *Oscar Bronner*.[106] Here for the first time the doctrine of essential facilities was before the European Court and subject to a full analysis by Jacobs A-G, whose opinion was subsequently substantially followed by the Court. In Austria, Mediaprint was a publisher of daily papers with a market share of some 46.8 per cent.

---

[104] *Maritime Container Network* [1994] OJ L104/34: an appeal to the CFI was rejected (Case T-229/94 [1997] ECR II-1689: [1998] 4 CMLR 220).

[105] Case T-504/93 [1997] ECR II-923: [1997] 5 CMLR 309.

[106] Case C-7/97 [1998] ECR I-7791: [1999] 4 CMLR 112. The case should be read in conjunction with the authoritative earlier analysis of the issues set out by John Temple Lang in 'Defining Legitimate Competition: Companies' Duties to Supply Competitors and Access to Essential Facilities' [1994] Fordham Corp L Inst 245–313. See also Bergman, Case note [2000] 21 ECLR pp. 59–63.

Bronner meanwhile published a single newspaper with a share of national circulation of 3.6 per cent. Bronner claimed that access to Mediaprint's countrywide home delivery system was the only method available to it of ensuring nationwide punctual house delivery (since postal delivery was not viewed by it as an adequate alternative). Mediaprint justified its refusal to grant access to its system to Bronner on grounds that its home delivery service had been established only with its considerable investment, had little spare capacity to incorporate new publications, and moreover that Bronner did have a choice of other methods to obtain national circulation.

Jacobs A-G stressed the importance of not extending the doctrine in an undesirably wide manner. He emphasized the principle that in general it is pro-competitive (and in the consumer interest) to allow a company to retain for its own use facilities which it has developed for its own business. Otherwise, its incentive to invest in efficient facilities is reduced. The purpose of Article 82 is not to protect the position of individual competitors but to prevent the distortion of competition. To allow the doctrine of essential facilities to lead to the granting of access to such facilities might assist short-term 'static' competition but might well change the 'dynamic' long-term competition in a detrimental way through the removal of appropriate incentives to invest. Moreover, in the current case Bronner had other alternative methods of distribution even if it were uneconomic for it to set up a rival home distribution service. He feared that too broad a definition of the doctrine would leave both the Commission and courts involved in widespread regulation of prices and conditions.

In a relatively short judgment the ECJ agreed with the substance of the Advocate General's opinion. Newspapers could be distributed by post or through sales in shops and kiosks, and it was for Bronner to prove that (as it had not) it was not economically viable for a rival home delivery scheme to be set up with a circulation comparable to that of the Mediaprint system. In other words, the main limitation to a broad use of the doctrine of essential facilities set out in *Bronner* comes through the requirement of *indispensability*—a well-known criterion in cases concerning refusals to grant access to intellectual property rights like *IMS*. Only if there are no alternatives or substitutes for the facility and it is unreasonably difficult for a competitor to replicate it, would the dominant company be obliged to grant access to it. In response to the questions raised by the Austrian Court under Article 234, the Court ruled that national courts should decide cases of this kind on the basis that the exceptional circumstances of the *Magill* case were not present.

10. REFUSAL TO SUPPLY INTEROPERABILITY INFORMATION

The Commission dealt for the first time with the refusal to supply interface or interoperability information in the context of the IBM settlement, discussed in section 7.1 of this chapter. This special form of refusal to supply refers to the information that software producers need from competitors in order to make products that can be compatible with other systems or programmes. One of the most highly publicized litigation in this area in recent times—not least because of the phenomenal fines imposed by the Commission on the dominant company—has been the *Microsoft* saga. There, Microsoft was accused, inter alia, of abusing its position of dominance through its refusal to disclose interoperability information to competitors which needed it to create workgroup servers compatible with Microsoft Windows' desktops and servers operating systems. After a lengthy investigation, the Commission issued a decision which found Microsoft in breach of Article 82 EC and ordered the company to license the interoperability information to its competitors.[107] Microsoft appealed and the Court of First Instance delivered its much-awaited judgment in September 2007.[108]

The Court tuned its ruling to the traditional approach used in previous cases concerning refusals to supply information like *Magill* and *IMS* and upheld most of the Commission's findings. First, the Court referred expressly to the fact that the interoperability information was indispensable for Microsoft's competitors if these were to market their products viably. Secondly, it concurred with the Commission that the refusal to supply was likely to eliminate competition in the market of work group server operating systems. Thirdly, and in relation to the condition that the refusal to supply should prevent the emergence of a new product in the market for which there was potential consumer demand, the Court agreed with the Commission that Microsoft's actions limited technical development to the prejudice of consumers— even though a distinct new product was not identified. The Court observed that if Microsoft competitors were given access to the interoperability information, it would not be in their interest to merely reproduce Microsoft's operating systems but to develop products that, by virtue of their differentiation and special features would compete with Microsoft's and would offer broader consumer choice. Finally, and on the issue of objective justification, the Court rejected Microsoft's first argument that the technology in question was protected by intellectual property rights. If the mere fact of holding an intellectual property right could constitute an objective justification, then a refusal to license could never come under the scope of Article 82—a result at variance with established case law. Furthermore, the Court seemed prepared to accept that a refusal to license could be objectively justified if the dominant company could demonstrate that a significant negative effect on its incentives to innovate would ensue as a result. This was Microsoft's second line of justification. However the Court ruled, on the facts, that Microsoft had failed to demonstrate such an effect and hence concluded that the behaviour of the company could not be objectively justified.[109]

---

[107] [2005] 4 CMLR 965.   [108] Case T-201/04 [2007] 5 CMLR 11.

[109] For an excellent and critical commentary of the *Microsoft* judgment, see D. Howarth and K. McMahon, ' "Windows has Performed an Illegal Operation": The Court of First Instance Judgment in *Microsoft* v. *Commission*' [2008] 29 ECLR 117.

11. TYING PRACTICES

The essence of tying is that the supplier holds a dominant position in a 'tying' product, usually in short supply, which enables him to impose on his customer an obligation to acquire the second product, 'the tied product', at a price often above current market price, even though it is available elsewhere on better terms. There are numerous cases on this practice in United States antitrust law, where the practice is prohibited under section 3 of the Clayton Act. There are only a few exceptional circumstances in which it can be justified as normal business practice, for example where for technical reasons the tying product, perhaps a piece of equipment, will only work properly if used in association with another item.[110] Generally, however, tying arrangements are unlawful under US antitrust law, though a 'rule of reason' approach is applied to 'technological tying' when a novel product is involved. A related practice is 'full-line forcing', when the supplier refuses to supply a customer except with its full range of a particular product, e.g. a range of perfumes or paints. A quite separate practice is that of offering to sell two items together to a purchaser for a total price less than that paid for the items purchased separately, known as 'mixed bundling', which was one of the main issues in the *GE/Honeywell* merger case (see Chapter 16, fn. 77).

Example (d) in Article 82 refers to the making of contracts 'subject to acceptance by the other parties of supplementary obligations which, by their nature or according to commercial usage, have no connection with the subjects of such contracts'. It was established in *Tetrapak (No. 2)*[111] that, even in cases where the two products are closely associated, this alone will not constitute a 'natural link' justifying tying practices. Tetrapak had argued that if the product formed part of what could be regarded commercially as a 'integrated service' which customers acquired from both the filling machinery and the requisite cartons for aseptic milk products, no breach of Article 82(d) occurred. The European Court, however, confirming the ruling of the Court of First Instance, held that so long as there existed independent manufacturers who specialized in the manufacture of non-aseptic cartons, and so long as there were no intellectual property reasons preventing such manufacturers from starting to make aseptic cartons, Tetrapak had no right to treat the manufacturing equipment and the cartons as an integrated service.

Tying cases under Article 82 may also involve reliance by the owner of the 'tying' product on intellectual property rights as seen in previous sections. Tying, of course, can and often does occur without the supplier having to rely on intellectual property rights, though the practice is considerably more commercially effective if based on such a foundation, particularly where the intellectual property right has a substantial life, for example a copyright.

---

[110] As in, e.g., *US* v. *Jerrold Electronics* and *Dehydrating Process Co.* v. *A.O. Smith Corporation*, described in A. D. Neale and D. G. Goyder, *The Antitrust Laws of the USA* (3rd edn, Cambridge University Press, 1981), pp. 279–80. See also *US* v. *Microsoft*, 253 F. 3d 34 DC Circ. 2001.

[111] Case C-333/94P [1996] ECR-5951: [1997] 4 CMLR 560.

A variant of the simple refusal to deal involves the imposition on the customers of the dominant company of onerous conditions, such as exclusivity. An example of this which is a minor case but nevertheless significant, was the refusal of *Deutsche Bahn*[112] in late 2000 to respond to the request of a smaller German rail company, GVG and its partner (Swedish State Railway) for the loan of an engine suitable for operating a new rail service from Berlin to Malmo, in circumstances where Deutsche Bahn had ample engines available for loan and there was no other source of suitable traction so that without Deutsche Bahn's assistance the new service could not operate. Moreover even if the engine could be made available, Deutsche Bahn were insisting that GVG should hire Deutsche Bahn's own staff for operation of the entire service, although GVG had its own qualified staff available. The Commission issued a statement of objections with regard to Deutsche Bahn's refusal, although it was anticipated that the dispute would be settled.

Another example occurring in a different context is where Nordion,[113] a Canadian company, was the only company apart from a Belgian company (IRE) able to supply the world market for Molybdenum 99, a source of the material needed for radio-pharmaceutical material used in nuclear medicine. Nordion had contracts to supply a number of European purchasers, but insisted they entered into requirements contracts preventing them from purchasing the material from IRE or other sources. IRE complained to the Commission and after investigation Nordion agreed that the requirements contract was abusive and that it would not enforce its exclusivity clauses.

Exclusivity was also the issue in a case involving ice-cream freezer cabinets which arose from the attempt by Masterfoods, a subsidiary of Mars, to contest the practice of Unilever and its subsidiary Van den Bergh Foods to lease out freezer cabinets in Ireland only on condition that they were used exclusively for Unilever icecream. The Commission ruled[114] that the use of such exclusivity clauses by a dominant company was abusive, a conclusion that was subsequently upheld by the Court of First Instance.[115]

In more recent times, abusive tying has been considered again in the *Microsoft* case. There, the Commission took the view that by tying the Windows Media Player with the Windows PC operating system, Microsoft had breached Article 82 EC. The Court upheld the Commission's analysis, which included the enumeration of four factors that determine the abusive nature of a tying practice. First, the undertaking should have a position of dominance in the market for the tying product. Secondly, the tying and the tied product should constitute separate markets. Thirdly, consumers should not have a choice to obtain the tying product without the tied product. Finally, the practice should foreclose competition. On the facts, all these conditions were found to be satisfied. It was clear that Microsoft had a dominant position in the tying market (PC operating systems); that there was separate consumer demand for media players (the tied product); that consumers were unable to acquire the Windows operating

---

[112] IP/01/1415 15 October 2001.   [113] Annual Report (1998) at para. 74: [1998] 5 CLMR 142.
[114] [1998] OJ L246/1: [1998] 5 CMLR 530.
[115] Case T-65/98 [2003] ECR II-4653: [2004] 4 CMLR 14.

system without the Windows Media Player and that the bundling practice would lead to a weakening of competition. Furthermore, Microsoft was unable to provide any objective justification for the tying practice. This kind of analysis is very similar to the one provided in the 2005 Discussion Paper of DG Competition on exclusionary abuses.[116]

12.   OTHER FORMS OF ABUSIVE CONDUCT

12.1   ACQUISITIONS BY DOMINANT COMPANIES

Apart from the principal forms of abuse there are a number of other miscellaneous examples which have been the subject of Commission decisions (formal and informal) and which illustrate the inherent flexibility and wide range of application of the Article.

The first example has to be the well-known case of *Continental Can*, the facts of which are set out in Chapter 16.[117] At the time of the case there was no European Community Merger Regulation (ECMR) in existence, but nevertheless the Commission became concerned that in some circumstances a company with existing dominance could further abuse it, not by any of those abuses involving pricing or refusals to deal, but simply by acquiring other undertakings in the same market. This would enable it to have additional market power and leverage over its competitors. There was no need for the Commission to prove, said the European Court, that the increase in dominance brought about by the merger would necessarily lead, as a matter of causation, to any particular abuse being introduced; an increase in market share alone would be sufficient in these circumstances to constitute abuse.

This approach may well today seem unduly harsh, given the substantive criteria laid down in Article 2 of the EC Merger Regulation,[118] requiring that the merger must have the result of 'significantly impeding' competition in the Common Market. The decision is however a reminder that, had no merger regulation ever been adopted, Article 82 might well have been developed through Commission and Court jurisprudence along lines possibly even more stringent than those contained in the Merger Regulation, even if this is now an argument that is of hypothetical rather than practical significance.

Nor is the reach of Article 82 limited to the acquisition of majority control. It is clear from the *BAT/Reynolds*[119] case (also dealt with in Chapter 16) that the abuse may consist of the acquisition even of minority control provided it gives the acquirers some influence on the commercial policy of the target. The existence of well-established systems of both Community and Member State merger control make it unlikely that in practice Article 82 will be used in the context of acquisitions.

---

[116] At para. 183.   [117] See section 1.2.
[118] See Reg. 139/2004, [2004] OJ L24/1.   [119] See Ch. 16, section 1.4.

12.2 IMPOSITION OF UNREASONABLE TERMS

Article 82(a) states that the imposition of unreasonable terms and conditions, whether directly or indirectly, is an abuse. This has been of particular relevance to the Commission's approach to national schemes for encouraging the recycling of packaging waste. The 2001 Annual Report sets out some of the principles which it has applied in recent cases, notably that of the *German Green Dot Scheme (DSD)*.[120] Under German laws, DSD operated a nation-wide collection scheme, under which undertakings paid DSD a licence fee and were thereby authorized to place a 'green dot' on their packaging. DSD then agreed to collect this on its behalf. DSD held 82 per cent of the national market for organizations authorized to carry out such services in return for a fee. The term of the licence fee required payment to DSD for every package bearing the green dot and was not limited to those packages which were actually collected by DSD. This restriction meant that existing barriers to entry to market were raised even higher, and provided a disincentive to licensees to make their own disposal arrangements for part at least of their packaging waste. No commercial justification was shown for the clause and DSD was required by the Commission to replace these arrangements with a contract under which the fee was calculated by reference to packaging waste actually collected by DSD.[121]

12.3 NATIONALITY DISCRIMINATION

Discrimination on the grounds of nationality is of course forbidden under Article 12 (formerly Article 6) of the Treaty but may also be treated as an abusive practice under the Article 82. The *GVL* case has already been referred to in the section on collecting societies, as an example of discrimination on grounds of nationality by the German collecting society. In *1998 Football World Cup*[122] a notional fine of €1,000 was imposed on the French organizers of ticketing arrangements for the World Cup, for giving preference in the allocation of tickets to those members of the public able to provide an address in France, and for imposing unfair conditions on football supporters in other EEA countries, under which their applications for tickets could only be made through their own national associations (which had far fewer tickets to distribute). Likewise in the *Corsica Ferries* case[123] tariffs set for the pilot service provided to ships had favoured those provided for ships of a particular nationality, a tendency also common to the

---

[120] [2001] OJ L166/1: [2001] 5 CMLR 609. In *Alsatel* (fn. 25, Ch. 13) the terms of the rental agreement for telephone equipment was likewise held abusive because of the penalty imposed on the hirer, if it sought to extend the equipment, was excessive.

[121] The Commission adopted two decisions in this case: one dealing with the Art. 81 aspects ([2001] OJ L319/1) and another one dealing with the Art. 82 aspects of the case ([2001] OJ L166/1). These decisions were subsequently upheld by the Court of First Instance in Cases T-289/01 and T-151/01, respectively, judgment of 24 May 2007 (not yet reported).

[122] [2000] OJ L5/55: [2000] 4 CMLR 963.

[123] Case C-18/93 [1994] ECR I-1783 ('the *Corsica Ferries (No. 1)* case'). See Ch. 21, p. 565.

numerous cases already referred to in Section 4.4 above with regard to landing fees at airports in certain Member States.

12.4 ABUSE OF LEGAL PROCEEDINGS

In the *Hilti* case it was held that a dominant company which sought to obtain in respect of a licence required to be granted under national patent law requirements, a royalty six times that finally awarded by an independent expert was itself abusive. Moreover, even the bringing of legal proceedings can itself in certain situations be abusive. In *ITT Promedia* v. *Commission*,[124] the Court of First Instance upheld the Commission ruling, following a dispute in Belgium over the right to publish telephone directories, that the bringing of legal proceedings could be abusive. In this case Belgacom had originally held a State monopoly for their publication but this had been abolished by statute in 1994. ITT Promedia decided to enter the market and sued Belgacom for failing to provide it with subscriber data needed for compilation of its directory. This claim was settled but Belgacom then issued counter proceedings in connection with an earlier agreement with ITT for the supply of other subscriber data to Belgacom. ITT Promedia complained to the Commission that Belgacom by its counterclaim was seeking to abuse its dominant position so as to drive ITT from the Belgian market. The Commission and the Court of First Instance both rejected ITT's claim but stated the bringing of litigation could be abusive if:

(1) the legal action could not reasonably be characterized as an attempt to establish the bona fide rights of the dominant company and

(2) if it had been conceived in the framework of a plan whose goal was to eliminate competition to the dominant company.

FURTHER READING

A. ALBORS-LLORENS, 'The Role of Objective Justification and Efficiencies in the Application of Article 82 EC' [2007] 44 CMLRev 1727.

W. BISHOP, 'Price Discrimination under Article 86: Political Economy in the European Court' [1981] 66 MLR 282.

A. CAPOBIANCO, 'The Essential Facilities Doctrine: Similarities and Differences between American and European Approaches' [2001] 26 ELRev 548.

D. S. EVANS and A. J. PADILLA, 'Tying under Article 82 and the *Microsoft* decision' [2004] 27 World Comp 503.

I. FORRESTER, 'Article 82: Remedies in Search of Theories' [2004] Fordham Corp L Inst Ch. 10.

E. FOX, 'What is Harm to Competition? Exclusionary Practices and Anti-Competitive Effect' [2002] Antitrust Law Journal 371.

---

[124] Case T-111/96 [1998] ECR I-2937: [1998] 5 CMLR 491.

D. HOWARTH and K. MCMAHON, '"Windows has Performed an Illegal Operation": The Court of First Instance's Judgment in *Microsoft* v. *Commission*' [2008] 29 ECLR 117.

A. JONES, 'Distinguishing Predatory Prices from Competitive Ones' [1995] EIPR 252.

U. MÜLLER and A. RODENHAUSEN, 'The Rise and Fall of the Essential Facilities Doctrine' [2008] 29 ECLR 310.

O. ODUDU, '*British Airways plc.* v. *Commission*' [2007] 44 CMLRev 1763.

D. RIDYARD, 'Essential Facilities and the Obligation to Supply Competitors' [1996] ECLR 438.

B. SHER, 'Price Discounts and Michelin II: What Goes Around, Comes Around' [2002] ECLR 482.

B. SHER, 'The Last of the Steam-Powered Trains: Modernising Article 82' [2004] ECLR 243.

C. STOTHERS, 'Refusal to Supply as an Abuse of Dominant Position: Essential Facilities in the European Union' [2001] ECLR 256.

J. TEMPLE LANG and R. O'DONOGHUE, 'Defining Legitimate Competition: How to Clarify Pricing Abuses under Article 82 EC' [2002] 26 Fordham ILJ 83.

15

ARTICLE 82: ITS RELATIONSHIP WITH ARTICLE 81

1. THEIR COMMON FEATURES AND DIFFERENCES

1.1 SIX DISTINCTIONS BETWEEN THE ARTICLES

The case law of the European Court and of the Court of First Instance has clarified the meanings of both these Articles in their application to a wealth of differing circumstances and sectors. The great majority of cases have been concerned with one rather than both Articles, but in some decisions the relationship of the Articles to each other has been a central feature.

No account of EC competition law should disregard the important interaction between these two Articles. At first sight the possibility that such interaction could be significant might seem remote. Although their drafting has some shared characteristics, their individual scope and purpose appear to be mutually exclusive; whereas Article 81 prohibits agreements or concerted practices between two or more undertakings, the primary target under Article 82 is action by a single undertaking abusing its market dominance, without the need to prove any agreement or concerted practice involving another undertaking. One of the main problems encountered by the Commission in enforcing Article 81 is proving the existence of the relevant agreement or concerted practice between two or more undertakings in the absence of unequivocal written evidence. This problem of identification does not arise under Article 82.

Five further important distinctions between the Articles should be noted:

(1) Since it is necessary under the terms of Article 82 to establish that the abuse occurred in a market comprising a substantial part of the Common Market, the chief difficulty in such cases (rather than proof of an agreement or concerted practice) is to define accurately the relevant geographic and product markets to which the dominance applies. Such dominance must be either over the entire Common Market or over a single Member State or group of Member States, or possibly a substantial part of a single Member State. By contrast, under Article 81, although the Commission must still carry out economic analysis to identify the markets where the agreements or practices have their effect, their delineation is normally less critical to the outcome

of the case, especially where they have as their *object* the restriction of competition, as opposed to *effects* cases.

(2)   Article 82 provides no sanctions of voidness for illegality against the prohibited conduct, for there is no equivalent of Article 81(2). On the other hand, since Article 82 is directly enforceable in the courts of Member States (confirmed by the 1974 European Court decision in *Belgian Radio and Television* v. *SABAM*[1]) the offending clauses in any contractual provision imposed by way of abuse may be declared void and unenforceable by national courts against contracting parties. Moreover, *Magill*[2] shows that a compulsory licence may be ordered against the dominant company found to have abused its position by refusal to grant one. In *Tetrapak (No. 2)*[3] sweeping remedies were allowed to its customers: the company was required to supply any of them through the Tetrapak subsidiary which the customer chose and at the price made available generally. This was combined with a prohibition against Tetrapak refusing orders from dealers and a requirement upon it that carton discounts be granted solely on the basis of quantities ordered.

(3)   Since the prohibited action is an 'abuse' of existing market power, logically there can be no exceptions of the kind available under the 'four conditions' contained in Article 81(3). If the dominant company wishes to raise arguments of the kind considered by DG Comp when reviewing the application of these four conditions, it will have to do so by contesting the Commission's claims that the acts which it admits to performing are an 'abuse', and establishing that they are no more than the normal use of its economic strength within the boundaries of legitimate competition, or justified on other grounds. As seen in Chapter 14, a reasoning based on objective justification and proportionality has been developed in some Article 82 EC cases in order to infuse a measure of flexibility to the prohibition set out in that provision. However, whilst there is a right in 'refusal to deal' cases, for example, to rely on 'commercial justification' as a defence, this is considerably more limited in scope than the exemptions made available under Article 81(3).[4] The same would be true of any attempt by a dominant company to rely on the doctrine of proportionality to defend a response to strategic moves by a non-dominant competitor.

---

[1]   Case 127/73 [1974] ECR 51 (the Court's judgment dealing with the direct effect in national courts of Art. 82) and 313 (the Court's judgment dealing with the issue of whether SABAM was exploiting its dominant position as a copyright authority in Belgium): [1974] 2 CMLR 238 is a consolidated report of both judgments.

[2]   Ch. 14, pp. 344–8.

[3]   See fn. 30, Ch. 13 The availability of damages as a remedy under Arts. 81–2 is considered in Ch. 20.

[4]   Only the 2005 Discussion Paper of DG Competition considers systematically and in detail three possible heads of justification for abusive behaviour: the existence of an objective and external justifying cause (referred in the Discussion Paper as an 'objective necessity defence'); the protection of the legitimate commercial interests of the dominant company and the efficiency defence. The last head of justification applies in cases where ostensibly abusive behaviour may be justified by the efficiencies it produces. It is noteworthy that in considering these efficiencies, the Discussion Paper outlines conditions very similar to those listed in Art. 81(3) EC. See also the discussion on objective justification and proportionality in Ch. 14, section 6.4.

(4) Whilst a finding of a breach of Article 81 will necessarily involve some restriction of competition, a breach of Article 82 can occur when the abuse of dominance is simply 'exploitative', i.e. an advantage obtained for the dominant company at the expense of the consumer without any effect on the competitive process or the structure of the market in which the dominant company operates.

(5) Under Article 81, with an agreement or concerted practice either an 'object' to restrict competition or an appreciable 'effect' on competition must be shown. By contrast, if a dominant enterprise is alleged to have committed abuse the focus normally is on the action of that dominant company (whether it affects the structure of competition in the market or is exploitative of consumers), whether or not the dominant company showed intent to restrict competition by its actions or otherwise to breach the Article.

1.2 THREE SIMILARITIES BETWEEN THE ARTICLES

Notwithstanding these basic differences between the two Articles, their similarities in both language and position within the overall scheme of the Treaty are significant. Article 83 (which provided the legal basis for Regulation 17/62 and for the current enforcement Regulation 1/2003) requires the Council to adopt regulations or directives to give effect to the principles set out in both Articles. Article 84, dealing with the interim obligations of Member States pending adoption of such Regulation, also refers to both Articles. Moreover, Article 85 obliged the Commission as soon as it took up its duties to ensure the application of the principles laid down in both Articles. Regulation 1/2003 therefore applies to both Articles, and given that the same procedural powers are available to the Commission in Article 82 cases as in Article 81 cases, its powers to conduct investigations under Articles 20 and 21 of Regulation 1/2003 and the range of sanctions available, including penalties, fines, and termination of prohibited conduct, are therefore the same.

Three other important substantive similarities should be noted:

(1) In both cases the conduct challenged must be such as to 'affect trade between Member States'. Accordingly, the recent 2004 Commission Guidelines on the Notion of Effect on Trade provide guidance on the interpretation of this requirement for both Article 81 and 82 cases.[5]

(2) The examples of abusive conduct given in 82(a) to (d) include examples identical, or at least very similar, to those referred to under Article 81 as the subject matter of prohibited agreements or concerted practices. Only (c) in Article 81 ('the sharing of markets or sources of supply') is omitted from Article 82, since for that 'sharing' two or more undertakings must be involved. The types of conduct referred to are simply examples; the width of the definition of those agreements or concerted practices which have as their object or effect the prevention, restriction, or distortion of competition

---

[5] See Ch. 7, Section 1.3.

on one hand, and the definition of abusive conduct on the other, is not limited in either case by the nature of the examples set out. In *Gottrup Klim* v. *DLG*[6] the European Court held that the test for whether a provision in the rules of an agricultural cooperative prohibiting its members from participating in other cooperatives in direct competition with it was in breach of Article 81(1) or Article 82 (if it had a dominant position) was the same, namely whether it was limited to what was necessary to ensure that the cooperative could function properly.

(3) The scope of Article 82 is not limited to abuses by single corporate groups. It can be utilized in the case of abuse 'by one or more undertakings' so that, as with Article 81, relationships between undertakings may concern the Commission in both cases, although normally these are more important in Article 81 cases. It was emphasized in the judgment of the European Court in *Compagnie Maritime Belge*[7] that the same conduct or practices engaged in by more than one undertaking can both involve a breach of Article 81 and of Article 82; the language of the court was as follows: 'it is clear from the very wording of Article [81] and Article [82] that the same practices may give rise to an infringement of both provisions. Simultaneous application of Articles [81] and [82] of the Treaty cannot be ruled out a priori.' Fennelly A-G in his opinion had reached the same conclusion in different words 'Articles [81] and [82] do not exist in watertight compartments.' However, and as discussed in section 2.1 of this chapter, the Court of First Instance was careful to emphasize in *Italian Flat Glass*[8] that the Commission must not simply 'recycle' the facts that constitute an infringement of Article 81 EC in order to find that the practice in question also constitutes a breach of Article 82 EC. In other words, it is necessary to show that the facts give rise to two *separate* infringements: one of Article 81 EC and another of Article 82 EC. Cases involving exclusivity obligations described in section 1.3 of this chapter provide sound examples of concurrent breaches of the two provisions.

1.3 ISSUES OF EXCLUSIVITY INVOLVING BOTH ARTICLES

Cases involving exclusivity obligations can raise closely linked issues involving both Articles. In *Almelo*[9] the European Court had to advise a Dutch court under Article 234 on a contract between SEP, a consortium of electrical generators, and Almelo, a local distributor, under which Almelo was required to obtain all its electricity from SEP and was banned from importing it from sources outside the Netherlands. The Court ruled that both Article 81 and 82 applied to the exclusivity requirements imposed on Almelo by the agreement, given the dominant position of SEP in the Dutch market for electricity generation.

The two Articles were also well entwined in the *Masterfoods* saga (considered also in Chapter 19). The exclusivity in this case related to the supply by Unilever (through

---

[6] Case C-250/92 [1994] ECR I-5641: [1996] 4 CMLR 191.   [7] Ch. 14, fn. 16 and p. 321.
[8] Cases T-68, 77–78/89 [1992] ECR I-1403 [1992] 5 CMLR 302 at para. 360 of the judgment.
[9] Case C-393/92 [1994] ECR I-1477.

its Irish subsidiary Van den Bergh Foods), of ice-cream freezer cabinets to small retail outlets in Ireland. These outlets only normally had room for a single freezer and therefore it was not practical for them to have freezers for other makes of impulse ice cream. The freezer cabinets, in which Unilever retained ownership, were supplied free of charge or at a nominal rent provided they were used *exclusively* for Unilever ice creams. A new entrant to the Irish market, Mars, through its subsidiary, Masterfoods, challenged the agreements under both Articles. The Irish Supreme Court held in favour of Van den Bergh, but Mars appealed in respect of both Articles to the Irish Supreme Court and also referred the dispute to the Commission. After considerable delay, whilst the Commission sought to resolve the dispute by negotiation, a Commission decision[10] was eventually issued in 1998 which held that the exclusive supply arrangements for these ice-cream freezers in Ireland constituted a breach of both Articles. The Commission decision was later upheld by the Court of First Instance, which found that the non-compete clause contained in the distribution arrangements was in breach of Article 81(1) and did not meet the conditions for exemption in Article 81(3).[11] Furthermore, the Court agreed with the Commission's analysis that Van den Bergh had a position of dominance in the relevant market and that the exclusivity clause had, in fact, the effect of preventing retailers from selling other brands of ice cream and of precluding competing manufacturers from gaining access to the market. As a result, Van den Bergh had also abused its position of dominance in the market.

2. CASE LAW ON THE RELATIONSHIP BETWEEN ARTICLE 81 AND 82 EC

2.1 *CONTINENTAL CAN* AND *ITALIAN FLAT GLASS*—COLLECTIVE DOMINANCE EMERGES AS A CONCEPT

The first opportunity for the European Court to comment on the relationship between the Articles came in the *Continental Can* case. As the summary of the case in Chapter 16 indicates,[12] the Court emphasized that both Articles had been included in the Treaty for the same reason: to ensure that both Article 2, and Article 3(1)(g) could be implemented. They should be interpreted in a purposive way to ensure that the implementation of one Article did not frustrate the purposes of the other. The important result of the approach in this case was to provide the Commission with jurisdiction over those mergers entered into by companies already holding a dominant position. This jurisdiction did not prove of great value to the Commission in practice and, as explained in Chapter 16, was rendered less important by the introduction of the first EC Merger

---

[10] [1998] OJ L246/1: [1998] 5 CMLR 530.
[11] Case T-65/98 *Vand den Bergh Foods* v. *Commission* [2003] ECR II-4653: [2004] 4 CMLR 1.
[12] See Ch. 16, pp. 385–7.

Regulation, which entered into force in 1990.[13] The long-term result of the *Continental Can* case, however, has been to make it more likely that Article 81 and Article 82 will be treated as two parts of a whole (or as two sides of the same coin) rather than as largely unrelated.

Whilst in the great majority of cases proceedings brought by the European Commission, or by parties in national courts, relate to one or other of the Articles, Article 82 does expressly refer to the possibility of abuses being practised by more than one undertaking, often referred to as 'joint' or 'collective' dominance. If this occurs, and there is also some form of agreement or concerted practice between the parties, then as already mentioned there could be a breach of both Articles. In the majority of cases where the Commission have alleged a horizontal cartel against a group of companies with an aggregate market share of a sufficient level for market dominance to be alleged, the Commission has not sought to raise Article 82 arguments, contenting itself with proceedings under Article 81. However, in *Italian Flat Glass*,[14] the Commission sought to show that it was legally possible to link agreements and concerted practices referred to under Article 81 to the joint abuse of dominant position referred to in Article 82. It undoubtedly felt that a decision in its favour in this area would provide an important weapon to enable it to deal with oligopolistic markets, which always present the greatest problem for competition authorities. Oligopolists often manage to adjust their relationships with competitors to mutual advantage without the need to enter into agreements or concerted practices because oligopolies are naturally transparent markets. To bring them collectively within the scope of Article 82 for the purposes of imposing a fine or preventing abusive conduct is a much more difficult substantive task for the Commission.

Against this background the facts in *Italian Glass* might at first sight have appeared to provide an encouraging scenario. Three companies supplied glass in Italy, both to the car industry (its primary customer) and to non-automotive users, principally the construction and furnishing industries. These three major companies between them held 95 per cent of the car-industry glass market and 79 per cent of the non-automotive market, and it was alleged that the arrangements they had made for the exchange of different categories of product were of such scope and permanence as to constitute 'structural' links rather than merely concerted practices of the kind normally found in Article 81 cases. The Commission imposed fines on the three companies under Article 81, but also made a separate finding that the companies were in breach of Article 82 'by abusing their collective dominant position through conduct whereby they deprived customers of the opportunity of getting suppliers to compete on prices and terms of sale, and whereby they limited outlets through the setting of quotas for automotive glass'. The Court of First Instance,[15] however, found a number of errors in the way in which the Commission had handled the case, in particular that it had given insufficient

---

[13] See Reg. 4064/89, now replaced by the current EC Merger Regulation (Reg. 139/2004 [2004] OJ L24/1).

[14] [1989] OJ L33/44: [1990] 4 CMLR 535.

[15] Cases T-68, 77, 78/89 [1992] ECR II-1403: [1992] 5 CMLR 302.

weight to the activities and market power of wholesalers in the non-automotive sector. On the main substantive issue under Article 81 the Court found on the evidence that one of the three companies, Vernante Pennitalia, had not acted in breach of Article 81 though two other companies had done so. Although the Court then went on to over-rule the Article 82 findings against all three companies, it provided a useful definition of the concept of collective dominance. The key passage in this part of the judgment reads as follows:

There is nothing in principle to prevent two or more independent economic entities from being, on a specific market, *united by such economic links* that, by virtue of that fact, together they hold a dominant position vis-à-vis the other operators on the same market. This could be the case, for example, where two or more independent undertakings jointly have, through agreements or licences, a technological lead affording them the power to behave to an appreciable extent independently of their competitors, their customers and ultimately of their consumers. However, it should be pointed out that for the purposes of establishing an infringement of Article [82], it is not sufficient...to 'recycle' the facts constituting an infringement of Article [81], deducing from them the finding that the parties to an agree-ment or to an unlawful practice jointly hold a substantial share of the market, that by virtue of that fact alone they hold a collectively dominant position, and that their unlawful behav-iour constitutes an abuse of that collectively dominant position.[16]

It followed from *Italian Flat Glass*, that for two or more companies to hold a position of joint dominance, it would be necessary for them to be *independent* undertakings that are united by certain *economic links* and able to present themselves as a common entity that can behave independently from competitive pressures in the relevant market.

2.2 THE *CMB* CASE—THE DEVELOPMENT OF COLLECTIVE DOMINANCE

Legal commentators then spent considerable time and ingenuity in seeking to inter-pret the phrase 'united by such economic links'. It is important to bear in mind that the example given by the Court of First Instance of undertakings having a techno-logical lead in a particular market as the results of agreements or licences between them was clearly not meant to be exhaustive. Some light on the proper interpret-ation of this phrase was later shed by the subsequent European Court decision in *Compagnie Maritime Belge*.[17] Under the provisions of Council Regulation 4056/86, shipping lines are allowed a block exemption for certain activities of their liner con-ferences in respect of services to or from Community ports. The regulation allows agreements concerning matters such as rate-fixing, coordination of timetables, allo-cation of sailings between members, regulation of carrying capacities for individual members, and allocation of cargo or revenue between members. Nevertheless, under

---

[16] Paras. 358, 360.
[17] Cases T-24/93 etc [1996] ECR II-1201: [1997] 4 CMLR 273; on appeal, Cases C-395 and 396/96P [2000] ECR I-1365: [2000] 4 CMLR 1076.

Article 8, if the conduct of a conference benefiting from these exemptions has effects which are incompatible with Article 82, the Commission is expressly authorized to withdraw the benefit of the block exemption from those members of the conference. Action was taken by the Commission against three liner shipping conferences, operating routes between Continental North Sea ports such as Rotterdam, and West Africa on the grounds of activities which were not covered by the Regulation. These included entering into loyalty contracts outside the scope of the Regulation with shippers and with other conferences. Members of the conferences were found by the Commission to have collectively abused their dominant position by:

(1) attempting to enforce agreements under which members of the conference had exclusive rights to ship goods on the route to Zaire

(2) making loyalty agreements with certain customers in return for lower shipping rates (a form of exclusive rebate)

(3) introducing a system of 'fighting ships' targeted at particular competitors seeking to enter the market.

These actions had been separately identified from breaches of Article 81; in the Court's view the Commission was correct to treat them under Article 82 as examples of collective dominance by the members of the conference. The Commission was also right, in the Court's view, to find that the members of the conference held a dominant position collectively as a result of their combined market share of more than 90 per cent, strengthened by other circumstances such as the support for the arrangements received from the government of Zaire, the length of time the route had been operated by the conference, and its large size, especially in relation to the size of its competitors. The members of CEWAL used their legitimate links within the framework of the authorized liner conference to participate jointly in activities which went far beyond its legitimate goals; they were thus able to present a common front to any would-be competitors and organize actions in practice equivalent to the unilateral action of a single dominant firm. In dealing with the Article 82 issues, the Court placed particular emphasis on abuses (2) and (3). These contracts provided for substantial rebates where a shipper used members of the conference for 100 per cent of their shipping requirements. If shippers did not meet this obligation, their name was put on a 'blacklist' and they received less favourable service. The members of the conference argued that loyalty arrangements are permitted specifically under Regulation 4056/86, but the Court ruled that the loyalty agreements made were not within the framework of the Regulation, and could be imposed on customers because of the high market share of CEWAL and the lack of a choice of less restrictive discount and bonus schemes.

The final finding of abuse involved the procedure of designating specific sailings by CEWAL members closest to the sailings of competitors as 'fighting ships', involving the joint setting of freight rates for these to match or under-cut the new entrants, with the sharing of any resultant trading loss or earnings between members of the conference. The Court observed that the main purpose of the 'fighting ship' system had been to remove CEWAL's only competitor on the relevant market, and this was ruled a disproportionate response to the conduct of the new entrant, even though without having achieved its objective.

This *CMB* decision seems to make clear that the agreement linking the collectively dominant parties can itself be legitimate, authorized by Community legislation, and not necessarily subject to attack under Article 81, in contrast to the allegedly anti-competitive agreements between the three Italian companies in the *Flat Glass* case which were the basis for the claim in that case of collective dominance. In view of the terms of Article 8 of Regulation 4056/86 this is not a particularly surprising finding.

The judgment of the European Court in *Compagnie Maritime Belge* was especially significant in the clarification of the expression 'economic links' which had so troubled commentators since *Italian Flat Glass*. Not only it noted that an agreement in principle exempted by a block exemption could constitute an economic link for the purposes of a finding of collective dominance—as relevant to the facts of case—but also held, at para. 45 that:

The existence of a collective dominant position may therefore flow from the nature and terms of an agreement, from the way in which it is implemented and, consequently, from the links or factors which give rise to a connection between undertakings which result from it. Nevertheless, *the existence of an agreement or of other links in law is not indispensable* to a finding of a collective dominant position; such a finding may be based *on other connecting factors* and would depend on an economic assessment and, in particular, on an assessment of the structure of the market in question. [emphasis added]

It seemed therefore that an economic link need not be an agreement or even a link in law but may arise from market structure. This statement of the Court broadened considerably the possibilities for the use of the notion of collective dominance as a tool to control oligopolies—where the natural relationship of interdependence that arises in such markets could be easily construed as an economic link.

More surprising, perhaps, is the emphasis placed by the Court of First Instance, though not emphasized by the European Court on the appeal, on the duty of proportionality on the shipping companies in respect of their 'fighting ships' scheme. Some commentators have suggested that to introduce the concept of proportionality into Article 82 is potentially dangerous, since it places the dominant company in a dilemma as to whether a particular commercial reaction to a specific competitive threat will be deemed 'proportionate'. It is said that to argue that a penal provision such as Article 82 should only apply when undertakings can clearly be shown to have acted in breach of normal competitive principles measured objectively, and that the duty to act proportionately imposes too heavy a burden upon them. The weakness in this argument is that, notwithstanding the use of the word 'objective' in *Hoffman-La Roche*, there is inevitably an important element of 'drawing the line' in assessing many aspects of potentially abusive conduct considered under the various sections of Chapter 14, for example in the essential facilities cases. It may be that the phrase 'proportionate' is less appropriate to the assessment of actions of commercial undertakings given that the doctrine derives originally from German law where its application was to legislation. If the term were changed to 'reasonable reaction' to competitor activities, this may provide a better test in a commercial context, though it is unlikely that the outcome of particular cases would be altered on this semantic basis alone.

3. THE INFLUENCE OF MERGER DECISIONS ON THE CONCEPT OF COLLECTIVE DOMINANCE

The development of the concept of collective dominance was significantly influenced by court judgments in merger cases, and not just with those specifically dealing with Article 82. Despite the absence of a direct reference to joint dominance in the first Merger Regulation (Regulation 4064/89), the European Court soon interpreted Article 2 of that regulation—which laid down the substantive test to declare the compatibility of proposed concentrations with EC law—as allowing the prohibition of mergers that contributed to the creation of a position of *collective* dominance in the Common Market or a substantial part of it.[18] Despite the clear differences between Article 82 and merger cases, the legal principles underlying the concept of collective dominance in these two quite different categories of case appear to be nevertheless the same. Proof of this is the fact that the Community judicature has made reference to the notion of collective dominance developed in merger cases when dealing with Article 82 EC cases.[19] The new EC Merger Regulation (Regulation 139/2004) has introduced a broader substantive test for concentrations (as discussed in Chapters 16 and 17) which allows for the control not only of concentrations that contribute to the creation of a position of dominance (or collective dominance) but *also* those which significantly impede competition in the Common Market. As a result, mergers that produce unilateral or non-coordinated effects can now come under the scope of the EC Merger Regulation. However, the concept of joint dominance remains a very important one in merger cases and rulings in this area are bound to continue having a cascade effect on Article 82 EC cases.

The leading cases on collective dominance under the Merger Regulation are *Kali & Salz*,[20] *Gencor*,[21] and *Airtours*;[22] details of the facts of the cases can be found in Chapters 16 and 17. The *Gencor* decision emphasized the width of the concept, which was not

---

[18] Case C-68/94 and C-30/95 *France* v. *Commission* and *Kali & Salz* [1998] ECR I-1375: [1998] 4 CMLR 829. Art. 2 of Reg. 4064/89 clearly provided that mergers that contributed to the creation or strenghtening of a position of *individual* dominance by the entity resulting from the concentration would be incompatible with EC law (see Ch. 16, Section 8.5).

[19] See for example the judgment in Case C-395 and C-396/96P *Compagnie Maritime Belge* (fn. 17 above) at para. 41 and in Case T-228/97 *Irish Sugar* v. *Commission* [1999] ECR II-2969: [1999] 5 CMLR 1300 at para. 46.

[20] Cases C-68/94 and 30/95 [1999] ECR I-1375: [1998] 4 CMLR 829.

[21] Case T-102/96 [1999] ECR II-753: [1999] 4 CMLR 971.

[22] Case T-342/99 [2002] ECR II-2585: [2002] 5 CMLR 317.

necessarily dependent upon the existence either of economic links between the parties of a structural nature or commercial agreements of any kind, a point later confirmed in *Compagnie Maritime Belge*—as discussed in Section 2.2. The essential core of this concept was held to be 'the relationship of interdependence existing between the parties to a tight oligopoly within which, in a market with the appropriate characteristics, in particular in terms of market concentration, transparency and product homogeneity, those parties are in a position to anticipate one another's behaviour and are therefore strongly encouraged to align their conduct in the market'.

The Commission's success in the *Gencor* case however was not repeated in *Airtours*. Here the Court of First Instance rejected an attempt by the Commission to broaden the concept of collective dominance so as to cover any situation of an oligopolistic nature, when it would be rational for the major participants in the relevant market (in this case the shorthaul foreign package holiday market in the United Kingdom) individually to restrict the supply of such holidays. In a decision which annulled the Commission's block on the merger, the Court laid down that there had to be three elements present if collective dominance was to be established by the Commission:

(1) Each member of a dominant oligopoly must have the ability to know how the other members are behaving so as to be able to monitor sufficiently, precisely, and quickly whether they are adopting a common policy (whether this involves price rises or capacity reductions), which means that there has to be enough transparency for this in the market.

(2) There must be an incentive to maintain tacit coordination between all the members of the oligopoly over a reasonable period of time, which means in turn that there must be an awareness by each member that any departure from the common policy by one member will provoke retaliation from the others, usually by matching any price cuts or capacity increases.

(3) It must be established that the 'foreseeable reaction' of current and future competitors, as well as those of consumers, would not jeopardize the results expected from the common policy.[23]

The outcome of the *Airtours* case may force an amendment not only to the approach in merger cases where the proposed concentration creates or strengthens a position of collective dominance but also to the Commission's 1998 Notice on access agreements

---

[23] The *Airtours* criteria are now reflected in the 2004 Guidelines on the assessment of Horizontal Mergers ([2004] OJ C31/03) at paras. 41–57) and also in the 2005 Discussion Paper on Exclusionary Abuses (at paras. 44–50). The Court of First Instance applied these criteria loosely in Case T-464/04 *Impala* v. *Commission* [2006] ECR II-2289: [2006] 5 CMLR 19, where it annulled a Commission decision that had cleared a merger on the grounds that it did not lead to the creation of a position of collective dominance. The judgment of the Court of First Instance has, however, been recently set aside by the European Court of Justice and the case referred back to the Court of First Instance (see Case C-413/06P *Bertlesmann AG and Sony Corporation of America*, Judgment of 10 July 2008, not yet reported). Essentially, the European Court has taken the view that the Court of First Instance misconstrued the legal criteria necessary to establish collective dominance.

in the telecommunications market. The Notice states that for collective dominance to apply it is sufficient if the undertakings have the kind of independence which often comes about in oligopolistic situations, without the need for any other economic links, such as co-operation agreements. After *Airtours* this statement is unquestionably too broad and requires the qualifications laid down by the Court of First Instance in that case. Furthermore, the same conclusion can be extended to Article 82 EC cases. Although *Compagnie Maritime Belge* did not make an express reference to oligopolistic interdependence as an economic link, this inference could be easily made when the Court alluded to links deriving from *market structure* in its judgment—particularly when read in conjunction with the *Gencor* decision. However, if the same limitations laid down in *Airtours* are to apply to collective dominance cases under Article 82 EC, it becomes clear that joint dominance cannot be so easily used as a mechanism to control oligopolies as previous rulings appeared to suggest.

4. COLLECTIVE DOMINANCE IN A VERTICAL RELATIONSHIP

Normally in a case of alleged collective dominance the undertakings will be in competition with each other and in a horizontal relationship. In *Irish Sugar*,[24] however, the Court of First Instance confirmed that that there is no inherent reason why collective dominance cannot exist between undertakings even when the relationship is vertical, as for example, between a patentee and its licensees or between a supplier and its distributors. Irish Sugar had itself for several years had a distributor, SDL, which was a wholly owned subsidiary of SDH. Irish Sugar held 51 per cent of the shares in SDH for several years before later acquiring the remaining 49 per cent from its owners. Over the period between 1985 and 1990, half the board of SDH were representatives of Irish Sugar but the other half represented the minority shareholders in SDH. The Irish Sugar chief executive and several of its board members were amongst those who sat on the SDL board. SDL worked closely with Irish Sugar; it was given responsibility for technical services and consumer promotions and marketing whilst the supply obligations were the responsibility of Irish Sugar. Commercial policy including the important topic of pricing and discounts was shared between the parties and SDL undertook that it would purchase all its sugar, subject only to availability, from Irish Sugar. The Court concluded that, by reason of these connecting factors which existed between those two undertakings, they had the power to adopt a common market policy in the relevant market—an essential component in the definition of collective dominance. The Court of First Instance made the finding of abuse only against Irish Sugar although both it and SDL were held to have been collectively dominant. It is however

---

[24] Case T-228/97 [1999] ECR II-2969: [1999] 5 CMLR 1300, on appeal Case C-497/99P [2001] ECR I-5333: [2001] 5 CMLR 1082.

an unsatisfactory case because of the facts cited by the Commission; it is possible that Irish Sugar actually controlled SDL at all relevant times (even when holding only 51 per cent of the shares in SDH), a situation to which the 'group economic entity' concept should have applied.

5. THE RELEVANCE OF INDIVIDUAL OR BLOCK EXEMPTIONS TO ARTICLE 82

The mere existence of an agreement which prima facie falls within the prohibition of Article 81(1), but which has received exemption and to which a dominant company is party, is clearly not going to be allowed to prevent the utilization of Article 82 by the Commission. This issue arose in the earlier *Tetrapak (No.1)* case,[25] where the Court of First Instance had to decide whether to confirm a Commission decision which raised the question, namely what should happen where the dominant company had entered into an agreement subject to Article 81(1) but within the terms of a later block exemption regulation that effectively removed the prohibition. The resolution of this potential conflict between Articles 81 and 82 was ultimately the only issue before the Court, other matters dealt with in the decision of the Commission relating to the existence of dominance and relevant markets having been conceded by Tetrapak during the hearing.

Tetrapak's argument ran along the following lines. Whilst it was admittedly dominant in relevant markets, namely the production of machinery for filling aseptic UHT milk cartons and the cartons themselves, by acquiring the benefit of an exclusive licence in favour of its competitor Liquipak through take-over it had not breached Article 82 because the agreement was in terms permitted by the then Patent Block Exemption Regulation 2349/84. Such an exemption was a 'positive' action of the Commission in terms of the *Walt Wilhelm* judgment,[26] and should not, therefore, lead to any liability under Article 82, since the Commission had in its discretion the alternative remedy of withdrawing the exemption under the terms of the block exemption regulation.

The Court of First Instance nevertheless upheld the Commission's decision that the acquisition of the licence was a breach of Article 82. It pointed out that the withdrawal of the block exemption could only operate in a prospective way, not in respect of the past. The two Articles were independent legal instruments which, within the overall scheme of the Treaty, addressed different situations. The acquisition by a company with a dominant position of an exclusive licence was not per se an Article 82 abuse, but the circumstances of the acquisition and the effect it might have on the structure of competition in the relevant market must be taken into account. The Court supported

---

[25] Case T-51/89 [1990] ECR II-309: [1991] 4 CMLR 334. The facts are more fully set out in Ch. 14, Section 7.6.

[26] Case 14/68 [1969] ECR 1: [1969] CMLR 100.

the Commission's conclusion that in this case the acquisition of the particular licence for the packaging of the aseptic milk containers not only strengthened Tetrapak's substantial existing dominance but prevented or at least delayed the entry of new competition into the market. The take-over of Liquipak was simply the means by which Tetrapak had acquired the Liquipak licences and the mere fact that the licences themselves had received a block exemption could not render inapplicable the prohibition of Article 82. The Court also pointed out that block exemptions are merely secondary legislation, being a specific application of the grounds for exemption set out in Article 81(3) to particular categories of agreement; by contrast, Article 82 is primary legislation in the Treaty, which takes precedence over such secondary legislation.

The position would differ if an individual exemption had been granted to a particular licence agreement because, if exemption had been sought for an individual agreement in this way, the Commission would have to take account of the particular circumstances in which it was made. The second negative condition of Article 81(3) itself refers to the requirement that the parties to such individual agreements shall not be afforded by it the 'possibility' even of eliminating competition for a substantial part of the relevant products. Unless these circumstances had altered by the time an Article 82 allegation was later made the earlier findings of the Commission would be relevant and taken into account. By contrast, with a block exemption there is by definition no case-by-case examination of the circumstances of the parties to those agreements and no positive assessment of the overall market situation. The benefit of block exemption is therefore different from any form of negative clearance from Article 82, which had a binding effect upon the Commission; it is not automatically held back from companies which have a dominant position, and therefore cannot take into account in advance their position on relevant markets in respect of any particular agreement.

FURTHER READING

A. ALBORS-LLORENS, 'Collective Dominance in EC Competition Law: Trojan Horse or Useful Tool?' *Cambridge Yearbook of European Legal Studies* [2003] pp. 151–72.

V. KORAH, '*Gencor v. Commission*: Collective Dominance' [1999] ECLR 337.

G. MONTI, 'The Scope of Collective Dominance under Article 82 EC' [2001] 38 CMLRev 131.

B. SUFRIN, 'Oligopolistic Markets and EC Competition Law' [1992] YEL 59.

R. WHISH, 'Collective Dominance' in D. O'Keefe and M. Andenas (eds.), *Liber Amicorum for Lord Slynn* (Kluwer, 2000).

16

MERGERS (1)

1. THE ORIGINS OF COUNCIL REGULATION 139/2004

1.1 THE NEED FOR MERGER CONTROL

Competition authorities tend to regard control over mergers and acquisitions by large and powerful companies as one of their most important priorities. Such authorities are concerned not only with the conduct of undertakings but also with the possible effects on market structures, and especially on the degree of concentration (and consequent increase in market power) which mergers may bring about in particular product and geographic markets. They naturally prefer, therefore, that such mergers are not allowed to occur without careful scrutiny of their likely effects on the competitive process: preferably before they occur, rather than afterwards. In the absence, however, of any rules for ensuring such scrutiny, two possibly undesirable consequences may occur. Undertakings which are prevented from making anti-competitive agreements with each other by the prohibition contained in Article 81(1) may simply determine that, to achieve the objectives of such agreements, they will merge their business operations into a single unit, thereby avoiding the reach of that Article: they may also, by their merger, increase the market power of their combined undertaking in a particular product or geographic market and thus reduce the scope for competition within it. Any competition authority, therefore, with inadequate substantive and procedural control over major merger proposals operates under a severe disadvantage.

Nevertheless, there seems little doubt that those responsible for drafting Articles 81 and 82 did not intend that this should give control over mergers to the Commission. Neither the actual wording of the Articles nor the evidence of those who participated in the negotiations leading up to the Treaty or in its early administration support any contrary argument. Nevertheless, concern within DG Comp over this apparent gap in its powers was felt even during its first decade of active operation when, as we have seen, it had a variety of other pressing problems to which prior attention had to be given, in particular those relating to vertical agreements. In a memorandum in 1966[1]

---

[1] 'Le problème de la concentration dans le Marché Commun', *Etudes CEE* (Series Concurrence No. 3, 24 (1966)). As a statement of principle this has now been overruled by the *Philip Morris* decision (fn. 6) and

it admitted that the concentration of undertakings following transfer of shares or assets was not covered by Article 81, which ceases to apply once the integration of two or more undertakings has gone beyond the stage of temporary assistance and cooperation to a stage of full-scale merger where both policy direction and management have been centralized in a single body. The possible utilization, therefore, of Article 82 in a suitable merger case was not overlooked by the Commission and, in spite of considerable doubts even within DG Comp itself, an opportunity arose in the early 1970s. It was then decided to seek a ruling from the European Court that Article 82 did enable the Commission to issue a decision prohibiting a merger where the merger itself strengthened pre-existing dominance in a particular market.

1.2 *CONTINENTAL CAN* AND ITS CONSEQUENCES

The case chosen for this purpose was *Continental Can*.[2] The American company of that name had acquired an 85.8 per cent holding in a German company, SLW of Brunswick. In the following year, Continental Can formed a Delaware corporation known as Europemballage Corporation which opened an office in Brussels and soon afterwards, with financial help from its parent, acquired 91.7 per cent of the shares of a Dutch company, TDV. SLW was the largest producer in Germany of packaging and metal closures whilst TDV was a leading manufacturer of packing material in Benelux. In its decision[3] prohibiting acquisition by SLW of TDV, the Commission stated that it took into account not only the market share which the Continental Can group would as the result of the mergers control in Germany and Benelux, but also the group's advantages over its competitors resulting from its size and economic, financial, and technological importance. In the view of the Commission, all these factors gave the company room for independent action, conferring on it, at least in respect of the German market, a dominant position for lightweight containers for preserved meats, fish and shellfish as well as in respect of the market for metal closures.

The Court held in a relatively brief judgment that the factual evidence failed to support the Commission's conclusion that Continental Can held a dominant position in the German market. In simply assigning tin cans for fish and tin cans for meat to separate markets and assuming that a high market share within each area involved market power, the Commission had failed to consider the possibility and ability of producers shifting from the manufacture of one product to another, e.g. from fish cans to meat cans or vice versa. It also failed to consider whether large buyers would decide to manufacture their own cans if the price of Continental's cans was too high. The Commission had not prepared adequate evidence relating to the suitability of other types of containers or the probable entry by other companies into the markets if

inevitably, therefore, this part of Ch. 16 deals with Art. 81 as well as with Art. 82. The position under the ECSC Treaty was, of course, different (see Ch. 3, p. 29).

[2] Case 6/72 *Europemballage and Continental Can* v. *Commission* [1973] ECR 215: CMLR 199. On the question of the basis for the Commission's jurisdiction over this case, see Ch. 22.

[3] [1972] CMLR D11.

Continental Can utilized their market dominance to raise prices. Its market analysis was simply insufficient to support its conclusion.

Nevertheless, whilst the Commission suffered a defeat on the facts, on the main issue of principle it gained a surprising victory. The ECJ chose to interpret Article 82 in a purposive way to give effect to the spirit of the Treaty of Rome and to ensure consistency between Articles 81 and 82. The Court referred to the then terms of Article 3(f)[4] and concluded that, as the result of it providing for the institution of a 'system' to protect competition within the Common Market from distortion, there was an underlying principle that competition must not be eliminated. Its existence was also supported by the principles in Article 2 relating to the harmonious development of economic activities. Articles 81 and 82 had, therefore, been included in order to preserve the principles set out in these two Articles. It was not to be supposed (said the Court) that the Treaty should in Article 81 prohibit certain agreements, decisions, and concerted practices that might restrict but would not eliminate competition, while at the same time allowing Article 82 to permit already dominant undertakings, simply by making further acquisitions, to strengthen their position to the extent that any serious possibility of competition in the relevant market would be eliminated. Such a diversity of legal treatment could open a breach in the whole structure of competition law that would jeopardize the proper functioning of the Common Market. Articles 81 and 82 had to be interpreted in a manner which reflected the fact that they were both inserted to achieve the same ends, those set out in Articles 2 and 3(f).

The Court went on to say that Article 82 applied not only to practices directly prejudicing consumers, but also to those that prejudiced consumers indirectly through interference in the structure of markets. It referred to the risk that, if individual undertakings obtained a sufficiently powerful position in markets, all those who remained would become dependent on the dominant undertaking with regard to their market behaviour. There was no need for the Commission to show any cause or connection between the dominant position and the abuse of it. An increase in market share might alone be sufficient to constitute an abuse.

There is perhaps no better example of the difference between the approach adopted by the European Court to the interpretation of the Treaty of Rome and that which would have been adopted by any English court than this decision, whose outcome was a surprise to many, although received gratefully by the Commission. Unfortunately, though the Commission won the victory relating to the applicability of Article 82 to mergers by companies already holding a dominant position which, therefore, gave it in principle better standing for the future on such issues, the task of winning the subsequent campaign to obtain effective substantive and procedural control over mergers proved more difficult.

The relationship between the *Continental Can* decision and the scope and content of the first draft of the Merger Regulation issued a few months after the decision of the Court (at the request of Member States) was therefore more psychological than

---

[4] Now 3(1)(g) since the Treaty of Maastricht.

substantive. A Council Regulation was essential to merger control, because the use of Article 82 simply on the basis of the *Continental Can* decision would not have provided the Commission with the desired ability to control the creation of a new dominant position as opposed to the ability to prevent an undertaking with an existing dominant position from strengthening it still further, as under the rather unusual facts of *Continental Can*. Such a Regulation was also essential to make pre-notification of major mergers mandatory, so that any necessary powers of the Commission could be exercised before the merger took place rather than being employed in the always more difficult and sensitive task of unscrambling it after completion. Moreover, interim measures (subsequently adopted in some Article 81 and 82 cases) were no real substitute for a regulation containing full procedural powers to control mergers, equivalent to those already provided for other competition cases.

1.3 EARLY DRAFTS OF THE MERGER REGULATION

The original 1973 draft that appeared shortly after *Continental Can* provided a basic scheme of control, though significantly it refers not to Article 82 but to Article 308 of the Treaty as the authority for its enactment.[5] The lengthy recitals refer to the importance of preventing concentration in markets within the Community. For this reason, prior notification of major mergers over a specified threshold was essential. The only mergers to be excluded from its control would be those between undertakings with a joint turnover of less than 200 million units of account and where the market share of goods or services affected would in no Member State exceed 25 per cent. This was, of course, an extremely low threshold. Article 1 of the Regulation, in terms strongly reminiscent of Article 81, stated that control would apply over all transactions that had the direct or indirect effect of conferring power on the combined undertaking to hinder effective competition. It also provided that consideration should be given to exempting those mergers 'indispensable to the attainment of an objective which is given priority treatment in the common interest of the Community'. The threshold for compulsory notification was set at 1,000 million units of account, calculated on the joint turnover of the undertakings, unless the target undertaking had a turnover of less than 30 million units of account. Decisions had to be rendered within a time limit of twelve months and were subject to review by the Court, just as any other decision of the Commission. The Regulation would apply to both agreed and contested mergers, since it applied to 'transactions' as well as to 'agreements'.

With hindsight, the scope of the proposed new Regulation was undoubtedly too broad. It would have brought within its scope a very large number of mergers, far more than the staff of DG Comp (either in 1973 or even in their increased numbers of later years) could have dealt with within the time limits proposed, save perhaps on

---

[5] Article 308 reads: 'If action by the Community should prove necessary to attain...one of the objectives of the Community and this Treaty has not provided the necessary powers, the Council shall, acting unanimously on a proposal from the Commission and after consulting the Assembly, take the appropriate measures.'

what would have been a demonstrably inadequate basis. In any case, political opposition by Member States in the Council ensured that the original 1973 Regulation was not adopted. Subsequent realization within the Commission that the scope of the draft Regulation would need to be modified so as to affect only a smaller proportion of mergers led to new drafts of the Regulation being put forward to the Council in 1982, 1984, and 1986, but even these initially failed to overcome the political deadlock. Important changes in later drafts included a reference to the fact that competition had to be shown to be limited at Community level (rather than Member State level) before the Commission could intervene. Unless the market share in the goods or services covered by the merger exceeded 20 per cent either in the entire Common Market or in a substantial part of it, the merger was to be deemed compatible with the provisions of the Treaty, it being presumed that the merger was incapable of hindering effective competition. The joint turnover jurisdictional threshold was raised from 200 million to 500 million, and subsequently to 750 million ECU.

1.4 THE *PHILIP MORRIS* CASE

Commissioner Sutherland, responsible at the time for competition policy, indicated publicly on a number of occasions from 1985 onwards that failure by Member States to break the deadlock would leave the Commission no alternative but to rely on Articles 81 and 82 for the purposes of merger control. Whilst initial reactions by Member States to this suggestion were sceptical, given the many substantive and procedural difficulties involved, the *Philip Morris* judgment[6] of the European Court in November 1987 caused them to realize that control based on a new Regulation might be far better than the unpredictable consequences of that case.

The case involved an agreement by Philip Morris to acquire a 30 per cent interest in its competitor, cigarette manufacturer Rothmans, from its South African owners, Rembrandt, though the voting rights to be obtained by Philip Morris were limited to 24.9 per cent. Both groups kept the right of first refusal should the other wish to sell, and there were other arrangements to ensure that Philip Morris had neither board representation nor managerial influence over Rothmans. The Commission had given exemption to these proposals, and the Court upheld its decision in the face of a challenge by two other tobacco companies, BAT and R. J. Reynolds. It ruled that the acquisition of an equity interest in a competitor did not of itself restrict competition, but might serve as an instrument to that end. Article 81 would then become applicable to the relevant agreement.

The central section of the Court's judgment on this legal issue reads as follows:

That will be true in particular where, by the acquisition of a shareholding or through subsidiary clauses in the agreement, the investing company obtains legal or *de facto* control of the commercial conduct of the other company or where the agreement provides for

---

[6] Cases 142 and 156/84 *BAT and R. J. Reynolds* v. *Commission and Philip Morris* [1987] ECR 4487: [1988] 4 CMLR 24.

commercial co-operation between the companies or creates a structure likely to be used for such co-operation. That may also be the case where the agreement gives the investing company the possibility of reinforcing its position at a later stage and taking effective control of the other company.[7]

1.5 FINAL NEGOTIATIONS FOR THE REGULATION

The decision, though welcome to the Commission, nevertheless left many problems for it. These included the effect of Article 81(2) on the agreement, the lack of time limits or jurisdictional thresholds, and uncertainty as to the exact range of mergers affected. However, perhaps the most important outcome of the case from the Commission's viewpoint was its effect in concentrating the minds of the more unwilling Member States, now fearful of the use of the *Philip Morris* precedent to attack mergers under Article 81, on the terms of the draft Regulation.

In March 1988 a new draft Regulation was therefore presented to the Council, which for the first time included some of the main features of the Merger Regulation that would ultimately be adopted. The criteria for assessment also included for the first time language familiar from both Articles 81 and 82 of 'compatibility' with the Common Market. A merger that gave rise to or strengthened a dominant position in the Common Market or a substantial part of it would not be regarded as compatible. A long list of factors relating to the competitive structure of relevant markets was set out for consideration in connection with the assessment of compatibility. The new threshold for world turnover was 1,000 million ECU, with a minimum of 50 million ECU Community turnover for the target company.

These new proposals seemed to break the deadlock, and the arrival of Sir Leon Brittan as the new Commissioner with responsibility, inter alia, for competition brought new impetus. Early in 1989 the Commission responded to Member State criticisms by raising the thresholds for jurisdiction considerably, namely to 5 billion ECU for aggregate world turnover and to 250 million ECU aggregate Community turnover for each of at least two companies involved (with the intention that both figures should be reduced later after experience of the operation of the Regulation). In addition, the exception for mergers between undertakings both having a substantial proportion of their Community turnover in the same Member State was reduced from three-quarters to two-thirds.

When France took over the presidency of the Council at the end of June 1989, it made clear that it regarded agreement on the final text of the Regulation as being a high priority; the succeeding six months of its presidency saw the final difficult stage of the negotiations edge forward to completion. An important difference lay between those Member States that wanted the criteria expressly limited to competition issues (especially Germany and the United Kingdom) and those, such as France, which wanted social and industrial policy issues to remain among the criteria that could be applied.

[7] Paras. 38–9.

Both Germany and the United Kingdom also sought to keep the right of national competition authorities to retain jurisdiction in those cases where major national interests and markets were involved. On the other hand, the majority of Member States, as well as industrial and commercial interests within them, were attracted by the possibility of a 'one-stop shop' for large-scale mergers with a Community dimension and the original merger regulation (Council Regulation 4064/89) came into force on 21 September 1990.

1.6 INITIAL STEPS TOWARDS REFORM

Although Commission resources devoted to merger control increased steadily after 1990 the Commission had difficulty in coping with its caseload within the mandatory time limits. Many of the cases involved major multinationals and a large number of relevant product and service markets of considerable complexity. Even to establish the relevant facts and issues will always be hard enough, but to apply the merger control criteria in a fair and consistent way to such a large number of cases, whilst fully complying with the procedural requirements of the Regulation, proved to be a substantial challenge.

   A number of measures were taken by the Commission to cope with this situation, including:

- a new simplified procedure for routine cases
- added emphasis on the pre-notification procedures, including the publication of 'Best Practice' principles
- a tendency to declare notifications incomplete (often as a tactical device to give further time for the Commission to consider difficult cases).

Perhaps the most significant consequence of the pressures of the caseload on Commission officials was the increasing tendency to encourage, at an early stage in the case, offers of concessions and obligations, even before the Commission had itself fully identified the competition issues which the case presented. This often happened when the parties were seeking to obtain early clearance and hoping that by offering early concessions, they would avoid being required to undergo an in-depth inquiry. Moreover, the Commission was still concerned that its jurisdiction was inadequate, in that a large number of concentrations with important cross-border effects did not meet the turnover requirements of Article 1 and, therefore, had to be reviewed by one or more national competition authorities. A wide ranging consultation was undertaken by the Commission with the publication of a Green Paper in December 2001.

1.7 THE 2002 CRISIS

The pressure for reform further increased as the result of three successive adverse judgments of the CFI between June and October 2002 (discussed in Chapter 23, Section 4) which not only annulled Commission decisions which had prohibited mergers but contained severe criticisms of both procedural and substantive aspects of its work.

The areas where the Green Paper itself had already indicated the possibility of change included:

- the amendment of Article 1(3) thresholds to include all cases where the parties have to obtain clearances from at least three Member States' authorities
- the replacement of the existing criterion of dominance in Article 2 by the test of whether the merger will lead to a 'substantial lessening of competition'
- greater flexibility in the use of referrals to and from Member States
- procedural improvements allowing the parties or the Commission on occasion to 'stop the clock' and thus allow more time for analysis of appropriate remedies.

In a major speech in Brussels on 7 November 2002, soon after the last of the three adverse CFI rulings, Commissioner Monti announced that he would shortly be submitting a package of proposed reforms to the Regulation. After a year of negotiations, including lengthy discussions on whether the substantive test should be changed, a new Merger Regulation (Council Regulation 139/2004) was adopted in January 2004. It came into force on 1 May 2004.[8]

2. MERGER REGULATION 139/2004: THE COMMISSION'S JURISDICTION OVER CONCENTRATIONS WITH A COMMUNITY DIMENSION

2.1 THE REGULATION: ITS JURISDICTIONAL SCOPE

The purpose of the Regulation[9] is to subject mergers of a certain size to review by the Commission. The Commission's jurisdiction over such mergers is exclusive (subject to certain exceptions). The Commission assesses whether a merger is compatible with the Common Market and is required to prohibit it if it would significantly impede effective competition.

The Commission has jurisdiction over a range of concentrations which are of a very substantial size and which take wider effect than simply within an individual Member State. It is therefore not normally concerned with companies that have a relatively small turnover within the Community; on the other hand, if large multinationals—even

---

[8] Council Reg. 139/2004, [2004] OJ L24/1.

[9] The Regulation is referred to below on some occasions for convenience as the Merger Regulation. All the cases decided under the Merger Regulation and its predecessor can be found on the DG Comp website under 'Mergers-Cases' in both alphabetical and numerical order.

those whose primary activities are, say, in Japan or the United States—have sufficient turnover within the EU, their acquisitions or joint ventures may fall within the jurisdiction of the Merger Regulation, even if at first sight they have little material connection with the Community. This objective is ensured by the minimum jurisdictional figures first proposed in early 1989 and still in force:

(1) at least €5 billion combined worldwide turnover for all the undertakings, and

(2) at least €250 million Community turnover for at least two undertakings involved, but

(3) *no* jurisdiction if more than two thirds of the Community turnover of each of the undertakings concerned is achieved within one and the same Member State.

Article 1 lays down this basic jurisdictional principle, supported by Article 5, which contains necessarily detailed provisions to allow the calculations to be made in individual cases. Turnover for ordinary trading companies is defined so as to cover all sales of goods and services but excluding value added tax and sales tax; for insurance companies and banks different methods of calculation relating to insurance premiums and banking income are provided. To the turnover of both the bidding and the target company are to be added the turnover of its parent and its subsidiary companies forming part of the same group. However, if the acquisition is simply of part of a company's business, for example where a division manufacturing a particular product is being sold rather than the entire company, then the relevant turnover in calculating the seller's worldwide and EU turnover is only that of the division being sold, not the entire company (Article 5(2)). In joint ventures, however, extremely small transactions may be caught since in all cases the turnover of both parents is relevant. In order to prevent the artificial splitting up of a major purchase into a series of transactions each of which remains below the jurisdictional threshold, the Commission may aggregate all transactions made between the parties over a two-year period.

   Provided that the combined world turnover of €5 billion can be established, the next task is to assess the Community turnover for the undertakings concerned. Here the requirement is that at least two of the undertakings concerned have a turnover in the Community of at least €250 million. If this level of turnover has been achieved in the financial year relevant to the transaction, then the Community turnover requirement will be satisfied unless each of the companies has its main business focus and turnover in the same Member State (when that Member State would have the right to assess the validity of the transaction). The technical legal requirement is that the relevant companies should not achieve more than two-thirds each of their aggregate Community-wide turnover within one Member State. For example, suppose that two large chemical companies, R and S, situated in France and England respectively wish to merge, each having a Community turnover of €3,000 million. If R has three-quarters of its turnover, i.e. €2,250 million, in France and €750 million in England, whilst S has only half (€1,500 million) of its turnover in France and the other half (€1,500 million) in England, there will be a Community dimension to the transaction.

This is because, whilst R achieves more than two-thirds of its aggregate Community turnover in France, the same cannot be said of S, which only has half of its turnover in France and the other half in England. A similar conclusion would have been reached if each company had more than two-thirds of its aggregate Community turnover in France and England respectively. It would only have been if both companies R and S had achieved more than two-thirds of their respective Community turnovers in the same Member State that the transaction would not have Community dimension. If the Community turnover requirements are not met then the concentration in question will not have a Community dimension, however large the aggregate world turnover of the undertakings. It is, nevertheless, important to realize that undertakings may fall within the Merger Regulation on the basis of their turnover even if they have minimal or even no assets within the Community (as in *Gencor/Lonrho*[10] and *Boeing/McDonnell Douglas*[11]).

It had originally been intended that the jurisdictional thresholds would be revised in 1993, but this did not occur. In 1997 the Council of Ministers reached agreement on further extensions to the jurisdictional thresholds; the main objective was to bring within them some concentrations involving undertakings with a reasonably large turnover in at least three Member States but whose aggregate world and Community turnover fell below the original thresholds. In March 1998 an alternative set of jurisdictional thresholds was introduced.[12] These alternative thresholds remain in force so that the requirements for a concentration with a Community dimension are also met if:

(1) the combined aggregate worldwide turnover of all the undertakings concerned is more than €2,500 million

(2) in each of at least three Member States, the combined aggregate turnover of all the undertakings concerned is more than €100 million

(3) in each of at least three Member States included for the purpose of point (2), the turnover of at least two of the undertakings concerned is more than €25 million each and

(4) the aggregate Community-wide turnover of each of at least two of the undertakings concerned is more than €100 million.

unless each of the undertakings concerned achieves more than two-thirds of its aggregate Community-wide turnover within a single Member State.

2.2 THE IDENTIFICATION OF RELEVANT TURNOVER

Before going on in Section 3 of this chapter to consider the definition of 'control' and 'decisive influence', it is sensible first to understand the correct approach for deciding which undertakings, of those involved in particular transactions, should have their

---

[10] Case IV/M.619 [1996] 4 CMLR 742. On appeal Case T-102/96 [1999] ECR II-753: 4 CMLR 971.
[11] Case IV/M.877 [1997] OJ L336/16.   [12] Art. 1(b) of Reg. 1310/97.

turnover taken into account for the purpose of the calculation of the thresholds set out in Article 1. The choice of turnover as a criterion for jurisdiction would seem at first sight to present fewer problems than the alternatives of market-share percentages or asset values. Unlike market shares, turnover figures are found in the published accounts of public companies, which are in most cases the undertakings involved in transactions potentially subject to the Merger Regulation. Compared to market share calculations, their assessment is relatively straightforward; turnover is defined in Article 5(1) of the Merger Regulation as 'the amounts derived by the undertakings concerned in the previous financial year from the sale of products and provision of services falling within the undertaking's ordinary activities'.

Nevertheless, in determining whether a particular transaction is a concentration of Community dimension because the turnover thresholds are met, it may sometimes be less than obvious how to identify the undertakings which are relevant for this purpose. The Commission has published a Jurisdictional Notice[13] which provides detailed guidance on this and other issues.

The Jurisdictional Notice points out that the thresholds are purely quantitative and based on turnover calculation only, rather than market share, because the aim is to provide 'a simple and objective mechanism' that can be easily handled by the companies involved so as to determine whether a transaction is of Community dimension and, therefore, notifiable. Its purpose is to measure the economic strength of the undertakings concerned as reflected in turnover figures, regardless of the sector or sectors where the turnover was achieved and whether those sectors will themselves be affected by the transaction in question. Clearly it is important to exclude from these figures any intra-group turnover.

Sometimes such identification of the relevant undertakings may be quite simple. Thus:

(1) If A acquires the whole of the assets or share capital of B, then A and B alone are the relevant undertakings whose turnover is taken into account.

(2) If either A or B is a member of a corporate group (as defined in Article 5(4) of the Merger Regulation), the other companies in that group will be treated as part of that undertaking.

(3) If A and B merge to form a separate undertaking, C, then A and B are the relevant undertakings.

The Jurisdictional Notice considers some complex situations.[14] It stresses that it is the concept of 'acquiring control' that determines which undertakings are to be taken into account. It is necessary to look at both the 'acquiring' and 'acquired' side of the transaction; on the 'acquiring' side, one or more companies may be obtaining sole or joint control of the assets of subsidiaries of the target and normally the turnover of all these undertakings will be included in the calculation of thresholds. On the 'acquired' side, by contrast, the seller of such assets or subsidiary companies will not be included,

---

[13] [2008] OJ C95/01.   [14] Para. 133ff.

apart from the actual turnover of the businesses sold, provided that after the sale it has no continuing links with the newly merged entity.

Further complexities may arise if an existing joint venture acquires control of another undertaking, or where changes of shareholding occur in an undertaking so that sole control becomes joint control, or vice versa. If B is acquired by an existing joint venture, XY, only the turnover of XY and B will be relevant, provided that XY itself is a full-function joint venture, with sufficient financial and other resources to carry on business on a lasting basis. On the other hand, if XY is regarded by the Commission as simply a vehicle for the acquisition of B by X and Y (so that XY has itself no existing commercial character or identity) it is the turnover of X and Y (and their respective corporate groups) which will be aggregated with that of B.[15]

Where the transaction involves changes in the shareholdings held by separate undertakings in an existing joint venture company, as when a joint venture moves from joint control to sole control, the relevant undertakings will be the acquiring shareholder and the joint venture itself, but not the selling company.

Other situations where the identification of the relevant undertakings may present difficulty include that where the number of shareholders in a joint venture is reduced by only some of them selling their holdings, whilst the remainder are reduced to the status of minority shareholders without having any element of decisive influence, either individually or collectively. In this situation it is likely that this latter category will no longer be considered as relevant to the turnover calculations. In every case however the Commission will analyse not only the legal rights of the parties, but also the actual way in which those rights have been exercised. When a joint venture is split up between its members or demerged, the turnover taken into account will be that of the individual members and of the parts of the joint venture business that each will be acquiring.[16]

The Jurisdictional Notice also deals with a number of other situations where corporate control may pass but where the identification of the relevant undertakings may be difficult. These include an exchange of assets, when a swap is arranged between two undertakings. Even if the transactions are regarded by the parties as interdependent, they will be treated for the purpose of the Regulation not as a single concentration, but as two separate transactions: for each of them the acquiring company and the acquired companies or assets will be relevant. Even the acquisition of control by individuals (such as management buy-outs) may sometimes fall within the scope of the Regulation, provided that the individual concerned has sufficient economic activity of his own to effect a lasting change in the structure of the undertaking acquired. The Jurisdictional Notice also explains the principles for calculating the turnover of investment funds and state owned companies. In the latter case, the Jurisdictional Notice provides that a state-controlled company should be treated as being 'independent' (i.e. only its turnover is relevant) unless other state-controlled companies 'are under the same independent centre of commercial decision-making' in which

---

[15] Paras. 145–7.   [16] Paras. 148–50.

case their turnover should be considered as part of the group of the state-controlled company which is directly involved in the transaction.

Many detailed problems can arise on the calculation of turnover and the Jurisdictional Notice deals with a wide range of these, including the following issues:

- geographical allocation when goods are sold or services provided (In the majority of cases the place of sale is attributed to the place where the customer is located because, in most circumstances, that is where the turnover is generated and where competition with alternative suppliers takes place. Thus, for example, in the case of the sale of package holidays, competition for the sale of such holidays through travel agents takes place locally, even though the holidays may be enjoyed in a number of distant locations. The essential point is that the turnover is earned locally and that is where the turnover is to be counted.)
- adjustment for divestments or acquisitions since the date of the relevant audited accounts
- aggregate calculations when successive acquisitions have taken place within a two-year period
- adjustments for exchange rate variations.

2.3 ARTICLES 5(3) AND 5(4)

Article 5(3) sets out special rules to apply if the undertakings are financial, such as banks or insurance companies. In the case of banks, turnover is replaced by 'income' which is primarily the income received by way of interest, dividends, commissions, and net profits on their financial operations. In the case of insurance companies, turnover is replaced by the aggregate of their premiums received and reinsurance premiums paid out.

In applying the rules to calculate turnover it is important to remember that under Article 5(4) aggregation applies not simply to the companies directly involved in the transaction but to all those companies which they control or by whom they are controlled. The relevant definition of control is found in Article 5(4) and includes:

(a) the undertaking concerned;

(b) those undertakings in which the undertaking concerned directly or indirectly:
- owns more than half the capital or business assets; or
- has the power to exercise more than half the voting rights;
- has the power to appoint more than half the members of the supervisory board, the administrative board or bodies legally representing the undertakings; or
- has the right to manage the undertaking's affairs;

(c) those undertakings in which the undertaking concerned has the rights or powers listed in (b)

(d) those undertakings in which an undertaking as referred to in (c) has the rights or powers listed in (b)

(e) those undertakings in which two or more undertakings as referred to in (a) to (d) jointly have the rights or powers listed in (b).

As a result of the very specific wording of Article 5(4) problems may arise in cases when an undertaking has the de facto ability to exercise control over another company in spite of the fact that it does not hold a shareholding above 50 per cent. Its acquisition of less than a 50 per cent holding may have conferred de facto control and, in this case, under Article 3 (discussed in Section 3 below), a 'concentration' may have been deemed to have occurred. It is not necessarily the case, however, that the same answer will be reached under Article 5(4) for determining whether the turnover of the acquiring company in this case is also to be included in the calculation made for assessing relevant turnover.

The problem arose in an early case under the original merger regulation—*Arjomari/ Wiggins Teape*.[17] Arjomari had a 39 per cent shareholding in Wiggins Teape and the remaining shares were widely dispersed. The major shareholder in Arjomari itself was another company, GSL, but its holding was less than 50 per cent. In turn a third company owned a large but not a majority shareholding in GSL. A Community dimension for the case in respect of world turnover calculations would only exist if all of the three companies were each deemed to form part of the relevant acquiring group.

The Commission placed weight on the fourth ground for qualification under Article 5(4)(b), namely that the undertaking 'has the right to manage the undertaking's affairs'. It took the pragmatic view that, whereas the first three examples given under (b) gave legal control of the business of the company, there must also be under the fourth heading the right to include companies which, without having this legal right of control, nevertheless de facto could be proved in the past to have shown the ability to manage the affairs of that undertaking. The Commission, therefore, examined the voting record at past annual general meetings and found that in practice the voting rights actually exercised, for example by GSL, fell short of 50 per cent by a small fraction. As it could not be shown, therefore, that de facto it had the ability, for example, to appoint the members of the board of Arjomari, it could not be considered under Article 5(4). Had it been shown that in practice it had exercised more than 50 per cent of the votes cast then, regardless of its actual shareholding, it would have been considered to have qualified under the fourth heading of Article 5(4)(b). Since GSL itself could not qualify, the third party holding the substantial share interest in GSL similarly could not qualify. By contrast, in *Eridania/ISI*,[18] an almost equivalent shareholding held in Eridania by Ferruzzi was shown in practice to confer the ability to control Eridania, given the large discrepancy between the Ferruzzi shareholding and the very small shareholdings held by all other members. Even, therefore, in what is supposed to be the purely objective assessment of turnover, the Commission will have to exercise an element of judgment in difficult cases.

---

[17] Case IV/M.25 [1991] 4 CMLR 854.   [18] Case IV/M.62 [1991] 4 CMLR 663.

By the same token, if the undertaking making the bid for another company does not have a sufficient shareholding in it to maintain an absolute majority at shareholder meetings, it may nevertheless qualify if it has contracts with other companies giving it the right to manage them. In *Accor/Wagon-Lits*,[19] Accor had management contracts in a number of relatively small companies owning hotels. The owners of these companies entered into contracts with Accor under which Accor managed the hotels under their own trading names on a long term basis. The Commission decided that the owners of these hotels had virtually withdrawn from management and merely exercised the proprietary rights of shareholders. Accor was, therefore, allowed to include the turnover of these companies in calculating whether it had achieved sufficient turnover to be of Community dimension (which it was apparently anxious to do), and the jurisdiction of the Commission was held to be established.

3. THE MEANING OF A 'CONCENTRATION'

3.1 THE MEANING OF 'CONTROL'

It is an essential element of any scheme of merger control that an exact definition of that particular transaction which gives jurisdiction shall be given, hence the importance under the Merger Regulation of defining a 'concentration'. According to Article 3(1) the term covers the case where two separate undertakings merge into a single body, and also the more common situation where one person or undertaking acquires 'direct or indirect control' of the whole or part of another. 'Control' is defined in Article 3(2) as 'rights, contracts or any other means which either separately or in combination... *confer the possibility of exercising decisive influence on an undertaking*' (emphasis added) whether this occurs through share ownership, voting or management agreements, or through any other form of rights operating on the undertaking. Also to be considered is the extent to which the acquiring company has rights which affect the commercial strategy and detailed financial management of the company acquired, as opposed to those rights which relate simply to proprietary protection of its investment. It could include an acquisition either of 100 per cent of the shares of a target company or a lesser percentage sufficient in practice to enable such 'decisive influence' to be exercised. It can also cover cross-shareholdings, cross-directorships and a variety of other means of exercising control.

3.2 THE MEANING OF 'CONCENTRATIVE' JOINT VENTURES

Only those joint ventures falling within the definition of 'concentrative' were covered by the original merger regulation, being those which performed on a lasting basis all

[19] Case IV/M.126 [1992] OJ L204/1: [1993] 5 CMLR M13.

the functions of an 'autonomous economic entity' and which did not have as their object or effect the coordination of the economic activities of their parents. However, now the Merger Regulation applies more widely, covering all 'full-function' joint ventures, even those where there is an element of coordination of the activities of the parents. Reference, therefore, to 'concentration' includes all full-function joint ventures that have a Community dimension. It is, however, important to be aware that, under Article 2(4), when there is an element of coordination this is appraised under the criteria of Article 81(1) and (3), taking into account in particular the activities retained by the parent companies in the same or related markets as those in which the joint venture operates, as well as the degree to which this coordination could allow the possibility of eliminating competition in relevant markets (see Chapter 18 for the treatment of joint ventures under the Merger Regulation).

3.3 THE MEANING OF 'DECISIVE INFLUENCE'

The definition of 'decisive influence' has arisen in a number of decided cases. What is clear is that it is not necessary for the bidder to acquire full legal control of the target in order to obtain 'decisive influence'. An acquisition of a minority shareholding may be sufficient and the test is less demanding than that applied under Article 5(4), already considered in the context of deciding which companies' turnovers are to be included. In *Eridania/ISI*,[20] Eridania increased its shareholding in ISI to 65 per cent by purchasing 15 per cent from another shareholder, a sugar beet growers' cooperative, Finbieticola, which retained 35 per cent. The Commission decided that before the transaction had occurred Eridania exercised joint control with Finbieticola because the ISI board of directors, on which Eridania had no absolute majority, exercised a number of important rights, including the appointment of a managing director and the making of decisions on the sale of plants and on plant closures. After the transfer, the rights retained by Finbieticola had been considerably reduced and merely enabled it to veto major changes to the structure of the company, such as the issue of new capital or a transfer of its head office. It was held, therefore, that, as a result of the 15 per cent transfer of shares, Eridania had now acquired sole control in place of the previous joint control with Finbieticola. The transaction was therefore notifiable.

We have already discussed the *Arjomari/Wiggins Teape* case[21] in connection with the definition of Article 5(4)(b). The case is also relevant to the assessment of 'decisive influence'. Here the 39 per cent shareholding that Arjomari had obtained in Wiggins Teape was considered by the Commission sufficient to constitute sole control over Wiggins Teape because there were no other shareholders who individually owned more than 4 per cent of the share capital. In practice, therefore, this 39 per cent holding was considered more than sufficient to give Arjomari de facto control over the operations of Wiggins Teape, even though a shareholding of 45.19 per cent held in Arjomari by Groupe Saint Louis, as explained above, was deemed insufficient to constitute 'control'

[20] See fn. 18.   [21] See fn. 17.

for the purposes of Article 5(4), in the absence of showing that such control had actually been exercised at past general meetings.

3.4 JOINT CONTROL

Under the Regulation concentrations may also occur where joint control has been created by the transaction. This is illustrated by the *MBB/Aerospatiale* case[22] where Aerospatiale and MBB formed a joint venture to carry out their helicopter businesses which was held by the Commission to give them joint control. Aerospatiale received 60 per cent of the equity and MBB 40 per cent. Under the terms of the relevant agreement all strategic decisions for the joint venture required the unanimous consent of both partners at the supervisory board level. Management of the joint venture was to be exercised by two managing directors acting on a basis of unanimity. Where joint control is obtained the shareholdings of both parties can be aggregated in looking at total turnover, for the purposes of determining whether the concentration has a 'Community dimension'.

It is clear that where two firms each hold 50 per cent in their target company they will have joint control of it. It does not necessarily follow that three or more undertakings acquiring a target will themselves *all* be deemed to acquire joint control. The Commission will only accept the existence of joint control where there is no likelihood that 'shifting alliances' may change the identity of those who jointly control the target. Joint control will normally only be admitted to exist if under the terms of the shareholders' agreement major strategic decisions are subject to veto rights. For example, in the *Paribas/MTH/MBU* case[23] both Paribas and MTH acquired a 40 per cent interest in MBU, a newly created joint venture. Both Paribas and MTH had a veto over decisions made in shareholders' meetings in spite of the fact that each held only a minority interest in the company. Although the theoretical possibility of changing alliances existed, the veto rights were held sufficient by the Commission to establish joint control. A similar decision was arrived at in the Volvo/Renault trucks and buses merger where the parties each acquired a 45 per cent holding in each other, a strong situation of common interest which together with other factors led to a de facto permanent common control situation, thus effectively establishing a single economic entity between the two parties.[24] It is also sufficient to establish a 'concentration' if the bidder is an existing joint controller which acquires a further holding in the target company bringing it from 50 per cent to a higher percentage, as in the *ICI/Tioxide* case[25] (where ICI increased its shareholding from 50 per cent to 100 per cent).

Article 3(5), however, provides for certain situations in which a concentration is not deemed to arise, namely:

(1) where the acquisition of the 'decisive influence' is purely temporary and obtained by a financial institution or insurance company with a view to immediate

22 Case IV/M.17 [1992] 4 CMLR M70.   23 Case IV/M.50 [1991] OJ C277/18.
24 Case IV/M.4 [1991] 4 CMLR 297.   25 Case IV/M.73 [1991] 4 CMLR 792.

disposal, with the disposal itself taking place within a year of acquisition, or some reasonably short extension if disposal was not possible within the original period set

(2) where a liquidator or receiver acquires control of a company

(3) in special cases involving financial holding companies engaged in reconstruction.

The Commission's Jurisdictional Notice provides guidance on its approach to the interpretation of the many difficult issues that can arise in defining whether a concentration has come into existence. It emphasizes that in this process qualitative rather than merely quantitative criteria have to be taken into account, in considering both legal and factual issues.

3.5 THE ISSUE OF PHYSICAL LOCATION

In *Gencor/Lonrho*,[26] the CFI held that a 'concentration with a Community dimension' does not necessarily have to be one where the undertakings concerned are resident or established in the European Community or have their production assets located there. The test of jurisdiction is one of turnover, i.e. sales carried out within the Common Market, applying the jurisdictional principles laid down in the *Woodpulp* case (see Chapter 22, Section 2.3). Application of the Regulation is justified under public international law when it is foreseeable that a proposed concentration will have an immediate and substantial effect on the Community.

4. NOTIFICATION OF CONCENTRATIONS

4.1 THE TASK OF NOTIFICATION

The Regulation is administered by the Directorate General for Competition ('DG Comp') of the European Commission in Brussels. There is a Deputy Director General for Mergers who is responsible to the Director General of DG Comp, who in turn reports to the Commissioner for Competition. DG Comp is divided into Directorates responsible for particular sectors of the economy, and within each Directorate is a mergers unit responsible for reviewing mergers in that industry sector. These units are supported by a team responsible for the formulation and coordination of merger policy. However, the final decision in relation to any particular case is that of the Commission itself. Commission officials who deal with mergers are drawn from the Member States (and sometimes from third countries) and have specialist legal, economic and accountancy qualifications and experience, as well as experience in the administration of competition cases. Whilst the majority are career EC employees,

---

[26] Case T-102/96 [1999] ECR II-753: 4 CMLR 971.

some are national experts seconded for two or three years from their Member States' competition authorities.

Notification involves provision to DG Comp of a substantial quantity of information about the transaction contained in the document known as Form CO, whose outline and structure can be found as an annex to Regulation 802/2004. This document will include details of the method proposed for effecting the concentration, of the relevant corporate groups, their recent accounts, and a full explanation of their ownership and control and of any existing relevant link between the parties. A full analysis of all the 'affected markets', including both product and geographic dimensions, will also be needed together with detailed assessment of the market shares held by the parties and information as to actual or potential barriers to entry. 'Affected markets' are defined as relevant product markets, where the individual or combined market shares of the parties amount to 15 per cent or more for parties in a horizontal relationship and to 25 per cent or more in a vertical relationship. Further information will be needed in appropriate cases on matters such as the degree of vertical integration; distribution systems; research and development expenditure; and the existence of cooperation agreements and the licensing of patents and know-how may also be relevant. For relatively small-scale agreements which nevertheless meet the requirements of the thresholds for jurisdiction, there is a provision for short-form notification. In addition the Commission has adopted a simplified procedure for handling the most straightforward cases, which permits it to adopt a short-form clearance decision at the end of Phase I (see Chapter 17, Section 3.6).

4.2 THE NEED FOR PRE-NOTIFICATION

In the pre-notification stage DG Comp will receive inquiries from undertakings and their professional representatives as to whether a particular transaction (probably not yet finally agreed) falls within the scope of the Regulation and, if so, what kind of information will be required by the Commission in order to carry out its first stage inquiry both into jurisdiction and, if satisfied on this, into merits. The DG Comp officials may well then express a preliminary non-binding view on whether the transaction does or does not fall within the jurisdiction of the Merger Regulation, and any likely problems that are anticipated with it. At this stage time is not running against the parties but both the parties and DG Comp will be aware that once notification has become mandatory there is then only a short period in which the first phase investigation has to be carried out and a decision reached whether to clear it at that point or pass the case on to the 'second phase'. The Best Practice Guidelines (published in January 2004 and available on the website of DG Comp under the heading 'Mergers') state that even in straightforward cases it is appropriate to have pre-notification contact with DG Comp, in particular to reduce the risk of lodging an incomplete Form CO. A draft Form CO is often shown to the Commission at this stage to ensure that its requirements in the case are being fully met. The Commission may reject a Form CO if it believes that the information contained in it is incomplete or misleading.

Once notification has been made and jurisdiction established, the Commission publishes in the Official Journal and on its website the fact of the notification indicating the names of the parties and the nature of the concentration. The possible outcomes following notification are dealt with under Article 6. Article 6(1)(a) provides for the possibility that the concentration notified does not for some reason fall within the scope of the Regulation at all; for example it may be that the turnover on either the world or EC basis is insufficient. Another alternative is under Article 6(1)(b) where jurisdiction of the Commission is satisfied, but where the merits of the case notified 'do not raise serious doubts as to its compatibility with the Common Market'. In this situation the case proceeds to clearance at the end of the first stage and is not further examined. Only approximately 5 per cent of notified cases proceed to the second phase under Article 6(1)(c). The content of Form CO and the detail of the notification process is considered further in Section 3 of the next chapter.

5. CRITERIA FOR ASSESSMENT OF A CONCENTRATION

5.1 COMPATIBILITY OF CONCENTRATIONS WITH THE COMMON MARKET: ARTICLE 2(1)

An important feature of the Merger Regulation is that the assessment of a concentration is not identical to the assessment applied to agreements under Article 81 or abuses of a dominant position under Article 82.

After deciding whether a particular transaction falls within the Regulation, the substantive criteria for assessing that transaction are crucial. The formula chosen in Article 2 is whether the concentration is 'compatible' with the Common Market. Criteria of this kind can be defined either in a broad manner, including not only competition issues but also social and industrial policy, or they can be more specific and limited to particular issues, for example the effect on competition in the relevant product and geographic markets. Contrary to what may have been expected, the Regulation as adopted did not reflect a compromise between the two approaches; the criteria are firmly based on competition issues, although the language of Article 2 suggests that other factors might be taken into account in a particularly evenly balanced case. The Article sets out the rules to be applied by the Commission by way of three separate subclauses whose relationship to each other is not immediately obvious. Article 2(1) lists several factors to be considered in deciding upon 'compatibility':

- the need to maintain and develop effective competition within the Common Market in view of, among other things, market structures and actual (or potential) competition from other undertakings

- the economic and financial power and market position of the parties and also of their suppliers and consumers (and their access to alternative supplies)
- legal and other barriers to entry
- trends of supply and demand in relevant markets
- the interests of intermediate and ultimate consumers
- development of technical and economic progress, provided that it is to consumers' advantage and does not form an obstacle to competition.

5.2 THE CHOICE: 'DOMINANCE SIGNIFICANTLY IMPEDING COMPETITION' OR 'A SUBSTANTIAL LESSENING OF COMPETITION'?

In the critical clauses (Article 2(2) and (3)) the original version of the Merger Regulation stated that 'a concentration which creates or strengthens a dominant position as a result of which competition would be significantly impeded' was incompatible with the Common Market. From 1 May 2004 these articles were amended to state that 'a concentration which would significantly impede effective competition...in particular as a result of the creation or strengthening of a dominant position' is incompatible. The reason for the choice of dominance as the original criterion was that it had already become a familiar concept under Article 82 and thus the subject of a number of Community Court decisions. Moreover, since in Article 2 the additional requirement had been added that this dominant position should significantly impede competition, it seemed an adequate basis for the assessment of any kind of concentration falling within the scope of the Regulation. On the other hand, it was not the test applied in any other important jurisdiction at that date. The USA has since 1914, in the Clayton Act, adopted the criterion of prohibiting mergers where their effect might be 'substantially to lessen competition'; and this wording has been adopted with minor variations in Australia, Canada, and South Africa and, most recently, in the United Kingdom under the terms of the 2002 Enterprise Act. Nevertheless, the majority of Member States followed the lead of the Community in adopting the dominance test for national merger control.

The debate over the suitability of the criterion adopted was sparked into life by the Commission's publication of the Green Paper on the review of the Regulation in December 2001, on which extensive consultation then took place with Member States, industrial and commercial concerns, and many law firms with experience in this area. The Green Paper itself took a conservative approach, stating that the experience of the Commission in applying the test had not revealed 'major loopholes' in its application and pointing out that there were many similarities between the two types of criterion and that the same outcome normally occurred whichever criterion was applied to the same facts. The only concession which the Commission did make in respect to its support for the status quo was an admission that, in a merger between the second and third largest undertakings in the market where neither would have dominance (in view of the relative strength of the largest undertaking), these undertakings might nevertheless be able to raise prices by exercise of their market power following their merger. In this situation the 'substantial lessening of competition' test would clearly be applicable whilst by contrast the test of dominance would not, unless collective dominance could be proved.

5.3 THE DEFINITION OF COLLECTIVE DOMINANCE IN *AIRTOURS*

The weakness in the Commission's position however was then dramatically illustrated by the subsequent *Airtours* ruling of the CFI in June 2002, and the criticisms of the Commission's approach by the CFI in its judgment. The CFI focused on two principal weaknesses in the Commission's decision. First of these was that its definition of collective dominance was so general that it could be applied to any market regarded as oligopolistic regardless both of: (i) the degree to which the parties had the incentive and ability to practise tacit coordination on output or price as well as the ability to retaliate effectively against any undertaking which decided to cheat; and (ii) the ability of consumers to react against such moves. The second criticism was that the Commission's analysis of the relevant market was itself faulty, since the finding of collective dominance was not supported by the evidence in respect of barriers to entry, transparency, volatility of market share, and levels of demand for the package holidays concerned.

The old dominance test was capable of application in two situations, neither of which could be established on the evidence in *Airtours*. These were:

(1) where there is a *unilateral* effect of the merger, that is the effect simply of A becoming dominant or increasing its dominance through having acquired B, leading to an increase in prices or reduction in output, without reference to the ability of other undertakings in the market to coordinate their behaviour and future commercial strategy as a result of the merger

(2) where the effect of the merger is to enable such coordinated behaviour by undertakings, in circumstances where it can be shown that they will then have collective dominance with the merged undertaking, usually referred to as '*coordinated effects*'.

The dominance test did not however apply to a third situation, where say the second and third largest undertakings in the market merge (without becoming dominant) and there is no likelihood of *coordinated* effects as a result of the merger, but where the small numbers of players remaining in the market means that it will nevertheless lead to undesirable consequences such as price rises for consumers. By contrast the 'significantly impede effective competition' test introduced by the new Merger Regulation can be applied to this situation in a relatively straightforward manner.

5.4 ARTICLE 2(2) AND (3)

After substantial debate between the Member States, Article 2(2) and (3) were changed
and now read as follows:

2(2) A concentration which would not significantly impede effective competition in the
Common Market or in a substantial part of it in particular as a result of the creation or
strengthening of a dominant position shall be declared compatible with the Common
Market.

  (3) A concentration which would significantly impede effective competition in the
Common Market or in a substantial part of it in particular as a result of the creation
or strengthening of a dominant position shall be declared incompatible with the
Common Market.

Accordingly, whilst dominance remains an important consideration in assessing
mergers, it is no longer a prerequisite for a merger to be prohibited.

Whilst the Article as a whole emphasizes the assessment of competition and structural issues, Article 2(1) provides a reminder to the Commission that in its analysis
it should not overlook the many other factors to be taken into account in making its
overall assessment, not all of which are purely structural. Article 2 in subclauses (2)
and (3) provides the formal legal framework within which the final decision has to
be made. However, the approach adopted by the Commission in its application of
Article 2 has not been characterized by formal textual analysis.

5.5 THE APPLICATION OF THE CRITERIA

Formal Commission decisions under Articles 81 and 82 concern agreements already
made and implemented and abuses of dominant position that have already occurred.
The focus of concern for the Commission under Article 81 is not only the formal content of an agreement but the way in which it has actually operated; under Article 82
the focus is on the effect of the practices by the alleged dominant company over a
period of time in the past. By contrast, assessment of concentrations under the Merger
Regulation necessarily looks to the future, seeking to answer the question 'what effect
will this transaction have, if implemented, on competition in the relevant geographical and product/services sector?' The fact that the focus is on the future effect of the
concentration, rather than on the imposition of penalties for past misconduct, means
that the approach under Article 2 inevitably differs in a number of respects from that
adopted under Articles 81 and 82. Underlying the approach of the Commission under
the Merger Regulation is the importance of identifying those cases, probably only a
small percentage of the total number notified to it, whose implementation might result
in serious damage to competition in the relevant market.[27] Sometimes the result of

---

[27] By contrast, if the target company's market share would, absent the concentration, fall into the hands
of the bidder anyway, a 'failing company' finding by the Commission may be justified, Cases C-68/94 and
30/95 *France v. Commission (Kali and Salz)* [1998] ECR I-1375: 4 CMLR 829.

the Commission's examination may lead to a total prohibition of the transaction; in a greater number, conditions may be imposed on the transaction which substantially reduce the adverse consequences.

Clearly an advantage of the existence of the Merger Regulation could be the removal of the need to consider the use of, for example, Article 82 in subsequent cases if the Commission, in exercising its merger control jurisdiction, has been able to prevent the creation or strengthening of dominant positions which might subsequently be used in an abusive manner. That being said, in cases where the Commission wishes to prohibit a merger on the basis that it might permit the merged entity to behave in the future in a manner which would constitute an abuse of a dominant position (e.g. a refusal to supply, or abusive tying) the courts have insisted that any such prohibition must be based on particularly 'plausible' evidence and must also take into account the 'deterrent effect' of Article 82 on any such putative future behaviour.[28]

In conclusion, therefore, proving a significant impediment to effective competition under the Merger Regulation can be difficult for the Commission, since it requires the prediction of future developments from the starting point of a present situation where some of the facts may be undisputed but others may be controversial. The test applied is essentially one based on a combination of economic theory and past experience. The burden of proof is upon the Commission and not upon the parties and, if the Commission does provide evidence which, on the basis of the test stated above, would reasonably allow a conclusion of such an impediment, it is for the parties then to show that in the particular case this conclusion can be challenged.

5.6 THE MERGER REGULATION IN PRACTICE

Since the Merger Regulation came into force and up to 31 October 2008 over 3,900 cases have been notified under it to the Commission, of which 186 (just under 5 per cent) went into a second-phase investigation. Of these, twenty received a blocking decision (three of which were later annulled by the CFI), whilst eighty-seven received conditional clearance. In addition 174 of those cleared at the first phase were also made subject to conditions. The build up of notifications of concentrations with a Community dimension has been impressive; until 1995 the annual total was less than one hundred, but this had risen to 224 in 1998 and then to well over 300 in both 2000 and 2001, reducing slightly thereafter as mergers and acquisition activity slackened worldwide but peaking in 2007 at over 400.

It is therefore the second phase cases that tell us most about the application of the criteria for assessing transactions under the Merger Regulation, and a number of these cases are referred to in the course of this and the next chapter. For detailed analysis of their application, however, reference should be made to one or more of the specialist text books listed in the Bibliography.

---

[28] See Case T-5/02 *Tetra-Laval v Commission* [2002] ECR II-4381; [2002] 5 CMCR 1182.

6. DEFINITION OF THE RELEVANT PRODUCT OR SERVICE MARKET

6.1 THE COMMISSION'S GENERAL APPROACH

The Commission had, prior to 1990, considerable experience of market analysis in Article 81 and 82 cases. The number of cases reaching it, however, under the Merger Regulation and the short time-limits in which decisions have to be prepared have forced on it the development of a more methodical approach to market definition. There are many sectors, for example those for petroleum products, pharmaceuticals, and banking, in which the Commission has developed considerable expertise and precedent in its market analysis.

Given the importance of market definition in merger cases it is perhaps surprising that the Regulation itself gives no directions to the Commission on how it is to approach the task of defining relevant markets, though the Commission's Notice on Market Definition (published in 1997) states the general approach of the Commission in this respect to all cases under Articles 81 and 82, as well as under the Merger Regulation. If, for example, in a particular case the combined shares of the target and bidder under one definition of the product market were to be 70 per cent but under another definition 30 per cent, a finding of dominance is obviously far more likely in the first than the second situation. The Commission will normally seek to apply the SSNIP test wherever possible, which is explained in paragraphs 15 to 17 of the Jurisdictional Notice. The parties will have completed Form CO (section 6) which asks them to identify 'affected markets' in both a product and geographic sense, but their choice will not be binding on the Commission. Often it is the parties who are seeking a broader market definition in which the combined market shares will be lower, while DG Comp seeks a narrower market in order that market shares can be established which are substantial.

There are many cases where the Commission does not need to make a detailed analysis of the markets and choose between possible alternatives, because it can reach a decision that a clearance can be given to the concentration, even on the assumption that the narrowest possible market definition (giving the highest possible market share) will not raise any problems: an example is the *PepsiCo/General Mills* case.[29] Easy generalizations about the approach of the Commission to the definition are of limited value; experience of cases to date, however, does show the importance of the following factors:

(1) The Commission has generally adopted narrow product-market definitions (for the reasons stated above), while the parties have striven for acceptance of broader markets; though there have been some cases where it has defined markets

---

[29] Case IV/M.232 [1992] OJ C228/6.

narrowly and concluded as a result that there was not an overlap between the parties' commercial activities.

(2) The Commission is, however, quite prepared in making this assessment to take into account all factors that, in a commercial sense, may render other products interchangeable or substitutable by the consumer.

6.2 ISSUES OF DEMAND AND SUPPLY SUBSTITUTABILITY

At the first stage the emphasis is on the 'demand side' approach to the substitutability of products. The Commission will look at the essential physical characteristics of products, their prices and their intended use by purchasers. It will also look at the circumstances in which they are marketed and the nature of the buyer. For example, in *Magneti Marelli/CEAC*,[30] the starter batteries used as original equipment for new cars and those used as replacements in used cars were identical but were, nevertheless, adjudged to be in separate markets. This was not only because of the price differences between them, but also because of the fact that the manufacturers were required to supply very large numbers of batteries on a just-in-time basis to car manufacturers under stringent conditions, which differed very much from supplying a wide range of dealers and garages with a variety of replacement batteries for stock for resale to motorists from time to time. A similar decision was reached in *Knorr-Bremse/Allied Signal*[31] where the original equipment market for air-brake systems was held distinct from the supply of such products in the after-market.

In *Aerospatiale-Alenia/De Havilland*,[32] an analysis of this kind was applied to the turbo-prop commuter-aircraft market. The parties had argued that all aircraft with between twenty to seventy seats constituted the same product market. DG Comp, however, analysed the different end uses to which such turbo-prop aircraft were put, and came to the conclusion that there were three categories of plane which were essentially purchased by different categories of buyer. After taking evidence from a number of customers for the aircraft it became clear that, for different types of route, aircraft with different seat capacities were required. This information enabled the Commission to find that there were actually three sub-markets, namely those aircraft with twenty to thirty-nine seats, those with forty to fifty-nine seats and those with sixty seats and over. Similar emphasis on customer requirements can be found in a case involving buses manufactured in Germany, *Mercedes Benz-Kässbohrer*.[33] Here the Commission found that the total bus market in Germany is composed of three types of bus: city buses for local use, inter-city buses, and touring coaches. It is important to note, however, that this finding did not stop the Commission, at a later stage in its examination of the transaction, from looking at the degree of substitutability on the supply side which enables the bus manufacturers to switch with relative ease from the manufacture of one bus type to another.

---

[30] Case IV/M.43 [1992] 4 CMLR M61.   [31] Case IV/M.377 [1993] 5 CMLR 535.
[32] Case IV/M.53 [1992] 4 CMLR M2.   [33] Case IV/M.477 [1995] 4 CMLR 600.

The end use of products is clearly relevant, and physical differences between the products which mean that different end uses are possible are likely to lead to the establishment of separate markets. This issue arose, for example, in *Renault/Volvo*,[34] where the Commission found that trucks of over sixteen tons were a distinct market from those of a smaller size because only the larger category could be used for long-distance haulage.

Whilst the substitutability of particular products by other products is always relevant to market definition, the Commission will normally focus on the ability of manufacturers to switch to alternative products only at a later stage, when it comes to deal with the assessment of dominance (see Section 8 below). However, the Commission's practice is not always consistent. For example, in *du Pont/ICI*,[35] the Commission defined the market by reference only to the end-use applications for the intermediate product, nylon fibre, and by reference to the requirements of the purchasers of that particular product. It found that nylon fibres for carpets, on the one hand, are not substitutable by nylon fibres used for textile and other industrial applications on the other. The Commission found no competitive overlap between the two markets; it, therefore, focused only on the nylon fibres used for carpet manufacture. The proposed merger gave rise to serious doubts as to compatibility in that specific market alone. It was also suggested that polypropylene fibres were a substitute for nylon fibres for carpet manufacturers but, after examining the evidence from such customers, the Commission found that they cannot generally switch between the two types of fibres merely as a result of variations in the price ratio between them. Moreover, examining price trends over a period of time showed the Commission that the prices for nylon fibres did not in practice influence prices for the polypropylene fibres.

In some major second-phase cases where there was adequate time for examination of both sides of the relevant market, the Commission has brought both the demand and the supply into the product market analysis. One example is *Nestlé/Perrier*,[36] where a variety of soft drinks were established as not being in practice recognizable by French consumers as substitutes for bottled water. In another case involving consumer products, *Proctor & Gamble/VPS*,[37] the Commission was faced by an argument by P&G that, in the feminine-hygiene markets, sanitary towels and tampons constituted a single product market. The Commission, however, made a finding based on a variety of demand and supply-side factors that the two products represented separate products. Their conclusion was based primarily on an assessment of differences with regard to the use of the products, consumer preferences (including factors such as comfort, security, and morality) and detailed study of the relevant price movements and usage patterns, coupled with the views of retailers involved in the markets.

Even in the first-phase cases, detailed examination of consumer demand characteristics may be required. *SKB/Block Drug*[38] involved the proposed acquisition by a

---

[34] See fn. 24.   [35] Case IV/M.214 [1995] 5 CMLR M41.
[36] Case IV/M.190 [1993] 4 CMLR M17.   [37] Case IV/M.430 [1995] 5 CMLR 146.
[38] Cases Comp/M.2192 (decisions of 11 January 2001).

major pharmaceutical company of a smaller undertaking specializing in the sale of toothpaste for users with sensitive teeth. The combined market shares for this specialist product in the United Kingdom were substantial, but were far lower if toothpaste were regarded as a single general relevant market. On the supply side, it was clear that manufacturers could switch production easily between different types of toothpaste, and that many brands, aimed at a range of different user priorities, shared a common range of ingredients. Many users with sensitive teeth did not purchase the specialist product aimed at them, preferring brands or types which offered 'total care', i.e. a range of features. Given all these factors, the Commission ruled at the end of the first phase that there was only a single general market in the United Kingdom, and cleared the merger.

Of course, market-definition problems are not limited to consumer products. *Alcan/Pechiney II*[39] involved the proposed acquisition by a producer of flexible packaging materials of a competing business. Flexible packaging is produced by converting plastic and cellulose films, aluminium foils, and paper into packaging products. Flexible packaging customers include food and pharmaceutical companies, who tend to define markets narrowly by reference to the qualities of the packaging materials. For example, producers of portioned processed cheese would not consider the flexible packaging used by a manufacturer of confectionery or crisps to be an appropriate flexible-packaging substitute. However, the flexible-packaging producers could produce a wide range of flexible-packaging materials for a wide variety of different end uses (including cheese foil, pharmaceutical packaging, dairy lidding, confectionery packaging) on the same machinery. Given these supply-side substitutability factors, the Commission considered that the market was wider than flexible packaging for processed cheese and cleared the merger at the end of the first phase.

The Commission will normally pay considerable attention to industry practice in assessing markets. Nevertheless it is prepared on occasion to depart from conventional industry analysis or official classification. In *Ciba-Geigy/Sandoz*,[40] it declined to follow the World Health Organization's 'Anatomical Therapeutic Classification' of pharmaceutical drugs; instead in its market analysis it gave principal emphasis, in the case of over-the-counter drugs, to the requirements of patients and, in the case of prescription drugs, to the views of prescribing doctors. A transaction that involves undertakings active in a large number of separate product or service markets may require analysis by the Commission of the competitive situation in all of these, and the pharmaceutical industry has provided some complex investigations of this kind (for example the *Glaxo/SKB* case[41]).

A market definition is reached by the Commission in the context of the facts of the case found at the time when its investigation is being carried out. Since these facts may subsequently change the CFI has confirmed in *Coca-Cola* v. *Commission*[42] that a

---

[39] Case COMP/M.3225 (decision of 29 September 2003).
[40] Case IV/M.737 [1997] OJ L201/1.   [41] Case IV/M.1846 (decision of 8 May 2000).
[42] Cases T-125 and 127/97 [2000] ECR II-1733: [2000] 5 CMLR 467.

market definition by the Commission in an earlier case is not binding on the Commission in a subsequent case and that the Commission must carry out a fresh analysis.

The Commission's Annual Report on Competition Policy is a useful source of information on the experience of the Commission in analysing the major cases of a particular year. For example, its 1999 Annual Report emphasized that market defin-ition may itself be influenced by changes in commercial practice, often brought about by the changing requirements of customers. For example, whereas in the past the Commission had regarded *standard* mail services and *express* mail services as having distinctly separate characteristics, it had now recognized that there had been a certain shifting and blurring of the boundaries between them, in that even users of the stand-ard postal services now had certain delivery guarantees available.

The case of *Tetra/Sidel*[43] shows that the Commission may intervene to block a mer-ger even if the parties are technically operating in different product markets. Here, Tetra Laval was the market leader in carton packaging, where it had a world market share of some 80 per cent, whilst Sidel was the world leader in the PET (plastic) pack-aging market, with some 60 per cent. The Commission felt that these two markets, though separate, were closely related and likely to converge in the next few years. The effect, therefore, of the merger would be to reduce the likelihood of Sidel being able to increase the share of PET packaging for fruit juices and dairy products in substitution for cartons; this in turn would increase Tetra's ability to control developments in both markets and to increase prices to consumers. This decision, however, was annulled by the CFI, and the CFI's judgment was upheld by the ECJ. The judgments are discussed in Chapter 17.

7. DEFINITION OF THE RELEVANT GEOGRAPHIC MARKET

7.1 THE COMMISSION'S GENERAL APPROACH

In parallel with establishing the relevant product market it is necessary for the Commission to identify the relevant geographic market. The range of possibilities is that a single Member State (or even a region within a Member State) is the geographical market or perhaps two or more Member States; another alternative is the European Community as a whole and, for some costly and highly technical products, the mar-ket may now be worldwide (for example, in *Aerospatiale/Alenia/De Havilland*,[44] where the market was found to be commuter aircraft manufactured worldwide). The Commission's Notice on Market Definition (1997) already mentioned is a valuable source of information in explaining its approach to this task.

---

[43] Case Comp/M.2416 (original Commission decision): [2002] 5 CMLR 1182.
[44] Case IV/M.053 [1991] OJ L 334/42: [1992] 4 CMLR M2.

With consumer products the geographic market chosen as relevant has often been individual Member States because the basis for distribution is often national, and the imperfections of the Single Market have meant that it is often necessary for a single manufacturer to treat individual Member States as separate markets. Differing local specification requirements corresponding to local consumer wishes and the existence of different legislation prescribing requirements for the goods may also be relevant. As Sir Leon Brittan explained in an address to the Centre for European Policy Studies in Brussels in October 1991 in discussing the *Magneti/Marelli/CEAC* case[45] on car batteries:

no legislation exists preventing the import and sale of batteries into France. Thus, one might expect the geographic reference to be wider than a single Member State. However, when the Commission examined this problem it discovered that due to the existence of consumer brand loyalty and the lack of a cross-border distribution and marketing infrastructure imports would not be likely to enter France in response to an increase in demand, more likely the price would increase. The market was thus considered national. Many Community markets have developed on national lines for hundreds of years. Manufacturing, marketing, and purchasing patterns were national in scope. The removal of regulatory barriers does not in itself create a true single market overnight. The establishment of a true Common Market in business terms with major cross-border distribution and marketing infrastructure occurs gradually. The Commission recognizes and accepts this.

7.2 THE RANGE OF POSSIBLE GEOGRAPHICAL MARKETS

In *American Cyanamid/Shell*,[46] the parties had claimed that the relevant geographic market for the herbicides which they sold was Community-wide. In favour of this argument they cited:

(1) centralized production facilities for manufacturing active chemical ingredients and a tendency to the creation of centralized formulating facilities to produce the finished product

(2) the presence of a large number of multinationals in this market throughout the EC

(3) the use of international brand names rather than national names and

(4) low transport costs relative to the high value of the products.

The Commission, nevertheless, found that the markets were still national. It pointed out that, although manufacturing is centralized, marketing and distribution operations in the herbicide industry were still generally organized on a national basis. In addition, the range of products sold and their individual chemical formulations varied in accordance with the different crop patterns for each country. Moreover, the existing scheme of regulation for the industry encouraged a national approach to marketing because each Member State used its own certification standards. Although there was

---

[45] See fn. 30.   [46] Case IV/M.354 [1993] OJ C273/6.

a Community regulatory regime covering the marketing of plant-protection products, classification of products, labelling, and packaging, this would only promote Community-wide trading in the long term.

In *Mannesmann/Hoesch*[47] the Commission found that the market for steel gasline pipes was limited to Germany because the conditions of competition there were different from those in other Member States. There was only a low level of imports (less than 10 per cent), an absence of harmonization of technical standards, and a purchasing policy of German customers in favour of German products; all this indicated to DG Comp that the relevant geographic market for these pipes was Germany alone. Similar considerations apply in the vehicle-building industry as illustrated both by *Mercedes/Kässbohrer*[48] mentioned above and by *Volvo/Renault*,[49] where one of the reasons for considering the markets for buses to be national was the existence of local specification requirements differing substantially between Member States.

Another factor is the existence of other barriers to entry for companies wishing to penetrate national markets. Some of these can exist within a single Member State, such as the basic ratio of value to cost of transport. Goods that have a heavy weight or significant volume in relation to their value will not normally be economic to transport large distances, whether across national boundaries or within a single country. In the Community, of course, there is the additional problem in some cases of language under which expense may be incurred in preparing labelling, instructions, and in organizing after-sales service across borders. In *Viag/Continental Can*,[50] a case involving two companies manufacturing cans and glass bottles, the Commission held that since these products had only a small value and take up a great deal of space they cannot economically be shipped more than 200 kilometres, especially as in many cases deliveries have to be 'just in time', thus giving a great advantage to local suppliers. As a result, the Commission concluded that the market was not one of the whole Community but one of a number of regional geographic markets containing shipping distances not exceeding 200 kilometres.

Both parties in *Volvo/Scania*[51] were Swedish-based manufacturers of trucks and various types of bus and coach with a combined market share in Sweden of between 50 per cent and 90 per cent. Their combined market share for trucks over 16 tonnes was over 90 per cent. The parties claimed that the appropriate geographic market was not just Sweden, but either Scandinavia as a whole or, even possibly, the whole EC. The Commission, however, placed much weight on the barriers to entry that existed for any manufacturer seeking to enter the Swedish market, in particular the difficulty of establishing an adequate after-sales network. It was influenced by the fact that no other major manufacturer had been able to gain a substantial market share for such vehicles in Sweden over a considerable number of years. The relevant geographic markets were therefore national ones, such as Sweden, Finland, and Denmark.

---

[47] Case IV/M.222 [1992] 5 CMLR 117.   [48] See fn. 33.   [49] See fn. 24.
[50] Case IV/M.081 (decision of 6 June 1991).   [51] Case Comp/M.1672 [2001] OJ L143/74.

Operating in favour of expanding the geographic market definition are the harmonization of national legislation and introduction of Community legislation under which the barriers to cross-border entry are gradually broken down. Provided the market integration process implemented through the Commission's single market programme will, in the short term, lead to wider geographic markets then this may be taken into consideration when defining the relevant market. An example is the public procurement Directive referred to in *Mercedes/Kässbohrer*. Also relevant is the *Alcatel/Telettra* case.[52] There the merger involved the acquisition by Alcatel of a controlling interest in Telettra. Both companies were involved in the supply of telecommunications equipment in the Spanish market. The acquisition resulted in an aggregate market share of 80 per cent for both microwave and line transmissions. Moreover, the Spanish telecommunications operator, Telefónica, had a strong position in the Spanish market as a monopolist; it also had a minority shareholding in both companies and a known policy at that time of purchasing only from local suppliers. Notwithstanding these factors, the merger was cleared, largely because of assurances received from Telefónica that not only would it cease to hold any share interest in any of the companies, but would abandon its previous preference for local purchasing and would treat foreign suppliers equally. This was a decision taken in the knowledge that the Commission was itself in the process of seeking to liberalize the telecommunications equipment market throughout the Community. Had this general policy trend not been in evidence, the merger might well have been prohibited. It was only against the background of these changing conditions that the Commission regarded the high market shares of the two parties as no longer representing market dominance, because they would be counterbalanced by the power of a monopolistic purchaser willing to acquire its supplies from both local and foreign sources.

Some of the complexities that can arise in the analysis of the geographic market are well illustrated by *Totalfina/Elf Acquitane*.[53] This case involved a bid by one French oil company for another, and both were involved in the sale of a number of different petroleum products. The Commission identified these as including: petrol, motorway fuel sales, aviation fuel sales, domestic heating oil, liquid petroleum gas, sulphur, ethylene, and the transport of refined products by pipeline. In some cases, the whole of France was regarded as the relevant area, in others regional markets of various different configurations were identified, whilst for others they were drawn even more narrowly.

Finally, consumer preference itself remains in some markets a powerful argument for treating the market as national. Perhaps the best available example of this is *Nestlé/Perrier*.[54] Here Nestlé and Perrier between them were dominant in bottled source water in France and owned a number of the leading brands. Their total market share was some 60 per cent and their main competitor was BSN with some 22 per cent, the remainder of the market being shared by a number of small companies. There were

---

[52] Case IV/M.0422 [1991] 4 CMLR 778.   [53] Case Comp/M.1628 and 1647 [2001] 5 CMLR 682.
[54] Case IV/M.190 [1993] 4 CMLR M17: [1992] OJ L356/1.

no legislative barriers to entry to the French market if foreign manufacturers wished to enter, but it appeared that such attempts had always been unsuccessful. A relevant factor was that the great majority of sales were made to large supermarkets or hyper-markets, which were very aware of the loyalty of their customers to the well-known brands owned by the leading French companies. In their view it was unlikely that the French customers would switch to foreign brands because of their deep-seated and long-standing preference for the local product from French springs.

It should not be supposed, however, that in the majority of cases the Commission's decision would be in favour of national markets. For high-technology products and those with a very high capital cost, reflecting substantial amounts of research and development expenditure, it is quite likely that markets will be at least Community-wide, if not worldwide. Such markets will be found for example in communications, computers and large scale transport; see for example *GE/Honeywell*,[55] *Boeing/McDonnell Douglas*,[56] *Digital/Phillips*,[57] and *Blackstone/Acetex*.[58] In some 70 per cent of all its cases, however, the Commission has not needed to reach a firm decision on market definition, because the outcome of the case will, in its view, be unaffected by it.

8. THE PROHIBITION OF MERGERS

8.1 APPLICATION OF THE 'SIEC' TEST

As discussed above, the substantive test under the original merger regulation turned on whether the merger could create or strengthen 'dominance'. The new test is whether the merger will 'significantly impede effective competition'. As Recital 25 to the Merger Regulation explains, the introduction of the new test is to permit the Commission to prohibit mergers in oligopolistic markets which do not create or strengthen dominance but may nevertheless have non-coordinated effects that restrict competition. The practical effect of the test is to expand the scope of the Merger Regulation. This is confirmed by the final sentence of Recital 25 which says:

The notion of significant impediment to effective competition in Articles 2(2) and (3) should be interpreted as extending, beyond the concept of dominance, only to the anti-competition effects of a concentration resulting from the non-coordinated behaviour of undertakings which would not have a dominant position on the market concerned.

In other words, the Commission can now prohibit all mergers which have anti-competitive 'unilateral' or 'coordinated' effects.

A unilateral-effects case is one where the merged entity will have the ability, alone, to behave independently of competitors and customers ('single-firm dominance'

---

[55] Case Comp/M.2220 (decision of 3 July 2001).
[56] Case IV/M.877 [1997] OJ L336/16: 5 CMLR 270.   [57] Case IV/M.129 [1991] 4 CMLR 737.
[58] Case Comp/M.3625 (decision of 13 July 2005).

cases) or where the market structure is highly concentrated and the merger eliminates the competitive constraint exercised by one of the merging parties on the market as a whole so that prices may rise even though the merged entity will not itself be 'dominant' ('non-coordinated effects' cases).

A 'coordinated effects' case is where the market structure is highly concentrated and the behaviour of one firm has an appreciable effect on overall market conditions such that the firms on the market are interdependent. In these circumstances the firms could enjoy a position of 'collective dominance' where it is economically rational for them to tacitly collude in ways which substantially reduce competition between them.

The Commission also distinguishes between 'horizontal mergers' (i.e. mergers between competitors which have 'unilateral' or 'coordinated' effects) and 'non-horizontal mergers' (i.e. mergers between companies in closely related markets who are not competitors but whose merger might have anti-competitive 'vertical' or 'conglomerate' effects).[59]

The remainder of this chapter examines how the Commission assesses mergers between competitors (i.e. 'unilateral' and 'coordinated effects' cases) and mergers between companies with a 'vertical' or 'conglomerate' relationship. Finally, it discusses the 'efficiency' and 'failing firm' defences raised by merging companies.

8.2 DOMINANCE OF A SINGLE COMPANY

Once the product and geographic markets relevant to the merger have been determined, the degree of dominance which it will confer in those markets has to be considered next. The concept of dominance is familiar from Article 82 and the definitions contained in the *United Brands*[60] and *Hoffmann-La Roche*[61] cases continue to apply, though their application to individual cases may pose difficulties. The essential element of dominance is the ability to behave independently of its competitors, customers and consumers; in other words to be largely free from the pressures imposed by competition as to price, quality and conditions of business. A degree of dominance cannot be measured, as with a thermometer, in any particular market, but has to be assessed in the light of several factors. The principal factors involved in merger cases are:

(1) The aggregate of the *market shares* which the combined undertakings will have, provided that these are of a relatively durable nature rather than merely temporary. Just as when assessing the relevant market itself, the concept of dominance has to strike a balance between existing facts and likely future developments. Future

---

[59] The Commission has published guidelines on horizontal and non-horizontal mergers. For horizontal mergers see "Guidelines on the assessment of horizontal mergers under the Council Regulation on the control of concentrations between undertakings" [2004] OJ C31/5 and for non-horizontal mergers see "Guidelines on the assessment of non-horizontal mergers under the Council Regulation on the control of concentrations between undertakings" [2008] OJ C265/6.

[60] Case 27/76 [1978] ECR 207: 1 CMLR 429.   [61] Case 85/76 [1979] ECR 461: 3 CMLR 211.

developments that are not likely during the next two or three years are generally too remote to be considered. Case law has established that a market share of 50 per cent or more may in itself be evidence of a dominant position.[62] It is clear from the recitals to the Regulation that a combined share of less than 25 per cent raises no presumption of dominance, but rather a presumption of non-dominance. Between 25 per cent and, say, 40 per cent the presumption is relatively low,[63] but once past 40 per cent the presumption increases gradually until once up to, say, 65 per cent or 70 per cent it may be difficult to refute unless the circumstances are extremely unusual as, for example, in *Alcatel*.[64]

(2) The relationship of the market share of the merging undertaking to those of other competitors will clearly be relevant. If, for example, the merging companies have 40 per cent and 20 per cent respectively and no other company has more than 5 per cent, the gap itself in market share will make it far easier for the combined entity to operate free of the pressures of competition. On the other hand, if there was a competitor in that market also with a 30 per cent share, genuine competition could at least be anticipated from that source to the two merging companies. That fact alone might not be sufficient to enable the concentration to be cleared; other factors would have to be examined relating to the respective strengths of the undertakings, such as their individual product range, the quality of their research and development in a technical industry, the strength of the customer base and the way in which market shares had developed in the past. Also relevant would be the strength of the various buyers in the relevant markets.

(3) It is clear that certain sectors are likely to be characterized by *volatility of market share*, whereas others, perhaps the more traditional industries, may show a marked degree of stability. In an industry subject to innovation and where R&D plays an important part in the competitive struggle, market shares are likely to vary and are a less certain indicator of market power, as the trend data will show. On the other hand, a case such as *TetraPak/Alfa-Laval*[65] is an example of an acquiring company with a market share exceeding 90 per cent maintained consistently for a considerable number of years in the sale of aseptic carton-packaging machines for milk, supported by a wide range of technological advantages over all its competitors.

(4) Commercial strengths of various kinds can in general play an important part in buttressing the benefits of substantial market share. Intellectual property rights may, as in the *TetraPak* case, be relevant since, if they cover a wide range of the necessary technology for entry into the industry, licences may not be available from the

---

[62] Case C-62/86 *AKZO v Commission* [1991] ECR I-3359 [1993] 5 CMLR 215 at para. 61 and Case T-221/95 *Endemol v Commission* [1999] ECR-II 1299 at para. 134.

[63] But in the *Rewe/Meinl* case (Case IV/M1221, decision of 3 February 1999) the bidder's market share in the Austrian food retail market was only 37 per cent but, nevertheless, dominance was found as a result of the particular features of that market, e.g. the bidder's strong position in major urban centres and in Eastern Austria.

[64] See fn. 52.   [65] Case IV/M68 [1992] 4 CMLR M81.

dominant company, or may be available only on disadvantageous terms. Such a company as market leader for a number of years may also be skilled at making aggressive use of its patent rights to discourage competition. In consumer products the ownership of well-known trade marks may also play an important role in giving a strong market position. Other factors to be taken into account in the analysis of commercial strengths include:

(a) the forecast of likely product demand and changing patterns of raw material supply and product development in the industry, the time and cost required to enter the market, including the time required for testing and licensing of new products, and the possibility of the need to incur high initial start-up costs

(b) whether there are over-capacities in neighbouring geographic and product markets

(c) whether the market is in general over-or under-supplied

(d) the development of Community harmonization of technical standards, and Directives on public procurement

(e) whether the undertakings concerned hold a 'portfolio' of a substantial number of brands in the same geographic market.

8.3 NON-COORDINATED EFFECTS CASES

Where a merger results in the removal of an important competitive constraint on one of the merging parties, competition in the market will typically be significantly impeded where the merged entity obtains a dominant position. However, it may be that a merger in an oligopolistic market could, without creating a dominant position, involve the elimination of important competitive constraints that the merging parties previously exerted upon each other, together with a reduction of competitive pressure on the remaining competitors, such that there is a significant reduction of competition even though there is little likelihood of coordination between the members of the oligopoly.

In deciding whether a merger is likely to produce anti-competitive, non-coordinated effects, the Commission will have regard to the following issues:

(1) Are the merging firms close competitors? If customers consider the merging firms' products to be particularly close substitutes (for example, products which a substantial number of customers regard as their first and second choice) then the merger could generate a significant price rise. A price rise is more likely where the merging parties' products are 'differentiated' from those of their rivals (for example, their products have a better brand image or a higher technical specification than their rivals' products). However, such a price rise is unlikely to occur if rival firms produce close substitutes to the products of the merging parties.

(2) Can customers switch to alternative suppliers easily? If customers have difficulties switching to other suppliers because there are few alternative suppliers or

switching costs are high, then they may not be able to protect themselves against a price rise. This could be the case, for example if, in the past, customers have sourced their products primarily from the two merging companies.

(3) Could competitors increase supply if the merged firms were to increase prices? When market conditions are such that competitors of the merging parties are unlikely to increase supply if prices rise, the merger may increase the merged firm's incentive to significantly impede effective competition by making it easier for it to reduce output or raise prices. This is likely to be the case when barriers to entry are high or existing competitors cannot expand production easily because, for example they suffer from capacity constraints.

(4) Will the merged firm be able to hinder expansion by competitors? It may be that the merger will enable the combined entity to restrict others from competing effectively. For example the merging parties may be the only two companies with the relevant technologies, or access to the relevant raw materials, which rivals or potential rivals need in order to expand or compete. In making this assessment the Commission may also take into account the financial strength of the merged entity relative to its rivals.

(5) Will the merger eliminate an important competitive force? Some firms have more of an influence on the competitive process than their market share might suggest. For example, a pharmaceutical firm with a relatively small market share today may nevertheless be an important competitive force if it has promising products under development which are likely to make a major impact on the market once introduced. Effective competition could be significantly impeded by a merger between two important innovators with 'pipeline' products related to a specific product market even if, together, the merged entity may not 'dominate' the market alone.

8.4 COORDINATED EFFECTS: THE EARLY DAYS

There are a number of national competition law systems in the EC, including both Germany and the United Kingdom, under which mergers can be prevented or subjected to conditions either if they are seen to enable single undertakings to acquire an undue degree of market power, or if the merger will have coordinated effects (i.e. the outcome of the transaction will be to place two or more companies in a position of collective dominance). Although Article 82 expressly provides that it can apply when 'one or more' undertakings have a dominant position the terms of the original merger regulation, however, did not contain explicit wording that it also applied to a situation of collective dominance. Clearly the absence of such a provision could have been an embarrassment to the Commission, given that there are a number of important product markets, in Member States and in the Community, with notably oligopolistic features and which could be rendered even less competitive if further concentration took place which allowed or facilitated coordination between the leading players in the relevant markets.

The Commission's desire to face this challenge head on was not surprising. The first indication of the Commission's willingness to examine the coordinated effects of a merger was found in *Alcatel/AEG-KABEL*,[66] though the doctrine was not actually utilized to block or restrict the terms of the concentration in that case. The most important early precedent in this respect was *Nestlé/Perrier*,[67] in 1992. The relevant facts were that Nestlé and Perrier had between them some 60 per cent of the French bottled mineral water market, whilst BSN had 22 per cent and the remainder of the market was shared by a number of much smaller companies with far more limited access to the relevant springs from which the water had (under French law) to be obtained. Nestlé sought to acquire Perrier and was willing in view of its large market share to give up the Volvic brand to BSN, which would have brought their market shares more in line, but still in aggregate leaving these two large companies with a share of 82 per cent. The decision reads:

Para. 120. The reduction from three to two suppliers (duopoly) is not a mere cosmetic change in the market structure...the reduction from three to only two national suppliers would make anti-competitive parallel behaviour leading to collective abuses much easier.

Para. 121. The mineral water suppliers in France have developed instruments of transparency facilitating a tacit co-ordination of pricing policies...

Para. 123. Their reciprocal dependency thus creates a strong common interest and incentive to maximise profits by engaging in anti-competitive parallel behaviour. This situation of common interest is further reinforced by the fact that Nestlé and BSN are similar in size and nature, both active in the wider food industry and already co-operate in some sectors of that industry.

Having made these findings as to the nature of the market, the conclusion which the Commission reached (in para. 131) was that 'the market structure resulting from the merger...would create a duopolistic dominant position on the French bottled water market which would significantly impede effective competition and would be very likely to cause a considerable harm to consumers'.

The remedy adopted was to require Nestlé to divest itself of a major brand, not to BSN, as had been proposed by Nestlé, but to a third party, so as to weaken the duopoly power of the two major companies.

The facts in this case were clearly strong enough to provide an ideal base for establishment of a collective dominance (or coordinated effects) doctrine. It has been used subsequently in a number of cases, although it has not always resulted in the blocking of the concentration. An example of a case where it was considered is *Pilkington/SIV*[68] in 1993. This concentration consolidated the position of Pilkington as the second largest company in the European float glass market, the other participants, apart from the market leader St Gobain, being considerably smaller.

Although the Commission acknowledged that the industry had been subject to a number of cartels in the past, it ultimately cleared the concentration on the basis of the differing sizes and market shares of the remaining enterprises and the existence of

---

[66] Case IV/M.165 [1992] OJ C6/23.   [67] See fn. 36.   [68] Case IV/M.358 [1994] OJ L158/24.

chronic excess capacity, as well as the anticipated 'maverick' aggression expected from Guardian, one of the smaller companies. The Commission argued that chronic excess capacity made collusion less likely because of the high profits that could be earned from cutting prices to win marginal additional sales.

8.5 COORDINATED EFFECTS: *KALI UND SALZ*

A serious challenge to the Commission's application in merger cases of the principles of coordinated effects was raised before the ECJ in an appeal by France and a French company against the Commission's 1994 decision in *Kali und Salz/MDK*.[69] In that second-phase case, the Commission had attached several conditions to its clearance of the merger of the two companies which, between them, would control the entire German market for agricultural potash, and would also have a 23 per cent share of this market in the rest of the Community. It was claimed by the Commission that the merged companies' trading links with the French company (which held 37 per cent of the EC market outside Germany) would lead to oligopolistic collective dominance in that market; for this reason the severance of those trading links was made a condition for clearance of the concentration.

The ECJ had to decide whether, in the circumstances of this particular case, the Commission had been correct in its determination that the transaction would lead to a situation of collective dominance. The Court laid down four elements which the Commission would have to establish in order to justify such a finding. These were: (1) sufficiently substantial and stable existing market shares for the parties; (2) a sufficient increase in total market share as a result of the merger itself; (3) conditions present in the market, including barriers to entry, which would be likely to encourage mutual interdependence; and (4) existence of structural links between the parties. On the facts of this case, the Court ruled that the structural links that did exist had insufficient influence on the competitive conduct of the parties to bring about collective dominance.

8.6 COORDINATED EFFECTS: *GENCOR* AND *AIRTOURS*

In the *Gencor/Lonrho* case,[70] Gencor held 46.5 per cent of Implats which carried out the activities of the Gencor Group in platinum mining in South Africa. Lonrho similarly held some 73 per cent of a company called LPD, engaged in the same business. The merger proposal would have given Implats control over LPD and left the platinum market to be supplied only by this group and by one major rival, Amplats. The CFI upheld the decision of the Commission that this concentration would have led to collective dominance for these two large companies in the world's platinum and rhodium markets. In an important development however the Court stressed that structural links between the parties did not have to be shown; it was enough if 'the relationship

69 See fn. 81.   70 See fn. 10. For the Court's assessment of the extraterritorial issues, see Ch. 22.

of interdependence was existing between the parties to a tight oligopoly within which in a market with the appropriate characteristics...these parties were in a position to anticipate one another's behaviour and, therefore, were strongly encouraged to align their conduct in the market'. In other words, the issue was whether the characteristics of the market were conducive to tacit coordination of their activities.

In September 1999, in *Airtours/First Choice*, after a second-phase proceeding the proposal by Airtours to take over First Choice was blocked on the ground that the merger would have left the three largest travel companies in the United Kingdom holding 80 per cent of the short-haul package holiday market, a structure which would have enabled them to act in a collectively dominant manner. Airtours, however, successfully appealed against this decision to the CFI on the grounds that the Commission analysis of this market was faulty.[71] In its judgment the CFI severely criticized the quality of the Commission's economic reasoning and laid down that, before a finding of collective dominance could be made, three conditions had to be established:

- sufficient market transparency for each undertaking to be aware precisely and quickly of the way in which each other's market conduct was evolving

- the situation of tacit coordination must be reinforced by the presence of long-term incentives on the parties not to provoke retaliation by departing from their current policies

- the results expected from these common policies must not be at risk from foreseeable reactions from competitors or consumers.

In 2008 the CFI's approach was endorsed by the ECJ in its judgment in the *Impala* case, concerning Commission clearance of a joint venture between Sony and Bertelsmann. The ECJ overturned a CFI judgment annulling the clearance, and in so doing approved the Airtours criteria, and in particular the need to establish market transparency.[72]

Coordinated effects as a feature of merger analysis by the Commission does not of course limit itself to pricing. It can also extend to coordination over capacity, since an industry where it was possible to keep tight control over the building of new production facilities or the provision of additional services would be likely to be one where price levels could be maintained at a higher level than would be the case if such coordination on capacity did not occur. This issue arose in *UPM-Kymmene/Heindl* and *Norske Skog/Parenco/Walsum*.[73] Heindl was a German company which sold its manufacturing assets (producing paper for magazines and newspapers) to two Swedish companies, UPM and Norske Skog. Whilst the market shares of the companies were all below 15 per cent it was suggested that the newly merged companies could tacitly coordinate with the other major manufacturers in these markets in the building of new plants, both by delaying capital investment and by the allocation of building new capacity between them over time, possibly on a rota basis. An analysis of the paper manufacturing business however convinced the Commission that such coordination

---

[71] Case T-342/99 [2002] 5 CMLR 317. [72] Case C-413/06 P, 10 July 2008 (not yet reported).
[73] Case Comp/M.2499 [2002] 5 CMLR 1309.

was highly unlikely. Each individual plant would necessarily represent a major investment; and the company entitled under such arrangements to come in first with such
an investment would have a large commercial advantage over its rivals. Moreover, any
participant which desired to break ranks and increase its capacity prematurely would
find that effective retaliation by the other companies would be difficult, as the capacity increase for the industry as a whole would be irreversible (unlike a price cut). The
only punishment possible in the longer term would be retaliatory increases in capacity
which in turn would tend to bring prices down further. The transactions were therefore cleared.

8.7 COORDINATED EFFECTS: THE HORIZONTAL
MERGER GUIDELINES

As we have seen, any lingering doubts that the Merger Regulation applies to coordinated effects cases were dispelled with the adoption of the 'significant impediment to
competition test' introduced in January 2004 by Regulation 139/2004. In February
2004, the Commission published its Horizontal Merger Guidelines[74] which effectively
codify the principles set out in the *Airtours* judgment. The Horizontal Guidelines
make it clear that a merger in a concentrated market may significantly impede effective competition if it increases the likelihood that firms are able to coordinate their
behaviour, even without an agreement, or if it makes tacit coordination easier, more
stable or more effective for firms that were already coordinating before the merger.
Such coordination could involve the companies maintaining prices at a high level,
limiting production, or dividing customers between themselves.

When assessing whether a merger is likely to produce coordinated effects, the
Commission will consider whether the market's characteristics are oligopolistic.
Relevant factors are that:

- the market has few players
- the product at issue is homogenous (for example a commodity product)
- demand and supply conditions are relatively stable
- key information relating to matters such as prices, capacities and production
  levels is transparent
- there is no or little innovation or technological development; market participants
  are relatively symmetric in terms of costs structures, market shares, capacity
  levels and degree of vertical integration
- there are cross-shareholdings, joint ventures or other structural links between
  firms
- barriers to entry are high and buyer power is low.

Evidence of past coordination is treated with particular importance by the Commission.

---

[74] See fn. 59.

Where many or all of these features are present, the Commission will assume that coordination between market participants is possible and will then examine whether:

(1) the coordinating firms can monitor, to a sufficient degree, whether the terms of coordination are being adhered to (for example because price rises are announced)

(2) there is some form of credible deterrent mechanism that can be activated if deviation is detected (for example, the cancellation of a supply contract in another market)

(3) outsiders (sometimes called 'maverick competitors') who are not participating in the coordination, and customers, cannot jeopardize the outcome of the coordination (for example, in the case of mavericks, by increasing capacity sufficiently to render the co-ordinated behaviour unprofitable).

9. VERTICAL AND CONGLOMERATE MERGERS

9.1 THE HARM THAT CAN BE CAUSED BY NON-HORIZONTAL MERGERS

In its Guidelines on non-horizontal mergers,[75] the Commission has made clear that non-horizontal mergers are generally less likely to significantly impede effective competition than horizontal mergers. When announcing the Non-horizontal Merger Guidelines in 2007, Competition Commissioner Kroes recognized that 'the majority of vertical and conglomerate mergers do not raise problems, and they can bring about efficiency gains that benefit both businesses and consumers'. In that context, the Commission has also stressed that the mere fact that a competitor may be harmed because a merger creates efficiencies cannot in itself give rise to competition concerns. A vertical or conglomerate merger is unlikely to raise competition concerns unless the merged entity has a significant degree of market power (which does not necessarily amount to dominance) in at least one of the markets concerned. As a general rule of thumb, provided the market is not unduly concentrated, if the merged entity will have a combined market share of less than 30 per cent the Commission will presume that the vertical or conglomerate merger poses no threat to effective competition.

The main concern raised by vertical and conglomerate mergers is that they might lead to foreclosure of rivals or of customers. For example in a conglomerate merger, the merged entity may acquire the opportunity to increase sales of a product in one market through its market power in a closely related market. Such a strategy could

---

[75] See fn. 59.

be implemented through 'tying' where customers that purchase one good (the tying good) are required to also purchase another good from the producer (the tied good). In certain circumstances, this practice may lead to a reduction in competitors' ability or incentive to compete in either the 'tied' or 'tying' product market.

In a vertical merger, one party to the merger may integrate with an important customer in the downstream market. Because of this downstream presence, the merged entity may foreclose access to a sufficient customer base to its actual or potential rivals in the upstream (or 'input') market and reduce their ability or incentive to compete. In turn, this may raise downstream rivals' costs by making it harder for them to obtain supplies of the 'input' under similar prices and conditions absent the merger. This may allow the merged entity to raise prices on the downstream market.

Similarly, in a vertical merger, one party to the merger may acquire an important supplier of raw materials in the upstream market. Because of this upstream presence, the merged entity may be able to restrict access to the raw materials, thereby raising its rivals' costs by making it harder for them to obtain supplies of the raw material under similar prices and conditions as absent the merger. This may lead the merged entity to profitably increase the price charged to consumers, resulting in a significant impediment to effective competition.

In vertical and conglomerate cases, the Commission will examine first whether the merged entity would have the ability after the merger to foreclose its rivals; secondly, whether it would have the incentive to do so; and thirdly, whether a foreclosure strategy would have a significant detrimental effect on competition downstream.

The analysis is particularly speculative, since it attempts to predict the future commercial conduct of the merged firm. The CFI has made it clear that the more speculative the prediction of the loss of future competition the greater the evidential requirements to support it. The quality of the evidence is particularly important since the evidence must support the Commission's conclusion that the economic developments which the Commission has predicted are plausible.[76]

9.2 CONGLOMERATE MERGERS IN PRACTICE: *GE/HONEYWELL*

The most recent major case involving the analysis of conglomerate effects is *GE/ Honeywell*.[77] This merger involving two major US corporations was cleared by the US Department of Justice, with very limited conditions attached. The bid involved the takeover by GE, a dominant manufacturer of large commercial and regional aircraft engines, of Honeywell, a leader in the production of flight management systems, jet-engine starters, marine gas turbines, and other avionic products. The Commission's concern related principally to the future ability of the combined enterprise to strengthen its dominance by its ability to 'bundle', that is to offer discounts to

---

[76] See Case T-5/02 *Tetra-Laval v Commission* [2002] ECR II-4381, [2002] 5 CMLR 1182 at para. 44.

[77] Case Comp/M2220 (decision of 3 July 2001): DG Comp Competition Policy Newsletter 2001, No. 3, p. 5.

its airline customers, which would provide a major incentive to purchasers of GE aero-engines to link these with purchases of avionic products from Honeywell. In addition, the Commission feared that GE's aircraft-financing subsidiary, GECAS, would impose its 'GE only' policy on customers seeking to lease new planes. The merger was therefore blocked.

On appeal, the CFI upheld the Commission's prohibition decision but, in relation to the conglomerate effects aspects of the case, it held that the Commission had not investigated sufficiently rigorously whether the merged GE/Honeywell entity had (a) the ability and (b) the incentive to behave in the manner predicted by the Commission.[78]

9.3 VERTICAL MERGERS IN PRACTICE: *GE/HONEYWELL*

The *GE/Honeywell* judgment also allowed the CFI to review the Commission's analysis of the merger between GE's aero-engine manufacturing business and Honeywell's upstream engine starter business. The Commission had decided that the merger would strengthen GE's dominant position in the market for large commercial aircraft engines because it would give GE the ability and incentive to disrupt or delay supplies of engine starters to GE's aero-engine competitors. The Court accepted that such conduct would be in the merged entity's commercial interests but noted that the Commission had not taken into account the deterrent effect of Article 82 when analysing GE's incentives to behave in that way. As a result, the Commission's finding that GE's dominant position would be strengthened by this vertical acquisition was overturned.[79]

An example of the Commission imposing conditions on a merger to remedy vertical foreclosure concerns is the acquisition of Pfizer's Consumer Healthcare Division by Johnson & Johnson. Without the divestiture remedies of assets used for the production of raw materials for nicotine patches, the Commission claimed that the merger would have given Johnson & Johnson control over key inputs for such patches produced by its main competitor, GSK.[80]

10. THE 'EFFICIENCIES' DEFENCE

A factor not specifically mentioned in Article 2 is that of efficiencies. Parties to mergers may put forward as one of their principal arguments that the merger will bring about important efficiency gains that the parties could not realize on their own, whether through economies of scale or scope or through improvements in geographical coverage, distribution systems, or research and development. The Commission has consistently opposed attempts to include such considerations within Article 2, in a number of major cases including *Aerospatiale* and *Kässbohrer/Mercedes Benz*; and even when

[78] Case T-210/01 *General Electric v Commission* [2005] ECR II-5575: [2006] 4 CMLR 686.
[79] Ibid.
[80] *Johnson & Johnson/Pfizer Consumer Healthcare* Case Comp/M.4314 (decision of 11 December 2006).

efficiencies have been acknowledged as a likely outcome, they have been rejected as a defence because of the failure by the parties to show that they will be passed on to consumers (as in *Accor/Wagon-lits*). In its Horizontal Merger Guidelines the Commission has made it clear that for it to conclude that, as a consequence of efficiencies, there are no grounds for declaring the merger to be incompatible with the Common Market, the efficiencies have to be substantial, timely, and benefit customers (and not just the merging parties); be merger specific (and not be capable of being realized through less anti-competitive alternatives); and be verifiable. The burden of proof to establish these cumulative conditions rests on the notifying party.

11. THE 'FAILING COMPANY' DEFENCE

If an undertaking being acquired would go out of business apart from the acquisition, it has normally been assumed that clearance would be given to the transaction, even if the consequence was that the acquirer remained in, or would establish, a dominant position as a result. This is known as the 'failing firm defence'. In *Kali und Salz*,[81] three conditions were laid down for the clearance of such acquisitions:

- that, in the absence of the acquisition, the target (failing company) would become insolvent in the near future

- that there was no other potential acquirer whose substitution would have been less harmful to competition

- that the market share of the target would in any case have gone to the acquirer upon its disappearance from the market.

In *BASF/Pantochin/Eurodiol*,[82] however, the Commission stated that the third of these conditions could be ignored if, in the absence of the acquisition, the plant capacity of the insolvent undertaking would have been lost from the market, especially if (as in this case) the loss would have also had serious environmental consequences and caused supply shortages leading to immediate higher prices.

FURTHER READING

S. Baxter, F. Dethmers, and N. Dodoo, 'The *GE/Honeywell* Judgment and the Assessment of Conglomerate Effects: What's New in EC Practice?' [2006] 2 ECJ 141.

D. Bailey, 'Standard of Proof in EC Merger Proceedings: A Common Law Perspective' [2003] 40(4) CMLRev 845.

---

[81] Cases C-68/94 and 30/95 [1998] ECR I-1375: 4 CMLR 829.
[82] Case Comp/M.2314 [2002] OJ L132/45.

P. D. Camesasca, 'The Explicit Efficiency Defence in Merger Control: Does it Make the Difference?' [1999] ECLR 26.

C. J. Cook and C. J. Kerse, *EC Merger Control* (4th edn, Sweet & Maxwell, 2006).

L.-H. Röller and M. de la Mano, 'The Impact of the New Substantive Test in European Merger Control' [2006] 2 ECJ 9.

J. S. Venit 'The "Merger" Control Regulation: Europe Comes of Age or Caliban's Dinner' [1990] 27 CMLRev 7.

R. Whish, 'Substantive Analysis under the EC Merger Regulation: Should the Dominance Test be Replaced by "Substantial Lessening of Competition"' in *EU Competition Law & Policy Developments and Priorities* (Hellenic Competition Commission, 2002).

17

MERGERS (2)

1. REFERRALS OF CONCENTRATIONS BETWEEN THE COMMISSION AND MEMBER STATES

1.1 THE 'ONE-STOP SHOP'

It is clear that one of the principal reasons for the acceptance by Member States of the Merger Regulation was the value placed by both the Commission and by business interests throughout the Community on the concept of the 'one-stop shop' for larger concentrations having both a substantial world and Community turnover. No longer would it be necessary to seek approval from several national authorities within the European Union in such circumstances; the decision of the Commission, and the Commission alone, would be decisive. Article 21(1), therefore, provides that only the Commission may take decisions in respect of concentrations that have a Community dimension. Nevertheless, when the final terms of the Merger Regulation were being negotiated in 1989, several EU countries emphasized the rights of continuing involvement of Member States in certain situations where the particular concentration could have an impact on their economy or on a local market.

When the original Regulation 4064/89 was first introduced, it was intended that review by Member States of Community dimension mergers and Commission review of non-Community dimension mergers would happen only in 'exceptional circumstances'. That regulation permitted Member States to request (but only after the transaction had been notified to the Commission) that a concentration which would have adverse effects on a local market be referred back to that Member State for review. Member States could also take measures in respect of Community dimension mergers to protect 'legitimate interests' including public security, plurality of the media and prudential rules. Article 296 of the EC Treaty also permits Member States to take 'measures' to protect their national defence interests.

As for non-Community dimension mergers, as we have seen, these do not fall within the jurisdiction of the Commission. Nevertheless, the original merger regulation permitted Member States to ask the Commission to examine whether a merger would have adverse effects within the territory of the Member State (or States) concerned. This provision was included at the behest of those Member States which, in the 1980s, did not have their own merger control laws.

However, since then merger control laws have been introduced in all Member States except Luxembourg and there has been a consequent increase in the number of transactions which, although not of 'Community dimension', are subject to multiple notifications in Member States. Accordingly, revisions were made to the merger referral system contained in Regulation 4064/89. These changes, introduced in Regulation 139/2004, allow for parties to a transaction, before notification, to request that a non-Community dimension merger be reviewed by the Commission or that a Community dimension merger be reallocated to the Member States. Guidelines have also been published describing how the case referral system works.[1] The underlying principle is that jurisdiction should only be re-attributed to another competition authority if the latter is 'the more appropriate authority' for dealing with the merger having regard to 'the specific characteristics of the case as well as the tools and expertise available to the authority'.[2]

In this section we review the exceptions to the 'one-stop shop' principle, and, in particular, those provisions of the Merger Regulation which allow for a reallocation of jurisdiction before notification (Articles 4(4) and (5)) and those which provide for a reallocation of jurisdiction post-notification (Articles 9 and 22). In the second section of this chapter we review the legitimate interests exception contained in Article 21(4) of the Merger Regulation and the 'national defence' exception and the application of Article 296 of the EC Treaty to industry defence mergers.

1.2 PRE-NOTIFICATION REFERRALS FROM THE COMMISSION TO MEMBER STATES (ARTICLE 4(4))

From the introduction of Regulation 139/2004 to 31 December 2007, thirty-two Community dimension mergers were referred to Member States prior to notification (one partially, thirty-one in their entirety). Not one request for such a referral was refused.

In order for such a referral to be made there must be indications 'that the concentration may significantly affect competition' in a market (or markets) and that market (or those markets) must be within a Member State and 'present all the characteristics of a distinct market'.

In practice mergers which are likely to affect markets which are national (or narrower) in scope will be referred to the relevant Member State. An example is the *Total/Petrofina* merger which involved the acquisition of local oil storage markets in France.[3]

If the merger is likely to affect competition in more than one Member State a referral is less likely. However, if a merger gives rise to competition concerns in a number of Member States but the concern is founded on a series of distinct geographic markets and the investigation can be handled by each Member State's authority independently

---

[1] Commission Notice on Case Referral in respect of concentrations [2005] OJ C56/2.

[2] Ibid., at para. 9.

[3] Case Comp/M.1464 (decision of 26 March 1999). The case was decided under Art. 9(3) of the Reg. 4064/89 but the principles are the same.

and without the need for coordination, then the merger may be referred. An example is the *Leroy Merlin/Brico* merger[4] where the Commission decided to refer Leroy Merlin's acquisition of Brico DIY stores to the French, Spanish and Portuguese authorities on the grounds that these national authorities were best placed to assess the impact of the transaction on the local distribution of DIY items in their countries.

The request for referral is made voluntarily by the parties by way of a reasoned submission (Form RS) before notification. Form RS requires the submission of a significant amount of information (including 'indications' that the merger may significantly affect competition in a distinct market). Copies of the request are sent to the national competition authorities which have fifteen working days to agree or object to the proposal. If they agree, the Commission then decides (within twenty-five days of submission of Form RS) whether to agree to the referral request.

1.3 PRE-NOTIFICATION REFERRALS FROM THE MEMBER STATES TO THE COMMISSION (ARTICLE 4(5))

From the introduction of Regulation 139/2004 to 31 December 2007 134 non-Community dimension mergers were referred from the Member States to the Commission prior to notification and four requests were refused. The reason for the greater popularity of requests for referrals from Member States to the Commission is probably twofold. Companies prefer the simplicity of one notification procedure rather than multiple Member State procedures. Also, as we have seen, for a Community dimension case to be referred from the Commission to the Member States, the requesting parties have to provide indications that the merger may significantly affect competition in a market within a Member State. This is not an attractive 'admission' to have to make even though the Commission has stressed that such an indication is without prejudice to the outcome of the investigation.[5]

In order for an Article 4(5) referral to be made the transaction must be a 'concentration' (within the meaning of Article 3) which is 'capable of being reviewed' under the national merger-control laws of at least three Member States. This language ensures that if a merger does not need to be notified to a national authority but, nevertheless, as a matter of national competition law, that authority has jurisdiction to review the merger (for example, the OFT in the UK where merger notifications are voluntary) that Member State will count towards one of the three required.

A good example of a merger referred from the Member States to the Commission even though it did not have a Community dimension was *Reuters/Telerate*.[6] This transaction did not have a Community dimension but was capable of being reviewed under the national merger control laws of 12 Member States and one EFTA State. Reuters and Telerate were the only two global suppliers of software used by financial institutions

---

[4] Case Comp/M.2898 (decision of 13 December 2002). The case was decided under Art. 9(3) of Reg. 4064/89 but the principles are the same.

[5] Commission Notice on Case Referral in respect of concentrations [2005] OJ C56/2 at para. 17.

[6] Case COMP/M.3692 (decision of 23 May 2005).

and other consumers of real-time market data. The US Department of Justice and the Commission both had concerns about the transaction and both required remedies in order to approve the transaction. The transaction clearly had effects beyond the territory of one Member State and it was therefore appropriate for the Commission (rather than the national competition authorities) to scrutinize it. The Article 4(5) procedure thus permitted the parties to avoid multiple filings in Europe but also had the result that the Commission and the Department of Justice worked together on a common remedy offered by the parties to secure clearances of the transaction in both jurisdictions within the same timeframe.

As with the Article 4(4) referral procedure, a request that review of a merger be reassigned from Member States to the Commission is made voluntarily to the Commission on Form RS before notification of the transaction to any of the Member States. Copies of the request are sent to the national competition authorities who have fifteen working days in which to object. If any one Member State objects, then jurisdiction is not transferred and all the relevant Member States retain the competence to review the merger. If none of the national competition authorities objects then the transaction must be notified to the Commission in accordance with the same procedures applicable to Community dimension concentrations.

1.4 POST-NOTIFICATION REFERRALS FROM THE COMMISSION TO MEMBER STATES (ARTICLE 9)

Under Article 9(1) of the Merger Regulation, a Member State may request the Commission to grant it jurisdiction over a concentration which has a Community dimension. Article 9(1) was contained in the original Regulation 4064/89 (when it was known as 'the German clause', because it was included at the particular request of Germany). A case can be referred to a Member State under Article 9 if the merger threatens to significantly affect competition in a market within that Member State which presents all the characteristics of a distinct market. If the Commission does not consider that such a distinct market or threat to competition exists, then it will reject the request and deal with the case itself. If it does consider that competition in such a market is threatened, then it may, should it so choose, refer the whole or part of the case to the national competition authority. However, if the distinct market within the Member State does not constitute a substantial part of the Common Market, the Commission has no discretion and must refer all (or the appropriate part) of the transaction to the Member State.

Until 31 December 2007 67 requests had been accepted under this Article, 31 in their entirety and 36 in part only. The greatest numbers of requests have been made by Germany, the United Kingdom, and France.

The United Kingdom was the first successful applicant under this Article in the *Tarmac/Steetly* case,[7] in early 1992. This involved a proposed joint venture of a

<hr/>

[7] Case IV/M.75 [1992] 4 CMLR 343.

concentrative nature between these two UK companies which would have effectively pooled their building materials activities, including the supply of bricks, clay roofing tiles, concrete and masonry products. The aggregate world and EC turnover of the parties meant that the case had a Community dimension, but the United Kingdom successfully sought a reference back under Article 9(3) reasoning that the case concerned specific 'distinct markets'. These were:

(1) the manufacture and sale of bricks in the North East and South West of England

(2) the manufacture of clay tiles throughout Great Britain.

Following this request the Commission gave two decisions: the first accepted the UK request and set out an assessment in detail of local markets in Great Britain, confirming that there would be a particular local problem in both the north-east and south-west of the country because the combined aggregate market share of Tarmac and Steetly was 80 per cent or more with little potential for new entry, particularly given the cost of transporting such heavy goods as bricks from other parts of the United Kingdom. Jurisdiction was also ceded with regard to tiles but here the market to be investigated was national because, as lighter products, they could be transferred widely throughout the country. Again there was a significant entry barrier to this market: the need to own adequate clay reserves in order to manufacture tiles. The second Commission decision of the same date dealt with the remaining products covered by the joint venture, namely concrete blocks, structural concrete products, and masonry products. The Commission concluded that in respect of these markets the merger was compatible with the Common Market.

   The United Kingdom was, however, denied its request in 1999 to take back the concentration involving Electricité de France's bid for London Electricity,[8] largely on the basis that the regulatory control which the UK wished to exercise over the combined company could already be exercised under existing statutory powers. A more unusual case, also involving the United Kingdom, was the 1999 *Airtours/First Choice* travel services merger.[9] Here, the Office of Fair Trading decided against requesting an Article 9 reference back on the ground of lack of sufficient effect of the merger on competition in the UK travel agency market, but the Commission, believing the case raised collective dominance issues, nevertheless, instituted a second-phase investigation, which led to a 'blocking' decision that was eventually annulled by the CFI.

   Where 'partial' referrals are made, the 'split' will normally be on a geographical basis, but can be more complex. Thus in *Shell/DEA*[10] and *BP/E.on*[11] a reference back in both these parallel cases was made to the German BKA of downstream retail petroleum markets in Germany while the Commission conducted a second-phase examination of broader upstream markets, such as the supply of ethylene to a number of West European markets.

---

[8] Case IV/M.1346 (decision of 27 January 1999).   [9] Discussed in Ch. 16.
[10] Case Comp/M.2389 (decision of 20 December 2001).
[11] Case Comp/M.2533 (decision of 20 December 2001).

An example of a case where the Commission decided that the merger would affect competition in a distinct market that did not constitute a substantial part of the Common Market is the *Strabag/Walter Bau* merger which involved Strabag acquiring Bau's road building business. One of the markets affected by the transaction was the Hamburg regional market for asphalt which was referred to the German BKA.[12]

1.5 POST-NOTIFICATION REFERRALS FROM MEMBER STATES TO THE COMMISSION (ARTICLE 22)

Article 22 permits one or more Member States to request the Commission to scrutinize a non-Community dimension merger which nevertheless affects trade between Member States and threatens to significantly affect competition within the territory of the Member State or Member States making the request.

This referral option can be useful to a Member State which prefers that a case normally falling within its national jurisdiction is actually dealt with by the Commission in Brussels. It may be because the resources, or the substantive legal provisions of the local competition authority, are thought to be inadequate or inappropriate or, alternatively, because the issues concerned are believed by the Member State to be primarily of Community interest. Once jurisdiction has been decided, the Commission will proceed to deal with the case in the normal manner as if it was an investigation into a concentration with a Community dimension.

Member States without well-established merger-control procedures or institutions have used the provisions of this Article to request the Commission to handle several important cases: these have included *British Airways/Dan Air*[13] (referred by Belgium), *RTL/Veronica/Endemol*[14] (referred by the Netherlands), *Kesko/Tuko*[15] (referred by Finland), and *Blokker/Toys 'R' Us*[16] (also referred by the Netherlands). Each of the last three cases resulted in an outright prohibition of the proposed concentration; in the *Kesko* and *Endemol* cases the Commission's decisions were upheld by the CFI, which approved both its substantive and procedural findings.

The first joint references were made in 2002. In *Promatech/Sulzer*[17] concerns over the Western European market for rapier weaving machines led to a second-phase inquiry which led to undertakings being given by the parties for the disposal of businesses in Italy and Switzerland; the reference in this case was by no fewer than seven Member States. Seven Member States also requested that the Commission review the *GE Engine Services/Unison Industries*[18] merger which raised issues in the worldwide aero engine market. Clearance was given after a first-phase inquiry.

In the period until 31 December 2007, the Commission had received nineteen requests under Article 22. Since all Member States except Luxembourg now have national merger control authorities to review concentrations that do not have

---

[12] Case Comp/M.3754 (decision of 23 June 2005).   [13] Case T-3/93 [1994] ECR II-121.

[14] Case IV/M.343 on appeal Case T-221/95 [1999] ECR II-1299: [1999] 5 CMLR 611.

[15] Case T-22/97[1999] ECR II-3775: [2000] 4 CMLR 335.   [16] Case IV/M.890 [1998] OJ L316/1.

[17] Comp/M2698 (decision of 24 July 2002).   [18] Comp/M2738 (decision of 17 April 2002).

Community dimension, references by individual Member States to the Commission in the future are less likely.

2. MEMBER STATE PROTECTION OF LEGITIMATE AND DEFENCE INTERESTS

2.1 THE LEGITIMATE INTEREST EXCEPTION—ARTICLE 21(4)

Article 21(4) presents a different focus on the exceptions to the 'one-stop shop'. Here the emphasis is on the nature of a 'legitimate interest' entitling Member States to intervene, whereas under Article 9 the emphasis is on the competition in the distinct local market in the Member State which the concentration would affect. Under Article 21(4):

Member States may take appropriate measures to protect legitimate interests other than those taken into consideration by this Regulation and compatible with the general principles and other provisions of Community law. Public security, plurality of the media and prudential rules shall be regarded as legitimate interests... Any other public interest must be communicated to the Commission by the Member State concerned and shall be recognised by the Commission after an assessment of its compatibility with the general principles and other provisions of Community law before the measures referred to above may be taken...

This provision simply recognizes that Member States have the power to intervene in certain aspects of concentrations that affect them on grounds other than those covered by the Merger Regulation, but does not give Member States the power to authorize concentrations which the Commission may have itself prohibited under the Merger Regulation. A case showing that 'legitimate interest' additional to those specifically mentioned may be accepted by the Commission is that of *Lyonnaise/Northumbrian Water*.[19] The Commission accepted in March 1995, at the request of the United Kingdom, that the UK system established for the regulation of the water industry did represent such a national legitimate interest. Following privatization of the water and sewerage industry in the United Kingdom in 1989, legislation made mergers between water enterprises above a certain size automatically referable to the Commission for assessment. The criterion, which the Commission is required to apply in such cases, is whether the water regulator (the Director General of Water Services) can continue to make comparisons between different water enterprises (each of which has a regional or local monopoly) in maintaining the principle of 'comparative competition' to maintain competitive pressures on them in lieu of actual competition. The regulator uses these principles for a number of purposes, in particular to obtain comparative data

---

[19] Case IV/M.567 [1995] 4 CMLR 614. At the time of the case the relevant UK competition authority was the 'Monopolies and Mergers Commission' which was renamed the 'Competition Commission' by the 1998 Competition Act with effect from 1 April 1999.

on operating and capital costs to enable quinquennial price reviews for each water (or water and sewerage) authority.

The EC decision in March 1995 went beyond simple recognition of this legitimate interest and contained suggestions to the United Kingdom as to how it was to carry out its assessment of the legitimate interest. The decision included a direction to the UK authorities along the following lines:

the control exercised by the UK authorities is aimed at ensuring that the number of inde-pendently controlled water companies is sufficient to allow the Director General of Water Services to exercise his regulatory functions ... in order not to go beyond the interest pursued by the UK regulatory legislation other issues in relation to mergers between water compan-ies can only be taken into account to the extent that they affect the control regime set out above ...

In the event the UK Competition Commission prepared a report on the *Lyonnaise/ Northumbrian* merger which concluded that the merger could be expected to operate against the public interest, in that it would prejudice the principle of comparative com-petition, but recommended that remedies by way of price reductions and other condi-tions be imposed if the merger was allowed to proceed. Following negotiations terms for reducing prices and other conditions were agreed between the parties, the water regulator and the Secretary of State, and were accepted by the Commission which then proceeded to give a formal clearance under Article 6(1)(*b*).

In 1999 a dispute arose under this Article between the Commission and Portugal, which had tried to block a proposed merger in the banking sector (*BSCH-Champalimaud*).[20] The Commission itself adopted decisions against the Portuguese measures, referring to the exclusive jurisdiction it possessed under Article 21 and on the basis that the 'prudential' grounds, stated by Portugal to justify its actions, were unjustifiable and, in any case, had not been notified to the Commission. Subsequently, revised terms of the merger were agreed and Portugal withdrew its opposition.

2.2 THE DEFENCE EXCEPTION—ARTICLE 296 OF THE EC TREATY

For completeness there should also be mention of those merger cases involving mili-tary equipment dealt with by Member States under Article 296 of the Treaty of Rome. Generally jurisdiction over such cases is not 'referred back by the Commission', because the terms of this Article provide that the Member State is entitled to take 'measures' to protect its national jurisdiction in defence-related matters, which the Treaty and the Merger Regulation do not control. Among the principal cases decided under this heading was *General Electric Company/British Aerospace/VSEL*[21] in 1995. The two competing bidders were each seeking to acquire VSEL, builder of the UK Trident

[20] Cases Comp/M.1680, 1724, and, later, 1799.
[21] Case IV/M.529 [1994], Case IV/M.528 OJ C368/23; [1994] OJ C348/6. The relevant Monopolies and Mergers Commission reports are CM2851 (*British Aerospace/VSEL*) and CM2852 *GEC/VSEL*, both pub-lished in 1995.

nuclear submarines. The UK Government, relying on Article 296, notwithstanding that both bids were of Community dimension, instructed the companies not to notify the military aspect of their bids to the Commission. A notification to the European Commission was, therefore, made solely of the non-military aspects of the bid, which were relatively minor and were soon cleared. In fact the non-military aspects of VSEL's business, mainly the production of equipment for oil and gas rigs, represented only about 2.5 per cent of its total business. The UK authorities then took over the preparation of the report into the two bids as to the military aspects; their reports were published in May 1995 clearing the British Aerospace bid but recommending by a four to two majority that the GEC bid should not be permitted. Exercising his statutory discretion, however, the Secretary of State rejected the recommendation concerning the GEC bid, which was ultimately successful.

In a 1999 sequel to these cases, the European Commission gave a first-phase clearance[22] to proposals to merge the non-military business of Marconi Electronic Systems (part of GEC) with British Aerospace finding, in this case, the relevant market to be worldwide. With regard to the military business of the companies, the Commission confirmed again that Article 296 applied.

In 2001, although the joint venture between European Aeronautic Defence and Space Company and Nortel Networks[23] was cleared by the Commission under its normal procedures, the UK, because of concern over defence and security aspects of the case, exercised its powers under this Article to obtain behavioural undertakings from the parties relating to the confidentiality of sensitive information and the development of certain defence technology. There are also examples of mergers of defence related businesses where no Article 296 measures were adopted by any Member State and the Commission ruled on the entirety of the transaction. One such example is *Northrop Grumman/TRW* which involved military aircraft and military command and control systems.[24]

3. MERGER REGULATION INVESTIGATORY PROCEDURES AND POWERS

3.1 TIME LIMITS

Time is an important element in all competition cases. The decisions which competition authorities, such as the Commission, have to take often involve examination of activities and agreements of undertakings stretching back over a considerable number of years. It may take the authorities a number of years to reach decisions in complex

[22] Case IV/M.1438 (decision of 25 June 1999).
[23] Case Comp/M.2546 (decision of 10 October 2001).
[24] Case Comp/M.2781 (decision of 13 September 2002).

cartel and dominance cases under Articles 81 and 82, which are often then followed by appeals to the CFI and the ECJ. The Article 82 case of *Magill*[25] took some ten years to resolve, from the first complaint to the Commission to the final ECJ decision.

For mergers, which often raise difficult competition law issues, this kind of time-scale is completely unrealistic. Such transactions are particularly sensitive to even short delays. Volatility of stock exchange prices and the difficult personal and corporate relationships that may develop between bidder and target mean that, in many cases, delay of even a few months may be fatal to the completion of the transaction. Time limits in national merger-control systems are, therefore, normally quite strict and, in the case of the Commission, the original time limits suggested as far back as 1973 of twelve months for the Commission to handle a case have now been reduced to six months for virtually all difficult in-depth review cases. Since many of the transactions now reaching DG Comp are so complex, requiring the analysis of numerous product or service markets often in highly technical areas (such as energy, telecommunications or electronic equipment), the task of the Commission in giving its decisions within the mandatory time limits is onerous. Because of the longer time likely to be taken in pre-notification discussions in such cases, the total period for resolving them may well exceed considerably the official periods for the first and second phase cases provided for in the Merger Regulation.

3.2 THE FRAMEWORK OF A COMMISSION INVESTIGATION

The procedural rules governing the investigation are set out in Regulation 802/2004 (the 'Implementing Regulation'). The structure of the Implementing Regulation is as follows: the recitals state that the Implementing Regulation has been modified as compared with its predecessor to make it consistent with the substantive amendments to the merger control regime contained in Regulation 139/2004. In particular, it seeks to place greater emphasis on the calculation of time limits and on the parties' and third parties' additional rights of information and right to a hearing before the Commission. Articles 1 to 6 deal with notifications by the parties, who start the time limits running when the relevant Form CO is lodged. In certain cases a 'short-form notice' may be used. Articles 7 to 10 set out details of the time limits authorized by Articles 9 and 10 of the Merger Regulation. The first phase cannot last longer than twenty-five working days after notification, though this is extended to thirty-five working days in cases where the parties put forward commitments to remedy concerns raised by the transaction or a Member State makes an Article 9 request to transfer jurisdiction to it. The second phase is limited to an additional 90 to 125 working days (in cases which are particularly complex and commitments are offered). These time periods are longer than the four months period for second phase investigations which applied under the original merger regulation. Articles 11 to 16 deal with the hearing of the parties and

---

[25] [1989] 4 CMLR 757 (Commission decision); Case 214/91 [1995] ECR I-743: 4 CMLR 718 (ECJ decision).

of third parties with a legitimate interest in the outcome of the case. A distinction is drawn between:

(1) parties submitting the notification, always including the bidding company or companies

(2) other involved parties, that is parties to the concentration other than those notifying such as, for example, the seller of a business or an undertaking which is a target of a hostile bid

(3) third parties with a sufficient interest; they may include customers, suppliers, and competitors, or members of relevant management, union or consumer organizations.

Articles 14 and 15 provide for oral hearings with the notifying parties to be held in private to supplement the written submissions normally filed. Involved parties and third parties are likewise able not only to make their views known in writing, but also to have a hearing if they have applied in writing. Articles 17 and 18 deal with matters relating to access to the file, use of documents and rules regarding the safeguarding of confidential information.

Also in 2004 a number of the internal organization and working procedures of DG Comp were revised and new checks and balances introduced in order to strengthen the economic analysis and fact finding processes which had been severely criticized by the CFI (see for example the discussion of *Airtours* in Chapter 16, Section 8.6). These changes included:

- the creation of the post of a 'Chief Competition Economist' within DG Comp, with a team of economists working for him who are involved in all major cases

- the appointment in such cases of a 'peer review' panel of experienced officials, to review provisional conclusions of the investigating team and provide a necessary 'fresh pair of eyes'

- allowing companies involved an earlier opportunity to have access to the file and to review third-party submissions made to the Commission in connection with the case

- the holding of regular 'state of play' meetings between the Commission and the parties during the process, so that the parties are kept fully aware of the progress of the investigation and the thinking of the Commission on the merits of the case

- the publication of revised and expanded guidelines on 'Best Practices' in the conduct of such cases.

3.3 MODIFICATION BY THE PARTIES OF THE ORIGINAL CONCENTRATION PLAN

Articles 19 and 20 of the Implementing Regulation are significant, since they contain provisions to cover the situation where the parties seek to offer commitments to remedy competition concerns raised by a merger. A number of cases have occurred, for example *du Pont/ICI*,[26] where the commitments offered by the parties have been received by DG Comp so late in the second phase that the Commission has had great difficulty in conducting a proper analysis of the effects during the remaining few weeks of the time permitted for the second investigation phase. Article 19 requires any commitments put forward to the Commission by the parties be submitted within not more than twenty working days from the date of receipt of notification by the Commission or, in second phase cases, not more than sixty-five working days from the date on which the second phase investigation was initiated. Articles 21 to 25 complete the Implementing Regulation and deal with a number of technical matters, such as method of transmission of documents, the acknowledgement of receipt of documents and the definition of 'working days'.

3.4 FORM CO

Annexed to the Implementing Regulation is Form CO with appendices. This is a complex form which requires considerable legal, financial and economic input and, in all likelihood, the assistance of specialist consultants. Among the requirements of this form are:

- Section 1—An executive summary of the transaction including its strategic and economic rationale.
- Section 2—Extensive background information as to the parties and their representatives.
- Section 3—Details of the concentration, its timing, method, structure, and a list of market sectors involved in the concentration together with financial details of turnover in each Member State as well as Community-wide and worldwide turnover.
- Section 4—Ownership and control of the undertakings involved including personal and financial links and previous acquisitions of the parties.
- Section 5—Copies of all relevant documentation including agreements, public bid documents, reports and accounts, analyses, studies or surveys etc prepared for any member of the board of directors.
- Section 6—This, perhaps the most demanding section, requires market definitions of both product and geographic markets, from which the market power of the new entity arising from the concentration is to be assessed, as already discussed in our treatment of product and geographic market definitions.
- Sections 7 and 8—These sections require further details of many aspects of these markets, including market share, price levels, market entry, demand, research and development, trade associations, and general conditions.

[26] Case IV/M.214 [1995] 5 CMLR M41.

- Section 9—A summary of the overall market context and of any efficiency gains generated by the concentration.
- Section 10—Requests additional information to analyse the cooperative effects of joint ventures.

In practice it is essential in all cases to hold pre-notification discussions with the officials of DG Comp, who are quite prepared to express preliminary views on the likely main issues that will arise as a result of notification of the concentration, and may even be prepared to indicate whether the concentration plan as originally proposed will be acceptable or not. 'Best Practice Guidelines' have been published on the DG Comp website. Notification will be required prior to implementation of the concentration and following the conclusion of the agreement or the announcement of a public bid, or the acquisition of a controlling interest (Article 4(1) of the Merger Regulation). The mention of these various alternatives indicates the Commission's awareness that 'decisive influence' can be obtained in a number of different ways; some with the agreement of the target and some in a hostile manner. In an effort to be more flexible, the Commission will also accept notifications where the undertakings concerned can demonstrate a good faith intention to conclude an agreement or, in the case of a public bid, where they have publicly announced an intention to make such a bid.

The parties making the acquisition make the notification, which must be in one of the official languages of the European Union; the accurate completion of all parts of Form CO which the Commission has not agreed to waive in the particular case is of great importance, since there are fines and penalties for incorrect completion, and the form is likely to play a considerable role in the presentation of the bidder's case. For concentrations where no significant competition issues are raised, a simplified procedure has been introduced for which a much smaller amount of data has to be provided.

Pre-notification discussion with DG Comp is of particular importance in merger cases because:

- it enables the parties to the proposed concentration to become aware at an early stage of the likely concerns of the Commission
- it may enable the parties in such circumstances to adjust their proposals in a way that will facilitate clearance at first phase
- it may enable the Commission to waive the need for the parties to complete certain sections of Form CO which may be irrelevant to a particular case
- it will reduce the risk of the Commission returning the notification of Form CO as incomplete (which is now occurring more often).

3.5 THE INQUIRY PROCESS: POWERS OF THE COMMISSION

During the concentration's examination, the transaction is suspended. The only exception is contained in Article 7(2) under which a public bid (or a transaction involving a series of securities purchased on a stock exchange) which has been properly notified to the Commission under Article 4 can be completed, provided that in the meantime the bidder does not exercise the voting rights attached to the securities acquired, or does so only to protect the full value of the investment made on the basis of a derogation granted by the Commission. Once the official notification has been made, the DG Comp team allocated to the case begins an intensive three weeks of analysis of the information provided, while also seeking information from a wide variety of other sources, including suppliers, customers, trade associations, and public authorities. Consultations will also take place widely within the Commission itself and with Member States. Quick visits or surveys may be made in relevant parts of the Community to obtain information, and urgent information requests under Article 11 of the Merger Regulation sent out to interested parties. As already stated, the outcome of the inquiry may be one of three alternatives, either:

(1) that the concentration for some reason does not fall within the scope of the Regulation, e.g. because it is not a full-function joint venture or, although a 'concentration', its turnover falls below the required thresholds under Article 1

(2) that the concentration is regarded as compatible with the Common Market at the end of this first phase

(3) that the concentration raises serious doubts as to its compatibility with the Common Market and so has to go into a phase two investigation.

3.6 THE SIMPLIFIED PROCEDURE

The far greater number of concentrations with a Community dimension which are now being notified led to the publication in 2000 of a Notice, which was updated in 2005, setting out the simplified procedure dealing with cases which do not raise competition concerns. The categories of cases which fall within the simplified procedure (and which now amount to some 25 per cent of all cases) are as follows:

(1) when the acquisition involves joint control of a joint venture and the assets and turnover of the joint venture are less than €100 million within the EEA territory

(2) when the transaction is between parties not engaged in business activities in the same product or geographical market or related upstream or downstream markets

(3) even when the parties do not meet the conditions of (ii), if the total market share of the parties is less than 15 per cent for horizontal and 25 per cent for vertical relationships

(4) when a party acquires sole control of an undertaking over which it already has joint control.

3.7 POWER TO IMPOSE CONDITIONS AND
OBLIGATIONS—ARTICLE 8(2)

Even during a first-phase inquiry, the parties are free to put forward remedy proposals to eliminate competition problems raised by the concentration which would otherwise lead to a second phase detailed investigation. As we have seen, such proposals have, under Article 19 of the Implementing Regulation, to be notified to the Commission within twenty working days from receipt by the Commission of the notification, so as to give the Commission an opportunity to analyse the proposals put forward and ensure that they actually resolve the relevant competition problems, and thus eliminate the 'serious doubts' which would otherwise lead to a second-phase inquiry. Usually a first-phase undertaking, or conditions of this kind, involves a relatively simple divestment of part of the business of the bidder or target, such as occurred in *Owen-Illinois/BTR Packaging*.[27]

The power of the Commission to attach conditions and obligations to a decision following a second-phase investigation is contained in Article 8(2) of the Merger Regulation. The requirement of this Article is that the conditions and obligations have to ensure that the undertakings involved comply with the commitments that they have made to the Commission when modifying their original concentration plan, so as to render the concentration compatible with the Common Market. The parties must put forward any proposals not later than sixty-five working days from the date on which the second phase inquiry was initiated.

3.8 THE ADMINISTRATIVE POWERS OF THE COMMISSION

The Commission has the same powers in investigating concentrations as it does under Regulation 1/2003 for Article 81 and 82 cases, including the powers to carry out 'dawn raids' and to ask Member State competition authorities to carry out investigatory tasks. These powers, however, are only rarely used in merger cases. Commission officials are entitled under Article 13(2) of the Merger Regulation:

(1) to examine the books and business records of the parties

(2) to take or obtain copies of, or extracts from, these books and business records

(3) to ask for oral explanations on the spot

(4) to enter premises for the purposes of their investigation

(5) to seal business premises and books or records for the period necessary for the inspection.

Failure to notify a concentration with a Community dimension can lead to the imposition of a fine as can the provision of incomplete or misleading information in Form CO. In June 2002, Deutsche BP was fined €35,000 for unintentionally but negligently supplying incomplete information relating to an acquisition. Obstruction by parties of the Commission's attempt to seek information can be penalized under Articles 14 and 15 by fines and periodic penalty payments. In January 2008 E.on was fined €38 million for breach of a seal during an inspection.[28] Professional secrecy is protected under Article 17, under which the Commission and the competent authorities of the Member

---

[27] Case IV/M.1109 (decision of 21 April 1998).   [28] IP/08/108 Press Release 30 January 2008.

States and their relevant officials are prevented from disclosing information that is within the category of professional secrecy; information obtained from investigations relating to a particular concentration may not be used as part of any other investigation which the Commission or a Member State may wish to carry out.

There are important rights of defence under Article 18 of the Merger Regulation and the Commission is required to give those concerned, particularly the parties to the concentration, the opportunity of making known their views on the statement of objections which the Commission will provide if it has serious doubts as to whether the concentration should be cleared. This requirement is supplemented by the provisions of the Implementing Regulation, in particular Articles 14 to 16. The combined effect of the Implementing Regulation and the Merger Regulation is that in broad terms third parties and the parties concerned have the same rights of hearing and access to relevant documents as under Regulation 1/2003 for Article 81 and 82 cases.

Article 19 of the Merger Regulation sets out the advisory role that Member States play in the Commission's administrative procedure. The Advisory Committee (which is made up of experts in competition law from the relevant Member States—typically officials from the Member States' national competition authorities) can provide its opinion on the Commission's draft merger decision. Although the Commission is required to take the 'utmost account' of the Advisory Committee's opinion, the Commission is not bound to follow it. There have been a number of occasions when both the majority and minority opinions of the Advisory Committee have been published, e.g. in *Varta/Bosch*.[29]

3.9 THE BLOCKING OF MERGERS

Article 8(3) of the Merger Regulation entitles the Commission, following a second-phase decision investigation, to state that the concentration is incompatible with the Common Market without reference to any conditions. There have so far been twenty cases in this category,[30] and in other cases the likelihood of such a decision has led to the withdrawal of the notification.

Such total prohibition decisions reflect the Commission's view that the effect of the merger will be to give the merged entity such a degree of power in relevant markets as, to use the language of the Regulation, 'would significantly impede effective competition'. In some cases, there may simply be no remedy to the competition problems raised that is acceptable to the parties. *Volvo/Scania*[31] represents one of those cases; Volvo offered a number of commitments, including the opening up of its dealer network in Sweden for heavy lorries to third parties, but none was regarded by the Commission as adequate.

---

[29] Case IV/M.012 [1992] 5 CMLR M1.
[30] Although three of these decisions have subsequently been annulled by the CFI. See Section 7 below.
[31] Case Comp/M.1672 [2001] OJ L143/74.

In other cases, there may have been a greater possibility of suitable conditions being agreed, but the parties may have failed to submit their proposals at a suitably early stage or have failed to meet the strict time limits required under the Regulation. Thus, in *GE/Honeywell*,[32] the Commission would have been willing to clear the merger had GE been prepared to dispose of a sufficiently large percentage of its shares in its aircraft leasing subsidiary, GECAS, to an independent purchaser, but GE failed to agree such proposals within the time limits of the second phase. The merger was therefore blocked. It is important to be aware that the total number of mergers so far blocked by the Commission represents a tiny percentage of the cases falling within the Regulation, and that over 90 per cent of all concentrations notified to the Commission are cleared unconditionally.

Under Article 10(5) of the Merger Regulation a judgment of the ECJ or CFI annulling the whole or part of the Commission decision, as in *Kali und Salz*,[33] enables the periods for phase one and phase two laid down in the Regulation to start again. In such a case the parties are required to submit a new notification or to certify that there are no changes in market conditions requiring such a new notification.

4. REMEDIES—CONDITIONS AND OBLIGATIONS IMPOSED AS THE PRICE OF CLEARANCE

4.1 THE PURPOSE OF REMEDIES

As we have seen in the previous chapter, the outcome of a merger notification to the Commission is not necessarily that the transaction is either blocked or cleared in its entirety. In between 5 and 10 per cent of all cases notified, the result is a clearance subject to conditions and obligations agreed between the Commission and the parties to the merger. Some of the most important and high-profile cases dealt with by the Commission over the last eighteen years have been resolved in this way; and those who advise the parties in any case other than the most straightforward have to keep the possibility of such an outcome, at the end of either the first or second phase, in mind right from the early stages of the pre-notification procedure.

Articles 6(2) and 8(2) of the Merger Regulation refer to the Commission attaching to the phase one or phase two decision 'conditions and obligations intended to ensure that the undertakings comply with the commitments they have entered into vis-à-vis the Commission with a view to rendering the concentration compatible with the Common Market'. It is important to understand that the Commission cannot impose these 'conditions' and 'obligations' on the parties without their agreement.

---

[32] Case Comp/M.2220 (decision of 3 July 2001). See DG Comp Competition Policy Newsletter (2001) No. 3, p. 5.

[33] Cases C-68/94 and 30/95 [1998] ECR I-1375: [1998] 4 CMLR 829.

During both first and second phases, the parties may decide that they should put forward certain suggestions to the Commission, which they believe will enable the substantive criteria contained in Article 2 to be met, by reducing the impact of the merger on competition in the relevant markets. Negotiations will then take place over both the principle and the detail of the proposals; if the Commission is not satisfied that the proposals go far enough, it may request the parties' agreement to more stringent terms.

Although the Commission, therefore, cannot impose a remedy consisting of particular conditions and obligations on the parties, it has two important means at its disposal under the Regulation for putting pressure on them. At the first phase, it can threaten the parties with a full-scale second phase investigation under Article 6(1)(c), rather than simply dealing with the proposed merger under Article 6(1)(b). Beyond that, once the case has actually entered the second phase, the threat can be that a blocking decision will be reached, unless the parties come up with an adequate package of proposals to meet the perceived problems in some or all of the affected markets.

Over the period in which the Regulation has been operative, there has been extensive case law which illustrates how the Commission will exercise its discretion in such situations. Moreover, its experience was summarized in a Notice published on 2 March 2001,[34] which also drew on the experience of US antitrust authorities. This notice has now been replaced by a new Remedies Notice which was published in April 2007.[35]

A fundamental principle underlies the whole subject of remedies. This is that the package of remedies agreed must, by their combined effect, eliminate the competition concerns identified by the Commission, so that conditions of effective competition will be maintained on a lasting basis in the relevant markets. The Commission, in applying this principle, will necessarily have to examine every aspect of the merger, including the structure and special characteristics of the relevant markets.

4.2 STRUCTURAL AND BEHAVIOURAL REMEDIES—THE CASE LAW

It was originally thought that the Merger Regulation only empowered the Commission to accept *structural* remedies from the parties, involving the disposal by the bidder or target undertaking of part of its existing business activities or divisions, such as factories, distribution networks, research and development laboratories, or intellectual property rights, including patents and trade marks. Remedies involving restrictions of a *behavioural* nature were not thought permissible. This limitation, however, was removed by the CFI in *Gencor v. Lonrho*;[36] it confirmed the Commission's belief that it was inappropriate in the context of Article 2 merely to require undertakings to abstain from abusing a dominant position, but ruled that, in certain circumstances,

---

[34] [2001] OJ C68/3.   [35] [2008] OJ C267/1.
[36] Case T-102/96 [1999] ECR II-753: [1999] 4 CMLR 971.

behavioural undertakings might prove, either in combination with structural remedies or even on their own, the most effective way of preventing the creation or strengthening of a dominant position.

Behavioural remedies may involve the licensing of technology, the guarantee of products supplied to third parties, access to key infrastructure or the termination of existing exclusive contractual arrangements. They must be capable of being implemented effectively within a short period, without the later need of additional monitoring by the Commission, and must be described by the parties to the Commission in sufficient detail to ensure that their impact can be fully assessed. An important difference between the two types of remedy is that a structural remedy is of immediate effect and should not be capable of being reversed in the future, while a behavioural remedy will normally operate only for a fixed period of time (often three or five years) and can be varied or terminated as the result of a major change of circumstances.

An example of a case where behavioural conditions were imposed is *Boeing/McDonnell Douglas.*[37] The Commission found that the takeover by Boeing of one of its main rivals in aircraft manufacture on the world market would strengthen its existing dominant position. It proved impossible to find third parties of sufficient commercial stature to acquire the McDonnell Douglas business, so that finally the conditions agreed by Boeing involved not disposals, but acceptance that, inter alia:

- it would guarantee customer support to all purchasers of McDonnell Douglas' aircraft of the same quality as that given to its own customers
- it would not discriminate against purchasers of McDonnell Douglas' aircraft if they later decided to purchase other aircraft from third parties
- it would not enter into any additional exclusive arrangements with airlines for a ten-year period, nor enforce certain existing exclusive agreements
- it would license certain patents to third parties on a non-exclusive basis.

Nestlé/Ralston Purina,[38] by contrast, provides an example of a remedy package that included both structural and behavioural elements, in a case involving pet food markets in several Member States. Nestlé, the bidder, was required as a condition of clearance to grant an exclusive licence for a long period to a third party for its 'Friskies' brand in Spain, as well as to dispose of a production site near Barcelona. If, however, this proved impossible, alternatively it could divest Ralston Purina's 50 per cent interest in a joint venture in Spain. In Italy and Greece it had to grant exclusive licences of its rights under the 'Chow' brand. In *Pernod Richard/Diageo,*[39] the conditions agreed also included the disposal of certain brands acquired by these two bidders from the purchase of the worldwide wines and spirits business of Seagram; brands of rum and whisky had to be transferred to purchasers because of the bidders' dominant position in Iceland and other national markets.

---

[37] Case IV/M.877 [1997] OJ L336/16: [1997] 5 CMLR 270.
[38] Case Comp/M.2337 (decision of 27 July 2001).
[39] Case Comp/M.2268 (decision of 8 May 2001).

It is important to be aware of the difference between 'conditions' and 'obligations' within a 'remedy package'. Where an 'obligation' is breached, the Commission may revoke the clearance decision acting pursuant to Article 6(3) in first phase cases or Article 8(3) in second phase cases. The parties may also be subject to heavy fines (up to 10 per cent of worldwide turnover) or periodic penalties (as provided for in Article 14(2)(d) and 15(1)(c) respectively). Where a 'condition' is breached the consequences are even more severe. Not only may heavy fines be imposed but the clearance decision is no longer valid.

Once the parties have reached agreement with the Commission officials as to the remedies in their case, the Commission will proceed to 'market test' them by asking Member States, competitors, and other interested parties if they believe that they are adequate to restore effective competition. Such consultation may even extend in some cases to foreign competition authorities, for example in the USA, Canada or Japan, with whom the European Community has a formal Treaty of Co-operation (see Chapter 22).

4.3 DIVESTITURE—A STRUCTURAL REMEDY

The Commission's wide experience to date has enabled it to produce for the parties in cases involving structural remedies a model form of commitment, which they are required to follow as closely as possible. In addition to the principal conditions, it will contain a number of detailed obligations, whose aim is to ensure that disposals are promptly and effectively carried out, as the price of clearance for the transaction.

The buyer of the assets being disposed of cannot be freely chosen by the parties to the merger. The Commission will insist in the decision that it has to approve the buyer as suitable: being a viable existing or potential competitor; independent of the parties; with appropriate financial resources and expertise; and whose purchase will not itself raise Merger Regulation issues (if the transaction is of a Community dimension). In some cases, the Commission has gone even further, insisting that the buyer of the assets must be identified before the merger can be cleared and must also have signed a legally binding contract to acquire them. This is known as the 'upfront buyer' condition (as, for example, in the case of *Robert Bosch/Rexroth*).[40]

Whilst the more common structural remedy is disposal of one or more of the target businesses, the Commission may judge it more appropriate in some cases for one or more of the businesses owned by the bidder to be disposed of as, for example, happened in *Exxon/Mobil*[41] and *Bayer/Aventis*.[42] The divestiture may even include businesses where there is no apparent competitive concern, so as to ensure that the buyer acquires a viable package of assets that can compete with the merged undertakings.

If the original proposals of the parties turn out to be impractical within the short time-scale permitted (which may be a period of a few months and rarely exceeds a

---

[40] Case Comp/M.2060 (decision of 13 December 2000).
[41] Case IV/M.1383 (decision of 29 September 1999).
[42] Case Comp/M.2547 (decision of 17 April 2002).

year), they may in default be required to divest another valuable business or business asset in its place (known as the 'crown jewels' solution).

In the event of a remedy involving divestiture, the parties will have to agree to maintain the viability of the business pending its sale, and to refrain from any steps which could make it less attractive to a purchaser. A trustee will have to be appointed to manage the business pending sale and supervise its disposal. If initial attempts to effect the sale fail, the appointed trustee will be placed under considerable pressure to complete the sale within the time limit, either by lowering the price or by adding attractive additional assets to the original business being disposed of.

The Commission has, on rare occasions, agreed to modify the original conditions imposed if the parties can show that every effort has been made to carry them out, e.g. to dispose of part of the business acquired to a non-competitor. In *Pirelli Edizone/Telecom Italia*,[43] the sale of the Blu mobile telephone company to a number of competing mobile operators was ultimately agreed to, even though the original conditions had required disposal to a purchaser not already in the mobile telephone business, it having been shown that no such purchaser was available.

5. ANCILLARY RESTRAINTS

5.1 THE CONCEPT

The Community law doctrine of ancillary restraint refers to restrictive clauses whose presence is, in a commercial sense, essential to the particular transaction to which they are connected and without which that transaction would probably not take place at all. A very common type of ancillary restraint is the restrictive covenant which, on a sale and purchase of a business, binds the vendor not to compete with the purchaser for a number of years so that the purchaser will obtain the full value of the goodwill and assets for which he is paying. It is clear that the terms of the restrictive covenant in this situation have to be reasonable in the light of the overall transaction and this will affect its scope, its geographical coverage, and the period of time for which it is applicable. In the general context of a sale it must also be necessary in a commercial sense for adequate protection of the purchaser.

It may be that restrictions contained in transactions which qualify as concentrations within the terms of the Merger Regulation may technically be outside the reach of Article 81(1). Since, however, the Merger Regulation itself prohibits application of Regulation 1/2003 in respect of such concentrations, there needs to be a provision for negative clearance for such clauses in merger cases. For this reason Recital 21 and the final sentences of Articles 6(1)(b) and 8(2) of the Merger Regulation provide that the decision declaring the concentration compatible shall also cover restrictions directly related and necessary to the implementation of the concentration.

---

[43] Case Comp/M.2574 (decision of 29 September 2001).

5.2 THE 2005 NOTICE

In March 2005,[44] the Commission published a new Notice replacing its earlier Notices of 1990 and 2001. The 2005 Notice reflects the principle of self-assessment introduced by Regulation 1/2003 in relation to the analysis of restrictions under Article 81(1) and provides that the Commission will not assess ancillary restraints in the course of its substantive decisions, so that the parties will have to make their own assessment of such restraints, with any dispute being resolved by national courts. However Recital 21 of the Merger Regulation does state that the Commission should, at the request of the undertakings concerned, expressly assess the ancillary character of restrictions if a case presents 'novel and unresolved questions giving rise to genuine uncertainty'. Such questions are defined by the Recital as those 'not covered by the relevant Commission notice in force or a published Commission decision'. In practice, most forms of ancillary restraint are covered by the 2005 Notice and self-assessment is very common.

In making their assessment, the parties can, of course, make use of the guidance which the new Notice provides. The main principles stated in the Notice are that:

(1) The duration of non-competition clauses in favour of the purchaser are generally limited to two years in cases involving the transfer of goodwill alone, and to three years where know-how is also protected.

(2) The geographical scope of such clauses is generally limited to the territories where the vendor offered goods or services immediately before the transfer, unless the vendor had already invested in other territories with a view to immediate entry.

(3) Non-solicitation and confidentiality clauses are to be assessed in the same way as non-competition clauses though, in some cases, confidentiality clauses concerning technical know-how may be accepted for longer than three years.

(4) Non-competition clauses between the parents of a joint venture and the joint venture can be justified as a general rule for the lifetime of the joint venture.

(5) Licences of intellectual property rights (including know-how), purchase and supply agreements (the latter normally for a maximum of five years) and service and distribution agreements would also be allowed to extend where necessary to cover the transitional period of a new joint venture from dependency to autonomy.

Contractual provisions which do not constitute ancillary restraints and which infringe Article 81(1) may be capable of benefiting from block exemptions, such as Regulation 2790/99.

5.3 NON-COMPETE CLAUSES

The first example of an ancillary restraint is a non-competition clause which protects the goodwill acquired by the purchaser. The Notice stresses that it is the purchaser

---

[44] [2005] OJ C56/24.

which requires such protection and that it is rare that a vendor can reasonably seek to impose any similar restriction on its purchasers. In all cases, however, such clauses must be limited to a duration, geographic area, and subject matter which are necessary for the protection of the party receiving their benefit.

As stated above, the period of two years is normally the most allowed for transfers of goodwill alone, extended by a further year if know-how is also transferred. In some cases, however, there may be reasons why there is special loyalty between the vendor and its customers and, in these circumstances, sometimes these limits can be extended. The vendor's covenants can bind its subsidiaries and agents, but cannot bind third parties, such as distributors and resellers.

An example where the parties sought to impose non-compete clauses with excessive coverage was *Tesco/Catteau*.[45] The Commission here objected to the unlimited geographic scope of a non-compete agreement given by the Catteau family on the sale to Tesco of certain supermarket businesses in Continental Europe, and limited those obligations to specific defined regions in France and Belgium. Moreover, in the same agreement, the members of the Catteau family bound by the restrictions included not only the named principals and vendors but also other members of their family, not all of whom were necessarily shareholders in the relevant company. The Commission also refused to recognize non-compete obligations unlimited in time, holding that a maximum term of three years would be reasonable in the light of Tesco's lack of experience in these continental markets and the fact that no technical know-how, and only limited commercial know-how, were being transferred to Tesco by the Catteau family.

5.4 INTELLECTUAL PROPERTY RIGHT LICENCES

The second example of an ancillary restraint is that of licences for intellectual property rights (IPRs) and know-how. In a number of concentrations, and particularly in full-function joint ventures, an important issue may be the transfer of IPRs by the parents to the joint venture. The parent companies, however, may not be willing to assign these rights absolutely since they may need to retain them for their own trading purposes. The parent companies may, therefore, only be prepared to grant licences to the purchaser of the joint venture to use these rights for the specific purposes for which the joint venture has been set up, or in relation to the assets of the business that the purchaser has acquired.

Such licences are normally regarded as ancillary to the purchase agreement and need not be limited in time. The Notice indicates that simple or non-exclusive licences of IPRs are normally acceptable as necessary and ancillary and can be limited as stated above to certain fields of use. On the whole, territorial restrictions will not normally be looked on favourably though field of use restrictions in non-exclusive licences may be acceptable. Restrictions in licence agreements going beyond this do not obtain the benefit of the negative clearance provisions and they should be assessed on their

---

[45] Case IV/M.301 [1993] 4 CMLR 238.

merits under Article 81(3). They may benefit from the block exemption for Technology Transfer Agreements (Regulation 772/2004, discussed in Chapter 12). Similar principles are applied to licences governing trade marks, business names, and similar rights. On occasion vendors may wish to retain control of IPRs for activities other than those being transferred and to provide appropriate licences to enable the purchaser to have the full benefit of the assets being transferred. Alternatively, if the IPRs are to be transferred with the business, it may be reasonable to require the purchaser to licence these back to the vendor to allow the vendor to continue activities outside the scope of the transfer.

5.5 PURCHASE AND SUPPLY AGREEMENTS

The third category of ancillary agreement is purchase and supply agreements. The Notice acknowledges that the sale of a business or undertaking may cause problems to the new owner, since the business transferred may find the transfer causes a disruption of its normal sources of supply or the distribution of its product. It is often, therefore, necessary to maintain, at least for a transitional period, links between the vendor and purchaser of the business under which raw materials continue to be supplied by the vendor to the purchaser. The legitimate aim of such obligations to ensure continuity of supply of such products is recognized and accepted provided that it is not made a permanent feature. The Commission does not, however, look favourably on general clauses governing exclusive purchase or exclusive supply, because such exclusivity is not normally necessary to permit the implementation of the concentration. Alternative and less restrictive methods for ensuring reasonable supplies to the purchasing company for its new acquired asset will have to be considered. The arrangements must in any case only be enforced for a reasonably limited period, normally up to five years. Insofar as a vertical agreement between the parties is not ancillary and infringes Article 81(1), it may be capable of exemption under Article 81(3) and, in particular, the block exemption Regulation 2790/99.

Examples of ancillary supply agreements can be found in *ICL/Nokia*,[46] where a provision that the vendor (Nokia) and the business transferred by it to ICL would make available to each other any supplies required in the course of their trading for one year was treated as ancillary. A similar provision was approved in the *Courtaulds/Snia*[47] joint venture whereby the parent companies agreed to supply their joint venture on a non-exclusive basis with some products essential to the activities taken over. The Commission, however, rejected the original proposed duration of the supply agreement, because it regarded it as excessive in the context of the replacement of the original dependent relationship with the parent companies by the new joint venture.

Finally, it should be noted that in some full-function joint-venture cases examined under the Merger Regulation rather than under Article 81, the Commission appears to take a more generous view of non-competitive covenants than it does in Article 81 cases.

---

[46] Case IV/M.105 [1991] 4 CMLR 817.   [47] Case IV/M.113 [1992] 4 CMLR 349.

6. THE RELATIONSHIP BETWEEN THE MERGER REGULATION AND ARTICLES 81 AND 82

Articles 81 and 82 came into effect as part of the Treaty of Rome on 1 January 1958, and have played a key role in the development of the Community as central pillars of the Community's constitutional structure. Later regulations, such as the Merger Regulation, have no legal basis to nullify or amend these Articles. Nevertheless, whilst this cardinal principle has to be maintained, it is important to be aware of the practical differences in the application of these Articles which the adoption of the Merger Regulation has brought about.

Before adoption of the Merger Regulation in December 1989 both Articles 81 and 82 had been applied to mergers and acquisitions of shares, albeit in limited circumstances as described in the previous chapter. No procedural regulations were, however, ever adopted by the Commission or Council to support the application of these Articles in this way. It was the inadequacy, therefore, of these two Articles to provide an effective system of merger control that led ultimately to the adoption of the Merger Regulation which states, in Article 21(1), that Regulation 1/2003 has no application to concentrations as defined in Article 3 except in relation to joint ventures that do not have a Community dimension and which have as their object to effect the coordination of the competitive behaviour of undertakings that remain independent.

Articles 81 and 82 do, however, also have direct effect in national courts. The question, therefore, has been asked whether they can be used to block concentrations in those courts. It would seem that Article 81 cannot be used in such a way although it can be used in respect of minority shareholdings or joint ventures which fall short of being concentrative.[48] The position under Article 82, however, is different since the acquisition of a competitor by a dominant company may be an abuse of a dominant position[49] and the Article can be implemented immediately in national courts without the need for specific Community legislation. In principle, therefore, it seems that a party could challenge a concentration (whether it had a Community dimension or not) in a national court under this Article. In practice however, the national court judge may well hesitate to consider the merits of the concentration which is challenged given the complexities of such an assessment and it would require a strong case, perhaps one involving the very high market shares found in *Continental Can*, before any national court is likely to intervene on the plaintiff's behalf. If the concentration was being reviewed by the Commission or a national competition authority, a stay of the national court proceedings by the judge would seem a likely outcome.

---

[48] See Ch. 16, Section 1.4.
[49] Case 6/72 *Europemballage and Continental Can v Commission* [1973] ECR 215: [1973] CMLR 179.

7. APPEALS TO THE CFI AND ECJ

7.1 COMPETITION LAW APPEALS IN GENERAL

The CFI and ECJ have both dealt extensively with competition cases arising under Articles 81 and 82. These cases reach them by one of two main routes:

(1) By way of appeal against a Commission decision and/or against a fine imposed for a breach of one or both of these Articles. Such cases reach the CFI initially under Article 230 which allows an appeal from the Commission in the following circumstances:

   (a) lack of competence or authority;

   (b) infringement of an essential procedural requirement;

   (c) infringement of the terms of the Treaty or any rule of law relating to its application; or

   (d) misuse of powers.

   A further appeal can take place, on a point of law only, to the ECJ. Examples of such cases would be those brought on appeal from decisions under Article 82 by the Commission, such as *Magill*.[50]

(2) By way of request from a national court for a preliminary ruling under Article 234 of the Treaty, as for example in the *Delimitis*[51] and the *Hag*[52] cases.

Article 230 of the Treaty clearly applies to decisions by the Commission under the Merger Regulation and the Regulation recognizes the rights of the parties in this respect. Article 21(2) states that 'subject to review by the ECJ, the Commission shall have sole jurisdiction to take the decisions provided for in this Regulation'. Article 16 furthermore provides that the ECJ has unlimited jurisdiction to review decisions when the Commission has fixed a fine or periodic penalty payments under Articles 14 or 15 of the Regulation.

It is not only actual parties to merger decisions who are entitled to appeal. Under Article 230(2) of the Treaty a person may also appeal in respect of a decision which, 'although in the form of a regulation...addressed to another person, is of direct and individual concern to the third party'. A third party with a legitimate interest may also bring an action before the CFI, as for example in *Impala v Commission*.[53] The third party must then show that the relevant decision is capable of affecting its interests by bringing about a specific change in its legal position. Finally, the appellant has to show that it is 'individually concerned'. This means that the decision must be shown to have

---

[50] See fn. 25.   [51] Case C-234/89 [1991] ECR I-935: [1992] 5 CMLR 210.

[52] Case 192/73 *Van Zuylen* v. *Hag* ('*Hag 1*') [1974] ECR 731: 2 CMLR 127; Case 10/89 *CNL-Sucal* v. *Hag* ('*Hag 2*') [1990] ECR I-3711: 3 CMLR 571.

[53] Case T-464/04 [2006] ECR II-2289, overturned on appeal Case C-413/06 P, 10 July 2008 (not yet reported).

affected it by reason of its own particular characteristics which distinguish it from all other persons.

7.2 APPEALS UNDER THE MERGER REGULATION

The early cases involving appeals to the Courts in Luxembourg involved third parties. In the first case employees of Perrier challenged the substantive decision of the Commission in 1992 in *Nestlé/Perrier*.[54] The employees were concerned that the acquisition would result in a loss of several hundred jobs and they asked the Court to suspend the Commission's decision. The Court ruled that the employees were entitled to raise an appeal but it refused to grant them an order for interim measures suspending implementation of the decision. The Court noted that under Recital 13 of Regulation 4064/89 the Commission was required to engage in an appraisal of the merits of a concentration within the general framework of the achievement of the fundamental objectives referred to in Article 2 of the Treaty, including that of strengthening the Community's economic and social cohesion referred to in Article 130(a).

The first ruling by the CFI came in the *Zunis Holding* case[55] in 1993 where shareholders in a target company, the subject of a 1991 Commission decision *(Mediobanca/ Generali)*,[56] complained about the Commission's finding that the acquisition of shares by Mediobanca up to a total percentage of 12.84 per cent did not constitute a concentration within the meaning of Article 3 of the Merger Regulation. The applicant shareholders tried to obtain an order from the Court that the Commission should reopen proceedings on the basis of late and new information about secret shareholder agreements, which the applicants suggested rendered the influence of Mediobanca greater than had been thought appropriate by the Commission itself. The Court found that, since the Commission's decision did not place any of the applicants as minority shareholders in Generali in a position different to any other shareholder, they were not individually concerned by the decision.

Appeals were brought to the CFI by Air France against two decisions of the Commission in respect of the acquisition by British Airways of Dan Air and TAT European Airways.[57] In the first case, the Commission had ruled that the acquisition was outside the scope of the Regulation because the turnover did not reach the required figure. The Commission's decision had not been taken formally after a full first-stage inquiry but given informally. It was, nevertheless, held to be an action with legal effect because of the effect it had on the position of the parties. Air France was held entitled to appeal to the CFI because the decision given was of direct and individual concern to it as a competitor in the relevant market; it lost, however, on the merits.

The number and importance of appeals against merger decisions to the CFI is now on the increase. As we have already noted, in *Gencor*,[58] both substantive and procedural

---

[54] Cases T-96/92 [1995] ECR II-1213 and T-12/93 [1995] ECR II-1247.
[55] Case T-83/92 [1993] ECR II-1169. On appeal to ECJ, Case C-480/93 P [1996] ECR I-1: [1996] 5 CMLR 219.
[56] Case IV/M.159 [1994] 4 CMLR M1.   [57] Cases T-2 and 3/93 [1994] ECR II-121, 323.
[58] See fn. 36.

issues were raised, including the right of the Commission to exercise jurisdiction when the parties have no assets within the Community. In *Coca-Cola* v. *Commission*[59] Coca-Cola sought not to have the Commission's decision annulled (as the Commission had found in favour of the concentration in which Coca-Cola was involved), but to have certain findings of the Commission overruled, which it believed could be prejudicial to it in future cases. These included a finding that it held a dominant position in the British market for cola drinks, but the CFI held such a finding was unappealable in that, as the concentration in question had been unconditionally cleared, it had no legal effect on the appellant.

The first major substantive appeal against a Commission decision under the Merger Regulation was in the *Kali und Salz* case (discussed in Chapter 16 at Section 8.5). Here, both the French government and a French company had challenged the decision; whilst the French company only challenged the conditions attached, the government attacked the whole decision. The Court's decision in March 1998 clearly showed that it was prepared to examine the detailed reasoning of the Commission and its interpretation of the provisions of the Merger Regulation. The outcome of the Court's decision was the complete annulment of the decision, not simply the removal of the conditions; the Court stated that, if the decision itself was annulled, the conditions attached to it were also invalid. In the event, the Commission finally issued a fresh decision to clear the concentration, even though it was impossible after the passage of four years to reinstate the original commercial relationship of the parties.

It is noteworthy that in this case the ECJ had been prepared to grant interim orders to the parties to preserve the status quo. For example, one of the conditions was that the merged entity (K&S) was required to withdraw from an export cartel set up in Vienna for exports outside the Community, in which both SCPA and K&S had a 25 per cent interest. At the request of SCPA the President of the CFI suspended the withdrawal of K&S from the export cartel because neither of the other shareholders in the cartel organization was willing to buy out the K&S shares. The cartel would automatically dissolve under its provisions upon notice of termination by any one of the shareholders, unless one of the other shareholders was willing to acquire the shares of the withdrawing party, and such an imposed dissolution was felt to be unfair on SCPA until its substantive hearing on the merits of the decision had been heard.

The review by the CFI is detailed and meticulous. The CFI scrutinizes the evidence to ensure that it provides a proper factual basis for the conclusions contained in the Commission's decision. Several high-profile CFI judgments have criticized the Commission for not having sufficient evidence to support some of the theories of harm used to prohibit proposed mergers.[60]

So far as issues of economic assessment are concerned, the CFI recognizes that the Commission has a certain discretion but, as the ECJ explained in *Tetra Laval*, 'that does

---

[59] Cases T-125 & 127/97 *Coca Cola Company* v. *Commission* [2000] ECR II-1733: [2000] 5 CMLR 467.

[60] See, for example, Case T-342/99 *Airtours v Commission* [2002] ECR II-2585: [2002] 5 CMLR 317; and Case T-5/02 *Tetra Laval v Commission* [2002] ECR II-4381: [2002] 5 CMLR 1182, discussed in Section 7.3 below and Ch.16, Section 8.6.

not mean that the Community Courts must refrain from reviewing the Commission's interpretation of information of an economic nature. Not only must the Community Courts, inter alia, establish whether the evidence is factually accurate, reliable and consistent but also whether that evidence contains all the information which must be taken into account in order to assess a complex situation and whether it is capable of substantiating the conclusions drawn from it.'[61]

In an interesting recent development, the CFI has allowed Schneider to recover damages for procedural defects in the merger process amounting to a breach by the Commission of Schneider's rights of defence.[62]

7.3 THE EXPEDITED APPEAL PROCEDURE OF THE CFI: *SCHNEIDER AND TETRA*

The CFI has now introduced a system for hearing appeals (not limited to competition cases) on an expedited basis, adopting written procedures but with a full oral hearing, and this has increased the number of appeals brought. Whilst the *Airtours* decision had been dealt with under the normal procedure (and therefore took nearly three years), both *Schneider/Legrand* and *Tetra/Sidel* in autumn 2002 were dealt with under the new procedure as was ENI/EDP/GDP in 2005.[63] In *Schneider*[64] the Commission's analysis of the many national markets in Europe for electrical equipment was found inadequate except for that dealing with the French market; and in respect of that national market its decision was adjudged procedurally unfair, since it differed from the statement of objections in its description of the impact which the combination of the businesses of the two parties would have. In *Tetra/Sidel*[65] the decision of the Commission was based on a theory of leverage; Tetra had a strong position in the manufacture of cartons and carton packaging machinery whilst Sidel manufactured plastic (PET) bottles as well as the machinery used for shaping the raw plastic forms into bottle shapes. There was some limited overlap between the products (milk, fruit juice, and tea and coffee drinks) that could be sold in either form of container. The Commission's decision had been based on its perception that Tetra would be likely to use its dominance in the carton business to discourage packagers from shifting from the use of cartons to that of plastic bottles for their requirements and would practise 'mixed bundling' by offering discounts to such packagers on their future carton purchases, on condition that they also acquired their plastic bottle machinery from Sidel rather than from other manufacturers. Whilst the CFI confirmed in its decision

---

[61] Case C-12/03P *Commission v Tetra Laval* [2005] ECR I-987 at para. 39. See also Case C-413/06 P *Bertelsmann and Sony v Impala*, 10 July 2008 (not yet reported).

[62] Case 351/03 *Schneider Legrand v Commission* [2008] 4 CMLR 1533, on appeal Case C-440/07.

[63] Case T-87/05 *EDP v Commission* [2005] ECR II-3745, [2005] 5 CMLR 1436.

[64] Case T-310/01 [2002] ECR II-4071. See DG Comp Competition Policy Newsletter (2002) No. 3, p. 7 on the expedited appeal process.

[65] Case T-5/02 [2002] II-4381: [2002] 5 CMLR 1182, upheld on appeal to the ECJ Case C-12/03 [2005] ECR I-987.

that the Regulation could be applied to conglomerate mergers and that leverage from a position of dominance in one market to another related market could be the basis for intervention, it found, on the evidence available to the Commission, that this case had not been proved in that it fell far short of establishing that the consequences of the merger justified an adverse decision.

Decisions are now regularly given under the expedited procedure on appeals from the Commission. Not all appeals, however, are held under the expedited procedure, as it is not appropriate in more complex cases. The benefit of the expedited procedure is that a judgment can be produced within eight to ten months from the original Commission decision rather than the two- to four-year period typically experienced. Moreover, although the majority of these cases involve appeals by the parties against Commission decisions blocking a merger or imposing onerous conditions upon them, others have been brought by third parties objecting to the decision of the Commission to clear a concentration or to attack conditions considered too lenient.[66]

FURTHER READING

D. BAILEY, 'Damages Actions under the EC Merger Regulation' [2007] 44(1) CMLRev 101.

—— 'Standard of Proof in EC Merger Proceedings: a Common Law Perspective' [2003] 40(4) CMLRev 845.

O. BUDZINSKI, 'An Economic Perspective on the Jurisdictional Reform of the European Merger Control System' [2006] 2 ECJ 119.

M. HARKER, Cross-border Mergers in the EU: The Commission v the Member States' [2007] 3 ECJ 503.

M. MOTTA 'EC Merger Policy and the Airtours Case' [2000] ECLR 199.

---

[66] See e.g. *Impala v Commission*, fn. 53.

18

JOINT VENTURES AND
HORIZONTAL COOPERATION
AGREEMENTS

1. INTRODUCTION

1.1 WHY JOINT VENTURES ARE FORMED

There are many situations in which a business undertaking, looking at possible developments of its future commercial activities, will decide that it needs a partner (or even more than one) to share opportunities and risks in a particular project. Whilst the natural desire to 'go it alone' may be strong, it often has to acknowledge that the development of existing products (let alone the research and development (R&D) required to produce new ones) may demand investment too great for its own resources. It may, for example, have adequate personnel but inadequate finance; alternatively, whilst finance may not be a problem its staff may lack the required expertise. This is particularly likely in areas of quickly developing high technology such as electronics, computers, media, and telecommunications. The sheer pace of technical and technological development, coupled with an increasing liberalization of many markets throughout the European Union, means that even companies with a powerful position as incumbent national operators in their own home telecommunications market have found that they need partners for developing new services and for finding customers for them on a cross-border basis.

The task of choosing such a partner is never easy but will necessarily involve careful consideration of the known abilities and resources of the undertakings which themselves might be expected to be their chief rivals in this new field. Such undertakings may be existing rivals or potential competitors. The undertaking being considered for partnership may not be a competitor, actual or potential, but may have expertise in a totally different area which may offer the possibility to combine and to create novel products or services. The degree of cooperation proposed may be quite limited, e.g. the operation of joint-purchasing arrangements or shared laboratory work, or alternatively may be very extensive, e.g. a proposed merger of the parties' entire interests in a particular field with a consequential need to give up their individual business in that market in favour of the new joint enterprise. A national telecommunications operator may have in place an existing communication network, through which it is seeking to provide not only conventional voice telephony services, but also a range of new services, which may include video conferencing and business-data transmission, as well as the provision of digital-television services or cable or satellite services. Its potential partner or partners may have customers and expertise in all these areas but, as newcomers, lack access to a sufficient communication network. A joint venture may well be the best solution in these situations.

What will be required in each case is a structure that is adequate and appropriate to support the task that the joint venture will fulfil. In each case, there would at least seem to be the need for:

- the creation of either a separate legal undertaking, or at least a recognizable joint committee or informal organization clearly identifiable as separate from its parents
- the transfer by the parents to the new undertaking of personnel and assets (often including intellectual property rights)
- the allocation by formal decision to the new undertaking of responsibility for carrying out its allotted functions
- effective joint control by the parents of the joint venture.

1.2 CONTROL OF A JOINT VENTURE

Shared control of a joint venture by its parents can be achieved in a number of ways and this will vary according to the circumstances of the individual case. It may be based on retention of ownership or rights to the use of some or all of the assets of the joint venture such as plant, machine tools, patents, trademarks, and know-how. How the joint venture is to be controlled is often set out in the constitution of the joint venture or may be reflected in the composition of its board of directors or managing committee.

The essence of joint control is that the parent companies must agree on decisions concerning the activities of the joint venture because of their respective rights of ownership in the joint venture or because the terms of contracts or the provisions in the joint venture's constitution require joint agreement on matters of strategic importance to the joint venture. If one of the parent companies alone can decide on the commercial activities and strategy of the joint venture then there is no joint control and it will be deemed to control the company.

In the majority of situations joint control is based on the terms of the agreement between the parent companies, as will be illustrated by a number of the cases considered in this chapter. The constitution of the joint venture will contain the provisions required by each party to ensure that they retain sufficient legal rights to ensure that cooperation is required between them over its business strategy. It is important however to distinguish rights which are typically given to *shareholders* as compared with rights relating to the *managerial* and *commercial aims* of the joint venture. The latter decisions are taken by the governing body, normally the board of directors, of the joint venture. It is at this level that one looks for involvement by the parent companies if the requirement of joint control is to be satisfied. The possession simply of powers referable to the rights of shareholders, e.g. as to the issue of new shares or ultimate closure of the business, do not alone give sufficient control to constitute joint control. If therefore there are several participants in a joint venture it may be that only some of them will, by virtue of their larger shareholding or other rights conferred on them by the joint-venture agreement, be considered to have the necessary elements of joint control required by the Merger Regulation.

1.3 THE DISTINCTION BETWEEN JOINT VENTURES THAT ARE CONCENTRATIONS AND THOSE THAT ARE NOT

Having established the essential elements of a joint venture, next it is important to understand when a joint venture is treated as a 'concentration' and therefore potentially subject to the substantive and procedural provisions and timetables of the Merger Regulation, as already described in detail in Chapters 16 and 17. The detailed requirements for a 'concentration' are set out in the next section of this chapter but, in broad terms, require that:

(1) parent companies are acquiring joint control of the joint venture

(2) the aggregate turnovers of the parent companies of the joint venture reach the thresholds for world and EC turnover, set out in Article 1

(3) the joint venture itself is 'full-function', performing on a lasting basis all the functions of an autonomous economic entity.

If a joint venture satisfies (1) in respect of the required element of joint control and (2) in respect of turnover but fails to satisfy the requirements of (3), it will not be regarded as a 'concentration'. It will however be potentially within the scope of Article 81(1), provided that it falls within the specific conditions set out in that Article. It may also be subject to provisions of national merger control in those countries whose laws classify joint ventures as mergers by reference to the acquisition of shares rather than by reviewing the scope and autonomy of the joint venture.

The treatment of joint ventures under EC competition law has changed over the years. Initially, all joint ventures which might affect trade between Member States, and which had as their object or effect restriction of competition within the Common Market, were subject to Article 81(1) and (3); however, the treatment of such joint ventures changed when the Merger Regulation came into force in September 1990 and, for the first time, brought within its definition of 'concentration' certain categories of joint ventures.

Originally, the only joint ventures that were treated as 'concentrations', and therefore within the scope of the Merger Regulation, were those known as 'concentrative' joint ventures, which (as a *positive* matter) performed on a lasting basis all the functions of an autonomous economic entity and (as a *negative* matter), did not give rise to coordination of the competitive behaviour of the parents amongst themselves, or between the parents and the joint venture.

For a variety of reasons, the parties to such agreements and their lawyers often sought to frame joint-venture agreements and arrangements in ways that could be brought within the definition of 'concentrative' rather than 'cooperative'. Over the early years during which the Merger Regulation operated the Commission moved in favour of broadening the definition given to the concentrative joint venture, but many full-function joint ventures did not qualify to be dealt with under the terms of the Merger Regulation, but remained subject to Article 81 and its more protracted timescale for assessment. This situation was changed in March 1998 by amendment to Regulation 4064/89 and is encapsulated in the current Merger Regulation, with the result that *all* full-function joint ventures are now dealt with under the procedural rules and timescale of the Merger Regulation. This means that the Commission examines:

(1) the establishment of the joint venture itself and its structural aspects in accordance with 'the significant impediment to competition' test contained in Article 2(2) of the Merger Regulation

(2) the cooperation aspects of the joint venture in accordance with Article 81 (as imported into the Merger Regulation by virtue of its Article 2(4)).

1.4 THE EFFECT OF REGULATION 1/2003 ON JOINT VENTURES

Under Regulation 1/2003 (and as described in detail in Chapter 19), the EC notification system, established for so many years under Regulation 17/62, has been abolished and Article 81(1) and (3) is now enforced primarily by national competition authorities and national courts, freeing up the Commission to deal with major cases affecting a number of Member States, such as large-scale European cartels.

The introduction of Regulation 1/2003 did not directly affect the operation of the Merger Regulation and its treatment of joint ventures that are 'concentrations'. Those joint ventures which fall within that definition continue to be dealt with in the manner described in Sections 2 and 3 of this chapter. However, the Regulation has had serious consequences for those joint ventures which are not concentrations and are dealt with under Article 81. Instead of being able to satisfy the Commission that the relevant joint venture is either outside Article 81(1) or should benefit from an individual exemption under Article 81(3), parties now have to make their own judgment as to whether the formation of the joint venture and terms of the agreements to which it is subject, are compatible with Article 81, without any certainty that ultimately a national court or competition authority, or even the Commission itself, will be of the same opinion. In other words, an important element of legal certainty, which the former system of notification under Article 81 provided, has been lost.

Joint ventures often involve substantial investment and far-reaching integration by the companies involved. The existence of the compulsory prior notification scheme provided by the Merger Regulation for full function joint ventures is clearly more satisfactory for the parties than the self-assessment regime (with its risk of a later adverse decision by a national court or competition authority) which applies to other types of joint ventures under Article 81.

2. THE DEFINITION OF JOINT VENTURES WHICH ARE CONCENTRATIONS UNDER THE MERGER REGULATION

2.1 THE MERGER REGULATION ARTICLE 3(1) AND (2): DEFINITION OF A CONCENTRATION

As explained in Chapter 16, after many years of negotiation, the terms of the original Merger Regulation were finally agreed by the Member States and came into force in September 1990. The new regulation provided not only a different substantive test for the assessment of concentrations, but, in comparison to the old procedures under Regulation 17, provided a more streamlined and timely assessment of individual cases. From the start, it was the intention certain joint ventures would be able to benefit from the new and speedier procedures of the Merger Regulation and would no longer be subject to the slower processes under Articles 81(1) and (3).

The term 'joint venture' covers a wide range of activities, from the kind of market-sharing and price-fixing arrangements closely akin to a cartel at one extreme to an agreement at the other to merge completely the activities of the participants in a particular product or service whilst the parent companies cease to operate in that market themselves. While the former still need to be analysed under Article 81(1) and (3), the latter would more appropriately be treated as a concentration. It was necessary for the Merger Regulation to set out the criteria for deciding which joint ventures would in future be treated under the criteria appropriate to those of the Merger Regulation, which in turn would lead to a more favourable procedure and timescale being available for their assessment.

In order for a joint venture to be reviewed under the original Regulation, it had to meet not only the world and EC turnover requirements contained in Articles 1 and 5, but also had to:

- be legally under the joint control of two or more parties
- be formed on a lasting basis to carry out all the functions of an autonomous economic entity (the *positive* condition)
- not have as its object or effect the coordination of activity, either between its parent companies or between the parent companies and the joint venture (the *negative* condition).

Any joint venture unable to meet both the positive and negative conditions would be described not as 'concentrative', but as 'cooperative' and would fall within the jurisdiction of Article 81 and of Regulation 17/62[1] with its considerably longer and more unpredictable procedures and time limits.

Between 1990 and 1998, the interpretation and application of the negative condition, in particular, caused considerable difficulties both for the Commission itself and also for the parties to such joint ventures. In Commission 'Interface Notices' published in 1990 and in 1994, attempts were made to clarify the distinction; professional legal skills became increasingly utilized to frame joint ventures in such a way as to emphasize the 'concentrative' elements and to downplay the 'coordinating' effects or objectives. The procedures and timetable of the Merger Regulation were regarded as so much superior to those operated by the Commission under Article 81 that such efforts were regarded as necessary; in many cases, however, they were not successful in convincing the Commission that a particular joint venture should indeed be treated as a concentration.

2.2 THE EFFECT OF REGULATION 1310/97

The definition of a 'concentration' for the purposes of EC merger-control law was however changed in important respects by Regulation 1310/97, which came into effect on 1 March 1998. This eliminated the 'negative' condition referred to above and expanded the classification of joint ventures falling within the Merger Regulation by limiting the requirements to those of joint control and the 'positive' requirement of full-function. The revised text of Article 3(4) of the Merger Regulation reflecting this major policy change now simply reads as follows:

The creation of a joint venture performing on a lasting basis all the functions of an autonomous economic entity, shall constitute a concentration within the meaning of paragraph 1(b) of Article 3.

Definition of joint control and the definition of a full-function joint venture are found in the Commission's Consolidated Jurisdictional Notice.[2] It should always be remembered however that a Commission Notice has no legislative force and represents simply guidance as to the current practice of the Commission (rather than hard law), which can on occasion be overruled by decisions of a Community court. Sometimes, the Commission has even been known to depart from the approach of its own Notice.

2.3 JOINT CONTROL

In many cases joint control of the joint venture is based not upon shareholding alone but upon the detailed terms of the shareholders' agreement between the companies; a majority shareholder may extend to one or more minority shareholders a contractual right to take part in the control of the joint venture. If two undertakings each hold half of the equity of a joint venture, even without further agreement between them, both will be obliged permanently to cooperate so as to avoid reciprocal blocking votes on

---

[1] Now Reg. 1/2003.   [2] [2008] OJ C 95/1.

decisions affecting the joint venture's commercial activities. The same would apply to joint ventures with three or more parents if each of them had a right of veto relating to strategic decisions on the business policy of the joint venture. A joint venture with a complex structure may alternatively find itself controlled by a substantial number of undertakings that between them control a majority of the capital or hold together the requisite voting rights. In such cases joint control could only be presumed if the convergence of their economic interests supports the notion of a common policy of the parent companies towards the operation of the joint venture.

Paragraphs 62 to 82 of the 2008 Jurisdictional Notice provide guidance as to the notion of joint control. Joint control may exist even where there is no equality between the two parent companies in votes or in representation in decision-making bodies or where there are more than two parent companies. This is the case where minority shareholders have additional rights which allow them to veto decisions which are essential for the strategic commercial behaviour of the joint venture. These veto rights may be set out in the statute of the joint venture or conferred by agreement between its parent companies. The veto rights themselves may operate by means of a specific quorum required for decisions taken in the shareholders' meeting or in the board of directors to the extent that the parent companies are represented on this board. It is also possible that strategic decisions are subject to approval by a body, e.g. supervisory board, where the minority shareholders are represented and form part of the quorum needed for such decisions.

These veto rights must be related to strategic decisions on the business policy of the joint venture. They must go beyond the veto rights normally accorded to minority shareholders in order to protect their financial interests as investors in the joint venture. This normal protection of the rights of minority shareholders is related to decisions on the essence of the joint venture, such as changes in the statute, increase or decrease of the capital, or liquidation. A veto right, for example, which prevents the sale or winding up of the joint venture, does not confer joint control on the minority shareholder concerned.

In contrast, veto rights which confer joint control typically include decisions and issues such as the budget, the business plan, major investments, or the appointment of senior management. The acquisition of joint control, however, does not require that the acquirer has the power to exercise decisive influence on the day-to-day running of an undertaking. The crucial element is that the veto rights are sufficient to enable the parent companies to exercise such influence in relation to the strategic business behaviour of the joint venture. Moreover, it is not necessary to establish that an acquirer of joint control of the joint venture will actually make use of its decisive influence. The possibility to use this influence and, hence, the mere existence of the veto rights, is sufficient.

In order to acquire joint control, it is not necessary for a minority shareholder to have all the veto rights mentioned above. It may be sufficient that some, or even one such right, exists. Whether or not this is the case depends upon the precise content of the veto right itself and also the importance of this right in the context of the specific business of the joint venture.

In the case where a new joint venture is established, as opposed to the acquisition of minority shareholdings in a pre-existing company, there is a higher probability that the parent companies are carrying out a deliberate common policy. This is true in particular where each parent company provides a contribution to the joint venture which is vital for its operation (e.g. specific technologies, local know-how, or supply agreements). In these circumstances, the parent companies may be able to operate the joint venture with full cooperation only with each other's agreement on the most important strategic decisions, even if there is no express provision of any veto rights. The greater the number of parent companies involved in such a joint venture, however, the more remote is the likelihood of this situation occurring.

Even in the absence of specific veto rights, two minority shareholders may acquire joint control if, for example, they act together either on the basis of a legally binding agreement to vote together or, very exceptionally, on a de facto basis. De facto joint control can occur where, for example, two shareholders (who together have a majority of the votes in the company) each provide a specific and important contribution to the joint venture vital for its operation. For example, one company may supply technology and the other vital raw materials. In these circumstances, the parent companies will have a high degree of mutual dependency in attaining the strategic objectives of the joint venture and, in this way, effectively jointly control it.

2.4 PERFORMANCE OF THE 'POSITIVE CONDITION': FULL-FUNCTION JOINT VENTURES

To qualify as a concentration, the joint venture must perform on a lasting basis all the functions of an autonomous economic entity, i.e. be capable of performing all the same functions (e.g. R&D, manufacturing, sales, etc.) that other independent undertakings in the same market would be carrying out. The 2008 Jurisdictional Notice contains helpful guidance on the concept of full-function joint ventures,[3] but it is important to be clear that the Notice does not give guidance as to the way in which the substantive provisions of the joint venture and their effect on competition should be assessed; the Notice is concerned solely with the categorization of the individual joint venture in order to decide whether it is to be dealt with under the Merger Regulation or under Article 81.

The approach of the Commission to the interpretation of 'full-functionality' is set out in paragraphs 91 to 109 of the Jurisdictional Notice.

In essence, a full-function joint venture is one which operates on a market, performing the functions normally carried out by undertakings operating on the same market. In order to do so the joint venture must have a management dedicated to its day-to-day operations and access to sufficient resources including finance, staff and assets (tangible and intangible) in order to conduct on a lasting basis its business activities within the area provided for in the joint venture agreement. Joint ventures which satisfy this requirement bring about a lasting change in the structure of the market.

---

[3] Paras. 91–109.

A joint venture is not full-function if it only takes over one specific function within the parent companies' business activities without its own access to the market. This is the case, for example, for joint ventures limited to R&D or production. Such joint ventures are auxiliary to their parent companies' business activities. However, the fact that a joint venture makes use of the distribution network or outlet of one or more of its parent companies normally will not disqualify it as 'full-function', as long as the parent companies are acting only as agents of the joint venture.

The strong presence of the parent companies in upstream or downstream markets is a factor to be taken into consideration in assessing the full-function character of a joint venture where this presence leads to substantial sales or purchases between the parent companies and the joint venture. The fact that the joint venture relies almost entirely on sales to its parent companies or purchases from them only for an initial start-up period does not normally affect the full-function character of the joint venture. Such a start-up period may be necessary in order to establish the joint venture on a market. It will normally not exceed a period of three years, depending on the specific conditions of the market in question.

Where sales from the joint venture to the parent companies are intended to be made on a lasting basis, the essential question is whether, regardless of these sales, the joint venture is geared to play an active role in the market. In this respect the relative proportion of these sales compared with the total production of the joint venture is an important factor. As a general rule of thumb, if the joint venture achieves more than 50 per cent of its turnover from sales to third parties then this will be an indication of full functionality. Another factor is whether sales to the parent companies are made on the basis of normal commercial conditions. If they are, then the joint venture may still be full-function provided more than 20 per cent of its sales are made to third parties. A purely outsourcing arrangement will not typically be full-function.

In relation to purchases made by the joint venture from its parent companies, the full-function character of the joint venture is questionable in particular where little value is added to the products or services concerned at the level of the joint venture itself. In such a situation, the joint venture may be closer to a joint sales agency. However, in contrast to this situation, where a joint venture is active in a trade market and performs the normal functions of a trading company in such a market, it normally will not be an auxiliary sales agency but a full-function joint venture. A trade market is characterized by the existence of companies which specialize in the selling and distribution of products without being vertically integrated in addition to those which are integrated, and where different sources of supply are available for the products in question. In addition, many trade markets may require operators to invest in specific facilities such as outlets, stockholding, warehouses, depots, transport fleets, and sales personnel. In order to constitute a full-function joint venture in a trade market, an undertaking must have the necessary facilities and be likely to obtain a substantial proportion of its supplies not only from its parent companies but also from other competing sources.

Furthermore, the joint venture must be intended to operate on a lasting basis. The fact that the parent companies commit to the joint venture the resources described above normally demonstrates that this is the case. In addition, agreements setting up a joint venture often provide for certain contingencies, for example, the failure of the joint venture or fundamental disagreement between the parent companies. This may be achieved by the incorporation of provisions for the eventual dissolution of the joint venture itself or the possibility for one or more parent companies to withdraw from the joint venture. This kind of provision does not prevent the joint venture from being considered as operating on a lasting basis. The same is normally true where the agreement specifies a period for the duration of the joint venture where this period is sufficiently long in order to bring about a lasting change in the structure of the undertakings concerned, or where the agreement provides for the possible continuation of the joint venture beyond this period. By contrast, the joint venture will not be considered to operate on a lasting basis where it is established for a short finite period. This would be the case, for example, where a joint venture is established in order to construct a specific facility such as a power plant, but it will not be involved in the operation of the plant once its construction has been completed. In practice, a minimum period of ten to fifteen years will be sufficient to be 'long lasting' but a period of three years will be too short.[4]

Two cases demonstrate some of these principles in practice. In *Electrabel/Energia Italiana/Interpower*,[5] Interpower was acquired jointly by Electrabel and Energia. Interpower was required to sell most (between 85 and 95 per cent) of its electricity to its parents and it would have neither its own customers nor its own commercial strategy. Accordingly the Commission found that the joint venture was not full-function. By contrast in *Adecco/Manpower/Vediorbis*,[6] three temporary work agencies set up a joint venture for the provision of extranet services between temporary work agencies (including the parents) and companies employing temporary staff. Despite the fact that a relatively high proportion of the joint ventures' revenues were expected to come from its parents, the joint venture was considered to be 'full-function' since it would provide its services independently of its parents and, under the same conditions, to other temporary work agencies as well.

The Jurisdictional Notice also makes clear[7] that changes in the activities of a joint venture may constitute a new concentration or render a 'non-full-function' venture 'full-function' and therefore subject to review under the Merger Regulation. For example, if the parents of a production joint venture (which was originally set up to produce only for its parents) decide that it will start selling a substantial proportional of its output to third parties, then the joint venture may well become 'full-function' and a concentration arises.

---

4 Case M.3858 *Lehman Brothers/Starwoord/Le Meridien*, 20 July 2005.
5 Case M.3003 (decision of 23 December 2002).
6 Case M.3419 (decision of 5 November 2004).   7 At paras. 106–9.

2.5 THE ABOLITION OF THE 'NEGATIVE CONDITION'

The abolition from 1998 of the negative requirement of 'no coordination between the parties to the joint venture' has greatly simplified the characterization of joint ventures, i.e. whether they are concentrations or not. However, this does not mean that the Commission will ignore the issue of coordination when deciding as a substantive matter whether to grant a clearance to the transaction. In its substantive analysis, the Commission will consider not only whether the concentration itself significantly impedes effective competition (under Article 2(2)), but will also examine whether coordination of the competitive behaviour of the parent companies (or between the parent companies and the joint venture itself) is likely, as a direct result of the creation of the joint venture. Article 2(4) and (5) of the Merger Regulation reads:

To the extent that the creation of a joint venture constituting a concentration pursuant to Article 3 has as its object or effect the coordination of the competitive behaviour of under-takings that remain independent, such coordination shall be appraised in accordance with the criteria of Article 81(1) and (3) of the Treaty, with a view to establishing whether or not the operation is compatible with the common market.

  In making this appraisal, the Commission shall take into account in particular:

— whether two or more parent companies retain to a significant extent activities in the same market as the joint venture or in a market which is downstream or upstream from that of the joint venture or in a neighbouring market closely related to this market;

— whether the co-ordination which is the direct consequence of the creation of the joint venture affords the undertakings concerned the possibility of eliminating competition in respect of a substantial part of the products or services in question.

3. JOINT VENTURES WHICH ARE CONCENTRATIONS: THEIR TREATMENT UNDER THE MERGER REGULATION

3.1 ARTICLE 2(1) TO (3): THE APPLICATION OF THE NORMAL MERGER REGULATION CRITERIA TO JOINT VENTURES

In recent years approximately 300 concentrations have been annually notified to the Commission on Form CO and, of these, approximately half are joint ventures. Under the provisions of Article 6(1), the Commission has in each case to examine the notification to see if the transaction in question falls within the scope of the regulation. If the joint venture, once the criteria set out above have been applied, can be classified as a concentration and the appropriate turnover of the parties under Article 1 and Article 5 satisfies the Community dimension test, the Commission implements its 'first-phase' proceeding. If for any reason a notification cannot be classified as a concentration of Community dimension, the application will be rejected, although the joint venture may require assessment under Article 81 or, possibly, require notification under national competition law.

First-phase proceedings normally last twenty-five working days, though in some circumstances they can be extended by a further ten working days. By the end of this period, the Commission will have determined whether the case raises serious doubts as to its compatibility with the Common Market (Article 6(2)). If serious doubts have not been raised, the concentration will be declared 'compatible' and cleared; this may be on the basis that it has not raised any competitive issues at all even though, because of the combined turnover of the parties calculated under Article 1, the transaction had to go through the process of notification to the Commission under the Merger Regulation. Alternatively, the Commission may have granted clearance after the first-phase examination in return for commitments by the parties to amend or remove particular clauses in the joint venture agreement which are regarded as unnecessarily restrictive of competition. Commitments would not only relate to clauses in the agreement, but might also require divestiture of assets in order to eliminate the problem of creating or strengthening a dominant position.

If serious doubts are raised, the joint venture will pass into the second phase under Article 6(1)(c) and will be dealt with like any other concentration by way of further detailed examination. An example of the way in which such cases are dealt with is *Smith & Nephew/Beiersdorf.*[8] The Commission found that the proposed 50/50 joint venture would involve a substantial horizontal overlap between the parties' respective products in bandages and other wound care items. In particular, there were overlaps in several national markets in the EC for a number of such products. To remove the concerns of the Commission, the parties agreed to divest themselves of some trademarks and business activities in those Member States to third parties. The Commission was also concerned initially with possible 'spillover effects' from the joint venture into other markets in which both companies were engaged, but after detailed investigation concluded that the risk was minimal.

Another example is the *Thales/Finmeccanica/AAS/Telespazio* case[9] where Thales and Finmeccanica acquired joint control of AAS and Telespazio. AAS was a leading manufacturer of telecommunication satellites. Since Thales was one of only two producers worldwide of travelling wave tubes (a key component of telecommunications satellites) the Commission had serious concerns about the transaction and initiated phase-two proceedings. The in-depth investigation revealed that Thales' ability to restrict access to travelling wave tubes for rivals of AAS was constrained, in particular by the buying power of its customers and the strength of its rival, and the Commission cleared the transaction unconditionally.

It is important to emphasize that the criteria which are applied under the Merger Regulation to the concentrative aspect of joint ventures are no different to those which

---

[8] Case JV/54 (decision of 30 January 2001).   [9] Case M.4403 (decision of April 2007).

apply to all other 'concentrations with a Community dimension' under the Regulation. The arrangements for a joint venture are often very complex; this places major pressure upon both the parties and the Commission to ensure that the full investigation of the case is carried out within the appropriate time limit applicable under the Merger Regulation. The relevant product or service markets for the joint venture will be analysed and findings made as to the markets in which the parent companies already operate and those in which the joint venture is intended to operate. These markets may be the same as those in which the parents operate, or may be related, or, occasionally, may be totally distinct, though this is unusual.

Thus, for example, in the *Shell/BASF* joint venture case,[10] an analysis was made of the complex arrangements to be made under which the joint venture would operate in Western Europe in the polyethylene business on behalf of both of its parent companies, Shell and BASF. The joint venture was to operate a number of factories previously operated by the parents, receive supplies of raw material from both of them, and in turn utilize the production from the factories to supply a number of those other factories which the parent companies would retain. The markets for various categories of polyethylene produced by the two parent companies was analysed by the Commission, which reached the conclusion that, because there was a high degree of supply-side substitutability between the various companies producing the basic product and the number of other major companies with shares in the relevant markets, the creation of the joint venture would not give the parties a dominant position in them, nor in the related markets of polyethylene technology.

The examination, therefore, of a joint venture between X and Y which qualifies as a concentration under the Merger Regulation takes place in exactly the same way under Article 2(1) to (3) as an examination of an acquisition by X of Y, in terms of the effect that the concentration is likely to have on effective competition in relevant markets. In addition, as described above, a joint venture may also (in certain cases only) be subject to the special rules of Article 2(4) and (5), which relate to the possibility of the concentration having as its object or effect the coordination by the parties of their future activities in the same or related markets.

3.2 ARTICLE 2(4) AND (5): THE APPLICATION OF THE SPECIAL RULES APPLICABLE TO COORDINATION BETWEEN THE PARTIES TO JOINT VENTURES

In many cases of joint ventures that are concentrations, the problem of the coordination of the commercial activities of the parent companies, through the operation of the joint venture, will not be regarded as significant. If, however, a concentration does raise such issues, the application of Article 2(4) and (5) will come into play and officials of DG Comp familiar with the relevant sectors will seek to apply the principles of Article 81(1) and (3) to it.

---

[10] [1998] OJ C81/5. Case IV /M1041 (decision of 23 December 1997).

Article 2(4) and (5) applies to the subsequent assessment of the joint venture in the following circumstances:

- when a joint venture performs all the functions of an independent economic entity
- when either its object or effect is, inter alia, to coordinate the competitive behaviour between undertakings that remain independent.

Whilst there has not yet been a Commission decision blocking a joint venture because of the degree to which it enabled coordination of competitive behaviour of the parent companies without meeting the four-fold requirements of Article 81(3), it is the task of the Commission in such cases to apply all the conditions contained in Article 81(1) and (3) to the particular case.

In particular, the Commission will have to consider whether, as a matter of fact, two or more parent companies continue to trade to a significant extent in either:

- the same markets as those in which the joint venture will be operative
- an upstream market
- a downstream market
- a neighbouring market, which is closely related.

For example, if the proposed joint venture was to operate an oil refinery, the investigation by the Commission would examine whether the parent companies were retaining commercial activities, inter alia:

- in the oil-refining business itself
- in the oil-exploration or tanker business
- in the retail-fuel business (service stations)
- in, for example, chemical manufacturing where certain processes and products similar to those in the oil industry might also be utilized.

As a matter of prediction, the Commission will have to assess whether it would be possible for the parents to utilize the joint venture to eliminate competition in respect of a substantial part of the role of the products or services, i.e. in any of the possible markets considered above. The possibility may be provided either by the actual terms of the joint venture agreement or as the result of the existing commercial strengths and experience of the parties and their existing alliances; alternatively, a combination of these factors may lead to such a conclusion that coordination is likely. Having established whether the coordination is a possible consequence of the establishment of the joint venture, the Commission next has to consider whether the coordination which the operation of the joint venture would permit will itself actually enable such an elimination of competition to which Article 81 refers.

It is important to be clear about the nature of the 'coordination' with which Article 2(4) and (5) is concerned. It applies only to coordination involving undertakings 'which remain independent'. If only one of the parent companies is active in the relevant market, the Article does not normally apply even if that market is the one in which the joint venture is to operate; the likelihood of coordination between the joint venture and that parent is taken for granted and is not enough to warrant the application of Article 2(4) and (5), as the joint venture is insufficiently 'independent' from that parent. If, by contrast, both parent companies are active in the same market, the consequences of such coordination need not, however, be identical or symmetrical for them for the Article to apply. It is sufficient that there is some degree of effect on the conduct or interrelationship of the parent companies. Moreover, when the Article applies, all the factors relevant to Article 81(1) and (3) can be considered.

3.3 CASE LAW UNDER ARTICLE 2(4) AND (5)

In a number of cases, mainly involving telecommunications, the Commission has paid careful attention to the application of Article 2(4) and (5). A number of joint-venture concentration cases, under the Merger Regulation, raise issues of coordination and examples of such cases can be found in the Annual Reports of the Commission and the regular Commission publication 'Competition Policy Newsletter'. An example is *Telia/Telenor/Schibsted*.[11] Telia and Telenor were the national telephone authorities in Sweden and Norway respectively; Schibsted was a Norwegian publishing company. Both Telia and Telenor already competed on the Swedish market for website production and Internet gateway services. The Commission did not contest their submission that the joint venture did not have as its object the coordination of their activities on these markets, but was concerned to examine its effect. The function of the joint venture was to provide website production sites and Internet gateway services in Sweden, so as to provide users with easier access. The joint venture would be controlled as to 40 per cent each by Telia and Schibsted and 20 per cent by Telenor.

The Commission found that two main markets were relevant. The first was the production of websites and here the aggregate share of all the parties was less than 10 per cent. Even if the parent companies were to choose to coordinate such activities, they would still not be able to have a restrictive effect on competition and concerns under Article 2(4) were therefore not relevant here. The second relevant market was the dial-up Internet access market for Swedish consumers; here both Telia and Telenor had existing substantial market shares of between 25 per cent and 40 per cent and 10 per cent to 25 per cent, respectively.

The Commission felt, however, that the relevant national markets were growing so fast that these existing percentages were too ephemeral to be of much value, and that the growth in the markets would, notwithstanding any coordination of the parties' conduct, make restrictions on competition unlikely. There was therefore no reason under Article 2(4) not to clear the joint venture.

Another example is provided by the *Wegener/PCM* case[12] in which two Dutch newspaper publishers created a joint venture which would publish a new 'national-regional'

---

[11] Case JV/1 (decision of 27 May 1998).   [12] Case M.3817 (decision of 7 July 2005).

daily newspaper in the Netherlands. Its nineteen editions would combine a 'national segment' with 'local news'. By publishing newspapers, Wegener and PCM would remain active, together with the joint venture, on the market for national advertising space in daily newspapers. Since the combined market share of Wegener and PCM (including their joint venture) amounted to 45 to 55 per cent, and their main rival, De Telegraaf, had 30 to 40 per cent, the Commission considered that the creation of the joint venture could lead to the coordination of the competitive behaviour of Wegener, PCM and their joint venture. To address the Commission's concerns, the articles of association of the joint venture were changed to ensure its independence from its shareholders and Wegener committed, for the duration of the joint venture, to refrain from selling or offering national advertising space in its daily newspapers in any combination whatsoever (whether with the daily newspaper of PCM or with the joint venture).

4. ARTICLE 81 AND JOINT VENTURES WHICH ARE NOT CONCENTRATIONS

4.1 INTRODUCTION

Prior to the Merger Regulation the Commission could only deal with joint ventures as agreements under the provisions of Article 81. In each case, it had to apply the normal rules explained in detail in Chapters 6 to 8, and to ask in respect of the joint venture agreement whether:

- there was an agreement between one or more undertakings
- whether it might affect trade between Member States
- whether it had as its object or effect the prevention or restriction of competition within the Common Market.

If Article 81(1) was applicable, then Article 81(3) also had to be considered as the participants might have argued, in order to obtain an exemption, that the benefits to be expected from the joint venture would outweigh any restrictions on competition that it may involve. The parties to the joint venture would therefore have had to satisfy the Commission under Article 81(3) that it:

- contributed to improving the production or distribution of goods or to the promotion of technical or economic progress
- whilst allowing consumers a fair share of the resulting benefit
- whilst not imposing on the undertakings concerned restrictions not indispensable to the attainment of these objectives
- nor affording such undertakings the possibility of eliminating competition in respect of a substantial part of the products in question.

The Commission soon came to recognize from its cases that there are almost an infinite number of ways in which two or more undertakings can choose to cooperate with each other. As already mentioned, at one end of the spectrum the degree of cooperation may be very limited, e.g. an agreement to share transport or storage facilities or to run a common training course to provide employees with relevant skills or qualifications; at the other end of the spectrum the degree of cooperation may be so considerable and close that it virtually takes on the character of a cartel, e.g. by the exchange of current commercial data on prices and customers leading to a partial or total elimination of competition between the parties. Alternatively the closer cooperation required between A and B may take the form of the establishment by them of a third undertaking, C, in which are vested activities which A and B no longer wish to carry out for themselves. They are thus able to withdraw from that particular market whilst the integration of their interests in the provision of the particular goods or services is irretrievably committed to the new entity, their joint venture.

Between these extremes lie a variety of different forms of cooperation which involve to a greater or lesser degree a commitment to each other, but involve more than the mere sharing of facilities, whilst still falling short of a full integration of their assets and interests in a particular product or service market.

4.2 APPLICATION OF ARTICLE 81(1) TO JOINT VENTURES: BASIC PRINCIPLES

Following modernization, the assessment of joint ventures under Article 81 needs to be conducted by the parties involved themselves. In making such an assessment, the following questions are relevant:

- whether the parents themselves are in actual or potential competition with each other
- whether the parents operate in the same market as the joint venture, or in upstream, downstream, or related markets
- what functions is the joint venture intended to perform: are they limited, e.g. sales and marketing alone, or R&D alone, or covering a wide range of objectives similar to those of an independent company (of course, in the latter case, the joint venture might qualify as a 'concentration' under the Merger Regulation rather than be subject to Article 81)
- what freedom of action is left to the parent companies and whether they retain the right to compete fully with the joint venture or, more normally, would agree with each other to respect the proposed exclusivity of the joint venture in a particular market and not compete with it
- what restrictions are placed on the joint venture as to its right to grant licences of any intellectual property which it might itself develop in the course of its work to third parties.

In July 1968, when joint ventures were first being routinely assessed by the Commission under Regulation 17/62, the Commission published a Notice on cooperation between undertakings.[13] This sought to describe the categories of cooperative agreements or joint ventures which it stated should not be regarded as restricting competition under the terms of Article 81(1). They included a range of the more limited categories of cooperation.

Unlike a Regulation, a Notice does not create legal rights or obligations, but simply contains the current policy views of the Commission which may well be subject to change at a later date, as has proved the case with a number of the Commission's Notices. The purpose of this particular Notice was to make clear that certain categories of cooperation having a relatively minor effect on competition were prima facie deemed not to fall within the terms of Article 81(1). However, it became clear that the Commission would take a cautious attitude to arrangements which involved cooperation going beyond the categories listed in the Notice. In the great majority of decisions adopted by the Commission in the 1960s and 1970s it tended to apply Article 81(1) in a broad manner to the particular agreement, but would then exempt the agreement in question under Article 81(3). This policy choice had the advantage that, through individual case examination, the Commission acquired detailed knowledge of the workings and operation of joint ventures. Exemption would in accordance with Regulation 17/62 and Article 8(1), be for a limited period only and could have conditions attached, e.g. the parties could be required to notify the Commission on an annual basis of the turnover figures for the joint venture and of the occasions on which, for example, it had refused to make supplies of products or to grant licences of technology which it had developed.

4.3 APPLICATION OF ARTICLE 81(3) TO JOINT VENTURES: BASIC PRINCIPLES

Throughout the 1970s and 1980s the Commission was gradually developing its technique of analysis of the often complex contractual arrangements entered into by the parents of the joint venture. On many occasions the parties to joint ventures would not have notified them to the Commission, being satisfied that they had no appreciable effect on competition, nor effect on trade between Member States, or possibly being prepared to take the risks of non-notification, even though not fully satisfied on these matters. On the occasions when agreements were notified to the Commission, it would almost always continue (certainly up to the end of the 1980s) to claim that Article 81(1) was being infringed, even though it would then go on to grant exemption under Article 81(3), on some occasions after requiring certain restrictions to be taken out of the joint venture agreement.

In determining whether the joint venture satisfied the positive conditions of Article 81(3) that it made a contribution to the production or distribution of goods

---

[13] [1968] CMLR D 45.

or to promoting technical economic progress, a number of possible factors were taken into account. Of obvious significance would be the ability of the joint venture to develop a new product, such as a drug, which neither of the parent companies had the resources themselves to develop within a realistic timescale. Such considerations might now (though not in earlier years) enable the Commission to grant the joint venture a negative clearance on the grounds that it could not be said realistically to restrict competition. In the sectors where technology was of prime importance such as communications, satellites, computers, or the media, the ability to provide new products and develop new technology responding to demand by customers for new services, often on a worldwide basis, was taken into account. The improvement of quality, the ability to realize scale economies, and the enhancement of standards of safety were also likely to be taken into account.

The second condition of Article 81(3) requires that from the production or distribution improvement or the technical or economic progress users will derive 'a fair share of the resulting benefit'. A criticism sometimes made of the Commission has been that it has not in all cases gone analytically enough into the question of whether users will actually benefit. The Commission has tended rather to make the assumption that, if the first condition as to improvements or progress is satisfied, competition will itself automatically ensure that the benefit will pass through to consumers. In some cases the benefit is not simply a reduction in price or improvement in quality but the creation of a product or service not previously available (e.g. in Beecham/Parke, Davis,[14] the potential benefit was the availability of a new drug to prevent damage to blood circulation not previously available on the market).

Turning to the negative conditions under Article 81(3), the first is that the restriction 'does not impose on the undertakings restrictions not indispensable to the attainment of these objectives'. This condition, although expressed negatively, could also have been expressed positively, i.e. that the restriction is one which is essential (indispensable) to the attainment of the commercial objectives of the joint venture. In general the Commission has been fairly liberal in its interpretation of this condition, in that it has only opposed restrictions proposed by the parties when it appeared that these went well beyond the needs of the parties to protect their legitimate interests within the framework of the joint venture. In other words the restriction will only be deleted (or even in extreme cases cause the exemption to be refused) if it is more than a logical and reasonable consequence of the particular relationships into which the parties are entering. If, by contrast, the restriction is seen to be designed to give the parties a more secure position protected from competition than existed before, they will be challenged to justify it.

On occasion the Commission has asked therefore whether the joint venture could have been achieved in a simpler and less restrictive way, e.g. by a licensing agreement rather than by the formation of a subsidiary company accompanied by a number of restrictions on the parents from competing with that company. BP/Kellogg[15] was a good example of the need for quite broad restrictions to protect the interests of the

---

[14] [1979] OJ L70/11: [1979] 2 CMLR 157.   [15] [1986] 2 CMLR 619.

parties if they have each committed themselves to the joint venture as the way in which they would in future promote a particular aspect of their business. The parties will be allowed to protect themselves to a proportionate extent against any breaking of the essential logic of that relationship. An area, however, in which the Commission is particularly quick to intervene—if they feel restrictions are being extended too far—is when it is sought to limit the freedom of action of the parties following the termin- ation of the joint venture. A non-competition clause between the parents is usually considered to be indispensable, as it is unreasonable to expect that the parents should allow the joint venture to compete with the parents themselves or that the parents themselves should, in spite of the new relationship between them, compete with each other in the same sector and in competition with their own joint venture. Of course, in those cases where negative clearance was appropriate, i.e. where the joint venture had no appreciable effect on competition, such clauses would not in themselves lead to a finding that Article 81(1) and (3) was applicable, since such restrictions would be treated as ancillary to the joint venture, as clauses whose presence was commercially essential if the joint venture was to proceed at all.

The Commission is not however normally prepared to agree a long period in which, after the termination of the joint venture, the parents seek to prevent direct competi- tion between them. Clearly there may need to be a transitional period when the existing arrangements are run down, resources allocated to the joint venture are re-transferred and fresh licensing arrangements made to permit an orderly return to the status quo. Quite often then, the grant of exclusive intellectual property rights under licence by the parties to each other may be justified, though in some other cases the Commission may prefer the rights to be non-exclusive. The Commission's attitude will turn very much on the circumstances of the particular case, especially the degree of competition in the relevant markets.

The final condition for an Article 81(3) exemption is that the parties should not be able to eliminate competition for a substantial proportion of the products (goods or services) in question. The Commission will carry out analysis of the relevant mar- ket conditions which include both the market shares of the parties in Member States and the Community as a whole in the light of the respective market shares of their competitors. For example, in *Mitchell Cotts/Sofiltra*,[16] it was clear that whilst Sofiltra was strong in the French air-filter market (having more than half) it was very weak in the United Kingdom, whereas with Mitchell Cotts the reverse was the case, even though its market share in the United Kingdom was considerably lower than that of Sofiltra in France. The Commission is always concerned that, after the joint venture has come into full operation, the use of it by the parents should not provide them with a mechanism for reducing or eliminating competition for at least a substantial num- ber of the products. Collaboration therefore across a very large geographic market will prove harder to justify than if limited to a particular Member State or small group of Member States.

---

[16] [1987] OJ L41/31: [1988] 4 CMLR 111.

Clearly this condition overlaps to some extent with the assessment at the earlier stage of whether the agreement has as its object or effect the restriction of competition in the Common Market. The difference is that at the first stage the Commission is looking broadly at the overall effect of the agreement, whereas at this second stage in examining the application of Article 81(3) it is more concerned with the detail of the restrictive clauses and their effects on the markets concerned. The characteristics and strength of other companies involved in the relevant markets will be important; if the competition faced by the joint venture is severe and its creation seems a logical commercial response to the competition which the parents would face, without giving them a dominant position in that market, the likelihood of an exemption is greater.

In looking at the early application by the Commission of Article 81(3) to joint venture cases, two particular features should be noted. First was the general unwillingness of the Commission to accept that Article 81(1) did not apply at all. Second, which to some degree counterbalanced the first, was that it was rare for a joint venture to be refused an exemption under Article 81(3); in most cases the control imposed by the Commission in this respect did not extend beyond the required amendment of certain restrictive clauses to reduce the effect on competition or to limit their effect to what is regarded as indispensable in the reasonable interests of the parties.

In the second half of the 1980s, rather than starting from the presumption in all cases that almost any joint venture notified to the Commission was likely to have a sufficient effect on competition to fall within the terms of Article 81(1), it began to issue decisions in which the fact that the parties' current commercial activities and their actual and potential resources were in such different sectors meant that their joint venture fell outside Article 81(1) altogether.

Probably the first case in which this can be noted was *Optical Fibres*[17] in 1986 and a similar approach is found later in the *Odin* case[18] of 1990. On the other hand, an earlier case, *ICI/Wasag*,[19] illustrated the point that there can be joint ventures whose effect on competition in particular markets is potentially so serious that they have to be prohibited, rather than merely required to alter the most anti-competitive clauses in the joint venture agreement.

4.4 THE COMMISSION 2001 NOTICE: NEW GUIDELINES FOR HORIZONTAL COOPERATION AGREEMENTS

In 1993 the Commission published a substantial notice setting out its assessment of joint ventures under Article 81 based on its experience up to that time. Since then, however, that Notice has been rendered largely redundant. As we have seen, the range and type of joint ventures which are now classified as concentrations has been broadened and, moreover, the Commission's own approach to cooperation joint ventures has itself undergone change, leading to a more liberal treatment of this category of agreement.

---

[17] [1986] OJ L236/30.   [18] [1990] OJ L209/15: [1991] 4 CMLR 832.   [19] [1979] 1 CMLR 403.

For these reasons a more recent set of guidelines which came into effect on 1 January 2001, is now the most authoritative source of guidance as to the way in which the Commission will treat a variety of categories of joint venture which do not fall within the jurisdiction of the Merger Regulation. These new guidelines replace both the 1968[20] and 1993 Notices. The guidelines for horizontal cooperation agreements have become increasingly important since the modernization of Article 81, the introduction of Regulation 1/2003 and the 'self-assessment' regime which has followed as a consequence. The horizontal guidelines should be read alongside the Commission's guidelines on the application of Article 81(3) of the Treaty[21] which were introduced as part of the modernization package in 2004.

A horizontal agreement is one that is made between undertakings at the same level in a particular market, often either actual or potential competitors with each other. The intended scope of the guidelines to include all joint ventures that potentially generate efficiency gains means that they apply not only to the specialization and R&D agreements described in the next section, but also to exclusive purchase and selling agreements as well as to a variety of other cooperative arrangements. Agreements on industry standards and on environmental control are also included.

The new Horizontal Guidelines are intended to assist companies and their advisers when assessing their horizontal cooperation agreements under Article 81. This cooperation can take a number of forms: R&D, joint production, joint purchasing, joint selling (referred to in the Guidelines as 'commercialization agreements'), standardization, and environmental agreements. The Commission accepts that since such agreements can generate economic benefits, or alternatively lead to competition problems, it should provide a legal framework for their balanced assessment which will itself be based to a greater extent than previously on economic criteria as well as on the existing case law of the ECJ and the CFI. Not all horizontal agreements are, of course, covered: only those that potentially can produce efficiency gains. They do, however, cover vertical agreements made between competitors. Nor do they seek to cover more complex arrangements covering a number of different areas and methods of operation, nor specific sectors such as agriculture or transport, where special considerations may have to be taken into account.

At the outset there are a number of examples given of agreements that will normally fall outside Article 81(1) altogether. These include those between undertakings which are not competitors with each other, or have no effect on relevant competition, or which involve the undertaking of a project which neither party could individually carry out. In determining whether competition would be affected, the Commission will look at the nature of the market, and the likely effect of the cooperation on prices, quality, or variety of goods or services. Also of concern will be the extent to which the agreement would allow a high degree of common costs to the parties when they combine to manufacture or purchase jointly either an important intermediate product or items which will form a high proportion of the input costs of the final product.

[20] See fn. 13.   [21] OJ [2004] C1/97.

Certain categories of agreement will however almost always fall within Article 81(1). These include those that restrict competition between the parties by price fixing, output limitation, or sharing of customers or markets, all of which are regarded as a direct interference in the competitive process, damaging to customers because they are compelled to pay higher prices or are restricted from access to a full range of choices. In cases that fall on the borderline, important considerations will be the existing market share of the parties in relevant markets, entry barriers, buyers' countervailing power and the nature of the products themselves.

The case of *European Night Services*[22] illustrates the importance placed by the CFI on the accuracy of the Commission's analysis of such factors. In this case, four railways authorities from different Member States had formed a joint venture (European Night Services) to provide overnight passenger rail services between the United Kingdom and the continent through the Channel Tunnel. The Commission in its decision had found that the agreement underlying the joint venture had a sufficiently appreciable effect on competition to bring it within Article 81(1). It had granted an eight-year exemption under Article 81(3) subject to the imposition of a number of conditions requiring, inter alia, the shareholders to provide 'equivalent services on the same terms' to any other international grouping of railway undertakings.

The CFI, however, annulled the decision, finding that the Commission had overstated the market share of ENS in transport services between the UK and the continent in which it was competing with air, coach, ferry, and car transport. Its total share of business and leisure services in all forms of transport was only 7.4 per cent. In the circumstances of the case this could not be deemed to have an appreciable effect on competition in that market, and therefore Article 81(1) did not apply.

In cases where Article 81(1) does apply the Guidelines then direct the attention of the parties to the content of Article 81(3) and the four conditions which it contains which have to be satisfied. Economic benefits have to be weighed against the degree to which competition is restricted by the agreement and the market power of the participants. Interestingly reference is made to the relevance of efficiency gains, which have of course to be shared with customers and cannot in any case justify the elimination of competition to any major extent.

4.5 JOINT PURCHASING AND JOINT SELLING

Arrangements for *joint purchasing*, if made between SMEs, are nearly always regarded as pro-competitive. They often have both a horizontal and vertical element covering both the arrangements between purchasers and those with their suppliers. Since joint purchasers can themselves become independent sellers in downstream markets both the purchasing and the downstream market have to be analysed. The Commission will ask whether the joint purchasers are competitors in one or more selling markets and if they can achieve market power by coordinating their conduct, which may lead to

---

[22] Cases T-374–5, 384 and 388/94, [1998] ECR II-3141: 5 CMLR 718.

restriction of competition. If they are however active in different downstream markets fewer problems will arise. The issue of whether the potentially lower prices that can be obtained by joint purchasing will be passed on to purchasers in that downstream market will also be considered.

Joint selling arrangements are viewed with some suspicion under the Guidelines because it is felt by the Commission, on the basis of considerable case-law experience, that it is likely to lead to the fixing of common prices by the parties. There may be cases where the parties could not afford to enter a particular market or sector without the reduction of costs that the agreement may make possible; but the fear of the Commission is that inevitably such arrangements lead to coordination on pricing, not only of the goods or services covered by the joint selling agreement, but in respect also of sales outside the scope of the agreement. Other risks encountered are the exchange of information between the parties which may lead itself to a reduction of competition between them and the possibility that common costs enabled by the agreement may influence pricing coordination even if no direct breach of Article 81 occurs. For these reasons examples of individual exemptions for joint selling agreements are rare. The Commission issued a Statement of Objections to the English Football Association Premier League in connection with its joint selling of the TV and other media rights to Premier League matches. The case was settled but only after the FA Premier League agreed to sell the broadcasting rights in a larger number of packages and that no single buyer could purchase all packages.[23]

4.6 STANDARDIZATION AND ENVIRONMENTAL AGREEMENTS

Agreements on *standards* are also dealt with in the Guidelines. These are defined as agreements having as their primary objective the definition of technical or quality requirements with which current or future products, production processes or methods may comply. Some of these will clearly fall outside Article 81(1), for example where the agreement is voluntary and operates transparently, or is part of a wider agreement to ensure product compatibility, as for example when they are the result of coordination by recognized standards authorities operating in a non-discriminatory manner.

Borderline cases will be those where the parties have joint control over production or innovation and thereby restrict their own ability to produce individual products, or where they lose part or all of their freedom to develop alternative standards or the ability to test their own products for compliance. High market shares, however, are not necessarily relevant. Article 81(1) is sure to apply if the standard is being used as a means aimed at excluding actual or potential competition, for example when a trade association sets a standard and then applies pressure to third parties not to market products which fail to comply with it.

In the application of Article 81(3) to such agreements, the Commission will endorse a positive approach to those which promote economic penetration within the Common

---

[23] See Commission Press Release IP/06/356, 22 March 2006.

Market, provided that the information needed to develop the standard is made available to all those wishing to enter the market and if an appreciable part of the industry is involved. Standards clauses should not however have the effect of limiting innovation and should always be applied in a non-discriminatory manner.

The Guidelines also apply to *environmental agreements* under which undertakings combine to achieve pollution control or other environmental objectives (which may include standards or authorized processes). These will normally be sympathetically regarded, if no precise individual obligations are placed on parties or if the obligation upon them is merely to attain an industry-wide environmental target. Borderline examples are those which cover an industry at national and Community level, and also appreciably restrict the parties' ability to decide on the characteristics of their own products or the processes by which they are manufactured. Any grant of special status or exclusivity will be scrutinized very carefully by the Commission and, of course, any suspicion that the agreement serves as a cover to disguise cartel activity will lead to a full-scale investigation followed, if proved, by the imposition of fines on its members.

5. JOINT VENTURES WHICH ARE NOT CONCENTRATIONS: BLOCK EXEMPTIONS FOR SPECIALIZATION AND R&D AGREEMENTS

5.1 INTRODUCTION

Two categories of joint venture have received special treatment from the Commission, to which, on the basis of its early case law experience, it was able to apply block exemptions covering at least some of the simpler varieties of agreement within these categories, which do not normally present a serious threat to competition. These categories are:

(1) specialization agreements

(2) R&D agreements.

The particular features of each of these are described below, together with some relevant cases and the relevant block exemptions (Regulations 2658 and 2659/2000), which came into force on 1 January 2001 and will expire at the end of 2010. The Guidelines on horizontal cooperation agreements also deal with these categories of agreement.

5.2 SPECIALIZATION AGREEMENTS: EARLY CASE LAW

A specialization agreement is essentially an allocation of the products to be produced by the parties, so that each can specialize in manufacturing part of a range of goods. Thus, for example, in the case of two motor manufacturers, one might agree to limit its activities to cars of 2,000cc and less and the other to cars of an engine capacity above that level. This allocation is normally combined with close technical cooperation and a mutual obligation to supply each other with the specialized products produced, so that each can sell the full range in those territories allocated for distribution, often on an exclusive basis. This kind of agreement may lead to a reduction in the number of producers of a particular model or type of product, but may enable both companies to realize the benefit of longer production runs and better use of their manufacturing capacity, leading in turn to a reduction of the fixed costs for each product, and thus the final price to the consumer. It may well also have the advantage of improving product quality, as the result of the combination of technical cooperation and specialization.

There is, of course, a wide range of detailed provisions to be tailored to meet the facts of each particular commercial situation. An example of the kind of agreement approved by the Commission in its early years which may serve as a useful model for the kind of cooperation being considered here is the *Jaz/Peter* case.[24] Jaz was a French company specializing in electric clocks and alarm clocks, whilst Peter was a German company specializing in large mechanical alarm clocks. Under the arrangements, each agreed to supply the other with its special range of products and spare parts and not to supply any other customers. Each agreed that the other would be entitled to sell the small range of combined products in its own territory, Jaz in France and Peter in Germany. Each agreed not to buy from third parties any clocks or watches of the type covered by the agreement. The effect of these arrangements was to allow each of the two companies to manufacture in much larger quantities than before the range of clocks in which they specialized, and still to sell the whole range of clocks and watches in its own territory. The increase in production led to a reduction in costs, but the agreement did not include any pricing restrictions as prices were to be determined by the individual companies.

Clearly the agreement restricted competition. A purchaser in France could not now choose between goods supplied by Jaz or Peter, since in France Jaz was the only distributor for the entire range of clocks, and Peter the only distributor for this range in Germany. On the other hand, the fact that both companies could produce a greater volume of clocks meant that prices could be and were reduced during the period of the agreement. The exchange of technical information between the parties also proved of mutual benefit; the Commission also found that none of the restrictions went beyond the level that was required to support the specialization agreement. When the parties applied for renewal of the exemption in 1977, they were able to show that Jaz had quadrupled its production of pendulum and electric alarm clocks, and that Peter had increased its production of large mechanical alarm clocks by two and a half times. Not surprisingly, a further exemption was granted. An important element in the Commission's decision was that customers had at all times an adequate choice of such clocks made by competing manufacturers; even such an example of the benefits of

---

[24] [1970] CMLR 129.

cooperation may have been blocked if not for the substantial competition in the relevant markets, as required by the second negative condition in Article 81(3).

A slightly different form of specialization is where the parties combine, not to split a product range between them, but to allocate responsibility for the production and development of individual components for a product they wish to produce jointly. *ACEC/ Berliet*[25] is one of the earliest examples of such a case. ACEC, a Belgian company specializing in electric transmissions, had developed a low-weight and high-yield model particularly useful in commercial vehicles and buses. They entered into a collaborative arrangement with Berliet, a French company, which had experience in the manufacture and selling of buses. Responsibilities were divided on the basis that they would cooperate for ten years in the joint development of a bus which would have the ACEC transmission, but the basic structure of the Berliet bus. When a prototype had been made, ACEC would supply its transmission equipment in France only to Berliet, and Berliet would purchase only electric transmissions made by ACEC, though remaining free to sell its buses incorporating such transmissions anywhere in the world. ACEC would deal with Berliet on a 'most favoured client' basis and would guarantee performance by the transmission and continued availability of spare parts.

Restrictions on competition were clearly inherent in the arrangement, as third parties engaged in the manufacture of electric transmissions were no longer able to sell them to Berliet; nor were some bus manufacturers now able to buy the ACEC transmission. However, the restrictions which ACEC and Berliet had accepted were, in the view of the Commission, reasonable, given the commitment which each had entered into with the other.

If successful, the specialization would permit the manufacture of buses in longer production runs, giving a reasonable chance of producing a new model that simplified the mechanical construction and would give better performance and comfort to its users. Though the outcome of the technical research could not be predicted with certainty, the fact that it was being carried out on a collaborative basis by two specialist companies increased the chances of a positive outcome; there was a sufficient degree of probability that the results would be successful to justify the collaboration and the restraints ancillary to it. ACEC remained free throughout to make contracts with other bus manufacturers outside France, and such buses would be able to compete with those produced by the joint venture. Formal exemption was therefore granted by the Commission.

In *Prym/Beka*,[26] Prym was a German company with over 4,000 employees which decided that its capacity for production of sewing needles was inadequate; it entered into an agreement with a much smaller company in Belgium, Beka, employing only 350 people, that Prym would no longer make sewing needles and would transfer the relevant parts of its plant and equipment to Beka, provided that Beka guaranteed to supply all Prym's requirements. Prym would take a 25 per cent interest in the share capital of Beka and would agree not to purchase its needles elsewhere, unless Beka

---

[25] [1968] CMLR D35.   [26] [1973] CMLR D250.

proved unable to supply its requirements. Originally the agreement also contained market-sharing restrictions, both by definition of end-users and on a geographical basis, but the Commission insisted that the exemption was conditional on the removal of these restrictions. The advantages of the specialization agreements were that the Belgian plant could be more intensively used, increasing by at least 50 per cent its production of needles, whose unit cost was substantially reduced. Though this was not a true specialization agreement (since Prym itself was not allocated a specific product in whose manufacture it would specialize) the effect of the new arrangements for centralizing production at Beka's factory had many of the same advantages and was therefore accepted within Article 81(3), subject to the deletion of the clauses dealing with the allocation of markets.

A more unusual case involved the allocation of markets in the nuclear industry: *United Reprocessors*.[27] An agreement was made between three undertakings, in the UK (British Nuclear Fuels), France (the Commissariat à l'Energie Atomique), and Germany (KEWA). The agreement notified involved setting up a joint subsidiary company to cover the market of the reprocessing of nuclear fuels. It was agreed that they would not invest in any other business for this purpose and would allocate all their reprocessing work between the three companies. Other restrictions were also accepted including an obligation on KEWA not to build a new reprocessing plant until the throughput of the French and United Kingdom plants reached certain levels. In granting an exemption, the Commission held that the coordination of capital investment between the three companies would ensure that uneconomic plants would not be set up, and would enable the companies to wait until market conditions were more favourable, as well as reducing costs through increasing the production of the existing reprocessing plant. Dealing with a product as delicate and dangerous as nuclear waste, it was seen as essential by the Commission that the reprocessing service should be firmly established. Benefits arose for consumers because the proposed improved stability of the reprocessing service should result in lower electricity costs. The Commission, however, insisted that it should be closely involved in periodically reviewing the arrangements in order to ensure that consumers continued to receive their proportionate share of resulting savings. It also insisted on participating in the monitoring of the throughput of the reprocessing work of the French and United Kingdom plants.

The terms of the decision suggest that the Commission had major doubts about the effect on competition of such an arrangement, and that only the combination of the stringent conditions and the fact that this was a particularly sensitive industry in which to insist on completely free competition justified an exemption. The Commission indeed acknowledged in its decision that for a period competition would actually be reduced.

---

[27] [1976] 2 CMLR D1: cf. *KEWA* [1976] 2 CMLR D15, a similar decision granting exemption to a joint subsidiary set up to reprocess nuclear fuels in Germany by four companies and which would itself be one of the shareholders in United Reprocessors.

Some specialization agreements that were notified to the Commission under Regulation 17 involved particularly advanced technology, where the investment costs are particularly high, and where a substantial element of R&D is involved. *Bayer/Gist-Brocades*[28] was an example. Both Bayer, a German company, and Gist-Brocades, a Dutch company, were large drug manufacturers. Each produced raw penicillin and intermediate penicillin products for processing into ampicillins and other semi-synthetic products. In order to increase overall production, a specialization agreement was entered into under which Gist-Brocades would specialize in the production of raw penicillin, whilst Bayer would concentrate on intermediate products. The majority of the raw penicillin to be produced by Gist-Brocades would then be forwarded to Bayer for processing into intermediate products, although Gist-Brocades would retain some of the raw penicillin for traditional penicillin preparations. Both companies kept the freedom to carry out their own R&D, subject to an obligation to exchange information; various non-exclusive licences for the use of specific chemical processes relating to the production of penicillin were also granted. Although the companies were both large, with substantial financial resources and knowledge of the market, the Commission agreed that production could be carried out more economically as a result of the specialization.

Exemption was granted but with one important amendment. The individual factories were to have been transferred to joint subsidiary companies in which both parties would have a 50 per cent interest and an equal number of directors. Inevitably this would have led not only to joint research, but to joint control over the production and total investment in the individual plants. The Commission felt that this would restrict competition between the companies beyond what was essential to the specialization proposals. The proposal to form joint subsidiaries was therefore abandoned, each company administering the arrangements through their existing corporate structure. Having thus eliminated the restrictions that appeared too wide to be indispensable to the arrangement, the Commission ruled that the exemption could be granted. The specialization agreement would increase availability on world markets of both raw penicillin and intermediate products. The Commission fixed an eight-year period for the exemption but attached conditions, so that it could continue to check the results of cooperation on the competitive process in the relevant markets.

Another variety of specialization agreement notified to the Commission under Regulation 17 was brought about by the economic recession of the 1970s and early 1980s. The more generous treatment afforded to crisis cartels at that time illustrates the concern of the Commission in such situations not to be seen to take too rigid a stance, and to be accommodating where there was a genuine long-term substantial fall in demand and consequent excess production capacity. An alternative to a crisis cartel is an agreement whereby 'swaps' are made between major companies enabling them to eliminate production capacity they no longer require and to specialize in those fields where they remain strong. The process is illustrated by *Imperial Chemical Industries/*

---

[28] [1976] 1 CMLR D98. A subsequent extension of the exemption was granted until 1995.

British Petroleum Chemicals.[29] Both ICI and BPC had manufacturing plants producing PVC (polyvinylchloride) and low-density polyethylene (LDPE). Arrangements were made under which ICI disposed of its modern LDPE production plant in the UK and all related technical information and patents to BPC, whilst in return BPC sold its most modern UK production plant for PVC and related technical information to ICI. The notified agreement related simply to a swap of individual plants enabling ICI in the future to specialize in PVC and BPC in LDPE, neither continuing in the production process of the other product.

As a result of the agreement, BPC and ICI were each able to increase the capacity and the usage of their more modern plant thereby reducing unit costs, always an essential feature in specialization agreements. In the long run, a more healthy industrial structure was likely to be promoted, and although in the short term, the agreement would not improve competition, the Commission was satisfied that in the longer term effective competition would be maintained and consumers not deprived of a range of choice.

5.3 INTRODUCTION OF BLOCK EXEMPTION REGULATION 417/85 AND ITS SUCCESSOR NO. 2658/2000

As the result of the Commission's experience gained in this area it felt able to introduce a block exemption for certain agreements of this kind. Regulation 417/85, as later amended by Regulation 151/93, applied to a variety of specialization agreements including both the type seen in *Jaz/Peter* and in *ACEC/Berliet*. In its reliance on market share thresholds, the Regulation anticipated the approach later to be adopted by the Block Exemption Regulation for Vertical Restraints (Regulation 2790/99) of maximum market share percentages, though the percentages actually adopted by the two regulations were criticized subsequently for being too low.

The 1985 block exemption was available when the products in question together with other products manufactured by the undertakings and regarded as equivalent by reason of their characteristics, price, and intended use did not represent more than 20 per cent of the market either in the Common Market or a substantial part of it. Moreover, the aggregate turnover of the participating undertakings could not exceed €1 billion. These figures applied when the parties engaged in specialization simply for the purpose of manufacture, but if the parties (or a third party on their behalf) were also responsible for distribution the maximum market-share figures applicable were only 10 per cent though the maximum aggregate turnover figure itself was not reduced. This block exemption was replaced from the end of 2000 by the new Block Exemption 2658/2000.[30]

The single most important change found in the new block exemption is that the maximum turnover requirement has been removed. A market-share threshold, however, still remains at the comparatively low figure of 20 per cent, even though transitional

---

[29] [1985] 2 CMLR 330.   [30] [2000] OJ L304/3: [2001] 4 CMLR 800.

relief is given if the share remains at a figure no higher than 25 per cent for two years, or no higher than 30 per cent for one year.

The scope of the block exemption is now wider. Previously it was limited to reciprocal obligations not to manufacture products nor to have them manufactured by other parties or to manufacture products or have them manufactured only jointly. The current block exemption applies not only to such reciprocal specialization but also to unilateral specialization (often known as 'outsourcing agreements') under which one party agrees to cease production of particular items whilst a competitor agrees to supply it to them. Joint production arrangements are also covered by the exemption, which extends, moreover, to ancillary clauses required for the commercial implementation of the agreement, but without constituting its primary purpose, such as the assignment or licensing of intellectual property rights.

The reason that cross-supply clauses are required to be included in such agreements is that these should prevent them being utilized as a means of partitioning territorial markets for the product in breach of Article 81; exclusive purchase and supply clauses are also permitted, in order to facilitate the use of the exemption for outsourcing agreements (Article 2). The parties may set limits to the agreed amount of products and may set the capacity and production volumes of a production joint venture (Article 4). Prices of the products so produced can also be fixed, provided that the joint venture is also responsible for distribution. Joint distribution is allowed, or distribution by a third party so long as it is not a competitor in the relevant market.

The benefit of the block exemption can be withdrawn by the Commission if it believes that a particular agreement is having effects incompatible with Article 81(3), especially if:

- the agreement is not yielding significant results in terms of rationalization or consumers are not receiving a fair share of its benefits or
- the products which are the subject of the specialization arrangements are not subject to sufficient competition.

There is no long list of permitted 'white' clauses, and the list of 'black' clauses is short, referring merely to any agreements which, directly or indirectly, have as their object or effect:

- the fixing of prices
- the limitation of output or
- the allocation of customers or markets.

5.4 SPECIALIZATION AGREEMENTS: THE GUIDELINES

There are some twenty-five paragraphs in the Guidelines concerning specialization agreements and these focus mainly on agreements which are not within the scope of the new block exemption. The section also considers a range of joint-production agreements. As always the first task is the assessment of the relevant market and the strength of the parties within it relative to the specialization agreement. If the parties are not competitors (or even if they are, but cooperation with competitors is the only commercially viable way of launching a new product), then Article 81(1) is unlikely to apply. Borderline cases are those where the market share of the parties exceeds the threshold contained in the block exemption, but where their market power is still restricted; for example, where the concentration ratios of the market are low and there are no existing links between a significant number of competitors. Any specialization agreement, however, that involves agreement by the parties on output directly related to the joint production, or sets prices for them, is likely to fall within the scope of Article 81(1). A number of case studies provide further illustrations of the approach of the Commission to this type of agreement, as with each other category of agreement considered in the Guidelines.

5.5 R&D AGREEMENTS: THE 1968 NOTICE ON CO-OPERATION BETWEEN ENTERPRISES

Not all joint ventures fall neatly into a distinct category. Nevertheless, R&D agreements form a distinct group which can be recognized without difficulty; the main purpose of such agreements is to arrange for the carrying out of a number of functions, all of which are essential steps in the lengthy process from the first creative step of the inventor to the delivery of a finished product to customers at a competitive price. They are more common, and more important in their economic and commercial effects, than specialization agreements.

The development of a new product actually begins with basic research carried out in a laboratory or workshop, often taking years rather than months to complete. If the research proceeds successfully, the next stage is to apply its findings to the development of a product that could be saleable, either in competition with existing products serving the same function or as a novel product without immediate competitors. Once development has been completed which, especially in high-technology areas, may take several more years, the remaining stages follow a pattern. Production facilities are first set up and manufacturing commenced, coupled with the setting up of distribution systems and suitable promotion, especially for a consumer product. Once the product is on the market, backup arrangements are necessary to provide service and support for guarantee claims, whether the product is a consumer or a capital item.

The Notice on Co-operation between Enterprises in 1968[31] was initially thought to exempt many R&D agreements from Article 81 altogether. The Notice proved a disappointment, limiting its scope to assist only a narrow group of R&D agreements. It accepted as being outside Article 81 agreements providing simply for exchange of experience and research results without any restriction against the undertakings carrying out their own R&D. Agreements of such a pure and limited nature are, however, rare. If there is no right to mutual access to the results, or if the practical exploitation

---

[31] See fn. 13.

of its results is covered by the agreement, then a restraint on competition may occur. Whilst it is possible to have an arrangement under which there are major and minor participants in the research project, who may receive access to the results in proportion to the degree of their participation in the research work, a restraint of competition again arises if some of the participating enterprises are unable to exploit the results, either totally or to an extent that is not proportionate with their participation. Moreover, if there is any restriction on granting licences to third parties, competition is again likely to be affected, though it is permissible to require a majority decision of the participants for the grant of any individual licences.

5.6 EARLY CASE LAW ON R&D AGREEMENTS

From this Notice alone, one might have assumed that an agreement which imposed no restrictions on the parties' R&D and development activities would not normally be in breach of Article 81(1). *Henkel-Colgate*[32] showed that such an assumption would be wrong. The two companies involved were both important in the detergent market, Colgate holding some 10 per cent of the EC market and Henkel nearly three times that amount. In three of the Member States their combined market share was over 50 per cent, but they had major competitors, notably Unilever and Proctor & Gamble. The proposed jointly owned company was to be limited to R&D, and not involved with distribution and marketing. It was apparent that in this particular industry the 'cutting edge' of competition lay principally in the ability to improve the technical quality of the product, which, of course, had the effect of placing great importance on their capabilities for R&D. The practical effect of the agreement was to eliminate the likelihood that the firms concerned would carry out their own research, since each party was almost bound to encourage the joint subsidiary to exploit any successful progress which it might make on its own. Any successful results from the collaboration would improve the competitive position of the two parties jointly, whilst eliminating competition in this area between themselves.

In view of the size and strength of both Henkel and Colgate, an unfavourable reaction from the Commission was not unexpected but, perhaps surprisingly, an exemption was given to the agreement limited to R&D on the basis that it might enable technical and economic progress and contained no restrictions that were not indispensable to the arrangements proposed. The proceeds of the collaboration would be available to both on payment of a royalty not to exceed 2 per cent of the net price of the product and on a non-exclusive basis. Licences to use the information could only be granted if both parties agreed, but this limitation was felt to be an inherent consequence of the setting up of the joint research organization for the benefit of the two participants. In order, however, to prevent the joint research from leading to further integrated activities between such substantial companies (such as market-sharing or arrangements over production and sales policies), the Commission imposed stringent conditions on

---

[32] [1972] OJ L14/14.

the exemption granted. These included an obligation to pass full information to DG Comp on their policy relating to the licensing of patents and know-how resulting from the joint research, and the provision of information about changes in the shareholding in the joint venture or in other links between the two companies.

Continuing experience with such R&D agreements gradually taught the Commission that, although in nearly all cases it was eventually possible to grant exemption to the agreement, it was often necessary to impose detailed conditions on their operation. This required the Commission to become involved in monitoring the agreements between the parties. In many other cases under Article 81(3), however, once the Commission had rendered a favourable decision it was not concerned with the details of its operation, unless it received complaints that the agreement was not being carried out in accordance with its notified terms.

The need for joint research into long-term problems too difficult for individual companies to undertake was also illustrated in the *Beecham/Parke, Davis* agreement.[33] Here the parties proposed to carry out joint research into drugs to prevent the impairment of blood circulation, none being available at the time. The time-scale for the work was considered to be at least a decade. Testing alone would be extremely lengthy, and neither company thought it worthwhile to undertake the required investment alone. A joint research programme was set up, to be followed if successful by a development programme. The development programme was expected to last five years before any marketing would be possible. The arrangements involved cross-licensing arrangements for patents on a non-exclusive royalty-free basis, and neither party was prevented from carrying out its own research. The parties agreed that they would exchange information relating to any improvements in manufacturing processes for a term of ten years after the product was marketed. Marketing would be carried out by each party individually.

Exemption was granted for ten years, and the Commission indicated that a determining factor in this decision was the fact that the new product was to be 'pharmacologically and therapeutically different from all known medicine' so that it was not an issue of improving production of existing products but of creating a new product. Even for companies as large as Beecham and Parke, Davis such R&D would stand a better chance of proceeding if carried out on a joint basis. Moreover, both parties remained free to use the results of the R&D independently and could grant licences to third parties without obtaining the prior consent of the other party. Deleted from the agreements was an obligation to pay royalties for cross-licences since the burden of royalty payments proposed would have been a considerable disincentive for the parties to compete with each other.

It has, however, also always been a major concern of the Commission to prevent an apparently harmless R&D agreement from becoming a market-sharing arrangement. This concern arose in the case of *Carbon Gas Technology*,[34] which involved a joint venture between three companies, Deutsche BP, Deutsche Babcock, and a

---

[33] See fn. 14.   [34] [1984] 2 CMLR 275.

German company, PCV, for developing coal gasification. The possible conversion of coal into gas had major industrial and economic significance for Europe in view of its dependence on imported oil. This venture limited to R&D appeared to have important strategic consequences for the European Community and was approved, but only subject to strict conditions. The commercial logic of the venture was that PCV specialized in basic process technology and the manufacture of the equipment required for conversion; Deutsche Babcock were the specialists in constructing large-scale plant in which such equipment should be placed; whilst BP's expertise was in refining oil, with a technology similar to that of gasification. The cooperation between these three large companies would effect considerable savings of both time and money, and it was likely that any technical advances made in improving the process would ensure a share of the benefit for consumers, given the active competition with other fuels.

The parties accepted restrictions on their activity by agreeing to refrain from competition with the joint venture, which meant that in practice they would not compete with each other. If any of them withdrew from the joint venture for a period of five years they agreed not to disclose any know-how that had belonged to the joint venture, whether the know-how originated from the parent company or from the joint venture itself. The exemption was granted on condition that all licensing agreements between the joint venture and its parents were submitted to DG Comp for approval, to prevent them from being used for market-sharing arrangements for sale of the equipment or plant for coal gasification within the Common Market. This was considered a real possibility given the individual strength and contacts of the three companies in their specialized fields.

5.7 INTRODUCTION OF BLOCK EXEMPTION REGULATION 418/85 AND ITS SUCCESSOR 2659/2000

It was noteworthy that, although the enactment by the Council of Regulation 2821/71 had given the Commission the power to issue a block exemption for R&D agreements, legal and political difficulties prevented this until a draft was finally published in early 1984, which, after amendment, was adopted as Regulation 418/85, effective from 1 March 1985. Its content was much more highly detailed than the equivalent block exemption for specialization agreements already mentioned which came into force on the same day. It provided only a limited exemption for a very basic type of R&D agreement, which might well not infringe Article 81(1) in any event. The block exemption was often found inadequate for more ambitious schemes especially if linked with distribution of the resulting product. It was generally regarded by lawyers as having too narrow a basis to be of much value to proposed R&D joint ventures. It was replaced from the end of 2000 by the new Block Exemption 2659/2000.[35]

---

[35] [2000] OJ L304/7: [2001] 4 CMLR 808.

The most important changes that the new block exemption introduced were as follows:

- the thresholds for the aggregate market shares of the parties (previously 20 per cent except where joint distribution was included, in which case it was 10 per cent only) were raised to 25 per cent with no separate lower threshold for joint distribution
- where a production joint venture was established, production targets could be set
- where a distribution joint venture is established, sales targets and prices could be set
- no framework agreement has to be entered into between parties defining the scope of the R&D and the field in which it is to be carried out.

The content of this exemption is rather more complicated than that of the specialization block exemption, and a summary of its individual articles may therefore be helpful. It applies to the following categories of R&D agreements:

- joint R&D of products or processes and joint exploitation of their results
- joint exploitation of the results of R&D previously carried out by prior agreement between the same undertakings
- simple joint R&D without subsequent joint exploitation.

In addition, ancillary clauses directly related to the main agreement and necessary for their implementation, such as an obligation not to carry out independently, or with third parties, R&D in the same field during the term of the agreement, are exempted (Article 1).

If the agreement is simply for joint R&D each party must be free thereafter to exploit the results, and all parties must have access to the results of the work. Any joint exploitation must relate to results protected by intellectual property rights which substantially contribute to technical or economic progress and which are decisive for the resulting manufacturing of products or application or processes (Article 2).

The period of exemption for non-competing manufacturers is the period of the R&D and for subsequent joint exploitation for seven years from the time when the contract products are first put on the market within the Common Market; if, however, the parties are in competition the threshold already mentioned of 25 per cent must not be exceeded, nor can an agreement even between non-competitors continue to enjoy exemption after the end of the initial seven-year joint-exploitation period if their combined market share has itself come to exceed 25 per cent. There is limited transitional relief in Article 6 to qualify the market-share rules. A market share of over 25 per cent but only up to 30 per cent can have a two-year relief following the year in which the threshold was first exceeded, whilst a share of over 30 per cent can have a transitional period of one year, provided that the aggregate of these two periods of relief cannot extend beyond a total of two.

Article 5 contains the important 'black list' of R&D agreements which do not enjoy the benefit of the block exemption. The equivalent article in the previous block exemption 418/85 (Article 6) had applied where the parties had, by the agreement, been restricted from certain acts or required not to do certain things; in the new block exemption the criterion is the object of the parties in making the agreement, including:

- limiting the output or sales of the parties
- fixing prices
- restricting the parties from entering into R&D in unconnected fields during the agreement or after its expiration in the same or connected fields
- no-challenge clauses
- restrictions on passive sales for the contract products in territories reserved for other parties
- the requirement not to grant licences to third parties to manufacture the contract products or apply the contract processes in cases where exploitation by the parties themselves does not take place.

As already stated, however, the parties do have the right to set production targets, sales targets, and fixed prices in cases of joint production and distribution respectively.

The new regulation gives the Commission wider powers of withdrawal of the block exemption. No fewer than five examples are given of situations where the effects of R&D agreements may be incompatible with the conditions laid down in Article 81(3), namely where:

- the existence of the agreement substantially restricts the scope for R&D by third parties, because of limited research capacity elsewhere
- its existence substantially restricts access of third parties to the market for the contract products
- without an objectively valid reason the parties do not exploit the results of their R&D
- the contract products are not subject to effective competition in the Common Market
- the existence of the agreement would eliminate effective competition in R&D in a particular market.

5.8 R&D AGREEMENTS: THE GUIDELINES

As with the Guidelines to specialization agreements referred to above, the Guidelines here are also set out as a supplement to the Block Exemption. A wide range of agreements is covered including those providing for full R&D cooperation, for joint improvement of the existing technology, the development of new products, the outsourcing of some R&D activities, and the commercialization of R&D already carried out. The only universal requirement is that the 'centre of gravity' of the cooperation lies in R&D. The Commission accepts that such agreements can bring about a wide range of technical or economic progress referred to in the first condition of Article 81(3) by leading to, for example, quicker development of products, cross-fertilization of ideas and experience, cost reductions, and the encouragement of lively SMEs. A corresponding disadvantage which such agreements might bring about might be restrictive effects on output, innovation, or price.

Importance is placed on the identification of the likely effect of the cooperation. This could range from the making of minor improvements to an existing product, or the creation of a new product which might in time come to be regarded as a substitute for an existing product, to the development of an entirely new product such as a vaccine to cure a previously untreatable disease. There will in addition to the market for the product being developed be a market for the relevant intellectual property technology. It may also prove necessary for the Commission to analyse the degree of present and potential competition in this market. It will also be important to identify relevant 'R&D poles', meaning particular clusters of investment in the industry directed towards developing a new product for technology. If there are a number of these then horizontal cooperation in R&D is less likely to have an anti-competitive effect.

Many R&D agreements will fall outside Article 81(1) especially if they are entered into by undertakings not themselves competitors or if they are mainly carried out through outsourcing, or only involve pure research activities. There is however more risk of Article 81(1) applying if the R&D is likely to be mainly directed to the launch of a new product, if the parties are existing competitors or if exclusivity of access is given to the results of the cooperation, unless the other party to the agreement is itself an academic body or research organization.

6. RECENT TRENDS IN JOINT VENTURE PROPOSALS

6.1 THE CHANGING BACKGROUND

One of the main changes in recent years has been the increase in the number of joint ventures notified to the Commission under the Merger Regulation and, until 2004, under Article 81, from those sectors of the economy where technological development is moving forward at speed. It has been particularly noticeable in the telecommunications and energy sectors. The Commission has sought through the use of directives under Article 86(3) of the Treaty to liberalize national markets for fixed line and mobile telephony, as well as the market for corporate telecommunications services of all kinds and other forms of advanced data communication. It has also used its jurisdiction over proposed joint ventures under the Merger Regulation (and, previously, under Article 81) to the same ends, in telecommunications markets and increasingly in energy markets. National telephone operators in the Community have been forming alliances with one or more other foreign operators so as to be able to put together both national and international services of a 'seamless' nature, meeting current demands from international business for integrated services. In bringing in so-called 'global partners' to give their operations a fully international dimension, their motives are partly defensive, i.e. to protect their own market shares in national markets, but in part aggressive, seeking a share of the potentially profitable 'value-added' services which many large corporate groups are now seeking to obtain. Such alliances which are normally of a non-concentrative nature are not always long lasting and may shift as commercial pressures and opportunities fluctuate. Nevertheless, it is essential for the Commission to be able to control the basis on which they are drawn up and to eliminate restrictions from them which do not fall within the proper scope of Article 81(3).

In paragraph 55 of the 1995 Annual Report of the Competition Directorate, the Commission stated that 'the application of the basic competition rules to these alliances has become one of the major challenges for EU competition policy in recent years. The Commission must ensure that the current restructuring process will lead to competitive and growth-oriented market structures; its policy aimed at liberalizing telecommunications is generating new services and products at competitive prices for consumers, reducing costs for the industry and creating new jobs.' However, it states that these efforts would serve little purpose if new and restrictive agreements, practices, or market structures were allowed to develop which prevented competition from emerging on liberalized markets or, equally, if telephone-operating companies could engage in abusive behaviour aimed at preserving their dominant position in individual markets.

6.2 TELECOMMUNICATIONS JOINT VENTURES: SOME CASE LAW

An example was the ATLAS joint venture between the national telephone operators of France and Germany, *France Telecom* (FT) and *Deutsche Telekom* (DT).[36] Their joint venture was owned by the two parties in equal shares in order to enable them jointly to provide sophisticated communication packages, comprising both voice data communication and also rather less complex 'packet switching' data services for smaller customers, including for example point of sale information for retail chains or transfer systems for banks operating cash machine networks. The potential markets for such services are very large and the fact that both participants retained a vital monopoly of their domestic telecommunications markets and infrastructure, and were seeking through the joint venture to extend their control over national markets further, made it seem initially that an exemption under Article 81(3) might be difficult to obtain.

[36] [1996] OJ L239/29, [1997] OJ L47/8: [1997] 4 CMLR 89.

The Commission granted an exemption, but in such a way as to use the leverage of the exemption request to further its own policy priorities with the two governments concerned, thus enabling liberalization of French and German telecommunications markets to occur more quickly than would otherwise have been the case. Conditions imposed on the parties under the exemption decision included:

(1) applicable only to the formation of ATLAS and the appointment of FT and DT as reciprocal exclusive distributors in their own territory, an exemption period limited to five years from the date on which French and German governments grant the first licences in their countries for the construction or ownership of alternative infrastructures for liberalized telecommunication services

(2) for the inclusion in the joint venture of the national public switched data network of FT and DT, an exemption period expiring on the same date as (1), but not starting until the date on which both countries first fully liberalized all their telecommunication services (which under existing directives was due to occur on 1 January 1998)

(3) a guarantee of open access to domestic public switched data networks of both companies even after integration into ATLAS on a non-discriminatory and 'transparent' basis to all service providers, including the implementation of any new standardized interconnection standard

(4) non-discriminatory treatment of third-party competitors in respect of the availability of facilities related services such as interconnection rights

(5) arms' length dealing between the joint venture and its parent companies, to be externally audited

(6) separate service contracts for the services to be provided by FT and DT in acting as exclusive distributors for ATLAS and for providing their own services, identifying prices and rebates.

FT and DT were to remain potential competitors of ATLAS and to receive important R&D licences from ATLAS. The Commission's view was that the benefits of those joint ventures on such terms would include the provision of better technology at an earlier date. The opportunity of building a 'seamless' trans-European network, including better link-ups between the public switched networks of the parties and their other networks should also in its view enable better technical harmonization for Member States which would also be of benefit to consumers. It was felt that the parties to the joint venture would face substantial competition in all their markets if the liberalization occurred as scheduled within the shape of the directives. The joint venture, however, could not proceed unless all these conditions were satisfied.

Closely linked to the ATLAS exemption was that for *Phoenix*[37] (later renamed Global One) under which FT and DT also acquired a 10 per cent interest each in Sprint, a major US telecom operator, so as to be able to provide telecommunications and data

---

[37] [1996] OJ L239/57: [1997] 4 CMLR 147.

services worldwide. A number of the restrictions initially placed on the parties in both cases were cut down so as to minimize the risk that the joint venture's strong starting position would enable it to weaken competition from its competitors. The Global One joint-venture exemption was granted for a term of seven years from the date of coming into effect of the condition of (2) above. A number of other similar joint ventures in the telecommunications sector have also been approved and several joint ventures between major airlines for code-sharing and other forms of cooperation have also been notified and cleared with conditions.

6.3 B2B EXCHANGES

An increasingly important form of joint venture is the 'electronic exchange' or the 'business to business' (B2B) Internet marketplace. Not all these Internet exchanges, of course, are joint ventures, and of those that are some will be concentrations covered by the Merger Regulation, because they are full-function and come within Article 3(2) of that Regulation. Others, however, will fall under the jurisdiction of Article 81(1), and are likely to take one of two main forms.

The first of these is proprietary, when the market place for buying and selling in a given sector of the economy is established jointly by leading participants in that sector. One example considered by the Commission is *My Aircraft.Com*,[38] which although categorized as a concentration because of its full-function nature, could easily have been structured as a joint venture within the scope of Article 81. It had been established by two major US companies, Honeywell and United Technologies, to provide an electronic marketplace for companies involved in the manufacturing and selling of aerospace products and services and to supply management functions for all participants in that industry. It would have to compete with other similar exchanges in the same sector. Giving its first decision and affirmation in this e-commerce area, the Commission indicated that it expected to have to consider a large number of such cases in the future, under both the Merger Regulation and Article 81.

The second form is that of the independent trading exchange, run by an independent undertaking and not causing any 'concentration' to occur, which is open to a wide variety of participants on the basis of the rules which are laid down. They can be used for a number of purposes, including the provision of:

- secure sites where buying and selling of products or commodities can take place on a routine basis, probably integrated with the IT management systems of the participants
- information in connection with a particular sector, and the provision of other services such as risk management or quality certification
- auction and exchange services for the participants.

---

[38] Commission Press Statement IP/00/912 of 7 August 2000.

The Commission is well aware of both the pro- and anti-competitive risks of such exchanges and has tried through public consultation and other means to apply established principles of Community competition law to this new phenomenon.[39] The increased price transparency of such exchanges can, in principle, assist the competitive process, but equally it has the potential for increasing collusion between the parties, especially as 'cheating' on price agreements can with such exchanges be easily detected by other participants.

6.4 ENERGY JOINT VENTURES

Using competition law to open energy markets has been one of the features of the Commission's policy approach to joint ventures in the energy sector. A good example is the *Dong/DUC* case involving the Danish gas market.[40] Dong is the incumbent Danish gas supplier. DUC is a joint marketing consortium made up of Denmark's main gas producers (Shell, AP Møller and Chevron). Under gas supply agreements with Dong, DUC contracted to sell sufficient gas to satisfy not only all Danish demand but also additional volumes to sell to Sweden and Germany. After intervention by the Commission and the Danish competition authority, the DUC members agreed to market their gas production individually. Dong agreed that it would release the DUC members from their obligation to offer all their gas first to Dong. In order to facilitate the entry of new gas suppliers in competition with Dong, the DUC members also agreed to offer a substantial amount of gas (approximately 17% of the total gas production of the DUC members) to new customers.

Large gas-field projects involve substantial costs and substantial risks which individual energy companies may not be able to support on their own. The result of the Commission's intervention was to allow the DUC producers to continue to produce gas jointly. But at the same time, by introducing more competition in the marketing of the gas in Denmark, the Commission was of the view that Dong's market power would decrease and that gas prices would fall accordingly.

FURTHER READING

J.-P. GUNTHER, S. RAB, and P. BELMIN, 'Joint Selling v. Joint Production: a Rational Distinction?' [2005] ECLR 39.

J. KIRKBRIDE and T. XIONG, 'The European Control of Joint Ventures: An Historic Opportunity or a Mere Continuation of Existing Practice?' [1998] ELRev 37.

T. PICK, 'Sub-contracting Agreements under EU Competition Law—Applicability of Article 81 EC' [2002] ECLR 154.

[39] DG Comp Competition Policy Newsletter (2001), No. 3, pp. 14–16.
[40] Commission Press Release IP/03/566 of 24 April 2003.

19

ENFORCEMENT OF COMMUNITY LAW BY NATIONAL AUTHORITIES

1. INTRODUCTION: THE ORIGINAL DIVISION OF RESPONSIBILITY

1.1 THE NEED FOR MEMBER STATE PARTICIPATION IN COMMUNITY COMPETITION POLICY

The previous chapters in this book have explained the emergence of Community competition law as a mature and far-reaching body of rules, affecting businesses of all kinds in practically every sector of the economy. The task of enforcing these rules effectively in a Community of twenty-seven Member States is far beyond the ability of the Commission and Community Courts alone, even if they were granted substantial new resources. It is therefore vital that Member States themselves play a full and effective role in the application of the competition rules, not only of national law but those of the Community. Competition rules are applied both by national courts and by national competition authorities; this chapter and the next will describe the way in which their involvement has greatly increased in recent years. To understand the relationship of Community and national law in this area, it is necessary first to appreciate the original structure of the Treaty and relevant secondary legislation on this issue, and then to see the development of relevant legal principles through case law, leading in 2004 to a radical decentralization of the application of Articles 81 and 82.

Two major factors can be identified as having contributed to this movement. The first is the accretion of additional responsibilities to DG Comp as a result of new legislation and other developments. These comprise the European Community Merger Regulation and the heavy case-load that this has brought, including a large number of joint ventures, and the Article 86 jurisdiction, including the need to issue directives in many sectors formerly dominated by State controlled enterprises and State aid. A second important factor is the creation and growth in recent years of national competition authorities in all Member States, and their greater ability and willingness to work in cooperation with the officials of the Commission in resolving cases that have both Community and national significance.

These developments culminated in a White Paper produced by the Commission in April 1999 proposing a modernization programme under which responsibility for enforcing the provisions of Article 81 and Article 82 would in future be shared more equally between the Commission, which would lose its monopoly for the granting of individual exemption under Article 81(3). The competition authorities of Member States would be linked in a close network for the exchange of information and the coordination of their activities with each other and the Commission. National courts too would be able under the new arrangements to play a more significant role, as we shall see in the following chapter. These proposals, after extensive consultation, were converted into legislation by Regulation 1/2003 which from 1 May 2004 replaced the longstanding Regulation 17/62 which has played such an important role in the development of Community competition policy.

1.2 THE TERMS OF THE TREATY OF ROME

Before examining the detailed provisions of the Regulation it is important to understand how the original division of responsibility operated, as between the Commission and national competition authorities. It was never the case that responsibility for enforcing Articles 81 and 82 lay with the institutions of the Community alone. The inadequate resources of the Commission in general, and of DG Comp in particular, especially in the early years, would have made this impractical, quite apart from any other considerations. In any case the relevant provisions of the Treaty embodied the principle that the competition policy originally referred to in Article 3(f) was to be jointly implemented with Member States, both national courts and competition authorities playing an important role in its enforcement alongside the Commission. Whilst the primary role of such national competition authorities was to enforce their own domestic competition laws, their other responsibility would be to help the Commission to ensure that Community law on this subject was effectively and uniformly enforced.

That this was the original scheme of the Treaty is clearly shown by the terms of Article 83(2)(e). In referring to the regulations or directives to be adopted by the Council 'to give effect to the principles set out in Articles [81] and [82]' this mentions the areas in which in particular such regulations or directives shall operate, including those necessary 'to determine the relationship between national laws and the provisions contained in this Section or adopted pursuant to this Article'.[1] The exact pattern of cooperation could not be foreseen at that early stage; working out the consequences for the Common Market of the terms of Article 81, let alone Article 82, would take at least a decade, as we saw in Part I above.

Since the provisions of the Treaty relating to competition applied only to activities which 'affect trade between Member States', Member States remained free to enact

---

[1] The 'Section' referred to original Arts. 85–90 inclusive (now Arts. 81–6), the 'Article' to original Art. 87 (now Art. 83).

legislation to cover purely domestic issues.[2] In fact, when the Treaty came into force in 1958 limited legislation existed in Member States, ranging from the relatively sophisticated but untried (Germany) to the non-existent. Over the intervening fifty years all Member States have established national competition authorities, whose primary task is the application of national competition law to local cases outside the scope of Articles 81 and 82, but which must also cooperate on a procedural level with DG Comp on a range of Community cases. Many of these national competition authorities had the necessary powers to apply both these Articles within their national boundaries from an early stage, in recognition of the need to decentralize their application, and the remainder (including the United Kingdom) changed their law in response to the modernizing Regulation 1/2003. This development was aided by the choice in many Member States of a structure for national competition law which is either identical to that of the Community or at least contains many similar features. In Section 4 of this chapter the main features of national competition authorities are reviewed.

At the time of the signature of the Treaty, however, all these developments lay in the future. Articles 84 and 85 laid down basic ground rules to govern the immediate future until the adoption of Regulations under Article 83 by the Council. During this interim period, Member States were free to apply both Articles 81 and 82, including the exemption provisions of 81(3), whilst for its part the Commission was entitled to apply the Treaty provisions in this area 'in co-operation with the competent authorities in the Member States, who shall give it their assistance'. The terms of Regulation 17/62, however, ensured that the control of the development of Article 81 would rest firmly with the Commission, for the terms of its Article 9(1) provided that 'subject to review of its decision by the Court of Justice, the Commission shall have sole power to declare Article 81(1) inapplicable pursuant to Article 81(3) of the Treaty'. This key right to grant individual exemption under Article 81(3) was to be the monopoly of the Commission. No national court nor national competition authority was to share it. The importance of a consistent application of Article 81(3) was considered too vital to be weakened in any way by sharing its application with Member States, many of whom had limited experience of the operation of competition law, or were believed to be insufficiently committed at this early stage to the principles of competition in their national markets. So far as the application of Articles 81(1) and 82 were concerned, national courts and competition authorities were allowed to initiate action against an undertaking provided that the Commission itself had not formally initiated proceedings under Regulation 17. However, in the details of procedural arrangements a considerable degree of cooperation with national authorities was preserved.

1.3 REGULATION 17/62 AND THE NEED FOR COOPERATION

Article 10 referred to the contact required between DG Comp and the 'competent authorities' of Member States. They were entitled to receive copies of applications for

---

[2] Though the scope of such domestic legislation would in time be restricted by the wide interpretation given by the European Court to that very phrase. See Ch. 7, Section 1.

notification and exemption and the main supporting documents. Article 10(2) set out the principle that administrative procedures shall be carried out in close and constant liaison with these competent authorities, and paragraph (3) provided for the creation of an Advisory Committee on restrictive practices and monopolies to provide the forum in which national authorities could express their views on the procedure. As mentioned in Chapter 4, this is still the forum in which Member States become involved in individual decisions, the views of the Advisory Committee being influential though not decisive. DG Comp preferred naturally to receive the blessing of at least a majority of the Advisory Committee to a proposed decision. If there was substantial opposition within the Committee, the proposals might then have to be taken back for reconsideration in either major or minor respects. However, when DG Comp was convinced that its approach to a particular case was correct, it sometimes persevered in taking a proposed decision to the full Commission even if the vote or opinion of the Advisory Committee had been adverse.

The necessary consequence of such involvement for Member States in the decision-making process of the Commission was an obligation to cooperate with the administrative and investigatory procedures of the Commission. Articles 11 to 14 of the Regulation contained a number of provisions setting out how this help was to be provided. Thus:

(1) Under Article 11(1) the Commission could obtain 'all necessary information' from both governments and competent authorities of Member States as well as from undertakings and associations within those Member States. This was an essential power enabling the Commission to inform itself about the facts and issues relating to a particular complaint or pending case.

(2) Article 13(1) provided that the competent authorities of Member States could be asked to conduct investigations which the Commission itself could conduct, including the examination of books and business records, the taking of copies or extracts, and the requiring of oral explanations 'on the spot' of the contents of these documents. This power was not much used.

(3) Article 14 gave the Commission necessary powers to carry out its own investigations, but with the help of the competent authority which was entitled to (and normally does) escort the Commission officials on their investigations. In the United Kingdom this authority is the Office of Fair Trading. Member States were required under Article 14(6) to give all necessary assistance to the officials authorized by the Commission to make such investigations.

These investigations, often sprung as a surprise by way of a 'dawn raid', generally involved physical inspection of the books and files of undertakings. They could happen on a voluntary basis (under Article 14(2)) and in practice companies usually chose to cooperate, or following a formal decision of the Commission to that effect under Article 14(3), in which case the company was legally obliged to submit to the investigation.

1.4 EUROPEAN COURT CASE LAW ON 'DAWN RAIDS'

The exact nature of the Commission's powers under Article 14 was the subject of several cases in the European Court of Justice involving the chemical industry. In the *Hoechst*[3] and *Dow*[4] cases the rights of the Commission to carry out searches necessary for the particular stated objectives of its own decision were examined. If the national undertaking seeks physically to bar access to the Commission, its officials cannot use force to obtain entry to business premises without a national court order. The national court must make an order in favour of the Commission if satisfied that the necessary causal link exists between the proposed investigation and its stated objective. In the *Solvay* and *Orkem* cases[5] the Court drew a distinction between the making of factual and objective enquiries of undertakings in the course of such an investigation (which is allowed) and the asking of questions to which replies may force those undertakings to make statements which necessarily admit a breach of the law (not permitted). It was therefore inherent in Regulation 17 that the competent national authorities were to some extent involved in the administrative, fact-finding, and investigatory processes as well as in the decision-making of the Commission.

In a more recent case (*Roquette*)[6] the European Court has confirmed that national courts are entitled to verify that any coercive measures, such as forcible entry, which the Commission may seek under Article 14 are not 'arbitrary or disproportionate', but is not entitled to demand evidence from the Commission's file as to the grounds for its suspicions that a breach of Article 81 or 82 may have occurred. The Commission must provide the national court with a detailed description of the essential features of a suspected infringement and the involvement of the undertaking against which such coercive measures are sought. It must also indicate the exact matters to which its investigations relate and the need for the particular search. If the national court remains unconvinced by the Commission's evidence, it cannot simply dismiss it as 'arbitrary' or 'disproportionate' but must give the Commission a further opportunity to produce support for its case.

1.5 OTHER MEANS OF MEMBER STATE INVOLVEMENT

Member States are also involved, through the Advisory Committee, in reviewing proposed drafts of new Regulations, including those putting forward proposals for new block exemptions. They have a chance to express their views on these after entering into consultations over the terms of the draft documents with a wide variety of national interested parties and pressure groups. Views of Member States are also made known to the Commission through a number of other formal and informal channels. As a result, although Member States do not customarily initiate individual policies or

---

[3] Cases 46/87 and 277/88 [1989] ECR 2859: [1991] 4 CMLR 410.
[4] Cases 85, 97–99/87 [1989] ECR 3137, 3165: [1991] 4 CMLR 410.
[5] Cases 374/87 and 27/88 [1989] ECR 3283, 3355: [1991] 4 CMLR 502.
[6] Case C-94/00 [2002] ECR I-9011: [2003] 4 CMLR 46.

issue their own suggested drafts for Regulations or for block exemptions, they do have an important role and exercise influence in the framing of policies culminating in both actual decisions and new Regulations. It would therefore be unfair to suggest that the Regulations eventually issued by the Commission, following this lengthy process of consultation, involve some kind of diktat on Member States imposed from above.

2. ARTICLE 81(3) AND THE ISSUE OF SUPREMACY

2.1 THE *WALT WILHELM* CASE AND ITS THREE RULES

The Commission, with the enactment of Regulation 17/62, had firmly established its exclusive right to grant individual exemptions under Article 81(3), in addition to its right under the Treaty, once authorized by the Council, to issue category (block) exemptions. It also had its preferred, but not exclusive, position with regard to the exercise of jurisdiction over Article 81(1) and Article 82. Clearly the principle of the supremacy of Community law dictated that a Commission decision that a particular agreement was prohibited by Article 81 was binding on national courts and authorities. However, difficulties arose in two other situations. First, could a stricter national competition law be applied to prohibit an agreement if the Commission had found it to be outside the scope of Article 81(1), either because the jurisdictional criterion of an effect on trade between Member States was absent, or because the Commission considered there to be no restriction on competition within the meaning of Article 81(1)? Secondly, was an agreement exempted by the Commission under Article 81(3) capable of prohibition by national law, or did the grant of an exemption by reason of the primacy of Community law preclude the possibility of prohibition by national law? In general it was clear that agreements must satisfy both Article 81 and national law (the 'double barrier') but this might not be so where the Commission had granted an exemption. Because of the very wide interpretation placed by the early European Court decisions on the concept of 'trade between Member States', this question took on increasing importance; not many agreements of commercial significance, it seemed, would on the basis of such cases be outside the range of Community law, and it thus became important that the European Court of Justice provide an authoritative ruling.

Article 234 of the Treaty provides the appropriate means of obtaining a preliminary ruling on issues of Community law arising in cases being heard in national courts. Its purpose, and a very necessary one, is to ensure that Community law is interpreted in a like manner in all Member States. It was through a preliminary ruling under this Article that a Berlin Court obtained guidance in early 1969 on the relationship between national law and Community law, in the context of parallel investigations being carried out by both the Commission and the German cartel authority (Bundeskartellamt). In recent years, as resources and experience of national competition authorities have increased, and there has occurred the expansion and refinement of national competition laws substantially based on the principles and language of Articles 81 and 82, so has the willingness and ability of these authorities to work more closely with the Commission. This in turn has made possible the creation of the network of national competition authorities which, as we shall see in the next section of this chapter, formed an essential part of the modernization programme. But all this was far in the future at the time of the *Walt Wilhelm* case.[7]

The background to the case was that certain major manufacturers of aniline dyes had entered into discussions over price increases for their product in circumstances which led to strong suspicion that an agreement had actually been concluded between them as to the timing and level of future increases. Investigations carried out by the Commission led eventually to the bringing of the *Dyestuffs* case.[8] In the meantime, the Bundeskartellamt had begun its own investigation of agreements in which German companies had apparently been involved, and Wilhelm was one of the directors of Bayer involved in this investigation. His claim was that the Bundeskartellamt should desist from carrying out its own investigation whilst DG Comp was carrying out investigations for the Commission into the same matters. The Kammergericht in Berlin referred to the European Court of Justice the issue of whether the Bundeskartellamt could continue with its investigations, or whether under Community law it was required to suspend them pending completion of the investigation being carried out by DG Comp.

The Court pointed out that Community and national laws considered cartels and restrictive agreements from a different point of view; whilst Article 81 regarded them in the light of the obstacles which they would present to trade between Member States, national legislation had its own individual priorities and considerations; though there might be some overlap and interdependence between the two separate investigations, there was no reason in principle why the same agreements could not be the object of two separate parallel proceedings. However, to ensure that the general aims of the Treaty were respected, such simultaneous investigation could only be allowed on the national level if three conditions were satisfied:

(1) The national application of the law must not prejudice the full and uniform application of Community rules, or of the full effect of the measures adopted in the implementation of those rules ('the uniformity rule').

(2) To ensure in any conflict between Community and national rules that Community law takes precedence (to protect the effectiveness of the Treaty), Member States should not introduce or retain any measures which would prejudice this aim (the 'practical effectiveness rule').

---

[7] Case 14/68 *Walt Wilhelm* v. *Bundeskartellamt* [1969] ECR 1: CMLR 100.

[8] Case 48/69 *ICI* v. *Commission* [1972] ECR 619: CMLR 557; several related cases are also reported in [1972] ECR.

(3) Individual Member States must take appropriate measures to avoid any risk that a national decision on an issue of competition law might conflict with Commission proceedings still in progress (the 'parallel proceedings' rule).

Whilst these principles gave a clear answer to the Berlin Court as to the proper procedure in the *Walt Wilhelm* case, their application to other circumstances of potential conflict was far from clear, as commentators then noted.[9] As already stated, if the agreement or practice is forbidden by Article 81(1), then the requirements of both uniformity and practical effectiveness underline the impossibility of allowing national law to provide an exemption for it.

Walt Wilhelm did not deal directly with the converse case, where the agreement or concerted practice is found by the Commission, for whatever reason, to be outside the scope of Article 81(1). It would seem in principle that the national authority should be free to intervene if it wishes to invoke national law with regard to the domestic effects of the agreement or practice. The intervention in such circumstances is in an area where the Commission either has no jurisdiction under the Treaty or has elected on policy grounds not to exercise any jurisdiction. With regard to the problem of conflict between parallel national community investigation and proceedings, the Commission stated as early as its *4th Annual Report*[10] that the onus was firmly on the national authorities to avoid the risk of conflict, an obligation that could be complied with so long as the national authorities had early consultations with the Commission or even suspended proceedings whilst the Commission investigation was completed.

Whilst acknowledging that the principles in the *Walt Wilhelm* decision provided an answer to some questions, the Report also acknowledged that the Court's decision failed to provide answers to the most difficult issue, of the status of an agreement granted exemption by the Commission under Article 81(3) when a national authority nevertheless wished to declare it illegal in whole or part. The Commission in its *4th Annual Report* purported to read into the *Wilhelm* decision a rejection by the Court of the argument that exemption by the Commission withdraws only the Community barrier to a restrictive agreement under Article 81(1), leaving unimpaired the national authority's power to prohibit such agreement under its own law (the 'double barrier' theory). However, such rejection can only be found, if at all, implicitly in the Court decision and is not expressly stated in it.

It was clear therefore that in respect of Article 81(3) there were two situations for which the *Wilhelm* case provided incomplete guidance. First, where the Commission had given an individual exemption to an agreement or concerted practice which a national authority in a Member State wished either to reject completely or to make subject to some restriction or condition. The second problem arose when there was a Regulation in force containing a block exemption for particular forms of agreement, from which the Member State wishes to derogate.

---

[9] Including K. Markert, 'Some Legal and Administrative Problems of the Co-Existence of Community and National Competition Law in the EEC' [1974] 11 CML Rev 92.

[10] (1974) pp. 27–31.

To provide an answer in these situations, it is necessary, whilst bearing in mind the terms of the judgment of the European Court in *Wilhelm*, also to consider the inherent nature of the exemption process for individuals and groups respectively. Although the 'four conditions' to be applied by the Commission are in principle identical for both individual and block exemptions, they are applied in a different way. On one hand, if the exemption flows from an individual decision (which is properly described as administrative or possibly quasi-judicial) it is given on the basis of the particular facts disclosed in the course of the Commission's administrative procedure, rather than from a 'legislative' decision that a particular category or class of agreement both having certain 'plus' (or 'white') features and lacking certain defined anti-competitive 'minus' (or 'black') elements should be exempt. In the latter case, the facts of the individual cases benefiting from the block exemption will never need to be disclosed to DG Comp, since the very concept of the block exemption, emphasized by the recitals to the enabling Council Regulation 19/65, is to provide a legislative solution to the 'mass problem' by excluding the need to notify a large number of separate agreements.[11]

In the *Walt Wilhelm* case the Court refused to accept the argument of the Advocate General that the application of a stricter national law to an individual agreement, possibly overruling the effect of an exemption given by the Commission under Article 81(3), did not prejudice Community law because each system was concerned essentially with the same objectives. Whilst the reasons for its refusal to follow him are not explicitly stated in its judgment, the main difference in the approach of the Court is found in this key section:

Article [81] of the EEC Treaty applies to all the undertakings in the Community whose behaviour it governs either by prohibitions or by means of exemptions granted—subject to conditions which it specifies—in favour of agreements which contribute to improving the production or distribution of products or to promoting technical or economic progress. While the Treaty's primary object is to eliminate by this means the obstacles to the free movement of goods within the Common Market and to confirm and safeguard the unity of that market, it also permits the Community authorities to carry out certain positive, though indirect, action with a view to promoting a harmonious development of economic activities within the whole Community, in accordance with Article 2 of the Treaty.[12]

This passage clearly gives the Community both a positive and a negative function in carrying out its responsibilities. It is hard to see how the grant of an individual exemption by the Commission should not be treated as such a 'positive' act, grounded on both the investigation of the relevant circumstances affecting a particular agreement, and the finding that on balance its preservation is desirable in the public interest of the Community. To quote an early commentary on this issue:

signature of the Treaty by the Member States implies their acceptance of competition policy (as formulated and implemented by the Community authorities) as one of the means of

---

[11] See also the *Tetrapak (No. 1)* judgment of the Court of First Instance discussed in Ch. 14, p. 350, for comment on the difference between block and individual exemptions under Art. 81(3).

[12] [1969] ECR I-14: CMLR 100, 119.

achieving the aims set out in Article 2 of the Treaty and that accordingly the positive aspects of the policy must be given the same weight as its negative aspects. Balance must be struck between too little competition at the expense of the consumer and too much competition leading in certain circumstances to inefficiency. If it is right that the Commission's actions should not be frustrated by the application of incompatible national legislation in relation to the former, it must also be right that the Commission should have an equally free hand in relation to the latter. The driver must have the use of the accelerator as well as the brake.[13]

A separate distinction has been suggested between exemptions granted purely for 'public policy reasons', when the Commission's decisions would have to be respected by national courts and authorities, and other cases, when a national authority or court would be free to impose further requirements. It is difficult to see how this distinction could be applied even to individual exemptions, where one has the advantage of a specific finding as to the relevant facts, as it will be hard to distinguish those cases where the public policy element is so great that the exemption should be respected by national courts. In every case where an exemption is granted, the fact that the agreement or practice must comply with all the four conditions contained in Article 81(3) makes it difficult to deny that an element of public policy enters into this assessment. Public policy must enter into an assessment as to whether, for example, an agreement contributes to improving the production or distribution of goods or the promotion of technical or economic progress, but is also likely to be relevant to the assessment of whether consumers receive a fair share of the resulting benefit. An important element in the opinion of Advocate General Roemer is the statement that:

If national authorities thwart the Community exemption through the application of a national rule of prohibition, they no more threaten the objectives of the Treaty than do the parties to that agreement when they refrain from applying it, which can occur at any time. This conclusion applies as a general rule because in principle cartels cannot be considered as instruments of the organisation of the Common Market.[14]

This is surely misleading. If an individual agreement is no longer applied by the parties to it, this has no precedential value, nor does it affect any other agreement between the same or any other parties. On the other hand, an individual exemption has value as a precedent and may affect other persons and Courts in Member States which may take it into consideration in future cases, as well as the parties to the agreement. It reflects a 'positive' policy of the Commission under the Treaty; it is difficult to see how the status of a block exemption cannot equally be described as 'positive' and 'an act of policy' within the spirit of Articles 2 and 3(1)(g) of the Treaty. Indeed, the involvement of Member States in the legislative process leading up to the enactment of block exemptions by way of Regulation is, as we have seen, substantial even though they do not control the final terms in which they are produced. National competition authorities, and Member States themselves, should not therefore be entitled to disregard their

---

[13] D. Barounos, D. Hall, and J. R. James, *EEC Antitrust Law: Principles and Practice* (Butterworths, 1975), pp. 142–3.

[14] [1969] ECR I-23: [1969] CMLR 100, 110.

terms merely because they prefer a different and stricter solution for their national legislative purposes.

2.2 THE *BMW* AND *VOLKSWAGEN* CASES

It had been hoped that the case of *BMW* v. *ALD Autoleasing*[15] in 1995 would provide the European Court with an opportunity to remove any remaining doubts on this issue. BMW in Germany had sought to prevent its official dealers from selling cars to leasing companies outside their own exclusive territories, issuing a circular ordering them to discontinue such sales to companies like ALD which had established a substantial leasing business throughout Germany. ALD challenged the circular alleging, that it was in breach of Article 81(1) and not within the permitted set of contractual restrictions allowed by Regulation 123/85. The Bundesgerichtof referred the case to the European Court on two issues: first on the application of the terms of Regulation 123/85 to BMW's prohibition on its dealers from making such sales to leasing companies outside their territory, and secondly, if such a restriction was permitted by the exemptions contained in 123/85, whether the German courts could prohibit the practice under national rules against supply boycotts. In his opinion Tesauro A-G came down firmly on the side of the supremacy of Community law, stating that 'to reconcile the primacy of Community law with the possibility of prohibiting an agreement which had been exempted by and under Community law seems to me a desperate undertaking, even a diabolic one'. Unfortunately the European Court, after agreeing with the opinion of the Advocate General that the proposed ban by BMW on its dealers selling to leasing companies was not protected by Regulation 123/85, gave no ruling on the possible conflict between a Community exemption under that Regulation and a German prohibition of the same practice under national law.

In the companion case of *Bundeskartellamt* v. *Volkswagen*,[16] the Advocate General (though not the Court) considered whether a negative clearance by the Commission of an agreement under Article 81(1) left a Member State free to restrict or prohibit that agreement. He suggested that this might depend on the basis for the grant of negative clearance; if clearance was granted after a finding that the agreement contained no appreciable restriction of competition, after balancing the various relevant circumstances, then the Member State should not act against that judgment by the Commission. On the other hand, if the negative clearance had been granted simply because the agreement did not affect trade between Member States, then the Member State was entitled to act in regard to the agreement as a case where the Commission had disclaimed any jurisdiction over it.

---

[15] Case C-70/93 [1995] ECR I-3439: [1996] 4 CMLR 478.

[16] Case 266/93 [1995] ECR I-3477: [1996] 4 CMLR 505. Whilst both these cases dealt with block exemptions, it had been hoped that the judgments would be sufficiently broad to deal with the issue of individual exemptions, too.

2.3   THE NEW REGULATION RESOLVES THE ISSUE

The outcome of this long and important debate has however now been resolved, not by any decision of a Community Court, but by the new Regulation 1/2003[17] that replaced Regulation 17/62 from 1 May 2004. The most important single Article in this new Regulation is Article 3, which establishes the supremacy of Community competition law whilst still allowing a limited degree of freedom to national competition authorities in the application of their national law.

Under its original terms as set out in early drafts the supremacy of Community law in this context was absolute; the text proposed at this time read simply:

Where an agreement, a decision by an association of undertakings or a concerted practice within the meaning of Article 81 of the Treaty or the abuse of a dominant position within the meaning of Article 82 may affect trade between Member States, Community competition law shall apply to the exclusion of national competition laws.

The sweeping nature of this proposal raised numerous objections from Member States. The Commission soon acknowledged that it would be satisfied with a less absolute provision provided that the essential core of the text conferring supremacy on Community law remained intact. After long negotiations the final text adopted makes clear that national competition authorities still retain some freedom to apply their own competition laws alongside Articles 81 and 82. Thus the text of the new Article 3 as finally adopted reads:

1. Where the competition authorities of the Member States or national courts apply national competition law to agreements, decisions of associations of undertakings or concerted practices within the meaning of Article 81(1) of the Treaty which may affect trade between Member States within the meaning of that provision, they shall also apply Article 81 of the Treaty to such agreements, decisions or concerted practices. Where the competition authorities of the Member States or national courts apply national competition law to any abuse prohibited by Article 82 of the Treaty, they shall also apply Article 82 of the Treaty.

2. The application of national competition law may not lead to the prohibition of agreements, decisions by associations of undertakings or concerted practices which may affect trade between Member States but which do not restrict competition within the meaning of Article 81(1) of the Treaty, or which fulfil the conditions of Article 81(3) of the Treaty or which are covered by a Regulation for the application of Article 81(3) of the Treaty. Member States shall not under this Regulation be precluded from adopting and applying on their territory stricter national laws which prohibit or sanction unilateral conduct engaged in by undertakings.

3. Without prejudice to general principles and other provisions of Community law, paragraphs 1 and 2 do not apply when the competition authorities and the courts of the Member States apply national merger control laws nor do they preclude the

---

[17] [2003] OJ L1/1.

application of provisions of national law that predominantly pursue an objective different from that pursued by Articles 81 and 82 of the Treaty.

The effect of these rules (which apply also to national courts as explained in the following chapter) is as follows:

(i)   A national competition authority which applies national competition law to an agreement, decision or concerted practice 'which may affect trade between Member States' must also at the same time apply Article 81 (paragraph 1). If dealing with abuse of a dominant position, it must also apply Article 82.

(ii) In the course of such application national competition authorities may not prohibit under national law agreements, decisions or practices that will either fall outside Article 81(1) or meet the requirements of Article 81(3) whether by individual or block exemption (paragraph 2).

(iii) National competition authorities may however apply national competition law, and paras 1 and 2 do not apply even if national law is stricter than the corresponding Community law (a) in the case of unilateral conduct engaged in by undertakings, and (b) in the application of national merger control law, and (c) in applying national law that predominantly pursues a different objective from those of Articles 81 and 82, provided in all cases that the application of national law is itself not in breach of general principles of Community law.

This compromise protects the right of national competition authorities to adopt sanctions under national law for unilateral acts or practices by undertakings which Community rules might not be able to reach, because of the fact that Article 82 applies only to dominant companies. Let us suppose that a market investigation by the Competition Commission in the United Kingdom under the Enterprise Act 2002 produces a finding that several companies in a particular sector, for example brewing, have separately adopted practices relating to exclusive supply or refusal to deal with particular wholesalers, but where none of the brewers can be legally characterized as individually dominant and between whom no agreement or concerted practice can be shown. Under the Enterprise Act the Commission would then be able to impose sanctions against these non-dominant companies individually, not by way of fines (as might have been appropriate following proceedings by the Office of Fair Trading) under the United Kingdom Competition Act Chapter 1 or Chapter 2 (equivalent to Articles 81 and 82) but by way of a varied range of remedies which may be of a different kind (as listed in Schedule 8 of the Enterprise Act). Moreover, measures taken primarily by way of consumer protection in such a case or any other (either under the Competition Act or Enterprise Act) would also be permitted under the terms of this Article.

3. NATIONAL COMPETITION AUTHORITIES AS ACTIVE ENFORCERS OF COMMUNITY LAW

3.1 THE DEBATE ON NATIONAL COMPETITION AUTHORITY PARTICIPATION

The original role envisaged under Regulation 17/62 for the national competition authorities of the Six was very limited, especially as only one Member State at that time, Germany, could be described as having an effective authority with both a full substantive law and the resources to enforce it. Through the Advisory Committee established under that Regulation the Member States could render some help to the Commission in enforcing its Community rules. But it was certainly not anticipated initially that they would play an active part themselves in enforcing Community competition law both because of lack of resources and of the legal powers under national law for the enforcement of such rules at a time when their own national laws were only starting to emerge.

Gradually however over the last fifteen years or so, and with the expansion of the Community from its original membership of six to twenty-seven Member States, the landscape has changed. Not only did the Commission begin to find that national competition authorities were now more willing and able to help it enforce competition policy but it realized that its own resources were more than fully stretched in dealing with major Community-wide cases, particularly cartels, and that maintenance of its monopoly over the grant of individual exemptions (both formal and informal) under Article 81(3) was no longer sensible or indeed possible. The Commission had taken on substantial new responsibilities under the Merger Regulation, including the review of many major joint ventures, an increased caseload under State aid, and more work under Article 86 including the preparation of directives under Article 86(3) in order to liberalize sectors formerly dominated by national monopolies in transport, telecommunications, and energy. The decision in *Automec (No. 2)*[18] had enabled it to give priority to cases with a high Community interest and to consider the allocation of responsibility for dealing with cases not in that category to national competition authorities with the necessary powers.

In an article surveying these developments, a former Director General of DG Comp, Claus Dieter Ehlermann, stated his surprise that the debate on fuller use of national competition authorities for Community law enforcement did not begin until the early 1990s.[19] In this article he describes the steps taken by the Commission after *Automec (No. 2)* to seek greater participation by national competition authorities and

---

[18] Case T-24/90 [1992] ECR II-2223: 5 CMLR 431.

[19] 'Implementation of EC Competition Law by National Antitrust Authorities' [1996] 17 ECLR 88–95. See also P. Marsden [1997] 17 *ECLR* pp. 234–41. For a later view, see C.-D. Ehlermann [2000] 37 CML Rev 537–90.

to establish ground rules for their extension of jurisdiction. The working party chaired by Jean Dubois in 1994 led to a number of comments in the 1994 *Annual Report*[20] of the Commission as to how it was hoped this decentralization would proceed, as follows:

The [Dubois] Report applies three criteria to identify the cases that might be dealt with by a national authority. First, their effects must be located mainly within a single Member State. However, if an agreement or practice implemented mainly in a Member State raises a question of Community interest, the Commission will initiate proceedings on the basis of Article 9(3) of Regulation 17/62. Secondly, the case must involve infringements of Article [81(1)] that probably do not satisfy the criteria of Article [81(3)]. The case may also involve infringements of Article 82, which are often detected following a complaint. Thirdly, protection at national level must be effective. Such effectiveness depends on various factors; the prime requirement is that there must be adequate legislation. Adequate legislation means legislation that is satisfactory from the point of view of the substantive competition rules. It should be noted in this respect that some national legislations do not provide for the possibility of their competition authorities applying Articles [81] and [82] of the Treaty directly, and that some national legislations are based on concepts of competition other than those Articles. However, national legislation should also provide for effective investigatory powers and for the possibility of effectively penalizing infringements of the competition rules. Yet a legislative arsenal is not sufficient; there must also be the will and means of using it. Each national authority must, therefore, not only have rules of substance and procedure, but also the necessary human and material resources. In addition one must not overlook the possibility of conflicts of interest, particularly in cases involving public enterprises.

3.2 THE 1997 NOTICE ON COOPERATION

As part of the same process, the Commission published a Notice at the end of 1997[21] on cooperation with such authorities, intended to operate in parallel with the equivalent 1993 Notice on cooperation with national courts. The 1997 Notice emphasized again the special nature of the role played by competition authorities, primarily concerned with monitoring and enforcing the law rather than resolving disputes between individuals and undertakings, without the constraints that courts are necessarily under from the fact that the conduct and timing of cases are controlled not by them but by the parties. The Commission believed that the competition authorities of Member States were often better placed to deal with cases with a Community element than the courts. They often have the ability to acquire detailed and precise knowledge of relevant markets, especially those with distinctive national features, and to carry out investigation, particularly where the impact of the practices or agreements is largely within their own territory. Nevertheless, there would always be a large number of cases for which the Commission would continue to take jurisdiction, either because of the degree of Community interest or because of the importance of the economic or legal issues raised.

[20] pp. 38–9.   [21] [1997] OJ C313/3.

3.3 THE MODERNIZATION WHITE PAPER OF 1999

The Commission was by now well aware that reform would have to take a more funda-mental character. Senior officials met therefore during 1998 and 1999 on a regular basis, but in some secrecy, to debate the future of the Directorate General for Competition within the Commission, and in particular the need for it to adapt in order to meet the challenge of expected major enlargement in 2004. The outcome of the deliberations of this working group turned out to be far more radical than had been anticipated. The White Paper setting out its detailed proposals that was published in April 1999 sparked off a lively debate in industrial, commercial, political, legal and administra-tive circles and at all levels about the practicality of the new proposals.

The central theme of the White Paper was that, while the monopoly over the grant-ing of individual exemptions granted to the Commission by Regulation 17/62 had been appropriate in its day, it was no longer possible for the Commission to operate it under its present and likely future workload. Even with increased resources, which were by no means guaranteed, it would not be able to operate such a centralized system of con-trol. It would be necessary for it rather to focus on those tasks to which priority had to be given, namely the investigation and enforcement of sanctions against widespread cartels and abuses of dominant position within the Community, whilst sharing with national competition authorities and courts the enforcement of Articles 81 and 82. The Commission had of course contributed to its own predicament by the wide inter-pretation which it had applied to Article 81(1) and to the very small number of formal decisions which it had proved able to issue each year. But the notification system which Regulation 17/62 had adopted would in any event have ultimately proved unsatisfac-tory, even if the Commission had been granted greater resources and had not been given the extra responsibilities mentioned above, in particular the application of the Merger Regulation.

The White Paper acknowledged that a consequence of Regulation 17/62 had been an over-emphasis on the legal content of agreements, without sufficient attention being paid to their economic effect, or to the market power of the undertakings concerned. It argued that, whilst the removal of the availability of individual notification by the Commission would to some degree reduce legal certainty for undertakings entering into such agreements, this could be minimized by the fact that there had been four decades of Community experience in the application of Articles 81 and 82, and that case law had clarified many aspects of these Articles. Moreover, the current range of block exemptions starting with Regulation 2790/99 with its emphasis on market share thresholds and limited 'black' lists of forbidden clauses provided a much greater degree of certainty than their earlier counterparts. The Commission's regular prac-tice of publishing extensive guidelines could also play an important role in assisting undertakings; the possibility of issuing additional block exemptions was also to be considered.

In place of the notification system, the new system proposed would be that of 'exception légale' under which the application of paragraphs (1) and (3) of Article 81 would be combined, so that agreements, decisions and concerted practices would either be 'valid' (having applied both paragraphs (1) and (3)), or 'void' under paragraph (2), because they fell within paragraph (1) without being able to benefit from the provisions of paragraph (3). This change would allow the application of Article 81 in its entirety both by national competition authorities and national courts, without having any longer to suspend investigation or judgment while the Commission decided whether an exemption should be granted.

3.4 ADOPTION OF REGULATION 1/2003 AND THE MODERIZATION PACKAGE

On the whole the reception of these unexpectedly far-reaching proposals was favourable; it was recognized that the Commission had made a real attempt to face the problems that it confronted and its past inadequacies, and had sought to produce a blueprint for the future which offered a genuine prospect of a more effective way of applying competition policy. After considerable debate in the Community institutions and elsewhere it was finally agreed at a Council meeting on 26 November 2002 that the new Regulation 1/2003 embodying these proposals should come into force on 1 May 2004, thus allowing some seventeen months for the necessary preparatory work. This consisted of the drafting and adoption of a procedural implementing Regulation and six Notices and Guidelines, and also the further strengthening of the existing network between the Commission and national competition authorities. This date was also chosen so as to coincide with the date of admission of ten new members, whom it was obviously sensible to admit simultaneously with the introduction of the new rules.

The full 'modernization package' of measures consisted of the following:

- Council Regulation 1/2003 on the implementation of the rules on competition laid down in Articles 81 and 82 of the Treaty, and accompanying Joint Declaration[22]

- Commission Regulation 773/2004 relating to the conduct of proceedings by the Commission pursuant to Articles 81 and 82 of the EC Treaty[23]

- Commission Notice on cooperation within the Network of Competition Authorities[24] (see Section 5.4 below)

- Commission Notice on cooperation between the Commission and the courts of the EU Member States in the application of Articles 81 and 82 (see Chapter 20)

- Commission Notice on the handling of complaints by the Commission under Articles 81 and 82 of the Treaty

- Commission Notice on informal guidance relating to novel questions concerning Articles 81 and 82 of the Treaty that arise in individual cases

---

[22] [2003] OJ L1/1.   [23] [2004] OJ L123/18.
[24] All six Notices and Guidelines are published in [2004] OJ C101.

- Guidelines on the effect on trade concept contained in Articles 81 and 82 of the EC Treaty (see Chapter 7)
- Guidelines on the application of Article 81(3) of the Treaty (see Chapter 8).

When the new regulatory framework was more or less in place, and a few months before it came into force, the Court of Justice gave a message of encouragement to national authorities in taking up their new role, in the form of a preliminary ruling reinforcing the importance of their competition law enforcement role. In its ruling it confirmed that such authorities are obliged, where a national law conflicts with Community law, to disapply the national law, and indeed to ensure that it is disapplied by all other relevant State bodies.[25]

4. THE NEW ROLE FOR NATIONAL COMPETITION AUTHORITIES

4.1 INTRODUCTION

Regulation 1/2003 gave national competition authorities a completely new role, conferring far greater responsibilities and jurisdiction on them than could ever have been anticipated in the early days of the Treaty of Rome. To understand their place in the new order, it is necessary both to examine the way in which such authorities are organized under national law, and the functions which they perform under the terms of the new Regulation.

It would perhaps have been convenient at this point to include detailed descriptions of the competition authorities in each of the Member States, setting out the national legislation governing their activities and the separate individual bodies found in each of them, upon which the task of administering the national law falls.[26] However, this would produce not only a section of unwieldy length, but also one that is of considerably less interest than it might have been some years ago. This is because there has been widespread convergence, in particular during the four years since Regulation 1/2003 entered into force, in the laws of nearly all Member States, mainly in response to that Regulation and the impact of the modernization programme. Some of the change that took place was of course legally required under the terms of the Regulation. But much of it, affecting a range of substantive, procedural and institutional issues, has taken place as 'soft' convergence, meaning that it has been undertaken voluntarily by the Member States.

---

[25] Case C-198/01 *Consorzio Industrie Fiammiferi v AGCM*, [2003] ECR I-8055: [2003] 5 CMLR 829.

[26] There are numerous sources of information about the current national competition legislation and national competition authorities on the websites both of the Commission and of the individual authorities, some of which provide English language versions of their legislation.

What therefore seems more relevant is to explain the organization, first of the United Kingdom's own competition law authorities as set up under the 1998 Competition Act and the 2002 Enterprise Act, and then to indicate in general terms the constituent elements common to the national competition authorities of the other Member States.

4.2 UNITED KINGDOM COMPETITION AUTHORITIES

For many years after the United Kingdom joined the Community in 1973, the structure of UK Competition Law and its component authorities remained largely unchanged. The Director General of Fair Trading was responsible for maintaining a register of restrictive agreements under the Restrictive Trade Practices Acts 1976 and 1977 which might then be called before the Restrictive Practice Court for an assessment of whether they should be declared unenforceable as in breach of that law. Mergers and sectoral references, known as 'monopoly references', were made by the Secretary of State or by the director general of Fair Trading in cases considered appropriate to the Monopolies and Mergers Commission under the 1973 Fair Trading Act. If the MMC after investigation found adverse effects to the public interest in such a case they would make a report to this effect to the Secretary of State for Trade and Industry on an advisory basis and the Secretary of State could then, in conjunction with the Office of Fair Trading, determine appropriate remedies. A Competition Act of 1980 allowed investigation of anti-competitive practices by individual undertakings but proved in practice ineffective.

Such legislative inactivity in national competition law for over twenty years came to an end eventually with the election of a Labour Government in 1997; since then both substantive and procedural changes have been substantial. The effect has been to bring UK substantive law into a much closer relationship with Community competition law and policy, and to bring about elimination in most cases of ministerial rights to intervene. This involved giving greater responsibilities to both the Office of Fair Trading and the Competition Commission which from 1 April 1999 replaced the Monopolies and Mergers Commission, though performing the same functions. A Competition Appeal Tribunal has been established which deals with appeals both from the Office of Fair Trading under the terms of the Competition Act and with judicial review applications in respect of decisions of the Competition Commission in merger and market investigation cases heard under the Enterprise Act.

The combined effect of the two Acts can be summarized as follows. Chapter 1 and Chapter 2 of the Competition Act reproduce the precise terms of Articles 81 and 82 and authorize the Office of Fair Trading to impose fines for undertakings found in breach. Appeal lies against any such finding or against the fine imposed to the Tribunal which is a separate body, and has already rendered a number of important decisions in appeal cases.[27] Appeals can be brought to the Tribunal only by the parties to the decision

---

[27] These are reported in the Competition Appeal Reports (Comp AR). See P. Collins 'Some Reflections on the First Seven Years of the Competition Appeal Tribunal' [2007] CLJ 307. The Tribunal and the courts

or by a third party with a 'sufficient interest' in the view of the Tribunal. Moreover, monetary claims can also be made to the Tribunal by those who have suffered financial loss as a result of any formally established infringement of either Chapter 1 or Chapter 2 of the Act or of Articles 81 or 82. All such actions for monetary compensation are described generally as 'follow on actions'. Claims for compensation can also be brought by groups of consumers through specific bodies which represent them, again once a decision has been given confirming a breach of either the United Kingdom or EC competition law not still subject to appeal. From the Tribunal itself, in all cases, appeal lies to the Court of Appeal on points of law only. Criminal proceedings can also be brought against individuals who dishonestly enter into cartel agreements, leading to a range of penalties including both fines and imprisonment.

The Office of Fair Trading not only investigates alleged breaches of Chapters 1 and 2 of the Competition Act, but also determines whether particular mergers or market investigations should be referred to the Competition Commission for examination. These cases are no longer governed by the Fair Trading Act 1973, in which the criterion applied had in principle always been 'the public interest' as defined by section 84 of that Act, although the effect on competition had normally been the prime element in the assessment. Under the Enterprise Act the criterion is now whether the merger will lead to a 'substantial lessening of competition' or in a market investigation, whether there are features of that sector which restrict competition. One of the most important provisions of the Act is the removal of the power of the Secretary of State to make decisions in mergers and market investigation cases. Henceforth, the decision to make a reference will be that of the Office of Fair Trading, now a body corporate, of which the present Director General is both chairman and chief executive, and the decision of the Competition Commission, in such cases, will normally be final. The Secretary of State retains the right of decision only in cases involving a special 'public interest' such as national security or defence, or where Parliament has specifically approved a particular public interest as relevant to the case. In such cases the Competition Commission will, in most respects, render a report but this will not be determinative and will simply be advisory to the minister, as was previously the case under the Fair Trading Act (except in those cases where no public interest finding had been made, when the Competition Commission's report had always been determinative).

Appeals from decisions of the Office of Fair Trading under the Competition Act or the Competition Commission under the Enterprise Act in respect of mergers or market investigations all go to the Tribunal. In the case of the Competition Act it is a full rehearing of the case, but in the case of appeals on mergers or market investigations under the Enterprise Act, it is of more limited scope by way of judicial review, with appeal of matters of law in all cases from the Tribunal to the Court of Appeal. The jurisdiction of the Tribunal extends to England and Wales, Scotland, and Northern Ireland.

in dealing with cases under the Competition Act are required by s. 60 to apply the Treaty of Rome and the principles and case law laid down by the ECJ and CFI, to ensure consistency with EC law. They must also 'have regard' to any relevant decision or statement of the Commission.

The competition laws of the United Kingdom are thus administered by a number of different bodies each with its separate function, as follows:

(1) the *political* function of the Secretary of State for Trade and Industry, who under the new regime introduced by the two Acts referred to above has a considerably reduced role, since he makes decisions only in special 'public interest' cases

(2) the *administrative* or *executive* function performed by the Office of Fair Trading, which investigates complaints from third parties or on its own account, and can render decisions imposing fines and banning agreements and practices under the Competition Act, Chapter 1 and Chapter 2, equivalent to Articles 81 and 82, as well as under Articles 81 and 82 themselves, and which also makes references to the Competition Commission in respect of mergers and market investigations

(3) the *decision-making body* in merger and market investigation cases, the Competition Commission

(4) the *specialist appellate* body, the Competition Appeal Tribunal, with its dual role of hearing appeals by way of full rehearing from decisions of the Office of Fair Trading under the Competition Act and also by way of judicial review from the Competition Commission under the Enterprise Act, dealing with both procedural and substantive issues in respect of merger and market investigation references

(5) the *Courts of First Instance*, which retain jurisdiction in competition cases, though potentially subject to transfer to the Competition Appeal Tribunal on some occasions, under provisions of the Enterprise Act (see Chapter 20, Section 4.3)

(6) the *higher courts of law*, namely the Court of Appeal and the House of Lords, which will hear appeals on points of law arising from decisions of the Competition Appeal Tribunal.

4.3 NATIONAL COMPETITION AUTHORITIES IN OTHER MEMBER STATES

Whilst there is obviously considerable variation in detail between the legislative provisions operating in each Member State and between the institutions that each have established to apply national competition law, nevertheless a common pattern can be seen in each of the Member States, which is required by the nature of the subject matter of competition law cases. It is possible to identify six common elements in the law of these Member States which correspond in broad terms, though not in detail, to the structure of the UK system. Thus within each Member State we can find:

(1) A *comprehensive law or laws* setting out the substantive and procedural rules. These statutes will have been amended on a number of occasions and in particular as a result of the modernization Regulation 1/2003. They are now all closely modelled in

both structure and language on Articles 81 and 82, although in some Member States there are additional or supplementary rules extending the scope of national law beyond these Articles. For example, in Germany and Austria, the definition of 'dominance' is rather more specific in terms of market share than that contained in Article 82. In some countries, including Sweden, Finland, and Ireland, the right to claim damages for breach of the competition rules is expressly preserved in the governing statute. In Estonia, France, Ireland, and the United Kingdom criminal sanctions of imprisonment can be imposed on individuals concerned, in addition to the fines to be imposed upon undertakings (in all Member States) and individuals (in some Member States). A number of Member States have adopted national block exemptions parallel to those of the Community, and one or two have even added additional block exemptions to national legislation (such as that applicable in the Netherlands to certain aspects of retail trade). In addition Regulation 1/2003 requires national law to include the power to apply Articles 81 and 82 as part of domestic law.

(2) An *administrative body* equivalent to the Office of Fair Trading in the United Kingdom often named as the 'Competition Authority' or 'Competition Commission' which has primary responsibility in the Member State for implementing national competition policy. It will carry out investigations into suspected breaches and will have powers to make 'dawn raids' on undertakings and to obtain information from third parties. It will have close links on a day-to-day basis with the European Commission and will exchange a large amount of information with them on pending cases. It will normally appoint its national representative on the Advisory Committee in Brussels. It may also have power itself to impose decisions involving fines and prohibition orders against undertakings for breach of national law or for breach of Articles 81 or 82; alternatively (in some or all cases) it may have to pass the case on to another body, which alone has the required authority to make binding decisions.

(3) The *decision making body* which in some jurisdictions may be the same as, and in others may be quite separate from, the administrative body referred to under (2). Thus, for example, in Austria, in some cases the Federal Competition Agency, and in other cases the Federal Antitrust Prosecutor, bring prosecutions before the Cartel Court which can then alone issue binding decisions on undertakings. In Belgium, whilst the Competition Service can carry out investigations, only the Competition Council can impose fines. In Finland the Market Court imposes fines which are proposed to it by the Competition Authority and similar arrangements prevail in Sweden; whilst the Swedish competition authority can impose injunctions against infringement of national law, only the Stockholm District Court can impose a fine. In Germany on the other hand the Federal Cartel Office (the Bundeskartellamt) is both the administrative and decision making body and a similar situation prevails in the Netherlands, Italy, and Greece.

(4) The *appellate body*—a court or tribunal which has specialized experience in such cases—to which, in many Member States, the rulings of either the administrative body or the decision-making authority in competition cases can be appealed. Whilst in the

United Kingdom such appeal is to the Competition Appeal Tribunal, this is unusual; in most cases the appeal is to one of the regular courts. Thus, in the Netherlands the appellate court is the Rotterdam District Court, in Sweden the Stockholm District Court and above it the Market Court, and in Finland it is the Market Court and the Supreme Administrative Court. In France we find this role reserved for the Paris Court of Appeals (and for appeals from the Minister of Economics, as in merger cases, to the Conseil d'État). In Germany the specialist court of appeal is now the Higher Regional Court in Düsseldorf, in Poland it is the District Court in Warsaw, and in Bulgaria the Supreme Administrative Court. There is frequently a further right of appeal on points of law to higher courts, and requests can be made to the European Court of Justice under Article 234 for opinions on matters of either EC law or on matters of national law which are identical to those arising under Community law (as in the *Oscar Bronner* case[28]).

(5) There is often a further body established with solely *advisory powers* which is responsible for preparing reports on the operation of national competition laws and procedures, which are then forwarded to the heads of competition authorities and to the responsible minister in the national government. Not many Member States possess this type of body but those that exist can have important influence on the development of national law through their reports. In Germany the Monopolies Commission plays this role and in Austria the Competition Commission. It is possible that in time other Member States may also find this type of body useful for carrying out reviews of national substantive and procedural law.

(6) *Political institutions*: in some Member States the minister with political responsibility for the administration of national competition law may retain substantial powers to intervene, and in other countries he is only entitled to intervene in a limited range of cases. Thus in Germany the Minister for Economic Affairs has the right to intervene to overrule a merger decision of the Bundeskartellamt on grounds of national interest but has only done so on a handful of occasions during the last fifty years. In France it is the Minister of Finance that makes all decisions in merger cases (though not in other competition cases) where the role of the Conseil de la Concurrence (Competition Commission) is solely consultative. In Portugal a number of important decisions are also made by the Minister but they are still subject to appeal to the Supreme Administrative Court. By contrast in the Netherlands and in Sweden there is no ministerial right to intervene in competition cases.

---

[28] Case C-7/97 [1998] ECR I-7791; [1999] 4 CMLR 112. See also Case C-280/06 *AGCM v. Ente Tabacchi Italiani* [2008] 4 CMLR] 277, where a reference on the interpretation of an Italian legal provision was held admissible on the basis that Italian law required the provision in question to be interpreted in accordance with Community law.

5. NATIONAL COMPETITION AUTHORITIES UNDER REGULATION 1/2003—THE NEW ERA

5.1 INTRODUCTION

The main principles which underlie the Regulation and the modernization programme have already been discussed, but the radically new nature of the functions which the programme conferred on such authorities can only be fully appreciated in the context of an examination of the detailed terms of the Regulation. It is the responsibility of Member States to designate those bodies[29] (which could either be administrative or judicial in nature or with a combination of these functions) which are to be its competition authorities, as indeed they had to do in the past under Regulation 17/62.

The terms of the Regulation need to be read against the background of lengthy-recitals which lay out its main principles. These include:

- the importance of ensuring that national competition authorities can apply Articles 81 and 82 in their entirety, including for the first time cases arising under Article 81(3), and that they also do so in all cases where trade between Member States is affected

- the consequent need for a network joining all such authorities and the Commission through which a high level of cooperation can be maintained and sufficiently detailed information exchanged

- the retention of the Commission's right (after consultation with the Member State affected) to intervene and take over cases in which an authority is already acting

- the right of a national competition authority to suspend an investigation into a case if it discovers that another Member State's authority is already dealing with it

- the general principle that authorities should avoid decisions that are in conflict with those of the Commission or other national authorities

- the option for authorities to assist other Member States' authorities by carrying out investigations on their own territory and on their behalf.

5.2 THE CONTENT OF REGULATION 1/2003

Article 1 of the Regulation is the replacement for Article 1 of Regulation 17/62 but differs from it in the important respect that the whole of Article 81, as well as Article 82, now becomes of direct effect and that no 'prior decision' of the Commission is required for the application of Article 81(3).

---

[29] On the question of the 'designation' of national competition authorities see C. Kerse, *EC Antitrust Procedure* (5th edn, Sweet & Maxwell, 2005), Ch. 5, p. 259.

Article 2 confirms that the original burden of proof that Article 81(1) or Article 82 applies remains with the Commission or other competition authority seeking to enforce the prohibition but that the undertaking which seeks to show that Article 81(3) is available to exempt its agreement has itself that burden of proof.

Article 3 contains the rules of supremacy as between national and Community law described in the previous section of this chapter. This enables national authorities to apply national law of a different or stricter character in three cases; namely in merger control, in control of unilateral conduct, and in applying national law with a predominantly different objective such as consumer protection or environmental protection laws. The decisions which a national competition authority can take are specified in *Article 5,* namely those:

- requiring an infringement to be ended
- ordering interim measures
- accepting commitments
- imposing fines and penalties
- determining that no grounds for action exist.[30]

Articles 7 to 10 set out the Commission's decision-making powers. As well as the powers that existed under Regulation 17/62, there is an express power under *Article 7,* where necessary, to impose not only behavioural, but also structural remedies, and also to close a case by taking formal commitments from the undertakings under investigation. The power to impose structural remedies has not yet been used and is expected to remain an option of last resort. On the other hand frequent use has been made of the possibility, under *Article 9,* to take commitments, in markets ranging from energy supply through football broadcasting rights to soft drinks.[31] One power not mentioned is the power to provide informal guidance on novel questions, which is the subject of one of the Commission Notices, and which has not yet been used.

Articles 11 and 12 deal with the vital issue of the cooperation required from authorities throughout the network and commits both the Commission and the authorities to apply the competition rules of the Community in close cooperation. Such close cooperation is of great importance in preserving uniform interpretation of EU law in the new decentralized system, which was a main concern raised following the modernization proposals. *Articles 13 to 16* deal with other aspects of the authorities' role, and to some extent that of national courts. Their impact on national authorities is discussed further in Part 5.3 below.

---

[30] In so doing a national authority is obliged to disapply any national law that conflicts with Community law: Case C-198/01 *Consorzio Industrie Fiammiferi v AGCM,* see fn. 26; A. Kaczorowska 'The Power of a National Competition Authority to Disapply National Competition Law Incompatible with EC Law—and its Practical Consequences' [2004] ECLR 591.

[31] See e.g. J. Lawrence and M. Sansom, 'The Increasing Use of Administrative Settlement Procedures in UK and EC Competition Investigations' [2007] CLJ 163.

The power of the Commission to carry out its own investigations has been extended under *Articles 17 to 21* and national authorities already had an obligation to provide necessary information to the Commission to enable it to carry out its duties, and to assist it with its dawn raids, if necessary obtaining the required court orders from national courts. Obtaining the court order will be mandatory in the case of searches of domestic premises as opposed to the more normal practice of searching business premises. *Article 17* reproduces the already existing power to investigate particular market sectors, but has already been used much more frequently than its predecessor power in Regulation 17/62, with inquiries being made into aspects of energy and financial services markets and also into pharmaceuticals. Regular use is also made of the new power under *Article 19* to interview consenting individuals in connection with an investigation.

A fresh power conferred on national authorities by *Article 22* is to carry out within their own territory investigations for other national authorities in order to establish whether there has been an infringement of Articles 81 or 82.

Finally *Article 29(2)* entitles an authority to withdraw the benefit of Commission block exemptions in its territory, if it discovers that agreements which have enjoyed the benefits of such exemption have effects in the territory (or part of it) which have all the characteristics of a distinct geographic market. This power had already been included in Regulation 2790/99 on vertical restraints and this provision means that it now applies to all block exemptions.

5.3 CASE ALLOCATION BETWEEN THE COMMISSION AND NATIONAL AUTHORITIES

A key question that arose as soon as the shape of modernization became clear was how cases were to be allocated as between all the available authorities. A Joint Declaration by the Council and Commission on the functioning of national competition authorities was therefore adopted at the same time as the Regulation, to provide national authorities with guidance on how to operate in cooperation with both the Commission and other such authorities. Member States accepted that their own authorities may operate with different systems of enforcement, but that they are all independent from each other and entitled to mutual respect; all would have full legal authority to apply Articles 81 and 82. The Commission itself would be responsible for ensuring that the Treaty and the Regulations made under it were observed by all authorities but would exercise its powers with utmost regard for the essentially co-operative nature of the network. The Joint Declaration was supplemented by a more detailed Commission Notice,[32] and it is that Notice which is now the chief source of guidance.

According to that Notice any given case may be dealt with either by a single national authority or several acting in parallel, or the Commission. The Commission will itself

---

[32] Commission Notice on cooperation within the Network of Competition Authorities [2004] OJ C101/3.

normally deal with cases if there are effects on competition in more than three Member States. In other cases individual authorities can assert jurisdiction if the agreement or practice substantially affects that jurisdiction, and if moreover that Member State is in a position to gather the necessary evidence, bring the infringement to an end and apply effective sanctions. If more than one authority is potentially involved, case allocation will be discussed between them and if appropriate one Member State nominated as the lead authority. If the same case is investigated by more than one authority, one of them will normally take a formal decision whilst the others stay their proceedings, or alternatively both will deal with the case in close cooperation.

Article 13 of the Regulation outlines the rights of an authority to suspend or reject proceedings in a case because another Member State is already dealing with it. This however is an optional, not a mandatory, obligation. Situations may arise where both Member States are keen to continue with their respective investigations and it may be necessary for consultation to take place, officially or unofficially, through the network to avoid conflicting decisions being rendered by two authorities.

There may be circumstances in which the Commission will wish to exercise its powers under *Article 11(6)* of the Regulation to take over a case, but it does not appear ever to have done so yet and, once the initial case allocation has taken place, it will only do so if:

- network members envisage that there will be conflicting decisions in the same case or decisions in conflict with existing case law (either of the Commission or of Community Courts) or

- members are unduly protracting proceedings or

- a similar problem has arisen in several Member States and there is need for a Commission decision in order to clarify the competition policy of the Community or

- none of the authorities concerned objects.

The Commission, nevertheless, in cases not covered by *Article 11(6)* will not normally adopt a decision itself in conflict with a decision of a national competition authority, provided it has been kept fully informed of the case under the provisions *of Article 11(3) and (4)*.

In practice, despite the fears expressed by some at the outset, case allocation seems to have run smoothly in the first four years, with a pragmatic and common sense approach on the part of those involved having apparently averted any major disputes or clearly undesirable allocation decisions.

5.4 THE EUROPEAN COMPETITION NETWORK

To some extent the necessary close connection between the Commission and the national authorities had already been developed but the Regulation required even further cooperation. Well before May 2004 a European Competition Network (ECN), made up of the Commission and all the (then) twenty-five national competition authorities, was active. Its nature and functioning is described in the same Commission Notice that governs case allocation but its activities go well beyond case allocation.

The network operates not only between national authorities, but also between the many competition officials who work for those authorities and are in regular contact with each other through electronic and other means of communication. Each of the participating authorities, and the Commission itself, keeps the others fully informed of important general developments and particular cases. The Regulation requires each authority to give the Commission at least thirty days' notice of the adoption of any infringement decision, the acceptance of a commitment from an undertaking or the withdrawal from an undertaking of a block exemption, sending copies of the relevant documentation. While this is compulsory, the authority may also, at its option, supply the same information to the authorities of other Member States with whom they are entitled to exchange information on cases of mutual interest. Moreover the authorities are free to consult the Commission at any time on any case involving the application of Community law.

The exchange of information which underpins the network is covered by *Article 12*. *The Spanish Banks* decision,[33] which dealt with the interpretation of Article 20 of Regulation 17/62, made it clear that information provided by the Commission to national authorities could not be used for cases under national law but only as a starting point for the authority to commence its own investigations. The terms of *Article 3* will considerably reduce the difficulties caused to authorities and the Commission by that judgment, since in many cases the national authority will be applying both national law and Community law in parallel, where *Article 12(2)* provides that confidential information from the Commission can be used. Only in cases where an authority is applying national law alone will it have to carry out its own investigation and obtain its own evidence, without being able to rely on evidence from the Commission.

A number of national authorities apply sanctions not only upon undertakings but also on individuals, usually directors or employees who have been involved in cartels or other prohibited restrictive practices. In these cases confidential information from elsewhere can only be used in evidence to impose sanctions (of fine or imprisonment) on individuals if both the transmitting and receiving authority have sanctions of a similar type. If not, the information can only be used if it has been collected in a way which respects the same levels of protection of the rights of defence of the individual as is the standard for the recipient authority, and then only for the application of fines, not for imprisonment.[34]

Article 16(2) provides that authorities cannot take decisions that run counter to existing Commission decisions but this does not apply to conflicts between two authorities of Member States. *Article 15* provides the authorities with the opportunity of assisting their own national courts in competition cases though their involvement

---

[33] Case 67/91 [1992] ECR I-4785.

[34] A number of national competition authorities including the UK now have statutory powers to disclose information to other foreign authorities on a mutual basis, where the case is sufficiently serious. See Enterprise Act, ss. 243–4.

is limited to the presentation of written observations, though these may be oral with the court's consent.

While much of the cooperation described here is mandated by Regulation 1/2003, what is done within the ECN in fact goes far beyond what is legally required. There is very frequent and informal contact at all levels, both on a personal basis and through a variety of different working groups and different types of meetings. This has led a degree of voluntary or 'soft' harmonization on a range of procedural and substantive issues that would not have been possible on the basis of legal instruments alone. Indeed, the speed and extent of the process of convergence of Member States' substantive and procedural law is striking and is one of the outstanding successes of the modernization programme. In this way the national systems have come to resemble one another far more closely than was the case just a few years ago.[35]

FURTHER READING

P. COLLINS, 'Some Reflections on the First Seven Years of the Competition Appeal Tribunal' [2007] Comp LJ 307.

C. D. EHLERMANN, 'Implementation of EC Competition Law by National Antitrust Authorities' [1996] 17 ECLR 88.

D. GERBER and P. CASSINIS, 'The Modernisation of EC Competition Law; Achieving Consistency in Enforcement' [2006] 27 ECLR, Pt I, 10–18, Pt II, 51–7.

A. KACZOROWSKA, 'The Power of a National Competition Authority to Disapply National Competition Law Incompatible with EC Law—and its Practical Consequences' [2004] ECLR 591.

J. LAWRENCE and M. SANSOM, 'The Increasing Use of Administrative Settlement Procedures in UK and EC Competition Investigations' [2007] Comp LJ 163.

F. MONTAG and A. ROSENFELD, 'A Solution to the Problems? Regulation 1/2003 and the Modernization of Competition Procedure' [2003] 2 ZWeR 107.

DANIEL REICHELT, 'To What Extent does the Co-operation within the European Competition Network Protect the Rights of Undertakings?' [2005] CMLRev 745.

J. VENIT, 'Brave New World: The Modernization and Decentralization of Enforcement Under Articles 81 and 82 of the EC Treaty' [2003] 40 CMLRev 545.

---

[35] See 'Results of the questionnaire on the reform of Member States' national competition laws after EC Regulation No. 1/2003', a document produced by the European Competition Network's working group on cooperation issues, available on DG Comp's website.

20

NATIONAL COURTS AND THE DIRECT APPLICATION OF COMMUNITY LAW

1. INTRODUCTION AND EARLY CASE LAW

1.1 *HASSELBLAD* AND *BRT* V. *SABAM*

The enforcement of Community competition law was clearly not to be left solely to the institutions of the Community itself; the terms of the Treaty, the wide variety of relevant issues arising in different parts of the Community, and the limited resources of the Commission in general and DG Comp in particular all favoured the greatest possible involvement not only of national authorities, as described in the previous chapter, but also of national courts in enforcing Articles 81 and 82. The Commission had from its earliest days encouraged Member States' courts to receive hospitably private actions of this kind, hoping that, as in the United States, the burden of public enforcement could be lightened by the increased use of private actions. The Court and Commission had not hesitated to state in their decisions that enforcement of competition policy is not simply a matter of public law but also of private law enforcement. However, implementation of these developments has taken much longer than was originally hoped, and it is only in the last few years that momentum has begun to gather, with the publication in 2005 by the Commission of a Green Paper, followed up by a White Paper in 2008.

A major factor in the slow development of private litigation in this area has been the easy availability of an alternative remedy, namely the complaint to DG Comp which, at first sight, appeared to have many attractive features. The Commission for many years showed a willingness to give priority to the handling of complaints, even in fairly trivial matters, over certain of its other responsibilities; the wide powers of investigation and discovery under Regulation 17 and the apparent cheapness of involving its services (not to mention the relative informality with which it could be done) all seemed to undertakings and their lawyers good reasons for approaching the Commission rather than instituting litigation in national courts. The Commission also had the advantage that, if it offered an administrative remedy, this would be applicable throughout the Community rather than merely in the Member State where court action had been started.[1] Formal decisions by the Commission as the result of its investigation of the complaint would be accepted and respected by all national courts within the Community, although the informal 'comfort letters' to which the Commission had increasingly been resorting were less satisfactory.

The United Kingdom Court of Appeal underlined the importance of the complaint procedure in the *Hasselblad* case.[2] It ruled on a point of law, albeit only by a majority of two to one, that the public interest in ensuring that the Commission was not frustrated in its duty of enforcing the provisions of Articles 81 and 82 was sufficient to provide a defence of 'public interest' against a claim for defamation brought by a party which had been the subject of a complaint, here Hasselblad. The Master of the Rolls referred to the risk that if an action in defamation could be brought in the United Kingdom in connection with the subject matter of a complaint, the substance of that complaint might have to be simultaneously considered by, on one hand, the Commission and the European Court of Justice and, on the other hand, by the UK courts.

The increasing volume of the Commission's work meant that its perceived obligation to give priority to complaints was beginning to become an embarrassment. The importance to it, therefore, of the 1992 *Automec (No. 2)*[3] judgment was considerable. Automec was an Italian motor dealer which BMW refused to continue to supply following the expiration of its contract; it made a complaint against BMW to the Commission under Article 82. The Court of First Instance upheld the right of the Commission to give different degrees of priority to cases in the light of the degree of 'Community interest' that the case presented. Here the Italian court was already involved in a case brought by Automec against BMW which involved the contractual relationship between the parties within the framework of the then block exemption for motor dealing (Regulation 123/85). The Court of First Instance ruled that the Commission was acting within its powers in saying that the dispute between the parties was best resolved by the Italian court, which in any case could make a reference under Article 234 of the Treaty if any issue of Community law arose. The Court therefore upheld the Commission's decision to refuse to conduct a full investigation into the complaint on the ground that the case did not have the required degree of Community interest. This has provided it with a great element of discretion in determining whether to intervene in cases that may not have a sufficient element of 'Community interest'.

Some advantages could still be obtained by undertakings bringing the matter before the national courts: after all, the Commission was unable to award an ex parte injunction, nor could it award compensation to the complainant (nor legal costs) or consider

---

[1] Though UK Courts on occasion claim jurisdiction in intellectual property cases to give judgments which have effects outside their own territorial jurisdiction: see for example *Pearce v. Ove Arup* [1997] FSR 641 and *Coin Controls v. Suzo* [1997] FSR 660.

[2] *Hasselblad (GB) v. Orbinson* [1985] 1 All ER 173: 2 WLR 1: QB 475.

[3] Case T-24/90 [1992] ECR II-2223: 5 CMLR 431. The Commission was given further guidance on its rights in Case T-114/92 *BEMIM v. Commission* [1995] ECR II-147: [1996] 4 CMLR 305 and in Case T-5/93 *Tremblay* [1995] ECR II-185: [1996] 4 CMLR 305 by the Court of First Instance, upheld in the latter case by the Court of Justice, Case C-91/95P [1996] ECR I-5547: [1997] 4 CMLR 211.

claims under related heads, such as unfair competition or breach of copyright, at the same time as the main substantive complaint under Article 81 or 82. The foundation for private actions in national courts was laid by the important European Court case of *Belgian Radio and Television* v. *SABAM*[4] which established two important principles. The first was the direct applicability, and therefore enforceability, in national courts of both Articles 81 and 82. Whilst the direct application of the Treaty had been confirmed in a number of earlier cases, in particular the European Court case of *Van Gend en Loos*[5] in 1963, this application of Articles 81 and 82 was confirmed for the first time in unequivocal terms here, as well as the obligation of the national courts to enforce their provisions.

However, the legal position was also affected by the provisions of Article 9(3) of Regulation 17, which stated that 'authorities' of Member States have jurisdiction and competence to apply Articles 81(1) and 82[6] so long as the Commission had not 'initiated any procedure' under that Regulation. It was originally thought that this expression meant not only all legislative and executive agencies but also all courts and judicial bodies. This view was later shown to be incorrect: in the *BRT* v. *SABAM* case the meaning of the latter words was limited to courts 'especially entrusted to apply domestic competition law or to ensure its application by domestic authorities'. This would, for example, include the tribunal set up under UK competition legislation, the Competition Appeal Tribunal, to hear appeals from the decisions of the Office of Fair Trading and Competition Commission.

1.2 *DELIMITIS* AND *MASTERFOODS*

The rights of national courts in applying Community law were then considered in detail in the *Delimitis* case,[7] the facts of which were discussed in Chapter 10. The chief issue in this dispute between a brewery and its trade customer was whether the exclusive purchasing block exemption then in force covered the exact terms of the arrangements between them. The German court in the Article 234 reference had also raised a number of questions as to how it should exercise its jurisdiction over the parties in the application of Article 81. In an impressively clear judgment, substantially assisted by the opinion of Van Gerven A-G, the following principles were laid down:

(1) The national Court could interpret and apply a block exemption (such as Regulation 1984/83) but must do so in a strict rather than a flexible manner.

(2) The Commission and national courts shared the competence to apply Articles 81(1) and 82, and could therefore declare an agreement void under Article 81(2) if it

---

[4] Case 123/73 [1974] ECR 51, 313: 2 CMLR 238.

[5] Case 26/62 [1963] ECR 1: CMLR 105. This case involved not a competition law point, but the issue of whether the Dutch Government's imposition of an increased rate of import duty on ureaformaldehyde in breach of Art. 12 of the Treaty of Rome could be challenged in the Dutch courts by an undertaking claiming to have been prejudiced by the tax.

[6] But not Art. 81(3).   [7] Case 234/89 [1991] ECR I-935: [1992] 5 CMLR 210.

was clearly in breach of 81(1) and unlikely to obtain any Commission individual exemption (taking into account both the previous decisions of the Commission and the terms of relevant block exemptions).

(3) The Commission had exclusive jurisdiction to grant exemption under Article 81(3), and national courts could not do so.

(4) If a national court believed that the contract in dispute might be the subject of an individual exemption from the Commission, it could suspend the proceedings or adopt interim measures to protect the interests of the parties. The national court could, in this situation, seek information and assistance from the Commission, which was itself bound under Article 10 of the Treaty by a duty of sincere cooperation with the national court. Alternatively, the national court could make a reference under Article 234.

That the process of national litigation could be frustrated to a major degree by parties seeking a decision on Article 81 or 82 issued from the Commission in the course of that litigation, was later dramatically shown by *Masterfoods*.[8] Here Irish proceedings between Masterfoods (as plaintiffs) and HB Ice Cream (as defendants) were on appeal from the High Court to the Supreme Court but under a ruling from the ECJ under Article 234 had to be suspended while a Commission decision on the same issue (to the opposite effect from the Irish High Court decision) was appealed by HB Ice Cream to the CFI. This ruling was not surprising since it reflected the supremacy rules contained in *Walt Wilhelm* and *Delimitis*, but it emphasized the difficulty of seeking simultaneously to encourage undertakings to resolve competition law disputes in national courts, whilst retaining the monopoly of the Commission in determining the grant of individual exemptions under Article 81(3).

1.3 THE 1993 NOTICE ON CO-OPERATION WITH NATIONAL COURTS

Following *Delimitis* and in the light of the greater freedom accorded to it in choosing the priority of complaints for investigation under *Automec (No. 2)* the Commission felt that it was important to issue a general Notice indicating how in its view such cooperation should take place and spelling out the principles from *Delimitis* in more detail. The 1993 Notice on Co-operation with National Courts[9] not only therefore set out the division of responsibility from that case but also provided some guidance to national courts on how they should handle a variety of different situations that might arise. The Treaty did not intend to create new remedies in national courts to ensure observance of Community competition law, but it must be possible for every type of action available under national law to be available also to enforce Community law

---

[8] Case C-344/98 [2001] 4 CMLR 449. For commentary on this important case, see L Kjølbye, Casenote [2002] 39 CML Rev 175–84 and S. O'Keefe, 'First Among Equals: The Commission and the National Courts as enforcers of EC Competition Law' [2001] 26 ELR 301–11.

[9] [1993] OJ C39/6.

with direct effect, and subject to the same conditions of admissibility of evidence and procedure. Parties to competition cases in the national courts should have a right to obtain injunctions to prevent infringement of their interests under Community competition rules and a right to compensation for infringements of those rights, when these are also available under national law.

The Commission acknowledged in its Notice that its own resources were inadequate to carry out its many responsibilities and that it was having to give priority to cases of particular political, economic, or legal significance to the Community. Other cases it would prefer dealt with by national courts, which had the advantage of being able, unlike the Commission, to award damages and costs to injured parties and to hear simultaneously claims under both national and Community law. In reaching their decision national courts should always take into account prior decisions or statements of the Commission, though mere administrative letters to parties known as 'comfort letters', were clearly not binding on the courts.[10] When the possibility of individual exemption arose, the national court must act with care, and must normally suspend its proceedings until the Commission had either granted exemption or indicated that it would not do so. To assist national courts further the Commission indicated that it would be willing to provide factual information about relevant market studies and economic data in its possession or about the progress of cases pending before it. It said that it would also try to give priority to those decisions where the outcome of a dispute in a national court depended on it; advice on points of law might also be made available, if requested, though these would in no sense be binding on the national court.

1.4 THE BASIS FOR PRIVATE DAMAGES CLAIMS

The issue of whether an undertaking financially damaged by an agreement or concerted practices entered into in breach of Article 81(1) or by practices prohibited by Article 82 could recover damages in UK courts took some time however to resolve. The Commission itself had often expressed the wish that its public enforcement of the Articles, limited in scope by its overall lack of resources, should be supplemented by private actions brought by litigants in national courts. It referred to the requirements of Article 10 imposing the general obligation of cooperation on Member States in ensuring fulfilment of Treaty obligations, including those arising from decisions of Community institutions including Community courts.

The traditional approach of English courts was to say *ubi remedium, ibi jus*—in other words to look for an existing procedural 'pigeon hole' into which a new category of substantive claim can be fitted rather than to accept the new substantive claim in its own right. Since UK courts, unlike those of the United States, have traditionally been unfamiliar with the concept of awarding damages for the breach of economic laws embodying principles similar to those of Articles 81 and 82, the search to find a

---

[10] The Perfume Cases (*Procureur de la République* v. *Giry and Others*), Cases 253/78, 37 and 99/79: [1980] ECR 2327, 2481, 2511: [1981] 2 CMLR 99, 143, 164.

suitable *remedium*, or cause of action, has proved troublesome. Community law has undoubtedly laid down the *jus*, but places the onus on the Member State to determine how the *remedium* is provided in its own courts.

Three principal suggestions were put forward for the basis of such action, in the course of an extensive debate. First, that the action should be in the form of a claim for wrongful interference in contractual relationships; secondly, that it was a new form of tort, the solution preferred by Lord Denning in early cases, which is not covered by any existing cause of action; thirdly that it was an action for breach of statutory duty, the statute being the 1972 European Communities Act under which the Treaty of Rome became part of United Kingdom law. The relevant sections would be 2(1) and 3, under whose combined effect the UK courts are required not only to give legal effect to the Treaties, as interpreted by the Courts in Luxembourg, but also to provide for the enforcement of 'remedies and procedures' without further enactment in the United Kingdom so as to give legal effect to them.

This last solution seems in principle the most satisfactory, subject to one technical difficulty, namely that under UK law the civil right of action for a statutory breach is not normally available if the statute in question provides an alternative remedy, for example a fine or penalty. However, this argument should not prevail over the express terms of Community case law; in practical terms, whether the right of action is for breach of statutory duty (in the traditional sense) or for breach of the Treaty provisions incorporated in UK law by the 1972 Act may not make a great difference.

1.5 THE *GARDEN COTTAGE* CASE

This issue was discussed by the House of Lords in 1983 in *Garden Cottage Foods Ltd.* v. *Milk Marketing Board*,[11] although strictly it did not form part of the ratio of the case. The Board had a statutory function to sell milk, butter, and cheese. Garden Cottage had been buying butter from the Board since 1980 and had resold most of it to a Dutch purchaser. In 1982 a new distribution policy was introduced under which Garden Cottage was no longer able to buy direct from the Board but had to buy from one of four distributors approved by the Board. The result of the introduction of these four preferred distributors was to reduce Garden Cottage's profits on the resale of butter, as it would have difficulties in competing with the prices that the four preferred distributors, with their privileged position as direct purchasers from the Board, could quote to customers. Proceedings were started against the Board on the ground that the refusal to supply Garden Cottage with butter in bulk was an abuse of the Board's dominant position. At first instance, Parker J refused to grant any interim relief, such as an injunction, pending trial, as he thought that it would be difficult to frame the

---

[11] [1983] 3 WLR 143: 2 All ER 770: 3 CMLR 43: [1984] AC 130. The Court of Appeal hearing is reported at [1982] All ER 292: QB 1114.

terms of an injunction against the Board, and that in any case damages might provide an adequate remedy for Garden Cottage.

The Court of Appeal, however, allowed the appeal by Garden Cottage and granted an interim injunction against the Board preventing it from confining its sale of bulk butter to any particular category of persons and also from discriminating between their different customers save in accordance with normal practice. In addition to allowing the application for the injunction, Denning and May LJJ indicated that they would be in favour of allowing a claim for damages in such circumstances, whilst Shaw LJ expressed doubts. Faced with so important a decision against it, the Board not surprisingly decided to appeal and achieved some success. The House of Lords decided by four votes to one that the injunction granted by the Court of Appeal should be discharged. Lord Diplock for the majority emphasized that in principle the Court of Appeal should not interfere with a trial judge's decision on an application for inter-locutory relief unless the judge had reached a decision that was clearly wrong on the facts or law, or where fresh evidence or a change in circumstances had emerged. In the view of the majority, none of these situations applied to the present case so that the original order by Parker J refusing the injunction should be restored. Lord Wilberforce disagreed, being in favour of allowing the injunction to maintain the status quo, which he considered would be more just, and indicated that in his view damages would not be a complete remedy for Garden Cottage, as it would be out of the butter market for a considerable period of time.

In the course of the hearing, the House of Lords entered into a general discussion of the rights of parties in United Kingdom courts under Articles 81 and 82. None of the courts below, nor the House of Lords, found any difficulty in accepting the principle laid down in *BRT* v. *SABAM* that under these Articles individuals had directly enforceable rights in national courts. The plaintiffs' claim could be categorized in English law probably as a breach of a statutory duty 'imposed not only for the purpose of promoting the general economic prosperity of the Common Market but also for the benefit of private individuals to whom loss or damage is caused by a breach of that duty'. However, the legal question then before the House of Lords was whether to interfere in an existing grant of an injunction on an interim application. The question of whether damages would be payable if Garden Cottage were successful in their case strictly did not arise as an issue. Nevertheless, the majority of the House saw no reason why damages should not be granted for a breach of Article 82 as a breach of statutory duty, although it did not reach a final decision on this issue. Lord Wilberforce, however, had considerable doubts; whilst he agreed that Community rights had to be enforced in national courts, he felt that a complainant under these Articles was not necessarily entitled to compensation so that the grant of damages by a national court might enlarge, rather than merely enforce, the rights of a claimant.[12]

---

[12] It is clear that, if damages would not be an adequate remedy for a breach of Arts. 81 or 82, an injunction may be granted: *Cutsforth* v. *Mansfield Inns* [1986] I All ER 577.

2. REMEDIES AVAILABLE IN THE UK COURTS BEFORE *CREHAN*

2.1 PROGRESS AT THE ECJ: *FRANCOVICH* AND *BRASSERIE DU PÊCHEUR*

The prospects of UK courts enforcing private claims to damages in competition law cases was however soon to be considerably enhanced by developments in Community law in cases dealing with other issues. The well-known European Court cases of *Francovich* v. *Italy* and *Brasserie du Pêcheur*[13] arose as a result of breaches by Member States, Italy and Germany respectively, of their obligations under Community law. The Court judgments in these cases laid down rules under Community law setting out the circumstances in which national courts should award damages against Member States to private litigants who had been injured by such breaches. These were as follows:

(1) when the defendant Member State has infringed a rule of Community law intended to confer specific rights to the plaintiff (whether an individual or undertaking) and

(2) when the defendant Member State's breach is sufficiently serious and

(3) when the plaintiff can show direct causation between the Member State breach and its own financial loss.

These three principles were to be implemented by national courts, which were instructed to ensure also that the legal conditions for making such claims were not less favourable than those governing similar domestic cases, nor so restrictive as to make it impossible or excessively difficult to make a successful claim.

These cases did not however directly address the question of whether by parity of reasoning damages could also be claimed for a breach of Community competition law, by a plaintiff that could show financial loss caused by such a breach by a private party rather than by a Member State. Van Gerven A-G soon afterwards gave strong support to this principle in his opinion in *Banks* v. *British Coal Corporation*,[14] citing earlier European Court jurisprudence. Unfortunately however the Court did not deal with this issue and decided the case on other grounds.[15]

2.2 LATER HIGH COURT CASES

The influence of the trend of these Community cases on the English judiciary was however noticeable in an important case arising on the issue of whether plaintiffs in

---

[13] Cases C-6 and 9/90 *Francovich* [1991] ECR I-5357 [1993] 2 CMLR 66. Case 46/93 *Brasserie du Pêcheur* v. *Germany* [1996] ECR I-1029: 1 CMLR 889, AER (EC) 301. For a detailed analysis of the pre-*Crehan* position, see C.-D. Ehlermann and I. Atanasiu (eds.), *European Competition Law Annual 2001* (Hart Publishing, 2002), especially W. van Gerven pp. 53–89.

[14] Case C-128/92 [1994] ECR I-1209: 5 CMLR 30.   [15] See further C. A. Jones, cited at fn. 32.

competition private law actions could rely on prior findings in Community proceedings. In *Iberian* v. *BPB*[16] Spanish importers of plasterboard into the UK complained that their business had in the late 1980s been damaged by practices of BPB which had been found by the Commission (upheld on appeal to both the Court of First Instance and the European Court) to be in breach of Article 82 and led to a fine. The practices consisted primarily of granting special discounts to builders' merchants in the United Kingdom and Northern Ireland who agreed to deal exclusively with BPB and not to buy imported Spanish board. BPB claimed that for the purpose of civil proceedings in the United Kingdom the plaintiffs would have to prove afresh all the relevant facts of the case without being able to place any reliance on the previous findings of the Commission or the Community Courts. The plaintiffs argued that this would make it in practice almost impossible for any plaintiffs to recover civil damages especially as the various Community proceedings had taken nearly a decade. Laddie J upheld the plaintiffs' arguments largely on the grounds of policy, stating that English courts should respect the decision of Community institutions in order to ensure consistency of treatment and avoid the risk of conflicting decisions from the Community and national courts and authorities.

In many of the cases coming before the UK courts at this time, plaintiffs who had entered into standard-form contracts (often in the beer-supply business) sought to defend against actions by their brewery landlord for payment of arrears of rent of their licensed premises, or in respect of beer supplied, by counterclaiming for damages, on the grounds that the tenancy agreement was itself in breach of Article 81 because of the restrictions imposed on them by its terms, principally from obtaining cheaper supplies of beer on the open market. In all these cases the traditional view of the High Court was maintained, namely that the parties to a contract which is illegal (for so agreements in breach of Article 81 were characterized) were not entitled to recover damages, regardless of whether they had any element of bargaining power on their side or had been forced into the acceptance of an onerous contract in standard form. *Gibbs Mew* v. *Gemmell*[17] may serve as a typical example. Gibbs Mew, a small brewer, had bought some pubs from Centric, a small company. One of the tenants, Gemmell, was in arrears with his rent and was sued by Gibbs Mew. Gemmell's defence was that the lease was not covered by the current block exemption for exclusive purchasing (Regulation 1984/83) and he counterclaimed for damages in restitution of the sums he had paid for beer. Gibbs Mew had obtained summary judgment in the High Court and to overturn it Gemmell had to persuade the Court of Appeal that one of his claims under Article 81 was arguable, not necessarily at that stage that it was right. On the critical issue of whether Gemmell was entitled to sue as a co-contractor, the Court

---

[16] [1996] 2 CMLR 601: [1997] EurLR 1. Following the decision by Laddie J on the interlocutory issues, the substantive claim by Iberian under Art. 82 was settled. See also Ch. 14, fn. 32. It has been suggested that the UK Courts might have taken a different attitude if the Commission decision had not been appealed to and upheld by a Community Court. However, such an attitude would appear to be not only in breach of Art. 10 but also inconsistent with the respect which the UK courts are required to give to findings of fact made by the UK Office of Fair Trading in rendering decisions under the Competition Act 1998.

[17] EurLR 588.

ruled that he had no such right. Article 81 was directly effective but was designed primarily to protect third party competitors. It was irrelevant that in block exemptions the Commission might pursue wider policy objectives of redressing inequalities in bargaining power; the grounds for exemption under Article 81(3) could not define the scope of Article 81(1) and, as the contract was illegal, neither party was entitled to recover damages from the other.

A further difficulty which was raised by the Courts in the case of plaintiffs seeking to enforce a Community right for damages was the ruling in *Passmore* v. *Morland*[18] that, since Article 81(1) is phrased as an 'effects based' prohibition, the prohibition itself can be made to 'vanish' if there is a change in circumstances. The actual change of circumstances in this case was that the tenancy agreement originally made by Passmore, the tenant, with a multiple-pub owner, Inntrepreneur, was subsequently assigned over by the latter to Morland, a much smaller brewery. The Court of Appeal held that even if the terms of the original tenancy had been in breach of Article 81 the prohibition vanished once the effects of the agreement changed, as a result of the assignment to a new owner with a far lesser degree of market power vis-á-vis the tenant as well as in the beer market generally. The assessment of an agreement under Article 81(1) therefore is not a 'once for all' affair but one which depends on the circumstances at the time when the plaintiff's claim is brought.

3. REMEDIES AVAILABLE IN THE UK COURTS AFTER *CREHAN*

In a number of previous beer-supply actions, High Court judges had refused to make references to the European Court under Article 234 on the issue of whether co-contractors, such as Messrs Gemmell or Passmore, were under Community law entitled to damages from their brewery landlord, notwithstanding the strict rule of illegality that prevailed under UK law. Finally however such a reference was made in *Crehan* v. *Courage*[19] with results that were to have a major impact on the ability of plaintiffs to bring private actions for damages for breach of competition law in the UK and indeed other Member States.

The facts in *Crehan* were broadly similar to those in the earlier two cases. Crehan was a tenant under a lease with Courage, a large brewer, and owed it substantial sums for beer supplied. He claimed that his contract obliged him to buy beer exclusively from Courage and that this prevented him from purchasing any quantities on the open market at a lower price. He alleged also that Courage sold its beer at lower prices to independent pub tenants than to tied tenants like himself, and therefore claimed

---

[18] [1999] 1 CMLR 1129; 1 EurLR 501. The decision is not without criticism. See G. Cumming [2000] 21 ECLR 261–6 and Preece [2000] 21 ECLR 433–6.

[19] Case C-453/99 [2001] ECR I-6297: [2001] 5 CMLR 1058.

damages against Courage. It was likely that the particular restriction in this lease did infringe Article 81(1) and an earlier notification for individual exemption for this and other similar restrictions in Courage agreements had been withdrawn. The case therefore directly raised the question of whether Crehan was barred from suing Courage simply because he was a party to the contract prohibited by Article 81 rather than a third party damaged by such a contract.

In a relatively short and clear judgment the European Court had no difficulty in deciding in favour of the tenant's right to sue, notwithstanding the fact that he was a co-contractor with Courage. Its findings were that:

(1) a party to a contract liable to restrict or distort competition within the meaning of Article 81(1) can rely on the breach of the Article to obtain relief from the other contracting party

(2) Article 81 precludes a rule of national law under which a party to a contract in breach of Article 81 is barred from claiming damages for loss caused by performance of that contract, on the sole ground that he is a party to the contract himself

(3) nevertheless, national law may bar him from claiming damages if he bore 'significant responsibility' for the distortion of competition contained in the contract.

The Court stated that the principal reason for the decision was the importance in its view of ensuring the 'full effectiveness' of Article 81. If individuals could not claim damages in such situations, the practical effect of the Article would be put at risk and it was necessary to provide effective protection for plaintiffs in respect of their rights under the Treaty.

The Court also laid down criteria which would be relevant to the assessment of 'significant responsibility'. National courts should take into account:

• the economic and legal context in which the parties had made the contract

• the respective bargaining power and conduct of the parties

• whether the plaintiff found himself in a markedly weaker position than the other party, such as seriously to compromise or even eliminate his freedom to negotiate the terms of trade and his capacity to avoid the loss or reduce it to any extent

• in the case of a network of similar contracts, a party contracting with a person controlling the network cannot be held to have 'significant responsibility' for the contract, especially if the contract terms were imposed on him by the controller.

It is significant that in its ruling the Court is being consistent with the equivalent United States authority, the Supreme Court decision in *Perma Life Mufflers*[20] where it was ruled that a plaintiff who was a co-contractor was entitled to claim treble damages under the Sherman Act from the other party to the contract. In this case where contractual restrictions had been placed on a franchisee of car exhaust systems, the

---

[20] *Perma Life Mufflers v. International Parts Corp* 392 US 134 [1968].

contract had included a requirement on it to purchase all specified products from the other party, to operate only from approved locations and to sell at prices fixed by the franchisor without any right to sell competing products. The justification set out in the 6–3 majority opinion given by White J in that case was the importance of ensuring that the principles of the Sherman Act were respected, even if the plaintiff and defendant were both parties to the contract.

4. THE IMPACT OF REGULATION 1/2003 ON NATIONAL COURTS

4.1 THE RECITALS OF REGULATION 1/2003

Notwithstanding the outcome of the *Crehan* v. *Courage* litigation however, the use of national courts as the forum for the resolution of competition law cases between private parties would still have remained considerably restricted by the combined effect of the *Delimitis* and *Masterfoods* judgments already referred to. The effect of these cases was that the national courts could not rule in any case already in the hands of the Commission (other than to raise issues with the Court of Justice under Article 234) nor assess the application of Article 81(3) to the merits. As a result a number of private actions that had been brought in UK courts had to be suspended while the assessment of Article 81(3), in respect of the agreement in dispute, was carried out by the Commission; this normally would have the result of delaying a substantial resolution of the case by years rather than months. Leading examples of this were *MTV Europe* v. *BMG Records*[21] and *Williams* v. *Welsh RFC*.[22]

This situation could only be altered if the Commission were to yield up its monopoly over the granting of individual exemptions under Article 81(3). This required a radical reorganization of the entire framework and balance of power between the Commission on the one hand and national courts on the other, and the reform implemented by Regulation 1/2003 which took effect in May 2004 at last brought about this important change. The effect of the Regulation is that national courts are now able, alongside national competition authorities, to have a more important role than before in applying the content not only of their own national law but also of Articles 81 and 82 in their entirety.[23] Agreements can be reviewed as a whole by national courts on the basis of 'exception légale' which means that they are concerned

---

[21] [1997] EurLR 100: 1 CMLR 867.

[22] [1999] EurLR 195. See also J. Groning, 'National Judges in a Modernised Community Law System' in *European Competition Law Annual 2000: The Modernisation of EC Antitrust Law* (Hart Publishing, 2001), pp. 580–92.

[23] For confirmation of this in the context of Spanish Court proceedings, see C. Fernandez and P. Gonzalez Espejo [2002] 23 ECLR 163–171.

only with a single issue, namely: is the agreement valid or void under Article 81? In answering that question the court of course has to consider both whether the agreement falls within the scope of Article 81(1) and if so whether it can benefit from the terms of Article 81(3).

A number of the recitals and clauses in the new Regulation directly affect national courts. Recital 3 acknowledges that the limitations which Regulation 17/62 placed on the courts have hampered the application of Commission competition rules and Recital 4 records the need for the courts to be able to apply 81(3) directly to the dispute before them. Recital 7 refers to the essential part played by the courts in being able to award damages to the 'victims of infringement'. Recitals 21, 22, and 27 emphasize three obligations which the new system places upon them, namely:

- to cooperate with the Commission and to be able to ask it for information or opinions on points of Community law whilst keeping both it and national competition authorities 'sufficiently and well informed' of their proceedings (recital 21)
- to avoid conflicts with the proceedings and decisions of the Commission and other national competition authorities (recital 22)
- to ask for additional information from the Commission if required in connection with requests by it to enter private homes in order to search for business records (recital 27).

4.2 THE RELEVANT ARTICLES OF REGULATION 1/2003

The Regulation itself spells out the responsibilities and powers of national courts which are bound by Article 3, and it is supplemented by the Notice on the cooperation between the Commission and the courts of the EU Member States,[24] which is one of the six accompanying Commission guidance notices to the Regulation and replaces the 1993 Notice. It updates that Notice in the light of subsequent case law such as *Crehan* and *Masterfoods* and of the modernization Regulation, and provides detailed practical guidance on how this cooperation should work.

On the question of the supremacy of Community law Article 3 allows both national courts and competition authorities an element of freedom in connection with unilateral conduct engaged in by undertakings (whether or not dominant) and also in connection with the application of legislation that predominantly pursues objectives different from that covered by Articles 81 and 82. National courts are able to apply Articles 81(1) and 81(3) together as confirmed by Article 6. No longer do cases have to be suspended merely because one of the parties has notified the agreement in dispute to the Commission; the court now has full jurisdiction to determine whether the agreement complies with Article 81 as a whole. The limitations contained in *Delimitis*

---

[24] [2004] OJ C101/4.

therefore no longer apply. The effect of the *Masterfoods* judgments however remains important and Article 16(1) emphasizes this[25] by stating that:

When national courts rule on agreements, decisions or practices under Articles 81 or 82 of the Treaty which are already the subject of a Commission decision, they cannot take decisions running counter to the decision adopted by the Commission. They must also avoid giving decisions which would conflict with a decision contemplated by the Commission in proceedings it has initiated. To that effect, the national court may assess whether it is necessary to stay its proceedings. This obligation is without prejudice to the rights and obligations of Article 234 of the Treaty.

In these new circumstances it is essential for the courts to be in close touch with the Commission as well as with their own national competition authorities (Article 15). They may, under Article 15(1), ask the Commission to send them information or to offer its opinion on questions relating to the application of Community competition rules to the case before it. Member States must, under paragraph (2) of the same Article, ensure that copies of any written judgment of national courts relating to Articles 81 or 82 are forwarded to the Commission once the parties themselves have received the full written judgment. The national court must accept participation in competition cases from both national competition authorities and the Commission, by means of written submission in any case and with its specific consent by way of oral presentation; relevant documents must be forwarded by the court to these parties if necessary and relevant to the assessment of the case. The court itself may be designated by a Member State as a 'competition authority', this being likely when it hears appeals on such cases from national competition authorities.

4.3 THE COMBINED EFFECT OF *CREHAN* AND OF THE NEW REGULATION

The combined effect of the new Regulation and of the *Crehan* decision, means that national courts in Member States now have jurisdiction in the following situations:

(1) to apply Article 81(1) by declaratory judgments and to state that the agreement is outside its scope or within it (*Delimitis*)

(2) in parallel, to apply Article 81(3) dealing with all the four conditions and leading to a decision by the Court that the agreement or certain restrictions within it is/are void or that it is wholly or partially (as a result of severance) valid (Regulation 1/2003, Article 6)

---

[25] The scope of the obligation imposed by this principle remains uncertain in the absence of any European Court cases on the point. In the judgment that finally ended Mr Crehan's long-drawn out quest for damages, the House of Lords, concerned with the law prior to Reg. 1/2003 but following *Masterfoods*, interpreted it narrowly, holding that it only applied where the Commission had taken a decision on the same factual case and not just in a similar case, *Inntrepreneur v. Crehan* [2006] UKHL 38.

(3) to apply Article 82 (the position is unchanged since the Article has direct effect (*BRT* v. *Sabam* and *Delimitis*))

(4) to award an injunction to restrain a breach of competition law or to prohibit an act or practice in breach (*Crehan; Cutsforth* v. *Mansfield Inns*)

(5) to give an interim injunction (normally an inherent power of the court)

(6) to award damages to parties injured financially as a result of breach of competition rules whether or not they are co-contractors, except where the plaintiff has 'significant responsibility' for the restriction in breach of the rules (*Crehan*).

As already explained in the previous chapter however, the power to award damages is in the United Kingdom shared between the High Court and the Competition Appeal Tribunal (CAT) as a result of provisions in the Enterprise Act 2002.[26] Under these, in cases in which there has already been a decision of either the Office of Fair Trading or the Competition Appeal Tribunal that a breach of a Chapter 1 or Chapter 2 prohibition has occurred, or where there is a decision of the European Commission (no longer subject to appeal) that Article 81 or 82 has been infringed, the injured party can bring a claim for damages to the CAT for an award of a sum of money in compensation. Moreover under section 16 of the Enterprise Act the Lord Chancellor has the power, not yet used, to make rules, by secondary legislation, which will entitle the High Court to transfer to the CAT part of any case which relates to competition infringement issues and can later retransfer such matters to the High Court. The principle underlying this provision is that the CAT should be allowed in appropriate cases, where it is likely to be more familiar with the background to the case, to assess what, if any, damages should be paid for the competition law infringement, and to relieve the High Court judge dealing with the case of that responsibility.

5. THE GREEN AND WHITE PAPERS ON PRIVATE DAMAGES CLAIMS

5.1 THE NEED FOR FURTHER ACTION

Despite the importance of the extension of jurisdiction of the national courts and other reforms introduced by Regulation 1/2003 in equipping them to play a fuller part in competition law enforcement, it was clear that more would be needed if private damages claims being brought were to increase in number. Many factors discouraging such actions remained, and the Commission was aware that further initiatives

---

[26] Sections 18 and 19 permitting monetary claims to the Tribunal both by individuals or undertakings or by consumer bodies on behalf of groups of consumers.

on its part would be necessary if it was to achieve its aim of stimulating more private enforcement of Articles 81 and 82.

Well before the Regulation had entered into force it had commissioned a study with a view to obtaining a clear picture of the existing situation in respect of damages claims[27] based on competition law infringements, and in particular identifying the main obstacles to the bringing of such actions.

The results of the study, published in 2004,[28] showed a picture characterized by the authors as 'one of astonishing diversity and total underdevelopment'. In all in the then twenty-five Member States there had only ever been around sixty judged cases for damages actions, twelve based on Community law, thirty-two on national law, and six on both. Of these only twenty-eight had resulted in damages being awarded. Reasons identified in many jurisdictions for such low levels of litigation included:

- lack of clarity as to the legal basis for claims and as to which court is competent
- lack of the necessary judicial expertise in the relevant courts
- lack of provision for collective or class actions that allow a large number of small claims to be grouped together
- the burden and high standard of proof imposed on the plaintiff, in particular as to causation and damage
- difficulties in obtaining evidence (with the notable exception of the United Kingdom, Ireland and Cyprus where broad pretrial discovery is available)
- impossibility for plaintiffs to question witnesses
- limitations on relying on infringement findings by the Commission, national authorities or other courts
- the 'passing on' defence (discussed in Section 5.5 below)
- the difficulty of assessing the damage suffered, and restrictions on the amount of damages, and on the interest, that can be awarded
- lengthy proceedings and short limitation periods
- high costs.

It will be noticed that none of these factors are remedied by Regulation 1/2003, and it is interesting that the inability of national courts to apply Article 81(3) does not feature in the list of obstacles. Rather, the hindrances to damages actions are attributable almost entirely to characteristics of national judicial systems and national rules of evidence and procedure. The accuracy of this conclusion is borne out by the fact that over four years have now passed since the Regulation entered into force, and there appears to have been only a slight increase in such claims so far. For this reason

---

[27] Private enforcement can also include claims for other forms of redress, such as an injunction or restitution, but this study, and the Green and White Papers that followed it, were confined to damages actions.

[28] Study on the conditions of claims for damages in case of infringement of EC competition rules: comparative report (2004), available on DG Comp's website.

the Commission in December 2005 took the next step, which was to publish a Green Paper on competition damages actions.

5.2 ANTITRUST LITIGATION IN THE UNITED STATES

Before considering what the Commission has proposed in order to encourage more damages claims in Europe, it is worth describing briefly the main features of the US antitrust damages litigation landscape, not least because the current Competition Commissioner Neelie Kroes and her services have been adamant that it is not their intention to introduce a US-style litigation culture to European competition law, but to develop a model which ensures 'respect for European legal systems and traditions'.[29] So what is it that they are so keen to avoid?

In the US the courts have for over 100 years been actively involved in antitrust enforcement in a way that has never been the case in Europe, and it is estimated that around 90 per cent of US antitrust cases consist of private enforcement actions. Since 1890 judges have been able to award treble damages, meaning that the plaintiff can receive up to three times the value of the damage he actually suffered. The class-action system allows lawyers to bring actions on behalf of a large group of plaintiffs, some of whom may be unaware of or uninterested in the claim, because if they do not actively 'opt out' then they can be included as claimants. Lawyers are able to work on a 'contingency fee' basis, taking a proportion of any award obtained, and such litigation imposes a heavy burden on the defendant, including onerous discovery rules requiring the production of vast numbers of documents. Nor are unsuccessful claimants required to pay the defendant's costs, though if successful the claimant may recover his own costs. Availability of trial by a jury of laymen contributes to uncertainty as to the outcome of a case. All of these factors combine to produce a high volume of litigation, much of which is settled even where the claim is unmeritorious, because the burden of litigation on the defendant, and the incentives to litigate for plaintiffs and lawyers, is so high.[30]

5.3 THE 2005 GREEN PAPER

The Green Paper[31] set out a range of options for reform on a large number of issues. It starts by setting out its reasons for taking up this cause:

Damages actions for infringement of antitrust law serve several purposes, namely to compensate those who have suffered a loss as a consequence of anti-competitive behaviour and to ensure the full effectiveness of the antitrust rules of the treaty by discouraging

[29] Commission Press Release IP/08/515, 3 April 2008.

[30] Those wanting to go beyond this necessarily simplistic summary of the US system may look at, e.g, C. A. Jones, *Private Enforcement of Antitrust Law in the EU, UK and USA* (OUP, 1999).

[31] COM(2005) 672 final, and 77 page accompanying Commission Staff Working Paper SEC(2005)1732, both available on DG Comp's website.

anti-competitive behaviour, thus contributing significantly to the maintenance of effective competition in the Community.

What is not made explicit here, but certainly true, is the pragmatic point that, in the light of the size of the Community and the Commission's limited resources, it is essential to ensure that as great a part of the enforcement burden as possible is taken up through private litigation.

The many issues covered in the Green Paper include rules on disclosure of evidence, the relevance of fault on the part of the defendant in establishing liability, calculation of damages and the availability of punitive damages, the role of the 'passing on' defence (discussed below in Section 5.5), class and collective actions, the impact of costs rules, limitation periods and rules on causation, and questions of jurisdiction and applicable law.

As might be expected of a document touching so closely on the sensitive issue of national judicial and legal systems, the Green Paper provoked lively and impassioned debate on almost all the issues it raised. Apart from the concerns raised in the context of competition law, the debate also prompts the question of the extent to which it is desirable to create special rules in this area, when many of the same issues arise in other areas, for example, in claims based on product liability or environmental law infringements.

Almost all reponses were broadly in favour of facilitating damages claims,[32] but many took issue with some of the options set out. A common theme of responses was a reluctance to depart from the principle, common throughout Member States, that damages represent compensation for damage suffered. Proposals to provide for the award of multiple or punitive damages, or to remove the 'passing on' defence, were therefore unpopular.

Following the debate the Commission took a long period for internal reflection. It faced a delicate task in deciding on its next steps, not least because there was some doubt surrounding the extent to which it, alone or with other Community institutions, had the power to introduce some of the changes it was suggesting, and in some areas it was clear that ultimately it would be for Member States to decide whether or not to adopt changes to their laws and procedures.

5.4 THE 2008 WHITE PAPER

The White Paper,[33] when it finally appeared in April 2008, was relatively conservative, and a number of its proposals were made tentatively, with some also being expressed as subject to further consultation. The Commission repeats its commitment

---

[32] Many regard this as self-evidently a good thing in principle. For a refreshing look at the arguments against encouraging private enforcement see W. P. J. Wils, 'Should Private Antitrust Enforcement be Encouraged in Europe?' (2003) 26 World Comp 473 and the reply from C.A. Jones, 'Private Antitrust Enforcement in Europe: A Policy Analysis and Reality Check' [2004] 27 World Comp 13.

[33] COM(2008) 165 final, and a 98-page accompanying Commission Staff Working Paper SEC(2008) 404–6, both available on DG Comp's website.

to improving conditions for victims of anti-competitive conduct to bring damages actions, and proposes:

- allowing representative actions to be brought by designated bodies such as consumer groups (as is already possible in the United Kingdom), and also collective actions, on an 'opt-in' basis, meaning that a claim can only be brought on behalf of those who have actively agreed

- giving national courts greater powers than most of them currently have to order disclosure of evidence (though, in the interests of maintaining the attractions of applying for leniency, not of statements made by a cartel member in the context of a leniency application)

- preventing courts from taking decisions that conflict with a final decision of any national competition authority

- exempting cartel members who have been granted immunity from joint and several liability in respect of the conduct of the other cartel members

- extended and more flexible limitation periods.

It still remains to be seen to what extent such reform can be implemented through binding Community legislation, such as a regulation or directive, as opposed to non-binding guidance. In any case, implementation by Member States will be key in ensuring its effectiveness.

5.5 THE 'PASSING ON' DEFENCE

Two of the issues left unanswered in the *Crehan* case and featuring in both the Green and White Papers are the 'passing on defence' and the 'indirect purchaser' issues. In many cases, if there has been a price-fixing agreement between A and B, purchaser C may have had to pay a higher price to A and/or B for goods covered by that agreement than he would have done had that cartel not existed. On the other hand C may simply have increased the price he charges to D to whom he resells the products, which may have been sold on either as he purchased them from A or B or having had value added in some way. In this situation, the question arises: can A and B be sued by either or both of C or D?

Under the US case law, C is still entitled to sue A and B even if he has 'passed on' a higher price to D. The only exception would be when his contract with D had been made on a 'cost plus' basis, where by definition he will have suffered no loss (the *Hanover Shoe* decision). On the other hand as a logical consequence of *Hanover Shoe*, D as merely an 'indirect' purchaser from A or B is not entitled to sue either of them (this being decided by the well-known *Illinois Brick* case).[34] The justification given by the Supreme Court for the *Hanover Shoe* decision is that to allow the 'passing on'

---

[34] *Hanover Shoe v. United Shoe Machinery Corp* 392 US 481 [1968]; *Illinois Brick Co v. State of Illinois* 431 US 720 [1968].

defence would be to give anti-trust offenders an opportunity to retain their unlawful profits and to considerably increase the burden on plaintiffs seeking compensation by forcing them to produce a detailed analysis of their business accounts showing their purchases, sales, prices and profits. The decision in *Illinois Brick* is simply the logical consequence of *Hanover Shoe*; if the 'passing off' defence is not allowed to the wrong-doer then it would be unfair that indirect purchasers could recover from him in addition to the direct purchaser, leading to the situation where multiple damages will be paid, which have already (under US law) been subject to trebling!

It is however far from certain that UK courts, or those of other Member States, will follow the US case-law precedents. The normal UK approach to damage claims of all kinds is to require the plaintiff to show both a cause of action (here 'an illegal contract') and a causal link between the defendant's wrongful act and the plaintiff's losses. If no loss can be shown by the direct purchaser, it is likely however, that the UK courts, having declined to make a finding in his favour, would in contrast be willing to accept suits by indirect purchasers, provided they can show that they have incurred loss; but this is likely whether or not the 'passing off' defence itself is permitted by UK courts.[35]

The European Commission's White Paper recommends retaining the 'passing on' defence, which is consistent with the European tradition of treating damages as compensation, as opposed to punishment or deterrence. At the same time it proposes a partial change in the burden of proof to assist indirect purchasers: such a claimant would benefit from a rebuttable presumption that the entire overcharge was passed on to him. While this would strengthen the position of such claimants, it may be objected that it would put direct purchasers at a considerable disadvantage.

This and many other issues remain to be resolved in the years to come. Some of these are explored further in Part III of this book.

FURTHER READING

S. DRAKE, 'Scope of *Courage* and the Principle of Individual Liability for Damages: Further Development of the Principle of Effective Judicial Protection by the Court of Justice' [2006] 30 ELRev 841.

C. D. EHLERMANN, 'The Modernisation of EC Antitrust Policy: A Legal and Cultural Revolution' [2000] 37 CMLRev 537.

J. GRONING, 'National Judges in a Modernised Community Law System' in *European Competition Law Annual 2000: The Modernisation of EC Antitrust Law* (Hart Publishing, 2001) 580.

A. JONES and D. BEARD, 'Co-Contractors, Damages and Art. 81: The ECJ Finally Speaks' [2002] 23 ECLR 246.

---

[35] A. Jones and D. Beard, 'Co-Contractors, Damages and Art. 81: The ECJ Finally Speaks' [2002] 23 ECLR 246.

C. A. JONES, *Private Enforcement of Antitrust Law in the EU, UK and USA* (OUP, 1999).

C. A. JONES, 'Private Antitrust Enforcement in Europe: A Policy Analysis and Reality Check' [2004] 27 World Comp 13 (reply to Wils, below).

O. ODUDU and J. EDELMAN, 'Compensatory Damages for Breach of Article 81' [2002] ELR 327 [2008] ECLR 33.

W. P. J. WILS, 'Should Private Antitrust Enforcement be Encouraged in Europe?' [2003] 26 World Comp 473.

21

MEMBER STATES AND EC COMPETITION RULES

1. ARTICLES 81 AND 82: OBLIGATIONS OF MEMBER STATES

Although the provisions of the Treaty can have direct application to persons and undertakings, the majority of the Articles of the Treaty of Rome are directed towards Member States, either stating principles which they are required to observe, or laying down specific tasks for performance by them. By contrast, Articles 81 and 82, which lay down the main principles of competition law, are not directed primarily towards the Member States, but to individual undertakings and associations of undertakings.

If the activities of Member States were confined simply to the exercise of the traditional powers of governments,[1] such as the conduct of foreign affairs and defence, and the implementation of education, housing, and social policies, then their involvement with Articles 81 and 82 might indeed be limited. In fact, however, all Member States are also involved in a wide variety of both industrial and commercial activities, often in direct or indirect competition with private undertakings; moreover Member States also finance in part or whole the operations of many public undertakings, bodies, authorities, and utilities which have many dealings with other undertakings, even if not directly in competition with them. These activities might include the grant of a monopoly by statute for the public supply of gas, water, electricity, or telephone services, the provision of pilotage or marine environmental services, and television or radio transmission.

The framers of the Treaty anticipated the problems that would arise if the public undertakings of Member States and commercial undertakings in which they might become involved were not made subject to the common rules of competition. Thus, Articles 81 to 89, which comprise the first Chapter of Part 3 entitled the 'Policy of the Community', have a substantial effect on the activities of governments of all Member States; a number of leading European Court and Court of First Instance decisions have dealt with the extent to which the administrative and legislative activities of Member States are subject to them. The approach of the Courts has been founded on the basic

---

[1] Insofar, of course, as the Treaty of Rome or successor treaties have not placed them wholly or partly in the hands of Community institutions.

framework of the Treaty, in particular Article 10, which emphasizes the obligation of Member States to take all appropriate measures to ensure fulfilment of their Treaty obligations which include, under Article 3(1)(g), support for 'a system ensuring that competition in the internal market is not distorted': they must also accept obligations which result from action taken under the Treaty by the institutions of the Community, including actions taken against undertakings under Articles 81 and 82. The second part of Article 10 places on them a positive obligation to facilitate the achievements of the Commission's tasks, and a requirement to abstain from any measures which could jeopardize the attainment of Treaty objectives. The Treaty on European Union adopted at Maastricht contains a further requirement that under Article 4(1) the activities of Member States shall include an obligation 'to support the general economic policies in the Community, in accordance with the principle of an open market economy with free competition'.

It would, therefore, have been reasonable to expect Member States to refrain from legislative or administrative policies that offered undertakings a means of escaping their obligations under the competition rules. On the whole this has been the case, but we shall see that certain exceptions exist to this general principle.

2. NATIONAL LAWS AFFECTING PRICE-FIXING: SOME LEADING CASES

2.1 THE FIRST RULE: MEMBER STATES MUST NOT LEGISLATE TO CREATE OR PROTECT AGREEMENTS OR GIVE PRIVILEGES IN BREACH OF ARTICLE 81 OR 82

In dealing with national legislation that might conflict with the competition rules of the Treaty, and in particular with Articles 10, 81, and 82, the case law of the Community Courts has made it clear that in such cases there are two aspects to be considered, which are quite distinct. The first is whether the Member State has itself by its own legislative or administrative measures, or by a combination of them, breached its obligations under Article 10 in a way that might have rendered ineffective the competition rules applicable to undertakings; this could have been by requiring or favouring the adoption of agreements, decisions or concerted practices contrary to Article 81 or by reinforcing their effect, or depriving its own national legislation of its official character by delegating to private traders responsibility for decisions affecting economic markets or by granting them privileges that would lead to a breach of Article 82. This principle was established in *Inno* v. *ATAB*,[2] an Article 234 reference from the Belgian Court of

---

[2] Case 13/77 [1977] ECR 2115: [1978] 1 CMLR 283. See J. Temple Lang, 'The Duties of Co-operation of National Authorities and Courts under Art. 10' [1998]: 23 EurLR 109 and [2001] 26 EurLR 84 and H. Schepel 'Delegation of Regulatory Powers to Private Parties under EC Competition Law [2002] 39 CMLR 31–51. See

Cassation concerning the validity of a Belgian statute which required retailers to sell cigarettes and tobacco only at the official price. The official price was the price notified to the authorities for purposes of the assessment of excise duty, together with value added tax. The statute had the effect of preventing retailers from competing with each other on price and would have enabled their trade association to take advantage of its dominance in the Belgian market which, under the protection of such legislation, it would have little difficulty in exploiting and abusing. The European Court of Justice referred back to the principles embodied in Articles 3(1)(g) and 10 of the Treaty, and from their combined effect found no difficulty in reading into the Treaty an implied duty on Member States not to adopt or maintain in force any measure which could deprive Article 82 of its effectiveness. The Court also stated that Member States should not enact measures enabling private undertakings to escape from the constraints imposed by the competitive scheme of the Treaty; it added that any national measure which had the effect of facilitating the abuse of a dominant position capable of affecting trade between Member States would generally be incompatible with Articles 28 and 30 on the free movement of goods.

The freedom of Member States to enact legislation reducing or eliminating price competition was the central issue in a later case (*Leclerc Books*),[3] where a French court sought a ruling of the European Court of Justice under Article 234 on whether the Treaty prohibited the establishment of a system within a Member State to control the price at which books, whether locally published or imported, could be sold only at a price of not more than 5 per cent below the official price named by the publisher or importer. The French government was held to be entitled to enact resale price maintenance legislation for books published in France so long as no Community sectoral policy had been adopted relating to the pricing of books, and so long as the legislation did not conflict with other provisions of the Treaty, notably Articles 28 and 30. On the basis of these latter articles, however, the Court ruled that price restrictions imposed on books imported into France would be illegal, since they would rank as being of 'equivalent effect' on imports; the only exception would be if it were established that the original exports of the books had been for the sole purpose of circumventing the legislation by subsequent reimportation.[4] The argument of the French government that the legislation in its entirety was indispensable to protect both specialist book shops and books as a cultural medium against the likely reduction in variety and availability of books if unrestricted price competition was allowed failed to convince the Court, and the exceptions contained in Article 30 were held not to apply here so as to effect any qualification to the prohibitions in Article 28.

---

also Case C-198/01 *C.I.F.* v. *Autorita Garante della Concorrenza del Mercato* [2003] ECR I-8055: [2003] 5 CMLR 829.

[3] Case 229/83 [1985] ECR 1: 2 CMLR 286.

[4] The issue of whether the reimportation was genuine or artificial, i.e. simply to avoid the effects of the French law, would be for the national court to decide. Its companion case is Case 231/83 *Leclerc Petrol* [1985] ECR 305: 2 CMLR 524, officially *Cullet* v. *Leclerc*. See also Case C-9/99 *Échirolles Distribution* [2000] ECR I-8207.

National legislation was also considered in two cases by the European Court in which, although the legislation did not actually require anti-competitive conduct in breach of these Articles, it nevertheless provided considerable support for private agreements of such a kind. Both cases were Article 234 references from Belgian courts. The first was the *Flemish Travel Agents* case[5] where a Royal Decree required travel agents not to depart from official tariffs and not to share commissions with their customers. Standard forms of agreement between such travel agencies and tour organizers were ruled by the Court to constitute a breach of Article 81. Under the Decree, a travel agent which complained of 'cheating' by other travel agents could obtain an injunction against them and ask for their operating licences to be withdrawn. The judgment of the Court was unequivocal, that Belgium was in breach of Article 81. The second case, *Van Eycke* v. *ASPA*,[6] led to a less clear-cut answer. Here the Royal Decree provided that the holders of deposits in savings accounts were only entitled to tax relief on the income if interest rates did not exceed 7 per cent. Mr Van Eycke alleged that the decree merely confirmed an existing restrictive agreement between the banks. The Court ruled that in such a case the central issue was whether the legislation merely confirmed the method of restricting interest rates which the interbank arrangements had set out, or whether it went further. Finding ambiguity in the evidence on this issue, the Court referred it back to the national court.

The issue of the enactment by Member States of legislation reducing or eliminating price competition also arose in the air transport sector. As noted in Chapter 7 (at p. 132), the European Court decided in *Nouvelles Frontières*[7] that Member States and the Commission remained free, in the absence of any Community rules, to adjudicate under the terms of Articles 84 and 85 respectively on the admissibility of agreements and practices and the abuse of dominant position. In these circumstances it was uncertain whether Member States were entitled to continue to create and enforce domestic legislation covering such matters as tariffs, charter flights, discount fares, and the general terms and conditions upon which air travel was provided to other countries within the Community. It could have been argued, by analogy with *Leclerc Books*, that until a Common Community policy on air transport had been adopted by the Council, Member States retained jurisdiction in this area, even if the effect might be to permit agreements or practices by individual undertakings which were inconsistent with the provisions of Articles 81 and 82. Since the adoption of a number of Community regulations dealing with air transport, this issue is less important, apart from the continued absence of Community jurisdiction over routes from or to destinations outside it.[8]

It is clear however that a Member State does retain the freedom to determine the prices to be charged for particular goods and services, if it does so as manifestly an exercise of governmental authority in a sector where this power has not been removed

---

[5] Case 311/85 *VZW Vereniging van Vlaamse Reisebureaus* v. *VZW Sociale dienst van de Plaatselijke en Gewestelijke Overheidsdiensten* [1987] ECR 3801: [1989] 4 CMLR 213.

[6] Case 267/86 [1988] ECR 4769: [1990] 4 CMLR 330.

[7] Cases 209–213/84 *Ministère Public* v. *Asjes* [1986] ECR 1425: [1986] 3 CMLR 173.

[8] See Ch. 7, p. 133.

from it as the result of Community legislation, as for example by the regulations form-ing the Common Agricultural Policy. In *Cullet* v. *Leclerc*, France had fixed maximum prices for retail sales of petrol, but this was not adjudged a breach of Article 10 by the Court of Justice; there was no attempt to achieve this result by delegating the respon-sibility for fixing prices to suppliers or retailers of the product by means of industry wide agreements.

The national legislation introduced may have had an impact on the relevant profes-sional or trade bodies which is simply too limited to allow a conclusion that the State has thereby delegated to them the task of fixing prices or terms of business. Examples of such legislation can be found in some Italian cases. In *Conte* v. *Rossi*[9] architects were allowed to set their fees for professional services and have them endorsed as appropri-ate by their association in cases where they had to sue for their recovery. When Conte was sued by Rossi for her fees he claimed that the endorsement given by her associ-ation represented a 'decision' prohibited by Article 81. The Court of Justice however ruled that this was not so; the endorsement only had legal effect if the debtor failed to dispute it and was in any case not binding upon the local court. However, in different circumstances the Commission fined the *Belgian Architects' Association* for setting a fixed fee scale.[10]

In both *Arduino*[11] and *Cipolla*[12] the tariff in issue was that of members of the Italian Bar, which set both maximum and minimum fee levels for their services. But again it was clear that the legislation fell short of allowing the Bar to adopt a 'decision' that would bind their members. The legislation did not contain either procedural arrange-ments or substantive requirements capable of ensuring that the Bar was exercising an authority fully delegated to it by the State; any draft tariff produced by the Bar had to be approved by the Minister for Justice, who himself after consulting two public bod-ies could then amend the draft. Moreover the local court in assessing such fees was also allowed to depart from the tariff, in exceptional circumstances.

Moreover, if the government measure simply consists of a prohibition of a particular practice, and in its self-contained form has no requirement of any agreement or prac-tice to be entered into, then again there can be no breach of Article 10, as in the case of *Meng*,[13] where German law had forbidden the sharing of commission by insurance brokers with their clients. If however there is some real link between national legisla-tion and the subsequent autonomous conduct of the undertaking in then entering into a related agreement or practice relating to prices or conditions of business, Article 81 may have been breached; if so, anyone suffering financial loss may have a claim under the principle of *Francovich* discussed in the previous chapter, so long as the breach of Community law is regarded as sufficiently serious.

---

[9] Case C-221/99 [2001] ECR I-9359: [2002] 4 CMLR 269.

[10] Decision of 24 June 2004, not published. See Commission press release IP/04/800 which describes the case and also refers to similar cases brought by the French and UK authorities against national architects' bodies.

[11] Case C-35/99 [2002] ECR I-1529: [2002] 4 CMLR 866.

[12] Case C-94/04 *Cipolla* [2006] ECR I-11421.   [13] Case C-2/91 [1993] ECR I-5751.

2.2 THE SECOND RULE: UNDERTAKINGS DO NOT ESCAPE ARTICLE 81 OR 82 MERELY BECAUSE OF STATE ACTION AFFECTING THEIR MARKETS

The second aspect of the rule relates to the undertakings themselves, and whether they have acted with sufficient autonomy to have themselves breached Article 81 or 82 or whether the terms of the legislation relating to their conduct left insufficient freedom to them for their actions to be characterized as independent.

Undertakings cannot claim that Articles 81 and 82 do not apply to them simply because national legislation or executive action has reduced the degree of competition within the market. The leading cases, like *Inno/ATAB,* dealt with the cigarette and tobacco markets, in Belgium and Holland respectively. In *Fedetab*[14] the Belgian legislation imposing strict price control at the retail level considerably reduced the scope for competition. Excise duty in fact comprised some 70 per cent of the price of an average packet of cigarettes. In this situation, the legislation laid down strict requirements for the affixing to every packet of the exact price upon which the relevant duty had been calculated in order to reduce the scope for fraud. These laws, of course, also considerably reduced the scope for competition but the European Court ruled that competition could have remained in three important areas, namely profit margins for both wholesalers and retailers, rebates, and terms and conditions of supply including credit terms. These were all areas where in a competitive market variations would have been anticipated, as particular undertakings sought to increase their market share by improving the terms offered to their more favoured customers, but which under the rules of the relevant trade association had been suppressed so as to exclude the element of uncertainty which such competition would have brought. Fedetab's appeal against the decision of the Commission that its recommendation to members as to standard terms of business and prices to be charged contravened Article 81(1) was therefore rejected.

To similar effect was the Court's decision in the later *SSI* case[15] relating to Dutch legislation, along similar lines but involving not only regulations relating to excise taxes but the permitted level of price increases by Dutch manufacturers and restraints on their profits. Once again, while the Court accepted that this legislation had considerably affected the climate of competition, it held that its terms did not prevent all aspects of competition between those engaged in the trade. Competition would still have been possible (had the relevant trade associations not prevented it) on such promotional matters as giving additional discounts or rebates, and providing more favourable terms and conditions of sale. A decision finding breaches of Article 81(1) by the association of Dutch tobacco dealers was therefore also upheld.

It will be comparatively rare for government involvement through legislation or administrative action to be so all-pervasive as to eliminate the possibility of

---

[14] Case 209/78 [1980] ECR 3125: [1981] 3 CMLR 134.
[15] Cases 240–2, 260–2, 268–9/82 [1985] ECR 3381: [1987] 3 CMLR 661.

competitive activity to such an extent that Articles 81 and 82 can no longer have any application. The only case in which this has been found to occur was the *Sugar Cartel* case[16] where the Italian government limited competition with regard to imports into Italy of sugar in no fewer than four major respects. There is no other recorded case in which all these conditions have applied, and it seems unlikely that defendants will be allowed to rely on this precedent save in the most unusual circumstances. Even though in the *SSI* case the Dutch authorities had held formal consultations with the cigarette industry on its agreed objectives, including the guarantee of substantial tax revenue for government and stable income for retailers, the Dutch government had not gone to the extent of suggesting to undertakings that they should support those objectives by anti-competitive arrangements.

In the majority of cases, as we have seen, the defence of State compulsion (as in *Fedetab*, for example) has been dismissed on the ground that the State action left sufficient 'breathing space' in which the undertakings could operate without being required to act in contravention of Articles 81 or 82.[17] However, if the State action was sufficiently compelling and allowed no room for manoeuvre, it would provide a defence to the undertaking, against both Commission proceedings and any private action by an injured third party.[18]

It can also be said with confidence that if Member State governments merely encourage undertakings to establish prices and regulate industry by methods reducing or eliminating competition, this is no defence if the legislation is permissive rather than strictly mandatory. Nor will it be any defence to show that there is governmental ratification for the implementation of schemes to regulate prices and other industry conditions that were originally agreed between the undertakings themselves. Justification for this statement can be found in the twin French cases of *Pabst and Richarz KG/ BNIA*[19] and *BNIC* v. *Clair*.[20]

In the first, the *Armagnac* case, this famous brandy was produced under the auspices of the trade association BNIA, whose function was to regulate the affairs of the industry and in particular to regulate quality and control the terms upon which it was sold, as well as providing technical and research assistance to the growers. The association had a chairman appointed by the French Ministry of Agriculture, twelve delegates representing producers and co-operatives, and another twelve representing

[16] Case 40/73 [1975] ECR 1663: [1976] 1 CMLR 295. Details of this case are set out in Ch. 9, p. 176.

[17] For a recent example in the highly regulated telecommunications sector see Case T-271/03 *Deutsche Telekom v. Commission*, 10 April 2008 (not yet reported).

[18] There is, however, an argument based on European Court decisions in other fields that an undertaking which seeks to rely on State action as a defence against a claim of anti-competitive behaviour must itself take the risk that the State was not authorized by Community law to compel such action.

[19] [1976] OJ L231/24: [1976] 2 CMLR D63. The Commission's comment on this case in the *6th Annual Report* (1976), p. 68, was that it showed 'where associations or undertakings entrusted with certain statutory powers act beyond their powers and take measures to regulate the market, the object or effect of which is to promote the uniform conduct of its members, they cannot evade the rules of competition and hold the State responsible for their actions'.

[20] Case 123/83 [1985] ECR 391: 2 CMLR 430.

wholesalers, distillers, and brokers. All sales of armagnac were graded from 0 to 5, the most expensive variety being grade 5, VSOP Napoleon at least five years old. Forty per cent of industry production was sold in France, and 60 per cent was exported either in bottles or in bulk. The majority of exports were in bulk, and the association had authority to issue certificates of age for these. The association effectively controlled all movements of bulk armagnac and was fully informed of the stocks of various ages and grades held by the members of the association.

Concern had apparently been felt that some German importers had sold the brandy under a false trade description, claiming lower grades to be grade 5. The association, purporting to deal with this abuse, imposed a ban upon bulk deliveries of grades 4 and 5. German importers, who had become used to receiving bulk deliveries of the higher grade, complained to the Commission that this restriction was in breach of Article 81. It was claimed that, whatever the alleged justification for the interference by the association in trading practices, its effect would be artificially to reduce the supply and increase the price of the higher grades of brandy. In 1976 the Commission ruled that the decision of the association was a breach of Article 81; it pointed out that the effect of the ban on bulk supplies was far in excess of the measures that would have been necessary to carry out the quality protection obligations assigned to BNIA by the relevant French decrees. The objective of BNIA's decision appeared rather to be to restrict competition within the Common Market and to increase the price of the highest grades by reducing their availability on the German market. The Commission ruled that other administrative and legal means to stop unfair practices or false trade designations were available, and those should have been applied in a way that was proportionate to the disclosed problem, rather than by the exercise of powers to prevent altogether bulk deliveries of the two highest grades.

In 1982 the Commission ruled that similar practices fixing the price of cognac by a similar professional association responsible for that industry was likewise in breach of Article 81, this being confirmed by the 1985 European Court decision in *BNIC v. Clair*. Here, the association also had the function of acting as a joint trade organization between the various interests in the cognac industry. It provided technical details and information as to the supply and demand for the products, it supervised maintenance of industry standards, and subject to government supervision was entitled to implement rules for the marketing of cognac, including prices and terms of payment.

A committee representing the various interests in the trade, similar to that in the armagnac industry, decided prices and conditions of sale. A committee decision had to be approved by a three-quarters majority of the members of the association, who included delegates of wine growers, dealers, brokers, workers, and technicians. Once the rules had thus been adopted, the association was entitled to apply to the French Minister of Agriculture to extend the agreement compulsorily for a specified period to all members of the trade, whether or not they were participants in the joint trade organization. Once the ministerial decree had been made, any contract failing to comply with it would be void. In the relevant year, a minimum price of wines for distillation into cognac had been fixed, but Clair had made contracts for sale to various growers at prices below those allowed. BNIC claimed that this agreement was void; Clair responded by arguing that the price-fixing was contrary to Articles 81 and 82. The French court before whom the case came made an Article 234 application to the European Court to determine whether this form of price-fixing was covered by Article 81(1).

The European Court answered in the affirmative.[21] The Court ruled that any agreement which had the object or effect of restricting competition by fixing minimum prices for the purchase of a semi-finished product (wine) could affect trade between Member States, even if the semi-finished product was not itself traded between Member States, as long as it formed the basis of a final product (cognac) marketed elsewhere in the EC. The fact that the agreement had been concluded within the framework of a public law, with the 'blessing' of government, could not affect the application of Article 81; nor would the fact that the persons who signed the agreement were themselves largely appointed by a government minister on the nomination of the relevant trade organization be considered relevant.

2.3 MANDATORY TARIFFS FOR SECTORS OF THE ECONOMY

More recently, however, there have been disturbing signs that these principles laid down in earlier cases are being diluted in situations where Member States have laid down mandatory tariffs for particular sectors, after consultation with industry representatives. Such tariffs have been fixed, for example, for German road hauliers and inland waterways and for Italian road hauliers.[22] The common feature of these cases was that the members of the Consultative Committee consulted by the Member State for the implementation of the detailed tariffs were not only industry representatives, the majority being public authority members not engaged in the industry who were required by the national statute to act in the interests of all users, including small and medium-sized businesses (SMEs in Community jargon) and economically weak areas. Nevertheless, the Member State retained a right in all cases to overrule decisions of these committees if it disagreed with their findings. Some concern must be felt at the risk that, notwithstanding these theoretical safeguards in the process leading up to the publication of the mandatory tariff, the interests of members of the industry may

---

[21] In a further Art. 234 case involving the cognac industry the Court predictably ruled that a levy on a French wine-grower for exceeding his production quota was a private arrangement subject to Art. 81. The French government was held in breach of Art. 10 by adopting and extending to non-members of the relevant trade association the burden of such production levies and restrictions: Case 136/86 *BNIC* v. *Aubert* [1987] ECR 4789: [1988] 4 CMLR 331.

[22] Case C-185/91 *Reiff* [1993] ECR I-5801: [1995] 5 CMLR 145. Case C-153/93 *Germany* v. *Delta* [1994] ECR I-2517: [1996] 4 CMLR 21. Case C-96/94 *Spediporto* v. *SMG* [1995] ECR I-2883: 4 CMLR 613. A similar approach was adopted by the Court in Cases C 140–2/94 *Bassano* [1995] ECR I-3257: [1996] 4 CMLR 157 concerned with the granting of licences in an Italian town authorizing the opening of retail shops.

in practice predominate, so that the outcome may be remarkably similar to a price cartel for the industry.

In some cases however the element of public interest in the determination of the tariffs may be minimal, and in such cases it is likely that the Court of Justice would rule both that the Member State was in breach of Article 10 and that the undertaking or association was in breach of Article 81. This occurred in relation to customs agents' tariffs in Italy. In *Commission v. Italy*[23] the Court had held that the law requiring the agents' association to fix their charges was unenforceable, because its terms included little or no 'public interest' in the fixing of the charges; indeed the association was given a freedom to draw up the tariffs and conditions of business in a way damaging to competition between them. In *Commission v. CNST*[24] the association was subsequently itself held in breach of Article 81 because the tariff made large increases to the minimum charges previously in force and introduced rules that curtailed the freedom of agents to reduce their costs or to offer reductions in charges to their customers.

2.4 THE *ALUMINIUM CARTEL* CASE

In the light of the above, it will not come as a surprise that mere governmental encouragement without any statutory basis provides no defence to a claim under Article 81 or 82, as the *Aluminium Cartel* case[25] shows. The Commission decision, issued in 1984, concerned agreements between major Western producers of aluminium which ensured that during the years 1963 to 1976 all Eastern Bloc source material passed into the hands of the leading Western producers, who prevented their competitors from obtaining the benefits of metal at lower prices, removing a major source of price competition from Western markets. The original scheme for preventing the marketing of Eastern Bloc aluminium in the West, in a way which would reduce the overall level of prices, had been entered into with at least the tacit support of the British government, which had been concerned with the risk that the market price for aluminium would be substantially reduced by Eastern Bloc material at a time when there was no UK law limiting the agreements that could be made with regard to such foreign source material, this being several years before the entry of the United Kingdom into the European Community and its acceptance of the Treaty, including Articles 81 and 82. The Commission held that the encouragement given by the British government did not provide any defence to a charge under Article 81, although it might be a factor reducing the culpability of defendants and therefore relevant to the assessment of whether any fine should be imposed, and if so how large.[26]

---

[23] Case C-35/96 [1998] ECR I-3851: 5 CMLR 889.
[24] Case T-513/93 [2000] ECR II-1807: 5 CMLR 614.
[25] See Ch. 9, p. 177, for a fuller account of the facts of the case.
[26] In the event, no fines were imposed on the participants to the agreement.

3. ARTICLE 86(1) AND (2): PUBLIC UNDERTAKINGS SUBJECT TO THE TREATY RULES ON COMPETITION

3.1 THE PURPOSE OF THESE ARTICLES

It is not only by legislative or executive acts that Member States may become involved in interference with the normal working of competition. Member States are themselves involved in the provision of public services in many ways, either through nationalized industries or public corporations of many kinds. Their right to preserve their own balance of public and private enterprise is specifically retained under Article 295.[27] It is, however, undoubtedly true that if public undertakings were treated by Member States in a more favourable manner than other enterprises, considerable damage could be done to the process of competition in national markets in ways that would affect trade between Member States. For this reason, Article 86 was included in this part of the Treaty; unlike Articles 81 and 82, it is specifically aimed at Member States, but its function is to clarify the application of the competition rules to them, rather than to restrict their application. This Article has a close connection with Article 10. Moreover, Article 86 applies not only to competition rules but to a number of other Treaty obligations of Member States, including the adjustment of State monopolies (Article 31), free movement of labour (Article 39), the right of establishment (Article 43), and freedom to provide services (Article 49). Therefore Article 86 is normally necessarily applied in connection with another Treaty Article. Undoubtedly, however, its major significance and use, of increasing importance during recent years, has been in connection with breach by public undertakings in Member States of the rules contained in Articles 81 and 82.

Article 86 contains three paragraphs. The first lays down the broad principle:

(1) In the case of public undertakings and undertakings to which Member States grant special or exclusive rights, Member States shall neither enact nor maintain in force any measure contrary to the rules contained in this Treaty, in particular to those rules provided for in Article [12] and Articles [81 to 90].

The second paragraph contains a relatively narrow exemption to the basic principle contained in paragraph (1). Three cumulative conditions have to be satisfied before it comes into operation:

  (i) the undertakings concerned must have been entrusted with the 'operation of a service of general economic interest' or 'having the character of a revenue-producing monopoly'

---

[27] Art. 295 reads 'This Treaty shall in no way prejudice the rules in Member States governing the system of property ownership'.

(ii) the application of the Treaty rules would obstruct the performance in law or fact of the particular tasks assigned to it

(iii) in any case the development of trade must not be affected (if the exemption were otherwise available) to an extent contrary to the interests of the Community.

The third paragraph, dealt with in Section 4 of this chapter, provides the Commission with important powers to issue directives and make decisions relevant to liberalization of particular national markets and to prevent breaches of competition law by Member States.

3.2 PUBLIC UNDERTAKINGS AND UNDERTAKINGS WITH SPECIAL OR EXCLUSIVE RIGHTS

Two categories of undertaking are affected by these rules, namely 'public undertakings' and public, quasi-public, or private undertakings to which 'special or exclusive rights' have been granted. The general rules therefore apply, inter alia, to all public bodies which possess an identity independent from that of the Member State itself; this appears to exclude only actual departments or ministries of the government forming an integral part of the executive or administrative function of the State.[28]

Help in interpretation of the meaning of 'public undertaking' in Article 86(1) is obtained from Article 2 of Commission Directive 2006/111 on 'transparency of financial relations', introduced under the authority of Article 86(3), defining it as follows: 'Any undertaking over which the public authorities may exercise directly or indirectly a dominant influence by virtue of their ownership of it, their financial participation therein or the rules which govern it'.[29] That definition covers a very wide range of bodies, including large-scale nationalized industries responsible for the production and distribution of gas and electricity, national railway authorities, and many other public bodies, large and small, engaged in public economic activity. It includes the provision of services, even if these also involve the sale of goods.

The second category of undertaking mentioned in Article 86(1) is narrower since, although public undertakings could often be described as enjoying 'special' or 'exclusive' rights, the phrase refers to undertakings not actually public but which have nevertheless been granted such special privileges in order to carry out functions regarded as important by Member State governments. This category includes bodies authorized to operate State television and broadcasting services,[30] and bodies with rights to prescribe standards for particular sectors, such as agricultural produce. It also covers bodies authorized to run ports, airports, or other public facilities, and private operators of telecommunication services provided that the special rights which they

---

[28] See A. Pappalardo, 'Measures of the States and Rules of Competition of the EEC Treaty' [1984] Fordham Corp L Inst 515–41.

[29] [2006] OJ L318/17, replacing the original Commission Directive 80/723.

[30] See, e.g. Case 127/7 *BRT* v. *SABAM* 3 [1974] ECR 313: 2 CMLR 238, and Case 155/73 *Sacchi* [1974] ECR 409: 2 CMLR 177.

have been granted have been accorded only to a limited number of undertakings. In the United Kingdom, the Drivers and Vehicles Licensing Office in Swansea and Her Majesty's Stationery Office, both now privatized, would qualify, as would bodies with the right to supervise activities in particular sectors (such as the Meat and Livestock Commission) and bodies such as the Law Society or the General Medical Council responsible by statute for regulating particular trades or professions. 'Special rights' have also been defined by Directive 94/46, referred to in the context of the telecommunications industry in Section 4 below.

The 1984 European Court decision in *IAZ International Belgium* v. *Commission*[31] concerned a trade association granted such statutory rights by the Belgian government for approving appliances for connection to the public water supply, evidenced by the award of official certificates of conformity. The association used its rights in a way designed to force all manufacturers and importers of washing machines to become members, by making difficulties in the granting of such certificates to parallel importers and firms which preferred to import appliances without joining the association. Applying Article 86, the Court held that the association was subject to Article 81 notwithstanding its statutory functions.

A similar conclusion was reached in *RTT* v. *GB/INNO*,[32] where the Belgian national telephone company had legal powers to give licence approvals to telephone equipment imported for sale by third parties, but made qualification by them unduly onerous. Their actions were challenged by GB/INNO, a supermarket chain, importing cheaper forms of equipment which were in competition with RTT's more expensive equipment. The European Court held that it was a breach of Articles 82 and 86 for an enterprise such as RTT having a dominant position in one market (the operation of a telephone service) to reserve for itself ancillary activities (approval of equipment) which might enable it to foreclose other competitors from that market, given that any safety or other technical objective could be achieved by the publication of specifications rather than by licensing. Such standards could, moreover, be better enforced by an independent body, rather than by RTT as a national telephone operator.

Merci Convenzionali Porto di Genoa v. *Gabrielli*[33] provided the European Court with a further opportunity to define the types of undertaking caught by Article 86(1). Merci Convenzionali held exclusive rights under Italian law to operate the Port of Genoa and made excessive charges for its monopoly stevedoring services provided to Gabrielli, a company importing steel. The Court held that the port undertaking was one with 'exclusive rights' under 86(1) and that a Member State could not reserve jobs in stevedoring operations carried out by it for Italian nationals alone; such reservation was a breach not only of Article 39 but also of Article 82 since the port was a substantial part of the Common Market and was operated in a manner which was abusive. The

---

[31] Case 96/82 [1983] ECR 3369 [1984] 3 CMLR 276 (also known as *Anseau-Navewa* v. *Commission*).
[32] Case C-18/88 [1991] ECR I-5941.
[33] Case C-179/90 [1991] ECR I-5889: [1994] 4 CMLR 422. A similar case involved monopoly stevedoring rights in La Spezia, Case C-163/96 *Silvano Raso* [1998] ECR I-533: 4 CMLR 737.

abuses included charging excessively high prices and refusing to make use of modern technology in its operations.

Subsequent legislation adopted by the Italian government dealing with the arrangements for the use of temporary labour in the port were also struck down by the Commission as in breach of Articles 82 and 86, since it enabled the port authority to grant a monopoly in the supply of such labour to a single undertaking, which would thereby gain an advantage over all its competitors (*Community* v. *Italy*).[34] Italian legislation was also ruled to infringe these Articles in the *Piloting Tariffs* case[35] where, following an adverse decision by the European Court on the pilotage charges in the port of Genoa in *Corsica Ferries (No. 1)*[36] the amending legislation was also held by the Commission to be discriminatory against non-Italian shipowners.

3.3 THE LIMITED EXEMPTION IN ARTICLE 86(2)

The exemption from the competition rules contained in Article 86(2) for bodies entrusted with the operation of services of general economic interest or having the character of revenue-producing monopolies, has some similarities to Article 81(3); it is, however, a far more difficult exemption to obtain. The three cumulative conditions listed above have been strictly construed by the Community Courts, and are applicable to a relatively narrow range of bodies. Indeed some bodies falling within Article 86(1) would not meet the requirements for exemption under 86(2), though it is also possible that some private undertakings which would not fall under 86(1) (as neither 'public' nor having 'special or exclusive rights') might nevertheless qualify for exemption under (2) if carrying out tasks of sufficient 'general economic interest'.

This means that the scope of the exemption is limited to activities of a public undertaking which have a direct relationship with its main statutory functions and are not, for example, simply commercial activities which are ancillary to them. To obtain the benefit of this restricted exemption, however, the undertaking must show that there is an inherent conflict between the task imposed upon the undertaking and the application of the Treaty rules. That this is a substantial burden is clearly illustrated by the *Telespeed (British Telecom)* case[37] decided by the European Court in 1985. The Commission's decision was that British Telecom, at that time 'a public corporation established by statute holding a statutory monopoly on the running of telecommunication systems in the United Kingdom',[38] was abusing a dominant position within the meaning of Article 82. The abuse of its dominant position had occurred through the prohibition against private message-forwarding agencies in the United Kingdom transmitting messages, whose originators and recipients were resident in other countries, through the British network. This could be done at a cheaper rate than sending the messages direct between two other countries. It is interesting that the appeal against

---

[34] [1998] 4 CMLR 73.   [35] [1998] 4 CMLR 91.   [36] Case C-18/93 [1994] ECR I-1783.

[37] Case 41/83 [1985] ECR 873: 2 CMLR 368, reported under the name of *Italy* v. *Commission*.

[38] The quotation is taken from an account of the case at p. 96 of the *15th Annual Report* (1985). The case related to practices of British Telecom between 1975 and 1981, before its privatization.

the Commission's decision was not brought by British Telecom itself, which accepted the Commission decision, but by the Italian government which obviously regarded it as a precedent relevant to its own public undertakings.

Amongst the arguments raised by the Italian government was that Article 86(2) protected BT in acting to prohibit the activities of such independent agencies, so as to protect the services of general economic interest which BT was required by statute to carry out. The European Court rejected this argument, on the ground that in taking action against the private agencies BT was acting not in an official capacity, but simply in its commercial capacity, like any other undertaking engaged in business. The management of public telecommunications equipment and the placing of that equipment at the disposal of consumers against payment of a fee was inherently a business, not a governmental, activity. The rules under which telex messages were forwarded had been prepared by British Telecom alone and were not laid down by statute. They clearly formed an integral part of its business strategy and activity.

The leading case on the interpretation of the exemption under paragraph 2 is *Corbeau*.[39] Paul Corbeau ran a business in Liège which undertook to collect letters from the sender's home address to be delivered into a local area by the next morning, essentially a 'rapid delivery' service claimed to be superior to that of the normal post. Corbeau was prosecuted under Belgian law which gave the official post office exclusive rights to collect, transport, and deliver all mail in Belgium. The Liège Court sought guidance under Article 234 on the compatibility of this law with Article 86. The European Court ruled that it was contrary to Article 86 for Belgian law to prohibit competitors to the Post Office from providing services that the Post Office did not offer, with additional features such as collection from the sender's address, greater speed or reliability of delivery and distribution, and the possibility of changing the destination of a letter in the course of transit. Creators of such special services should not therefore face prosecution unless it could be shown that their existence would compromise the whole economic basis and equilibrium of the general postal service. Whether Corbeau's service was such a threat to the Belgian postal services was a matter for the national court to decide with the burden of proof firmly on the Post Office. The test laid down here is not very different from that provided in the *Telespeed* case referred to above, though in that case it was absolutely clear that BT's activity in prohibiting the activities of private message-forwarding agencies was not needed to protect the financial equilibrium of a universal telephone service.

Although a number of Italian measures concerning ports have been found illegal, as mentioned above, one of the rare findings of a service qualifying as one of 'general economic interest' and exempted by Article 86(2) was made in *Corsica Ferries (No. 2)*.[40] The services provided were local mooring operations in La Spezia and Genoa. The Court of Justice ruled that the provision of a general mooring service, available at all times and in all conditions, was within this definition, especially as the charges

[39]   Case C-320/91 [1993] ECR I-2533: [1995] 4 CMLR 621.
[40]   Case C-266/93 [1998] ECR I-3949: 5 CMLR 402.

payable had been subjected to widespread consultations with all affected parties and were based on objective local and national criteria. In any case the arrangements were justified under Article 46 of the Treaty on public security grounds.

3.4 THE GRANT OF EXCLUSIVITY

The necessity for providing exclusivity to a public undertaking has been challenged in several cases. In *Höfner and Elser* v. *Macrotron*[41] the German legal monopoly for employment recruitment held by an official body was reviewed. Whilst legally only the Bundesanstalt für Arbeit was allowed to act as an employment agency, in practice private bodies competed with it because the official body was clearly unable to cope with the volume of business. The client of a private employment agency refused to pay their charges on the basis that the activities of such an 'unofficial' agency were illegal. The reference under Article 234 to the European Court by the Munich Oberlandesgericht produced a finding that the legal status of the Bundesanstalt für Arbeit did not prevent it being an 'undertaking'; finding jobs for applicants was an economic activity. The fact that this body could not in practice handle the demands in a modern economy for employment services meant that its dominant position, under law, became illegal, nor did it require any special privileges under Article 86(2) in order to carry out its duties. Whilst it was an undertaking with responsibility for the operation of a service of 'general economic interest', the exemption under 86(2) only arose when application of Community competition rules would actually interfere with those responsibilities. Here it was not competition rules that made it impossible for the duties to be carried out, but the inadequacy of the institution, which had encouraged private companies to enter into competition with it.

In two Italian cases involving similar facts (*Job Centre Co-op*[42] and *Carra*[43]) national law had provided that only undertakings registered with the Ministry of Employment were allowed to operate as employment agencies for temporary workers. The Court of Justice found in both cases on Article 234 references that such a prohibition was in breach of the Article, if it created a situation where public placement offices were manifestly unable to satisfy demand for such services but it was impossible for private agencies to operate. The Court emphasized that national courts should refuse to implement such legislation without waiting for its formal withdrawal.

Exclusivity was also an issue in the *ERT* case.[44] ERT had an exclusive right to broadcast its television programmes in Greece and sought to prevent potential operators from competing with it, in particular DEP and the Mayor of Thessaloniki which had set up a local television station, TV 100. The Court found that the grant of that exclusive right would infringe Article 86 'if those rights are liable to create a situation in which that undertaking is led to infringe Article [82] by virtue of a discriminatory

---

[41] Case C-41/90 [1991] ECR I-1979: [1993] 4 CMLR 306.
[42] Case C-55/96 [1997] ECR I-7119: [1998] 4 CMLR 708.
[43] Case C-258/98 [2000] ECR I-4217: [2002] 4 CMLR 285.
[44] Case C-260/89 [1991] ECR I-2925: [1994] 4 CMLR 540.

broadcasting policy which favours its own programmes, unless the application of Article [82] frustrates its performance of the particular tasks entrusted for it'. Whereas in *Höfner* the facts showed that the exclusivity itself was an abuse, in ERT no such finding was made; what the Court made clear is that the possibility of abuse is sufficient to infringe Article 86, even if ERT had not taken any active steps to abuse the dominant position which Greek law had given it.

The Court has not been disposed to interpret Article 86(2) broadly, even where the functions performed by the undertaking are central to the proper functioning of the economy of a Member State. In *Züchner* v. *Bayerische Vereinsbank*,[45] Züchner was a customer of this German bank and queried whether it was entitled to agree with all other banks in the Federal Republic of Germany a uniform service charge for transfers of sums of a similar amount to other Member States. The bank argued that by reason of the special nature of the services which banks provide, especially in regard to transfer of capital, they should be considered as undertakings 'entrusted with the operation of services of general economic interest within the meaning of Article 86(2)'. Although the Court accepted that the transfer of funds from one Member State to another normally carried out by banks is an operation which has a public element, it ruled that banks do not come within the classification of Article 86(2), unless in performing such transfers they can be shown to operate a service of general economic interest with which they have been entrusted through measures adopted by government. The Court declined to make such a finding.

The same principle arose in the *Ijsselcentrale* case.[46] Local distributors of electricity in Holland complained to the Commission that an agreement between the four Dutch generators of electricity (all owned by local authorities) and their joint venture SEP violated Article 81. The restrictive clauses in the agreement not only provided for coordination of their activities but prevented imports and exports by any undertaking other than SEP and required the generators to impose similar restrictions on their local distributors, who in practice passed these obligations on to their own customers; these included large industrial concerns who might well have wished to import electricity, for example, from Germany. The Commission ruled that although the supply of electricity was a service of general economic interest, it could be carried out satisfactorily without the control of import and export required by the agreement; in other words, the restrictions were in the terminology of Article 81(3) 'not indispensable to the attainment of its objectives'.

The mere grant by the State to an organization of exclusive rights does not necessarily mean that there will automatically be a breach of the Article, as is illustrated by *La Crespelle*.[47] Here the French government had granted to some fifty approved bovine insemination centres throughout France exclusive rights in particular regions

---

[45] Case 172/80 [1981] ECR 2021: [1982] 1 CMLR 313.

[46] [1991] OJ L28/32: [1992] 5 CMLR 154 (the Commission decision) upheld on appeal by the Court of First Instance Case T-16/91 [1992] ECR II-2417: [1997] 4 CMLR 453 and by the European Court (save on one minor ground) Case C-19/93P [1995] ECR I-3319: [1997] 4 CMLR 392.

[47] Case C-323/93 [1994] ECR I-5077.

of the country. Another unofficial establishment with similar objects opened in the Mayenne area and was sued for damages by the local official centre. The defence to the claim was that the exclusive rights were in breach of Article 86(2). The justification given by the French government for them was that the long-term programme for improving the quality of breeding stock would be damaged if the centres (which were non-profit making) had to engage in price competition with other centres and were thereby forced to reduce their extensive research programmes. A procedure did exist for enabling orders from farmers or breeders for semen from outside France to be supplied through the centres. The Court of Justice upheld the legality of the exclusive arrangements under an Article 234 reference.

3.5 SERVICES OF GENERAL ECONOMIC INTEREST—A DEFINITION

In recent years concern has been expressed by a number of Member States, and especially France, that sufficient consideration had not been given in the application of Article 86(2) to the need for a broad and sympathetic definition of the phrase 'services of general economic interest' and their social function. A new Article 16 was introduced into the Treaty by the Treaty of Amsterdam emphasizing that the Community and Member States should each 'take care that such services operate on the basis of principles and conditions which enable them to fulfil their missions'. While the terms of the new Article do not alter the language or legal effect of the phrase, its existence means that in practice that the Commission has now had to adopt a more cautious approach to its interpretation.

This is shown by its Communication on Services of General Interest published in 2001,[48] which defined them as covering both market and non-market services, which Member States have classified as of general interest and subject to specific public service obligations, having an economic nature but not necessarily profit-making. The Commission acknowledged that to compile a comprehensive list of these services would be difficult and that Member States should be left to determine their exact scope. States remained free to lay down—by way of non-discriminatory legislation—standards of security, quality, and regularity on all operators. The Commission was at pains to emphasize that in its liberalization programmes it had always sought to maintain their 'public-sector obligation' content and that these programmes had themselves often improved the quality and affordability of such services. Since then the issue has been considered predominantly in the context of the State-aid rules, where it is important in situations where States seek to justify financial support for those who provide such services.[49]

While national courts are entitled to apply the first two conditions of Article 86(2), the determination of the third issue, whether the development of trade has been affected

---

[48] [2001] OJ C17/4: 4 CMLR 882.
[49] A Green Paper in 2003 was followed in 2005 by the adoption of a package of State aid measures, including an Art. 86(3) decision, see *35th Annual Report* (2005).

by the practices to an extent contrary to the interests of the Community, appears to be for the Commission alone to decide. This issue remained in doubt until the *Ahmed Saeed* case, confirmed later by guidelines published in 1991 on the application of EC competition rules to the telecommunications sector. It is clear that the national court can decide that competition rules apply to the organization with a responsibility for general economic services and that it does not need protection from the competition rules to carry these out. However, if the national court believes that protection is required, then it must pass to the Commission the responsibility for determining if the derogation from these rules is likely to affect trade to an extent contrary to the interests of the Community, by showing that trade between Member States in the relevant market has been sufficiently affected.[50]

4. ARTICLE 86(3): DIRECTIVES AND DECISIONS OF THE COMMISSION

4.1 THE INITIAL USE OF SUCH DIRECTIVES: TELECOMMUNICATIONS

This provision has become increasingly important over the last fifteen years, as the Commission realized that if Article 86 was to be an effective means of improving the competitiveness of vital sectors of the economies of Member States, then it would need to use its powers to address appropriate directives and decisions to them. The Commission has freedom here to act without the formal consent being required of the Council or any other Community institution, though it uses its power with discretion and only after extensive consultation.

The initial principal use of directives was in telecommunications; the Commission had for some time viewed with concern the practices of Member States in granting special or exclusive rights to national telecommunications organizations in drawing up specifications for the installation and operation of terminal equipment such as telephone exchanges. In order to remedy the situation it adopted Directive 88/301 which set out a number of principles for Member States to observe in order to improve the competitive situation applying to this equipment and to bring to an end existing breaches of the Article. The Directive provided that:

(1) Member States should withdraw such exclusive or special rights from their own favoured undertakings relating to telecommunications terminal equipment.

(2) Member States should ensure that undertakings have the right to import, market, connect, and maintain terminal equipment.

---

[50] Case C-157/94 *Commission v. Netherlands* [1997] ECR I-5699: [1998] 2 CMLR 373; Case C-159/94 *Commission v. France* [1997] ECR I-5815: [1998] 2 CMLR 373. M. Ross [2000] 25 EurLR 22–38.

(3) Type-approval specifications should be drawn up by bodies independent of the operation of telecommunications network or terminal providers.

(4) All contracts for leasing or maintenance of such equipment should be terminable on not more than a year's notice, thus preventing the use of long-term contracts as a means of shutting out new competitors for longer periods.

The validity of this Directive was challenged by France and other Member States. Eventually the issue reached the European Court of Justice[51] which upheld the right of the Commission to deal with breaches of Article 86 by such a Directive which specified in a general way the obligation which the Treaty imposed on Member States. It was not necessary, said the Court, for the Commission to utilize Article 226, which applied only when specific infringements of the Treaty had occurred. Nor was it necessary for the Commission to obtain from the Council separate measures under Articles 83 or 95 of the Treaty. Dealing with provisions (1) and (2) above, it upheld the requirement by the Commission that exclusivity should no longer be permitted for telecommunications operators since restrictions issued for this purpose by Member States would in any case be in breach of Article 28. Point (3) relating to type approval was also approved. The Court did, however, annul the prohibition in the Directive on special rights (largely because of failure by the Commission to provide an adequate definition of this category) and also those relating to long-term contracts under (4). The reason for this latter ruling was that the practice of long-term contracts was one adopted by independent undertakings rather than Member States and should, therefore, be dealt with under Article 81 or 82 rather than Article 86. Directive 88/301 was amended by Directive 94/46 in the light of this Court decision so as to incorporate a full definition of 'special rights', namely rights granted to a limited number of undertakings through any legislative, regulatory, or administrative instrument which, within a geographical area:

limits to two or more the number of such undertakings, otherwise than according to objective, proportional and non-discriminatory criteria, or designates, otherwise than according to such criteria, several competing undertakings, or confers on any undertaking or undertakings, otherwise than according to such criteria, any legal or regulatory advantages which substantially affect the ability of any other undertaking to import, market, connect, bring into service, and/or maintain telecommunication terminal equipment in the same geographical area under substantial equivalent conditions.

The related but even more significant Directive 90/388 was enacted in 1990 dealing with telecommunications services themselves.[52] This provided for the abolition of monopoly rights in the provision of such services and opened them up to competition; the arrival of digital networks and other technical advances had made possible

---

[51] Case C-202/88 *France* v. *Commission* [1991] ECR I-1223: [1992] 5 CMLR 552.

[52] This Directive was also challenged by some Member States, with an identical outcome to that in the earlier case referred to in fn. 51, in Cases C-271, 281, 289/90 [1992] ECR I-5833 (*Spain and Others* v. *Commission*).

enormous improvements in the quality, variety, and commercial value of these services, and liberalization of the market was essential if users were to benefit fully from them. It was necessary that each Member State set up an independent authority to carry out the regulatory functions previously dealt with by the national telephone authority. The Directive in its original terms provided that monopoly rights could be retained by Member States in four areas, namely:

(1) voice telephony services to the general public

(2) satellite services

(3) mobile telephony

(4) radio and TV broadcasts.

However, these services were brought within the scope of the Directive by amending legislation following the pattern set out in the 1995 Commission Green Paper, which set out its general policy towards liberalization of the telecommunications sector. Directive 94/46 brought satellite station equipment and satellite communication services within the scope of both Directives 88/301 and 90/388. A later Directive, 95/51, provided for the abolition of all restrictions on the transmission of telecommunications services on cable TV networks (apart from voice telephony services) from 1996, making possible the interconnection of all cable TV networks, and national public telephone networks. By Directive 96/2 mobile telephones were also brought within the scope of Directive 90/388, and Member States had thereafter to abolish all special or exclusive rights for incumbent national operators, enabling new entrants to set up rival systems, including access to suitable frequencies on equal terms with the incumbents. By bringing down in this way the cost to the public of mobile services, an important step was taken towards the complete liberalization of voice telephony.

The final and most important liberalization in this first stage was introduced by the 'Full Competition Directive' (Directive 96/19), taking effect from 1998. By that date any exclusive rights within a Member State for the provision of voice telephony services had to be abolished, and rules introduced to make competition with the incumbent national operators fully effective. For example, interconnection rules had to be transparent and non-discriminatory, and access for new entrants facilitated. Transition periods for adjustment were granted to the smaller Member States with less developed or smaller telephone networks. In 1999 the Services Directive was amended so as to require telecommunications and cable networks owned by the same undertaking to be operated as separate legal bodies.

The Commission later adopted the consolidating Directive 2002/77[53] which took effect in July 2003 and incorporated all the previous directives made under either

---

[53] [2002] OJ L249/21: [2002] 5 CMLR 1142. This Directive applies to all electronic 'networks' and 'services' rather than merely telecommunications 'networks' and 'services', reflecting technological convergence in recent years.

Article 86(3) or Article 95. Also in 2002 a second package of liberalization legislation was adopted, but this time in the form of Council and Parliamentary measures relating to the regulatory framework for telecommunications. Greater powers were vested in national regulatory authorities to apply the relevant rules within their own territories, rules which are now becoming more closely linked to competition policy, rather than regulatory principles, as the degree of competition in this sector increases. In November 2007 the Commission proposed a third package of liberalization measures, again to take the form of Council and Parliament Directives, including the proposal to create a new 'European Telecom Market Authority'. While Commission Directives are clearly no longer the instrument of choice in this area, their importance in enabling the Commission to start up the liberalization process cannot be overstated.

4.2 OTHER RELATED INITIATIVES OF THE COMMISSION

The Commission has not however been solely dependent on Article 86(3) and other Directives for liberalization of this market, and has also used its opportunities in cases under Articles 81 and 82 and above all under the Merger Regulation to move its policy of liberalization forward. It also took the initiative in 1998 and 1999 to investigate the charges made by fixed line operators and the interconnection charges between fixed and mobile operators throughout the Community, which resulted in significant price reductions for these services.

It also opened major sectoral inquiries under Article 12 of Regulation 17/62 into local loop unbundling, mobile phone 'roaming charges', leased lines and the provision of sports content over third-generation mobile networks. The Commission has also brought a large number of infringement actions under the directives against Member States, and Annual Reports record significant decisions of the Court of Justice in favour of the Commission in this sector. An important example of such cases was the decision rendered against France in 2001,[54] in which the French rules for financing the universal service elements of its telecommunications system were adjudged unfairly weighted against new entrants and lacking a sufficient degree of transparency and proportionality.

4.3 COUNCIL AND EUROPEAN PARLIAMENT DIRECTIVES—OTHER SECTORS

Directives were also issued by the Council (rather than the Commission) for both the electricity and gas sectors (96/92 and 98/30 respectively), under which national markets were opened up for the first time to new suppliers from abroad. These were superseded by a second package of directives adopted in 2003, but continuing concerns related to rises in wholesale prices, limited customer choice and entry barriers

---

[54] Case C-146/00 *Commission v. France* [2001] ECR I-9767.

led the Commission in 2005 to open sector inquiries into the electricity and gas markets. Final findings from these inquiries were announced in January 2007, together with proposals for a third legislative liberalization package of Council and Parliament measures. Individual enforcement measures, against both Member States and energy companies, and under merger review proceedings as well as Articles 81 and 82, continue to play a key role in this sector.

In the case of postal services, Directive 97/67 was issued jointly by the Council and the European Parliament requiring certain postal services to be opened to competition for the first time, and accompanied by a Notice from the Commission spelling out in detail the way in which the competition rules should be applied in the sector.

In looking across the whole range of markets traditionally dominated by national incumbents, including telecommunications, energy, and postal services, towards which the Community's liberalization policies have been directed, it is noteworthy that Article 86(3) has played, at an early stage, a leading part in establishing important principles and in putting pressure on Member States to accept the principle of change, even if in recent years the role of Council and Parliament Directives has become correspondingly greater. In its 2001 Annual Report[55] the Commission however fired a warning shot towards the Member States, in the context of opposition to its attempts to complete full liberalization in the gas and electricity sectors. It mentioned that Article 86(3) remained available as a means by which the Commission could advance its policies without first having to obtain Member State approval through the Council, if this should seem the only way forward. As we have seen, this has not yet so far occurred.

It should be emphasized that Article 86(3) has not given the Commission unlimited general freedom to impose legislation on Member States. The Court of Justice has in the various cases referred to above made it clear that the Commission is not entitled to impose new obligations, but only to determine the obligations already imposed on Member States by the Treaty with regard to public undertakings or undertakings granted special or exclusive rights. Its power is more limited than the Council's powers to issue directives through normal Community procedures in conjunction with the European Parliament and the Commission. The Commission has therefore used its powers under Article 86(3) sparingly and only where its awareness of the existence of many infringements by Member States of fundamental rules of the Treaty makes it necessary, to avoid having to bring a large number of infringement proceedings and to provide operators in the sector with the required minimum amount of legal certainty. Such Directives are moreover only introduced after considerable consultation and dialogue with the institutions of the Community, Member States, and other interested parties.

---

[55] Para. 94.

4.4 COMMISSION DECISIONS UNDER ARTICLE 86(3)

The nature of 'decisions' issued under Article 86(3) is quite different from that of directives. Decisions are given in specific cases where a Member State appears to be in breach of the Treaty rules, and particularly of Articles 81 and 82 or the terms of an Article 86 Directive. Such decisions have affected a number of sectors. The first such decision is recorded in the *15th Annual Report*,[56] declaring a Greek law requiring all public property to be insured with a particular state-owned insurance company to be incompatible with the Treaty. Subsequent *Annual Reports* record several other examples. In December 1993 the Commission, following complaints from shipping lines, issued a decision requiring Denmark to bring to an end a refusal to grant access to port facilities at Rødby in Denmark, or alternatively to construct new facilities for such lines on land adjacent to the existing port so that competitive services between Denmark and Germany could be instituted. Rødby had been owned and managed by the State-owned Danish Railway Company which had exclusive rights to organize rail traffic in that country. The Commission found[57] that there was no objective justification for the refusal of the Danish authorities to provide port facilities either in the existing port or on the adjacent available land in order to strengthen the joint dominance of the Danish and German State railway companies on the existing ferry route from Rødby. This case had elements in common with earlier Article 82 cases on access to essential facilities (see Chapter 14, Section 9).

Liberalization in the mobile-telephony sector led to infringement proceedings against both Italy and Spain for raising barriers to entry against would-be competitors with the incumbent national operator. A formal decision was taken in the case of Italy[58] for discriminating in favour of Telecom Italia Mobile, the State operator, against Omnitel Pronto Italia by requiring Omnitel to pay a substantial entry fee for their licence although no equivalent payment was required from Telecom Italia. The decision of the Commission provided that Italy must either insist on an equivalent payment from the incumbent operator or adopt corrective measures in favour of Omnitel that would be equivalent in economic terms. In other words, the decision placed the Italian government under an obligation not to undermine the competition introduced by the requirement of other directives to authorize the second mobile telephone operator. In reaching its decision the Commission relied on the European Court's judgment in the 1991 *Terminal Equipment* case on Directive 88/301.[59] In 1996 an equivalent decision was rendered against Spain in respect of the initial licence fee imposed on Airtel Movil as the public operator, Telefonica, had been granted its licence without an initial licence fee.[60]

The landing fees structure at Brussels Zaventem airport also provoked intervention by the Commission.[61] The airport operated a discount system on landing fees based on

[56] (1985) pp. 201–2.   [57] *1993 Annual Report*, p. 471.
[58] *1995 Annual Report*, p. 54: [1996] 4 CMLR 700.   [59] See fn. 52.
[60] *1996 Annual Report*, p. 55.   [61] [1996] 4 CMLR 232.

the minimum number of daily arrivals related to a particular size of aircraft. The effect of the discount structure was that only a carrier based at the airport and having a very large number of arrivals and departures could gain the benefit of these discounts. This rule favoured Sabena which had by far the largest number of movements, but the scale was not cost-related and did not follow the recommendations of the ICAO as to the criteria for assessment of landing fees, which are a significant part of an airline's operating costs. The Commission found that the airport authority was applying dissimilar conditions to other airlines than Sabena, placing the majority of them at a competitive disadvantage in breach of Article 82(c). Since it was a Member State which had established the relevant fee system, this State measure infringed both Articles 82 and 86. *Annual Reports* record successful action taken against other Member States in respect of discriminatory landing fees charged at national airports, including Portugal[62] and France in 1999 and Spain in 2000.

Although the use of Article 86(3) decisions has been rarer in recent years, in 2004 the Commission adopted such a decision finding that Germany had infringed Articles 82 and 86 through provisions in its postal regulatory framework that allowed it to extend its market power from reserved services, where it had special rights, into the market for mail preparation, where it had no such rights, and thereby to discriminate against certain types of commercial service providers in the postal sector.

The most recent case of this kind occurred in 2008, when the Commission made a finding against Greece for giving a public undertaking special rights amounting almost to a monopoly to extract lignite, which in Greece is the cheapest fuel for producing electricity. As a result of this privileged access the undertaking was able to exclude or hinder market entry, thereby maintaining its dominant position in the wholesale electricity market.

FURTHER READING

J. FAULL and A. NIKPAY (eds.), *The EC Law of Competition* (2nd edn, OUP, 2007), Ch. 6. by J. L. Buenida Sierra.

L. HANCHER, 'Case note on Corbeau' [1994] 31 CMLRev 105.

L. HANCHER, 'Community, State and Market' in P. Craig and G. de Burca (eds.) *The Evolution of EU Law* (Oxford: OUP, 1999).

J. HOLMES, 'The Control of State Action' in V. Korah (ed.), *Competition Law of the European Community* (Lexis Nexis, 2004).

M. Ross, 'Article 16 and Services of General Interest: From Derogation to Obligation' [2000] 25 ELRev 22.

---

[62] [2002] 4 CMLR 31.

J. TEMPLE LANG, 'The duties of co-operation of national authorities and courts under Art. 10' [1998]: 23 *EurLR* 109 and [2001] 26 *EurLR* 84.

H. SCHEPEL, 'Delegation of Regulatory Powers to Private Parties under EC Competition Law' [2002] 39 *CMLR* 31.

P. SLOT, 'Applying the Competition Rules in the Healthcare Sector' [2003] *ECLR* 580.

22

INTERNATIONAL ASPECTS OF EC COMPETITION LAW

1. INTRODUCTION

This chapter examines the three main ways by which the Community has been able to surmount the limitations of its territorial legal jurisdiction in order to address foreign anti-competitive activity that has an impact either on competition in Europe or on the competitiveness of European companies abroad.

The first method involves applying EC competition law in what some might view as an 'extraterritorial' manner, that is, to foreign undertakings themselves, when their actions have an anti-competitive impact in Europe. This is different, of course, from the direct application of the principles contained in Articles 81 and 82 in countries that are members of the EEA. In such situations, this is simply domestic enforcement of the European regime by the governments of those countries, rather than extraterritorial enforcement of EC law by the Community institutions themselves.[1] While the 'effects-based' rationale for extraterritorial enforcement is generally recognized (if not wholly accepted) as a matter of public international law, the European institutions do not generally justify their foreign enforcement activities on this ground. Indeed, they do not describe such enforcement as 'extraterritorial' at all. Rather than reaching out to foreign conduct on the basis that it *affects* trade within the common market, the European institutions have laboured to explain that when they have enforced their law against a particular foreign actor, they have done so on the basis that the foreigner is responsible for conduct that is actually occurring *within* Europe.

The first section of this chapter describes the various legal tests and contortions of reasoning in which the Commission and the Courts have had to engage in order to achieve this result. The section then examines some of the problems that this can cause both for European enforcers and for foreign undertakings engaged in commerce

---

[1] The EEA Agreement effective from 1 January 1994 ensures that the EC Treaties and secondary legislation made by the Council and Commission are also applied in parallel to Norway, Iceland, and Liechtenstein, known as the three EFTA States. The EEA Agreement contains provisions which match as closely as possible the equivalent clauses of the Rome Treaty including those dealing with competition policy. Arts. 53 and 54 of the EEA Agreement are the equivalent to Arts. 81 and 82 of the Rome Treaty. The EFTA Surveillance Authority is responsible for ensuring the application of the Agreement, subject to the jurisdiction of the EFTA Court.

in an increasingly interconnected global economy, particularly where the 'effects' test for jurisdiction appears to be gaining greater acceptance amongst other competition authorities than the test employed by the Community's own institutions. The section also reminds readers of the Commission's own initial preference for justifying its international enforcement activities in terms of the 'effects' test, a preference which is increasingly reasserting itself, particularly in merger cases. The section concludes that, to the extent that unilateral enforcement action against foreign anti-competitive conduct is necessary and feasible, the difficulties that the 'European' test for jurisdiction presents for effective and acceptable enforcement will lead the Community inevitably to rely more on the effects test, rather than on its own creative 'European' model.

The second method of addressing foreign conduct with anti-competitive consequences for Europeans grows out of the limitations of the first. No matter which test is used to justify extraterritorial application of laws, purely unilateral enforcement will always be an uphill and lonely struggle against undertakings that will be keen to remain at a distance. The most obvious problem is an evidentiary one though: while it may be clear what anti-competitive harm a foreign activity may do to the common market, the evidence of the activity itself may reside in another country. No matter how powerful they may seem, European Commission officials cannot simply arrive in another sovereign jurisdiction and commence a dawn raid. Nor will sending information requests to foreign undertakings guarantee as full a response as may be desired, or indeed any response at all.

The only way that the Commission can get the evidence that it requires is by combining forces with the competition authority that is responsible for the undertakings' 'home' jurisdiction, or the jurisdiction where the evidence required is thought to be located. This is why the Community institutions have been building bridges across various political borders so that the Commission can exchange information with, and benefit from the enforcement powers of, the American, Canadian, Japanese, and other governments. Bilateral enforcement efforts based on such international agreements can help authorities to address conduct that harms competition and consumers within their respective jurisdictions. The Commission has also noted how such enforcement cooperation can help trade.[2] In particular, the European Commission can use 'positive comity' commitments that trigger foreign enforcement activity against foreign conduct which may not be harming competition and consumers in Europe, but may be preventing European undertakings from entering a particular foreign market. At the same time, of course, it is important to note that the American and Canadian authorities can use the same instruments to incite European enforcement action against European undertakings that may be harming American or Canadian exporters or investors.

The second section of this chapter thus examines the main aspects of the bilateral agreements that the Community has signed with its counterparts in other jurisdictions

---

[2] Communication to the Council, submitted by Sir Leon Brittan and Karel Van Miert, 'Towards an International Framework of Competition Rules', COM (96) 296 final, 18 June 1996 (hereinafter, 'Commission Communication').

and some of the benefits and limitations of these commitments from the perspectives of both the enforcers and the private sector. In particular, it examines concerns that have been raised by undertakings to ensure that exchanges of information among competition authorities do not jeopardize the confidentiality of business information.

The third method employed by the Community to address foreign anti-competitive activity stems from the limitations of the first two methods. Unilateral extraterritorial enforcement and bilateral enforcement cooperation would not be necessary, so goes the argument, if the Community's trading partners would only make sure that they were addressing anti-competitive conduct in their own markets which may also be distorting competition in the common market, or which may be impeding European companies' abilities to access those foreign markets. This was the primary rationale for the Community's quest for a global solution to international restraints of trade and competition in the mid to late 1990s. The third and final section of this chapter thus examines the various proposals that the Community made in this regard along with some competition commitments already present and arising on the global stage, particularly through the work of the International Competition Network.

2. EXTRATERRITORIALITY AND THE EFFECTS TEST

2.1 THE PRINCIPLE OF EXTRATERRITORIALITY

By definition, extraterritorial enforcement conjures up images of a law being applied beyond the territorial ambit of its sovereign legitimacy. It is not surprising then that this is tolerated only in the exception, and even then remains tainted by a somewhat pejorative connotation. To counter this, perhaps, the long arm of American antitrust law is only extended into another country's territory when it can be justified objectively. The American authorities and courts thus permit the application of many US laws (including antitrust laws) to foreign actors where the latter's conduct could be seen to have a 'direct, substantial and reasonably foreseeable' effect on US commerce.[3] There are various attractions to this test; for one thing, an action's effects are presumably something that is capable of being determined objectively. The 'directness' and 'substantiality' of that effect ought to be capable of proof through analysis of economic evidence. Resort to legal argument will be required to demonstrate the 'reasonable foreseeability' of such effects, but even then, it will be hard to argue with the facts, and again, economic evidence would be useful to identify which consequences were likely to be foreseen. Some cases of extraterritorial enforcement will be easier to justify than others. In the case of cartel activity at least, price increases will have been the primary

---

[3] Foreign Trade Antitrust Improvements Act of 1982 (7 *Sherman Act*, 15 USC 6a).

rationale for the activity in question. Even if clever defence counsel can credibly deny this, such effects would be hard to deny as being 'reasonably foreseeable' consequences of the activity. It may become more difficult to display the effects with other conduct—such as exclusive purchasing commitments or a particular merger transaction—but this does not mean that the effects test itself is any less relevant or applicable to these situations as well.

Despite the initially appealing logic of the effects test, American legal incursions have been met with blocking statutes in many countries, who simply will not tolerate their citizens—whether corporate or corporeal—being prosecuted or sued under the laws of another government.[4] This is particularly so when the actions occur wholly within the 'home' territory, when they may or may not be illegal under domestic law, or may even have been authorized by the domestic government. While the Community institutions themselves have not erected blocking statutes, they have made clear their distaste for extraterritorial enforcement in the Commission Communication and otherwise. This policy stance has meant that the Commission has had to find other justifications when it has wanted to address foreign conduct with anti-competitive effects within Europe.

The next section examines how the Community has been, for the most part, wary of using extraterritorial enforcement in the true sense of the word. Rather than allow itself to be perceived as reaching out and applying EC law within another sovereign territory, the Community institutions have instead devised various legal tests that seek to bring the conduct and the culprits *within* the ambit of EC law.

The European Commission, Council, and Courts have all provided various grounds by which EC competition law can be applied to foreign undertakings whose conduct has anti-competitive effects in the common market. As mentioned above, the criteria differ, but the result is the same; by typifying the activity in question as being domestic, the conduct is seen to fall within European legal jurisdiction, and no resort to 'extraterritorial' enforcement is required. Nevertheless, while an eminently neat legal solution may appear to have been devised, the contortions that are required to label some conduct as European and other conduct as not raises problems both for businesses and for enforcers.

2.2 THE GROUP ECONOMIC UNIT DOCTRINE

The most established basis in EC competition law for asserting jurisdiction over foreign companies is the doctrine of the 'group economic unit'.[5] This test attributes to foreign parents responsibility for the anti-competitive activities of a subsidiary that is present and active in Europe and over which they supposedly exert some control; and owing to the supposed control that the parent can exert and should have exerted over

---

[4] In Canada, the Foreign Extra-territorial Measures Act, RSC CL F-29 (1985) and in the UK, the Protection of Trading Interests Act, 1980, Ch. 11.

[5] Case 48/69 *ICI* v. *Commission* [1972] ECR 619: CMLR 557, Case C-73/95P *Viho Europe BV* v. *Commission* [1996] ECR I-5457: [1997] 4 CMLR 419.

the subsidiary, the parents and other relevant members of the group may be brought within the jurisdiction of European law.

This method of asserting jurisdiction is not of course unproblematic. In its reasoning, the Court has emphasized the corporate structural relationship between the parent and the subsidiary and merely considered the parent's *ability* to control the latter, rather than *whether* that control was actually exercised. Consequently the facts of each case do not need to be analysed other than to set out the relevant corporate organization chart, and show where control could and, presumably, should be exercised. In a post-Enron world, it is perhaps natural to seek to attribute corporate responsibility where control is possible, and thus should have been exercised. However, it is still at least arguable that European jurisdiction over foreign undertakings should be based on a role that is more active than that. After all, the European subsidiary is present in Europe, and available to be fined. Where the subsidiary is being wound down, however, or has insufficient assets to satisfy a judgment against it, enforcers will naturally want to seek the controlling mind of the company group, whether or not it actually controlled the anti-competitive conduct in question. Whether the parent should be entitled to rely on a defence that it was not involved in the subsidiary's daily activities and should not therefore be responsible for all of its actions raises difficult issues that would benefit from further clarification by the Commission and the Court.

2.3 THE CONCEPT OF IMPLEMENTATION OF AN AGREEMENT: *DYESTUFFS* AND *WOODPULP* (NO. 1)

Where matters have become rather more confused, however, is with the rejection by the Court of the Commission's use of the effects doctrine itself to justify asserting jurisdiction against foreign cartel members. The conflicting policy interests involved are most clearly displayed by a brief account of the arguments of the various parties, Advocates General, and interested governments in the *Dyestuffs* and *Woodpulp* cases.

ICI was alleged to have assisted in concerted practices relating to price increases for various dyestuffs by giving price instructions to its wholly owned subsidiary incorporated in Belgium, although itself as a parent company demonstrably neither directly present in nor trading with the Community. The arguments relied on by the Commission in support of the imposition of a fine on ICI rested on three separate though related bases: firstly, that ICI by its actions, notably the giving of such instructions for performance by its subsidiary, had *actually been itself engaged* in the concerted practices, treating the subsidiary company as if it were simply the agent of the parent; and secondly was that ICI was present within the Community *by reason of the corporate control* it was entitled to exercise over its subsidiary (the 'group economic unit' argument). The third ground was that in any case the actions taken by ICI had *produced effects* within the Common Market.

Interestingly, Advocate General Mayras came down in favour of acceptance only of the third argument. He conceded that under international law the Community could exercise jurisdiction outside its territorial bounds, but based its right to take action simply on the effects doctrine, for the application of which he laid down three conditions, namely that the effects must be (a) direct and immediate, (b) reasonably foreseeable, and (c) substantial. It did not extend to enable the Community to implement 'coercive measures or indeed any measure of enquiry, investigation or supervision outside the territorial jurisdiction of the authorities concerned where execution would inevitably infringe the internal sovereignty of the State on whose territory they claim to act'. The Court was careful to avoid either specific acceptance or rejection of the findings of the Advocate General, but based its decision against ICI on the second argument raised, namely that of the 'group economic unit' theory. It said: 'The fact that a subsidiary has separate legal personality is not sufficient to exclude the possibility of imputing its conduct to the parent company... In the circumstances, the formal separation between these companies, resulting from their separate legal personality, cannot outweigh the unity of their conduct on the market for the purposes of applying the rules on competition.'[6]

In reaching its decision the Court implicitly rejected the argument of the UK government contained in a well-known aide-memoire of October 1969 to the Commission. It is argued that the attribution of the activities of even a wholly owned subsidiary through its parent company involved an unacceptable rejection of its separate corporate status; in the view of the UK government, ICI could not possibly be held liable for the activities even of its subsidiary on the Continent. In other words it rejected the whole 'group economic unit' argument. However, this view had changed by the time of the *Woodpulp* case.

In the *Woodpulp* case, the Commission prosecuted a foreign cartel for raising prices within the Common Market.[7] The accused were producers of bleached sulphate pulp established outside the Community who had entered into price-fixing arrangements. The producers were exporting either directly to purchasers within the Community or though branches, subsidiaries, agencies or other establishments in the Community. The Commission established jurisdiction by concluding that the *effect* of the agreements and practices on prices announced and/or charged to customers and on resale of pulp within the EEC was not only *substantial* but *intended* and was the primary and direct result of the agreements and practices. The producers appealed the decision, claiming that it involved an incorrect assessment of the territorial scope of Article 81. The Court did not refer specifically to the effects test in its judgment. Instead it ruled that the conduct infringing Article 81 consisted of two elements, the formation of the agreement and its implementation. Wholly ignored was the logical third step: that of

---

[6] [1972] ECR 662–3: CMLR 629. The 'group economic unit' concept was further confirmed soon afterwards in both Case 15/74 *Centrafarm BV* v. *Sterling Drug Inc.* [1974] ECR 1147: 2 CMLR 480, and Cases 6–7/73 *Istituto Chemioterapico Italiano and Commercial Solvents Corporation* v. *Commission* [1974] ECR 223: 1 CMLR 309. Advocate General Warner at ECR 264: 1 CMLR 321, stated that it is difficult but not impossible for a subsidiary to rebut the presumption of de facto control by its parent.

[7] Cases C-89, 104, 114, 116–17, 125–29/85. *Ahlstrom and Others* v. *Commission* [1988] ECR 5193: 4 CMLR 901. See Ch. 7, pp. 92–3.

the anti-competitive effect. The Court simply stated that 'the producers in this case *implemented* their pricing agreement within the common market. It is immaterial in that respect whether or not they had recourse to subsidiaries, agents, sub-agents, or branches within the Community in order to make their contacts with purchasers within the Community'.[8] In *Woodpulp*, since the cartel agreement had been 'implemented' within the Common Market—through a marketing organization run by the parties in a Member State—it became a European matter and was thus subject to European competition law.

Of course, the fact that the Court did not expressly reject the effects test means that its application as a legal basis for jurisdiction is still possible. Whether or not there is any significant difference in fact between the two tests is the subject of some debate. Van Gerven A-G, along with other commentators, has found that the two doctrines can 'lead to different results in a narrow but significant group of cases'.[9] For example, there are doubts whether the implementation doctrine would establish jurisdiction in cases of direct sales by companies to customers within the Community in the absence of any type of marketing organization, or in respect of refusal to supply or collective boycotts entered into outside the Community by undertakings established outside the Community. Similarly, the implementation doctrine's insistence on there being some form of activity by the accused parties on the ground in the Community means that a wholly foreign cartel agreement which raises prices, but does so through arms'-length sellers, may arguably not be implemented in a sufficiently 'European' manner to attract European jurisdiction. As such, considerable harm may be done to consumers that would be able to be addressed if the effects test were used instead. At the same time, though, the fact that the Commission does not require any proof of anti-competitive effect in order to justify an assertion of jurisdiction means that some conduct that should not be investigated at all may come under DG Comp's magnifying glass. This would happen in the case of business practices that are clearly implemented in the common market, and which may appear to harm competition, but where no anti-competitive effect in Europe can be proven. A network of vertical restraints, or an export cartel, that may harm foreign competitors or foreign consumers, respectively, are obvious examples. Such conduct would not attract a fine or other remedial measure unless there was evidence of a substantive offence, of course, but it is at least arguable that the Commission is free to assert jurisdiction over any undertakings with operations in Europe without any evidence that their conduct actually has an anti-competitive impact within the common market. Without a requirement of having to prove reasonably foreseeable anti-competitive effects resulting from their conduct, too many companies may be brought within the scope of an initial investigation.

[8] Cases C-89, 104, 114, 116–17, 125–9/85. *Ahlstrom and Others* v. *Commission* [1988] ECR 5243: 4 CMLR 941 (emphasis added).

[9] W. Van Gerven, 'EC Jurisdiction in Antitrust Law Matters: The *Woodpulp* Judgment' [1989] Fordham Corp L Inst 451–83; J. P. Griffin, 'Foreign Governmental Reactions to U.S. Assertion of Extra-territorial Jurisdiction' [1998] 19 ECLR 64–73.

Who is to say that the Court is wrong in not simply using the effects test to justify extraterritorial enforcement? Other competition authorities are also reluctant to admit that they enforce their laws extraterritorially. The American authorities have rarely admitted that they enforce their laws in an 'extraterritorial' manner, even when they are clearly prosecuting foreign undertakings or individuals for foreign activity that has harmful effects in the United States. They focus on the harm to United States commerce.[10] Presumably, such reasoning would bring much of the same type of conduct within the ambit of European law. However, the European Court has preferred to eschew any proof of anti-competitive harm in order to allow the Commission to assert jurisdiction, and instead has preferred to create a legal fiction that focuses on creating the impression that a foreign agreement is actually European. From an enforcement approach this may be a more effective way of addressing harmful effects that occur but are difficult to establish. However, it seems that the chance of either inadequate or inappropriate enforcement is higher under the current Community regime.

2.4 THE MERGER REGULATION: CONCENTRATIONS WITH A COMMUNITY DIMENSION

The third way of bringing foreign undertakings within European jurisdiction exists by virtue of the Merger Regulation.[11] Indeed, as Article 1 makes clear, the Regulation itself will only apply where a concentration has what is defined is a 'Community dimension', in terms of involving the requisite amount of sales within Europe.[12] Article 5(1) goes on to specify that Community turnover consists of 'products sold and services provided to undertakings or consumers, in the Community'. As such, unlike the Court's approach in *Woodpulp*, no distinction is made between sales made directly, or made through a branch, agent, subsidiary or distributor within the Community by a foreign undertaking. Defining business activity in this manner avoids any admission that what is really going on is the extraterritorial application of European law to foreign undertakings. After all, their sales are 'in' Europe and thus, the merger's effects are also likely to be there, at least to the extent of those sales.

It is difficult to distinguish the effects test from the turnover test in this regard, and indeed, the Commission has been quite explicit in linking the two concepts. In the *Gencor* case, the Commission blocked a merger between two companies incorporated in South Africa that would have led to 'the creation of a dominant duopoly in the platinum and rhodium markets as a result of which competition would have been significantly impeded in the common market'.[13] The Commission justified

[10] In *F. Hoffman-La Roche Ltd. V. Empagran* S.A. 124 S Ct. 2359 (2004) the United States Supreme Court restricted the extraterritorial application of U.S. antitrust laws by holding that purchasers in foreign markets who claimed injury from antitrust violations could not sue in U.S. courts simply by alleging that they were harmed by conduct which also injured consumers in the U.S.
[11] Council Regulation (EC) No 139/2004 on the control of concentrations between undertakings, [2004] OJ L 24/1.
[12] See Ch. 16, Section 2.
[13] Case T-102/96 *Gencor Ltd* v. *Commission* (1999) ECR II-753: 4 CMLR 971, at para. 91.

exercising its jurisdiction using language usually associated with the effects test stating that 'application of the regulation is justified under public international law when it is foreseeable that a proposed concentration will have an immediate and substantial effect in the Community…It is therefore necessary to verify whether the three criteria of immediate, substantial and foreseeable effect are satisfied in this case'.[14] The Court found that the 'concentration would have the direct and immediate effect of creating the conditions in which the abuses were not only possible but economically rational'.[15] The Court concluded that 'it was in fact foreseeable that the effect of creating a dominant duopoly position in a world market would also be to impede competition significantly in the Community, an integral part of that market.'[16] The underlying rationale for the turnover tests in the Merger Regulation is indistinguishable from the 'effects' test.

A similar situation arose in the *Boeing/McDonnell-Douglas* case,[17] where the Commission exercised its jurisdiction over a merger between two US corporations on the basis that both parties exceeded the Community turnover requirements. Commissioner Mario Monti commented that the Court had made clear that the Commission's application of EC competition law to foreign undertakings in such cases was in accordance with the principles of public international law where the merger produced direct, substantial, and foreseeable effects within the Community.[18] The propriety of the effects test has thus been clearly accepted in the context of merger control.

From this description of the three tests, it might be concluded that the logical way for EC competition policy to develop in this area would be to accept the effects test more fully, at least in order to supplement the 'group economic unit' doctrine and to replace, where inconsistent, the peculiar 'implementation' doctrine. Without a firm statement in this regard from the Community institutions, however, this will have to evolve gradually. The coherence and effectiveness of EC competition law enforcement would, however, benefit from the formal adoption of the effects test sooner rather than later. This is particularly the case as the occasions when the Commission needs to reach beyond its borders increase. When it takes jurisdiction over a merger there is a clear, and effects-based, rationale. For the credibility of EC law within Europe and internationally, both among undertakings and other competition authorities, this approach needs to spread to the non-merger area of EC law enforcement. The Community's credibility amongst other competition authorities is important, not least because the occasions where the Commission needs the help of such comrades-in-arms in order to address truly foreign conduct far outnumber the situations where it can handle such conduct itself. The next section examines this in more detail.

---

[14] Paras. 90, 92.   [15] Para. 94.

[16] Para. 100.   [17] Case IV/M877 [1997] OJ L336/1: [1997] 5 CMLR 270.

[18] M. Monti, 'Co-operation Between Competition Authorities—A Vision for the Future', The Japan Foundation Conference, Washington DC, 23 June 2000, at p. 2, available at <http:www.europa.eu.int>.

3. ENFORCEMENT COOPERATION THROUGH BILATERAL MEASURES

3.1 THE NEED FOR COOPERATION

The Community has recognized that it cannot merely rely on its own legal concepts and procedures to act against foreign business conduct that harms the common market. There are a number of reasons for this. First of all, if such conduct does not harm competition or consumers within Europe, it is difficult to use the 'European' tests to address foreign conduct, even if it may be impeding the ability of European competitors to access and compete in foreign markets. The effects doctrine would be no easier to apply in such cases as well, of course. Finally, extraterritorial enforcement brings with it a great many political 'negative externalities' as it necessarily involves the perception of enforcement activity in another sovereign territory.

This section examines how the Community has tried to address the limitations of unilateral extraterritorial enforcement by developing increasingly detailed enforcement co-operation agreements with foreign governments. To some extent such arrangements merely offer a formal framework within which a great deal of informal cooperation has already been occurring between the European Commission and foreign authorities. To that extent, though, the agreements provide an important imprimatur of legitimacy to such ad hoc cooperative enforcement activities, as well as a formal mechanism through which they can be channelled and intensified. The exchange of confidential information about a particular international case is a very important way of ensuring that the best-placed authority can effectively address it. Even more important mechanisms, like positive comity for example, have been created for authorities to use to request enforcement action in another State. Positive comity is particularly helpful when it allows the Community to induce another authority to enforce its laws in its own jurisdiction, for example, to address business practices that impede the entry of European competitors, provided that there is evidence of harm to competition in the market of the requested authority. The next subsections examine the main aspects of the agreements that have been signed to date, the benefits they provide, and some of their limitations.

3.2 BILATERAL AGREEMENTS MADE BY THE COMMUNITY

To bridge the divide between national competence and international anti-competitive activity, governments have negotiated legal assistance treaties, which are usually of a bilateral nature. The Community and the US entered into their first antitrust cooperation agreement in 1991.[19] This agreement provides for forms of cooperation that have

---

[19] [1991] 4 CMLR 823. Following a successful challenge by France to the Commission, on the basis that the Agreement should have been made by the Council (Case C-327/91 [1994] ECR I-3641: 5 CMLR 517) the Agreement was ratified in 1995 by the Council [1995] OJ L95/45.

become fairly standard in most similar accords between other jurisdictions. It contains what are known as passive, or traditional, comity provisions, which permit an active communication of information and a consideration of a trading partner's interests, but do not involve any 'triggering' of enforcement activity in another jurisdiction. This latter action, by contrast, can only arise when a positive comity request is made, and one country asks another to begin enforcement proceedings in its own jurisdiction.

In terms of traditional comity, the 1991 Community/United States Agreement provides that the authorities will notify one another when practices or enforcement activities would affect the other party to the Agreement. The Agreement also contains fairly basic provisions to allow information to be exchanged between the authorities and permitting them to coordinate their enforcement activities in accordance with 'traditional comity', explained in more detail below. However, it is important to note that in complying with such commitments the Agreement cannot be interpreted inconsistently with US or Community legislation. Perhaps most important in this regard are rules which protect the confidentiality of information that is gathered in investigations. The 1991 Agreement also contains certain basic provisions to provide positive comity that are examined in more detail below. In 1998 the Community and United States entered into a separate accord expressly supplementing these positive comity commitments. In particular, they specified the conditions under which the party requesting enforcement action should suspend its own enforcement activities and let the requested party 'take the lead', so to speak.[20] This suspension arrangement was limited, however, to competitor-only complaints dealing with allegations of export restraints, i.e. where the anti-competitive activities at issue do not harm the requested or requesting parties' consumers (or harm them only incidentally) and the primary problem is exclusionary conduct directed at the requesting party's competitors.

The Community and Canada also entered into a cooperation agreement in 1999[21] which is broadly similar to the first Community–US accord of 1991 and which provides for reciprocal notification of cases under investigation by either authority, coordination by the two authorities of their enforcement activities, positive and negative comity provisions and the exchange of information between the parties, while also not affecting either party's confidentiality obligations with respect to such information. Other accords have also been signed with Japan, Brazil, Israel, Mexico, Korea, South Africa, Ukraine, and Russia, and EEA countries have signed cooperation agreements with the Commission, which are also designed to ensure that they align their enforcement regimes with European law.[22]

---

[20] [1998] OJ L173/26: [1999] 4 CMLR 502.   [21] [1999] OJ L175.

[22] Japan: Agreement between the European Community and the Government of Japan concerning cooperation on anti-competitive activities, [2003] OJ L183/12; Israel: Euro-Mediterranean Agreement establishing an association between the European Communities and their Member States, of the one part, and the State of Israel, of the other part, [2000] OJ L147/3 (this contains competition provisions at Ch. 3); Mexico: Economic Partnership, Political Coordination and Cooperation Agreement between the European Community and its Member States, of the one part, and the United Mexican States, of the other part, [2000] OJ L276/44 (competition provisions at Title V, Art. 11); Korea: Memorandum of Understanding on cooperation between the Fair Trade Commission of the Republic of Korea and the Competition Directorate General

Despite the lack of any formal arrangement, the Commission also cooperates informally with many other authorities, in particular Australia and New Zealand. Many of these informal contacts come about as a result of the Commission's participation in regional and multilateral meetings of competition authorities, at the OECD, the International Competition Network (ICN), or the World Trade Organization (WTO).[23]

The closest cooperation relationship to date that the Community has with foreign governments, though, is that with its major trading partner, the US. Indeed, the two parties have begun designing a blueprint for future cooperation by issuing 'best practice guidelines' with respect to their cooperation in merger cases.[24] They have proposed that their investigation timetables run in parallel to increase the effectiveness of cooperation and that merging parties be given the possibility of meeting with them together to discuss timing issues. Companies are encouraged to waive confidentiality so that the authorities can exchange information and allow joint Community/ US interviews of the companies involved. Points are designated for when it would be appropriate for direct contacts to occur between senior officials. The best practices guidelines also stress that the outcome of an agency's investigation will not be affected by an undertaking's decision to abide by only some of the agency's recommendations. Therefore companies are still left with the discretion to decide to what extent they cooperate regarding confidentiality waivers, transaction timings, and notification decisions.

3.3 THE PRINCIPLE OF NOTIFICATION

Notification is an essential principle of a cooperation agreement which ensures coordination by providing for the reciprocal notification of competition cases under investigation which might affect the important interests of the government of the other authority. The US–Community agreement provides guidance on the particular

of the European Commission (2004), available at <http://ec.europa.eu/comm/competition/international/ bilateral/kr2_en.pdf>; South Africa: Agreement on Trade, Development and Cooperation between the European Community and its Member States, of the one part, and the Republic of South Africa, of the other part, [1999] OJ L311/3 (competition provisions, Title III, Section D); Ukraine: Partnership and Cooperation Agreement between the European Communities and their Member States, and Ukraine—Protocol on mutual assistance between authorities in customs matters, [1998] OJ L49/3 (competition provisions at Title VI); Russia: Agreement on partnership and cooperation establishing a partnership between the European Communities and their Member States, of one part, and the Russian Federation, of the other part, [1997] OJ L327/3; and the EEA Treaty but also: Council Reg. 2894/94 concerning arrangements for implementing the Agreement on the European Economic Area, [1994] OJ L305/6.

[23] OECD Members have agreed a non-binding Hard-core Cartel Recommendation based on the above agreements, which sets out the kind of enforcement cooperation that Members should provide in addressing such practices. The International Competition Network is a network of competition authorities with the aim of improving worldwide cooperation. It does not exercise any rule-making function but serves as a forum to establish best practices to be implemented by individual agencies whether unilaterally, bilaterally or multilaterally. The work of the ICN is considered at the end of this chapter.

[24] 'EU and US issue best practices guidelines concerning bilateral co-operation in merger cases', Brussels 30 October 2002, (IP/01/1591).

situations where these effects and interests may occur, but it is still general enough to cover most enforcement situations. These include cases that are relevant to the enforcement activities of the other party, or involve anti-competitive activities carried out in significant part in the other party's territory, or involve a merger or acquisition in which one or more of the relevant undertakings is a company incorporated under the laws of the other party, or where the anti-competitive practice involves conduct encouraged or approved by the other party or involves remedies that would require or prohibit conduct in the other party's territory. In practice the number of notifications made under this agreement has risen gradually each year.

3.4 TRADITIONAL COMITY

Traditional comity is the 'general principle that a country should take another country's important interests into account in its own law enforcement in return for their doing the same'.[25] While this principle does not provide an obligation to take another country's interests into account, it does help to avoid conflicts about the application of extraterritorial jurisdiction. For example, although the *Boeing/McDonnell Douglas* merger highlighted the different approaches taken by the United States and the Community to merger control (or at least to the exclusive purchasing agreements at the heart of the case itself) and the difficulties of cooperation in the face of such different standards, the Commission did take the US government's concerns relating to important US defence interests into consideration to the extent consistent with Community law, and limited the scope of its own enforcement action accordingly to commercial aircraft.[26] Comity has also played a part in the Department of Justice decisions on the international telecommunications joint ventures between *BT/MCI*[27] and *Sprint/France Telecom/Deutsche Telekom*.[28] It is thought that the Department of Justice would have prohibited the *BT/MCI* transaction if it had not been for the competitive policies and safeguards that were being incorporated into the UK telecommunications regulatory regime, whilst the absence of such safeguards in the *Sprint* case meant that the DOJ imposed more stringent conditions. For example, the substantive requirements imposed on MCI were devised to 'avoid direct US involvement in BT's operation of its telecommunications network in the UK on an ongoing basis, minimizing the potential for conflict with UK authorities'.[29]

3.5 POSITIVE COMITY

This principle applies where undertakings from one party to a cooperation agreement are being harmed by the anti-competitive practices occurring within the territory of

---

[25] M. Janow, *Antitrust Goes Global* (Brookings Institutions, 2000), p. 33.
[26] DG Comp Competition Policy Newsletter, Vol. 3 No. 2 Summer 1997, pp. 29–31.
[27] [1994] OJ L223/36: [1995] 5 CMLR 285.
[28] Case Comp/M 1741 [1996] OJ L239/57: [1997] 4 CMLR 147.
[29] J. McDavid, *Antitrust Goes Global*, op. cit. p. 182.

another party. As the injured party cannot itself initiate extraterritorial enforcement proceedings (because of the absence of evidence of harm to competition in its own market) it has to rely on the other party taking action on its behalf.

The most public informal case of positive comity involved investigations by both the DOJ and the Community of the practices of A.C. Nielsen, a US company that tracks retail sales. Following a complaint by Neilsen competitor IRI, the Department of Justice investigated Nielsen's practices of bundling or tying the terms of contracts in one country with those in other countries. Specifically the authorities were interested in whether Nielsen offered customers more favourable terms in countries where the company had market power as a way of ensuring that the customers would agree to use Nielsen in countries where it faced significant competition. The US notified the Community of the problem and let the latter take the lead in the investigation since the conduct mostly affected Europe and the Commission itself 'showed a firm intention to act'.[30] The Commission subsequently found that Nielsen had indeed implemented various exclusionary practices designed to impede IRI from entering the European market. As a result, Nielsen gave undertakings to the Commission to address the concerns of both the Community and the United States. The two authorities had cooperated extensively throughout the process.

Formal use of the positive comity mechanisms has been limited to the referral in the *SABRE-Amadeus* case.[31] After having started its own investigation, the United States Department of Justice asked the European Commission to investigate possible anti-competitive conduct by Amadeus, the dominant computer reservation system in Europe, which might be preventing the US-based SABRE computer reservation system from competing effectively in certain European Member States. The DOJ justified the referral, and importantly the temporary suspension of its own investigation, by stating that it believed that the Commission was in the best position to investigate the matter. The exclusion of a US competitor was a concern for the United States, but it justified the referral to the Community because European consumers were also affected by the conduct, which took place within the Commission's jurisdiction.[32] The US government's concerns, and those of SABRE, were largely resolved when the European Commission issued a Statement of Objections to member airlines of the Amadeus network, particularly Air France. This is the only time to date that there has been resort to formal positive comity procedures.

3.6 THE ISSUE OF CONFIDENTIALITY

Both the Community/United States and Community/Canada Agreements have a confidentiality provision whereby parties can refuse disclosure of any information if it is prohibited under the law of the party that holds the information or if it would be incompatible with the important interests of the party that holds it. Therefore there

---

[30] J. Rill, C. Wilson, and S. Bauers, *Antitrust Goes Global*, op. cit. p. 193.
[31] Ibid., p. 195.   [32] Ibid., p. 197.

is a significant amount of discretion that is left open to the parties as to how far their cooperation extends. This is also a reflection of the importance of such information to the companies involved. They will want to be assured that any information exchanged will not be made known to competitors of the company and will only be used for the purpose for which it has been exchanged.

In addition, the Community distinguishes between confidential *business* information and confidential *agency* information. Confidential business information is information obtained in the course of an investigation (including business or trade secrets) and cannot be disclosed to the United States unless the relevant company expressly agrees. Confidential agency information relates to the investigation itself (including procedural aspects) and can be disclosed to the United States. The United States on the other hand does not make such a distinction and prohibits the disclosure of *any* information that it holds without the consent of the undertakings involved, except in relation to administrative or judicial actions or proceedings.

Therefore, a waiver of confidentiality is almost always required from parties involved in a Community/United States investigation. Past experience has shown that waivers are more readily given in merger cases where companies involved will cooperate in order to get expedited clearance for their merger.[33] However, reports have also shown that there has also been an increased level of information-sharing between the Community and the United States in cartel cases including one company providing a waiver allowing the two authorities to exchange views regarding confidential evidence.[34] These developments are all the more important as the effectiveness of cooperation in cartel cases depends greatly on the ability of the agencies involved to share confidential information.

Particular problems also arise with respect to the differences in the regimes in the EU and Canada. The Community, for example, will restrict disclosure of confidential information to the Canadians in much the same way as it distinguishes between business secrets and other agency information. However, in Canada information is protected if it is held by the Competition Bureau and was obtained under the powers provided by the Competition Act. Information provided voluntarily to the Competition Bureau (including business secrets) is not protected, however. Therefore it would appear that information provided by the Community to Canada could be released or accessed under an Access of Information request under Canadian law, as it was not obtained using Canada's competition law. To try to address this, the Canadian Commissioner for Competition has issued a specific Communication of Confidential Information which states that such shared information would also be covered by Canada's confidentiality provisions. The question for undertakings, of course, is whether this assurance is enough. Companies should also note that confidential information in the hands of the Competition Bureau could be disclosed to the Community

---

[33] M. Monti, 'Co-operation Between Competition Authorities—A Vision for the Future', The Japan Foundation Conference, Washington DC, 23 June 2000, see fn. 18.

[34] B. Sweeney 'Combating Foreign Anti-Competitive Conduct: What Role For Extraterritorialism?' [2007] 8(1) Melbourne Journal of International Law 35.

where the purpose is to receive reciprocal assistance regarding a Canadian investigation. However, the authority to do this is somewhat ambiguous and as a result the
Commissioner has proposed amendments to the Competition Act in order to give
formal status to such a disclosure of information.[35]

The OECD has also examined the need for a requirement for comparable downstream protection of information, as a way of reconciling business needs for confidentiality and the authorities' need for information. Downstream protection would
assure undertakings involved in investigations that any foreign cooperating agency
would have in place comparable protections for shared information through a case-
by-case examination and assurance that adequate protection exists for the particular
information being sought.[36]

3.7 SUBSTANTIVE DIFFERENCES IN LAW

Another restriction on the utility of positive comity results from substantive differences
in the parties' laws. Positive comity—and indeed cooperation itself—can only apply
where the anti-competitive conduct is illegal in the jurisdiction of the requested party.
The US authorities still approach vertical arrangements in sufficiently different a way
from the Community that cooperation may not work when 'westward' (Community
to United States) positive comity requests are made about such restrictions. European
competition law prohibits arrangements that may significantly restrict competitors'
access to a market. US competition law, however, takes further factors into account and
requires that the arrangement must substantially lessen competition as well. As such,
it is not likely to be the case that the United States will act against vertical restraints—
even when expressly requested to do so by the Community—absent evidence that the
arrangements substantially lessen competition, despite the fact that they may impede
the ability of a European company to enter the US market.[37]

As has been pointed out by one American lawyer, 'it is not realistic to expect one
government to prosecute its citizens solely for the benefit of another. We should not
expect the principle of positive comity to impact dramatically on the proposition that
laws are written and enforced to protect national interests.'[38] Fundamentally, the application of positive comity is dependent on the good will and trust of the parties, factors
that do not always come to the fore when their own political and economic interests
are affected. However, this self-interest can also induce cooperation, as the reciprocal
nature of such agreements tends to make them self-enforcing. This was illustrated in
the Community's willingness to cooperate in the *SABRE-Amadeus* matter in order
to reap the benefits of such cooperation in subsequent cases. As Alexander Schaub
explained, the American request's effect on the dynamic of trans-Atlantic cooperation was 'important...psychologically. We have given our people the instruction to

---

[35] L. Hunter and S. Hutton, 'EU-Canada Co-operation' in *European Antitrust Review* (2002).
[36] OECD Global Forum on Competition—'Information Sharing in Cartel Cases', [CCNM/GF/
COMP/2002], 30 January 2002, available at <http://www.oecd.org>.
[37] P. Marsden, *Antitrust Goes Global*, pp. 117–36.
[38] J. R. Atwood 'Positive Comity: Is it a positive step?' [1992] Fordham Corp L Inst 86.

consider this as a priority case because we are aware of the fact that how we handle American positive comity requests will certainly determine largely how the US authorities will handle our future requests.'[39]

The trust implicit in the use of positive comity—particularly when one authority suspends its own enforcement activities—is most likely to work between jurisdictions that have well-developed, mature competition law systems, and a history of international contacts. It is least likely to work when the requesting party 'does not have the resources, the experience or legal infrastructure to undertake a requested investigation',[40] or, as has been noted above, does not prohibit the particular practices under its own law.

3.8 THE LIMITATIONS OF BILATERAL COOPERATION

The inherent limitations of bilateral enforcement cooperation have led the Community to push for wider and deeper commitment from their trading partners. Three limitations stand out in particular. First, the fact that cooperation is subject to various restrictions, and is voluntary in any event, has led the Community to push for binding commitments between governments to help one another battle international anti-competitive practices. Second, the fact that cooperation to date has been primarily of a bilateral nature has meant that enforcers are simply not able to keep up with the increasing prevalence of international anti-competitive activity. Even the development of a wider patchwork of individual agreements among countries would not constitute a web that would be broad enough, or strong enough, to capture all international cartels, let alone other forms of anti-competitive activity. As such, the Community has urged that whatever binding commitments are negotiated be of a multilateral nature, so that they stamp out anti-competitive conduct throughout the world. Third, the fact that countries may have inadequate resources or differing legal regimes means that it will be difficult for their governments to act against anti-competitive conduct, and cooperate in that regard with one another. As such, the Community is pressing for all governments to agree to 'common approaches' that they will take to anti-competitive conduct. Authorities that have already made a commitment to cooperate with one another agree with one another a great deal more than they disagree, however when there is conflict between their substantive laws or enforcement approaches, no amount of comity or cooperative spirit will bridge the gap.[41]

The next and final section reviews some of the Community's proposals for such binding, multilateral rules, examines some existing 'competition' rules of that nature, and evaluates the extent to which they will be able to help induce individual competition authorities to address conduct in their markets which is either harming

---

[39] A. Torres, 'E.U. Gives Priority to US Airline Reservation Case' (9 September 1997) citing Alexander Schaub, <http://www.insidetrade.com>.

[40] M. Janow, *Antitrust Goes Global*, p. 41.

[41] *General Electric/Honeywell*, Case No. COMP/M.2220 (3 July 2001).

competition in Europe or impeding the ability of European companies to enter and expand in such foreign markets.

4. PROPOSALS FOR MULTILATERAL MEASURES

4.1 THE COMMUNITY'S APPROACH

The Community has admitted that one of its 'main reasons' for recommending 'the adoption of international rules on competition' has always been 'as part of the Community's strategy on market access: anti-competitive practices are keeping our firms out of third country markets but they cannot, in the absence of proper enforcement measures in those third markets, be tackled effectively without international rules'.[42] The Commission had noted that European companies were not doing as well overseas as their foreign competitors were doing in Europe. As Karel Van Miert has noted in Annex B of the Van Miert Report:

[our] strict competition policy guarantees companies from third countries that access to the Community market will not be compromised as a result of restrictive practices by European companies seeking to protect their traditional markets.

But this guarantee calls for reciprocity! If other countries are less vigilant than we are with regard to the anti-competitive behaviour of their companies, access to their markets for Community products will be blocked.[43]

Strict reciprocity would require that foreign countries adopt the European enforcement model. The Community has not called for this expressly. However, in 1994, Van Miert commissioned a 'Group of Experts' to 'consider these issues and contribute towards a European Community approach based largely on *our experience* on the integration of the internal market'.[44] In July 1995, the Experts issued their report, which found that purely domestic competition law enforcement was unable to address all aspects of market-closing business conduct. In addition, they found that international competition law enforcement efforts were being hampered by the non-binding nature of existing agreements, the differences between—and gaps within—existing competition laws, and the fact that many countries did not even have a competition regime at all. On the basis of this report, in June 1996 Brittan and Van Miert issued a joint 'Trade and Competition' Communication from the Commission to the European Council, the Community body responsible for negotiating international treaties.[45]

---

[42] Commission Communication, Annex at p. 2 (see fn. 2).

[43] European Commission, *Competition Policy in the New Trade Order: Strengthening International Co-operation and Rules*, Report of the Group of Experts (Luxembourg: OOPEC, July 1995), p. 3 (the 'Van Miert Report') (emphasis added).

[44] The Van Miert Report. Annex B, 'Text of letter of convocation'. External experts included Professors Immenga, Jenny, and Petersmann of Germany, France, and Switzerland respectively and Commission experts Ehlermann, Pons, Abbott, Lamoureux, Marchipont, and Jacquemin.

[45] See fn. 2.

This Commission Communication recommended that WTO Members negotiate a binding agreement to enact, enforce, and cooperate in enforcing competition laws, in accordance with common minimum international standards. The Commission has since done a great deal of work in setting out what those standards should look like. Not surprisingly, early proposals had a distinctly European flavour.

In the mid-1990s the Community made a detailed set of proposals for global rules on exclusive arrangements. One of its first proposals was ready in 1996, when the European Commission suggested that '[a] common approach to vertical restrictions could be found by concentrating on restrictions that create barriers to market access. The [WTO]...could examine to what extent competition authorities could take into account the international dimension and weigh the effects on domestic competition of market access restrictions'.[46] This suggestion resembles European competition policy's approach of concentrating on arrangements of a 'Community dimension' that restrict trade between Member States. This was no accident, of course. Sir Leon Brittan argued that for 'the next stage in the logical process of opening up world markets to trade and competition...what the Community has gone through these last forty years is of considerable relevance to the challenge facing the wider world'.[47] This was to apply to issues of both process and of substance. With respect to procedures, for example, the Van Miert Group of Experts had recommended that WTO rules should comprise 'a list of minimum principles... [which] should be incorporated into the national law of the participating countries in much the same way as European Directives: each country would have an obligation as to the result to be achieved, but would not be obliged to amend its current legislation if it already contained these principles or if it was open to similar interpretation'.[48] As to the substance of the common rules, the Van Miert Group recommended that in analysing exclusionary arrangements, '[a] "rule of reason" approach is desirable...Vertical agreements raise...difficulties since opinions differ as to the conditions under which they are acceptable from a competition perspective.'[49] They did not propose leaving each Member completely free to conduct its own analysis, though. Foreseeing 'disputes over international rules of reason', the Van Miert Group recommended a WTO agreement to 'define minimum standards for national rules of reason and rules of conflicts of jurisdiction'.[50] Their specific proposal was for a formula that would 'prohibit agreements where their restrictive effect on competition is not offset by an advantage for the consumer and/or where they constitute a barrier to market access'.[51] As in European competition law, this would establish a competition offence that had a form of efficiency defence, as well as a separate offence of impeding market access.

[46] Commission Communication at p. 11 (emphasis added).

[47] L. Brittan, 'A Framework for International Competition', Address to World Economic Forum, Davos (3 February 1992) in *International Economic Insights*, Issue 3 (March/April 1992), pp. 21–2.

[48] The Commission's Experts Group recommended EU law as one of the principles: 'As regards the control of dominant positions, a regime similar to that of Article [82] of the...Treaty appears appropriate insofar as it focuses on the abusive behaviour of enterprises in a dominant position'. Van Miert Report at p. 22.

[49] Van Miert Report at pp. 21–2.   [50] Van Miert Report at p. 25.

[51] Van Miert Report at pp. 21–2 (emphasis added).

4.2 THE US APPROACH

Across the Atlantic, however, the United States had been historically against multilateral disciplines on how governments should enforce their competition law. When such rules had been proposed in the 1940s, the US Congress refused to sign up to them, out of a fear that multilateral rules would lead to a watering down of US standards.[52] When WTO competition rules were being discussed again in the late 1990's, then Assistant Attorney General for Antitrust Joel Klein issued 'A Note of Caution with respect to a WTO Agenda on Competition Policy'.[53] He submitted that the binding nature of WTO commitments would mean that governments would only be able to agree on the most general standards. This would inevitably be far less than was present in the purely hortatory *UNCTAD Set*, or the Model Law Programme it was developing, and would not provide any guidance to countries in the early stages of developing a competition law regime.[54] Moreover, fixing such norms in international law might inhibit the policy competition between regimes and the resulting evolution that allows competition policy analysis itself to keep up with the changing nature and effect of business practices. Agreeing minimum standards could even allow anti-competitive conduct to restrict trade if it enabled countries with lax enforcement regimes to hide behind an inadequate but nevertheless global benchmark. That was a real risk if, as seemed likely, a negotiation of binding rules involved a multilateral barter down to the lowest common denominator.

While American antitrust enforcement moreover would be likely to satisfy a common international standard, there was a concern that its coherence, rigor and the finality of its decisions would be put into question if subjected to international challenge and review by trade officials and diplomats unfamiliar with competition policy. Whether the US government signed up to WTO competition rules or not, Klein argued, a minimalist approach at the global level could well thwart its own and other international efforts to get governments to increase their enforcement activities. The way forward, Klein submitted, was through the continued refinement and expansion of enforcement cooperation agreements between governments. Cooperation among enforcers could improve their understanding of each other's laws and enforcement approaches and thereby bring about a convergence of legal positions of both substance and procedure. In the longer term, this would better help to create and support an international code of binding rules of the highest, rather than the lowest, calibre. A virtuous circle could then evolve among competition laws, bilateral cooperation, and multilateral code building.

---

[52] D. Wood, 'Remarks on Regulatory Co-operation for Effectiveness and Compliance: Joint Action among Securities, Banking and Antitrust Regulators' in *1997 Proceedings of the American Society of International Law* (1998), pp. 223, 228–31.

[53] J. Klein, 'A Note of Caution with Respect to a WTO Agenda on Competition Policy', presented at the Royal Institute of International Affairs, Chatham House, London, 18 November, 1996 (available at <http://www.usdoj.gov>).

[54] UNCTAD Secretariat, 'Continued Work on the Elaboration of a Model Law or Laws on Restrictive Business Practices', Draft, 21 August 1995 (available at <http://www.unctad.org>).

The DOJ did not prevail, however. At the WTO's first Ministerial Conference to consider the issue, then US Trade Representative, Charlene Barshefsky, announced that the US government was 'willing to go along with others who wish to begin a modest work program in the areas of investment and competition, as part of a balanced overall agenda for the WTO'.[55] WTO Members then accepted the Community's proposals to form a WTO Working Group 'to study issues raised by Members relating to the interaction between trade and competition policy, including anti-competitive practices'.[56]

During the discussions at the Working Group in the late 1990s, governments learned a lot from each other's enforcement experience, and were generally supportive of the need for competition rules. The Community had also amended some of its more European-sounding proposals to align them more with generally acceptable 'trade' and 'competition' principles. As a result, the work plan at the WTO was to 'focus on the clarification of: core principles, including transparency, non-discrimination and procedural fairness, and provisions on hard-core cartels; modalities for voluntary cooperation; and support for progressive reinforcement of competition institutions in developing countries through capacity building'.[57] These are to a large extent 'motherhood and apple pie' issues about which agreement was thought possible. Such was not to be the case. All work on this subject at the WTO ceased after the failure to reach agreement on a broader negotiating work plan, including the liberalization of agricultural trade and other areas, at the WTO's Cancun Ministerial in 2003.[58] Regardless, it is at least arguable that competition laws and their enforcement are already subject to WTO commitments to be non-discriminatory and transparent.[59] It is beyond the scope of this chapter to consider the ramifications of those particular proposals of the EC.[60] However, an examination of some of the existing competition rules at the WTO may indicate some of the kinds of concerns that might be raised in future negotiations for rules on competition law enforcement.

4.3 THE 1996 WTO *REFERENCE PAPER*: PRO-COMPETITIVE REGULATORY PRINCIPLES

Soon after the end of the Uruguay Round of trade negotiations, governments recognized that prohibitions of discrimination in world trade might not be sufficient to ensure that formerly publicly run sectors became competitive. This was particularly

---

[55] Statement by Ambassador Charlene Barshefsky, 9 December, 1996, WT/MIN (96)/ST/5 (available at <http://www.wto.int/english/theWTO_e/minist_e/min96_e/st5.htm>).

[56] WTO, Singapore Ministerial Declaration, Conf. Doc. WT/MIN(96)/DEC/W, 13 December 1996 (96–5315), (hereinafter, 'Singapore Declaration'), para. 20 (available at <http://www.wto.org>).

[57] WTO, Doha Ministerial Declaration, WT/MIN(01)/DEC/W/1 (14 November 2001) at para. 25 (emphasis added) (available at <http://www.wto.org>).

[58] P. Marsden, 'Competition after Cancun—A Personal View', Competition Law Insight (October 2003).

[59] *GATT* Art. III and *GATS* Art. XVII.

[60] For such a consideration, see P. Marsden, *A Competition Policy for the WTO* (Cameron May, 2003).

the case for the telecommunications markets. As a US government submission explained:

the negotiating parties [accepted] that a grant of *de jure* market access and national treatment was insufficient to grant *de facto* or effective market access, absent commitments by governments to regulate former monopolies in a pro-competitive manner, because such former monopolies have both the ability and the incentive to dictate anti-competitive terms of market entry for new competitors.[61]

A right of general entry had to be provided to new competitors, whether domestic or foreign, through pro-competitive 'asymmetric regulation' of major domestic suppliers.[62] Trade negotiators thus provided a *Reference Paper on Pro-competitive Regulatory Principles* to require that WTO Members ensure that their large incumbents provide sufficient entry points on satisfactory terms so that their competitors could connect to their networks.[63]

The approach in the *Reference Paper* is part competition policy, part regulation.[64] It protects competition by requiring that governments prohibit major suppliers from engaging in anti-competitive practices that frustrate market entry. It promotes competition by requiring that major suppliers provide their competitors with market access, for example, by allowing other firms to connect to their telecommunications networks on non-discriminatory terms and conditions, in a timely manner and upon request.[65] 'Major suppliers' are those with the power to 'materially affect the terms of participation (having regard to price and supply)' due to their control over 'essential facilities' or their 'position' in the market.[66] Examples of anti-competitive practices include 'anti-competitive cross-subsidisation' and 'use of information' obtained from competitors with anti-competitive results'.[67] As the *Reference Paper* imposes regulatory obligations, certain competition policy-related concepts are left undefined, including 'anti-competitive', 'essential facilities', and 'use' of one's position. Furthermore, a supplier can be 'major' without being what competition authorities would consider to be 'dominant'. Each signing Member undertakes to have its regulator, which can be a competition authority, adhere to these commitments.[68] When a Member has made the *Reference Paper* part of its specific commitments under the General Agreement on Trade and Services (*GATS*), any failure to adhere to it can be the subject of WTO dispute settlement.

---

[61] Communication from the United States, 'The Impact of Regulatory Practices, State Monopolies, and Exclusive Rights on Competition and International Trade' WT/WGTCP/W/83 (14 August 1998) (hereinafter 'US Communication 83') at p. 11 (available at <http://www.wto.org>).

[62] US Communication 83 at p. 12.

[63] Negotiating Group on Basic Telecommunications, *WTO Reference Paper on Basic Telecommunications* (24 April 1996) (hereinafter 'Reference Paper').

[64] *Reference Paper*, Arts. 1.1 and 2.2, respectively.   [65] *Reference Paper*, Art. 2.2.

[66] *Reference Paper*, Definitions.   [67] *Reference Paper*, Art. 1.2.

[68] *Reference Paper*, Art. 2.5.

The *Reference Paper* is more detailed than any other binding multilateral 'competition' rules. As such, trade negotiators are seeking to test the applicability of its principles to other formerly 'public' sectors with monopolistic or oligopolistic characteristics, including postal and courier, air transport, and energy as well as non-public sectors such as 'distribution' services. A 'built-in agenda' to this end is firmly in place and discussions continue.[69]

One of the most important aspects of 'unfinished business', of course, is to determine the meaning of the competition terms that are strewn throughout the *Reference Paper*. Competition law in America, Australia, Canada, and even the Community only imposes similar obligations on firms to help their competitors when at least four conditions have been satisfied: first, the firms have been found to be 'dominant', as opposed to being merely 'major'; second, they have been proven to be abusing their dominant position by, for example, refusing to deal with their competitors, and third, this has been proven to have had the effect of lessening competition substantially,[70] or of eliminating it all together.[71] In addition, the preferred model in both Europe and the United States appears to be one where governments only intervene to order the owner of an essential facility to provide its competitors with access to it if, in addition to the above three conditions, it is not possible (or at least not economically feasible) for the competitors to develop a competing facility.[72] Of course, as a matter of logic, if a facility truly is 'essential' for competition to exist, then the elimination of competition is the only logical result of any denial of access to it. In any event, the *Reference Paper* does not require evidence of 'elimination' or 'substantial lessening' of competition. It focuses purely on the denial of access to a facility that is controlled by a supplier that is 'major' either on its own, or with other providers.

It is more than a little unfortunate that the *Reference Paper* set such an obviously regulatory approach that is so different from current practice under the laws of most WTO Members, particularly when the American and European approaches to essential facilities have been converging towards one another and when governments generally have been favouring the use of competition law disciplines rather than regulation. Any one of the four conditions required by the competition law analysis set out above is far more rigorous than the criterion to which Members have committed themselves in the *Reference Paper*. Since the *Reference Paper* influences how Members intervene in their markets, this divergence needs to be resolved sooner rather than later. This is particularly important because of the use of the provisions of the *Reference Paper* in dispute settlement procedures.

---

[69] WTO Secretariat, 'Distribution Services—Background Note by the Secretariat' S/C/W/37, 10 June 1998 at p. 14; Inside US Trade, 'US presses for alternative negotiating methods for *GATS*', 20 August 1999 (available at <http://www.wto.org>).

[70] US Sherman Act, 15 U.S.C., s 2; Australian Trade Practices Act 1974 (consolidated), s 46; Canadian *Competition Act*, R.S.C. 1985, c. C-34, as amended, ss 78–9. See, e.g. *MCI Communications Corp v. AT&T*, 464 US 891(1983).

[71] Case C-7/97 *Bronner v. MediaPrint* [1998] ECR I-7791 [1998]: 4 CMLR 112.

[72] *MCI Communications Corp v. AT&T, Bronner*.

4.4. APPLICATION OF THE *REFERENCE PAPER*—MEXICAN TELECOMS

The US has used the *Reference Paper* already to effect considerable changes to the business environment in Mexico. The case in question arose after an American telecoms provider, Sprint, had partnered with Mexico's largest supplier of telecommunications services, Telmex, to provide mobile telecommunication services in the United States and Mexico. AT&T and MCI had to settle for deals with lesser Mexican players and could not benefit from Telmex's considerably larger network. They called upon the US Trade Representative to help them achieve the kind of access enjoyed by Sprint. The resulting American WTO complaint requested that Telmex be required to provide these US firms with non-discriminatory access as provided for under the *Reference Paper*.[73] After only a few months of the pressure of strained trade relations with the United States, the Mexican telecoms regulator COFETEL issued a set of 'Asymmetric Regulations for Telmex'. These ordered Telmex to provide its long distance competitors with access to its network at cost.[74] The United States then withdrew its WTO complaint.

It is interesting to note that at no point did AT&T, MCI, or the USTR make a public request for the Mexican competition authority to investigate Telmex's activities, and of course they had no incentive to do so. Their allegations would have had to survive a rigorous market analysis and satisfy a competition law standard—that competition in the relevant market had been proven to have been 'diminished, impaired or prevented',[75] before the Mexican competition authority would have intervened. The complainants and the USTR obviously thought that they stood a much better chance of success if Geneva-based trade panellists reviewed their complaint under the pro-competitive rules of the *Reference Paper*. They would not have to find evidence of 'harm to competition' but simply a failure by Mexico to honour its commitment to *promote* competition by increasing foreign entry. From the point of view of international trade policy, the use of this standard, combined with the threat that Mexican products would be barred from the vast American market, makes Mexico's capitulation and imposition of 'asymmetric regulations' on its 'major supplier' not at all surprising.

While the initial Mexican case was settled through bilateral 'negotiation', a WTO dispute settlement panel had an opportunity to explain what the *Reference Paper*'s pro-competitive regulatory principles actually meant. In April 2004, a WTO Dispute Settlement Panel reviewed the above situation and found that the Mexican law created a situation in which Telmex was involved in 'anti-competitive practices' as defined under the *Reference Paper*.[76] The panel found that Telmex's state-approved pricing

---

[73] *Mexico—Measures Affecting Telecommunications Services—Request for Consultations by the United States*, WT/DS204/2, 17 August 2000 (available at <http://www.wto.org>).

[74] Inside Trade, 'USTR backs off Mexico WTO threat in wake of telecom company deal', 1 June 2001 (available at <http://www.insidetrade.com>).

[75] *Ley Federal de Competencia Económica*, Diario oficial de la federacion (24 December 1992) Arts. 8 and 10.

[76] Mexico, Measures affecting telecommunications services, WT/DS204/R, 2 April 2004.

practices had 'effects tantamount' to a price-fixing cartel.[77] The panel expressly found that 'the object and purpose of the Reference Paper commitments made by members supports our conclusion that the term "anticompetitive practices", in addition to the examples mentioned...includes horizontal price-fixing and market-sharing agreements by suppliers which, on a national or international level, are generally discouraged or disallowed'.[78] As such, the Panel found that it was 'aware that, pursuant to doctrines applicable under the competition laws of some members, a firm complying with a specific legislation requirement of such a member (e.g. a trade law authorizing private market-sharing agreements) may be immunised from being found in violation of the general domestic competition law'. Nevertheless this so-called state action doctrine could be swept aside when considering WTO commitments: 'International commitments made under the GATS "for the purpose of preventing suppliers...from engaging in or continuing anticompetitive practices" are, however, designed to limit the regulatory powers of WTO members'.[79] As such, 'a requirement imposed by a member under its internal law on a major supplier cannot unilaterally erode its international commitments made in its schedule to other WTO members'.[80] While the panel's decision was not appealed by Mexico, the decision is not without its critics who have questioned whether it accords with the *Vienna Convention on the Law of Treaties*, and criticized its 'competition policy' analysis.[81]

Given the vagueness of its terms, however, problems of interpretation are likely to arise in any dispute-settlement proceeding. To minimize the possibility of regulation being introduced when it is not appropriate, the meaning, application and even the propriety of pro-competitive regulation are matters that have to be decided as a matter of urgency. Being part of the *GATS*, it is natural for the *Reference Paper* to have more to do with promoting 'market access' than with protecting the competitive process. It is closer to entrant-friendly *ex ante* regulation than to competition law, which disciplines anticompetitive behaviour after it has been proven likely to harm competitors or consumers. Of course, a bias towards entry is to be expected in any trade agreement, and should not necessarily be condemned, particularly when it applies to sectors that are controlled by former public monopolies and where mandated access is essential for competition to exist at all. The question most relevant to the development of further 'competition' rules at the WTO, though, is how appropriate the *Reference Paper* is as a template for opening up other sectors. This is particularly the case for those sectors where the role and effect of government regulation is minimal or has long since ceased to operate.

These are all difficult issues that WTO Members, and dispute settlement panellists, will not be able to ignore. It is to be hoped that the Multilateral Competition Agreement that the Community now so ardently seeks from its WTO colleagues will eventually provide a much needed 'competition policy' anchor to help to determine how these existing terms will be interpreted and applied in the telecoms and other sectors.

---

[77] Ibid., para. 1.41.   [78] Iid., para. 1.16.   [79] Ibid., para. 1.23.   [80] Ibid.

[81] P. Marsden, 'WTO decides its first competition case, with disappointing results' Competition Law Insight (May 2004) at p. 3.

4.5 THE INTERNATIONAL COMPETITION NETWORK (ICN)

What is more likely to provide such guidance at a much earlier date, however, is the work that competition authorities themselves are doing under the auspices of the ICN, referred to earlier.[82] There will still need to be a binding agreement in place, most likely at the WTO, to ensure that competition principles prevail over mere demands from companies for access to their rival's supply or customer base. Such an accord is likely to take a great deal of time for governments to negotiate, however, and for dispute settlement panellists at the WTO to interpret in any substantive manner.

In the meantime, the officials from DG Comp at the European Commission, and from over one hundred other competition authorities around the world have been meeting to learn from one another's expertise through the virtual network, the ICN. They share experience learned from actual cases and develop 'best practice guidelines' about how they should enforce their laws (in particular, in a non-discriminatory manner) and how they should co-operate with one another to address anti-competitive conduct with international effects.[83] They have addressed topics relating to harmonizing procedures and reducing costs and burdens (to both business and governments) associated with multi-jurisdictional merger review. They have begun an international competition law advocacy programme to help explain the importance of competition policy to governments that may be resistant to such arguments, or at least may pay little heed to the policy advice of the competition authority in their jurisdiction. They have examined the substantive analytical framework underpinning merger control analysis, evaluating the propriety and applicability of the three main tests: 'substantial lessening of competition', 'dominance', and 'public interest'. Their work programme also involves reviewing merger notification thresholds, discussing approaches to unilateral conduct, improving cartel investigations and more generally the implementation of competition law.

This process will help competition authorities to understand the concerns that other governments have about extraterritorial enforcement, and its limitations, and should provide a stable but flexible basis for international cooperation at the bilateral, regional, and multilateral levels.

FURTHER READING

M. DABBAH, *The Internationalisation of Antitrust Policy* (Cambridge University Press, 2007).

C. NOONAN, *The Emerging Principles of International Competition Law* (Oxford University Press, 2008).

---

[82] P. Marsden, 'Tune in to the International Competition Network—not the WTO—for practical advances in International Anti-trust', [2001] (December) In Competition 3.

[83] See <http://www.internationalcompetitionnetwork.org>.

B. Sweeney, 'Combating Foreign Anti-Competitive Conduct: What Role For Extraterritorialism?' [2007] 8(1) Melbourne Journal of International Law 35.

M. D. Taylor, *International Competition Law* (Cambridge University Press, 2006).

B. Zanettin, *Cooperation between Antitrust Agencies at the International Level* (Hart Publishing, 2002).

PART III

CONCLUSIONS AND PROSPECTS

23

FIFTY YEARS OF THE TREATY OF ROME

1. THE COMMISSION'S TASK 1958–2008

1.1 THE BASIC PRIORITIES FOR THE COMMISSION

Over the fifty years since the Treaty of Rome was signed Community competition law has developed into a mature system, and the final part of this work considers that development. This chapter provides a general assessment of its achievements, and in the following chapter we look ahead to likely developments and changes that may be necessary for the Commission in general and DG Comp in particular to continue to meet their responsibilities and priorities in the coming years.

The framework of the Treaty of Rome (as subsequently amended) sets out the main objectives and tasks of its institutions; these tasks comprise principally the promotion, throughout the Community, of economic growth and expansion, an increase of its stability and living standards, and the maintenance of close relationships between Member States. The means whereby the objectives were to be achieved were a number of common policies laid down in Article 3 including, of course, in paragraph (1)(g) 'the institution of a system ensuring that competition in the Common Market is not distorted'. The characteristics of this system would necessarily have included:

(1) the establishment of primary rules, both substantive and procedural, of sufficient width, clarity, and certainty to ensure a reasonable degree of compliance in all economic sectors covered by the policy, which in turn could provide a stable foundation for business development, to apply both to horizontal and to vertical relationships

(2) the consistent application of competition policy throughout the geographical area of the Community, actively carried out not only by the institutions of the Community but by Member States themselves, to ensure that the implementation of the relevant provisions of the Treaty was both legally consistent and complete

(3) the even-handed application to both Member States and undertakings within the Community of the rules comprised in this system, within the framework of the Treaty and regulations made under it

(4) acceptance by the Council of Ministers and Member States that the human and financial resources provided for the effective implementation of the system by relevant Community institutions should be adequate for the considerable tasks involved.

1.2 THE CHANGING ECONOMIC BACKGROUND

Any attempt to make a balanced assessment must, of course, take into account not only periods of success and forward movement but also the problems encountered, both internal and external. Over this period the Commission has at certain times certainly faced considerable difficulties in both the economic and the political spheres. In particular, the economic background against which it operates has undergone disruption and substantial change. The early years of the Six, even up to the start of the 1970s, can be seen in retrospect as a comparatively calm period, remarkable for steady economic growth throughout much of the territory of the Community. The continuous growth of both the internal and external trade of the Community and rising standards of living in its individual Member States (other than a few clearly identifiable regions such as the southern part of Italy) contributed to the willingness of governments of Member States to agree readily to the grant of extensive powers to the Commission in this area of competition policy, in relation to both procedures and the application of substantive law. Even during the mid-sixties, when the Council remained largely inactive as the result of political deadlock, the powers already granted to the Commission and the decisions that towards the end of this time began to come from the European Court of Justice ensured that, in the area of competition law at least, progress continued.

All this changed during the early seventies. The sharp increase in oil prices in late 1973 led to nearly a decade of stagnation in economic growth and an acute increase in mutual sensitivity between Member States concerned about the effect of government involvement in sectors such as steel, textiles, and shipbuilding, where the economic consequences of the new era were most keenly felt. It was also unfortunate, as many commentators have pointed out, that the expansion of the Community to nine (including the United Kingdom) and then to ten Member States took place against such a background, accentuating problems as well as opportunities for the enlarged Common Market. Nevertheless the Community continued to expand, the entry of Spain and Portugal in 1986 bringing its membership to twelve. It became fifteen with the accession of Austria, Finland, and Sweden at the start of 1995, then twenty-five when Cyprus, Malta, and eight East European countries joined, and finally the current twenty-seven when Bulgaria and Romania joined at the start of 2007.

The development of competition policy continued steadily over the 1980s and 1990s. Under active Competition Commissioners, Peter Sutherland (for the period 1985–8), Sir Leon Brittan (1989–92) and Karel van Miert (1993–9), DG Comp was able to place greater emphasis on the positive aspects of its responsibilities. Special attention was paid to liberalization of air transport and some progress made in the enactment of both procedural and substantive regulations within whose framework progress could be made (if slowly) towards a greater freedom for airlines to fix their own fares, without having on all occasions to obtain government approval. Maritime transport was also given a block exemption, and a number of major cases brought against price-fixing and other anti-competitive practices within this sector.

Some of the most important changes in the jurisdiction of the Commission occurred at the end of the 1980s. The enactment in 1989 of Merger Regulation 4064/89 filled an important gap, allowing proposed concentrations that might enable dominant positions to be created or strengthened in particular sectors to be prohibited, or at least subjected to conditions which would reduce the likelihood of consequent damage to the competitive process in those markets. Moreover, the approval by the European Court of the use by the Commission of its powers under Article 86(3) to issue Directives, to put pressure on Member States to open up their telecommunications terminal equipment and services market in order to establish a functioning market within the Community for large-scale information technology, was vital. These decisions led in turn to the enactment of a number of Council Directives, particularly in the fields of energy and communication, designed to liberalize national markets traditionally dominated in most Member States by State-controlled national operators not subject to adequate outside competition, though there continued to be serious opposition to the full liberalization of the gas and electricity markets, especially from France.

The technological boom in particular in the communications, computer hardware and software, transport, and energy markets throughout the 1990s meant that pressures on the Commission further increased. There were a large number of joint venture proposals which had to be dealt with under either Article 81 or the Merger Regulation, and it became apparent that the original division by category of joint ventures into 'cooperative' (considered under Article 81) and 'concentrative' (considered under the Merger Regulation) was unworkable. New legislation had to be brought in to ensure that all full-function joint ventures could benefit from the fixed timetable of the Merger Regulation. The actual number of mergers with a Community dimension, now including of course all full function joint ventures, also increased to well over 300 a year, of which some 5 per cent raised serious doubts about their effects on competition in the relevant sectors and needed the more detailed assessment of the second-phase procedure.

Under Commissioner Mario Monti (2000–3), and continuing subsequently under the current Commissioner Neelie Kroes, the present era began: following harsh criticism of the Commission from the CFI, significant changes were made in the substance and procedure of merger control, and a switch was completed to a more economics-based, and less legalistic, approach in all enforcement activity, with the possible exception of Article 82 cases. By 2004 the number of Member States was to become so large that it was not possible for enforcement of Articles 81 and 82 to continue to be so heavily centralized with the Commission. The 'modernized' and decentralized enforcement system was enacted and took root, and national authorities became very much more active and better connected with one another and the Commission.

2. THE COMMISSION'S LEGISLATIVE PROGRAMME

2.1 THE INITIAL CHOICES

The very first *Annual Report on Competition Policy,* published by the Commission to cover the period to the end of 1971, drew on over a decade of experience in DG Comp in administering Articles 81 and 82. It chose to give priority to the following issues:

(1) It recognized the need to take action with special vigour against restrictions on competition and practices jeopardizing the unity of the Common Market, notably sharing markets, allocating customers and collective exclusive dealing agreements, and to prevent agreements which indirectly resulted in concentrating demand on particular producers.

(2) With regard to systems of distribution, any degree of exclusivity permitted must not prevent distributors and consumers from obtaining goods in other Member States 'on the terms customary in that State'.

(3) Heavy fines should be expected by those undertakings engaged in restrictions on competition causing serious damage to consumers' interests, and which were clearly forbidden.

(4) The Commission would reinforce the competitive position of undertakings by exempting (both by individual decisions and by means of a block regulation) positive forms of cooperation, particularly between small and medium-size businesses.

(5) The Commission did not intend to apply the prohibitions of Article 81 to restrictions on competition which had no appreciable effect on the Common Market.

The extent of the Commission's success in carrying out these aims has been considered in Part II above. In general, within the limits of its resources, the Commission has been reasonably effective. Experience has shown that, while in applying Articles 81 and 82 many difficulties have arisen, the Articles themselves are not flawed nor inadequate as a foundation for the establishment of the necessary system referred to in Article 3(1)(g) of the Treaty, save in the area of merger control for which a special Regulation has proved necessary. These two Articles, however, are merely the framework for the application of the detailed rules of the system and cannot by themselves provide answers to all the questions which arise in their implementation. To have expected DG Comp to administer a competition law in the form contained simply in those two Articles, even as supplemented by Articles 83 to 86, would clearly have been unreasonable, given that responsibility for the development of competition policy was assigned under the terms of the Treaty to the Commission and was not simply to be enforced through national courts or the European Court of Justice.[1] It is, therefore, to the legislation adopted by both Council and Commission, as well as to the case law of the Commission and Court, that we must turn for many of these answers.

2.2 BLOCK EXEMPTIONS

Once the implementation of Regulation 17 had brought about the early problem of mass notification, the major priority for DG Comp had to be the enactment of detailed regulations to lay down the exact criteria for block exemptions. As described in Chapters 10 and 11, the original approach of the Commission to block exemptions in the field of distribution was relatively simple, as exemplified by the original Regulation 67/67 which applied for just over fifteen years until replaced by Regulations 1983/83 and 1984/83 on exclusive distribution agreements and exclusive purchasing agreements respectively. These in turn were supplemented in 1988 by Regulation 4087/88 on franchising agreements. The tendency in each of these regulations was to extend the white (permitted) list of restrictions which could be included without losing the benefit of the exemption; although the intention of the Commission was to assist suppliers, wholesalers, and retailers to prepare agreements that could benefit from exemption, it had the unintended consequence of making the regulations far too complex and legalistic. By 1998 it was clear to the Commission that a new approach to the drafting of block exemptions might be necessary.

The new approach developed by the Commission was indicated in its *1998 Annual Report*[2] as follows:

The general idea is that there should be a single and very broad block exemption regulation covering all vertical restrictions of competition in respect of all intermediate and finished goods and all services. A limited number of restrictions would be excluded, such as price-fixing agreements for example. These would form a 'black list' of clauses that were not exempted by the regulation. The regulation would not seek to list the clauses that were exempted, as is done in the block exemption regulations currently in force, and this would immediately remove the straitjacket effect associated with the present 'white lists', which incite firms to force their agreements into a mould provided by the relevant block exemption regulation.

The main objective of this wide-ranging and flexible exemption regulation would be to give a measure of freedom and legal certainty to the very many firms that do not possess

---

[1] This policy differed from the choice made by the US when first enacting the Sherman Act in 1890. It is the decisions of Federal courts over subsequent years that have provided the corpus of legal principles and refinements by which the Act has been interpreted, without the assistance of delegated legislation in the nature of block exemptions that Art. 81 for its part appears to have expressly contemplated (by its reference to exemption for 'categories' of agreement).

[2] See pp. 21–2.

market power. Within the limits thus mapped out they would not have to be concerned for the validity of their agreements under Community law. To preserve competition on markets, and to confine the benefit of the exemption to firms with no great market power, the regulation would lay down market share thresholds beyond which the block exemption would no longer apply. The fact that these thresholds were exceeded would not mean that the agreements were necessarily unlawful, but only that they would have to be examined for compatibility on an individual basis.

The Commission had had difficulty when consulting about the introduction of a new composite regulation covering the transfer of technology a few years earlier, because of opposition to a proposed market share threshold of 40 per cent, beyond which a licensee holding such a share could not benefit from the block exemption, and it was only when that Regulation 240/96 was succeeded by Regulation 772/2004 that block exemption of technology transfer agreements became conditional on fulfilling market share thresholds.

The Commission first prevailed in including market share thresholds in the new distribution Regulation 2790/99 and this approach has been regarded as a successful reform. The new Regulation eliminated the special provisions for the beer and petrol sectors that had been contained in Regulation 1984/83. The Commission on principle dislikes sectoral block exemptions unless the characteristics of the sector are so special, and the lobbying power of its members so great, that a tailor-made block exemption is inevitable, as in the case of maritime transport. In the case of the car industry it was inevitable that Regulation 1475/95 (which itself had replaced Regulation 123/85) would be replaced by another Regulation (1400/2002) dealing alone with motor vehicles. However, the Commission's policy of increasing the commercial independence of motor vehicle distributors, and enhancing their ability to accept orders from outside their primary sales areas, had the effect of making the final terms of Regulation 1400/2002 even more complex. It also led the Commission to publish very detailed guidelines on the interpretation and application of the regulations. Lengthy Commission guidelines have also been a feature of other recent block exemptions.

In providing in 2000 revised versions also of the block exemption regulations covering specialization and R&D (Regulations 2658 and 2659/2000) the Commission has sought to utilize the same principles as under Regulation 2790/99, even though these two categories are essentially dealing with horizontal agreements between undertakings who may be actual or potential competitors. 'White lists' have again been omitted and market share thresholds for research and development agreements increased to 20 per cent whilst turnover thresholds were eliminated from the specialization agreement. Nevertheless, the drafting by undertakings of such horizontal agreements within the terms of the block exemption remains far less widespread than in the context of vertical agreements where the model of the new regulation has largely been followed, given its greater flexibility.

3. THE PROBLEM OF RESOURCES

3.1 STAFFING LEVELS OF DG COMP

In assessing the performance of DG Comp over the last fifty years a relevant fac-tor should be the degree to which adequate resources were provided to it from the Community budget. It is likely that resources allocated for expenditure on public pur-poses will always be regarded as inadequate by those responsible for administering them as well as by those for whose benefit they are administered; whether the pub-lic purpose be health, social security, education, or defence, the same principle holds good. By comparison with such major areas of public expenditure, the sums required for expenditure in enforcing competition policy are indeed small. Nevertheless, problems of inadequate resources still remain for such authorities. Governments in Member States moreover tend to take an ambivalent view towards their own com-petition authority. On the one hand they recognize the need for the existence of such authorities to deal with clearly anti-competitive agreements, practices, mergers, and monopolistic activities whose termination or prevention can be shown to benefit both the consumer and the general economy. On the other hand, governments are also con-cerned by the problems which competition authorities may cause, by threatening to challenge or investigate activities which individual ministries may regard as their own responsibility, and where the link between the authorities' intervention on the side of competition and consequent benefit is less obvious. This ambivalence is also found within the European Community.

The history of DG Comp does show a steady increase in the manpower provided to it, as the responsibilities placed upon it gradually grew. Thus from a handful of 'A' grade officials in its early years the total had risen after thirty years to 300, including 140 'A' grade officials, and by ten years later (1998) to 450. The current figure of total employment in DG Comp is around 800, of whom some half are 'A' grade officials. It should be remembered that about a quarter of the 'A' grade officials are concerned with State aid rather than competition issues. These numbers overall are not insignificant, though less than those of some national competition authorities.

On the other hand the history of DG Comp shows also a steady growth in its incre-mental responsibilities in not only State aid but also in the considerable amount of additional work brought about by the liberalization process under Article 86(3), and during the nineties the heavy workload introduced by the Merger Regulation, and by the leniency programme designed to assist in uncovering cartels. Many of the tasks more recently added, in particular the much greater number of major cartel cases, are extremely labour intensive, and the resources available in this respect have not always matched the demands placed upon DG Comp. This order of numbers was inadequate even for a Community of around 380 million people and fifteen Member States, and it was clear that DG Comp could not continue to function in the same way after 2004 in an enlarged Community of twenty-five or more.

3.2 THE ROOT OF THE PROBLEM—NOTIFICATION

From necessity therefore the Commission had always sought to improve its procedures and over the period leading up to 2004 these in many respects improved.
The Annual Reports show a continuing consciousness of, and preoccupation with,
the importance of minimizing the difficulties and delays inevitably imposed by the
institutional structure and bureaucracy of such an organization, not to mention the
difficulties caused by the necessity of supporting eleven official languages. The introduction of Regulation 1216/99 considerably reduced the number of notifications of
vertical restrictions; the new form of Regulation 2790/99 simplified the legal position
and reduced the number of notifications made. The Notice on Agreements of Minor
Importance was further extended in 2001 so as to eliminate the need to notify more
of the de minimis category of agreements and the Commission continued to take a
harder line with regard to complaints unless they had a clear Community interest.

But none of these procedural changes could compensate for the fundamental and
unavoidable weakness of the notification system operated by DG Comp. This system remained in outline unchanged from its original structure, even though many
detailed improvements had been made and internal time-limits adjusted, mainly as
a result of the pressures exerted by the Merger Regulation. The fundamental problem was that at any one time there was a considerable number of notified agreements
sitting in files awaiting decision by the Commission, whose status might remain in
doubt for some years whilst the parties probably continued to operate them without
any certainty as to the outcome of the notification (though doubtless as the decades
passed with a greater feeling of freedom). This of course was not necessarily of concern
to all companies which had made a notification; some preferred not to hear anything
from the Commission for a considerable period (if ever) on the assumption that they
would receive a 'comfort letter' in due course and in the meantime enjoyed the benefit of freedom from fines on an indefinite basis: they might even prefer this uncertain
status to being granted an exemption limited in time, possibly subject to reporting and
other conditions. Other notifying companies thought that if they later required a ruling, formal or informal, they could then apply sufficient pressure to the Commission
to ensure a response. The actual number of pending cases at any one time therefore did
not represent an equivalent number of dissatisfied companies unable to place reliance
on commercial arrangements they had made and notified. Even so, the size of the backlog of pending cases remained a problem for both DG Comp and many companies, in
particular those who wished to commit themselves to a substantial investment on the
assumption that a particular agreement would not be found void under Article 81(2).

3.3 THE HANDLING OF COMPLAINTS

A wide range of complaints regularly reach DG Comp from all parts of the Community
about agreements or practices, or abuses of dominant position, alleged to be in breach
of Article 81 or 82, and the original tradition of DG Comp was that all complaints, even
the comparatively trivial, were given priority and dealt with as promptly as possible.

Against a background of the substantial growth in its jurisdiction and the need to keep the backlog of cases under control, the *Automec (No. 2)* judgment[3] brought welcome relief from this burden. The Court laid stress on the importance of the Commission having the ability to set priorities and to use its discretion to decide those cases which were of principal relevance to the Community. The basis for a rejection of any complaint will be, as in *Automec (No. 2)*, that the issues are better dealt with by national courts or competition authorities applying either Community law or national law principles and rules. This decision enabled the Commission to begin to decentralize the administration of Article 81(1) and encourage national courts and competition authorities to deal with cases under Articles 81 and 82.

This change was of course assisted by the fact that during the 1980s and 1990s almost all Member States had either created new competition authorities of their own or had strengthened the powers and resources of their existing authorities. In nearly all cases national laws were closely modelled on or exact copies of the Community pattern. But the chief problem in the decentralization of the work remained: that of the Commission's monopoly on granting individual exemptions, which blocked decentralized application by both courts and competition authorities and left the Commission as the sole, real guarantor of compliance with the competition rules. This situation was all the more worrying as while the Commission was giving its attention to analysing these notified agreements, it was unable to investigate properly the complaints it received or to conduct the necessary own-initiative investigations into the most serious infringements. It was therefore primarily a question of resources that drove the Commission and the Community to adopt Regulation 1/2003 and thereby to effect a significant degree of decentralization of enforcement activity, as described in Chapter 19.

4. THE COMMISSION AND THE COMMUNITY COURTS

4.1 THE FIRST THIRTY YEARS (1958 TO 1988)

Regardless of the resources made available to DG Comp as a competition authority, its achievements can be assessed in another way. To every institution such as the Commission, opportunities are often presented by a random conjunction of events, quite separate from its own acts or decisions, enabling unexpected progress to be made in the implementation of its policies. The structure of the Treaty and the organization of the Commission have meant that from time to time such 'windows of opportunity' have arisen, mainly as the result of rulings of the CFI and ECJ. These cases have arisen either out of requests for preliminary rulings by national courts under Article 234, or following requests by undertakings for review of the legality of Commission decisions, under Article 230. The Chronological Table at the front of this book shows that

---

[3] Case T-24/90 [1992] ECR II-2223: 5 CMLR 431.

during the early years of the operation of the Treaty cases came only slowly, so that the first decisions of the Commission are not found until 1964 and the first decisions of the Court under Article 230 do not occur until the *Grundig* case in 1966. Looking at the cases decided in the years immediately after 1966, the Commission's preoccupation with vertical relationships (so often the subject of complaint by a distributor or licensee) is noticeable, especially those dealing with exclusive distribution, whilst only a minority of the decisions relate to cartels, trade associations, and other, mainly horizontal, relationships. This preoccupation with the vertical arose directly from the early policy choice made in the course of negotiations leading up to the adoption of Regulation 17, that the range of vertical agreements for which in practice notification would be needed would be very wide. Had the mesh of the net for notification been less fine, and fewer notifications thus required in the early stages of the Commission's work, more attention could have been paid at that vital time to horizontal agreements, and particularly to cartels allocating national markets. As it was, not until the end of the 1960s did the Commission and the Court get to grips with substantial horizontal cartels of the type found in the *Dyestuffs* and *Sugar* cases, which of course present much greater evidentiary problems.

During its early years the Commission's chief windows of opportunity came undoubtedly from the Court, which went out of its way to emphasize the importance that Articles 81 and 82 played in the overall scheme of the Treaty by giving broad interpretation in a number of leading cases to the essential elements of those Articles. The extent to which the Court had taken trouble to do this has been pointed out by an authoritative source. After stressing that the application of Article 234 always posed particular difficulties for the Court because of the risk that the findings of the national court were wrong or did not arise from the evidence established, or that the questions put to the European Court might have been inadequately phrased, Lord Slynn (then Advocate General and later the United Kingdom judge) pointed out some years ago that the Court nevertheless had in a number of ways given great assistance to the Commission in its task. It had treated as a priority from the outset the creation of a single market for Member States rather than focusing on issues of efficiency or even of consumer protection. To quote his words:

It is wholly consistent with this approach that the Court took a broad view of what constitutes a concerted practice...that it should treat as part of contractual arrangements what on the face of it could appear to be background or contextual material...that it should see one individual contract as part of a network rather than in isolation...that it should construe 'undertaking' broadly, 'relevant market' narrowly, often by reference to the nature of the product, of the end uses, or in relation to intraband rather than broader market considerations, that it should accept a narrow geographical base such as that of one or several Member States rather than by taking a broader region as the area appropriate for the relevant market; that it should define abuse in terms of its effect on competition rather than by balancing whether the allegedly abusive conduct might contribute to economic efficiency.[4]

---

[4] In an address 'EEC Competition Law from the Perspective of the Court of Justice' [1985] Fordham Corp L Inst 383.

The Court also made it clear that it would not intervene on applicants' behalf in the course of Commission investigations unless there were cogent grounds for doing so, nor would it annul Commission decisions on procedural grounds unless there was either a cardinal flaw in the process or a total inadequacy of economic analysis.

One must give credit to DG Comp for taking full advantage—in the early years at least—of the support which it received from the Court. As can be seen by a study of its individual decisions year by year, it fully utilized the width of interpretation accorded by the Court to the principal elements of Articles 81 and 82. It did not find itself handicapped, as have some national courts, by technical or narrow interpretation of its jurisdiction and powers. Moreover, the Commission did its best to pay attention not only to the words of the Court's decision but also to the rather broader 'signals' which the Court had apparently been trying to send to it as to the general conduct of its cases, *Continental Can* being a good example of a warning in that period that superficial analysis would not be tolerated even if the decision appeared on the facts to be (from the Commission's viewpoint) an obvious one.

4.2 THE PERIOD FROM 1989 ONWARDS

A new relationship however between the Community Courts and the Commission began in 1989. It had been clear for some time before that date that the ECJ was not an appropriate forum for the detailed review of Commission competition decisions, when appeals were brought by undertakings which had been subject to adverse decisions and often fines in addition. Inevitably the decisions of the Commission themselves were lengthy and involved much detailed factual as well as legal analysis.

The many other pressures on the ECJ, with its responsibility for dealing with disputes between Member States and between Community institutions, and other important constitutional issues arising under the Treaty itself through the mechanism of Article 234, meant that painstaking analysis of the facts of an alleged cartel or abuse of dominant position imposed unreasonable burdens upon it. What was needed was a rather less formal tribunal sitting in Chambers of not less than three or more than five members, able to involve itself closely in the often intricate details of the Commission's decision. Given the Commission's combined role as prosecutor, judge, and jury in competition cases,[5] it was clearly vital that confidence in the whole process be maintained by the availability of a thorough appellate forum, dealing with the detailed case as one of its essential responsibilities rather than as one of many equally important duties. As a result the Court of First Instance was set up in 1989.

The work of the CFI since 1989 has not disappointed the hopes of those responsible for its establishment.[6] Although its jurisdiction was not limited to competition

---

[5] For the purposes of Art. 6 of the European Convention of Human Rights the ECJ has held that the Commission itself is not a 'tribunal' (Cases C-209–15, 218/78 *Van Landewijck v. Commission* [1980] ECR 3125: [1981] 3 CMLR 134); but the fundamental rights of the parties to a Commission decision are preserved by the availability of an appeal to the CFI. See K. Lenaerts and I. Maselis, 'Procedural Rights and Issues in the Enforcement of Arts. 81 and 82' [2000] Fordham Corp L Inst 279–363.

[6] A. Johnston, 'Judicial Reform and the Treaty of Nice' [2001] 38 CMLRev 499, 503.

cases except in its initial four years, the majority of the Commission decisions against which an appeal was brought to it did involve alleged breaches of Articles 81 and 82. It has produced a number of notable judgments in competition cases, a large number of which, especially in cartel cases, have substantially upheld the decision of the Commission, even if on a number of occasions also fines have been marginally reduced, mainly on procedural grounds. There have also been some sharp defeats for the Commission where the CFI has not been afraid of expressing its disapproval of the procedures or findings of the Commission in language that is never less than precise and occasionally even savage.

Dealing first with appeals against decisions under Articles 81 and 82, amongst the numerous cases heard, there has been a reasonable number of successful appeals, often on procedural grounds. In *European Night Services*[7] the Court's decision was notable for its critique of a Commission finding that a joint venture set up to run night services through the Channel Tunnel by four national railway undertakings with less than 10 per cent of the relevant market share for transport services had a restrictive effect on competition within the Common Market. Another notable judgment overruling the Commission was *Bayer* (discussed in Chapter 6) in which it refused to apply the concept of 'agreement' to the unilateral refusal of supplies by Bayer to its wholesale distributors in France and Spain because of their practice of sending some of these supplies by way of parallel exports into higher price countries such as the United Kingdom. More recently in *GlaxoSmithKline* the CFI annulled a Commission decision under Article 81(3) on the grounds that the Commission had not applied properly one of the conditions for exemption set out in that provision. In the *Italian Flat Glass* case the court was also critical of some of the evidence relied upon by the Commission and its attempt to 'recycle' Article 81 evidence in order to use it under Article 82 as well. On the other hand it has broadly been supportive of the Commission's approach to, and decisions in, some complex and controversial Article 82 cases such as *Tetrapak (No. 2)*, *Magill*, *CMB* and *Microsoft*, described in Chapter 14.

The CFI also has, of course, to deal with appeals against the Commission's decisions under the merger regulations, the first of which came into force shortly after the formation of the Court itself. As we have seen in Chapter 17, the delay inherent in the normal appeal procedure for such cases meant originally that it was rarely worthwhile for dissatisfied undertakings to raise an appeal against a substantive finding of the Commission which had blocked or imposed onerous conditions on a proposed merger. Nevertheless, on occasions when a point of principle was at stake, appeals were brought. The case of *Gencor*, for example, laid down important principles on the definition of collective dominance under the regulation and on issues of extraterritoriality. Most influential however in recent years was the 2002 judgment in *Airtours*, where the Commission's blocking decision on a proposed merger in the UK foreign package holiday market was held unjustified because of undue reliance on the collective dominance theory, against a background of evidence which in the opinion of the CFI fell

[7] See Ch. 7, p. 108.

far short of proving that such a state of affairs existed. Moreover the language used by the CFI could only be described as severe.

This particular case had taken nearly three years from the date of the original Commission decision to the date of the CFI judgment. The arrival however of an expedited appeal procedure for cases which did not raise highly complex factual issues meant that three months later, two further cases under this new procedure were handed down, namely *Schneider/Legrand* and *Tetra Laval/Sidel*. The *Schneider* decision in particular had some common features with that of *Airtours* in that the fact-finding processes of the Commission were severely criticized, whereas the *Tetra Laval* case turned more on the question of burden of proof in a case where the adverse finding was principally based on the theory of economic leverage by a dominant company from one market to another. Nevertheless the combined effect of these three judgments (delivered in a space of just over four months) on the morale of the Commission and its Merger Task Force in particular was potent and led directly to the changes made to the merger control rules in 2004. The cases are described further in Section 5.3.4 below.

The relationship between the ECJ and the Commission is primarily felt in two ways. The first is in the treatment by the ECJ of appeals from the CFI which are of course limited to points of law in competition cases. In this respect the ECJ has in most cases upheld the CFI's judgment on issues of principle, even if on occasion it has placed a different emphasis when making its own findings.[8] The second relationship is the result of Article 234 cases, where one could name by way of example the *Bronner* and *Masterfoods* cases as laying down legal principles providing important assistance to the Commission. In the first case the outcome was a clear signal as to the limits of the doctrine of essential facilities which some commentators had thought had been extended too far in certain earlier Commission decisions. In the second case the Court confirmed the obligation of courts in Member States to suspend proceedings whilst the Commission was itself dealing with the same issue and even while further appeals from its rulings were still possible to Community courts.

5. THE ACHIEVEMENTS AND FAILURES OF THE COMMISSION

5.1 THE BACKGROUND

In this final section we seek to draw up a balance sheet for the Commission, which recognizes both its achievements and its failures. Taking first its achievements, the starting point must be the willingness of the Commission to adapt over a period of

---

[8] K. Lenaerts, 'The European Court of First Instance: Ten Years of Interaction with the Court of Justice', in *Liber Amicorum in honour of Lord Slynn: Judicial Review in European Union Law*, (Kluwer, 2000), pp. 97. Sometimes however it has firmly set aside the decisions of the CFI. See for example Case C-413/06P *Sony and Bertelsmann v Commission*, 10 July 2008 (not yet reported).

fifty years to the changing demands made upon it. The political and economic circumstances in which it operates have changed substantially over this period. The pace
of change in recent years has been particularly marked as the nature of the world of
business and industry has altered, under the combined force of globalization and the
computer and communications technological revolutions. Pressures on senior officials
of DG Comp have increased markedly, both in terms of the timescale within which
decisions, both formal and informal, are expected, and because of the controversial
and complex nature of cases before them, particularly those arising under the Merger
Regulation. The continuing enlargement of the Community has brought a perpetual
pressure on the Commission to find legislative and administrative solutions to enable
it to handle adequately the many areas for which it is responsible.

A continuing challenge therefore for the Commission has been to adapt itself to new
circumstances, both economic and political, prevailing not only in the Community
itself but in the world generally. It may not always have reacted as quickly as its critics
would have urged, but it has so far nevertheless shown impressive ability to find solutions to existing problems. Going back to the 1970s, its ability to adapt was shown in
its handling of crisis cartels in a number of industries. It showed itself sensitive to the
problems of particular sectors and undertakings at a time of economic difficulty following the rise in oil prices: cases from that time illustrate this flexibility.[9]

The Commission has also been able to apply Article 81(1) and (3) to a large variety of
new sectors including the media, communications, sport, and transport as well as to the
more traditional range of goods and services with which it had been concerned in its
earlier decades. It has not been afraid to apply Article 81(3) to situations even where some
novel factors have been brought into account, such as environmental gains, and even
where the parties were required to accept considerable restrictions on their freedom,
for example, the phasing out of production of certain less efficient models of household
goods, such as washing machines and refrigerators, on an industry-wide basis.[10]

As we have already noted, its realization that its approach to block exemptions in the
1980s and early 1990s had become too legalistic and negative, when a more liberal and
'effects based' style both of economic analysis and of drafting was more appropriate,
led to a marked simplification of approach in the block exemption on vertical restraints
in Regulation 2790/99. This trend was enhanced by the introduction of Regulation
1216/99 making retrospective notification possible for vertical agreements.

But of course in drawing up such a balance sheet it is important to remember that
it is not only DG Comp itself or even the Commission as a whole that can claim the
entire credit (or blame) for achievements or failures. On occasion it is the Council that
has played a decisive influence by enacting appropriate legislation to confer additional
powers on the Commission when it has received cogent argument that such new powers
were required, for example with regard to Regulation 1216/99. On other occasions it is

---

[9] See for example *Synthetic Fibres* [1985] 1 CMLR 787; *KEWA* [1976] 2 CMLR D15; *URG* [1976] 2 CMLR
D1; *International Energy Authority* [1984] 2 CMLR 186.

[10] *CECED* [2000] OJ L187/47: 5 CMLR 635. For a fuller exposition of this aspect of the Commission's
approach to Art. 81(3), see R. Whish, *Competition Law* (6th edn, Butterworths, 2008), pp. 153–5.

the outcome of Article 234 decisions of the ECJ in cases such as *Masterfoods* or *Crehan* which have clarified uncertainties or provided a powerful signal to the Commission as to the way in which legal developments should be driven. On the other hand let us give credit to the Commission for having on occasion itself provided the initiative and fresh thinking which has been a decisive factor in advances in policy or increased effectiveness of administration. In some cases it has clearly benefited from the experience of, and cooperation given by, competition officials in the USA and other nations, especially in the handling of cartels and of mergers, where jurisdictions have had a mutual interest in close coordination.

5.2 GREATER TRANSPARENCY

The first achievement that should be mentioned is the creation of a far greater measure of transparency for the work of DG Comp as a whole. It introduced in 1994 an EC competition policy newsletter published three times a year giving details of recent decisions and policy articles by officials. It has also published a number of guidelines to block exemption regulations and useful guides to procedure. It now also makes full use of modern technology: from the middle of 1996 it has had its own Internet website. This contains a wide range of information on the main aspects of competition policy, including a full set of press releases and the full text of current legislative provisions and policy documents and of Commission decisions. Up-to-date statistics on ECN activity, merger cases, and cartel fines are given and written submissions to public consultations are also made available. Separate sections set out speeches given and articles published by the Competition Commissioner or by the Director General of DG Comp. Given the large amount of current information often required by those involved in competition cases, this development is a great advance.

5.3 SUBSTANTIVE ACHIEVEMENTS AND FAILURES

It might seem neater to present separately first the Commission's achievements and then its failures. Nevertheless they will be considered together, as in some areas there has been great success on one front or during one time period, and failure or very little success on another, and a more coherent assessment can be provided by taking the two together.

5.3.1 Treatment of vertical agreements

As described in Chapter 10, the priority given by the Commission in its early years to distribution systems and its first block exemptions have been criticized. The exemptions relied not only on a list of 'black' prohibited clauses, but set out a lengthy list of other restrictions regarded as less significant on a permitted 'white' list, rather than allowing all such clauses to be permitted within the scope of the block exemption. This more liberal solution had to wait until Regulation 2790/99 which not only eliminated the 'white' list and sectoral provisions for beer and petrol, but consolidated a number of previous block exemptions. It was also the first time that block exemption was linked to market power, through the use of a market-share threshold, which was a very important step towards a more economics-based application of Article 81, both to vertical restraints and more broadly.

The problem of framing an appropriate block exemption for vehicle distribution has also remained a concern for the Commission. Although the current block exemption 1400/2002, the third to be adopted, is the one which grants the greatest degree of commercial freedom to dealers and imposes the most restrictions on vehicle manufacturers, nevertheless even this seems unlikely to solve the fundamental problem of imbalance of bargaining position between suppliers and dealers. The creation of a workable single Community market for cars, where consumers have a genuine range of choice for the purchase of different models from manufacturers in different Member States, still seems far off. Major car manufacturers have long treated their dealers, not as true distributors with freedom of operation in the conduct of their own business, but as quasi-agents with only a limited range of freedom and the likelihood of sanctions if they are too active in extending sales beyond their primary territory in their home State. Regulation 1400/2002 has brought some progress in this respect.

On the other hand it can certainly be regarded as a success that, following this early concentration on vertical agreements, the gradual development of the Single Market and the implementation of block exemptions covering a wider range of agreements of a vertical nature made it possible in the late nineties for some resources to be switched, in particular providing a more effective challenge to major cartels affecting a number of Member States, of the kind which in the past had not previously been challenged at all or only over a very lengthy period owing to lack of resources.

5.3.2 Cartels

Another achievement has been that the likelihood of such major cartels being discovered has been greatly increased as a result of the implementation of the original 1996 leniency programme, followed by revised versions in 2002 and 2006. This provides a real incentive for participants to approach the Commission to give them sufficient information enabling it either to carry out an investigation or to find an infringement of Article 81(1) (see Chapter 9).

Experience in earlier cases had shown the great evidential problem in such cases where there is no 'insider' to provide key information about the workings of a cartel, so that the prosecution can only proceed on the basis of piecing together fragments of documentary information from a number of different sources. Hence, the leniency programme is probably the most important factor in enabling a remarkable growth in the number of successfully prosecuted cases and the increase in the number and level of fines. Fines in 2002 reached nearly €1 billion, a fact proudly commented on by Commissioner Monti at the end of that year, a year which in other respects (particularly in regard to merger cases) had been particularly difficult for him personally and the Commission. Since then fine levels have continued to increase, reaching a total of €1.8 billion in 2006 and €3.3 billion in 2007.

5.3.3 The notification system for Article 81 and its abolition through modernization

The situation in which the original system for dealing with agreements restricting competition was introduced is now so unfamiliar to us, as we look back over more than four decades to its start, that it is important to remember why it was adopted. As explained in Chapter 4, at the outset the way in which Article 81 should be interpreted and applied was far from clear. Many forms of cartel had been regularly entered into by European businessmen prior to the Treaty of Rome without any realization that they were of damaging economic effect; on the contrary their impact on employment and levels of demand for goods and services was often genuinely, if incorrectly, believed to be stabilizing. The Commission could not therefore risk allowing decisions on the application of Article 81(1) and 81(3) to be left to national courts or authorities where these existed. The monopoly over the granting of individual notification was the natural method of maintaining the necessary degree of control for the Commission at this critical early stage.

A solution suitable therefore for the 1960s and 1970s turned out, nevertheless, to be unworkable and ineffective in the far more complex and demanding conditions of the final decades of the twentieth century. The Commission found itself, for both administrative and linguistic reasons, unable to issue more than a few formal decisions under Article 81(3). Although the actual number of such decisions eventually rose from single figures in each year to as many as forty-two in 1998 and sixty-eight in 1999, this still represented less than 10 per cent of the total number of cases dealt with in each year. Moreover, each formal decision was itself taking an unreasonably long time to be issued; for example the *1998 Annual Report*[11] records that of the eleven formal decisions issued in that year the shortest duration was over two years, the longest eight years and the average four years and ten months.

The problem was ultimately solved by the Commission's 'modernization programme', which abolished the notification system as a whole, and introduced significantly decentralized enforcement. The very name of this reform is a branding triumph for the Commission, and the various procedural changes brought to enforcement of Articles 81 and 82 were timely. As a former Head of the Commission's Legal Service has said, 'For the Community to have started with the authorization system and to evolve towards a legal exception system would be a natural and historically justified crescendo.'[12] This process took nearly half a century; during this time considerable experience has been gathered within the Community on how competition policy can be framed, consulted over, and finally put into effect, as a cooperative process between all of the many interested parties, including not only the Commission and its many Directorates General, responsible for different areas of its work, but also the

---

[11] See p. 28.

[12] Giuliano Marenco, 'The Modernization of EC Antitrust Policy', in C.-D. Ehlermann and I. Anastasiu (eds.), *European Competition Law Annual 2000* (Hart Publishing, 2001), p. 175. This volume is essential reading for all those interested in the background to the modernization programme of the Commission.

Council and other Community institutions, Member States, and their own competition authorities. Still, the Commission's central role remains key, as it alone is charged
with acting in the interests of the Community *as a whole*; its members are to be 'completely independent' in the performance of their duties, taking no instructions from
any Member State, government, or any other body.[13]

The many consequences and achievements so far of modernization and Regulation 1/2003 are described in Chapter 19. It will be seen there that the Commission
has received a number of new powers, and that its position therefore has been strengthened by the terms of the Regulation, notwithstanding the surrender of the monopoly
over applying Article 81(3). The only power which it sought during the negotiations,
but which was not granted, was that to issue under its own authority (rather than
under the authority of the Council) new block exemptions. It was felt ultimately by
Member States that this would give the Commission too wide a power and would be
inconsistent with the spirit of the new cooperative arrangements being made with
them. At the same time the reform opened up more possibilities for private enforcement, as described in Chapter 20. Finally, modernization has also indirectly achieved
very significant voluntary harmonization of national competition laws, the implications of which are explored in the following chapter.[14]

5.3.4 The Merger Regulation

Under the Merger Regulation the Commission has created an efficient system for
handling more than 300 concentrations of Community dimension each year. This has
provided both a firm timetable which normally allows even the most complex cases
to be resolved within six months while enabling the clearance of the remaining 95 per
cent through shorter and more simplified procedures, even if in some cases certain
conditions have to be applied. Because of its widely drawn turnover-based jurisdictional range, the Commission has in effect become a 'world competition authority', at
least in respect of all major companies which do substantial business in the EC as well
as elsewhere. Its achievements in this respect remain—notwithstanding the problems
that arose both with regard to its procedures and its substantive criteria for assessment
and which came to a head in 2002.

By that time, the application of the Regulation had been regarded as the Commission's
greatest success for nearly twelve years. DG Comp had apparently been able, admittedly only through massive efforts, to cope over the 1990s with handling an increase
from sixty cases in the first year to well over 300 per year by the end of the century. This
total included a number of complex mergers and joint ventures in major sectors such as
oil, chemicals, telecoms, finance, and aeronautics. The Commission had only blocked
eighteen cases over this period, these being the rare group of cases where no remedies

---

[13] John Temple Lang, 'How Much Do the Smaller States Need the European Commission? The Role of the
Commission in a Changing Europe' [2002] 39 CMLR 315–35.

[14] For a detailed account of the way in which the new system has functioned in its first four years see
E. Gippini-Fournier, 'The Modernisation of European Competition Law: First Experiences with Regulation
1/2003', Report to the FIDE Congress 2008, available at <http://www.ssrn.com/abstract=1139776>.

of a satisfactory nature could be suggested by the parties that would effectively eliminate the damage to competition that the merger would cause in relevant markets. In many others, structural or behavioural conditions—often of a complex nature—had been agreed as conditions for approval. While the application of the rules in certain mergers between major US companies had provoked some controversy and an 'agreement to disagree' over the assessment of the case, overall relationships with the US antitrust authorities continued to be close and cooperation worked well on a day-to-day basis. The tone of the tenth anniversary conference held in Brussels in September 2001, if not exactly triumphalist, at least was one of satisfaction at real achievement. Collective dominance had been upheld as a principle applicable to merger cases in *Kali und Salz* and *Gencor* (even if on the facts the Commission had been overruled by the ECJ in the first case) and it was clear that this doctrine would continue to play an important part in future cases. But the Commission was certainly not complacent and in its December 2001 Green Paper had put forward a number of suggestions of further improvements to the operation of the Regulation.

All this was changed however by the publication in June 2002 of the *Airtours* decision by the CFI, followed in October by the decisions in *Schneider* and *Tetra Laval*, which together proved very painful for the Commission and in particular its officials working on merger cases. Three blocking decisions were annulled in language highly critical of the Commission's economic analysis, fact-finding competence, and application of economic theories. Since the decisions are often treated collectively as a wholesale assault on the previously high reputation of the Commission for application of the Merger Regulation, it is important to distinguish between the separate grounds in each case for the annulment of the original decision. In *Airtours*, the blocking decision had been based on a finding that the UK short-haul foreign package-holiday market would, as a result of the proposed merger, create a market collectively dominated by three major undertakings, leading to a reduction in the availability of holidays and an increase in their price. The CFI found that the Commission's analysis was inadequate in a number of respects namely that it:

- failed to provide adequate evidence to support a finding that there was an existing tendency in the sector to collective dominance
- did not take account of current and past volatility in the market
- underestimated the foreseeable reaction of smaller tour operators, consumers, and hotel operators to any coordination between the three major players
- misinterpreted and misapplied some of the documentary evidence.

In *Schneider*, the two main criticisms were that:

- with regard to the French market (where dominance and effect on competition was clearly established) the Statement of Objections had failed to set out fully the case against the merger, so that the defendants had not been allowed an adequate opportunity of making their case

- with regard to the other national markets, the Commission had failed to do a full analysis of their individual state and the relevant strength of the parties within it.

In *Tetra Laval*, the Commission had relied on a theory of 'leverage', arguing that Tetra's admitted dominance in its main markets (aseptic carton packaging equipment) would allow it to offer juice and milk packagers special terms if they were to agree to purchase their stretched blow moulding machines required for the making of PET bottles from the target company, Sidel, thereby shifting demand away from Sidel's competitors. The CFI found that the evidence for this was weak and insufficient to justify a blocking decision. The Commission appealed to the ECJ, arguing that the level of the burden of proof imposed on the Commission was too high, but the ECJ confirmed the CFI's judgment.

In responding to these events, a sense of proportion was of course needed. Of well over two thousand cases already decided less than five per cent had been through the second phase examination reserved for concentrations that raise serious doubts about their compatibility with the Regulation. Of these probably only a dozen or so could be described as controversial in their outcome.

Nevertheless, it was clear that radical change was needed, and since 2002 many far-reaching and constructive changes have been implemented, in particular through the adoption by the Council of the replacement Merger Regulation 139/2004, with its new substantive test and a number of procedural improvements such as more flexibility in both time limits and the referral of cases from the Commission to one or more Member State authorities, or in the other direction. In addition DG Comp itself has been restructured and has changed its procedures significantly, successfully restoring its positive image within a fairly short time, and in particular allowing it to cope with the exceptionally large number of 402 notifications made in 2007. A fuller description of these changes is given in Chapters 16 and 17.

Notable recent successes in the merger area include a number of instances of 'economic nationalism' where the Commission stood firm against Member State governments which sought illegally to prevent or interfere with transactions that they regarded as contrary to their national economic interest. These cases are discussed in Chapter 24.

5.3.5 Article 82

One of the Commission's specific achievements in the area of abuse of dominance has been establishing the concept of essential facilities firmly in the jurisprudence of Article 82, applying it in a wide range of situations including harbours, airports, bank payment systems, and computer reservation systems. Notwithstanding the firm limiting signal given by the ECJ in *Bronner*, it has been able to utilize the concept in a wide variety of situations where dominant companies might otherwise have been able to foreclose access to competitors. This has been particularly valuable in the telecommunications sector, where by both Directives and Decisions under Article 86(3) it established strong criteria for national competition authorities in terms of the basis for competition in that sector between incumbents and new entrants.

However, the Article 82 case law of both Commission and Court is generally open to the criticism that, though it is extensive, there is still an unsatisfactory lack of clarity about the key concepts of dominance and abuse. As indicated in Chapter 13, the definition of dominance is one often difficult to apply to the facts of particular markets. The law appears moreover to have moved from a situation where an undertaking either is or is not dominant, taking market share and all other circumstances into account, to one where it may fall either into a category of dominance or of 'super dominance'. In the latter case its obligations not to engage in one of a number of particular practices may depend upon the actual market share which it holds and its relationship to the other members of that market, calculated on what appears to be almost a 'sliding scale'. It appears that the law has moved on quite a long way from the simple rule contained in the *ECS/AKZO* case where the possession of a regular market share of 50 per cent or more was deemed to constitute a presumption of dominance. In addition, this is the area of competition law in which the starkest divergences between EU and US law appear.[15]

The Commission has been able to bring a number of successful cases in this area, the most notable in recent years being its decision fining Microsoft almost half a billion euros for refusal to supply interoperability information to allow other producers' workgroup server operating systems to interoperate with Microsoft's Windows PC operating system, and for tying of Windows with its MediaPlayer software. In this case, as in a number of others such as *Michelin II*, *British Airways* and *Deutsche Telekom*, it has generally received broad support from the Community Courts when appeals have been heard. While the different categories of abuse have grown impressively (as the length of Chapter 14 indicates), there remains a broad suspicion that, particularly in cases concerned with pricing, the Commission's analysis of what constitutes abuse is unduly restrictive on dominant undertakings.

As far as intellectual property rights are concerned, whilst the Commission did not (contrary to fears originally expressed) take the outcome of the *Magill* decision of the ECJ as a basis for seeking compulsory licensing in a wide variety of situations, the CFI's 2007 judgment in *Microsoft* has raised fresh worries on this front.

The Commission is aware of the unsatisfactory state of the law, and DG Comp formally opened a review of its Article 82 enforcement policy with the publication of a Discussion Paper in December 2005, the main thrust of which was the need for an approach based on sound economic analysis and a focus on effects on consumer welfare. This has potential to earn the classification of achievement, but though the initiative provoked very many useful debates and has undoubtedly influenced the approach of individual officials it has yet to have any concrete outcome in the form of published guidance.

---

15 J. Vickers, 'Competition Law and Economics: a Mid-Atlantic Viewpoint' [2007] ECJ 1.

5.3.6 Bilateral and Multilateral Co-operation Agreements

Finally, the Community, at the initiative of DG Comp, has created strong bilateral cooperation agreements covering both traditional and positive comity with the USA, Japan, and Canada, and has strong links of various types with many other important antitrust jurisdictions. This has provided a good deal of information of value in particular cases, including cartels where proceedings had already taken place in the US and large fines imposed so that Community proceedings could subsequently follow aided by those earlier proceedings; it has also given valuable psychological support to the Commission, supplementing the work of existing multinational organizations such as OECD and the newer organization for cooperation between national competition agencies, the International Competition Network (see Chapter 22).

24

THE FUTURE OF EUROPEAN COMPETITION LAW

1. INTRODUCTION

1.1 LOOKING BACK: REFORMS SUGGESTED IN THE FOURTH EDITION

All the previous chapters of this fifth edition of *EC Competition Law* have dealt with the past development of the competition policy of the Community and with the variety of economic and legal issues with which it has had to contend. These include both procedural and substantive questions, some of long standing and some relatively new on the scene. In this final chapter it is time to anticipate the future progress of competition law and competition policy in Europe, and to seek to identify those current problems for which effective solutions will be required in the next few years.

At this point it is also salutary to look back at the equivalent chapter which closed the previous edition, in order to see whether the analysis five years ago of some of the reforming steps which the Commission and Council might take have actually come to pass. The main reforms identified as necessary in 2003 can be listed as follows:

- following the procedural modernization programme, the need for the Commission to retain its central role in both policy consultation and policy implementation, with the European Parliament retaining its present role and not being given increased powers in the competition law area

- integration of officials from the new Member States into DG Comp

- use of two- or three-year secondments of officials from these countries to DG Comp so that their national authorities could benefit from DG Comp's experience and expertise

- further legislation on the functioning of the modernized enforcement environment, to the extent that this proved a necessary supplement to the existing 'soft' instruments

- adoption of a practice similar to that of US 'Business Review Letters' to give companies guidance on the application of Articles 81 and 82 when necessary

- greater use by DG Comp of its powers to carry out sector inquiries so as to gain better knowledge of particular sectors and types of agreement which may raise competition issues
- a solution to the limitations that the *Bayer* judgment imposed on the use of Article 81 to combat the use of supply quotas by pharmaceutical companies
- revision of the technology transfer block exemption Regulation 240/96 to bring it into line with other, more economics-based, block exemptions
- continued surveillance of the liberalization process in telecommunications and energy markets and intervention if necessary
- measures whereby DG Comp regained trust in its conduct of merger control, following the criticisms made of it by the CFI in its *Airtours*, *Schneider/Legrand* and *Tetra Laval/Sidel* judgments, but without allowing it to become fearful of making blocking decisions
- restructuring of DG Comp to meet the criticisms contained in those judgments
- replacement of the dominance test by a more satisfactory substantive test for merger control
- procedural changes in merger control, including increased flexibility of the timetable
- more thorough approach by DG Comp to gathering data in merger cases
- investigation and assessment of mergers to be carried out by separate groups or, ideally, different bodies
- creation of three or four regional chambers of the CFI, to deal with competition appeals from the highest national courts and also Article 234 references on competition law.

1.2 THE PROGRESS OF REFORM SINCE 2003

European competition policy and the approach of DG Comp and the Commission generally towards their responsibilities in this area have changed out of all recognition over the last five years. In particular in 2004 three changes of major significance altered the shape and effectiveness of the competition policy of the Community in an irrevocable and fundamental manner. In this sense therefore the situation now is completely different from that of five years ago. These major changes have all been referred to in various chapters in Part II but it may be appropriate to recall them at this point:

- the implementation of Regulation 1/2003, replacing Regulation 17/62, as the principal basis for the modernization programme under which the administration of Articles 81 and 82 was decentralized and in large measure entrusted to national competition authorities and national courts, in particular by the introduction of the principle of 'exception légale' and the removal of the Commission's monopoly on granting individual exemption

- the introduction of a new revised Merger Regulation containing important changes in both substance and procedure, and designed in particular to respond to the criticisms of the Commission's procedures made by the CFI in its three critical judgments of 2002

- the enlargement of the Community by the accession of ten new Member States, eight from Eastern Europe, together with Cyprus and Malta, to be followed in 2007 by the accession of Bulgaria and Romania.

Looking back at the 'menu for change' identified five years ago and set out in Section 1.1, it is good to record that in many, if not all, respects there has been substantial movement in the direction of these rather optimistic suggestions. The main developments anticipated concerned the modernization programme, which has now become part of daily competition law life without raising insurmountable difficulties, and merger control. There, following the discouraging events of 2002, the considerable efforts of DG Comp and others have led to the Commission's position as a respected world-level competition authority being restored.

Moreover, as the list of achievements at the end of the previous chapter indicates, there have been some important and welcome reforms, or moves towards reform, that were not included in that list. For example Member States' procedural and substantive competition law rules have converged very significantly, to a large extent on a voluntary basis. Considerable efforts have also been made towards articulating a modernized and more economics-based approach towards the enforcement of Article 82.

The remainder of this chapter will deal with likely and desirable future developments in European competition law. We will consider in order the status of competition policy within the scheme of the Treaty as a whole, an issue brought to prominence during negotiation of the Lisbon Treaty (Section 2), outstanding issues raised by or related to the modernization programme (Section 3), the future of merger control (Section 4), cartel enforcement and damages actions (Section 5), abuse of dominance (Section 6), the role of economics and economists (Section 7), the new economy (Section 8), and finally the international dimension (Section 9).

2. COMPETITION LAW: ITS STATUS IN THE COMMUNITY LEGAL ORDER

Before turning to more concrete issues of likely and desirable future developments in the substance and procedure of Community competition law, it is appropriate to consider a fundamental issue of principle, which is the place of competition policy in the broader context of the Community Treaties. This issue has a small but real potential to cause far-reaching changes to the European competition law environment and the direction that policy may take in the future.

In June 2007 the European competition law community was shaken by news concerning the draft Lisbon Treaty, intended to adapt the Community Treaties in the light of various developments, not least among which was the accession of twelve new Member States since 2004. It emerged that, as part of the political trading inherent in the negotiation of any such Treaty, President Sarkozy of France had succeeded in having Article 3(1)(g) of the Treaty of Rome, which establishes the maintenance of competition as a main activity of the Community, deleted from the opening articles of the Treaty, with its essential content being transferred to a specific 'Protocol on the internal market and competition'. This remained the situation when the Lisbon Treaty was finalized and signed by all the Member States later in December that year.[1]

Opinions differ as to the effect, if any, that such a change would have on competition law enforcement. The strict legal position is that text in a protocol to a treaty has the same force as the text of the treaty itself, and certainly the Commission takes the view that the change does not portend any weakening in its position as enforcer of competition law.[2] On the other hand, commentators have evoked a number of potential dangers, mainly centred on the possibility that the Commission, and more importantly, the European Courts, will interpret the change in position of this key competition wording as meaning that they are now required to treat competition as a lower order Community task than it was previously. This might result, for example, in the endorsement of merger clearances on industrial policy grounds rather than maintenance of a focus, as has been the case in recent years, strictly on consumer welfare. Similarly, the change could weaken the pressure for market liberalization, and this could have a critical impact on policies such as the Commission drive to liberalize energy markets, and in particular to achieve ownership unbundling and the break up of infrastructure monopolies. Furthermore, Article 3(1)(g) has been cited by the Court of Justice in several seminal cases in the development of European competition law, including *Continental Can* and *Crehan*, which concerned conflicting policy objectives. It is by no means certain that the Courts will apply a protocol in the same way.

Whether or not the Lisbon Treaty eventually enters into force,[3] and whether these dangers do in fact materialize or not, these events are a salutary reminder of the crucial importance of communicating to citizens the benefits of a strong competition policy. The Commission was already well aware of the need to communicate to the

---

[1] The Constitutional Treaty, signed in 2004 but abandoned after French and Dutch popular referenda rejected its ratification, would, in contrast to the Lisbon Treaty, have given competition policy a clearly enhanced position in the Community legal order.

[2] Commissioner Kroes has even stated that the existence of a specific Protocol on competition policy would strengthen its position, 'Making Waves: Interview with EU Competition Commissioner Neelie Kroes' [2008] 22 Antitrust 2, 47.

[3] At the time of writing the fate of the Lisbon Treaty remains uncertain. It can enter into force only after ratification by all 27 Member States. Though 23 had ratified it by 1 September 2008, the Irish government is currently prevented from doing so because in a referendum in June 2008 the Irish voted against ratification.

population at large why European citizens benefit from the maintenance of competitive markets. This is evident, for example in the drafting of its press releases on individual decisions, and in various events that it organizes across the Community. Nevertheless, speaking at the time, President Sarkozy sought to rally popular support, saying 'Because as an ideology, as dogma, what did competition give to Europe? It has given less and less to the people who vote at European elections, and less and less to the people who believe in Europe.'[4]

While it is not in the Commission's power to control the attitude of the European Courts, nor to change the drafting of the Lisbon Treaty, it can and should be on its guard as to the potential difficulties it may face if and when this Treaty enters into force, and to the increased importance of ensuring it has political support when working close to the boundaries of established law. In addition this incident underlines the fact that the Commission and national authorities need to be alert to seize and to create opportunities to increase public understanding of their mission. There remains plenty of work to do in promoting the value of competition policy to citizens, and it is now clearer than ever that this is a key and not optional part of its work.[5]

3. MODERNIZATION: THE NEW ORDER

The new environment created by the modernization programme on 1 May 2004, though formally effecting only procedural reform, in practice also promoted a shift to a more economics-based interpretation of the law, most notably through the Commission's Notice on the application of Article 81(3). The new regime has now been in place for over four years, which is long enough to be able to conclude with some confidence that on the whole it is working well. Nevertheless, there is a perhaps surprising number of questions about the new regime, raised prior to 2004, that still remain partially or almost wholly unanswered. Some of these, and other related issues, are discussed in this section.

In 2009 the Commission is due to report to the Council and European Parliament on the practical functioning of Regulation 1/2003, and in particular on Article 11(6), which appears not to have been used at all, and Article 17, which provides for sector inquiries. The report can also be expected to consider Article 3, and in particular the question whether it is still necessary to allow Member States to apply to unilateral conduct national laws that are stricter than Article 82, as well as some of the other issues mentioned below.

---

[4] See sources cited in A. Riley, 'The EU Reform Treaty and the Competition Protocol: Undermining EC Competition Law' [2007] ECLR 703; see also F. Graupner, 'The Battle Over the Role of European Competition Policy: Now You See It, Now You Don't' [2007] 6 Comp LJ 89. Though certainly not an intentional reference to Monty Python's film *Life of Brian*, Sarkozy's words deserve a similar response to that given there to the question 'What have the Romans ever done for us?.'

[5] It is ironic that questions be raised as to the centrality of competition policy within the EU just at a time when the EU is playing a stronger leadership role than ever internationally (see Section 9 below).

3.1 THE EUROPEAN COMPETITION NETWORK

Working relationships between national authorities, and between those authorities and the Commission, were already good in 2004. Since then they have deepened considerably, and been extended to those of twelve new Member States, and the habit of working together on cases of mutual interest has been quite normal for some years now. Factors contributing to this have included the voluntary harmonization of substantive national laws in nearly all Member States to incorporate those principles found in Articles 81 and 82, the experience of successful case handling following exchange of information between Brussels and the Member States, as well as improved resources and standards of operation now to be found in the majority of national competition authorities. Important too has been a greater willingness on the part of DG Comp to trust individual authorities to handle cases that previously it might have sought to keep for resolution in Brussels.

The European Competition Network (ECN) is of course a tangible link based on an electronic communication web between Brussels and the national competition authorities, and between the individual competition authorities themselves. It is also however an intangible relationship between individual national and Commission officials, now that the original perceived subordination of the national authorities to an all-powerful DG Comp no longer applies. This has been replaced by an association, if not of equals, at least of organizations with a reasonable degree of mutual respect for each other's expertise. Personal relations are strong within this network and the Commission, which has until now given national authorities substantial leeway in their application of Community law, can perhaps now afford, to the extent that its resources permit, to become a little more interventionist in ensuring consistent interpretation of Articles 81 and 82.

And even at this stage there remains scope for increased contacts and closer cooperation, not least as increasing numbers of regulators are joining the ECN and taking part in its activities. This is clearly desirable in that at national level competition law issues arising in given sectors frequently fall within the remit of a sectoral regulator, whose approach should at least mesh broadly with those of its fellow enforcement agencies. In some sectors, for example that of telecommunications, it is anticipated that when markets are sufficiently competitive they will cease to be subject to a special regulatory regime and will instead become subject to general competition law rules. Integration of regulators into the ECN will contribute to smooth transfers of this sort. However, given the nature of their traditional role, regulators tend to have significantly different cultures from those of national authorities, even within the same Member State, and so their incorporation into the network does represent a challenge.

3.2 CONVERGENCE OF NATIONAL COMPETITION LAWS

One direct result of the quality of relationships within the ECN is the scope it provides for voluntary harmonization of national law and procedures. Voluntary or 'soft' convergence of national competition laws is one of the unexpected success stories of the modernization programme, and has already achieved near uniformity in a number of areas. While most substantive laws were already relatively similar across the Community in 2004, a striking degree of progress, going far beyond what is legally required by Regulation 1/2003, has taken place since then in terms of the procedural rules that govern national authorities Any attempt to do this through binding harmonizing legislation would have been much more burdensome procedurally, might have failed to command the necessary support from Member States, and even had it been adopted, implementation at national level might in practice have been slow. While important differences remain, for example as to the precise powers of officials when carrying out inspections, this outcome is very satisfactory and suggests scope for more progress towards harmonized procedural rules in the future.

The results of a questionnaire circulated within the ECN and answered by authorities from all twenty-seven Member States illustrates clearly the kind of progress that has already been made.[6] It indicates, for example, that in twenty-one Member States any national notification system for agreements either no longer exists or is in the process of being abolished, and that the authorities have some form of power to carry out sector inquiries in all Member States except Cyprus and Luxembourg. Similarly, the authorities in over three-quarters of Member States have, or expect soon to have, powers, when carrying out investigations, to seal business premises, books and records, and to inspect non-business premises. Only in Denmark and Estonia is there no planned or existing power to order interim measures. Whereas case closure by taking commitments was almost unknown at national level before 2004 it is now possible, or planned, everywhere except in Bulgaria, Estonia, and Malta.

The same voluntary process of harmonization has brought impressive progress also in the field of leniency programmes, under which cartel members, in return for informing the authorities about a cartel, earn immunity or a reduction in respect of any fine which they might otherwise have received. In 2004 only four Member States had leniency programmes. In respect of several of the rest it was asserted that such a thing was incompatible with their national culture, either because disloyalty (to fellow cartellists) was unthinkable, or because the award of leniency would be seen as unfairly rewarding wrongdoing. Despite the existence of such misgivings, by March 2008 leniency programmes were in operation everywhere except Malta and Slovenia. Having seen this approach work so effectively, it was an obvious step to seek to harmonize the content of these leniency programmes through a 'soft', non-legally binding instrument. The Commission and all the national authorities therefore agreed in 2006 on a 'Model Leniency Programme' setting out common elements that all were prepared to include in their programmes. Within a short time there had been significant progress in adopting the necessary measures at national level.

The success of soft convergence has given the Commission confidence in this working method, and the many working groups and meetings at different levels and involving different interest groups of officials have produced much useful work in the form

---

[6] The questionnaire concerned the position on 18 May 2007. The results are available on the ECN page of the DG Comp website.

of developing common approaches to particular industries and issues and resolving differences of opinion and approach.[7] In addition this network can play an important role in providing an example and supporting national authorities in taking action in circumstances where this might be politically difficult. This is a rich seam and there is plenty more to be extracted from it in the future. Over the coming years we can expect to see many more initiatives of this sort, allowing increasingly common approaches at the level of both substance and procedure to be achieved.

At the same time, though recent experience suggests that the voluntary approach works well in some areas, it has limits and its potential should not be overstated. One of the areas in which differences remain is that of court procedure and rules of evidence in litigation. The Green and White Papers on private damages actions in national courts highlight a number of these, and explain why they are a hindrance to the bringing of such actions. As discussed in Chapter 20, progress in adapting national law is needed if private damages actions for competition law breaches are to become common. While the level of convergence in national rules has been impressive insofar as they affect primarily national authorities, the rules governing national courts may prove less susceptible to such an approach. In Section 5 below possible legislative and other solutions are explored.

Finally, an issue on which there is unlikely to be harmonization over the next few years is that of the availability of criminal sanctions against individuals who participate in hard-core cartels, which exist in certain Member States, including the United Kingdom[8] and the Republic of Ireland. Whilst there is some evidence from the United States, with its long experience of the application of severe criminal sanctions including heavy fines and prison sentences for individual directors and managers of companies found to have participated in price-fixing or other horizontal cartel activities, that this can be a powerful weapon in the armament of antitrust authorities, it may not however be as effective in the European context.[9] In addition, given the Community's very limited competence in the area of criminal law, criminal sanctions are highly unlikely to be made available to the Commission.[10]

It is quite possible also that such criminal enquiries and proceedings may even delay for considerable periods or frustrate the bringing of proceedings under Articles 81

[7] This possibility was referred to by Professor Ehlermann as the 'bottom up' approach in which 'the law bubbles up', a familiar phenomenon and one of the great merits of a federal structure such as the United States, in his Introduction to *European Competition Law Annual 2000: The Modernization of EC Antitrust Policy* (Hart Publishing, 2001), p. xxii.

[8] Section 188, Enterprise Act 2002. See J. Joshua, 'The UK's New Cartel Offence and its Implications for EC Competition Law: A Tangled Web' [2003] 28 ELRev 620. The first terms of imprisonment under this provision were imposed on three executives on 11 June 2008 for their part in an international cartel in the marine-hoses market.

[9] The United States has the advantage of the Grand Jury investigation procedure and moreover the availability of contingent fees which facilitates the bringing of related civil proceedings for treble damages against the undertakings found to have participated in such activities, C. Jones, *Private Enforcement of Antitrust Law in the EU, UK and USA* (Oxford University Press, 1999).

[10] See further W. Wils, 'Is Criminalization of EU Competition Law the Answer?' [2005] 28 *World Competition and Economics Review* 117.

and 82 against the undertakings involved and the exchange of information between Member States under the terms of Article 12 of Regulation 1/2003, though there is not yet enough experience to know whether this will be the case. In the longer term, a further consequence of widespread criminal enforcement could be that the Commission, assuming it remained without such powers, could over time find its central enforcement role diminished.

3.3 POWERS YET TO BE USED

Well over four years after the entry into force of Regulation 1/2003 several of the powers there provided for have yet to be used by the Commission. It is instructive to consider why that might be, and in what circumstances they might be used in the future.

First of all, the Commission has never adopted a 'finding of inapplicability' under Article 10, by which it is empowered to state that a given agreement or other arrangement does not infringe Article 81 or, as the case may be, Article 82. Recital 14 of the Regulation provides that this may be done in 'exceptional cases where the public interest of the Community so requires . . . with a view to clarifying the law and ensuring its consistent application throughout the Community, in particular with regard to new types of agreement and practices that have not been settled in the existing case-law and administrative practice'. Nor has the Commission made use of the similar, but less formal, option of providing 'informal guidance' to an undertaking in accordance with Recital 38 and the relevant guidance notice,[11] which it is permitted to do where a case presents 'novel or unresolved questions for the application of [Article 81 or 82]'. It appears from unofficial statements made by Commission officials on public occasions that DG Comp has received at least a few requests for such measures, but that the cases in question have not satisfied the respective criteria, notably that they raise sufficiently novel legal issues.

Whereas it clearly right for the Commission to set the bar high in this respect, to avoid recreating the old notification system and consequent workload, it does seem surprising that not a single qualifying issue has yet been raised with the Commission. In practice it may be that the majority of difficult issues concern not the state of the law but rather the application of that law to the facts. It is also possible that companies are not attracted by the prospect of publication of an assessment of their commercial projects.

However, it does seem likely that at some point in the future it will be appropriate for the Commission to use one or other of these measures. Perhaps the occasion is most likely to be provided by an Article 82 case, where the disparity in approach between DG Comp's 2005 Discussion Paper and some of its previous case law might in a suitable case justify an official statement that, for example, particular conduct in specified circumstances does not constitute abuse.

---

[11] Art. 30 of Reg. 1/2003 requires the Commission to publish Art. 10 decisions, and the Notice on informal guidance provides that any such guidance will be published on DG Comp's website.

Another power that is apparently[12] yet to be used is Article 11(6), which allows the Commission to initiate its own proceedings, thereby relieving the national competition authorities of their competence in a particular case. The Commission has stated that it will only do this in exceptional circumstances. These might be present if a Member State had blatantly failed to act in a non-discriminatory manner, by favouring the activities of one or more of its undertakings regarded as 'national champions', leading to protests from other Member States. Alternatively it might happen when a Member State had genuinely attempted to bring proceedings under Article 81 or 82 against an undertaking but was obviously unable to collect the evidence required because the relevant conduct was found to be outside its territorial reach. In practice it seems that, to the extent that divergences in approach have been dealt with, this has so far occurred within appropriate working groups or sectoral subgroups of the ECN, where an informal resolution can be worked out in a non-confrontational setting. Article 11(6) was never intended to be used extensively, and the way in which the role of the ECN has developed in resolving such differences makes it even less likely that it will be used to any great extent, if at all, in the future.

3.4 BLOCK EXEMPTIONS

In principle, block exemption regulations have no place in the modernized world as they purport to exempt agreements that are, if they satisfy the four substantive criteria set out in Article 81(3), already exempt.[13] Logically they should be converted into guidelines, but so far they have not normally been allowed to lapse, as the legal certainty that they provide is so highly valued by business and its advisers.

When the technology transfer block exemption Regulation 240/96 expired it was replaced by Regulation 772/2004 which entered into force on the same day as Regulation 1/2003, and early indications are that the vertical restraints block exemption Regulation 2790/1999 will similarly be replaced in 2010. While it is true that Regulation 1459/2006 exempting air transport passenger tariff consultations and slot allocations was allowed to expire without replacement and block-exemption Regulation 4056/86 on liner shipping was repealed,[14] this happened not because of the logic of the introduction of the 'exception légale' approach to Article 81(3), but rather because exemption was no longer considered substantively justified.

Block exemptions can therefore normally be expected to be replaced when they expire, though in each case the Commission will consider seriously whether they remain justified in substance. For example, following its sector inquiry into the business insurance market the Commission appears to have serious doubts about the

---

[12] In this instance there is no publication requirement, but DG Comp officials confirm informally that there have not yet been any such cases.

[13] Even prior to modernization many senior Commission officials did not accept that block exemption regulations are of legislative character, but considered them rather just an exposition of the provisions of Art. 81(3) for enforcement purposes. See E. Paulis, 'Checks and Balances in the EU Antitrust Enforcement System' [2002] Fordham Corp L Inst.

[14] See Ch. 7.

continuing need for an insurance sector block exemption which exempts certain cooperation agreements between insurance companies. Unless the insurance industry can convince the Commission of the necessity to retain it, Regulation 358/2003 may be allowed to lapse when it expires in 2010.

The vertical-restraints block exemption on the other hand clearly remains substantively justified and is fully expected to be renewed on its expiry in 2010. While experience does not suggest that it needs major change, the Commission may well come under pressure to make it even more generous in the restrictions it allows. In particular, now that the US Supreme Court has ruled in *Leegin*[15] that resale price maintenance should be considered under the rule of reason rather than be subject to a per se prohibition (see Section 7 below), the Commission may come under pressure to review its own approach to this issue.

3.5 SETTING PRIORITIES IN 2008

Although modernization freed up significant resources through the abolition of notification, Regulation 1/2003 at the same time imposed new supervisory and coordinating duties on the Commission, which therefore continues to have to make decisions as to the priorities it adopts in the new role that it has played since 2004.

Enforcement action against major cartels with participants in a number of Member States currently has, and will continue to have in the coming years, the highest priority, but these cases impose such a burden on DG Comp's resources that it is still actively seeking new ways of reducing this burden. The most recent innovation is the introduction in June 2008 of a procedure for reaching settlements in cartel cases, with a view to obviating in some cases the need to go through the full investigatory and decision-making processes. The scope for private damages actions in national courts to relieve some of the enforcement burden is also under discussion, and both of these topics are covered in Section 5 below.

DG Comp will also be working on a number of Community-wide sectoral issues. The sector inquiries into aspects of retail and business financial services provision, and gas and electricity markets, closed in 2007 but left the Commission with much to follow up on. In the case of energy DG Comp opened several sets of infringement proceedings, and in resolving these will be keen not just to sanction anti-competitive conduct but also to promote the opening of markets. The financial services inquiry gave it a broad and detailed picture of aspects of this market, and it will be remaining generally vigilant here, at present being most active in the area of payment-card systems.

Telecommunications is another sector that will require continued supervision. Even though considerable responsibility was devolved to Member States in 2003 under the terms of the Framework Directive, the Commission is still keeping a careful eye on the process of liberalization, and bringing infringement proceedings and imposing fines when appropriate, in particular in respect of markets for the provision of mobile telephony and internet services.

[15] Ch. 10, fn. 30.

A sector inquiry into pharmaceutical markets will also require considerable DG Comp resources. At one time the Commission's focus in these markets was predominantly the use of supply quotas and dual-pricing systems by pharmaceutical companies. These companies seek to distribute their products throughout the Community but they come up against a lack of price harmonization between different Member States. This has led to wide differences of price imposed by national governments, which in turn leads to widespread parallel importing from 'low price' to 'high price' countries. The response by pharmaceutical manufacturers has been essentially unilateral, and the ECJ confirmed in *Bayer*[16] that there are problems in seeking to characterize it as a form of implied agreement or consensus with its wholesalers, who have at no time expressed consent to the limitation of supplies which the manufacturers would like to impose upon them. The Commission may be able to bring cases of this sort through the invocation of Article 82, though this will only be possible where the supplier has a particularly strong position in a national market with regard to the individual drug supplied, and on the basis of a narrow product market. In addition the ECJ's judgment in *Syfait II*[17] has placed further limits on such action.

The pharmaceuticals sector inquiry opened in January 2008 with, unusually, unannounced Commission inspections of company premises, apparently because it was feared that relevant evidence might be concealed or destroyed. The inquiry focuses not directly on parallel trade, but on concerns surrounding the use of patent rights to prevent or hinder market entry of new, and in particular generic, products. The Commission is seeking reasons for apparent low levels of competition in this sector, and is particularly interested in agreements, such as settlements in patent disputes, and also other conduct such as misuse of patent rights or vexatious litigation, that block market entry. As in other recent sector inquiries, companies in this sector have been required to respond to detailed questionnaires, and to supply large amounts of data. Sifting through all the evidence resulting from the 200 or so questionnaires sent out, preparing a report and taking any necessary specific enforcement action are likely to keep many officials busy for some time.

Sector inquiries provide DG Comp with a wealth of market information and it is clearly desirable that they be carried out where appropriate. Nevertheless, they impose a significant work burden on both DG Comp and the companies concerned, so it is right, and to be expected, that the Commission will continue to be carefully selective when deciding to open new ones.

3.6 THE COMMISSION'S RELATIONSHIPS
WITH NATIONAL COURTS

Courts, unlike competition authorities, do not choose their cases but have to react in respect of those cases which reach them as the result of the initiation of suit by plaintiffs. Regulation 1/2003 was intended to bring the Commission more into the process

---

[16] See Ch. 10.   [17] See Ch. 14.

of the application of Articles 81 and 82 in national courts. Article 15 of the Regulation sought to provide a framework within which the new relationship could work. It entitles the court to ask the Commission to transmit information in its possession to the court or to give its opinion on questions concerning the application of Community competition rules; national courts must allow national competition authorities to submit observations on the application of these Articles in cases coming before them; oral participation will be much rarer, whether by the Commission itself or by the national competition authority, and requires the specific permission of the court in each case. The national court can in due course be asked to send copies of documents relevant to the case to the national competition authority and the Commission, so that they can prepare submissions to the Court. So far, however, little use has been made of these provisions.

Member States are also required by Article 15(2) of Regulation 1/2003 to transmit copies of any national court judgments applying Article 81 or 82, but this is not yet done reliably in all cases. An improvement in this situation is highly desirable, in that it would provide a clear picture, which is so far not available, of the true state of private enforcement across the Community.

At the time of adoption of Regulation 1/2003 considerable concern was expressed at the burden which their new responsibilities might impose upon national courts and national judges. Two types of burden have been especially mentioned; the first is that the application of the conditions in Article 81(3) may require the judge to balance up policy issues involving not only the commercial interests of the parties and the operation of relevant commercial markets but broader social and environmental issues with which it is less familiar. The second possible burden is the sheer complexity and consequent long duration of some competition cases.[18] The need for specialization is a real one, and those Member States which do not yet have a reasonable number of judges with appropriate case-law experience and familiarity with economic concepts will certainly need to face up to it.

Though so far the small number of actions necessarily means that the feared unsatisfactory or inconsistent national court decisions, and conflicts between courts in separate Member States, as well as problems of 'forum shopping', have not materialized in any great number, in the long term these effects may well be felt. The ECJ has now confirmed that references may be made to it on questions of interpretation not only of Community law but also of national competition law where, as for example in

---

[18] If for example the agreement under challenge is a multi-party one as for example in the *Premier League* case [1999] UKCLR 258 concerning exclusive television rights to Premier League football matches, the consequence is likely to be (as Dan Goyder expressed it at a seminar at the European University Institute in Florence in May 2000) 'mountains of paper, many volumes of economic analysis and statistics, and endless lever arch files of correspondence and other documents, not to mention an excess of economic experts expounding at great length to perplex the court'. At that seminar many other papers on the likely problems of modernization were presented and some of the senior judges there said that they felt that the problem of handling large-scale competition cases at first instance or on appeal were little more onerous than those that they faced in other subject areas.

Belgium, Italy and the UK, that law provides that it shall be interpreted in accordance with Community law.[19] This may cause the number of references to increase.

Courts of course do not have the facility of an existing electronic or other form of network with the Commission nor with national competition authorities. However, an Association of European Competition Law Judges had already been established in 2002, and provides a useful forum within which judges can meet. Though it is limited in what it can achieve, because of judges' need to maintain independence both from each other and from other bodies, it can be expected to continue to play an important role in facilitating judicial education and exchange of experience.

3.7 THE JUDICIAL ARCHITECTURE OF THE COMMUNITY

Judicial architecture is not a new issue raised by Regulation 1/2003, but modernization, if it were eventually to lead to many more cases at national level, raises serious questions relating to the involvement of national courts, and in particular that of provision of a system of appellate courts through an appropriate 'judicial architecture'. So far, as already discussed, national litigation seems to have remained fairly rare, but the issue could become more urgent if and when the Commission has any degree of success in its drive to stimulate the growth of private enforcement.

If one sought an ideal court structure for the Community within which both Articles 230 and 234 could be applied within reasonable time limits to competition law cases as well as to others, there would be a group of three or four regional chambers of the CFI[20] to which appeals could be brought in competition cases from the highest national courts and, in addition, Article 234 references would need to be made to the CFI in Luxembourg rather than solely to the ECJ.

Prior to the entry into force of the Treaty of Nice in 2003, the appellate position was far from such an ideal. No appeal could be brought from any national court in a competition case to any Community Court, and Article 234 references could only be made to the ECJ and were taking normally up to twenty-one months, though this was not the fault of the ECJ. There was therefore the risk of major inconsistencies between the way in which civil actions in competition matters were dealt with and the outcome of such cases, in the different national jurisdictions. The IGC held at Nice at the end of 2000, making use of prior detailed preparatory work carried out by working parties appointed by the Community Courts, led to some significant amendments to the Treaty of Rome in the Treaty of Nice, which corresponded to some of the urgent needs

---

[19] Case C-280/06 *AGCM v. Ente Tabacchi Italiani* [2007] ECR I-10893. On the other hand the restrictive interpretation given by the ECJ in Case C53/03 *Syfait I* [2005] ECR I-4609 to the concept of 'court or tribunal' in Art. 234 EC has reduced the potential for preliminary references from certain national enforcement bodies.

[20] The earliest reference to the possibility of regional chambers of the CFI appears to be J. Weiler and J. Jacqué, 'On the Road to European Union: A New Judicial Architecture' [1990] 27 CMLR 185–207.

for reform which these working parties had already identified.[21] These included the following:

- a recognition that the CFI is not merely an attachment to the ECJ, but is a court that has its own jurisdiction recognized in the Treaty (Article 220)
- the Council may in future annex judicial panels to it (Article 225a) with jurisdiction to hear and determine cases at first instance, with an appeal to the CFI; so far only a European Union Civil Service Tribunal, for hearing staff cases, has been created under this provision, but the use of such panels could be extended in the future to other categories of case, including competition cases
- the CFI is also to have jurisdiction to hear and determine questions referred for a preliminary ruling under Article 234, in specific areas to be laid down by the Statute of the court.

In 2008 these possibilities, as far as competition law is concerned, remain just that, as no implementing measures have been taken. With the backlog of cases in the CFI continuing to grow, and the average length of time taken for proceedings increasing,[22] now would seem a good time to transfer some of its work to a specialized panel.

So far, there has not been any marked increase in the ECJ's workload, and indeed the average length of proceedings there has been steadily falling. However, if in the future numerous cases involving competition issues were to require determination under Article 234, these could then be referred to the CFI rather than the ECJ, unless under the qualifications contained in Article 225 the case 'required a decision of principle likely to affect the unity or consistency of Community law' so that it would go direct to the ECJ. An appeal would lie from the CFI's decision under Article 234 to the ECJ if 'there is a serious risk of the unity or consistency of Community law being affected'.

4. MERGERS

4.1 HEIGHTENED PRESSURE ON THE COMMISSION

The challenge posed to DG Comp by its defeat in the CFI in 2002 in the three high-profile cases of *Airtours*, *Schneider* and *Tetra Laval* has been described in Chapter 23. There is no doubt that not only the consequent legislative and operational changes, but

---

[21] See A. Johnston, 'Judicial Reform and the Treaty of Nice' [2001] 38 CMLR, 499–523, and also A. Dashwood and A. Johnston (eds), *The Future of the European Judicial System* (Hart Publishing, 2001). The text of the Treaty can be found at [2001] OJ C80/1; see also Bo Vesterdorf, 'The Community Court System Ten Years From Now and Beyond: Challenges and Possibilities' [2003] 28 ELRev 303. A similar debate over the need for specialist Community Courts took place over the need for a Patent Court to apply the Community Patent Convention, but this work has been abandoned for now.

[22] The CFI's 2007 Annual Report attributes this to 'the ever increasing complexity and diversity of actions brought before the Court of First Instance'.

also the severe shock to the confidence of the Commission which those three annul-ment judgments caused, had a long-term impact on its operation.

DG Comp generally became more cautious in its approach to those cases where a blocking decision or the imposition of onerous conditions was possible. The emphasis that the CFI placed on the necessity for thorough factual and economic analysis affected, and indeed should continue to affect, the way in which DG Comp approaches its review task. However, the sheer quantities of data that it now requires parties to provide, when combined with the complexity of the business and economic issues often raised, means that, although the timeframe for review was made more flexible in 2004, sticking to that timeframe is now a much greater challenge than it was in earl-ier years. This is particularly the situation where the identities of the undertakings or their nationality make the outcome of the case one with an inevitably high profile. The knowledge that the scrutiny to be given to any appeal by the CFI will be searching, as evidenced by the judgments in even the expedited cases, is itself a major incentive for the Commission to ensure that facts are fully investigated and the application of eco-nomic theories fully supported by them.

It was initially feared that all these circumstances might have the undesirable effect of making the Commission fearful of making blocking decisions. That would been an unfortunate outcome of the largely salutary message which the CFI decisions carried, which is that a competition authority which has in practice become a world compe-tition authority for merger control cannot have less than world class standards. This fear was then compounded in 2007 by concerns raised by the CFI's *Impala* judgment which overturned a Commission clearance decision and heightened the pressure on the Commission still further. In 2008 however, these fears receded substantially with the ECJ's annulment of that judgment, widely seen as injecting some realism into the standards to which the Commission is held in carrying out merger review.[23]

Despite this, officials are fully aware that whatever the outcome of a review, disap-pointed parties are still now more willing to go to the CFI than in the past. This may be to appeal against the Commission's decision on the usual basis of Article 230, but it may occasionally be to claim damages under Article 288. Schneider has already been successful in principle in obtaining damages in respect of the Commission decision that was the subject of the 2002 judgment, though the amount has not yet been set and the Commission has appealed against the award of damages to the ECJ.[24] While the rejection of a similar claim by MyTravel[25] underlines the fact that successful claims of this sort are certain to remain very rare, given the strictness of the legal criteria for awarding damages, this does provide one more reason for DG Comp to take its merger review work extremely seriously.

---

[23] See e.g. R. Brandenburger, T. Janssens and J. Aitken, 'Bertelsmann and Sony Judgment: Welcome Clarity for EC Merger Review from the EU's Highest Court', [2008] (July) GCP, available at <http://www.globalcompetitionpolicy.org>.

[24] Case T-351/03 *Schneider v. Commission* [2007] ECR, on appeal Case C-440/07P.

[25] Case T-212/03 *MyTravel v. Commission*, 9 September 2008 (not yet reported).

4.2 ECONOMIC NATIONALISM

Another front on which the Commission will have to continue to fight in merger control is the situations in which Member States seek to put national interests above the legal requirements of the Merger Regulation, often bringing them into conflict not only with that Regulation but also with other Treaty rules such as those on free movement. This has occurred with some frequency in recent years. One example was when the Italian government managed to create enough obstacles to dissuade the Spanish company Abertis from its merger with the Italian motorway operator Autostrade. It was difficult for the Commission to intervene effectively here, not least because the market concerned was a regulated one. On the other hand legal action was taken when, following the Commission's approval of the acquisition by the Italian bank Unicredit of the German bank HVB, Poland sought to obstruct the implementation of the transaction insofar as the purchase included Poland's top banks.[26]

The global credit crisis that struck towards the end of 2007, and the consequent economic downturn, can only increase temptation of national governments to attempt to protect their domestic industries in this way. The Commission must continue to be alert to any examples of such cases, and act decisively, to give a clear message to governments and others who might be hatching similar plans. Not only would any other course of action be damaging to the Community economy and to the Commission's authority, but ultimately such protectionist policies are not even in the long-term interests of the country concerned.[27]

5. CARTELS AND PRIVATE ENFORCEMENT

5.1 HIGHER AND HIGHER FINES?

While rigorous enforcement of the law against 'hard core' cartels has been given top priority by DG Comp for many years now, recent changes in the enforcement landscape mean that this picture is still a changing one.

As explained in Chapter 9, the introduction of a leniency policy in 1996, and its revision in 2002 and again in 2006, has been extremely successful in allowing DG Comp to step up the uncovering and punishing of cartel activity. Fine levels have shot up, reaching a total of €1.8 billion in 2006 and €3.3 billion in 2007. Although the total for 2008 will probably be lower, there is the potential under the new fining guidelines

---

[26] The court actions brought by Poland and the Commission respectively were finally dropped before judgment. See D. Gerard, 'Protectionist Threats Against Cross-Border Mergers: Unexplored Avenues to Strengthen the Effectiveness of Article 21 ECMR' [2008] 45 CMLRev 987.

[27] L. Sørgard, 'The Economics of National Champions' [2007] ECJ 49.

adopted in 2006 for fines to be even higher in the future.[28] At the same time the CFI appears to be treating appeals more strictly. Until recently companies almost always appealed against cartel fines because they were nearly certain to obtain at least a small fine reduction, and possibly quite a large one. However, since 2006 there have been enough instances not only of outright rejections of appeals, but also of small *increases* in fines, for the decision whether or not to appeal to have become a more finely balanced one.

The vertiginous escalation in the level of fines has been controversial. It has been criticized not only by those companies who are the targets of the fines, and their advisers, who might be predicted to be unhappy about them. But even a former European Court judge—and judges are usually reluctant to comment on such issues—has indicated that a point might be reached at which general judicial support for fines imposed by the Commission could no longer be assumed.[29]

Certainly, the issue is not straightforward. Firstly, it is not the case that there is a simple relationship between higher fines and less cartel activity. As fine levels rise, applications for leniency may become fewer. This might seem paradoxical, but if the starting point for fines is high enough, only full immunity will be attractive. If companies are too fearful of not being first and therefore entitled to full immunity, they may prefer to take the risk of detection. This is particularly true now that the Commission is applying the conditions for leniency more strictly than it has done in the past, and because damages actions are gradually becoming more common. Second, fines are imperfect as punishment and hence deterrent as they often do not penalize those responsible: the persons responsible have often retired or moved on from the company by the time the cartel comes to light, and a very heavy fine will have an impact mainly on shareholders, who have little control over cartel conduct, and ultimately maybe on employees, most of whom have even less.[30]

Significantly, though the Commission revised its fining guidelines in 2006 so as to provide, in theory at least, for very much higher fines than have ever been imposed in the past, it has not yet by any means made full use of its new powers, and the first few decisions based on the new guidelines resulted in fines that are not among the highest in recent years. While total fines of €1.38 billion were imposed in the car glass cartel in November 2008, in general it has not used to the maximum the possibilities of either the starting point based on turnover, or the multipliers available where the company in question has previously participated in a cartel. The Commission is treading carefully, apparently aware of the risk of a judicial backlash, and the need to reserve the full force of its powers for conduct that is exceptionally egregious.

[28] S. Völcker, 'Rough Justice ? An Analysis of the European Commission's New Fining Guidelines' [2007] 44 CMLRev 1285.

[29] Bo Vesterdorf, speaking on 22 May 2008 at the XVth St. Gallen International Competition Law Forum. But on the same occasion CFI Judge Nils Wahl warned that appealing against cartel decisions was no longer a 'risk-free business'.

[30] W. Wils, cited at fn. 10; M. Motta, 'On Cartel Deterrence and Fines in the European Union' [2008] ECLR 209.

5.2 SETTLEMENT

The success of the leniency programme has brought with it its own resource problems for DG Comp. There are simply too many of these often long-drawn-out, complex and resource-intensive cases to be properly dealt with. Not only does it often take several years for the Commission to reach the point at which it is ready to take a decision, but there are then frequently protracted appeals on a variety of, often procedural, points to the Court of First Instance, and then sometimes to the Court of Justice. Seeking a solution to this problem, the Commission introduced a settlement procedure.[31]

As from July 2008 this provides for some cases to be disposed of without the need for the full investigatory and decision-making processes to be gone through, and a possible 10 per cent reduction in the fine that would otherwise have been imposed. It may increase considerably the rate at which the Commission is able to dispose of cartel cases. However, it is untested as yet, and it remains to be seen whether the procedure is sufficiently attractive to companies to be successful.

Doubts about this stem, in part, from uncertainty as to how the system will work in practice. For example, it is not completely clear how the availability and functioning of the procedure will be affected where one or more of the companies concerned does not wish to settle. Another major concern that companies may have is that, if the administrative case is dealt with quickly, damages claims may be brought sooner, with particular disadvantages to members of a cartel who have settled, when other members have not. The effectiveness of this new procedure will depend largely on whether the outcome of the first few cases demonstrates convincingly that the benefits clearly outweigh the disadvantages to participating companies.

5.3 MULTIPLE LENIENCY APPLICATIONS

A source of continuing frustration to users of leniency programmes is the fact that applications frequently need to be made to a number of different authorities, each with differing procedural and substantive requirements. In combination with the time-critical nature and need for absolute secrecy of such applications, this makes the task extremely delicate. Applicants dream of mutual recognition within the Community, so that a single application would have effect with respect to all ECN members. However, this idea, under discussion at one time, has for now been abandoned due to the seemingly unworkable nature of a system that would require an authority receiving an application to check rapidly with twenty-seven other authorities whether they had already had an application in respect of the same cartel, while ensuring strict confidentiality.

Meanwhile the harmonization brought about through the Model Leniency Programme brings some relief. As well as promoting harmonization of national programmes it provides for a shorter 'summary application' to be made to national

---

[31] Commission Reg. 622/2008 [2008] OJ L171/3 and Commission Notice [2008] OJ C167/1.

authorities in certain circumstances. When an application is filed with the Commission before it has opened an investigation into the cartel in question, a summary application, which can be completed later if necessary, can be made to safeguard the company against the risk that the Commission decides not to deal with the cartel and one or more national authorities takes it up instead. The degree to which this system functions well will be an important factor in the effectiveness of the Community and national leniency regimes in the coming years. Also important will be the extent to which remaining differences between national systems, such as the question of whether leniency is available in the case of vertical infringements as well as traditional horizontal cartels, are resolved.

5.4 PRIVATE ENFORCEMENT

Private enforcement, through actions brought in national courts for damages or other forms of relief, is in principle available following any type of competition law infringement, including abuse of dominance and prohibited vertical agreements. Indeed, Mr Crehan's action, described in Chapter 20, is an example of the latter. However, in practice such claims are most likely to be made in the case of cartels, and so private enforcement will be considered here.

Whilst there have been many reasons why private damages actions have been rare, now at last there are signs that this situation is gradually starting to change. Some Member States such as Germany and Sweden have changed their law to facilitate such claims, which do seem now to be becoming more common. By way of a few examples, in Sweden as early as 2002 SAS were awarded a very large sum in damages against the Swedish Civil Aviation Administration for discriminatory pricing practices relating to Arlanda Airport, and substantial damages were recovered from companies found to have been participants in the vitamins cartel (referred to in Chapter 9). Damages litigation is ongoing in Germany in respect of a cement cartel, and in Spain the telecommunications incumbent Telefónica is facing damages claims following findings of abuse of dominance.

As described in Chapter 20, private damages actions as a means of competition law enforcement and provision of a remedy to those harmed have been the focus of much discussion, in particular since the Commission published its Green Paper in December 2005. Though the April 2008 White Paper took the debate a little further, very many questions remain open, not least that of the extent to which the Commission has the power to introduce or propose any changes that it decides are needed. While a completely separate approach to tort law for competition law claims is clearly undesirable, and not justified, some adjustments would be welcome.

One practical way forward suggested in the White Paper concentrates on facilitating 'follow on' actions in which the claim is based on a prior infringement finding by the Commission or a national authority, meaning that the plaintiff should only have to establish causation and the loss suffered. National rules on reliance on such prior findings currently vary considerably across the Community, and normally do not allow reliance on a decision of a foreign national authority. 'Stand alone' actions in which the infringing conduct has to be proved without reliance on such a finding are always going to be much more difficult to sustain and therefore rarer.

It would also be helpful to ensure the availability of some form of 'class action' or other form of joint action that facilitates claims in cases where relatively small losses have been suffered by large numbers of potential plaintiffs, for whom it would not be worthwhile to bring individual sets of legal proceedings. The White Paper recognizes the usefulness of such types of action, but suggests that they be brought only through recognized consumer groups, with the aim of preventing the proliferation of unmeritorious claims. An additional layer of complexity is added to this debate by the fact that, both at EU and national level, this cannot be considered as a purely competition law issue, as it is part of the broader issue of the availability of such forms of action.[32]

The White Paper also recommends giving powers to national courts, where these do not exist currently, to order parties, including third parties, to disclose specific categories of evidence. Such powers already exist in the UK, but in many other Member States they do not, and their introduction would facilitate the bringing of actions.

Finally, there is the challenge of ensuring that any strengthened culture of private enforcement coexists harmoniously with the leniency programme. A way will have to be found of ensuring that leniency applicants are not worse off, with respect to private damages actions, because of the evidence they have supplied, than other members of the cartel who have not cooperated with the Commission. The White Paper faces this issue, and suggests that those enjoying leniency might be spared joint and several liability for harm caused by fellow cartel members, but it remains to be seen how this might work in practice.

The Commission has a particularly delicate task in making progress in this area, as it, and the Council and Parliament, have limited powers to require reform of national court rules and procedures. It will be even more dependent on the support of Member States than in some other areas where it has introduced reform. Its White Paper reflects awareness of this in that its proposals are more conservative than some of the Commission's earlier proposals. Success will come if it continues to proceed diplomatically.

6. DOMINANCE

When DG Comp published its Discussion paper on the enforcement of Article 82 in December 2005 it recognized that this was the final step in applying a more modern, economics-focused approach to competition law enforcement. Enforcement of

---

[32] Collective redress mechanisms were mentioned in a Commission Communication 'EU Consumer Policy Strategy 2007–2013' COM(2007)99, and in November 2008 the Commission published a Green Paper on Consumer Collective Redress. In the UK the Civil Justice Council has published recommendations to the Lord Chancellor on improving the efficiency and effectiveness of collective actions, 'Improving Access to Justice Through Collective Actions', July 2008, available on the CJC's website.

Article 81 and merger control had already undergone change both at the level of law and practice, and now Article 82 was due to receive the same treatment.

This last reform task, discussed at the start of Chapter 13, has turned out to be much more intractable than those that had gone before. Though it generated considerable useful debate, it has still to result in any formal published guidance. This is due not only to the inherent difficulty of the relevant economics, which is itself intimidating, but also to other factors. To begin with, in contrast to the enforcement of Article 81 and the merger rules, which is based largely on legislation in the form of regulations which can be, and frequently are, amended through the appropriate institutional procedures, Article 82 stands alone. The Treaty does not expressly provide for implementing legislation, and nor does the abuse of dominance lend itself to such an approach. In the absence of any realistic prospect that a Treaty amendment to Article 82 will be made in the foreseeable future, change is dependent on the initiative being taken either by the European courts or the Commission itself.

One thing is clear, and that is that it will not be the European Courts that initiate a change of direction in the interpretation of Article 82, though they may well support such a change.[33] In a series of judgments, including several handed down after DG Comp had published its Discussion Paper, the Courts upheld Commission decisions based more on traditional legal rules than on analysis of the effects of the allegedly abusive conduct on consumer welfare. These may be some of the rare instances in which some officials will have been dismayed to see their decisions upheld with such reliability by the Courts. Reform-minded DG Comp officials might have liked to see judicial criticism of the Commission decisions in, for example, *Michelin (No. 2)* or *British Airways*, but the Courts appear determined to allow the Commission a broad discretion in how it approaches such cases. This is not the same as saying that the Courts would not support the Commission were it to take a different, more economic effects-based approach, and indeed such support would almost certainly be forthcoming.

Another factor hindering reform is the fact that even if the Commission were to publish some form of guidance, it cannot interpret the law in a way that is actually contrary to the Courts' case law. This means that any possibility of real change depends on the Commission adopting a different approach in its individual decisions, and obtaining endorsement of its new approach from the Courts.

Evidence of change in the Commission's approach can already be seen, for example by comparing a Commission decision of May 2003, fining the incumbent German telecommunications company Deutsche Telekom for charging its competitors and retail customers unfair prices for access to its local network, with a 2007 decision based on similar facts against the Spanish incumbent Telefónica. A striking difference, apart from the very much larger fine in the later case, is the treatment of the issue of effect on the market. Only eight paragraphs of the Deutsche Telekom decision are devoted to 'effect on the market' and on appeal the CFI dealt with the question in a

---

[33] In this respect the role played by the European Courts today is in striking contrast to the judicial activism apparent in the past in judgments such as *Continental Can*, that effectively made new law.

similarly summary way. The *Telefónica* decision in contrast has seventy-six paragraphs on 'impact on competition' and includes detailed consideration of much empirical evidence. Appeals are pending in *Deutsche Telekom* (to the ECJ) and *Telefónica* (to the CFI), and it would be very helpful if the resulting judgments could be couched in terms that took the reform process a little further.[34]

Moreover, morale is high in DG Comp following the wholehearted upholding by the CFI of its decision fining Microsoft, and it is currently working on many Article 82 investigations. It would be helpful if at least one or two of these resulted in decisions clearly based on the more modern approach, and these came before the CFI on appeal.

The importance of achieving the right balance between the goals of protecting competition and promoting innovation, and at the same time providing clear legal guidance, cannot be overstated. Many types of conduct characterized as abuse under Article 82 are perfectly legal when engaged in by non-dominant companies. If dominant companies are to be denied recourse to commercial strategies that are available to their non-dominant competitors, it is essential for companies to know firstly whether they are dominant and secondly what conduct they must avoid. If the Commission meets this challenge successfully it will have beneficial effects on the European business environment and the economy. If it fails, it is not an exaggeration to say that in the medium to long term this could cause significant damage either in terms of the chilling of innovation or in unhealthy monopolization in important markets.

7. THE ROLE OF ECONOMICS AND ECONOMISTS

Economics has for quite a number of years now been a prominent feature of the competition law landscape, and it may seem strange to include it as part of a chapter on future developments. However, even though the changes that have taken place so far can properly be characterized as revolutionary, there remains substantial scope for further change. While in the field of Articles 81 and in merger control economics have to a large extent taken centre stage, their role in the sphere of Article 82 is not as clearly established, and the prospects for change here were discussed above.

Moreover, even Article 81 continues to throw up issues which raise questions as to how far economic integrity should be given priority over the benefits of clear legal rules. The debate over whether retail price-fixing by suppliers to their distributors should be subject to a more or less absolute prohibition, or whether each case should turn on the economic effects of the particular arrangements in question, was played out in 2007 in the United States. It culminated in the Supreme Court's judgment in *Leegin*,[35] the effect of which was to extend the number of cases in which economic

---

[34] Case T-271/03 *Deutsche Telekom v Commission*, 10 April 2008 (not yet reported), on appeal Case C-280/08; COMP/38.784 *Telefónica*, appeals pending Cases T-336/07 and T-398/07.

[35] See Ch. 10, fn. 30.

analysis, rather than application of a simple legal prohibition, must be carried out. A similar debate can be expected to take place in Europe during the period leading up to the expiry in May 2010 of the current block exemption on vertical restraints. While the Commission has so far given no indication of sympathy towards the idea of amending the existing prohibition of such vertical price-fixing, there is a general current running in the direction of more economic analysis, and this will force it to respond seriously to such suggestions which are bound to be made.

The last edition of this book evoked the need to develop a new specialist profession, which would combine the training and best characteristics of the competition lawyer and the economist, and this concern remains valid. The growing importance of competition law as a mainstream commercial subject has meant that the large band of highly skilled antitrust lawyers in the US have now been joined by a smaller, but equally competent, group in the European Community and other jurisdictions around the world. Likewise, there are now far more economists (academics and consultants) with experience of working in the general area of competition and monopoly, who are often called in to help either the authorities or the parties in leading cases. There are now increasing numbers of talented and experienced practitioners and academics well equipped to apply the necessary blend of legal and economic expertise. They include both lawyers who are as much at home in discussing the latest econometric techniques and the merits of different kinds of consumer survey as they are with analysing the latest ECJ judgment on the scope of collective dominance, and economists who likewise are as well equipped to analyse the language of a block exemption as to discuss the cost of capital.

But the demands of competition law in the twenty-first century including the likely increase in the complexity of markets will require greater numbers of those who can combine in their training and practice the technical disciplines and analytical abilities of both professions. The evolving history of Community competition law has seen it become an increasingly broader-ranging and more sophisticated discipline, and has shown clearly that continuing development in this direction is in the interests of the undertakings which are the subject of investigation as well as of the competition authorities themselves.

8. THE NEW ECONOMY

Many traditional product and service markets exist, as in the past, but there is a continuing growth in the number of new markets in the new economy, which present increasing challenges to Commission administrators.[36] Life would be much simpler for them if there were a greater degree of stability in the range of markets, and the predictability of decisions would certainly be greater. We know however that the current

---

[36] C. Ahlborn, D. Evans, and A. Padilla, 'Competition Policy in the New Economy: Is European Competition Law up to the New Challenge?' [2001] 22 ECLR 156.

pace of technological change is set to continue, and even accelerate, with both prod-ucts and business methods becoming more complex. The characteristics of some new markets include the tendency of the most successful undertaking to acquire a large market share and apparent dominance, as the sector 'tips' in its direction and com-petitors find it hard to match its technical lead. However that product or service too—and consequently the manufacturer's 'dominance'—tends to have a fairly short life before it is replaced by a more advanced alternative which in turn captures consumer imagination and offers better value. The cost structure of such undertakings will typi-cally be one of high fixed costs and low marginal costs; they normally have to invest heavily to build up networks so as to gain the benefit in time of the network effect. The Commission is of course aware of the need to move beyond the simple rules of *ECS/Akzo* in assessing when prices of such dominant undertakings are excessive or preda-tory, and have shown willingness to apply the more appropriate criteria of long range incremental costs (LRIC) in such cases.[37]

The impact of the Internet on competition has already both been exagger-ated by some commentators and downplayed by others. From the viewpoint of the Commission it has had both positive and problematic effects, and the same has been true for national competition authorities, as the experience of the Bundeskartellamt (BKartA) has shown.[38] On the positive side, it has increased transparency and has put pressure on both buyers and sellers by enabling the creation of electronic markets of both a B2B and B2C character. It can for example remove the need for intermediar-ies, such as travel agents, between the supplier of services, airlines, and their custom-ers; it can transform the nature of distribution as the original distinction between wholesalers and retailers becomes blurred. In the words of the head of the BKartA, the Internet 'has no time for quiet contemplation' nor does it allow patterns of trade or existing economic concepts to stand still. But it also has the potential for misuse, if linked with exclusivity requirements or other anticompetitive practices in order to control the operation of electronic markets in favour of particular categories of buyer or seller.

The facility which electronic communications provide for the instantaneous exchange of information between undertakings is frequently utilized to assist the operation of cartels, though this is a high risk operation because of the difficulty (far greater than in the case of paper documents) of ensuring that e-mails and other types of electronic communication between participants are permanently deleted before any investigation takes place. In such cases the Commission and many other author-ities increasingly make good use of powerful software which can perform sophisti-cated searches of vast amounts of electronic data, and indeed similar techniques are employed by undertakings themselves when they need to establish whether or to what extent people in their organization have participated in cartels.

---

[37] See Ch. 14.
[38] U. Böge, 'E-Commerce and Competition' in Hellenic Competition Committee (ed.), *EU Competition Law and Policy: Developments and Priorities* (Athens, 2002), p. 63.

All these developments can only increase the value of competition lawyers who are not only at home with economic concepts and analysis, but also with the language and functioning of information technology.

9. THE INTERNATIONAL DIMENSION

Always an important dimension of the Commission's competition law activities, the significance of international cooperation has increased very significantly over the last few years. This is a natural consequence of globalization which is affecting so many forms of trade and commerce. The mere fact that more businesses are trading internationally acts as a powerful incentive for governments and competition authorities to join forces at one level or another in their competition law enforcement. At its lowest this may mean refraining from hindering other nations' enforcement activities; at the other end of the spectrum it may involve frequent and active cooperation and mutual assistance in such activities.

An even higher proportion of concentrations of Community dimension will involve undertakings with activities extending across many countries. Nor is it only legitimate business activity that tends to become increasingly global. While statistics on the actual level of illicit cartel activity are of course unavailable, it is a safe assumption that this too occurs more and more often on an international scale, both in terms of the participants involved and of the markets affected.

In merger cases cooperation enables the coordination of timetables and procedures when cases are proceeding in parallel, which is quite often the situation when proposed mergers are being examined concurrently on both sides of the Atlantic. In merger cases of course the parties often have an incentive to waive their rights to prevent competition authorities from disclosing confidential information, whereas in Articles 81 and 82 cases they are far less willing to do so. But even in the latter case considerable help can be provided by way of background information and advice on techniques for obtaining evidence. The trend towards globalization will certainly continue and means that cooperation between different jurisdictions will become even more necessary than at present.

The forum for the exchange of ideas and cooperation on an international scale that the International Competition Network (ICN) provides (described in Chapter 22), is steadily growing in importance. At one time it was thought unlikely to lead to agreement on international rules on antitrust of a substantive nature, but the scale of its ambition now can be judged by the fact that, having already done significant work in the fields of cartels and mergers, it has established a Unilateral Conduct Working Group, and so is now tackling one of the most difficult substantive areas of all.[39]

---

[39] The Group's 'Report on the Objectives of Unilateral Conduct Laws, Assessment of Dominance/ Substantial Market Power, and State-Created Monopolies' is available on the ICN website, where it is stated that the Report 'identifies growing agreement in many important areas, as well as areas of difference'.

Finally, it may be observed that, for a combination of two principal reasons, the Commission has come to enjoy a unique and leading role on the competition world stage. Firstly, the fact that not only within the European Union, but also in major economies around the world, there are competition laws inspired to a large degree by those of the Treaty of Rome, gives the Commission a special position in the international competition-policy community. For example, the Commission has been very active in assisting both China and Russia in preparing their new competition laws, and it has given similar assistance in a number of other jurisdictions.

In addition, enforcement in the United States has developed a very low profile in recent years. Since 2004 a number of Supreme Court judgments have systematically reduced the scope for findings of infringement both in the case of agreements and in respect of unilateral conduct, and it has been fifteen years since a plaintiff won an antitrust case in the Supreme Court. Challenges to mergers by the federal antitrust enforcement agencies have also become rarer and more frequently unsuccessful.[40] As a result there has developed at least the perception in some quarters that the European Commission has taken centre stage, an observation that was made in particular in 2006 when the CFI upheld the Commission's heavy fine on Microsoft. Competition Commissioner Kroes has wisely sought to play down the importance of such perceptions. Nevertheless the combination of these elements does place the European Commission in a position of influence at international level, which it will undoubtedly use actively and constructively over the coming years.

---

[40] W. Kolasky, 'Different Roads' [2008] (February) Global Competition Review 17.

SOURCES OF LAW AND BIBLIOGRAPHY

SOURCES OF LAW

While legal practitioners and officials will be aware of the sources from which detailed information about cases and competition policy can be obtained, students are often unsure where they should best look for this information. The Treaty of Rome is, of course, the essential starting point. It should be studied in one of the annotated editions published by the leading law publishers.[1] The official source of information is the Official Journal, published in all official Community languages, but in English since 1973 only when the United Kingdom became a Member State.[2] The series marked 'L' includes details of relevant legislation and of actual competition cases decided by the Commission, whilst series 'C' contains Commission Notices and Guidelines and other relevant items of information relating to the work of DG Comp. The complete text of the Regulations issued by the Commission or by the Council is essential, and one of the best collections of the material is the *EC Competition Law Handbook*, published annually by Sweet & Maxwell. It contains not only the text of all relevant documents and notices published by the Commission but also extensive lists of the decisions of the Commission and the judgments of the Court of First Instance and of the European Court of Justice.

An important source of official information are the *Annual Reports* of DG Comp, which have been published since 1971 and contain useful summaries of the facts and decisions of complex cases and a review of the work of the Commission in each year. The decisions of the Court of First Instance and the European Court of Justice often have to be read in full detail, and are found either in the official European Court Reports (ECR) or in the Common Market Law Reports (CMLR). The official reports of the Courts in Luxembourg are divided into ECR-I for the cases decided by the European Court itself and ECR-II for cases of the Court of First Instance. The ECR series is published only slowly, normally at least a year after the case has been decided, but does include the officially approved text of the Advocate-General's opinion in European Court cases and of the Court judgment. By contrast, the decisions reported in the CMLR appear with commendable speed on a monthly basis, with competition cases being contained in Volumes 4 and 5 for each year. The text of the judgments of the European Court and Court of First Instance is also available in electronic form from the website of the European Court of Justice (<http://curia.europa.eu/en/index.htm>). The decisions of the Commission can be found in the Official Journal and the EUR-Lex website (<http://eur-lex.europa.eu/en/index.htm>), provides immediate and free access to all the publications in the Official Journal. Reports of UK and Irish cases involving

---

[1] It is important to ensure that the copy purchased or consulted is fully up to date, incorporating not only the original treaties, but also the amending Treaties of the Single European Act (1987), the Treaty of Maastricht (1993), the Treaty of Amsterdam (1997) and the Treaty of Nice (2003). Students should also be mindful that the Treaty of Lisbon (2007), though at the time of writing not yet ratified by all the Member States, and its future uncertain following the negative Irish referendum in June 2008, may enter into force at some point.

[2] Some special editions of the Official Journal containing English texts of important regulations, directives, and other official notices and publications prior to 1973 were published at the time when the UK joined.

EC law can, since March 1997, be found in a new series of reports, European Law Reports, cited as Eur. LR. Finally, decisions of the UK Competition Appeal Tribunal are found in the Competition Appeal Reports (Comp AR).

In recent years DG Comp has made efforts to make its operations better known to the outside world, particularly to those who have to deal with it. It issues numerous press releases dealing with cases settled between the parties and the Commission, and other recent developments. It publishes, often in recognizable bright yellow covers, good general descriptions of the application of Articles 81 and 82 in particular contexts, and of its procedures and method of investigation. It also publishes updated collections of the various Regulations and Notices dealing with the Merger Regulation, as well as substantial memoranda on new block exemptions when these are introduced. Every four months it brings out an *EC Competition Policy Newsletter* containing speeches by senior officials as well as articles and case notes by officials of DG Comp, in English and French. This publication can be read on line at (<http://ec.europa.eu/comm/competition/publications/cpn/>). Moreover, since July 1996 DG Comp has been placing a wealth of information on its own website (<http://ec.europa.eu/comm/competition/index_en.html>) which contains details of its activities including press releases, full texts of current legislation, acts published in the Official Journal in the previous month, and a list, with references, of Commission decisions and, usually, the text of the decision. The most recent *Annual Report* can also be read there together with an updated list of other available Community publications on competition. This site has been well prepared and is carefully updated. It is therefore, of considerable value to those who, for either professional or academic reasons, need to keep in close contact with the operations of DG Comp.

Students will also find in their law libraries a variety of textbooks on the topic of European competition law, often of formidable length and scholarship. The Bibliography contains details of books of various kinds available on many aspects of competition law and whose number has substantially increased over recent years. The date of any publication must always be carefully considered in view of the continuing changes and development of competition policy, and the regular appearance of important new Commission or Court judgments changing the law in major or minor respects. This renders any book published at risk of becoming quickly outdated, whatever its original value. The Bibliography includes some of these books but does not purport to be exhaustive. The choice of titles is necessarily selective and the non-appearance in the list of any particular title does not constitute any comment upon its worth. Books in the Oxford European Community Law Library, to which this book belongs, are listed elsewhere.

Finally, there are also a number of excellent specialist periodicals on the subject of European Law which often contain articles on competition law; these include *Common Market Law Review* and the *European Law Review* as well as the long-established *Modern Law Review*. Other periodicals devote themselves exclusively to the subject of EC competition law, principally the *European Competition Law Review* and the *European Competition Journal*. Undoubtedly the best source of articles, however, written in depth by judges and advocates-general of the Community Courts and practitioners from many jurisdictions as well as senior officials of DG Comp and national competition authorities, is the annual volume containing the proceedings of the *Fordham Corporate Law Institute,* Fordham University, New York City. The articles in these volumes are prepared for the annual October conference of the Institute, organized for many years by Professor Barry Hawk, and are published annually in the summer following each conference. They combine in unusual measure the qualities of authority and of radical analysis and provide an invaluable source of information and research material. Also of great value are the annual publications of the *Robert Schuman Centre* at the European University Institute, Florence, prepared from the material provided by those attending by invitation each summer at seminars held on major topics in EC competition law.

BIBLIOGRAPHY

1. General Books on EC Law

ARNULL, A., DASHWOOD, A., ROSS, M., WYATT, D., SPAVENTA, E., and DOUGAN, M., *Wyatt and Dashwood's European Union Law* (5th edn, Sweet &Maxwell, 2006).

BARNARD, C., *The Substantive Law of the European Union* (2nd edn, Oxford University Press, 2007).

BEATSON, J. and TRIDIMAS, T. (eds.), *New Directions in European Public Law* (1st edn, Hart Publishing, 1997).

BREALEY, M. and HOSKIN, M., *Remedies in EC Law* (2nd edn, Sweet & Maxwell, 1998).

BROWN, L. and KENNEDY, T., *The Court of Justice of the European Communities* (5th edn, Sweet & Maxwell, 2000).

CAMBRIDGE YEARBOOK OF EUROPEAN LEGAL STUDIES (Hart Publishing, annually since 1998).

CRAIG, P. and DE BURCA, G., *EC Law: Text Cases and Materials* (4th edn, Oxford University Press, 2007).

CHALMERS, D., HADJIEMMANUIL, C., MONTI, G., and TOMKINS A., *European Union Law* (updated version and supplement), (Cambridge University Press, 2008).

DASHWOOD, A. and JOHNSTON, A. (eds.), *The Future of the Judicial System of the European Union* (Hart Publishing, 2001).

HARTLEY, T.C., *The Foundations of European Community Law* (6th edn, Oxford University Press, 2007).

LASOK, K., *Law and Institutions of the European Communities* (7th edn, Butterworths, 2001).

LONBAY, J. and BIONDI, A., *Remedies for Breach of EC Law* (1st edn, Wiley, 1997).

MATHIJSEN, P., *A Guide to European Union Law* (9th edn, Sweet & Maxwell, 2007).

OLIVER, P., *Free Movement of Goods in the EC* (4th edn, Sweet & Maxwell, 2002).

RUDDEN, B. and WYATT, D., *EU Treaties and Legislation* (9th edn, Oxford University Press, 2004).

STEINER, J., WOODS, L., and TWIGG-FLESNER, C., *Textbook on EC Law* (9th edn, Oxford University Press, 2006).

WEATHERILL, S., *Cases and Materials on EU Law* (8th edn, Oxford University Press, 2007).

2. Books on EC Competition Law (General)

ALBORS-LLORENS, A., *EC Competition Law and Policy* (Willan Publishing, 2002).

AMATO, G. and EHLERMANN, C.D., *EC Competition Law: A Critical Assessment* (Hart Publishing, 2007).

BELLAMY, C., CHILD, G., and ROTH, P., *Common Market Law of Competition*, 2 Vols. (6th edn, Sweet & Maxwell, 2007).

BISHOP, S. and WALKER, C., *The Economics of EC Competition Law* (2nd edn, Sweet & Maxwell, 2002).

EZRACHI, A., *EC Competition Law: An Analytical Guide to the Leading Cases* (Hart Publishing, 2008).

GERBER, D., *Law and Competition in Twentieth Century Europe* (Oxford University Press, 1998).

FAULL, J. and NIKPAY, A., *The EC Law of Competition* (2nd edn, Oxford University Press, 2007).

JONES, A. and SUFRIN, B., *EC Competition Law: Text, Cases, and Materials* (3rd edn, Oxford University Press, 2007).

JONES, C. and VAN DE WOUDE, M., *EC Competition Law Handbook* (reissued annually) (Sweet & Maxwell).

KORAH, V. L., *An Introductory Guide to EC Competition Law and Practice* (9th edn, Hart Publishing, 2007).

——*Cases and Materials on EC Competition Law* (5th edn, Hart Publishing, 2007).

LANE, R., *EC Competition Law* (1st edn, Longman, 2000).

LINDSTRUP, G. (ed.), *Butterworth's Competition Law Handbook* (14th edn, Butterworths, 2007).

MATEUS, A. and MOREIRA, T. (eds.), *Competition Law and Economics* (Kluwer, 2008).

MONTI, G., *EC Competition Law* (Cambridge University Press, 2007).

RITTER, L., BROWN, D., and RAWLINSON, F., *European Competition Law; A Practitioners Guide* (3rd edn, Kluwer, 2005).

ROBERT SCHUMAN CENTRE, *European University Institute, Florence* (eds., Ehlermann, C.D., and others), annual publication on 'European Competition Law' since 1995, including *The Modernization of EC Antitrust Policy* (2000) (pub. 2001) and *Effective Private Enforcement* (2001) (pub. 2003).

SAUTER, W., *Competition Law and Industrial Policy in the EU* (Oxford University Press, 1997).

WAELBROECK, M. and FRIGNANI, A., *European Competition Law* (New York: Transnational Publishers, 1999).

3. (a) Books on Special Aspects of EC Competition Law

ANDERMAN, S.D., and KALLAUGHER, J., *Technology Transfer and the new EU Competition Rules* (Oxford University Press, 2006).

BASEDOW, J., *Private Enforcement of EC Competition Law* (Kluwer International, 2007).

BLUM, F. and LOGUE, A., *State Monopolies under EC Law* (Wiley, 1998).

BUENDIA SIERRA, J., *Exclusive Rights and State Monopolies under EC Law* (Oxford University Press, 2000).

CAMERON, P., *Competition in Energy Markets* (Oxford University Press, 2002).

COOK, J. and KERSE, C., *EC Merger Control* (4th edn, Sweet & Maxwell, 2005).

CHRISTOU, R., *International Agency Distribution and Licensing Agreements* (3rd edn, FT Law and Tax, 1996).

EC Merger Control Reporter (Kluwer—looseleaf).

GERADIN, D., *Modernisation and Enlargement: Two Major Challenges for EC Competition Law* (Hart Publishing, 2004).

GOYDER, J., *EC Distribution Law* (4th edn, Hart Publishing, 2005).

JEPHCOTT, M., *Horizontal Agreements and EU Competition Law* (Oxford University Press, 2005).

JONES, C., *Private Enforcement of Antitrust Law in the EU, UK and USA* (1st edn, Oxford University Press, 1999).

KERSE, C.S. and KHAN, N., *EC Antitrust Procedure* (5th edn, Sweet & Maxwell, 2004).

KOMMINOS, A., *EC Private Antitrust Enforcement* (Hart Publishing, 2008).

KORAH, V.L., *Intellectual Property Rights and the EC Competition Rules* (Hart Publishing, 2006).

—— and O'SULLIVAN, D., *Vertical Agreements: Distribution under the EC Competition Rules* (Hart Publishing, 2002).

LEVY, N., *The Control of Concentrations between Undertakings*, Vol. 5 of 'Competition Law of the European Community' (Matthew Bender, 2002).

LINDSAY, A., *The EC Merger Regulation* (2nd edn, Sweet & Maxwell, 2006).

NAVARRO, E., FONT, A., FOLGUERA. J., and BRIONES, J., *Merger Control in the EU* (2nd edn, Oxford University Press, 2005).

O'DONOGHUE, R. and PADILLA, J., *The Law and Economics of Article 82* (Hart Publishing, 2006).

ODUDU, O., *The Boundaries of EC Competition Law: The Scope of Article 81 EC* (Oxford University Press, 2006).

ORTIZ BLANCO, L., *EC Competition Procedure* (2nd edn, Oxford University Press, 2006).

ORTIZ BLANCO, L., *Shipping Conferences under EC Antitrust Law* (Hart Publishing, 2007).

—— and VAN HOUTTE, B., *EC Competition Law in the Transport Sector* (1st edn, Oxford University Press, 1997).

SAECKER, F.-J., MONTAG, F., and HIRSCH, G., *Competition Law: European Competition Practice and Procedure* (Sweet & Maxwell, 2007).

STOTHERS, C., *Parallel Trade in Europe* (Hart Publishing, 2007).

SZYSZCZAK, E., *The Regulation of the State in Competitive Markets in the EU* (Hart Publishing, 2007).

TAYLOR, M., *International Competition Law: A New Dimension for the WTO?* (Cambridge University Press, 2006).

VAN DEN BERGH, R. and CAMESASCA, P., *EC Competition Law and Economics* (2nd edn, Sweet & Maxwell, 2006).

VOGELAAR, F., STUYCK, J., and VAN REEKEN, B. (eds.), *Competition Law in the EU, its Member States and Switzerland*, 2 Vols. (Kluwer, 2000 and 2002).

WESSELING, R., *The Modernization of EC Antitrust Law* (Hart Publishing, 2000).

WILLS, W., *Efficiency and Justice in European Antitrust Enforcement* (Hart Publishing, 2008).

(b) Books on Special Aspects of Subjects Related to EC Competition Law

ANDERSON, D. and DEMETRIOU, M., *References to the European Court* (2nd edn, Sweet & Maxwell, 2002).

BARNARD, C. and SCOTT, J., *The Law of the Single European Market* (Hart Publishing, 2002).

BERNITZ, U., *European Law in Sweden* (Stockholm University, 2000).

CORNISH, W. R., *Intellectual Property: Patents, Copyright, Trade Marks, and Allied Rights* (4th edn, Sweet & Maxwell, 1999).

De Burca, D. and Scott, J. (eds.), *The EU and WTO: Legal and Constitutional Issues* (Hart Publishing, 2001).

Evenett, S., Lehmann, A., and Steel, B. (eds.), *Antitrust Goes Global* (Washington DC: Brookings Institution, 2000).

Gormley, L., *Prohibiting Restrictions on Trade within the EEC* (North-Holland, 1985).

Norberg, S. and others, *EEA Law: A Commentary on the EEA Agreement* (1st edn, 1993, Fritzes, Stockholm).

Weiler, J., Slaughter, A. M., and Sweet, A. S. (eds.), *The European Court and National Courts* (1st edn, Hart Publishing, 1998).

4. Books on UK and EC Competition Law

Butterworths Competition Law Encyclopaedia—looseleaf, 3 Vols. (eds., Freeman, P. and Whish, R.).

Dabbah, M., *EC and UK Competition Law: Commentary, Cases and Materials* (Cambridge University Press, 2004).

Frazer, T. and Waterson, M., *Competition Law and Policy* (1st edn, Harvester Wheatsheaf, 1994).

Furse, M., *Competition Law of the UK and EEC* (6th edn, Oxford University Press, 2008).

Green, N. and Robertson, A. (eds.), *The Europeanisation of UK Competition Law* (Hart Publishing, 1999).

Livingston, D., *Competition Law and Practice* (1st edn, FT Law and Tax, 1995).

Middleton, K., *Blackstone's UK and EC Competition Documents* (5th edn, Oxford University Press, 2007).

Middleton, K., Rodger, B., MacCulloch, A., and Galloway, J., *Cases and Materials on UK and EC Competition Law* (Oxford University Press, 2003).

Rodger, B. and MacCulloch, A., *Competition Law and Policy in the EC and UK* (3rd edn, Cavendish Publishing, 2005).

Slot, P.-J. and Johnston, A., *An Introduction to Competition Law* (Hart Publishing, 2006).

Smith, M., *Competition Law: Enforcement and Procedure* (Butterworths, 2001).

Taylor, P., *EC and UK Competition Law and Compliance* (Sweet & Maxwell, 1999).

Whish, R., *Competition Law* (6th edn, Oxford University Press, 2008).

5. Other Works

Amato, G., *Antitrust and the Bounds of Power* (Hart Publishing, 1997).

Black, O., *Conceptual Foundations of Antitrust* (Cambridge University Press, 2005).

Bork, R., *The Antitrust Paradox: A Policy at War with Itself* (Maxwell Macmillan, 1993).

Dell, E., *The Schuman Plan and the British Abdication of Leadership in Europe* (1st edn, Oxford University Press, 1995).

Diebold, W., *The Schuman Plan: A Study in Economic Co-operation* (Praeger, 1959).

Duchêne, F., *Jean Monnet: The First Statesman of Interdependence* (Norton, 1994).

GEORGE, S., *An Awkward Partner: Britain in the Economic Community* (2nd edn, Oxford University Press, 1994).

MAYNE, R., *The Recovery of Europe* (1st edn, Weidenfeld & Nicholson, 1970).

MONNET, J., *Memoires*, trans. Richard Mayne (Collins, 1978).

MOTTA, M., *Competition Policy: Theory and Practice* (Cambridge University Press, 2004).

PERITZ, R., *Competition Policy in America; History, Rhetoric, Law* (Oxford University Press, 2001).

POSNER, R., *Antitrust Law* (2nd edn, University of Chicago Press, 2001).

RODGER, B., *Article 234 and Competition Law* (Kluwer International, 2008).

INDEX

abuse of a dominant position
  (Article 82) 35–6,
    314–69 *see also*
    dominance, concept of
acquisitions by dominant
    companies 366
'affect trade between member
    states' 109–10
barriers to entry 367
block exemptions 376–9,
    382–3
categories of abuse 315–16
collective dominance 382–4
Commission 315–16, 636–7
comparison of Articles 81 and
    82 109–10, 379–83
competition policy 21
compulsory licences 371
decisions 2
direct effect of Articles 82 533
directives 5, 315–16
discounts and rebates 327–33
discriminatory pricing 324–6
distribution 228
enforcement 37–8
essential facilities 315,
    358–62, 626–7
European Coal and Steel
    Community (ECSC) 30
examples 314
excessive pricing 316–19
exclusionary abuses 315,
    323–4, 332–3
exclusive licences 382–3
exclusivity 373–4, 382–3
exemptions 376–9, 382–3
exploitative abuses 315, 372
fines 30, 43
foreclosure 626–7
implementation of rules,
    cooperation over 37
intellectual property rights 293,
    315, 341–57, 627
interoperability information,
    refusal to supply 315,
    362–3, 627
interpretation 109
joint ventures 498–500
legal proceedings, abuse
    of 368

legislate to protect agreements
    or give privileges in
    breach of Articles 81
    and 82, states must
    not 553–6
market definition 370
member states, obligations
    of 552–76
Merger Regulation 366,
    379–85, 406–7, 447–8,
    454, 498–500, 586, 609
national competition
    authorities 45, 627
national competition laws
    enforcement 414, 517
    Regulation 17/62 45
    relationship with 38
nationality
    discrimination 367–8
nature of abuse 314–15
negotiation over Articles 81
    and 82 33–5
objective justification 371
one or more
    undertakings 373
patent licences, excessive
    royalties and 368
predatory pricing 319–24
preliminary rulings 315
pricing 315, 316–26, 554–5
proportionality 371
public undertakings, Article
    86(1) and (2) and 565–6,
    567–9
recycling of packaging
    waste 367
refusal to deal 315, 333–41,
    371
Regulation 17/62 45
Regulation 1/2003 637
restrictive agreements
    109–10
royalties 368
sanctions 371
sectors applied to 5
Sherman Act 21, 315
single firm dominance 20,
    405, 416–20
sliding scale 627
software licences 293

state action, undertakings do
    not escape Article 81 or
    82 because of 557–60
state monopolies 315–16
substantial part of common
    market 370
super-dominance 627
supremacy of EC law 514
telecommunications 315–16,
    626–7
terms, imposition of
    unreasonable 367
text of Article 81 36–9
Treaty of Paris 38
tying practices 364–6
vertical relationship 381–2
accession countries
conformity with EC
    competition law 4
officials from new member
    states, integration
    of 628
secondment from national
    competition authorities
    of new member
    states 628
**acquisitions by dominant
    companies** 366
advantages of competition 9
Advisory Committee
block exemptions 142
Merger Regulation 445
national competition
    authorities 505–7, 515
opinions 445
Regulation 17/62 50
advocacy programme 603
**'affect trade between member
    states', meaning of**
abuse of a dominant
    position 109–10, 372
appreciable effect 107
banking sector 106–7
block exemptions 65–6
capable of affecting
    trade 102–3
Commission
    guidelines 105–8, 110
comparison of Articles 81 and
    82 109–10

'affect trade between member states', meaning of (*Cont.*)
context 103
de minimis rule 103–4
early cases 101–2
economic context of agreements 103
Grundig case 55
guidelines 105–6
international aspects of EC competition law 578
language 109
legal context of agreements 103
market integration 106
meaning of 101–10
minor importance, agreements of 103–5, 107
national competition rules
boundaries with 102
enforcement 503–4
networks of agreements 102–3
'object or effect' of restricting competition, meaning of 118–23
prevention, restriction or distortion of competition 101
restrictive agreements 101–10, 372
single member states, effect in 101
trade associations 105–6
trade, meaning of 107–8
volume of trade, effect on 102–3
after-sales 231, 233, 239, 247
agents
appointment 199
commercial agents 199–201
commission 198, 199
Commission guidelines 203–4
del credere agents 199
description 79
distribution 198–204
economic unity between principal and agent 203
genuine agents 77–8
information 592
market integration 203–4
motor vehicle distribution and servicing networks 245, 248

non-compete clauses 204
Notice 1962 199–202
policy 201–4
stocking agents 199
undertaking, definition of 77–9
vertical restraint 203
agriculture 96–7, 99–100, 129–31
air transport
airports, domestic and international transport between Community 133
bilateral aviation service agreements 134
Chicago Convention 131–2
discriminatory pricing 326
essential facilities, refusal of access to 360–1
International Air Transport Association (IATA) 130–1
legal certainty principle 132
market integration 131
nationality discrimination 134
restrictive agreements 131–4
service agreements 134
tariffs 132
treaties and conventions 131–2
allocative efficiency, meaning of 9
ancillary restrictions 123–6
Commission guidelines 126
franchises 125
goodwill 126
intellectual property rights 125, 452–3
joint ventures, covenants on 125
justification 126
know-how licensing 275
Merger Regulation 125–6, 450–3
non-compete clauses 125–6
proportionality 126
research and development (R&D) agreements 495
restrictive agreements 123–6
rule of reason 156
subcontracting notice 275
technology transfer block exemption 281
trade association rules 124–5

vendors and purchasers 123–4
annual reports 67, 412, 610, 656, 657
anti-competitive agreements *see* restrictive agreements (Article 81)
appeals
cartels 646, 647
Competition Appeal Tribunal (CAT) 520–4, 533, 535–6, 545
Court of Appeal 521
Court of First Instance 455–9, 617–19, 642–4
European Court of Justice 455–9
expedited appeals 458–9
fines 646, 647
Merger Regulation 455–9
national competition authorities 520–2, 523–4
Office of Fair Trading 521
third parties 455–6
appreciable effect on competition 107, 372
Article 81 *see* restrictive agreements (Article 81)
Article 82 *see* abuse of a dominant position (Article 82)
Article 82 and Article 81, relationship between 37–9, 109–10, 370–83
abuse of a dominant position 370–82
affect on trade between member states 372
block exemptions 376–9, 382–3
case law 374–9
collective dominance 374–82
Commission Guidelines 372
compulsory licences 371
concerted practices 375–6
Continental Can 374–5
distinctions between articles 370–2
evidence 370
exclusivity 373–4
exemptions 382–3
GMB case 376–9

identification of agreement or
concerted practices 370
Italian Flat Glass 374–5
liner conferences, block
exemptions and 376–9
market definition 370
mergers 379–81, 454
negotiation over Articles 81
and 82 33–5
objective justification 371
oligopolies 375
price-fixing 376–9
proportionality 371
refusal to deal 371
refusal to grant licences 371
Regulation 1/2003 372
restrictive agreements 370,
372
sanctions 371, 372
similarities between
articles 372–3
six distinctions between
articles 370–2
substantial part of common
market 370
three similarities between
articles 372–3
Article 86 *see* public
undertakings, Article
86(1) and (2) and
**Association of European
Competition Law
Judges** 642
**associations of undertakings,
decisions by** 82, 83,
96–100
Australia 589
Austria 523, 524
**average avoidable costs
(AAC)** 323
average total cost (ATC) 320,
323
**average variable cost
(AVC)** 320, 323

**B2B (business to business)
exchanges** 500–1
banking sector 106–7, 396–7, 437
barriers to entry
abuse of a dominant
position 367
dominance, concept of 302
market power 13, 14
market share 14
Merger Regulation 405,
414–16, 422, 434

multilateral measures,
proposals for 596
predatory pricing 323
recycling of packaging
waste 367
beer
bilateral agreements 165–6
block exemptions 166
brand preference 227
distribution 221, 227
exclusive purchasing 227
exemptions 165–6
free houses 166
non-compete
agreements 166, 227
nullity 169–70
sites for retail outlets 227
remedies available in UK
courts 540–1
restrictive agreements 165–6
trade mark licences 290
tying 166, 220, 227
vertical restraints, block
exemption on 227
behavioural remedies 447–9,
526
Belgium 523
benefits, fair share of 151–2
Benelux Memorandum 31–2
best practice 390, 402, 442, 589
bilateral agreements
air transport 134
beer supply cases 165–6
block exemptions 57, 61,
62, 68
Commission 628
enforcement 587–92, 594
extraterritoriality 580
international aspects of
EC competition
law 579–80, 587–95
notification 47–8
patent licensing 264–5
bilateral enforcement 579–80,
587–95
Australia 589
bilateral agreements 587–92,
594
Canada, agreement with 588,
591–2
comity 587–8, 590–4, 628
commitments 594
common approaches,
agreement of 594
confidentiality 588, 589,
592–3

cooperation, need for 587
DG Comp 628
effects doctrine 587
European tests 587
exclusive distribution 205
extraterritoriality, effects test
and 580, 587
legal assistance treaties 587–8
limitations 594–5
mergers 589
multilateral meetings
of competition
authorities 589
multilateral rules, proposal
for binding 594–5
New Zealand 589
notification 589–90
regional meetings
of competition
authorities 589
United States 587–92
World Trade Organization
(WTO) 597
block exemptions 141–4 *see
also* distribution
agreements, block
exemptions and
abuse of a dominant
position 376–9,
382–3
advent 57–69
Advisory Committee 142
'affect trade', meaning
of 65–6
approval 141–2
Article 82 and Article
81, relationship
between 376–9, 382–3
beer supply cases 166
Belgian Tiles Cartel 58–9
bilateral agreements 57, 61,
62, 68
black list 142–3, 241, 247,
255–6, 271, 276, 283–4,
290, 490, 496, 621–2
cartels 58–9, 69
case law 57–60
category-type
exemptions 62–3
Commission 139, 141–2,
611–12, 620
consultation 141
copyright licences 291–2
Council 141–2
criteria 59, 638
current examples 141

block exemptions 141–4 *see also* **distribution agreements, block exemptions and** (*Cont.*)
DG Comp 65–9, 141–2, 611–12
distribution systems 57–9, 205–6, 209, 239–42, 611–12
dominance, concept of 652
drafting 141
duration 143
early case law experience 57–60
economic factors 63
enforcement 144–6
European Competition Network (ECN) 529
European Parliament 141–2
evolution 266–83
exclusive dealing agreements 256–7
exclusive distribution 59–60, 64–9, 205–6, 209
exclusive purchasing 209–10, 220
expiry 638–9
extensions 143
form 142–4
franchising 253, 255–8
grey list 143, 247, 271
Grundig case 63–4
guidelines, conversion into 638
hard-core restrictions 241, 247
horizontal agreements 59, 61, 62–3, 69, 113, 139, 141, 612
Hummel/Isbecque 57, 61, 64
industrial property rights 60
industry, attitudes of 66–7, 142
insurance 638–9
intellectual property rights, abuses by individual owners of 351–2
interested parties 66–7, 142
Internet sales 241
interpretation 143–4
know-how licensing 276–7
lapse 638
legal certainty 249
liner conferences 182–3, 321, 376–9
Maison Jallatte/Voss 57, 61, 64

maritime transport 136
market integration 69
market power 612
market share 14, 15, 143, 612
modernization 638–9
motor vehicle distribution and servicing networks 244, 245–9
multilateral agreements 58–9, 68
national competition authorities 139, 509–12, 517, 523, 527
national courts 139, 633
need for block exemptions 59–60
non-compete clauses 226, 252, 624
notification 60, 68–9, 147
opposition procedure 48, 141, 271
parallel imports 57, 60, 147–8, 242
patent licences 59, 61, 68, 263–4, 266–83, 351–2
preparation 141–2
recitals 142–3
Regulation 17/62 45, 48
Regulation 19/65 60–5
Regulation 67/67 68–9, 611
Regulation 2349/84 271–4
Regulation 1/2003 527
replacement 638–9
resale 60
resale price maintenance 639
research and development (R&D) agreements 494–6, 612
reviews 143
road, rail and inland waterways 136
scope 142–3
simplification 620
specialization agreements 489–91, 612
STM case 63–5
supremacy of EC law 509–12
time limits 143
trade mark licences 288, 290
transfer of technology 210–11, 278–87, 612, 638
transparency 621
vertical agreements 61, 63, 65, 69, 113, 139, 141, 612, 621–2

vertical restraints 227, 257, 638, 639
white list 142–3, 247, 255, 271, 276, 490, 612, 621–2
withdrawal 143, 496
brands
beer and petrol 227
franchising 252
inter-brand competition 18–19, 214–15, 228, 281
intra-brand competition 217, 224, 243–4, 281
single branding (non-compete) clauses 226
breach of statutory duty 536, 537
Bulgaria 524
burden of proof
concerted practices 91–2
damages 550
indirect purchaser issues 550
Merger Regulation 407, 428
national competition authorities 526
Regulation 1/2003 526
Business Review Letters 629
business to business (B2B) exchanges 500–1

Canada
bilateral agreements 588, 591–3
Competition Bureau 592–3
confidentiality 591–3
cartels 171–97 *see also* **liner conference cartels**
appeals 646, 647
benefits, analysis of 171
block exemptions 58–9, 69
categories of horizontal agreements 171–2
class actions 649
Commission 172–3, 622
criminal proceedings 506
crisis cartels 184–7, 488
damages 550, 648–9
defensive cartels 173–4
DG Comp 645–7
electronic communications 653
enforcement 580–1, 583–4, 639, 645–9
evidence 172–3, 649
extraterritoriality 580–1, 583–4

fines 622, 645–7
follow-on actions 648–9
goodwill 172
hard-core cartels 645
immunity 550, 646
international aspects of EC
        competition rule 654
joint and several liability,
        avoidance of 649
joint ventures 172
leniency
        programmes 179–82,
        622, 645–9
market-sharing
        agreements 176–7
Merger Regulation 421–2
Model Leniency
        Programme 647–8
multiple leniency
        applications 647–8
mutual recognition 647
national competition
        authorities 508, 517, 521
national competition
        laws 636–7
national courts 648–9
national markets,
        controlling 187–9
notification 623
price-fixing
        agreements 173–82
primary objectives 171
private enforcement 648–9
restraints of trade 172
settlements 647
shipping lines 182–4
supremacy of EC law 508
trade associations 172,
        189–97
United States, agreement
        with 592
White Paper 648–9
Cellophane fallacy 310
chambers of commerce or
        trade 97
Christmas Message 264–7
class actions 547, 549, 649
Clayton Act 21, 364, 404
clearances see also negative
        clearances
conditions 407, 446–50
European Coal and Steel
        Community (ECSC) 29
Merger Regulation 391, 407,
        446–50
obligations 446–50

restrictive agreements 29
three member states, from
        391
coal see European Coal and
        Steel Community
        (ECSC)
collecting societies, abuses of
        intellectual property
        rights by
copyright 352–7
excessive charges 355–7
free movement of goods 357
intervention, Commission's
        reluctance to 357–8
nationality
        discrimination 353–5,
        367
restrictive rules 352–7
secondary exploitation 355
collective bargaining 77, 79,
        115, 128–9
collective or joint dominance
abuse of a dominant
        position 374–82
Article 82 and Article
        81, relationship
        between 374–82
competition policy 20–1
Court of First
        Instance 618–19
definition 405
horizontal agreements 20–1
Merger Regulation 379–81,
        405, 625
oligopolies 20–1
tacit collusion 21
vertical relationships 381–2
comfort letters 138–9, 236,
        536, 614
comity
bilateral enforcement 579,
        587–8, 590–1
definition 590
extraterritoriality 590–1
international aspects of EC
        competition rule 579
merger control 590
positive 579, 587–8, 590–1,
        593–4, 628
substantial differences in
        law 593–4
substantially lessen
        competition test 593
traditional 590, 628
United States 590–1, 593–4,
        628

commercial agents 199
Commission see also Advisory
        Committee; DG
        Comp; notices
1958–2008 607–9
abuse of a dominant
        position 315–16, 626–7
achievements and
        failures 619–28
adaptation 619–20
administrative powers 444–5
'affect trade between member
        states' 105–8, 110
agents 203–4
ancillary restrictions 126
annual reports 412, 498, 610
Article 82 and Article
        81, relationship
        between 372
basic priorities 607–8
bilateral cooperation
        agreements 628
block exemptions 139, 141–2,
        210, 222–3, 225, 611–12,
        620
Business Review Letters,
        adoption of practice
        similar to US 629
cartels 172–3, 622
case allocation 527–8
caseload 390, 517, 532–3, 614
changing economic
        background 608–9, 620
changing role of
        Commission 138–9
comfort letters 138–9
complaint procedure 531–2
cooperation 526–8
Council 620–1
Court of First Instance 615,
        617–18
crisis cartels 620
damages 545–50
decisions 563, 575–6, 656–7
directives 563, 570–3, 609
distribution 150–1, 210,
        222–3, 225, 610
dominance, concept of 296,
        650–1
effectiveness 610–11
environment 165
European Competition
        Network (ECN) 528–30
European Court of
        Justice 615–19
exclusive competence 138–9

Commission *see also* **Advisory Committee; DG Comp; notices** (*Cont.*)
exemptions 138–9, 542–3, 610, 631
fines 610
franchising 258–9
general approach 408–9
general economic interest, services of 569–70
improving the production or distribution of goods or promoting technical or economic progress 150–1
inapplicability, findings of 637
informal guidance 637
information 503, 523
initiation of own proceedings 638
inquiry process 442–3
international aspects of EC competition rule 655
investigations 527
joint ventures 480–2, 498
jurisdiction 38, 391–8, 507, 509, 512, 609
legislation 610–12, 620–1
leniency notices 179–82
maritime transport 135–6
market definition 308–11
market share 380–1
merger control 38, 391–8, 408–9, 412, 442–5, 480–2, 498, 623–6, 643–4
minor importance, notice in agreements of 113
modernization 148, 629
monopolies 631
multilateral cooperation agreements 628
multinational organizations 628
national competition authorities 50, 503, 505, 507–12, 515, 517, 523
national courts 531–4, 542–4
new sectors, application of competition rules to 620
notification 623–4
parallel proceedings 503, 515, 517
patent licensing 264–7

political background 620
predatory pricing 323–4
'prevention, restriction or distortion of competition' 113
priorities 607–8, 639–40
Regulation 17/62 138
Regulation 1/2003 526–8, 637–9
research and development (R&D) agreements 496–7
resources 22–3, 139, 172, 503, 515, 517, 535, 613–15
restrictive agreements 138–9, 148, 152
role 39
self-assessments 159
specialization agreements 490–1
surrender of monopoly 139
timescale 620
Trade and Competition Commission 595–6
transparency 621
Treaty of Paris 38
vertical agreements 621–2
commission schemes 198, 331–3
commitments
bilateral enforcement 594
European Competition Network (ECN) 529
Merger Regulation 440–1
national competition laws 526, 635
Regulation 1/2003 526
World Trade Organization (WTO) 597–8, 602
common agricultural policy 129–30
Community dimension test
joint ventures 470–1
Merger Regulation 391–8, 430–1, 433–5, 438, 470–1, 585–6, 624
multilateral measures, proposals for 596
national courts 532
community legal order, place of competition law in 631–3
comparative competition 436–7
compensation *see also* **damages**
Competition Appeal Tribunal (CAT) 521, 535–6, 545

national competition authorities 521, 523
Competition Appeal Tribunal (CAT) 520–4
Court of Appeal, appeals to 521
compensation 521, 535–6, 545
fines 520–1
judicial review 521, 522
jurisdiction 521
national courts 533, 545
Regulation 1/2003 545
standing 520–1
Competition Commission 520–2
competition policy 19–23
abuse of dominant position 21
agents 201–4
collective or joint dominance 20–1
consistent application 607
development 608–9
DG Comp 22, 608–9
distribution 213–14
economic changes which affect policy, list of 22
enforcement 22, 632–3
essential elements of effective competition policy 21–2
even-handed application 607
Lisbon Treaty 632–3
merger control 21
purposes going beyond competition 9, 10–11
resources, availability of 22–3
restrictive agreements 19–20, 21
single firm dominance 20
Spaak Report 32–3
strong policy, importance of 632–3
treaties, place in context of 631–3
Treaty of Rome 34, 607
complaints
Commission 531–2
decentralization 615
DG Comp 614–15
national competition authorities 615
national courts 531–2, 615
priorities 615
Regulation 17/62 46
rejection 615

resources 614–15
standing 46
compulsory licences 262, 371,
       627
computers
   electronic
       communications 529,
       634, 642, 653
   interface or interoperability
       information, refusal to
       supply 342–3, 362–3
   Internet 341, 653
   memory bundling 341–2
   reverse engineering 347–8
   Software Directive 347–8
   software licences 292–3
   websites
       DG Comp 657
       distribution 225
concentrations see also Merger
       Regulation; mergers
   business to business (B2B)
       exchanges 500–1
   concentrative joint ventures
       462–5, 471–2, 609
   definition 398–401, 474–5
   joint ventures 398–9, 470–97
   negative condition, abolition
       of 470
   not concentrations, joint
       ventures which
       are 475–97
concerted practices
   Article 82 and Article
       81, relationship
       between 375–6
   burden of proof 91–2
   cartels 196–7
   circumstantial evidence 96
   definition 83, 88–96, 174–5
   distribution chain 95–6
   documentary evidence 88, 95
   early case law 88–91
   evidence 88–9, 91–2, 95–6
   group economic units 80
   horizontal agreements 89–90,
       95
   identification 370
   information, giving and
       receiving 91, 94
   meetings, attendance at 95
   multi-party agreements 159
   national competition
       authorities 509
   number of undertakings
       involved 83

oligopolies 89–90
parallel conduct 88–9, 91–3,
       96
parallel imports 96
prices 89–90, 93, 95, 174–5
refusal to supply 92
restrictive agreements 82, 83,
       85, 88–96
supremacy of EC law 509
trade associations 196–7
United States antitrust
       law 88–9
Woodpulp case 92–3
conditions
   exemptions 167–8
   extraterritoriality 583
   fines 449
   Merger Regulation 407, 420,
       422, 427, 428, 443–50,
       609, 644
   negative conditions 147,
       152–5
   onerous conditions,
       imposition of 365
   positive conditions 146–53
   research and
       development (R&D)
       agreements 492–3
   restrictive
       agreements 144–56
   tying 365
confidentiality
   agency information 592
   bilateral enforcement 588,
       589, 592–3
   business information 592
   Canada, agreement
       with 591–3
   cartels 190
   European Competition
       Network (ECN) 529
   international aspects of EC
       competition rule 580,
       654
   mergers 444–5, 654
   OECD 593
   trade associations 190
   United States, agreement
       with 589, 591–2, 654
   waiver 592
conglomerate effects 417,
       425–7, 459
consumer preferences 309, 310,
       415–16
consumer welfare 11, 12, 650
container transport 155

contingency fees 547
contractual relationships,
       damages for wrongful
       interference with 536
cooperation
   bilateral enforcement 587
   joint ventures 463–5, 476,
       509
   motor vehicle distribution
       and servicing
       networks 243–4
   national competition
       authorities 526–8, 579
   Regulation 1/2003 526–8
cooperatives 97
coordinated effects of
       mergers 405, 416–17,
       420–5
   early days 420–1
   Gencor and Airtours 422–4
   horizontal merger
       guidelines 424–5
   Kali und Salz 422
   tacit coordination 424
copyright
   block exemptions 291–2
   collecting societies, abuses
       of intellectual property
       rights by 352–7
   duration of protection 293
   exclusive licences 291
   films 291–2
   freedom to provide
       services 291
   licences 290–3, 344–50
   refusal to licence 344–50
Council of Europe 25–6
Council of Ministers
   block exemptions 141–2
   Commission 620–1
   DG Comp 67–8, 140
   directives 573–4
   legislation 620–1
Court of Appeal 521
Court of First Instance
   appeals 617–19, 642–4
   backlog 643
   chambers, establishment of
       regional 630, 642
   collective dominance 618–19
   Commission 615, 617–18
   establishment 617
   judgments, text of 656
   judicial architecture of
       Community 642–3
   judicial panels 643

Court of First Instance (*Cont.*)
 jurisdiction 617–18, 642–3
 Merger Regulation 455–9,
  617, 644
 national competition
  authorities 522
 preliminary rulings 642–3
 time limits 642
 Treaty of Nice 642–3
credit crisis 645
criminal offences
 cartels 521, 636–7
 multilateral measures,
  proposals for 596
 national competition
  authorities 521, 523
 national competition
  laws 636–7
 Regulation 1/2003 637
crisis cartels 184–7
 Commission 620
 recession 184–5
 restructuring
  agreements 184–5
 specialization
  agreements 488
cross-elasticity of demand 14,
 305

damages *see also* **compensation**
 basis for claims 535–6
 breach of statutory duty 536
 burden of proof 550
 cartels 549, 648–9
 causes of action 550
 causation 550
 Commission 545–50
 contingency fees 547
 enforcement 639
 Germany 648
 Green Paper 545–50, 636
 indirect purchaser issues 549,
  550
 jury trials 547
 leniency notices 182
 low levels of litigation, reasons
  for 546
 Merger Regulation 644
 national competition
  authorities 523
 national competition
  laws 636
 national courts 535–7, 543,
  545–50
 obstacles to actions 546–7,
  636

 passing on defence 547,
  549–50
 price-fixing 549–50
 punitive damages 547
 Regulation 1/2003 545–6
 remedies available in UK
  courts 538–42
 representative actions 547,
  549
 Sweden 648
 time limits 549
 United Kingdom 535–6, 550
 United States, antitrust
  litigation in the 547, 550
 White Paper 545–50, 636
 wrongful interference
  with contractual
  relationships, damages
  for 536
dawn raids
 case law 506
 enforcement 144
 leniency notices 181
 Merger Regulation 444
 national competition
  authorities 505–6, 523,
  527
 Regulation 1/2003 527
 use of force 506
de minimis **rule** 103–4, 145
decisions
 abuse of a dominant
  position 2
 Article 86(3) 575–6
 associations of undertakings,
  decisions by 82, 83,
  96–100
 Commission 2, 563, 575–6,
  656–7
 definition 98–100
 European Court of
  Justice 617
 member states, obligations
  of 575–6
 public undertakings, Article
  86(1) and (2) and 563
 recommendations 100
 special rights 576
 text 656–7
 trade associations 82, 83,
  96–100
decisive influence test
 definition 393–4, 399–401
 Merger Regulation 393–4,
  399–401
decompilation 292–3, 347–8

defence industry 127, 437–8
defence, rights of 445
definition of competition 8–9
definition of market *see* **market
  definition**
del credere **agents** 199
**demand cross-elasticity,
  definition of** 14
**demand elasticity, definition
  of** 14
**demand
  substitutability** 309–10,
  409–12
Deringer Report 43, 48
designs 300
DG Comp *see also* **Advisory
  Committee;
  Commission**
 'A' grade officials 613
 additional
  responsibilities 502
 annual reports 67, 656, 657
 bilateral enforcement 628
 block exemptions 65–9,
  141–2, 611–12
 cartels 645–7
 caseload 48, 52–3, 502, 613
 competition policy 22, 608–9
 complaints 614–15
 Council 67–8, 140
 directives, adoption of 40–1
 early years 40–56, 65–9
 Economic and Social
  Committee (ESC) 67
 economics 12
 enforcement 144–6
 European Court of Justice 68
 European Parliament 67
 exemptions 140
 financial services sector,
  inquiries into 639
 fines and periodic penalty
  payments 41
 first ten years 65–9
 future, debates on 517
 Grundig case 53–6, 68
 inspections 640
 institutions, relationship
  with 67–8
 International Competition
  Network (ICN) 603
 investigations 49–50, 52
 joint ventures 472
 Merger Regulation 38405,
  401–2, 442–3, 472,
  624–6, 630, 643–4

national competition
　　authorities
　　additional
　　　　responsibilities 502
　　case-load 502
　　cooperation 504
　　future, debates on 517
　　Regulation 17/62 50
　　resources 503
　　secondment from new
　　　　member states 628
notification 614
officials from new member
　　states, integration
　　of 628
parallel trade 640
pharmaceutical sector,
　　inquiry into 640
press releases 657
procedural framework 40–5
publications 657
Regulation 17/62 41–53, 140
regulations, adoption of 40–1
resale price maintenance
　　(RPM) 216
resources 41, 68, 503, 613–15,
　　639
sanctions 41
sector inquiries 630, 639–40
staff 41, 140, 613
telecommunications sector,
　　inquiries into 639
transparency 621
vertical agreements 52–3
website 657
direct application of EC
　　law 531–50
direct effect of Articles 81 and
　　82 525, 533
directives
　　abuse of a dominant
　　　　position 5, 315–16
　　Commission 5, 40–1, 315–16,
　　　　563, 570–3, 609
　　Council 573–4
　　energy sector 574, 609
　　European Parliament 573–4
　　initial use 570–3
　　member states, obligations
　　　　of 570–4
　　national competition
　　　　authorities 503
　　postal services 574
　　public undertakings, Article
　　　　86(1) and (2) and 563

special or exclusive rights 574
telecommunications 570–3,
　　609
Director General of Fair
　　Trading 520
directorate general see DG
　　Comp
discounts and rebates
　　abuse of a dominant
　　　　position 327–33
　　British Airways 329–33
　　commission schemes 331–3
　　discount, definition of 327
　　discrimination 325–6, 331,
　　　　332
　　early cases 327–9
　　effect of limiting
　　　　competition 331
　　'English clause' 328
　　exclusionary abuse 332–3
　　exclusive distribution 219
　　fidelity rebates 219, 327–33
　　Hoffman 327–9
　　Michelin 327–9
　　Michelin II 329–33
　　parcel services 331
　　postal services 331
　　quantity rebates 328, 330
　　rebate, definition of 327
　　tying 327–8, 330
　　volume rebates 330, 332
discrimination see also
　　discriminatory
　　pricing; nationality
　　discrimination
　　discounts and rebates 331,
　　　　332
　　essential facilities, refusal of
　　　　access to 360–1
　　World Trade Organization
　　　　(WTO) 598–9
discriminatory pricing
　　abuse of a dominant
　　　　position 324–6
　　airport charges 326
　　European Coal and Steel
　　　　Community
　　　　(ECSC) 30
　　Irish Sugar 325–6
　　market forces 324
　　Napier Brown v British
　　　　Sugar 325
　　price squeeze 325
　　rebates 326
　　supply and demand 324

Tetrapax (No 2) 325–6
United Brands 324–5
distortion of competition see
　　'prevention, restriction
　　or distortion of
　　competition'
distribution agreements and
　　practices 198–230
　　see also distribution
　　agreements, block
　　exemptions and;
　　selective distribution
　　abuse of a dominant
　　　　position 228
　　agents 198–204
　　beer supply 221
　　Commission 610
　　concerted practices 95–6
　　direct representation 198
　　early years 205–7
　　end-users 225
　　exclusive distribution 187,
　　　　205–9, 214–15, 217–20,
　　　　226
　　exclusive purchasing 208–9
　　exemptions 228
　　foreclosure 228
　　franchising 250–4, 258
　　improving the production or
　　　　distribution of goods or
　　　　promoting technical or
　　　　economic progress 147,
　　　　148–52
　　integration with
　　　　organization 198
　　inter-brand
　　　　competition 214–15,
　　　　228
　　market integration 228
　　motor vehicle distribution
　　　　and servicing
　　　　networks 243–9, 622
　　national markets,
　　　　controlling 187–8
　　non-compete clauses 214–15,
　　　　219–20, 226
　　parallel networks 221
　　policy since 1999 213–21
　　Regulation 1983/83 209–10
　　resale price
　　　　maintenance 215–17,
　　　　225
　　tying 221
　　vertical restraints, green
　　　　paper on 210–14

distribution agreements, block exemptions and 57–9, 209–10, 213–14, 611–12
beer 227
black-listed clauses 224–6
buyer as to where or to whom he may sell, restrictions on 225
Commission guidelines 210, 222–3, 225
end-users
  parts, sale of 226
  selective distribution 225
  wholesalers prohibited from supplying 225
fixed or minimum resale prices 225
legal certainty 210
hard core restrictions 223, 224
intellectual property rights 224
intra-brand competition 224
market definition 222–3
market share 222–4
national authorities, withdrawal by 227–8
non-compete clauses 226
parallel networks 226
parts, sale of 226
petrol 227
policy 213–14
Regulation 1983/83 209–10
Regulation 2790/99 221–8
repairs 226
selective distribution 225
single branding (non-compete) clauses 226
websites 225
white list 221–2
wider scope of agreements 223–4
divestiture 444, 449–50
dominance, concept of 295–312
assessing dominance, factors involved in 302, 311–12
barriers inherent in nature of market 302
barriers to entry 302, 312
block exemptions 652
Commission 296, 650–1
competitive price level, measurement of 312
consumer welfare, effect on 650

control of product or service market, total 300
cross-elasticity of demand between substitutable products 305
Discussion Paper on Exclusionary Abuses 295–6, 299
economic effects-based approach 650–1
economic strength 295–8, 312
enforcement 649–50
essential facilities 300
exclusive legal rights, undertakings which hold 299
geographical market, definition of 296, 300, 303–4
Hoffmann-La Roche 296–9
intellectual property rights 299–300, 302
licence of patent rights 299–300
liner conferences, price-fixing by 301, 302
lower market shares, companies with 301–2
market definition 295, 296, 300–10
market power 296, 298, 303, 313
market share 296–303, 312–13
marketing strategies 312–13
mergers 308, 389, 391, 630
national legislation conferring monopolies 300
patent licences 299–300
predatory pricing 302
prices 301, 302, 312–13
problems in assessing dominance 311–12
product market definition of 296, 303, 304–5
  total control 300
qualitative criteria 302, 312
quantitative criteria 312
registered designs 300
relevant market, definition of 295, 296, 302–3
review of Article 82 295
service market, definition of 304–5

sliding scale approach 312
small markets, applicability to 299–300
substitutability 304–5
super-dominant companies, special responsibility of 301, 312
technological change 653
United Brands 296–9
vertical restraints 652
double barrier theory 507, 509, 520–1
dynamic efficiency, meaning of 9

ECN *see* **European Competition Network (ECN)**
Economic and Social Committee (ESC) 67
economic nationalism 626, 645
economics
'affect trade between member states' 103
block exemptions 63
changing background 608–9
competition policy, list of changes affecting 22
DG Comp 12
economic strength 295–8, 312
economic welfare and legal certainty 10–11, 14–15, 151–2
expansion 608
improving the production or distribution of goods or promoting technical or economic progress 147, 148–52
market power 12–13
market shares and market definition 13–14
Merger Regulation 457–8, 633
nationalism 626, 645
new economy 652–3
oil prices 608
profession, establishment of new specialist 652
progress, definition of economic 148–9
role 12–15
technological change 653
undertaking, definition of 74–5, 79

ECSC *see* **European Coal and Steel Community (ECSC); Treaty of Paris (ECSC Treaty)**
effects doctrine 578–87, 650–1
efficiency
  allocative efficiency, meaning of 9
  dynamic efficiency, meaning of 9
  improving the production or distribution of goods or promoting technical or economic progress 150–1
  Merger Regulation 425, 427–8
  productive efficiency, meaning of 9
  refusal to deal 340–1
electronic communications
  cartels 653
  European Competition Network (ECN) 529, 634
  lawyers 654
  Internet 653
  national courts 642
  searches 653
employees as undertakings 77, 79
employers' associations 97
energy
  directives 574, 609
  Euratom 128
  International Energy Authority (IEA) 158–61
  joint ventures 501
  liberalization 630, 632
  Lisbon Treaty 632
  Merger Regulation 501
enforcement *see also* **bilateral enforcement**
  abuse of a dominant position 37–8
  block exemptions 144–6
  cartels 639, 645–9
  competition policy 632–3
  cooperation 37–8
  damages 639
  dawn raids 144
  de minimis rule 145
  decentralization 139
  DG Comp 144–6
  dominance, concept of 649–50

European Coal and Steel Community (ECSC) 28–9
  extraterritoriality 578–87
  international aspects of EC competition rule 579–80, 587–603, 654
  Lisbon Treaty 632
  minor agreements, notice on 145–6
  modernization 146
  national competition authorities 139, 146, 502–30
  national courts 139, 146
  negative clearances 145
  notification 144–6
  'prevention, restriction or distortion of competition' 111
  Regulation 17/62 144
  Regulation 1/2003 139, 144
  resources 22–3
  restrictive agreements 144–6
  road, rail and inland waterways 136
  settlements 639
  United States 655
  vertical agreements 145
'English clauses' 219, 328
entry, barriers to *see* **barriers to entry**
entry, powers of 506
environment
  Commission guidelines 165
  horizontal agreements 484
  joint ventures 484
  Merger Regulation 484
  restrictive agreements 164–5
  trade associations 165
essential facilities, refusal of access to
  abuse of a dominant position 315, 358–62, 626–7
  air routes 360–1
  Bronner 361–2
  discrimination 360–1
  dominance, concept of 300
  ferries 358–60
  Harbour cases 358–60
  indispensability requirement 362
  transport sector 358–62
  tying 358

World Trade Organization (WTO) 600
Estonia 523
Euratom 128
European Broadcasting Union (EBU) Rules 162–4
European Coal and Steel Community (ECSC) 27–30 *see also* **Treaty of Paris (ECSC Treaty)**
  abuse of a dominant position 30
  central control 28
  clearances 29
  competition articles 27–9
  creation 27
  duration 27
  enforcement 28–9
  fines or penalties 29, 30
  High Authority 27, 28–31
  merger control 29–30
  negotiation over Articles 81 and 82 33–5
  predatory pricing 30
  price discrimination 30
  prohibited practices 27
  restrictive agreements 28–9, 37, 127–8
  sanctions 29, 30
  Schuman Plan 30
  state aid 30
  Treaty of Rome 127–8
European Competition Network (ECN) 528–30
  block exemptions 529
  case allocation 529
  Commission 528–30
  commitments 529
  confidential information 529
  electronic communications 529, 634
  fines 529
  informal resolution 638
  information, exchange of 529
  integration of regulators 634
  investigations 529
  modernization 634
  national competition authorities 528–30, 634
  national competition laws 635
  officials 529
  Regulation 1/2003 528–30
  sanctions 529
  voluntary or soft harmonization 530

European Convention on
    Human Rights 25
European Court of Justice
    1958–1988 615–17
    1989 onwards, period
        from 617–18
    appeals 455–9
    Commission 615–19
    decisions, review of 617
    DG Comp 68
    fines 45
    interpretation 616–17
    investigations 617
    judgments, text of 656
    judicial architecture of
        Community 642–3
    length of proceedings 643
    Merger Regulation 455–9
    notification 616
    preliminary references 51, 68,
        315, 507–8, 615–16, 643
    'prevention, restriction
        or distortion of
        competition' 112
    Regulation 17/62 45
    vertical agreements 616
    workload 643
European Economic
    Community (EEC),
    origins of 31–9
European Parliament
    block exemptions 141–2
    DG Comp 67
    directives 573–4
    Regulation 17/62 42–4
European Patent Office
    (EPO) 263
evidence see also burden of
    proof
    Article 82 and Article
        81, relationship
        between 370
    cartels 172–3, 649
    circumstantial evidence 96
    concerted practices 88–9,
        91–2, 95–6
    fines, reduction in 179–80
    international aspects of EC
        competition rule 579
    leniency notices 179–82
    market definition 307
    Merger Regulation 407, 418,
        426, 457, 459
    national courts 535, 649
    Regulation 1/2003 638
    restrictive agreements 370

excessive pricing
    abuse of a dominant
        position 316–19
    Competition Act 1998 318
    definition 316–17
    early cases 316–17
    predatory pricing 318
    profit margin 317–18
excise duty 557
exclusionary abuses 315, 323–4,
    332–3
exclusive dealing
    agreements 251, 256–7
exclusive distribution 208–9
    bilateral agreements 205
    block exemptions 59–60,
        64–6, 205–6, 209
    'English' clause 219
    foreclosure 219
    inter-brand competition 219
    intra-brand competition 217
    loyalty rebate clauses 219
    market integration 217
    national markets,
        controlling 187
    non-compete clauses 219–20,
        226
    notification 207
    parallel imports 66, 218–19
    patent licensing 263–8, 270,
        271
    pharmaceuticals 218
    quantity forcing 219
    Regulation 67/67 68–9, 205–7
    territorial protection 217–19
    vertical restraints 217–18
exclusive licences
    abuse of a dominant
        position 382–3
    copyright licences 291
    intellectual property
        rights 262–3, 351–2
    patents 351–2
    technology transfer block
        exemption 279
exclusive purchasing
    beer supply 220, 227
    block exemptions 209–10,
        220
    distribution 208–9
    franchising 254
    national markets,
        controlling 187
    non-compete clauses 208–9
    patent licensing 264
    petrol 121–2, 227

Regulation 67/67 208–9
'prevention, restriction
    or distortion of
    competition' 121–2
tying agreements 209, 220
exclusive rights
    dominance, concept of 299
    public undertakings, Article
        86(1) and (2) and 563–9
    software licences 292
    telecommunications 570–2
exclusive supply
    agreements 254, 258
exclusivity
    abuse of a dominant
        position 373–4
    Article 82 and Article
        81, relationship
        between 373–4
    Grundig case 56
    multilateral measures,
        proposals for 596
    public undertakings, Article
        86(1) and (2) and 567–9
exemptions see also block
    exemptions
    abuse of a dominant
        position 382–3
    Article 82 and Article
        81, relationship
        between 382–3
    beer supply cases 165–6
    Commission 138–9, 610, 631
    conditions 167–8
    DG Comp 140
    directly applicable legal
        exception system 159
    distribution 228
    duration 167–8
    European Broadcasting
        Union (EBU)
        Rules 162–4
    financial cases 164
    franchising 250
    joint ventures 475, 477,
        479–80, 499
    market share 154–5
    Merger Regulation 475, 477,
        479–80
    multi-party
        agreements 157–8
    national competition
        authorities 504–5, 507,
        509–12, 515, 517–18
    national courts 534, 542–4
    negative clearances 44

P&I clubs 162
parallel imports 153–4
public undertakings, Article
    86(1) and (2) and 562–3
Regulation 17/62 42, 44, 46–9
Regulation 1/2003 542–4
reporting requirements 168
research and
    development (R&D)
    agreements 492–3
restrictive agreements 42,
    44, 48–9
retrospectivity 42
review of contacts 167–8
road, rail and inland
    waterways 137
selective distribution 242–3
software licences 293
specialization
    agreements 485–6, 488
supervision 167–8
supremacy of EC law 507,
    509–13
telecommunications 499
television rights 162–3
time limits 48–9
exhibitions 196
exploitative abuses 315, 372
export bans 68, 119–20, 122–3,
    167
extraterritorial enforcement
    bilateral enforcement 580,
        587
    cartels 580–1, 583–4
    comity 590–1
    conditions 583
    Dyestuffs 582–5
    effects test 578–87
    European test 579
    group economic unit
        doctrine 581–4, 586
    implementation of an
        agreement, concept
        of 582–5
    International Competition
        Network (ICN) 603
    Merger Regulation 585–6
    price-fixing 582–4
    unilateral enforcement 580
    United States 580, 585
    Woodpulp (No 1) 582–5

failing company defence 428
fair share of benefits
    benefit, definition of 151
    consumers 151

improving the production
    or distribution of
    goods 151–2
joint ventures 478
Merger Regulation 478
promoting technical or
    economic progress 151–2
restrictive agreements 147,
    151–2
trade associations 152
fairness 10
ferries 358–60
fidelity rebates 327–33
field of use restrictions 293,
    452–3
films 291–2
financial cases
    banking sector 106–7, 396–7,
        437
    DG Comp 639
    exemptions 164
    information 191, 193–4
    Merger Regulation 396–8
    networks 164
    price-fixing 164
    restrictive agreements 164
    trade associations 191, 193–4
fines and periodic penalty
    payments
    abuse of a dominant
        position 29, 30, 43
    appeals 646, 647
    cartels 622, 646, 647
    Commission 610
    Competition Appeal Tribunal
        (CAT) 520–1
    DG Comp 41
    European Coal and Steel
        Community (ECSC) 29,
        30
    European Competition
        Network (ECN) 529
    European Court of Justice 45
    evidence 179–80
    guidelines 646
    heard, right to be 51
    immunity 180–2, 646
    increase 645–6
    jurisdiction 445
    leniency notices 179–82, 622
    Merger Regulation 444, 449,
        455
    misleading or incomplete
        information 444
    national competition
        authorities 520–1, 522

natural justice 51–2
notify, failure to 444
Office of Fair Trading 520–1,
    522
price-fixing 174
reduction 179–80
refusal to deal 334
Regulation 17/62 43, 51–2
restrictive agreements 29
supremacy of EC law 514
warnings 51
Finland 523
follow-on actions 648–9
force majeure 160–1
foreclosure
    abuse of a dominant
        position 626–7
    distribution 219, 228
    horizontal agreements 18–19
    Merger Regulation 425–6
    restrictive agreements 20
    tying 365–6
    vertical agreements 18–19
foreign competition authorities,
    consultation with 449
Form A/B 53
Form CO
    contents 441–2
    joint ventures 470–1
    Merger Regulation 402–3,
        408, 439, 441–2, 470–1
Form RS 432
forum shopping 641–2
France 524
franchising 249–59
    ancillary restrictions 125
    block exemptions 253, 255–8
    brands 252
    Commission
        Guidelines 258–9
    distribution
        franchising 250–4, 258
    early years 249–52
    elements 249–50
    exclusive dealing
        agreements 251, 256–7
    exclusive purchasing
        agreements 254
    exclusive supply purchasing
        agreements 254, 258
    exemptions 250
    identity and reputation of
        network, maintenance
        of 254
    industrial franchise
        agreements 259

franchising (*Cont.*)
  intellectual property
    clauses 255–6, 257–9
  know-how 254, 256, 258–9
  location 254
  no-challenge clauses 255–6
  non-compete clauses 226,
    254, 258
  parallel imports 254
  patent licensing 252
  premises, specified 254–5
  production franchising 250
  promotion 254
  Pronuptia case 252–5
  resale prices 254, 255
  selective dealing
    agreements 251
  selective distribution
    agreements 251, 257
  service franchising 250
  trade marks 250, 251, 258
  types of restrictions 250–3
  varieties of business-format
    franchising 250
  vertical restraints 257, 259
free houses 166
free movement of goods 262,
  264, 266, 345, 357
freedom to provide
  services 262, 291
full-function joint
  ventures 463, 465–9,
  500, 609
full-line forcing 364
future of EC competition
  law 629–55

General Agreement on
  Trade and Services
  (GATS) 599
general economic interest,
  services of 562, 565–70
gentlemen's agreements 82, 174
geographical market
  consumer preferences 415–16
  definition of relevant
    market 412–16, 417–19
  definition 14, 296, 300,
    303–4, 309
  dominance, concept of 296,
    300, 303–4
  Merger Regulation 412–16,
    417–19
  range of possible geographical
    markets 413–16
  relevant market 309

German clause 433
Germany 26, 523, 524, 648
globalization 654
goodwill 123–6, 172, 451–2
Greece 523
group economic unit doctrine
  concerted practices 80
  definition 80–1
  extraterritoriality 581–4, 586
  independent economic
    policymaking, capable
    of 80–1
  Merger Regulation 585–6
  restrictive agreements 80–1
guarantees 234–5, 239

heard, right to be 51
hearings, Merger Regulation
  and
  oral hearings 440, 458
  right to a hearing 439
  third parties 440
High Authority 27, 28–31
horizontal agreements *see also*
  cartels
  block exemptions 59, 61, 62–3,
    69, 113, 139, 141, 612
  categories 171–2
  collective or joint
    dominance 20–1
  concerted practices 89–90, 95
  cooperation
    agreements 460–502
  definition 83–4, 481
  foreclosure 18–19
  environmental
    agreements 484
  examples 481–2
  inter-brand competition
    between
    manufacturers 18–19
  joint purchasing
    agreements 482–3
  joint selling
    agreements 482–3
  joint ventures 480–4
  Merger Regulation 480–4
  minor importance, notice on
    agreements of 121
  notice 480–4
  'prevention, restriction
    or distortion of
    competition' 113, 121
  Regulation 17/62 69
  resale price maintenance
    (RPM) 215

restrictive agreements 83–4
standardization
  agreements 483–4
trade mark licences 288
vertical agreements,
  difference
  between 18–19
horticultural cases 166–7
human rights 25

immunity 180–2, 549, 646
importance of EC competition
  law 3–5
improving the production or
  distribution of goods or
  promoting technical or
  economic progress 147,
  148–52
inapplicability, findings of 637
indirect purchaser issues 549,
  550
indispensability
  requirement 362
industrial policy 10, 632
industrial property rights 60
information *see also*
  confidentiality
  Commission 503, 523
  concerted practices 91, 94
  economic assessments 457–8
  European Competition
    Network (ECN) 529
  exchange 190–4, 503, 523,
    580
  financial information 190–4
  fines 444
  international aspects of EC
    competition rule 580
  interoperability information,
    refusal to supply 315,
    362–3, 627
  Merger Regulation 402, 439,
    443–4, 630
  misleading or incomplete
    information, fines
    for 444
  national competition
    authorities 503, 505,
    523
  national courts 534
  obstruction 444
  third parties 439, 523
  trade associations 190–4
inherently restricted, markets
  where competition
  is 116–18

injunctions 535, 536–7, 545
inland waterways 136–7
inquiries
  financial services sector 639
  Merger Regulation 442–3
  pharmaceutical sector 640
  sectors 630, 635, 639–40
inspections 640
institutions *see also*
    Commission; DG Comp
  Council of Ministers 67–8,
    140–2, 573–4, 620–1
  European Parliament 42–4,
    67, 141–2, 573–4
  resources, adequacy of 608
  Treaty of Rome 34
insurance
  block exemptions 638–9
  P&I Clubs 162
  International Group 162
  restrictive agreements 161–2
  standard terms 161–2
  undertaking, definition
    of 76–7
integration *see* **market**
    integration
intellectual property rights
    see also **intellectual**
    property rights,
    licensing of
  abuse of a dominant
    position 315, 341–57,
    627
  ancillary restrictions 125,
    452–3
  block exemptions 351–2
  collecting societies, abuses
    by 352–7
  compulsory licences 627
  copyright 291–3, 344–50,
    352–7
  decompilation 347–8
  distribution 224
  dominance, concept of
    299–300, 302
  early cases 341–3
  excessive charges 355–7
  field of use restrictions 452–3
  franchising 255–6, 257–9
  free movement of goods 345,
    357
  IBM settlement 341–3
  IMS Health 348–9
  implicit tying 343
  individual owners, abuses
    by 341–52

interface or interoperability
    information, refusal to
    supply 342–3, 347–8,
    362–3
interim measures 349
intervene, Commission's
    reluctance to 357–8
Magill case 344–8
memory bundling 341–2
Merger Regulation 452–3
motor vehicle spare parts,
    refusal to supply 343–4
nationality
    discrimination 353–5,
    367
notice 452–3
patents 341, 351–2
pharmaceuticals 348–50
proportionality 351–2
registered designs 300
restrictive rules 352–7
reverse engineering 347–8
secondary exploitation 355
Software Directive 347–8
spare parts, refusal to
    supply 343–4
substitutability 346
supremacy of EC law 345
Technology Transfer
    Agreements, block
    exemption for 453
television listings 344–8
Tetrapak (No 1) 350–2
intellectual property rights,
    licensing of 261–94
compulsory licences 627
copyright licences 290–2
exclusive licences 262–3, 279,
    351–2
exploitation of such
    rights 262–3
free movement of goods 262
free movement of
    services 262
innovation 261
joint ventures 479
know-how licensing 274–9,
    294
Merger Regulation 452–3,
    479
nature of intellectual property
    rights 261–2
non-exclusive licences 262
patents 262, 263–74
plant varieties 293–4
quantitative restrictions 262

refusal to licence 344–51
software licences 292–3
sole licences 263
technology transfer 210–11,
    277–87, 289–90
trade marks 287–90, 293
inter-brand competition
  distribution 214–15, 228
  exclusive distribution 219
  foreclosure 18–19
  horizontal agreements 18–19
  technology transfer block
    exemption 281
  vertical agreements 18–19
interchangeability 409
interface or interoperability
    information, refusal to
    supply 342–3, 362–3
interim measures
  intellectual property rights,
    abuses by individual
    owners of 349
  Merger Regulation 387, 457
  national courts 534, 536–7
  predatory pricing 320
International Air Transport
    Association
    (IATA) 130–1
international aspects of
    EC competition
    law 578–604
  affecting trade within EU 578
  bilateral
    enforcement 579–80,
    587–95
  cartels 654
  comity 579, 590–1, 593–4,
    628
  Commission, importance
    of 655
  confidentiality 580, 654
  effects test 578, 579
  enforcement 579–80,
    587–603, 654
  evidence 579
  extraterritoriality 578–86
  globalization 654
  information, exchange of 580
  International Competition
    Network (ICN) 603, 654
  jurisdiction 578–9
  mergers 654
  multilateral measures,
    proposals for 595–603
  national competition
    authorities

International Competition
    Network (ICN) 603,
    654
International Energy Authority
    (IEA) 158–61
International Group of P&I
    Clubs 162
Internet 241, 653
interoperability 293, 315,
    347–8, 362–3, 627
interpretation
    abuse of a dominant
        position 109
    block exemptions 143–4
    European Court of
        Justice 616–17
    national competition law,
        preliminary references
        on 641–2
    nullity 168
    Regulation 17/62 45
    restrictive agreements 66,
        73, 109
intra-brand competition
    distribution 217, 224, 244
    exclusive distribution 217
    free riders 243
    motor vehicle distribution
        and servicing
        networks 244
    selective distribution 243
    technology transfer block
        exemption 281
investigations
    checks and balances 440
    Commission 527
    Competition
        Commission 521
    entry, powers of 506
    European Competition
        Network (ECN) 529
    European Court of
        Justice 617
    framework 439–40
    Implementing
        Regulation 439–41,
        444, 445
    Merger Regulation 438–46
    national competition
        authorities 444, 505,
        508–12, 521, 527, 528
    Office of Fair Trading 521
    procedures and
        powers 438–46
    Regulation 17/62 49–50, 52
    Regulation 1/2003 527, 528

separate groups or bodies,
    by 630
supremacy of EC law 508–12
Ireland 523
Italy 523

joint dominance see collective
    or joint dominance
joint purchasing
    arrangements 482–3
joint selling agreements 188–9,
    482–3
joint ventures see also joint
    ventures, Merger
    Regulation and
    ancillary restrictions 125
    cartels 172
    choice of partners 460–1
    concentrative, meaning
        of 398–9
    control of joint
        ventures 461–2
    cooperative joint
        ventures 463
    covenants 125
    exemptions 499
    full-function joint
        ventures 463
    horizontal cooperation
        agreements 460–502
    joint control 400–1, 461–2
    full-function joint
        ventures 399, 453–4
    managerial and commercial
        aims 461–2
    Merger Regulation 392, 395,
        399–401, 453–4, 624–5
    national competition
        authorities 502
    parents, control by 461–2
    'prevention, restriction
        or distortion of
        competition' 114
    Regulation 1/2003 463–4
    restrictive agreements 462
    self-assessment 464
    shareholder rights 461–2
    significant impediment to
        competition test 453
    telecommunications 499
joint ventures, Merger
    Regulation and 462–501
    abuse of a dominant
        position 498–500
    appreciable effect on
        competition 479

blocking joint ventures 473
business to business (B2B)
    exchanges 500–1
case law 474–5
changing background 497–8
Commission 480–2, 498
Community dimension
    test 470–1
concentrations 470–5
    business to business (B2B)
        exchanges 500–1
    definition 474–5
    distinction between non
        concentration joint
        ventures and those that
        are 462–3
    negative condition,
        abolition of 470
    not concentrations,
        joint ventures which
        are 475–97
concentrative joint
    ventures 462–5, 471–2,
    609
Consolidated Jurisdictional
    Notice 465–9
cooperative joint
    ventures 464–5, 476–7,
    609
coordination 465, 472–5
criteria 464, 470–2
DG Comp 472
dissolution 469
energy joint ventures 501
environmental
    agreements 484
exemptions 475, 477, 479–80
fair share of resulting
    benefit 478
first-phase proceedings 471
Form CO 470–1
full-function joint
    ventures 463, 465–9,
    500, 609
horizontal cooperation
    agreements 480–4
intellectual property rights,
    licences of 479
Interface Notices 465
joint control 465–7
joint purchasing
    agreements 482–3
joint selling
    agreements 482–3
jurisdiction 465–9, 498
legal certainty 463–4

minority shareholders, veto rights and 466–7
negative clearances 478–9
negative conditions 464–5, 470, 477
non-compete clauses 479
not concentrations, joint ventures which are 475–97
notice on horizontal cooperation agreements 480–4
notifications 463–4, 470–1, 497–8
parents, control by 466–7
positive condition joint ventures, performance of 464–5, 467–9, 477–8
product market 472
reasons for formation 460–1
recent trends 497–501
Regulation 1310/97, effect of 465
Regulation 1/2003 463–4
relevant market 472, 474
research and development (R&D) agreements 491–7
restrictive agreements 463, 464–5, 475–84
reviews 464, 469
second-phase 471
self-assessment 476
service market 472
shareholder agreements 465–6
significant impediment to competition test 470
specialization agreements 484–91
standardization agreements 483–4
turnover 464, 470–1, 477
veto rights 466–7
judgments
declaratory judgments 544
text of 656
transmission of 641
judicial architecture of Community 642–3
judicial review 521, 522
judiciary
Association of European Competition Law Judges 642
Court of First Instance 643

judicial architecture of Community 642–3
national courts, communication between 642
jurisdiction
Commission 38, 391–8, 507, 509, 512, 609
Competition Appeal Tribunal (CAT) 521
Court of First Instance 617–18, 642–3
European test 579
fines 455
international aspects of EC competition rule 578–9
joint ventures 498
Merger Regulation 389–98, 401, 430–1, 433–5, 455, 498
national competition authorities 44, 507, 509, 512, 516, 521, 527
notice 394–6, 401
'prevention, restriction or distortion of competition' 111, 113
Regulation 1/2003 528
Treaty of Paris 38
jury trials, damages and 547

know-how
ancillary restrictions 275
Block Exemption Regulation 556/89 276–7
duration of protection 274, 276
franchising 254, 256, 258–9
licences 274–9, 284, 294
patent licences 274
plant varieties 294
restrictive covenants 123
sale of businesses 123
subcontracting notice 274–5
technology transfer block exemption 278–9, 284
vendors and purchasers 123

language 109, 442
law reports 656–7
lawyers
electronic communications 654
profession, establishment of new specialist 652

legal assistance treaties 587–8
legal certainty
air transport 132
block exemptions 249
distribution 210, 249
economic welfare or efficiency 14–15
joint ventures 463–4
market power 14
market share 14, 15
Merger Regulation 463–4
motor vehicle distribution and servicing networks 249
national competition authorities 517
legal proceedings, abuse of 368
legitimate interest exception 436–7
leniency programmes
Commission 179–82
damages 182
dawn raids 181
evidence 179–82
fines 179–82, 622
joint and several liability, avoidance of 649
Model Leniency Programme 647–8
multiple leniency applications 647–8
mutual recognition 647
national competition laws 635
notice 179–82, 622, 645–6
price-fixing 179–82
settlements 647
tariffs 181
whistleblowing 179
licences see also intellectual property rights, licensing of
compulsory licences 371, 627
refusal to licence 293, 344–51, 371
research and development (R&D) agreements 492, 493–4
leverage theory 626
liner conference cartels 182–4
block exemptions 136, 182–3, 321
capacity 182
consortia 136
dominance, concept of 301, 302

liner conference cartels (*Cont.*)
    exemptions 135–6
    predatory pricing 321
    price fixing 136, 182–3, 301,
        302, 376–9
    proportionality 378–9
    rate-fixing 183–4
    Regulation 4056/86 135, 183
    super-dominance 301
    tariffs 183
    Transatlantic
        Agreement 183–4
    UNCTAD Code of
        Conduct 182–3
Lisbon Treaty 632–3

maintenance 243–4
maritime transport *see also*
        liner conference cartels
    block exemptions 136
    cartels 182–4
    Commission guidelines 136
    container transport 155
    essential facilities, refusal of
        access to 358–60
    exemptions 135–6
    ferries 358–60
    nationality
        discrimination 134–5
    P&I clubs 162
    price fixing 136
    Regulation 4056/86 135
    Regulation 870/95 136
    restrictive agreements 134–6
    trade, definition of 108
    tramp service vessels 135
market *see* market definition;
        market integration;
        market power; market
        share
market definition 13–14
    abuse of a dominant
        position 370
    Ahmed Saaed 305–6
    Article 82 and Article
        81, relationship
        between 370
    Cellophane fallacy 310
    Commission Notice 308–11
    consumer preferences 309, 310
    demand cross-elasticity,
        definition of 14
    demand elasticity, definition
        of 14
    demand
        substitutability 309–10

distribution 222–3
dominance, concept of 295,
    296, 300, 302–8
economics 13–14
evidence 307
false substitutes 310
geographic market 14, 309,
    412–16, 417–19
Hilti 306–7
market elasticity 14
market power 14, 308
market share 14, 15, 307–8
mergers 308, 408–19
notice 302–3, 408
potential competition 309
product market 13–14, 306–7,
    309
relevant geographic
    market 309
relevant market 13–14,
    306–7, 309, 408–12,
    417–19
relevant product
    market 13–14, 306–7,
    309, 408–12, 417–19
secondary markets 308
service market
    definition 408–19
SSNIP test 309–10
substitutability 13–14, 307,
    309–10
supply side
    substitutability 309, 310
Tetrapak (No 2) 307–8
United States 309
market integration
    'affect trade between member
        states' 106
    agents 203–4
    air transport 131
    block exemptions 69
    distribution 217, 228
    Grundig case 55, 68
    patent licensing 266
    predatory pricing 316–17
market power 12–14
    assessment 13
    barriers to entry or
        expansion 13, 14
    block exemptions 612
    dominance, concept of 296,
        298, 303, 313
    economics 12–13
    innovation 13
    legal certainty 14
    market definition 14, 308

market share, assessment
    of 13, 14
oligopolies 16
perfect or pure
    competition 16
perfect or pure
    monopolies 15–16
significant market
    power 12–13
single firm dominance 20
time scale 13
vertical agreements 622
market share
    30% cap 222–3
    assessment 13, 14
    barriers to entry 14
    block exemptions 14, 15,
        143, 612
    cartels 176–7
    commercial strengths 418–19
    Commission Notice 380–1
    distribution 222–4
    dominance, concept of
        296–303, 312–13
    economics 13–14
    exemptions 154–5
    legal certainty 14, 15
    market definition 14, 15,
        307–8
    market power 13, 14
    merger control 14, 385, 394,
        402, 415–22, 425
    minor importance,
        agreements of 104–5
    motor vehicle distribution
        and servicing
        networks 247, 249
    multi-party
        agreements 157–8, 161
    oligopolies 380–1
    'prevention, restriction
        or distortion of
        competition' 112
    research and
        development (R&D)
        agreements 493–4
    restrictive agreements 20,
        154–5
    selective distribution 240,
        241
    specialization
        agreements 489–90
    technology transfer block
        exemption 278, 282–5,
        287
marketing strategies 312–13

Marshall Plan 24–5
member states and EC
    competition
      rules 552–76
    Articles 81 and 82, obligations
      of member states
      under 552–3
    decisions 575–6
    directives 570–4
    positive obligations 552–3
    price-fixing 553–61
    public undertakings 552–3,
      562–70
    Treaty on European
      Union 553
memory bundling 341–2
Merger Regulation 384–428
    see also **joint ventures,**
      Merger Regulation and
    abuse of a dominant
      position 366, 379–85,
      406–7, 447–8, 454, 586,
      609
    administrative powers of
      Commission 444–5
    Advisory Committee,
      opinions of 445
    affected markets, definition
      of 402
    Airtours 405–6
    ancillary restraints 125–6,
      450–3
    appeals
      Court of First Instance
        and European Court of
        Justice 455–9
      expedited appeals 458–9
    application of the
      criteria 406–7
    Articles 81 and 82,
      relationship
      between 379–81, 454
    assessment, criteria for 389,
      403–7
    banks 396–7, 437
    barriers to entry 405, 414–16,
      422, 434
    behavioural remedies 447–9
    best practice 390, 402, 442,
      589
    bilateral enforcement 589
    blocking of mergers 445–7,
      454, 625–6, 644
    breach of conditions and
      obligations 449
    burden of proof 407, 428

cartels 421–2
Clayton Act 404
clearances
    conditions 407, 446–50
    obligations 446–50
    three member states, from
      391
collective dominance 379–81,
    405, 625
comity 590
commercial strengths 418–19
Commission 38, 515, 517,
    623–6
    administrative
      powers 444–5
    Advisory Committee,
      opinions of 445
    annual reports 412
    caseload 390
    general approach 408–9
    inquiry process 442–3
    jurisdiction 391–8
    pressure on 643–4
commitments 440–1
Community dimension,
    concentrations with
      a 391–8, 430–1, 433–5,
      438, 585–6, 624
comparative
    competition 436–7
compatibility with Common
    Market 389, 403–4
competition policy 21
concentrations, meaning
    of 398–401
concessions, offers of 390
conditions, imposition
    of 407, 420, 422, 427,
      428, 443–4, 446–50,
      609, 644
confidentiality 444–5
conglomerate effects 417,
    425–7, 459
consumer preferences 415–16
Continental Can 385–7
control
    definition of 393–4,
      396–400
    joint 400–1
coordinated effects 405,
    416–17, 420–5
Court of First
    Instance 455–9l, 617,
    644
credit crisis 645
crisis in 2002 390–1

criteria for assessment 389,
    403–7, 624
damages 644
dawn raids 444
decisive influence
    definition of 393–4,
      399–401
    ways of obtaining 442
defence exception 127, 437–8
defence, rights of 445
demand
    substitutability 409–12
deterrence 407, 425
DG Comp 384–5, 401–2,
    442–3, 624–6, 630,
    643–4
discussions before
    notification 442
divestiture 444, 449–50
dominant position 308, 389,
    391, 630
early drafts 387–8
economic assessments 457–8
economic nationalism 626,
    645
efficiencies 425, 427–8
end use of products 410
European Coal and
    Steel Community
    (ECSC) 29–30
European Court of Justice,
    appeals to 455–9
evidence 407, 418, 426, 457,
    459
expansion of competitors,
    hindering 420
extraterritoriality 585–6
failing company defence 428
failure to notify 444
field of use restrictions 452–3
final negotiations 389–90
financial undertakings 396–8
fines
    conditions and obligations,
      breach of 449
    European Coal and Steel
      Community (ECSC) 30
    failure to notify 444
    jurisdiction 455
    misleading or incomplete
      information 444
first-phase inquiry 443–4
foreclosure 425–6
foreign competition
    authorities, consultation
      with 449

Merger Regulation *see also*
    joint ventures, Merger
    Regulation and (*Cont.*)
Form CO 402–3, 408, 439,
    441–2
Form RS 432
future effect 406–7, 417–18
GE/Honeywell 426–6
Gencor and *Airtours* 422–4
geographic market
    consumer
        preferences 415–16
    definition of
        relevant 412–16, 417–19
    range of possible
        geographical
        markets 413–16
German clause 433
goodwill 126, 451–2
group economic unit
    doctrine 586
hearings
    oral hearings 440, 458
    right to 439
    third parties 440
horizontal mergers 417,
    424–5, 428
impeding competition,
    dominance
    significantly 404–5
Implementing
    Regulation 439–40,
    444, 445
industrial policy 632
information 402, 439, 443–4,
    457–8, 630
innovation 420
inquiry process 442–3
intellectual property
    rights 452–3
interchangeability 409
interim measures 387, 457
investigations
    checks and balances 440
    framework 439–40
    Implementing
        Regulation 439–41,
        444, 445
    national competition
        authorities 444
    procedures and
        powers 438–46
    separate groups or bodies,
        by 630
joint ventures 392, 395,
    624–5

concentrative, meaning
    of 398–9
joint control 400–1
full-function 399, 453–4
jurisdiction 389–91, 391–8,
    401, 430–1, 433–5, 455
Kali und Salz 422
languages 442
legitimate interest
    exception 436–7
leverage theory 626
Lisbon Treaty 632
location, issue of physical 401
management 397–8
market analysis 408
market definition
    geographic market 412–16,
        417–19
    notice 408
    relevant product
        market 408–12, 417–19
    service market
        definition 408–19
market share 385, 394, 402,
    415–22, 425
market transparency 423
misleading or incomplete
    information, fines
    for 444
modification by parties of
    original concentration
    plan 440–1
national competition
    authorities 389–91,
    430–6, 444, 505, 515, 517
national courts, use of
    Articles 81 and 82 to
    block mergers in 454
need for merger
    control 384–5
negative clearances 450,
    452–3
non-Community dimension
    mergers 430–3, 435–6,
    454
non-compete clauses 125–6,
    450–1, 453
non-coordinated effects
    cases 417, 419–20
non-dominance, presumption
    of 418
non-horizontal mergers 417,
    425–6
notice 125–6
notification 387, 390, 401–3,
    439–40

discussions before
    notification 442
failure to notify 444
incomplete 390
languages 442
multiple notifications 431–3
Official Journal,
    publication in 403
post-notification
    referrals 433–6
pre-notification
    referrals 402–3, 431–2
short-form 402
statistics 407
time limits 439
obligations, offers of 390,
    443–4, 446–50
obstruction, fines for 444
Official Journal, publication
    in 403
oligopolies 380, 405, 416,
    419–20, 424–5
one-stop shop 430–1, 436
oral hearings 440, 458
outsiders (maverick
    competitors) 425
partial referrals 434
Philip Morris case 388–9
pipeline products 420
post-notification
    referrals 433–6
preliminary non-binding
    views 402
product market, definition
    of 408–12, 417–19
professional secrecy 444–5
prohibition of
    mergers 416–26
public interest 437
purchase and supply
    agreements 453
recitals 387
referrals 391, 430–6
reform 631
Regulation 1/2003,
    application of 450, 454
relevant geographic market,
    definition of 412–16,
    417–19
relevant product market,
    definition of 408–12,
    417–19
remedies 446–50
    conditions, imposition
        of 407, 420, 422, 427,
        428, 443–4, 446–50

divestiture 444, 449–50
foreign competition
    authorities, consultation
    with 449
fundamental principle 447
market test 449
Notice 447
obligations, offers of 390,
    443–4, 446–50
purpose 446–7
structural and behavioural
    remedies 447–50
restrictive agreements 384–5,
    454
restrictive clauses 450–3
restrictive covenants 450–1
reviews 432–3, 455, 644
scope 379–80
second-phase inquiry 444
service market
    definition 408–12
SIEC test 416–17
short-form notice 439
significantly impede effective
    competition test 405,
    416–17, 424, 431–2
simplified procedure 390,
    402, 443
single-firm dominance 405,
    416–20
SSNIP test 408
stay of national
    proceedings 454
structural and behavioural
    remedies 447–50
submission, request for
    reasoned 432
substantial lessening of
    competition 391, 404–6
substantial size 391–2
substitutability 409–12, 414,
    419
supply agreements 453
supply
    substitutability 409–12
supply where price rises,
    increase on 420
surveys 443
switching to alternative
    suppliers, difficulties
    of 419–20
tacit coordination 424
Technology Transfer
    Agreements, block
    exemption for 453
third parties

appeals 455–6
hearings 440
information, right to 439
threshold 387–93, 402
time limits 391, 408, 438–9,
    444, 446, 449–50
turnover 387–97, 585–6, 624
tying 426
unilateral effect of the
    merger 405, 416–20
vertical agreements 384–5
vertical and conglomerate
    mergers 425–7
vertical effects 417
visits 443
mergers *see also* **Merger**
    Regulation
Clayton Act 22
competition policy 21
confidentiality 654
coordinated effects 424–5
international aspects of EC
    competition rule 654
market definition 308
market share 14
technology transfer block
    exemption 278
United States 589, 625, 654–5
waiver 592
Messina Declaration 32
minor importance, agreements
    of
'affect trade between member
    states' 103–5, 107
appreciable effect 107
automatic exception 105
de minimis rule 103–4
enforcement 145–6
horizontal agreements 121
market share 104–5
notice 104–5, 107, 113, 145–6
'prevention, restriction
    or distortion of
    competition' 112–13,
    121
Regulation 1/2003 105
turnover 104–5
vertical agreements 121
minority shareholders 466–7
misleading or incomplete
    information, fines
    for 444
modernization 633–43 *see also*
    Regulation 1/2003
background 609
block exemptions 638–9

Commission, role of 148, 629
economics-based
    interpretation of
    competition law 633
enforcement 146
European Competition
    Network (ECN) 634
list of measures 518–20
national competition
    authorities 503, 508,
    517–19, 522–3
national competition laws,
    convergence of 634–6
notification 623–4
'prevention, restriction
    or distortion of
    competition' 112
priorities in 2008,
    setting 639–40
restrictive agreements 146
soft instruments 629
technology transfer block
    exemption 281–2
monopolies
Monopolies and Mergers
    Commission
    (MMC) 520
national laws 300
perfect or pure
    competition 15–16
postal services 321–2
revenue-producing 563, 565
state monopolies 315–16,
    563, 565
telecommunications 571–2
Treaty of Rome 35
World Trade Organization
    (WTO) 600
motor vehicle distribution
    and servicing
    networks 243–9
after-sales 247
agents 245, 248
availability clause 247
block exemptions 244, 245–9
cooperation 243–4
hard-core restrictions 247
historical background 243–5
intermediaries 245, 248
intra-brand competition 244
legal certainty 249
location cause in respect
    of cars and light
    commercial
    vehicles 248
maintenance 243, 248

motor vehicle distribution and
    servicing networks
    (*Cont.*)
manufacturers and
    dealers, relationship
    between 243–4
market share thresholds 247,
    249
new vehicles 248
parallel imports 244–7
prices 249
qualitative criteria 246, 248
quantitative criteria 243–4,
    246, 248
Regulation 123/85 245
Regulation 1475/95 245, 246
Regulation 1400/2002 245–9
repair 248
spare parts 248
vertical agreements 622
vertical restraints 246
motor vehicles *see also* motor
    vehicle distribution and
    servicing networks
intellectual property rights,
    abuses by individual
    owners of 343–4
spare parts, refusal to
    supply 343–4
multilateral measures,
    proposals for
barriers to entry 596
Commission Trade
    and Competition
    Communication
    595–6
Community dimension,
    arrangements with
    a 596
criminal offences 596
enforcement 594–5
exclusive arrangements,
    global rules on 596
international aspects of
    EC competition
    rule 595–603
International Competition
    Network (ICN) 603
Multilateral Competition
    Agreement 602
rule of reason 596
standards 596–7
United States 597–8
Van Miert Group of
    Experts 595, 596
Van Miert Report 595, 596

World Trade Organization
    (WTO) 596–604
multi-party agreements
block exemptions 58–9, 68
Commission 628
concerted practices 159
exemptions 157–8
force majeure 160–1
International Energy
    Authority (IEA) 158–61
market shares 157–8, 161
notification 47–8
restrictive agreements 157–61

national competition
    authorities *see also*
    Regulation 1/2003,
    national competition
    authorities under
abuse of a dominant
    position 45, 514, 517,
    627
active enforcers, as 515–19
Advisory Committee 505–7,
    515
advisory powers, bodies
    with 524
'affect trade between member
    states', meaning
    of 503–4
appeals 520–2, 523–4
Austria 523, 524
Belgium 523
block exemptions 139, 227–8,
    509–12, 517, 523
Bulgaria 524
cartels 508, 517, 521
coercive measures 506
Commission
    Advisory Committee 505,
        515
    case load 517
    cooperation 50, 523
    information exchange 503,
        523
    jurisdiction 507, 509, 512
    Merger Regulation 515,
        517
    parallel
        proceedings 508–12
    resources 503, 515, 517
    white paper 503
compensation 521, 523
Competition Act 1998 520–1
Competition Appeal Tribunal
    (CAT) 520–4

Competition
    Commission 520–2
complaints 615
comprehensive law or laws
    setting out substantive
    and procedural
    rules 522–3
concerted practices 509
cooperation 579
Court of Appeal, appeals
    to 521
Court of First Instance 522
criminal proceedings 521,
    523
criteria 516
damages 523
dawn raids 505–6, 523
debate on national
    competition authority
    participation 515–16
decision-making bodies 522,
    523
DG Comp
    additional
        responsibilities 502
    case-load 502
    cooperation 504
    future, debates on 517
    resources 503
    secondment from new
        member states 628
directives 503
Director General of Fair
    Trading 520
distribution 227–8
division of
    responsibility 502–7
double barrier theory 507,
    509
enforcement 139, 146, 502–30
Enterprise Act 2002 520–1
entry, powers of 506
Estonia 523
European Competition
    Network (ECN) 634
exception légale 517–18
exemptions 504–5, 507,
    509–12, 515, 517–18
fines 520–1, 522
Finland 523
foreign competition
    authorities, consultation
    with 449
France 524
Germany 523, 524
Greece 523

growth and creation of
     authorities 502
information 503, 505, 523
international aspects of EC
     competition rule 579
investigations 444, 505,
     508–12, 521
Ireland 523
Italy 523
joint ventures 502
judicial review 521, 522
jurisdiction 44, 507, 509, 512,
     516, 521
legal certainty 517
member states, national
     competition authorities
     in other 522–5
Merger Regulation 389–91,
     430–6, 444, 502, 515, 517
modernization
     programme 503, 508,
     517–20, 522–3
Monopolies and Mergers
     Commission
     (MMC) 520
multilateral meetings 589
national courts 641
need for member state
     participation 502–3
Netherlands 523, 524
network of national
     competition
     authorities 508
new member states,
     secondment from 628
new role for national
     competition
     authorities 519–24
Notice on Cooperation
     1997 516
notification 505, 517–18
Office of Fair Trading 505,
     520–2, 523
original division of
     responsibility 502–7
other means of member state
     involvement 506–7
parallel proceedings 508–12
Poland 524
political institutions 524
Portugal 524
practical effectiveness
     rule 508–9
preliminary rulings 519
procedural rules 522–3
public interest 521

regional meetings 589
Regulation 17/62 504–5,
     515, 517
regulations 503, 504
resources 613
restrictive agreements 508,
     514, 517–18, 520
Restrictive Practices
     Court 520
secondment from new
     member states 628
Secretary of State
     political function 522
     removal of power of 521
soft convergence 519
substantial lessening of
     competition 521
substantive rules 522–3
supremacy of EC law 507–14,
     519
Sweden 523, 524
technology transfer block
     exemption 283
third parties, information
     from 523
Treaty of Rome 503–4
uniformity rule 508–9
United Kingdom 520–2
use of force 506
national competition laws
abuse of a dominant
     position 38
'affect trade between member
     states' 102
cartels 636–7
commitments 635
common approaches,
     development of 636
convergence 634–6
criminal sanctions against
     hardcore cartels 636–7
damages actions, obstacles to
     bringing 636
differences in laws 37
European Competition
     Network (ECN) 635
legislate to protect agreements
     or give privileges in
     breach of Articles 81
     and 82, states must
     not 553–6
leniency programmes 635
modernization 634–6
monopolies 300
notification, abolition of 635
price-fixing 553–61

Regulation 17/62 41–2
restrictive agreements 37
sector inquiries 635
voluntary or soft
     convergence 634–6
working groups and
     meetings 635–6
national courts *see also*
     Regulation 1/2003,
     national courts and
Association of European
     Competition Law
     Judges 642
block exemptions 139, 633
breach of statutory duty 536,
     537
BRT v *Sabam* 531–3
cartels 648–9
comfort letters 535
Commission 531–5
complaints 615
Community interest, cases
     with 532
Competition Appeal Tribunal
     (CAT) 533
complaint procedure 531–2
damages 535–7, 545–50
Delimitis 533–4
direct application of EC
     law 531–50
direct effect of Articles 81 and
     82 533
early case law 531–7
electronic network 642
enforcement 139, 146
evidence 535, 649
exemptions 534
forum shopping 641–2
Garden Cottage case 536–7
Hasselblad 531–3
inconsistent decisions 641–2
information 534
injunctions 535, 536–7
interim measures 534, 536–7
interpretation of national
     competition law,
     preliminary references
     on 641–2
judges, communication
     between 642
judicial architecture of
     Community 642
judgments, transmission
     of 641
Masterfoods 533–4
mergers, blocking 454

national courts *see also*
    Regulation 1/2003,
    national courts and
    (*Cont.*)
national competition
    authorities, observations
    of 641
Notice on Cooperation with
    National Courts 534–5
nullity 169
policy issues, balancing 641
preliminary references 641–2
public interest 532
Regulation 17/62 533
remedies available in UK
    courts 536–42
specialization 641
stay of proceedings 535
technology transfer block
    exemption 281–2
United Kingdom 535–6
wrongful interference
    with contractual
    relationships, damages
    for 536
national markets, cartels
    controlling 187–9
national markets, protection
    of 175, 177
nationality discrimination
abuse of a dominant
    position 367–8
air transport 134
collecting societies 353–5,
    367
maritime transport 134–5
national champions 638
Regulation 1/2003 638
road, rail and inland
    waterways 137
ticketing arrangements 367
Treaty of Rome 34
nature and aims of
    competition 10–12
negative clearances
enforcement 145
exemptions 44
horticultural cases 166
joint ventures 478–9
Merger Regulation 450,
    452–3, 478–9
Regulation 17/62 43–4, 46,
    51–2
negative proceedings 512
Netherlands 189–90, 523, 524
networks

'affect trade between member
    states' 102–3
European Competition
    Network
    (ECN) 528–30, 634–5,
    638
financial cases 164
identity and reputation of
    network, maintenance
    of 254
International Competition
    Network (ICN)
    603, 654
motor vehicle distribution
    and servicing
    networks 243–9
national competition
    authorities 508
Regulation 1/2003 528–30
restrictive agreements 84–6
new sectors, application of
    competition rules
    to 620
New Zealand 589
no-challenge clauses 255–6,
    267, 268, 290
non-compete clauses
agents 204
ancillary restrictions 125–6
beer 166, 227
block exemptions 226, 252
distribution 214–15, 219–20,
    226
exclusive
    distribution 219–20,
    226
exclusive purchasing 208–9
franchising 226, 254, 258
joint ventures 479
Merger Regulation 125–6,
    450–1, 453, 479
patent licensing 268–9
petrol 227
selective distribution 242
non-coordinated effects
    cases 417, 419–20
notices
abuse of a dominant
    position 315–16
agents 199–202
cooperation 491–2, 516,
    527–8, 534–5
cooperative joint
    ventures 477
horizontal cooperation
    agreements 480–4

intellectual property
    rights 452–3
leniency notices 179–82, 622,
    645–6
market definition 302–3,
    308–10, 408
minor importance,
    agreements of 104–5,
    107, 113, 145–6
national competition
    authorities, cooperation
    with 516
national courts, cooperation
    with 534–5
Regulation 1/2003 527–8
remedies 447
research and
    development (R&D)
    agreements 491–2
subcontracting 274–5
telecommunications 315–16
notification
abolition 635
bilateral enforcement 47–8,
    589–90
block exemptions 60, 68–9,
    147, 624
cartels 623
comfort letters 614
Commission 623–4
directly applicable legal
    exception system 159
discussions before
    notification 442
enforcement 144–6
European Court of
    Justice 616
exclusive distribution 207
failure to notify 444
Form A/B 53
incomplete notification 390
joint ventures 463–4, 470–1,
    497–8
languages 442
Merger Regulation 387,
    390, 401–3, 407, 431–6,
    439–40, 442, 444,
    463–4, 470–1, 497–8
modernization 623–4
multilateral agreements 47–8
multiple notifications 431–3
national competition
    authorities 505, 517–18
national competition law 635
Official Journal, publication
    in 403

opposition procedure 48
post-notification
    referrals 433–6
pre-notification
    referrals 402–3, 431–2
Regulation 1/2003 43, 46–8,
    51–3, 624
resources 614
restrictive agreements 147,
    623–4
short-form 402
specialization
    agreements 488–9
statistics 407
time limits 47–9, 52–3, 439
Treaty of Rome 35
United States 589–90
vertical restrictions 614
workload 48, 52–3, 614
nuclear energy 128
nullity 167–8

'object or effect' of restricting
    competition, meaning
    of 118–23
objections 53–4
obligations, offers of 390,
    443–4, 446–50
obstruction, fines for 444
occupational pension
    schemes 128–9
OECD (Organisation for
    Economic Co-operation
    and Development) 593
OEEC (Organization for
    European Economic
    Co-operation) 24–6,
    33–5
Office of Fair Trading 505,
    520–2, 523
Official Journal 403, 656, 657
officials
    'A' officials 613
    European Competition
        Network (ECN) 529
    new member states,
        integration of officials
        from 628
oil prices 608
oligopolies
    Article 82 and Article
        81, relationship
        between 375
    cartels 190–1
    collective or joint
        dominance 21

concerted practices 89–90
    definition 16
    market power 16
    market share 380–1
    Merger Regulation 380, 405,
        416, 419–20, 424–5
    single firm dominance 20
    trade associations 190–1
    workable competition 17
    World Trade Organization
        (WTO) 600
opposition procedure
    block exemptions 48, 141, 271
    notification 48
    patent licensing 271
    Regulation 17/62 48
    technology transfer block
        exemption 280
Organisation for Economic
    Co-operation
    and Development
    (OECD) 593
Organization for European
    Economic Co-operation
    (OEEC) 24–5
origins of EC competition
    law 24–39
    Benelux Memorandum 31–2
    Council of Europe 25–6
    European Economic
        Community
        (EEC) 31–9
    Germany 26
    Messina Declaration 32
    negotiation over Articles 81
        and 82 33–5
    Organization for European
        Economic Co-operation
        (OEEC) 24–5
    Schuman Plan 26–31
    Spaak Report 32–3
    text of Articles 81 and
        82 36–9
    Treaty of Paris 26–31, 33–4
    Treaty of Rome 31, 33–5
Organization for European
    Economic Co-operation
    (OEEC) 24–6, 33–5

P&I clubs 162
parallel proceedings 508–12
parallel trade
    block exemptions 57, 60,
        147–8, 242
    concerted practices 88–9,
        91–3, 96

DG Comp 640
distribution 66, 218–19, 221,
    226
    exclusive distribution 218–19
    exemptions 153–4
    franchising 254
    Grundig case 54–5
    motor vehicle distribution
        and servicing
        networks 244–7
    non-resident parties,
        restrictions by 122
    pharmaceuticals 122, 640
    'prevention, restriction
        or distortion of
        competition' 119–20,
        122
    refusal to deal 339–40
    restrictive agreements 86–8,
        147–8, 153–4
    selective distribution 242
    single market imperative 12
parcel services 321–2, 331
parts, sale of 226
passing on defence 547, 549–50
patents
    abuse of a dominant
        position 368
    abuse of rights 341, 351–2
    bilateral agreements 264–5
    block exemptions 142–3,
        263–4, 266–83, 351–2
    Christmas Message 264–7
    Commission 264–7
    compulsory licences 262
    dominance, concept of
        299–300
    European Patent Office
        (EPO) 263
    exclusive distribution
        agreements 263, 271
    exclusive licensing 263–8,
        270, 271, 351–2
    exclusive purchasing
        agreements 264
    extension of agreements 268
    franchising 252
    free movement of goods 264,
        266
    know-how licensing 274
    licences 262, 263–74, 278–9,
        284, 351–2
    Maize Seed case 267–71
    market integration 266
    no-challenge clauses 267, 268
    non-compete clauses 268–9

patents (*Cont.*)
   opposition 271
   Regulation 17 264-6
   royalties 368
   supplies, agreements
      requiring use of
      unpatented 268
   technology transfer block
      exemption 278-9, 284
   territorial protection 271
   Windsurfing case 271-3
pension schemes 128-9
perfect or pure competition 16
perfect or pure monopoly 15-16
performing rights
      societies 352-8, 367
periodic penalty payments
      see fines and periodic
      penalty payments
periodicals 657-8
petrol 121-2, 227
pharmaceutical sector 12, 218,
      348-50, 640
plant varieties 166-7, 294
Poland 524
policy purposes going beyond
      competition 9, 10-11
Portugal 524
postal services 321-2, 331, 566,
      574
potential competition 309
practical effectiveness
      rule 508-9
predatory pricing
   abuse of a dominant
      position 319-24
   Akzo case 319-22
   average avoidable costs
      (AAC) 323
   average total cost (ATC) 320,
      323
   average variable cost
      (AVC) 320, 323
   barriers to entry 323
   Commission Discussion
      Paper 323-4
   Compagnie Maritime Belge
      case 321
   definition 319
   Deutsche Post case 321-2
   dominance, concept of 302
   European Coal and Steel
      Community (ECSC) 30
   excessive pricing 318
   exclusionary abuses 323-4
   interim measures 320

liner conferences 321
loss-making prices 317
market integration 316-17
parcel services 321-2
postal monopolies 321-2
profit margin 317-18
preliminary rulings
   abuse of a dominant
      position 315
   Court of First Instance 642-3
   European Court of Justice 68,
      507-8, 522-3, 615-16,
      641-3
   national competition
      authorities 519
   national competition laws,
      interpretation of
      641-2
   supremacy of EC law 507-8
press releases 657
'prevention, restriction
      or distortion of
      competition'
   'affect trade between member
      states' 101
   assessment clause, Article
      81(1) as a 111, 113-14
   cases on
      interpretation 112-15
   collective bargaining 115
   Commission Notice on
      agreements of minor
      importance 113
   enforcement 111
   European Court of
      Justice 112
   exclusive purchasing
      agreements by petrol
      stations 121-2
   export bans 119-20, 122-3
   hardcore restrictions 113,
      114, 120-1
   horizontal agreements 113,
      121
   inherently restricted, markets
      where competition
      is 116-18
   joint ventures 114
   jurisdictional clause, Article
      81(1) as a 111, 113
   legitimate objectives,
      justification by 116
   market analysis 122-3
   market share 112
   meaning of 110-23
   Meca-Medina cases 115-16

minor importance, notice on
      agreements of 112-13,
      121
   Modernization
      Programme 112
   non-economic
      justifications 116
   non-resident parties,
      restrictions by 122
   'object or effect' of restricting
      competition, meaning
      of 118-23
   parallel imports 119-20, 122
   professional service, public
      interest and 115
   public interest 115
   restraint of trade 111, 117
   restrictive agreements 110-23
   rule of reason 111-12, 114,
      116
   Sherman Act 111, 121
   sport 116
   strict or liberal
      interpretation 110-12
   vertical agreements 112, 121
   Wouters case 115-16
price-fixing 173-82
   abuse of a dominant
      position 554-5
   Aluminium Cartel case 561-2
   Article 82 and Article
      81, relationship
      between 376-9
   cartels 173-82, 190, 191,
      194-6
   concerted practices,
      definition of 174-5
   damages 547, 549-50
   defensive cartels 173-4
   early cases 173-5
   excise duty 557
   export agreements 174
   extraterritoriality 582-4
   financial cases 164
   fines 174
   gentlemen's agreements 174
   leading cases 553-61
   legislate to protect agreements
      or give privileges in
      breach of Articles 81
      and 82, states must
      not 553-6
   leniency notices 179-82
   liner conferences 182-3, 301,
      302, 376-9
   maritime transport 136

member states, obligations of 553–61
national laws 553–61
national markets, protection of 175, 177
passing on defence 549–50
preprinted recommended prices 225
resale price maintenance 173, 554
restrictive agreements 555–6
sectors of economy, mandatory tariffs for 560–1
state action, undertakings do not escape Article 81 or 82 because of 557–60
tariffs for certain sectors of economy, mandatory 560–1
trade associations 190, 191, 194–6, 557, 558–60
prices *see also* **predatory pricing; price-fixing**
abuse of a dominant position 315, 316–26
competitive price level, measurement of 312
concerted practices 89–90, 93, 95
discrimination 30, 324–6
dominance, concept of 301, 302, 312–13
dual pricing 154–5
European Coal and Steel Community (ECSC) 30
excessive pricing 316–19
motor vehicle distribution and servicing networks 249
pharmaceutical sector 640
resale price maintenance (RPM) 173, 215–17, 225, 254, 255, 554, 639
restrictive agreements 154–5
selective distribution 235–6
telecommunications 573
trade associations 98
prior authorization principle 35
product differentiation 17–18
product market
definition 296, 303, 304–5, 408–12, 417–19
dominance, concept of 296, 300, 303, 304–5

joint ventures 472
market definition 13–14, 306–7, 309
Merger Regulation 408–12, 417–19, 472
relevant market 472
substitutability 304–5
total control 300
productive efficiency, meaning of 9
profession, establishment of new specialist 652
professional secrecy 444–5
prohibition principle 35
promoting technical or economic progress 147, 148–52
proportionality
abuse of a dominant position 371
ancillary restrictions 126
Article 82 and Article 81, relationship between 371
intellectual property rights, abuses by individual owners of 351–2
liner conferences 378–9
refusal to deal 337–41
restrictive agreements 152
restrictive covenants 123
Protection and Indemnity Clubs 162
protectionism 189
public interest
Competition Commission 521
Merger Regulation 437
national competition authorities 521
national courts 532
'prevention, restriction or distortion of competition' 115
professional service 115
television rights 163
public undertakings, Article 86(1) and (2) and 562–70
abuse of a dominant position 565–6, 567–9
decisions of Commission 563
definition of public undertakings 563
directives of Commission 563
exclusive rights 563–9

exclusivity, grant of 567–9
exemptions 562–3
general economic interest, services of 562, 565–70
limited exemption in Article 86(2) 565–7
member states, obligations of 552–3, 562–70
obstruct performance in law or fact, application of Treaty rules would 563
postal services 566
purpose of articles 562–3
revenue-producing monopolies 563, 565
special rights 563–5
trade associations 564
treaty competition rules, subject to 562–70
World Trade Organization (WTO) 598–9
punitive damages 547
purchasers *see* **vendors and purchasers**
pure competition 16

qualitative criteria
dominance 302, 312
motor vehicle distribution and servicing networks 246, 248
selective distribution 239–40, 242
quantitative criteria
dominance 312
motor vehicle distribution and servicing networks 246, 248
selective distribution 234, 236, 239–40
quantitative restrictions 262
quantity forcing 219
quotas 630

rail transport 108, 136–7
R&D agreements *see* research and development (R&D) agreements
rate-fixing 137, 183–4
rebates *see* discounts and rebates
recession 184–5, 189
recycling of packaging waste 367
reform
2003, progress since 630–1

reform (*Cont.*)
  Business Review Letters,
    adoption of practice
    similar to US 629
  future of EC competition
    law 629–55
  suggested and action
    taken 629–30
refusal to deal or supply
  abuse of a dominant
    position 315, 333–41,
    371
  Article 82 and Article
    81, relationship
    between 371
  Commercial Solvents 333–5
  concerted practices 92
  copyright 344–50
  efficiency
    considerations 340–1
  fines 334
  goods or services 333–41
  interface information 362–3
  interoperability
    information 315, 362–3,
    627
  licences 293, 344–51, 371
  objective justification 337–41
  occasional customers,
    treatment of 336–7
  parallel trade 339–40
  proportionality 337–41
  selective distribution 237–9
  shortages 338
  software licences 293
  spare parts 336, 343–4
  United Brands 333–4
regional meetings of
  competition
  authorities 589
registered designs 300
Regulation 17/62
  abuse of a dominant
    position 43, 45, 46
  Advisory Committee 50
  amendments 44–5
  Articles 1–9 46–9
  Articles 10–14 49–50
  Articles 15–25 51–3
  block exemptions 48
  Commission 138
  complaints, standing for 46
  contents 45–53
  Deringer Report 43, 48
  DG Comp 41–53, 140
  enactment 44–5

  enforcement 144
  entry into force 44
  European Court of Justice 45
  European Parliament 42–4
  exemptions 42, 44, 46–9,
    51–2
  fines and penalties 43, 51
  heard, right to be 51
  horizontal agreements 69
  implementation 52–3
  interpretation 45
  investigations 49–50, 52
  national competition
    authorities 45, 49–50,
    504–5, 515, 517, 525, 526
  national courts 533
  national laws, review of 41–2
  negative clearances 43–4,
    46, 51–2
  negotiations 41–2, 46–7
  notification 43, 46–8, 51–3
  objections, statements of 53
  opposition procedure 48
  patent licensing 264–6
  procedural framework
    40–4
  recitals 45
  Regulation 1/2003 525, 526
  replacement 45
  restrictive agreements 42–9
  standing 46
  Treaty of Rome 45
  vertical agreements, time
    spent on 52–3, 69
Regulation 1/2003 *see also*
  Regulation 1/2003,
  national competition
  authorities under;
  Regulation 1/2003,
  national courts and
  abuse of a dominant
    position 637
  Article 82 and Article
    81, relationship
    between 372
  Commission
    inapplicability, findings
    of 637
    informal guidance 637
    initiation of own
    proceedings 638
    obligations of 639
  criminal sanctions 637
  damages 545–6
  enforcement 139, 144
  evidence 638

  inapplicability, findings
    of 637
  informal guidance 637
  informal resolution 638
  joint ventures 463–4
  judicial architecture of
    Community 642
  Merger Regulation 450, 454,
    463–4
  minor importance,
    agreements of 105
  national champions,
    discrimination in favour
    of 638
  notification 624
  powers yet to be used 637–8
  practical function 633
  supremacy of EC law 513–14
  unilateral conduct 633
Regulation 1/2003, national
  competition authorities
  under 503, 513–14,
    518–19, 522–3, 525–30
  behavioural remedies 526
  block exemptions, withdrawal
    of 527
  burden of proof 526
  case allocation 527–8
  Commission
    case allocation 527–8
    cooperation 526–8
    decision-making 526
    initiation of own
    proceedings 638
    investigations 527
    Joint Declaration 527
    Notice on
    cooperation 527–8
  commitments 526
  content 525–6
  cooperation 526–8
  dawn raids 527
  decentralization 630–1
  decision-making 526
  direct effect of Articles 81 and
    82 525
  European Competition
    Network 528–30
  implementation 630–1
  informal guidance 526
  initiation of own proceedings
    by Commission 638
  investigations 527, 528
  Joint Declaration 527
  jurisdiction 528
  national courts 544

networks 528–30
Notice on cooperation 527–8
other authorities,
    investigations for 527
Regulation 17/62 525, 526
searches 527
structural remedies 526
supremacy of EC law 526
terms 525
**Regulation 1/2003, national
    courts and** 542–5,
    640–1
Crehan 544–5
Commission
    cases already with 542–4
    exemptions 542–3
    guidance 543
Competition Appeal
    Tribunal, High Court
    and 545
    compensation 545
    conditions 544–5
    damages 543, 545
    decentralization 630–1
    declaratory judgments 544
    Enterprise Act 2002 545
    exception légale 542–3
    exemptions, Commission
        monopoly over 542–4
    implementation 630–1
    injunctions 545
    national competition
        authorities 544
    recitals 542–3
    unilateral conduct 543–4
    victims 543
    written submissions 544
regulations
    DG Comp 40–1
    national competition
        authorities 503, 504
relevant market
    definition 295, 296, 302–3,
        412–16, 417–19
    dominance, concept of 295,
        296, 302–3
    geographic market 309,
        412–16, 417–19
    joint ventures 472, 474
    market definition 13–14,
        306–7, 309, 412–16,
        417–19
    Merger Regulation 412–19,
        472, 474
    product market 13–14, 306–7,
        309, 408–12, 417–19, 472

service market 472
specialization
    agreements 490–1
remedies *see also* **compensation;
    damages; remedies
    under Merger
    Regulation**
beer supply 540–1
behavioural remedies 447–9,
    526
Brasserie du Pêcheur 538
causation 538
Crehan 540–2
damages 535–42
Francovich 538
illegality 540
injunctions 535, 536–7, 545
prior findings in EC
    proceedings 539
restrictive
    agreements 539–40
significant responsibility,
    definition of 541
structural remedies 447–50,
    526
supremacy of EC law 514
United Kingdom 535–42
**remedies under Merger
    Regulation** 446–50
conditions, imposition
    of 407, 420, 422, 427,
    428, 443–4, 446–50
divestiture 444, 449–50
foreign competition
    authorities, consultation
    with 449
fundamental principle 447
market test 449
Notice 447
obligations, offers of 390,
    443–4, 446–50
purpose 446–7
structural and behavioural
    remedies 447–50
repairs 226, 248
representative actions 171–2,
    547, 549
resale price maintenance (RPM)
block exemptions 639
culture imperative of
    protecting small
    booksellers 216–17
DG Comp 216
distribution 215–17, 225
fixed or minimum 225
franchising 254, 255

free riders 215–16
horizontal agreements 215
preprinted recommended
    prices 225
price-fixing 173, 554
rule of reason 639
United States 639
vertical agreements 215
resales 60, 234, 235–6
**research and development (R&D)
    agreements** 491–7
ancillary clauses 495
block exemptions 281, 285,
    494–6, 612
Commission
    Guidelines 496–7
conditions 492–3
early case law 492–3
exemptions 492–3
joint ventures 491–7
licences 492, 493–4
long-term research 493
market sharing
    arrangements 493–4
Merger Regulation 491–7
monitoring 493
Notice on Cooperation
    between
    Enterprises 491–2
purpose 491
restrictive agreements 492, 497
technology transfer block
    exemption 281, 285
resources
block exemptions 68
Commission 22–3, 139,
    172, 503, 515, 517, 535,
    613–15
competition policy 22–3
complaints handling 614–15
DG Comp 41, 68, 613–15, 639
enforcement 22–3
institutions 608
national competition
    authorities 613
notification 614
staffing levels 613
workload 613
restraint of trade
cartels 172
common law 4
goodwill 172
'prevention, restriction
    or distortion of
    competition' 111, 117
restrictive covenants 4

restriction of competition *see*
       'prevention, restriction
       or distortion of
       competition'
restrictive agreements (Article
       81) 35–9
  'affect trade between member
       states', meaning
       of 101–10
  agreements, meaning of 82–8
  agriculture 129–31
  air transport 131–4
  ancillary restrictions 123–6
  appreciable effect on
       competition 372
  Article 82 and Article
       81, relationship
       between 370, 372
  assessment clause, Article
       81(1) as an 111, 113–14
  associations of undertakings,
       decisions by 82, 83,
       96–100
  Bayer case 86–8
  beer supply cases 165–6
  black clauses 19
  broad scope of Article 81 82–3
  change in circumstances 44
  clearances 29
  collective bargaining 128–9
  Commission
       changing role of 138–9
       Guidelines 148, 152
  comparison of Articles 81 and
       82 109–10, 370–83
  competition policy 19–20, 21
  concerted practices 82, 83,
       85, 88–96, 370
  conditions for escaping
       prohibition 144–56,
       167–8
  container transport 155
  defence 127
  definition of competition 8
  direct effect of Articles 82 533
  disapplication of Article 81(1)
       prohibition 138–70
  effect of restrictions on
       undertakings 152–4
  enforcement 144–6
  environmental cases 164–5
  Euratom 128
  European Coal and
       Steel Community
       (ECSC) 28–9, 37, 127–8
  evidence 370

  exceptions 126–38
  exemptions 42, 44, 48–9
  fair shares of benefits 147,
       151–2
  financial cases 164
  fines 29
  foreclosure 20
  gentlemen's agreements 82
  group economic units 80–1
  Grundig case 54–5
  horizontal agreements 83–4
  horticultural cases 166–7
  identification 370
  implementation of rules,
       cooperation over 37
  improving the production
       or distribution of
       goods 147, 148–51
  individual conditions
       for escaping
       prohibition 148–56
  industry, attitudes of 66–7
  insurance 161–2
  interpretation 66, 73, 109
  joint ventures 462–3, 464–5,
       475–84
  jurisdictional clause, Article
       81(1) as a 111, 113
  legal exception principle 45
  legislate to protect agreements
       or give privileges in
       breach of Articles 81
       and 82, states must
       not 553–6
  maritime transport 134–6
  market analysis 147, 154–5
  market share 20, 154–5
  member states, obligations
       of 552–76
  Merger Regulation 384–5,
       454, 463, 464–5, 475–84
  modernization 146
  multi-party
       agreements 157–61
  national competition
       authorities 508, 514,
       517–18, 520
  national competition laws,
       differences in 37
  necessity 152
  negotiation over Articles 81
       and 82 33–5
  network agreements 84–6
  notification 147, 623–4
  nuclear energy 128
  nullity 168–70

  objectives and effects of
       agreements 148, 372
  parallel imports 86–8, 147–8,
       153–4
  pharmaceutical companies,
       use of quotas by 630
  'prevention, restriction
       or distortion of
       competition', meaning
       of 110–23
  prices 154–5, 555–6
  proportionality 152
  provisional validity
       doctrine 42
  quotas 630
  register 520
  Regulation 17/62 42–4, 46–7
  remedies available in UK
       courts 539–40
  research and development
       (R&D) agreements 492,
       497
  restrictive agreements 370
  Restrictive Practices
       Court 520
  retrospectivity 43
  road, rail and inland
       waterways 136–7
  rule of reason 156
  Sherman Act 21
  state action, undertakings do
       not escape Article 81 or
       82 because of 557–60
  structure of Article 81 73–4
  supremacy of EC law 508, 514
  technical or economic
       progress,
       promoting 147, 148–51
  television rights cases 162–4
  text of Articles 81 and
       82 36–9
  trade associations 82, 83,
       96–100
  Treaty of Rome 128
  undertaking, concept of 74–9
  unilateral conduct 84–7
  vertical agreements 83–4
  voluntary agreements 82
  white clauses 19
  width of coverage 126–37
restrictive covenants
  know-how 123
  goodwill 123–4
  Merger Regulation 450–1
  proportionality 123
  restraint of trade 4

sale of businesses 123
vendors and
    purchasers 123-4
restructuring
    agreements 184-5
reverse engineering 292, 347-8
road, rail and inland
    waterways 136-7
royalties 279, 368
RPM *see* **resale price**
    maintenance (RPM)
rule of reason
    ancillary restrictions 156
    joint ventures 114
    multilateral measures,
        proposals for 596
    'prevention, restriction
        or distortion of
        competition' 111-12,
        114, 116
    resale prince
        maintenance 639
    restrictive agreements 156
    trade associations 196
    tying 364
    United States 156, 639

sale of businesses 123-4
sanctions *see also* **fines**
    abuse of a dominant
        position 371
    Article 82 and Article
        81, relationship
        between 371, 372
    DG Comp 41
    European Coal and Steel
        Community (ECSC) 29,
        30
    European Competition
        Network (ECN) 529
    supremacy of EC law 514
Schuman Plan 26-31
searches 527, 653
Secretary of State
    political function 522
    removal of power of 521
sector inquiries 630, 635,
    639-40
selective dealing
    agreements 251
selective distribution 230-49
    after-sales services 231, 233,
        239
    block exemptions 225,
        239-42, 252
    comfort letters 236

cross-supplies 225, 241
early cases 231-4
end-users 225
exemptions 242-3
franchising 251, 257
free riders 243
guarantees 234-5, 239
Internet sales 241
intra-brand competition 243
market share 240, 241
non-compete clauses 242
parallel networks 242
perfume and cosmetics 235-7
policy 242-3
prices 235-6
product type 240-1
qualitative criteria 239-40,
    242
quantitative restrictions 234,
    236, 239-40
refusal to deal 237-9
refusal to honour
    guarantees 234-5
resales 234, 235-6
retailers making active
    or passive sales to
    end-users, prohibition
    on 225
sole distributors 231-2
specialist dealers 231-2
wholesalers 230-2
self-assessments
    Commission guidance 159
    joint ventures 464, 476
    Merger Regulation 476
service agreements 134
service market 304-5, 408-12,
    472
settlements 639, 647
severance 168-9, 280, 286
shareholders
    joint ventures 461-2, 466-7
    Merger Regulation 466-7
    minority shareholders, veto
        rights and 466-7
    rights 461-2
Sherman Act
    abuse of a dominant
        position 315
    'prevention, restriction
        or distortion of
        competition' 111, 121
    restrictive agreements 20
    trade associations 189, 195
shipping *see* **maritime transport**
SIEC test 416-17

significant impediment to
    competition test 390,
        402, 404-5, 443, 453, 470
significant market power 12-13
single-firm dominance 20, 405,
    416-20
single market imperative 10-12
small markets, applicability
    of dominance concept
    to 299-300
social functions, performance
    of 75-6, 79
social security fund cases 76-7,
    79
social welfare 11, 149-50
Software Directive 347-8
software licences
    abuse of a dominant
        position 293
    decompilation 292-3
    duration of protection 29
    exclusive rights 292
    exemptions 293
    field of use 293
    inter-operability 293
    refusal to supply 293
    reverse engineering 292
    Software Directive 292-3
    technology transfer block
        exemptions 292
sources of law 656-8
Spaak Report 32-3
spare parts 248, 336, 343-4
special rights 563-5, 570-2,
    574, 576
specialist profession,
    establishment of
    new 652
specialization
    agreements 484-91
    block exemptions 489-91,
        612
    case law 484-9
    Commission
        Guidelines 490-1
    crisis cartels 488
    cross-supply clauses 490
    definition 484-5
    examples 485-9
    exemptions 485-6, 488
    joint ventures 484-91
    market share
        threshold 489-90
    Merger Regulation 484-91
    notification 488-9
    relevant market 490-1

specialization agreements
        (*Cont.*)
    swaps 488–9
    technology transfer block
        exemption 281
sport 116, 164
SSNIP test 309–10, 408
staff 41, 140, 613
standard terms 100, 161–2
standardization
        agreements 483–4
state action 557–60, 602
state aid 30, 35
state monopolies 16, 315–16,
        563, 565
stay of proceedings 454, 535
steel *see* European Coal and
        Steel Community
        (ECSC)
stocking agents 199
structural remedies 447–50,
        526
subcontracting notice 274–5
substantial lessening of
        competition 391,
        404–6, 521, 593, 600
substantial part of common
        market 304–5, 370
substitutability
    consumer preferences 309
    cross-elasticity of
        demand 305, 309–10
    demand 305, 309–10, 409–12
    false substitutes 310
    intellectual property rights,
        abuses by individual
        owners of 346
    market definition 13–14, 307,
        309–10
    SSNIP test 309-10
    supply side
        substitutability 309,
        310, 409–12
    United States 309
super-dominance 301, 312, 627
supply side substitutability 309,
        310, 409–12
supremacy of EC law 507–14
    abuse of a dominant
        position 514
    block exemptions 509–12
    BMW and Volkswagen
        cases 512
    cartels 508
    concerted practices 509
    consumer protection 514

double barrier theory 507,
        509
Enterprise Act 2002 514
exemptions 507, 509–13
fines 514
intellectual property rights,
        abuses by individual
        owners of 345
investigations 508–12
national competition
        authorities 526
negative proceedings 512
parallel proceedings 508–12
practical effectiveness
        rule 508–9
preliminary rulings 507–8
public policy 511
Regulation 1/2003 513–14,
        525
remedies 514
restrictive agreements 508,
        514
sanctions 514
trade between member
        states 507
uniformity rule 508–9
Walt Wilhelm case 507–12
Sweden 523, 524, 648
switching 419–20

tacit coordination 424
tariffs
    air transport 132
    leniency notices 181
    liner conference cartels 183
    mandatory sectors 560–1
    price-fixing 560–1
technology *see also*
        computers; technology
        transfer
    decompilation 347–8
    dominance, concept of 653
    economics 653
    electronic
        communications 529,
        634, 642, 653–4
    improving the production or
        distribution of goods or
        promoting technical or
        economic progress 147,
        148–52
    interface or interoperability
        information, refusal to
        supply 342–3, 362–3
    Internet 241, 653
    memory bundling 341–2

promoting technical
        or economic
        progress 147–52
    reverse engineering 347–8
    Software Directive 347–8
    technical progress, definition
        of 148–9
    tying 364
technology transfer
    active sales 284
    ancillary rights 281
    black list 280, 282–6
    block exemptions 210–11,
        277–87, 292, 453, 612,
        636
    customer restrictions 283–4
    exclusive licences 279
    grey list 280, 281, 282, 284
    inter-brand competition 281
    intra-brand competition 281
    know-how licences 278–9,
        284
    licences 210–11, 277–87,
        289–90
    market share 278, 282–5, 287
    merger control 278, 453
    modernization programme of
        Commission 281–2
    national competition
        authorities 281–2,
        286–7
    national courts 281–2
    non-compete clauses 283
    opposition procedure 280
    passive sales 284
    patent licences 278–9, 284
    recitals 278–9
    Regulation 240/96 278–80,
        282
    Regulation 772/2004 281–7
    research and development
        agreements 281, 285
    royalties 279
    severance 280, 286
    software licences 292
    specialization
        agreements 281
    territorial restrictions 278,
        279, 283–4
    trade mark licences 289–90
    travaux préparatoires 277–8,
        282–3
    vertical agreements 281
    vertical restraints 210–11
    white list 279–80, 281, 282,
        284

telecommunications
  abuse of a dominant
    position 315–16, 626–7
  Commission notice 315–16
  DG Comp 639
  directives 570–3, 609
  exclusive or special
    rights 570–2
  exemptions 499
  Full Competition
    Directive 572–3
  inquiries 639
  joint ventures 499
  leasing or maintenance 571
  liberalization 639
  monopolies 571–2
  prices 573
  sectoral inquiries 573
  terminal equipment 570, 609
  type-specific
    specifications 571
television rights
  European Broadcasting
    Union (EBU)
    Rules 162–4
  exemptions 162–3
  listings 344–9
  public interest 163
  restrictive agreements 162–4
  sporting events 164
terms
  P&I Clubs 161–2
  imposition of
    unreasonable 367
  national competition
    authorities 525
  Regulation 1/2003 525
  standard terms 161–2
territorial protection 217–19,
  271, 278–9, 283–4
textbooks 656, 657
third parties
  appeals 455–6
  hearings 440
  information 439, 523
  Merger Regulation 439–40,
    455–6
  national competition
    authorities 523
time limits
  block exemptions 143
  Court of First Instance 642
  damages 549
  exemptions 48–9
  Merger Regulation 391, 408,
    438–9, 444, 446, 449–50

notification 439
trade associations
  'affect trade between member
    states' 105–6
  agriculture 96–7, 99–100, 130
  ancillary restrictions 124–5
  associations of undertakings,
    decisions by 82, 83,
    96–100
  business organizations 97
  cartels 172, 189–97
  categories 97–9
  chambers of commerce or
    trade 97
  constitutions 97–8
  cooperatives 97
  decisions 82, 83, 96–100
  definition 96–7
  economic or commercial
    purpose 96
  employers' organizations 97
  environment 165
  expulsion 124–5
  fair share of benefits 152
  prices 98, 557, 558–60
  public undertakings, Article
    86(1) and (2) and 564
  recommendations 100
  restrictive agreements 82, 83,
    96–100
  rules 98, 99, 100, 124–5, 557,
    558–60
  small associations 124–5
  standard contracts 100
  termination of membership,
    rules for 98
trade associations, cartels and
  97, 189–97
  certification 195–7
  concerted practices 196–7
  confidential information 190
  Dutch trade association
    cases 189–90
  financial information,
    exchange of 191, 193–4
  information, exchange
    of 190–4
  oligopolies 190–1
  price-fixing 190, 191, 194–6
  protectionism 189
  recession 189
  rule of reason 196
  rules 190
  Sherman Act 189, 195
  standards 195–7
  statistics 191

trade fairs and
  exhibitions 196
trade, effect on see 'affect trade
  between member states'
trade fairs and exhibitions 196
trade marks
  beer supply 290
  block exemptions 288, 290
  confusion 289
  early cases 287–90
  franchising 250, 251, 258
  Grundig case 54–5
  horizontal agreements 288
  licences 251, 258, 287–90, 293
  no challenge clauses 290
  Regulation 772/2004 289–90
  technology transfer 289–90
  territories, allocation of 289
  Trade Marks Directive 293
trade, meaning of 107–8
trade policy 10
trade unions 77
training and practice 652
transparency 621
transport see also air transport;
    maritime transport
  essential facilities, refusal of
    access to 358–62
  inland waterways 136
  motor vehicle distribution
    and servicing
    networks 243–9
  motor vehicle spare parts,
    refusal to supply 343–4
  rail transport 108, 136
  road transport 136
  trade, meaning of 108
treaties and conventions see
    also Treaty of Paris;
    Treaty of Rome
  air transport 131–2
  competition policy 631–3
  Council of Europe 25
  legal assistance treaties 587–8
Treaty of Nice 642–3
Treaty of Paris (ECSC Treaty)
  abuse of a dominant
    position 38
  Commission, sharing of
    jurisdiction with
    member states of 38
  contents 27
  High Authority 27–31
  member states, sharing
    of jurisdiction with
    Commission of 38

Treaty of Paris (ECSC Treaty)
(*Cont.*)
origins of EC competition
law 26–31, 33–4
ratification 27
Schuman Plan 27, 31
Treaty of Rome 37–8
Treaty of Rome
abuse of a dominant
position 35–6
competition policy 34, 607
contents 34–5
contrasting Articles 81 and
82 37–9
entry into force 38
European Coal and
Steel Community
(ECSC) 127–8
framework 607
institutions 34
monopolies 35
national competition
authorities 503–4
nationality discrimination 34
notification principle 35
objectives 607
origins of EC competition
law 31, 33–5
primary rules, establishment
of 607
prior authorization
principle 35
prohibition principle 35
Regulation 17/62 45
restrictive agreements 35–6,
128
sources of law 656
Spaak Report 32
state aid 35
subordinate legislation,
enactment of 35
travaux préparatoires
(preparatory works) 32
Treaty of Paris 37–8
turnover
banks, income of 396–7
identification of relevant
turnover 393–6
joint ventures 464, 470–1, 477
Merger Regulation 386–96,
464, 470–1, 477, 585–6,
624
minor importance,
agreements of 104–5
tying practices
abuse of a dominant
position 364–6

beer 220, 227
Clayton Act 364
conditions, imposition of
onerous 365
definition 364
discounts and rebates 327–8,
330
distribution 221
essential facilities, refusal of
access to 358
exclusive purchasing 209, 220
foreclosure 365–6
full-line forcing 364
integrated services 364
Merger Regulation 426
natural link 364
petrol 227
rule of reason 364
technological tying 364

undertakings *see also* **public
undertakings, Article
86(1) and (2) and**
agents 77–9
associations of undertakings,
decisions by 82, 83,
96–100
borderline cases 74–5
collective bargaining 77, 79
concept of 74–9
definition 74–9
economic activities, engaged
in 74–5, 79
employees 77, 79
insurance 76–7
pension funds 76–7
public character, functions of
a 74–6, 79
social functions, performance
of 75–6, 79
social security fund
cases 76–7, 79
trade unions 77
unilateral conduct 84–7, 543–4,
633, 654–5
United Kingdom
beer supply 540–1
Brasserie du Pêcheur 538
causation 538, 550
causes of action 550
Competition Act 1998 318,
520–1
Competition Appeal Tribunal
(CAT) 520–4, 533,
535–6, 545
Competition
Commission 520–2

Court of Appeal 521
courts of first instance 522
Crehan 540–2
damages 535–42, 550
Director General of Fair
Trading 520
Enterprise Act 2002 520–1,
545
excessive pricing 318
Francovich 538
higher courts 522
illegality 540
injunctions 536–7
Monopolies and Mergers
Commission
(MMC) 520
national competition
authorities 520–2
Office of Fair Trading 505,
520–2, 523
prior findings in EC
proceedings 539
remedies 536–42
restrictive
agreements 539–40
significant responsibility,
definition of 541
United States
abuse of a dominant
position 315
agreement between EU and
US 587–90
best practice guidelines for
mergers 589
bilateral enforcement 587–92
Business Review Letters 629
cartels 592
class actions 547
Clayton Act 21, 364, 404
comity 590–1, 593–4, 628
concerted practices 88–9, 592
confidentiality 589, 591–2
contingency fees 547
damages 547, 550
demand substitutability 309
enforcement 655
extraterritoriality 580, 585
jury trials 547
market definition 309
mergers 589–92, 625,
654–5
multilateral measures,
proposals for 597–8
notification 589–90
rule of reason 156, 639
Sherman Act 20, 111, 121,
189, 195, 315

substantially lessen
    competition test 593
unilateral conduct 655
World Trade Organization
    (WTO) 597–8
use of force 506

Van Miert Group of
    Experts 595, 596
Van Miert Report 595, 596
vendors and purchasers,
    ancillary restrictions
    on 123–4
goodwill 123–4
know-how 123
restrictive covenants on
    vendors 123–4
sale of businesses 123–4
vertical agreements
abuse of a dominant
    position 381–2
block exemptions 61, 63, 65,
    69, 112, 121, 139, 141,
    612, 621–2
collective dominance
    381–2
Commission 621–2
definition 83–4
enforcement 145
European Court of
    Justice 616
foreclosure 18–19
horizontal and vertical
    agreements, difference
    between 18–19
inter-brand competition
    between manufacturers
    18–19
market power 622
Merger Regulation 384–5

minor importance, notice on
    agreements of 121
motor vehicle
    distribution 622
'prevention, restriction
    or distortion of
    competition' 112–13, 121
Regulation 17/62 52–3, 69
resale price maintenance
    (RPM) 215
restrictive agreements 83–4
technology transfer block
    exemption 281
vertical restraints
agents 203
beer and petrol 227
block exemptions 227, 257,
    638, 639
Commission guidelines 203,
    217–18
distribution 210–14, 217–19
dominance, concept of 652
exclusive distribution 217–19
franchising 257, 259
green paper on 210–14
motor vehicle distribution
    and servicing
    networks 246
technology transfer, block
    exemption for licences
    for 210–11
visits 443
volume of trade, effect on 102–3

websites
DG Comp 657
distribution 225
whistleblowing 179
wholesalers 225, 230–2
workable competition 16–17

World Trade Organization
    (WTO)
bilateral cooperation 597
commitments 597–8, 602
discrimination 598–9
essential facilities 600
examples of anti-competitive
    practices 599
General Agreement on
    Trade and Services
    (GATS) 599
International Competition
    Network (ICN) 603
lowest common
    denominator 597
Mexican Telecoms reference
    paper 601–2
Multilateral Competition
    Agreement 602
multilateral measures,
    proposals for
    596–604
monopolies 600
oligopolies 600
policy competition 597
pro-competitive regulatory
    principles 598–600
publicly run sectors 598–9
reference papers 598–602
regulation 599
standards 597
state action doctrine 602
substantial lessening of
    competition 600
United States 597–8
wrongful interference with
    contractual relationships,
    damages for 536
WTO *see* World Trade
    Organization (WTO)